# On a Field of Red

# ON A FIELD OF RED

*The Communist International and the Coming of World War II*

Anthony Cave Brown

and

Charles B. MacDonald

G. P. PUTNAM'S SONS
NEW YORK

The authors gratefully acknowledge permission from the following to reprint
material in this book:

Norma Millay Ellis for lines from Sonnet cxxii by Edna St. Vincent Millay,
from *Collected Poems,* copyright © 1934, 1962 by Edna St. Vincent Millay and
Norma Millay Ellis. Published by Harper & Row, Publishers, Inc.

Random House, Inc. for lines from "Spain 1937" by W. H. Auden, copyright ©
1940, renewed 1968 by W. H. Auden. From *The English Auden: Poems, Essays
& Dramatic Writings,* by W. H. Auden, edited by Edward Mendelson.

Maps by Steve Hardeman

Library of Congress Cataloging in Publication Data

Cave Brown, Anthony.
  On a field of red.

  Includes index.
  1. Communist International: I. MacDonald, Charles
Brown, date. joint author. II. Title.
HX11.I5C37      324'.3      80-17231
ISBN 0-399-12542-6

Printed in the United States of America

# Contents

# Authors' Note

In writing about the Communist International—more generally known as the Comintern—that organization created by the early leaders of Soviet Russia to bring about the downfall of the capitalist states and engineer the world revolution of the proletariat, the authors have made no effort to provide a formal history of the Comintern. Nor have we set out to examine any changes that the activities of the Comintern may have wrought in the social fabric of western civilization.

What we have concerned ourselves with are the intrigues and subversive operations of the Comintern, attempted both with and without the assistance of the Soviet intelligence services, in three countries—the United States of America, Great Britain, and Germany—and how Comintern policy in concert with Soviet revolutionary diplomacy contributed to the coming of World War II. We have thus focused on the narrow but decisive front of Soviet efforts to undermine the capitalist democracies and, coincidentally, of the efforts of the democracies not only to protect themselves but also to undermine Soviet Bolshevism. Those efforts on both sides created a very thick stew from which Nazism and world conflict emerged.

Since Comintern doctrine specified that the world was indivisible and that what happened in Peking, New Delhi, or Madrid had its effects in Washington, London, and Berlin, we found it necessary on occasion to go beyond the geographical boundaries of the United States, Britain, and Germany. So, too, if the operations of the Comintern were to be seen in proper perspective, we considered it necessary to place them against the historical backdrop of the tumultuous events of the era, such events as the Russian Civil War, the great famine, the doctrinaire disputes culminating in the purges and the murder of Leon Trotsky, the changes of government in Washington and London, the great depression, the rise of Adolf Hitler, and the first direct confrontation of Fascism and Bolshevism in Spain.

The canvas is thus vast, a reach dictated not by our ambition but by the nature of the events and the immense cast of characters involved in them. If the canvas is surreal, it will be understood that nothing about Communism is simple or tranquil; it lends itself not to pastoral beauty but to tumult and upheaval on vast, consequential, and sometimes virtually incomprehensible scales.

We have also attempted to show that there exists a serious inaccurate historical assumption: the belief that the Cold War began with the end of World War II. The Cold War began not with victory over the Fascist powers but that night in Petrograd during the October Revolution of 1917 when Communism emerged triumphant out of the Commencement Hall of the Smolny Institute for Young Ladies of the Nobility.

The authors gratefully acknowledge the kind assistance of the following:

David Donovan, literary executor of the William J. Donovan estate; Lucy Maguire of Donovan, Leisure, Newton and Irvine, New York: Richard Fletcher of London; Carol Anderson, U.S. Army Center of Military History; Penny Crumpler, U.S. Army Engineer Library; the patient staff of the U.S. Army Library in the Pentagon; Linda Morcock and Edward Grimsley, Federal Bureau of Investigation; Robert Howie, Atomic Energy Commission; Gene Wilson, Central Intelligence Agency; William C. Cunliffe, Edward J. Reese, Charles Shaughnessy, and John E. Taylor, Modern Military Records Branch, National Archives; Tim Nenninger, Old Military Records Branch, National Archives; and Patricia Dowling, Dr. Milton Gustafson, and Dr. Gerald Haynes, Diplomatic Branch, National Archives.

Special gratitude goes to our editors, Peter Israel and Elisabeth A. Jakab; to our copy editor, Fred Sawyer, and to Gypsy da Silva.

We also acknowledge with deep appreciation the assistance of a former specialist in Soviet affairs for the CIA, William Colligan.

—ANTHONY CAVE BROWN
—CHARLES B. MACDONALD

# Foreword

In late 1977, Major General Edwin L. Sibert, chief of intelligence during World War II, first to General of the Armies Omar N. Bradley and then to General of the Armies Dwight D. Eisenhower, talked about problems of counterintelligence that he had encountered in the period 1944–1946 during the great campaign in Northwest Europe and during the occupation of Germany. General Sibert said:

> As our intelligence operations developed, we began to see that there was an intelligence service in Europe—a substrata of society would be an accurate term for it—far more proficient and omnipresent than that of the Germans.
>
> That was the *apparat* of the old Communist International, which Lenin formed back in 1919 to spread the world revolution of the proletariat. Those *apparats* were everywhere, even in our own ranks and those of the Allied armies.
>
> It was plain to me that the members of the *apparats* were loyal not to their own leaders or capitals but to Stalin and the Kremlin.
>
> They became a matter of concern to me because they were armed, disciplined, and experienced underground fighters. We had to consider the possibility that if there was a war between Russia and the United States at the conclusion of World War II, as many thought there

would be, we would find these people fighting us in our rear as they had fought the Germans.

I brought the matter to the attention of both Bradley and Eisenhower, and Bradley asked me to prepare a paper on the subject of the Communist International in a hurry. I gave the problem to my chief of counterintelligence, but when we began to look for people who knew anything about this phenomenon, we found that there was nobody in the higher command who knew very much about the International.

In the end, we had to go to British intelligence and to the records of the German intelligence services and to employ two Belgian trade unionists who were familiar with the problem. We had four million men, and we could not find one who could write a five-page report on the International.

Well, the report was prepared, and we paid for it, but when I put the bill in to the fiscal people, they wrote back to me to ask why I had found it necessary to make a report on an Allied organization!

IN MEMORIAM
Major General Edwin L. Sibert, United States Army, Retired
1897–1977

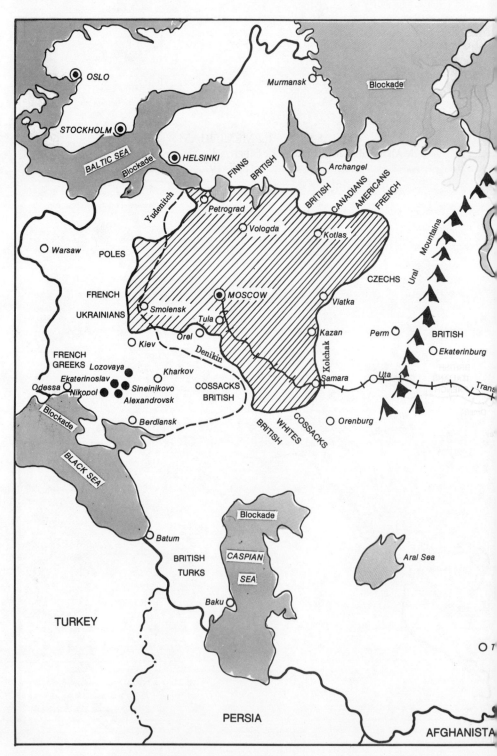

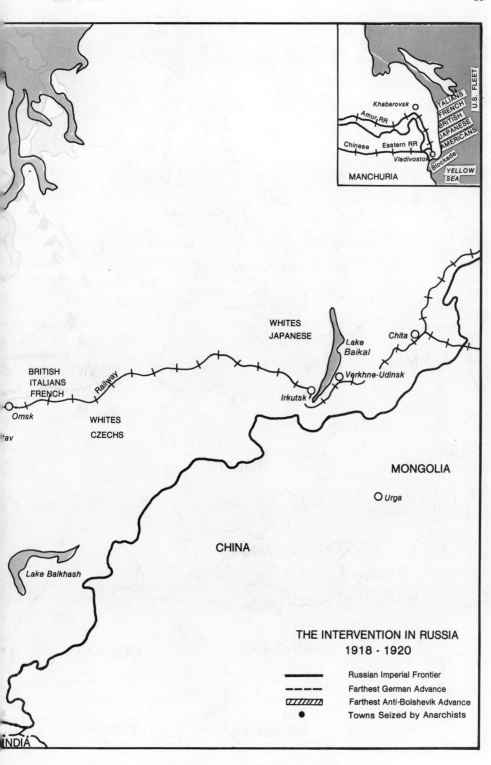

MANCHURIA

Khabarovsk

Amur RR

Chinese    Eastern RR

Vladivostok

Blockade

YELLOW
SEA

ITALIANS
FRENCH
BRITISH
JAPANESE
AMERICANS

U. S. FLEET

WHITES
JAPANESE

Lake
Baikal

Chita

BRITISH
ITALIANS
FRENCH

Railway

Verkhne-Udinsk

Irkutsk

Omsk

WHITES

CZECHS

av

MONGOLIA

Urga

CHINA

Lake Balkhash

INDIA

## THE INTERVENTION IN RUSSIA
### 1918 - 1920

———— Russian Imperial Frontier

- - - - Farthest German Advance

///////// Farthest Anti-Bolshevik Advance

● Towns Seized by Anarchists

## FARTHEST ADVANCES
### WORLD WAR II
—— GERMAN ADVANCE
- - - U.S.S.R. ADVANCE

# THE GERMAN CAMPAIGN IN RUSSIA

MOSCOW

Kuybyshev

Smolensk

Tula

Voronezh

SOCIALIST REPUBLICS

Stalingrad

Kharkov

Rostov

Odessa

BLACK SEA

# Prologue

As the Grossmünster's bells in Zurich tolled two o'clock on the afternoon of March 16, 1917, Vladimir Ilyich Ulyanov, alias Lenin, finished a lunch of boiled beef in a one-room flat at 14 Spiegelstrasse, next door to Halpern's sausage factory. The flat was furnished with kerosene lamps, a dining table covered with worn oilcloth, two chairs, two iron cots, and a second table piled high with books and pamphlets written by the Socialist theoreticians of the period and with back issues of *Iskra (The Spark)*, a newspaper of the European Socialist movement that Lenin had founded in Leipzig. Lenin's wife, Krupskaya, a plain, stout woman, was washing the plates and pots and talked about the storm that was rattling the tiles.

At forty-seven, Lenin was short and burly, running slightly to fat and balding. His suit was short in the sleeves, unpressed, and the coat would not button over his stomach. Putting on a worn and dirty overcoat and bowler, he intended spending the afternoon in the reading room of the Wasser Kirche, the municipal library beside the Zürichsee, reconstructing a manuscript called "Imperialism," which had been lost in the post, and preparing notes for a lecture. But as he was about to open the door, he heard a pounding of boots on the iron staircase outside. The door flew open, and one of his disciples, Moisei Warszawski (alias Bronski), burst in with the news that Lenin had waited for two decades to hear and for which he had spent two decades preparing himself: the revolution of the proletariat—the word derived from the Roman *proletarius*, the lowest social class— had begun in Russia.

Nonsense, said Lenin crossly; it was inconceivable that the revolution could have started without his knowledge.

Rain and sleet were falling as Lenin and Bronski hurried from 14 Spiegelstrasse to Brenner's newsstand. The reports, Lenin insisted, were drivel. There had been so many of them in the past. And what had they amounted to? German canards!

At Brenner's they picked up the *Züricher Post* and the *Neue Zürcher Zeitung*. Nothing! Bronski looked closely at the mastheads. They were, he said, the first editions; they would have to go to Krauss's on the Pfauzenplatz, where the late editions would already have arrived.

As they hastened through the streets, there were whitecaps on the Zürichsee, and at Krauss's there were headlines in the *Züricher Post*. A dispatch datelined Berlin announced that the Russian Army had mutinied, that civil war was erupting in Petrograd, that the czar was about to abdicate.

"If the Germans are not lying," Lenin declared, "then it's true."

The chief of staff of the German command on the Russian front, General Erich Ludendorff, whose forces had shattered the czar's armies in East Prussia in the Battle of Tannenberg, had conceived a stratagem in which such Russian Bolshevik revolutionaries as Lenin might be useful. If somehow Ludendorff could incite revolution in Russia and through it establish a government amenable to Germany, that would not only end the nightmare of a two-front war but would also put at Germany's disposal Russia's vast reserves of grain, oil, and ore. Germany then could mount a grand *Kaiserschlacht* (literally, kaiser's battle) to achieve victory on the western front. With that majestic ambition in mind, Ludendorff had arranged to provide Lenin and the Bolsheviks with the gold they needed to bring about revolution in Russia; but when the revolution came in March 1917 (February by the old-style calendar in use in Russia at the time), Ludendorff's scheme miscarried: the moderate Socialists seized the power, and their provisional government was dedicated to continuing the war with Germany. If Ludendorff was to salvage the grand stratagem, there had to be a second revolution.

From Bern in the last week of March 1917 came a message from the German ambassador, Baron Gisbert von Romberg: "Prominent revolutionaries here wish to return to Russia via Germany, since they are afraid to go via France because of U-boats." Passing the telegram to the chief of the Great German General Staff, Field Marshal Paul von Beneckendorff und von Hindenburg, the German foreign minister, Arthur Zimmermann, noted: "Since it is in our interests that the influence of the radical wing of revolutionaries should prevail in Russia, it seems appropriate to authorize transit."

There would be little delay in the response from the German General Staff, for from all indications, the United States of America was about to enter the war; and only if peace or even an armistice could be achieved quickly on the Russian front would the Germans be able to shift enough troops to mount a grand *Kaiserschlacht* to defeat Great Britain and France before American troops could arrive in strength. It was obviously worth the cost of transporting a few grubby, impoverished revolutionaries from Switzerland across Germany through Scandinavia to Russia. To Zimmermann went a telegram: "No objections to transit of Russian revolutionaries traveling as a group and reliably escorted."

Just after eleven o'clock in the evening of April 16, 1917, a holy day, a Baldwin steam locomotive pulling five coaches arrived at the platform of the Finland Station in Petrograd. As a brass band of the workers' militia, the Red Guard, struck up the "Marseillaise," Lenin stepped out onto the platform. Above the triumphant notes of trumpets, the thump of drums, the sound of hissing steam and grinding brakes rose the cheers of a great crowd. A guard of honor of Red sailors, men who had been "the cudgel of the revolution," presented arms. Lenin inspected them, uttered a few words of salute, then in company with a flock of Bolshevik functionaries moved down the platform to the czar's waiting room. At the doors a vibrant Red feminist, Alexandra Kollontai, presented Lenin with a bouquet of roses. Inside, he addressed the crowd: "Dear Comrades, Soldiers, Sailors, and Workers: I am happy to greet in you the victorious Russian Revolution, to greet you as the advance guard of the international proletarian army . . . The Russian Revolution created by you has opened a new epoch. Long live the worldwide Socialist Revolution."

As searchlights from the Peter and Paul Fortress danced over a dark, frosty sky, as bands played and the crowd cheered, Lenin climbed into the hatch of a Rolls-Royce armored car and was driven to the home of the prima ballerina, Kesenskaya, whose palace had become a Bolshevik headquarters. At almost the same moment, in the Marinsky Palace, a man who was destined to become the leader in the provisional government, Alexander Kerensky, received the news of Lenin's arrival with gloom. "Just you wait," he told a colleague. "Lenin has come and now the real thing will begin." While at the American Embassy, the military attaché, Colonel James A. Ruggles, was preparing a cablegram to be sent to Washington: "Sinister elements," he advised, "are taking control of the revolution."[1]

In New York City on March 16, 1917, Lev Davydovich Bronstein, alias Leon Trotsky, was reading in a three-room, $18-a-week rental apartment on Vyse Avenue in The Bronx. A man who would come to be called "a four-kind son of a bitch but the greatest Jew since Jesus Christ,"[2] Trotsky had lived there with his wife and three children since arriving in New York in the first days of 1917 as a political refugee. The telephone rang. It was Louis Fraina, an Italian-American Bolshevik, Trotsky's "side partner in New York,"[3] telephoning from *Novy Mir*, a Bolshevik newspaper with offices at 77 St. Mark's Place, where Trotsky worked as an editorial writer and adviser. There were, said Fraina, serious bread riots in Petrograd; perhaps Trotsky should come to look at the dispatches.

Hurrying to the newspaper's offices, Trotsky found the rooms jammed with the leaders of New York's revolutionary society, chattering in various tongues. Going immediately to the copy desk, Trotsky found dispatches telling a story far more momentous than bread riots: Czar Nicholas II had abdicated, and Prince Lvov was forming a provisional government. To get away from the babble, Trotsky went to his office, a dingy cubbyhole at the back of the basement, and there began to write an article: "The revolution of the proletariat in Russia has begun." Then he added as an afterthought: "It is but the beginning."

Soon thereafter a mysterious finger beckoned Trotsky, as it was beckoning Lenin's disciples around the world. Having returned some books to the public library, paid back taxes, three months' back rent, and household bills, Trotsky, on March 27, 1917, along with his family and some twenty followers, embarked on the Norwegian steamer *Christianifjord*. A large, boisterous crowd of New York Socialists was at the dock to wave goodbye. Also on hand was a large number of newspapermen, detectives, and intelligence agents.

On May 4, 1917, Trotsky arrived at the Finland Station in Petrograd much as had Lenin: to the acclaim of bands and crowds as if his were the second coming. One of the ministers of the provisional government, Matvei Skobolev, embraced him, kissed him, and exclaimed: "Dear and beloved teacher!" People in the crowd hoisted him to their shoulders and carried him past dancing red flags to the czar's waiting room. There Trotsky spoke. Russia, he cried, had "opened a new epoch, an epoch of blood and iron."

As chairman of the Military Revolutionary Committee of the Bolshevik Party, Leon Trotsky opened the tactical campaign to seize the power of the Russian state with a series of stealthy moves beginning on Monday and ending on Thursday of the first week of November 1917 (October by the old-style calendar, hence the name, October Revolution). In that brief period, Trotsky succeeded, as he himself would put it, in "crowding out the government step by step."[4] The climax came when the premier, Alexander Kerensky, fled the capital in a car provided by the American ambassador and when a squad of Red Guards charged into the cabinet room of the Winter Palace to arrest the vice-premier and the other ministers. The sinister elements had taken control of the Russian Revolution.

At that hour—2:40 A.M. on November 8, 1917—a Congress of Soviets was in temporary recess at Bolshevik headquarters in the Smolny Convent for the Daughters of the Nobility, the delegates refreshing themselves at the samovars. When the chairman of the congress, Lev Kamenev, one of the party's inner circle, received a telephonogram reporting that the government had fallen, he quickly sent stewards to reconvene the congress. The delegates began immediately to file back into the great white and gold Commencement Hall, where in other times young ladies of the nobility had assembled in white beneath shimmering chandeliers, carrying rosaries and sprigs of olive and chanting the praises of the Romanovs.

At 3:10 A.M., Kamenev mounted the tribune to look out over a forest of rifles and bayonets half-obscured by a dense blue-gray cloud of tobacco smoke. The Winter Palace, he cried, had fallen! All ministers of the provisional government except for Kerensky had been captured and interned for their own safety in the Trubetskoy Bastion of the Peter and Paul Fortress. The Military Revolutionary Committee was "in full possession of the capital." Applause erupted "heavier than a cannon salute."

At 8:40 P.M. that evening, Chairman Kamenev again mounted the tribunal in the Commencement Hall, rang a little bell, and called the delegates to order. The hero of the hour was soon at his side: Lenin. As Lenin prepared to speak, a bearded, ragged mass of 800 people seated below him burst into a tumult of applause. When he was at last able to be heard, his first words—"we shall now proceed to construct the Socialist Order"—produced a fresh outburst of jubilation.

Lenin's next words set alarm bells ringing in the great chancelleries of Europe. Speaking in a brittle, piercing voice, he repudiated the czar's pledge to Britain and France to make no separate peace with Germany and invited the Allied governments to join with Russia in immediate negotiations with Germany "for a just, democratic peace." Calling upon the workers and soldiers of the Allied countries, he enjoined them to rise up against their leaders, establish soviets (revolutionary councils of workers of peasants), and "help us carry through the business of peace and therewith the business of liberating the toilers and the exploited masses . . . from all slavery and all exploitation." Private ownership of land, he declared, was to be abolished; the entire economic, industrial, and commercial life of Russia was to be nationalized; and the new government rejected any responsibility for debts incurred with foreign powers by previous regimes, thereby wiping out at one stroke obligations totaling at least $2.7 billion.

As Lenin concluded his remarks, the entire assembly and Presidium rose as one and with "exalted faces and blazing eyes" began to sing. As Trotsky would record it: "The Bolsheviks have dared to do it. They alone have dared. Pride surges up of its own accord. Eyes shine. All are on their feet. No one is smoking now. It seems as though no one breathes. The Praesidium, the delegates, the guests, the sentries, join in a hymn of insurrection and brotherhood." The sound rolled out through the windows "to the autumn trenches, that patchwork upon unhappy, crucified Europe, to her devastated cities and villages, to her mothers and wives in mourning."

The song that rose from their throats was the "Internationale," the hymn of the revolution:

> Arise, ye prisoners of starvation!
> Arise, ye wretched of the earth!
> For Justice thunders condemnation,
> A better world's in birth.

*Book One*

# CONFRONTATION: 1917–1933

# PART I
## The Changing of the Guard

*Chapter One*

In 1903, when Lenin first established the notion of the world revolution of the proletariat and first presented the world with what Trotsky would call the "finality of 'tomorrow,' with all its stern tasks, its cruel conflicts and countless victims," Europe was ruled with plumy elegance by monarchs and princes supported and controlled by men whom the Bolsheviks called "the moneybags." The Romanov czar, Nicholas II, governed Russia; Edward VII of the House of Saxe-Coburg (whose dynastic name was later changed to Windsor) held the British throne; the Hohenzollern monarch, Wilhelm II, ruled Germany and Prussia; the head of the House of Hapsburg, the Emperor Franz Josef, occupied the throne of the Austro-Hungarian Empire; and King Victor Emmanuel III of the House of Savoy sat with crown and scepter amid the splendors of the Medicis at the Castro Pretorio in Rome. All those dynasties were intermarried; almost all were related by blood or marriage to Queen Victoria of England; and behind them, exercising power in the provinces, was a host of grand dukes, serene highnesses, princes, and barons.

Then in 1914 came the madness of the Great War, and by 1917, the world had long suffered. The great powers—Germany and the Austro-Hungarian Empire on one side and the Allies (Britain, France, Italy, and Russia) on the other—were locked in mortal combat. In 1917 the European monarchs were shocked by the ease with which the two revolutions in Russia had swept away the most autocratic of the princes, Nicholas II. The revolutionary government, established by a small band of political eccentrics, was not expected to endure, but Russia's civil unrest had momentous implications for the warring powers. On the western front in France and Belgium, the opposing systems of zigzag, timber-revetted trenches fronted by tangles of barbed wire had varied little in either direction since 1914, for the forces were too evenly matched for decision. On the Allied side, hope had at last stirred when on the 4th of July, 1917, a battalion of fresh young American soldiers paraded down the Champs-Elysées to cheers of near delirium from war-weary Parisians, but it would be a long time before this infusion of new blood would be transmuted into decisive force at the front. Yet if Russia should withdraw from the war and sign a separate peace with Germany, the Germans would be able to transfer a great number of troops to the west. Somehow, by whatever means, the Allies had to keep Russia in the war, thus maintaining the eastern front.

For a brief period, that looked to be no difficult task; for despite the solidarity exhibited at the Smolny Convent, Lenin's writ ran little farther than the boundaries of Petrograd, the capital, and even within the city, as bands of Red Guards looted the wine stores, Lenin felt compelled to proclaim a state of siege. So fragile did his hold appear to be that the chief of an American military mission in Petrograd, Brigadier General William V. Judson, reckoned that a single regiment of stout men could seize power in twelve hours. And even though the Bolshevik Revolution was swift and bloodless in some provincial cities, there were powerful blocs of resistance throughout the country, particularly among the fiercely independent Cossacks of the Don, the Kuban, and Orenburg and among nationalist separatists in the Caucasus, and the Ukraine; an opposition that would in time come to be known collectively, in contrast to the Reds, as the Whites.

As Lenin and Trotsky were aware, the Bolsheviks numbered no more than 300,000 among a population of 150 million, 80 percent of whom were peasants who would withhold active support to see if the Bolsheviks made good their promises of bread, land, and, above all, peace. Lenin immediately ordered the commander in chief of the Imperial Army, General Nikolai N. Dukhonin, to contact German headquarters to arrange an armistice; when Dukhonin ignored the order, he sent a trainload of tough revolutionary sailors to seize his headquarters at Mogilev. After the sailors lynched Dukhonin and tossed his corpse on their bayonets much as schoolboys toss one of their fellows on a blanket, their leader, a thirty-two-year-old naval lieutenant, Nikolai V. Krylenko, proclaimed himself head of the Army. With Krylenko's order to cease fire, some 6 million Russian soldiers began to leave the trenches.

So convinced was Lenin that the proletarian masses of Germany and the other western capitalist countries would follow the Russian lead and end the war that he had no concern about terms that the Germans might seek to impose. On December 3, 1917, at Brest Litovsk, a fire-blackened ruin on the Polish prairie, a Bolshevik delegation headed by a bearded revolutionary intellectual, Adolf Joffe, began armistice deliberations with the Germans. Knowing that Germany's one hope of victory lay in a truce in the east which would allow them to mount a grand offensive in the west, the Germans presented no obstacles. On December 15, 1917, as the delegations put their signatures to an armistice, German troop trains were already streaming westward with the vanguard of 600,000 soldiers that Erich Ludendorff needed for the *Kaiserschlacht*.

With radio intelligence revealing that German troop trains were leaving Russia daily for the west, Britain, France, and Italy began to search for some means of restoring a front in the east. The French provided support for a Rumanian army of 2 million men, while the British sent a mission to Novocherkassk, the capital of the Don Cossacks, to establish contact with their ataman, General Aleksei M. Kaledin, who had proclaimed his opposition to Lenin and his fealty to the Allies. Forming what was virutally an independent state, Kaledin hoped to unite all White forces in South Russia for a march on Moscow and Petrograd to destroy the Lenin government.

On December 1, 1917, American, British, French, and Italian representatives met in Paris to discuss support for General Kaledin's movement. Yet even though the British, French, and Italian representatives agreed to lend support, the American participant, President Woodrow Wilson's closest adviser, Colonel Edward M. House, demurred. "I consider it dangerous," said House, "for the reason that it is encouraging internal disturbances without our having any definite program in mind or any force with which to back up a program."[1]

The British nevertheless moved immediately to send war materials valued at $100 million to Kaledin's group. When intelligence revealed that other White forces were forming in the Ukraine, Transcaucasia, and Kurdistan, the British and French, even as a Russian delegation returned to Brest Litovsk to begin negotiations to turn the armistice into a treaty of peace, decided in Paris on December 23, 1917, to divide Russia into "zones of influence." Known as the Convention of 1917, the agreement assigned to France the region between the Rumanian frontier and the Crimea, while the British were to take charge in the area between the Crimea and the Caspian Sea, which contained one of the world's richest deposits of oil. (Almost immediately a British brigade set out on the 600-mile march across desert and mountains from Baghdad to take the great oil port of Baku.) In addition, the two governments began preparing a joint expeditionary force to move to the North Russian port of Murmansk, ostensibly to prevent the vast stocks of war stores, which had earlier been shipped to the czar's armies, from falling to the Germans.

These plans were grandiose, but the British and French means were limited, for the threat of the *Kaiserschlacht* made it impossible for them to pull sizable forces from the western front. Where to find the troops for operations in Russia? The only sources appeared to be Japan and the United States, but could either or both be persuaded to participate? It was soon clear that Japan, with unconcealed imperial ambitions, was anxious to send forces into Siberia, but the United States quickly expressed doubt about cooperating in any military adventure in Russia.

The British, in particular, began immediately to exert pressure on the American president, Woodrow Wilson, and in yet another effort to reestablish an eastern front, they turned to other tactics, which they called "special means."

Tall, slim, quick, somewhat puffy in the face from too much night-clubbing, thirty-year-old Robert Hamilton Bruce Lockhart was what the Scots call "a Scot of the Scots." The product of a severe, classical, Calvinist education, Lockhart had been well on his way to making a fortune in rubber in British Malaya when he offended a rule of British imperial conduct by taking as his mistress the beautiful ward of the sultan of Negri Sembilan. There was a "resounding scandal,"[2] and he was sent back to England to allow passions to cool. Upon his return to London in 1911, Lockhart decided to enter His Britannic Majesty's Consular Service. After he was posted to Petrograd in January 1912 as a vice-consul, golden reports of his work began coming back to his superiors in London; but again there were romantic entanglements, and again Lockhart found himself on the way home.

When the Bolsheviks seized power and Lenin announced his intention of concluding a separate peace with Germany, Lockhart was summoned to No. 10 Downing Street, the official residence of Prime Minister David Lloyd George. The prime minister was impressed. "Lockhart," he said, "obviously belongs in Petrograd, not London."[3] As the French ambassador to Russia, Joseph Noulens, was later to remark, Lockhart at that point became "one of those whom the British government employs, with rare felicity, for confidential missions, and whom it reserves, should the occasion arise, for disavowal."[4]

As Lockhart left London for Petrograd aboard the British cruiser *Iphigenia,* he had no license to attempt the overthrow of the Bolshevik government, but he was authorized to support any Russian faction that would continue the war against Germany. The British government having terminated formal diplomatic relations with the Lenin government, Lockhart was to head a three-man mission to establish unofficial relations and to serve as a general political *rapporteur.*

Lockhart arrived in Petrograd on the evening of January 30, 1918, at a time when the peace negotiations at Brest Litovsk appeared to be breaking down. As the head of the British secret service in Russia, Commander Ernest T. Boyce had learned through antibolshevik agents who had tapped the telegraph wire leading from Brest Litovsk to the Smolny Convent, the Germans were demanding a brigand's peace. Eighteen of Russia's richest provinces were to become independent states under German protection: the territories Russia held in Finland, the Baltic States, and Poland, as well as Belorussia, the Ukraine, and part of the Baku oil basin. If Russia acceded to the German demands, it would lose no less than 26 percent of its population, 27 percent of its arable land, 32 percent of normal agricultural output, 26 percent of its railroad systems, 33 percent of its industry, including 73 percent of its iron and steel production and 75 percent of its coal. The Germans intended in one stroke to establish their frontier from the White to the Black Sea and to acquire all the raw materials needed to compensate for an Allied naval blockade and to mount Ludendorff's *Kaiserschlacht.*

As Lockhart established his mission on Palace Quay across the Neva River from the Peter and Paul Fortress, Lenin sent Trotsky to Brest Litovsk with orders to use "the incalculable capacity of the Slav for interminable conversation."[5] The best course, as Lenin saw it, was to delay until revolutionary ferment inside Germany came to a boil. At long last, after exhausting that interminable conversation, Trotsky rose during the afternoon of February 9, 1918, to announce that the Russian government would sign no peace. Whether Germany accepted or not, the Soviet government considered the war to be at an end; there existed between the two countries, he said, a state of "no war, no peace." With an eye to revolutionaries all over Europe, but particularly to those in Germany, he added: "We are waiting in the belief that other peoples will soon follow our example."[6]

*"Unerhört!"*—"Unheard of!"—exclaimed General Max Hoffmann and ordered the eighty German divisions still in the east to prepare to advance. "We are going to start hostilities against the Bolsheviks," he declared, "before they turn the whole of Europe into a pig sty."[7] At noon on February 18, 1918, the German soldiers rose from their trenches and began to march in two great columns toward Petrograd and into the Ukraine.

To Lenin, there was only one weak hope left—to ask help from the Allies in exchange for a promise to resume the war—and to that end he sent a representative, Lev Kamenev, to London. But he had reckoned without the antipathy that the Bolshevik regime had by that time aroused in the west. There was widespread suspicion that Lenin and Trotsky were nothing more than German agents of influence in Russia and that they had deliberately acted against the Allies by enabling the Germans to withdraw their troops from the east. There was also a growing belief among western leaders that the new Russian rulers were less ineffective political eccentrics than inveterate intriguers, clever men with immense intellectual capabilities sharpened over the years by innumerable underground battles with the police forces of half the world, men who believed utterly in the political, economic, and social tenets of Marxism. They were coming to recognize, too, that Bolshevism might be no local phenomenon peculiar to revolutionary Russia but an exportable commodity with immense political and spiritual appeal, particularly to the nationalists who were beginning to emerge in every corner of the British and French empires. In fact, Bolshevik agents were at work within the Allied armies, urging the troops to lay down their arms, overthrow their governments, and help form a world soviet.

In London, the British quickly arrested Kamenev and sent him off on a packet bound for Norway, while in the meantime, a Russian delegation empowered to accept the German terms entered the officers' mess of the Citadel in Brest Litovsk on Sunday morning, March 3, 1918. Signatures were affixed at 5:50 P.M., and the Soviet delegation, having accepted one of history's more brutal settlements, withdrew without ceremony or cordiality. With German armies still hovering only seventy-five miles from Petrograd while awaiting ratification of the treaty by the Council of People's Commissars, Lenin moved his government to Moscow and the Kremlin, the old walled city grouped around the fifteenth-century Assumption Cathedral.

Bruce Lockhart followed the government, moving into the Hotel Elite on Red Square across from the main gate of the Kremlin. From that point Lockhart's activities would reflect the stern attitude of his government toward the Bolshevik regime. The change coincided with the arrival from London of a British agent named Sidney George Reilly.

Born Sigmund Georgievich Rosenblum just outside the Black Sea port of Odessa on March 24, 1874, Reilly had emigrated to England and anglicized his name upon being recruited as an agent in the British Secret Intelligence Service, known in Whitehall by the designation MI-1C. He early established a reputation for skill and daring by penetrating Bolshevik and Anarchist sects made up largely of Russian exiles which had sprung up in London before the outbreak of war. MI-1C subsequently sent Reilly to Petrograd, where he was equally at home in high society and the political underground and where he prospered financially as commercial agent for a firm of German naval architects, Blom und Voss.

In London early in 1918, the chief of MI-1C, Captain Mansfield Smith-Cumming, a one-legged sea dog with a long background in intelligence, briefed Reilly for a new assignment in Russia. As with most of the operations of the British secret service, mystery still beclouds the details of this episode. Although Reilly was apparently at no time a member of Lockhart's small staff, he was in close contact with the chief of the British secret service in Russia, Commander Boyce, and he was probably a member of a clandestine group known only as the Mission, which through arrangement between MI-1C and the Foreign Office was permitted to use the premises of the British Consulate. The evidence would suggest that Reilly's business was to serve as liaison between the British secret service and counterrevolutionary organizations in both Moscow and Petrograd.

Reilly's principal contact was a particularly determined enemy of Lenin's, Boris Viktorovich Savinkov. An educated man of considerable charm, Savinkov was a revolutionary extremist with a long record as an assassin, who in 1917 had joined Alexander Kerensky's provisional government. When Lenin seized power, Savinkov went to Novocherkassk to join the staff of Ataman Kaledin and participate in Kaledin's planned march on Moscow. It was at Novocherkassk that Savinkov encountered Reilly, whom he had known when Reilly was in Petrograd as the agent for Blom und Voss. Using false Cheka (secret police) credentials provided by Reilly, Savinkov returned with him to Moscow. In the capital, Savinkov served as an intermediary between Kaledin and Lockhart as part of the British scheme to provide arms and munitions to Kaledin to overthrow Lenin.

Under Reilly's plan, Lenin, Trotsky, and the rest of the Bolshevik leadership were to be arrested when in early July 1918 an All-Russia Congress convened in Moscow. White forces were simultaneously to seize twenty-three of the major cities of European Russia, including the ports of North Russia, where—Reilly and Savinkov hoped—Allied troops would land and march down the railroad tracks to Petrograd and Moscow. Lettish troops were to occupy the Kremlin, while a White army then operating in the Baltic provinces was to move on to Petrograd from the west.

What became known as the Reilly Plot was clearly a formidable undertaking, but there were reasons to believe that it had some chance of success. The Red Army was little more than a rabble of shirtless, bootless fanatics; and in early March 1918 the British battleship *Glory* and the cruiser *Cochrane* appeared at the North Russian port of Murmansk to land 200 British bluejackets. Later that month the French heavy cruiser *Amiral Aube* landed a company of French marines, the vanguard of an Allied force of some 17,500 troops under the British general Frederick C. Poole. Although empowered only to guard the Allied war stores near Murmansk, Poole quickly sent his men marching 300 miles down the Murmansk-Petrograd railroad, removed the Bolshevik soviet that ruled the province, replaced it with a mildly Socialistic government, hoisted the old blue and white ensign of the czars, and issued currency bearing the likeness of Catherine the Great which had been printed in London.

The plot gained added support when in May 1918 Lockhart met in secret conference in Moscow with representatives of all Russian political parties except the Monarchists and the Bolsheviks. The group decided that if the rebellion succeeded, the new government would be headed by a Directorate of Three, and if that government should prove unable to rule, it would be supplanted by a military dictatorship under an admiral who had recently appeared, with British connivance, among White forces in the foothills of the Ural Mountains along the boundary between European and Asiatic Russia, Alexander V. Kolchak.[8]

By mid-June 1918, as a heat wave hung over Moscow, the atmosphere was strange and uncertain. While the delegates began to assemble for the All-Russia Congress, the nobility and the upper and middle classes—the classes that were soon to be sentenced to death—went about their daily routines seemingly unaware of peril. They visited their cafés and restaurants, complained about the Bolshevik press, and went to the trotting races, to the ballet where Tamara Karsavina still enchanted, and to the opera where all agreed that Chaliapin's voice was never better.

On July 4, 1918, as Lockhart set out to attend the opening session of the congress, there was in the air an almost palpable sense of intrigue and murder, plot and counterplot. Driving to the Bolshoi Theater on Sverdlov Square, he remarked that there were more soldiers in the streets than was usual. Inside the theater, he went to the box where often he had sat to hear Chaliapin sing. Below him were the delegates: 678 Bolsheviks, mainly soldiers in uniform, and 269 Social Revolutionaries, mostly peasants in blouses, pantaloons, and boots, an assembly that looked remarkably out of place amid the theater's rich decor.

A heated discussion was in progress—the Social Revolutionaries were attacking the Bolsheviks for sending parties of soldiers into the countryside to appropriate grain for the cities. The high, shrill voice of Maria Spiridonova, a leader of the Left Social Revolutionaries, suddenly cut through the noisy debate. An extremely feminine figure, she was the more electrifying because of her past: she had killed one of the czar's leading state counselors; she had been sentenced to a lifetime of solitary confinement by the czar's courts; and she had been raped into insensibility by a troop of Cossacks. Yet there she stood like a phantom in black and pince-nez beneath the great crystal chandeliers. To Lenin personally she directed her words. "I accuse you," she cried, "of betraying the peasants, of making use of them for your own ends." Turning to her followers, she continued: "In Lenin's philosophy, you are only dung—only manure." Turning again to the tribunal, she shouted: "In my hand you will find the same pistol, the same bomb, which once forced me to defend—"[9]

A storm of shouted oaths and threats drowned out her words. As Lockhart watched apprehensively, a group of Cheka agents surrounded the Left Social Revolutionaries. Concerned that the theater might be sealed and all in it prevented from leaving, Lockhart rose and made for the street; but as he hurried down a corridor, someone stopped him: it was Sidney George Reilly, in disguise and carrying the credentials of a Cheka agent. He had heard, said Reilly, that the Left Social Revolutionaries were about to stage an insurrection and urged Lockhart to go back with him to see what would happen. As the two entered the box, a hand grenade exploded below them, killing two of the Bolshevik delegates and injuring six others. In the pandemonium that erupted, the Cheka agents appeared to be engulfed.

Hurrying to an exit, Lockhart and Reilly found that the turmoil had spread to the square outside. Their final impression as they departed was of Maria Spiridonova trying to make herself heard above the tumult. Lenin, she was shouting, was a German agent, and the German ambassador, Count Wilhelm von Mirbach-Harff, was raping the Ukraine.

Throughout the next day and well into the afternoon of July 6, 1918, an aura of impending counterrevolution hung over the capital like a gathering summer storm. Then the storm broke.

Close to three o'clock in the afternoon of July 6, 1918, a Left Social Revolutionary, Jacob Blumkin, who had been living in the Hotel Elite just down the hall from Lockhart, entered the German Embassy in Moscow with a companion. Producing Cheka credentials, the two men explained to the guards that they wanted to check security arrangements. Walking up the grand staircase of the palace to the ambassador's office, they produced pistols and shot Count von Mirbach-Harff. A few hours later, in Kiev, the German commander in chief in the

Ukraine, Field Marshal Hermann von Eichhorn, was assassinated when a bomb thrown by a Left Social Revolutionary exploded in his landau.

The two murders were done at the order of Spiridonova as part of a plot to provoke the Germans into marching upon Moscow to overthrow the Lenin regime and—so the plotters had it—appoint as the new rulers of Muscovy the only party that had consistently opposed the Bolsheviks: the Left Social Revolutionaries. But the Germans were not to be taken in: They had achieved their goals in Russia through the Treaty of Brest Litovsk, and they had more pressing problems on the western front where the *Kaiserschlacht* was falling short of its goals. When Lenin called at the Embassy to proffer his government's apologies, the German government duly accepted them.

Maria Spiridonova's insurrection appeared to have no connection with Savinkov's, but it served to trigger Savinkov's, probably prematurely. Backed by a regiment from the Pokrovsky Barracks, augmented by sailors on leave from the Fleet, counterrevolutionists—whether Spiridonova's or Savinkov's, or both— seized the headquarters of the State Bank, the Central Telephone and Telegraph Offices, the main Moscow train stations, and headquarters of the Cheka at 22 Lubyanka. In Petrograd, counterrevolutionists marched on the Smolny Convent but were unable to capture it. In twenty-three provincial cities, the counterrevolutionists struck with varying degrees of success.

In Moscow, the very ease of the first successes bred overconfidence, and when the insurrectionists later came up against opposition, they were unprepared for it. In the early evening a force marched on the Bolshoi Theater, but the mere presence of a few platoons of Red Guards was sufficient to turn it back. The appearance of two Lettish regiments loyal to the government and a force of armored cars prompted many of the counterrevolutionists either to melt away or to surrender. By midnight the counterrevolution had been "suppressed so quietly and completely that the great majority of citizens of Moscow did not know that it had happened." [10] In view of the outcome in Moscow, General Kaledin's force of Don Cossacks never began to march.

The only genuine success—however temporary—was achieved by Boris Savinkov himself. He led the forces that took over the rail center of Yaroslavl, 160 miles northeast of Moscow, where the railroad from the capital branched, one line going to Petrograd, the other to Archangel. The very choice of Yaroslavl as an objective would indicate that Savinkov expected that the Allied forces in North Russia would support him by landing at Archangel and driving south down the railroad. But no help came, and after two weeks of heavy fighting, the White forces at Yaroslavl were forced to surrender.

In the end, all that Maria Spiridonova, Reilly, and Savinkov accomplished was to set off what became known as the Terror. On the theory that Russia was engaged in a class war demanding far more ruthlessness than did conventional military conflict, Lenin himself authorized the Cheka to establish concentration camps, to seize anybody even remotely suspected of connection with counterrevolutionary organizations, and to execute them without trial. To a party functionary in the provinces, Joseph Stalin, Lenin telegraphed: "We are liquidating [the insurrection] mercilessly this very night, and we shall tell the people the whole truth; we are a hair's breadth from war. . . . Everywhere it is essential to crush mercilessly these pitiful and hysterical adventurers who have become tools in the hands of the counter-revolutionaries." [11]

Thousands upon thousands were swept up in a gigantic purge: members of the nobility, the aristocracy, the oligarchy, the bourgeoisie, and all of them were dragged before hastily created Special Revolutionary Tribunals.

"The Bolsheviks," Lockhart notified the British Foreign Office, "have established a rule of force and oppression unequalled in the history of autocracy"; aside from those executed "without even the mockery of a trial," thousands were "left to rot in the prisons under conditions to find a parallel to which one must turn to the darkest annals of Indian and Chinese history." [12]

Despite the harsh repression of the Terror, by midsummer of 1918 the young Bolshevik regime felt threatened from every direction. By the terms of the Treaty of Brest Litovsk, Finland had become independent, and German forces were in full control of the Baltic States—Estonia, Latvia, and Lithuania—the Polish territories, Belorussia, and the Ukraine. Apart from General Kaledin's Don Cossacks, there were strong White armies in the northwest threatening Petrograd and along lower reaches of the Volga, in the lower reaches of the Urals, and in Siberia. Little more than 400 miles east of Moscow was a strong force of 60,000 men known as the Czechoslovak Legion, which had fought against the Germans and had been on the way to Vladivostok for transfer to the western front when British and French agents had connived to turn the force to help the Whites. In the far north, British troops had seized another port, Archangel, and General Poole had again manipulated the local soviet into proclaiming a separate state; and in the far east, Japanese troops were landing at Vladivostok.

Sorely pressed, Lenin on July 29, 1918, took what appeared to be a grave step: he declared war on the western allies. "War has come once again," he declared, "and the enemy is Anglo-French imperialism." [13] Foreign Commissar Georgi Chicherin followed with an announcement that "a state of war" existed between the Soviet Republic and the governments of France, Great Britain, and the United States. The declarations sent Allied diplomats in Moscow, including the American consul general, DeWitt Clinton Poole, hastening to Chicherin's office at the corner of Spiridovka Street and Patriarch's Lane. Did a true state of war exist? Were all relations to be severed?

Even to officials trained in the vague diplomatic language of the Congress of Vienna, Chicherin's response was the height of obfuscation. In much the same manner as Trotsky declaring at Brest Litovsk a state of "no war, no peace," Chicherin declared that "there existed a state of defense rather than a state of war." He went on to explain that "In the new order of ideas established by my government, such a declaration need not entail a rupture of relations" and that the Soviet government wished to maintain relations with the Allied powers. [14]

The activities of the British worried Chicherin most of all. He sent a note to Poole, asking what the British had in mind. "Is it Britain's aim," he asked, "to destroy the most popular Government the world has ever known, the Soviets of the poor and the peasants?" He had to assume, wrote Chicherin, "that Great Britain intends to restore the worst tyranny in the world, odious Tsarism." Or, he continued, did Britain intend merely to seize a part of Russian territory?[15]

The confrontation continued when before daylight on August 5, 1918, Cheka agents forced their way into the British and French consulates, arrested close to 200 staff employees, and threatened to shoot them. The members of the foreign diplomatic community were released only after sharp protests from the British and French governments. Counting on diplomatic immunity for protection, Lockhart made no effort to leave Moscow, but Reilly—born a Russian—knew that he was in peril and with false Cheka credentials finessed his way past all controls to Petrograd. Disguised as a Norwegian seaman, he boarded a Norwegian freighter off the nearby naval base of Kronstadt.

On August 30, 1918, two incidents occurred that threw Bolshevik officials into even greater turmoil. In early morning, as the chief of the Cheka in Petrograd, Moisei S. Uritsky, was entering his headquarters, a military cadet shot and seriously wounded him. That evening, a few minutes after eight o'clock, as Lenin ended a speech to the workers of the Mihelson factory in Moscow, left the podium, and with short, rapid steps made his way through a clamoring and adoring crowd to an exit, a man named Novikov suddenly blocked his way while a woman, Fanny Kaplan, a Right Social Revolutionary, produced a pistol and fired three times. Gravely wounded, Lenin collapsed.

While guards seized the couple, others put Lenin into a car and drove him to the Kremlin, where he appeared to rally. He managed to walk up to his third-floor flat in one of the czar's old offices, but there he collapsed into a chair. When doctors arrived, they declared that his injuries might be fatal. A surgeon, Dr. Vladimir N. Rozanov, found that one bullet had shattered his left shoulder; a second had penetrated the apex of the left lung and passed between the spine and the gullet, missing the main arteries by a millimeter and coming to rest near the right sternoclavicular joint; the third had entered the right lower throat and was lodged close to the carotid artery. There was severe hemorrhaging into the left chest cavity, which caused such heavy pressure on the heart that during Dr. Rozanov's examination, Lenin's pulse and heartbeat were sometimes indiscernible.

As Lenin struggled for his life, the titular head of the Soviet state, President Yakov M. Sverdlov, took charge and intensified the Terror while the official Soviet news agency issued a statement to all party newspapers: "Each drop of Lenin's blood must be paid for by the bourgeoisie and the Whites in hundreds of deaths. The interests of the revolution demand the extermination of the bourgeoisie. They have no pity; it is time for us to be pitiless."[16]

At 3:30 A.M. on August 31, 1918, the Cheka arrested Lockhart in his suite in the Hotel Elite, took him at gunpoint to a room in the Lubyanka, and brought him face to face with Fanny Kaplan. The head of the Moscow Cheka, Jacob

Peters, conducted the interrogation, trying to establish a link between Lockhart and Kaplan. When at length he admitted failure, guards took Fanny Kaplan from the room and while she was in a state of fanatical ecstasy, dispatched her with a single bullet in the nape of the neck.

When daylight came, Foreign Commissar Chicherin, concerned about official British reaction, arranged Lockhart's release, and as Lockhart made his way back to the Hotel Elite, all Russia was caught up in a red blur. In Petrograd, the Cheka shot out of hand 512 hostages, including military officers, industrialists, and members of the aristocracy; at the nearby Kronstadt naval fortress, 500 hostages shot; in Moscow, sixty; in Perm, eighty shot; in Penza 154; in Nizhni Novgorod, forty-one. Proclaimed the deputy commander of the Cheka, Martyn Latsis, "we are engaged in exterminating the bourgeoisie as a class."[17]

Certain that Sidney George Reilly had had a hand in the shooting of the Cheka chieftain in Petrograd, and believing him to have taken refuge in the former British Embassy just off Palace Square in Petrograd, the Cheka stormed the old building, killed the naval attaché, Captain Francis N. A. Cromie, arrested everybody else, and ransacked the building for documents. In London, the British government moved swiftly to retaliate, arresting the "Plenipotentiary for Great Britain of the Russian People's Government," Maxim Litvinov, and twenty of his staff and throwing them into Brixton Prison. Foreign Minister Arthur Balfour demanded that the perpetrators of the "abominable outrage" in the old Embassy be punished, otherwise "His Majesty's Government will hold the members of the Soviet government individually responsible and will make every endeavour to secure that they shall be treated as outlaws by the governments of all civilized nations and that no place of refuge shall be left to them."[18] The War Cabinet instructed the First Lord of the Admiralty to send a special task force—five cruisers attended by nine destroyers and seven minesweepers—to the Baltic to be prepared to bombard Petrograd and instructed at least one British ambassador—not without a touch of irony—to inform his host government that a state of "no war, no peace" existed between Great Britain and the Soviet Republic.

The British response had no effect on the Cheka, which, having failed to catch Reilly, moved again against Lockhart, rearresting him on September 4, 1918. But concerned that Lockhart's execution might precipitate war with Britain, or at least reprisals against Litvinov, Chicherin again intervened, arranging Lockhart's transfer from the Lubyanka to the Kavaleria Korpus in the Kremlin. There Lockhart was provided a small flat formerly belonging to one of the czarina's ladies-in-waiting. Although informed that in time the Revolutionary Tribunal would prefer capital charges, Lockhart was treated well; he was given books to read and was allowed to receive his current mistress.

Under banner headlines, the official press on September 9, 1918, told of the discovery of a "sensational plot" involving "Allied complicity" to overthrow the Soviet government. Lockhart, said the account, had met at noon on August 14, 1918, with "the commander of one of the Soviet detachments in Moscow" in order "to organize a rebellion against the Soviet government in connection with the British landing on the [Murman Coast]." Although in Lockhart's pay, the Russian officer had betrayed him, disclosing "the whole scheme" to the Soviet authorities. Letters "on official British government notepaper" and bearing Lockhart's signature had been discovered, and it was claimed that in them he delegated the Russian officer "to act on behalf of the British government." The newspaper account stated that acting on this information, the Soviet police, on August 31, 1918, had broken up a conspiratorial meeting and had arrested Lockhart, although "some of the conspirators escaped and are now at large." [19]

In the sternest language, Foreign Minister Balfour demanded Lockhart's release, to which Chicherin replied that he would not be intimidated by imperialist robbers, murderers, and plotters. Yet that was bombast, for once Lenin recovered from his wounds sufficiently to be moved to the country to convalesce, Chicherin agreed to exchange Lockhart for Litvinov and his staff. Although Lockhart was put over the frontier on October 14, 1918, the Revolutionary Tribunal had the last word, sentencing both him and Reilly to death in absentia.

In London, the British government received Lockhart coolly but not without interest: he had, after all, behaved quite as well as Chinese Gordon had a generation earlier at Khartoum. But as with Gordon, Lockhart's crime was to have failed, and as French Ambassador Noulens had predicted, the government disavowed him. Once he had made his report, he was placed on the half-pay pension of a vice-consul and invited to take a long holiday on the Scottish moors.

## Chapter Two

Well before daylight on Sunday morning, November 25, 1917, eighteen days after Lenin and Trotsky had seized power in Russia, the first train to cross the Russo-Finnish frontier since the Bolshevik Revolution arrived at the Finland Station in Petrograd. Out of the gloom a British officer approached three men struggling with heavy luggage. Was one of them, he asked, Captain Pirie of the 4th Hussars? One was. Another was Sergeant Joseph Franklin, United States Marine Corps, a presidential messenger bearing secret mail for the American ambassador, and the other was a special agent of President Woodrow Wilson, Edgar Grant Sisson.

Learning that there was no vehicle from the American Embassy at the station, Sisson and Franklin accepted an invitation to ride into the city with the British officer. As they climbed into a Rolls-Royce tourer with open sides and canvas top, a spotlight shone on the Union Jack flying from the hood of the car. "The city is quiet," said the British officer. "The bolsheviks have control. We may hear shots, but they will mean nothing. Patrols fire into the air to keep their fingers warm, or just for deviltry." [1]

As the chauffeur drove through empty streets, ice chains rattled on the tourer's wheels, and flames from wood fires of Red Guard outposts flickered on dirty snow on the Field of Mars and Palace Square. Upon request, the driver dropped Sisson and Franklin at the Hotel de l'Europe, a long-renowned inn. Entering the great marble reception hall, the two men found it lit only with kerosene lanterns, and even though Sisson had made reservations, the lone receptionist explained that under orders of the Red Guard, the hotel could accept no new residents. He referred them to the command post of the Red Guard in the Hotel Astoria. There they found the reception hall littered with sleeping Red Guards. When the commander saw Sisson's and Franklin's laissez-passers, he showed them to an unheated room that had a bed but no mattress. By that time it was past four o'clock in the morning. Provided with a few blankets, the two men spread them on the carpeted floor, stretched out, and went to sleep.

It was ten o'clock when they awoke, yet it was only just getting light, for there were only five hours of daylight during a Petrograd winter. Washing face and hands in icy water, they descended and took their baggage into the street to find transport to the American Embassy, where a marine guard apologized that there had been no transport at the station: such was the chaos on the railroads that nobody knew when a train would arrive.

Sisson went immediately to the office of Ambassador David R. Francis, where he produced his Letter of Instructions from the president. It read in part: "We want nothing for ourselves and this very unselfishness carries with it an obligation of open dealing. Wherever the fundamental principles of Russian freedom are at stake, we stand ready to render such aid as lies in our power, but I want this helpfulness based upon request and not upon offer. Guard particularly against any effect of officious intrusion or meddling, and try to express the disinterested friendship that is our sole impulse."

When President Wilson wrote that letter on October 23, 1917, the provisional government of Alexander Kerensky had been in power. By the time Edgar Sisson reached Petrograd, the situation had so changed that Sisson would come to interpret his instructions far differently.

When called into the president's service upon the declaration of war against Germany in early 1917, Edgar Sisson was editor of the New York magazine *Cosmopolitan*. An accomplished writer of the far right, Sisson was severe in manner and prim and austere in appearance. Wearing a pince-nez, he resembled the very people he most detested: the Jewish Bolshevik terrorists.

Sisson's mission to Russia was an outgrowth of an earlier visit to Petrograd of a distinguished American, Elihu Root, a United States senator and former secretary of state and secretary of war, who had gone to Russia as an expression of the interest of the old republic for the new. Even though Catherine the Great had refused for thirty-three years following the American Revolution to recognize the United States, considering the new government to be dangerously revolutionary, the United States became the first country to recognize the new provisional government in Russia. Wilson sent teams of railroad experts to help restore the Russian transportation system, agronomists to help regenerate agriculture, and extended credits worth $325 million. Yet Wilson's overtures were less altruistic than he indicated in his letter of instructions to Sisson, for the underlying goal was to keep Russia in the war and prevent German reinforcement of the western front.

Sisson was on the high seas when Lenin and Trotsky seized power, an event that produced a sharp change in President Wilson's attitude toward Russia. The American press turned markedly hostile toward the Lenin regime as well, as did the State Department, the U.S. Army's Military Intelligence Division, the Treasury, and big business. Not only was there concern about the Bolsheviks making a separate peace with Germany, there was also the matter of Lenin's repudiation of foreign debts and investments, which for the United States involved, with interest, more than $636 million. As with Catherine the Great and the American Revolution, so Americans also feared the spread of the Bolshevik Revolution.

As laid down by President Wilson before the change in government, Sisson's mission was essentially propagandistic, as Sisson himself put it, to "sell" the United States to the Russian people in much the same way that a public relations man might "sell Quaker Oats and Ivory Soap."[2] To Sisson the change in Russian governments merely made his propaganda mission all the more important, so that he moved immediately to establish in Petrograd an official United States propaganda agency, the Amerikanski Bureau.

The Amerikanski Bureau occupied a suite of baronial proportions in the Hôtel de l'Europe, while Sisson opened branches in Moscow, Chita, Omsk, Ekaterin-burg, Kiev, Voronezh, Tambov, Odessa, and Tiflis. He employed both Americans and Russians in all the bureaus to distribute pamphlets and films subtly extolling the United States, and he had the cooperation of the thirty branches of the Russian Manufacturing Association, the 450 branches of the All-Russian Trade and Industry Association, the 700 branches of the Russian Cooperative Society, and the 650 branches of the Society of Municipal Employees. He also established a film division which distributed American motion pictures to 175 cinemas and virtually monopolized the four principal cinemas in Petrograd.

As the advent of the Bolshevik government convinced Sisson of the increased importance of his propaganda mission, so it convinced him also to broaden his mission to include intelligence. Having established such an extensive network of bureaus throughout European Russia, he was in an ideal position to become well informed about the country; and as he himself was later to note, he became involved "in one of the oddest minglings of double crossing and the matching of wits . . . that history can show."

If the United States was to begin an active struggle against the Lenin regime, the decision would be attributable in important degree to the work of Edgar Sisson and to one of the classic intelligence mysteries of the twentieth century: the Sisson Documents. The affair began for Sisson when the head of the American Red Cross in Russia, Colonel Raymond Robins, approached him with a set of documents which seemed to show that Lenin, Trotsky, and other Bolshevik leaders had been "the accredited and financed agents of Germany at the moment of their entrance into Russia." If the documents were authentic, they also seemed to provide considerable evidence that Lenin had executed the treaty of peace with Germany as part of the bargain struck with General Ludendorff for funds.

Since forgery for political ends was a major industry in Petrograd at the time, Sisson was from the first suspicious of the documents, particularly when Robins refused to reveal how or where he obtained them; but a few days later, on February 5, 1918, Ambassador Francis called Sisson to his office to tell him that the night before, a Petrograd journalist, Eugene Petrovitch Semenov, had shown him a letter written to Trotsky by the original head of the Bolshevik delegation at Brest Litovsk, Adolf Joffe, which contained a passage indicating that Trotsky was controlled by the Germans. In the letter, dated January 13, 1918, Joffe noted that the Germans were anxious "that complete harmony should prevail on the entire Russian front" so that they would "be in a position to take up their operations on the Western front on a very large scale."[3] Was the letter authentic? Or was it a forgery planted in an attempt by counterrevolutionaries to poison relations between the United States and the Soviet regime?

In checking, Sisson determined that the Bolsheviks had actually carried out actions requested in the letter. Checking further, he queried the British intelligence chief, Commander Boyce, about Semenov, whereupon Boyce said Semenov was "dependable and intelligently hostile to the Bolsheviks." Semenov, revealed Boyce, was the point of contact between two separate counterrevolutionary organizations that were operating against the Smolny Convent: the Brotherhood of Russian Truth, which was obtaining wiretaps on Bolshevik communications at the convent, and a group of Army and Navy officers who were operating inside the convent to reproduce documents. There could be no doubt that the wiretaps, at least, were authentic, for Boyce had run checks on them.

Following that conversation, Sisson entered into a full intelligence agreement with Boyce, to include providing part of the funds for the Smolny operation. It was a fateful alliance. It quite clearly provided Sisson with more intelligence material; but it was also destined to put Sisson under deep suspicion, for in time there would be charges that the documents passed to Sisson were forgeries, planted by the British Secret Intelligence Service to try to influence President Wilson to intervene against the Bolsheviks.

When Boyce left Petrograd for London, Sisson decided on a way to check the authenticity of the documents. Meeting with Semenov and the head of the wiretapping group, a Colonel Samsonov, Sisson arranged to obtain each day a list of the communications passing through Smolny. He would tick those he wanted to see for purposes of authentication, whereupon Semenov would arrange to remove the originals from the files, photograph them overnight, then return them to the cabinets. The procedure soon produced new items that appeared to show that Lenin and his colleagues were still taking German orders. Yet those documents and others were still photocopies which might be easily forged. The only way to make sure once and for all that they were authentic, Sisson decided, was to burgle the convent and obtain originals of documents of which he already had photographic copies.

According to Sisson's own version of events (a version confirmed independently by Semenov),[4] Semenov failed to greet the project "with any cries of enthusiasm at the outset." Yet Colonel Samsonov supported the project. As he and others of his group were aware, security at Smolny was poor. Journalists and diplomats were able to enter and depart the building virtually at will, and there were no restrictions on the naval and military officers who had been stealing and photographing documents. Once word came that Lenin intended to move the capital to Moscow, security appeared to deteriorate even further.

With Semenov won over, Sisson determined that the time to act was while the documents were being prepared for shipment to Moscow. When that time came, Semenov chose a Saturday night, March 2, 1918, when he calculated that the guards would be drunk. Entering a room where cases of documents were stored, Semenov's men painted signs on the cases indicating that they contained bullion. Once the guards smashed the cases to get at the bullion and found only paper, they left the cases open and the door to the room unlocked.

After dark the next evening, Semenov and his group delivered to Sisson "rather more than half the letters" that Sisson "had listed as desirable."[5] For two hours, Sisson, his assistant, Arthur Bullard, and some seven or eight Russians "sat around a large table, listing, checking, and reading" the stolen documents. When Sisson was satisfied that he had what he wanted, he "clasped each man by the hand, thanked him, and wished him safety and whatever good luck there could be in a clouded land." He also handed over $7,500 to be used to help the plotters to escape if detected. As Semenov would recall, Sisson declared: "I have nothing further to do here; I am going back."[6] Having made arrangements to use the Norwegian diplomatic pouch to get the documents out of Russia, on April 3, 1918, he reached Oslo, retrieved the documents, sent a 300-word cable to Washington, prepared a final report on his operations for the president, and prepared to leave for home.

Arriving in Washington on May 9, 1918, Sisson reported immediately to the chairman of the Committee on Public Information, George Creel, and to Secretary of State Robert Lansing, presenting them with both a report on what he would call "the German-Bolshevik conspiracy" and the documents he had acquired. That same evening, Creel took Sisson's report and the documents to the White House and gave them to President Wilson. There before the president lay the fruits of an incredible burglary: documents partly in Roman, partly in Gothic, and partly in Russian Cyrillic script. There were documents purporting to have originated in the offices of the German General Staff, the German Imperial Bank, the German secret service, and the German counterespionage service in Petrograd.

If the documents were authentic and Sisson's thesis was correct, the *Kaiserschlacht* had come about as a result of a cosmic German-Bolshevik plot. According to Sisson, the documents showed:

—that the heads of the bolshevik government—Lenin, Trotsky, and their associates—were German agents;

—that the Bolshevik Revolution was encouraged by the German General Staff and financed by the German Imperial Bank and other German financial institutions;

—that the treaty of Brest Litovsk was a betrayal of the Russian people by Lenin and Trotsky;

—that, in short, the bolshevik government was not an independent Russian government at all but a German puppet government acting solely in the interests of Germany and betraying the Russian people and Russia's allies for the benefit of the Imperial German Government.[7]

Those explosive accusations reached the White House even as President Wilson, under pressure from the British and the French, was trying to make up his mind about committing the United States to participate in military actions against Russia. The documents were circulated widely within the administration, and after the president in the summer of 1918 had reached his decision, the Committee on Public Information released a selection of the documents to the press and in October 1918 published them, along with an introduction by Sisson, in the pamphlet *The German-Bolshevik Conspiracy*. As a later scholar and ambassador to the Soviet Union, George F. Kennan, would note, publication was "made officially, in a United States government publication" and "there could be no question that the government backed the authenticity and significance of the material."[8]

Publication of excerpts of the documents and of the documents themselves produced a storm. It was a time when Americans, including their statesmen, saw Lenin as the embodiment of evil, who had embraced "a violent and total break with the past" to destroy "man's social and political heritage."[9] RUSSIANS SELL OUT TO THE GERMANS, read a headline in the New York *Times*; BOLSHEVIKI YIELD RUSSIA'S RICHES TO BERLIN.[10]

Yet as the years passed and wartime emotions cooled, most American scholars would come to accept that the Sisson Documents were forgeries. Was that indeed the case? What were the documents, and what did they contain?

As published, the Sisson Documents numbered sixty-eight state papers appearing to have emanated from Russian and German government agencies. Of that total, fifty-three were said by Sisson to have been taken from Bolshevik files during the raid on the Smolny Convent. The remainder were what were called the Alexeyev documents, provided by an agent of the former chief of staff of the czarist Army, which were unimportant, or odds and ends which Sisson had collected from various sources. Of the fifty-three Smolny documents, fifteen were originals and the rest photocopies.

If the documents were authentic, they clearly supported Sisson's accusations, for they included:

An order of the Imperial German Bank "allowing money to Comrades Lenin, Trotsky, and others for the propaganda of peace in Russia."

A protest to Lenin that "steps were not taken to destroy" the order.

A letter from the German General Staff "insisting" upon the election to the Central Committee of the Bolshevik Party of, among others, Lenin, Trotsky, Zinoviev, and Kamenev.

Notice from the Imperial German Bank that 50 million rubles in gold had been "put at the disposal of the representatives of the People's Commissars . . . to cover the cost of the keep of the Red Guards and the agitators in the country."

A series of documents showing that the Germans intended through connivance of Lenin and Trotsky to obtain control of Russian finance, industry, and markets and to exclude Britain, France, and the United States from all trade in coal, metallurgy, machine tools, oil, chemicals, and pharmaceuticals.[11]

The first attack on the authenticity of the documents came from the New York *Evening Post* during the course of the first newspaper publication in September 1918, an attack that was based on "confusion between the [old] Russian calendar and the German calendar";[12] there was a difference of thirteen days between the two. There followed a letter to President Wilson from the official Soviet government spokesman in New York, a Finnish-American, Santeri Nuorteva, branding the documents "brazen forgeries," but when Nuorteva was summoned to Washington by the Committee on Public Information, he proved to be uncertain and evasive and confessed to being "on the Bolshevik payroll."[13]

The most serious charge against the authenticity of the documents came from the British government, which had received copies of all Sisson's documents and more. On September 19, 1918, shortly before publication of the official pamphlet, Ambassador Walter Hines Page cabled from London that "the War Office, the Foreign Office, the Postal Censor and the Admiralty examined the material carefully and in a general way reached the decision that the documents which appeared to be genuine were old and not of any particular value, and those which had propaganda value were of doubtful character."[14]

Concerned by the British findings, George Creel decided, before publishing the documents in the official pamphlet, to submit them to expert analysis. Since publication date was but a few weeks away, the examination would have to be quick. At Creel's request, the National Board for Historical Research appointed two scholars to study the documents, who reported back at the end of eight days that "We have no hesitation in declaring that we see no reason to doubt the genuineness or authenticity of these fifty-three documents."[15]

Among the scholars who subsequently launched the strongest attacks on the documents, George F. Kennan stated that "unquestionably the documents were forgeries from beginning to end." He determined that to be the case because of "a number of their characteristics: in their historical implausability, in their implausability from the standpoint of government usage, and in a whole series of glaring technical weaknesses (handwriting, dating, language, form, etc.)." There were, said Kennan, three general reasons why he considered the documents to be forgeries:

No proper governmental inquiry was ever made into their authenticity.

The person or persons who produced the documents were well informed on what was going on inside the Smolny Institute . . . and were able to weave fact and fiction together in an unusually skillful and baffling manner.

There was just enough truth behind the general thesis that the Bolsheviki had "accepted German gold" to throw many people off the track and, apparently, to cause the Bolsheviks themselves to refrain from any attempt to refute the documents.

On the other hand, there was a considerable body of evidence in support of the authenticity of the Sisson Documents. The Bolsheviks did, for example, seek to refute the documents, for the propagandist Nuorteva was an official Bolshevik spokesman. Furthermore, when escaping from Russia in 1920, the man instrumental in obtaining most of the documents, the journalist Eugene Semenov, made a sworn statement to the American consul in Archangel accounting for their origin. After arriving in Paris in 1921, Semenov wrote an article for a Russian émigré newspaper setting out in detail the full story of how the documents were obtained. At the request of the U.S. Army's Military Intelligence Division and of J. Edgar Hoover of the Department of Justice, Edgar Sisson read and confirmed both the sworn statement and the article.[16]

In addition, contrary to Kennan's statement, the United States government did conduct a detailed investigation, not specifically into the Smolny documents provided by Sisson but into a similar set of thirty-nine documents acquired by representatives of the State Department in Russia. Those so closely resembled the Smolny documents in source, content, and form that, as the State Department put it, "the two stand or fall together."[17]

In a covering memorandum with the documents, the State Department referred to thirty-six other documents which its representatives had seen but had been unable to obtain; synopses of those documents were included. If authentic, the thirty-nine documents and the synopses of the others made clear that the director of the German Secret Intelligence Service, Colonel Walther Nicolai, and his chief representative in Russia, Rudolf Bauer, controlled the October Revolution and the Lenin government that emerged from it.

If the documents were genuine, they showed a degree of German direction of Lenin and Trotsky and German interference in Bolshevik affairs representing, if not total control, at least something close to it. That explained why the State Department made careful efforts to determine their authenticity. Much of that task was assigned to two handwriting experts on the staff of the Military Intelligence Division, Captains Harvey Given and James B. Green, whom the State Department described as "professional experts in handwriting of more than twenty years standing." Given and Green concluded: "We can find nothing that would in any wise indicate that any one of the documents in question is not genuine or did not originate from the institution indicated on the document itself."[18]

That report would appear to have been conclusive; but given the climate of the times—forgery was rife, and it was by no means beyond the resources of a first-rate intelligence service to assemble a combination of men and typewriters to create such a collection of documents—the State Department continued its inquiry by submitting the documents to the man who had brought the first collection to the United States, Edgar Sisson. Sisson found that historically and chronologically the second set of documents fitted the period to which they were related and that some of the signatures were the same as those on some of the Sisson Documents.

The State Department also considered the nature of the criticism that had been leveled at the Sisson collection. That criticism, a study revealed, had been directed exclusively at that part of the Sisson Documents known as Annex 1, which consisted of synopses of fifteen documents for which there were neither originals, photocopies, nor authenticated copies. In denouncing the entire Sisson collection as forgeries, the State Department found, the Bolshevik propagandist Nuorteva had in fact attacked only the synopses in the annex, for which Sisson had made no claims.

Further corroboration of the authenticity of the documents came from the former representative of the German intelligence service in Petrograd, Rudolf Bauer. To a representative of the State Department, Bauer revealed that the German General Staff had assisted in transporting to Petrograd not only Lenin but also Trotsky and other Bolshevik leaders and that in the aftermath of the October Revolution, he had "collaborated at Smolny" with the Bolshevik leadership. Following the revolution, Bauer said, he sent a staff of seven officers to Petrograd "personally to conduct the beginning of the Bolshevik work" in order to bring about "the complete fall of the Russian front." The group was supervised by a Major Guise from the German ambassador's staff in Stockholm, who made periodic visits to Petrograd for that purpose.[19]

A final piece of evidence, apparently overlooked by the State Department, emerged with declassification of the files of the Military Intelligence Division in the 1970s. It was a telegram dated April 15, 1918, from a certain Buckey, the division's representative in Rome.[20]

The telegram consisted of digests from the Italian intelligence service's wireless intercept and cryptanalytical branch, which revealed that between April 6 and 9, 1918, the Italians intercepted and unbuttoned a series of coded radio messages between the Germans and the Bolshevik government. The messages collectively demonstrated that even six months after the revolution, Lenin's government was still receiving orders from the Germans and was still requesting policy guidance. One of the intercepted messages corresponded exactly with the text of one of the German instructions to the Bolsheviks contained both in the State Department and Sisson collections of documents.

That substantially was the case for the authenticity of the documents but there was also the word of the head of the Committee on Public Information, George Creel. Sisson, wrote Creel, had resigned "a highly-salaried post to serve the Committee with its much lower government pay." Within a few weeks, Creel was "pleased with his sound judgment and executive ability." The documents which Sisson acquired, noted Creel, "while plausible enough . . . lacked substantiation, and he [Sisson] used them, very properly and wisely, only as a starting point." [21]

Sisson's principal point of contact, noted Creel, was Semenov, who was "head of a compact anti-German organization that had its representatives in the Smolny Institute." Many of those men were "clever and brave enough to hold positions on naval and military staffs and even in the Commissariat for Foreign Affairs" and thus had access to all files.

After Sisson brought the documents to Washington, wrote Creel, the government in the interval between Sisson's arrival in May and the time when they were sent to the printer in the fall submitted them "to every known test by various agencies of government, experts on ink, paper and typewriter type faces being called in." Even when "authenticity had been proved to the satisfaction of all, publication was still postponed out of the hope that the Bolsheviks would yet break away from their treacherous alliance." Instead of that, "the partnership intensified" and "the president ordered publication."

Publication of the documents, said Sisson, "brought about the first direct interference in our domestic affairs by Communist agents." The technique they used, he said, apparently referring to attacks on the authenticity of the Sisson Documents, was "much the same as that employed ever since: bold attack on whatever is said or done against them and the unceasing repetition of lies until they take on the look of truth."

What, then, was to be made of that queer and complicated affair? As is often the case in controversy, the truth probably lay somewhere between Creel's unqualified acceptance of the Sisson Documents and the view of those who attacked them, to the effect that:

There was no British plot to influence Wilson in favor of military intervention in Russia by planting false documents on Sisson, although the British probably did provide Sisson some documents on an opportunistic basis.

The Smolny documents were authentic; for apart from all else, there was too little time between February 27, 1918, when Sisson first mentioned the idea of a Smolny raid to Semenov, and March 2, 1918, when the raid was carried out, to manufacture sixty-eight documents, even in Petrograd, where forgery was a major industry.

President Wilson refused to permit a vigorous debate on the authenticity of the documents lest that expose the fact that a high American official had engaged in burglary and espionage in Russia.

There was a conspiracy between Lenin and Ludendorff—although Trotsky was not at first a party to it—that severely damaged Allied prospects for victory. Lenin was not, however, as Sisson claimed, a German agent; he was merely a consummate politician engaged in a marriage of convenience.

Whether the documents were forged or authentic, what really mattered was the effect they had, if any, on the evolution of American policy toward the Bolshevik regime. The chronology of events between January 1918, when Wilson and his administration first began to feel Allied pressure to join in an expedition to Russia, and July 1918, when Wilson finally made up his mind as to what he was to do, would suggest that the documents did have an effect. Until the end of May 1918, Wilson's position was consistent: he wanted nothing to do with any military undertaking in Russia. Then for the first time he began to consider seriously proposals to send American troops both to North Russia and Siberia. After that date, he agreed to permit massive arms shipments to the Whites in Siberia and tacitly encouraged the various war schemes of his allies against the Russians while appearing to disapprove of intervention. Within the Wilson administration, the reaction to the Sisson Documents was even more pronounced: the official attitude toward the Lenin regime hardened to the point that for many years all propositions that the United States recognize Bolshevik Russia were rejected. All trade, credit, and finance was officially disapproved, and Soviet representatives in the United States were regarded as criminals and treated as potential subversives.

The Sisson Documents thus produced an American antagonism for Russia that had few if any precedents in international intercourse during the previous century.

## Chapter Three

On May 14, 1918, two trains were drawn up at the railway station in Chelyabinsk in the eastern foothills of the Urals. One carried Hungarian soldiers freed from a prisoner-of-war camp in Siberia on their way back to Hungary. The other carried soldiers of the Czechoslovak Legion, a force created originally from a Czechoslovak minority living in Russia, then augmented by captured Czechoslovaks who wanted to turn against the Germans; the men were on their way to Vladivostok to board ship for passage to France to continue the fight against the Germans in the hope that the peace settlement would produce an independent Czechoslovakia.

When a Hungarian threw a piece of railroad coupling at the Czech train, mortally wounding a Czech soldier, hundreds of Czechs poured from their cars and lynched the Hungarian. A melee followed. When Lenin learned of it, he countermanded his order granting the Czechs passage to Vladivostok, directing instead that they be organized into labor battalions or conscripted into the Red Army. Vowing to fight their way to Vladivostok, the Czechs seized a necklace of frontier towns along the Trans-Siberian Railroad leading toward Vladivostok, raided local armories, and joined counterrevolutionary White forces gathering for war with the Reds.

The British propaganda machine quickly threw its vast and clever powers behind the Czechs. A rising young British statesman, Winston Churchill, spoke of the danger of the Czechs "being done to death by treacherous bolsheviks"[1] and likened them to the Scottish Archers of Louis XI, the Irish Brigade of Sarsfield, and the Swiss Guard of Louis XVI, those small bands of noble and heroic men who had stood and fought the forces of darkness and evil against impossible odds.[2] Yet the Czechoslovak Legion was, in reality, the strongest and best-armed military force in Russia, and its soldiers, far from being noble, were often no less brutish and murderous than were their adversaries.

The massive political warfare campaign generated by the western press demanding that the western powers send military forces to rescue the Czechs was but one of the pressures bearing down on President Wilson, who had so recently seen Sisson's report and the Sisson Documents; there were also domestic pressures, influential and demanding. Among them were banks and businesses with interests in Russia, including General Electic, the New York Life Insurance Company (which stood to lose over $67 million through Lenin's nationalization of the company's Russian subsidiary), the National City Bank of New York ($180 million), and thirty to forty other major industrial and capital concerns which had lost money and through various lobbies clamored for presidential action. A hundred different voices in the press and the Congress joined in a chorus demanding "intervention," a euphemism for military invasion. Only the military appeared to be against involvement in Russia: "Stay out of Russia altogether," advised the U.S. Army's chief of staff, General Peyton C. March.[3]

To those pressures the plight of the Czechs introduced, as Secretary of State Lansing put it, "a sentimental element into the question of our duty."[4] Meeting during the afternoon of Saturday, July 6, 1918, with Lansing, Secretary of War Newton D. Baker, Secretary of the Navy Josephus Daniels, and General March, the president announced that he had decided to send a reinforced regiment to North Russia and a light division to Siberia.

Just over a week later, on July 17, 1918, the president sat alone at his typewriter to compose a lengthy aide-mémoire for the Allied embassies, explaining the rationale for his fateful decision. In language redolent of weariness, anxiety, regret, and apology, he stated that "Military action is admissible in Russia . . . only to help the Czecho-Slovaks consolidate their forces and get into successful cooperation with their Slavic kinsmen and to steady any efforts at self-government or self-defense in which the Russians themselves may be willing to accept assistance."[5] It was a roundabout, politically conscious way of saying that he had acquiesced only because of the popular demand for help for the Czechoslovak Legion but that at the same time he wanted to see an end to the Bolshevik regime;

on the other hand, if that was to be accomplished, the Russian people, with minimal American—and Allied—help, would have to do the job themselves.

The American Expeditionary Force to North Russia consisted of the three battalions of the 339th Infantry Regiment, a battalion of engineers, and two companies of medical troops, a total of approximately 4,500 men. The infantry-men were mainly young conscripts, most of them of Polish-American origin, from Michigan and Wisconsin. They were noticeably callow and bewildered by their British uniforms, weapons, equipment, and rations, and few of them knew anything of North Russia or of their mission.

Sailing from England on August 25, 1918, the troops in all of three transports were soon afflicted by the Spanish influenza virus that was ravaging the world. By the time the transports reached Arctic waters, several hundred had been stricken and an officer and fifty-two men had died. As the men debarked at Archangel on September 4, 1918, in a dismal rain, ninety-two of them were so ill that they had to be brought ashore on stretchers.

It was a strange, exotic, Dantesque world in which the Americans found themselves. The troops of the Allied North Russian Expeditionary Force strolling down wooden sidewalks along Trotsky Prospekt beneath the gold, green, and white spires of the cathedral were polyglot and polychrome: Royal Marines in scarlet and khaki, French colonials in sky blue, Polish legionnaires in horizon blue, Norman marines with red pompons on their hats, Breton gunners wearing kepis, plumed British yeomanry, French-Canadian artillerymen, Italians, Serbs. The Russians who had congregated there seemed to be of infinitely varied extraction: German, Polish, Finnish, Lettish, Prussian, Lithuanian, Ukrainian. There were *starets* (holy men) and Diaghilev dancers, Muscovy dandies with tiny waists and long cigar holders, old retainers from the Winter Palace trudging behind their masters' carriages and carts, Mongols, Cossacks, carpetbaggers, and a troop of deformed dwarfs performing outside bars to earn their fare to New York.

In Archangel and Murmansk and the surrounding territory, the Americans soon discovered, the British commander, General Poole, had established, in effect, a British protectorate. A short, squarish man who wore a soft field cap, British Warm, jodphurs, riding boots, and spurs, and carried a crop, Poole believed implicitly that the British soldier was superior to all others. Having spent most of his career on the frontiers of the empire, he practiced with other nationalities that quaint mixture of patronage, paternalism, and ferocity that was characteristic of a long line of imperial soldiers. In the manner of British viceroys throughout the world, Poole manipulated and arranged the local political scene, soon convincing the head of the Murmansk soviet, Alexis M. Yuriev, a former ship's oiler and donkeyman, to declare independence of Moscow. After sending secret agents into Archangel to establish liaison with White leaders planning a coup d'état, Poole on the morning of August 2, 1918, staged an unopposed landing there and as at Murmansk, soon established his authority over a government headed by a moderate socialist, Nikolai Tchaikovsky, which called itself the Supreme Administration of the North. As with Yuriev, Poole convinced Tchaikovsky to renounce allegiance to Lenin's government.

General Poole's dealings with Colonel Stewart and his troops were from the start just as high-handed. Hardly had the men reached their barracks when Poole summoned Stewart and ordered him to prepare the regiment to move immediately into the line. While one battalion performed guard duty in Archangel, the other two were to join Allied drives under way down the railroad toward Vologda and up the Northern Dvina River toward Kotlas (Kirov), drives ostensibly aimed at establishing contact with the Czechoslovak Legion, which was thought to have turned toward the Arctic ports.

Colonel Stewart argued vigorously for time to put his command in order. Aside from the deprivations of illness, the men needed training and time to acclimatize. Moreover, he pointed out, the enemy was the Germans, not the Bolsheviks, and his orders were to engage in military operations only if the Russians themselves asked for assistance.

In response to that protest, Poole produced Tchaikovsky to ask Stewart for military assistance and showed him a message from Ambassador Francis to Secretary of State Lansing advising that he would "encourage American troops to obey the command of General Poole in his efforts to effect a junction with the Czechoslovaks."[6] At that point, Stewart considered that he had no alternative but to accede to Poole's demands. Within twenty-four hours of arrival in Archangel, two battalions were on the way to the front under British command while the other was performing guard duty. Stewart himself was "given quarters in a steam-heated building, modern and roomy, where he enjoyed considerable comfort and no authority."[7]

As it turned out, General Poole's days as viceroy to the Supreme Administration of the North were numbered. When Ambassador Francis informed Washington of Poole's methods, his telegram came to the attention of the president, who on September 9, 1918, directed Secretary of State Lansing "to tell the British government that unless Poole changed his whole attitude in dealing with the local government at Archangel, the American troops would be entirely withdrawn from his command."[8]

Not quite a month later, on October 10, 1918, General Poole announced that he had orders to return to England "for consultations." Although he asked Tchaikovsky to write a letter to the War Office asking that he be returned to Archangel, Tchaikovsky provided only a personal letter thanking him for his services. With that, General Poole boarded the naval yacht *Salvator*, saluted the crimson flag of Tchaikovsky's Socialist government, and sailed away.

President Wilson, meanwhile, informed Allied governments that no more American troops would be sent to Murmansk and Archangel and that "as far as our cooperation is concerned . . . all military effort in northern Russia [should] be given up except the guarding of the ports themselves and as much of the country round them as may develop threatening conditions." It was "plain," said Wilson, "that no gathering of any effective force by the Russians is to be hoped for."[9] It was a way of saying that his unstated objective in sending American troops to North Russia—to rally Russian opposition to the Bolshevik regime and restore the eastern front—was beyond reach.

Yet as the sky above Murmansk and Archangel began to turn a mustard yellow from ice crystals in high-altitude winds sweeping up from the Aral Sea, a harbinger of the Arctic winter with its breathtaking cold, near perpetual darkness, and intensely beautiful aurora borealis, American troops were still in the line. Along with their colleagues of various other nationalities, they began to build log blockhouses protected by great coils of barbed wire that soon would be buried in deep snow.

As evidence that a state of war still existed, an occasional crack of a sniper's rifle, the thud of mortars, and Bolshevik agents crept to the lips of the fireports to whisper to shivering soldiers hunched over their braziers: "The war with Germany has ended. Why are you not going home to be with your families? Why are you fighting the Russian Workers? They are your friends and allies."[10]

A native of Mount Calm, Texas, and a graduate of the United States Military Academy, William Sidney Graves had been on the General Staff in Washington through much of the World War, but at last, in mid-July 1918, he obtained an assignment that seemed to promise his joining the fight in France: commanding general of the 8th Infantry Division, in training at Camp Fremont, near Palo Alto, California. Yet hardly had General Graves become established at his new post when he received on the afternoon of August 2, 1918, a secret coded message from the War Department which when decrypted, revealed an order to "proceed to Kansas City, go to the Baltimore Hotel, and ask for the Secretary of War, and if he was not there . . . to wait until he arrived."[11] Graves found a train leaving in two hours. Unable to get Pullman accommodations, he was thoroughly fatigued by the time he reached Kansas City. As he arrived at the station, a porter met him with word that Secretary of War Baker was awaiting him in an anteroom. Their meeting was brief; the secretary had to catch a train that was leaving momentarily. Graves, said the secretary, was to command an American military force in Siberia. Baker handed him a sealed envelope. "This," he said, "contains the policy of the United States in Russia which you are to follow. Watch your step; you will be walking on eggs loaded with dynamite. God bless you and good-bye."[12]

When Graves reached his room in the Hotel Baltimore, he opened the envelope to find that it contained a copy of President Wilson's aide-mémoire to the Allied embassies, which had not yet been publicly released. After reading the document carefully, he went to bed. Although confident that he understood American policy, he still had trouble going to sleep. What was the policy of other nations? Why was he not given more information on what was happening in Siberia? One section of the aide-mémoire, in particular, stuck in his mind: ". . . the solemn assurance to the people of Russia, in the most public and solemn manner, that none of the Governments uniting in action in either Siberia or in Northern Russia contemplates any interference of any kind with the political sovereignty of Russia, any intervention in her internal affairs. . . ."

In the busy days that followed, Graves learned that the War Department was ordering to Vladivostok from the Philippines the 27th and 31st Infantry Regiments, a field hospital, an ambulance company, and a telegraph company, and that he was to send 5,000 men from Camp Fremont to bring the regiments to a full strength of approximately 9,000. Yet by the time he sailed from San Francisco on the U.S. Army transport *Thomas*, on the evening of August 14, 1918, he had received little more information about the situation in Siberia. He was, he would note later, "pitchforked into the melee at Vladivostok."[13]

It was just that at Vladivostok: a melee. While Graves was less than two days out of San Francisco, troops of the 27th and 31st Regiments had reached the port to step ashore on docks "piled with rotting war materials" against a backdrop of a city that aspired to the title "Lord of the East," with "imposing stone edifices and glittering church domes faced upon a background of overtopping hills."[14] There had been some Japanese troops in Siberia since April, the Americans discovered, and a few days earlier, large numbers of Japanese, a British battalion, and a small contingent of French officers had disembarked; but in advance of those, a vanguard of Czechs, arriving by way of the Trans-Siberian Railroad, had fought a pitched battle with Red Guards in Vladivostok's streets and established control. "White Russians by the trainloads" had piled into the city, with one after another among them professing to be the head of a new White government. "All public utilities were still out of order. The air reeked from ruin and neglect. Beneath bullet-riddled fronts along broad Svetlandskaya, piles of chipped stone and splintered glass still lay unswept from the streets."[15]

The vast region known as Siberia, extending over 4,000 miles from the Urals to Vladivostok, was a caldron. It was a region where the inhabitants were almost as wild as the vast stretches of untamed wilderness, as wont as not to take the law into their own hands. The population in the sparsely settled region had increased enormously: thousands of refugees from European Russia, former prisoners of war (Germans, Austrians, Hungarians), Chinese adventurers and bandits out to capitalize on the confusion, and hundreds upon hundreds of refugees from the czarist police, many of whom until the October Revolution had been residing in the United States. Amid that swollen population, secret agents everywhere: German, British, French, Japanese, Red, White. There were at least nineteen governments professing to be in control, all of them at that point ostensibly antibolshevik—Mensheviks, Left Socialist Revolutionaries, Right Socialist Revolutionaries, Monarchists—but at such odds that they sometimes tried to impose customs restrictions on each other. By the time American troops arrived, there still existed local soviets but not a single regional government loyal to Lenin. The Allied intervention contributed enormously to the upheaval, for contrary to President Wilson's exalted expression of neutrality, the British and French were openly trying to restore the eastern front and unseat the Bolsheviks, while the Japanese were engaged in raw imperialism.

As the first American troops reached Vladivostok, the senior Japanese commander, General Khuzo Otani, insisted to the senior American commander, Colonel Henry D. Styer, that all the Allied governments had placed their troops under his command. There was at least some truth to that, for President Wilson had agreed to subordinate American troops to Japanese command; but nobody had informed Colonel Styer of it, and when he cabled Washington for instructions, he received only a noncommittal reply saying that when General Graves arrived, he would have the proper instructions.

When General Graves did arrive, in September 1918, he had no more knowledge of Wilson's agreement to subordinate the troops to Japanese command than had Styer, and he refused, citing the instructions from his president to maintain strict neutrality. He ordered Colonel Styer's regiment into barracks at Khabarovsk, the northernmost point of the Trans-Siberian railroad, where it bore west to skirt the northern reaches of Manchuria. He stationed part of his other regiment in a town on the railway a few miles north of Vladivostok and held the rest of his troops in the port. In view of President Wilson's stricture of neutrality, there was little for the men to do except guard war stores, and that was no trying assignment. Who would steal rotting bales of cotton or crated automobiles for which there was no fuel? So the autumn passed and so too the grueling winter, but while the troops were often idle, their commander, General Graves, was fully occupied trying to counter criticism of his neutrality.

Ill-concealed conflict early developed with the State Department, whose diplomats were soon passing optimistic reports on a new government headed by Admiral Alexander Kolchak that had emerged in Eastern European Russia, while Graves was contending that the government could not last. State Department officials in Washington, while resenting President Wilson's refusal to take a more active role against the Bolsheviks, considered that Graves had far more latitude than he was willing to exercise.

The Kolchak government protested repeatedly against Graves' ardent neutrality. With the American consul at Kolchak's headquarters, Ernest L. Harris, openly advocating cooperation with Kolchak, what was wrong with Graves? So too the American Red Cross representative in Siberia, Dr. Rudolf Teusler; while shipping stores of Red Cross supplies to Kolchak, he spoke openly of the need to support him as an alternative to Bolshevism, comments that were all the more embarrassing to Graves because Teusler was Mrs. Wilson's cousin. The heads of the British and French military missions also protested, with the head of the British mission, Major General Alfred F. W. Knox, being particularly outspoken and working openly to get Graves relieved. The Japanese joined the chorus, often displaying their hostility to the American policy by causing trouble between their soldiers and the American troops.

General Graves' legion of detractors would have had his head except for strong support from antiinterventionists in the War Department, particularly Secretary of War Baker and the U.S. Army's chief of staff, General March. "Keep a stiff upper lip," March wrote Graves. "I am going to stand by you until hell freezes over." [16] The president, too, stood by him.

As opposed to Bolshevism as was anybody in the administration, Wilson nevertheless saw no solution in American military involvement in a Russian civil war: not only would it evoke violent protest from the American public but in his view the western powers were incapable of sending enough troops to do a job that only dedicated antibolshevik Russians could do for themselves. Yet the president also resisted bringing the American troops home, for that surely would precipitate collapse of the antibolsheviks and cement the Japanese position in Eastern Siberia. Besides, by that time, the British statesman Winston Churchill had imparted a new spirit to the antibolshevik campaign, a campaign conducted with such personal fervor that the British press promptly christened it "Mr. Churchill's private war."

## Chapter Four

On March 20, 1918, Winston Leonard Spencer Churchill, forty-four years of age and the minister of munitions in His Majesty's Government, visited the headquarters of the British Army in France in the downs near Saint-Omer. There the British commander in chief, Field Marshal Sir Douglas Haig, gave Churchill an intelligence briefing that was at once intriguing and distressing.

For some weeks, Haig related, there had been signals intelligence suggesting that the German armies in Flanders were being reinforced by as many as thirty divisions freed from the eastern front by the armistice concluded at Brest Litovsk. With a massive German offensive obviously in preparation, an indication developed on March 11, 1918, that it was imminent, for on that date the Radio Section of the U.S. Army Signal Corps had by chance detected that the Germans had suddenly placed in service an entirely new radio code.

All available specialists, said Haig, had been assigned the task of breaking the new code. That project had been helped by a second stroke of fortune when two days later the U.S. Army Signal Corps had intercepted a message sent in the old code, one the Allies had previously broken. The message was from a unit that had received a signal in the new code but had yet to master it and was unable to decipher the message; the unit asked that the message be repeated in the old code. By comparing the original message in the new code and the repetition in the old, the Allies were soon able to read the new code even before the Germans themselves were generally familiar with it. [1]

With the new code broken, British intelligence was able to establish that the Germans had massed 110 divisions against fifty-seven defending British divisions, and at some points along the line the British were outnumbered by four bayonets to one. British intelligence also learned that the Germans were aiming not at their usual objective—the French capital, Paris—but at the Channel ports. In both Haig and Churchill that realization resurrected an ancient British fear: a Teuton army facing them across the Narrow Seas.

In a somber and worried mood, Churchill left Haig to travel on to a ruined village about seven miles behind the front to dine at the headquarters of a longtime friend, the commander of the 9th Division, Major General Henry Tudor, whose division stood astride one of the main routes to the Channel ports. Much of the dinner conversation concerned the Russian defection and the grave position in which it placed the Allied armies. Never in the modern history of great powers, said Churchill, had there been such treachery.

Shortly after 10:00 P.M., Churchill left Tudor's mess and rode in a blacked-out staff car to a damaged farmhouse where he was to stay the night. The evening was cool and pleasant, still except for the sound of the car's motor and the occasional sizzle of a star shell or parachute flare.

At a few minutes after 4:00 A.M., Churchill awoke with a start. He would never be able to say what had disturbed him. Perhaps it was the extraordinary tension in the atmosphere, some premonition. Yet the night remained still, and a glance out a window revealed that a heavy ground fog had gathered. He was still lying awake on his camp cot when at exactly 4:30 A.M. the predawn twilight erupted in flickering flashes that resembled the Northern Lights and in a storm of rumbles and explosions that reminded Churchill of an angry Vesuvius. The field telephone at his bedside rang; it was Tudor announcing that the German offensive had begun and that German infantrymen were already through the first maze of barbed wire.

"Exactly as a pianist runs his hands across the keyboard from treble to bass," Churchill would write later, "there rose in less than one minute the most tremendous cannonade I shall ever hear."[2] It was the harbinger of "the greatest onslaught in the history of the world."[3] Over 6,000 German cannon were firing; gigantic land mines planted under British trenches by molelike sappers were erupting with earth-trembling explosions; 800 aircraft, 600 tanks, and three-quarters of a million men were on the move. It was the *Kaiserschlacht*, the offensive with which Ludendorff intended to end the World War in German victory.

Although Churchill asked permission to remain at Tudor's headquarters to watch the offensive unfold, his personal assistant, the Duke of Westminster, urged him to leave lest he be captured. After a quick breakfast, he departed for Dieppe, where he boarded a destroyer for England. By evening the Germans had overwhelmed Tudor's headquarters and cut the retreat roads to the Channel ports.

Churchill arrived in London shortly after noon on March 23, 1918. That same evening he entertained the chief of the Imperial General Staff, Sir Henry Hughes Wilson, and Prime Minister David Lloyd George at his home on Eccleston Square. "I never remember in the whole course of the war," he would record later, "a more anxious evening."[4] So real was the likelihood that France would be knocked out of the war and the British out of France that it produced, in Churchill's words, "a lasting imprint on British political history."[5] The specter of losing the war and even of invasion of the British Isles hung over the gathering.

.    .    .

The battle then joined in France turned out to be one of the greatest clashes of arms in the entire bloody course of the Great War. In it, Britain would lose 28,182 killed, 181,339 wounded, and 93,403 missing and captured, a total of more than 300,000 men, and it would turn out to be but the first of five great German offensives. In the end, Allied arms, infused with fresh blood from the New World, would prevail, but in the words of the Duke of Wellington after Waterloo, it was "a damned serious business . . . the nearest-run thing you ever saw in your life." That alone would have been sufficient for the British to condemn Lenin for treachery and respond accordingly, but there were yet other reasons for the hostility with which the British ruling class regarded the Bolshevik regime.

Besides the inbred aversion of the aristocracy and the oligarchy for Marxism, there were fears for the empire. Covering a quarter of the globe, a population of almost 600 million made the empire at least three times larger than either Russia or the United States. Yet that vast dominion of subject peoples ruled by a king, by a few agile brains, and by the bayonets of a few regiments with illustrious flags was peculiarly susceptible to infection from Bolshevism, that "plague bacillus," as Churchill was to label Lenin's dogma. If the infection should fester among the working classes of the homeland and the empire, the very institutions that combined to give Britain its special strength would be imperiled: the Parliament, the church, the schools, the banks, the commerce, the Navy, the Army, the Mercantile Marine. So, too, the royal traditions and even the monarch, King George V, and his dynasty.

For Winston Churchill himself there were multiple reasons behind his implacable antipathy to Bolshevism: it was a detestation intrinsic to his ancestry, his education, his career, his politics, his class. For the man who would emerge as the world's leading antibolshevik spokesman for the next thirty years was himself a member of the purple that he so cherished. He had gone to Harrow, which had educated eight of Britain's forty-odd prime ministers and countless other imperial leaders. He had attended the Royal Military College at Sandhurst, in the Surrey woods near London, where the aim was to make "truly superior persons."[6]

He had served in the 4th Hussars, a very tribal regiment crammed with young bluebloods, and he had joined the Carlton Club, a central citadel of toryism and privilege. He had fought for the empire on foot and horse in the Punjab, the Malakand, the Tirah, against the dervishes on the Nile, and at Khartoum. He had been a lieutenant with the Light Horse, and he had been present at the capture of Pretoria and at long-forgotten imperial battles. He had been undersecretary for the colonies and president of that most colonial of British political institutions, the Board of Trade. As home secretary, he had directed the hunting down of Bolsheviks, Syndicalists, Maximalists, Communists, Nihilists, and Anarchists, that small host of leftist sects that lurked about the alleyways of London. He had been chancellor of the Duchy of Lancaster and as First Lord of the admiralty had presided over warships carrying the Union Jack majestically about the world.

Churchill's detestation of the red was not only political; it was also personal. He called Bolsheviks "vipers" and "baboons"; and on Lenin he delivered a master-piece of invective: "Implacable vengeance, rising from a frozen pity in a tranquil sensible, matter-of-fact, good-humored integument! His weapon logic; his mood opportunist. His sympathies cold and wide as the Arctic Ocean; his hatreds tight as the hangman's noose. His purpose to save the world; his method to blow it up."[7]

For Churchill, the grim reality of the Bolshevik threat had already been demonstrated by the abdication of Czar Nicholas II. Yet that was but the beginning, for Bolshevism would soon demonstrate its inability to live with royalty, even royalty deposed.

In July 1918, the Cheka was holding Nicholas II and his family in Ekaterinburg (Sverdlovsk), a mining and rail town in the eastern foothills of the Urals. While the Romanovs idled away their time in the House of Special Designation, as the Cheka called a two-story villa in which they were held, their ultimate fate presented Lenin with a grave problem. Through German agents with whom he had dealt before his return to Petrograd, he had assured Kaiser Wilhelm II, first cousin of the czarina, that no harm would befall either Nicholas or his family, an assurance that had been basic to German support of the Bolsheviks. Yet there were some among the Bolshevik hierarchy who disapproved that promise. Trotsky, for example, recalling the words of the Jacobin Jean Paul Marat—"Woe betide the revolution which has not enough courage to behead the symbol of the *ancien régime*"—demanded that the czar be brought before a revolutionary tribunal at which Trotsky himself would play the role of chief prosecutor.

Aside from his promise to the kaiser, Lenin had to consider warnings from the American and British governments of dire political dangers if the Soviets should harm the czar. The British even offered to help Lenin resolve his dilemma by "rescuing" the imperial family.

The approach of the Czechoslovak Legion toward Ekaterinburg, which would almost certainly result in liberating the czars, compelled Lenin to come to a decision. In the second week of July, he summoned the regional commissar for war at Ekaterinburg, Chaya Goloshchokin, to Moscow for consultations, where in meetings with the head of the Cheka, Feliks Derzhinski, and the chief of the Moscow branch, Jacob Peters, the decision was taken: the czar was to die.

As determined by one of the triumvirs of British intelligence at the time, Basil Thomson, whose report on the matter to the United States government would be made public only in 1978, the Bolsheviks dared not allow the czar to live; as Lenin put it, "The worldwide bourgeoisie would have used his name to crush the communistic party and check its growth in all countries."[8] The death warrant, Thomson would determine, was sealed on July 16. "It was," Thomson reported, "simply an order of the Soviet Republic to execute 'Nicholas Romanoff, the Bloody, and all his family.'" It was signed, "Soviet of Workmen's, Peasants' and Soldiers' Deputies"; plainly nobody wanted his signature on it.

At one o'clock in the morning of July 17, 1918, the chief of the Cheka guard at the House of Special Designation, Yakov Yurovsky, awakened the czar. The Czechs, he said, were expected to break into the town before daybreak. "It would be better for you and your family," Yurovsky said, "to come down into the cellar, as there may be fighting in the streets and stray bullets may come through the windows."

In a dining room lit by stable lanterns, the imperial family assembled: the czar, the czarina, the fourteen-year-old Czarevich Alexis, and the grand duchesses— ages seventeen to twenty-one—Olga, Tatiana, Maria, and Anastasia. With them were four members of the royal suite, including the czarevich's physician, Dr. Yevgeny Botkin, and a maid, Anna Demedova.

With the czarina on his arm, the czar led the way into the cellar, a half-basement with windows, while one of the duchesses carried the hemophiliac czarevich. When one of the soldiers raised his lantern to light the way, he noticed that the Grand Duchess Tatiana was carrying her Pekingese dog, which was licking her face.

With a number of the soldiers, Yurovsky followed down the stairs. As the imperial family clustered at one end of the cellar, two of the soldiers drew their revolvers, "the first intimation to the prisoners of their impending fate." Crossing herself, the czarina covered her face with her hands and along with the other ladies, fell to her knees. Yurovsky, his face pale, drew out a paper and by the light of a lantern held by a soldier, began to read the writ of execution. The czar stepped quickly to a position in front of the others, "as if to shield them, and said something that was drowned by Yurovsky's voice echoing in that small chamber."

Concerned lest some appeal by the czar have an effect on the soldiers, "Yurovsky drew his revolver and shot the czar through the brain." That set off wild shooting by the soldiers; in a matter of moments all the imperial family had fallen, and only Tatiana and the maid, Demedova, remained alive. Wounded, Tatiana had fainted; "her little dog was on her body barking furiously" until one of the soldiers killed it. Using a cushion, Anna Demedova flayed at the muzzles of the weapons, sending bullets ricocheting against the walls. A bullet fired point-blank killed her. When the Grand Duchess Tatiana cried out "Mother! Mother!", three soldiers bayoneted her body and beat out her brains with their rifle butts.

Wrapping the corpses in blankets, the soldiers loaded them into a truck in the courtyard and drove to the Isetsky mine in the forest of Kopchiki, about twelve miles northeast of Ekaterinburg. There Yurovsky's men built a pyre, drenched it with petrol, placed the corpses on top, and set it afire. When the fire died out hours later, they drenched the remains with sulphuric acid, then smashed the bones and scattered them in the forest. All that White forces found later were several strips of petticoat, stays from a corset, a few precious stones, some jewelry, some false teeth, one of the czar's military decorations, a finger, a few small charred bones, a piece of the lower part of a human spine, and the skeleton of a small dog with a bullet hole in the skull.

The Romanovs were gone. To a stunned and horrified world, the question was, which of the royal houses would be next?

• • •

Of Erich Ludendorff, his doctor would say: "He was a man blind in spirit. He had never seen a flower bloom, never heard a bird sing, never watched the sun set. I used to treat him for his soul."[9] He grew up under the influence of a colorless middle-class father who had served as a reserve officer in the Franco-Prussian War and so prided himself on the experience that his study contained no books, no paintings, nothing but mementos of the campaign: a sword, a cartridge for a *mitrailleuse*, a piece of wallpaper from Château Bellevue near Sedan. Once Ludendorff entered the Army through the hard school of the cadet corps, his work became both his profession and his obsession. He was a young major general when early in the World War disaster threatened on the eastern front; too junior to assume direct command, he was well served by that system of dual commanders unique to the German Army, whereby elderly officers or those of royal blood were accommodated in their desire for the ceremonial attributes of command while as chief of staff, a younger, more capable officer wielded the actual authority on the battlefield. Having settled on Ludendorff to go to the eastern front, the General Staff called the elderly Field Marshal von Hindenburg from retirement to serve as titular commander on that front; when von Hindenburg in 1916 assumed the post of chief of the General Staff of the Field Armies and focused on the western front, the key figure still was Ludendorff. Since it would be awkward to have a chief of staff to a chief of staff, he took the title of first quartermaster-general, a traditional post in the Prussian Army that contrary to the title, had little to do with supply.

On September 28, 1918, at the behest of the kaiser, who wanted "an open and unequivocal declaration of military possibilities,"[10] Ludendorff left the field for Imperial Headquarters in the Belgian mineral springs resort of Spa. In his suite on the second floor of the Grand Hotel Britannique, he began to consider what he would tell the kaiser on the morrow.

There would be little that was good to report. All five blows of the *Kaiserschlacht* had failed and at tremendous cost, and almost everywhere the German armies were in retreat before an Allied force swollen by ever-increasing divisions of fresh American troops. Indeed, everything was going badly. Bulgaria had already asked for terms, and Turkey and the Austro-Hungarian Empire were also looking for a way out of the war. German politicians were faltering, members of the Reichstag demanding extensive changes in the Cabinet. The very fact that the kaiser had called for a candid report on the military situation indicated that his will was weakening. The year before there had been a mutiny in the Fleet, and every report from inside Germany spoke of impending revolution on the home front.

Dwelling on accumulated miseries, real and imagined, Ludendorff felt hopeless. The instrument of power—his beloved Army—was broken, yet there was no end to the labors the government wanted it to perform. He felt betrayed and as he himself would later put it, stabbed in the back. Striding about the suite, he railed at politicians, Freemasons, Jews, Jesuits, the kaiser, his own staff, the Navy for its blind faith in the overrated submarine. As his anger mounted, he came to a conclusion: there was but one way out, an armistice, a chance for the Army to regroup, and with not a moment to lose lest the Army on the western front collapse at any moment. Ludendorff, the man of iron will, had lost his nerve.

That evening, pale and shaken, he went to the suite below to talk with von Hindenburg. He saw no alternative, said Ludendorff, to telling the kaiser that he should seek an armistice. That would mean falling back behind the German frontier in the west and probably relinquishing Alsace and Lorraine to France, but since the Allied powers were obsessed with fear of Bolshevism, they might be persuaded to let Germany hold on to its gains in the east. As was usual when von Hindenburg's chief subordinate proposed something, von Hindenburg agreed.

Telling the kaiser the doleful news the next day, they suggested that Germany make a direct approach to President Wilson on the basis of Fourteen Points which the American president had earlier proposed as starting points for achieving peace. So informed by his military chiefs, the kaiser felt obliged to concur, but since he saw no prospect of any Allied statesman's treating with the current German government, he appointed a new chancellor, Prince Max of Baden, who had established an international reputation for moderation.

When the peace feeler went out, the German authorities found that Wilson was far less inclined to quick acceptance than they had supposed. Having at long last entered the war, the American public was in no mood to let the Germans off without punishment. However war-weary Britain and France, their leaders were of a like mind and grew increasingly bitter over Wilson's failure to consult them before responding to the German approach. Under pressure generated at home and abroad, Wilson equivocated, and as several notes passed between Washington and Berlin over the next few weeks, his position became increasingly firm. On October 23, 1918, he noted that "the only armistice he would feel justified in submitting for consideration would be one leaving Germany incapable of renewing hostilities."[11]

By that time, Ludendorff had recovered his nerve. As so often in the era of mass armies, he had depended too much on reports that crossed his desk, too little on his own observations in the field. The troops, he had discovered, still had fight in them. Furthermore, the kind of harsh armistice that Wilson was proposing had never entered his thinking. He urged the kaiser to reject the terms and get on with the war.

The man whose collapse of will had precipitated the crisis had turned around too late, for his demand that the kaiser seek an armistice had unalterably furthered the malaise that afflicted the home front. There was no room in the government, the new chancellor, Prince Max of Baden, told the kaiser, for both him and Ludendorff. On October 26, 1918, the kaiser summoned Ludendorff to Berlin and announced curtly that his resignation would be acceptable. Deeply hurt, Ludendorff returned to Spa to take leave of his colleagues and in time went to Sweden in temporary self-imposed exile.

Yet Ludendorff's dismissal did nothing to alter the sense of disillusionment that the news of impending defeat had brought to the German nation. Even as the armies at the front were regaining their spirit, the people at home saw no hope; they were "suddenly blinded by too much light after too long a darkness."[12] Cries of betrayal echoed through the corridors of the Reichstag and across the country, and as a clamor arose for the kaiser's abdication, the fabric of German society began to fall apart.

Nine months had passed since the war in Russia had ended with the treaty of Brest Litovsk and eight months since Adolf Joffe had arrived as the first Soviet representative (the Bolshevik equivalent of ambassador) to Berlin. One of Joffe's first acts was to negotiate with the German Foreign Ministry for the release of a German Bolshevik, Karl Liebknecht, the son of a man who had been a friend of Karl Marx, from Luckau jail. Liebknecht had formed an organization called the Spartakusbund, after the Roman gladiator who had freed the slaves during the Third Servile War in 72 B.C., a name which Liebknecht chose to symbolize the modern wage slave at war with his capitalist masters. At one of the early meetings of the Spartakusbund in 1916, Liebknecht had denounced the war, the government, and the kaiser and had gone to jail under a four-year sentence for contumacy.

Released from prison, he returned in the role of vindicated prophet to a Berlin in ferment, where in every machine shop, every *Bierstube*, every *Kaffeehaus*, workers reduced to a food ration averaging only a thousand calories a day were demanding peace. It was a milieu made for a Liebknecht and for a Joffe, who from the old Russian Imperial Embassy at 7 Unter den Linden, where the Red flag with gold hammer and sickle had replaced the Cross of St. Andrew, was dispensing 10 million rubles to produce a revolution and a dictatorship of the proletariat.

But Joffe was too openly interested less in diplomacy than in revolution; his days in Germany were numbered. The excuse to get rid of him came when porters at the Friedrichstrasse railroad station dropped a Russian diplomatic box, which split open and spilled leaflets across the platform, leaflets designed to incite revolution among the workers. While apologizing for the "accident" to the diplomatic box, the German Foreign Ministry ordered him to leave Berlin and terminated diplomatic relations with Russia.

When Joffe departed on November 19, 1918, he could note that revolution was already under way, and in Moscow Lenin was jubilant. "Things have so accelerated in Germany," Lenin declared, "that we must not lag behind . . . The international revolution has approached within a week to within a distance that it is to be reckoned with as an event of the immediate future."[13]

As in Petrograd, the revolution began with the sailors. Disturbed over the prospect of an armistice, on October 28, 1918, the German Naval High Command ordered the entire High Seas Fleet to assemble in Schillig Roadstead and await secret orders. The orders quickly became known to the crews of the battleships *Helgoland* and *Thüringen*: the Fleet was to make a night attack against Britain's Grand Fleet, which was in the English Channel off Dunkirk. Rumors spread throughout the Fleet that the kaiser was soon to arrive aboard his flagship, the battleship *Baden*, to lead them in one last glorious *Götterdämmerung* against the British, in which the kaiser and his officers would fight to the death. As an officer aboard the *Helgoland*, Lieutenant Friedrich Fikentscher, would record: "A state of indescribable confusion and despair prevailed among the crews." The cry passed from deck to deck, from ship to ship: "So near peace! So near death!" Agitators among the crews "demanded with boundless fury that the ships be prevented from going out and succeeded at once in winning the timid and stupid to their side."[14]

Some of the crews refused to take their ships through the locks; others doused the boilerroom fires; and aboard the *Thüringen*, 400 men rioted. Although the rioters were arrested, the rest of the crew took to its hammocks. On other ships, there was sabotage in the power systems for raising anchors, operating the guns and ammunition hoists, powering the signal equipment, and lighting the ships. Over the next few days, as officers sought to regain control, agitators liberally disbursing rum kept passions inflamed. Red flags appeared on some mastheads, and loyal and disloyal ships trained their guns and torpedo tubes on each other.

The commander in chief of the Fleet made preparations to sink the *Thüringen*, but at the last moment before torpedos were to be launched, the mutineers surrendered. By late evening of October 31, 1918, the mutiny appeared to be under control, but as 500 arrested sailors were transferred by packet boats to be held in brigs ashore, they shouted to dockworkers that they were about to be shot. The story spread rapidly up and down the Baltic coast. Within hours sailors, soldiers, and workers began to form soviets; they seized control of Kiel, Bremen, Hannover, and most of the main Baltic ports. Red flags appeared over the town halls of Hamburg, Cuxhaven, Lübeck, and many another northern city.

By November 9, 1918, the revolt had spread to Berlin, where workers from the factories throughout the city went on strike and marched by the thousands on the Reichstag to demand the kaiser's abdication. Among the demonstrators was Liebknecht, pulled through the streets by a group of soldiers in a flower-bedecked carriage.

Liebknecht in time made his way to the Imperial Palace, which was deserted except for a caretaker. Going to the balcony from which the kaiser was accustomed to address his subjects, he proclaimed to an imaginary audience: "The day of liberty has dawned. A Hohenzollern will never again stand at this place . . . I proclaim the free socialist republic of Germany . . . the new order of the proletariat."

In a final act of contempt for the monarchy, Liebknecht went to the kaiser's bedchamber where, as a young correspondent for the Chicago *Daily News*, Ben Hecht, reported, he undressed to his combinations. "Some of its buttons were missing," noted Hecht, "and the flap on the seat was baggy from too much laundering." Liebknecht climbed into the kaiser's bed, and Hecht "heard the royal bedsprings creak as Liebknecht stretched out his legs."[15]

In the Reichstag on that tumultuous day, Social Democrats withdrew their support from Prince Max's government in order to be free to contend with the Bolsheviks for leadership of the revolution, and by nightfall, the authority of the state had passed to the mob. Although the government tried to calm the demonstrators by announcing that a delegation headed by a prominent politician, Matthias Erzberger, had already left Berlin for the western front to arrange an armistice, neither that news nor the start of a light snowfall stilled the vast crowds.

At Imperial Headquarters in Spa, Erzberger found von Hindenburg determined that the General Staff should play no part in the armistice negotiations. Believing that the Allies would prefer to treat with civilians in any case, Erzberger set out for the Forest of Compiègne in France in a car draped with white flags and carrying a soldier on the runningboard to blow a bugle to clear the lanes of sheep and goats. For his troubles, he would eventually be murdered, while the German General Staff could maintain that the Army had never capitulated and, by inference, that "the laurels of victory had been snatched from its pure brow by the dirty fingers of democracy."[16]

There remained the problem of the kaiser, for without his abdication, a Bolshevik revolution as complete as that in Russia appeared inevitable. To Ludendorff's successor, General Wilhelm Groener, fell the task of informing the kaiser at a Crown Council in Spa on the morning of November 9, 1918, that he no longer had the allegiance of the Army. What, demanded the kaiser, had become of the *Fahneneid*, the ancient oath of the Teuton knights which required every soldier to obey the emperor even unto death? "Sire," Groener responded, "the oath on the colors is now but a fiction."[17]

Perhaps after a good meal and a cigar, said the kaiser, the situation would look better. Yet when the Crown Council resumed, there was only added gloom, for word had come that Prince Max of Baden, looking down in Berlin on tens of thousands of striking workers waving red flags, had proclaimed that the kaiser had already abdicated, then handed his powers as chancellor to a Social Democrat, Friedrich Ebert, who had formed a provisional government and promptly proclaimed a republic.

The next morning, Wilhelm II presented his baton for the last time as Emperor of Germany, King of Prussia, and Supreme War Lord, released his officers from their oath, and climbed aboard his cream-and-gold train for exile in Holland. The second of Europe's great dynasties had fallen. Would another follow? The answer quite clearly was yes, for events had long been under way in the Austro-Hungarian Empire indicating that, like those of the Romanovs and the Hohenzollerns, the days of the Hapsburgs were numbered.

Ever since 1867, when the Emperor Franz Josef had been compelled to accept the concept of the Dual Monarchy, whereby as head of the House of Hapsburg he ruled as emperor of Austria and as king of Hungary, it had been said that only respect and love for the emperor held the empire together. Even though the total size of the empire was smaller than the state of Texas, it embraced, in addition to Austria and Hungary, the regions of Bohemia, Moravia, Slovakia, Galicia, Transylvania, Slavonia, Croatia, Bosnia, Dalmatia, Herzegovina, and Carniola and encompassed no less than ten ethnic groups, thus making it peculiarly susceptible to new political doctrines. Amid a population of some 62 million, there were 10 million Germans, 10 million Magyars (Hungarians), 5 million Poles, and from 1 to 2 million Czechs, Slovaks, Slovenes, Croations, Rumanians, Ukrainians, Romansch, and Italians, among whom the Czechs and Slovaks made common cause, as did the so-called South Slavs: the Croatians, Serbians, and Slovenes. As it was said, Franz Joseph kept those diverse peoples united as an empire by maintaining each ethnic group "in a condition of even and well-modulated discontent." So long as the emperor lived, quipped the patrons of the coffee houses in Vienna, Budapest, and Prague, "conditions [might be] hopeless but not serious."[18]

On November 21, 1916, in the sixty-eighth year of his reign and the eighty-seventh of his life, the emperor died a gentle death. Since the original heir-apparent, the Archduke Franz Ferdinand, had fallen to an assassin's bullet in 1914 at Sarajevo in Bosnia, the event that had set off the Great War, the successor was the son of Archduke Otto, twenty-nine-year-old Karl I. That Karl was hardly the man to fill the old emperor's shoes was symbolically apparent at his coronation as Charles IV of Hungary when the great crown of St. Stephen came down so low on his small head that it covered his eyes, and the royal mantle appeared to weight down the young monarch's boyishly narrow shoulders.

For the new ruler, the obvious first goal was to bring peace to a realm that was suffering mightily from the Allied naval blockade. There had never been much support for the war in any case: the ultimatum to Serbia had been a German-backed bluff that had miscarried, and once the threat of the czar's legions had been turned back, what possible excuse was there for continuing to fight? For the Germans within the empire, the ever-increasing highhandedness of the kaiser in the supposedly equal alliance of the Central Powers was galling, and for the Slavs, there was never any enthusiasm for fighting their Russian big brothers.

Nationalist passions were already stirring. Exile groups in the Allied capitals representing the Czechs, Slovaks, and South Slavs were becoming increasingly vocal; for the moment they might be demanding autonomy within the empire, much like that enjoyed by the Magyars; but if the war went on, that might change. For the Poles, it had already changed; from Paris, the Polish National Council was calling for a united and fully independent Poland. Although the Allied powers were sympathetic, they were unwilling at first to encourage separatism, for if the Austro-Hungarian Empire should break up, there would be no place for the German portion of it to go but into the arms of Germany. Nobody wanted to see a postwar Germany strengthened by new lands and new peoples.

For a time it looked as if the example of the Bolshevik Revolution in Russia would reorient the winds of change within the empire from nationalism to social revolution; for the winter of 1917–1918 was bitter beyond recall, and so depleted were the food stocks, particularly in the Austrian capital of Vienna, that starvation had passed from threat to reality. As the government further reduced the food ration in Austria, 200,000 workers residing in the "rent barracks" of the capital stayed away from their jobs, as did another 95,000 in the industrial towns of Lower Austria. On January 18, 1918, the movement spread to Budapest, paralyzing the Hungarian railroads and bringing much of Hungary's industry to a standstill. In some of the factories, the workers formed soviets, but in general the strikers were apathetic: what most of them wanted, it turned out, was not social change but bread.

When in early February 1918 the Central Powers signed a separate peace with the Ukraine, the news broke the strikes. The Ukrainians, so the word had it, would open their bulging granaries; the bread peace, the people called it. Yet in the end few would see anything of a Ukrainian cornucopia, and the misery created by the *Hungerblockade* would continue, but by that time the focus of change within the empire had shifted almost totally to accommodate nationalist aspirations.

Although the Bolshevik Revolution in Russia had seemed to demonstrate that people might control their own destiny, President Wilson's Fourteen Points raised the issue of self-determination, not by revolution but by plebiscite. So, too, the Bolshevik Revolution and Lenin's prompt overtures for peace raised the issue of Allied survival in the war with the Germans, which led to Allied support of the Czechoslovak Legion inside Russia in hope of reestablishing an eastern front, a support that was tantamount to accepting the aspirations of the Czechoslovak exiles for an independent state and thus a breakup of the Austro-Hungarian Empire.

Long accustomed to varying fortunes and shifting allegiances, the Hapsburg Empire was no stranger to change, and there were changes the Emperor Karl might accept and still survive. Relinquishing the Italian and Rumanian territories, for example, would matter little; even giving up those regions populated by the Poles or the South Slavs. Yet Austria, Hungary, and the regions of Bohemia and Moravia were the core of the empire and vital to its survival; and when the Allied governments recognized Czechoslovakian nationalistic aspirations, that foreshadowed the departure of Bohemia and Moravia and eventually Slovakia.

On October 6, 1918, the Poles in Warsaw proclaimed their intent to establish a separate state. On the 21st the Austrian Germans in the parliament in Vienna formed a national assembly and on the 30th proclaimed independence. A few days later, a newly formed democratic government in Budapest declared an independent Hungary.

From the Schönbrunn Palace in Vienna, the Emperor Karl groped for some means of retaining power, even if it meant presiding over no more than a rump German-speaking Austrian state. Yet so great was the possibility that the Bolsheviks might take advantage of the interregnum to seize power that the members of his Cabinet convinced him to swim with the democratic current, to sign a manifesto accepting in advance whatever form of government the people might establish while personally renouncing "all participation in the affairs of the state."[19] Thus, while avoiding abdication, Karl might remain free to accept recall.

Yet if the emperor were to survive to accept recall, it appeared propitious to get away from the palace and the charged atmosphere of the capital, where only clever manipulation by the authorities was preventing Red Guards from coalescing and the Bolsheviks from seizing power. At seven P.M. on a foggy November 11, 1918, the imperial family and its retinue boarded seven automobiles in the inner courtyard of the palace, took a back road out of the park surrounding it, and traveled to the royal hunting lodge of Eckartsau. From there, Karl resisted pressure from Budapest to abdicate the Hungarian throne, agreeing only to repeat his pledge to the Austrians, renouncing any role in the Hungarian government. In time, Communist accusations that Karl was continuing to hold court at Eckartsau would prompt the new government in Vienna to demand either that he abdicate and live on as a simple citizen in the republic or that he depart Austria for all time. Still refusing to renounce the purple, Karl left by train on March 23, 1919, for exile in Switzerland.

When Winston Churchill on January 10, 1919, formally assumed the duties of Secretary of State for War and Air in the government of David Lloyd George, the fate of three of Europe's five remaining major royal houses had thus already been determined, and to Churchill there was reason to be concerned for the fate of his own beloved House of Windsor. So convulsive had been the effect of the long war, he would later note, "that a tremor, and indeed a spasm, shook the foundations of every State," and the revolutionary doctrines emanating from Moscow "seemed to millions of people in every land to offer prospects of moving forward into a bright new world of Brotherhood, Equality, and Science."[20]

In Britain, the discontent was most apparent in the armed forces. At large truck and mechanical depots at Kempton and Grove Park, for example, the troops were for some days beyond authority, forming soviets and spreading revolutionary slogans among working people living nearby. At Luton, forty miles north of London, rioting troops burned the town hall. At Belfast in Ireland and Glasgow in Scotland, rioters proclaimed soviets, and two brigades of infantry had to be moved in to restore order. In France, at Calais, the main port of entry for British troops to the Continent, 4,000 rioting troops seized control of the port, met the leave boats, and persuaded large numbers returning from home leave to join them. Two divisions on the way to serve as occupation forces in Germany had to be turned back to restore order.

Churchill himself was a witness to the most serious disturbance when on February 8, 1919, 3,000 soldiers waiting for a train at Victoria Station to take them back to France mutinied and marched on the Horse Guards' Parade, one of the entrances leading to King George V's residence, Buckingham Palace. As Churchill from his office window watched the Household Cavalry and the

Grenadiers head off the disaffected soldiers, he noted that "A very grave issue has arisen at the physical heart of the State." [21]

## Chapter Five

Soon after Winston Churchill assumed his duties as Secretary of State for War and Air, he delivered a speech at the Mansion House in London in which he expressed his views on Bolshevism and the Bolshevik leaders. "Russia," he declared, "is being rapidly reduced by the Bolsheviks to an animal form of Barbarism." The Bolshevik leaders, he said, were able to maintain power only "by bloody and wholesale butcheries and murders." So disrupted was the economy that "enormous numbers . . . will die of starvation during the winter." Civilization, he declared, "is being completely extinguished over gigantic areas, while Bolsheviks hop and caper like troops of ferocious baboons amid the ruins of cities and corpses of their victims." [1]

As he soon made clear at a meeting of the Cabinet, he saw Bolshevism as such a threat to Western Europe, Britain, and the British Empire as to warrant a major military campaign against it. As would soon be revealed, Churchill wanted:

To strengthen Allied forces in Archangel and Murmansk for a drive on Kotlas to link with White forces and the Czechoslovak Legion driving northwestward on Kotlas from Omsk.

To use the still-powerful German Army to prevent the Reds from expanding westward.

To persuade Canada to send troops to Siberia and the United States and Japan to increase their forces in order to bolster White armies operating generally along the border between European and Asiatic Russia.

To land more British troops in South Russia and to persuade France and Greece to assist, thereby to strengthen White forces for a march on Moscow.

To seize and hold the railroad between Batum on the Black Sea and Baku on the Caspian, thereby to control Russia's oil resources and prevent the spread of Bolshevism into the Near East and India.

To send a military mission and supplies to a White army in Northwest Russia and the Baltic States to support a march on Petrograd.

To maintain the naval blockade against Russia.

To coordinate all operations through the Allied Supreme War Council, of which the United States was a member.

Churchill's scheme encountered immediate opposition from Prime Minister Lloyd George. How could such a grandiose undertaking be justified in the wake of the long, debilitating war with Germany; how to gain support for it from an electorate that was one-quarter Socialist and thus sympathetic to the Bolsheviks?

Furthermore, Lloyd George believed, just as foreign intervention had bolstered the Jacobins after the French Revolution, so Allied military operations could but strengthen support for the Bolsheviks.

The prime minister nevertheless made no effort to prevent Churchill from traveling to Versailles, where the Allied leaders were assembling to write a peace treaty designed to assure the world a millennium of peace, and presenting his war plan to the Allied Supreme War Council. The key figure at Versailles, Churchill knew, would be the American president.

Thomas Woodrow Wilson arrived at the French port of Brest on January 18, 1919, aboard the cruiser *George Washington*. The first American president to visit the Old World in his official capacity, there was considerable alarm in his delegation over intelligence warnings that Bolsheviks and Anarchists would line the rail route to Paris with mutilated and gassed veterans of the French Army, but the intelligence turned out to be wrong: the president's journey was a triumphal progress, and when he arrived at the Palace of Versailles, the French premier, Georges Clemenceau, an odd figure in black skullcap, crumpled morning suit, and dusty boots, embraced him and announced that all Europe looked to America to lead the world "into a new and more splendid ethical era." That was also Wilson's hope, for he had brought with him a plan for a world parliament, the League of Nations, a proposal so inspiring that when Secretary of the Navy Josephus Daniels read a draft, he compared it to "one of the Parables of Jesus and almost as illuminating and as uplifting"; it was, Daniels thought, a "time for church bells to peal, for preachers to fall upon their knees, for statesmen to rejoice, and for angels to sing, 'Glory to God in the Highest.'"[2]

Yet the United States was still in an age of glorious innocence. However forewarned by the founding fathers, Washington and Jefferson, Wilson was hardly prepared for the intricate schemes, the whispered conversations in corridors and salons, with which he was soon confronted. There were, for example, the French: the French commander in the Rhineland had tried to inveigle the local American commander into supporting a scheme to revolutionize the German province of the Rhineland-Palatinate, and establish a state independent of Germany and favorable toward France.[3] Then there were the Danes, asking for bits of Schleswig-Holstein; the Italians wanting pieces of Bavaria and Austria; the Dutch slices of Hannover; the Belgians a part of Westphalia; the Lithuanians pieces of East Prussia; the Poles all of Upper Silesia, the richest coalfield in Europe. And then came Winston Churchill with his portfolio of plans for war with Russia. He asked the Peace Council to make a clear expression of policy: either abandon the White generals, which would create "an interminable vista of violence and misery,"[4] or provide sufficient strength to enable Allied commanders in conjunction with the White forces to destroy the Bolshevik regime and restore the country to moderate government.

Wilson was unimpressed with Churchill's plea. "The existing Allied forces could not stop the Bolsheviks," he declared, and none of the Allied powers was prepared to send more troops. That created "a cruel dilemma." If Allied soldiers were withdrawn, "many Russians might lose their lives," yet the fact had to be faced: "Some day or other the Allied troops would be withdrawn; they could not be maintained there forever and the consequences to the Russians could only be deferred."[5]

Yet Churchill argued so persuasively that, in the end, Wilson failed to dismiss the plan outright. While he personally opposed intervention, he said, he "would accept the decision of the other powers with respect to the preparation of joint plans."[6]

Trying to find an alternative to intervention, Lloyd George proposed inviting Russian Reds and Whites to come to Versailles to arrange what he called a "Truce of God." When Clemenceau objected to having Bolsheviks in his country, Lloyd George proposed an alternative site: the Princes Islands in the Sea of Marmara, about ninety minutes by steamer from Constantinople. Wilson undertook to draft the invitations, apparently unaware of the peculiar history of the islands: Byzantine emperors had used them as a place of exile for fallen royalty, who were often blinded before banishment; and more recently the Turks had used them "to exile all the pariah dogs which had formerly infested the streets of Constantinople." By tens of thousands the dogs had been shipped and left to devour one another and ultimately to die out. "To Bolshevik sympathizers," noted Churchill, "the place seemed oddly chosen for a Peace Conference. To their opponents, it seemed not altogether unsuitable."[7]

Wanting no peace conference in the Princes Islands or anywhere else, Clemenceau tried to sabotage the conference by directing his Foreign Ministry, which had the task of dispatching the invitations, to send no invitation to the Bolsheviks. Yet when the Lenin government learned of the proposal through an announcement broadcast wild by radio, the Bolsheviks promptly agreed to come; for it was obviously to Lenin's advantage to seize on any device that might rid his country of Allied arms and halt, even if but temporarily, the advance of the White armies. Yet in the end none of the White leaders who received invitations accepted, so that nothing came of Lloyd George's proposed conference.

Still hoping for some kind of accommodation with the Bolsheviks, Lloyd George thought he saw an opportunity in a visit to Russia proposed by Wilson's principal adviser, Colonel House. At House's suggestion, Secretary of State Robert Lansing, on February 18, 1919, directed an idealistic twenty-eight-year-old State Department intelligence officer, William Christian Bullitt, to go to Moscow for a firsthand look at the Bolshevik regime. When Lloyd George learned of the mission, he directed his secretary, Philip Kerr, to pass to Bullitt for transmission to Lenin terms which Britain was prepared to accept in return for an end to the fighting with Russia.

Contrary to a rumor that swept Britain, the terms favored the western powers. All de facto governments were to retain control of the territories they currently claimed, which would have left Russia dismembered, and Allied troops were to withdraw only after the bulk of Russian forces had been demobilized and their arms destroyed, which would have left Lenin at the mercy of the Allied forces. Lloyd George's intent was clear: if Lenin accepted the terms, Russia would be broken up into a group of lesser states posing no threat to the British Empire.

When Bullitt and two companions—a young captain and a crusading writer, Lincoln Steffens—reached Petrograd on March 8, 1919, Foreign Commissar Chicherin and his deputy, Maxim Litvinov, met and accompanied them to Moscow for an audience with Lenin. When Lenin agreed to relinquish—at least temporarily—large segments of the country in order to get Allied bayonets and cannon off Russian soil, Bullitt became flushed with enthusiasm. "The Soviet Government is firmly established," Bullitt telegraphed to Versailles. "Perhaps the most striking fact in Russia today is the general support which is given the government by the people in spite of their starvation." He ventured that "No government save a socialist government can be set up in Russia today except by foreign bayonets, and any government so set up will fall the moment such support is withdrawn."[8] Bullitt's colleague, Lincoln Steffens, was equally enthusiastic: "I have seen the future," he would note, "and it works."[9]

Those were hardly the evaluations of the Bolshevik regime that the Allied leaders wanted to hear. After agreeing to receive Bullitt and hear his report, Wilson reconsidered and declined on the grounds that he had a headache. Feeling betrayed, Bullitt resigned from the Foreign Service, while possibly with Churchill's connivance, Lord Northcliffe's *Daily Mail* broke the story of the Bullitt mission, revealing to Lloyd George's embarrassment that an Allied representative had discussed a treaty with Lenin.

That revelation so weakened Lloyd George's position in opposition to increased military action in Russia that it, in effect, removed the last obstacle to Churchill's getting on with his private war against the Soviet regime. That Churchill proceeded to do with speed, efficiency, and enthusiasm, sending to Russia seven general officers and some 2,000 other "advisers" to take charge of the battles to ring and capture Moscow and Petrograd and in the process to root out the dread plague bacillus of Bolshevism.

In North Russia, William E. Ironside, one of the most able and intelligent of the younger general officers in the British Army, succeeded General Poole in command of the North Russian Expeditionary Force.

An immense man—6 feet, 4 inches tall, well over 200 pounds—Ironside was at once a first-rate military politician, a compassionate soldier, an excellent tactician, and an accomplished linguist. American officers and men warmed to him, for unlike General Poole, he eschewed imperial swagger. Nor did Ironside have any illusions about the nature or the complexity of his assignment. As he noted in his diary as the Great War ended on November 11, 1918, "Now the German menace is over . . . we find ourselves opposed to the Bolsheviks only . . . We are now backing a White Russian Counter-Revolution against the Bolsheviks."[10]

Yet to execute the assignment, Ironside had only some 20,000 troops, whose morale was plummeting. A French battalion had shown signs of mutiny; British troops were displaying various signs of discontent; the Russian civilian and military population was becoming increasingly anti-British; and American soldiers wondered aloud why they had to remain after the war with Germany had ended.

To the mortification of the British, whose military tradition included a long record of raising loyal and obedient native forces, mutiny first developed in the Slavo-British Legion, a White Russian regiment commanded by British officers. A battalion of the legion quartered at the Alexander Nevsky barracks in Archangel refused to obey orders to leave for the front and on December 11, 1918, opened fire on British and American soldiers sent to break the rebellion. When the rebels at last surrendered, the overall White Russian commander in the region, General Eugene Miller, had thirteen of the leaders lined up against a wall and shot. When the others at last left for the front, they promptly went over to the Reds. A few weeks later another battalion of the same force refused to participate in a counterattack. To the even greater mortification of the British, the next mutiny occurred in one of Britain's most illustrious regiments, the Yorkshires. Refusing to undertake operations south of Archangel, the men threatened their officers and under the leadership of two sergeants formed a soviet and demanded to discuss their grievances with General Ironside. Although Ironside agreed to talk, he refused the demands, ordered the two sergeants arrested, and condemned them to the firing squad. They were spared only upon receipt of an order from London announcing that as part of a series of reforms instituted by Churchill in hope of restoring order in mutinous units, King George V had ordered a general amnesty for all British soldiers then under sentence of death.

The malaise came close to afflicting the American troops too. At one point men of Company I, 339th Infantry, refused to load sledges and prepare to move to the front, but after hearing a reading of the Articles of War and a few calming words from a newly arrived overall American commander, Brigadier General Wilds P. Richardson, the men backed down.

Agitation among the American troops nevertheless continued. Leaflets passed among them asking, "Why are we here?" and "What are we fighting for?" Letters from home deplored their casualties and reported "discussion and criticism of the policy of the expedition not only in the press but also on the floor of the Senate." The majority of the people in North Russia, one leaflet declared, appeared to prefer Bolshevism to British intervention, yet "the American military presence was only supporting British commercialism and imperialism in the region."[11]

There was, in fact, considerable reason behind the concern of American troops about British imperial designs, and it had a profound effect on Wilson. On April 24, 1919, a secret letter went out to American commanders in North Russia. While admonishing the commanders not "to divulge the exact nature of your instructions" to British commanders, the letter noted that "we shall insist . : . that all military efforts in Northern Russia be given up." Any commander receiving orders or instructions from "superior Allied authority, the execution of which would be in contravention to our Government's Policy," was to "express your regret that instructions from your Government prevent compliance."[12]

The implication was clear: the United States intended to get out of North Russia. On June 2, 1919, the American troops began to go home, and before the summer was over, all but a few officer observers would be gone.

The new American policy meant that there was to be no American participation in North Russia in implementing Churchill's new war plan. Yet despite the loss of American support, General Ironside began, as the long Arctic winter neared an end, to plan and mount one of Churchill's key operations. That was for White Russian forces under Miller to drive with British support southeastward on Kotlas to link with White Russian forces operating on the eastern fringe of European Russia. The key figure in that grand scheme was the self-styled Supreme Ruler of All-Russia, Admiral Kolchak.

Alexander Vasilievich Kolchak was a tall Crimean Tatar of considerable physical strength, intelligence, and ability. At the time of the czar's abdication in 1917, he had been commander in chief of the Black Sea Fleet; and to the American naval attaché at Petrograd, Captain Newton A. McCully, he was one of the really formidable Russian figures of the period.

At McCully's suggestion, Kolchak visited Washington in the early summer of 1917 as the guest of the United States Navy. Received by President Wilson and Secretary of State Lansing, he impressed both much as he had impressed McCully. As significantly, Admiral Kolchak came to the attention of British naval authorities in Washington, who were among the guests at a dinner in Kolchak's honor at the Army-Navy Club on Farragut Square when Kolchak received the news that Lenin had overthrown the provisional government.

When he announced that he would return immediately to Russia, the British offered him transport on a cruiser leaving San Francisco by way of Japan for Vladivostok. Learning in Japan of the armistice negotiated at Brest Litovsk, Kolchak informed the British ambassador that he would be unable to serve the Bolshevik regime and asked for a commission in the British Army. He was on his way to Mesopotamia to help the British fight the Turks when British authorities notified him that the Russian ambassador in Peking thought he could best serve White Russia in Siberia. Going to Vladivostok, Kolchak established contact with the head of the British Military Mission in Siberia, General Knox, who was equipping White and Czech forces in Siberia with British field guns and rifles.[13]

As Kolchak reached Vladivostok, the Allies were in the process of establishing a second major military force on the territory of the former Russian Empire. In addition to the 60,000 Czechs of the Czechoslovak Legion, there were already in some part of Siberia 70,000 Japanese troops, 9,000 Americans, and some 2,000 British troops, and there would eventually be some 10,000 Canadians, French, Italians, and Poles. There were also some 190,000 White Russian forces scattered along the Trans-Siberian Railroad between Vladivostok and Omsk, where the

White forces had established an antibolshevik government known as the All-Russian Directory.

The fighting front lay generally along the boundary between European and Asian Russia on vast, naked plains between the Urals and the Volga, some 6,000 miles from Vladivostok. It was a strange war: "over vast reaches of territory, armies consisting of hundreds of thousands of men might suddenly disperse and evaporate." It was "a war in which there were no real battles, only raids and affrays and massacres, as the result of which countries as large as England and France changed hands to and fro." [14]

To General Knox, the most powerful and influential Allied officer in Siberia, Admiral Kolchak was the ideal man to serve as arbiter of the vast ghost war, a man who could unify all the diverse antibolshevik forces into a single fighting force capable of destroying Lenin and the Bolshevik government. Knox was delighted when in mid-November 1918 the All-Russian Directory picked Kolchak to be minister of war, and Knox may have had a hand in elevating him beyond that post, for on the night of November 17, 1918, rightist officers within the All-Russian Directory staged a coup d'état while British machine guns of the 25th Middlesex Battalion covered the streets of Omsk with fire. From the coup d'état Kolchak emerged as the supreme authority, designating himself as the Supreme Ruler of All-Russia and Chief Commander of All-Russian Forces of the Land and the Sea.

In a rare display of unity for the Russians of the time, General Miller in North Russia, General Nikolai N. Yudenitch in Northwest Russia, and General Anton I. Denikin in South Russia all acknowledged Kolchak as their supreme commander. Allied support quickly followed, the British granting Kolchak a loan of $45 million and President Wilson directing the United States Army to turn over 25,000 rifles to him and promising another 75,000 as soon as shipping was available.

From Paris, the Supreme War Council telegraphed its desire "to restore peace within Russia by enabling the Russian people to resume control of their own affairs through the instrumentality of a freely elected constituent assembly," and since the Allies were convinced that they would be unable to achieve that goal "by dealing with the Soviet Government in Moscow," they were "disposed to assist the Government of Admiral Kolchak and his associates with munitions, supplies, and food to establish themselves as the Government of All-Russia." The Supreme War Council trusted, the telegram continued, that when Kolchak reached Moscow, he would "summon a constituent assembly elected by a free, secret, and democratic franchise as the supreme legislature for Russia." In regions already controlled by Kolchak, free elections were to be held immediately. Kolchak's government would also have to pay Russia's war debts, recognize the independence of Poland, Finland, Latvia, Estonia, Lithuania, and Rumania, and join the League of Nations to "cooperate with the other members in the limitation of armaments and of military organizations throughout the world." [15]

With General Knox dictating felicitous democratic phrases and guiding the pen,

Kolchak on June 4, 1919, wired Paris that he was "happy to note that the policy of the Allied powers toward Russia is in perfect agreement with the task which the Russian Government has imposed upon itself."[16] Provided that assurance, Wilson granted the new government a loan of $10 million from the presidential emergency war fund, increased the supply of rifles by 100,000, and authorized clandestine shipment of large numbers of machine guns, pistols, boots, and personal equipment. Through Knox, the British advised Kolchak that they were sending seventy-nine shiploads of war materials, including nearly a hundred aircraft. They were also providing a Royal Air Force fighter-bomber squadron and a military mission of some 2,000 men.

Yet even as Kolchak and Knox planned the great march on Kotlas to establish a unified front with Ironside and Miller, ominous reports began to filter through to the west. Word from naval and military observers reaching Washington revealed that although Allied confidence in Kolchak himself was justified, the Supreme Ruler of All-Russia was "surrounded by dishonest and incompetent subordinates." An officer attached to the corps that was to lead the drive on Kotlas reported that the Japanese intelligence service, the Hall of Pleasurable Delights, had more influence over the corps staff than did Kolchak, and that the commanding general was "too drunk most of the time to be responsible for anything." The dominating influence at the corps headquarters, the officer reported, was the chief of staff's mistress, a former cabaret entertainer known as "Masku, the Gypsy," who served as the quartermaster general and controlled the treasury. Although Kolchak nominally had ten corps under his command, others reported, none had more than "2,000 bayonets"; the corps commanders were inflating their strengths in order to obtain extra rations and pay, which they either kept for themselves or sold on the black market. Reports of great battles with the Bolsheviks were "fairy tales"; the truth was that the battles were "all maneuvers—one side maneuvers until it outflanks the other side, whereupon the army outflanked retires."[17]

In South Russia, the White general who had emerged in 1918 to lead the counterrevolution against Lenin, Ataman Kaledin, had vanished from the scene, dead by his own hand following a disastrous defeat in the field. But a new czarist general had emerged to take his place: thirty-seven-year-old Anton Ivanovich Denikin, a lean, tall, hard-riding aristocrat with a hawklike nose and jet black eyes. By the spring of 1919, Denikin controlled, or was in alliance with, formidable forces: a large force of Don Cossacks, two Greek divisions, a brigade of Polish volunteers, and several brigades of French colonial troops. A Cossack ataman, Grigorev, commanded large Cossack partisan bands, and a Ukrainian Nationalist leader, Simon Petlyura, controlled sizable forces. Denikin's own forces—known as the Volunteer Army—numbered 51,400 men. Although French support ended when the French troops mutinied and had to be withdrawn— Bolshevik wharfingers helping them on their way by shoving their ships off from the quays at Odessa—a familiar British figure arrived to carry the Allied banner:

Major General Frederick C. Poole, late of Archangel, one of the seven general officers that Churchill sent to Russia that spring to implement his war scheme.

As Miller and Kolchak prepared to march on Kotlas, Denikin gathered his forces to begin a drive northward aimed eventually at Moscow. For that drive Churchill provided more than $350 million in military equipment and aid as well as a British tank battalion and two squadrons of Royal Air Force fighters and bombers. Behind Denikin's force also stood two British infantry divisions of about 36,000 men guarding the Batum-Baku railroad line and the oil fields between the Black and Caspian seas.

But yet again there was something ominously wrong. While Denikin himself was honest and reasonably efficient, his staff was not. Theft, wastage, spoilage, inefficient distribution, and poor maintenance were commonplace. Not infrequently equipment simply rotted on the quays, and Red saboteurs had little difficulty infiltrating depots and blowing up the stores. One British observer reported that while the supply of uniforms far exceeded the number of Denikin's troops, only 25 percent of the men wore uniforms; the rest could be seen on nearly every official and bureaucrat in South Russia. Denikin's officers appropriated hospital beds and bedding for their own homes, and the same observer saw "girls who were emphatically not nurses, walking the streets of Novorossisk wearing regulation British hospital skirts and stockings." [18]

On the fourth front, the Baltic, whence Churchill intended a drive on Petrograd, conditions were little different. There the commander, General Nikolai Nikolaevich Yudenitch, was a Baltic Russian who was so gross that, much as Henry VIII had had to be winched onto his horse, so he had to be hoisted into his automobile. Churchill nevertheless provided Yudenitch with a wealth of war supplies.

In the meantime, lest there be any doubt on the part of Admiral Kolchak and the White Russian generals that Britain meant business in the conflict with Lenin, the War Cabinet passed a forceful and momentous resolution. "In fact," the resolution stated in part, "a state of war did exist between Great Britain and the Bolshevist Government of Russia." [19] Yet much as had Lenin at an earlier time, the Cabinet failed to follow up with a declaration of war.

## Chapter Six

On the first of April 1919, the Premier Regiment of the Don Cossacks formed into tribal squadrons and with swords at the present and battle pennants fluttering, clattered into the great square in Omsk in front of Admiral Kolchak's headquarters. The admiral awaited them on the reviewing stand, a marvelous figure in gray Cossack ceremonial robes, wearing the sword and the black-and-orange lanyard of a Knight of the Order of St. George ("Through Darkness into Light"). Just to Kolchak's right and slightly behind him stood General Knox in the dark green of the Royal Irish Rifles, the collar of a Knight Commander of the Most Honourable Order of the Bath around his throat. Grouped about the two were Kolchak's ministers and members of his military staff wearing either morning dress or uniforms with the quaint high-pointed helmets of the Tatars and Don Cossacks. Here and there among them were Czechoslovak officers wearing British warms and black trews.

Wheeling in precise formation, the Cossack squadrons came to a halt in long lines before the Supreme Ruler of All-Russia. With a great cheer, the men dismounted and stood silent at the bridles of their ponies as the Metropolitan—a giant in robes of brocade, silk, mohair, and gold filigree—appeared with his priests to pronounce the High Invocation and to lead the Supreme Ruler and the Premier Regiment in prayer. Kolchak himself made a short speech, whereupon the Cossacks at a signal from their commander mounted, gave three hurrahs, and wheeled away to the music of "D'ye Ken John Peel," played by the band of the Hampshire Regiment, which had come over 3,000 miles from Vladivostok aboard the Trans-Siberian Railroad for the ceremony.

It was the ceremonial beginning of Kolchak's drive on Kazan, the capital of the Tatars, whence one column was to proceed toward Moscow, a second was to turn northward toward Kotlas to link with Miller's forces driving down from Archangel, and a third was to wheel southwest across the Black Plain in the direction of Tsaritsyn (Stalingrad, then Volgograd), there to link with Denikin's cavalry. If the drives were successful, the White armies would soon hold a common front forming an arc about Moscow extending from the White Sea to the Black Sea.

That spring of 1919, the people's commissar for war, Leon Trotsky, was aboard a special five-car train, a mobile headquarters which contained a map room, signals center, armory, library, and dining and sleeping compartments and was equipped with a printing press and an automobile. It was drawn up on a siding at Penza, a regional market town on the Moscow-Syzran and Gorki-Don Basin railroads, whence Trotsky intended to direct the opening phase of his campaigns against Miller in the north, Kolchak in the east, and Denikin in the south.

On the eve of battle, Trotsky's military assets were few. The men of the Red Army, Trotsky himself admitted, were ignorant, drunken, ridden with syphilis, and "numbed with religion."[1] Desertions were legion: in the first year of civil war, close to 3 million soldiers would simply disappear. Those who remained knew little about military discipline. "Look at them!" Lenin exclaimed while reviewing a military parade marking the first anniversary of the revolution. "They march like bags of sand!"[2]

Personal weapons were in the majority of cases hopelessly antiquated, and most of the artillery pieces had been outdated at the start of the World War. Such supply service as there was rested on malfunctioning railroads. Although the Reds controlled the bulk of the armament industry, all but two of the powder factories were closed because of the effects of the Allied naval blockade; military-industrial production constituted only 13 percent of the 1913 figure. Since the currency was almost without value—13,000 Red rubles were equal to one 1913 imperial ruble— the soldiers received little compensation other than their food and clothing. Medical service was either nonexistent or so primitive as to represent a hazard to survival, and there was no mail service at all.

Although Allied support afforded Trotsky's opponents better arms and equip-ment, the Whites had much the same problem with desertions as did the Reds. Peasants conscripted by whichever side had no taste for fighting; they wanted only to return to their villages. Neither side did much to rally the peasantry to its cause: peasants who experienced Bolshevik discipline often took to the woods as guerrillas to fight the Reds, yet how could they support the Whites, for as often as not, the Whites would take away the lands the peasants had seized and return them to the large landowners?

Trotsky did have three factors going for him. One was the hard core of dedicated Bolsheviks who had constituted the original Red Guard; these men could be counted upon to provide backbone, discipline, and organization for the Red Army. The second factor was geography, for with Red territory little larger than medieval Muscovy, Trotsky was the spider at the center of its web, able to operate on short internal lines radiating from Moscow, capable of rushing the maximum amount of supply and manpower to the critical point in the shortest time. The third was Trotsky himself, supremely confident of his intellectual powers and the righteousness of his cause, utterly tireless with himself and ruthless with his staff. He was young, fit, a curious combination of cold technician and impetuous romantic. He cared not that he had read only the basics of strategy and tactics, for he was convinced that he was a revolutionary general of an unusually high order.

By midnight of June 3, 1919, Trotsky was ready to deliver his first blow against Admiral Kolchak. His agents having detected the main force of cavalry in Kolchak's left wing encamped on a flat, open steppe near Kazan, he ordered his Red Cossack cavalry and his horse artillery forward on muffled hooves. Far to the rear, well beyond the sight or hearing of any White forces, Trotsky positioned a hundred aircraft, an assortment of British, French, and Russian biplanes.

A few minutes after sunrise on June 4, 1919, an hour when, as Trotsky calculated, the White Cossacks had removed the tethers and hobbles from their mounts and were grooming them for the day's march, eleven flights of aircraft came in low, engines roaring, the pilots firing machine guns, dropping brilliant flares and small bombs, and zooming just over the heads of the horses. As the horses reared and fled in terror, Trotsky's artillery opened fire, thus making it impossible for the White Cossacks to retrieve their mounts. When the artillery lifted, Red cavalrymen charged from hiding places in nearby woods and copses.

By noon, the head of Kolchak's left column had been decapitated, and Trotsky's infantry had begun to hit both flanks of the column to the echo of the Red battle cry: "Proletarians! To horse!" It was the first of a series of reverses that began to afflict Kolchak's forces everywhere, in some places forcing the White armies back as much as 120 miles. As General Knox put it, "general situation from military point of view most unsatisfactory and uncertain, largely due to panic . . . and also quarrels between the chiefs."[3]

To the British commander at Archangel, General Ironside, and his Russian colleague, General Miller, the news of Kolchak's reverses east of Moscow appeared to eliminate any hope of a linkup at Kotlas. Even if Kolchak should be able to rally his troops, the level of the water in the Dvina River had dropped so low that a flotilla of British riverboats would be unable to operate, and without them, there would be no chance of breaking through. Besides, Lloyd George, while agreeing to continue to supply war matériel to the White Russians, had bowed to a critical press and opposition in the House of Commons and decreed that like the Americans, the British were to pull all their troops out of North Russia, whatever the outcome of the White Russian offensives, before another winter set in.

For a time Ironside and Miller tried to conceal British preparations for withdrawal lest panic envelop Archangel, but it proved impossible to keep the preparations secret for long. Alarm and indignation followed, a spate of appeals, petitions, deputations. Yet in time alarm gave way to apathy. When the British offered either to evacuate the White troops to Murmansk or to England or to leave British war stores so that the Whites could continue to fight, General Miller elected to stay. Many civilians bought up gold, valuables, and Bolshevik currency and left with their families for nearby villages, where they planned to stay until the Bolsheviks came and conditions reverted, as they believed they would, to what they had been before 1917.

The last British troops departed both Archangel and Murmansk on September 26, 1919. The Supreme Authority of the North was destined to survive another five months before General Miller fled to exile in Paris, Red troops entered Murmansk and Archangel, and the Cheka set about determining who would die and who would go on living.

For all Kolchak's reverses east of Moscow and Miller's dismal prospects in North Russia, White forces elsewhere in the summer of 1919 appeared to be close to major successes. In South Russia, for example, Denikin had seized all the major cities and advanced as far north as Orel, only 200 miles from Moscow. So impressive were Denikin's victories that by midsummer Churchill was considering how Britain might secure trading concessions in Denikin's rear, an indication that Mr. Churchill's private war may have been conducted for other than altruistic aims, an idea which General Denikin would comment upon with some bitterness in later years in his memoirs.[4] In setting out the case for the War Office to justify support of the operations in South Russia, Churchill specifically cited the opportunity for future British trade.

Lloyd George was far less impressed. "Everything indicated," he noted, "that General Denikin was surrounded by persons of reactionary tendencies, and it was quite possible that he might be beaten, not by the Bolshevist army in front of him but by the forces behind him."[5] That was a prophecy difficult to contradict, for Denikin with 50,000 men was in no way capable of policing the vast territory encompassing hundreds of thousands of square miles that his army had nominally conquered. Everywhere there were disparate political groups, all professing antibolshevism but all practicing private gain.

Yet Lloyd George seemed incapable of suppressing Churchill. At the end of August 1919, he sent him a note declaring that "Russia does not want to be liberated. Whatever she may think of the Bolsheviks, she does not think it worthwhile sacrificing any more blood to substitute for them men of the Yudenitch type. Let us therefore attend to our own business and leave Russia to look after hers."[6]

Churchill ignored him. With news that Deniken had taken Orel, Churchill penned a note of triumph to the foreign secretary, Lord Curzon, quoting the British commercial secretary at Odessa as saying: "[The Bolsheviks] may pass like a heap of snow melts under a hot sun, leaving behind only the dirt which it has gathered."[7] There was further encouragement in the news from Northwest Russia where British motor torpedo boats had sneaked into the Russian naval base at Kronstadt, which guarded the seaward approaches to Petrograd, and had sunk three ships, while Yudenitch's army was preparing to drive on Petrograd from positions only thirty-five miles from the former capital. "Victory is in sight," the Imperial General Staff informed Churchill in early October 1919. "The Bolshevik power is showing unmistakable signs of complete collapse at an early date."[8]

In Moscow on October 14, 1919, the Politburo met in an atmosphere of extreme crisis. As Lenin, seemingly fully recovered from his wounds, remarked, there was "a military threat of the utmost danger" and announced "the actual conversion of Soviet Russia into a military camp."[9] For Moscow, he established a Committee for Defense of the Capital and endowed it with extraordinary powers, and after first contemplating abandoning Petrograd, he sent Trotsky hurrying north in his command train to take charge of the defense.

At Petrograd, the crisis was acute. Advance patrols of General Yudenitch's army had appeared near Tosno on the Nicholas Railroad linking Moscow and Petrograd and seemed about to cut that vital line. Three days later four British-supplied tanks took the czar's summer palace about fifteen miles south of Petrograd at Pavlovsk and then the Mulkhovo Heights on the very outskirts of the city. So certain was Churchill that Petrograd was about to fall that he directed the Imperial General Staff to send a senior British general to Yudenitch's headquarters at once to ensure that Yudenitch established in Petrograd "a decent, enlightened, and humane administration."[10]

Meanwhile, the British Baltic Fleet supported Yudenitch's drive by attacking a naval base at Krasnaya Gorka, just outside Petrograd, and bombarding it for three days, killing over a hundred Red sailors and fostering a cry of outrage in the British press. Under that criticism, Lloyd George directed the Admiralty to call off the bombardment and accused Churchill of "misrepresentation of the Russian situation." That in turn sent Churchill to the House of Commons where on November 6, 1919, he delivered another of his ornate Edwardian polemics against Lenin: "Lenin was sent into Russia by the Germans in the same way that you might send a phial containing a culture of typhoid or cholera to be poured into the water supply of a great city, and it worked with amazing accuracy . . . [for] he set to work with demoniacal ability to tear to pieces every institution on which the Russian State and nation depended." [11]

When Churchill finished, colleagues crowded around him to praise his performance, and even his severest critic, H. A. L. Fisher, would write in his diary that night: "Winston brilliant." The erstwhile foreign secretary, A. J. Balfour, told Churchill in the lobby, "Winston, I admire the exaggerated way you tell the truth." [12]

Yet Churchill's oratory did nothing to change the opinion of Lloyd George, who kept Churchill in the Cabinet only because he considered he would be more dangerous on the other side of the House. Two days later, Lloyd George declared his policy. "Bolshevism," he said, "cannot be suppressed by the sword." He continued: "We cannot . . . afford to continue so costly an intervention in an interminable civil war. . . . Russia is a quicksand. Victories are usually won in Russia, but you sink in victories; and great armies and great empires in the past have been overwhelmed in the sands of barren victories." [13]

As if to prove Lloyd George's words, apparent impending victory by General Yudenitch's army at Petrograd turned out to be illusory. Rumor—and some subsequent evidence—had it that Trotsky bought him off. Yet that was reckoning without Leon Trotsky's ruthlessness, seething energy, and boundless perseverance. In the few brief days left to him, he ordered hurried completion of tanks, directed revolutionary tribunals to string up or shoot deserters, used the Terror to lash the reluctant people of Petrograd and the soldiers into a frenzy of defense. So it was that as Yudenitch's British-supplied tanks lumbered out of the Mulkhovo Hills, only eleven miles from the Winter Palace and the Smolny Convent, the Red Army turned them back into the hills and beyond.

For the coup de grâce, Trotsky employed that feature of warfare which Churchill so much admired: "Craft, foresight, deep comprehension of the verities . . . stratagems, devices, manoeuvres." [14] Aware that Yudenitch was wholly dependent for supplies on lines of communications running through Estonia, he arranged for Foreign Commissar Chicherin to grant Estonia peace on the favorable terms its leaders had been demanding. The Estonians duly cut Yudenitch's communications and as the troops fell back, disarmed them and set them to work in labor camps.

Yudenitch himself made his way to the Estonian capital of Reval, where he learned that the Cheka had placed on his head a bounty of half a million gold rubles. Before daylight on January 27, 1920, on orders of Estonian authorities, he was arrested as he lay in bed with his wife at the Hotel Commercial, but he would soon be released at the insistence of the British and French military missions and eventually make his way to Paris. Yudenitch, Estonian authorities subsequently determined, had stashed away almost $1.25 million in a personal bank account in Stockholm.

Trotsky, meanwhile, had returned to Moscow the hero of the hour, accepted the Order of the Red Banner, and then turned his talents as a soldier and organizer to finishing off Admiral Kolchak, whose forces had never recovered from the debacle at Kazan. They continued to fall back in the direction of the seat of the All-Russian Directory behind the Urals at Omsk, where the Cabinet and the ministries engaged in meeting after meeting and issued multiple drafts and recriminations, all leading to nothing but eventual dissolution. British and French military missions still existed but had little advice to give or anybody to give it to. The Czechoslovak troops had long since refused to fight and occupied themselves with controlling a 1,200-mile stretch of the Trans-Siberian Railroad to ensure their eventual repatriation. Hostile guerrilla bands, composed of peasants angered by the harsh methods of both sides in trying to conscript them, roamed the countryside.

There were White forces in the east still to be defeated nevertheless, and to do it Trotsky turned again to stratagems. Even before he had left to rally the defense of Petrograd, he had sent agents to meet secretly with representatives of the Polish government at a small railroad station sixty miles east of Pinsk, there to lull the Poles with hints of peace and enable him to slip his cavalry divisions away to fight Kolchak. At the same time, Bolshevik agents were at work fomenting trouble between Kolchak's generals and within the ministries.

The stratagem with the Poles having succeeded, Trotsky assembled a fleet of the world's first four-engine bombers, Ilya Muromets, designed by the aviation pioneer Igor Sikorsky. At dawn on November 2, 1919, those bombers flew in at low level in a repeat of the tactic designed to panic the mounts of the White cavalry. Again the tactic succeeded, sending the mounts rearing and neighing in terror and leaving Kolchak's cavalrymen without mounts and in most cases without their sabers and rifles.

By the end of the day, Kolchak's troops were retreating in disorder, and not quite a fortnight later, on November 14, 1919, Admiral Kolchak, with an imposing convoy of seven trains, whose cargo included the state gold reserve, abandoned Omsk. It was the start of one of the most disastrous retreats of all time. During a six-week, 1,500-mile trek between the Tobol River and Irkutsk near Lake Baikal, tens upon tens of thousands would die of typhus, cholera, cold, continued fighting, and starvation, perhaps as many as a million people.

Controlling the railroad stations, the Czechs saw to it that they had sufficient rolling stock and that their trains had priority. Others who were able to find a space on a train, including Kolchak himself, made the journey by widely spaced leaps and bounds as progress of the Czech trains permitted. Few of the ordinary soldiers found a space; they had to proceed on foot alongside the railroad tracks, the *trakt*, "a ridged and undulating ribbon of frozen snow."[15] There were sometimes fights for scarce fuel at pumping stations; points and signals froze; locomotives left unattended even briefly froze and their boilers burst. Naked corpses lined the tracks where they had been thrown from hospital trains to make space and clothes available for the living. Guerrillas attacked, and all the while pursuing Red troops nibbled at the rear guards.

Within the Directorate, a faction representing itself as the Political Center, hoping to strike a deal with the Bolsheviks, revolted. As fighting broke out in Irkutsk between the Political Centrists and forces loyal to Kolchak, the Political Centrists gained control and sent a delegation back down the railroad in hope of reaching quick accommodation with the Reds. The bait they intended to use consisted of Kolchak and the state gold reserve.

When a train that included a second-class passenger car carrying Kolchak and his entourage reached the edge of Irkutsk, the Political Centrists seized the admiral and took him to the town prison where a commission interrogated him at length in hope of obtaining details about his associates to use in ingratiating the Political Centrists with the Bolsheviks. The interrogation was still proceeding when word came that White forces bent on rescuing him were approaching the town. In a panic, the Political Centrists took Kolchak to the edge of the Angara River, shot him, and shoved his corpse under the ice.

In South Russia, General Denikin was also in difficulty, in large measure occasioned, as Lloyd George had predicted, by forces behind him. By late summer of 1919, a peasant turned Anarchist, Nestor Ivanovich Makhno, had assembled a force in Denikin's rear variously estimated at from 15,000 to 40,000 hard-fighting, hard-drinking, often brutal men, whose enemies were anybody and everybody. While Denikin was advancing on Orel, Makhno was seizing his supply points and cutting his supply routes. As Denikin was to write later, Makhno's depredations "had the effect of disorganizing our rear and weakening the front at the most critical period of its existence."[16] As Denikin tried to continue beyond Orel on to Moscow, the Red Army counterattacked; with reserves exhausted and supply lines cut, he had no choice but to fall back.

By March 1920 all that was left of Denikin's army had reached the Crimean Peninsula, about 40,000 men, and only about 26,000 of them adequately armed. The Crimea "was seething with political passions" and so vitriolic were the recriminations that Denikin resigned his position in favor of one of his senior commanders, General Baron Pyotr Nikolayevich Wrangel, and went aboard a British destroyer for eventual exile in the United States.

Winston Churchill finally had to admit defeat. In a letter to the chief of the Imperial General Staff, Field Marshal Wilson, he said that he understood that the cause was lost: "I am convinced that very great evils will come upon the world, and particularly upon Great Britain, as a consequence of the neglect and divided policies of this year on the part of the Allies and of ourselves. We shall find ourselves confronted almost immediately with a united Bolshevik Russia, highly militarized and building itself up on victories easily won over opponents in disarray."[17]

Then Churchill added: who was this Wrangel?

Baron Wrangel was probably the best of Denikin's generals, politically as well as militarily; indeed, quite possibly the best of the White generals. Trotsky's successor as commissar for war, Mikhail Frunze, would note that "In Wrangel, our country unquestionably had a most dangerous opponent. In the various operations in which he took part, Wrangel demonstrated not only tremendous energy but a complete grasp of the situation."[18] One of Churchill's observers in the Crimea, Colonel C. S. Ford, reported on a visit to Wrangel: "One could not have easily passed him . . . as an ordinary personality. . . . His quick, energetic movements and stiffly erect bearing [suggested] a spirit of boundless energy and an iron will contained in a wiry, tireless body."[19]

Although Wrangel had assumed command of a defeated force, he believed that because of the restricted access to the Crimea across isthmuses from the mainland, he would be able to hold out. He planned to establish a Fortress Crimea with the Grand Duke Mikhail, then in Siberia, as a figurehead czar. The new regime was to be founded on the basis of land reform, religious freedom, an end to land taxation, and a general spirit of equality.

Alas for Wrangel, time had run out; he had lost the support of the British.

In March 1920, Churchill left London for a two-week holiday in France. While he was away, Lloyd George summoned the Cabinet for a decision ending all further support to the Whites. Soon thereafter, he invited Soviet representatives to London to discuss an end to the fighting and a start of trade. When two representatives, Lev Kamenev and Leonid Krassin, arrived in May 1920, Lloyd George promised that as part of any trade agreement, he would withdraw all support from Wrangel and seek to persuade him to enter into peace negotiations with the Soviet government. He had already informed Wrangel that he would try to arrange amnesty with the Bolsheviks for the troops and their families.

Wrangel declined Lloyd George's advice; a promise of amnesty from the Bolsheviks no doubt looked more attractive in London than it did in Sevastopol. Shortly thereafter, Wrangel went over to the offensive.

His move was not the act of desperation it might have appeared to be. In the first place, the Crimean Peninsula was incapable of producing enough food for his men and their dependents. In addition, Polish troops had recently driven into the Ukraine and in May had taken Kiev. Backing the fortunes of the Poles, the French offered Wrangel support if he could link up with the Poles; there was also hope of uniting with Cossack forces that were still holding out against the Red Army.

It was to no avail. French support turned out to be more moral than material, and in early October 1920 the Poles agreed to an armistice. Falling back into the Crimea, Wrangel's army and the families of the soldiers—a total of 146,000 men, women, and children—boarded British, French, and Italian ships. Wrangel himself was the last to board; reaching the top of the gangplank, he faced toward the north—toward Moscow and Petrograd—and made the sign of the cross. Mr. Churchill's private war was at an end.

# PART II
## The Clarion

*Chapter Seven*

At 9:10 A.M. on January 24, 1919, only a few weeks after the end of the World War, the chief of the United States Army's intelligence service, Brigadier General Marlborough Churchill, a member of President Woodrow Wilson's delegation to the peace conference at Versailles, received an "advice" of fateful importance: a report broadcast on Moscow Radio in which Lenin announced establishment of "the general staff of the world revolution of the proletariat" to be known as the Communist International, or, more commonly, by its acronym, the Comintern. The Comintern was to hold its founding congress in Moscow in March 1919; all the world's Socialist parties were invited to send delegates.

In summarizing the objectives of the Comintern, Lenin attacked the great capitalist powers that had so recently emerged victorious from the most savage war in history. As an economic system, Lenin declared, capitalism was moribund, and even though the capitalist leaders had brought the world to ruin in the war, they were at that very moment plotting to force the working classes of the world into a new "rule of kings and bankers" that would bring yet another calamity upon the world. Thus the Communist International—sometimes also known as the Third International—was established. (The First International, an international association of Socialist workers, was founded in London in 1864, the Second International in Paris in 1889.) The Third International aimed to destroy the political power of capitalism and replace all its institutions with soviets of the

85

proletariat in which all the assets of all nations would be placed at the service of the working classes. The concept of the state itself would eventually be destroyed and replaced by a world soviet of proletariat nations with headquarters in Moscow, a soviet that would end war forever. To achieve that goal, said Lenin, "There must be a common fighting organ for the purpose of directing and maintaining premanent coordination and systematic leadership of the Communist International, a center in which the interests of the communist movement in each country would be subordinated to the common interest of the international revolution." Using what would become the familiar idiom of the Comintern, Lenin issued a clarion call to all parties of the left:

> WORKERS OF THE WORLD! In the struggle against imperialist barbarism, against monarchy, against the privileged estates, against the bourgeois state and bourgeois property, against all kinds and forms of class or national oppression—UNITE! Under the banner of the Workers' Soviets, under the banner of revolutionary struggle for power and the dictatorship of the proletariat, under the banner of the Communist International—WORKERS OF THE WORLD! UNITE![1]

In the United States, the announcement was dismissed at first as the jabber of political eccentrics who had managed by accident to seize the power of Russia and who would be ejected the moment the Russian people came to their senses; but in Britain, the Privileged Bodies, as the British people called their leaders, could have heard few announcements with greater apprehension. In the fearful conflict just ended, 14 million people had died, almost all of them Europeans; the combatants had expended close to $282 billion; and all Europe, that great center of industry, finance, culture, and political power, was in tumult. The terrible expenditure of blood and gold had brought no peace; on the contrary, it had brought disillusionment, hunger, unemployment, revolution, the collapse of all known standards, and a general sense of great despair. As Churchill wrote, "Appetites, passions, hopes, revenge, starvation, and anarchy ruled the hour."

Palpably the world was no tranquil place; plainly the preconditions for a successful world revolution of the proletariat existed. Kings and empires had been swept away, leaving no established order in their place. There was brutal civil war in Russia; machine-gun fire swept the streets of German cities; Britain, France, Italy, and the United States seethed with reactionary disturbances. Japan was bent upon carving an empire from the smoking ruins of the old Occidental order; France frothed with hatred and vengeance for Germany; Germany stood sullen and conspiratorial behind the Rhine, only temporarily defeated. As trade wars developed, Britain and France watched Japan and the United States suspiciously and anxiously, and the United States watched Japan's imperial ambitions with a conviction that one day there would be war. Red revolutions were brewing in

Hungary, Saxony, Thuringia, Bavaria, and the Ruhr. The British Army had mutinied in France; the French Army had mutinied in France and Russia; the Greeks were about to make war on the Turks; Georgia, Armenia, and Azerbaijan were, with British encouragement, seceding from Russia; Finland and the Baltic States of Latvia, Estonia, and Lithuania had already broken away from the rule of Moscow; the Irish were at war with the British; the armies of two new nations, Poland and Czechoslovakia, fought each other over frontier matters; and the Russians were contemplating an invasion of Rumania. Turkey invaded Russia, and Britain invaded Turkey; the Russians and the British invaded Persia; the French invaded Syria; and the British invaded Mesopotamia. There was a jihad against the British in Afghanistan and revolution against the British in Waziristan; a Balt seized Mongolia, Russia seized Mongolia from the Balt, and Japan seized large parts of Asiatic Russia from the Russians. Mexico quivered with civil war; Panama was about to attack Costa Rica; and the Haitians were about to fight the United States. In many parts of the world, there was famine; almost all normal communications had been destroyed; the British were blockading Russia and Germany; and an influenza pandemic was killing millions. There was inflation, recession, depression; the world commodity exchanges were disordered; and there was such suspicion of money that the barter system was being used throughout Eurasia. At the Hall of Mirrors in Versailles, where the world's statesmen were trying to make a peace fit for heroes, those who believed in omens saw the sign that to peasants meant the world was coming to an end: an eclipse of the sun.

Into the midst of that grim carousel burst Lenin's announcement. An American journalist, Louis Fischer, would record how the Muscovy clarion "sent a thrill through humanity" and how it "shook the upholders of privilege, tradition, empire, white supremacy."[2] Lenin seemed to be standing there in the gloom, offering the world a shining vision of a revolutionary utopia where there was to be peace, land, work, food, security, education, medicine, art, music, clothes, housing, holidays, and happiness, a vision of a world brotherhood of man united in wealth and power with the world's bountiful treasures at its disposal.

Looking at their leaders, the nations saw aged men with snowy hair under tall silk hats, men wearing snug Chesterfields with astrakhan collars, cynical men with elegant whispers and conspiratorial nods, brokers of destiny with watery, crafty, rheumy old eyes. Yet in Moscow there was youth: Lenin was forty-seven when the revolution came; Leon Trotsky and Joseph Stalin were thirty-eight; and the leaders of the Comintern, Gregori Zinoviev and Lev Kamenev, were thirty-four. To the multitudes it seemed that for the second time in history a portentous star had appeared in the east; and unless the established order found an alternative to Bolshevism, it seemed that all Europe would become Bolshevik within a year. Yet what could the established orders offer as an alternative? How were the statesmen to restore pastoral tranquility to a world in disorder in time to prevent the alien cult from engulfing Europe? As the Russian Communist Party prepared for the First

Congress of the Comintern, the men arranging the destiny of the world had no answers.

If Lenin was the strategist of the world revolution of the proletariat, so Trotsky was the tactician. Together they decided that the revolution could be no gentle process of transmutation, but could be obtained only through intrigue and violence that would have to persist until capitalism was rooted out and destroyed. The soil of the new world was to be nourished, as in the case of the French Revolution, with the blood of the Purple. And there had to be organization, and to provide that organization, Lenin and Trotsky selected one of Bolshevism's most faithful and brilliant disciples, Gregori Evseevich Radomilsky, alias Apfelbaum, alias Gregori Zinoviev.

Born in 1883 in the Pale of the Settlement of Imperial Russia, that part of the empire to which the czar had banished Jews, Zinoviev was a product of the very class he intended to destroy, and like so many leading Bolsheviks, a journalist; his first job in Russia after the Bolshevik Revolution was as a senior member of the party newspaper, *Pravda*. In making him chief of the Comintern, Lenin also appointed him to the important and powerful post of chairman of the Petrograd Soviet.

Although Zinoviev was a compelling orator, he was one of the ugliest men in the Kremlin. The English sculptor Clare Sheridan, who visited the Kremlin in 1920 to sculpt the Communist leaders, provided a rare portrait of the man who was to lead the world revolution of the proletariat: "[Zinoviev] arrived—an hour late—in the frame of mind of a man who means to spend the rest of his life trying to recover that hour. He was restless and impatient; he sighed and groaned, looked up and down, looked out of the window, and then at the newspaper. He seemed arrogant rather than vain. His face was thick, his neck short, his chest pulpy, his hair curly, his lips petulant, his eyelids heavy. The effect was of a shrewd, fat, middle-aged woman."[3]

Under Zinoviev, the Comintern was to become a vast bureaucracy devoted first to the propagation of the Communist faith and then to political warfare against the capitalist powers. Lenin himself laid down its fundamentals: since capitalism was to him an illegal and immoral conspiracy against the people, and since the capitalists held the political power of the great nations outside Russia, the Communist International would have to fight illegality with illegality by creating what would come to be called "the Communist underground."[4] Although the Soviet government would provide the Comintern with headquarters, funds, even personnel, and although the Comintern would serve the objectives of the Soviet government, the government could not accept responsibility for the Comintern's actions, which, it was said, would be determined not by the Soviet government but by the Comintern's own Executive Committee. As with any secret service, the government might have to disown any connection with the Comintern.

To be successful, Lenin decreed, the organization of the Comintern in Russia would have to be highly centralized and highly disciplined. Any disobedience for whatever reason was to be dealt with by what would come to be called "pitiless courts." Although the Comintern was to be responsible for its own discipline, as time passed, the Soviet secret services, which would come to use the political world created by the Comintern for their own special purposes in the field of espionage, would be available to ensure that Communists at home and abroad maintained ideological excellence. From the start, the Comintern would be protected by Lenin's secret service, the Cheka, whose symbol was a sword hanging over the head of a snake.

With the Cheka playing such an important part in the Comintern's activities, it followed that the Comintern would assume some of the personality of the Cheka; and since all secret services derive much of their personality from that of their founder or director, the methods of the Comintern were likely to be unusually severe, cold-blooded, agile, and determined. For the first chief of the Cheka was a forty-one-year-old ideological fanatic who was neither Russian nor proletarian but a Pole and an aristocrat, Feliks Edmundovich Derzhinski.

When Lenin in 1917 made Derzhinski the guardian of the Bolshevik Revolution, he was already a dying man: as a result of eleven years in one of the czar's prison mines, his health was wrecked, he had tuberculosis, and his heart had been weakened. His features were sepulchral, his skin was the color of alabaster, and his cheeks blossomed rose-red when he coughed, which he did constantly, day and night. He spoke softly, almost in a whisper, and often gave the impression of being gentle, even kindly. Yet at heart he was an icy scientific Bolshevik theocrat, as utterly pitiless as any cardinal of the Inquisition.

Clare Sheridan later wrote,

> This modest, unassuming figure was a great surprise. As I analyzed him that first hour, he made a curious impression upon me. He was calm and sphinx-like, except his eyes, which seemed to be swimming in tears. His face was narrow and his nose transparent. . . . He provoked in me subconsciously a feeling of pity, and yet God knows, by all the laws, it should have been just the contrary.[5]

After Derzhinski had gone, Sheridan would recall feeling "so affected I could neither think nor work, but sat for a while meditatively." She "felt some strange vibrations lingering . . . like the faint odour of the world hate that encircled him . . . Call his malady by any name one chooses, he was dying, choking, suffocating from thought-waves of hatred."[6]

Sheridan might have better understood Derzhinski had she appreciated the fact that he worked to Lenin's principle: "The scientific conception of dictatorship means neither more nor less than unlimited power resting directly on force, not limited to anything, nor restrained by any laws or absolute rules." Upon that basis, the world utopia was to be created: and for that purpose the proletariat gathered at the Kremlin.

On March 2, 1919, fifty-two men and women assembled in the former Imperial Court of Justice in the Kremlin to establish the Comintern. But for a *cordon sanitaire*, including a naval blockade, that Britain and other western powers had thrown up about Russia to prevent the plague bacillus of Communism from spreading, more would have been present. As it was, only five foreign delegates attended—those from Socialists parties of Germany, Austria, Sweden, Norway, and Holland—and even they spoke only for themselves.

It was nevertheless that small, revolutionary incubus, that unrepresentative gathering of political eccentrics, that Lenin proposed to employ to generate a world revolution of the proletariat. As if to emphasize that it was to be a revolution from below, no attempt had been made to restore the courtroom to its imperial grandeur. The only indication that the occupancy of the Kremlin had changed was the discernible outline where the czarist eagle had hung on the wall and the badge of the Comintern in its place: a brawny workman in a cloth cap smiting at the chains of capitalism binding the world. The only color in the dingy, dusty room was the blood-red of banners proclaiming in Russian Cyrillic the slogan of the Comintern: WORKERS OF THE WORLD! UNITE! YOU HAVE NOTHING TO LOSE BUT YOUR CHAINS! Except for the lavish chandeliers, it might have been a drab trade union hall anywhere in the world.

Almost all the men and women present were wanted by various police forces for such crimes as contumacy, subversion, draft evasion, treason. They were earnest but uneasy, listening and nodding as if at some literary or medical conclave where they were to respond to some uncertain and dangerous proposal. They fidgeted, smoked, coughed, chewed sunflower seeds. They became genuinely attentive only when Lenin appeared on the dais and began to speak and then not so much for the significance of his words or his delivery, which was lackluster, but because of the aura of mystery that surrounded the man. England, America, France, and Germany, said Lenin, had built a great wall around Russia, but he knew that the masses of workmen around the world sympathized with the Bolshevik cause. Already, he said, the world soviet of the proletariat was closer than anyone knew. As his words droned on, an uninspired actor addressing an almost empty theater, his most fateful words almost escaped attention: "We are not living in a state but in a system of states, and existence of the Soviet Republic side by side with capitalist states for a long time is unthinkable. One or the other must triumph in the end. Before that end supervenes, a series of frightful collisions between the Soviet Republic and the bourgeois states will be inevitable."[7]

As Lenin ended his remarks, the heavy oak doors flew open and into the room strode Leon Trotsky, commissar for war, fresh from the battlefields, bringing with him a whiff of gunpowder, blood, and strife. Immaculate in a leather suit, breeches, cap, and riding boots and carrying a crop, Trotsky mounted the tribunal, strode over to Lenin, and embraced him warmly and sincerely.

In a voice ringing with fire and bile, Trotsky began to read the manifesto of the Comintern, which he had written aboard his warrior's train. "Seventy-two years ago," he said, "the Communist Party proclaimed its program to the world in the form of a Manifesto written by the greatest heralds of the proletarian revolution, Karl Marx and Frederick Engels."[8] Then as now, he continued, Communism was baited by "lies, hatred, and persecution of the possessing classes who rightfully sensed their mortal enemy in Communism."

"The war," Trotsky declaimed, "was unleashed through the direct and conscious provocation of Great Britain," but then the United States had "assumed the role which England had taken in previous wars, namely: weakening one camp by playing it against another, intervening in military operations only to such an extent as to guarantee her all the advantages." From the "moral savagery" of those two powers, said Trotsky, from their "war of blood and muck," had sprung the world's first parliament, the League of Nations: "Is all toiling mankind to become the bond-slaves of victorious world cliques who, under the firm-name of the League of Nations and aided by an 'international' army and 'international' navy, will here plunder and strangle some peoples and there cast crumbs to others, while everywhere and always shackling the proletariat—with the sole object of maintaining their own rule? Or," he went on, "shall the working class of Europe and of the advanced countries in other parts of the world take in hand the disrupted and ruined economy in order to assure its regeneration upon socialist principles?"

The speed of Trotsky's speech quickened; his audience was fast becoming entranced. The last war had been for colonies, he cried, and the colonial populations had been drawn into the war on an unprecedented scale. "Indians, Negroes, Arabs and Madagascans fought on the territories of Europe—for the sake of what?" Never before had "the infamy of capitalist rule in the colonies been delineated so clearly." As a result, he shouted, "open insurrections and revolutionary ferment" had arisen in all the colonies. "In Europe itself, Ireland keeps signaling through sanguinary street battles that she still remains and still feels herself to be an enslaved country." In "Madagascar, Annam and elsewhere" bourgeois troops had been called upon to "quell the uprisings of colonial slaves . . . [and] in India the revolutionary movement . . . had recently led to the greatest labor strikes in Asia, which the English government has met by ordering its armored cars into action in Bombay."

Socialist Europe, Trotsky proclaimed, "will come to the aid of liberated colonies with her technology, her organization and her ideological influence. Colonial slaves of Africa and Asia! The hour of proletarian dictatorship in Europe will strike for you as the hour of your own emancipation!" Systematically and with fury, Trotsky proceeded to lay down the course of Communist policy for the next half century, perhaps longer.

In the capitalist states, Trotsky declared, "The whole course of capitalist development has acted to undermine political democracy."

> The peasant in Bavaria and Baden who still cannot see beyond the spires of his village church, the small French wine producer who is being driven into bankruptcy by the large-scale capitalists who adulterate wine, and the small American farmer fleeced and cheated by bankers and Congressmen—all these social layers thrust back by capitalism away from the mainstream of development are called upon, on paper, by the regime of political democracy to assume the direction of the state. But in reality, on all the basic questions which determine the destinies of the peoples, the financial oligarchy makes the decision behind the back of parliamentary democracy.

On the other hand, he said, the new Russia offered "a broad organization which embraces the working masses independently of trade or level of political development already attained." It was "working-class self-rule," a "flexible apparatus . . . capable of attracting into its orbit ever newer layers, opening wide its doors to the toiling layers in the city and the country."

Thus the vision of scientific Socialism, a new Elysium to replace the decadent, crumbling, despicable old order. Yet how was the proletariat to realize that lustless paradise? Join the Comintern! Establish a Cheka! Build a Red Army! "Under the banner of Workers' Soviets, UNITE! Under the banner for revolutionary struggle for power, UNITE! Under the banner of the International, UNITE! WORKERS OF THE WORLD! UNITE!"

One of the great speeches of the century was at an end. For all its dogmatic obscurities, for all its vituperation and bombast, Trotsky's presentation of the Comintern Manifesto was a major event in the history of mankind, a clarion call to change the entire structure of human society. Deeply moved, the little group of revolutionaries rose and sang the hymn of the Comintern, the "Internationale":

> Arise, ye prisoners of starvation!
> Arise, ye wretched of the earth!

Trotsky then strode from the hall for the marches of Asia to continue the war against the counterrevolutionary Whites. Thereupon the congress elected a Committee of Five to act as stewards of the Comintern until a second congress should meet and elect a representative international executive committee. The stewards were: Gregori Zinoviev, chairman; Angelika Balabanov, a dwarf with a beautiful face, known to all the police forces of Europe as a "particularly elusive and dangerous clandestine"; Vatislav Vorovsky, who had helped organize Lenin's journey across wartime Germany; and two men who were to act as Zinoviev's functionaries. In time that tiny committee would swell to become a full-scale secret and political warfare service with a headquarters staff in Moscow of at least

2,500 people bound together by the iron discipline of the Bolsheviks and watched over closely by the Cheka and the secret police organizations that would succeed it.

Their business done, the delegates left the court of justice for the czar's throne room where Zinoviev and Vorovsky waited to bid them Godspeed. A photographer was on hand to take their picture. As the delegates assembled in a phalanx on the richest carpets of Bukhara and Transcaucasia, the photographer fussed, postured, and rearranged them until he could see them all with his lens. Some stood, some sat. Winged collars prodded ample jowls. Their suits were nicely pressed, their mustaches nicely trimmed, their hair nicely oiled. They could have been comfortable shopkeepers from any town in Europe or America. They looked exactly like the class the Comintern was sworn to destroy.

The photographer at last disappeared under a black cloth draped over a four-legged Kodak. Magnesium powder in a flashpan exploded with a blinding puff. The session was over, and so was the congress. The delegates dispersed to begin the world revolution of the proletariat.

## Chapter Eight

Since revolutionary ferment was such a prevalent condition of the times, Lenin had ample reason to believe that a world revolution of the proletariat was imminent. Declared Gregori Zinoviev in the first issue of the Comintern journal: "Old Europe is rushing toward its revolution at breakneck speed. In a twelve-month period we shall already have begun to forget that there was ever a struggle for Communism in Europe, for in a year the whole of Europe will be Communist."[1]

Within two weeks of the founding of the Comintern, on March 21, 1919, as if to underscore Zinoviev's words, the first soviet state outside of Russia was established in Hungary. At the head of the revolution was a thirty-three-year-old Transylvanian Jew, Béla Kun. A junior officer in the Austro-Hungarian Army that fought alongside the Germans in Russia, Kun had been captured and interned in a prisoner-of-war camp at Tomsk in Siberia, where he became indoctrinated with Bolshevism. Upon release from prison, he came to know Lenin in Petrograd. Lenin sent him in November 1918 to Budapest to found, with Soviet funds, the Hungarian Communist Party. Even though the Comintern was still in its formative stage, Béla Kun thus became one of its first agents.

Kun was "a plump little man" who was "endowed with an inexhaustible capacity for puffing out Marxist slogans."[2] Exuding an aura of support from neighboring Red Russia, he inevitably attracted followers in a country torn by defeat and stunned by harsh conditions imposed by the Allied leaders, particularly Georges Clemenceau of France, who took a special delight in dismembering the old Austro-Hungarian Empire. Yet even so, Kun's disciples were few, mainly men like himself who had been indoctrinated in Bolshevism in Russian prison camps.

Kun nevertheless began immediately to conspire against the all-party government of Count Mihály Károlyi, who had engineered the dissolution of the Austro-Hungarian monarchy of the Emperor Charles and had established a republic. In what was clearly a disruptive move, Kun demanded that the government pay every demobilized soldier 5,400 crowns. Since that would have produced catastrophic inflation, Károlyi refused. When Kun and his small band of Communists took to the streets in bloody clashes with the police, Károlyi responded by throwing Kun and his principal lieutenants into jail.

There they might have languished indefinitely but for Clemenceau's persistent efforts at Versailles to dismember Hungary. According to the terms of the armistice, division of the old Austro-Hungarian Empire was to be determined by plebiscite, but when Rumanians, Serbs, and Czechs occupied great sections of the territory and sent Magyar refugees fleeing to Budapest, the Allied powers accepted the divisions as a fait accompli. When Károlyi refused to allow Hungary to be used as a base for interventionist operations against Russia—having "had enough of war"[3]—the French demanded in the name of the victorious powers that the Hungarian Army withdraw from still more territory, including districts indisputably populated by Magyar majorities.

In the atmosphere of despair produced by that treatment, many a Hungarian leader began to dwell on the possibility that as Lenin had proclaimed, world revolution was coming; and one basic idea took hold: the only hope for Hungary was Russia. When Károlyi called on the Socialists to form a new government, they looked enviously on Béla Kun's Russian support and called on him to join them. Released from prison and appointed commissar of foreign affairs, Kun moved swiftly to take over. Nobody dared challenge a man who could invoke the support of Lenin himself; it was time "to see what could be salvaged of St. Stephen's Kingdom under the Hammer and Sickle!"[4]

On the night of March 21, 1919, Kun proclaimed a dictatorship of the proletariat, a "Government of the Glorious Light." The action produced in Prime Minister Lloyd George the utmost anxiety. In a note to President Wilson, he stated that unless the Allied powers offered the defeated states sensible terms providing an alternative to Bolshevism, "all Eastern Europe will be swept into the orbit of the Bolshevik revolution and within a year we may witness the spectacle of three hundred million people organized into a vast Red Army" ready with German support "for the renewal of the attack on Western Europe."[5]

Within a matter of weeks, the apocalypse that Lloyd George predicted looked for a moment to be under way. Using the Hungarian Embassy as a base, Kun's agents, on April 18, 1919, precipitated an uprising in Vienna, but it attracted no general support. A more professional revolutionary effort followed, engineered by a Budapest lawyer, Ernst Bettelheim. Acting in the name of the Comintern, Bettelheim removed the old leadership of the Communist Party in Vienna and replaced it with a directorate designed to serve as the general staff of the revolution. Throwing "thousand-crown notes around like water,"[6] Bettelheim emulated Trotsky's tactics in Petrograd, organizing small teams to seize control of the state by capturing a few of the most important government buildings and creating committees to spread revolution in the Army. Agents were supposed to bring out industrial and transportation workers along with sympathetic soldiers on June 15, 1919, while Kun concentrated a corps of Hungarian troops on the Austro-Hungarian frontier, only two hours' march from Vienna; but, for all the preparations, the revolution failed to prosper. Most of Bettelheim's Hungarian crowns had gone into the wrong pockets, the plans were betrayed to the government, and on the night before the uprising was to begin, the police arrested the entire leadership of the Communist Party and more than a hundred agitators. The next morning in the Ringstrasse, where Communist masses were supposed to have gathered, loyal Austrian battalions stood, and when some 4,000 Communists began a march on the prison to release their comrades, the police opened fire, wounding eighty and killing twenty. The revolution collapsed.

Inside Hungary, Kun had considerably more success in establishing his authority, which, he quickly revealed, was to be absolute. On the day after he declared a "government of the glorious light," when a three-man delegation of veterans called to remind him of his earlier demand for 5,400 crowns for every demobilized soldier, Kun dismissed the veterans peremptorily. "Now shut up with your demands for 5,400 crowns," he shouted, "or instead of 5,400 crowns you will get 5,400 machine gun bullets."[7]

Kun's "main scheme was simple enough," reported a British agent, Sir Basil Thomson. "The State was to take over the ownership of all public and private property, every citizen was to receive a fixed wage and to pay a fixed price for every commodity."

The administration of the new regime consisted of a directorate of five, including Kun, and a series of soviets down to local level, with each having the power to change or annul any action of the soviet below it. The right to vote was limited to workers of both sexes who were eighteen or over and who were actually working; employers, people with private incomes, merchants, priests, lunatics, and criminals were disenfranchised. The country's thirty-two banks were nationalized under the jurisdiction of the Commissariat of Finance, and nobody could withdraw more than 2,000 crowns (about $750) a month. All jewelry and other valuables exceeding a worth of 500 crowns became the property of the state. Businesses employing more than ten persons were nationalized and run by councils of employees, while smaller businesses were subject to strict controls.

Kun's government was "in direct telegraphic communication with Lenin three or four times a week if not oftener." As Sir Basil Thomson reported to London, Kun and the other members of the directorate acknowledged Moscow as the "centre of the World Revolution" and obeyed all Moscow's instructions.

Yet to Sir Basil, at least, "the realm of the glorious light" appeared to have produced only "one happy class": the commissars, who were "enjoying themselves to the full." They were "exactly like a lot of mischievous schoolboys let loose in a shop of a scientific instrument maker." The result, said Sir Basil, was "a sort of compound of 'Alice of the Looking-Glass' and a bad dream, and, like a dream, it will pass."

It would, indeed, pass, for it soon became evident to most Hungarians that Allied leaders, Clemenceau in particular, would not tolerate a "Petty Russia on the Danube."[8] Dismayed at the thought of a soviet so close to France, Clemenceau encouraged the Czechs and Rumanians to continue their advance. True to the promise that the Red Army would go to the assistance of any revolutionary state that needed help, Lenin sent troops to help Kun by diverting the Rumanian Army, but they were ragtag battalions in bark slippers, tattered uniforms, and outmoded weapons, herding cows, goats, and horses as they went, and were soon put to flight.

Promising that the Rumanians would withdraw from all Magyar territory if the Hungarians ceased to contest annexation of the lands populated by Czechs and Rumanians, Clemenceau called on Kun to pull his army back on Budapest. "Determined to play Lenin in Brest-Litovsk,"[9] Kun pretended to agree and ordered withdrawal, but then, in the hope that the withdrawal had put the Rumanians off guard, he ordered the Hungarian Red Army to attack. It was a stratagem hardly worthy even of a schoolboy, and within a few days the Rumanians were in Budapest.

On the eve of the capital's fall, Kun appealed to Lenin for more help, but Lenin was fighting for his life against the Allied and White Russian armies and could spare nothing. Blaming defeat on a lack of revolutionary ardor among soldiers and workers, Kun resigned on August 1, 1919. The Hungarian people, he declared, needed "to taste a really ruthless and horrible bourgeois dictatorship before they will become revolutionaries."

A man given to quick tears, Kun appealed between sobs to his ambassador in Vienna to arrange asylum for him. As he crossed the frontier, Gregori Zinoviev in Moscow bewailed "the greatest tragedy." The Comintern's first foreign soviet had lasted but 133 days; it had collapsed, said Zinoviev, "under pressure from imperialist bandits . . . aided by the gold of the imperialists and the bayonets of their executioners." Although Kun would continue for some years to try to foment revolution in Austria and Germany, he would in time be called to Moscow and charged with deviationism and would languish and die in a Bolshevik jail.

As German sailors mutinied at Kiel in November 1918 and strikes and dissident marches occured in Berlin, a Socialist uprising swept Munich, led by a bearded theater critic and romantic, Kurt Eisner, who had visions of establishing "a realm of light, beauty, and reason." So widespread was the uprising that King Ludwig III abdicated and his heir, the Duke of Brunswick, renounced the throne, thus ending the Wittelsbach dynasty, which had ruled Bavaria since 1180. Eisner established what he called "a government of kindness," but he was to have little time to perfect it. Elections in January 1919 produced an overwhelming victory for the middle and strident demands for Eisner's resignation, and as Eisner made his way to the Landtag on February 21, 1919, to proffer it, a young, anti-Semitic, rightist count, unaware that Eisner was about to resign, shot him in the back and killed him.

The assassination plunged Munich into a state of hysteria, aggravated when a waiter, Alois Lindner, marched into the Landtag and shot down two delegates and a member of the Cabinet, whom he thought were responsible for Eisner's murder. Amid violent tumult, the city's politics took a sharp swing to the left. A Bolshevik minority declared a general strike; Red Guards occupied public buildings, banks, and centers of communication and learning; hostages were taken; and the streets swarmed with soldiers in armored cars calling over their bullhorns: "Revenge for Eisner."[10]

Out of the maelstrom emerged a Socialist poet, Ernst Toller, who announced that he would establish "a dictatorship of love."[11] As Toller and a muddled band of idealists surrounding him plotted a takeover of the government, Lenin acted to move professional revolutionaries to Munich. Among them was Dr. Eugene Leviné.

Born in 1883 in Petrograd of wealthy parents, Leviné went in 1903 to Heidelberg to study law. There he became involved with Russian revolutionaries who were busily plotting the assassinations—with an occasional success—of czarist dignitaries. When Leviné in time returned to Russia he was eventually jailed for distributing arms. Upon his release, he became a Socialist preacher, trudging from village to village in the Vitebsk region, in the process contracting swamp fever and a particularly severe form of conjunctivitis that left him partially blind.

At the end of 1907, he was arrested as a revolutionary spy and beaten almost to death at the jail in Minsk. His mother bought his half-dead body from his jailers and took him back to Germany, where he lived in Heidelberg again, partially blind, partially deaf, and tubercular.

He turned to writing revolutionary short stories that became inspirational classics in the German working class movement. One that became particularly celebrated, "The End of a Revolutionary," contained what would turn out to be a prophetic account of a revolutionary's execution:

> Some, indifferent and cool as always, take the coffin. The four prisoners stand erect and bare-headed in the icy cold wind. The black iron gate opens with a creak. A unit of soldiers with their lieutenant come out. They draw up facing the prisoners. From one window comes the subdued sound of the funeral march of the Russian revolutionaries: "You have fallen a victim in the fatal struggle." The coffin slowly sways toward the black gateway. The four are still bare-headed in the yard. The lieutenant shouts, "Away from the windows, I'm going to shoot." Fire! The shots ring out. We draw back into the damp cells. Outside, behind the bars, the dusk falls. From far, far away we can hear the hearse rumbling down the street. Rest in peace, comrades. Now you are free.[12]

Expecting never to return to czarist Russia, Leviné obtained German citizenship in his mother's maiden name, representing himself as the son of a wealthy Russian family with good connections in the scientific world. Joining Karl Liebknecht's Spartakusbund, Leviné moved to Mannheim, where he spread pacifist ideas with subtlety and infiltrated the workers' movements with skill. It was in March 1919 that he received orders from the Comintern to go to Munich and help emulate in Bavaria the triumph of Bolshevism in Hungary.

In Munich, Leviné quickly discerned that the revolutionary movement was perilously threatened by the military monks of the German General Staff, particularly by a bullet-headed General Franz Xaver Ritter von Epp, leader of the paramilitary Freikorps in Bavaria. As representatives of the left gathered in the former home of the Bavarian kings, the Wittelsbach Palace, Leviné warned that von Epp was sending agents into the city to incite the revolutionaries to premature action and decapitate the movement. When on April 3, 1919, leftists in Augsburg, spurred by von Epp's agents, demanded the immediate proclamation of a Bavarian Soviet Republic, the Spartakists under Leviné's leadership prudently refused to participate; but the poet Ernst Toller, intoxicated by the heady smell of power and by the prospects of a Socialist Bavaria at last independent of Prussia, was not to be restrained. On April 7, 1919, he formed a Revolutionary Workers' Council and proclaimed a Soviet Republic of Bavaria. As churches rang their bells in celebration, large red posters appeared throughout Munich announcing that "the toiling population has become the master of its own destiny" and acclaiming "the abolition of the accursed epoch of capitalism." Declaring a national holiday, Toller announced that diplomatic relations had been established with Soviet Russia and Soviet Hungary.

The proclamations were grand but the results a sham. The soldiers of the Munich garrison had remained in their barracks under the tight control of Ritter von Epp, and as Leviné declared: "In the factories the workers toil and drudge as ever before for the capitalists. In the offices sit the same Royal functionaries. In the streets the old armed guardians of the capitalist world keep order."[13]

For a time it seemed that Leviné would flee, but even though convinced that General von Epp soon would strike, he decided to try to capture the revolution. The Spartakists, he declared to Toller, will be "at your side when the fight breaks out," but in exchange for that assistance, Toller would have to accept Communist orders, for "we will only take over if you are ready to carry out our programme."[14] After only three days, Toller's government collapsed, and Leviné formed a Committee of Twenty to take control. As he sent Red Guards into the streets to arrest von Epp's agents, one who was caught in the net was a corporal of infantry, Adolf Hitler, but some officers of the corporal's old regiment, who had thrown in their lot with the Spartakists, persuaded Leviné to let him go.[15]

As Leviné's government began to function, fervid crowds gathered outside the Wittelsbach Palace to watch the functionaries come and go, to listen to the proclamations, to join the Red Army or the Red Guard. Proclamation after proclamation issued from the Wittelsbach Palace: soldiers who supported the revolution would receive an extra five marks pay per day; the bourgeoisie was to surrender all arms and to appear at their banks with keys to their safe deposit boxes; the banks were to dispense funds to the workers but not a pfennig for the bourgeoisie without written authority from the government. "Revolution cannot be made with safe, compassionate hearts," Leviné declaimed. "It demands a stern, relentless will." Seizing hostages and holding them in the Luitpold High School as a means of enforcing his decrees, Leviné telegraphed Lenin: "We have the pleasure of informing you that the bogus Soviet Republic has collapsed and a real proletariat rule has been established in its place."[16]

Yet the real proletariat rule was destined to be short-lived. By April 30, 1919, General von Epp had drawn a tight circle around Munich. Sensing the end, Leviné's Red Army commander ordered execution of the hostages in the high school, and before a horrified Ernst Toller could intervene, at least twenty were shot. That night students slipped through the lines to tell von Epp of the atrocity, and the next morning, the first day of May, the Freikorps attacked.

The troops encountered little opposition, and the people cheered their coming. By May 3, 1919, Munich was secure, but since sixty-eight of von Epp's troops had died in the process, there had to be a reckoning and there ensued a brutal White terror that claimed at least a thousand lives. It was, reported the French military attaché, "a savage debauchery, an indescribable orgy."[17]

When General von Epp put a price of 10,000 marks on Eugene Leviné's head, Leviné was soon betrayed. Charged with high treason, he could offer only the classic defense of the revolutionary: he had lost. "Sooner or later," he told the court, "other judges will sit in this hall and then those who have transgressed against the dictatorship of the proletariat will be punished for high treason."

The sentence was inevitable: death by firing squad. On June 6, 1919, Leviné's wife, Rosa, passed an hour with her husband in his cell; as she was ushered out, Leviné was led away. In the courtyard of the jail, a lieutenant of infantry positioned him against a wall, and just as Leviné had written in "The End of a Revolutionary," shouted to other prisoners to get away from the windows. Facing the firing squad, Leviné refused a blindfold. "Long live the world revolution!" he cried, then as the firing squad took aim: "We communists are all dead men on leave."[18]

In 1904, in a lecture before the Royal Geographical Society in London, the English geographer Sir Halford Mackinder recalled that in the Middle Ages, Europe had been confined to its boundaries and constantly threatened by mobile horsemen from the great Euro-Asiatic landmass to the east, but then with the conquest of the seas, Europe had "emerged upon the world" and succeeded in "wrapping her influence round the Euro-Asiatic land-power which had hitherto threatened her very existence." Yet change, said Sir Halford, again was coming, for the railroad was restoring mobility to Euro-Asia and returning the great landmass to its former "pivot position." An alliance of the two great powers in that Euro-Asian heartland, Russia and Germany, either through political liaison or military conquest, would upset the balance of power "in favour of the pivot state." If there should be a melding of the vast industrial power of the two nations, their technological genius, their manpower and raw materials, "the empire of the world would then be in sight."[19]

Although Lenin may have been unaware of what came to be known as Mackinder's "heartland theory," he nevertheless demonstrated almost from the moment of seizing power in November 1917 an appreciation of what might be achieved by a union of Russia and Germany. From the start he worked unceasingly through his agents (he called them "phantomas"), through his secret services, and through the Comintern to revolutionize Germany and establish a dictatorship of the proletariat with the strongest ties to Moscow. Without such an alliance, said Lenin, Russia would always be liable to attack by the capitalist powers, and during the time of the perils in 1918, he insisted that the only way the Soviet Republic could survive would be through a parallel revolution in Germany. To procure that revolution, he had sent one of his most able phantomas, Adolf Joffe, to Berlin, and when Joffe was expelled and the Germans broke diplomatic relations with Russia, he dispatched a team of his most able revolutionaries to infiltrate Germany: Karl Radek, one of the most powerful men in the Comintern; Nikolai Bukharin, second-in-command of the Comintern; Christian Rakovsky, a Bulgarian who was a signatory at the founding of the Comintern; and a mysterious man called Ignatov, who probably was Alexander Shpigelglas, an official of the Cheka's Foreign Department who had a record of assassinations during the Terror.

Lenin's phantomas arrived in Berlin in December 1918 in time to attend the founding congress of the Communist Party of Germany, called by Karl Liebknecht. To Radek and his Russian colleagues, conditions in Germany appeared to be ideal for revolution. They could see, as did a German diarist, Count Harry Kessler, that "Germany lay prostrate," that the continuing Allied naval blockade "achieved a casualty list of 700,000 children, old people, and women," and that people were "reeling deliriously between blank despair, frenzied revelry, and revolution."[20]

Yet Liebknecht's closest associate, Rosa Luxemburg, a short, stout Polish woman who walked with a limp, saw those very conditions as unpropitious for revolution. Although there was a lot of noise in the streets, the masses were too concerned about finding food, clothing, firewood, and work to trouble themselves with politics, and without the support of the masses, she saw no hope that revolution would succeed. So, too, many deserters and ex-soldiers were waving red flags, but thousands of others had formed themselves into well-armed private armies (Freikorps) that would march to the tune of the government, and there were still powerful regiments loyal to the General Staff, led by officers disgusted and angered since their return from the front by rude, humiliating treatment at the hands of revolutionary soldiers and sailors. Nor was the party leadership itself ready for revolution, said Luxemburg; it lacked organization and was sustained only by a spirit of fanatical revolutionary romanticism and utopianism. A revolution, she said, would fail.

Her arguments made little sense to Karl Radek. Well aware of Lenin's maxim that only through a revolution in Germany could the revolution in Russia survive, he had no concern for the fate of the German proletariat. Even if the revolution should fail, it still would serve to distract Britain, France, and the United States from their war against Russia. Radek used all his powers of persuasion to insist that the German workers rise to "chase out" Friedrich Ebert's government and establish "a genuinely revolutionary government in its place."[21]

How the Army would react to an uprising was soon demonstrated when some 3,000 sailors, calling themselves the People's Marine Division, occupied the Imperial Palace and demanded 80,000 marks as the price for leaving. Having promised Chancellor Ebert that he could rely upon the Army against the Bolsheviks, General Groener called up artillery to shell the palace. He drove the revolutionaries out, killing seventy, but in the process he set off a tragedy that would come to be known as "Spartakus Week."

Angered, Liebknecht and the leaders of other left-wing groups on January 4, 1919, called out the masses for a march to the Siegesallee, the Avenue of Victory lined with statues of all the rulers of Prussia and Brandenburg. By the tens of thousands, the workers trudged through slush and snow but with a curious lack of unity or verve. Whether Liebknecht intended it or not, armed revolutionaries joined in. On the first day, they seized all the railroad stations, which slowed the arrival of Army reinforcements, and most of the newspaper offices. They placed machine guns on the Brandenburg Tor to command the government quarter and from hastily established mortar pits shelled Army artillery positions.

The actions of Liebknecht and the other left-wing leaders appeared to indicate that the success of the revolutionaries took them by surprise. "The masses stood shoulder to shoulder from the Roland to the Viktoria . . . [and] far into the Tiergarten," reported a Communist newspaper, Rote Fahne, on January 7, 1919. "They were armed and they were waving red flags . . . standing there at 9 o'clock in the morning in the mist and the cold [but] meanwhile the leaders were merely sitting and talking." When twilight came, "sadly the masses went home."[22]

Liebknecht spent part of the day drinking beer in his Lokal, and when he at last went to party headquarters at ten o'clock that night, he attempted revolution by decree. He issued "a revolutionary manifesto" in which he declared that he had "dismissed" the Ebert government and that his Revolutionary Committee had "provisionally taken over" the government of Germany. With that declaration, Liebknecht vanished into the workers' suburb of Neukölln, where he had a safe house, and nothing more was heard of his Revolutionary Committee. Rosa Luxemburg, she who had advised against revolution, was the only leader to act with vigor and enthusiasm. "Act!" she cried. "Disarm the counter-revolution, arm the masses, occupy all important positions. Act quickly! The revolution demands it!"[23]

Yet for all Rosa Luxemburg's show of enthusiasm, the revolution was dying out. As Count Kessler noted on the 9th: "I made my way to the upper part of Unter den Linden. To the rat-tat-tat of distant machine guns, life proceeded almost normally. A fair amount of traffic, some shops and cafés open, street-vendors peddling their wares, and barrel-organs grinding away as usual."[24]

Approximately 1,200 people died during Spartakus Week, although nobody could be really sure of the figure, for police would be pulling corpses from the Landwehr Canal running through the heart of the city for weeks. At least 3,800 people were wounded.

Karl Liebknecht spent the first days after the end of Spartakus Week reading fairy tales to the young daughter of the household in which he was hiding, then, upon word that police were looking for him nearby, he left in disguise for the home of a relative in the bourgeois district of Wilmersdorf. There Rosa Luxemburg joined him, along with another Spartakist, Wilhelm Pieck. Luxemburg appeared undaunted by the collapse of the revolution; when the defense minister, Gustav Noske, announced that order had been restored, she wrote out a manifesto on the kitchen table: "'Order rules in Berlin.' You stupid lackeys! Your 'order' is built on sand. Tomorrow the revolution will rear ahead once more and announce to your horror amidst the brass of trumpets: 'I was, I am, I always will be!'"[25]

Well that might be, but neither Rosa Luxemburg nor Karl Liebknecht would see it. Somebody betrayed them to the police, and while they were having supper on the evening of January 15, 1919, a troop of horse guardsmen took them into custody. It was rumored that their betrayer was Wilhelm Pieck, that he had revealed their whereabouts in return for his own freedom. If true, it was an early manifestation of Pieck's ability to survive: as a leader of the German Communist Party, he would escape purges by both Hitler and Stalin to become one of the highest officials of the Comintern and in 1949 to become president of the Democratic People's Republic of Germany.

The horse guardsmen took Luxemburg and Liebknecht to headquarters of the Guards Cavalry Division in the Hotel Eden. There they interrogated them brutally and then put them into separate cars, supposedly to be taken to the Moabit prison for further questioning. Neither of them arrived. Six officers drove Liebknecht into a dark alley off the Tiergarten, where they killed him with a single bullet in the head. Other officers took Rosa Luxemburg to the Liechtenstein Bridge, killed her with a shot in the nape of the neck, and tipped her body into the Landwehr Canal.

Except for Karl Radek, Lenin's other phantomas made their way uneventfully back to Russia. Radek was arrested and held for a time in Moabit prison, where he may have been questioned by agents of the British intelligence service, but when the police were unable to prove that he had had any part in the Spartakus uprising, they put him under house arrest in the home of a friend, a German baroness. In time, the German foreign minister, Count Ulrich von Brockdorff-Rantzau, arranged for his release out of concern that his continued retention might alienate the Russian government. Von Brockdorff-Rantzau saw Germany and Russia as partners in misfortune, and as would soon emerge, he had important business to transact with the Russian foreign commissar, Georgi Chicherin.

*Chapter Nine*

Early in 1920, rumors that the Red Army was about to march into Poland, take Warsaw, then Berlin, jump the Rhine, and seize Paris spread throughout Europe. The old soldier, Erich von Ludendorff, not only heard those rumors but also read reports to the same effect from the German intelligence service, which, like the Great General Staff, had been outlawed at Versailles but still existed. If Germany was to stand any chance of stopping that thrust by the Red Army, there had to be a change in the harsh conditions the Allied powers had imposed at Versailles. How was a nation limited to a purely defensive army of 100,000 men, no heavy artillery, no warships, no submarines, no aviation to be expected to quarantine that plague bacillus of which Churchill spoke?

"Bolshevism," said General Max Hoffmann to a correspondent of the Washington *Post* over coffee at the Hotel Eden, "has ceased to be a regional problem and is now a world problem." There would have to be, said the whiskered old general, "an international army to march on Moscow." Only with the occupation of Moscow, Hoffmann continued, stirring his *Kaffee-mit-Schlag,* could the regime of Lenin and Trotsky be "unhorsed" and the commissars sent along "the shortest way to oblivion."[1]

Ludendorff and Hoffmann were being more opportunistic than realistic, seizing on the specter of Red invaders as a device to restore German power. Surely it would be no easy task for an army bearing rusty Mausers and shod with bark to march all the way to the English Channel. Yet Ludendorff, in particular, could see no Russian weaknesses; he conjured instead visions of Red cohorts camped in the Rosengarten in Berlin and defecating at the base of the Siegessäule, the great monument to German prowess on the battlefield.

Apparently unnerved by the prospect, Ludendorff sent for Lieutenant Colonel W. Stewart Roddie, a British secret agent whom he had met at one of the *thé-dansants* held for Allied military observers at the Hotel Adlon. Germany, Ludendorff told Roddie, was in great peril. As soon as the ground was hard enough following the *rasputitza*—the mud that comes with the first spring thaws—the Red Army intended to march through Poland and use its bayonets to support a Red revolution in Germany. So well would the Communist underground prepare the way that the Red Army might be able to occupy Warsaw without a fight. "Tell Churchill this," said Ludendorff. "We are standing at the crossroads, and a decision has to be come to. Either the world is going down under Bolshevism or the world is going to kill it."[2]

To prevent the Red Army from conquering Germany, Ludendorff told Roddie, the western powers would have to join the Germans to form a powerful army to march on Petrograd and Moscow to seize "the Bolsheviks' power bases." To effect the plan, he said, he would have to meet with Churchill, and since time was short, the meeting would have to take place soon. "We are no longer climbing up a mountain," Ludendorff said. "We are actually moving down the inner slope of a crater."

Was there no other way, asked Roddie, for Germany to avoid defeat? The only alternative, Ludendorff responded, was for Germany to find a dictator, a man of iron. Did Ludendorff have such a man in mind? No, but he had no doubt that one would emerge when the occasion demanded.

Colonel Roddie took his notes to London where he composed a letter to Churchill. Churchill in turn presented the letter at a meeting of the Cabinet, where the proposal created a stir. To H. A. L. Fischer, president of the Board of Education and an influential voice, the idea "that Winston should meet Ludendorff" was alarming. "Really," he wrote Lloyd George, "these Huns are very impudent."[3]

Churchill himself, while cautious, looked on Ludendorff's suggestion with more favor. "In my view," he wrote a colleague, "the objective which we should pursue . . . is the building up of a strong but peaceful Germany which will not attack our French allies, but will at the same time serve as a moral bulwark against the Bolshevism of Russia." On the other hand, he noted, since the end of the war, every suggestion by the War Office designed to bring about "the recovery, stability and tranquilisation of Europe" had "fallen on deaf ears."[4]

So that suggestion too would fall on deaf ears. Churchill would have to wait for thirty years before his vision of an Anglo-German alliance against Russia would be realized. In the meantime, Ludendorff's warning that an iron messiah would emerge from the chaos of German defeat would have been demonstrated as having been all too accurate.

The Bolshevik leaders did, indeed, intend a military campaign against Poland and Western Europe during the spring of 1920. To prepare the way for it, they arranged a congress to convene on February 5, 1920, in Amsterdam, the founding congress of the Western European Bureau of the Comintern. Once organized, the Western European Bureau was to plan what the Comintern called its "spring action": coordinating subversive actions and popular uprisings throughout Western Europe with an attack by the Red Army on Poland that was to proceed through Poland to link with a Red German Army; the other governments having been paralyzed by subversion and uprisings, the combined Russian and German armies were to assist the revolution of the proletariat to sweep Western Europe.

Some thirty representatives of various European Communist parties were to attend the conference along with two Americans, Louis Fraina, the international secretary of the American Communist Party, and a Comintern courier, Harry Nosowitsky, who was also an agent of the British intelligence service and of the Bureau of Investigation of the U.S. Department of Justice. Although the Comintern intended the congress to be "the most secret and important congress held by International Bolshevists" up to that time,[5] it was from its inception a masterpiece of insecurity and ineptitude.

There was, for example, the matter of funding. Recognizing that to stage the congress would require a considerable sum of money and that the Soviet government would be unable to transmit funds through normal channels, Moscow dispatched a special courier with twenty large diamonds concealed in the heels of his shoes. He vanished, never to be heard of again. When the Dutch organizer of the conference, Sebald Justinius Rutgers, left Moscow for Amsterdam, he too carried a number of diamonds and pearls; but in passing through Germany, he became so concerned that German authorities might detect the stones that he entrusted them to two officials of the Red underground in Berlin, known as Soviet 22, who promised to send them along later. Rutgers later was "greatly surprised when, after sending several letters to the German Comrades for these stones, he finally received an answer to the effect that he could not have [them] because the German Communists had sold them for four million marks" to finance their own revolutionary propaganda.[6]

As the date for the Amsterdam congress neared, Rutgers had only the proceeds from the sale of three stones, most of which had already been spent in advance of the arrival of the delegates. Without personal means, many of the delegates would be unable to pay their hotel bills or purchase their return fares, which would enable the Dutch police to arrest some of them on charges of vagrancy and hotel fraud and expel them from the country.

There was also the matter of $8 million which the head of the Comintern, Gregori Zinoviev, promised to deposit in Amsterdam and elsewhere to finance the spring action. Those funds either never were sent or were funneled through the German Communist Party, which, as with Rutgers' jewels, appropriated them.

As the delegates began to arrive at Dutch border crossing points early in February 1920, the Dutch police were fully alert to their coming. The police held many of them for checks of credentials—most of which were forged—and those who got through were painfully aware that they were the objects of intense surveillance by the police and counterintelligence agents. On the opening date of the congress, February 5, 1920, few of them showed up at the conference site, the Heystee Building on the Heernscgragchat, and those who did found an empty room with a note pinned to the beige of the chairman's table advising them to return to their hotels and await instructions as to a new location that presumably would be unknown to the police.

The congress opened two days late in Rutgers' home in Amersfoort, some thirty miles from Amsterdam. Yet the delegates were unable at first to focus on the critical issues, for a spokesman for the British delegation promptly took the floor to accuse the American delegates—Fraina and Nosowitsky—of being police agents. A British agent may well have planted that story in an effort to wreck the congress, but Fraina was able to cite the fact that his peers in New York had recently acquitted him of similar charges, whereupon he successfully sprang to Nosowitsky's defense. That issue at last dispensed with, the delegates stumbled one by one through various resolutions, the most important of which declared that the Western European Bureau should "create favorable agitation in countries of Western Europe in such a manner that on arrival of Soviet armies . . . no opposition shall be offered to occupation and that in those countries a Soviet republic shall be proclaimed as a consequence of measures taken by the [Western European] Bureau."

The next day so many Dutch police were swarming about Rutgers' house that the delegates found it impossible to continue their session. They split into sections to meet at a variety of locations, including the homes of Dutch Communists, but on February 9, 1920, the Dutch police wrecked the congress completely by arresting everybody they could find. Louis Fraina managed to escape, a fact duly noted by a number of other delegates. Nosowitsky was among those detained; interrogated at length, he was finally put aboard a steamer bound for England and upon arrival of the ship at Folkestone was again taken into custody, an event— British authorities were pleased to note—that was obviously observed by a known British Communist aboard the ship. Nosowitsky in time made a full report on the congress to the British security chief specializing in antiradical activities. To maintain Nosowitsky's cover, British authorities charged him with possession of a false passport, sentenced him to a month at hard labor in Wormwood Scrubs, then turned him loose to continue his work as a courier for the Comintern and as a spy for the British intelligence service and the American Bureau of Investigation.

Under instructions from the Comintern to proceed from Amsterdam to Moscow for the Second Congress of the Communist International, Fraina, in company with a British Communist, John T. Murphy, managed to sneak across the Dutch-German frontier. Making their way to Berlin, they checked in with the Red underground, Soviet 22. Soviet 22 was supposed to arrange their passage along an underground railway leading through Sweden and Finland to Russia, but since there was martial law, most civilian travel was prohibited, and Soviet 22 abandoned Fraina and Murphy to their own devices.

Although the two eventually crossed the frontier into Schleswig-Holstein on foot, the Danish police arrested them and deported them to Germany. There the German police, alerted by the American commissioner in Berlin, were waiting. The Americans intended to offer Fraina return to the United States in exchange for his turning informant against the Comintern, but for once his stars were smiling: while the policemen guarding him supped—they were in the pay of Soviet 22—Fraina and Murphy simply walked out into the night through an unlocked door. They made their way to Hamburg, where Soviet 22 got them aboard a ship repatriating Russian prisoners of war to Revel. Five days after arriving in Estonia, Fraina and Murphy finally reached the promised land, where, Fraina was soon to discover, new troubles awaited him.

Lenin's plan for an attack on Poland by the Red Army was thwarted by the founder and president of the Polish Republic, Marshal Josef Pilsudski. Having formed an alliance with the head of the Ukrainian Nationalists, Symon Petlyura, Pilsudski on April 25, 1920, struck first, sending a Polish army of 200,000 men driving into the Ukraine. With the help of the Nationalists, the Poles in less than two weeks seized the capital, Kiev.

Lenin reacted with fury. To lead the main drive of a counteroffensive, he called on the Red Army's foremost soldier, General Mikhail N. Tukhachevsky, only twenty-seven years of age but already a hero of a score of battles and a dedicated Bolshevik. A supporting drive was to be launched by a second army under the experienced cavalryman General Semyon M. Budyenny.

General Tukhachevsky issued a call to arms: "Soldiers of the workers revolution! Fix your glance towards the West. In the West will be decided the fate of the world revolution. . . . On our bayonets we will carry happiness and peace to the working masses of mankind. To the West! Close ranks! Forward march! The hour of attack has arrived. To Vilna, Minsk, and Warsaw—march!"[7]

Opened on May 15, 1920, the Red Army's drive quickly began to push the Poles back, and once the Reds recaptured Kiev, the Poles fled in disorder. The march was soon progressing at the rapid pace of twelve miles a day, and Budyenny's cavalry reached the outskirts of Lvov, almost at the traditional western boundary of the Ukraine.

In desperation, the Polish premier, Wladyslaw Grabski, appealed in early July 1920 for help from the western allies. The response from both Britain and France was weak, a proposal that Grabski seek an armistice by agreeing to accept an eastern boundary for Poland along what would later become known, after the British foreign minister, Lord Curzon, as the Curzon Line, roughly a north-south line through Brest Litovsk, to the west of which the population was made up almost entirely of ethnic Poles. It was the same line that the Supreme War Council had proposed as an eastern boundary but which the ambitious Poles had rejected. Grabski rejected it again.

On the next day, July 11, 1920, Lord Curzon made the same proposal to the Russians but strengthened it with a specific warning to Lenin that if the Red Army crossed the ethnic boundary, Russia faced the prospect of British military intervention. This impelled Lenin to rethink his position. It was one thing to endure relatively small contingents of foreign troops on the periphery of a country the size of Russia, quite another to come face to face with major western armies on the plains of Central Europe. Even if Lord Curzon was bluffing, the British Fleet might well move to bombard Petrograd.

Lenin might also have noted that for all the success of Tukhachevsky's and Budyenny's armies, the Polish peasantry had failed to rise in support of their liberation; indeed, had done quite the opposite, had responded with a fervor to a call to arms from Marshal Pilsudski. Nor for all his successes against the White armies was Lenin by any means master of his own house; there were still dissident forces to be conquered, still foreign troops on Russian territory, and there was a growing hunger in the streets. To a man the Politburo urged Lenin to back down to await a more propitious time for exporting the revolution to the west.

On the other hand, in the aftermath of the carnage of the Great War, all of Europe—and even the United States—appeared to Lenin to be so close to revolution as to need but a push to go over the brink. Lord Curzon, Lenin finally decided, was bluffing. On July 24, 1920, Tukhachevsky's army crossed the line into ethnic Poland and a few days later took the Polish rail and textile center of Bialystok. There the head of the Cheka, Derzhinski, quickly installed a provisional government of Polish Communists, which immediately nationalized the big textile mills and railroad-servicing shops and issued proclamation after proclamation informing the population of 100,000 on proper Socialist behavior.

And still the Red Army continued to march. A few days later Derzhinski followed in the wake of the advance to a point where from a house on a hilltop he could see the spires of Warsaw. On August 13, 1920, an advance guard took the village of Radzymin, only twelve miles from the capital.

Would the British intervene?

Winston Churchill strongly urged intervention. "All my experience," he declared, "goes to show the advantage of attacking these people. They become very dangerous the moment they think you fear them."[8]

In an article in the London *Evening News* called "The Poison Peril from the East," Churchill hinted again at Anglo-German cooperation, urging the Germans "to build a dyke of peaceful, lawful, patient strength and virtue against the flood of red barbarism from the East, and thus safeguard their own interests and the interests of their principal antagonists in the West."[9]

The article invoked the wrath of the London *Times*, which declared that "Mr. Churchill clearly ought not to remain a member of the Government of whose peace policy he disapproves." Yet that was before the threat to Warsaw became palpable; when it did, the *Times* reversed course, urging that the country invoke "the same unanimity and the same courage with which we faced the crisis of 1914." The British ambassador in Warsaw, Lord D'Abernon, wired the foreign secretary that if Poland were to be saved, Britain and France would have to send an expeditionary force of at least 20,000 men without delay. The London *Daily Herald*, a Socialist newspaper financed by Lenin with diamonds smuggled in the centers of a pound of chocolates by a London socialite jazz-band leader and Socialist, Edward Meynell, declared in a banner headline: BRITAIN PLUNGING INTO WAR WITH SOVIET RUSSIA. The prime minister summoned the two representatives of the Soviet trade mission, Leonid Krassin and Lev Kamenev, to No. 10 Downing Street and warned that unless the Red Army stopped its advance, the British Fleet would sail for the Baltic within three days.

That ultimatum turned out to have little real determination behind it. On August 7, 1920, the day the ultimatum was to expire, Lloyd George agreed to withdraw it if Krassin and Kamenev would assure him that they would do all they could to persuade Lenin to halt the Russian advance. To the Commons, where an atmosphere of crisis prevailed, Lloyd George declared that no British troops would be sent to Poland but that "if Russia tried to destroy Polish independence," Britain would send "military stores and advisers" and "would exercise an economic pressure" to force Russia "to release her stranglehold on the life of the Poles."[10]

The lack of determination demonstrated by the British government reflected two hard facts of life: first, after four years of warfare, the British people had no stomach for continued fighting, and second, the British working man wanted no part of a war with a government that presumably represented the working man of Russia. As the government debated the question of aid to the Poles, the secretary of the Labour Party, Arthur Henderson, called upon all British Socialists to stage protest demonstrations. Massive rallies followed throughout the country, carrying with them a barely veiled threat that if war should begin, a general strike would ensue. On August 9, 1920, at the instigation of Ernest Bevin, secretary of the dockworkers' union (who was destined at the end of World War II to become Britain's foreign secretary), the Labour Party Executive met with the Parliamentary Party in the House of Commons and passed a resolution stating that "the whole industrial power of the organized workers" would be mustered against a war with Russia. Within a few days workers had established 350 "Councils of Action"—Lenin, correctly, called them soviets—and were ready on signal to call a general strike. Bevin warned Lloyd George that "if war with Russia is carried on directly in support of Poland, there will be a match set to an explosive material, the result of which none of us can foresee."[11]

The British workingman may not have been prepared to support the world revolution of the proletariat—a resolution to join the Comintern was defeated by 2,940,000 votes to 225,000—but quite clearly he was determined that his country conduct no military campaign to undo the Russian Revolution. If Poland were to survive, there would have to be some way other than British intervention to achieve it.

Late in July 1920, French General Maxime Weygand, who had been chief of staff to the Supreme Allied Commander, Marshal Ferdinand Foch, arrived in Warsaw to advise Marshal Pilsudski on defense of the capital. In surveying his assets, it was soon obvious that what the Poles needed more than advice was guns and ammunition, but General Weygand learned also that Pilsudski had one cardinal advantage: the Poles could read the ciphers the Russians used to exchange messages between Tukhachevsky's and Budyenny's armies. Through that means, Weygand and Pilsudski learned that both Russian armies had outrun their primitive supply lines and were short of almost everything, including food. They also learned that a serious disagreement had developed in regard to the Red Army's strategy.

At the order of the chief political officer of the Revolutionary Military Council, Joseph Stalin, Budyenny's army was advancing not in support of Tukhachevsky's drive on Warsaw but instead independently to take the city of Lvov. With the Poles concentrating for a stand before Warsaw on the Vistula, Tukhachevsky needed Budyenny's help if the capital were to be taken. Although Tukhachevsky pleaded with Red Army headquarters to provide reinforcements and the headquarters ordered Budyenny to join him, Stalin directed Budyenny to ignore the order.

Although the Poles upon Weygand's advice had been preparing a counterattack to hit Tukhachevsky's north flank, Pilsudski through signal intercepts learned that his opponent's weak point was his center. There, along the axis of the Warsaw-

Brest Litovsk road, Pilsudski, on August 16, 1920, launched his principal thrust. Breakthrough was swift, whereupon Pilsudski turned northward to encircle the bulk of the Russian forces by linking with the drive planned by Weygand from the north.

Caught between the Polish pincers, Tukhachevsky's command disintegrated. Some 30,000 Russians fled across the frontier into East Prussia, there to be disarmed by the Germans. Before Tukhachevsky could rally his forces, the Poles had captured 66,000 prisoners, and Russian casualties totaled 150,000 men.

It was a victory that would be called one of "the decisive battles of the 20th century," for much as Charles Martel's victory at Tours in A.D. 732 had turned back the Muslim surge into Europe, so the Battle of Warsaw was "a check to Communism's first overt westward thrust."[12] In the fighting that followed, the Russians lost another 200,000 men before agreeing on October 12, 1920, to an armistice. In the Treaty of Riga on March 18, 1921, the Russians accepted an eastern boundary for Poland that gave the Poles large areas of Belorussia and the Ukraine, almost 52,000 square miles of territory to the east of the Curzon Line.

Winston Churchill was at his most jubilant. Something "sudden, mysterious and decisive" had occurred, he would later write. Lenin had barked his shins on Polish nationalism, and "Europe, her liberties and her glory [were] not to succumb to Communism."[13]

However costly and unsatisfactory the settlement of the Russo-Polish War for the Bolsheviks, the fact remained that for the first time since soon after the October Revolution, the Lenin regime faced no major organized military opposition inside European Russia. Yet there was still to be no end to crisis, for the long months of civil war had aggravated the problems of the body politic. Even as early as 1919 famine had begun to appear in many parts of the Soviet Republic, and even as the fighting against the White armies and Poland ended, there was to be no quick relief. Seed grain having been used for food, railroads having been devastated, old patterns of supply and demand having been destroyed, the country was in "a terrible economic ruin."[14] Soldiers long absent from their villages and needed to till the fields failed to come home; factories were idle for lack of raw materials; and tens of thousands were dying of malnutrition.

All the while "a brutal regime of terror and governmental suppression" continued; and to the general populace, government officials appeared to pay less attention to trying to alleviate the harsh conditions than to pursuing internal quarrels, intrigues, and power struggles that penetrated even to lower levels of the administrative apparatus. "Little by little," noted an American observer, "the deceived masses, still hungry, cold, oppressed, opened their eyes" and came to understand "that the situation was not the consequence of the struggle against the Whites but the inevitable consequence of a Communist regime."[15]

The big trouble began in the cradle of the revolution, Petrograd, at the Troubochny Works, where workmen accompanied by wives and children took to the streets, crying "Down with the Communists and Jews" (belief was widespread that the Bolshevik Revolution was an international Jewish conspiracy). They marched first to the Laferm Factory, where thousands swelled their ranks, then to the Baltic Shipbuilding Works, where thousands more joined in.

Although the chief of the Petrograd Cheka ordered the commander of the local Red Guard to break up the demonstration, the troops refused to march, and some Red Guard detachments joined the demonstrators. When at the direction of the Petrograd Politburo, the commandant of the 6th Soviet Military School sent cadets from his cavalry and machine-gun classes to put down the disturbance, the students fired their weapons into the air and allowed the workers to disarm them. Men of the 11th Reserve Regiment, sent to the center of the demonstration, also allowed the workers to take their weapons. Sailors aboard warships in the harbor— they had been the "cudgel" of the October Revolution—threw their weapons overboard.

When a local commissar by the name of Antseliovitch drove into the district to try to persuade the mob to disperse, the crowd dragged him from his car and sent him fleeing for his life. The crowd was kinder to the chairman of the Communist Party's Central Executive Committee and the titular head of state, Mikhail Ivanovich Kalinin, who happened to be in Petrograd at the time, and agreed to hear him, but he accomplished nothing. By late afternoon, work had stopped at virtually every plant in the city, and the workers filled the streets.

The next day, February 25, 1921, the government forbade all public assembly, ordered a curfew, and proclaimed martial law, but despite these decrees, a crowd again assembled, and leaders of the demonstration demanded that the government restore personal, press, and religious freedom, return all forms of private enterprise, and call a constituent assembly. The authorities refused to parley; a few loyal Red Guard units fired into the crowd; the Cheka began arresting people on any pretense; and the prisons soon were full. The next day, the 26th, there were no more demonstrations, but the workers still stayed away from the plants, while rumors swept the city. It was said that the counterrevolutionary Boris Savinkov was in the harbor aboard the warship Poltava and that the Grand Duke Nikolai Nikolaievitch, the czar's cousin and one of the few Romanovs to escape the royal massacre, had arrived in Riga as a preliminary to forming a new government.

To that point there had apparently been no contact between the workers and the sailors at the great fortress of Kronstadt. Built by Peter the Great on Kotlin Island in the Gulf of Finland about sixteen miles off the coast, Kronstadt was the main base for the Red Baltic Fleet. The base and its sailors had a long history of mutiny: in 1825 against Nicholas I, in 1882 against Alexander III, and in 1905 and 1917 against Nicholas II. On the 27th a message reached leaders of the workers' demonstration from the fortress inviting them to send a delegation to discuss mutual interests.

In Anchor Square in Kronstadt on March 1, 1921, sailors and representatives of the workers staged a boisterous convention aflame with counterrevolutionary fervor. One by one they shouted approval of fifteen resolutions. "Inasmuch as the present Soviets do not represent the will of the peasants and workmen," the resolutions began, there had to be elections by secret ballot to form new soviets.[16] The principal grievance appeared to be the Cheka, which in the words of the resolutions, had "brought the workers, instead of freedom, an ever present fear of being dragged into the torture chambers [which exceeded] by many times: the horrors [of] the gendarmerie administration of the Tsarist regime."[17]

The sailors sent a copy of the resolution to Lenin with a demand for an audience. Lenin promptly denounced the leaders of the revolt as "an indefinite conglomerate or union of ill-assorted elements" with whom he would never parley. The White generals and foreign elements, he declared, were behind the outbreak, and he ordered Trotsky to Petrograd to put down the revolution.

It was no minor force that Trotsky faced at Kronstadt. In the fortress and aboard the mutinous ships, the rebels possessed at least sixty-eight machine guns and 135 cannon, and their ranks, including sailors, soldiers, and armed workers, numbered approximately 40,000 men. There well might have been more had not Trotsky, aware that most of the troops of the Petrograd garrison sympathized with the rebels, ordered commanders to confiscate the soldiers' greatcoats and boots, without which the troops were unable to go out in the snow and subfreezing temperature.

To subdue the fortress, Trotsky had about 150,000 men but "a really reliable" core of only 20,000 officer cadets, and behind the attackers he posted machine-gun units of the Cheka.[18] Since the only way to reach the fortress was across the frozen waters of the gulf, devoid of cover or concealment, casualties were bound to be high. The defenders repulsed Trotsky's first assault, launched in darkness on March 8, 1921, and turned back others at terrible cost, perhaps as many as 25,000 killed. Yet in the end Trotsky assembled warships whose crews were loyal to bombard the fortress from the seaward side while launching yet another assault over the ice. As defeat appeared imminent, the leader of the revolt and about 8,000 others, some accompanied by wives and children, abandoned the fortress and escaped over the ice into Finland. On March 18, 1921, all resistance ceased, and revolutionary tribunals went to work executing all who were captured.

Despite the government's claims that the rebellion was the work of White generals and foreign elements, the uprising clearly had been spontaneous, for had it been preplanned, it would surely have been timed with the spring thaw when Kronstadt would have been invulnerable to all except attack by warships. As determined by the American consul in Vyborg, Finland, Harold B. Quarton, who interviewed survivors from Kronstadt, there had been no prior agitation among the sailors, no antibolshevik propaganda, no foreign funds. "The sailors rebelled," Quarton reported, "because of sympathy for their brother-workmen and because of the economic conditions under which they were oppressed."[19]

Lenin himself clearly recognized the Kronstadt Rebellion for what it was, a genuine uprising in the face of oppression and harsh economic conditions; for the government moved swiftly to ameliorate those conditions through what became known as the New Economic Policy. In the place of food requisitioning, peasants were assessed a specified amount of their crops to be furnished the state as a tax, and once having met that obligation, they were free to dispose of what was left on the open market. Instead of equal pay, wages were fixed to reflect ability, effort, and degree of responsibility. While large industries, transport, public utilities, the financial system, and natural resources remained the province of the state, shops and many small industries were permitted to operate for private profit, which gave rise to a new class of small businessmen. Even state-owned enterprises traded with each other and sought to expand through profits.

Although Lenin admitted that the New Economic Policy was a form of state capitalism, he maintained that it was only a strategic retreat, a temporary recourse from the goal of pure Communism occasioned by the rigors of war. To the chaste, the new policy was nevertheless seriously disturbing. The workers, peasants, soldiers, and sailors themselves had forced a revision within the world's first Communist state that the White armies, for all their foreign support, had been unable to achieve.

## Chapter Ten

Born into the nobility in the Baltic provinces, Baron Roman Nikolaus von Ungern-Sternberg fought in the ranks at Port Arthur in the Russo-Japanese War, where he received multiple wounds and was mentioned in dispatches. When the war ended, relatives persuaded him to attend military school; with considerable difficulty he finally managed to pass the officer's examination. Joining a Cossack regiment in Siberia, he established a reputation for eccentricity: eating with his men, sleeping with them on the floor, and joining them in debauchery, during which on one occasion he received a saber blow to the head, which added to his unpredictable behavior. In the World War, he served for a time as a squadron commander in the czarevich's own regiment of Nerchinsk Cossacks, again incurred multiple wounds, and was awarded the Cross of St. George for valor.

Because of his wounds, he left the czar's army and by the time of the Bolshevik Revolution had become established with a wife and child on an estate in Siberia. In the flush of freedom that came with the revolution, vassals on the estate burned the manor house and murdered Baron von Ungern-Sternberg's wife and child. Although the baron escaped, the experience destroyed even the faint vestiges of aristocratic mien and gentleman's demeanor that, with apparent difficulty, he had previously maintained.

Even in the Wild West atmosphere that prevailed in Siberia at the time, von Ungern-Sternberg's slovenly appearance, irascible temper, and licentious antics were a scandal. There were some drinking bouts that ended with his slaying a companion, and when he entered a café, "other occupants retired, for he was an expert with his gun."[1] Beneath unkempt yellow hair, he wore a long, reddish mustache "with waving ends, at which his nervous fingers pulled continually. He had the eyes of a vulture, with trembling pupils. Behind his broad cranium the calculating cruelty of madness smoldered."[2]

On the night of February 3, 1921, Baron von Ungern-Sternberg, accompanied by thirty-five men, some Russians, others Siberian tribesmen, crept past the carcasses of spavined dogs half-buried in windblown snow up to the eastern gates of the wall around the little city of Urga (Ulan Bator), capital of Outer Mongolia. It was a city of sharp contrasts. In some sections there were Russian-type houses of wood or adobe, neatly set off by painted wooden fences, in others, crude earthen yurts, black stovepipes protruding from domed roofs; elsewhere monasteries and atop a high hill beyond the Tula River, the golden-domed palace of the Jebtsundamba Khutukhtu, the "Living Buddha," filled with rich trappings as befitted an Oriental despot, before whose walls thousands of pilgrims prostrated themselves day after day in reverent respect for the divine reincarnation.

Arousing the people through reverence and awe, the Khutukhtu before the start of the World War had thrown off the yoke of Manchurian conquerors. Although he had established an independent feudal monarchy, so unsure was he in respect to his Chinese neighbors that he had sought and obtained close association with Russia as a protectorate. Yet when Russia became preoccupied with the war against Germany and then its own civil war, the Chinese had come back. It was the Chinese garrison in Urga that Baron von Ungern-Sternberg and his little band would have to deal with.

Late that night, "after the din of copper temple bugles, drums, and conches, and the rising and falling chant of praying lamas had ceased, and all the place lay silent,"[3] von Ungern-Sternberg and his men slipped up on the sentries at the eastern gate, slit their throats, and made their way into the city. Catching the Chinese soldiers asleep, they killed brutally; those Chinese who survived abandoned their weapons and fled into the night. At dawn, when they rallied and tried to retake the city, they were too late; the baron and his gang had by that time enlisted recruits from the Mongols in the city, anxious again to throw off the Chinese yoke.

In the days and weeks that followed, hundreds flocked to von Ungern-Sternberg's banner, and he began to create not only his own army but his own Mongolian state. He established the Khutukhtu as a figurehead chief of state, and with gold looted from the banks of Urga and other treasures provided by the Khutukhtu, he created a mixed force of Russians and Mongolians with which he intended to move into Siberia and thence, leaving a trail of blood behind him, drive down the Trans-Siberian Railroad to Moscow.

Siberia was "a witch's cauldron of blood, politics, pillaging, and intrigue."[4] With a coating of Russian adventurers and political exiles superimposed on a half-primitive native population, the inhabitants were almost as wild as the countryside. With the coming of revolution and war, lawlessness was rampant. Whites and Bolsheviks fought each other, while guerrillas, wanting no part of either, fought both in a war that made up in wanton brutality what the forces lacked in size and armament.

It was a perfect setting for a madman such as Baron von Ungern-Sternberg. It was a perfect setting too for other wild adventurers. Such as Gregori Mikhailovich Semenov, a former colleague of von Ungern-Sternberg's in the czarevich's Nerchinsk Cossacks, and Ivan Pavlovich Kalmykov, who had once served with Semenov in the Caucasus. Armed and supplied by the Japanese, Semenov, Kalmykov, and other lesser figures like them well served the goal of their benefactors, which was to keep Siberia in turmoil while the Japanese established a government subservient to Japan. In the process, they murdered, raped, robbed, and pillaged in such a brutal reign of terror that they drove many a White sympathizer into the arms of the Bolsheviks or the guerrillas.

By the time von Ungern-Sternberg emerged on the scene in Urga, much had changed. Semenov and Kalmykov, for all their support from the Japanese, were confined to small corners of Siberia, and Japanese hopes for a permanent influence in Siberia were nearly bankrupt. The last of the White armies in European Russia had been defeated, and the Czechoslovaks and all Allied troops had left Vladivostok, including the Americans, a last contingent having sailed on April 1, 1920. Of some sixteen groups calling themselves "governments" that had emerged in Siberia, all had disintegrated, but another had arisen and was fast establishing control over the entire primitive land.

That government was the Far Eastern Republic, essentially the creation of one man, Alexander Krasnoshchekov. Born in Kiev Province in 1880 to humble Jewish parents (the real family name was Tobelson), Krasnoshchekov had become a revolutionary as a student and at the age of eighteen was arrested, imprisoned, and subsequently exiled to the Maritime Province of Siberia. There he continued his revolutionary activities as a protégé of Leon Trotsky and eventually, like his mentor, made his way to the United States. Settling in Chicago, Krasnoshchekov went on to earn a degree in law from the University of Chicago, but with news of the Kerensky Revolution, he left for Russia, landing almost penniless in the summer of 1917 at Vladivostok.

Following the Bolshevik Revolution, he dedicated himself to establishing Bolshevism in Siberia. He was for a time markedly successful, but with the arrival first of the Japanese, then Allied troops, he recognized that at that point not militancy but patience was required. He took to the hills, where Japanese troops searched for him in vain.

Obtaining a passport identifying him as a merchant, Krasnoshchekov in time came down from the hills and in disguise traveled west beyond Lake Baikal. Convinced that the Allied powers would not tolerate a Bolshevik regime in Siberia, he conferred at Omsk with representatives of the Red Army and through them obtained the sanction of the Lenin government to establish a democratic buffer state in Siberia. With six Mensheviks and Left Social Revolutionaries as colleagues, he returned to Siberia to the town of Verkhne-Udinsk, a few miles east of Lake Baikal, there to take the first step toward his goal.

To the Lenin regime, Krasnoshchekov's proposal for a buffer state was welcome. Since he was an old associate of Trotsky's, there was no questioning his ultimate loyalties, and at the time the Red Army was in no condition to press on to the

Pacific. On the other hand, the time would come when the Bolsheviks would be capable of taking over friendly autonomous governments and binding them firmly to Moscow. Lenin warmly welcomed the news that on April 6, 1920, at Verkhne-Udinsk a new government came into being: the Far Eastern Republic.

As the position of the Japanese-supported White armies deteriorated under widespread and continuous Bolshevik forays and uprisings, the Japanese finally agreed to an armistice. Pulling their troops back to the Maritime Province, they nevertheless held onto their White satraps, Semenov and Kalmykov, for there still might come a time when force might accomplish their aims in Siberia. That time appeared to have come with the emergence in late spring of 1921 of Baron von Ungern-Sternberg and his little army in Urga.

The Bolshevik leaders in Moscow also welcomed the emergence of the mad baron in Outer Mongolia, for to the Soviet leaders, von Ungern-Sternberg represented an unanticipated assist—"a godsend"[5]—to a plot already in the making to take control of Outer Mongolia as a buffer state against China. Even as the Balt staged his brilliant coup against the Chinese in Urga, Lenin and Trotsky were entertaining representatives of a revolutionary but nonbolshevik group of Mongolians, a group numbering less than a hundred members but one that might still be utilized for Moscow's design. The representatives had come in response to an invitation adroitly playing on Mongolian resentment of the czar's previous manipulation of their country and on concern about Japanese and Chinese ambitions. The Russian people, the Soviet government proclaimed, had "re-nounced all treaties with the Japanese and Chinese governments which deal with Mongolia. Mongolia is henceforth a free country." How better to ensure that status than to "enter into diplomatic relations with the Russian people" and "send representatives of the Mongolian people to meet the advancing Red Army?"[6]

Bolshevik machinations against Mongolia had begun on a modest scale in 1919 when one of Lenin's phantomas, Ivan Maisky—who was later to be the Russian ambassador to the Court of St. James's—surveyed the scene. There was, Maisky found, not even the rudiments of a Communist Party. It was a bleak, desolate land of some 700,000 people, mainly sheep herders and nomads. Strongly nationalistic and united in devotion to the Khutukhtu, they feared and hated the Chinese and the Japanese and saw the Russians as only the lesser of three evils. By the time Maisky left in 1920, he had helped form two revolutionary cells totaling altogether no more than twenty to thirty people and calling themselves the Mongolian People's Party. The party was revolutionary, not after the Bolshevik pattern but only in a devotion to nationalism, independence, and modernization. Yet to Maisky—and to Lenin and Trotsky—that was enough for a start.

Even as von Ungern-Sternberg announced his intent to invade Russia and liberate the country from Bolshevism, a Soviet-sponsored First Congress of the Mongolian People's Party met in a Russian town just north of the Mongolian frontier, Kyakhta. No matter that only twenty-five Mongolian delegates attended; the congress on March 13, 1921, proclaimed creation of a Mongol People's

Provisional Revolutionary Government. The government called for a program that would have done credit to any democracy: ending feudalism and slavery, establishing an equitable tax system, and forming a constitutional, parliamentary monarchy under the Khutukhtu. Not a word about Socialism, Communism, or the dictatorship of the proletariat.

In keeping with the Bolshevik design, that government was soon to be installed in Urga on the tips of Russian bayonets, but there had to be at least a pretense that the bayonets were in the hands of Mongols. Thus the formation at Kyakhta of a People's Revolutionary Army; no matter that it consisted of only 400 men, it served the design. Given the honor of striking the first blow, the little force crossed the frontier on March 18, 1921, and captured the town of Kyakhta Maimaicheng. That established the Mongol People's Provisional Revolutionary Government on Mongolian soil.

Baron von Ungern-Sternberg had by that time accumulated a force of about 20,000 men, mixed Russians and Mongols. Promised weapons and other supplies by the Japanese, in early June 1921, he set out on his trail of blood for Moscow, while the Japanese planned to complement his drive with renewed attacks from the east by Semenov and Kalmykov.

The Mongol People's Provisional Revolutionary Government promptly called for help, and the Red Army dutifully responded. So swiftly was von Ungern-Sternberg's absurd little army defeated that the complementary drives by Semenov and Kalmykov never got under way. Although the baron fled, Red Army patrols hunted him down. Brought before a special tribunal, he defiantly confirmed his oath to wreak vengeance on the Bolsheviks. When his judges reputedly told him that he might buy his freedom simply by singing the first verse of the "Internationale," the baron replied that he would sing it only if the judges first sang the anthem of Imperial Russia. On November 5, 1921, they shot him, "and the worn blue Mongolian shirt, with the star of St. George's Cross hanging from the collar sank into the muddy puddles of the Russian prison yard at Ekaterinburg,"[7] but a short distance from where the Romanovs had met their tragic end.

Every attempt to take over the government of a country by Comintern-directed revolutions of internal Communist parties had failed: in Hungary, in Austria, in Bavaria, in Berlin. It was simple to analyze the basic reason for the failures: no powerful Red Army to back up the revolutionaries. That was not to be repeated in Mongolia. In addition, since the Bolshevik leaders had learned from their failures in Western Europe, there would be no fanatical, overnight attempt at revolution; there would be instead a new strategy of gradualism, a slow, methodical building of a broad base of Comintern agents operating behind the scenes in the Mongol People's Provisional Revolutionary Government. The first arrivals were Mongols who had earlier been trained in revolutionary doctrine at the Lenin School for foreign revolutionaries in Moscow or at a similar school at Irkutsk. Then there were the Buryat Mongols, an ethnic group inhabiting a region just north of Outer Mongolia, whose language closely resembled that of the Khalka Mongols, who made up the bulk of the population of Outer Mongolia; calling on the Buryat Mongols to serve as interpreters, the Bolsheviks had a ready channel for transmitting Soviet ideas, methods, and institutions into the Mongol government.

The Buryat Mongols were happy to assist in the belief that they were liberating their brothers, the Khalka Mongols, from Chinese domination and in the belief that once that was accomplished, all the Mongol peoples might be united in an independent Greater Mongolia. By the time the Buryats awoke to the fact that they were gaining control of Outer Mongolia not for creating an eventual union with the Khalkas in a Greater Mongolia but for establishing a Soviet-dominated satellite state, it would be too late.

For with Red Army bayonets still present in Urga, the Bolsheviks began to install their own people in the government as advisers. In every bureau, there would be a Khalka Mongol who was ostensibly the chief, a Buryat adviser, and a Soviet adviser; but the Mongol was in reality only a figurehead, the Buryat only a go-between, and the Russian the true chieftain. As an American consul stationed in North China would report as early as October 1921: "There may be a Mongolian Government, but the authority is the Russian Soviet Commandant."[8]

For the Russians, there nevertheless remained the problem of the Living Buddha, the Khutukhtu, for such devotion did he command from the people that the government could never be a total puppet of Moscow so long as he continued to reign. Fate would soon solve that problem, for in 1924 the Khutukhtu would die of natural causes. The Soviet-controlled government swiftly convened the First Great Khuraldan (parliament), which at Moscow's bidding declared Mongolia to be a People's Republic. A new constitution nationalized all natural resources, abolished the titles of princes and nobles, ended the ruling rights of the reincarnated saints, and separated the church from the state.

For the first time, the Soviet Union had established a subservient satellite state outside the boundaries of Imperial Russia. It was the Comintern's first success in the struggle for the world revolution of the proletariat, achieved not through internal struggle of the Mongolian masses but through application of and manipulation by external forces. It was a new method, but it had succeeded, and in the years to come, the world would see it repeated many times over.

In the meantime, in October 1922, the last Japanese troops left Siberia, and there remained only the formality of Krasnoshchekov's Far Eastern Republic dissolving itself. That done, the Soviet state absorbed all of Siberia and extended its hegemony to the shores of the Pacific.

## Chapter Eleven

A few minutes past nine o'clock in the evening of May 10, 1923, a former White Russian intelligence officer, Captain Maurice Conradi, beckoned the headwaiter to his table in the restaurant of the Hotel Cecil in Lausanne, Switzerland. Had all ladies, Conradi asked, left the restaurant? When told that they had, Conradi pointed to three men sitting at a table beneath palm trees by the orchestra. Were they, he asked, Russians, and if so, was one of them V. V. Vorovsky? The headwaiter became uneasy, for one of the three men was indeed Vorovsky, secretary of the Comintern and the Soviet plenipotentiary to the Quirinal Palace and the Holy See, and there had been rumors that Vorovsky was to be murdered. The headwaiter nevertheless confirmed that one of the three was Vorovsky. At that Captain Conradi asked if he might have another glass of *fine*. Bowing slightly, the headwaiter clicked his fingers and a wine steward appeared to pour Conradi a brandy. Returning to his stand, the headwaiter considered calling the hotel detective, but he approached the idea too late.

Having finished the brandy quickly and nervously, Captain Conradi walked to the table where the three men sat, took out a revolver, and shot Vorovsky just above the right ear. Collapsing, Vorovsky died immediately. Turning on the other two men—one was registered as Ahrens, head of the Soviet Telegraph Service, the other as Divilkovsky, an assistant to Vorovsky—Conradi fired twice, wounding both men gravely.

He was about to fire again when something distracted him. Turning, he walked over to the headwaiter, placed his weapon on the headwaiter's reservations stand and announced: "There is my revolver. I have done my task. Now call the police." He lit a cigarette and for twenty minutes awaited arrival of the police. To a waiter he remarked: "What I have done tonight will ring around the world."[1]

It was no exaggeration, for through the medium of Conradi's crime, the Lenin government and its methods—indeed Bolshevism itself—were to be placed on trial in perhaps the most extraordinary court hearing of the early twentieth century.

One of the founders of the Bolshevik movement who had helped organize Lenin's journey across Germany in 1917, Vatislav Vorovsky had also been among the founders of the Comintern. Having occupied his post in Rome for some time, Vorovsky had come to Switzerland to attend a conference called by the Allied powers to arrange a final peace settlement for the Near East and Turkey. Aristocratic in appearance, possessed of fine features and good manners, Vorovsky was nevertheless a highly trained clandestine and thus could hardly have been unaware that in Lausanne he was in grave danger.

Nor could he have been unaware that he was unwelcome in Switzerland. The Allied powers had made it clear that he would not be permitted to attend the current phase of what was to be a prolonged conference, and Swiss authorities informed him that since he had no official role in the conference, he held no diplomatic status. If he refused to leave the country, they would withdraw his visa. Despite rumors of a plot against Vorovsky, the Swiss police ruled that because he held no official status, they could provide him no special protection.

Two days before Vorovsky's assassination, a man called Glardon, leader of a Swiss Fascist organization, La Ligue de Lausanne, had called at the Hotel Cecil with several members of the organization's Executive Committee. Although Glardon demanded an audience with Vorovsky, Vorovsky instead sent Ahrens.

He would give the Soviet party forty-eight hours in which to leave Switzerland Glardon told Ahrens; if not, "there were 40,000 men who were ready to help put Vorovsky over the border into France."[2] In a country like Switzerland, Glardon said, the citizens had a right to assist the governmental authorities.[3] Although the Swiss police learned of Glardon's threat, they still conducted no more than routine protection of Vorovsky and his party.

Taken to police headquarters, Maurice Conradi declared under interrogation: "This evening I have done an act of justice which I do not regret, for one must have the courage to deliver Europe from the Bolshevist plague."[4] Conradi denied any association with La Ligue de Lausanne. Since tensions were increasing between Britain and Russia, the police pressed him to establish if he had contacts with western intelligence services, but he denied any. He also denied association with the Brotherhood of Russian Truth, which had an office in Geneva.

In making that denial, Conradi came close to lying. When police searched his room in the Hôtel de l'Europe, they found an envelope postmarked in Geneva on May 9, 1923, containing 100 Swiss francs and a letter from Arcadius Polounin, secretary of the Czarist Red Cross in Switzerland, which did have connections with the Brotherhood of Russian Truth. Under interrogation, Polounin admitted that he had known Conradi since 1919.

Brought face to face, Polounin and Conradi admitted that they had plotted to kill the Soviet foreign commissar, Georgi Chicherin, and the foreign trade minister, the former trade representative in London, Leonid Krassin, when the two visited Berlin in April 1923. Polounin had provided the funds while Conradi went to Berlin to do the killing, but for some reason Chicherin and Krassin had failed to appear. When Conradi returned to Switzerland, he and Polounin had decided to kill Vorovsky instead. Polounin provided the pistol and ammunition and 100 francs to finance Conradi's escape.

When both Ahrens and Divilkovsky, surviving their wounds, demanded access to Vorovsky's effects, asking specifically for a safe deposit box number and key, the Swiss police became suspicious. Investigating, they discovered that just before the murder Vorovsky had deposited cash, gold, and precious stones worth $1.6 million. In addition to other duties, Vorovsky, the police learned, had been a paymaster for the Comintern. The Swiss government immediately froze the assets.

While Vorovsky's body was being conveyed to Moscow, there to be cremated and the ashes placed in the Kremlin wall, the Bolshevik propagandist Karl Radek accused the British secret service, the Swiss police, the Brotherhood of Russian Truth, and La Ligue de Lausanne of complicity in the murder. Foreign Commissar Chicherin sent the Swiss government a strongly worded note demanding the severest penalties for Conradi and Polounin and the immediate return of "Vorovsky's estate" while claiming that either the British or the French had been behind the affair. In an appeal to the workers of the world, the president of the Comintern, Zinoviev, asked that "this bloody challenge . . . not be left unanswered" and called upon the workers "to form stronger organizations to bring about revolutionary success east and west."[5]

The Swiss government refused to be intimidated. In a diplomatic note, the government expressed official regret for the murder and its having occurred on Swiss soil, disclaimed all responsibility, denounced Soviet allegations as being "audacious and arrogant," and stated that "pending investigations," Vorovsky's "estate" would be held by the Swiss government.[6] When Vorovsky's companions, Ahrens and Divilkovsky, were fit to travel, the government added, they would be formally expelled from Switzerland as agents of the Comintern.

The trial of Maurice Conradi and Arcadius Polounin opened at the Montbenon Casino in Lausanne on November 5, 1923. Since there was no dispute over the facts of the assassination, it was clear from the outset that Bolshevism was also on trial; if the accused were acquitted, then Bolshevism would have been found guilty. Some of the lawyers and much of the Swiss press called it "the trial of the century," while the case's "international political importance" prompted a rising young American diplomat, Joseph C. Grew, to send daily reports on it to Washington.[7]

In an opening statement, Conradi declared that he had decided "to shoot one of those Red dogs" as revenge for the murders by the Cheka of his uncle and his father, who had been prosperous chocolate manufacturers in Petrograd. Polounin in turn stated that he aided and abetted Conradi because of the horrors he had seen while inside Red Army lines on an intelligence mission for General Wrangel. That was the line the defense took: that the Reds were butchers and that in seeking vengeance, Conradi and Polounin—Conradi, in particular, having lost his father—had reacted as many a man would have reacted. It was what the French called *un crime politique.*

The Swiss prosecutors confined themselves primarily to trying to show that Conradi and Polounin were receiving a fair trial according to Swiss law, leaving to a lawyer from Moscow, Maître Tchernov, the task of upholding Bolshevism. The course Tchernov would take was apparent from the testimony of the first witness, General Eugene Dostovalov, formerly on the side of the Whites. Dostovalov passionately denounced his former cohorts and went on to say that the only real Russian patriots were "now on the side of the Bolshevists" and "the only government that can exist in Russia today is that of the Soviets." Under cross-examination, General Dostovalov admitted that he was hoping to obtain an appointment in the Red Army.

An Italian Socialist deputy, Fabrizio Maffi, a man well known at headquarters of the Comintern in Moscow, painted a saintly portrait of Conradi's victim. "Vorovsky was not a thug," Maffi declared. "He was a man of kindness and intelligence who was *persona grata* at the Quirinal and the Vatican. He was a model father and husband and a Roman Catholic." Along the same line, the editor of the French Communist newspaper, *Humanité*, Charles Rappoport, testified "that Lenin and the other Commissars are leading a simple life devoted to work," while Professor Klutchinikov of Moscow University maintained that "the educational situation" in Russia was "flourishing."

Throughout the proceedings, White Russians kept to one side of the courtroom, Reds to the other, like parties in a divorce action. Conradi and Polounin sat quietly and seemingly indifferent, as if the affair concerned somebody else. From time to time a Russian Orthodox priest in a tall gold hat passed messages to them. All the while the president of the court, Maître Fonjallaz, listened quietly, occasionally taking notes, apparently unconcerned that the testimony had little to do with the charges against the accused.

On the third day, a moment of drama that sent correspondents from *Izvestia* and *Pravda* hurrying from the court to file their stories: testimony from two Americans who claimed to have served in the United States Army during the Siberian intervention. Identified as "Sydney Grierson" and "Charles H. Smith," they testified that "all White generals in Siberia were bandits, pursuing exclusively their personal enrichment." In overcoming Admiral Kolchak's forces, "Grierson" continued, the Bolsheviks had covered themselves with glory.

Who, in reality, were the two Americans? Word came from the American window on Russia in Riga that Grierson was in fact Major Sidney Graves, son of the former commander of the American expeditionary force in Siberia, Major General William S. Graves. Smith had yet to be identified but "seems to have proceeded [to Lausanne] from Moscow, where he had just received a gold mine concession." The report continued: "It has been confidentially reported that he has the financial support of Major General Graves, father of Major Graves, in the gold mine concession."[8]

There followed to the witness box a veritable parade of soldiers, ex-soldiers, and civilians: a Cossack with legs bowed by years in the saddle; an aide-de-camp to the former minister of war; a clerk with the *Stavka* (czarist military high command); some civilians obviously of the Comintern, others just as obviously members of various White Russian organizations, such as the Brotherhood of Russian Truth, the League for the Regeneration of Russia, or the Superior Soviet of the Throne Occupant. All came before the court either to praise Lenin or to damn him, to applaud the Bolsheviks or to condemn them, to salute the Red government or to denounce it.

Polounin's employer, Dr. George Lodigensky, chief of the Czarist Red Cross, testified that at a hospital in Kiev where he served, patients "were driven naked into the streets where they were hunted by the Reds and then shot." He said he had personally seen a house where the Reds had confined the intellectual leadership of Kiev; it was "bathed with blood," there was "flesh on the walls," and nearby ditches "were full of decomposing bodies." He offered photographs of the slaughter as further evidence. Under cross-examination by Maître Tchernov, both he and Crosier denied that they had helped plan and finance Conradi's and Polounin's unsuccessful attempt at assassination in Berlin.

A Russian then living in Paris, Madame Marie Kallasch, decried the fact that "The Bolshevists systematically persecute the Church, assassinate its priests, and conduct mass executions of them." She contended that they denied religious education in schools and homes. At religious feasts and festivals, she said, children dressed up as priests sang songs "ridiculing religion," and commissars distributed to children "obscene and injurious literature describing the Orthodox Church."

Maître Tchernov attacked that testimony vigorously. "I solemnly affirm," he declared, "that Madame Kallasch's statements regarding the persecution of religion are false, as the churches are open and the bells are ringing." He asked the court to telegraph the Swiss Red Cross in Moscow to verify his remarks. As Maître Fonjallaz subsequently announced, the churches were indeed open and the bells ringing.

Undeterred by that apparent contradiction, the parade of witnesses continued until at last, exhausted by the length and passion of the testimony, the court adjourned for the weekend. Few in attendance noted that during the course of the trial, the sixth anniversary of Lenin's revolution had passed.

When the court reconvened on November 12, 1923, the lawyers began their summations.

A prominent Communist attorney from Geneva, Maître Volti, representing Vorovsky's widow, spoke first. He asked the jury to take no notice "of the grave insults that have been hurled at the Russian people and its authorities. The Russian Revolution will not be judged by this court," he declared, "but by the tribunal of history." There had been those at the time, he said, who condemned the French Revolution, "whose influence on social relations in Europe is recognized by everyone today."

Another Swiss attorney, Maître Dicker, representing the deceased, noted that the trial was being held in the Swiss canton of Vaud. "It is impossible," he said, "for a Vaudois jury to judge the Russian Revolution. In order to do so, it would be necessary to know Russia and its history." By means of revolution, he said, Russia had just shaken off three hundred years of oppression, and "there have never been revolutions without floods of blood." It was Kerensky, Dicker said, who had originally taken the czar and his family into custody, so that Conradi and Polounin, having served as officers in an army loyal to Kerensky, were as guilty of the murder of the czar as was any officer of the Red Army. Demanding the maximum sentences, he concluded: "Switzerland's honor is at stake."

The Russian, Maître Tchernov, representing the wounded Ahrens and Divilkovsky, concentrated on defense of the Bolshevik Revolution and his country. "We who were not imprisoned," he declared, "also ate herring soup and bread mixed with straw and mud. We also swept the streets and the roofs. We also suffered from the cold. All that is in the past, but if it were to begin all over again, the Russian people would be ready to suffer anything." If Russia were to be judged, he said, it should be the Russia of today, of November 1923. That Russia, he declared, "is not a paradise but a poor country. Nevertheless it is in a state of reconstruction and business people are going there. A new Russia has been born. The civil war is ended. The cause of the Whites is lost."

Another Swiss, Maître Magnenat, representing Vorovsky's daughter, called Conradi "a Russian of the most reactionary kind" and Polounin "too vile a person for any right thinking Swiss to consort with." Vorovsky, on the other hand, he said, "was a Roman Catholic of noble family . . . a model husband and an excellent father."

The final summation for the prosecution rested with the attorney general fo th canton of Vaud, Maître Capt. In the trial's most forceful speech, Capt declared that the question before the jury was "whether anyone has a right to commit a crime in the struggle against a certain political regime now existing in a great European country" even though that might be "a regime which we believe is contrary to true civilization." Based on personal vengeance and "a desire to strike at the Soviet government," Capt said, Conradi and Polounin had committed murder. "Those two men," he declared, "had no right to kill anybody, especially on foreign soil, in order to combat a despotic and terrorist government." Whatever the Bolshevik regime might be, he said, "it does not justify assassination in a foreign country," for, "What would become of States if each citizen should decide on his own authority that a chief is a tyrant and should determine, also on his own authority, to kill this leader?" Maître Capt concluded with a plea for punishment of the crime. "Your judgment, Gentlemen of the Jury," he said, "will be that of the entire country. When you have spoken, Switzerland will have spoken."

The counsel for the defense was next. In a lengthy speech, the attorney for Polounin, Maître Aubert, argued that when Polounin conspired with Conradi, he was acting under "an irresistible impulse." In Russia, Aubert declared, Polounin had been twice condemned to death by the Cheka, and while he was in prison, the authorities had treated his wife and children brutally. Those experiences, Aubert said, had impelled Polounin to act against "the infamous Bolshevist executioners," and the fact that nobody else could or would stand up to the Bolsheviks further consumed him. "It is the lack of Europe's moral courage toward Bolshevism," Aubert continued, "the lack of the collective sentiment for justice, which permitted Bolshevism to develop." When collective justice fails, he said, "individual justice arises."

In conclusion, Aubert made an impassioned appeal:

> The Bolshevists have killed the noblest human sentiments. Every human being who still has a heart should be filled with sentiments of disgust for the Bolsheviks. How then is it possible to pretend that Polounin is guilty? Cursed are those who invented this regime. The conscience of the world would revolt if these two officers, Conradi and Polounin, were convicted. . . . Remember, Gentlemen of the Jury,

. . . everyone awaits from you a verdict freeing the defendants, a
verdict relieving the conscience of the world through a complete
condemnation of Bolshevism.

The summation by Conradi's attorney, Maître Schopfer, was an echo of
Aubert's. Conradi had acted, Schopfer said, under "violent provocation and
irresistible impulse." That alone should be sufficient for acquittal, he maintained,
but there was an additional consideration: "If Conradi and Polounin are
convicted, the crimes committed by the Bolshevists would be justified, and it
would imply the recognition of Soviet Russia as a civilized state. Never since the
beginning of the world," he concluded, "has there existed a regime similar to that
of the Bolshevists. The case of Conradi is an instance of the revolt of a free
conscience against tyranny."

At half past three o'clock in the afternoon of the eleventh day of the trial,
November 16, 1923, the members of the jury withdrew. Two hours and twenty
minutes later, they returned. As the president of the court reminded them, to
obtain conviction under Swiss law, at least six members of the panel of nine would
have to vote guilty. That, said a spokesman for the jury, they had failed to do. On
the condition that Conradi and Polounin pay half the costs of the trial, Fonjallaz
declared the two acquitted. The Soviet government, contended the western press,
stood condemned of crimes against humanity.

# PART III

## The American Cockpit

*Chapter Twelve*

On the day the Comintern was formed, March 2, 1919, the State Department's leading expert on Russian affairs, Raymond E. Murphy, an Edwardian figure with muttonchops and a Prince Albert coat with silk facings, was at his desk amid those symbols of the Edwardian calm in which the United States Foreign Service worked: the palms, the statues of long-dead consuls, the great oil portraits of former secretaries of state, the spittoons, the rocking chairs, the great bookshelves heavy with leatherbound volumes on protocol, and the cool marble corridors. The letter before Murphy had been found by an official messenger, who had discovered it lying on the silver tray at the reception desk, left just as visiting diplomats left their cards, beside the Visitors' Book beneath a great plaque of remembrance to the horses and mules killed in the World War. To Murphy, who believed in the elegances prescribed for diplomatic intercourse by the Congress of Vienna, the letter came as a rude shock.

Written not in copperplate, as was the custom, but on a typewriter with an imperfect face, the letter stated:

RUSSIAN SOCIALIST FEDERATED REPUBLIC
People's Commissariat of Foreign Affairs
Office of the People's Commissar,
January 2, 1919,
No. 9/k

Moscow, corner of Spiridovsky and Patriarch's Lane,
House number 30/1
Telephone number 4-22-96.

It is hereby announced that Russian citizen Ludwig Christian Alexander Carlovitch Martens, who resides in the United States of
America, is appointed the representative of the People's Commissariat
of Foreign Affairs in the United States.

(signed) People's Commissar
for Foreign Affairs:

G. *Tchitcherine.*

Acting Secretary of the Office:

F. Shenkin.[1]

That was all: none of the plumy elegance that normally attended the
presentation of credentials of a new ambassador in a major capital. Cold, formal,
brisk, the note was by the standards of the times insulting, illustrative of the new
Soviet regime's contempt for the traditional forms of diplomacy.

Murphy promptly sent the letter to Attorney General T. W. Gregory,
requesting such information as existed concerning "this man Martens and his
business in this country."[2] The task of investigating Martens went to J. Edgar
Hoover, who had just been appointed head of the General Intelligence Division, a
unit of the Bureau of Investigation established to watch and report on the
activities of political extremists, particularly those of the left. A similar task of
investigation outside the United States fell to the director of the U.S. Army's
Military Intelligence Division, General Marlborough Churchill.

The report was hardly calculated to make Martens acceptable to the United
States in any capacity. Born in South Russia of German parents, he was arrested as
a revolutionary in 1896 and served three years in one of the czar's prisons before
being deported to Germany. While a soldier in a German engineer regiment, he
met Lenin and Trotsky in Berlin and began to engage in revolutionary activities
against the czar and eventually returned to Russia. In 1906 he went to London as a
Bolshevik organizer and while active in Russian revolutionary and Italian
Anarchist circles, joined an Austrian Bolshevik, Cheslaw Bielinski, to establish an
engineering shop in High Street, Hoxton, a poor neighborhood where the two
manufactured a prototype of a machine gun which they tried to sell to the British
Army but without success. The business failed, they were unable to pay the rent,
they were evicted and their goods placed under a debtor's lien. It was at that point
that Martens fell afoul of Scotland Yard.

The young Winston Churchill was at the time the home secretary, responsible
for the nation's internal security. There had been a prolonged series of violent

social disorders, sometimes involving radicals but as often as not involving British workers protesting against work conditions and pay, which Churchill put down with considerable firmness, even—some would say—with harshness.

During the night of December 16, 1910, residents of Houndsditch, a grimy working class neighborhood, reported strange sounds coming from beneath a jeweler's shop, the domain of a jeweler who, rumor had it, was fencing jewels stolen from wealthy Russians. When the police arrived to investigate, they were met by a fusillade; three policemen were killed and two severely wounded before the burglars made off. A short while later, other policemen located them, barricaded in a building, where they again opened fire. Since British police carried no firearms, Churchill authorized the dispatch to the scene of a detachment of Scots Guards from the Tower of London, some horse artillery, and detachments of armed police. Churchill himself hurried there to direct the operations.

In the gun battle that followed, the house caught fire. One man burned to death and two others surrendered, but the leader, a man known only as Peter the Painter, escaped. Since the other three men had been close associates of Ludwig Martens, the theory was that Peter the Painter was Martens. Although Scotland Yard took Martens into custody, he was quickly released.

When the war began in August 1914, he registered at the Harrow Road Police Station as enemy alien XA-137, but even though he had served in the German Army and had a record of revolutionary associations, he was not detained. When he asked on December 21, 1914, to be allowed to go to the United States, the Home Office raised no objection and granted him Exit Permit 15009, whereupon he sailed three days later aboard the SS *St. Louis* from Liverpool.

Those developments indicated that Martens may have been working for Scotland Yard and was sent to the United States to report on activities of anti-British radicals who were making mischief in American ports over loading arms and munitions bound for Britain. That postulation was strengthened by the fact that even though Martens could show no evidence that employment awaited him in the United States, American authorities in London granted him an entry permit. During the voyage, Martens would say later, he made the acquaintance of an English engineer, John Gibson, a graduate of the Technical University in Moscow and the New York representative of the Demidov Iron and Steel Works of Perm, Russia; Gibson offered Martens work as a draftsman and clerk at his New York office in the Hotel McAlpin, and when Gibson was recalled to London, Martens remained as Gibson's representative in New York.

While working for Gibson, Martens became reacquainted with Leon Trotsky, then in exile in New York and working for the newspaper *Novy Mir*. Martens himself began to contribute articles to *Novy Mir*. Leaving Gibson's employ, Martens joined the man designated by the Soviet government as its official propagandist, Santeri Nuorteva, in founding the Russian Soviet Government Information Bureau. He also obtained a new post as vice-president of a prominent engineering firm, Weinberg and Posner, which position he held at the time he presented Chicherin's letter to the State Department.

That the United States had not recognized the Soviet government and continued to regard the ambassador from Alexander Kerensky's government as the legitimate Russian representative in Washington deterred Martens not at all. On March 21, 1919, he announced publicly that he had been appointed "by the Russian Socialist Federal Soviet Republic to be its official representative in the United States."

Martens also revealed the text of a memorandum that had accompanied the letter to the State Department announcing the desire of the Soviet government to establish trade relations with the United States. The Soviet government, according to the memorandum, was "prepared to place at once in banks in Europe and in the United States gold to the amount of $200 million·to cover the price of initial purchases." Among goods needed "in great quantities" were railroad equipment, agricultural implements, tools, factory equipment, electrical supplies, automobiles, trucks, chemicals, medicines, clothing, food, and the like. In return Russia was prepared to sell various raw materials, including furs, timber, flax, grain, metals, and minerals. Yet a prerequisite to trade, said Martens, was withdrawal of American troops from Russia and recognition of the Soviet government by the United States.

As American businessmen began to call at offices of the Russian Information Bureau in the World Tower Building on West 140th Street, J. Edgar Hoover and Marlborough Churchill were instructed to look into Martens' claim that he had access to $200 million in gold. They soon determined that Martens himself was often so short of funds that he sometimes had difficulty paying his rent and meeting his payroll. Although he had limited credit at the Guaranty Trust, a leading New York bank, that had been granted only because the bank's officials hoped that if Martens did succeed in establishing fruitful trade relations with the United States, they might redeem large holdings of currently worthless Nicholas and Kerensky rubles. Most Russian assets outside Russia, they learned, were either in the hands of Kerensky's representatives or held by banks as security for loans, debts, and old rubles.

Nor did Russia appear to have sizable holdings of noble metals. Although Russia had once been one of the world's two leading producers of those metals, production had dropped catastrophically during and after the revolutions and the civil war. As of October 1917, the gold reserve of the Russian State Bank had been 1.3 billion gold rubles, but by 1919 only an estimated 380 million was left. Since all traders with Russia insisted on gold deposits, foreign trade (which was minimal in any case because of the naval blockade) was hardly a remunerative source of funds, and the Russians were unable to increase output from the mines, either because they had been blown up or because mining equipment had worn out.

Some State Department experts speculated that the Bolsheviks may have obtained gold from private holdings; they may have plundered the gold reserve of the Rumanian State Bank, which was sent to Petrograd for safekeeping in 1916; and they may have found some gold when they murdered the czar and his family.

Although Lenin had issued a decree confiscating all articles of gold and all precious stones belonging to private owners, churches, convents, monasteries, and palaces, State Department observers believed little revenue would have resulted. The czar's treasury was immensely valuable, but that was being used primarily by the Comintern to finance its outside agents. Martens himself retained a well-known American Communist lawyer, Morris Hillquit, in an effort to obtain control of Imperial Russian and Kerensky government funds in the United States, estimated to total $187 million, but the venture was unsuccessful.

The State Department also noted that while Martens lured American business-men with "attractive business propositions having no ostensible connection with politics," his colleague, Nuorteva, engaged "in an aggressive effort to win public sympathy on the side of unlimited recognition of the Soviet Republic and of its principles of government, as well as the lifting of the blockade and the withdrawal of all American troops in Russia and Siberia." So successful was Nuorteva in creating the impression that Martens was officially received and accredited by the United States government that the State Department on two separate occasions in mid-1919 felt compelled to make public announcements to the effect that, "Mr. Martens has not been received or recognized as the representative of the Government of Russia or any other government."

As the activities of the Russian Information Bureau continued, a special committee of the New York State Legislature, created to investigate political extremism and sedition, subpoenaed Martens to appear. Aside from verifying his prior radical activity in Russia, Germany, and Britain, the committee established that:

> Martens subscribed to the doctrines of the comintern, including overthrow of the United States government.
>
> The Russian Information Bureau propagated revolutionary doctrine through funds derived from the Soviet government.
>
> Martens maintained liaison and control over various socialist groups in the United States, including the International Workers of the World, an extremist and often anarchical trade union.
>
> Martens subsidized so-called "Soviet schools and universities" in the United States, including the Smolny Institute, established in Chicago with funds provided by Martens.
>
> Martens had established collegiate socialist organizations and a system for distributing radical literature among college and university students.
>
> Martens had established "an elaborate counterespionage organiza-tion" in the United States in order "to install agents in government offices, hotels, railroads, newspaper offices, etc., to keep advised of anti-Bolshevik activities."
>
> Martens had been spending "large sums of money" in lobbying with a view to obtaining the assistance of Congressmen and government officials.

Yet how were those charges to be proven when every indication was that Martens and his bureau were in serious financial difficulty? Instituting a new investigation into Martens' funding, the Department of Justice soon determined that at least one source of the bureau's finance was a system of couriers operating between New York and Russian and Scandinavian ports. Among some two dozen men and women engaged in the activity was—on at least one occasion—the writer and poet Carl Sandburg.

By 1920 Sandburg had already made an impression on American letters but was not yet the distinguished figure of twentieth-century American literature he was later to become. The son of poor Swedish immigrants, he had become a newspaperman in Milwaukee, where he served as secretary to the Socialist mayor before moving on to Chicago and the staff of the *Daily News*.

In 1918, Sandburg left New York for Oslo, from where he was to report on a soviet republic established by the Red Army in Finland for a feature syndicate with which Martens was associated, the Newspaper Enterprise Association. While awaiting a return steamer, he was approached by a man who asked him to transport to the United States a small sum in Norwegian kroner to his wife in Chicago, a trunk of documents and propaganda material, and two money drafts destined for Santeri Nuorteva. One of the drafts was for $3,000, the other for $5,000.[3]

When Sandburg returned to New York aboard the SS *Bergensfjord* on Christmas Day, 1918, port authorities searched him—the port was still operating under various war emergency acts—and found the propaganda material and the drafts. When questioned, he "refused to reveal . . . who gave him the drafts or to whom he was to deliver the same in this country, stating that he was bound to secrecy and would only give this information to a member of the President's cabinet."[4] Although the drafts were held in the custody of the assistant U.S. attorney's office, Sandburg himself was allowed to proceed.

A second source of Martens' income, the Department of Justice determined, was the international diamond market. Some evidence of that developed on April 6, 1920, when a German aircraft carrying a Comintern agent, Fritz Platten, and his wife was forced down near Kovno, Lithuania. When Lithuanian authorities searched the two passengers, they found coded messages written on pieces of silk sewn into their clothing. When decoded, one message referred to an urgent need for funds for the Comintern in France and Italy and noted that the best way to send funds was in the form of precious stones and jewelry. "Large pearls sell well," noted one message intended for the head of the Comintern, Gregori Zinoviev. The messages named a small diamond merchant in the New York diamond bourse and another in Los Angeles, who were prepared to negotiate stones and jewelry.[5]

Yet neither the courier system nor the mails was sufficient, the Department of Justice believed, to finance expenditures as large as those of the Russian Information Bureau, an estimated $150,000 a year. In the continuing search for Martens' source, the Bureau of Investigation's New York office took another look at his relationship with the Guaranty Trust Company. Turning up information about a "confidential luncheon" attended by Nuorteva, Raymond Robins, the former representative of the American Red Cross in Petrograd, who was known to be pro-Bolshevik, and two members of the foreign department of the Guaranty Trust, Henry C. Emery and Charles Sabin the New York office determined that Sabin "had given Martens considerable funds out of his personal resources."

Sabin and the Guaranty Trust Company were anxious to create the impression that the Soviet government would survive, thereby interesting American manufacturers in trading with the Bolsheviks and "bringing pressure on the administration to recognize Soviet Russia." Aside from the large number of worthless rubles held by the Guaranty Trust, for which there appeared to be no satisfactory solution unless the United States recognized the Soviet government, the bank also held the equivalent of $6,540,000 belonging in whole or in part to the Russian Imperial government while at the same time it had claims against that government for $7,540,000. Thus in hope of strengthening the Soviet government in order eventually to satisfy the bank's claims, Sabin may have been financing Martens or granting him credit against the funds belonging to the Russian Imperial government.

By late spring of 1920, the Department of Justice considered that there was adequate proof to support a variety of charges against Ludwig Martens, not the least of which was that as an agent of the Comintern he was an agent of the Soviet government. At about the same time, the State Department issued a formal ruling on the nature of the relationships between the Soviet government, the Russian Communist Party, and the Comintern. The Russian Section, headed by the former American consul in Moscow, DeWitt Clinton Poole, asserted that

> The inter-relation of the Bolsheviks, the Russian Soviets [government], and the Third International is such, in fact, that while the three may be distinguished theoretically, in practice they represent a single movement, backed by the administrative machinery and the resources of Soviet Russia. This is important, especially from an international viewpoint, because the aim of the Communist or Bolshevik Party is world-wide revolution, and the purpose of the Third International is to propagate revolution and Communism throughout the world. Therefore, while the Soviet institutions, as such, may agree to abstain from subversive propaganda abroad, neither the Russian Communist Party nor the Third International would be bound thereby.[6]

To Martens, it was soon apparent, as he remarked in a message to the Soviet foreign commissar's deputy, Litvinov, that "a terrific campaign" was being conducted against him. American authorities, he reported, "had launched all the Sherlock Holmes in New York to find out all about his work."[7]

Alarmed by that activity, Martens for a time disappeared. When detectives of the Bureau of Investigation finally found him at the Hotel Lafayette in Washington, he asked to be put under the protection of the Senate Foreign Relations Committee. Having formed a subcommittee to investigate Martens and his activities, the Foreign Relations Committee welcomed the request. Ordinary courtesies apart, the subcommittee treated him delicately, for the senators were conscious that Soviet authorities were currently holding at least two Americans in Moscow jails.

However carefully members of the subcommittee trod, they came up with a damning, if discreetly worded, indictment. Martens' "letters of credence [as ambassador]," they reported after extensive interrogation and deliberation, "were not in a form to warrant his assumption of diplomatic privilege."[8] None of Martens' trade offers had proved to be more than tentative, so that to the subcommittee the conclusion appeared "inescapable" that "the entire fabric of trade negotiations which Martens unrolled was part of an ingenious scheme of propaganda to create sympathy, based upon cupidity, for the Russian Soviets" and to produce "by indirect means the admission of Soviet Russia into the companionship of international relations which other means had failed to secure."

The entire matter appeared to the subcommittee to be "shrouded in some mystery." Martens' communications to and from the Soviet government were "almost invariably carried by couriers—whose names were withheld from the committee" who brought in "at least $150,000" in violation of the Trading with the Enemy Act, for, the subcommittee contended, Martens was not Russian as he claimed to be but German and thus at the time he entered the country, an enemy alien.

"Martens' activities," the subcommittee concluded, "have been of a nature to render him more suitable for investigation and action by the Department of Justice than by the Committee of the Senate." For that, the Department of Justice was ready under the provisions of the Act of Congress of October 16, 1918, which provided that aliens "who believe in or advocate overthrow by force or violence of the Government of the United States or of all forms of law" or who were "members of or affiliated with any organization that entertains a belief in, teaches or advocates the overthrow by force or violence of the Government of the United States or of all forms of law" should be taken into custody and deported.[9]

Before deportation papers could be served and Martens taken into custody, the Soviet foreign commissar, Georgi Chicherin, ordered him to Moscow. Attended by a flock of agents from all the government's investigative bureaus, Martens boarded ship in New York on January 22, 1921. Upon arrival in Moscow, he told the press that he regretted his "expulsion" from the United States, but, "There are no grounds," he declared, "for any anxiety as to our future relations with America."[10]

## Chapter Thirteen

Ludwig Martens' activities provided an example of a Soviet functionary's carrying out a basic Marxist tenet: that if the Soviet government were to survive and nourish the world revolution of the proletariat, Soviet representatives would have to collaborate with capitalism while at the same time helping history to do its work. The deputy chief of the Comintern and trade plenipotentiary in London in 1920, Lev Kamenev, expressed the tactic another way when he declared that capitalism, lured by the prospect of profit in helping the Soviet government develop Russian industry, would at the same time "dig for itself its historic grave."[1]

There were other variants of what the Program of the Communist International, adopted at the Second Congress of the Communist International, called "economic maneuvering,"[2] the use by the Soviet government of trade favors or the prospect of them as a means of influencing governments to grant diplomatic recognition. Lenin had used that type of maneuvering to great effect in 1920 to induce Britain to end Mr. Churchill's private war, and in that same year, displaying almost Confucian subtlety, Lenin used the same tactic to try to extract recognition from a hostile United States and to bring the United States and Japan—Russia's principal enemy in Asia—into collision, thereby enabling Russia to get on with domestic rehabilitation and external revolution in the west without concern for war in the east. As exemplified by what came to be known as the Vanderlip Affair, that immense game of chess was played at a time of serious tensions between the Soviet government and Japan, whose troops were still on Soviet territory in great strength, and between the United States and Japan, who appeared to be at a point of clashing over the issue of trade in Asia.

Washington B. Vanderlip was a man of uncertain age and nationality; he looked about fifty and talked and dressed like an American who had spent most of his adulthood in wild parts. Vanderlip described himself as a gold prospector, and although he said he spent four years in the Siberian wilderness, he found no gold, so that when he arrived in Los Angeles in 1912, he had "no means of moment, and no fixed income or tangible resources of any kind."[3]

Yet Vanderlip did have a silver tongue. When he met Santeri Nuorteva in New York in 1919, he persuaded Nuorteva to grant him a visa to go prospecting in Russia, which Nuorteva was pleased to do because he knew that Moscow was anxious to get the old gold mines working. Returning to California, Vanderlip managed to persuade a group of the state's more prominent businessmen to attend a meeting: the publisher of the Los Angeles *Times*, Harry Chandler; the multimillionaire oil magnate, Edward Doheny; an executive of the Title and Trust Company, O. F. Brant; and the presidents or their personal representatives of the Union Oil Company, California Mutual Insurance, and a major chain of grocery stores owned by H. Jevne.

At the meeting Vanderlip provided letters of recomendation from leading New York bankers, including the president of the National City Bank of New York, Frank A. Vanderlip, one of the wealthiest men of the period, whom Washington Vanderlip described as his cousin. (Frank Vanderlip would confirm that Washington Vanderlip was a distant relative but said that the two had never met.)

At a second meeting, Vanderlip gave a glowing account of "the great possibilities for investment of capital in Siberia." If the syndicate would provide him with $25,000, he would "leave at once for Siberia and try to locate mining, coal, and if possible, oil properties."[4] Eleven executives who were present—and the oilman, Edward Doheny, who was not—each contributed $2,000.

With the syndicate's money in his pocket, Vanderlip left the United States, but not for Siberia. He went first to Stockholm, where he met with one of the Soviet trade representatives to London, Leonid Krassin, and then to Copenhagen, where he saw the Soviet representative in Denmark, Maxim Litvinov. It would emerge later that in talking with Litvinov, Vanderlip said that in addition to representing his syndicate, he was the personal representative of U.S. Senator Warren G. Harding, who had recently been nominated as the Republican candidate for the presidency and from whom, if he were elected president, Lenin expected improved relations between the United States and Russia. (When Harding learned of Vanderlip's representation, he stated that he had never met the man and until that moment had never heard of him.)

On August 30, 1920, Vanderlip called at the American Legation in Copenhagen. Introducing himself as "the representative of twelve corporations and individuals residing in Los Angeles," he told an official, T. W. Anderson, that he was on his way to Moscow as guest of the Lenin government "to see what is possible in the way of commencing trade with Siberia." The syndicate that he represented, Vanderlip said, intended through a subsidiary, the Los Angeles Steamship Company, to transport rubber from Singapore to manufacture automobile tires in Vladivostok and "to commence a passenger and freight trade in the Pacific Ocean which will compete with the Japanese companies."[5]

Litvincv had offered, Vanderlip told Anderson, to send gold bullion to the Los Angeles syndicate with all packing, freight, and insurance paid, whereupon the syndicate was to sell the gold to the United States government at commission and then extend a credit to the Russian government equivalent to the amount realized in the sale of the gold, less a discount. Litnov guaranteed, Vanderlip said, to use the credit solely for purchases in the United States and proposed to eliminate one of the principal reasons professed by President Wilson for refusing to recognize Lenin's regime: the large war debts which the United States contended Russia had amassed in the United States before the October Revolution.

Anderson was by that point already suspicious of Vanderlip. If nothing else, the plan to manufacture tires in Vladivostok and to open trade that would "compete with the Japanese companies" would have been sufficient to alert him: to create trade squabbles that might serve to break down the united embargo against Russia had long been recognized as a basic objective of the Russian Information Bureau in the United States. The United States government, he told Vanderlip, had "repeatedly expressed its opinion that no credence is to be given to any statements of the Soviet government, which has so often violated the most solemn agreements." Apparently undeterred, Vanderlip left the legation for the voyage across the Baltic to Petrograd to negotiate what he would later describe as the biggest business deal in the history of the world.

As Washington B. Vanderlip disappeared for a time inside Russia, many agencies and governments, including the State Department, the Department of Justice, Scotland Yard, the Foreign Office, and the French and Japanese governments, were anxious to determine just what was happening and what kind of support he actually had. Neither was easy to ascertain. The one apparent fact— and that not really positive—was that Vanderlip was an American. He was also apparently a mining engineer of some experience. Almost certainly the bankers' references which he presented to establish his credentials with the Los Angeles syndicate had been provided by the Guaranty Trust of New York, the bank which was hoping to redeem large holdings of worthless rubles. Nor was it impossible that Vanderlip received some form of endorsement from Senator Harding, for some of Harding's principal backers for the presidency were members of the syndicate. Harding may well have suggested, however indirectly, that Vanderlip look into the Russian trade situation, for there was considerable concern lest the British steal a march on American capital by establishing trade relations with Russia.

In the second week of November, 1920, Vanderlip resurfaced in the Latvian capital, Riga, aboard the private train of the head of a special commission to purchase locomotives in the west, Professor Yuri V. Lomonosov. Seeing an opportunity to impress the businessmen he represented with the riches available to the Russians for trade, Vanderlip told a group of newspapermen that one of the coaches on the train was carrying so much gold that the axles had broken.

At subsequent stops on Vanderlip's journey home, he boasted of the immense concessions he had obtained. In Stockholm, he announced that Lenin had granted him oil, mining, and fishing concessions over 400,000 square miles of Siberia for a period of sixty years. In Copenhagen, he said that the value of the business he had transacted was $3 billion. He did further service for the Russian Information Bureau when he told the Stockholm *Dagensnyheter*—which called him "the American billionaire Vanderlip," obviously confusing him with his distant relative—that "The reports of uprisings and street fighting [in Moscow] are utterly untrue . . . and I believe that they root in French and British propaganda conducted with a view to preventing legitimate American business in the Russian market."[6]

As Vanderlip pursued his journey back to the United States, he continued to leave a trail of bombast. In London, he told the press that "A bill authorizing the resumption of American trade with Russia is assured of passage in the Republican Congress in December, if necessary over President Wilson's veto." It was absurd, he said, "to think that I would undertake such a gigantic undertaking and that the capitalist group behind me . . . would be interested unless it had assurances of favorable action by the American Government."[7]

While the press appeared inclined to take Vanderlip's proclamations seriously, official Washington was entertaining doubts. As late as November 12, 1920, noted Marlborough Churchill's Military Intelligence Division, the Communist journal *Krasnaya Gazetta* stated that negotiations with Vanderlip were yet to be completed. "The belief is said to obtain in some well informed quarters that there is a string attached to any understanding Mr. Vanderlip may have reached with the Soviet Government in the form of demand for recognition of the Soviet regime by the United States Government."

The controversy surrounding Vanderlip and his transactions intensified when in mid-December 1920 the official Soviet newspaper, *Izvestia,* announced that Vanderlip as "representative of the Central American Syndicate" had promised to supply the Russian government with: "100 ocean steamers, 2,000 river steamers, tugboats and motor boats, 100 airplanes, 300 electric locomotives, 5,000 ordinary locomotives, 2,500 passenger and 50,000 freight cars, 5,000 tramway cars, 3,000 complete telegraph and telephone installations, 5,000 automatic signal apparatuses, 800 pumps, 250 machines for washing gold, 350 locomotives for narrow gauge railways."[8]

The magnitude of the proposed deal made Russian policy abundantly clear. Not only did Lenin aim at obtaining recognition from the United States, he also wanted to promote friction among the western powers and between the United States and Japan. By granting an apparent concession to Vanderlip, Lenin told a conference of Communist Party officials on October 9, 1920, "we aggravate the relations between Japan and America."[9] Using the British Socialist-writer H. G. Wells as a means of informing the press, Lenin planted the idea that the United States had proposed, in exchange for the concessions in Siberia, to sign "a defensive alliance [with Russia] against Japanese aggression in Siberia."[10]

There were some indications that the attempt to promote friction was succeeding. Upon hearing of Vanderlip's $3 billion deal, the Japanese Foreign Office notified the State Department that "the Japanese Government is in no way bound to take cognizance of any such private agreement,"[11] and the French government declared that should any of the funds involved in the transaction pass through its jurisdiction, the government reserved the right to attach them.

The Vanderlip Affair had by that time advanced to the stage of a cause célèbre. Governments, diplomats, secret agents, journalists, bankers hung on his words, for it appeared that he might be provoking a trade war between the major capitalist states. Yet when Vanderlip arrived in Washington on January 12, 1921, he vigorously defended his mission as "a purely industrial and commercial project" with nothing political about it. Immense benefits, he maintained, would follow for the entire country. If, he concluded, "our State Department will cooperate with us in keeping it out of politics."[12]

Politics nevertheless did intrude, for to the Russians, politics was what the Vanderlip Affair was all about. In a news agency bulletin, the official Soviet trade agency declared that if the concessions to Vanderlip were to be ratified, the United States would have to do something to improve relations with Russia. The implication was clear: if the $3-billion deal were to be consummated, Russia had to be rewarded with American recognition of the Lenin regime.

Yet again Vanderlip appeared to be unperturbed, and on April 6, 1921, the Washington *Post* announced that he was back in Moscow, again as guest of the Lenin government, still seeking the key to the door of Siberia. The dispatch, datelined Paris, said that Vanderlip was "practically dictator of the commercial and economic policy of Russia" and was "forcing the soviets to denationalize all factories, mines, and oil fields." Vanderlip, the dispatch noted, was said to be living in Lenin's house.[13]

Whoever sent that dispatch apparently got his information from the exuberant Vanderlip himself, for there was no truth to it other than that he was, indeed, back in Moscow. Far from living in Lenin's quarters or exercising any influence in the Soviet regime, he was back in the government guest house, the Sugar King's Palace, doing nothing but waiting, interminably waiting. Lenin refused every overture for an audience but finally wrote him a letter in which he noted that he was "very glad to hear of President Harding's favorable views as to our trade with America" and thanked Vanderlip for "the part played in this respect by your syndicate and also . . . your personal efforts."[14]

Lenin's letter was a dismissal, and with it, Vanderlip disappeared from the world scene. In retrospect, his activities were nothing more than those of a confidence man of ability and imagination, but Lenin had used them skillfully for his own ends. At a time when it was by no means sure that the major capitalist powers— Britain, France, Germany, and the United States—would not combine to destroy the weak, unstable Soviet regime, he had used Vanderlip to set the powers squabbling among themselves, to deceive the European governments into believing that the United States was gaining a marked advantage in Soviet trade. So, too, at a time when there were still powerful Japanese forces at Vladivostok, he had used Vanderlip and the reputed concessions to him to sow considerable distrust between the two principal powers in the Pacific, the United States and Japan. To such an extent had Lenin inflamed the commercial rivalry among the great powers that when the time came, he would be able to make a deal with Germany that would be highly favorable to him in all three fields that were of serious concern to Russia: military, political, and economic.

Another demonstration that the Bolsheviks viewed trade as a weapon developed in 1924 when the Soviet government established an official trade organization in New York: Amtorg. The activities of that organization also reflected the Bolshevik theory that in dealing with capitalists, trickery was justified, for capitalism was amoral and socially illegal. In that spirit, Amtorg quickly became a major center of

Soviet industrial espionage in North America. Although the Bureau of Investigation regarded Amtorg from the start with suspicion, it was not until two years later, in 1926, through a tax dispute with the Internal Revenue Service that enabled revenue lawyers to audit Amtorg's books, that substantial light was thrown on that dark hive of commerce and revolution at 164 Broadway.

The Amtorg Trading Corporation was incorporated under the laws of New York State on May 23, 1924, as a result of a merger of two similar organizations, owned by the Soviet government, which were engaged in the importing and exporting business on a commission basis. The new organization was described as "a domestic corporation whose stock is held by a Russian corporation which is financed by the Russian State Government."[15] Its officials were Russians, "sent to the United States on visa to supervise the office and accounting records." For selling Russian products, chiefly furs, and for purchasing American products for export to Russia, Amtorg collected a commission of 2½ percent. The remaining 97½ percent of the sale price of Russian goods was credited to the Russian corporations on whose account the goods were sold. After deduction of expenses from the 2½ percent commissions, Amtorg paid a "so-called excise or license tax" of 60 percent of net profits to the Soviet government in exchange for being allowed to do business in Russia. All business appeared to be conducted with various Russian syndicates or with the Russian State Importing and Exporting Company—known as Gostorg—all of which were owned and operated by the government.

The Internal Revenue Service determined that between January 1, 1924, and the fiscal year ending September 30, 1926, Amtorg on a gross income of $5,223,056 remitted to the Soviet government "for the privilege of importing and exporting" the sum of $481,805. The tax deficiency owed the United States for the period was $66,307.

Within the Bureau of Investigation, there was considerable doubt that any of the tithe of $481,805 was actually transmitted to Russia. Through clever bookkeeping, officials of the bureau believed, that money was retained to finance subversive activities in the Americas. Although that was never proven, so dubious were Amtorg's activities by 1930 that the company's chairman, Peter A. Bogdanov, was called before an internal security subcommittee of the House of Representatives to explain. When the committee alleged that Amtorg had been "engaging in communist activities," Bogdanov indignantly threatened to curtail and even to discontinue Soviet purchases in the United States. The accusations, he declared, were "absolutely without foundation" and damaged Amtorg's "substantial credit position."[16]

In a public address soon after the committee hearings, Bogdanov insisted that "The fundamental element in the foreign trade policy of the Soviet Union is the peaceful development of economic relations with other countries of the world on the basis of mutual benefits." Russia wanted to trade with the United States in particular, he said, because "it is considered in the Soviet Union that the United States has attained the highest achievements in industrial technique."[17]

As would be revealed later by a former Amtorg official, Robert Pitcoff, who defected in 1934, Amtorg's interest in American "industrial technique" went beyond a mere appreciation of the quality of American goods to a desire to build on that industrial technique. Amtorg, Pitcoff revealed, maintained a continuous scrutiny of American industry. "There were commissions that were studying glass," he told a House Committee on Un-American Activities. "There were commissions that were studying aviation . . . the chemical industry . . . the manufacture of paper and such things as that. Almost every industry was studied by these commissions."

It was also clear that Amtorg provided cover for high-level Soviet intelligence officers in the United States, and there was at least one firm associated with Amtorg that acted as a large-scale intelligence procurement agency for the Soviet government. That was the Amtorg Bookstore, established on Liberty Street in New York soon after the founding of Amtorg by a Soviet agency commonly known as Mezhkniga, whose primary activity was to export Soviet literature and import foreign literature.

From time to time over the years, the bookstore would ostensibly be closed down, usually in the wake of probing into its affairs either by some Congressional committee or by the Bureau of Investigation, only to reappear shortly under some new name but usually with the same assets and much the same staff. It eventually came to be known as the Four Continents Book Corporation, which the State Department described as "a Soviet agency for the acquisition of American publications of interest to Soviet agencies" whose activities lay "in the field of intelligence acquisition."[18]

The State Department estimated that over a period of five years, only 6 percent of Four Continents' business involved bringing Soviet literature into the United States, while in the same period, the company purchased about 130,000 American technical magazines, manuals, newspapers, and books. Over a slightly longer period, the State Department noted, Four Continents or its predecessor agencies acquired 80,993 patent descriptions from the U.S. Patent Office, purchased some 4,250 documents from the U.S. Government Printing Office, including documents on atomic energy, scientific and mathematical tables, mineral resources of Alaska, and detailed maps of Alaska and strategic areas within the United States. Through the War Department, the National Bureau of Standards, the Bureau of Mines, the Weather Bureau, the Geological Survey, and the Department of Commerce, Four Continents obtained data and publications on the topography of the Philippines and nautical charts of the Atlantic and Gulf coasts, the Pacific and Alaskan coasts, and the coasts of Puerto Rico, the Virgin Islands, the Philippines, and Hawaii. There were also detailed charts of harbors showing port details, such as lighthouses, landmarks, and floating aids to navigation. Under the direction of Mezhkniga, said the State Department, there were fifty-seven agencies like Four Continents operating in various countries around the world.

As with the yearnings of capitalism for new markets, so the Soviet government freely exploited capitalism's publication of its activities. As with trade, that practice might be exploited to help capitalism, as Kamenev had put it, to "dig for itself its historic grave."

## Chapter Fourteen

In 1920, a Hearst newspaperman, Floyd Gibbons, began writing a novel called *The Red Napoleon*. A Bolshevik warrior resembling Leon Trotsky lands in Manhattan at the head of a Red expeditionary force and in great battles reduces New York, that capital of capitalism, to ruins. Although the United States Army wages a gallant fight against the Red hordes, the defenders are forced back on Washington and beyond. As the Red Napoleon establishes a provisional capital of the Red Union of America at Newark, New Jersey, the president of the United States, from a temporary capital in St. Louis, broadcasts a Christmas message and to give heart to heroic fighters still holding out in the rubble of Wall Street and Governors Island, George M. Cohan sings "Give My Regards to Broadway." In the end the forces of darkness and evil fail to triumph: the United States Navy defeats the combined Red fleets of Britain, France, Germany, Japan, and Russia in a super-Trafalgar off Cuba, the president returns to the White House, the odious Red forces are ejected from Wall Street, and Old Glory flies again over the Battery.

The work was an immense popular success, for its publication came at a time when it seemed to many that the Bolsheviks might seize power in the United States as they had done in Russia. That host of sects known as the radical left seemed to have run amok. It was a time when American politics took on some of the aspects of the class warfare that had preceded the Russian Revolution. So serious had the outbreak of disturbances become by May Day, 1919, the great international Socialist holiday, that the United States Army and the New York National Guard prepared a siege plan to deal with the "possibility that radical agitation which is now being pushed by fiery propaganda" might "erupt into violence."[1] The plan called for using artillery in the streets of New York, just as it had been used in the streets of Moscow and Petrograd.

As a wave of bombings, murders, strikes, and riots swept the country, the War Department General Staff prepared for the president a special study entitled, "Estimate of the Radical or Revolutionary Situation in the United States."[2] The study asserted that within the country some 1,142,000 men and women were members of or associated with left extremist groups. Most were armed, and most were employed in or associated with such industries as mining, port operation, textiles, lumber, railways, farms, and steel and metal trades, which if shut down could paralyze the country. "Thousands of agitators and propagandists" were at work, "'borers from within,'" most of them clandestine, out "to undermine morale, foment disorders and disseminate their doctrines by insidious methods."

The objective, the staff declared, was "overthrow of the government of the

United States by force and violence" and installation of a revolutionary government. As the staff observed, the methods of achieving that goal could have been excerpted from a manual prepared by the Comintern: a strike in some branch of essential industry; a general strike by all workers in a specific area, such as New York City, to tie up transportation and deny the food supply; seizing public utilities and transportation; forming bands of armed strikers (a Red Guard); organizing and seizing power with local revolutionary councils; occupying railway terminals to prevent passage of federal troops to restore order; and spreading propaganda among sympathetic workers, pacifists, "Parlor Bolsheviks," and soldiers and sailors. "This may seem far-fetched and impossible," the study warned, "but when one realizes that a small armed minority of 600,000 Communists control the entire Russian people, this possibility becomes more than food for thought." The American revolutionaries, the study continued, were directed and controlled by "the Communist Party of Russia" through the medium of the Comintern, which "exercises a more powerful influence on radical activities in the United States than any other body," and which through propaganda had convinced "the average laborer in this country . . . that government by the workers has been a success in Russia."

During Fourth of July celebrations in New York, more than 11,000 policemen were on round-the-clock duty against threatened bomb attacks on federal, state, and city buildings, the Stock Exchange, banks, and the homes of prominent citizens. In Chicago, two companies of federal troops deployed to protect key points in the city; in Boston, troops guarded all federal buildings; in Philadelphia, the streets teemed with policemen; similar states of alert existed in Oakland and San Francisco. A wave of Anarchical bombings struck eight cities, including Washington, and within a year 4 million workers at one time or another were out on strike.

In that atmosphere, concern for the reliability of the armed forces grew. The deteriorization of morale in the American force at Archangel, while only partially due to Bolshevism, and the various disturbances in the British and French forces at the end of the war shocked the War Department, for the events had shown that soldiers were as liable to radical infection as were civilians. Considerable alarm and vigilance spread when the Bureau of Investigation intercepted an instruction from the Comintern's Fifth Congress to Communist parties throughout the world "to commence an insistent and regular propaganda in the 'Bourgeois armies'" and another to two American Communist leaders, James P. Cannon and Alexander Bittelman, to form a "military commission" to carry out the Comintern's instructions "in the strictest secrecy" in the United States.[3] In the event, incidents in the American armed forces would be few, but such was the effect of the Red Scare of 1920 that it swept the country into a state of collective hysteria without precedent and sent both citizens and government looking for new Praetorians to defend the established order against hostile forces looming on all frontiers and especially from within.

• • •

Among the new Praetorians was J. Edgar Hoover, who at age twenty-four had impressed U.S. Attorney General A. Mitchell Palmer. His credentials, Palmer believed, were excellent: he was distinctly bourgeois, the class that the Bolsheviks had sentenced to death. Born in the capital, Hoover had attended Central High School and had worked at night for $30 a month as an indexer at the Library of Congress to help pay his way through college. Here, thought Palmer, was no wild blueblood, no frothy intellectual dabbling in advanced ideas; here was a sound, steady, systematic young man with the mind of a high-grade clerk and the eye of an assiduous policeman. In due course, Palmer made Hoover chief of the General Intelligence Division, the new department created to provide law enforcement agencies with intelligence about radical movements and individuals, especially Communists and Anarchists. With that assignment, Hoover began what would turn out to be a life-long crusade against Communism, and in pursuit of his crusade, he went to war with the weapon of the political warrior: the police files.

For J. Edgar Hoover, a single individual, a woman amply represented in the police files, came to personify the attitude of the extremists and the capacity of a few determined and clever people to disrupt the orderly pursuit of social change. She was an Anarchist writer, Emma Goldman, born in 1869 in Russian Lithuania, who emigrated to the United States at the age of fifteen, lived briefly in Rochester, New York, and New Haven, Connecticut, while working at menial jobs, and at the age of twenty-one, moved to New York City. There she met a fellow Russian, Alexander Berkman, a leader in the Anarchist movement in the United States who edited an Anarchist journal, *The Blast*. The two were lovers and collaborators in Anarchist work until 1892 when Berkman, during the course of a steel strike in Pittsburgh, tried to murder the steel baron Henry Clay Frick, seriously injuring him in the process. While in prison for fourteen years, Berkman wrote *Prison Memoirs of an Anarchist*, which Emma Goldman, having founded a publishing company called Mother Earth, brought out. In the book Berkman expressed the philosophy which he and Goldman shared:

> Society is a patient; sick constitutionally and functionally. Surgical treatment is often imperative. The removal of a tyrant (such as Frick), of an enemy of the People, is in no way to be considered as the taking of a life . . . [as] murder. To remove a tyrant is an act of liberation, the giving of life and opportunity to an oppressed people. . . . It is the test of a true revolutionist—nay, more his pride—to sacrifice all merely human feeling at the call of the People's cause. If the latter demand his life, so much the better.[4]

Only a year after Berkman's imprisonment, Goldman also went to jail, sentenced for inciting a riot in Union Square. Upon her release, she quickly came to the attention of the police again, first for worshipful articles about Gaetano Bresci, an Italian Anarchist who murdered King Umberto of Italy on July 29,

1900, then for possible complicity in the assassination of the twenty-fifth president of the United States, William McKinley, shot on September 6, 1901, as he stood in a receiving line at the Pan-American Exposition in Buffalo by an Anarchist, Leon Czolgosz, who approached him holding a pistol concealed by a handkerchief, declared the president to be "an enemy of good working people," and fired twice.

Czolgosz in his confession declared that he had been influenced by the writings of Emma Goldman and by speeches she had made in Cleveland. During his interrogation, he denied ever having met her, but in later testimony he indicated obliquely that he had in fact met her when she spoke in Cleveland shortly before the attack on the president and that it was she who had put the idea into his head. That Goldman had made such a suggestion either directly or indirectly could never be proven, but Abraham Isaak, editor of an Anarchist newspaper, *Free Society*, stated in a published article that Czolgosz was at the railway station when Miss Goldman left Cleveland on July 18, 1901, and that "Emma Goldman pointed Czolgosz out to Isaak at the station as being a young man who desired to speak to Isaak."[5] It was subsequently established that Emma Goldman had been in Buffalo shortly before Czolgosz shot the president, thus raising the possibility that she had spied out the land at the Pan-American Exposition.

Although authorities arrested Goldman in connection with the murder and questioned her for two weeks, they "were compelled to release her because of lack of evidence linking her in any way with the assassination."[6] There was, nevertheless, no doubt where her sympathies lay: in an article in *Free Society* on the eve of Czolgosz's execution, she sought to justify his act. "And my heart goes out to you in deep sympathy," she wrote, "and to all those victims of a system of inequality and the many who will die the fore-runners of a better, nobler, and grander life."[7]

Following Czolgosz's execution, Goldman entered upon a period of relative seclusion. For fifteen years she continued to preach Anarchism through books and articles and occasionally in speeches, but she was rarely in trouble with the police again until 1916, when she went to jail briefly for publicly advocating contraception, debate on which was considered to be an offense against public morals. As a new wave of Anarchist bombings swept the country—there were bombings of St. Patrick's Cathedral and the 110th Street subway station in New York, and of courthouses, municipal buildings, and churches elsewhere—the authorities considered that Goldman's leadership of the Anarchist movement and her open advocacy of violence made her intrinsically responsible; but there was nothing under existing law that they could do about it.

With the entry of the United States into the World War, Goldman was again out of prison, and she and Berkman began openly to oppose the conscription laws and emergency powers acts. Since their activities were clearly seditious, they were arrested, tried, fined $10,000 each, and sentenced to two years at hard labor at a federal penitentiary.

By the time they had served their sentences, the United States government possessed a legal means for dealing with aliens considered to be undesirable: the

Act of Congress of October 16, 1918, whereby aliens advocating overthrow of the government "by force or violence" might be deported. The Department of Justice on October 27, 1919, brought Goldman and Berkman to Ellis Island for deportation hearings. The charges against them sustained, the government directed that Goldman and Berkman, along with 247 other extremists, be deported to Russia. Before dawn on December 21, 1919, the USS *Buford,* a U.S. Army transport, arrived off Ellis Island. As the deportees, including three women and one sixteen-year-old-boy, filed aboard a tug, some began to chant, "Long live the revolution in the United States!" but "a few of them wept and most of them seemed downcast."[8]

Emma Goldman was defiant. "This is the beginning of the end of the United States Government," she told newspapermen. "We, the first American political refugees, will yet live to see America truly brave and truly free, and we will be recalled by this land to rejoice with her people in the triumphant achievement."[9]

As Goldman and Berkman arrived at the Finland Station in Petrograd on January 22, 1920, they were aglow with ecstasy. "Soviet Russia!" exclaimed Goldman; "Sacred Ground! Magic People! You have come to symbolize humanity's hope. You alone are destined to redeem mankind. I have come to serve you!"[10]

But that was not to be, for they soon found that their Elysium was no paradise. There were, they discovered, no less than thirty-four different grades of food rations, the best being reserved for party officials in the Smolny dining room. They learned of nightly raids by the Cheka, of "the taking of hostages . . . not exempting even old parents and children of tender age." Conducted by the secretary of the Comintern, the dwarf, Angelika Balabanov, to see Lenin, Goldman demanded to know why the Cheka was hounding Anarchists in the Ukraine, a common topic at the time. "Who told you such yarns?" responded Lenin; there were no idealistic Anarchists in Soviet jails, he said, only bandits. "Even in capitalist America," Emma Goldman retorted, Anarchists were "divided into two categories, philosophic and criminal." Did free speech exist in Soviet Russia? "Free speech," Lenin answered, "is a bourgeois prejudice, a soothing plaster for social ills . . . In the present state of Russia, all prattle of freedom is merely food for the reaction trying to down Russia. Only bandits are guilty of that, and they must be kept under lock and key."[11]

Although Lenin urged Goldman and Berkman to work for the Comintern, they politely but firmly declined. They had never worked for any institution, they said, only for a cause; they had seen Lenin's vision of the future, and for them it did not work. When they begged to be permitted to leave the country, they were allowed to do so only when it became apparent that they would make more trouble than they were worth. Yet where were they to go? They were stateless, and American authorities made it clear that they would not be allowed to return to the United States.

At length they were put across the frontier near Pskov. To the U.S. Army's intelligence officer in Riga, Major T. Worthington Hollyday, they offered to talk in exchange for permission to reenter the United States, but Hollyday expressed no interest. Together the two began to wander about Europe until, in time, they parted. The promise to which they had devoted their passion and their lives—world revolution—had failed them. In a fit of grief and madness, Alexander Berkman killed himself on a capitalist playground, the French Riviera, while Emma Goldman eventually died an old woman in exile in Toronto.

## Chapter Fifteen

The Anarchism to which Emma Goldman brought many a convert was a political theory holding that man was essentially good but was corrupted by artificial institutions, that justice and equality could be realized, not by government but only through free contracts between individuals, in essence a society without government. Although the belief was Utopian in concept, Goldman, Berkman, and others of their time brought to the movement a streak of militancy and violence that produced in many in the United States and elsewhere an almost paranoid fear of Anarchism, with which Communism seemed to be synonymous. It was in that electric atmosphere that one of the most celebrated trials of the twentieth century occurred, a case of special importance in the history of the Comintern, for it established the tactics the Comintern was to employ in similar cases for years to come.

At three o'clock in the afternoon of Thursday, April 15, 1920, the paymaster of the Slater-Morrill Shoe Company of South Braintree, Massachusetts, Frederick A. Parmenter, left his office accompanied by a guard, Alexander Berardelli, carrying two boxes containing a weekly payroll of $15,776.51. As they were walking up Pearl Street, two men who had been loitering in the vicinity accosted them, seized the payroll, and fired, killing Berardelli and mortally wounding Parmenter. A car that had been waiting nearby drew alongside and the two assailants jumped in.

Two days later the car was found abandoned in thick woods outside the town of West Bridgewater, its license plates missing. A check revealed that the car had been stolen in November 1919 in nearby Needham and the original license plates replaced with others stolen from another vehicle; the numbers of the plates on the getaway car at the time of the killings, as noted by witnesses, were the same as those on the stolen plates.

Not quite a fortnight later, on May 5, 1920, four men appeared at the home of Simon Johnson, a garage keeper in West Bridgewater not far from the site where the getaway car had been abandoned. Although it was 9:30 in the evening, the men wanted Simon to open his garage so that they might retrieve a car that had been left for repair. Suspicious that the men should arrive after hours to pick up a car that, Simon had already remarked, had no license plates, Johnson told his wife to notify the police while he procrastinated in order to keep the men at the scene.

At length, the men agreed to come back the next day; two of them left on a motorcycle with a sidecar while the other two waited for a trolley. As the trolley arrived, the police also boarded and as they approached the two for questioning the men appeared to go for weapons. Taken into custody, one man was found to be armed with a .32 caliber Colt automatic pistol, the other with a .38 caliber Harrington & Richardson revolver, both fully loaded.

The men turned out to be Italian immigrants prominent in the Anarchist movement, Nicola Sacco, a factory worker, and Bartolomeo Vanzetti, a fish-monger. Under questioning, they denied that they had been at Simon Johnson's house, but with the killings of Parmenter and Berardelli still much in mind, the police also asked where they had been on the day of the killings, April 15, 1920. Vanzetti was unable to remember, and although Sacco said he was at work that day in his factory in Stoughton, Massachusetts, the story failed to check out. Neither did accounts of when and where they had procured their weapons.[1]

Suspicions aroused, the police produced eyewitnesses who identified Sacco and Vanzetti as two of five men who had made off in the getaway car and Sacco as the man who had shot down Berardelli. Both men had been seen in the vicinity of the shootings earlier in the day, Vanzetti as he got off a train from Plymouth at the East Braintree station and later, around noon, sitting in "a large dark car" at one end of Pearl Street, and Sacco in the vicinity of the scene of the shootings during the late forenoon and early afternoon.

Ballistics experts soon determined that the bullet that had proven fatal to Berardelli had been fired from Sacco's automatic and that the Harrington & Richardson carried by Vanzetti appeared to be a revolver belonging to Berardelli, who had recently had a new hammer put in it by a gunsmith in Boston. Vanzetti's revolver had a new hammer, and no revolver was to be found at the scene; even though as a guard Berardelli was accustomed to carrying his while on duty.

Indicted for highway robbery and murder in the first degree, the two men were to have been tried in December 1920, but the Commonwealth of Massachusetts granted a stay at the request of defense attorneys to permit some documents to be brought from Italy. (During the course of the stay, Vanzetti was indicted, tried, and convicted of an earlier attempt at highway robbery.) The Sacco-Vanzetti trial began half a year later on June 1, 1921, before Judge Webster Thayer in the Superior Court of Norfolk County at Dedham.

In the course of a trial lasting six weeks and ending on July 14, 1921, one of the longest and costliest murder trials in the history of the Commonwealth, the prosecution called approximately sixty witnesses, the defense a hundred. The burden of the prosecution's case rested upon the two alleged murder weapons, a cap found at the scene that resembled one that witnesses said Sacco wore and which fit him, and identification of the defendants by multiple witnesses at the scene and in the getaway car. The defense in turn produced other witnesses who had been at or near the scene who testified that neither of the defendants had been present, testimony which the prosecution succeeded in large measure in contra-dicting. Sacco maintained—and produced witnesses in support—that on the day of the shootings he was in Boston applying at the Italian consul's office for passports to enable him and his family to return to Italy, while Vanzetti produced witnesses to testify that on the day of the murders they had seen him or bought eels from him at his fish stall in Plymouth.

Taking the stand, both men admitted making false statements to the police at the time of their arrest. They were frightened, they said, by the antianarchist atmosphere prevalent at the time. In introducing the subject of radicalism, the defense attorneys violated a dictum from Judge Thayer, delivered out of hearing of the jury at the start of the trial, that neither side was to make any reference to Vanzetti's prior conviction or to the radical views and activities of the defendants. Although "no reference was made to these features of the case by the state,"[2] the principal attorney for the defense, Fred H. Moore, introduced testimony on several occasions to the effect that Sacco and Vanzetti were active Italian Anarchists and that having refused to register under the Selective Service Act, they had fled to Mexico to avoid prosecution. Under questioning by Moore, both Sacco and Vanzetti delivered "lengthy speeches concerning their radical beliefs and activities." In answer to prosecution protests, Attorney Moore maintained that the testimony was essential to establish the whereabouts of his clients at the time of the shootings, but government officials wondered if it was not instead "for the purpose of propaganda."[3] Indeed, both men testified that "they intended to prove that the real cause of their arrest and prosecution was due to the fact that they were two active propagators of anarchistic ideas."[4] U.S. government observers at the trial also noted that the witnesses for the defense "were practically all persons well known in the radical movement in the United States."

At the conclusion of the presentations of evidence, neither defendant filed a request for specific instructions to be provided the jury by Judge Thayer, and at the conclusion of the judge's charge to the jury, neither defendant took any exception to the charge or any part of it. After deliberating five hours, the jury found both men "Guilty of Murder in the First Degree." Judge Thayer subsequently sentenced both to die in the electric chair.

Organized by prominent Anarcho-Communists "assisted by a myriad of Italian anarchistic agitators,"[5] the Sacco-Vanzetti Defense Committee began to press immediately for a new trial, and as the committee succeeded in obtaining stay after stay of the executions, a massive outcry against the verdicts and the sentences swept the left-wing political communities of the world. Sacco and Vanzetti, so the story had it, were being sent to the electric chair not because they were murderers but because they were Anarchists. With such considerable skill as to suggest careful orchestration by the Communist International, the campaign played upon raw emotions, seeking to involve the case in various extraneous matters such as racial prejudice and the United States government's antiradical campaign. Various subcommittees of the Sacco-Vanzetti Defense Committee sprang up across the country: Detroit, Pittsburgh, Philadelphia, New York City (two subcommittees), Chicago, San Francisco.

Overseas, the outcome of the trial produced, in the understated words of the

American ambassador in Paris, "a certain effervescence in communist and anarchist circles."[6] Demonstrations developed at American legations in Argentina, Belgium, Chile, Cuba, England, France, Holland, Italy, Mexico, Panama, Portugal, Spain, and Switzerland. Mobs damaged American government buildings in Brest, Oporto, and Lisbon, and bombs damaged American embassies and consulates in Paris, Lisbon, Rio de Janeiro, Sofia, Marseilles, Buenos Aires, and Montevideo. There were riots in which a score of people were killed and many more injured. The volume of letters and telegrams, most of them addressed to President Warren G. Harding in the White House, was immense, ranging from semi-illiterate manifestos issued by Socialist groups around the world to fervent expostulations from eminent intellectuals, such as Anatole France, Romain Rolland, and Henri Barbusse.

On April 9, 1927, Judge Thayer formally decreed that the executions were to take place during the second week of July 1927. So loud and vociferous were the protests greeting his announcement around the world that the governor of Massachusetts, A. T. Fuller, while declining to grant clemency on his own authority, afforded a reprieve of thirty days so that a special independent investigating committee might review the evidence. Composed of the presidents of Harvard University, A. Lawrence Lowell, and of the Massachusetts Institute of Technology, Samuel W. Stratton, and of a former judge of probate, Robert Grant, the committee found no grounds for upsetting the verdict of the court.

It was a decision, noted the Manchester *Guardian*, that "has been awaited all over the civilised world with an interest that was by no means confined to sympathizers with the revolutionary ideas professed by the two prisoners." Which was testimony to the emotion that the appeals of the radicals had aroused through the years. "To say that the innocence of the accused was taken for granted by all those who had championed them," the *Guardian* continued, "would be going too far." What many did believe was that despite admitted facts in the case pointing to guilt, the jury had been "improperly influenced" by "the revolutionary views expressed by the accused, the trial having taken place at a time when public opinion throughout the country was violently inflamed against 'radicals' of every description."[7]

When Sacco and Vanzetti at last went to their deaths on April 23, 1927, the reaction of the Communist press and the Comintern reiterated what many had already discerned, that the campaign was directed not so much toward saving Sacco and Vanzetti as toward inflaming the people of the United States and the world against governmental institutions and capitalist society. In death, Sacco and Vanzetti lost none of their value to the revolutionary cause, for they became martyrs.

Yet however blatantly propagandistic, however vituperative, however virulent, however vindictive, the tracts, newspaper articles, denunciations, and protests so effectively implanted the notion that American justice in the case was unfair that well into the second half of the twentieth century demands would still be heard in responsible circles for an inquiry into the case. As late as 1961, when new ballistics tests conducted with modern equipment again showed that the gun found on Sacco had fired the bullet that killed Berardelli, a widespread belief still remained that the two had died for their political beliefs. The distinguished American scholars Samuel Eliot Morison and Henry Steele Commager in their monumental history, *The Growth of the American Republic,* averred that the evidence against Sacco and Vanzetti was "slight and their alibis were sound." When the men were executed, they wrote, "a cry of horror at the injustice of it went around the world, and those citizens of Massachusetts who loved justice . . . hung their heads in shame."[8] Edna St. Vincent Millay wrote the lines:

> As men have loved their lovers in times past
> And sung their wit, their virtue and their grace,
> So have we loved sweet Justice to the last,
> Who now lies here in an unseemly place.[9]

As repercussions from the case faded, the United States government conducted a detailed survey into the propaganda methods of the Comintern and its objectives. In a study headed by the man who had been a military intelligence official in the Baltic States during the Kronstadt uprising, Robert F. Kelley,[10] the State Department noted that the Comintern clearly saw the Communist movement in the United States as one of the most important in the world. As Lenin's eventual successor, Stalin, put it: "The American Communist Party is one of those few Communist Parties in the world upon which history has laid tasks of a decisive character from the point of view of the world revolutionary movement."[11]

As early as 1920, the Comintern directed that to achieve the basic objective of "overthrow of the North American bourgeoisie," the American party was to stage "a general political strike and an armed revolt of the proletariat."[12] When that had still to be accomplished by 1931, the Comintern directed that the American Communist Party "must more comprehensively and popularly expose the nature of the capitalist system as a whole and the necessity for overthrowing it." The party was to "make use of all current events (oppression in the factory, unemployment, police brutality, oppression of Negro workers and foreign born, corruption in government, war preparation) in order to expose the whole system and mobilize the masses in the struggle against capitalism."[13] In preparing the way "for the revolutionary mass battles of the American proletariat in the not very distant future," American Communists were thus to utilize the same tactics they had pursued—in concert with sympathizers, both witting and unwitting—in the case of Sacco and Vanzetti.

## Chapter Sixteen

In the minds of J. Edgar Hoover and General Marlborough Churchill, the case of John Silus Reed symbolized a seemingly inexplicable aspect of Communism: its appeal to the very class the Communists would destroy. The son of a prosperous businessman in Portland, Oregon, a product of private schools and Harvard University, Reed had wealth and privilege and well might have become a Republican senator, a banker, or president of some big corporation, but in 1913, at a time when the silk workers of Paterson, New Jersey, had gone out on strike, Reed happened to be a guest in the home of a rich socialite, Mabel Dodge, who lived on Fifth Avenue in New York. There Reed met the leader of the Paterson strikers, "Big Bill" Haywood, head of the militant labor union, International Workers of the World. Enthralled by Haywood's description of the courage, determination, and solidarity of the silk workers in the face of violent police counteraction, Reed visited Paterson, mingled with the strikers, wrote an article about them for the Socialist journal *The Masses*, and even briefly went to jail for them.

Reed emerged from jail a changed man. The gilded youth had become a boisterous idealist, so inspired by what he had seen among the grim mills of Paterson that he organized a mass protest of intellectuals at Madison Square Garden. In 1916 he made his first trip to Russia, briefly visiting the trenches on the Russian side of the eastern front, then later the German side of the western front. He came home convinced that the war was nothing more than a struggle between rival capitalist interests from which only the bankers and armament manufacturers would profit.

Upon return to New York, he began to practice an aspect of extreme Socialism that the prim J. Edgar Hoover so deplored: sexual license. He formed a *ménage à quatre* with his wife-to-be, Anna Louise Bryant, Eugene O'Neill, and Emma Goldman. He also attached himself to Communist groups forming around such Socialist luminaries as Jay Lovestone, William Z. Foster, and Earl Browder, while at the same time lodging comfortably and elegantly in that temple of the establishment, the Harvard Club.

Soon after Kerensky's revolution, Reed left again for Russia, arriving on August 19, 1917, in Petrograd with messages of support for the revolution from the American Communist movement. Within a week he had embraced Lenin and Bolshevism. He was present in Petrograd the night Trotsky seized power so easily and smoothly and was also present at Lenin's creation of the Socialist state at the All-Russian Assembly of Soviets. He reported vividly if none too accurately on those events; intercepted by the postal censor in New York, his telegrams provided a useful addition to information about the revolution reaching Washington from more sober government sources. On the basis of those dispatches, Reed wrote what Trotsky would consider to be a brilliant account of the seizure of power and the establishment of the Soviet state, *Ten Days That Shook the World.*

Trotsky found the vivacity of the young American highly agreeable in contrast to the stern, stolid Bolshevik theologians with whom he usually dealt. When Reed prepared to return to the United States where he intended to help found the Communist Labor Party, through means of which he hoped to establish the Soviet Republic of North America by overt legal means, Trotsky provided him credentials as an organizer of the Bureau of International Revolutionary Propaganda, a predecessor of the Comintern. As Reed produced those papers for scrutiny by the founding conference of the Communist Labor Party in Smolny Hall in Chicago, his stature among the comrades was assured.

Returning again to Petrograd for *The Masses,* Reed reported unfavorably on the conduct of American soldiers at Archangel, which earned him the enmity of the American diplomatic and intelligence community in Russia and an indictment in Washington under the Espionage Act. By the time he left Russia, American intelligence officers in Petrograd suspected that he might be serving as a Communist courier, which may have been why Finnish intelligence officers boarded his steamer when it called at the Finnish port of Abo. The Finns discovered a man hiding in the coal bunkers who said he was James Gormley, an American donkeyman employed by a British steamship company. He was an Irish-American, he said, age thirty-one, and had jumped ship at Oslo because he had fallen in love with a Finnish girl whom he had accompanied to Helsinki; but she had deserted him and because he was penniless, he had stowed away aboard the steamer in hope of getting to New York.

The Finnish officials put little credence in the story. Asking to see Reed's hands, they remarked that, "No sailor could have such fine hands."[1] Nor was Reed at all penniless. When they opened his baggage, they found 102 diamonds, $500, £60 Sterling, 10,000 German marks, 2,400 Swedish crowns, 900 Finnish marks, 500 Danish crowns, and a strip of microfilm (the first recorded instance of microfilm found on a suspected clandestine). The diamonds, Reed would later admit, were intended for Ludwig Martens in New York.

A packet of letters found upon Reed eventually reached the desk of J. Edgar Hoover. Written by Emma Goldman while she was en route to Petrograd, crossing Finland, and living in Petrograd and Moscow, the letters, as Hoover noted, made "rather spicy reading," and included an indication that Goldman had had a child by Reed.[2] They also contained ecstatic approbations concerning life in revolutionary Russia and pleas to ask mutual friends in New York to send gold, clothes, and food instead of paper money.

Of greater interest to Hoover than the letters was the fact that upon Reed's return to the United States, his relations with his Communist colleagues took a strange turn. Because Reed disagreed with the basic Bolshevik doctrine calling for overthrow of the American government by any means, including armed insurrection, he was accused of the crime—serious in Bolshevik circles—of deviationism. Rumors soon began to circulate in New York to the effect that he was guilty of other crimes, that he had misappropriated Soviet funds and that he was an informant for the American government.

That Reed was involved in peculation would never be proven. The more serious allegation, that he was a secret American agent, would also never be proven, but it was true that on at least one occasion he provided American authorities with an important piece of information. To an American naval intelligence agent, Fred P. Rogers, talking with Reed at his home in Patchen Place in New York, Reed revealed that "Trotsky's personal agent in the United States"[3] was a man named Jacob Gruzenberg. That information was of special importance, for Gruzenberg would prove to be Mikhail Borodin, the Comintern's first organizer in the United States.

Reed's motive in betraying Borodin was hard to fathom. He may have been concerned that Borodin was trying to incite open revolution in the United States, which Reed believed was premature and would discredit the entire Communist movement in the United States. Or he may have believed that Borodin was embezzling Comintern funds.

When John Reed left New York again late in 1919, traveling under false papers provided by Ludwig Martens, he was heading for the Second Congress of the Communist International as the official delegate of the Communist Labor Party, which had emerged as one of two rival American Communist groups. Reed's party was American-oriented, while its rival, the American Communist Party, dominated by immigrants, mainly Russians, held to strict Bolshevik principles as laid down by Lenin and Trotsky. Every effort to bring the two groups together had merely produced more altercations. Like the delegate of the American Communist Party to the Second Congress, Louis Fraina, Reed believed that the party that succeeded in winning the recognition of the Comintern would be the party to survive.

Born in Galdo, Italy, in 1892, Louis C. Fraina came to the United States from Italy with his Orthodox Jewish parents when he was four and grew up in one of the worst of the New York slums. Frail and slight of stature, Fraina as a youth joined the American Socialist Party, a forerunner of the American Communist Party. He later worked closely with Trotsky in New York and so impressed radical circles that when Trotsky left for Petrograd after Kerensky's revolution, many saw him as the leader of the Communist movement in the United States. While earning a living as managing editor of *Modern Dance Magazine*, Fraina established in New York what he called the "Bolshevik Information Bureau." That organization had no rival until the first Soviet political representative to the United States, Ludwig Martens, with the help of the Finnish Bolshevik Santeri Nuorteva, opened the Russian Information Bureau, the first official Soviet agency to operate in the United States.

Conflict between a man of Fraina's ambition and Martens and Nuorteva, each of whom wanted for himself the privilege of representing Lenin in America, was inevitable, and so was intrigue. Nuorteva began the intrigue when he reported that Fraina's organization was riddled with deviationists. In Petrograd, Trotsky refused to accept that contention and sided openly with Fraina against Nuorteva. Out of that situation grew mutual antipathy between Fraina and Nuorteva, which the Bureau of Investigation quickly perceived and which it began to manipulate for its own purposes.

The Bureau of Investigation first became aware of the nature of Fraina's ambition and extremism when in 1918 its agents intercepted (and stopped) a telegram that Fraina attempted to send to Trotsky in Petrograd: "Bolshevik Information Bureau organized here two months ago to interpret actions of commissaries [i.e., the Lenin government] and arouse solidarity of American workers with Russian proletariat. Widespread sympathy of American workers with you. Have taken steps to organize Red Guard."[4]

On the strength of that telegram, which by the war emergency acts that were still in effect, was seditious, agents of the bureau raided Fraina's home at 3246 Kingsbridge Ave. in New York but found nothing incriminating. When they questioned Fraina, he coolly replied that before composing the telegram to Trotsky, he had sent another to President Wilson asking permission to form the Red Guard, which turned out to be true.

A few months later, in March 1919, agents of the bureau who had infiltrated Fraina's Bolshevik circles reported that at a meeting in New York, he proposed founding a "Revolutionary Legion of Americans." He intended to seize five Russian ships impounded in New York Harbor to transport the legion to Russia to fight for Lenin. If that failed, he intended using the legion in the course of labor disturbances in the United States to oppose the police and federal troops.

Indicted in Illinois in September 1919 for alleged "criminal anarchy,"[5] Fraina went underground. Managing to stay a jump ahead of the police, he continued to maintain an active if limited role in Communist affairs; but at the same time his antagonist, Nuorteva, saw in Fraina's new vulnerability a chance to rid himself of his rival.

At some point before Fraina's indictment, Nuorteva had set out to place an agent within the New York office of the Bureau of Investigation: Ferdinand Petersen, like Nuorteva a Finn. At Nuorteva's instructions, Petersen trailed his coat before the bureau's counterradical expert, Jacob Spolansky. Spolansky ostensibly took the bait and arranged for an agent of the Military Intelligence Division to interview Petersen, who stated—as directed by Nuorteva—that he was a disillusioned ex-Bolshevik who still had connections with Ludwig Martens' bureau. Little time elapsed before the Bureau of Investigation employed Petersen as Special Agent FF-22 at a per diem of $5 to inform against Martens and his bureau.

What neither Martens, Nuorteva, nor Petersen realized was that Petersen had deceived nobody, least of all the chief of the New York office of the Bureau of Investigation, Frank Burke. Aware of the rivalry between Fraina and Nuorteva, Burke plotted to use Petersen to exploit it. Having fabricated a number of canceled checks drawn by the Bureau of Investigation in favor of Fraina, Burke left them lying on a desk where he knew Petersen would see them. Petersen predictably reported the discovery to Nuorteva.

Nuorteva just as predictably passed the information to Martens, and together the two filed a complaint with the American Communist Party demanding that the party investigate Fraina's association with the Bureau of Investigation. The accusation shook the world of American Communists. Fraina, the Communist Party's Executive Committee decreed, would have to appear before "a pitiless party court,"[6] which met in secrecy some time in January 1920 in a private home in Brooklyn. Martens and Nuorteva were present as observers "to watch the interests of the [Martens] Bureau." Also present was another observer, Harry Nosowitsky, the agent of the British intelligence service and Special Agent N-100 for the Bureau of Investigation.


Harry Nosowitsky was thirty-two years old at the time, a former assistant surgeon in the czar's navy. He had first come to the attention of the British intelligence service in early February 1918 when, along with other Russian naval officers, he was rescued by British sailors from the Russian patrol boats *Rasveet* and *Probeet*, whose crews had mutinied near Liverpool. When Nosowitsky offered his services to the Royal Navy, he was employed as a translator in the naval intelligence section. After the war, he obtained employment, probably with the help of naval intelligence authorities, with the Cunard Steamship Company. In 1919 he was serving aboard the transatlantic liner *Mauretania*, and at some stage, probably with the assistance of the British intelligence service, contacted the Bureau of Investigation in New York and offered his services as an informant. His assignment was to penetrate the Martens bureau.

Approaching Ludwig Martens, Nosowitsky offered his services as a courier, to which Martens agreed; but Nuorteva was suspicious of him, which accounted for Nosowitsky being denied membership in the Communist Party. Yet Nosowitsky soon established such an excellent record for smuggling jewels and propaganda materials from Europe to New York for Martens that he was permitted to associate freely with officials of the Martens bureau.

Nosowitsky soon ingratiated himself further with the Communist officials in New York when in late 1919 a way had to be found to get Louis Fraina out of the country and back again, in keeping with instructions from the Comintern for him to attend the founding congress of the Western Bureau of the Comintern in Amsterdam and then to go on to Russia for the Comintern's Second Congress. In view of the criminal indictment pending against Fraina in Illinois and the intensified police surveillance that that generated, arranging the trip would be a difficult assignment, yet Nosowitsky agreed to take it on and to accompany Fraina to Europe. The alacrity with which Nosowitsky accepted the task should have aroused suspicions: how, for example, was he able to obtain an extended leave of absence from his job with the Cunard Line? It was with considerable facility that Nosowitsky also obtained a passport for Fraina, presumably through the British, for it was a Canadian passport in the name of a Dr. Ralph Snyder of Montreal. Yet neither Martens, Nuorteva, nor anybody else raised a question.

It was at that point that Ferdinand Petersen produced his information about the canceled checks in the New York office of the Bureau of Investigation. To Nuorteva, the information could have come at no more opportune time, for if Fraina were allowed to proceed to the conference in Amsterdam, his status within the Comintern would be enhanced. Nuorteva insisted that Fraina should be tried immediately. To add strength to the other charges against Fraina, Nuorteva claimed that it had been Fraina who had provided the evidence that had enabled the Department of Justice to deport the Anarchists and Communists who had left the United States aboard the USS *Buford.*

Fraina's "trial" was a lengthy affair (the transcript—a copy of which was quickly in the hands of the Bureau of Investigation even though only three copies were made—covered eighty-two pages of foolscap).[7] The proceedings throughout reflected less an aura of dedicated conspirators sitting in solemn tribunal to enforce the iron discipline necessary to overthrow the government of the United States than the rivalries, animosities, pettiness, and provincialism that featured the American Communist movement at its birth.

The case against Fraina rested on four allegations by Petersen:

• Petersen had seen Fraina in and about the anti-radical department of the Bureau of Investigation and on one occasion had seen him leaving the office of an official of that department, Charles Scully.

• Scully had told Petersen that Fraina was a paid agent.

• Petersen had seen canceled checks drawn in favor of Fraina on the account of the Department of Justice.

• Fraina ran a string of subagents in Boston, Philadelphia, and Washington and that in Scully's office Petersen had seen reports of those agents countersigned by Fraina.

Those were the gravest of charges, so grave that Fraina's fate seemed predetermined; but hardly had Petersen given his testimony backing up the charges when with no apparent objection from the others in the room, Fraina suddenly found himself with a defender: Harry Nosowitsky. Where, Nosowitsky demanded, was there any documentary evidence of the checks and the subagent reports? Petersen replied that he had succeeded in making off with copies but when subsequently arrested by federal agents, they had been taken from him. Petersen had, indeed, been arrested, but Nosowitsky managed to suggest effectively that both the checks and the reports were fabrications, purposely left about for Petersen to discover in order to exploit the rivalry between Fraina and Nuorteva and create dissension within the Communist movement.

Probing the relationship between Petersen and Nuorteva, Nosowitsky got Petersen to admit that Nuorteva had offered him a thousand dollars to "get the goods on Fraina." He even managed to induce Nuorteva to admit that from time to time he had paid Petersen small sums. Then Nosowitsky blew the case apart: on the dates when Petersen claimed to have seen Fraina at the offices of the Bureau of Investigation, he declared, Fraina was either in Chicago attending the founding congress of the American Communist Party or had been participating in party meetings in Boston. Since the three judges making up the tribunal had been with Fraina at those functions, all knew that there was no possibility Petersen could have seen Fraina on any of the dates anywhere in New York.

The pitiless court ended around two o'clock in the morning with Fraina's acquittal. Within two days he was aboard the SS *Lapland* bound for Southampton and, he well might have hoped, high office in the Comintern. Yet no high office was to come to Louis Fraina.

Delayed by attendance at the congress in Amsterdam and the peregrinations to elude the police that followed, Fraina arrived in Petrograd just in time for a ceremonial opening of the Second Congress of the Communist International. John Reed, he discovered, had reached Petrograd ahead of him and brought with him the old charges that had been leveled against him in New York, to which two who had attended the Amsterdam congress added the charge that Fraina was not only an American spy but also an agent of the British intelligence service. It was Fraina and Harry Nosowitsky, they maintained, who had betrayed the Amsterdam meeting to the police, which was why they had been able to escape while most of the other comrades had gone to prison.

The Comintern's "cadre section," which was responsible for foreign operations and discipline, appointed an investigating committee to look into the charges. The committee took evidence from all those in Petrograd who had come either from Amsterdam or the United States, examined the stenographic record of Fraina's Brooklyn "trial," and when the delegates to the Second Congress moved on for the business meetings of the congress in Moscow, interrogated Fraina at length. Members of the committee agreed unanimously in the end that Fraina was innocent of all charges.

Yet hardly had that decision been announced when Santeri Nuorteva arrived in Moscow and promptly raised new allegations about Fraina's infidelity. Fraina himself went to the president of the Comintern, Zinoviev, to demand that Nuorteva be silenced, whereupon Zinoviev gave Nuorteva forty-eight hours in which to present whatever new evidence he had against Fraina.

Lenin himself demanded an immediate hearing, for if the revolution in the United States were to proceed, the squabbles among the American Communists had to be brought to an end. Recalling earlier charges that he himself was a German spy, Lenin also had a certain sympathy for Fraina's predicament, so that when yet a third "court" cleared Fraina, Lenin directed the Comintern's Executive Committee to issue a strong statement exonerating Fraina and requiring Nuorteva to "retract publicly, in the press, all the accusations made by him against Fraina."[8] Although Fraina was duly seated in the Second Congress, his troubles were destined to continue.

Like Fraina, John Reed also soon found that the altercation between the two American Communist parties was the least of his concerns, for the Russian leaders of the Comintern, Reed discovered, had adopted a strict new attitude. Persuaded that the revolutionary tide had begun to recede, Lenin insisted upon absolute obedience of the world's Communist parties to the dictates of Moscow. Those Communists who in the past had seen no need to compromise, no need to participate in "bourgeois parliaments," no need to work from within "reactionary trade unions," at that point had to recognize, as he had done, that tactics of compromise and maneuver were essential.[9] That was not to sit well with Reed. He also objected to the fact that even though the Second Congress was far more representative than the founding congress (delegates from thirty-seven countries were represented), Russian delegates still dominated and pushed through various resolutions binding all Communist parties to the will of the Comintern.

Throughout the Second Congress, Reed clashed with Zinoviev and Radek, whom Reed saw as Zinoviev's court jester and who had become secretary of the Comintern after Angelika Balabanov had developed an acute case of apostasy. Reed found Zinoviev and Radek overbearing, ill-mannered, and imperious. The major controversy was over Zinoviev's insistence that American Communists had to join a new union, the American Federation of Labor, which was far less radical than Reed's beloved International Workers of the World, and secure control of the union by working from within, not, as Reed and the Communist Labor Party wanted, to try to destroy it overtly from without. Elected as the American representative to the Comintern's Executive Committee, Reed repeatedly differed with the Comintern's leaders. At one session, he "peremptorily offered his resignation" but "was persuaded by his fellow-delegates to withdraw his resignation and offer his apologies to the committee."[10]

That Reed still stood high with Soviet officials was nevertheless demonstrated when he went to Foreign Commissar Chicherin to request an entry visa for another American, William Burgess Estes, and Chicherin promptly granted it. Estes was a dentist who would declare later that he had known Reed while working in military intelligence in New York in 1918. Having "secured authentic information to the effect that John Reed's life was in danger," Estes had sent word to Reed "by devious ways" that he "would never be allowed to leave [Russia] alive again."[11]

Soon after arriving in Moscow, Estes became aware that he was being watched by the head of the Cheka's Foreign Directorate, Solomon Grigoryevich Mogilevsky. Estes also learned that Reed was in the early stages of disillusionment with Communism. At their first meeting, Reed remarked that "things were not going as well [in Russia] as world communism would have us to believe."[12] The conversation went no further, for at that point Mogilevsky entered the room and Reed fell silent.

A few weeks later, Mogilevsky personally arrested Estes, charging him with being an American intelligence agent. As the two entered the Cheka's interrogation room, Mogilevsky remarked that "the floor of this room is soaked with the tears of persons pleading for mercy, but this is no place for mercy. This is a place to exterminate counter-revolutionists." Before the interrogation began, Reed arrived to serve as interpreter. "Do not worry," he told Estes; "everything will come out all right. I will help you all I can."[13]

Estes was still being detained when with other members of the Comintern's Executive Committee, Reed left Moscow in early September 1920 to attend a Congress of the Nations of the Orient, held at Baku in the Crimea and designed to unleash a jihad against the western colonial powers in the near and mideast.

Traveling to Baku with Zinoviev and Radek in a special train, Reed was "infuriated" by Zinoviev's and Radek's conduct during the long journey, in particular by "lavish meals and sexual orgies."[14] Reed was also upset by the conference itself, which he found to be less a revolutionary congress than a disorganized jamboree involving delegates of myriad nationalities milling about with little direction by the Soviet organizers.

Back in Moscow, William Burgess Estes was sentenced to death, and John Reed would be unable to fulfill his promise to help him. On October 17, 1920, John Silus Reed died of typhus, and as the Bolshevik press announced, his remains were interred "in the sacred precincts before the walls of the Kremlin, where so many revolutionaries have already found a resting place."[15]

What happened to Reed during his last days would be something of a mystery. Other than William Estes' story that "John Reed's life was in danger" and that Reed knew it, there was little to suggest that he might have been murdered. One report had it that upon his return from Baku, Reed again offered his resignation and that Zinoviev and Radek threatened to "destroy" him, but his illness was from all indications genuine. The mystery was over the extent of Reed's disillusionment with Communism.

As told by Angelika Balabanov, she who had become disenchanted with "the hypocrisy of Bolshevik policy and of Lenin personally,"[16] Reed, shortly before his death, was "in a terrible state of depression." He had become "profoundly disillusioned and disgusted" by the methods of Zinoviev and Radek, and his experience at the Second Congress and at Baku had "confirmed his worst fears" and brought "his moral sufferings and indignation to a high point." He had returned from Baku "a totally broken man, even physically." Thereafter, according to Balabanov, he wanted only "to go back to America and to work there in the revolutionary movement as an independent honest revolutionary."[17]

Reed's wife, Anna Louise Bryant, who had a closer connection with American military intelligence than the Comintern would have wished, told the American military observer in Riga, Major Hollyday, that her husband had been "carried away by Communism when he first went to Russia," but when "he got in close touch with the situation," he found so few Communists and "so many who used Communism as a means to get comfortable positions, extra food, homes, etc.," that he had become "disillusioned." Had she been with him, she said, "he would never have gone to the extreme that he did."[18]

Louis Fraina, on the other hand, with whom Reed was reconciled on his deathbed, discounted all stories about Reed's disillusionment. "As one of the two or three Americans who saw him shortly before his death," Fraina declared, "I can affirm that Jack Reed kept all his loyalty to the Soviet Union and communism."[19]

Reed's true position probably lay somewhere in between. In an article written shortly before his death, he indicated that at the next congress of the Comintern he intended to fight the Comintern's dictum that American Communists work from within the labor movement. That and his remark to Balabanov that he intended to continue work as a revolutionary in the United States would indicate that he had no intent to break with the Comintern, yet his remarks to his wife and to Estes and his other remarks to Balabanov would indicate that he was obviously dismayed with the Comintern and the direction that Communism had taken in Russia.

Even though three "courts" had cleared Louis Fraina of the charges leveled against him in the United States, the Comintern's Executive Committee nevertheless decided soon after John Reed's death that Fraina should not return to New York but that he should go to Mexico City, there to establish a bureau from which to conduct operations against the United States. To finance the venture, the Orgbureau, which controlled operations and funding, granted him cash in the amounts of £600 and $60,000. Using a cobbled (dead man's) passport in the name of a film distributor, he gave credence to his cover while passing through Germany by buying a print of a film, *The Arabian Nights*. When he got to London, his calvary began anew.

According to a British representative of the Comintern in the pay of the American government, Fraina upon reaching England contacted his former British traveling companion, John T. Murphy. Worried about carrying large sums of cash on his person, he entrusted part of the funds provided by the Orgbureau to Murphy and other British Communists. He never saw the money again. When he reported the loss to the Comintern's Executive Committee, he was, according to the informant, "exonerated from all blame in this matter."[20]

From London, Fraina went to Montreal to establish contact with a former Socialist organizer in San Francisco of Japanese extraction, Sen Katayama, who was to be his assistant in Mexico City. As the two proceeded on a roundabout route to Mexico City, Canadian Communists reported to the Comintern that they were "very skeptical of [Fraina's] honesty,"[21] and hardly had Fraina set up the bureau in Mexico City when Katayama wrote a letter to Zinoviev—it was intercepted by American military intelligence as it passed through Riga—in which he complained that "we are bankrupt. We have not even enough funds for current salaries." Katayama also referred darkly to "financial mismanagement."[22]

To that communication, Zinoviev reacted sternly, demanding that Fraina provide the Executive Committee a detailed accounting of the funds provided by the Orgbureau. That Fraina did, noting that from the period October 15, 1920, when he was still in Moscow, until July 8, 1921, when he was fully established as the Comintern's representative in Mexico City, his expenses, including his own salary of $45 a week, had exhausted the £600 and $40,700 of the $60,000; the remainder, he reported, was that lost in London.

By that time, late 1921, Santeri Nuorteva had managed to reestablish himself in the favor of Comintern officials in Moscow and had been put in charge of the Anglo-American Department of the Foreign Commissariat. At that point, neither Zinoviev nor Lenin was inclined to defend Fraina and turned his case over to Nuorteva. Free at last to ruin his old enemy, Nuorteva used accusations of treachery and peculation to compel Fraina to resign from the Comintern and the Communist Party.

Taking $4,200, the remains of the Comintern funds—the only substance to the charges of embezzlement—Fraina went into hiding. Changing his name to Joseph Charles Skala, he eventually made his way alone to New York, where he eventually saved enough money to send for his wife and child. Working by day as a proofreader, Fraina at night wrote articles on economic theory, and when the first was accepted for publication, he used a new name, Lewis Corey. Such a reputation did he build as Lewis Corey, the economist, that eventually he obtained a position as professor of political economy at Antioch College in Ohio. Yet in time his Communist past came back to haunt him; while Communists spread tales of his "embezzlement," rightists ignored the fact that he had long ago denounced Communism and complained that he was poisoning the minds of innocent students. He nevertheless held on at Antioch for ten years until 1952 when he became caught up in a campaign by the United States government to deport alien Communists. While awaiting the outcome of an appeal, the man who would have been the American Trotsky died on September 16, 1953, of a cerebral hemorrhage.

## Chapter Seventeen

The Comintern's first organizer in the United States, Mikhail Borodin, the man allegedly betrayed by John Reed to an American naval intelligence agent, was born Mikhail Markovitz Gruzenberg into a rabbinical family in Belorussia in 1884. Arrested by the czarist police as a Bolshevik revolutionary in 1908 and given an option of prison or exile, he departed for the United States. "A man with shaggy black hair brushed back from his forehead, a Napoleonic beard, deep-set eyes, and a face like a mask,"[1] Borodin studied law at Valparaiso University in Indiana and in August 1918 heeded the call of the Russian Revolution to return to Russia. In Petrograd and Moscow, he established close contact with Lenin, Trotsky, and Zinoviev and soon became an organizer for the Comintern. In mid-1919, named to head the bureau of the Comintern in Mexico City, Borodin left for New York by way of Western Europe, traveling on a diplomatic passport and bearing papers signed by Lenin and Trotsky appointing him as Soviet representative (ambassador) in Mexico City. In the first of a series of mishaps involving Borodin and Comintern funds, Swiss police confiscated half a million Nicholas rubles that Borodin placed in a safe deposit box in a Swiss bank; the funds, said the police, were intended to finance Bolshevik propaganda.

As Borodin's steamer entered New York harbor, police came aboard. In a moment of panic, he threw overboard a packet containing jewels intended for Ludwig Martens and worth a million rubles. It turned out that he had been prudent, for awaiting him at customs was the head of the Chicago office of the Bureau of Investigation, Jacob Spolansky, who had known Borodin in Chicago by the name of Jacob Gruzenberg and learned from sources in Russia that Borodin would be arriving with a consignment of jewels. Like Borodin a Russian émigré, Spolansky had broken with the Russian revolutionary movement when the Bolsheviks came to power; recruited into the U.S. Army military intelligence in 1918, he had transferred to the Bureau of Investigation, where hunting down American Communists became his specialty.

When Spolansky searched Borodin's luggage, he found no trace of the jewels, and without the jewels, there was no reason to hold Borodin. Shadowed by agents of the Bureau of Investigation, Borodin continued to Chicago to see his family, then returned to New York on September 25, 1919, where, in the language of his dossier in files of the U.S. Army's Military Intelligence Division, he "was lost sight of." [2]

Borodin had in fact left the United States to take up his duties in Mexico City, arriving at the end of September 1919. His presence and purpose were soon known to American authorities, thanks to an informer on his staff.

"Gruzenberg"'s presence in Mexico City had a "twofold object," "to make bolshevik propaganda and effect a union of all Latin-American countries, and to secure a sum of money which amounted to $2½ million dollars which was at that time in the hands of agents on the Island of Santo Domingo, and which was to be used to make propaganda and buy government officials in Mexico, Central and South America, and Cuba." [3]

American officials had long been concerned about Communist use of Mexico as a base of operations against the United States, for as one intelligence officer observed, Mexico provided "excellent material for Bolshevism in its militant forms." Mexican officials, he declared, would "follow any leader who pays" and "Moscow knows this. . . . As a flank attack on the United States, it is a stroke of genius." [4]

Yet for the moment, at least, there was no need for alarm, for Borodin was too preoccupied with trying to recover the $2.5 million, which he required to finance his operations in Latin America. To accomplish the task, he sent first one agent, then another to Santo Domingo to get the funds, but the word was that the Communists in Santo Domingo refused to hand over the money. In the end, it would appear that the first agent, a Mexican-American clergyman named Rafael Mallen, absconded with the funds to Havana.

By that time, Borodin was growing desperate for funds. A personal reserve fund of $10,000 was about to run out, and Ludwig Martens in New York, under tight police surveillance, was having his own troubles getting funds and was unable to help; Borodin saw no alternative but to return to Moscow and try to get money there.

In the Soviet capital, Borodin had considerable explaining to do: he had, after all, lost in one way or another no less than three large treasures. Although he managed to clear himself, Zinoviev decided against returning him to Mexico, sending him instead as an interim measure to attend the organizing congress of the Western European Bureau of the Comintern at Amsterdam. Zinoviev named as the new representative to Mexico a Hindu Nationalist and Socialist, Mahendra Nath Roy, whom Borodin himself had converted to Bolshevism in Mexico City.

The calamities befalling the early Comintern disciples and agents in the United States—John Reed, Louis Fraina, and Mikhail Borodin—demonstrated the fragile nature of the Comintern's penetration. To Gregori Zinoviev and other officials of the Comintern, it was also apparent that despite all the Comintern's efforts, the rival Communist factions in the United States had achieved no true unity. After considerable bickering, the American Communist Party and the Communist Labor Party had merged as the Communist Party of America, but as a letter from the Comintern delicately put it, there were "still existing difficulties."[5] To solve those "still existing difficulties," the Comintern sent the first of its agents with no previous tie to the party in the United States, a Pole, H. Valetski, and a Hungarian, Josef Pogany, who had been Béla Kun's war minister and who was to become the Comintern's permanent resident in the United States.

Part of the troubles besetting the American Communist movement were attributable to early raids and arrests. Although many were indicted, few were sentenced, and fewer still served time, but the governmental clampdown nevertheless drove the party underground. To the factional dispute over a degree of independence for the American party as opposed to slavish adherence to the Comintern was added the question of whether the party should adopt a restricted program that would enable it to operate openly and legally or whether an underground arm should still be maintained to do the dirty work of revolution.

By the time Valetski and Pogany arrived, the Communist Party of America consisted of four factions: two in the open, the Workers' Party and the United Toilers of America, which were creatures of two underground factions known by the derisive names pinned on them by their opposite number: the Liquidators, from an epithet Lenin had hurled at the Mensheviks, who wanted to do away with the underground, and the Geese, from the legendary cackling geese who were said to have saved ancient Rome, which saw an underground apparatus as essential to the party's survival and the achievement of its revolutionary objective.

Few of the small band of active American Communists—some 6,000 to 8,000 at the time—disagreed with the fundamental objective of the Comintern, which was to establish what was called the "Soviet Republic of America," yet persistent interference and dictation from Moscow proved irritating, especially when transfusions of Soviet money were usually accompanied by demands that the party render Russia—not the international Communist movement—some particular service, usually in the field of industrial espionage. And the demands for unquestioning obedience to the Comintern were unrelenting and utterly binding.

As laid down at the Second Congress of the Third International, every party belonging to the Comintern had to subscribe to irrefutable dicta:

> The Comintern was established solely to organize joint action by the proletariat to overthrow capitalism and establish dictatorships of the

proletariat, which were then to form an international soviet republic which would "completely abolish all classes and realize Socialism, the first stage of Communist society."

The "essential task" of the Communist International was "to fight by every means including armed force for the overthrow of the international bourgeoisie and for the creation of an International Soviet Republic."

There would be no federalism; the goal could be obtained only if all parties "in fact and effect" became "one unified Communist party throughout the world."

The Russian party was the model for all others because "of its iron discipline and its strict organization."

All parties were subordinate to the Comintern's Executive Committee, which was the "general staff" of the world-wide revolution and which had the authority to expel individuals, groups, and even national parties.

To reinforce the Comintern's strictures, Lenin at the Second Congress had introduced what became known as his twenty-one points. They provided that parties would be admitted to membership only if they were genuine Bolshevik parties with "highly centralized organization," governed by "iron discipline," and possessed of "the fullest power and authority and the most far-reaching prerogatives." They had to be prepared to conduct "periodical purges," to expel "all unreliable elements" in order to cleanse the system of "petty bourgeois elements which infiltrate into it."

On the matter of illegality, Lenin left no room for equivocation. "Communists," he declared, "can have no confidence in bourgeois legality." They were "obliged everywhere to create a parallel illegal organization which at the decisive moment will help the party to do its duty in a revolution." In countries where "emergency laws" interfered with the spread of "Communist ideas" in the armed forces, the work had to be "carried on illegally." Refusal to undertake the work would be tantamount to a dereliction of revolutionary duty.

A member of a Communist Party was also a member of the Comintern, whether he or she wanted to be or not, obligated to obey the Comintern's rules, orders, and dogma. The American Communist thus was bound to Moscow at least as tightly as the American Catholic priest to Rome. What was more, the disciplinarians of the party not infrequently resorted to menace and violence, and if for one reason or another neither of those weapons could be used, there was always excommunication. To the Communist, that was far more intimidating than to the Catholic, for it meant not only that he was shunned within the party but also outside it, where as an ex-Communist he was often deprived of a means of livelihood in the bourgeois world he had sworn to destroy.

So it was that Valetski and Pogany made the journey from Moscow to New York, their mission resembling that of the old inquisitor generals of the Holy Office of Rome, who traveled to the most distant parts of the world to persuade heretics to return to the faith. Like their predecessors in the Inquisition, they used that minatory combination of the soft voice, the gentle touch, and the flash of the hard eye. Yet the representatives of the Comintern were foredoomed in their mission, not only because of the mulishness of the factions but also because the defenders of the republic were at work.

By the time Valetski and Pogany arrived, the factions had already decided to hold a conciliatory convention. Taking extraordinary precautions to prevent the Bureau of Investigation from intervening, they arranged to meet near Bridgman, a village some fifteen miles from St. Joseph, a mineral springs resort in a fruit-growing region along the shores of Lake Michigan. Posing as representatives of a choral society coming for a holiday, two advance men rented a large wood-frame Victorian farmhouse and several cottages that were on the property; amid rural hills and woods and fronting on the lake, it was properly secluded.

As part of the security precautions, none of the delegates—including the visitors, Valetski and Pogany—was told where the convention was to be held. They were advised merely to present themselves on August 13, 1922, at a district meeting of the Workers' Party in Philadelphia. There one of the organizers took them by train to Cleveland, whence another conducted them by boat to Detroit, whence a third guide took them by rail to Grand Rapids and yet a fourth by rail to St. Joseph and Bridgman.

One of the delegates was particularly disturbed not to know where he was headed. He was Francis A. Morrow, a shipyard worker in Camden, New Jersey, known to the Communists as "Comrade Day" and to the Bureau of Investigation as Special Agent K-97. Reaching Grand Rapids and being given a ticket to St. Joseph, Comrade Day discerned that the trip might be nearing an end and managed to post a letter to his wife, who promptly passed the word to the Bureau of Investigation, which just as promptly ordered Jacob Spolansky from Chicago to St. Joseph.

As some eighty delegates to the convention began their first session on August 17, 1922, they laid down strict rules to assure secrecy. They met in a wooded hollow with lookouts posted on surrounding hills. All had to rise at six in the morning and retire at ten at night; they were not to "leave the grounds, talk to strangers, take notes, keep incriminating documents on their persons, mail letters, or bathe in Lake Michigan except at certain periods."[6]

To Valetski and Pogany, the depth of the schism in the American Communist movement was quickly apparent. Factional arguments raged in the woods through the day and by a dim kerosene lantern into the night. Although the Geese had more delegates, several unattached delegates joined the Liquidators, so that every vote might have ended in deadlock had not Francis A. Morrow sided with the more extreme Geese. In the end, the Geese emerged in control of a new Central Executive Committee, which assured continued life for the underground arm of the party, but to win they had to agree to a compromise assigning the main task of revolution to the open arm of the party.

Unknown to the delegates, Spolansky and a colleague, Edward Shanahan, had arrived in St. Joseph on August 19, 1922, where a query to the sheriff produced the information that the likeliest spot for a meeting of the type Spolansky described would be in Bridgman. At the village, the postmaster revealed that "a bunch of foreign-looking people" had arrived a few days earlier and had walked off in the direction of Lake Michigan.

Dressed in overalls, Spolansky and Shanahan early the next morning found the house where the delegates had just finished breakfast. On the pretext of wanting a drink of water, they moved among the delegates. Spying familiar faces—one of them was William Z. Foster, later to be a Communist candidate for president of the United States—Spolansky realized that they had found their quarry and returned to Bridgman to raise a posse.

What Spolansky failed to realize was that William Z. Foster had also recognized him. No sooner had Spolansky and Shanahan left than Foster revealed what had happened. There appeared to be no recourse but to flee. The exodus began that night, with priority given to the safety of the two representatives of the Comintern, those under immediate threat of jail, and aliens, while a group made up of delegates having American citizenship stayed behind to hide the records of the convention.

Counting Spolansky and Shanahan, the posse consisted of four government agents, the Bridgman sheriff, and some twenty villagers. They struck at dawn. Among those taken was the national secretary of the party, Charles E. Ruthenberg, and Special Agent K-97. Although held in the Bridgman jail with the others, Morrow managed, without breaking his cover, to inform Spolansky of the location of two sugar barrels full of documents buried on the rented property. Unearthed, the barrels were found to contain "a registration of all the delegates, checks, instructions from Moscow, texts of the speeches, and an assortment of similarly revealing papers."

The documentation was useful when at the end of the year the government prosecuted William Z. Foster and Charles E. Ruthenberg for treason, but the end result was hardly worth Special Agent K-97's having to come into the open as a prosecution witness. Ruthenberg was sentenced to five years in jail but was freed on appeal and died before a hearing could be held. Foster's trial resulted in a hung jury.

Over the years that followed, the American Communist movement was destined to remain fractured and unruly and to insist on a degree of independence from Moscow until at last, in 1940, it would withdraw—at least ostensibly—from the Comintern. Yet in the meantime, the work of the Comintern to establish a disciplined underground in the United States would continue. One who would be in the forefront of that effort used numerous aliases—such as Alexander Stevens, Steve Lapin, Pete Stevens, Steve Miller—but he was most generally known by the name J. Peters. One of the most mysterious—and possibly the most effective—of all Comintern agents in the United States in the period up to the American entry into World War II, Peters was born in Czechoslovakia as Alexander Goldberger. After serving in the Great War in the Austro-Hungarian Army, he entered the United States in February 1924, using his real name and accompanied by his brother and his mother.

The Bureau of Investigation developed little definite information on Peters' early history as a Comintern agent other than that he served the Comintern underground as a controller and the Soviet intelligence service as a political intelligence agent and that he worked with the American Communist Party's underground. The most important information concerning Peters was less definite: that he was a member of the Otdel Okhrany, or OO (Security Department or Section), which was a branch of the Russian intelligence services concerned with preventing the penetration of overseas Comintern organizations by such hostile services as the Bureau of Investigation.[7]

There were a number of indications that that was the case. According to a letter from "Control 50" of the Western European Bureau of the Comintern in Berlin to "Most Respected Comrade Bratman-Brodovsky" in Paris, which was intercepted and sent to Washington by the American military attaché in Paris, Control 50 had established an "OO chairman" in France and another in the United States," the appointment of the American chairman coinciding almost exactly with Peters' arrival in the United States.[8] If Peters was the OO chairman, he occupied a position of "unlimited authority" in his territory and had the assignment of seeing to it "that in every governmental and hostile institution and organization there are on hand hired agents" to whom "the existence, substance, and tasks of the OO must not be known."

The theory that Peters was the OO chairman in the United States was strengthened by the fact that he was in Vienna in June 1923 when a "Committee of Action" laid down certain rules for the conduct of principal officers of the OO and their "hired agents." In regard to terror, for example, the Committee of Action declared "the principle of its absolute inadmissability" in OO operations; terror was instead to be "replaced by a systematic doing away with the counter-revolutionary and treasonable element." The only time that terror might be used was when there was "assurance of entire success," and should such an undertaking fail, the instructions noted ominously, "the responsibility is taken by each member of the OO individually."

"The entire organization of the OOs and their work," noted the Committee of Action, "have a strictly conspirative character," and to assure that no OO activity should become known, "the members of the OO shall in no case maintain relations with their comrades, who are occupying a legitimate party, public, or governmental position. Every connection with each other of the members of the OO and the OOs among themselves and with other organs is made with special couriers . . . All the matters and the correspondence of the OO are conducted with the aid of the oral code. No archives are kept; all materials which have been used are destroyed."

The OO was thus among the most secret of Communist organizations. While there was some evidence that the Bureau of Investigation for long had an informant within the Communist Party of America's Central Committee, there would be no indication of penetration of the OO. Yet the OO organization had at least one weakness: unable to do the work alone, the chairman had to have at least one intermediary to serve as a contact with the "hired agents." The man whom the OO chairman—presumably Peters—chose as his intermediary was Jay David Whittaker Chambers.

Whittaker Chambers came of age at the end of the Great War at a time when many of his generation accepted the notion that Britain and France had tricked the United States into the war, that the war had been fought largely to consolidate capitalism, that patriotism was futile, that military institutions were inherently stupid. Deeply cynical and disillusioned, Chambers was a man of intellect and talent. The American writer and editor Clifton Fadiman, who knew Chambers when he was a student at Columbia University, felt that Chambers was a "brilliant poet" who, had he concentrated on his writing, would have been "a renowned literary figure."[9]

Yet as Fadiman would note, Chambers "seemed to consider school as a sort of side line." It was a time, said Fadiman, when "many students at Columbia . . . were wild with ideas about changing the world." Many, like Chambers, "turned towards Communism as a solution," but as most became more mature, they "swung back and away." Not Chambers; not, at least, for a long time.

Upon leaving Columbia, Chambers spent several months in Germany, France, and the Low Countries studying "the aftermath of war" and "formed the definite opinion that there was something basically wrong with the condition of the world." When he returned to the United States, he began to read the works of the British Fabian Socialists, Sidney and Beatrice Webb; the British labor historian, economist, and Socialist, G. D. H. Cole; and the French social philosopher, Georges Sorel. He also read a pamphlet by Lenin, "A Soviet at Work," and as he would later state, all combined to persuade him "that the theories of Karl Marx and the tactical directions of Lenin offered the best explanation and solution for the social crisis."[10] Chambers made up his mind to join the Communist Party.

Admitted to party membership early in 1924, his first job for the party, for which he received no compensation, was to collect money from newsstands from sale of the Communist newspaper, the *Daily Worker*, and to recover unsold copies. Yet from that humble start, Chambers was destined to progress up through the party's ranks until he became a leading courier for both the Comintern and the OO.

## Chapter Eighteen

Having campaigned against Woodrow Wilson on a pledge of "a return to normalcy," Warren Gamaliel Harding became in 1921 the twenty-ninth president of the United States. The new secretary of state was Charles Evans Hughes, an able and distinguished lawyer who had been governor of New York, an associate justice of the Supreme Court, and in 1916 the Republican candidate for president. Yet for all the ability of the new secretary and the desire of the president to begin trading with Russia, normalcy in regard to Russia would remain elusive, and the situation was complicated by a new, vast, and lamentable factor: plague and famine in the Volga Basin threatening the health and lives of perhaps 35 million people. Should the United States provide assistance, thereby helping to perpetuate a detestable regime, or should the United States allow the trouble to run its course, with all the pitiful consequences that might entail?

Was the situation as catastrophic as the Russians in their quest for help apparently wanted the world to believe? Or were the Bolsheviks using the crisis as another tool in attempt to obtain recognition by the western governments in order to establish trade? What, too, of a growing contention that American citizens were languishing in Russian prisons; would the American people sanction assistance, however humanitarian, to a government that persecuted not only its own subjects but Americans as well? Would it not be better to deny assistance on the theory that the economic situation in Russia had grown so desperate that the crisis of famine and plague would topple the Bolsheviks and rid the world of an oppressive regime?

A New York consultant in industrial economics, organization, and management, Royal B. Keeley, early in 1918 met Russian professor, Yuri M. Lomonosov, who had come to New York the previous year to purchase railway locomotives and equipment for the provisional government and who, at Lenin's direction, had remained with the same objective following the October Revolution. After several meetings, Lomonosov invited Keeley to visit Russia, where "every opportunity would be given for the investigation of the Russian industrial and economic situation in preparation for the future trade which he was sure would develop between Russia and America."[1]

Traveling together, Keeley and Lomonosov arrived in Petrograd on September 18, 1919. From that moment Keeley began keeping a detailed diary which, as the days and weeks passed, began to reflect a national catastrophe in the making. When typed the full diary would consist of seventy-two pages of single-spaced and closely packed foolscap. Keeley himself may have provided a copy of the diary to the American military observer in Riga, which for all the major western democracies had become a listening post with antennae directed toward the Soviet Socialist Republic.

Communism, Keeley observed in one entry, had failed "absolutely." Lenin's regime, he wrote, had no support among the peasants and little more among the workers. Russian industry, he observed, had collapsed; raw materials were virtually nonexistent; there was impending and actual famine, "incompetency and graft in the Red Army," and a widespread breakdown of law and order. Without

"American administrative ability and capital," Keeley saw "a return to barbarism."[2]

The rate of inflation, noted Keeley, was astronomical. In six months prices for black bread had increased by 260 percent, for wheat flour by 275 percent, sugar by 490 percent, salt by 675 percent, vegetable oil by 515 percent, milk 550 percent, meat 300 percent. So short or unavailable through sale or barter were the necessities of life that "It seems that all conditions work together to make criminals, thieves, liars and scoundrels of all. Everybody is a law breaker."[3]

As noted in the diary, Keeley on December 13, 1919, wrote a "personal memorandum" to Lenin in an effort "to give him an unprejudiced view" of the country's condition; but as he was to observe, Lenin and his colleagues "plainly did not like these criticisms and to face the cold facts. What they like is praise and flattery overlooking the difficulties."[4]

Shocked and depressed, Keeley on March 1, 1921, applied to the authorities for permission to leave the country. As a consequence, the commissar for internal affairs, Alexei I. Rykov, contacted him with a request that he take with him when he departed "data on the natural resources of the country" in the hope that he could "interest American capital" in developing the resources. When Keeley assented, he was invited to several conferences where officials provided him the data, then was granted a visa authorizing him to leave Russia on May 12, 1921.

Meanwhile, at about the time Keeley applied for his visa, a man named Jonas Lied arrived in Moscow. Lied "professed to be acting for the British Foreign Office"; that appeared to the American military observer in Riga to be unlikely. As noted in Riga, Lied claimed to have "secured large concessions [in Russia] and expects to make millions of pounds out of them," and in pursuing that objective, he had done what the observer in Riga called "a rather mean thing": he had reported to the office of the Soviet foreign commissar that Keeley was "spreading pessimistic reports about Russian industries."

Why Lied took that step was uncertain. It may have been a result of a personal vendetta; he could have been concerned that Keeley's reports would interfere with his own undertakings; or it could have been a by-product of an incipient trade war between certain sections of American and British commerce hopeful of new riches to be found in trade with Russia.[5] In any event, as Keeley was preparing to leave Russia by way of Latvia, agents of the Cheka arrested him.

Keeley vanished without trace until discovered by chance by a representative of the French Red Cross in a Moscow prison; he had been neither charged nor tried. Soon thereafter British authorities passed to the American military attaché in London two intercepts of Russian radio messages. The first noted that Keeley "secretly compiled memoirs concerning the position of industries in Russia" with "descriptions that were maliciously slanderous." Keeley, the message concluded, "has been brought to trial."[6] The second message noted that during the course of trial, Keeley had "produced no documents and made no statements to justify his conduct." He was sentenced "to two years imprisonment for having published libellous statements regarding Soviet Russia."[7] Keeley at that point became a member of a little band of Americans whose presence in Russian cells provided a focal point for the opposition of a large segment of the American press and public to helping the victims of the Russian famine.

Beginning in 1918 and increasing in 1919, there had been numerous reports in the European and American press of famine in Russia, reports that were sufficiently credible to prompt President Wilson to authorize the head of the American Relief Administration, Herbert Hoover, whose organization was already feeding millions in Western Europe, to look into the possibility of relief for Russia. One of the first official indications to reach Washington of the brutal nature of the famine and its probable widespread extent came in December 1919, when an official of the American Relief Administration in Reval, Estonia, Van Arsdale Turner, reported to the State Department on a tour he had made through some 20,000 square miles of Northwest Russia recently taken from the Red Army by General Yudenitch.

Of the prewar population of the agricultural lands around Pskov, Turner reported, only 20 percent remained; the rest had simply vanished. Agriculture in the region was unable to support even that drastically reduced population, for the Red Army had confiscated seed grains and killed most of the cattle and horses to feed its troops; there was no fertilizer; and the transportation system had collapsed. Political commissars having seized all currency, the region was reduced to a barter economy. The population, reported Turner, was "on the verge of starvation, with the percentage of deaths among children under ten years of age running to more than 25%."[8]

As the United States was eventually to ascertain, the plight of the Pskov region was like that in much of European Russia. By midsummer of 1921 the food shortages had become so severe that certain elements within the Politburo saw no recourse but to appeal to the west for help, but others believed that would be an admission of the failure of Communism and preferred to see the peasants die. In the end the two factions compromised: the government itself would not at first ask for help but would sanction an ostensibly unofficial appeal from the renowned Russian novelist and short-story writer, Maxim Gorki, directly to the director of the American Relief Administration.

As that appeal came, Herbert Hoover had already gained an idea of how the Russians might react to offers of American help when in August 1920, following the Red Army's defeat before Warsaw, he had sent two members of his Relief Administration to accompany the Polish delegation to armistice talks that first opened in Minsk. The two—Maurice Pate and Herschell C. Walker—were to arrange relief operations in that part of Poland still occupied by the Red Army and to investigate the need and practicality of providing relief for children in Russia. Although the Relief Administration's European headquarters in London informed Moscow of Pate's and Walker's coming and their purpose, the Russians professed, when the delegation reached Minsk, to have had no advance notice of Pate's and Walker's presence and promptly arrested them.

That the Russians had acted deliberately and with advance knowledge was soon to become apparent when, after three days of vehement protests by the two Americans, the Russians agreed to allow them to proceed to Moscow. Their guard during their confinement and their trip appeared to be a man "of almost bovine stupidity" and "totally ignorant of the English language," but upon arrival in Moscow, he turned out to be an intelligent member of the Foreign Commissariat who spoke impeccable English.[9]

There could be no operations by the American Relief Administration either in Red-occupied Poland or in Russia, the Foreign Commissariat informed Pate and Walker. If the Americans wated to contribute relief supplies, the Soviet government would be pleased to accept them for distribution through its own facilities.

That requirement made clear the true purpose behind the Russian position. As the Soviet representative in New York, Ludwig Martens, pointed out, the Soviet government had no wish for "charity." The government wanted instead "to be allowed to purchase in foreign markets those essential supplies of medicine, soap and other necessities for lack of which men, women and children in Soviet Russia are now suffering." Relief, he said, "would be unnecessary if the foreign governments would remove their ruthless blockade against the resumption of normal commerce."[10]

Opponents of relief for Russia in the United States received proof of long-held contentions that the Russians had imprisoned American citizens when in November 1920 Nuorteva announced that the Soviet government held six Americans on charges of espionage.[11] They were: a Greek-American, Xenophon Kalamatiano, and ex-newsman Henry J. La Marc, both implicated in the early scheme devised by the British agent Sidney George Reilly to stage a rebellion against the Lenin government; John Reed's acquaintance, William Burgess Estes, who had been sentenced to death for espionage; a member of the New York publishing firm of Boni and Liveright, Albert Boni, who, Nuorteva said, had been "asked by American authorities in Berlin to do political spying in Russia, which promise he was busy fulfilling when arrested"; a major in the United States Army, Merion B. Cooper, supposedly shot down while flying over Russian territory for the Polish Air Force during the Russo-Polish War; and an official of the American Red Cross, Emmett Kilpatrick, whom the Lenin government had arrested in South Russia and denounced for having spied for the United States Army.

Blame for the predicament of the American prisoners, Nuorteva declared, rested squarely upon the government of the United States. He accused the United States of "absolutely and unreasonably refusing to release Russians detained for much more pardonable offenses in America."

As officials in Washington already knew, there were other Americans in Moscow jails. In leaving Russia in early September 1920, Pate and Walker had notified Washington of those six prisoners and two others: a former correspondent for the Associated Press, Mrs. Margaret Harrison, whom the Russians contended was a spy for the State Department, and an American soldier, presumably captured in Siberia, Thomas Hazelwood, who had reputedly gone mad.

On August 9, 1921, without prior Russian arrangements with American authorities and without public announcement, five men dressed in rags and looking like skeletons debarked from a train at Narva on the Russo-Estonian frontier. They proved to be Kalamatiano, Estes, Kilpatrick, La Marc, and Keeley. Why those five and not also Major Cooper, Margaret Harrison, Albert Boni, and Thomas Hazelwood went unexplained. So also the motive behind the release, although that could well be surmised; for the next day, August 10, 1921, Deputy Soviet Foreign Commissar Litvinov was scheduled to open discussions in Riga with officials of the American Relief Administration on aid to Russia, and Herbert Hoover had made clear that "the absolute *sine qua non* of any assistance" was "the immediate release of the Americans now held prisoner in Russia."[12]

Conducted unilaterally by the Americans, the discussions in the Latvian capital attracted a flock of newsmen from around the world and diplomatic representatives and intelligence agents from the other western nations, the diplomats and agents lured by alarm over what conditions the Americans might be about to agree to or what trade advantage they might seek in exchange for their assistance, for both the British and French governments were suspicious that the Soviets were exaggerating the severity and extent of the famine in an attempt to reestablish trade relations and diplomatic recognition. Aside from release of American prisoners, Hoover actually was demanding nothing more than freedom to distribute relief supplies without interference by the Soviet government, but to suspicious observers, the Soviets accepted Hoover's offer with disturbing alacrity.

The American press shared the concern. Lenin, warned the Washington *Post*, for example, "knows that Russia can not continue in the position which she now occupies but must in some way secure a place among the nations of the world, with diplomatic and trade relations, and he is working to that end, using the famine conditions as the lever with which to accomplish his object." At the same time, according to the *Post*, Trotsky still harbored "the notion that the world is ripe for revolution and that Russia is destined to lead [it]." The *Post* admonished Hoover to note that "the 600,000 bolshevist adherents in and about Moscow are kept well fed and comfortable" despite the famine and that Lenin would seize every opportunity to make political capital out of the relief measures.[13]

Radical and Communist sympathizers mounted a particularly vociferous attack against Hoover, for by proffering relief, he took away the weapon with which they had been bludgeoning him: his previous failure to provide relief for Russia. Hoover intended at that point, the radicals charged, to use relief supplies in Russia for political purposes.

As protests from both sides mounted and the discussions opened, the controlled Russian press began to publish for the first time detailed accounts of the horror of the famine, apparently to prepare the way for accepting at least some measure of American control over the relief operations. The Moscow journal *Economic Life* reported that peasants in the province of Samara had to substitute grass and acorns for wheat. For meat the population was reduced to eating "marmots, cats and dogs." The *Krasnaya Gazeta* said peasants were eating peat, hemp root, and "clay with iron oxide," and some were "grinding down" birch and lime wood to make a form of flour. The Moscow *Biednota* reported homeless children "rooting like hungry dogs in dunghills," and a population feeding "on leaves, marmots, offal, dead carcasses, and horses' hooves." The number of children in sixteen "starving regions," reported *Izvestia*, totaled 9,351,467, and the total of all ages facing starvation approached 22 million people.

At the same time the controlled press attacked the measures proposed for handling relief by the American Relief Administration as "nothing more or less than an attempt on the part of a capitalistic government to break down the Soviet regime."[14] On August 13, 1921, for example, *Pravda* branded "foreign schemes of relief as a cloak for intervention and the robbery of the last of Russia's wealth." The Comintern charged that the British and French governments were preparing "a war of extermination" against Russia, an effort, the British declared, to divert the attention of the Russian people from "the ruin at home" by spreading "false stories of perils from abroad."

Concerned about the possible consequences of unilateral American relief, the British and French formed an International Commission for Russian Relief, which met in Paris with official representation from Belgium, Britain, France, Italy, and Japan. Although the American Relief Administration was invited to send an official representative, Herbert Hoover declined, concerned that political considerations might assume more importance than relief; he sent only an unofficial observer.

Hoover was right. Fearful of Russia's use of the famine as a lever to obtain recognition and trade, the commission decided that nothing should be done until a delegation of some thirty experts in various fields could go to Russia and determine the true situation. If at that point it was decided that the governments should participate in relief, credits might be granted to the Soviet government but only if that government would "recognize its responsibility for the discharge of existing debts and other obligations and liabilities."[15]

The Lenin government reacted with predictable acerbity. The commission, noted Foreign Commissar Chicherin, proposed "instead of collecting bread, to collect statistical data"; the proposal was "a monstrous mockery against the starving masses."[16]

After conducting two more perfunctory meetings, the International Commission for Soviet Relief dissolved itself.

Herbert Hoover nevertheless proceeded with his plans. In what was either one of the great humanitarian acts of the era or one of the most extraordinary examples of political naiveté, he signed a document that virtually guaranteed the survival of

Lenin, his regime, and the Bolshevik ethos, and a delegation headed by the director of the European headquarters of the American Relief Administration in London, Walter Lyman Brown, presented Litvinov with a draft agreement based on the principles to be applied in distributing relief supplies. Basic to some twenty-seven conditions was the principle of freedom of action by the Relief Administration inside Russia, to which the Lenin government had earlier agreed but then had berated.

As enunciated in detail, that freedom involved diplomatic immunity and full liberty of movement for all American representatives and the right to employ Russian nationals, regardless of their political beliefs, to form local committees to distribute relief supplies, to use whatever ports the Americans chose, to distribute supplies in the name of the American Relief Administration, and to have priority on transportation and communications facilities. The Russians were to guarantee that they would "take every step to insure that relief supplies . . . will not go to the Army, Navy, or Government employees (to include the Cheka and officials of the Communist Party)" but only to recipients designated by the relief administration, to reimburse the administration in dollars or replace in kind "any misused relief supplies"; to bear the cost of transportation, storage, and distribution; and to "acquaint the Russian people with the aims and method of the relief work."

The draft agreement noted in conclusion:

> The Soviet authorities having previously agreed as to the absolute *sine qua non* of any assistance . . . to release all Americans detained in Russia and to facilitate the departure from Russia of all Americans so desiring, the ARA reserves to itself the right to suspend temporarily or terminate all its relief work in Russia in case of failure on the part of the Soviet authority to fully comply with this primary condition or with any condition set forth in the above agreement.[17]

To Deputy Foreign Commissar Litvinov, those conditions represented less agreement than dictate, but Walter Lyman Brown refused to bend, pointing out that the conditions were the same as laid down in Hoover's original offer, to which the Russians had agreed.

Asserting in almost every utterance that "food is a weapon,"[18] Litvinov drew out the negotiations, which led to prophecies and speculation that the conference was about to break down. Word that breakdown had actually occurred appeared in the European press amid warnings from many that negotiations with the Bolsheviks could never succeed. Yet in the end the threat of mass starvation and the effect that might have on the regime in Moscow proved overpoweringly persuasive to the Bolsheviks. While protesting to the last that the agreement was rife with capitalistic political intrigues, Litvinov on August 20, 1921, signed.

The dread that the specter of mass starvation held for the Soviet authorities was apparent not only in their acquiescence in that agreement but also in the strength of the decree that they issued "to all Commissariats, Revolutionary Military Soviets of the Republic, and District Executive Committees." The decree directed that "all requests or demands emanating from the American Relief Administration must be considered and dealt with within forty-eight hours of their receipt." If there was any question about the request or how to fund it, the request was to be met and deliberations conducted later. "Any infraction of this order," the decree concluded, "which might reflect unfavorably upon the prestige of the Soviet Government in view of the obligations taken upon itself . . . , will be visited with the severest punishment in accordance with revolutionary law." The document was signed by the president of Soviet Russia, Mikhail Kalinin.[19]

Despite that decree, not all went smoothly. Some of the difficulties were beyond the ability of Soviet authorities to remedy: the condition of the railroads, shortages of river craft, bad weather, inadequate roads in the provinces, a breakdown in community spirit and cooperation brought about by the famine itself, the migration from village to town that the famine had produced. Others were built into the Communist system: pilferage by stevedores and other workmen, a form of supplementing one's inadequate pay that was accepted throughout Soviet society; a sluggish, indifferent bureaucracy; an inability of commissars at local levels to accept change in their dictatorial authority. Nor was it easy for the Communist hierarchy at local levels to accept that relief supplies might be dispensed without counterrevolutionary intent, particularly when the Central Committee of the Communist Party warned the people to be wary lest Hoover attempt in Russia what the committee said he had accomplished in Hungary, the downfall of the government of Béla Kun. That apprehension led to many a Russian who worked for the Americans being thrown into jail on the vaguest of charges. So, too, the controlled press tried to ridicule the American contribution. It was only through profits from the war that the United States had become so rich that it could raise an entire generation of Europeans on their condensed milk. "The bearing of Hoover's emissaries," declared *Pravda* on September 21, 1921, "is in the style of the duke visiting the collier's hut."

With hundreds of employees involved, representatives of the American Relief Administration were not always masters of tact nor above making errors in judgment. Yet overall, given the huge nature of the undertaking, the inherent suspicions, and the primitive state of much of the country, the relief operations proceeded with a remarkable smoothness and dispatch. At a peak in the summer of 1922, the American Relief Administration was feeding more than 4,170,000 children and 6,300,000 adults. By the spring of 1923, as new crops grew in Russian fields, the program began to wind down, and the last American administrator departed in November 1923.

The total expenditure by the American Relief Administration exceeded $61 million, while other private American relief organizations contributed almost $5 million. The U.S. Congress had appropriated $20 million, and the rest represented voluntary contributions from the American people. The Soviet of

People's Commissars in a formal resolution thanked the people of the United States "in the name of the millions of people saved and in the name of all the working people of Soviet Russia and the Federated Republics" and declared "that the people inhabiting the Union of Soviet Socialist Republics will never forget the help given them by the American people, . . . seeing in it a pledge of the future friendship of the two nations."[20]

Amid that apparent aura of goodwill, Chicherin suggested that the time had come to discuss normal diplomatic, trade, and financial relations between the two countries. When Secretary of State Hughes replied on December 18, 1923, he made clear that the work of the unofficial American Relief Administration had changed nothing in regard to official relationships. The United States would be prepared to discuss recognition and trade, he said, only after Russia restored confiscated American property, paid the war debt, repudiated a Russian claim for $750 million against the United States for participating in the Allied blockade of Russian ports, and abandoned attempts to foment revolution in the United States.

One of the principal American advocates of recognition, Senator William Borah of Idaho, who called for recognition with such vehemence and persistence that the press called him "Bolshie Bill," demanded that the Harding administration reconsider that stand. That was impossible, Hughes replied in a public statement, so long as the Communists continued interfering in internal American affairs. The Department of Justice, for example, had only recently intercepted instructions from the president of the Comintern, Gregori Zinoviev, to an organization recognized by the Comintern as friendly and sympathetic, the Workers' Party of America, in which Zinoviev directed the party to form "fighting units" to receive instructions in marksmanship and demolitions. Zinoviev, according to Hughes, declared that those units "will give enormous results in the sense of preparing thousands of new propagandists, future leaders of the military forces of the party, and faithful fighters during the social revolution." Zinoviev had also declared, Hughes said, that "the red flag will fly over the White House."[21]

# PART IV
## The British Cockpit

---

*Chapter Nineteen*

Through the Treaty of Versailles, the British Empire had acquired 800,000 square miles of new territory and 13 million new subjects in Arabia, Africa, Asia, and the Pacific, so that King George V of the United Kingdom of Great Britain, Ireland, and of the British Dominions Beyond the Seas, Defender of the Faith, Emperor of India, ruled the largest empire in the history of mankind. In a sense of wonderment at what the empire had achieved, the 1919 edition of that imperial reference, Whittaker's Almanac, showed that the British Empire far exceeded the size of other nations:

| | |
|---|---|
| British Empire: | a. 13,355,426 |
| | p. 475,000,000 |
| China: | a. 2,446,855 |
| | p. 474,487,000 |
| United States of America: | a. 3,026,789 |
| | p. 122,775,046 |
| Russia (1914): | a. 7,626,717 |
| | p. 100,857,985. |

That immense demesne, announced the *Morning Post* in obvious pride, was content and happy and ruled securely from London, a conurbation of no more

179

than 620 square miles. It was at that point more incontestable than ever, the *Post* continued, that the sun could never set on the British Empire. In the Age of the New Imperium, it was possible to travel from Capetown to Alexandria, to British Columbia, to Newfoundland, to England, and from England to Gibraltar without passing from the shadow of the Union Jack. It was also possible to go by rail from Capetown to Cairo without once leaving British territory. And that, it seemed, was not the end of British acquisitions; even as the Bolshevik civil war was going on in Russia, the British were displaying interest in vast areas of North Russia.

In keeping with the old imperial adage that trade follows the flag, a British economic and commercial mission had arrived in Murmansk in the summer of 1918. According to the British foreign secretary, Arthur J. Balfour, responding to an American request for information about the mission, it was "a small commission of commercial experts to advise the Russians as to the best means of restoring and developing British trade relations and interests in Russia and of countering enemy [i.e., German] schemes of commercial penetration."[1]

That somewhat indirect answer may well have been true, but it was not the whole answer; and it failed to satisfy the United States government, which was endeavoring to persuade the Russian people that the Allies had invaded not for gain but for the Russians' own good. The Americans suspected that British capital intended to follow British bayonets and take control of North Russia in much the same way that the City of London in the seventeenth century had established the Hudson Bay Company in North Canada, formed a trade monopoly, and colonized the region. That the suspicions had at least some basis in fact became apparent in February 1919 with the arrival at Murmansk of a renowned British explorer of the Arctic and Antarctic, Sir Ernest Shackleton, a man cut from the same mold as the "Gentlemen Adventurers trading into Hudson Bay."

Shackleton, reported the American military attaché, Colonel Ruggles, had negotiated with the Supreme Administration of the North, the puppet government established by General Poole, on behalf of a British trading company capitalized at from one to two million pounds.[2] He had obtained leases on large tracts of Murmansk waterfront property and prospecting rights in some 81,000 square miles of nearby territory. In exchange for royalties on the products of mines and forests, on waterpower concessions, and on building sawmills, Shackleton obtained the right to build railways and to have the privilege of purchasing them at the lowest price offered should the Supreme Administration of the North ever decide to sell them. In return for the various concessions, Shackleton's company was to expend $125,000 annually for a period of five years for prospecting and was to import food and clothing to be sold to local inhabitants at "a small profit." Soon thereafter, Colonel Ruggles reported that Shackleton's company had expanded its requests to include large timber, commercial, railway, waterpower, and fishery rights, and that the commercial exploitation of the region was the real reason the British government was maintaining an Allied army there. It should also be noted, reported Ruggles, that Shackleton was in the uniform of a major of the British Army and was in North Russia in an official rather than a private capacity.

Then officials of the Hudson Bay Corporation themselves arrived in North Russia; they had come, it was reported to Washington, to take control of all import and export trade, and their first move was to export goods worth $14 million. As the commanding officer of the USS *Olympia*, Captain Byron C. Bierer, the American flag officer in North Russia, reported, the British "hoped that conditions would so shape themselves that they would be able to secure control or domination of the region."[3] Imperialism was plainly at work, and when President Wilson learned that the British were using American troops to help them establish themselves in North Russia, it contributed materially to his decision to withdraw Americans forces from the North Russian Expeditionary Force.

Nor was British exploitation confined to North Russia. Numerous reports reached American naval and military intelligence in Washington of British attempts to obtain control of the "oil puddles" of the Caucasus, one of the richest oil-bearing regions in the world; and an American mining engineer employed by the Ayan Corporation of London, which had large interests in the Aian Gomei Kaisha gold mining company of Japan, operating in Siberia, informed military intelligence that he was securing large numbers of gold mining claims for the British in Siberia. The British also, he reported, had begun to drill large petroleum oil deposits on the east coast of North Sakhalin, which were held under Russian titles by Japanese companies working with British capital.[4]

For all the terrible casualties of a war that had wiped out almost the entire succeeding generation of the British ruling class, the old imperial spirit was obviously still there; and if there was discontent in Egypt, in India, in Persia, in Kenya, in Ireland, on the Niger, it was the discontent of ambitious functionaries and politicians, for in the view from London, the king-emperor's subjects were as devoted, as loyal as ever. If there was fatigue, it had had no effect upon the mechanical genius and the adventuresome spirit of the island people; to add to London's sense of confidence, the airship R (for royal) 34 spanned the North Atlantic in ninety-seven hours and without landing turned around and flew back again in seventy-four hours, a journey that raised the possibility of new imperial political dimensions; the king-emperor might be in Montreal for a meeting with the governor-general one week, then out to Alexandria for conversations with the Arabian princes the next, and then on to Jerusalem to see the grand mufti before returning within a matter of hours to Windsor Castle in time for tea. It was a thrilling prospect: a Queen of the Skies with the flag of the Mercantile Marine fluttering from the captain's deck, potted plants in the stateroom, and Marconigrams bleating in and out of the wireless room, conveying imperial commands and receiving imperial advices from His Most Britannic Majesty's secretary of state for foreign affairs, the almighty Curzon, of whom the street wags sang:

My name is George Nathaniel Curzon,
I am a most superior person,
My cheek is pink, my hair is sleek,
I dine at Blenheim once a week.

George Nathaniel Curzon was 1st Marquess of Kedleston; his family motto was "Let Curzon Holde What Curzon Helde," and the family had held Kedleston Hall for 800 years. In the family chapel was inscribed the stately claim: "This ancient Family which has inherited a Good name and ample Possessions in this place before the NORMAN CONQUEST." Curzon believed absolutely in the imperial greatness. "Under Providence," he declared in a magisterial voice, "the British Empire was "the greatest instrument for good that the world has seen . . . there has never been anything so great in the world's history." As his family had held on to Kedleston Hall, so he intended that Britain should hold on to the empire for 800 years and more.

A Victorian of Victoria's times, Curzon was first undersecretary of state for India, then became viceroy and governor-general of India, a post of such eminence that its holder stood next to the king and before the heir-apparent in the British hierarchy. Curzon annexed Tibet, established a protectorate in Persia, planted the Union Jack on the sheikhdoms and emirates of the Persian Gulf, the Red Sea, and the Arabian fringes of the Indian Ocean, and constructed the Northwest Frontier Provinces of India. He was forever appearing in howdahs on the backs of elephants, descending from broughams, being borne through the surf to visit tribal rulers, arriving and departing in remote parts by imperial train, separating the Sikhs and the Jats, the Pathans, the Hindus, and the Muslims, clipping the claws of moneylenders, changing frontiers, presenting the Order of the Star of India or the Imperial Order of the Crown of India, arranging for the sons of the khans of Bukhara to go to Eton or Oxford or for the Rajput princes to attend Sandhurst. And he fashioned one of the world's most formidable police services, the Indian Special Branch, whose agents trapped Communist agitators and entered Russia to bribe the Musselmen or spy out the gradual seeping eastward of Russian rail and telegraph.

All that Lord Curzon did he did in the name of keeping Russia out of India, for like many a British patriarch, he had an obsession with the Russian threat and specifically with the threat to India, the second most precious jewel—after England—in the king-emperor's crown. Unless Britain held on to India, Lord Curzon believed, the British Empire would disintegrate as surely as had that of the moguls.

In 1919, Curzon became foreign secretary, a brisk figure in a Prince Albert coat with silk facings and an Indian pearl in his necktie, his papers in a case made for him at the command of the maharajah of Cooch Behar. As he came to office, the peril to his beloved India had never appeared greater, for in the wake of the October Revolution there had appeared, as Winston Churchill put it, "A world-wide conspiracy" against England and the empire, a marshaling of "sinister forces" and "the rascals and rapscallions of mankind" to undermine the unity of the empire in Ireland, in Egypt, in India, and wreck England's glory and heritage.

In the years just before the start of the Great War, there were on the west coast of the United States and in the imperial outpost of British Columbia some four to five thousand Hindus, most of them Sikhs who worked mainly as laborers on fruit and vegetable ranches and in lumber camps and sawmills. Scattered elsewhere in the United States was a sprinkling of more educated Hindus—university students, doctors, engineers, lecturers—many of whom showed "revolutionary and anarchistic tendencies."[5]

Shortly before the war clouds broke, a Hindu, Har Dayal, founded an organization called the Pacific Coast Hindustani Association, or Ghadr (freedom) Society. He also founded a newspaper in San Francisco called *Ghadr,* in which he stated in the first issue that "the object was to create a rebellion in India." From a counterespionage office in New York, the British took note of the organization with concern, as did American intelligence services, particularly when it was established that Har Dayal's organization was in touch with the Bolshevik organizers Santeri Nuorteva and Louis Fraina and "with various negro subversives" in organizations called the Star Order of Ethiopia and the Princes of Abyssinia.

Because of the activities of the Ghadr movement, Har Dayal was called upon in March 1914 to show cause why he should not be deported from the United States as an illegal alien and Anarchist. Jumping bail, he fled to Switzerland, leaving as editor of *Ghadr* and head of the movement "an out-and-out revolutionary from the frontier provinces of India," Ram Chandra. Two months later, in May 1914, two other Indian revolutionaries "of equal or even greater influence" arrived in San Francisco from Japan. As they joined forces with Ram Chandra, the Ghadr organization soon exercised "great power over the Hindus of the Pacific Coast."

When the war broke out, the Ghadr Society proclaimed that "the hour of India had come." Calling upon the membership to leave for India immediately to take part in the revolution against the British viceroy, the raj, the leaders arranged shipping for those agreeing to do so. Possibly as many as 200 departed in late August and September 1914 and got together in Yokohama with others from British Columbia, but when they reached India, "their expectations were sorely disappointed." They found no signs of revolt, and after "a few isolated outrages" in the Punjab, "the whole movement was soon suppressed."

To Ram Chandra and the other leaders of the Ghadr movement, the debacle indicated a need for closer liaison with the Germans. Two Hindu leaders soon arrived in New York from Germany, and a number of Hindus left the United States for Germany to become agents of the Berlin India Committee, which worked to create anti-British sentiment in the United States, throughout the Orient, and among Indian troops serving the British Army in the Sinai, Mesopotamia, Persia, and Afghanistan.

The German consul in San Francisco, von Brincken, cooperated with the Ghadr Society; and in May 1914, with his assistance, arms purchased by a German intelligence agent in New York were shipped from Los Angeles aboard the SS *Annie Larsen,* which rendezvoused at sea with the SS *Maverick,* to which the arms and six Hindu agents were transferred. Sailing for the wild, intricate waterways at the mouth of the Ganges, the *Maverick* awaited the arrival of Bengal revolutionaries led by Narendra Bhattarcharjya, alias Mahendra Nath Roy, who was later to become a leading agent of the Comintern. Upon receipt of the arms, the revolutionaries intended to attack the seat of the viceroy, Calcutta, but the maneuver "misfired owing to gross mismanagement."

So did several similar attempts, largely through clever intelligence work by British agents. By the spring of 1917, agents of the Bureau of Investigation, with British assistance, had accumulated sufficient evidence of malfeasance to begin arresting the Hindu revolutionaries, including Roy; and on July 7, 1917, American authorities arrested the entire leadership of the Ghadr Society. The trial that followed attained the sensational when a rival of Ram Chandra's for leadership of the Ghadr movement accused Chandra in open court of being a British spy and shot him down.

In the meantime, Roy had jumped bail and made contact with "General" Samuel Pearson, a departed South African veteran of the Boer War who manufactured glass coffins for a living in Scranton, Pennsylvania, and led an antiBritish conspiracy aimed at destroying the alliance between Britain and the United States. Between the start of the war and America's entry in 1917, Pearson formed several cover companies behind which at least a portion of a large and vigorous German espionage and political warfare apparatus functioned in the United States. Following American entry into the war, he became involved with the Socialist movement in Scranton and in New York with the Irish nationalist movement, Sinn Fein. He was so involved when contacted by Roy, who had established close relationship with Nuorteva and Fraina.

In February 1920, Pearson approached an officer of the Liberty National Bank in New York City, announcing that he was "a representative in this country of the Bolshevist Government" and expected momentarily to receive from the Soviet government $500,000 in gold rubles and bullion. He wanted to arrange a transaction to convert the gold into dollars in Sweden and obtain a credit with which to purchase an equivalent amount of goods for shipment to Russia. He was "a Bolshevist," Pearson told the bank official, "and hated the British." The bank declined to become involved, and when apprised of the approach, the Bureau of Investigation came to the conclusion that it was an attempt to finance the revolutionaries, Ludwig Martens, Santeri Nuorteva, and Mikhail Borodin, the last-mentioned of whom Mahendra Nath Roy was soon to join to participate in operations of the Comintern in Mexico City.

That was the first link—however tentative—that either the American or British intelligence services established between the Indian independence movement and the Comintern. More definite evidence would develop later, and the Comintern would be helped in its agitation by an event that in the words of Winston

Churchill was "without precedent or parallel in the modern history of the British Empire . . . an extraordinary event, a monstrous event, an event which stands in singular and sinister isolation."[6]

As the World War progressed, political opinion in India stirred and matured to a degree that surprised the British rulers. Much of it emerged from a sense of pride in the achievements of Indian troops, who turned out to be capable of fighting quite as well as those of the nation that ruled them. At the same time, the scope of the terrible war in Europe had left the Indian people with the sense that Europeans were no more capable of handling their affairs than they themselves had been during the eighteenth-century wars that had wrecked the Mogul Empire. So too the Russian Revolution demonstrated that the world's greatest autocracy could be pulled down overnight; why should the British autocracy in India endure?

Having pledged in 1917 and again in 1918 to give India self-rule within the empire, the British had contributed to Indian unrest by reneging on their promises. Fearing a rise of Indian nationalism, they contributed further when they restored or instituted repressive acts, such as the old Press Acts, which permitted the Heaven Born—as the Indians called their rulers—to suppress the press, and the Rowlatt Acts, which enabled them to dispense with juries and even with trials when subversion was involved, acts stemming directly from the raj's fear of Bolshevism. Although Bolshevism was unquestionably present in India and would play a part in subsequent disorders, it was at first poorly organized and generally ineffectual.

Indeed, the man who emerged in the forefront of the Indian campaign for freedom had no connection with Bolshevism: Mohandas Karamchand Gandhi, Gandhi of the Pure Soul, a mystic who had supported Britain in the war with Germany because he believed in the promises of independence. With the institution of the Press and Rowlatt Acts, with a failure of the harvest in 1918, and with millions of deaths in an influenza epidemic in the winter of 1918–1919, Gandhi turned against the British and called for *hartals*—strikes on the grounds of conscience—and violence erupted throughout the country. It was most marked in the Punjab among the Sikhs, who had provided Britain with some of the empire's most effective troops but who had also formed the core of the Ghadr movement in the United States.

For some days, as gurus excited the people's passions, there were wild disorders in the Sikh holy capital of Amritsar. Events approached a climax when the Sikhs killed five British administrators and bank managers and committed the unpardonable offense under the unwritten imperial laws of British India of molesting a *memsahib*, a representative of the British and Foreign Bible Society, Frances Marcella Sherwood. The raj promptly sent in military forces under Brigadier General Reginald Harry Dyer, who imposed martial law.

The Sikhs ignored the order. On April 13, 1919, several thousand gathered in a garden square in the center of Amritsar, the Jallianwalla Bagh, to demonstrate against the crown. Like most Indian crowds, the people gathered partly "out of conviction, partly in the hope of profit, partly for something to do."[7] Although some carried cudgels, nobody had firearms.

With about two hundred Baluchi, pastoral nomads from the Northwest Frontier, and Gurkhas, Tibeto-Mongolian killers with smooth, smiling faces, British officers under Dyer's direction surrounded the square, blocking three narrow exits with armored cars. A guru addressed the crowd, reciting a patriotic Sikh poem, which the crowd repeated after him as if in a liturgy, but there was no subversive call to arms, no exhortation to have at the Heaven Born. General Dyer nevertheless ordered his British officers to open fire. With rifles and with machine guns on the armored cars, the Baluchi and Gurkhas fired at point-blank range. For six full minutes they fired, killing 379 people—the Sikhs said 800—and wounding over 2,000, and "when dusk fell upon the carnage and the last survivors had left the square terrified and aghast, women and children crept around the garden searching for their menfolk." Because there was a curfew, all who could move had by nightfall dragged themselves away, and jackals and pi-dogs took over. "By ten o'clock there was scarcely a sound in the Jallianwallah Bagh but the rustling and gnawing of these animals, the moaning of the wounded, and the echoing voices of the British patrols outside, tramping with cocked rifles through the shuttered streets."[8]

The awful tragedy at Amritsar was soon front-page news around the world, and in Moscow Foreign Commissar Chicherin called a press conference in which he prophesied that the incident marked the beginning of the end of British rule in India. Although the world was "horrified" by the massacre, the British people "shaken and even remorseful,"[9] it took an official British commission investigating the tragedy seven months to report, and in the meantime General Dyer retained his command and even received a promotion. When the report was at last in, Dyer was finally relieved and called home, never again to be employed on military duties. Yet there was considerable sympathy for him nevertheless; a Tory newspaper, the *Morning Post*, organized a subscription for him and raised the princely sum of $100,000.

Not for another eight months was there a debate on the massacre on the floor of the Commons, and then Winston Churchill, who as secretary of state for war was the responsible minister, mitigated the issue by intimating that the Bolsheviks had been behind the disturbances that had preceded it. He deplored Dyer's actions and applauded the relief from command, but, he continued, the House should take note of "the world-wide character of the seditious and revolutionary movement with which we are confronted . . . the bloody and devastating terrorism which [the Bolsheviks] practise in every land into which they have broken, and by which alone their criminal regime can be maintained."[10]

Churchill's speech was something of a triumph, for the government survived the impact of the atrocity when conceivably it might have fallen. Yet it was nevertheless a disaster for Britain, for in India the name Amritsar assumed an emotional connotation not unlike the name Bastille in France. Declaring that there could be no cooperation with "a satanic government," Mahatma Gandhi called for a campaign of *dharma,* passive noncooperation with the raj, a campaign that shook the old bolts of British rule more seriously than had any event since the Indian Mutiny of 1857–1859. From the beginning of the Gandhi movement until the eventual end of British rule in India, the initiative would remain with the Indians, and "In a moral sense, thanks to the sacrifice in the Jallianwalla Bagh, they were free already."[11]

Soon after the Amritsar tragedy, Lenin and Trotsky attended a Comintern strategy conference. The recent defeat of Béla Kun's soviet in Hungary, noted Trotsky, showed that capitalism in Europe was not yet at a point where it could be destroyed by a frontal attack. Recent disturbances in the British imperial domains of India, Egypt, and Persia, he remarked, indicated that London might be more readily damaged by a Comintern attack "via the towns of Afghanistan, the Punjab, and Bengal." To make such an attack effective, Trotsky proposed establishing "a political and military headquarters for the Asian revolution."[12] Toward that end, the leadership decided to call a Congress of the Nations of the Orient to be held at Baku, the capital of Azerbaijan. When Moscow radio broadcast invitations to the conference, the news caused an excitement in western capitals not unlike that provoked by the announcement in early 1919 of the formation of the Communist International, for the Comintern was declaring a political war against the imperial powers through their colonies.

Despite British efforts to prevent any of the king-emperor's subjects from participating in the conference by sealing all ports and frontier posts under their control, 1,891 delegates attended, including Turks, Arabs, Hindus, Afghans, Persians, Kalmucks, Bashkirs, Kashgirs, Bukharans, Uzbekits, Dagestans, Chinese, Siberians, all the Caucasian and Tatar peoples, Russians, Hungarians, Bulgarians, English, French, Italians, Germans, and three Americans: John Reed, Louis Fraina, and a Russo-American Bolshevik Alexander Stoklitsky, a familiar figure at the Smolny Institute in Chicago until he vanished without a trace in 1923. The delegates were housed in the palaces and hotels of the Apsheron peninsula that, lizardlike, protrudes into the Caspian. The conference met in the seventeenth-century palace of the khans of Baku, while the eleventh-century mosque of Synyk-Kala was set aside for the use of Moslem delegates, who for all their adherence to Bolshevism, bowed each day not to Moscow but to Mecca.

Although represented as a congress called by the Oriental peoples themselves, it was from the first session on September 1, 1920, dominated by the Russians. They did allow a delegate from Azerbaijan to perform the ceremonial opening: "Comrades," declared Nariman Narimanov, "I have the honor to open today the never seen nor heard of, first in the world, Congress of the Nations of the Orient."[13] Narimanov then introduced the principal speaker, the president of the Communist International, Gregori Zinoviev.

Zinoviev's speech was agonizing in its effect on the congress. Since he spoke in Russian, which only a few understood, every sentence was laboriously translated into Persian, Turkish, and Uzbek, and the whole process consumed five hours. Since many of the delegates spoke none of the languages, they milled about the floor conversing in a babel of tongues, and Muslims from time to time left the floor in large delegations "to make their ablutions in the corridors." [14] Many of the delegates had brought with them samples of their native products—Bukhara silks, Turkestan cotton, rice sweets—and loudly traded them on the floor while Zinoviev spoke.

His purpose was to bring the delegates to an emotional peak so that they would unanimously proclaim a jihad against the colonial powers. Six colonial powers, he declared, America, Britain, France, Japan, Belgium, and Holland, which had a combined population of 437 million, ruled a group of eastern nations with a combined population of one and one quarter billion. "Comrades," Zinoviev cried, "remember what these robbers are doing in the world." At Amritsar, he said, "an unarmed crowd was lured under machine guns and was massacred." In a distorted reference to four cases in which Baluchi sepoys had compelled Sikhs to crawl past the spot where Frances Sherwood had been molested, he declared that "Armed English compelled the population of Amritsar to crawl on their fours in the streets of this town." That, he said, "is the method of the English 'civilized' imperialists . . . It is time to declare the real Holy War against the British capitalists." [15]

With much waving of caftans and ullulation, jihad was proclaimed, and two days later the delegates gathered in the center of Baku for a ceremonial start of the Holy War. Their ranks swollen by thousands of the native proletariat, they gathered under the Maiden's Tower where a scaffold and gallows had been erected and a Muslim hangman with traditional black robes, black mask, black gloves and fez sat dawdling with his prayer beads. On the gallows were effigies of British Prime Minister David Lloyd George, French President Alexandre Millerand, and American President Woodrow Wilson, "very well made, with black coats, decorations, and ribbons." After a brief speech by Zinoviev, the hangman uncorked a bottle of gasoline and placed it under the nostrils of each effigy so that "they could smell the petroleum which they have liked so much to receive from Baku." Pouring the gasoline over the effigies, he set fire to the likeness of Lloyd George, which fell to the ground aflame while "the crowd shrieked with joy." Millerand's head fell off and rolled from the scaffold, and Wilson "fell from his chair like a man whose heart was broken." [16]

As a last act before disassembling on the eighth day, the congress formed a Council of Action—as had Lenin in Petrograd in 1917—of the Organization of the Eastern Nations. The Council of Action was to direct the revolution of the Orient against the Occident.

Western intelligence circles were inclined to disavow any accomplishment by the Baku congress. A White Russian officer, Captain C. V. Inozemtzev, who had dressed in native garb to penetrate Baku on behalf of, among others, the American consular service, said it was "an absolute failure." The eastern delegates, he reported, "devoured all the rice offered them, stole a few carpets that were decorating the hall of the Congress, and left for their homes, unsatisfied with the principles of the Great Eastern Revolution dictated to them in Russian by Zinoviev, Radek, and Company." [17]

It was true that at one point Zinoviev came close to breaking up the congress by condemning the Muslim religion and declaring that the Muslim form of Communism was defective and had to be corrected. According to British and Turkish intelligence, noted the American Embassy in Constantinople, "Matters regarding oriental religion, caste, customs, etc., which the other delegates from the deserts and mountains of inner Asia carried burning in their hearts or written out in strange language in their flowing robes, were forbidden utterance by the presidium, since they largely conflicted with the rigid, narrow class dictatorship of Karl Marx." The congress, according to the American Embassy's report, failed to establish "effective practical means . . . for the Holy War against British, French, and American imperialism and capitalism, their colonial exploitation, the oppression of the 'subject' races, etc., concerning which Zinoviev and others spoke so eloquently." [18]

On the other hand, the eastern delegations had come to several agreements among themselves in private:

To unify all Asiatics to work in common for their liberation.

To obtain the assistance of the Russian Bolsheviks without being obliged to adopt Communistic principles or to abandon religious freedom.

To organize for distributing arms and ammunition to the Asiatic peoples and to adopt a unified command with a view to common action.

To form the Council of Action and to found a University of Marxism in Baku for the peoples of the Orient.

The Comintern for its part saw the congress as a success. Soon after the end of the conference, for example, Moscow allotted 750,000 gold rubles—at a time when the country appeared close to bankruptcy and threatened by a harsh famine—to extend the ranges of two radio stations from 12,000 to 20,000 kilometers, making them probably the most powerful transmitters in the world; one of them was at Nicolaev in Central Siberia, an installation that would obviously be of considerable utility in beaming propaganda to the colonial nations of Asia. [19]


## Chapter Twenty

Although the Communist International and the Council of Action of the Congress of Oriental Nations had openly declared war on the British Empire, it suited both Britain and Russia in 1920 to open trade negotiations. Having had suits tailored in Savile Row and hair trimmed and perfumed at the most imperial of all barbers, Trumper's of Mayfair, where King George V customarily had his hair cut, Lev Kamenev and Leonid Krassin met with Prime Minister Lloyd George at No. 10 Downing Street on the last day of May 1920 to conclude a trade agreement.

The British stipulated from the first that in exchange for their promise to cease all military and political operations against Russia, Soviet Russia would have to promise "to restrain all persons under its direct or indirect control from any act endangering the tranquility and prosperity of Great Britain, or intended to embitter the relations of the British Empire with other countries."[1] To the British government, that warranty applied as much to the Communist International as to the Soviet government, for in the British view, the Soviet government and the Comintern were "organically connected in such a manner as to form, to all intents and purposes, a single organization; that, therefore, obligations assumed by the Soviet government rest also upon the Communist International." Thus any activities of the Comintern directed against not only Britain but also the British Empire would constitute a violation of the pledge.

Although the Russian delegates, Kamenev and Krassin, readily agreed to the British stipulation, the British secretary of state for war, Winston Churchill, put no store by it. Following a meeting at the prime minister's residence, Churchill called to his office the director of British military intelligence, General Sir William Thwaites. "The more evidence you can secure to compromise Kameneff and Krassin," said Churchill, "the better. Pray keep me constantly informed."[2]

Despite postwar economies, the British intelligence apparatus in 1920 remained a formidable, hydra-headed instrument. In addition to Mansfield Smith-Cumming's MI-1C, charged with foreign secret intelligence, and MI-5, the counterespionage service operating at home and within the empire, there existed the intelligence organizations of the armed services, those of the Foreign, Colonial and Home offices, the diplomatic services, and the Special Branch of Scotland Yard. They were all linked to the police, governmental, and military intelligence services throughout the empire and also to the intelligence services of the United States, France, the Netherlands, Belgium, Italy, the Baltic States, and Poland.

Of particular interest was Britain's code- and cipher-breaking organization, the Government Code and Cipher School. Throughout the year that Lloyd George negotiated with Soviet trade representatives, the school provided him with most—and sometimes all—communications to and from the Soviet delegates and Moscow. Combined with information from Kamenev's and Krassin's mail, which was being read on a regular basis, those intercepts afforded Lloyd George with what he himself would describe as "a real insight into Bolshevist interests and policy."[3]

In both Churchill and the foreign secretary, Lord Curzon, those intercepts produced a mounting sense of outrage, particularly toward the chief Soviet delegate, Kamenev. As Lord Curzon exclaimed after reading a message from Soviet Foreign Commissar Chicherin to Kamenev: "With so colossal and finished a liar it is useless to cope." Even Lloyd George, who was normally unperturbed by the intrigues and mendacity of Bolsheviks, was on occasion stirred to anger. At one point he accused Kamenev of "a gross breach of faith" and told him that when he went on leave in September 1920, his return would not be welcomed,[4] but he did nothing to put a stop to the negotiations.

By late summer of 1920, Churchill was convinced that "A veritable plot is being hatched against England and France."[5] The intercepts showed that Kamenev was seeking to divide the two governments and through agents was trying to incite the industrial and trade unions to disturbances over shipping arms to Poland. The intercepts, declared Churchill in a note to Lloyd George, provided proof that Kamenev and Krassin had "repeatedly and flagrantly broken their undertaking to abstain from propaganda while in this country." He felt bound, he said, to call the attention of other members of the Cabinet to "the perturbation" afflicting British intelligence officers when they saw unfolding "what they cannot but regard as a deliberate and dangerous conspiracy aimed at the main security of the State" without the government taking any steps to counteract it.[6]

Like Churchill, the chief of the Imperial General Staff, Field Marshal Wilson, was deeply disturbed. As Wilson confided to his diary, he began to consider whether the prime minister might not be a "traitor," by which he meant a secret Bolshevik. How else, Wilson asked himself, explain Lloyd George's inaction? In a conversation with Churchill, Wilson warned that "we soldiers might have to take action if he did not," meaning either some stroke against Lloyd George or the Bolshevik delegates or both.

On August 26, 1920, Churchill again wrote to Lloyd George, declaring that "we are confronted with a treasonable conspiracy and our duty is clear." Kamenev and Krassin, he declared, "ought to be given their passports." Forget about a governmental trade agreement, urged Churchill, and permit "British subjects to trade freely [with the Russians] if they choose and if they can." He saw no reason why Britain should be "the official bear leaders to these ruffianly conspirators and revolutionaries" who while in London had been "trying to foment a revolutionary movement and intriguing and bribing on every side." "From a national point of view," he wrote, "their presence is most dangerous."[7]

When Lloyd George still declined to move against Kamenev and Krassin, Churchill called to the War Office Field Marshal Wilson, General Thwaites, and the directors of Naval and Home Office Intelligence and asked them to prepare papers immediately showing why Kamenev and Krassin should be expelled. With those papers in hand, Churchill convened another meeting in the predawn hours of September 2, 1920, at which he called for a Council of Ministers that same day where all concerned might read the intercepts and arrange for their publication. Yet again Lloyd George refused to act.

Even though Lloyd George failed to follow through on his dictum that Kamenev not return to London after taking home leave in September 1920, it suited the purposes of the Soviet government to do the British premier's bidding. While the principal object of Lenin's operations in Britain in the early 1920s was still to subvert the crown and empire and influence the British electorate in favor of Soviet Russia, Lenin was also anxious to keep abreast of developments in British technology. It was thus no accident that when Kamenev left London, he was replaced as a delegate to the trade talks by a senior Soviet intelligence officer, General Eduard Petrovich Berzin. That appointment represented the first known arrival of a major Russian intelligence figure—as opposed to a diplomatic or political warfare agent—in either Britain or the United States.

Several months after Berzin's arrival, on March 16, 1921, with a minimum of ceremony, Lloyd George and Leonid Krassin signed the Anglo-Soviet Trade Agreement, the first de facto recognition from one of the victors at Versailles for Lenin and the Soviet government. The principal clause in the agreement stated that both powers would "refrain from hostile action or undertakings against the other and from conducting outside of its own borders any official propaganda direct or indirect against the institutions of the British Empire or the Russian Soviet Republic respectively."[8]

To many—including Churchill—it was clear that the Soviet government would never honor that clause. Sensing that it would be but a matter of time before serious trouble developed with the Soviet delegation, an official of MI-1C on April Fool's Day 1921 opened a new file called "Violations of the Russian Trade Agreement." In a note to his chief, Mansfield Smith-Cumming, the official expressed a hope that the file would remain slender. To which Smith-Cumming replied with prescience: "It will not."[9]

A short while later, Krassin opened offices of the official Soviet trade agency, Arcos, at 49 Moorgate, in the City of London. From the offices in one direction stood St. Paul's Cathedral, in Christendom second only to St. Peter's in Rome as a testament to "the singular mercy of God." In the other direction, the Bank of England, the empire's teller, sitting upon a pile of ingots as a symbol of the triumph of Mammon and fiscal order. In that direction, too, the Royal Exchange, the great center of world commerce surmounted with an inscription from the Psalms: "The Earth is the Lord's and the Fullness thereof." There also the Mansion House and the Stock Exchange and around the corner, the *Times*. Yet the City of London, that bastion of capitalism, was also, as a bishop had once put it, "The south alley for Popery and usury, the north for simony, and the horse-fair in the midst for all kinds of bargains, meetings, brawlings, murders, conspiracies, and the font for ordinary payments of money, as well known to all men as the beggar knows his bush."[10]

It would soon be established whether the Russians knew their bush.

In the first entry in MI-1C's new file, there appeared a familiar name, Mahendra Nath Roy, the Indian who had first come to the attention of MI-1C through the Hindu conspiracy in the United States. Accompanied by an American wife, Roy had left the United States for Vera Cruz, where he established contact with the Comintern's representative in Mexico City, Mikhail Borodin, a fact that quickly became known to the U.S. Army's intelligence division, which described Roy to its foreign posts as a man with "noticeably large feet" who had "a Van Dyke beard," wore glasses, and made "a sucking noise through his teeth during pauses in conversation and when concentrating."

Roy next turned up in Moscow where, as revealed by a photograph in a Comintern magazine, he attended the obsequies for John Reed. He had gone to Moscow, British intelligence would determine, as a step in becoming a Comintern agent in a bid for $200,000 with which to found the Indian Communist Party and in an attempt to purchase poison gas bombs in Germany for use against the British in India as the first stage of an invasion of India through the Herat valley of Afghanistan, the ancient trade route from Persia to India.[11]

Captain Smith-Cumming at MI-1C passed a report on Roy's activities to Lord Curzon, with a note that the information came "from a reliable agent." The report, Smith-Cumming summarized, related to "intrigues between Bolsheviks, Afghans, and Indians for the favourite project of an invasion of India" and to a scheduled gathering "of Indian revolutionaries from various countries in Moscow for the further elaboration of the scheme." It remained to be seen, noted Smith-Cumming, "whether, in view of the Trade Agreement, Moscow cancels the proceedings."[12]

Since the alleged machinations appeared to antedate signing of the Trade Agreement, Lord Curzon let them pass without comment; but when MI-1C produced extracts reputed to be from two telegrams among a long series of messages sent by the Comintern's second-in-command, Nikolai Bukharin, to the Soviet deputy foreign commissar, Litvinov, then in Reval, Estonia, alarm bells rang. The source for the extracts was the same as for the report on Indian revolutionaries, one known to MI-1C as "BP-11." If authentic, the extracts showed that the Comintern had established clandestine centers of "germ cells" in London and Dublin and had decided to fund in the amount of just under a million dollars the Irish revolutionary secession movement, the Sinn Fein. If true, the information provided by BP-11 revealed that through the medium of the Comintern, the Soviet government, in direct violation of the political clauses of the Trade Agreement, was meddling in internal British affairs in a cynical and obvious manner.[13]

The reliability of the evidence for that apparent transgression obviously hinged on the credibility of BP-11. That came into question when, despite extensive inquiries, the intelligence service was "unable to discover anything more about these two germ cells." Although Lord Curzon found the evidence "damning" and apparently sufficient to justify abrogating the Trade Agreement, he admitted that "the file is quite imperfect" and asked MI-1C to "put up to me the entire case."[14]

Before MI-1C could develop more information, the director of intelligence at the Home Office, Sir Basil Thomson, sought to determine how the funds the Comintern was allegedly assigning to the Sinn Fein were being transmitted. As Thomson's agents conducted detailed inquiries through banks in the City of London, the Royal Navy intercepted all trawlers and small ships off the Irish coast. Yet neither endeavor turned up any sign of the funds or evidence that a

Communist germ cell existed either in Dublin or London. Thus Thomson notified the Foreign Office that he was "not convinced that the telegrams are authentic."[15] Not only was there no evidence of the money's having been transmitted but the Code and Cipher School had failed to intercept any reply from Krassin to Litvinov about the funds, and the Sinn Fein remained in serious financial difficulty.

That shook the confidence in BP-11 even of Mansfield Smith-Cumming, and when a new source of information opened up, MI-1C dropped BP-11. The new source was a confidential journal called *Ostinformation*, which Sir Basil Thomson described as "a publication issued periodically under the joint auspices of the German Foreign Office Political Intelligence Department and the German Special Police."[16] *Ostinformation* being a German source, there was reason to be suspicious of it, but when intercepts obtained by the Government Code and Cipher School verified some of *Ostinformation*'s material, MI-1C accepted the source as reliable. By September 1921, *Ostinformation* had provided sufficient material, in Lord Curzon's opinion, to show indisputably that the Soviet government was violating the political clauses of the Trade Agreement and was interfering in the internal affairs of the British Empire.

There appeared to be evidence that Lenin had appointed Mahendra Nath Roy as head of the Indian Communist Party and that the Comintern had made various arrangements for supplying Roy and his comrades with munitions, propaganda materials, and funds. There was also a report that Santeri Nuorteva, then holding the position of "Director of the Department of Propaganda under the Third International" had on June 26, 1921, declared that the Comintern was under the direct control and discipline of the Soviet authorities and that it controlled "176 Communist nuclei and labour organisations, comprising 40,000 subscribing members . . . in England, Scotland and Ireland, and that 890 agitators have graduated from the Manchester and Cardiff propaganda institutes."[17]

According to *Ostinformation*, "Comrade Stalin" had stated at an official meeting of the Comintern that a Communist takeover in India was absorbing "the whole attention of the Department of Propaganda." On June 1, 1921, *Ostinformation*'s report continued, Stalin in a formal report to the Central Committee of the Russian Communist Party declared that "the general guiding purpose" of the Comintern's Eastern Secretariat was to exert pressure "upon the political authority" of the Western European capitalist powers through their colonies, "discrediting them in the eyes of the native population and simultaneously preparing the latter to emancipate themselves from an alien yoke." The report concluded: "The problems connected with the class struggle in the West will be incomparably easier of solution if the external power of England can be undermined."[18]

The Soviet interest in India was all the more disturbing to Lord Curzon because of his having once served as viceroy of India. In a stern, formal note to Chicherin, he declared: "It is with profound disappointment that His Majesty's Government are obliged to register the fact that, although five months have elapsed since M. Chicherin's assurance was given, the hostile activities, upon the cessation of which the successful working of the agreement depends, still continue unabated. His Majesty's Government are, moreover, in possession of indisputable evidence that the objectionable activities are due to the direct instigation of the Soviet Government." [19]

Unhappily for Lord Curzon, the evidence turned out to be less indisputable than he claimed. Chicherin responded that only "a cursory glance" at the documents presented by Lord Curzon would be sufficient to show that they were "either unfounded or based on false information." The Soviet government, he said, had come across "a document published in Germany under the title 'Ostinformation,' published by an anonymous group of detectives and supplied mostly to counter-revolutionary [news] papers and to secret agents of various Governments anxious to obtain secret documents on Soviet Russia." That document, noted Chicherin, had much the same information in "practically the same wording" as that contained in Lord Curzon's note. That the allegations were false could be shown by indisputable proof that Stalin had been away from Moscow when he was reputed to have made his declaration of June 1, 1921, and that when Nuorteva was reputed to have made his declaration, he had been in prison.

The British diplomatic agent in Moscow, Robert Hodgson, was unable to disprove Chicherin's claims about Stalin and Nuorteva. After examining his own file of advices from *Ostinformation*, he telegraphed London: "Everything points to our having been unfortunate in the selection of some of the data advanced in support of our allegations." As an official of the Foreign Office notified Lord Curzon, he was unable to avoid "half-wondering whether there is not some foundation for the Bolshevik assertions," for "Berlin is certainly full of White Russians, all probably ready to make money by selling forgeries."

A week later, Mansfield Smith-Cumming, the almost legendary "C," chief of an organization that considered itself to be the world's greatest intelligence service, was compelled to admit that "the bulk of our information did come from, or is at any rate in suspicious identity with, tainted sources" and that "we can only substantiate 2 or possibly 3 of our charges." To which Lord Curzon exploded in rage: "I am positively appalled . . . at the entire history of this case."

Who was BP-11, the agent that had started MI-1C down the road to embarrassment?

Such slim evidence as existed indicated that BP-11 was a Volga German known as Gregory who worked in the coderoom of Litvinov's office in Reval and was, according to American military intelligence, an employee of the Cheka. MI-1C's chief in Reval had engaged BP-11 in February 1921, a most important connection "because about the same time Reval was made the transmission point for the despatch of propaganda funds and literature from Russia to Europe generally." For a time BP-11 apparently provided legitimate synopses of Litvinov's cable traffic to both British and American intelligence, which built up the early belief in his reliability.

At the instigation of a German industrialist, Hugo Stinnes, the situation at that point abruptly changed. Recognizing the importance of Russo-German trade and military cooperation, Stinnes had put agents to work in concert with the German General Staff and the German intelligence service (which had gone underground because of restrictions imposed by the Treaty of Versailles) to establish a German hegemony over Soviet trade. It was thus to Stinnes's advantage to wreck the Anglo-Soviet Trade Agreement, for among the European nations, only Germany possessed the industrial resources to take Britain's place in filling Russian orders.

While BP-11 was working for the British and Americans, a German intelligence agent persuaded him to insert false extracts in the synopses of Litvinov's cable traffic, designed to provide "evidence" of Russian perfidy in regard to the Anglo-Soviet Trade Agreement. Thus the two extracts telling of germ cells in London and Dublin and of Soviet funds for the Sinn Fein were apparently false. In shifting from BP-11 to *Ostinformation*, Smith-Cumming had merely exchanged one dubious source for another. The directors of *Ostinformation* were allied with the German General Staff, Hugo Stinnes, and German intelligence in the attempt to make a secret politico-military pact with Soviet Russia. Thus it was to the advantage of *Ostinformation*, as it was to Stinnes, to sabotage the Anglo-Soviet Trade Agreement.

In the face of Lord Curzon's rage over MI-1C's bumbling, the British intelligence system underwent a major purge. Sir Basil Thomson received a choice of resigning or being dismissed with a sharply reduced pension; he chose resignation and ended his public service in disgrace when he and a young woman were arrested in Hyde Park for violating public decency. Mansfield Smith-Cumming's career came to a happier end: he was invited to retire and made a Knight of the British Empire.

## Chapter Twenty-One

Clare Consuelo Frewen Sheridan was one of the most beautiful women of her generation, the granddaughter of the American financier and sportsman Leonard Walter Jerome, one of the richest men of the age. One of Jerome's daughters, Clara, married an Anglo-Irish banker and speculator, Moreton Frewen, to whom Clare was born, while another Jerome daughter, Jennie, married Lord Randolph Churchill, to whom Winston was born.

Clare Frewen moved in the highest social and political circles in England but chose to marry a virtually penniless British Army officer named Wilfred Sheridan, who was killed in action in France in 1915 and left her with a son to raise. Beginning a career as a sculptress, she obtained her first major commission from the inventor of wireless telegraphy, Marconi, as a result of which she received many more. In the summer of 1920, she suggested to a friend, identified only as "Fisher" but clearly connected with one of the British intelligence services, that she would like for the Soviet trade delegates in London, Kamenev and Krassin, to sit for her. Agreeing to see what he could do, Fisher telephoned a few days later to say that he had made an appointment for her with Krassin; but in the event, she was received not by Krassin but by Kamenev, of whom Clare Sheridan would write: "He had a neatly trimmed beard and pince-nez and an amiable smile. He might have been mistaken for a *bourgeois* French banker."[1]

Kamenev could hardly have been unaware of Sheridan's kinship with Winston Churchill, nor that she enjoyed the friendship of almost the entire constellation of British political figures of the period. Thus he may well have had ulterior motives in offering to sit for her in her studio, but if so, they were matched by her own: she was most certainly under assignment either from the British Secret Intelligence Service or from the British Security Service.

Although Clare Sheridan was at the time engaged to be married to one of Britain's leading aristocrats, the Earl of Wilton, she and Kamenev, who was in London without his family, were soon such constant companions that London society buzzed with speculation that they had become lovers. By her own account, they saw each other every day during August 1920, the time when Anglo-Russian relations were in crisis over the Russo-Polish War, and in the process she learned "a good deal about the new Russian regime, its aims, its methods, and the lies that were misrepresenting it abroad." When Kamenev had finished work, she would note, "he used to ask me to show him London." One day, while she was out, Kamenev "called at the studio and left a bunch of red roses" at the feet of her latest work, "Victory."

Throughout that period, Clare Sheridan reported to a man whom she would identify only as "Melbourne," later thought to have been Major Stewart Graham Menzies of the Life Guards, a friend of Churchill's and subsequently the director of the British Secret Intelligence Service. Melbourne proved to be intensely interested in all Kamenev's activities, his movements, his meetings. "A Russian atmosphere began to pervade my studio," she would write; "I felt myself beginning to be entangled in a web." She rationalized her reporting on the theory that if Kamenev had to be watched, it was "better for him that I were substituted in the place of some importunate paid third person."

The relationship between the two was just over a month old when Kamenev prepared to go on home leave, from which he was aware he would not return. Inviting Sheridan to go with him, he assured her that she would be the guest of the Soviet government and that he would arrange for Lenin and Trotsky to sit for her. Learning of the invitation, Melbourne encouraged her to accept and provided £100 toward expenses.

As Sheridan left St. Pancras Station early in September 1920, crisis still pervaded Anglo-Russian relationships. At the Comintern-sponsored Congress of the Nations of the Orient at Baku, the delegates had declared a jihad against the British Empire, and the Russo-Polish War continued with British and French help for the Poles. In such a time, noted an American intelligence report, it might be expected that Clare Sheridan would supply London with "very valuable reports."[2]

Her contact, Melbourne, escorted her to the Newcastle docks to catch the packet boat for Norway, and to avoid attention from newspaper reporters, she boarded only after Kamenev had preceded her. When the packet reached Oslo, the Soviet government's plenipotentiary to the Scandinavian states, Maxim Litvinov, met Kamenev. "'Who accompanies you?'" he asked. "'A spy?'" To dispel that or other talk, Sheridan assumed the role of Kamenev's secretary. She also lent a certain luster to the plenipotentiaries of the proletariat by dining with the Swedish crown prince, who subsequently sent his aide-de-camp to escort her to the docks to board the steamer for Reval, where she, Kamenev, and his party boarded a *wagon-de-luxe* for the rail journey to Moscow. At the junction point with the Petrograd-Moscow line, Kamenev's train awaited the arrival of the Petrograd Express, from which the president of the Comintern, Zinoviev, disembarked to join the party for the remainder of the trip to Moscow. Learning from Zinoviev that Lenin had agreed to sit for Sheridan, Kamenev woke her late at night to give her the news.

Clare Sheridan's delight over that development was tempered by the reception that greeted her at the station in Moscow. Kamenev's wife, who was Leon Trotsky's sister, was on the platform to meet her husband and was obviously unhappy over Sheridan's presence. She and her husband engaged "in animated and earnest conversation," and "by their gesticulations," Sheridan "judged they were disputing." In the end, "mercifully," she was "not abandoned on the siding." They entered "a superb open Rolls-Royce" and "drove at frantic speed amid frenetic hooting through half-deserted streets, like London on an early Sunday morning." At the Kremlin, they went to the Kamenevs' suite in the former apartments of Czar Nicholas II, where Sheridan was provided a room but where the hostility of Kamenev's wife continued. On the fifth day of her uncomfortable stay, she met the American journalist John Reed, in Russia for the Second Congress of the Comintern, who advised her to speak bluntly to Kamenev about her predicament. Taking his advice, she told Kamenev that she had to leave, that his wife hated her. Kamenev "looked rather foolish and rightly so," but the next morning he called for her in the Rolls-Royce.

Kamenev conducted Sheridan to the official Soviet guest house, the Sugar King's Palace, where she settled in with other guests that included Washington Vanderlip, Louis Fraina, Mikhail Borodin, and John Reed. Kamenev also secured her a studio in a former interviewing room in the Imperial Courts of Justice and a pass to enter the Kremlin.

While awaiting an appointment with Lenin, Sheridan occupied much of her time by recording detailed observations of her companions in the guest house or Soviet officials whom she met. Of Vanderlip, for example, she noted that he was not the well-known millionaire, "but the Russian authorities thought he was and treated him as an important person." In pursuit of "some great monopoly concession," he was, like Sheridan, "faced with a great deal of waiting. . . . The high-pressure standard clung to him; he moved jerkily, he spoke quickly."

One night, Clare Sheridan recorded, Borodin joined them in the drawing room, whereupon Vanderlip rose quickly and retired to his room. Borodin "had straight, rather long, shiny black hair that would not stay back, although he continually ran his fingers through it." After gazing at her at length through "half-closed eyes," he asked suddenly, "'What is your economic position? Do you belong to the petty bourgeoisie?'"

First Zinoviev and then the chief of the Cheka, Feliks Derzhinski, sat for Sheridan in her improvised studio in the Kremlin. She was in the drawing room of the Sugar King's Palace on October 6, 1920, darning her stockings and listening to Vanderlip recite poems by Rupert Brooke, when the officer in charge of the guest house burst in: "'Greetings from Comrade Kamenev,' he announced, 'and all is prepared for you to go and do Lenin in his room tomorrow from 11 till 4.'"[3]

At eleven o'clock the next morning, Sheridan entered Lenin's office in the Kremlin. Rising to greet her, Lenin had "a genial manner and kindly smile, which put one instantly at ease." As she began to work, he sat at his desk, occasionally interrupted by "a low buzz accompanied by the lighting up of a small electric bulb," indicating a telephone call. When speaking on the telephone, "his face lost the dullness of repose and became animated and interesting. He gesticulated to the telephone as if it understood." There were other interruptions by secretaries bringing letters or documents.

Lenin's power of concentration impressed his visitor immensely, "that and his ponderous and mighty brow that dominated all the rest and gave him an unbalanced look, as if his head were too big for his body." His expression, she observed:

> was always thoughtful rather than commanding . . . I saw in him the thinker, not the dictator. I imagine that he lived purely in the abstract and the intellectual, and he had no personal life at all. He looked very ill. The woman assassin's bullet was still in his body. One day his hand and wrist were bandaged; he said it was 'nothing,' but he was the colour of ivory. He took no exercise, and the only fresh air reached him through a small revolving ventilator in an upper window pane. I believe he sometimes took a day off in the country . . . but they must have been rare occasions.

In those days, Sheridan saw little of Kamenev. "He was different now," she would write. "His manner had a vague nervousness, as if he were not quite sure if I was worthy to be treated as a friend." One day he nevertheless sent a functionary to the Sugar King's Palace to make good on an earlier promise to provide her a fur coat. At a cavelike building in which hung hundreds of the rarest and richest furs, she was invited to take what she wanted. "'You have shared,'" announced the functionary, "'in the government distribution of bourgeois property to the people.'"

Sheridan's next subject was Leon Trotsky, who arrived in Moscow for a brief respite from the duties at the fighting fronts. From the first meeting, she was entranced with him:

> The thing that struck me as unusual . . . was that he had a charming manner but no smile. One is so accustomed to the social smile of greeting that the person who merely looks at one intensely seems more interesting. . . . He talked perfect French, asked what I thought about the light, and whether I would like his writing table moved into some other position. . . . He . . . pointed out that he was quite asymmetrical and snapped his teeth to show that his underjaw was crooked. He had a cleft in his chin, nose and brow, as if his face had been moulded and the two halves had not been accurately joined. Full face he was Mephisto, his eyebrows slanted upwards, and the lower part of his face tapered into a pointed and defiant beard. His eyes . . . had a curious way of lighting up and flashing like an electric spark; he was alert, active, observant, *moqueur*, with a magnetism to which he must have owed his unique position.

For a week the sessions continued, beginning usually in the early evening and extending late into the night, whereupon Trotsky would conduct Sheridan to the Sugar King's Palace. An attachment was growing. "'You shall make this your permanent studio,'" said Trotsky on one occasion. "'I like to feel that you are working here. As soon as you really have finished the bust, we will destroy it and start again.'" (American intelligence officials speculated that Sheridan became Trotsky's "mistress," although "this was doubted by competent British authorities" even though it was "well understood that her morals" were "not of the highest character.")[4]

When Trotsky insisted that Clare Sheridan remain in Russia, she replied that she had obligations in Britain and had to return, "but Russia—with its absence of hypocrisy—Russia with its big ideas—has spoilt me for my own world."

> 'Ah, that is what you say now; but when you are away. . . .' He hesitated. Then suddenly he turned on me with clenched teeth and flashing eyes; he shook a threatening finger in my face. 'If, when you get back, *vous nous calomniez*, as the rest have, I tell you . . . I will follow you to England and . . . I will. . . .' He did not finish his threat. I said: 'I am glad you have told me how to get you to England!' He went on: 'It is easy enough here to be blinded *par les saletés et les souffrances*, and to see no further, but people forget there is no birth without pain, and Russia is in the throes of a great *accouchement*.'

The bust at last completed, Trotsky invited Sheridan to accompany him on a trip to the front, but she questioned the propriety of her going. Having discussed it at length with Litvinov, she decided that her presence "would be explained only in one way, and it was a way that might do Trotsky harm as well as myself." Two days later she changed her mind, but when she telephoned Litvinov, she learned that Trotsky's train had just departed.

Although Sheridan intended to sculpt the foreign commissar, Chicherin, he proved to be elusive. When Litvinov conducted her to the foreign ministry, she found "a little man in a brown coat and trousers that did not match, [who] shuffled across the office and back again, bent and agitated." It was Chicherin. As she learned in time, he was "an abnormal man who lived always in the Foreign Office with closed windows and never went out." He "would frequently ring a 'comrade' at three or four in the morning for the most trivial information." That was the hour he finally proposed for sitting for Sheridan; it was, he said, his "'quietest time.'" To which she replied that unfortunately, it was her quietest time too. They never got together for a sitting.

When Clare Sheridan at last prepared to return to England, she discovered that "to get out of Russia was far more complicated than to get in." Inquiring about her passport, she learned that she would have to wait for it until her sponsor, Kamenev, returned from a visit to the front. A visit from Litvinov contributed to a growing uneasiness. Did she know, Litvinov asked, "'a certain person in England called—Melbourne?'" The way he asked it, Sheridan would note, "produced a shiver down my spine." And did she know, Litvinov continued, "'that he is in the Intelligence Service?'" Sheridan said she knew only that he worked in "a city office." Litvinov persisted: "'But he *was* in the Intelligence Service.'" When she admitted that he may have been during the war, Litvinov smoked a cigarette in silence, his "small eyes" scrutinizing her until she felt she was "the author of a murder."

When Kamenev returned from his journey, he called at the guest house, but as Sheridan tried to thank him for all he had done for her, he cut her short: "'We are glad to have amongst us *une femme artiste*; your nationality and your relations are nothing to us; there is only one thing we cannot stand.'" For the first time since Clare Sheridan had known him, "his face adopted a hard expression." Rising, he moved toward the window "in an abstract way and looked out. 'The only thing we cannot stand,' he continued, '*c'est l'espionnage!*'"

With Melbourne's £100 note in her pocket, which Kamenev refused to accept as partial payment toward the expenses, Sheridan, on November 6, 1920, prepared to leave Moscow. She carried with her the furs presented her as a gift from the Soviet state and also the heads she had sculpted. Upon arrival in London, she was met by Melbourne, who took charge of her diary and instructed her to report to the Foreign Office. Although she tried to return the £100 note to Melbourne, he insisted that she keep it. When the British government later released her diary for publication, she became a national celebrity, but inside herself, as she was to write, she was "in a very unsettled and tormented state," for "Russia with her mysticism, her art, her romance, her martyrdom, had seized my imagination . . . my reaction to Russia was sensual but artistic also, and almost religious." To the consternation of London society and especially to Winston Churchill, the woman who had set out for Moscow in the Praetorian spirit of a British intelligence agent had come back a Bolshevik.

## Chapter Twenty-Two

When the World War formally ended in the Hall of Mirrors at Versailles, the victors—and especially Britain—enjoyed the notion that the Anglo-Saxon world and its institutions were all-powerful and beyond challenge. Yet the reality was that Britain was a weary Titan carrying what the English poet Matthew Arnold called "the too vast orb of her fate." Among those who purported to recognize the fact was a gloomy, impoverished German don, Oswald Spengler, living in a garret overlooking a cemetery in Munich and writing a book, *The Decline of the West*.

According to Spengler's theory, the world's races went through stages: youth, power, maturity, and wisdom; then, largely through war, decline, senility, and finally submission to another race. Casting an eye upon Britain, Spengler noted that almost an entire generation of the British ruling class had perished in the war, creating an unnatural disturbance in the laws of succession that was not to be overcome. The same was true in Germany. Thus the Anglo-Saxon race had entered upon a period of irrevrsible decline in which it would inevitably give way to another more vigorous race, probably from the east.

Coming at a time when both the United States and Britain were disturbed by the power and vigor of the New Russia and its ideology, publication of *The Decline of the West* produced an enormous if apprehensive readership in both countries. It seemed to foreshadow the inevitable termination of Anglo-Saxon leadership in the world, and in conjunction with a vast and sudden increase in Jewish migration from Eastern Europe to the United States, it contributed to a wave of anti-Semitism. Within the intelligence communities on both sides of the Atlantic, the belief became widespread that the Lenin Revolution, Bolshevism itself, and the Comintern were all inspired by and dominated by Jews.

The dispatches of the American military observer in the Baltic States, Major T. Worthington Hollyday, reflected the suspicions and the nature of that anti-Semitism. A movement of some 1.2 million Eastern European Jews to the United States, assisted overtly and covertly by various Jewish relief organizations, presented, noted Major Hollyday, "a serious menace, because the chief supporters of Bolshevism in Russia are the Jews and many of the Jews who go to the United States are agitators or Bolshevik agents." He warned that sooner or later the influx would result in "a troublesome racial minority" and "filthy Jewish quarters in American cities" similar to the Jewish ghettos in Eastern Europe. To Major Hollyday it appeared odd that "the desirable emigrants" from Scandinavia and elsewhere in Northwestern Europe could enter only with great difficulty while it was easy for "any Polish or Russian Jews who take a notion to change his place of abode to America."[1]

A subsequent investigation revealed that much of the emigration was illegal. As reported by the Commission of the United States in the Baltic States early in 1921, for example, "the Lithuanian Government, which has a Ministry for Jewish Affairs, is inclined to wink at the illegitimate methods and to encourage this emigration."[2] A few weeks later, as civil war continued to rage in Russia, Major Hollyday reported that a Latvian newspaper had predicted that large numbers of Russian Jews were preparing to leave for America, Poland, and Palestine to escape what they believed would be "unheard-of Jewish pogroms" once the Lenin government was overthrown. Hollyday warned that "This will dump in the United States the most radical of radicals unless rigid passport control is maintained, and legislation passed for careful control, limitation and selection of persons entering our country."[3]

Many in the intelligence community in Washington shared Major Hollyday's concern; some even saw in the Jewish migration a plot for world domination. That view seemed to be confirmed by an intelligence survey of the Bolshevik leadership in Russia, which purported to show that among the top leaders were a Hungarian, two Poles, three Finns, nine Germans, nine Armenians, nineteen Russians, twenty-seven Letts, and 294 Jews.[4]

As anti-Semitism unparalleled in the history of the United States swept the country, establishmentarians—particularly New Englanders—demanded that the Congress pass an act sharply restricting Jewish immigration. Others formed patriotic organizations such as the American Defense Society, financed primarily by such wealthy Gentiles as John Jacob Astor and designed "to defend the United States against subversion" and "to educate radicals in American ways."[5]

In Britain, as a conference of International Zionists opened to discuss the founding of a Jewish state in Palestine, at which such prominent figures as Lord Rothschild, Judge Louis Brandeis of the United States Supreme Court, and Felix Frankfurter of the Harvard Law School were in attendance, the usually staid Tory newspaper, the *Morning Post*, which had close connections within the British government and secret service, began publishing a series of sensational articles which showed, according to the editor, that there had long existed, "like a canker at the heart of our civilization, a secret revolutionary sect, mainly of Judaic origin, bent on the destruction of all Christian empires, altars, and thrones,"[6] and which attempted to demonstrate that Bolshevism and the Comintern represented a Jewish conspiracy aimed at the destruction of the British Empire.

The articles that followed tried to show that Jews had established the Comintern, that its members were nearly all Zionists, and that the theory and practice of the Communist International lay not in modern Bolshevism but in various secret societies of history, beginning with the Freemasonry cells established in Germany by the Bavarian Adam Weishaupt. The French student of occult societies and practices, Copin Albancelli, the first article stated, wrote that "the occult power which works behind Revolutionary Freemasonry is the secret government of the Jewish nation." The ritual of the Knights Templars, the author wrote, closely resembled Jewish ritual, and in that ritual were the seeds of the

Jacobinical code of revolution which Trotsky and other Jews among the Bolshevik leadership so much admired.

In a book, *L'Entrée des Israélites dans la société française*, the article noted, the author, Abbé Joseph Lehmann, a Jew who had embraced Christianity, had presented "definite evidence" that "Hebraic antagonism against Christianity [had] led the Jews to utilize Secret Societies." Since the time of Moses, there had existed a cabal constituted as "the oral but secret custodian of the most sublime truths of the Hebraic religion," but the cabal, "abstruse on its speculative side, bad and wicked on its practical side," was known to only a small number of Israelites, and "Most honest Jews, occupied with their daily affairs and their patriarchal customs, although not loving the Saviour of the World and his Church, had no penchant for, nor pleasure in, this commerce with the Cabal and with magic." The cabal, according to the *Post*, had nevertheless succeeded, through control of certain of the organizations of Freemasonry, in penetrating France, Germany, Russia, and the United States.

The author of the *Post*'s articles then set out to show how the cabals were linked to Mikhail Bakunin and Karl Marx, the fathers of modern Anarchist and Bolshevik thought. Marx, said the *Post*, was a Jew; his patronym was Mordechai, his grandfather a rabbi in a line of rabbis stretching back into the sixteenth century, and his mother also descended from a long line of rabbinical ancestors. The family had practiced the Christian faith only because the Prussian government forced it to do so by edict. In consequence—the *Post* (using italics for emphasis) quoted the German revolutionary Wilhelm Liebknecht, an intimate associate of Marx—*"his whole life was a reply and a revenge."*

The bitter fight between Marx and Bakunin for control of the International Working Men's Association, which was founded in London in 1864 (the First International) and from which Lenin's Bolshevik movement flowed, was an issue not of politics but of race: Jew against Slav. Marx's victory, the *Post* contended, was attributable to the work of "Hebraic conspirators" who aspired to "the dominion of the world" and who intended, as Abbé Lehmann had written, "to disorganize at one blow Christian society."

Providing only the vaguest evidence for those assertions, the *Post* at that point revealed that the early articles had been but a prelude to a discussion of the "Protocols of the Learned Elders of Zion," which, said the *Post*, constituted "an amazing and cynical exposition of a scheme by which 'the learned elders of Zion'" sought "to overthrow the Christian order. In the light of recent events, it may be called the Bolshevist Bible."

The protocols purported to be a report of a series of twenty-four meetings held in secret in Basel in 1897 at the time of the first Zionist congress. The general object of the protocols, said the *Post*, was to establish "government of the world by a king of the blood of David."

One of the protocols, maintained the author of the *Post*'s articles, clearly established a link between Jews and Freemasons. There was thus, said the *Post*, "an inner or Jewish Masonry, the true governing power, and an outer or Gentile

Masonry [according to the protocols, 'these *goyim* (Gentile) cattle'] which blindly follows the lead of a direction it does not suspect."

The protocols claimed credit for the French Revolution: "In all corners of the earth the words 'Liberty, Equality, Fraternity,' brought to our ranks . . . whole legions who bore our manners with enthusiasm. And all the time these words were the canker-worms at work boring into the well-being of the *goyim*. . . . On the ruins of the natural and genealogical aristocracy of the *goyim*, we have set up the aristocracy of our educated class, headed by the aristocracy of money."

Tying the protocols to the Russian Revolution, the *Post* noted that the elders claimed that "our goal is now only a few steps off." The "fighting forces" for the final revolution were "Socialists, Anarchists, Communists, to whom we always give support," and the campaign was to be masked "under an alleged ardent desire to serve the working classes."

The ultimate weapon was to be "a great financial crisis which will reduce the workers to the verge of starvation and make them ripe for the most desperate acts. . . . [W]hole mobs of workers . . . will rush with delight and shed the blood of those whom, in the simplicity of their ignorance, they have envied from their cradles, and whose property they will then be able to loot. Ours they will not touch, because the moment of attack will be known to us, and we shall take measures to protect our own."

The *goyim* then would be "compelled to offer us international power of such a nature as will enable us without any violence gradually to absorb all the great forces of the world and to form a super-government."

There was to be no anarchy, according to the protocols, and the government was to be "just and orderly," even though there was to be "a natural division of society into classes" and the "Gentile 'cattle' are to work for their Jewish masters without any hope of liberation." A "system of education" would be established "calculated to wipe out of the minds of the *goyim* any recollections of their former state" and lead in time to establishing "the Jewish religion . . . as the universal faith." By such means, the elders intended "to produce a tranquil world."

Making no reference in any of the articles to the fact that scholars had already challenged the authenticity of the protocols with massive conviction, the *Post* passed to the question: are Bolsheviks Jews? Bolshevism, said the *Post*, "is derived primarily from the beatitudes pronounced by the Jew, Karl Marx, and its present fountain head in Moscow." According to the *Post*'s calculation "nearly all the Bolsheviks are Jews." Of fifty individuals—listed by both names and aliases— whom the *Post* contended were "responsible for the establishment of the present regime," forty were Jews, one was a Jewess, and another was suspected of being a Jew.

In concluding articles, the *Post* maintained that the Zionists, operating through the Freemasons, had been behind revolutions or conspiracies that followed the World War in Turkey, Portugal, Hungary, and Bavaria, and that President Wilson and the Paris Peace Conference were manipulated by eminent American and international Jews. The object, said the *Post*, was to enable the United States, controlled by the American Jewish business community, to supplant the British Empire, an ambition, according to the *Post*, not unlike that of the Bolshevik Jew working through the Comintern.

The *Post* also linked prominent British Jews to the conspiracy to overthrow the empire. "The stability of the British Empire," wrote the *Post*, "is the chief obstacle which those who aim at the overthrow of European civilization have to overcome." As Karl Marx had allegedly noted, Ireland was the empire's weakest link, and Lenin had reputedly said that without a revolution in Ireland, there could be no revolution in Britain. Disturbances then occurring in Ireland, said the *Post*, were engineered by New York Irish extremists working in concert with, and financed by, Jewish-Bolsheviks in Moscow and elsewhere. In recent years, the *Post* warned, "the struggle against the British Empire" had come under the control of "far more dangerous and subtle brains, and one is forced to the conclusion that the real directing force regards Irish independence not as an end in itself but as the means toward the accomplishment of the world-wide anarchy."

With those assertions, the series in the *Morning Post* ended, leaving London gasping in wonderment as to why the normally respectable Tory newspaper would publish it. Even taking into account the yellow journalism prevalent in the times, it seemed an incredible editorial decision. Yet no explanation was ever offered, only speculation that powerful members of the government, anxious to increase defense budgets, had convinced the paper to run the articles in an attempt to shock the empire into a more determined stand against Russia and the Comintern.

However the articles might have shocked some in London, it was soon evident that there was a ready market for them elsewhere. They were translated into all the great languages and quickly jumped the Atlantic, where Henry Ford's Dearborn *Independent* was the first to publish them. In a covering article, Ford denied that he was publishing the articles because he personally was anti-Semitic but because he wanted "to wake up" the "poor Gentile boob" and promote world peace by stopping "the international Jewish bankers . . . from financing armament."[7]

Unlike the British Jewish community, which accepted publication of the articles with indifference, the American Jewish leaders responded with spirit, eloquently turning the attack on their race into the service of a greater cause: the campaign to establish a Jewish homeland in Palestine. "These malevolent prints," declared a committee of Jewish leaders, represented "a mere recrudescence of medieval bigotry and stupidity," but noted that the time had come "to make answer to these libels." During the war, said the committee, the protocols in various forms and under various titles had been "clandestinely circulated, in typewritten form, among public officials an carefully selected civilians." Noting the publication in the London *Morning Post* and the Dearborn *Independent* and circulation of copies "with an air of mystery" among "various influential circles in the United States," the committee saw the protocols as "abominable charges that can only appeal to the credulity of a stunted intelligence."

"From the time of the destruction of the temple at Jerusalem by Titus," the committee wrote, "the Jews have had no political state." For centuries "they were forced to wander from land to land, to flee for refuge wherever they might find it against bitter persecution." They had been deprived of "even the shadow of civil or political rights," and it was "little more than fifty years since the Jews of Western Europe became politically emancipated." Constituting less than half of one percent of the world's population, more than half of them were on the verge of starvation, and in Eastern Europe, where most of them lived, they were not even permitted "to exercise the rights of citizenship," they were "hampered in every way in their efforts to earn a living," and "far from desiring to govern the world, they were content with the opportunity to live."

The man who had first published a full version of the protocols, Serge Nilus, said the committee, was "a Russian mystic and an ardent supporter of Czarism" who claimed in 1901 to have received the protocols in manuscript from "a Russian office-holder, a lady whose name is not given, and who . . . obtained them in a mysterious way." Nilus had never produced the manuscript nor revealed what language the alleged protocols were written in. He claimed to have shown them to a Russian grand duke, not further identified, then incorporated them in a book, *The Great in the Little*, a mystical work published in Russia in 1905. In a second book published in 1919, *It is Near, At the Door*, Nilus declared that he had learned from "Jewish sources" that the "Protocols were . . . a strategic plan for the conquest of the world . . . worked out by the leaders of the Jewish people during the many centuries of their dispersion."

Nilus contended that the protocols had been presented to the Council of Elders by Theodore Herzl at the time of the first Zionist congress, which Herzl summoned at Basel in August 1897. He contended further that the protocols "were signed by the Zionist representatives of the thirty-third degree of initiation, that they were secretly removed from the complete file of Protocols that pertained to the first Zionist congress, that they were taken from the secret vaults of the main Zionist office, which, it is said, 'at present is located in French territory.'"

The protocols as published, the committee noted, bore no signatures, nor was either the identity of any Zionist who reputedly signed them or the locations of the main Zionist office and secret vaults revealed. Yet it was "a matter of history," the committee noted,

> . . . that the first Zionist Congress was publicly held by Jews who came from various parts of Europe for the purpose of considering the misery of their brethren in Eastern Europe and of enabling them to find shelter in the Holy Land. Theodore Herzl was a distinguished journalist, a man of true nobility of character. He presided at the Congress, all of whose deliberations were held in the light of day. The insinuation that there was a thirty-third, or any other, degree of initiation in this organization is merely a malicious effort to bring the

Jews into parallelism with the Freemasons and thus to subject them to all the fanciful and fantastic charges that have from time to time been laid at the door of Freemasonry, oblivious to the fact that fifteen Presidents of the United States, including Washington, and many of the leading statesmen of Europe and America have been members of that order.

In upholding privilege and autocracy, the committee said, the protocols were fundamentally opposite to Jewish thought and aspirations. To maintain that they were genuine simply because of the onset of the Russian Revolution twelve years after their publication and thus to presume that Bolshevism was a Jewish movement was "absurd in theory and absolutely untrue in fact."

Contrary to the figures published by the *Morning Post* and reprinted by the Dearborn *Independent,* the committee maintained that "the originators of Bolshevism were exclusively non-Jews," and while it was true that there were Jews among the Bolsheviks, notably Trotsky, "they represent a small fraction of the Jews and of the followers of Bolshevism." Lenin, Chicherin, Bukharin, Krassin—none of them were Jews. In the Bolshevik Cabinet—the People's Commissars—only two out of twenty members were Jews, and in the Central Committee of the Communist Party, there were four Jews out of thirteen.

On the other hand, the leaders of the Mensheviks, who were "the sworn foes of Bolshevism," were "to a large extent Jews." The same was true of the other major opposition parties and the opposition newspapers. Noting that the Russian Jews "had been ruined by the coercive measures of the Soviets," that their property had been confiscated, and that they were "undergoing unspeakable hardships," the committee maintained that the Orthodox Jews, who were in the majority among the faith, remained "loyal to the faith of their fathers" and regarded the Bolsheviks "as the enemies of all religion."

As for the Bolsheviks, they looked upon the Jews "with comparatively few exceptions . . . as belonging to the hated bourgeoisie and as favoring capitalism." They denounced the Zionists "as counter-revolutionary, and many of them have been cast into prison and threatened with death." The Jews had "traditionally stood for religion, law, order, the family, and the right of property," all of which the Bolsheviks had denounced.

The protocols were manufactured, said the committee, "by those who are seeking to restore the Hapsburgs, the Hohenzollerns, and the Romanoffs on their former thrones." Publication of them in the United States and the whispering campaign that followed were "an attempt to drive into the solidarity of the citizenry of our country . . . the wedge of discord . . . in the hope of discrediting free government in the eyes of the European masses and thus facilitating the restoration of absolutism in government." The protocols, the committee asserted,

ARE A BASE FORGERY. THERE HAS NEVER BEEN AN ORGA-
NIZATION OF JEWS KNOWN AS THE ELDERS OF ZION . . .
OR BEARING ANY OTHER SIMILAR NAME. THERE HAS

NEVER EXISTED A SECRET OR OTHER JEWISH BODY ORGANIZED FOR ANY PURPOSE SUCH AS THAT IMPLIED IN THE PROTOCOLS. THE JEWISH PEOPLE HAVE NEVER DREAMED OF A JEWISH DICTATORSHIP, OF A DESTRUCTION OF RELIGION, OF AN INTERFERENCE WITH INDUSTRIAL PROSPERITY, OR OF AN OVERTHROW OF CIVILIZATION. THE JEWS HAVE NEVER CONSPIRED WITH THE FREEMASONS, OR WITH ANY OTHER BODY, FOR ANY PURPOSE.

Close on the report of the American Jewish Committee, a British journalist, Philip Graves, conducted a study of the protocols and called attention to a remarkable similarity between them and a political satire on Napoleon III published in 1864 by a French lawyer, Maurice Joly, *Dialogue aux enfers entre Machiavel et Montesquieu.* Subsequent journalistic and literary investigation tended to show that the protocols were fabrications of the czarist secret police, the Okhrana, based both on Joly's work and others. There were surely sufficient political reasons for the czars to welcome such a document, for they were constantly seeking justification for the May Laws of 1882, the pogroms of 1881–1882, and for the thirty-five years of *ratissages* within the Pale. A phenomenon of the Russian Revolution nevertheless was—and remained—a suspicion that it was made by Jews. The omnipresence of the controversy, the vastness of the problem created by the revolution, the activities of a Jewish minority: all would serve later to revive the mystery and the prejudice. As a consequence at least partly of that, it would be a long time—a terrible time—before the Zionists would arrive at Zion, that mythical idyll where, as the great Haskalah poet Micah Lebensohn had written, "the muses dwell, where each flower is a Psalm, each cedar a song divine, each stone a book and each rock a tablet."[8]

## Chapter Twenty-Three

Throughout the previous century, the prime ministers of Great Britain had borne the most illustrious names and ranks—such as the Duke of Wellington, Viscount Melbourne, Sir Robert Peel, Lord John Russell, the Earl of Derby, the Earl of Roseberry, the Marquess of Salisbury—all, except for an occasional Liberal, establishment Whigs and Tories. On December 6, 1923, there came an exception: on that date, as a result of a marriage of convenience between minority Liberal and Labour parties, King George V summoned to Buckingham Palace James Ramsay MacDonald, the son of an unmarried maidservant, a Socialist whose pacificism at the outbreak of the World War had led many to regard him as a traitor, and invited him to form a new government.

The shock produced by a Socialist occupying the post of the king's first minister—particularly at a time when Britain, the world's arbiter in economic and political thought, was still reeling from the effect of Lenin's revolution in Russia—was profound. No sooner had MacDonald kissed hands with the monarch than George V was at his diary to record the extraordinary event. "Today 23 years ago dear Grandmamma [Queen Victoria] died," wrote the king. "I wonder what she would have thought of a Labour Government."[1]

As MacDonald, having reserved for himself the post not only of prime minister but also of foreign secretary, settled into No. 10 Downing Street, other spirits in British politics expressed their concern. As Churchill put it: "The enthronement in office of a Socialist government" was "a serious national misfortune." The intelligence services were particularly uneasy, stunned by the new prime minister's words at the Royal Albert Hall on January 8, 1924, when he decried "the pompous folly of standing aloof from the Russians."[2] Britain, he declared, would grant full commercial, financial, and diplomatic relations to the new Soviet Republic.

MacDonald, ironically, enjoyed no favor with the Communists, who saw him as a traitor to the working class. From Moscow, Zinoviev instructed all Communists to support MacDonald "like a rope supports a hanging man" and announced that as a result of MacDonald's appointment, Britain, not Germany, had become the Comintern's principal target.[3]

Yet the new prime minister's most effective enemies were to be within the right-wing London establishment, particularly the intelligence community. Some of its most formidable names openly declared their dislike for and suspicion of him and contrived to route the intercepts of Russia's radio traffic so that they would cross neither MacDonald's desk nor those of his close associates. But the new prime minister was not to be intimidated. When the Labour Party's Advisory Committee on International Affairs proposed "suspension of the secret service and the revelation of its activities,"[4] MacDonald vowed not just to clip the wings of the intelligence service but to dissolve the Secret Intelligence Service, MI-1C, to which Captain Hugh Sinclair, who had succeeded Mansfield Smith-Cumming as its head, reacted by telling the prime minister that if he were to be unwise enough to follow that course, the intelligence service would simply go underground, and with the help of the banks and other institutions of the City of London, keep their staffs intact, and when MacDonald was replaced by a more patriotic premier, emerge to resume business.

The matter was still pending when on February 2, 1924, despite the most intense activity on the part of the Tories, MacDonald carried out a campaign pledge to grant Soviet Russia de jure recognition. He further exacerbated officials of the intelligence services by receiving as the Russian chargé d'affaires an old Bolshevik, Christian Rakovsky, who had been at the founding congress of the Comintern in 1919.

Disregarding evidence that MacDonald was as stern an opponent of Bolshevism and the Comintern as any Tory, and that he was as devoted a subject of the crown as any Liberal, the intelligence services with Tory backing set out on what looked to be "a prolonged criminal conspiracy"[5] against the MacDonald government.

Their ultimate goal was to bring down the government, and their first step was to wreck new conversations soon to begin in London designed to produce a new Anglo-Russian trade agreement, the agreement of 1921 having resulted, in Rakovsky's words, in "a fragile cease-fire rather than the desired peace treaty."[6]

The MacDonald government's desire for increased trade was based on the simple capitalist goal of capturing a potentially vast Russian market for British factories. The Russian motive was more complex. After nearly a decade of general war, civil war, Allied invasion and blockade, poor harvests, famine, and diplomatic and economic hostility and isolation, the Soviet government required trade and elimination of threats to Russia's existence in order to ensure success of the moderated form of private enterprise adopted in the wake of the Kronstadt Rebellion, the New Economic Policy. The Anglo-Soviet Trade Agreement of 1921 having established a precedent and MacDonald's Socialist government appearing to be sympathetic to new ties, the Soviets saw a real possibility of obtaining a broader agreement with Britain and thereby achieving in time a breakthrough to trade with other western powers.

What the Russians seemed to fail to realize was that MacDonald's was a minority government and survived in the face of a constant and palpable threat from the opposition benches only on sufferance. Since London was in fact two capitals—the City of Westminster being the capital of politics and the City of London the capital of finance—the City of Westminster was obliged to heed the voice of the City of London. Although a trade agreement might be negotiated without approval of the London bankers, it could never prosper without it.

And there had long been the closest association between the bankers and the intelligence services. Their executives spent considerable time together in opera boxes, on the grouse moors, and in their country houses. In wartime the intelligence services recruited extensively in the marble halls of the joint stock and merchant banks, and in peacetime the banks provided a kind of aftercare institution for secret service alumni. Both institutions were the most ardent supporters of the monarchy and the system; both were usually dominated by Tories; and both had a long history of suspicion of Russia, of which the war in the Crimea in 1853–1856 and intervention in the civil war in 1918–1920 were only the more recent violent manifestations. In 1924, both the banking and intelligence communities of Britain knew that Russia needed money to survive; thus both were determined to see that the Soviet government got no money except under conditions that would assure the demise of Bolshevism.

A few days before the trade conversations opened on April 14, 1924, in Lancaster House in London, the bankers—often called "the gnomes of London"— sent the prime minister a memorandum setting out the conditions under which they were prepared to restore the credit which they had withdrawn when Lenin had nationalized or expropriated almost the entire foreign investment and holdings in Russia. The Soviet government, said the bankers, would have to restore private property to foreigners, change certain aspects of the civil code, provide guarantees against future expropriations, and abolish the government's trade monopoly. Few could have seen those demands as acceptable to the Soviets, for apart from ideological matters, the demands would necessitate Russia's paying Britain some $4 billion in exchange for a line of credit of only about $300 million. So intimidated was Prime Minister MacDonald by the demands that he declined personally to take part in the conversations and in an opening ceremonial speech declared that "the successful conclusion of a treaty depended upon adequate compensation of bond-holders and former property owners in Russia."[7]

Addressing the subject of the bondholders early in the conversations, the Soviet representative, Rakovsky, proposed as a basis for discussion a figure of $200 million. To the banks, which had lost more money as a result of the Russian Revolution than any individuals or other institutions, that figure was unacceptable, for it represented only 16 percent of the face value of the bonds and only double their current depressed value on the London market. Although Rakovsky delivered a long, eloquent, and excruciating account of his country's financial problems, the banks treated him as they would any other financial delinquent.

Still seeking a basis for agreement, he proposed a three-year, $300 million loan guaranteed by the British government, but MacDonald refused. "The granting of direct credits to the Soviet Government," he told Parliament, "was inadmissible," but privately he told Rakovsky that he would "use his influence to help the Russians to raise a loan in the City" provided "an agreement in principle was reached with the bondholders."[8]

Rakovsky took little comfort in that promise, for he had concluded that Russia could never raise a loan in the City of London. When the prime minister for a second time rejected a demand for a government-guaranteed loan, the negotiations seemed to be about to founder, an appearance accentuated by clear opposition from the palace, the press, and the political opposition.

Partly through strong support from the undersecretary of the Foreign Office, Arthur Ponsonby, and partly through persistence and compromise on the part of Rakovsky, the MacDonald government in the end defied the opposition, executed one treaty, and prepared the way for another. Signed on August 8, 1924, a new commercial treaty was to replace the Anglo-Soviet Trade Agreement. In addition, the two sides agreed to hold further talks designed to lead to another treaty settling Russian debts to Britain through the means that the prime minister had twice rejected, a loan guaranteed by the British government. A decision on a proposal to exchange ambassadors was also deferred.

Communist officials were elated. The former trade negotiator, Lev Kamenev, at that point an official of the Comintern, acclaimed the commercial treaty as "a cornerstone in the development of the Soviet Union," while the foreign commissar, Chicherin, called it "an international recognition of the October Revolution as a basis for state structure."[9]

Those were premature judgments, for the treaty still had to be ratified; and while that might be perfunctory in the case of the Russians, in the case of the

British it was not. The opposition moved quickly to the attack. A Tory newspaper, the *Evening News,* for example, declared that "What Mr. MacDonald, Mr. Ponsonby and their fellow dreamers about Russia are doing is to pledge the British taxpayer to lend money to the conspirators who want that money to hasten the collapse of the British Empire."[10] Yet however virulent the campaign, it still might have failed had not the MacDonald government inadvertently handed its critics the weapon with which to do the job.

On July 25, 1924, a Scottish Communist, J. R. Campbell, who would later become a British representative on the Executive Committee of the Comintern, had published an article in the British Communist journal *Workers' Weekly,* in which he called on British soldiers employed in breaking strikes to disobey orders. Although the government immediately arrested Campbell under the Incitement to Mutiny Act, Attorney General Sir Patrick Hastings dropped the charges.

When Parliament convened on September 30, 1924, the opposition accused the prime minister of having ordered the attorney general to dissolve the charges under pressure from his party's left wing, whose support he required to remain in office. When Lloyd George's Liberals demanded an investigation, the Tories supported the demand, and MacDonald made the mistake of calling for a vote of confidence. In a vote clearly reflecting the unpopularity of the government's Russian policy, he lost by 364 votes to 198. By royal proclamation, Parliament was dissolved and a general election fixed for October 29, 1924.

A campaign replete with some of the most sensational charges in modern British history followed. From the start, the principal issue was the commercial treaty and the agreement to consider a government loan to Russia; and from the outset, the Tories, including Winston Churchill, who was seeking to retrieve a political career that had appeared to be at an end when in 1922 he had lost his seat in Parliament, tried to generate an atmosphere of Red peril.

Five days before the election came the first of two sensational charges when the *Daily Express* published a story probably leaked by the head of the counterintelligence service, MI-5, Colonel Sir Vernon Kell. It was an account of a debacle during the first Ludendorff offensive of March 1918 when the British 5th Army had collapsed and disintegrated, not just in the face of overwhelming German power but also—the story had it—because of sedition in the ranks.

Even after the passage of more than half a century, hard facts concerning the 5th Army's disaster would be almost impossible to come by. None of the official British histories would assign any role in the calamity to sedition, and the government would officially deny that it played any part. Yet as revealed in the *Daily Express* by a man who at the time had commanded a Canadian cavalry brigade on the 5th Army's front, a former war minister in Ottawa, a close friend of Churchill's, and a passionate enemy of Bolshevism, Major General J. E. B. Seely, sedition was at the root of the collapse. "For weeks before the German attack," Seely said, Bolshevik agents "were going about behind the lines" telling the soldiers "that it was a wicked capitalist war, and all they had to do was to give up fighting and the war would end." While according the agents no specific nationality, Seely said they were "in various disguises," and despite "the greatest vigilance on the part of our staff . . . a large number remained undetected until the attack."[11]

"When the attack fell on the dawn of a misty morning of March 21," Seely continued, "numbers of spies dressed in our uniform went about ordering troops to retire at once." In a number of cases, he said, troops fell back under the false orders, while "Close behind the lines other spies were running about telling the transport drivers, labour battalions, and everyone they could find . . . that their only chance of safety was to clear out as fast as they could." Seely himself had not "the least doubt . . . that seditious propaganda and the cry of the 'capitalist war' were the direct cause of the deaths of thousands of brave and loyal British soldiers."[12]

However far-reaching the effect of that story on the electorate, it was merely the forerunner of a greater thunderbolt known as the Zinoviev letter, which of all the political incidents of twentieth-century British history was perhaps the most mysterious. The most powerful men in Britain—including Churchill, the highest functionaries at the Foreign Office, the secret service, the press barons, and, perhaps, the gnomes of the City—were involved, but to what degree would never be established. Indeed, for every pen applied to the subject, there was a different version, and the truth of what went on would still be debated more than fifty years later. Only one thing was certain: the Tories were behind it.

On a Saturday morning, October 25, 1924, the day after the *Daily Express* broke the story of Red agitation in the 5th Army, readers of the *Daily Mail* found huge headlines proclaiming: CIVIL WAR PLOT BY MOSCOW REDS—MOSCOW ORDERS TO OUR REDS—GREAT PLOT DISCLOSED YESTERDAY—"PARALYZE THE ARMY AND NAVY"—AND MR. MAC DONALD WOULD LEND RUSSIA OUR MONEY!—DOCUMENT ISSUED BY FOREIGN OFFICE AFTER 'DAILY MAIL' HAD SPREAD THE NEWS.

Alongside 80-point headlines was a pen portrait of Zinoviev, which exaggerated his Semitic features, and an accompanying caption declared that his real name was Apfelbaum. Under the headlines and the portrait, an announcement from the editors:

> A 'very secret' letter of instructions from Moscow, which we publish below, discloses a great Bolshevik plot to paralyze the British Army and Navy and to plunge the country into civil war.
>
> The letter is addressed by the Bolsheviks of Moscow to the Soviet Government's servants in Great Britain, the Communist Party, who in turn are the masters of Mr. Ramsey MacDonald's Government. . . .
>
> The letter is signed by Zinoviev, the Dictator of Petrograd, President of the Third (Moscow) International, and is addressed to A. McManus, the British representative on the executive of this interna-

tional, who returned from Moscow to London on October 18 to take part in the general election campaign.

Our information is that official copies of the letter, which is dated September 15, were delivered to the Foreign Secretary, Mr. Ramsay MacDonald, and the Home Secretary, Mr. Arthur Henderson, immediately after it was received some weeks ago. On Wednesday afternoon copies were officially circulated by the Executive authorities to high officers of the Army and Navy.[13]

The text of what quickly became known as the Zinoviev letter followed, a long document which in some respects resembled the letter which Zinoviev had allegedly sent to the Workers' Party of America in 1923 calling for establishing "fighting units" trained in marksmanship and demolitions and expressing the hope that "the Red flag will fly over the White House." The letter accurately reflected, in somewhat different wording, pronouncements that had been handed down by the Comintern at its Fifth Congress, which had met in Moscow between June 17 and July 8, 1924, and at which a resolution had been passed addressed specifically to the small but well-organized Communist Party of Great Britain, calling for "creation of factory and plant cells," a swift "transition" from "simple propaganda" to "concrete military work," and "creation of cells in bourgeois armies."[14] "Armed warfare," the Zinoviev letter read, "must be preceded by a struggle against the inclinations to compromise which are embedded among the majority of British workers, against the ideas of evolution and peaceful extermination of capitalism." Only then "will it be possible to count on complete success of an armed insurrection."

The Russian chargé d'affaires, Rakovsky, promptly dismissed the letter as a forgery, but although he produced what he claimed to be evidence, it was unconvincing. A denunciation of the letter by Foreign Commissar Chicherin, was to some degree more convincing in that Chicherin was able to conjure up the ghost of the BP-11–*Ostinformation* affair of 1921. Chicherin claimed to have evidence that the letter had been forged by a group of cobblers in Berlin.

Evidence that the letter was genuine was little more impressive than that presented to prove it a forgery. It was mainly circumstantial: that it resembled other letters previously intercepted in London and Washington; that it reflected what was known to be current Comintern policy; that the Comintern had recently reinvigorated its efforts through Mahendra Nath Roy to subvert the crown in India; and that the letter had come into the hands of the British intelligence services through not one source but four, all of which were considered to be reliable.

The first of the sources had supplied the letter in a manner which had permitted the intelligence services to follow "its whole course from its origin until it reached our hands." The three other sources were "wholly independent" of each other. One had provided evidence that the Central Committee of the Communist Party of Great Britain had received the letter and discussed it at a recent meeting.

Another was a British secret agent who had obtained the minutes of a meeting of the "Russian Council of Commissars," at which Chicherin reputedly reported that Zinoviev, while maintaining that the text of the letter had been corrupted, acknowledged its authenticity. If the Zinoviev letter was, in fact, cobbled, the intelligence services would have had to be deceived by not one forgery but several forgeries provided through four different sources. [15]

Although that would appear to have been improbable and perhaps even impossible, it was a hypothesis not to be totally dismissed. As a disinterested study of the letter conducted later at Cambridge University would point out, "The intelligence services were considerably alarmed by some of the members and by some of the policies of the Labour government," and they had "showed themselves capable on this and other occasions of exceeding (though in far less spectacular ways) their ill-defined authority." [16]

In terms of the British election, it mattered not in the end whether the Zinoviev letter was genuine or fraudulent; for the government, the intelligence services, the press, and probably also the electorate could discern that even if the letter were a forgery, it was at least based upon actual official pronouncements of the Comintern. The letter, whatever its origin, linked the unease of the middle classes at the apparent sympathetic attitude of the MacDonald government toward the Soviet government, the dismay of the upper classes over the Anglo-Soviet agreements, and the alarm occasioned by dismissal of the charges against the Scottish Communist Campbell, and by the revelations about the 5th Army by General Seely.

The British electorate brought the MacDonald government down with a thundering crash: 419 seats for the Tories to 151 for Labour. Churchill himself obtained 20,000 votes to 3,700 for his opponent, whereupon the new prime minister, Stanley Baldwin, invited him to become chancellor of the exchequer, the second-highest post in the cabinet and a post held in 1886 in the government of the Marquess of Salisbury by Churchill's father, Lord Randolph Churchill. When asked if he would accept the post, Churchill would recall that he was tempted to reply: "Will the bloody duck swim?" but so august was the occasion, that he actually replied: "This fulfills my ambition. I still have my father's robes. . . . I shall be proud to serve you in this splendid office." [17]

The first move of the new government was to refuse to ratify the Anglo-Russian agreements, indeed, even to engage in any further discussions on agreements. The second was to investigate allegations by Ramsay MacDonald that the Zinoviev letter had been a plot. There was, the investigatory committee pronounced in November 1924, "not a shade of a shadow of a doubt as to the authenticity of the document." [18] Yet despite that solemn assurance, many would continue to believe that there had indeed been a Tory plot to bring down MacDonald's government and that Churchill's high office was a reward for his participation in it.

## Chapter Twenty-Four

In 1924, all Europe teemed with Russians dispossessed and exiled—either voluntarily or forcibly—by the Russian Revolution: Monarchists, aristocrats, landowners, industrialists, bankers, members of the arts, Anarchists, Mensheviks, Revolutionary Socialists, Syndicalists, counterrevolutionary Ukrainians, Armenians, Georgians, a vast flotsam and jetsam of humanity cast up by the tidal wave of revolution. A Special Refugee Committee of the League of Nations calculated that at least 844,000 citizens of the former Russian Empire were refugees, 150,000 in the Baltic states, 120,000 in other countries bordering on Russia, 400,000 in France, perhaps another 150,000 in Manchuria and China. The number may well have exceeded a million, almost to a man bitter over their losses and their exile and determined above all else to overthrow the Bolsheviks and go back home.

The exiles, or émigrés, were loosely organized into various counterrevolutionary movements, most notably Boris Savinkov's Brotherhood of Russian Truth, the organization which earlier had helped Edgar Sisson accumulate the Sisson Documents in Petrograd, and a Russian Inter-Forces Union, the latter headed by General Wrangel and consisting mainly of ex-soldiers and officers evacuated from the Crimea. At Warsaw in June 1921 and again the next month at Bad Reichenhall in Bavaria, representatives of the various émigré movements met to form a government-in-exile to be ready to assume power upon overthrow of the Bolsheviks. An American intelligence agent who attended the meeting in the Hotel Axelmannstein in Bad Reichenhall noted that "There were no disputations or discords . . . which was something unusual for a Russian gathering." Some 150 delegates, he reported, concluded their congress with "a most solemn mass and singing of Russian national hymns."[1]

The import of the founding of that congress, representing vast numbers of antibolshevik Russians, was hardly to be lost on the Soviet leadership. In an order to all agents of the Cheka, the chief of the secret police, Derzhinski, advised that there existed "a plot against Russia" financed by "foreign agents." The Cheka was to form "detachments ready to act on a moment's notice" and also to create an organization to penetrate the congress and the émigré organizations and liquidate their leaders.[2]

The new organization was the Osobyy Otdel (Special Department) under an official of the Cheka who was later to assume some prominence, Genrikh Yagoda. As a vehicle to perform the duties of penetration and liquidation, the Osobyy Otdel created a fictitious organization called the Municipal Credit Association, more generally known as the Trust. The Soviet Foreign Service, the Comintern, and the Red Army's military intelligence service, which was gradually expanding its activities in Western Europe, were to render all possible assistance. The principal targets were Savinkov's and Wrangel's organizations and an individual, the Russian Jew turned British secret agent whose machinations in 1918 against Lenin the Cheka had never forgotten, Sidney George Reilly.

There followed throughout Western Europe a violent subterranean conflict not unlike American gangster wars. The first action was against Boris Savinkov, then in Warsaw.

In the treaty ending the Russo-Polish War, the Poles had agreed to prevent Russian émigré organizations from establishing anti-Soviet cells in Poland and from conducting espionage and guerrilla operations against Russia from Polish soil. Among various Russian undertakings was a promise to pay the equivalent of $15 million in gold rubles as compensation for wartime damage to Polish property. Yet hardly was the treaty signed when Chicherin noted that Boris Savinkov was operating from Warsaw. Unless Savinkov and his associates were immediately expelled, Russia would refuse to pay the reparations.

Although the Polish president, Marshal Pilsudski, was a close personal friend of Savinkov's, he agreed to expel Savinkov on the condition that Russia without delay turn over $2 million of the reparations in gold. When Chicherin agreed, Pilsudski ousted Savinkov, his brother Victor, and various associates, among them some who were designated as officials in the government-in-exile founded at Bad Reichenhall.[3]

Yet Pilsudski waited in vain for the $2 million in gold, possibly because Chicherin, with some reason, feared that even though he had expelled Savinkov, Pilsudski still might pass some of the gold to Savinkov's Brotherhood of Russian Truth. When Chicherin finally responded to Pilsudski's protests, he claimed inability to pay in gold and asked Pilsudski to accept in its place $2 million in diamonds. A commission of Polish and Russian experts were soon "haggling in Moscow over the valuation of the diamonds offered."[4]

As the matter remained unsettled, the Brotherhood of Russian Truth was soon in serious financial difficulty. What was at first a crisis approached calamity when in 1924 the French and the Czechs, like the British, negotiated agreements with the Russians containing noninterference clauses and withdrew subsidies that their secret services had been providing the exiles. The former British agent Sidney George Reilly, then associated with the Brotherhood of Russian Truth, sold a personal collection of Napoleana and borrowed a thousand dollars from a British agent to enable him to go to New York, where he hoped to obtain a half-million dollars that he claimed the Baldwin Steam Locomotive Company owed him in commissions on railroad deals with the czar's government. He intended to use the money to support the Brotherhood of Russian Truth.

At the same time, Savinkov's health began to fail (he was an incurable morphine addict), yet he nevertheless went to Rome in search of a loan or subsidy from a renegade Socialist who had just become Fascist dictator of Italy, Benito Mussolini. He failed, not because Mussolini was unsympathetic but because Italy, too, had recognized the Bolshevik regime in Russia in hope of cashing in on Russian trade.

While Sidney George Reilly was staying at the Hotel Gotham in New York in July 1924, he received an urgent note from Savinkov in Paris. Savinkov said he was in contact with a Monarchist organization called the Trust and was preparing to return to Russia to lead the organization in a coup d'état. Reilly was upset: hopeful that he would soon solve Savinkov's financial problems through funds raised from rich members of the American Defense Society and similar organizations, he saw Savinkov as an irreplaceable leader who would be lost if the Trust should turn out to be a trap laid by the Cheka. Reilly promptly booked passage for Europe in hope of dissuading Savinkov from going to Russia.

In Paris, Reilly first saw Commander Ernest Boyce, chief of the British secret service in Petrograd at the time of the incident of the Sisson Documents and currently a member of the Russian section of MI-1C in Western Europe, specializing in counter-Comintern operations. Although Boyce said that the Trust appeared to be antibolshevik and pro-Monarchist and to exercise considerable power and influence in Russia, too little was yet known of the movement to permit a confident assessment to be made.

Visiting Savinkov, Reilly tried over several days to dissuade him from his journey but without success. His health broken and spirit weakened by long years of clandestine activities, Savinkov saw an alliance with the Trust as his last chance to do something decisive. Even if he should fall into the hands of the Cheka, said Savinkov, he was confident that the Trust would be able to obtain his release.

With an assistant, the assistant's wife, and two officials of the Trust, Savinkov left Paris on August 10, 1924. Nineteen days later the Soviet journal *Izvestia* announced that he had been captured in Russia and would be brought to trial. Other official announcements followed, the first to the effect that he had been sentenced to death, then that the sentence had been commuted to ten years' imprisonment, and finally that he had been freed. In reality, Savinkov on or about May 23, 1925 committed suicide by throwing himself from a window of the Lubyanka.

Savinkov's true fate would not be known for some time, but in any event, his failure to return had left the Brotherhood of Russian Truth leaderless. Into the breach stepped Reilly, who still had visions of being the Napoleon Bonaparte of Russia. His first task was to obtain American and British money. His first step toward that end was the Zinoviev letter.

When MI-1C had first obtained the Zinoviev letter, which was dated September 15, 1924, and passed it to the Foreign Office, the letter had produced little interest, for similar communications, dating back to 1921, had previously been intercepted. Yet on closer examination, the letter appeared to introduce new factors. If genuine, it revealed that a member of the Soviet delegation to the Anglo-Russian trade negotiations was under instructions to help the British Communist Party revolutionize Britain, clearly a violation of a noninterference clause that was integral to the negotiations. So, too, the letter arrived just as all anti–Labour Party forces in London, including officials of the Foreign Office, among them the permanent undersecretary, Sir Eyre Crowe, were looking for political weapons to turn against the Labour Party in the general elections. Since Crowe was the official responsible for MI-1C, he was particularly anxious to prevent a return of the MacDonald government and thus remove that government's threat to the intelligence services.

Although the Foreign office had received the Zinoviev letter on October 10, 1924, nineteen days before the general elections, Crowe allowed six days to pass before, on October 16, 1924, transmitting it to Prime Minister MacDonald, who was making a campaign appearance at Manchester, only five hours from London by train, where he obviously could have been reached earlier. When the prime minister saw the letter, he directed that if its authenticity could be established, a strong note of protest should be sent to Rakovsky, then the note and the letter released to the press.

Crowe instructed the head of the Foreign Office's Russian Department to prepare the note to Rakovsky, but because of an intervening weekend, the draft was ready only on October 20 and reached the prime minister three days later, only six days before the elections. Although MacDonald was at the time in Port Talbot in Wales, a place remote from London, it was not so remote but that the note could have reached the prime minister within a day of its being drafted.

When MacDonald finally saw the note, he approved it in principle but withheld his initials of approval until he could see a final draft. Again he directed that the authenticity of the letter be verified first, then the note delivered to Rakovsky, and only then were the note and the letter to be released to the press.

Crowe either failed to understand that the prime minister had not yet finally approved the note or else chose to ignore it. Nor did he follow the instructions to verify its authenticity. Instead, without further communciation with the prime minister, he sent the note to Rakovsky. A student of the affair would later observe that "The determination and haste of the Foreign Office in dispatching the Note, in contrast with their leisurely handling of the letter, gave rise to accusations that they were acting deliberately to undermine the Labour Government." Yet the official government committee that later investigated the affair concluded that Crowe "never anticipated the political consequences which in fact followed";[5] but in view of the nature of the note to Rakovsky, which was couched in language usually reserved in diplomacy for the penultimate stages before a formal declaration of war, that finding would be hard to accept.

Whatever Crowe may or may not have anticipated in quickly dispatching the note to Rakovsky, he failed to inform his prime minister of what he had done. Not until the evening of October 25, 1924, did MacDonald learn from a newspaper reporter, only four days before the general elections and at a time when he was still away from London, that the note had been sent and that the *Daily Mail* had obtained a copy of the Zinoviev letter and that morning had published its sensational story. MacDonald was understandably "staggered" by what he recognized as "a political bomb."[6]

Who gave the Zinoviev letter to the *Daily Mail*? And why?

Those questions were not to be answered immediately, for the editor of the *Daily Mail*, Thomas Marlowe, invoked the journalist's privilege of confidentiality of sources. Yet it would later emerge that Marlowe had learned of the existence of the letter on October 23, 1924, from a former director of Naval Intelligence, Admiral Sir Reginald Hall, clearly a man sympathetic to the intelligence services. Yet if that information was correct, who actually passed the letter to Marlowe?

Marlowe would state only that on the morning of October 24, 1924, he received copies of it from two separate sources. Other evidence later accumulated to suggest that one source was the deputy at MI-1C, a powerful figure in the London Conservative establishment, Lieutenant Colonel Frederick H. Browning, who was in charge of the economic section of the British secret service. The other source was probably also a member of the intelligence community, possibly Browning's superior, Captain Hugh Sinclair, or Colonel Sir Vernon Kell, who while head of the counterintelligence service, MI-5, had leaked the story of Red agitation in the 5th Army. As the Cambridge University study of the Zinoviev affair put it: "There seems little doubt . . . that the 'political bomb' which exploded in the last days of the Labour Government was planted by the intelligence community." The motives: "exaggerated fears of the Labour Government's susceptibility to Bolshevik pressure" and "the far more rational fear for the future of the intelligence services following a Labour election victory." The leak of the Zinoviev letter, the study concluded, "was intended to bring down the Labour Government."[7]

Still other questions: Was the Zinoviev letter a forgery? If so, who executed it, and why?

Despite the official investigating committee's finding in November 1924 that the letter was authentic, serious doubts persisted. Not until forty-two years later, on December 18, 1966, would they be resolved with a front page announcement by the *Sunday Times* of London: "One of the great unsolved mysteries of British politics is cleared up at last: the Zinoviev letter *is* a forgery."

A team of reporters for the *Sunday Times* based its case primarily on the diaries of an official of the Conservative Party's Central Office, Major Guy Kindersley, and of an employee in MI-5, C. Donald im Thurn, and on interviews, the most important of which was with Irina Bellegarde, widow of a former officer in the czar's Army who at the time of the Zinoviev letter was in exile in Berlin.

Irina Bellegarde revealed that in late summer of 1924, a friend named Gumanski told the Bellegardes, both of whom appeared to have been members of the Brotherhood of Russian Truth, that "a person in authority in London" had commissioned Gumanski through a go-between to produce what became known as the Zinoviev letter. While the *Sunday Times* failed to identify "the person in authority," the go-between was Sidney George Reilly.

In hope that the letter "might discredit the Soviet Union and ruin the developing rapprochement of the 'workers republic' with Britain," Bellegarde and other members of the Brotherhood of Russian Truth's forgery cell accepted the commission. Although Mrs. Bellegard maintained that the Zinoviev letter was the work of her husband and Gumanski alone, in that she was probably mistaken, for there was evidence that the Russian text, which later came into possession of the British Academy of Forensic Science, was in Reilly's handwriting and was the text from which Bellegarde and Gumanski worked. Having written a draft, Mrs. Bellegarde's account continued, Gumanski and Bellegarde obtained a specimen—one sheet only—of Comintern stationery through a man named Serge Drushelovsky. An underpaid agent of the Cheka, Drushelovsky, hungry for money, obtained the sheet from offices of the Comintern in the Soviet Embassy in Berlin and provided it without ideological commitment.

The final letter, said Irina Bellegarde, was composed in the Bellegardes' apartment in Berlin. In Mrs. Bellegarde's presence, Gumanski transferred the final draft by means of a Russian typewriter to the Comintern stationery, whereupon a Lithuanian friend who specialized in forging signatures copied Zinoviev's signature from a Communist Party circular.

There was a gap in the account by the *Sunday Times* between creation of the letter and October 10, 1924, when Captain Sinclair's MI-1C sent it to the Foreign Office. The letter sent was a copy, for according to the *Sunday Times*, "the original letter seems to have vanished very early in the affair." That was understandable, for it was logical to conceal or destroy the original Bellegarde forgery lest it be examined forensically.

As to who passed the letter to the *Daily Mail*, the *Sunday Times* turned to the diary of a London businessman who at the time had been working for MI-5, Donald im Thurn. Thurn's diary showed that on October 8, 1924, two days before the secret service sent the Foreign Office a copy of the letter, Thurn met a man whom he called "X." The man was almost certainly Sidney George Reilly. According to Thurn's diary, X asked for the meeting "to tell me that his old enemy Apfelbaum [Zinoviev] had boasted in Moscow a few days ago that he was entering on a great propaganda war in England." There was a letter, said X, that told the nature of the project.

By October 15, 1924, Thurn was apparently convinced that he would obtain possession of the letter, for on that day he met with the Conservative Party's treasurer and former chairman, Lord Younger. Also present was the current chairman of the Tories' Central Office, Lieutenant Colonel Sir Stanley Jackson. According to the diary, Thurn, Younger, Jackson, and one of Thurn's relatives put up the sizable sum of £10,000 to "guarantee against loss," which the *Sunday Times* took to mean payment for X.

As the *Sunday Times* noted, "Publication was the vital goal, but it was impossible until the Tories or a newspaper got a copy of the letter itself, preferably through a Government department since this would add veracity to the letter." Apparently under pressure from Thurn and Lord Younger, someone—presumably the permanent undersecretary at the Foreign Office, Sir Eyre Crowe—circulated copies to other government departments. That made the letter more available, whereupon Thurn leaked it to the *Daily Mail* along with word that the government soon planned to release the letter to the press in general, which, as the *Sunday Times* put it, meant that it was "endowed with impeccable authenticity." As the proprietor of the *Daily Mail,* Lord Rothermere, would acknowledge, publication of the letter won the Tories at least a hundred seats in Parliament.

The account by the *Sunday Times* was apparently correct except that it failed to tie Reilly into the plot with conviction. That was done by the author of Reilly's biography, *Ace of Spies,* Robin Bruce Lockhart, who had inherited the private papers of his father, Sir Robert Bruce Lockhart. According to the younger Lockhart, Reilly was the central figure in the affair in that he had procured the forgery. But if Reilly was X, he never got the £10,000. The Tories finally paid out the money in 1928 but to Thurn, not to Reilly, for by that time Sidney George Reilly had conducted his last intrigue.

Reilly must have obtained money from somewhere else, for soon after the escapade he appeared in New York, where he opened an office, employed a secretary, and sued the Baldwin Steam Locomotive Company for the $500,000 in commissions that he contended was owed him for railroad deals accomplished on behalf of the czar. When he lost the case, he begain raising funds for the Brotherhood of Russian Truth from the American Defense Society, the American Legion, and such rich capitalists as Henry Ford. He also began a one-man crusade against the activities of the Cheka in the United States, buttonholing politicians, writing to newspapers, pursuing the lecture circuit. It was said that he was personally responsible for torpedoing a Soviet attempt to raise a loan in Wall Street.

In January 1925, Reilly received a letter from the British agent Commander Boyce, who had left Paris to head MI-1C in the Baltic States. Boyce wrote that the apparently anti-Soviet organization, the Trust, had grown greatly in strength and merited Reilly's attention. In September 1925, Reilly went to Paris, where he met with Boyce and a group of counterrevolutionaries, including leaders of the Russian Inter-Forces Union, the organization of White émigrés formed by General Wrangel. Boyce reported that serious stresses and strains had developed inside the Russian Communist Party, making the time propitious for the Brotherhood of Russian Truth to enter into an alliance with the Trust and together overthrow the Soviet government. Should Reilly elect to become involved, said Boyce, neither the British government nor the secret service would acknowledge any association.

Although Reilly was "exhilarated"[8] by the proposal, he was still wary lest the Trust turn out to be a device of the Cheka. He nevertheless wrote to the Trust's representative in Helsinki, N. N. Bunakov, expressing interest in the movement and a willingness to cooperate in the Trust's activities. To Boyce he wrote that if he could "see the right people and the prospects of real action, [he was] prepared to chuck everything else and devote myself entirely to the [Brotherhood's] interests." He was, he said, "fifty-one yesterday and I want to do something worthwhile whilst I can."[9]

On September 21, 1925, Reilly set out for Helsinki, but still cautious about the

Trust, he stopped off in Berlin to see the czar's former forger, Vladimir Orlov, and an old friend, Serge Grammatikov, who was to have been prime minister in the government Reilly in 1918 had hoped to install in Moscow. When both spoke encouragingly of the Trust, Reilly went on to Helsinki.

In Helsinki, both Boyce's deputy and a woman who had investigated the Trust for Boyce also spoke enthusiastically of the Trust. Yet Reilly still might have remained cautious had not the Trust's man in Helsinki, N. N. Bunakov, lured him with financial bait.

According to a former high official of the British secret service long after this event,[10] Bunakov told Reilly that the Trust had acquired part of the Romanov crown jewels. To finance the counterrevolution, the Trust needed to sell the jewels in the United States but had no agent there. Would Reilly act as the agent?

The bait—for bait it was—was irresistible. Reilly agreed to go to Vyborg, a town on the Finnish side of the Russian frontier, to meet a senior official of the Trust, Alexander Yakushev. Reilly knew Yakushev of old: he was an official of the Cheka, but as Reilly also knew, Yakushev was one of Boyce's informants and was considered to be what the secret services of the period called a "radish"—a man who was red on the outside and white on the inside.

At Vyborg, Yakushev apparently convinced Reilly that the Trust was indeed a powerful anti-Soviet underground movement, for Reilly, who had the instincts of a stoat, accepted an invitation from Yakushev to go to Moscow to meet the leaders of the Trust and pick up the crown jewels. The Trust had so many people in high places, said Bunakov, that there would be no risk involved, yet the very fact that the leaders were in senior positions meant that they themselves were unable to leave the country with the jewels lest their abence be quickly noted. Reilly was to travel with a passport in the name of Nicholas Nikolayevich Steinberg. Although Yakushev had to return immediately to arrange the meeting in Moscow, two of his assistants would travel with Reilly.

Reilly crossed the frontier and may have reached Moscow, for Commander Boyce received a card from him postmarked in the capital, September 27, 1925; but that was the last that was to be heard of Reilly except for two announcements.

The first was a formal communiqué issued by the Soviet government:

> In the summer of 1925, a certain merchant carrying a Soviet passport with the name of Steinberg was wounded and arrested by the Frontier Guard while illegally crossing the Finnish frontier.
>
> During an inquiry a witness declared that his name was actually Sidney George Reily [sic] and that he was an English spy, a captain of the Royal Air Force, one of the chief organizers of "Lockhart's Plot," who by sentence of the Tribunal of December 3rd, 1918, had been declared an outlaw.
>
> Riley declared that he came to Russia for the special purpose of organizing terroristic acts, arson and revolts, and that when coming from America he had seen Mr. Churchill, Chancellor of the

Exchequer, who personally instructed him as to terroristic and other acts.

His written testimony is in the possession of the Government. Riley's evidence was entirely corroborated by material seized during further arrests.[11]

The second announcement was in the *Times*. All it said was: "Reilly—On the 28th Sept., killed near the village of Allekul, Russia by *Cheka* troops, Captain Sidney George Reilly, Military Cross, late Royal Air Force, beloved husband of Pepita N. Reilly."[12]

## Chapter Twenty-Five

Despite a program promoted by Churchill to combine fiscal purity with social amelioration, there were clear signs in Britain at the start of 1926 of the approach of a serious national crisis. As so often in the past, the immediate danger point was the coal mines, the mainstay of Britain's fuel and power. In demanding better hours, wages, safety, and conditions, the miners' leaders used words that led the government, especially such anti-Russian Tory diehards as Churchill, to conclude that capital and labor were on the brink of an unprecedented confrontation. Following a declaration by the mine owners that they were unable to meet the demands, all the mining unions struck. When the government proclaimed a state of emergency, the Trades Union Council called for a general strike to begin at midnight, May 3, 1926.

Crippling almost all industries, the general strike produced a sense of the gravest apprehension within the government. Since newspapers could be neither published nor distributed, people could but wonder how close the country was to civil war. Under Churchill's leadership, the government initiated skeletal public services and tried to fill the communications void by publishing a small newspaper, the *British Gazette*, and stepping up news reports on the British Broadcasting Corporation for those few who had radios.

Although the miners remained out for a calamitous eight months, the overall crisis passed when on May 12, 1926, the Trades Union Council called off the general strike. The financial consequences were nevertheless grave: Churchill put the loss at $295 million. Budgeting for a deficit of $180 million, he had to renege on an earlier promise to cut taxes. Quite clearly there had been a financial disaster (multiplying the figures by ten would give an indication of the impact of such a loss in 1980). It was thus with extraordinary anger that Chancellor of the Exchequer Churchill, the official most damaged politically by the strike, learned that not only had agents of the Comintern helped plan and execute the strike but that the Soviet government had helped finance it.

Still president of the Comintern at the time, Gregori Zinoviev proclaimed that the strike introduced "a new era in the English and the world workers' movement."[1] Leaders of the Comintern "hung on the telegraph wire waiting with tense impatience for every tiny item of news" about the strike, while Zinoviev created a special commission under Arnold Lozovsky, chief of the Profintern, the labor union branch of the Comintern, to do all possible to promote the strike.

The Comintern was said to have sent or offered a total of nearly $7 million to help the strikers, $6 million of it specifically designated for the miners (as against a little over $2 million furnished by the treasuries of the miners' unions). Not all the money got through: in some cases the strikers rejected it, and the government blocked some through special financial powers quickly enacted by Parliament. Yet large amounts of "Red Gold"—as the Comintern's rubles came to be called—did get through even as the Soviet government was virtually begging the British government and the City of London's banks and financial houses for credits. Home Secretary Sir William Joynson-Hicks, the Cabinet official primarily concerned with internal security, told the Cabinet on June 9, 1926, that he had "intimations"—a euphemism for secret intelligence, probably of cryptanalytical origin—that proved "the Russian government's direct participation in the organization and transfer of funds to Brtain."

Winston Churchill demanded that the foreign secretary, Sir Austen Chamberlain, take "positive action to counter Bolshevik intrigues against the country." Although opposed to "positive action"—breaking off all relationships with Russia—Chamberlain did send a petulant note to Foreign Commissar Chicherin, who rejected it on the grounds that since "the Russian government represented the will of the workers and peasants of the Soviet Union, it could not be expected to forbid the transfer of contributions by trade unions to their British counterparts."

That response so stirred British anger that the Cabinet took a fateful step, agreeing unanimously that the Russians' "malignant hostility to the British Empire" fully justified terminating relations between the two countries. The Cabinet also decided that the public should be fully informed of the "menacing character" of Russia's attitude, thereby preparing the way for what Churchill called retaining a free hand to take "any action it may think to be in the public interest."

Although Foreign Secretary Chamberlain failed to take those steps, a stream of public denunciations followed. On June 19, 1926, Churchill warned the City of London that the government would accept no responsibility for investments made in Russia. In a speech reeking of gunpowder, the secretary of state for India, Lord Birkenhead, expressed doubts "on the desirability of association with a state whose purpose in every part of the world" was to undermine "the historical greatness of this country." An influential Tory MP, Commander Oliver Locker-Lampson, introduced a resolution calling upon the government to cancel the trade agreement of 1921 and denounced the Bolsheviks as "an enemy" which "under the cloak of friendship" had replaced "weapons of steel" by "gold and propaganda" and had "suckled" the British Communist Party during the strike with "Soviet shekels."

The Soviet government could hardly have been unaware that its relations with Britain were approaching a critical stage, particularly after Chamberlain informed the current Russian chargé d'affaires in London, Gregori Rosengoltz, that "the gulf of principles" separating the two countries was "unbridgeable." At that point the Russian deputy foreign commissar, Maxim Litvinov, hastened to London to assure Chamberlain that there had been "fundamental shifts within the Soviet leadership" which produced "more of a Russian government and less of an international conspiracy." Yet that did little to ease the tension.

At the beginning of 1927, the diehards around Churchill, refreshed after the recess in the House for Christmas and New Year's, acted on the theory that one more puff of breath would blow away the Anglo-Soviet Trade Agreement and the Russian diplomatic and commercial missions in London. Events in China, where Britain had large financial, commercial, and political interests, provided the opportunity Churchill needed to revive the debate on Anglo-Soviet relations and to rekindle Tory passions against the Comintern.

In the early twentieth century, a string of Treaty Ports administered by Britain and other western powers formed a golden chain of priceless beads along the China coast, the greatest of them Shanghai, city of grand hotels and imposing banks (both built mainly by the British) where half China's trade and finance was conducted. The Treaty Ports were two worlds, the rulers and the ruled, existing side by side.

On the Oriental side, "bustle, crowds, smells and the incessant din of voices" in streets "filled with outdoor vendors, rickshaws, wheelbarrows, sedan chairs of the rich surrounded by bodyguards shouting for passage, coolies with twin loads bobbing from bamboo shoulder poles, thin dogs prowling underfoot for scraps and men squatting over open drains." On the occidental side, "neat streets lined by shade trees," tennis courts, cricket fields, and clubs to which no Chinese were admitted. "Every afternoon the Concession's elite rode out . . . in sedan chairs whose Chinese bearers wore the various uniforms of the consulates and mercantile companies—red facings on white for the British Consul, white on blue for Jardine Matheson's, the great British trading company."[2]

The two worlds appeared on the surface to live in amity, the exotic with the serene, but on the Oriental side there was actually passionate resentment at what was clearly inequity, injustice, and exploitation. Yet the Occidental side was typical of British outposts around the world, representing a way of life to which many a subject of the crown had grown fondly accustomed and had come to accept as a right of being British. Winston Churchill saw the outposts that way and was determined that the sun should not set on that little privileged world—at least not in his time. Yet Zinoviev was equally determined to see that the sun did set on it.

Following the Comintern's Second Congress in 1920, a Dutchman, Hendricus Sneevliet, apparently at Zinoviev's direction, went to Shanghai to help Chinese Marxists establish a Communist Party. Sneevliet earlier had helped found the Indonesian Communist Party, and probably with his assistance, Li Ta-chao, a

Hopei who had studied law and political science, founded the Chinese Communist Party in early July 1920 at a meeting in the Po Wen Girls' School in the French Concession of Shanghai. Although the man who would eventually rule China and claim to be "Founder of the Nation," Mao Tse-tung, attended the meetings, he was appointed to none of the party's organizations.

There were at first only intermittent contacts between the Chinese Communists and the Comintern, partly because of the Comintern's preoccupation with revolution in Germany and partly because the Chinese party seemed too small to be effective. In 1922 the party had only two hundred members and as late as 1925, only a thousand. Yet as Mao Tse-tung was said to have remarked at the founding congress, "The smallest spark can start the largest prairie fire."[3]

Deciding that the tiny party could achieve little without an alliance, Li Ta-chao, with the knowledge and encouragement of Zinoviev, approached Sun Yat-sen, a medical doctor turned revolutionary whose Kuomintang had evolved from a revolutionary league into a political party based on "Three Principles": Nationalism, Democracy, and the People's Livelihood. Hoping to learn something from Communist organizing ability and to benefit from the immense assistance the Communists might be able to glean from Russia, Sun welcomed Li Ta-chao's approach. In 1923 he sent his chief of staff, twenty-seven-year-old Chiang Kai-shek, to Moscow to study the organization of the Russian Communist Party and the Red Army. For Chiang, the visit "quickly removed all illusions as to the sincerity of his hosts,"[4] but the Comintern accepted him as a radical exponent of pro-Bolshevik politics and when he returned to China, sent an old hand with him, Mikhail Borodin.

To promote Communist revolution in China, Zinoviev established in Canton a Comintern general staff. The head man was Borodin; his military chief and adviser to the Kuomintang's military commander, Chiang Kai-shek, was General Vasili Blücher. In addition to Blücher, Borodin had the help of an imposing group of Communist luminaries, including Mahendra Nath Roy, who despite the fact that his revolution in India had failed, had been elected to both the Comintern's Executive Committee and its Presidium; an American, Earl Browder; the chief of the Profintern, Arnold Lozovsky, the man who had recently funnelled funds into Britain to try to turn the British general strike into a civil war; Jacques Doriot, French Communist leader who later was to recant and become one of Adolf Hitler's principal collaborators in France; and Nguyen That Than, alias Nguyen Ai Quoc, alias Ho Chi Minh, a Vietnamese who had been recruited as a Comintern agent by the Red Youth International in Paris. They were men who were as much strangers to the infinite mystery of China as were the British whom they had come to challenge.

When Borodin arrived on October 6, 1923, foreign investment in China amounted to about a billion dollars, and foreign capital owned large portions of China's principal industries and in some cases entire industries. In the textile industry, for example, of just over 1,100,000 spindles, the Chinese owned considerably less than half. The authorities—Chinese and foreign—exploited the workers ruthlessly. Denied the right to strike, they worked twelve-hour days seven days a week and looked to be a receptive target for revolutionary agitation.

One of Borodin's first moves was to establish control of the Kuomintang's military forces, which he essentially achieved within nineteen days of his arrival by placing Red Army advisers on the staffs of all Chiang Kai-shek's armies. Thereupon he set out to penetrate and take over the Kuomintang along classic Leninist lines. He established a Committee of Nine to run Kuomintang affairs, to which he and Li Ta-chao served as advisers; he insinuated a Chinese Communist, T'an B'ing-shan, as head of the Orgburo at the heart of the Kuomintang; he induced the Kuomintang congress to accept Chinese Communists as members; and he was said to have personally drawn up the Kuomintang's constitution and statutes, which the Kuomintang congress approved.

Under the control of the Central Executive, Borodin established eight sections: organization, propaganda, youth, labor, peasants, women, military affairs, and foreign policy. He pushed through the Kuomintang congress an ideology based on collaboration with Soviet Russia, collaboration with the Chinese Communist Party, and support for the workers and peasants. He established a party press and a propaganda department, in which Mao Tse-tung occupied the principal post. Through General Blücher, he helped Chiang Kai-shek create the Whampoa Military Academy, in which a Communist, Chou En-lai, received the post of assistant political director. Borodin also saw to it that the academy's curriculum incorporated Leninist revolutionary studies and that it turned out politically reliable graduates who were to come to dominate the staffs of the Kuomintang's armies.

As those armies began to advance and win victory after victory over the fragmented forces of the old warlords, they followed what had come to be a revolutionary doctrine: not molesting or preying upon the people. Weary of oppression, the people welcomed their coming, and with them came Communist functionaries who quickly occupied key positions in the local governments.

Meanwhile, under Borodin's direction, the Kuomintang began to strike at the foreign colonies, particularly those of the British, through the telling medium of labor agitation. Beginning early in 1925, Borodin organized a series of strikes that cost foreign investors huge sums. Disorders inevitably followed, beginning on May 25, 1925, when a Chinese worker in a Japanese-owned textile plant in Shanghai was killed in a quarrel with his Japanese foreman. Stirred by Communist agitators, students five days later staged a large demonstration in the city. When they tried to seize a police station on Nanking Road, a British officer panicked and ordered his troops to open fire. Twelve demonstrators were killed and eighty-two injured. The city was soon plastered with huge, luridly colored posters, pamphlets, and broadsides depicting the dead and wounded lying in a grisly pile at the entrance to the police station, above which flew the Union Jack: it was a second Jallianwallah Bagh.

Fanned by agitators, hatred of the foreigner spread. On June 23, 1925, as workers, students, and soldiers led by cadets from the Whampoa Academy staged a mammoth parade in Canton, they appeared to be about to attack the British and French Concessions on Shameen Island. British troops and French marines opened fire, killing fifty Chinese and wounding a hundred. A paralyzing boycott of the British in Hong Kong ensued, lasting fifteen months, denying goods and services, and emphasizing "to every foreigner in China his final vulnerability."[5]

Meanwhile, with the death of Sun Yat-sen on March 15, 1925, of cancer of the liver, a power struggle had begun within the Kuomintang. In a deathbed letter, Sun had expressed the hope that "In the great struggle for the emancipation of all the people in the world, our two countries [China and the Soviet Union] will walk hand in hand to victory."[6] Yet Sun Yat-sen's devoted disciple, Chiang Kai-shek, was to see to it that that was not to be, for in the power struggle within the Kuomintang, Chiang had allied himself with the forces of the right.

The struggle began to develop in intensity following the murder of the Kuomintang's finance minister, Liao Chung-k'ai, apparently by the anticommunist faction. A few days later ten prominent right-wing members met in the hills some fifteen miles west of Peking before the coffin of Sun Yat-sen in the Temple of the Azure Clouds and passed a resolution declaring that Mikhail Borodin was just another *tuchun* (foreigner) and like all other *tuchuns* should be expelled from China. The group further demanded expulsion of all Communists from the Kuomintang. In Canton another group emerged with similar views.

On the night of March 18, 1926, came the first open indication of Chiang Kai-shek's sympathies: amid growing tension and apprehension, the gunboat *Chung Shan*, commanded by a Communist, appeared off the Whampoa Academy. When Chiang learned that the crew had orders to arrest him, he moved first, arresting the twenty-five Chinese Communist tutors at the academy, including the assistant political director, Chou En-lai, and placing Russian advisers under house arrest. He then sent troops to disarm all Communists in the trade unions and to place headquarters of the unions under close surveillance.

Under Chiang's direction, the Kuomintang's Central Executive Committee, at a special meeting on May 15, 1926, took stern measures to prevent further Communist penetration of the Kuomintang. The committee adopted regulations requiring the Communists to uphold Sun Yat-sen's three principles, and to submit a list of names of their supporters within the Kuomintang. The regulations also forbade Communists to hold more than a third of the posts in the Kuomintang and the government; denied them the right to form organized groups within the Kuomintang; required that all Chinese Communist Party and Comintern directives be submitted in advance for approval of a special committee of the Kuomintang; and forbade members of the Kuomintang from joining the Communist Party without formal permission of the Kuomintang.

Returning hurriedly from a mission to Peking, Borodin managed for a time to keep the revolutionary front together through a combination of sweet reason and nimble diplomacy. Yet his edifice within the Kuomintang was clearly shaky, and in an effort to sustain it, he began again to play upon the hatred of foreigners that was endemic among almost all members of the Kuomintang.

The special target was the British. At Wanhsien in August 1926 and again in September, there were incidents in which Szechuanese troops murdered several Britons, and in reprisal British gunboats bombarded the city, killing over a hundred Chinese and providing Borodin with yet more fuel for anti-British propaganda. On January 3, 1927, the trade unions in Hankow conducted massive anti-British demonstrations, and in the key city of Shanghai more than 100,000 workers staged strikes and demonstrations. As Kuomintang armies approached, foreigners in Shanghai prepared for a siege; Britain, France, and Japan sent Army and Navy reinforcements and the United States 5,000 Marines. In Nanking on March 24, 1927, Kuomintang troops under obvious instigation rampaged through the city, looting and burning foreign homes and businesses and attacking foreigners wherever found.

In London, the turmoil in China provided Winston Churchill and his Tory colleagues with grounds for a resolution in the Cabinet instructing the foreign secretary, Sir Austen Chamberlain, to prepare a formal protest to the Soviet government citing evidence, including events in China, of Russian hostility toward Britain. What Churchill and his colleagues really wanted was expulsion of the Russian diplomatic and commercial missions and termination of relations between the two powers, but Prime Minister Baldwin stopped short of that in case it should imperil the peace of Europe.

The note delivered to the Russian chargé d'affaires in London on February 23, 1927, was nevertheless strong, a clear warning that unless the Russians "refrained from interference with purely British concerns," a breach would become inevitable. Yet the Russians declined to view the matter as serious. Replying three days later, the deputy foreign commissar, Litvinov, dismissed the implied threat as unlikely "to intimidate anyone at all," while the official Russian press called upon the British government to discipline Churchill and the diehards as "a prerequisite for regulating Anglo-Soviet relations."[7]

The Russian reaction further upset the British. In Parliament on March 3, 1927, Foreign Secretary Chamberlain said the protest note was "the last word" before a break in trade and diplomatic relations. Hastening to prepare the other European powers for such an eventuality, he called friendly ambassadors at the Court of St. James's to the Foreign Office to describe the "uncertain character" of Anglo-Soviet relations, then went to Geneva for a session of the League of Nations. There he found the German chancellor, Gustav Stresemann, and the French foreign minister, Aristide Briand, seriously disturbed lest "military action inevitably follow the termination of Anglo-Soviet relations."[8]

The Russians also were finally becoming concerned. Although Chamberlain denied that Britain had any aggressive intentions, the Russians were unconvinced.

Had Chamberlain and Stresemann made a secret agreement by which Germany would permit passage of British troops?

Meanwhile, another peal of thunder rang out of China.

## Chapter Twenty-Six

As the crisis in relations between Britain and Russia in 1927 deepened, reflective statesmen saw that in reality what appeared to be an ominous situation was but a new variant on a long recurring theme. Ever since Catherine the Great had helped to overthrow her own husband, Czar Peter III, to seize the power of the state, the British had traditionally regarded Russa as a rogue power; and before, during, and after that intriguing display of feminine infidelity, Britain had always reacted pugnaciously whenever the Russians had shown any interest in either India or China, where British commercial interests were large, their rule fragile, and their legal tenure doubtful. The British seemed never to understand that as deplorable as autocracy might be, it had always suited Russia; on their part the Russians could never quite comprehend why intrigues in such remote places as the Muslim khanates of Kokand, Bukhara, and Khiva, beyond which lay the frontiers of the British-dominated countries of India, Afghanistan, and Persia, were likely to set the bugles sounding in the Horse Guards Parade.

As serious as the Anglo-Russian crisis of 1927 was, it was thus but another incident in a prolonged imperial dispute, and neither power actually intended to make war on the other, even though it might suit various interests in both countries to make war eemaf1ineitble and imminent. Yet for all that, crisis there was, and there was always the possibility that it might get out of hand.

After months of intrigue, the Chinese warlord Chang Tso-lin, who was known as the Mukden Tiger, who wore a black satin skullcap bearing what was said to be the largest pearl in the world, and who was as suspicious of the Russians as of the British, decided to raid the Russian Embassy compound in Peking. As he sent 300 police and soldiers over the walls, the raid, as noted by American military intelligence, appeared to be "carefully planned and well executed,"[1] which suggested British involvement.

Chang Tso-lin's men found on the premises a number of Chinese Communists, some of whom tried to escape by scaling a wall separating the compound from the British Legation, only to be turned back by British sentries. The raiders seized nineteen of the Communists, including the founder of the Chinese Communist Party, Li Ta-chao, all of whom were charged with treason and executed by strangling.

Ransacking the offices, Chang Tso-lin's raiders appropriated vast quantities of propaganda materials, red silk identification badges with the Sickle and Star stamped on them, thousands of small Communist paper flags, quantities of weapons and small-arms ammunition, the names and addresses of 4,000 members of the Peking branch of the Communist Party, and a diagram showing the organization of the Kuomintang at home and overseas. The raiders prevented a clerk in the military attaché's offices from burning the Embassy's and the Comintern's codes and ciphers, so that those countries that had been tapping radio reports between Moscow and Borodin could in the future read Borodin's back traffic. There were stacks of secret reports from the Soviet intelligence service, from Russian military and Comintern commissions in Canton, and from Russian advisers with the Kuomintang armies, and messages to and from Li Ta-chao, the military attaché and subordinates in the provinces, and the Embassy and Moscow.

Of the greatest importance was "a resolution relating to the Bolshevization of China passed at the 7th Plenary Session of the Executive Committee of the International Communist Party, Moscow," which the Soviet military attaché had received only a few days earlier. It would be necessary, the resolution declared, "to organize anti-European riots" by "any measures" in order to bait the "foreigners" into retaliating, but care had to be taken to avoid provocations against the Japanese, who were in a position "to land large military forces in China very swiftly." The agitation should nevertheless be designed "to preserve the existing antagonism between the individual foreign powers."[2]

The documentation seized in the compound left no doubt "that most elaborate and detailed plans and preparations had been made for the overthrow of the government in Peking and for the establishment of a Kuomintang regime,"[3] and that Mikhail Borodin and the Comintern intended it to be a Communist regime. That was not to be lost on Chiang Kai-shek; on the night of April 12, 1927, he sent troops assisted by agents of the secret Green Society and police from the French Concession on a ruthless purge of the left. The Communists subsequently reported 300 of their number killed and 5,000 "disappeared."[4] Other purges followed throughout the five provinces then under Chiang's control. In Canton, for example, 2,100 were "arrested" and their ultimate fate unnoted. By the end of July 1927, "The revolution was turned from Red to right."[5]

Long years later the Communists were destined to come to power in China, but for the moment the victory belonged to Chiang Kai-shek, and the Comintern had incurred a disastrous defeat. Joseph Stalin, strategist of the Comintern's policy in China, was severely criticized by the Politburo, and Mikhail Borodin, tactician of that policy, left China hurriedly for Moscow. There Borodin was dismissed from the Comintern and reduced to working as editor of an obscure newspaper. The Moscow correspondent for the Manchester Guardian, Malcolm Muggeridge, was to see him at official functions on several occasions, sitting alone, "quietly drinking champagne, wearing an expression of oriental vacancy."[6] After a time, Muggeridge ceased to encounter him; when he inquired, he learned that on Stalin's order, Borodin had been shot as a British spy.

Evidence uncovered in the raid in Peking was in large measure responsible for a raid made by the London police on May 12, 1927. Without regard for the terms of the Anglo-Soviet Trade Agreement of 1921, in which the British had granted

Soviet trade representatives immunity from search and arrest, the police surrounded the offices of Arcos, the Soviet trade agency. For four days they occupied the offices, in the process removing several truckloads of safes and filing cabinets. To energetic protests made by the Russian chargé d'affaires, Gregori Rosengoltz, the foreign secretary, Chamberlain, replied that the raid was "not an administrative act but a process of law taken in pursuance of a magistrate's warrant" and under similar circumstances would have been directed "against any other company" operating in Britain. To which Rosengoltz retorted that the raid was suspiciously similar to that staged by Chang Tso-lin on the Russian compound in Peking. Both raids, Rosengoltz maintained, were intended to sabotage a $50 million loan that the Russian government was on the point of raising with the Midland Bank, one of London's leading counting houses. It was also, said Rosengoltz, an attempt by Winston Churchill and his diehard colleagues to undermine "the possibility of coexistence of two [differing] national economic systems" and to sabotage Russian efforts to improve relations "with business circles in Britain."[7]

The British government's official explanation of why the police were granted a search warrant was that a British employee of Arcos had seen on the premises a copy of a British Army signals training pamphlet. The pamphlet was marked "confidential," only a middle-grade security classification, but as with all classified documents, was stamped in red to the effect that it was an offense under the Official Secrets Act—an act providing for very severe penalties—for unauthorized persons to possess it. The pamphlet was hardly of sufficient importance to justify a raid that might lead to a breach of relations between Britain and Russia. Unless the British government wanted a breach in relations. Or unless there was something more serious but unrevealed behind the raid.

There was some indication that that was the case when in late November 1926 the British police arrested a German student, Georg Hansen, and a British Communist, Wilfred McCartney, on a charge of espionage. At their trial, held partly in camera, a renegade Communist turned king's witness, George Monkland, said McCartney had asked him to obtain "a secret manual of the Royal Air Force," aircraft performance reports, and data on "aeroplane appropriations." If he could get the material, said Monkland, he was to go to the offices of Arcos, ask for a certain individual, and hand over the information. Having done that, he would be rewarded with "a generous remuneration."[8]

At that point, reported the American military attaché, Colonel John R. Thomas, whom the British made privy to certain aspects of the case, Hall had provided Monkland with the Royal Air Force's manual and, most quarters assumed, the signals pamphlet. Yet, reported Thomas, "There is an undercurrent of belief in London that much of the information which the State does not wish revealed related to the shipment of British arms and ammunition to Lithuania and Poland."[9]

The British government may indeed have been motivated—in keeping with the "undercurrent of belief," as Colonel Thomas had put it—to conceal British shipment of arms and ammunition to Lithuania and Poland by arranging the expulsion of the Russians before they could find out about it. At the same time, there was no doubt that Arcos was indeed an espionage center employing British Communists, nor was there any doubt that Hansen and McCartney had been involved with Arcos.

Yet, long before those revelations, government leaders, at a Cabinet meeting on May 23, 1927, had determined that the intelligence taken from Soviet House was in itself insufficient to justify a rupture of relations; but there was other material to buttress the case, possibly some of it obtained as a result of the raid in Peking. So it was that on May 24, 1927, Prime Minister Baldwin went before a crowded and anxious House of Commons to tell of "a group of secret agents engaged in endeavoring to obtain highly confidential documents relating to the Armed Forces of Great Britain." It "became increasingly difficult," said Baldwin, "to resist the conclusion that the agents were working on behalf of the Soviet Government and that they obtained their instructions from members of the Russian Trade Delegation."[10]

Apparently recognizing that he had fairly weak evidence upon which to base a case for a break in diplomatic and trade relations, Baldwin noted that on numerous occasions the British government had been compelled "to draw the attention of the Soviet authorities" to breaches in the agreement between the two countries whereby both pledged to avoid interference in the internal affairs of the other and in relations with other countries. That was particularly true, said Baldwin, in the case of China and the Soviet emissary there, Mikhail Borodin.

Upon specific direction from the Soviet government, Baldwin continued, the Russian chargé d'affaires, Rosengoltz, had told the *Daily Telegraph* in London that "Borodin is a private individual who is not and never has been in the service of the Soviet Government" and thus it was "self-evident that the Soviet Government can in no way be held responsible for his actions and speeches." Deputy Foreign Commissar Litvinov, said Baldwin, had said much the same to the British chargé d'affaires in Moscow.

To the contrary, Baldwin continued, the British government held a telegram dated November 12, 1926, from the Soviet Foreign Office to the Soviet delegation in Peking, which stated that "Until a Soviet representative is appointed to Peking, Comrade Borodin is to take his orders direct from Moscow. The Far Eastern Bureau is to be informed that all its decisions and measures regarding questions of the general policy of the Kuomintang in China and of military-political work must be agreed on with Comrade Borodin."

Thus, said the prime minister, "The denials of any responsibility for Borodin's actions" were untrue and "made only in the hope of deceiving His Majesty's Government and the British public." He went on to cite similar evidence of Comintern activities elsewhere, including territories within the empire, and tied those activities to Arcos.

The preliminaries over, he came to the case at hand. His Majesty's Government, said Baldwin, had decided that "unless the House expresses its disapproval," to terminate the trade agreement with Russia and "require the withdrawal of the Trade Delegation and Soviet Mission from London and recall the British Mission from Moscow." The House approved the decision by 346 votes to 98.

As rumors of war spread throughout the London diplomatic corps, Gregori Rosengoltz left the British capital by train on June 5, 1927. During a two-hour stopover, on the morning of June 7 at the Central Station in Warsaw, the Soviet ambassador to Poland, Peter Voikov, took him to breakfast at the station buffet.

Shortly after ten o'clock, the two diplomats returned to the train. Awaiting the train's departure, they talked, Rosengoltz in his seat by a window, Voikov standing on the platform. Moments before the train began to move, a nineteen-year-old Russian-born Monarchist, Boris Korenko, approached Voikov. "This," he shouted, "is for Nationalist Russia, not for the International!" At almost point-blank range, he fired several shots from a pistol into Voikov's chest. Although police rushed Voikov to a hospital, within the hour, after telling his secretary to "remove the keys and papers from the pockets of his clothing," he died.[11]

The world diplomatic community was aghast. In view of the differences between Britain and Russia, the assassination could hardly have come at a moment of more tension in European affairs. Were the shots fired at the Warsaw Central Station to be, like that fired by Gavril Princip at Sarajevo, the start of a world war?

The Russian reaction was harsh. To the Polish ambassador in Moscow, Litvinov handed a strong note, declaring the crime to be another in a series aimed at disrupting Soviet foreign relations and "menacing peace." The raid on the Soviet compound in Peking, the occupation of Soviet House in London, and Britain's severance of relations, the note declared, "have encouraged the activity of terrorist groups among reactionaries who in their blind and impotent hatred of the working class make use of the method of political murder." Despite the expulsion of Boris Savinkov, Litvinov charged, Poland still harbored anti-Soviet White Russian groups. The Soviet government, he said, considered the murder "to be the result of the failure on the part of the Polish Government to take sufficient measures" to suppress the counter-revolutionary organizations.[12]

The Polish government promptly expressed condolences to Russian President Kalinin, and throughout Europe statesmen condemned the murder. But not for long, for the day after the assassination, Lord Northcliffe's *Evening News* in London, which was noted for intensive anti-Red campaigns and support of Tory diehards, published a startling allegation. Peter Voikov, charged the *Evening News*, was the man who as president of the Provincial Soviet Executive at Ekaterinburg in 1919 had signed the death warrants for Czar Nicholas and the members of his family, was "actually present to see the deed carried out," and had arranged for the gasoline and sulphuric acid which destroyed the corpses. Because of that record, reported the *Evening News*, virtually every country with which the Soviet Union maintained relations had refused to accept Voikov as a Soviet minister, and Poland had received him only after assurances from Moscow at the highest level that he had not been involved in the murders.

Although the Soviet government promptly denied the story, it appeared to have some substance. The New York *Times*, for example, reported that Voikov had been one of Lenin's closest friends, had traveled in the sealed railway carriage that had taken Lenin across Germany in 1917, and had been implicated in the murder of the royal family by Nikolai Sokolov, a former czarist judge who had been sent to Ekaterinburg to investigate the murders after White forces took the city.

With those revelations, sympathy for Voikov swiftly faded, and in Warsaw his corpse became a symbol of the official disdain with which most western nations viewed the Soviet government. When the Russian Embassy in Warsaw through the vice-dean of the diplomatic corps, Ambassador Laroche of France, invited the diplomatic corps to pay its last respects to the dead man, Laroche passed the invitation to the other embassies with the announcement that the French flag would fly at half-mast and that French diplomats would join the procession conveying Voikov's corpse to the train; but few of the other embassies accepted. They would "pay no attention whatsoever, privately or publicly, to the sad event."[13] The declining missions included all but five of fifty-four governments represented in Warsaw.

The Polish government nevertheless granted Voikov full honors. The cortege to the Central Station was escorted by five companies of lancers and infantry, the coffin was placed aboard a special train, and at every station between Warsaw and the Russian frontier local civil authorities presented their condolences to the widow and accompanying officers from the Russian Legation.

Those honors in no way placated the current Russian ruler, Joseph Stalin. In a second note to the Polish government, Litvinov, at that point the foreign commissar, accused Britain of connivance in Voikov's murder. In a communiqué issued at about the same time in Moscow, the Soviet government said that Britain had been involved in several plots against Russia, including one engineered by Sidney George Reilly, who had "confessed to having been sent on a terrorist mission to Russia and that Winston Churchill, the Chancellor of the Exchequer, personally had given him instructions."[14] The Soviet government, said the communiqué, had rounded up a number of terrorists who were "acting from abroad and on instructions and with funds from foreign intelligence services," had sentenced twenty to death, and had carried out the sentences.

The identity of one of the twenty suggested that the OGPU—as the Cheka had been renamed—may have actually uncovered a Royalist plot. For one was Prince Pavel Dolgorukov, in prerevolutionary days one of the wealthiest men in Russia. In exile he had taken refuge in Britain, where he was "widely known and admired," and maintained a residence in Upper Grosvenor Street in Mayfair, the richest section of London. In London the prince apparently came in contact with the Brotherhood of Russian Truth, for he had infiltrated Russia on at least two occasions before his final capture. On his second trip, it appeared that he was in touch in advance with the Cheka's front organization, the Trust. In Paris he met a man who professed to have influence with the Soviet Embassy and who secured him another bogus passport. The two left for Russia together with the intention of coming back with part of Prince Dolgorukov's family treasure, but as soon as they acquired it, Dolgorukov's companion arrested him. "The friend was an agent of the *Cheka* sent to lure the prince to his doom."

The list of those executed also included Prince Meschervsky, a close relative of one of the late czar's advisers, and General Kyril Naryshkin, one of the czar's aides-de-camp. All of those executed, according to the OGPU, had been connected with a Monarchist organization run by Reilly, presumably the Brotherhood of Russian Truth.

The world press roundly condemned the executions, but as was to be expected, the denunciations had no effect in Moscow, where as an accompaniment to the executions, Russian sabers rattled. The commissar for war, Klementi Voroshilov, announced "a decree of public safety [a form of martial law] to protect the republic" and warned the workers of the world that "class war is inevitable." The international situation, Voroshilov declared, was "acute" and "no slackening of the hostilities against us can be expected." He concluded with alarming words: "War is imminent."

When superimposed on the break in Anglo-Soviet relations and Voikov's assassination, Voroshilov's speech produced what the New York *Times* called "a surcharged atmosphere." The newspaper's headlines reflected it. On June 11, 1927: EXECUTIONS SPREAD TERROR IN RUSSIA; EUROPE IS SHOCKED—OGPU COMMUNIQUE EXPLAINS SHOOTING OF 20 AS ANSWER TO ANTI-RED ATTACKS—SOVIET ARMY COMMISSAR, BLAMING BRITAIN FOR ASSASSINATIONS, SAYS WAR IS INEVITABLE. On June 15, 1927: MOSCOW IN PANIC UNDER MAILED FIST—FOREIGNERS LEAVING—STATE OF SIEGE EXPECTED—EXECUTIONS NOW EXCEED 100—THOUSANDS SENT TO SIBERIA; SUICIDES INCREASING—ARMY IN UKRAINE IS INCREASED BY 300,000 BY CALLING UP RESERVES.

Yet to a few the clatter of Russian sabers had an empty sound. Back in London following the break in relations, the former British chargé d'affaires in Moscow, Sir Robert Hodgson, suggested that the Soviet leaders had no real expectation of British attack. The war talk, he said, was "a bullfrog's chorus," designed to stimulate acceptance of a five-year plan for an extensive expansion of heavy industry by a people that for a decade had been deprived of all the luxuries of life and many of the necessities.

As the hot summer dragged on, Hodgson appeared to be right. War Commissar Voroshilov soon changed his prediction of imminent war to war "in two years, one year, or possibly, though very unlikely, in a few months," and various calls for military readiness were couched in terms of industrial development. Posters proclaimed: "Our defense is extensive industrialization and reconstruction of the national economy." The short-term requirement, said Stalin, was for the people to rally around the Communist Party; for the long term, to develop "the national economy and expand both our military and civilian industries."

By autumn the bullfrog's chorus had died down to an occasional solitary croak. Britain, in any case, had never had any intention of going to war with Russia, indeed, hardly had the means to do so; and by the spring of 1928 Prime Minister Baldwin would begin to make guarded overtures toward restoring relations.

Yet hardly had the British negotiated a resumption of diplomatic and trade relations when still another major Comintern conspiracy came to light in the empire. On June 1, 1931, British police in Singapore arrested a Frenchman, Joseph Ducroux, alias Serge LaFranc, alias Dupont, a Comintern representative responsible for "organizing activities of the Comintern in the East Asia colonies"; he was "caught red-handed with members of the Malayan Communist Party."[15]

The discovery of a telegraphic address on Ducroux led to a raid on offices of the Pan-Pacific Trades Union Secretariat, a Comintern cover organization in Shanghai, and the arrest of the secretary, a Comintern agent known locally as Hilaire Noulens. The secretariat's archives revealed an extensive network of Comintern agents and subagents in Hong Kong, Shanghai, the British-protected sultanate of Brunei, the Australian-mandated former German colony of New Britain, and the great British naval base of Trincomalee in the crown colony of Ceylon. The archives also revealed that in one year alone—1925—the Comintern had spent $3¼ million, over three times its acknowledged income in that year, on operations in China alone.

If Britain wanted trade and diplomatic relations with the Soviet Union, the government obviously would have to learn to live with the machinations of the Comintern.

# PART V
## The German Cockpit

*Chapter Twenty-Seven*

At Pasewalk military hospital in Pomerania, a twenty-nine-year-old German corporal, Adolf Hitler, a messenger with the List Regiment of Bavaria, was recovering from temporary blindness incurred in October 1918 during a British attack employing mustard gas on a German-held hill outside Wervik, in Belgium near Ypres. Revolution was sweeping Germany, the House of Hohenzollern had fallen, and, the hospital chaplain informed Hitler, Germany had surrendered. "And so it had all been in vain," the corporal anguished. "In vain all the sacrifices and privations; in vain the hunger and thirst of months which were often endless; in vain the hours in which, with mortal fear clutching at our hearts, we nevertheless did our duty; and in vain the death of two millions who died." As Hitler would later recall: "Again everything went black before my eyes; I tottered and groped my way back to the dormitory, threw myself on my bunk, and dug my burning head into my blanket and pillows. Since the day I had stood at my mother's grave, I had not wept . . . But now I could not help it." [1]

Corporal Hitler had an exemplary military record: he had received the Iron Cross 2nd Class for bravery in the first battle of Ypres; a regimental certificate for bravery; the Iron Cross 1st Class, which was rarely awarded to the ranks, for bravery in the great *Kaiserschlacht* battles of 1918; he had been wounded in the thigh; and he had been gassed.

Discharged from Pasewalk near the end of November 1918, Hitler reported to the replacement battalion of his regiment in Munich. The barracks, he discovered, had gone over to the Kurt Eisner government and was devoid of discipline, a pigsty. Volunteering for any duty that might take him away from the barracks, he served for a time as a guard for prisoners of war and upon collapse of the Leviné insurrection, offered his services to a military tribunal investigating conduct of officers from the List Regiment who had supported Leviné. That work was Hitler's first experience in the half-world of intelligence that attends politics, and he performed so well that he was selected for a training course in what was called "civic thinking," a euphemism for counterrevolutionary activities.

From the training course, Hitler joined a special unit with diverse duties called Bavarian Group Command IV, where he was assigned to the propaganda section, which provided a cover for investigation of subversive political activities among the troops and for infiltration of workers' organizations to watch for revolutionary activities. As further training, he and his colleagues attended special indoctrination courses at the University of Munich, involving, as he himself put it, "certain historical, political, and economic theories" conveyed by "reliable nationalists." It was while attending those courses that Hitler made a critical discovery about himself: he had an unusually powerful gift of oratory.

As Professor Karl Alexander von Mueller would recall, he was leaving the hall after delivering a lecture when he found his way blocked by a group that "stood fascinated around a man in their midst who was addressing them without pause and with growing passion in a strangely guttural voice." Von Mueller "had the strange feeling that the man was feeding on the excitement which he himself had whipped up." The orator was a man with "a pale, thin face beneath a drooping, unsoldierly stand of hair, with close-cropped mustache and strikingly large, light blue eyes coldly glistening with fanaticism."

Years later, a committee appointed by the American Office of Strategic Services and headed by Dr. Walter C. Langer, would make a detailed study of Hitler's oratorical powers. "Even his greatest opponents," the committee concluded, "concede that he is the greatest orator that Germany has ever known."[2]

At that early stage of Hitler's career, he spoke in a conglomeration of high German and Austrian dialect, sometimes called "dumpling speech." Both then and later "his speeches were sinfully long, very repetitious, positively painful to read," but they "had an extraordinary effect upon his audiences." A British foreign correspondent, G. Ward Price, who for a number of years was accepted in Hitler's inner circle, described the technique: "The beginning is slow and halting. Gradually he warms up when the spiritual atmosphere of the great crowd is engendered. For he responds to this metaphysical contact in such a way that each member of the multitude feels bound to him by an individual link of sympathy."[3] "In Munich," noted the Langer Committee, "his shouting and gesturing were a spectacle men paid to see."

From a physical standpoint, Hitler was hardly one to inspire awe or even confidence. In height, he was "a little below average." His hips were "wide," his shoulders "relatively narrow," his muscles "flabby," his legs "short, thin, and spindly," and he was "hollow-chested to the point where it was said that he had his uniforms padded." An American writer, Dorothy Thompson, found him "formless, almost faceless, a man whose countenance is a caricature, a man whose framework seems cartileginous, without bones. He is inconsequent and voluble, ill-poised and insecure . . . the very prototype of the little man." Another American writer, Edgar Mowrer, saw him as a "provincial dandy" who "seemed for all the world like a travelling salesman for a clothing firm."[4]

Yet, for all that, there was no denying the power the man would exercise over millions, and even as Professor von Mueller first heard him speak, the rudiments of his oratorial power were already apparent. When the professor told Hitler's commanding officer, Captain Karl Mayr, of Hitler's striking talent, Mayr assigned him to an "enlightenment squad," which delivered nationalistic, anti-Marxist lectures to soldiers awaiting demobilization. The soldiers, Hitler soon found, were bitter, home from an animal-like existence in the trenches only to find their world in chaos. Hitler gloried in providing them targets for their hatred: the "November criminals," the "Jewish-Marxist world conspiracy," and the "sin and corruption of democracy and internationalism." In an odd, penetrating, hoarse voice that grew more mesmerizing with every speech, he spoke of "the fatherland's humiliation, the sins of imperialism, the envy of neighbors, the 'smearing of Germany's past,' the shallow, commercialized, and debauched West from which had come the [German] republic, the disgraceful dictated peace of Versailles, the Allied Control Commission, nigger music, bobbed hair, and modern art, but neither work, security, nor bread."[5]

Incensed at Bolshevik uprisings in Bavaria, the Ruhr, Hamburg, Berlin, Saxony, and Thuringia, Hitler railed about "Red squads of butchers," "murderous communists," the "bloody morass of Bolshevism." In Russia, he declared, Lenin and Trotsky had murdered more than 30 million people, "partly on the scaffold, partly by machine guns and similar means, partly in veritable slaughterhouses, partly, millions upon millions, by hunger."

In most of his speeches, he exploited the anxieties of the times by associating Bolshevism with the Jews, and by invoking ever more colorful diatribes against the Jews: ". . . at the heart of the towering structure of anxiety, black and hairy, stood the figure of the Jew: evil-smelling, smacking his lips, lusting after blonde girls, eternal contaminator of the blood." He saw Germany as "the object of a world-wide conspiracy, pressed on all sides by Bolshevists, Freemasons, capitalists, Jesuits, all hand in glove with each other and directed in their nefarious projects by the 'blood-thirsty and avaricious Jewish tyrant.'" The Jew "undermined governments, bastardized races, glorified fratricide, fomented civil war, justified baseness and poisoned nobility: 'the wirepullers of the destinies of mankind.'" No phrase was too lurid: "creeping venom," "belly worms," "adders devouring the nation's body."

On September 12, 1919, Hitler received an assignment that was to have fateful consequences: he was to attend a meeting of one of the small political groups that had sprung up in Munich and report on its activities. Known as the German Workers' Party, it had been founded that January by a machinist in the Munich railway yards, Anton Drexler, whose political theory was simple: "Good work, a full cookpot, and a fair chance for the children."

As Hitler entered the meeting place, a little beer hall on the Herrenstrasse, the Sterneckerbräu, he found the speaker to be an economist, Gottfried Feder, whose subject was: "How and by what means can capitalism be eliminated?" Hitler found the speech dull, the little group of some forty people "stifling in their absurd philistinism." When one of the audience in a discussion period demanded the secession of Bavaria from Germany, Hitler took the floor. "Man," whispered Anton Drexler to an associate, "he has a big mouth; we could use him." As Hitler stormed from the hall in disgust, Drexler hurried after him, asked him to return to another meeting and speak, and pressed into his hand a forty-page pamphlet entitled "My Political Awakening."

Before daylight the next morning, as Hitler was watching mice in his little barracks room chasing after morsels of bread he put out for them, he thought of the pamphlet and began to read it. From the start he was enthralled. In Drexler's account of his life he found elements of his own experience: "exclusion from jobs by union terrorism; earning a wretched living by semi-artistic work," and, finally, "the great illumination accompanied by feelings of intense anxiety—recognition of the role of the Jewish race as corrupters of the world."

Drexler followed up his invitation by sending Hitler a party card, and a new invitation to attend a committee meeting at a run-down restaurant, the Altes Rosenbad. In a back room, Hitler found Drexler and four others around a table. By the light of a cracked gas lamp, one of the group read the minutes of the last meeting and counted the party's treasury: seven marks, fifty pfennigs. Glancing through the few party directives, Hitler discovered that the group had no real program, yet when the men pressed him to join them, he found himself, to his surprise, assenting. The little club, he decided, could be shaped to his own needs. He had taken, as he would later note, the decisive step of his life: he had set his feet upon the political stage.

Hitler began immediately to transform the "timid, static group of club members into a noisy, publicity-conscious party of struggle." He established its headquarters in the Sterneckerbräu, for which the party paid a rent of fifty marks a month, and in cosigning the lease gave his occupation as "painter." He acquired a table, some chairs, a telephone, an old typewriter, a safe for membership cards and the treasury, and spent hours at the Munich public library looking for a drawing of a German eagle suitable for a party stamp.

With the help of Drexler, Hitler drafted a party program, which the two first presented to a growing membership at a meeting in the Hofbräuhaus in Munich on February 24, 1920. Consisting of twenty-five points, it was essentially anticapitalist, anti-Marxist, antiparliament, anti-Semitic, antidemocratic, and anti–Versailles Treaty. It contained the germ of what would become known as *Lebensraum:* living space for the German people to make up for the loss of German colonies. It also provided for limiting the work and other activities of Jews, and it specified that when the German Workers' Party came to power, the good of the state would transcend the rights of the individual.

Designed to check the spread of Bolshevism in Germany, the points represented essentially a combination of nationalistic and social revolutionary schemes. Thus the term, National Socialism, and a redesignation of the party as the National Socialist German Workers' Party, or more familiarly, as the Nazi Party, for which the symbol was the swastika—a word borrowed from Sanskrit, the ancient and sacred language of India—long a symbol of the Teutonic knights.

Leaving the Army on April 1, 1920, Hitler spent most of his time in the cellar of the Sterneckerbräu planning what he described as the aim of the Nazi Party: "the annihilation and extermination of the Marxist world view" by means of "an incomparable, brilliantly orchestrated propaganda and information organization" side by side with a movement of "the most ruthless force and most brutal resolution, prepared to oppose all terrorism on the part of the Marxists with tenfold greater terrorism."

On July 29, 1921, Adolf Hitler took over the leadership of the Nazi Party and assumed the title of Führer (leader). By that time, the party had begun spending lavishly on propaganda and recruitment and would continue to do so. Primarily through the former commander of the Freikorps that had saved Munich from Eugene Leviné, General von Epp, the party had raised 90,000 marks as downpayment on purchase of a racist biweekly, the *Völkischer Beobachter*, which became the official party newspaper. Donations for more general purposes came from comfortable and respectable members of the Munich bourgeoisie, from membership dues, from fees charged for party meetings at which Hitler spoke, from collections at rallies, but those funds alone were hardly sufficient to sustain his lavish expenditures, which were "so conspicuously out of all proportion [to the party's numbers] that there was every reason to look around for financial backers." Some of those were early party members who virtually ruined themselves financially in its support, and others were wealthy spinsters "emotionally shaken" by Hitler's personality, but those contributions were still insufficient to explain a rapid expansion of the party's *apparat* in 1922 and the creation of a private army, the Sturmabteilung (SA). Although there was some backing from powerful and wealthy individuals and institutions, such as the locomotive manufacturer Borsig, Consolidated Steel's Fritz Thyssen, the Daimler Company, and the Bavarian Industrialists' Association, it would subsequently be established that only in later years was the Nazi Party a major beneficiary of German industry. Yet the additional funds had to come from somewhere. In 1923, for example, Hitler was said to have gone to Zurich and to have returned "with a steamer trunk stuffed with Swiss francs and American dollars." There were apparently other mysterious sources of funds in Czechoslovakia, Hungary, and Latvia.

Who those sources were would never be satisfactorily explained; but soon after World War II, as U.S. Army intelligence officers were taking evidence in regard to trials of German officials for war crimes, there emerged an affidavit executed by a dying German nitrate magnate, Arnold Rechberg, who maintained that at a breakfast in Berlin in 1933 with a figure of political and military eminence, General Kurt von Schleicher, he had been told that Lenin's successor, Stalin, had provided Hitler with substantial funds on the theory that Hitler's rise would bring about civil war in Germany, from which the Communists would emerge as victor. That, Stalin believed, would lead to an alliance between German and Russian soviets that would make the Soviet Union invincible.[6]

In addition to the affidavit, Rechberg had prepared a long statement about the conversation for the New York *Times* (which did not publish it) and provided a copy for the U.S. Army's military intelligence service. In 1945, the head of the foreign section of the Nazi Party's intelligence service, the Reichsicherheitsdienst, SS-Brigadeführer Walter Schellenberg, would swear to his American captors that the story was true and would subsequently provide other details of it in his published memoirs.[7]

The man who might have confirmed or disavowed the information, General von Schleicher, would be unable to, for in 1934 at Hitler's command he had been murdered. Thus all that would be certain about Hitler's finances during his early days in politics was that powerful forces were behind him, for the Nazi movement was fast spreading; indeed, it had become so troublesome and minatory that in the states of Prussia, Saxony, Thuringia, Baden, and Mecklenburg it was proscribed.

Still confined primarily to Bavaria, the movement was nevertheless pervasive there. A stranger arriving in Munich, wrote a correspondent for the London *Times* on May 22, 1923, "might well imagine that the town was occupied by a foreign power." On "a Hitler field day bands of storm troops march about in strictly military formation"; they wore gray uniforms and carried Fascist standards, "usually red with a black *Swastika* emblazoned in the centre," and while many of the troopers were "lads from 17 to 20, professional men, business men, ex-officers, students, and farmers can be seen in the ranks." The "semi-military organization is not only tolerated but indirectly supported by the Government on the ground that its formation could be used to suppress any Communist rising." Whereas membership in the party had been estimated in December 1922 at only about 20,000, "the number of men wearing *Swastika* badges to be seen during a walk through the streets of Munich is amazing."

Hitler had adroitly welded some eighteen military, patriotic, and nationalistic societies in Bavaria into a single political entity. The political leader was Hitler; the spiritual head was Crown Prince Rupprecht of Bavaria; and the titular head was General Ludendorff.

In appealing to Winston Churchill to help form an international army to fight Bolshevism, Erich Ludendorff had predicted that unless the Allied Powers cooperated with Germany, some day "a man of iron" would arise to lead Germany. By 1923 Ludendorff appeared to have found his messiah in Adolf Hitler.

He had come to Ludendorff's attention early, soon after Hitler as a member of the enlightenment squad of Bavarian Group Command IV made his report on his first meeting with the German Workers' Party in the Sterneckerbräu. Seeing the little party as a possible start for rebuilding Germany's military power, Ludendorff called on Hitler's commanding officer, Captain Mayr, to urge that Hitler be allowed to join the party and build it up. Because Ludendorff in retirement still commanded great respect among the military, Mayr obliged and provided Hitler a small stipend for the purpose.

In the spring of 1920, in the course of a rightist attempt at a coup d'état, Hitler arrived in Berlin to confer with the leaders, only to find the attempt failing. He nevertheless took advantage of the occasion to call on General Ludendorff. From that point, the relationship of the two became ever closer. Vowing to unite all rightist nationalist groups throughout Germany, Ludendorff by the fall of 1920 had embraced Hitler as the political leader of a new party, to be founded with the National Socialist German Workers' Party as a nucleus. Not only had Ludendorff found his messiah; Hitler had found the war hero he needed as a front for his rise to power.

The extent of Ludendorff's commitment was apparent to the American assistant military attaché in Berlin, Captain Truman Smith, when in the fall of 1922 he went to Munich "to assess the reported developing strength of the National Socialist movement."[8] When Smith talked with Ludendorff, the former first quartermaster general told him that he had long believed that Bolshevism had to be crushed in Russia before it could be eliminated in Germany, but he had changed his mind: "Bolshevism," he said, "must first be crushed in Germany." Calling for Allied support for "a strong German government capable of combatting Marxism," he declared that such a government could be formed only "by patriotic men."[9]

Smith also obtained an audience with Hitler. "A marvelous demagogue," Smith would note. "I have rarely listened to such a logical and fanatical man." The purpose of the Nazi movement, Hitler told Smith, was "to oppose Marxism." Calling for Allied support, he said it was "much better for America and England that the decisive struggle between our civilization and Marxism be fought out on German soil rather than on American and English soil." Particularly disturbed about Hitler's anti-Semitism, Smith queried him directly about it, to which Hitler replied that he intended nothing more than "the withdrawal of citizenship and their exclusion from public affairs."[10]

As suggested by Captain Smith's question, Article 4 of the twenty-five points in Hitler's program was ominous: "None but members of the nation may be citizens of the State. None but those of German blood, whatever their creed, may be members of the nation. No Jew, therefore, may be a member of the nation."[11]

That article later provoked Truman Smith, by that time a colonel and the

American military attaché in Berlin, to conduct a survey of the modern history of anti-Semitism in Germany. Smith established that anti-Semitism was deeply rooted in both Germany and Austria and had become more vocal and organized through the work of an Austrian nobleman, Georg Ritter von Schoenerer, a leader in the Austrian parliament in the decade before the World War.

During his early years in Vienna, Smith noted, Hitler had displayed no strong anti-Semitic prejudices; indeed, he was on excellent terms with the Jews in the Männerheim Brigittenau, the flophouse where he lived and painted; they sometimes gave Hitler food, money, their old clothes. It was only after Hitler came to know von Schoenerer, whose godfather, Johann Prinz, who lived in Vienna, was also Hitler's godfather, that Hitler began to display antagonism toward Jews. It was quite clearly von Schoenerer, whom Hitler came to regard as "his hero,"[12] who turned Hitler against Jews. Hitler came to accept von Schoenerer's theory based on "a philosophic conception" of racism as conveyed by the German word *völkisch* which contains both racist and folk-nationalistic implications. That concept, Colonel Smith's survey noted, implied "the exact opposite of the American 'melting pot' theory." Neither von Schoenerer nor Hitler objected to a mixing of related racial stocks, but "both felt that for a European race to mix with an Asiatic or an African race would result in the blood of the 'lower' race gradually infecting the 'higher' and destroying the fundaments of the [higher race's] civilization."[13]

Smith noted that the Nazis not only held the Jew to be Asiatic and therefore nonassimilable but also "parasitic, i.e., that the Jews cannot build a state of their own but must live off the labors of some other race." The Nazis believed that "wherever the Jew appears in the midst of a foreign race, he provides only an infinitesimal portion of the agricultural and hand-working proportion of the host land but an unusually large proportion of the commercial element, and if long established, an unusually high percentage of the intellectual professions as well." They also believed that during the war, while the German people as a whole became impoverished, "the Jewish element . . . succeeded in markedly increasing their wealth, in gaining influence within the government, in the intellectual professions, and in control of the German cultural institutions such as theaters, universities, the kino, and the arts."

That "sharp and rapid increase in Jewish influence," noted Smith, produced a strong anti-Semitic reaction throughout Germany, but there was another contributing factor of equal importance: "the role of the Jews in the Russian, German, Bavarian, and Hungarian revolutions. That Trotsky, Liebknecht, Rosa Luxemburg, Kurt Eisner, and Béla Kun were simultaneously Jews and the leaders of the Communist revolutions with anti-National tendencies did not escape the attention of the German 'Racialists.'" To Hitler and other nationalist-racist leaders, Communism appeared to be "a Jewish phenomenon," and "the international tendencies of Communism appeared to converge exactly with the international tendencies of Jewry."

"Hitler has never disguised his intention," Colonel Smith concluded, "to perform ultimately a radical surgical operation on the Jews and remove them totally from German political, intellectual, and commercial life and ultimately, if possible, from the German soil."


## Chapter Twenty-Eight

Only a few days after the murders of Karl Liebknecht and Rosa Luxemburg at the conclusion of "Spartacus Week" in early 1919, the new provisional German Republic held its first elections for the Reichstag. They produced an overwhelming victory for the center, a rejection both of a return to the Hohenzollerns and of a leftist revolution. By a large majority, the assembly elected the incumbent chancellor, Friedrich Ebert, as first president of the Reich, whereupon Ebert cast about for a foreign minister whose first assignment would be to treat with vengeful Allied governments to turn the armistice into a peace.

Ebert's choice fell upon Count Ulrich Karl-Christian von Brockdorff-Rantzau, of the Holstein nobility, a man whose ancestry included a marshal of France, who—so it was said—had sired the Sun King, Louis XIV. Von Brockdorff moved into the foreign minister's office-palace at 75 Wilhelmstrasse in Berlin, where the great dancer, Barberina, had lived during the mid-eighteenth century, and began to mold a policy for the coming trial with the Allies. A man of labyrinthine methods, von Brockdorff devised a policy combining conciliation with menace: if the Allies refused a just peace in accord with President Wilson's Fourteen Points, Germany would seek a rapprochement with Bolshevik Russia. That would create the conditions for a realization of the Mackinder heartland theory so acutely feared, as von Brockdorff was aware, by Lloyd George.

Von Brockdorff's intent was hardly to be concealed from the Allied governments. A German alliance with the Bolsheviks was an obvious threat and one that had taken on new likelihood with the founding of the Comintern and the Bolshevik revolutions in Hungary and Bavaria. Adding to the unease, Lenin announced only a week before von Brockdorff departed for Versailles that Russia desired commercial and diplomatic relations with Germany.

As von Brockdorff began his journey on April 28, 1919, the proposals he intended to lay before the Allied representatives were scarcely those of a power admitting defeat: Germany would disarm to the same degree that neighboring countries disarmed; Germany was prepared to concede some territory, but only if the inhabitants established by plebiscite that that was what they wanted; and Germany would pay reparations only for damage to Allied civilians and their property. Von Brockdorff would demand return of Germany's Merchant Marine, then in the hands of the British, and of the African and Asian colonies, most of which the British were administering.

As the train carrying von Brockdorff and his party of 180 crossed the French frontier, the delegation soon had a foretaste of the reception that awaited them. The French compelled the train to creep along at ten miles an hour so that the Germans would get a long look at the devastated countryside of Northern France, and upon their arrival at Versailles, they were taken to a hotel surrounded by barbed wire and guarded by rude sentries and told to handle their own luggage. For five days they were kept waiting before at last being informed that terms would be presented them at three o'clock on the afternoon of May 7, 1919, in the Trianon Palace.

The date, von Brockdorff learned to his mounting anger, had been selected at the wish of the Americans, because it was on May 7, 1915, that a German U-boat had sunk the liner *Lusitania* with a loss of 128 American lives. His distress mounted further when he saw a diagram of the seating arrangement in the Hall of Mirrors; the German delegation's table was labeled *banc des accusés*. Nor was there to be, he learned, any discussion of the treaty; the Germans would simply be handed the terms and permitted fifteen days in which to study the 440 articles and submit their observations in writing.

When the dreadful day arrived, the sky was clear and the sun brilliant, the birds sang, and the scent of lilacs filled the air, a lyrical day hardly appropriate for humiliation. Yet as von Brockdorff took his seat at a table facing a half-circle formed by the Allied representatives, it was apparent that humiliation was to be the German lot.

"The hour has struck for the weighty settlement of our account,"[1] intoned Clemenceau, looking squarely at the bemonocled, haughty minister plenipotentiary of Germany. "You have asked for peace. We are willing to grant you peace."[2] Departing from his prepared text, he vehemently accused Germany of full responsibility for the war.

When Clemenceau directed that the white-bound treaty be handed the German delegation, von Brockdorff rose slightly and received it wearing black gloves. Speaking in the icy, polished style of Edwardian diplomacy, tinctured with irony, he declared: "We are deeply impressed with the lofty aims which have brought us together with you: to give the world quickly a permanent peace." The Germans, he said, had "no illusions about the extent of our defeat, the degree of our impotency." Nor had he any illusions about "the weight of hatred which confronts us here." Yet when the Allies demanded that "we acknowledge that we are the ones solely responsible for the war, such an avowal, coming from me, would be a lie." While the Hohenzollerns had their failings, von Brockdorff said, the truth was that not the Hohenzollerns but fifty years of capitalistic and imperialistic adventuring had brought on the war. He hoped, he said in conclusion, that the treaty was in such a condition that it could be "signed by all."[3]

As Count von Brockdorff left the room, Clemenceau was red with anger; Wilson was plainly appalled; and Lloyd George was smiling stiffly. In the face of overwhelming defeat and humiliation, they had seen cold, aristocratic arrogance.

Back at the hotel, von Brockdorff's worst fears were realized. It was a treaty, he discovered, of Carthaginian harshness. Among the more onerous of the terms were:

Germany to admit exclusive responsibility for the war.

Germany to pay reparations totaling some $120 billion.

Alsace and Lorraine to be ceded to France.

Eupen and Malmédy and surrounding territory to be ceded to Belgium, northern Schleswig to Denmark, and parts of northern Silesia to a new state of Poland.

Most of West Prussia, including Poznan and a corridor leading to the port of Danzig was to be ceded to Poland and Danzig to be made a free city.

The German Empire to be confiscated and placed under the mandate of the League of Nations, with Britain the principal administrator.

The Saar industrial region to be governed for fifteen years by the League of Nations and its coalfields to be administered by France.

The Rhineland to be occupied by the Allied armies for up to fifteen years and the left bank of the Rhine and the right bank up to a depth of thirty miles to be permanently demilitarized.

The German Army to be permanently reduced to 4,000 officers and 96,000 men and permitted no tanks, no artillery other than light cannon, and no aircraft; the German Navy to be similarly reduced and permitted no submarines.

The intelligence services and the General Staff to be abolished.

There was to be no discussion of terms; they were to be signed by 7:00 P.M. on June 23, 1919, and if they were not, Allied military forces would occupy Germany. The terms came as an unbelievable shock to the General Staff and to the Ebert government, for not even the most pessimistic of them had believed that President Wilson would lend his name to a treaty so destructive and malevolent.

In Versailles, von Brockdorff and his staff completed their counterproposals in writing on the last day permitted by the Allies and sent them to the Allied leaders. Yet neither Germany's anger nor von Brockdorff's cool barbs to the effect that lofty Wilsonian principles were obviously intended for the victors and not the vanquished made any impression. The treaty came back with an ultimatum: sign within five days or the armistice would be terminated. The only concession von Brockdorff could gain before departing to consult with his government was a two-day extension of the ultimatum.

In Weimar, where the Reichstag sat because of the turmoil in Berlin (whence the name, Weimar Republic), and where Count von Brockdorff-Rantzau arrived on June 17, 1919, the government was in much the same state of consternation as Trotsky had found in Petrograd when he had returned from Brest Litovsk. In favor of outright rejection of the treaty, President Ebert asked First Quartermaster General Wilhelm Gröner how the country would respond if the war were resumed. On no account, Gröner responded, would the German people support renewed war; although temporary local resistance might be possible, the people as a whole were too war-weary for sustained conflict. Rejection, he said, would mean war and war would mean civil war instigated either by the right or the left.

Just nineteen minutes before the ultimatum was scheduled to expire, the German delegation in Versailles handed Clemenceau Germany's acceptance of the terms, and four days later a German plenipotentiary, Johannes Bell, signed the treaty. "We commend our unhappy country to a merciful God," declared the president of the National Assembly, Konstantin Fehrenbach. Wrote the diarist Count Kessler: "A terrible time is dawning for Europe, a sultriness before the storm which will probably end in an even more terrible explosion than the World War."⁴ A first step toward that eventual explosion was soon under way in Berlin.

Through Baron Ago von Maltzan, a man who combined "the detachment and centuries-old philosophy of the Chinese and something also of their Confucian indifference to contemporary standards"⁵ and whose duties at the Foreign Office included Russian affairs, the German Cabinet had established one of those bureaus that like the Quakers, the Red Cross, and the Young Men's Christian Association sometimes serve as political conduits when all orthodox communication between hostile powers has broken down. That particular organization was the Reich Central Office for Military and Civilian Prisoners, which looked after Russian prisoners of war in Germany.

In November 1919, a Russian who had once worked as a distributor of Lenin's revolutionary journal, Iskra, Victor Kopp, arrived in Berlin as the representative of the Soviet Red Cross charged with the exchange of civilian and military prisoners. Kopp was not unknown in Berlin: he had been expelled as a Bolshevik revolutionary along with Adolf Joffe in late 1918. Although he was known to German police as a Comintern clandestine, the police were unaware that he was also a representative of the Western European Secretariat of the Comintern, which had been established in Berlin only a few weeks before Kopp's arrival at the express order of Lenin with the mission of transmitting the Comintern's secret directives to Western European Communist leaders.

The head of the Reich Central Office for Military and Civilian Prisoners was a German who had been born in Moscow, Gustav Hilger. He and Victor Kopp soon established amicable relations, and on April 19, 1920, the German and Russian governments signed an Agreement on the Repatriation of Prisoners of War and Civilian Internees, which provided for an exchange of commissions and thus represented a first step toward normalizing relations between the two countries. Why not turn those commissions, suggested Kopp, into consular offices? When Count von Brockdorff-Rantzau's successor, Dr. Walter Simons, came to office, he soon made it clear to the Soviet foreign commissar, Chicherin, that if "amends were made" for the assassination of the German ambassador in Moscow, talks could begin toward establishing trade or diplomatic relations or both.

That suited Lenin. As he declared to Chicherin: "I am not fond of the Germans by any means, but . . . Germany wants revenge and we want revolution. For the moment our aims are the same," but, he added, "when our ways part, [the

Germans] will be our most ferocious and our greatest enemies. Time will tell whether a German hegemony or a Communist federation will arise out of the ruins of Europe."[6]

Yet hardly had Dr. Simons uttered his conditions to Victor Kopp in Berlin when in March 1921 German Communists with Comintern assistance began insurrections in Saxony and Thuringia. "It really takes a considerable dose of self-control," noted Simons, "to negotiate with these people when they are trying to burn one's house down over one's head."[7] Simons nevertheless remained determined to establish some form of understanding with Russia, for Germany's need was great.

In January 1921, the Allied Supreme War Council at Versailles demanded that Germany pay reparations over forty-two years of 226 billion gold marks, a sum, as the German government replied, that was far beyond what even an inventive and industrious country such as Germany could pay. In response, French troops occupied the Rhine ports and Düsseldorf and Duisburg in the Ruhr industrial region. Five months later the Allied governments presented a second bill: one billion gold marks to be paid by May 30, 1921, or the entire Ruhr would be occupied. More than any other factor, these ruthless demands forced on the Germans a marriage of convenience with the Russians. The ceremony would be performed at the Ligurian resort of Rapallo.

Early in 1922, the British prime minister, Lloyd George, invited thirty-four countries to attend a conference in Genoa designed to find a means of restoring the economic and financial health of Europe. Among the countries solicited were Germany and Russia, the first time since the end of the Great War that those partners in misfortune had been invited into any gathering of the European family. Lenin himself planned to attend the conference, for in Moscow there was considerable excitement that Bolshevik Russia had at last been invited to participate in a great international gathering. In Chicherin's office in Patriarch's Lane, there were earnest conferences as to whether the invitation constituted de facto recognition of the Soviet government.

Lenin was particularly pleased over the prospect of meeting the American secretary of state, Charles Evans Hughes, yet such a meeting was foredoomed. Despite advices from various quarters urging Hughes to attend, if only to settle the burning issue of the great Russian debt to the United States, Hughes refused. "The economic restoration of Russia," he declared, "cannot be realized before the necessary measures are taken by those who chiefly are responsible for the present economic chaos in Russia."[8] He would not, he said, beg the Bolsheviks to pay their bills.

The refusal of Secretary Hughes to participate was but the first obstacle to the success of the conference. The Italian premier also declined to attend, and a new French premier, Raymond Poincaré, was determined to wreck it, for he wanted the Germans to fail in their reparations payments so that he would have an excuse to occupy the entire Ruhr, "expecting"—so Lloyd George told his mistress—"to find the roads there littered with gold as in some celestial city."[9] Lloyd George himself had been persuaded to sponsor the conference by the new German foreign minister, Walther Rathenau, one of Germany's most successful industrialists, who wanted it not in the interest of European amity but in the hope that he might avoid paying any more gold to "those howling wolves," the French. Suffering from a general debility—headaches, stomach upsets, and insomnia—Lenin in the end accepted the advice of Derzhinski, head of the Cheka, who feared Lenin's assassination, and decided against attending. The truth of an aphorism by the British diplomatist and diarist Harold Nicolson, that diplomacy by conference was "the most unfortunate diplomatic method ever conceived,"[10] was about to be tested.

Lenin sent a large delegation headed by Chicherin. On the way to Genoa, the delegation stopped in Berlin on the first day of April 1922 to be received by an imposing German delegation in frock coats headed by Rathenau. Hilger and Kopp having long ago executed the preliminaries, Chicherin promptly informed Rathenau that Russia was ready for an understanding with Germany. Talks began immediately. Since Rathenau was reluctant to commit himself finally in case a treaty signed with the Bolsheviks in advance of the Genoa conference should interfere with efforts to induce the French to provide some respite from the terrible burden of reparations, the arrangement was completed in secrecy and signing postponed. Yet there could be little question about German intentions.

The terms of the agreement were simple:

Diplomatic and consular relations were to be resumed immediately.

Economic and trade relations were to be based on the principle of most-favored nation.

The German government pledged to support efforts by private enterprise to enter into trade agreements with Russia.

Each country renounced all financial claims against the other. Although there were several lesser articles having to do with trade, there was no mention of the Comintern.

The protocol—provided it became a treaty—represented a triumph for both the partners in misfortune. For Russia it meant an end to frigid international isolation, a first step toward world recognition, and it meant a marriage of Russian resources to German industry. For Germany it meant a step toward economic health and a chance, with Russian collaboration, to rebuild German armies and military technology in Russia beyond the view of the Allied watchdogs enforcing the Treaty of Versailles. It was thus in a mood of considerable satisfaction that the two delegations set out for Genoa to meet the men whom Chicherin called "the moneybag conquerors."[11]

At the opening event of the conference, a reception in the Palace of the Doges, the two delegations consciously kept apart, yet that hardly mattered, for all eyes were on Chicherin and the other Russians in their diplomatic debut. The consensus had been that the Russians would behave loutishly, like the unwashed they represented, but the consensus was incorrect. The delegation appeared in frock coats and pinstriped trousers and "behaved exactly as diplomats were expected to behave." [12]

However felicitous the reception, the conference was a disaster, partly, at least, because Lloyd George, who believed that diplomats "were invented simply to waste time," [13] had made few preparations other than to rule that the official language would be French. There was neither a proper agenda nor even a clear definition of the objectives: Lloyd George mentioned in turn the need to attend to the Russian problem, the German problem, the European problem, war debts, reparations, to do *something* to restore the economic bloom to Europe's cheeks. As hundreds of delegates and their advisers and a large press corps crowded the ballroom of the Palace of the Doges, jabbering in many languages and propagating a score of ideas, Lloyd George presided in a kind of Celtic trance, alternating between statesmanlike pronouncements about the need for order and efforts at roguish good humor.

Delivering the opening address, the Italian foreign minister, Luigi Facta, tried to set a noble tone: there were no victors at the conference, no vanquished, only equals. Catching the mood, Lloyd George said that even coexistence with Communism was possible. Yet when it came Chicherin's turn to speak, he made it clear that living with Communism still might present difficulties. Employing flawless French and keeping to a text provided by Lenin, Chicherin parroted the standard Comintern line: an end to colonial empires; world demobilization and disarmament; the need not for a European conference but for a world conference to include representatives of workers' organizations, a conference to address not only Europe's problems but the problems of the subjugated colonial states and to consider such matters as redistributing the world's supplies of gold and petroleum.

Under orders from Premier Poincaré to wreck the conference, the French foreign minister, Jean Louis Barthou, rose to demand that Chicherin keep to the agenda. What agenda? Chicherin wanted to know; no agenda existed. Then keep to the subject at hand, demanded Barthou. Seeking to restore calm, Lloyd George suggested that Chicherin not insist "on his universal, ethereal, noble, but very questionable conference" since they all would enter "the kingdom where there are neither wars nor conferences" before Monsieur Chicherin's conference would ever convene. [14]

As the assembly recessed for the weekend, Lloyd George, in an effort to salvage the conference, invited Chicherin to his residence. Raising the old, troublesome question of Russia's huge debt to Britain—$3,357,000,000—he asked if something could be done about payment. Russia would meet its obligations to England when England met its obligations to Russia, Chicherin responded: when England paid for the damage done in intervening in Russia and prolonging the civil war, when England canceled the czarist debt of $2,766,000,000, when England granted Russia nonusurious credit terms.

Chicherin's meeting with Lloyd George worried the German delegation. Were

Britain and Russia about to conclude some financial and commercial deal at Germany's expense? Playing on the German concern, one of Chicherin's party told Baron von Maltzan that the Russians did, indeed, expect to conclude some kind of deal. Von Maltzan retired to his hotel downcast, for if Russia made a deal with Britain, he saw no hope for a treaty between Russia and Germany.

It was with considerable relief that von Maltzan at one o'clock in the morning received a telephone call from Adolf Joffe, a member of the Russian delegation. If the Germans wished to conclude the treaty with Russia, said Joffe, the Russians were ready. What about the talks with the British? asked von Maltzan. They were going fine, Joffe responded, but it was Easter and Lloyd George wanted to rest.

With the coming of daylight, the two delegations left for the nearby seaside resort of Rapallo. Meeting at the Hotel Bristol on that Easter Sunday, April 16, 1922, they put their seals to the treaty.


## Chapter Twenty-Nine

A few weeks after the Germans and Russians signed the Treaty of Rapallo, the London *Morning Post* published a startling story from its Paris correspondent. The Germans and the Russians, according to the article, had signed a "military convention" on May 3, 1922, in Berlin. Although both powers denied it, there was "no doubt" that "this preparation for a united offensive war between the bankrupts [the Germans] and the bandits [the Russians] on the one hand and the Western European Powers on the other has actually been carried out."[1]

According to the *Morning Post*, Germany had agreed to provide the Red Army with weapons and equipment for 180 infantry regiments; supply artillery for twenty Russian divisions; help the Red Navy reorganize its Black and Baltic Sea fleets and repair warships in German ports; train Russian officers and noncommissioned officers "in conformity with the requirements shown by the experiences of recent years"; furnish "with the least possible delay" 500 Junkers warplanes with spare parts; send technical teams to help the Soviet government rebuild its armament industry; and build new factories for the use of the German Army at Samara (Kuybyshev) and outside Petrograd.

Intelligence officers of the United States Army in Europe came to the conclusion that the report was false. In some ways, it was; but there was also considerable truth in it, and the true facts were even more lurid.

The genesis of that strange confederacy between aristocratic, monarchistic German generals and the ex-sergeant majors commanding the Red Army went back to Karl Radek's sojourn in Moabit Prison following his arrest for suspicion of complicity in the events of Spartakus Week in January 1919. When the head of the German intelligence service during the war, Colonel Walther Nicolai, called on Radek in the prison, Radek spoke passionately of the necessity of a Russo-German alliance against the Versailles powers to prevent them from creating an independent state of Poland, a region that had been an unwavering source of friction between the Teutons and the Slavs since the ninth century. Like the rest of the German General Staff, Colonel Nicolai was concerned by the threat that a sovereign Poland would pose to the rich coal district of Upper Silesia; he promptly passed word of Radek's proposal to the man responsible for eastern affairs in the Foreign Office, Baron von Maltzan, and the former military representative on the German delegation at Versailles, General Hans von Seeckt. Both men were aware—as had been the Iron Chancellor, Bismarck, before them—of the likely high cost of an alliance between Germany and Russia, but they also saw how badly it might be needed. They also believed that despite the Comintern's perpetual attempts to disturb the tranquillity of Germany, mutual concern about Poland provided the two powers with an incentive for an alliance.

Within a few months, General von Seeckt became commander in chief of the German Army and thus one of the most powerful men in the Reich. A Pomeranian nobleman of the time when Bismarck created the German Empire and established the First Reich as the chief power on the Continent, von Seeckt was the epitome of that queer age of guns and violins. He had begun his army career with the Emperor Alexander's 1st Regiment of Foot Guards, then in 1899 became a member of that corps d'élite, the General Staff, at a time when staff officers with their three-inch, wine-red stripe down the seams of their trews were regarded with admiration akin to idolatry, a time when traffic stopped in the streets to allow them to pass.

Taking command of the German Army at the occasion of its unparalleled humiliation, von Seeckt maintained a long-held reputation for inscrutability. While noting that he could "converse charmingly and entertainingly" when he chose, a newspaper reporter also noted that he could be "mysteriously taciturn and sinister" and often met "the most temperamental utterances and insidious questions only with the enigmatic stare of his eyes." They were "gray, cold, shrewd, penetrating eyes, one of which with a certain rigid stare transfixes one through the monocle." He was, concluded the reporter, a man of such shrewdness as to "forbid him to venture into dangerous experiments."[2]

The reporter's judgment as to von Seeckt's antipathy for dangerous experiments might have been correct under ordinary circumstances, but as he took charge of the German Army, the circumstances were far from ordinary. The Treaty of Versailles had abolished the General Staff and reduced the Army to a size smaller than that of little Belgium's, and Germany's peril was immense. In the west the French were itching to occupy the Ruhr, and in the east the Poles were just as anxious to occupy Upper Silesia. There were strong separatist movements in the Rhineland and Bavaria; a powerful Red Army of the Ruhr was poised to strike; and another Red Army of 103,000 men was threatening civil war in Saxony. There had already been Communist insurrections in Berlin, North Germany, and Munich; the Monarchists would soon attempt to seize power in Berlin, and in Bavaria a Fascist movement was growing under a still obscure agitator, Adolf Hitler.

To General von Seeckt, the issue was clear: unless the German Army and the

General Staff were restored to a measure of their former power and greatness to their traditional position as the palikars of the Reich, Germany would disintegrate into a patchwork of soviets, petty kingdoms, and French and Polish client states. Yet von Seeckt was fully aware that he could never persuade the Ebert government to defy the Versailles powers and restore the Army openly; that would be to invite economic sanctions, war, or forced occupation of the country. If the German Army were to be resurrected, it had to be done in secret.

Von Seeckt's first step was to establish within Reichswehr (armed forces) headquarters an organization called the Truppenamt, or Troop Department, which, as explained to vigilant Allied observers, was responsible for the administration of the Army. That was true; yet it was also true that deep within the Truppenamt, hidden behind the serried ranks of filing cabinets, was the embryo of the General Staff. From that point von Seeckt and a minute group of his most trusted colleagues worked unceasingly to rebuild the army that had come so close to conquering Europe from the Dniester to the Seine. Almost all the eighty officers whom von Seeckt picked for training to guide the mighty army of the future were of the old military caste, and all were submitted to the severest physical and intellectual testing prior to their selection.

Since the old Kriegsakademie—the "Red Den," where, it was said, a man who passed through that illustrious but stern institution never smiled again—had been discontinued under terms of the treaty, von Seeckt's young officers attended special courses conducted secretly in the country's great universities. The courses were difficult, and not all the candidates survived them to join that odd band of monks and chevaliers and gentleman killers that constituted the General Staff. General von Seeckt's objective was to preserve what he called the *Generalstabsoffiziermentalität*, and he succeeded under the noses of the suspicious bloodhounds of the Allied Control Commission, whose duty it was to track every spoor of revived German militarism.

So too with the Officer Corps. Allowed to have only 4,000 officers, von Seeckt paid the most careful attention to their selection, personally assessing character, ability, intelligence, and blood. Although he preferred patrician sons, especially of the East Elbian Junkerdom, he was no bigot; one of his appointments who was to become one of Germany's greatest generals was the bastard son of a Jew. As training progressed, von Seeckt personally pruned the candidates, for each officer had to be capable of assuming higher command at a moment's notice with no additional training. Such was the success of his recruitment policy that not a single officer betrayed his scheme.

General von Seeckt was similarly meticulous in the choice of noncommissioned officers, the traditional backbone of the German Army. By an odd oversight, the Treaty of Versailles had failed to specify the number of noncommissioned officers who might serve, so that of the 96,000 men authorized for the ranks, von Seeckt allotted to noncommissioned officers 44,000, each man selected on the basis of his ability later to become an officer. He also specified similarly high standards for privates, insisting on men of intelligence, physical fitness, and resource; for when a new day dawned, every man was to be capable of becoming either a noncommissioned officer or an officer.

Yet however carefully selected the officers and the rank and file, without new and continuing development of arms, equipment, and tactics, the force would stagnate. To avoid that, General von Seeckt turned simultaneously to German industry and to the Red Army.

Von Seeckt's first contact with the Bolsheviks occurred in April 1920, when to the relief of the German General Staff, the Russo-Polish War erupted. With a view to establishing a collaboration with a victorious Red Army, von Seeckt sought out the Russian, Victor Kopp, who was ostensibly working on prisoner exchange but was spending more time revolutionizing the Ruhr. The collapse of the Red Army before Warsaw delayed any Russo-German arrangement, but so shattering had been the defeat that it convinced Lenin of the necessity of rebuilding his proletarian army along German lines. When in the spring of 1921, he approached the German government secretly for military assistance, von Seeckt was ready.

Believing an approach from the Russians to be but a matter of time, von Seeckt had already formed within the Truppenamt an organization called Sondergruppe R—Special Group Russia—under Colonel Nicolai, whose task was to organize and supervise military relations with Russia. In September 1921, von Seeckt arranged a military convention through the Soviet trade commissar, Leonid Krassin, an agreement for mutual collaboration in the development of arms and munitions. The German chancellor and finance minister, Joseph Wirth, who was regarded in some circles as so sympathetic to the Bolsheviks as to be in effect a Soviet agent,[3] was aware of the arrangement, as was the foreign minister, Walther Rathenau, and the head of the Eastern Department in the Foreign Office, Baron von Maltzan; but few other members of the government were in on it.

In furtherance of the agreement, the Germans founded a private trading organization called the Company for the Promotion of Industrial Enterprises. Capitalized at the considerable sum of 75 million reichsmarks, the company established offices in Berlin and Moscow, the one in Moscow called Wiko-Z, or the Economic Commission, and located in the German Embassy. The company's chief tasks were to establish a Junkers aircraft factory near Moscow, capable of producing 600 all-metal aircraft annually, along with spare parts; to form a joint Russo-German company for manufacturing poison gas at Troitsk in Samara; and to arrange production of 300,000 artillery shells annually at Russian factories in Tula, Petrograd, and Schlüsselburg (Petrokrepost).

Of even greater importance was an arrangement for large numbers of German officers and men to undergo training in Russia in aviation and armor, for by 1920 the world stood on the brink of a new form of warfare first proposed by Colonel J. F. C. Fuller of the Royal Tank Corps, the man who had devised the plan for the first use of tanks to obtain a strategic decision. Known as Plan 1919, Fuller's proposal envisaged infantry pinning the enemy to the main front while motorized infantry and tanks executed deep encirclement drives on the flanks and while aircraft took out the enemy's headquarters with bombs.[4]

The Russo-German military convention enabled the German General Staff to action-test the new theory beyond the sight and knowledge of the Allied Control Commission at the great tank testing grounds on the silent steppe east of Kazan. Having developed the first panzer, the Germans installed in it a primitive voice-radio that enabled the tank commander to talk with pilots in aircraft overhead. With that development, Plan 1919 began to change into what the world would come to know as blitzkrieg.

Also of importance to the Germans was intelligence gained about Soviet military personalities, doctrine, and capabilities. Between 1925 and 1933, almost the entire Red Army High Command (more than 150 officers) spent from a month to a year in Germany studying German military techniques and in the process revealing inevitably something of themselves. Among them were the rising young officer General Mikhail Tukachevsky, and two others destined for High Command: Generals Georgi Zhukov and Konstantin Rokossovsky. Eminent German generals visited Russia in similar numbers.

It is an axiom of politics that where there is a free press, secrets do not remain secrets for long, and in the Germany of the 1920s, the press was free. How long would the Russo-German military convention stay a secret? As early as 1922, Lloyd George was aware of a secret military understanding between the two powers, but since he feared a German soviet more than he feared Germany rearmed, he chose not to reveal what he knew. Yet the secret was bound to come out eventually.

In late 1923, at a trooping of the colors at Königsberg Castle, the suspicions of the American military attaché, Lieutenant Colonel Creed Fulton Cox, were aroused. During a magnificent torchlight ceremony with massed bands, Colonel Cox noted that for every German soldier, there were three or four others of military age, bearing, and appearance wearing Army-type uniforms but with symbols and facings unfamiliar to him. Making inquiries, he learned that the men were in the Arbeits-Kommando, or AK; they had formerly served in the Army but were then employed as volunteer civilian laborers working for the Army on short-term contracts to build roads, dig ditches, and perform kitchen and clerical services. That explanation failed to satisfy Colonel Cox, for the men appeared to be members of some paramilitary force, which was forbidden by the Versailles Treaty. After further inquiry, he learned that the AK was also known as the Black Reichswehr, a term with connotations of clandestinity, and that they lived in the barracks with the regular troops, drew the same rations, engaged in drills and training, and received their pay not from some contractor but from the local Army paymaster.

The AK was, indeed, a paramilitary force, working in relationship to regular Army commanders in the same way as had the Trained Bands of the Dark Ages, units composed usually of peasants who worked on their liege lord's estate in peacetime and fought at his side in war. Using that ancient principle, von Seeckt had formed the AK to reinforce the ranks of his 100,000-man Army, particularly in units serving on the eastern frontier, and like the regular troops, they had taken the *Fahneneid*, that ancient and personal oath of allegiance. Like paramilitary forces, the *Fahneneid* had been expressly forbidden by the Treaty of Versailles.

By 1923, there had also reappeared in Germany the ancient Teutonic secret societies with all their mysticism, ritual, terror, and brutality. Although von Seeckt discouraged any connection between them and the Army, some officers used the societies to dispose of informants. In one such case, an AK named Wilms, who had informed the local police of the connection between the AK and the Army, was executed under orders of his commanding officer. Police inquiries into the murder revealed that the secret societies had infiltrated the AK, where they acted in much the same manner as the medieval *Femegerichte*, the secret courts of which Sir Walter Scott wrote in *Anne of Geierstein*. An important element in German criminal law in the fifteenth and sixteenth centuries, those courts consisted of "holy bands" sworn to "the utmost secrecy, who dispensed, by means of a system of terror, a brutal but efficient form of justice."[5]

When the story of Wilms' murder broke in the German press, a long trial followed, involving an eight-man group accused of the murder and in the process exposing the existence of the AK. The men were members of a group of 200 who worked on baronial estates, all of them ex-soldiers who "only awaited the signal to regain their command." They and others like them were an organic but secret part of the Army, and within each major component there existed a "Detachment for Special Purposes," charged with "watching and quietly removing such members . . . as were suspected of reporting or intending to report to the police . . . or alleged to carry information to the Allied Control Commission." There had been, the court was told, some twenty *Femen*, as the secret courts were called, and in each case the accused had been "put away."[6]

Although General von Seeckt survived the revelations of the Wilms case, so damaged was his reputation by it that any other revelation of imprudence was bound to ruin him. An ever-vigilant leftist press was to see to it that such a revelation would in time come about.

Just as the German Army was secretly struggling to regain its former power and authority, so too the German Navy was engaged in a weighty intrigue to regain its place as one of the world's first fleets. Yet as with the Army, so with the Navy: under the Versailles Treaty, the German Navy was permitted to have only those few battleships built before the turn of the century, a few inshore warships, and no submarines at all. On the last the treaty was explicit, for it specified that "The construction or acquisition of any submarine, even for commercial purposes, shall be forbidden in Germany."[7] The German Navy was also forbidden to experiment with or produce any of the weapons of underseas warfare, including torpedoes, mines, and acoustic detection devices. Stationing the most vigilant observers at German shipyards and naval munitions factories, the Allied Control Commission by 1923 was confident that all German submarine design and construction was at an end.

That was to overlook the business acumen of two German naval officers, Captain Walter Lohmann, who had served during the war in the Kriegsmarine's naval intelligence department, and Lieutenant Commander Wilhelm Franz Canaris, one of the founders of the Etappendienst, which had been the German Fleet's worldwide intelligence and supply organization. Starting in 1920, their connivance resulted in the saga of what became known as Lohmann Enterprises.

The corporation had its origins in the "Ruhr Funds," some 200,000 gold reichsmarks (about $50,000) thought to have come from the great industrial combine, Krupp. With the money, Lohmann established the Navis Corporation at 30 Lützowufer in Berlin and set out to transmute the Ruhr Funds into a fortune to be placed at the disposal of the German Navy for the clandestine rebuilding of the German fleet and the Etappendienst.

Although the German war minister, Otto Kessler, would reveal some facts about the Lohmann Enterprises to the Reichstag in 1927, it was not until after World War II when the Supreme Allied Commander, General Dwight D. Eisenhower, called for a report on clandestine German rearmament, that appreciable detail would emerge. The principal informant, Leopold Heinemann, reported that Lohmann was soon producing income for the Navy that far exceeded official appropriations.[8] Concealed in the military and naval budgets as *Sonderfonds*, or Black Funds, the first contributions came from proceeds of commodity deals in which the Navis Corporation bought on credit and sold long for gold or hard currencies, which Navis then used to engage in currency transactions and speculation. With some of the profits from those transactions, Lohmann established three groups of businesses.

The first group purchased small shipyards and shipping companies in Germany and Spain with the underlying purpose of building fast small craft that could be turned into motor-torpedo boats, yachts that could be converted to submarine chasers, and tankers that could become fleet oilers. One plant built in Spain partly with funds supplied by Lohmann and partly by the Basque millionaire Horacio Echeverria, built torpedoes and fire-control equipment. The group also provided facilities for fostering youthful interest in such naval matters as radiotelegraphy and seamanship.[9]

A second group revolved around the Phoebus Film Corporation, which produced "reliable" motion pictures intended "to procure the renewal of the German spirit" and "awaken an understanding for true German character abroad." Lohmann purchased a chain of cinemas which showed mostly Phoebus films, and the parent corporation provided cover for naval intelligence operations throughout the world.

A third group engaged in a variety of enterprises, such as investing in patents, including a new system for raising sunken ships; iron exploration in the Erzegebirge; and the building of a bacon rendering plant, primarily for sales to Britain in order to earn sterling for reestablishing the Etappendienst.

But their most important and expensive project involved the clandestine reforging of the Fleet's submarine arm, achieved primarily through Lohmann's financing of a Dutch submarine design company, Ingenieurskantoor voor Scheepsbouw (IvS) in The Hague. The first IvS project resulted in the sale of plans for submarines and minelayers to Japan and the building of the vessels in Japan under German supervision, thereby providing the Germans practical experience in modern submersible naval architecture and weaponry. The Turks bought two of IvS's 500-ton submarines; the Spaniards two 750-ton submarines; and the Finns a 100-ton submarine and three of 500 tons. In Spain, German torpedo engineers worked on such innovations as a splashless torpedo discharge system, while at the Soviet naval base at Kronstadt, others experimented with trackless electrical torpedos. In conjunction with the Finns, other engineers worked on submarine prefabrication and assembly and developed a 250-ton submarine that was destined to become the model for a subsequent German series, U1-U24. German sailors trained on the submarines built for foreign sale, thereby providing a nucleus for the crews of the World War II U-boat Fleet. As would be revealed only after the war, Lohmann sold Russia plans for the IvS "S"-type submarine, which served as the mainstay of the Red Navy's Submarine Fleet during the war.

Lohmann Enterprises also provided financing for an embryonic German Fleet Air Arm and some of the funds for preserving large airbases at Holtenau and Norderney; established a naval aviation bureau that became the nucleus of the Kondor long-range maritime reconnaissance squadrons of World War II; established a bureau to collect foreign military and technical journals; provided civil aircraft to enable naval pilots to train; funded clubs for ex-naval officers and airmen; and conducted costly experiments with remote-controlled aircraft.

In time, Lohmann Enterprises controlled twenty-eight companies and thirty-two naval institutions that would be able to provide the essential cadres for rebuilding the Kriegsmarine. In 1935, for example, it would be discovered that Germany was capable of building a submarine every eight days and floating numbers of them with trained crews. Yet Lohmann was destined to receive no gratitude from his country, for in 1927, when he dismissed one of the directors of the Phoebus Film Corporation, a scandal ensued. The sacked director went to the *Berliner Tageblatt* with a report on government funding of a major film production, which produced an outcry from the press and the left wing of the Reichstag for an end to *Sonderfonds*. When the government dropped credit guarantees, Phoebus went bankrupt, and when it emerged that Lohmann had switched assets from other companies to cover Phoebus, several of the companies were compelled to put a moratorium on cash transactions.

When the government appointed a commission to investigate Lohmann

Enterprises, it soon emerged that there were numbers of other Black Funds in scores of bank accounts. Most people assumed that Lohmann was guilty of peculation, and the war minister and the commander in chief of the Navy were forced to resign; but it would eventually be established that the suspicions of peculation leveled at him were unjustified. The man was utterly honest. "The main driving power and cause for my actions," he would later state, "was a quite natural, simple love for my Fatherland." As a man who kept some of Lohmann's accounts and later wrote a final report on the Lohmann Enterprises for the German armed forces High Command, Captain Walter Schüssler, would note: "The fact remains that the greater part of his undertakings were of considerable military value which especially now [1937] . . . is of importance for the basis of quick constructional work" leading to counteracting "the most disgraceful of peace treaties that the world had ever known." Yet as a member of the government's investigating committee put it: Lohmann "had too many pots on the fire and did not notice when some of them burned or boiled over."

## Chapter Thirty

On the 24th of June 1922, the kaiser's son, Prince Eitel Friedrich, made his way to the Friedenskirche in Potsdam, where the bones of the Emperor Friedrich Wilhelm IV and the Empress Elizabeth lay in a crypt before the altar. Present in the church were Field Marshal von Hindenburg and 150 novices of the Johanniten Order, a Monarchist society of Teuton knights founded by Friedrich Barbarossa, the Holy Roman Emperor of the Dark Ages who according to legend was asleep in a cave in the Bavarian Alps awaiting the call to come forth and restore Germany to greatness. Since the monarchy and its associated societies had been proscribed by the Treaty of Versailles, the gathering at the Friedenskirche was illegal. The prince, who was the Grand Master of the Johanniten Order, nevertheless led the novitiates in reciting the ancient oath, the *Fahneneid*.[1] The ceremony completed, Prince Eitel and the new members of the Johanniten Order repaired to the Horse Guards Club for lunch and the usual discussions on how to restore the Hohenzollern monarchy, to destroy the Bolsheviks in Germany, to terminate the Treaty of Rapallo with the Kremlin and the Treaty of Versailles with the Allies, and to eject the foreign armies from German soil.

Perhaps it was mere coincidence that the royal conclave occurred on the very day that the Black Reichswehr murdered Walther Rathenau.

The man who was in large measure responsible for the Treaty of Rapallo, Walther Rathenau, was a millionaire Jew; in the streets, the extreme right wing, pro-monarchy Freikorps, which existed largely to fight the Bolsheviks, sang a ditty about him:

*Knallt ab den Walther Rathenau,*
*Die Gottverflüchte Judensau.*

Shoot down Walther Rathenau,
He's a goddamn dirty Jew.

In May 1922, Chancellor Wirth had received information that an extremist right-wing group specializing in assassination, Organization C, had marked Rathenau for death. The gunmen were already in Berlin, Wirth's advices told him, and the attack might take place at any time. Although Wirth offered police protection, Rathenau declined it.

Walther Rathenau was the son of an ironmaster who had bought the European license for Thomas A. Edison's electric light bulb and later founded an immense combine, Allgemeine-Elektrizitäts-Gesellschaft (AEG), to which his son succeeded. During the World War, Walther Rathenau had headed a strategic raw materials department in the War Ministry. As a member of the European capitalist monopoly, he would write: "Three hundred men, all acquainted with each other, control the economic destiny of the Continent."[2] Intensely nationalistic, he had demanded that rather than agree to an armistice, Germany be called to arms in a *levée en masse,* and after the war he raised $5 million in support of the Freikorps.

Tall, with dark eyes, a bald head and gray-flecked black beard, Rathenau was widely distrusted and often disliked, for in the manner of a gamekeeper turned poacher, he was a capitalist turned liberal. His friend, the Austrian writer Stefan Zweig, noted that "In speaking with him, one felt stupid, faultily educated, uncertain and confused in the presence of his calm, deliberate and clear-thinking objectivity . . . there was something in the blinding brilliance, the crystal clarity of his thinking, just as there was something in the choice furniture and fine pictures in his home, that made one feel uncomfortable."[3]

When Joseph Wirth became chancellor in 1921, he first brought Rathenau into the Cabinet as reconstruction minister, a position Rathenau accepted largely because he believed that arguments against the Treaty of Versailles were futile, that the Germans had to "discover some means of linking ourselves to the world." It was that attitude that sealed his doom, for as a member of Organization C put it, "there was only one political common denominator that held the whole 'national movement' together at that time and . . . it amounted to this: 'We must make an end to . . . the Versailles Treaty and cooperating with the West.'"[4] So too his role as foreign minister in arranging the Treaty of Rapallo alienated the rightists, for they saw the treaty as a license for creeping Communism. In intelligence circles in Berlin, it was whispered that Rathenau had connived with Lloyd George to negotiate the treaty so that trade with Russia and the work it would produce for German factories would make it possible for Germany to pay the huge reparations.

The three men selected by Organization C to murder Rathenau were a twenty-one-year-old son of a Berlin magistrate, Ernest-Werner Techow, who was to drive the murder car, and two who were to do the killing, a twenty-five-year-old former naval lieutenant, Erwin Kern, and a twenty-five-year-old engineer, Herman Fischer. On June 24, 1922, a Saturday morning, about 11:40 A.M., as Rathenau left his mansion in Berlin-Grunewald in an open car, the assassins followed, also in an open car. As Techow pulled his car up alongside Rathenau's, Kern rested the butt of a long-barreled pistol in an armpit and opened fire, while Fischer threw a hand grenade decorated with a ribbon of red, white, and black, the colors of the extremist Monarchist societies.

Rathenau was mortally wounded. Three of Kern's bullets struck him, and the blast from the grenade tore away his jaw. Before his chauffeur could get him back to his home, he was dead.

The murder plunged Germany into an intense state of anger and turmoil. "The political feeling aroused by the assassination among the leaders of all Republican and Socialist parties, who lay the murder at the doors of the extreme Monarchistic secret societies," noted an American military observer, "is at this time very great, and we cannot tell what the next few days will bring."[5] As the Communists stirred the people against Monarchists, rightists, and Nationalists, so intense were emotions that even three days after the murder mass demonstrations were still occurring in Berlin, Lübeck, Breslau, Hamburg, and Darmstadt.

In the Reichstag, Chancellor Wirth spoke bitterly against the assassins and against people who supported and financed such terrorist groups as Organization C. He attacked Prince Eitel Friedrich and the Johanniten Order for holding their initiation ceremony and intimated that the Grand Master and other members of the order knew more about the Monarchist-militarist societies than they would reveal.

When the government finally acted, passing a law which provided for the death penalty for political assassins and for anybody belonging to or providing financial assistance to organizations advocating political murder, it merely added to the turmoil. Suspecting that the law was aimed as much at leftists as rightists, the Communists demanded the removal of all Monarchist officers from the Army and dispersal of all right-wing organizations, such as the Freikorps and Hitler's private army, the Sturmabteilung. Rightists just as strongly assailed the new law, and as the government tried to implement it, civil war had never seemed closer.

In Bavaria, Hitler emerged from a brief stay in prison for inciting a riot just in time to join the demonstrations against the law. It was nothing more, he cried at a rally, than "a means for reducing all criticism to silence."[6]

As the nation's emotions continued to run at full tide, police arrested the driver of the murder car, Ernest-Werner Techow. He had participated, said Techow, because he was told that Rathenau was "one of the three hundred Elders of Zion who were seeking to bring the world under the rule of the Jews," a reference to the ·Protocols of the Elders of Zion, which the *Völkischer Beobachter*, like newspapers in Britain and the United States, had recently published. In Techow's confession, he named the assassins, Edwin Kern and Herman Fischer. The subsequent odyssey of those two men would demonstrate the power and extent of the secret societies within Germany, for even though police blanketed the country with posters displaying their photographs and issued a million-mark bounty, there was no hint of their whereabouts.

Immediately after the murder, Kern and Fischer had gone to the Alexanderplatz to observe the public reaction, then taken a steamer on Lake Wannsee to Warnemünde, where they intended to catch the packet for Sweden. When they missed the boat, a member of Organization C gave them an address near Bad Kösen, about 150 miles south of Berlin, where they might hide.

By that time, voluntary subscriptions had increased the bounty on the two men to 4 million marks, but despite that large reward, they safely made their way by bicycle to Bad Kösen, where the owner of Burg Saaleck, a Dr. Stein, gave them sanctuary in one of the two turrets of the castle while Organization C maneuvered to get them out of the country. Arrangements were virtually complete when on the evening of July 16, 1922, a villager noted a light burning in the eastern turret of Burg Saaleck; aware that the entrance and staircase to the turret had long been boarded up, he informed the police.

Before daybreak the next morning, police entered the tower and started up the narrow stone staircase. As they neared the top, Kern appeared with the same pistol he had used to shoot Rathenau. The police retreated to await reinforcements. When over a hundred more policemen arrived, Kern and Fischer climbed out on the battlements to shoot it out. "We live and die for ideals," they cried. "Others will follow us."[7] They were soon dead and lying in the forecourt of the castle, their corpses protected from the steady rain by a tarpaulin. The first Fascist "soldiers" of the Fascist-Communist war had fallen.

As the first ambassador from the German Republic to Moscow, Count von Brockdorff-Rantzau, whose unhappy lot it had been to receive the Allied terms at Versailles, prepared to board his sleeping car at the Friedrichstrasse Station on the evening of October 30, 1922, he was in a mood of high optimism. The staff of the Wilhelmstrasse, as the Foreign Office was called, was on hand to see him off, and Baron von Maltzan presented him a bottle of French cognac from 1871, the year in which the German Empire had been established on the ruins of Napoleon III's dictatorship. The pretty gesture drew a polished quip from von Brockdorff: *"In hoc signo vinces!"*

The new ambassador's optimism was based on the fact that he had already established a friendly, even intimate, relationship with the Soviet foreign commissar, Georgi Chicherin. That kind of relationship boded well for the policy that von Brockdorff had in mind, one of countering the victorious Allied powers by a close relationship with the Russians, "to fight the ignominious *Diktat* of Versailles successfully from Moscow and possibly throw the whole infamy overboard."[8]

Arriving at the old Nicolas Station in Moscow on November 2, 1922, von

Brockdorff received immediate evidence that there would be testy moments in the new relationship, for except for a welcoming party from the German Embassy and a few station officials and porters, the platform was deserted. Although he would protest to Chicherin about the "insulting and shabby" reception, he was actually well aware that any Russo-German relationship was likely to be tempestuous and that the man who was to become his agreeable dinner companion, Chicherin, was a Bolshevik revolutionary first and a gentleman second.[9]

One of the great eccentrics of the Bolshevik Revolution, Georgi Vassilievich Chicherin had been born into a family of czarist diplomats. A wispy, sickly, chaotic man, Chicherin worked with a consuming passion to try to persuade the world that the proletarian revolution would precipitate no apocalypse. He was genuinely concerned with "the sorry conditions of the underprivileged, the cause of their social and economic inferiority, and the road which would lead the peoples of Russia and other countries to their final emancipation and enfranchisement."[10]

Thus dedicated, Chicherin acted, even while serving as foreign commissar, as advocate, confessor, apologist, and Praetorian for the organization that was charged with engineering the world revolution, the Comintern. He pursued the goals of the revolution with an abundance of energy that belied his bony little frame and in the process astonished the cynical, remote, superior diplomatic world that he lived in. In pursuing his cause, Chicherin worked by night and slept by day, keeping his staff at his side but doing most of the work himself. To those who complained, Chicherin would remark that while Moscow slept, most of the other great capitals were awake, and somebody had to be on duty in Moscow to guard the revolution.

As Count von Brockdorff-Rantzau was soon aware, that dedication to revolution included revolution in Germany. Near the close of the summer of 1923, he learned that Trotsky had met with other Bolshevik leaders, including Chicherin, and concluded that if revolution came in Germany, the Red Army should intervene "to assure the ultimate victory of the proletariat." When two leading German revolutionaries, Heinrich Brandler and August Thalheimer, visited Moscow, the Comintern hierarchs received them with ceremony while the official press proclaimed: "The fate of the German revolution is our fate; defeat of the German revolution is also our defeat."[11] In Berlin, police and military intelligence officers discovered on premises belonging to the German Communist Party large quantities of machine guns and munitions that had been purchased by the Soviet military attaché in Berlin, Mikhail Petrov.

When von Brockdorff protested, Chicherin replied that it was the work not of the Soviet government but of the Comintern. In the final analysis, demanded von Brockdorff, who directed Russian foreign policy, the government or the Comintern? In one memorable meeting, von Brockdorff told Chicherin that Germany was "no experimental rabbit which Moscow could use for the purpose of testing its ideas for saving the world"; if the Comintern continued its activities, the time would come when he would find that "the Moscow climate" no longer agreed with him.[12]

Chicherin was clearly aware of how much Germany needed Russia and thus that von Brockdorff's implied threat was essentially empty. Yet even had he seen it otherwise, there would have been little he could have done about it, for when viewed from Moscow, conditions in Germany were so conducive to revolution that whoever controlled Soviet foreign policy would have come to the same conclusion: it was time for a Comintern-supported revolt of the German proletariat.

In the fateful year of 1923, who could say in what direction Germany was heading? The Monarchists were trying to arrange a return of the Hohenzollerns; the Black Reichswehr was trying to create a Fascist state of thatched cottages and sturdy Teutonic peasants who would worship the solstices and Nordic runes; Adolf Hitler was trying to establish his own racially purged Fascist state; and the democrats were trying to hold the republic together while fighting a raging inflation that threatened to destroy all economic life. Using as an excuse German failure to deliver 200,000 telephone poles to France and Belgium under the reparations agreements, the French and Belgians sent seven divisions to occupy the Ruhr, that region of mines and smelters just east of the Rhine that was essential to the life of the German nation; and as President Friedrich Ebert's government encouraged the burghers of the Ruhr in a general strike and a campaign of passive resistance that quickly approached the dimensions of guerrilla warfare, an already tottering German currency collapsed to a degree never before known in modern society, not even in the debacle that had beset the Russian ruble after the October Revolution. In 1918, the value of the mark had stood at 4.20 to the dollar; by the fall of 1923, it took 6,014,300 marks to equal a single 1918 mark. The orchestra conductor Bruno Walter would recall that his fee for a concert, 130 million marks, was just enough to buy a small bag of salt; after a concert, the pianist Artur Schnabel paid half of his fee of 180 million for a sausage, but when he returned the next morning in hope of buying another, he found that overnight inflation had advanced at such a rate that he was short 32 million of the purchase price. Long-held family fortunes were wiped out overnight; pensioners and others living on fixed incomes were quickly destitute; profiteers and opportunistic foreigners who had gold or foreign currency bought up jewelry and real estate at ridiculously small real outlay. Except for the barter system, the basis of human industry was destroyed.

A nation so beset by economic malaise—so it seemed from Moscow—was obviously susceptible to revolution. When the general strike in the Ruhr spread to Berlin in August 1923, it seemed impossible that revolution could fail. Meeting on August 23, 1923, the Politburo and the Comintern's Executive Committee concluded that the time had come for revolution in Germany. Through the halls of the Russian proletariat echoed a new slogan: "Russian Youth, learn German! The German October is approaching!"

Masquerading as nature lovers on the way to a hiking tour in the Black Forest, a politico-military group under a Soviet secret police general, Peter A. Skoblensky, arrived in Berlin in the middle of September to help the German Communists and resident Comintern plenipotentiaries to organize the revolution; another arrival was a Soviet military intelligence officer, Walter Krivitsky, who came from The Hague, where he was posing as an art dealer. Russian commercial representatives throughout Western Europe received instructions from the Soviet government to establish wheat and gold reserves to support the German proletariat during the revolution, while the Russians stockpiled 4.5 million tons of wheat near their western frontier to be used should Britain and France institute a naval blockade against a newly established Soviet Reich. Victor Kopp, at that point head of the Foreign Commissariat's Department for the Baltic States and Poland, visited the capitals of those countries to ensure that should the Red Army have to intervene in Germany to protect the victorious proletarian revolution against military intervention by Britain and France, the Baltic States and Poland would remain neutral.

Under the plan as devised by Trotsky and Zinoviev, the revolution was to begin in Saxony and Thuringia, where the trusted Heinrich Brandler and August Thalheimer were to arm the proletariat and mobilize their "Red Centurions." The German October was to begin on November 7, 1923, the anniversary of the October Revolution in Russia.

What the Comintern's leaders failed to take into account was the possibility that before the revolution opened, something might happen to lessen the chaos that enveloped Germany. Yet even as the Comintern was taking the decision to engineer a revolution, President Ebert was appointing a new chancellor, a specialist in the economics of chocolate manufacture, Gustav Stresemann, and charging him with the task of bringing order to the republic. A portly man who to foreigners personified the wartime cartoons of the Hun—he was square, ponderous, beef-red, bald, bullet-headed, stiff, humorless, implacable—Stresemann was a nimble politician with considerable intelligence and courage.

He embarked on his mission by assigning the post of Reich commissioner of currency stabilization to the president of the Darmstadt Bank, Hjalmar Horace Greeley Schacht. Immediately stopping the mint from printing more money, Schacht lopped twelve zeros off the value of the existing currency; since the Reich lacked sufficient gold on which to base the currency and give it value, he turned to a psychological standard: the Rentenmark, which would be negotiable for Rentenbriefe, bills bearing interest, which would be guaranteed by the land values of the nation and the obligations of business, industry, and the banks. As was quickly pointed out, "there was no practicable way land values or industrial paper could cover the mark in this fashion unless people accepted the fiction that they could," but that the German people did. "With limits set on government borrowing, it was enough for millions of Germans, avid for any kind of stable currency, to fall upon the new marks, one of which could be had for 1,000 billion of the old ones."[13]

At the same time, Stresemann, who hated the Treaty of Versailles as much as any German, moved to end the campaign of passive resistance to French and Belgian occupation of the Ruhr. It was, in his view, accomplishing nothing other than to contribute to the currency crisis and to hostile relations with the Allied powers. If Germany were to regain its position in the family of nations, Stresemann believed, rapport would have to be established with the victorious powers.

Stresemann and Schacht thus brought hope to a people craving stability. Their policies also brought a considerable wealth to the German Communist Party. Because the Comintern had financed the German party in dollars, sterling, and gold, Schacht's policy of lopping off twelve zeros to create the Rentenmark had made the party rich, but its leaders were reluctant to risk those riches in a revolutionary contest of arms with a government that was demonstrating a marked ability to govern. So, too, the end of passive resistance in the Ruhr had allowed passions to cool, and the general strike was over.

"As obedient as corpses," some 400 German party leaders nevertheless assembled at Zinoviev's behest in the old Wendish capital of Chemnitz in Southeast Germany to hear the Comintern's call to the barricades. Fresh from Moscow, the Communist leader from Saxony, Heinrich Brandler, delivered the call, demanding a return to the general strike and ordering the arming of the proletariat. Yet Brandler saw immediately that the party leaders seated before him, "90 per cent good solid working-class men . . . people who had fought before, not just through words, but with firearms," lacked the old revolutionary zeal. As the issue approached a vote, it was clear that the Comintern's call to arms would be rejected.

Brandler's colleague from Thuringia, Ernst Thaelmann, also saw how the vote was heading. Leaving the conference, he rushed outside where messengers were waiting to depart for all parts of Germany with sealed instructions directing local party organizations to begin the revolution. "Clear off! Get going!" Thaelmann told the couriers. "It's all agreed!"[14]

When Thaelmann told Brandler what he had done, Brandler was appalled, for so decisive had been the vote against revolution that he saw no hope that a revolution would succeed. If the rank and file manned the barricades without the support of the party leadership, disaster was sure to follow. On Brandler's order, messengers rushed to the railway station to intercept the couriers and bring them back; they were successful in every case but one: the courier to Hamburg had caught his train.

Even as a motorcyclist hurried to Hamburg to cancel the instructions, the Hamburg Executive received the sealed orders, opened them, and in the belief that a national insurrection was about to begin, ordered the cadres to arms.

Although the Hamburg branch of the party had at the time 14,000 members, scarcely 200 responded to the call. Those few stormed police stations and over the next three days would continue to battle the police, but no mass uprising developed. "Thousands went past these fighters every day," noted Klara Zetkin, a lame grandmother who was a protagonist within the Comintern executive for women's liberation, but "they kept their hands in their pockets." The masses, she reported to Trotsky and Zinoviev, "remained dumb." [15]

The failure depressed the leaders of the Comintern. "We can accept defeat in battle," said Zinoviev, "but when a revolutionary party lands itself in a derisory position . . . it is worse than defeat." Occurring at a time of growing tensions within the Bolshevik Party in Russia between supporters of Stalin and adherents of Trotsky, it severely damaged Trotsky's position, for he stood condemned of having committed the grave political sin of so misjudging the situation as to attempt a revolution before the proletariat was ready.

Like the leaders of the Comintern, Adolf Hitler also judged that the German people were ready for revolution. By mid-October 1923, so inflammatory were his speeches—in his usual hypnotic style, he called for "a national revolution" to "cleanse" the "Jew-Marxist" capital, "that whore of a city, that pig sty, that Babel" [16]—and so crude and violent the depredations of his followers that Chancellor Stresemann called on the Bavarian government to restrain him. Yet that was hard for the Bavarian president, Eugene von Knilling, to do, for even among those Bavarians who deplored Hitler's methods, there was strong sympathy for his dream of a strong, rejuvenated Germany.

A former Hitler acolyte who had recanted, Gustav von Kahr, whom von Knilling had appointed as state commissioner with emergency powers to counter the grave political turmoil that beset the state, shared the president's reluctance to act, as did the head of the Reichswehr in Bavaria, General Otto von Lossow. When Berlin specifically ordered von Lossow to curb Hitler and ban his newspaper, he dallied at such length that General von Seeckt in Berlin dismissed him, which so angered von Knilling that in the name of the Bavarian government he assumed command of all Army units stationed in Bavaria. The officers in turn renounced the Weimar Republic and swore allegiance to the Bavarian government. It was mutiny, bloodless, but nonetheless mutiny.

A few days later, in an article in the *Münchener Zeitung*, Commissioner von Kahr attacked the Stresemann government, claiming that it was dominated by Marxists, and General von Lossow reportedly declared that there were but three choices for Bavaria: proceeding along the same old aimless way, seceding from the Reich, or marching on Berlin. Von Knilling, von Kahr, and von Lossow were agreed that the government in Berlin should be overthrown, but they would act only in concert with nationalist organizations throughout the country, not in conjunction with sectional extremist organizations such as Hitler's National Socialists.

For Hitler, the big concern was that the ruling triumvirate in Bavaria might proclaim Bavarian independence and return the Wittelsbach monarchy while doing nothing about Berlin. Even when the triumvirate refused to act in conjunction with the Nazis, Hitler incited his followers to action; on the evening of October 30, 1923, he told a wildly cheering audience: "We all feel that the hour has come and like the soldier in the field, we will not shirk our duty as Germans."[17] A few days later, he decided to strike on the following Sunday, November 11, 1923, the fifth anniversary of Germany's capitulation, a day on which government offices would be deserted, the guard at military and police posts reduced, and the streets relatively free of traffic, thus enabling his storm troopers to march unimpeded. Although the main thrust of the Putsch would be in Munich, where Hitler's private army would outnumber Army troops and the police almost two to one, there would be takeovers of key installations in all cities throughout Bavaria.

On November 7, 1923, von Kahr announced a mass patriotic demonstration to be held the next night in the Bürgerbräukeller in Munich, ostensibly to outline the aims of his regime but actually to make a show of unity in order to discourage any act by Hitler and the National Socialists. To Hitler, the meeting posed a crisis: was von Kahr about to announce a break with Berlin and return of the monarchy? Yet to Hitler the meeting also posed a remarkable opportunity: through a dramatic takeover of the gathering, he might convince von Kahr and von Lossow to join forces with him.

A large, rambling building containing a number of dining rooms and bars and a main hall seating 3,000, the Bürgerbräukeller was a half mile from the center of Munich, on the other side of the Isar. The main hall was packed and von Kahr was delivering a droning, pedantic lecture from the platform when Hitler arrived outside in a red Mercedes and entered an anteroom off the main hall to await the arrival of his storm troopers.

As the troopers arrived in trucks, the police in and around the Bürgerbräukeller melted away. Entering the main hall from the anteroom, Hitler and his entourage strode toward the podium. Pandemonium took over, tables overturned, some people made for the exits only to find them blocked by Hitler's brown-shirted troopers. When the press of the crowd blocked Hitler's way, he leaped upon a chair, yelled for quiet, and fired a bullet into the ceiling from his revolver. In the stunned silence that followed, Hitler shouted: "The national revolution has begun!" The hall, he said, was surrounded by armed men. "The Bavarian government and the national government have been overthrown, and a provisional government is being formed. The barracks of the *Reichswehr* and the state police have been occupied; the *Reichswehr* and the state police are already approaching under the swastika flag."[18]

Reaching the tribunal, Hitler beckoned von Kahr and von Lossow to join him in a side room. It was, Hitler told them, the first step in the national revolution. General Ludendorff, he said, was to lead the march on Berlin, and once the national government had fallen, there would be high posts for both von Kahr and von Lossow. Yet neither man would commit himself; what interested him, said von Kahr, was Ludendorff's position. Since Ludendorff had yet to arrive at the hall, Hitler appeared uncertain what to do; at length, he strode back to the tribunal in the main hall and began to harangue the crowd.

It was, one observer would note, "an oratorical masterpiece, which any actor might well envy."[19] The task, Hitler cried, was "to organize the march on that sinful Babylon, Berlin, for the German people must be saved."[20] The ruling triumvirate of Bavaria—von Knilling, von Kahr, and von Lossow—he intimated, was about to join the movement. "They are struggling hard to reach a decision," he declared. "May I say to them that you will stand behind them?" 'Ja! Ja!' roared the crowd."[21]

Hitler had left the podium to return to the side room when Ludendorff arrived at the main door of the hall. Hitler hurried to greet him and usher him to the side room. "Come along with us," said Ludendorff to von Kahr and von Lossow, "and give me your hand on it." Von Lossow was the first to agree; von Kahr quickly followed. As the group moved back into the hall to cheers of near delirium from the audience, Hitler was ecstatic. "Now," he cried, "I am going to carry out what I swore to myself five years ago when I lay blind and crippled in the army hospital: neither to rest nor sleep until .. . the present pitiful Germany had been raised to a Germany of power and greatness, of freedom and glory."[22] The crowd stood and began to sing the anthem, "Deutschland über Alles," some people with tears streaming down their cheeks.

Through much of the night, as Hitler's supporters took over one key center after another, it appeared that throughout Munich the Putsch was succeeding. Then came word that the storm troopers at the engineer barracks were having problems with the engineers; Hitler himself decided to to there, leaving Ludendorff in charge at the Bürgerbräukeller. Hardly had he left the building before von Lossow asked Ludendorff's permission to go to his headquarters, where he would have communications facilities to issue orders in support of the uprising. When Ludendorff approved, von Kahr also departed. Returning to the Bürgerbräukeller, Hitler was appalled, but Ludendorff rebuked him; von Lossow had sworn to support the Putsch, he said, and a German officer would never break his oath.

As was soon apparent, Ludendorff was mistaken, for a telegram signed by von Lossow was soon on its way to all posts of the government, the Army, and the police: "State Commissar General v. Kahr, Col. v. Seisser [head of the state police], and General v. Lossow repudiate the Hitler Putsch. Expressions of support extracted at gunpoint invalid."[23] As a dull, overcast dawn arrived with a biting chill in the air and occasional spasms of wet snow, Hitler's revolution was clearly in serious trouble. At those public buildgs still held by storm troopers, police and Army troops laid siege. Although Hitler's supporters held most of the bridges over the Isar, state troopers manning machine guns were emplaced nearby.

At the Bürgerbräukeller, some wanted to leave the city and retreat to the hills to begin a guerrilla war, but Hitler would have no part of that. As Ludendorff put it sarcastically, "The movement cannot end in the ditch of some obscure country lane."[24] The Putschists had to act boldly at once or else surrender ignominiously.

When Ludendorff suggested a march into the center of Munich to raise the siege at the war ministry, Hitler seized upon it. "We would go into the city," Hitler would explain later, "to win the people to our side, to see how public opinion would react, and then to see how Kahr, Lossow, and Seisser would react to public opinion." They would "hardly be foolish enough," he believed, "to use machine guns against a general uprising of the people."[25]

Close to noon on November 9, 1923, the parade formed. There was no band to lead it, merely a group of picked skirmishers and eight men carrying the swastika and black, white, and red flags, followed by Hitler with Ludendorff on his left and other leaders of the movement, including a corpulent World War fighter ace, Captain Hermann Göring, wearing a steel helmet decorated with a large white swastika and a leather coat carefully unbuttoned to reveal Germany's highest military decoration, the pour le Mérite. Behind them came military units marching four abreast, including Hitler's hundred-man bodyguard, and behind them, a motley collection of workers, veterans, students, shopkeepers, middle-aged businessmen, their only common mark being a swastika brassard on the left arm. There were close to 2,000 men in all.

As had been the case throughout the uprising, one side seemed reluctant to fire upon the other. When the strange procession reached the Ludwig bridge over the Isar, a small force of state police hesitated just long enough for the skirmishers to overrun them, the men shouting "Don't shoot at your comrades!" In the Zweibrückenstrasse, lined with people cheering and waving swastika flags, many joined the ranks of the paraders. In the Marienplatz, still festooned with swastika banners and with the Nazi flag still flying from the City Hall, a large crowd was singing patriotic songs. With Ludendorff leading the way, the procession turned into the Weinstrasse and headed toward the Odeonsplatz and one of Munich's most revered landmarks, the Feldherrnhalle, the Hall of the Generals. Turning into the narrow Residenzstrasse, where there was room but for eight men abreast, the marchers began to sing "O Deutschland hoch in Ehren [O Germany high in honor]." Up ahead, green-uniformed state police blocked the way. Hitler locked arms with a companion, Max Erwin von Scheubner-Richter, one of the men who had organized Hitler's treasury, but Ludendorff, supremely confident that no German would fire upon him, the old war hero, strode forward alone.

Bullets from the first fusillade killed von Scheubner-Richter but not before he helped Hitler's personal bodyguard drag Hitler to the pavement, pulling him down so sharply that his left arm was dislocated. Thirteen more of the marchers died, and in the return fire, four of the state police. Among the wounded was Captain Göring, his display of his honored medal having done nothing to safeguard him. After first following the veteran soldier's instinct to take cover, Ludendorff rose and walked with determination into the ranks of the police; arrested, he reacted with petulance and indignation.

A mad scramble for safety ensued. In agony from the dislocated arm, Hitler got away in a car accompanied by a medical officer, and after encountering machine-gun fire at various points within the city, made his way out of Munich in the direction of the Austrian frontier. Yet he had no intention of seeking refuge outside Germany, and when the car reached the village of Uffing, he directed the driver to stop and, with the medical officer, made his way on foot to the villa of one of his supporters, Harvard-educated Ernst Hanfstängl, whose mother was of an old New England family. There Hitler made a show of suicide but was easily dissuaded. Late the next day, November 11, 1923, the anniversary of the ignominy that drove him, he surrendered to the police.

When Hitler drew a sentence of a year in prison at Landsberg, some forty miles west of Munich, many began to talk of him in the past tense. He was "passion incarnate," said one, "a fanatic for Germany," but he had failed to understand "how to give his National Socialism any intellectual basis." The cause had been "still-born from the start"; [26] nothing went right for Germany. Yet, in Munich, defiant orders were already going out to the National Socialists: "The first period of the national revolution is over . . . Our highly revered Führer, Adolf Hitler, has again bled for the German people. The most shameful treachery that the world has ever seen has victimized him and the German people . . . The second phase of the national revolution begins." [27]

## Chapter Thirty-One

Von Brockdorff-Rantzau strongly protested the Comintern's intervention in trying to incite a German October. Dining with Chicherin, he warned that the Comintern's continuing interference in German affairs might produce a political reaction in Germany that von Brockdorff would be unable to control, for even though Stresemann's strongly antibolshevik government had fallen, Stresemann had entered the successor government as foreign minister and was inclined to accommodation with Britain and France. Continuing Comintern activity in Germany, said von Brockdorff, might well lead to Germany's joining some form of antibolshevik crusade by the great powers.

Chicherin responded that he was aware of the dangers of unrestricted Comintern revolutionary activity but that in keeping with the principles of Marxism and Leninism, his government had a duty to the world proletariat. Chicherin nevertheless arranged for von Brockdorff to have a talk with Trotsky, to whom von Brockdorff said that he could continue at his post only if "he had influence in Berlin and was trusted in Moscow"; [1] if the Comintern persisted in undermining his position with its activities in Germany, he would be compelled to go home, and with his departure, Russia would lose one of its few German friends.

The protests appeared to have some effect, for Trotsky promised to divert Russian industrial orders from France to Germany, thereby helping the German economic situation, and a few days later, on January 9, 1924, Chicherin handed von Brockdorff a formal note in which the Soviet government pledged to "take the most stringent measures against the Comintern agents and against any interference in Germany's domestic affairs by members of the diplomatic staff in Germany." Yet as both parties must have recognized, the exchanges represented little more than diplomatic double-talk, for the requirements of the two countries remained at once interrelated and antithetical. So long as their two positions remained the same, little would change.

In the early morning of May 3, 1924, two detectives of the Würtemberg criminal police, Gruener and Kasser, arrived at the Stettiner Station in Berlin in charge of a prisoner, Johannes Bozenhardt, a German Communist under indictment for treason. Learning that they had missed their connection for Stettin, where Bozenhardt was to stand trial, they decided, while awaiting the next train, to have breakfast. When Bozenhardt volunteered that he knew of a good restaurant nearby, they took a taxi to the address: 14 Lindenstrasse. Not until they were inside the foyer did the two detectives discover that Bozenhardt had led them not to a restaurant but to the offices of the Soviet Trade Delegation. Breaking away, he dashed up the stairs, crying that he was a Communist under arrest and needed help. Five employees emerged from their offices, seized the detectives, locked them in an office, and spirited Bozenhardt away.

When released, Detectives Gruener and Kasser went to headquarters of the Berlin police, where they laid out Bozenhardt's file before the director of the political police, a certain Weiss. Without consulting the German Foreign Office, Director Weiss moved to recapture Bozenhardt by raiding the premises of the Soviet Trade Delegation. Within two hours of Detectives Gruener and Kasser having made their complaint, some 200 agents descended on the offices. Finding no trace of Bozenhardt, they broke into desks and file cabinets and confiscated copies of revolutionary tracts intended for distribution among German troops and policemen.

The Soviet ambassador in Berlin, Nikolai N. Krestinsky, protested to Foreign Minister Stresemann; the raid, he said, violated the extraterritorial and diplomatic immunity of the trade mission. The complaint was without basis, Stresemann rejoined, for under the Russo-German trade agreement of 1921, no extraterritorial privileges had been afforded the delegation, and only the chairman and seven members of his staff had been granted diplomatic immunity. While acknowledging that the agreement permitted house searches only under extraordinary circumstances, Stresemann insisted that the participation of members of the mission in Bozenhardt's escape constituted extraordinary circumstances. To the German press, Stresemann issued a statement alleging that the trade delegation was a center of anti-German conspiracy conducted by the Comintern.

In Moscow, Chicherin told von Brockdorff-Rantzau that "the raid was evidence of a complete change of Germany's policy toward Russia . . . a change of alignment," and he recalled Ambassador Krestinsky from Berlin for consultations. That reaction produced a partial backdown in Berlin. The blame, said the head of the Foreign Ministry's Eastern Department, Baron von Maltzan, appeared to rest jointly upon the German police and the members of the trade delegation. Calling for arbitration before a committee drawn from the foreign diplomatic corps, he announced that pending arbitration, the director of the political police, Weiss, had been suspended and that the Germans would not make public the subversive pamphlets uncovered in the raid. Releasing the pamphlets was of litle concern, responded Chicherin, for if the Germans used them, the Soviet Foreign Commissariat might find it necessary "to reveal the secret military collaboration that existed between the Red and German Armies."

For all the apparent posturing on both sides, von Brockdorff-Rantzau was genuinely concerned over the incident. He saw it as an attempt by antibolsheviks in the Berlin government to torpedo the Treaty of Rapallo as a preliminary to establishing an anti-Soviet alliance with Britain, France, and the United States, and that might well destroy the policy of regeneration through alliance with Russia, which von Brockdorff still saw as Germany's only hope. So disturbed was von Brockdorff that he asked permission to leave his post in Moscow "for the reasons of health and the need to attend to family business connected with my estates in Schleswig Holstein."

That had the effect he had intended, for Stresemann promptly begged him to reconsider; if he resigned, said Stresemann, the Russians would attach more importance to the incident than it warranted. That the Russians were attaching great importance to the incident was already apparent in any case for on June 1, 1924, Chicherin handed von Brockdorff a note maintaining that the Berlin government had staged the Bozenhardt escape as a deliberate anti-Soviet provocation; if the German government wished to make amends, Weiss would have to be not suspended but dismissed, and the German government would have to recognize the extraterritoriality not only of the offices of the Soviet Trade Delegation in Berlin but also of regional offices in Hamburg, Königsberg, and Frankfurt.

Agreeing to stay as ambassador, von Brockdorff nevertheless asked to return to Berlin for consultations. There he emphasized to Stresemann and von Maltzan that if the menace from France and Britain were to be contained, "the fiction of strong political, possibly military, support by the Soviet Union" was essential, and if that were to be maintained, Germany should do nothing to undermine Chicherin.

The opportunity for a settlement came on July 14, 1924, when Chicherin arrived in Berlin to consult a specialist in pancreatic complaints, and in the process of undergoing medical tests, he discussed the latest German offer with von Brockdorff, who made a point of being in Berlin at the same time: since approximately a quarter of the Lindenstrasse building would appear to be required for legitimate trade activities, the German government would grant extraterritoriality to that portion of the building. When Chicherin agreed to settle for no less than 60 percent, the Germans acquiesced.

Honor satisfied, Chicherin returned to Moscow; Ambassador Krestinsky returned to Berlin; and the two nations resumed trade relations. All was again in apparent accord, but in the case of two parties having such antipodal objectives, it could hardly be expected to endure.

In the course of investigating Comintern intrigue in regard to the German October, the German political police arrested a man known to his German Communist colleagues as Hellmuth. Despite the name, the man was plainly not a German, and inquiries into his background established that he was in fact a general officer in the Soviet secret service, the OGPU: he was Peter A. Skoblensky, who had arrived in January in the disguise of a tourist but had been sent to organize a Special Department (OO), a secret operations and political warfare *apparat*. According to a German Communist, Feliks Neumann, who was Skoblensky's principal assistant and who turned state's evidence, one of the primary tasks of the OO was to assassinate prominent Germans, including Field Marshal von Hindenburg, General Ludendorff, and the commander in chief of the Army, General von Seeckt. Although Neumann claimed that the OO had come close on two occasions to shooting von Seeckt, the only person actually assassinated was a barber named Rauch, whom the OO suspected of being an informer. Yet even though the OO had killed but one man, the organization had conspired extensively against the state on behalf of the Comintern; he himself, Neumann swore, had received $35,000 from the Soviet Embassy in Berlin and various officials at the Soviet Embassy, and had spent about $200,000 to purchase explosives, munitions, and arms for the OO and the German Communist Party.

In October 1924, not long after the settlement of the crisis occasioned by the Bozenhardt affair, the German government announced that Skoblensky and fifteen other Communists would be placed on trial for their lives before the Court for the Protection of the Republic in Leipzig. While the Comintern executive in Moscow issued threatening protests, the OGPU went to work to procure hostages to be used as pawns for the life of Skoblensky.

On October 13, 1924, while traveling by train from Riga to Moscow, von Brockdorff-Rantzau's principal deputy in the German Embassy in Moscow, Counselor of Legation Gustav Hilger, struck up a conversation with three students: Karl Kindermann and Theodor Wolscht, who were German, and their friend, Max von Ditmar, an Estonian. Students at the University of Berlin, they confided that they were on their way to Asiatic Russia to gather economic intelligence for a German machinery manufacturer. Conscious of Russian sensitivity about anything that might be taken for economic espionage, Hilger warned them about Soviet regulations in that regard, gave them his calling card, on which he wrote his private address and telephone number, and suggested that they visit him upon arrival in Moscow.

As von Brockdorff would subsequently establish, von Ditmar was a member of the German Communist Party, whose acquaintance Kindermann and Wolscht had only recently made. In Berlin, von Ditmar had introduced the two youths to the first secretary of the Soviet Embassy, who suggested that they might avoid problems in Russia by joining the German Communist Party; both applied, but for some reason only Kindermann was granted membership. To finance the trip the two obtained $500 from the editor of the Berliner Tageblatt as an advance on a proposed series about student life in Asiatic Russia and additional comissions from various German firms to procure information about business possibilities in Siberia.

Shortly after arriving in Moscow, the students were arrested and indicted for suspicion of political and economic espionage, a capital offense. Despite persistent efforts, the German Embassy was able to learn little more about the young men or their fate until January 1925, shortly before Skoblensky was scheduled to go on trial in Leipzig. At that point, Chicherin informed von Brockdorff-Rantzau that the three students were members of the Fascist terrorist group in Germany, Organization C, which was responsible for the murder of Walther Rathenau. Chicherin also told von Brockdorff that he had learned that German police had recently arrested a friend and political associate of Joseph Stalin's, Arkadi Maslov, a powerful member of the Comintern's Orgburo, and the leader of the extreme left wing of the German Communist Party. Maslov was suspected of having helped direct the German October from Comintern headquarters in Moscow.

To von Brockdorff, it appeared obvious that the arrest of the German students was tied to the trial of Skoblensky and, for good measure, to the arrest of Maslov, which meant that Russo-German relations were about to enter another period of storm. One of the three sudents, von Ditmar, Chicherin told von Brockdorff, had turned state's evidence and revealed that they had planned to assassinate Stalin, Trotsky, Zinoviev, and Derzhinski. Von Ditmar had also revealed that the mastermind behind the plot was none other than von Brockdorff's assistant, Hilger. Although the OGPU refused to allow anyone from the German Embassy to visit the students, Chicherin's deputy, Litvinov, offered to call on them and report to von Brockdorff on their well-being. Upon his return, he provided von Brockdorff with a copy of a detailed "confession" by Kindermann. A few days later, Litvinov brought word that Wolscht and von Ditmar had confirmed what Kindermann had confessed.

On February 10, 1925, Skoblensky and the fifteen other Communist defendants went before the State Court for the Protection of the Republic in Leipzig. The chief witness for the prosecution was Feliks Neumann, whose testimony proved to be lurid, involving all the leading German Communists, including the party's deputies in the Reichstag, in plots to murder and to incite revolution on the dictate of the Comintern. After long weeks of sensational testimony on Soviet intrigue, the court on April 22, 1925, handed down its verdict: two of the defendants were found not guilty; thirteen received sentences ranging from six months to fifteen years at hard labor; and three others, including Skoblensky, were sentenced to death. The allegation that the Soviet government had plotted to overthrow the German Republic, the court declared, had been substantiated.

A few weeks later, in late June 1925, the trial of Kindermann, Wolscht, and von Ditmar opened before the Special Board of the Supreme Court of the Soviet Union. When Kindermann and Wolscht appeared in the dock, they showed signs of nervousness, depression, and emaciation (Kindermann had staged a hunger strike seven times, Wolscht twice). As the German court had depended primarily on the testimony of one man, Neumann, so the Russian court relied on the word of von Ditmar. Organization C, said von Ditmar, had instructed Kindermann and Wolscht how to use poison, which they were to administer at the first opportunity to Stalin, Trotsky, Zinoviev, and Derzhinski. Although von Ditmar offered no particulars on how two young foreign students were to meet and mingle long enough with the leaders of the world revolution of the proletariat to poison them, he was specific in how they were to get their intelligence information out of the Soviet Union: Organization C, he said, had arranged for them to send it through a contact in the German Embassy, whom they found to be upon their arrival in Moscow none other than the counselor of the legation, Hilger.

As the Moscow trial proceeded, Foreign Minister Gustav told his ambassador in Moscow that it was evident to everybody in Germany with the possible exception of the Communists that the trial of Kindermann and Wolscht was but "a companion piece" to the Leipzig trial and that the attempt to implicate Hilger was in retaliation for the way the Leipzig court had implicated the Soviet Embassy. The Moscow trial, he said, quite clearly jeopardized Russo-German relations at a time when the two nations had only recently begun a new round of political and commercial discussions of far-reaching character and importance; did the Russians really want to destroy this close relationship with Germany?

When von Brockdorff passed that admonition to Chicherin, it may have had some effect, for Hilger was never called as a witness, and even though the court found all three students guilty, there was no mention of involvement by Hilger, the German Embassy, or the German government. The judges did note that "fascist *provocateurs*" in Berlin were behind the students and that the students had conspired to kill not only Soviet leaders known to favor friendship with Germany but also German leaders, including General von Seeckt, who favored friendly relations with Russia.

That year of 1925, Adolf Hitler was in Landsberg Fortress where, with the accommodation of patronizing prison authorities, he was writing a book he would entitle *Mein Kampf*. Dedicated to a disciple, Rudolf Hess, a young ex-student whom Hitler had come to know at meetings of the German Workers' Party, the volume was conceived as an account of Hitler's "four and one half years of struggle."² As it turned out, it was a mixture of autobiography, ideology, and theory of tactics.

The style and content of the work revealed a man haunted by the images of adolescence: masturbation, copulation, sodomy, perversion, rape, contamination of the blood. It also displayed a preoccupation with snakes: "He who has not himself been gripped in the clutches of this strangulating viper will never come to know its poisoned fangs." From the pages "A curiously nasty, obscene odor emanated . . . particularly when Hitler wrote of sex, race, and Jews":

> The final Jewish goal is denationalization, is sowing confusion by the bastardization of other nations, lowering the racial level of the highest, and dominating this racial stew by exterminating the folkish intelligentsias and replacing them by members of his own race. . . . The folkish ideology must at last succeed in bringing about that nobler age in which men will no longer see it as their concern to breed superior dogs, horses, and cats, but in the raising of man himself.

Yet for all the work's obsession with twisted visions of procreation and race, it still purveyed a portrait of a man with a remarkably ossified ideology, an ideology destined to remain constant throughout his life. The four pillars of it were nationalism, anti-Semitism, antibolshevism, and the Darwinian theory of natural struggle for existence and triumph.

With bold clarity, Hitler revealed his life's purpose to be the elimination of Bolshevik Russia. "What is refused by amicable methods must be taken by force," he wrote. If a nation in Europe required land, it could be obtained "by and large only at the expense of Russia," and that meant that "the new Reich must again set itself on the march along the road of the Teutonic Knights of old." The German people, he wrote, required *Lebensraum*. Acquainted through Rudolf Hess with the heartland theory of Sir Halford Mackinder, he joined that theory of geopolitics with the theory of racial purity to come up with what would become the essence of his policy toward Russia:

> By handing Russia to Bolshevism, [fate] robbed the Russian nation of that intelligentsia which previously brought about and guaranteed its existence as a state. For the organization of a Russian state was not the result of political abilities of the Slavs in Russia, but only a wonderful example of the state-forming efficacy of the German element in an inferior race . . . For centuries Russia drew nourishment from this Germanic nucleus of its upper leading strata. Today it can be regarded as almost totally exterminated and extinguished. It has been replaced by the Jew. Impossible as it is for the Russian by himself to shake off the yoke of the Jew by his own resources, it is equally impossible for the Jew to maintain the mighty empire forever. He

himself has no element of organization but a ferment of decomposition. And the end of Jewish rule in Russia will also be the end of Russia as a state. We have been chosen by fate as witnesses of a catastrophe which will be the mightiest confirmation of the soundness of the folkish theory.

To help Hitler achieve the post of authority that he had to hold in order to embark on his crusade against Russia, he could have asked no more cooperative an ally—however unwitting an ally—than a meddling Communist International.

## Chapter Thirty-Two

In the words of Gustav Stresemann, the German people had no respect for leaders who wore top hats; they preferred generals of the old order, men who had taken the *Fahneneid*. In the turmoil of the early years of the 1920s, such a leader, Stresemann believed, would provide the bulwark the German people needed against *Kulturbolschewismus*, the detestable social and sexual free-for-all purveyed by Zinoviev as part of the elysium awaiting the German people once they had rid themselves of their bourgeois leaders. Yet for a long time the prospect of a military strong man's emerging to create that bulwark appeared to be remote; then, on February 28, 1925, at the age of fifty-four, the ex-saddlemaker and *Bierlokal* proprietor who had founded the democratic Weimar Republic, Friedrich Ebert, died suddenly of peritonitis.

When the Death's Head Hussars had pulled the gun carriage bearing the dead president through gray Berlin streets as they had once pulled the Hohenzollerns to their crypts in the Garrison Church at Potsdam, the political kingmakers began to cast about for a successor. Meeting over coffee at the Herrenklub, the kingmakers arrived at a candidate who had a seemingly irresistible name and reputation: Field Marshal Paul Ludwig Hans Anton von Beckendorff und von Hindenburg. Here, at last, was no statesman in top hat; here was a man who had commanded the triumphant legions that had symbolized the power and glory of the old Reich and the invincible days of the emperor.

To the kingmakers, von Hindenburg's entire career appeared to have prepared the old gentleman—he was seventy-eight at the time—for the fight against *Kulturbolschewismus*. He was of the East Elbian aristocracy that had produced and sustained the Great German General Staff, and he had fought with distinction in the Austro-Prussian War of 1866 and the Franco-Prussian War of 1870–1871. The coming of the World War had led to his exemplary partnership in command with General Ludendorff, which had produced resounding victories over numerically superior Russian armies at Tannenberg and the Mazurian lakes and which had come close to victory on the western front in 1918 with the *Kaiserschlacht*. Through geriatric craftiness, von Hindenburg had survived the fall of the emperor and a persistent cry by the Allied powers for his trial as a war criminal and, much honored, had gone into retirement on his great estate at Neudeck on the blue, hazy plains of East Elbia. It was there, where the old warrior lived in a mansion surrounded by battle flags, Teutonic pennants, Nordic axes, Prussian breastplates, stags' heads, models of cannon, piles of cannonballs, and a gallery of pictures of the Madonna, that Germany's greatest living hero received the call to perform a final service for the Reich.

When the politicans came to see him, he complained that he was old and tired and needed his rest. He was still a great bull of a man—6 feet, 5 inches tall and weighing 212 pounds—but his eyes were rheumy and he mumbled at length behind a great mustache. Yet his old comrade at the Herrenklub, Grand Admiral Alfred von Tirpitz, prevailed upon him, and *Der Alte*, as the people spoke of him, agreed to stand for election.

In the election, the old soldier prevailed by a vote of 14,655,000 to 13,751,000 for the Social Democratic candidate, Otto Braun, president of Prussia. Yet to those who looked closely at the results, something fateful had occurred at the polls: the Communist candidate, Ernst Thaelmann, had received just under 2 million votes, and had he agreed to side with Braun against von Hindenburg, the right would have been denied power.

As it was, on the Communist workers' holiday, May Day 1925, a special train bearing the new president of the Weimar Republic arrived at the Heerstrasse Station on the western fringe of Berlin. As the newly elected president rode slowly along the six miles to the palace, great crowds lined the route, manifesting what the American military attaché, Colonel Cox, called "the deep-seated respect in the hearts of the German people" for the old soldier and prompting Cox to speculate that the election of von Hindenburg, a professed Monarchist, "might be employed by the Monarchists as a stepping stone for the return of the Hohenzollerns."[1]

Yet there would be an indication at the swearing-in at the Reichstag that the old gentlemen might have less dedication to monarchy than to constitution. As noted by the Berlin diarist and boulevardier Count Kessler: "Hindenburg, standing on the spot where Rathenau's coffin had stood, swore the oath of office . . . and read a declaration from a piece of paper inscribed with such huge letters that it would have been possible, with the aid of an opera-glass, to read them from the gallery." To Count Kessler, "the impression was of a somewhat self-conscious old general enunciating unaccustomed and incomprehensible material," but he was also struck by the fact that "the emphasis laid . . . on the constitution's republican and democratic character . . . was stronger than expected."[2]

From time to time there had been plots to restore the monarchy, yet in the end, all the plans, including some for a constitutional monarchy, would be stillborn, in large measure because for all President von Hindenburg's sympathy for the monarchy, he insisted on adhering to the letter and spirit of the republican constitution. Thus, for all the turbulence in the infant republic and over vehement protests by extreme leftists and Socialists in the Reichstag, the matter of the disposition of the monarchy would be settled in a civilized manner.

Under a compassionate, even generous settlement dictated by the Reichstag, the royal family was compensated for properties taken by the state to a total amount of approximately $18.5 million. In addition, the kaiser, forty-nine members of the immediate royal family, and sixteen members of related families were permitted to keep 180,000 acres out of a total estate acreage of 290,000. The settlements with the twenty other princely families were in most cases as generous as those with the Hohenzollerns.

Yet despite that happy solution, the German princes would continue to conspire for their restoration but with decreasing fervor and effect. Under various pressures—financial, social, political—the dynasties that had ruled Germany for so many years and had given the Teutons a national purpose and identity would disintegrate. The mysticism through which monarchies flourish would evaporate in a welter of social, financial, and sexual scandals, leaving a void in the national ethos that the republican ministers, chancellors, and presidents would prove incapable of filling.

The first blush of relations between President von Hindenburg and Chicherin were promising for what had become known as the Spirit of Rapallo. Having returned to Berlin for further medical consultations, Chicherin accepted an invitation from von Hindenburg to tea. From Chicherin's viewpoint, in particular, there was much to discuss, for Germany had recently joined the Allied powers in the Pact of Locarno, one of several diplomatic devices of the period designed to keep the peace and one having particular import in that it represented at least a first step in a rapprochement between Germany and the Allied powers. In addition, the British were wooing Germany to join the League of Nations, that newly founded institution operating from the shores of Lake Geneva that had been established "to deliver mankind painlessly and inexpensively from the curse of war to the great advantage of all concerned."[3] In the view of a man who was emerging as the power in the Soviet government, Joseph Stalin, both the Pact of Locarno and the League of Nations were capitalist plots, the start of an alliance dominated by Britain to encircle and destroy the Socialist fatherland.

Yet when the two met, von Hindenburg and Chicherin agreed to avoid thorny issues. What mattered was that they had met and that there was no acrimony. That was reserved for talks between Chicherin and Stresemann, the latter again complaining about "perpetual and flagrant" interferences by Zinoviev and the Comintern in Germany's internal affairs.[4]

Suspecting—with considerable reason—that it was Stresemann who was leading Germany into a rapprochement with Britain and France, Chicherin replied curtly that he was on medical leave, that if Stresemann wanted to discuss official matters, he should talk with his deputy, Litvinov, who was in Berlin officially. In any case, said Chicherin, parroting the oft-used Soviet line, the Soviet government "could not be blamed for the actions of the Comintern just because its seat was in Moscow." While aware of the sham of that position, Stresemann realized that Chicherin himself had no control over Zinoviev and his bazaar of revolutionary idealists and even less over a sullen and sinister Feliks Derzhinski of the OGPU. That had been well demonstrated only a few weeks after von Hindenburg had taken his oath of office when officials of the OGPU on December 13, 1925, arrested the German consular agents in Baku, Poti, and Batum.

To the much-beleagured von Brockdorff-Rantzau in Moscow, it was clear that he was in for another of those seemingly inexplicable staged confrontations that the leaders in the Kremlin somehow required in order to maintain their pride and self-esteem. As von Brockdorff had done often in the past, he told Chicherin that unless the incident could be quickly settled, he would be forced to resign as ambassador; but Derzhinski refused to release the consuls. They had used their diplomatic privileges, he said, to travel about the Caucasus and spy on the Red Army.

In the negotiations for release of the consuls, the German government possessed a weapon that Stresemann was inclined to wield: at Chicherin's initiative, primarily because of concern over German rapprochement with the Allied powers, the German and Russian governments had recently concluded what Chicherin called "a reinsurance treaty," known as the Treaty of Berlin, which reaffirmed the understandings of the Treaty of Rapallo and assured that neither country would join the western powers either in a new war or in economic sanctions against the other; but the German government had yet to ratify the treaty. Whether at Stresemann's initiative or that of antibolshevik rightists in the government, a number of German newspapers in April 1926 published articles revealing that there were forty-four German citizens, including the three consuls and the students, Kindermann and Wolscht, in Soviet jails; and such public indignation did the revelation arouse that Stresemann passed word to Chicherin that something would have to be done or there would be no possibility of the German government's ratifying the treaty.

In Chicherin's absence from the Foreign Commissariat because of illness, his deputy, Litvinov, suggested that both countries clear the air by releasing all their prisoners, whereupon the Soviets acted to make sure that the Germans would return the two men they wanted back most: the secret service officer Skoblensky, and the high-level Comintern official Arkadi Maslov. The OGPU arrested a German engineer, Heinrich Scholl, who was working at the Junkers factory which was producing aircraft for the Russian and German air forces, and charged him with economic and military espionage. If Skoblensky and Maslov were released immediately, said Litvinov, the Soviet government would let Scholl go without a trial.

To von Brockdorff, the arrest of Scholl was an obvious attempt at blackmail, for if Scholl went on trial, the German military collaboration with Russia would be publicly revealed, which would probably block Germany's admission to the League of Nations. It probably would also be revealed that even as Germany had been protesting its poverty, the German government had secretly set aside 75 million gold marks to sustain its military relationship with Russia, funds that France, in particular, which was still far stronger militarily than was Germany, would maintain should have been spent on reparations. It "might sound good to the gallery," said von Brockdorff, "to declare proudly that one does not want to deal with extortioners, but such a declaration is contradictory *after* one has delivered oneself into the hands of the blackmailers."

Two days after receiving word from von Brockdorff, von Hindenburg pardoned and released Skoblensky, Maslov, and several other Comintern agents of Russian origin. The Russians, in turn, released their forty-four prisoners, including Kindermann and Wolscht, and the three consuls, and dropped the charges against Scholl. The exchange was completed in October 1926 at a place that the Russians may well have chosen for symbolic reasons: Brest Litovsk.

In the continuing struggle between right and left inside Germany, hardly did the government solve or paper over one crisis before another arose. At least two of them appeared to be the work of Comintern agents or sympathizers intent on bringing Germany back into the full embrace of the Treaty of Rapallo.

The first involved the principal architect of the Russo-German military relationship, General von Seeckt, a man of the right who saw restoration of the Hohenzollern monarchy as the only way to unite his country against Bolshevism and to restore the privilege and glory of the Army and the officer corps and, in time, of the empire itself. Von Seeckt considered a number of royal candidates for the throne before settling on the kaiser's grandson, who was also named Wilhelm, a young man immensely popular in North Germany and one whose name was in no way connected with the disasters of 1918.

Although the Treaty of Versailles forbade any member of the House of Hohenzollern to be connected in any way with the German armed services, von Seeckt began quietly tutoring Prince Wilhelm in military affairs. It was a course hardly to be concealed for long from a vigorous, highly partisan press. Three days after Germany joined the League of Nations, the Communist press revealed that Prince Wilhelm had taken part in maneuvers with the 9th Regiment's 1st Company, known as the "Traditional Company" because all Hohenzollern princes received their first military training in it. That news produced a sensation, for the presence of a Hohenzollern prince in the Traditional Company could hardly be interpreted in any way other than that the Reichswehr was kingmaking.

The revelation of von Seeckt's connivance came at a time when the Allied powers had indicated a willingness to bury the past provided there was no revival of German militarism and the monarchy with which it was identified. Thus not even *Der Alte*, von Hindenburg, with whom von Seeckt had served in the Great War, could protect the brilliant soldier against his critics and enemies. In September 1926, General von Seeckt tendered his resignation as commander in chief of the Army, but as he departed, he left behind an army that was qualitatively the finest in the world.

Even more than the crisis posed by the revelation of von Seeckt's intransigence, the second crisis clearly posed the possibility of rupturing the newfound German relationship with the country's recent enemies and thus of serving the Comintern's purpose. It emerged from publication by a leading British newspaper, the Manchester *Guardian,* on December 3, 1926, of a dispatch from its Berlin correspondent alleging "Russian involvement in the illegal activities of the German monarchists and counter-revolutionaries." Revealing details that could hardly have come from other than Soviet sources, the *Guardian* reported that the Reichswehr, under von Seeckt's leadership, had arranged for the Junkers aircraft company to build military aircraft in Russian factories, that for almost five years two Russian plants had been producing poison gas for the German Army, that German and Russian officers collaborated in training exercises in both Russia and Germany, and that Russian factories had produced munitions for the German Army.

When the story broke, Stresemann was in Geneva for talks with foreign ministers of members of the League of Nations. Convinced that British and French reaction to the revelation would be harsh, Stresemann asked his government for guidance. The response revealed that von Hindenburg's government would try to deal with the crisis by obfuscation. Soon after the end of the war, the government noted, "certain departments of the *Reichswehr"* had seized upon German participation in Soviet industrial development as an opportunity for altering the lack of ammunition and other defensive materials required by the German Army for the defense of East Prussia against Poland. To that concern had been added others generated by the Red Revolution in the Ruhr, the Communist disturbances in Saxony, Thuringia, and Bavaria, and the problems created for the Army by French and Belgian occupation of the Ruhr. Yet even during that "catastrophic" period, the collaboration with Russia had been limited, and "as soon as the authoritative departments of the Reich government found out about the facts," they ordered the Reichswehr to discontinue its contracts. It had been impossible to make "a complete break in a short time" lest the Soviet government take affront; thus the German government had arranged for the relationship "to disappear gradually" and "no actual military or political importance of any kind could be attributed to the whole matter."

The government's true position was quite to the contrary, for there was no intent to give up the military relationship with Russia. Although some minor enterprises were discontinued with attendant publicity, the principal fields of collaboration—Russian manufacture of aircraft, tanks, and poison gas—would continue. The German institutions that had been coordinating and monitoring the operations in Russia were closed down, thus providing apparent evidence that the collaboration had ended, but another institution, known as the "Home for German Employees," soon opened in Moscow to oversee the collaboration.

The world appeared to be lulled. In an opinion representative of the foreign press, the Washington *Evening Star* noted that the entire affair had been manufactured by the German left to force the resignation of the German government. A few months later, the British foreign secretary, G. L. Locker-

Lampson, would inform His Majesty's Government that he was "given to understand that the import into Germany, in contravention of Article 170 of the Treaty of Versailles, of arms and ammunition from Russia, has now ceased and all transactions in connection with such imports have been liquidated." The German government, he said, had "made it quite clear that they disapproved of these transactions and they have stopped them."

Locker-Lampson and other officials of the British government may or may not have believed that statement. It could have been that the British government was merely playing politics, for at that time there was such concern over the Comintern's activities in Britain and the empire that war between Britain and Russia appeared possible. Britain would hardly be inclined to do anything that might promote a Russo-German coalition.

## Chapter Thirty-Three

In 1927—the year in which war threatened between Britain and the Soviet Union over the activities of the Comintern, the year also in which Germany began work on missiles, the pocket battleship, the hydrogen-peroxide submarine, the 88-millimeter gun, the Stuka dive bomber, and important experiments connected with the science of atomic energy—the Allied Control Commission, which had been in Germany since 1919 to assure compliance with the terms of the Treaty of Versailles, packed up and went home. Before leaving, the commission warned that Germany "had never disarmed and had never had the intention of disarming."[1] Yet the declaration produced no Allied reaction, for in view of the difficulties with Soviet Russia, the British and French governments were not averse to having an armed Germany on the side of the Versailles powers.

Given the possibility of war between Britain and Russia, Germany's geographical position between the two possible antagonists posed special perils for the Reich. As the crisis began in February 1927, there were rumors that the Treaty of Rapallo and the recent Treaty of Berlin contained secret military protocols specifying that if either Germany or Russia were attacked by a third power or coalition of powers, one would come to the assistance of the other; but on March 7, 1927, the French journal *Excelsior* reported an interview in which the undersecretary at the German Foreign Office, Karl von Schubert, said that should Czechoslovakia or Poland require military assistance, Germany would permit foreign armies to cross German territory. Since Russia was the only country likely to attack Czechoslovakia or Poland, the Soviet government concluded that as a price for the Pact of Locarno, Germany had entered into some form of secret military arrangement with Britain and France.

In Moscow, von Brockdorff assured Chicherin that von Schubert had been misquoted, that Germany had no secret arrangements with the western powers. Although Chicherin himself appeared to accept that assurance, the Soviet government refused to let the matter rest. The article in *Excelsior,* declared *Izvestia,* "proved" that the Germans had concluded an anti-Soviet agreement at Locarno, and, the official journal maintained, Britain had promised Germany in exchange for support in a war with Russia parts of Silesia, the Baltic port of Danzig, and the Danzig corridor that afforded Poland an outlet to the sea but cut Germany off from East Prussia.

*"Erstunken und erlogen!"* ("Wild inventions and stinking lies!") declared Stresemann and instructed von Brockdorff to demand that the Soviet government stop publication of such scurrilous attacks; but before von Brockdorff could do that, the Russian ambassador in Berlin, Krestinsky, called at the Wilhelmstrasse to demand an official explanation of the von Schubert interview. How dare the Russians, of all people, stormed Stresemann, question the German foreign minister's veracity? If the Russian attitude continued, said Stresemann, further diplomatic conversations between the two countries might become "impossible."

It sounded like an argument in a schoolyard, and there was soon some evidence that that might be all that it was. On April 19, 1927, the chairman of the Soviet Council of People's Commissars, Alexis I. Rykov, remarked in a speech that Article 16 of the covenant of the League of Nations, to which Germany was a party, contained a passage that, while ambiguous, could be interpreted under certain circumstances as authority for Anglo-French forces to cross German territory. Although the dispute with Britain had produced "an extremely tense and alarming international atmosphere," Rykov noted that relations with Germany had for five years been "amiable" and that Stresemann had made "the most explicit official declaration to the Soviet government" that Germany had assumed no obligation to allow foreign troops to cross German territory.

Count von Brockdorff-Rantzau was soon so convinced that the war talk was nothing but an attempt by Stalin to obfuscate some kind of turmoil within the Soviet hierarchy, that on May 13, 1927, he departed for his annual leave at his estate in Schleswig-Holstein. Not quite a fortnight later, Stresemann informed him that the British government had severed diplomatic relations with Russia. Perhaps, suggested Stresemann, von Brockdorff should return to Moscow? In view of the crisis, the absence of the German ambassador might be interpreted as an indication that Germany was in league with Britain.

Von Brockdorff thought it better to avoid giving an impression of undue concern over the crisis; he recommended that Stresemann merely inform the Soviet government that Germany would maintain strict neutrality. That did, indeed, appear to placate the Foreign Commissariat, but on June 7, 1927, when a White Guard gunman murdered the Soviet diplomat Peter Voikov on the platform at the Warsaw Station, the Russians expressed new concerns. In Berlin again for medical treatment, Chicherin told Stresemann that there were indications of an Anglo-French-Polish coalition against Russia; that he was convinced the Polish leader, Josef Pilsudski, intended to manufacture a border incident to serve as an excuse for attacking Russia; and that the British and French would join Poland.

That, said Chicherin, would raise the question of Article 16 of the covenant of the League of Nations.

Discounting Chicherin's concerns and assuring the foreign commissar once again of Germany's neutrality, Stresemann seized the occasion to note that Russia would have no problem were it not for the activities of the Comintern. When, he asked, was the Soviet government going to recognize that the actions of the Communist International were antagonizing not only Russia's enemies but also Germany, upon whom the Russians depended for security? The Comintern, Chicherin admitted with a touch of sadness, was making foreign relations difficult, but, he said, there was nothing he could do about it.

With both Chicherin and von Brockdorff back in Moscow, the two dined again in early August 1927 in Patriarch's Lane and again engaged in a long evening of discussion. Calling attention to the impending admission of Finland to the League of Nations, Chicherin said that Britain and France were using the league to encircle Russia with hostile states, but when von Brockdorff offered his government's services as an intermediary with Britain, Chicherin declined. That added to von Brockdorff's belief that even though the British had been arrogant and provocative, the Soviet government was keeping the war scare alive for its own internal purposes.

Count von Brockdorff was nevertheless becoming discouraged over what seemed more and more to be diminishing prospects of accomplishing real rapport with the Soviet Union, a discouragement accentuated by the steady progression of an incurable cancer in his throat. Throughout his five years in Moscow, he had concealed his personal disdain for the Communist creed, but now that his days were numbered, he had come to the conclusion that he was wasting his time. Lenin's adoption of the New Economic Policy had provided hope that Russia might return to free enterprise, but that had failed to develop; and his hope that a Russo-German alliance would eventually erase the humiliation that Germany had suffered at Versailles had been dashed by Soviet exploitation of German misfortune through blackmail over Russo-German military collaboration. Meanwhile, Field Marshal von Hindenburg's government was revealing more and more a belief that Germany's future lay not in a beneficent relationship with Moscow but in some form of a strong nationalist—perhaps authoritarian—government. The time was approaching, von Brockdorff believed, when he should go home to Schleswig-Holstein.

There followed another of those incidents that had for so long served to strain Russo-German relations. On the fifth anniversary of the capture of a German Bolshevik revolutionary, Max Holz, who had led a guerrilla campaign against the Weimar Republic during the German October in 1923 and who was currently in a German prison, the Comintern official Nikolai Bukharin issued a statement in *Izvestia* commending the "revolutionary heroism" demonstrated by Holz and announcing that the Soviet government had awarded Holz the Order of the Red Banner. A few days later, the commissar for war, Voroshilov, made a speech at a dinner in the Kremlin honoring Holz and presented his decoration for transmittal by the German Communist leader Wilhelm Pieck.

Count von Brockdorff promptly protested to Chicherin, stating that the award was a deliberate affront. Unless personal and official amends were made immediately, said von Brockdorff, he would resign his post and leave for Germany. In support, Stresemann told the Russian ambassador, Krestinsky, that the German government considered the action a grave insult.

The Soviet government eventually apologized but hardly in the form that Stresemann and von Brockdorff wanted. The medal had been awarded, said the Russian note, without consultation with the Foreign Commissariat, but in any case, the award was not for Holz's work against the German gvernment but for services rendered an anti-French revolutionary before the signing of the Treaty of Versailles.

Yet however unsatisfactory the Soviet apology, Stresemann again urged von Brockdorff to remain at his post. Despite his serious illness and disillusionment, von Brockdorff acquiesced. He was thus still in Moscow when early in 1928 the Russians staged the most serious of the various incidents that had so sorely tried his patience over the years and that had kept Russo-German relations in almost constant turmoil.

To the consternation of German officials, the new incident occurred even as a representative of the Soviet Economic Commissariat was in Berlin trying to extend the Russo-German trade pact and to raise a new credit from German banks of $150 million to finance a long-term industrialization program. To achieve those objectives required the abundant trust of the German industrial and money barons, for even though the German economy had stabilized, the barons were markedly cautious about dealing with and assisting a power that was devoted to the destruction of capitalism.

Yet even as those delicate conversations were taking place, the OGPU on March 7, 1928, arrested five German engineers who were supervising the installation of turbines and mining machinery in the Don Basin industrial region and charged them with industrial espionage, sabotage, and conspiracy with foreign capitalists to wreck the communizing of the mines. That same evening Chicherin informed von Brockdorff that there would be a public trial, and as if to indicate that he himself was powerless to forestall a trial, he implored von Brockdorff "to use his influence to prevent a break of relations."

When news of the arrests reached Germany, the chimney barons of the Ruhr and elsewhere reacted with determination. The executive director of the giant electrical combine Allgemeine Elektrizitäts Gesellschaft (AEG), Felix Deutsch, whose firm employed four of the five engineers, telegraphed his old friend von Brockdorff that unless the charges were withdrawn, AEG was prepared to pull out of Russia. When relayed by von Brockdorff to Chicherin, the threat served to obtain the release of two of the engineers, but three others—Max Maier, Ernst Otto, and Wilhelm Badstieber—remained in custody along with fifty Russian engineers and technicians.

To get a first-hand report on the incident, Deutsch recalled his senior official in Russia, Franz Goldstein. The Soviet government, said Goldstein, had staged the incident to divert attention from a major decline in production, troublesome labor disturbances, and serious accidents in mines and plants in the Don Basin industrial region. Those misadventures were due not to sabotage or conspiracy but to the inefficient administration of Soviet officials, who were chosen less for their knowledge and abilities than for their standing in the Communist Party. The Soviet worker produced per day less than a third of what a German worker produced, and the thirty-hour week decreed by the government for mines and power industries further lowered production. The Bolsheviks, Goldstein explained, had boasted that through their Socialist system Soviet Russia would exceed the productive capacity of Western Europe in ten years and that of the United States ten years after that. There had been, instead, "a catastrophic decline" in industrial output. There had to be scapegoats, and the German engineers, along with many of their Russian associates, were the first.

In retaliation for the arrests, the German government suspended further talks on extending the commercial treaty and suggested that the existing treaty might be abrogated, but two months passed following the arrests before there was even any indication of the charges that would be lodged in the case. The first alleged that AEG had financed a counterrevolutionary organization in the Don Basin through a 3 percent commission on orders obtained in Russia and that AEG provided bribes to Soviet officials to obtain orders and to induce them to accept substandard machinery. The counterrevolutionary group, said the charge, worked to disorganize and destroy the mining industry in the Don Basin. There followed quickly an announcement in the Soviet press that the German engineer Badstieber had confessed he had bribed Soviet inspectors.

That the trial was of tremendous importance to the Soviet regime—it would serve as the model for show trials to be staged in the next decade—was apparent from the fact that the president of the court was no less a personage than the chairman of the Supreme Court, Andrei Y. Vyshinsky. Stalin himself in a speech printed in *Pravda* declared that the conspiracy represented "an economic counterrevolution," that the conspirators received funds from former Russian mine owners living abroad and "from counter-revolutionary anti-Soviet capitalist organizations in the West," and that the accused "operated and wrought destruction to our industry" on orders from those capitalist organizations. The plot in the Don Basin, he said, "marks another serious attack on the Soviet regime launched by international capital and its agents in our country."[2]

As the trial opened, von Brockdorff lodged one protest after another with Chicherin: the court's refusal to accept a German lawyer as defense counsel for the three Germans, the court's refusal to hear German witnesses, and the attitude of the prosecutor, V. N. Krylenko, his "sarcastic smile, showing polished teeth." All that deterred von Brockdorff from advising Berlin to sever diplomatic relations was the gloating that he was sure would follow in Britain, France, and the United States over the collapse of the Russo-German partnership.

As the trial unfolded, it proved to be a continuous indictment of capitalist industry and an unending paean to Socialist industrial planning and efficiency. The prosecution produced squads of witnesses to testify about inferior German workmanship, faulty dynamos, capitalist greed, while others took the stand to acclaim Socialist altruism, dynamos that worked, all-for-one-and-one-for-all. The facts of the case seemed to have little interest or relevance to the court; what mattered was proving the inferiority of capitalist industry vis-à-vis Bolshevik state planning. On the grounds that Soviet trial procedure had no place for "unrequested testimony," sworn affidavits from AEG were rejected by the court, as was evidence that neither AEG nor its employees had engaged in counterrevolutionary activity. When two of the German engineers, Maier and Otto, defended themselves with vigor, a principal government witness against Maier broke down and retracted his testimony.

As the trial approached an end, Prosecutor Krylenko began on June 29, 1938, to sum up. His summation made clear that for all the anticapitalist testimony during the trial, the Soviet government wanted to salvage the Russo-German trade relationship. Although, said Krylenko, there was "a distinct possibility that meetings of foreign members of the counter-revolutionary organization had taken place in the AEG's Russian Department," the AEG firm was not on trial. Otto, said Krylenko, was a former member of the Black Reichswehr's civilian organization, Stahlhelm, and of a proczarist organization, Friends of New Russia, which made him "politically untrustworthy" and which made it "entirely plausible that he had acted as liaison between the saboteurs and the Germans"; thus Krylenko demanded that Otto be sentenced to six months in prison. Badstieber, having confessed to bribery, should be given a suspended sentence; and because of the retraction of the testimony of the principal witness against Maier, charges against him should be dropped.

Four months after the arrests, the Soviet court presented its verdict. Thirty-seven of the Russians received varying prison terms; one had not been brought to trial because he had gone mad while in confinement; and eleven were condemned to death. Of the Germans, Badstieber was given a suspended sentence of one year, while Otto and Maier were acquitted.

Von Brockdorff thus had achieved his goal. He had obtained the release of all five of the Germans who had been arrested, and the Soviet government, obviously in concern for the political consequences of the trial and presumably having accomplished its domestic ends, had proved to be conciliatory. Hardly was the trial over before the Foreign Commissariat indicated that in the wake of the demonstration of the objectivity of proletarian justice, conversations leading to a new and broader commercial treaty should be resumed.

Yet for von Brockdorff, there was in the outcome no real triumph. So many things had by that time combined to convince him that the Spirit of Rapallo was dead: the brutality of the Soviet regime, the forcible and agonizing remodeling of Socialist agriculture (collective farms), the unending unpredictability of Soviet foreign policy. In view of his trying experiences in Russia, how could he maintain any hope that Russo-German collaboration would accomplish anything toward helping Germany recover from the humiliation of Versailles?

His service in Moscow, von Brockdorff believed, had achieved little with the possible exception of the threat of a Russo-German partnership's having helped Germany back into the circle of western nations. Aware that he was dying, he concluded that the time had come for him to leave Moscow; he had never liked the place much in any case. On July 18, 1928, he boarded the Berlin Express. There was nobody to see him off except his own staff, although he comforted himself in the belief that his long-time dinner companion, one whom he looked upon as a true friend, Chicherin, would have been there had not his diabetes confined him to his bed.

In one of von Brockdorff's last official acts, he engaged upon arrival in Berlin in a conference at the Foreign Ministry, which was attended by Chicherin's deputy, Litvinov, and Ambassador Krestinsky, designed to explore how relationships between the two governments might be improved. Upon yet another promise that the Comintern would be restrained, von Hindenburg's government entered into a new commercial treaty.

Thus it appeared that in Russo-German relationships, little had changed. Yet, in fact, everything had changed. Those arbiters of cooperation, Chicherin and von Brockdorff, were gone: with Chicherin so incapacitated by his diabetic condition that he was foreign commissar only in name, the foreign policy of the Soviet Union actually rested with a chubby little proletarian, Maxim Litvinov, while von Brockdorff was at last retired to his estate in Schleswig-Holstein, where he had so often threatened in his frustration in Moscow to go, and there, only a few weeks after his retirement, on September 8, 1928, he died of cancer.

## Chapter Thirty-Four

There was something unearthly about Heinrich Himmler. The British ambassador in Berlin, Sir Nevile Henderson, would write that "Himmler was the most enigmatical and elusive of all the Nazi leaders . . . it was scarcely possible to believe that this mild-looking and bespectacled young man with his somewhat deprecatory manner and the appearance of a provincial schoolmaster, could be the tyrant directly responsible for the persecution of the so-called enemies of the state. . . . But like a mole, he worked unceasingly underground, and his galleries were burrowed under the whole fabric of the German state."[1]

The son of a Munich tutor and the godson of Prince Heinrich of Wittelsbach, Himmler attended the University of Munich, where he studied strawberry mutations and raising chickens. As a youth, he was a solitary figure, a nature lover, striding up and down mountains, collecting wild flowers and butterflies, and engaging in earnest and passionate conversations on the alpine meadows about his hero, Henry the Fowler, King of the Saxons from 876 until 926. For his beloved Germany he envisaged a Teuton society based upon peasants among whom the men would be sturdy leaders conscious of "the world's lies and frauds" and the women would be "lively, clean-living . . . with true maternal instincts, free from the diseases of today's degenerate city women, strong and gracious, leaving the last word to the man in the everyday things of life." In that utopia, value would be placed "upon character, rather than knowledge," and the object would be to produce "men of healthy bodies, strong nerves, and strong wills."[2]

Such pastoral fantasies were common among German youth faced with the confusions created by the collapse of the imperial state, the "Judeo-democracy" of the Weimar Republic, and the bewildering intrigues of the Bolsheviks. Yet in Himmler they reposed in a man who intended to give practical expression to the Nordic dreamland; while continuing to attend Sunday mass at Munich Cathedral, he joined an organization called the Reichskriegsflagge, which soon placed itself under the leadership of Adolf Hitler and was in time to become the Praetorian Guard of the Third Reich, the Schutzstaffel, or SS.

The young Himmler rose swiftly in the hierarchy of the National Socialist Party. By early 1928 he had become the deputy to Reichsführer-SS Joseph Goebbels, a failed novelist and poet who was Hitler's chief propagandist. Himmler by that time had married a blonde, blue-eyed Valkyrie named Marga, who ran a private clinic for geriatrics, and with her money he had established a chicken farm near Munich. Yet the blush of happiness in the marriage was brief; his wife was eight years his senior, a divorcee, and a Protestant, and she was also cloying. To escape the sugary *Gemütlichkeit* domesticity of marriage to Marga, Himmler threw himself ever more deeply into his work with the SS. "You naughty soldier of fortune," wrote Marga from the farm. "You must come to this part of the world sometimes."[3]

Himmler had by that time become a devoted disciple of the Führer. It mattered not to him that in the elections for the Reichstag, only twelve Nazis had been elected to that legislature of 540 seats, that the National Socialist Party, with only 800,000 of 33 million votes, was the weakest party in the parliament; he believed, as did his chief, Goebbels, who was one of the twelve elected to the Reichstag, that the election was but a prelude to what was to come.

With passionate zeal, Himmler began to create an intelligence service with which to fight the party's enemies, particularly the Bolsheviks and the Comintern. It would in time become known as the Sicherheitsdienst, but it was still in an embryonic stage when Himmler in 1931 encountered a young former naval officer named Reinhard Tristan Eugen Heydrich. Born in Halle, a folkish town of steep-roofed, half-timbered houses in the Teutoburg Forest, Heydrich was the son of an opera singer father and an actress mother, who named him after characters in Wagner's operas. Heydrich excelled at everything he approached: unusually intelligent, he became an outstanding naval officer, athlete, and swordsman, a skilled linguist, and a proficient fighter pilot. He was also an exquisite violinist, a delight to hear and watch; it was said that as he played, he would weep. Heydrich also possessed what Himmler would call "an infallible nose for men—he saw the ways which friend or foe would take with a clarity that was absolutely amazing."

He was also amoral to such a degree that when he was eventually murdered in 1942 by British agents, a member of Himmler's order of chivalry, Sepp Dietrich, would remark: "Thank God that sow's gone to the butcher."[4]

Not long before coming to see Himmler, Heydrich had impregnated the daughter of one of the directors of the I. G. Farbenindustrie, a chemical trust and the most powerful business firm in Germany. When the girl's father insisted that Heydrich marry his daughter, he refused; he would never marry a girl of such easy virtue. Almost defiantly, he became engaged to a nineteen-year-old Valkyrie, Lina Mathilde von Osten. When the wronged girl's father brought the matter before the commander of the Navy, a court of honor was convened, and when Heydrich still refused to marry the girl, the Board of Admirals decided he lacked the honorable qualities to serve in the German Navy; the fearful words were stamped on his documents: "Dismissal for Impropriety."

Heydrich was at that point unemployed in a nation where there were 6 million others in the same predicament. Influential in the National Socialist Party, the beautiful Fräulein von Osten arranged for her fiancé to meet Himmler, who was immediately impressed by one who looked to be the personification of Himmler's racial ideal: Heydrich was tall, slender, blond, blue-eyed, with a lithely muscular build and an excellent leg for a jackboot. Although he spoke with a markedly high falsetto ring to his voice, that appeared to concern Himmler little. On the spot, he gave Heydrich twenty minutes in which to draft a plan for forming the Sicherheitsdienst. So impressed was he with what Heydrich produced that he subsequently adopted the plan, and on October 4, 1931, the party headquarters in Hamburg received a telegram: "Party Member Reinhard Heydrich, Membership Number 544916, will, with effect from October of this year, be carried on the strength of party headquarters as a member of the staff of the *Reichsführer-SS* Himmler with the rank of *Sturmführer-SS*."[5]

With the addition of Heydrich to the staff, Himmler was equipped to turn the Sicherheitsdienst into one of the phenomena of the early twentieth century, the Extraordinary Department of the National Socialist Party, a medieval brute cabal devoted to acquiring, by whatever means, the information needed to protect the faith.

As the decade of the 1920s neared an end, the problems that bedeviled the Weimar Republic were the same that had accompanied its birth: reparations, the Comintern, French hatred based on fear of German militarism, and a disordered political spectrum. Those problems were complicated by an economy functioning on foreign credit, a chronic disaffection throughout the republic, and the continued presence of foreign troops on German soil; but the large mass of the people saw some compensation in the economic boom of 1928. It was as unexpected and as welcome as an Indian Summer: unemployment dropped dramatically, production rose steadily, per capita income was the highest ever, and real wages for the first time reached their prewar level.

Yet as the man who continued to serve as foreign minister, Gustav Stresemann,

saw with more clarity than most, economic storm clouds were gathering; and
because the German economy was peculiarly dependent upon foreign investment,
a world economic crisis was likely to wreak particularly serious damage on
Germany. The arbiter of Germany's stability and the future of Europe, Stresemann
warned, was neither Communist nor capitalist but gold. Each year Germany had
to pay the Versailles powers 2.5 billion gold marks in reparations. Although there
had been some reduction in 1924, the requirement was still onerous and could be
met only by massive borrowing, mostly through short-term notes, and the
Versailles powers had as yet set no limit on the reparations. Largely through
personal diplomacy, Stresemann finally achieved in 1929, by means of a measure
known as the Young Plan, a limitation on reparations; the plan set total remaining
German payments at 121 billion Reichsmarks payable in fifty-nine annuities,
ended foreign controls on German industry, railways, and customs, and required
the Allies to complete evacuation of the Rhineland by June 1930, four and a half
years before the date set by the Treaty of Versailles.

Long in frail health, Stresemann lived to see accord reached on the Young Plan,
but on October 3, 1929, before the holding of a national plebiscite to determine
German adherence to it, he died of the second of two strokes.

Only three weeks after Stresemann's death, on October 24, 1929, the economic
storm that he had warned against struck with the resounding crash of the New
York Stock Exchange in what came to be called Black Friday. The catastrophe
that followed, the Great Depression, that vast spasm between the end of the
industrial revolution and the start of the technological age, dealt the Weimar
Republic, as Stresemann had feared, a devastating blow.

In the campaign preceding the plebiscite on the Young Plan, Adolf Hitler led
the opposition. "You will pay eighty gold marks a second for sixty years!" ran one
of Goebbels' slogans. "It means slave labor for three generations!" ran another.
Although the campaign failed, it drew 6 million votes, and Hitler moved
immediately to turn those votes into a political base for National Socialism. When
President von Hindenburg called for elections to the Reichstag, they took place in
an atmosphere of public disorder with Nazis and Communists brawling in the
streets. When the results were in, the Communists had increased their membership in the Reichstag from 54 to 77, but the Nazi membership had increased from
12 to 107 on a wave of more than 18 percent of the total vote. Flaunting the
triumph, the new Nazi delegates defied regulations to appear in the Reichstag in
the brown uniforms of the Sturmabteilung.

As if heaven-sent for Hitler's purposes, the Great Depression worsened, for no
measure taken by any of the affected nations would succeed in halting the
onrushing disaster. It was a worldwide epidemic of a kind never before seen. To
tens of millions of Germans, the only hope appeared to lie either with the extreme
right or the extreme left, for the government of the political centrist, Chancellor
Heinrich Brüning, appeared to be powerless. By the end of 1930, the unemployed

in Germany totaled 5 million; of every thousand of the population capable of working, 61 in France were unemployed, 110 in Japan, 186 in Britain, 207 in the United States, and 275 in Germany, and that was taking place in a nation still required to pay reparations.

In July 1931, the Darmstadt and National Bank, one of the four largest in Germany, collapsed in what was the largest bank failure in the history of Europe. The collapse of thousands of banks and businesses, large and small, followed. The first manifestations of anarchy, that stage of human affairs when all order and all purpose is lost, began to appear, and in the political shadows, the extremist leaders—on the right, Adolf Hitler, and on the left, Ernst Thaelmann, whose orders came from the Comintern—watched and waited.

Born in Hamburg, Ernst Thaelmann was a Stalinist, a Communist who believed implicitly not in Utopian Socialism but in the dedication of the Communist movement to the task of protecting the cradle of Socialism, the Soviet Union. He had attended the Third Congress of the Communist International, had participated in the Hamburg insurrection in 1923, and the next year had attended the Comintern Executive Committee's deliberations over the failure of the German October. Other than that, little was known of him, partly because Hitler would in time see to it that he was murdered. Yet Thaelmann was Hitler's chief competitor for power in Germany, and as the world economic crisis that Lenin long ago had predicted came to pass, Thaelmann's assignment was to ensure that out of it emerged a Soviet Republic of Germany.

To advance that purpose, the Red Army over the years had secretly sent several hundred advisers to Germany to train German Communists in the crafts of revolutionary warfare. In every major city, there were well-equipped Red Brigades, some even armed with cannon and all better organized and more battle-ready than had been Trotsky's centurions in Petrograd in 1917. As proclaimed by Thaelmann in 1931, the doctrine for people's revolution in Germany differed markedly from that which had gained power in Russia; rather than swift, carefully planned strikes by small bands of dedicated revolutionaries, there was to be general warfare by the masses with the Red Brigades leading the fight. Street brawling between the Red Brigades and Hitler's storm troopers was soon a way of life in German cities, and often when the police intervened, the two sides would combine to fight them off. Yet while their fervor might unite them against the authorities, it did nothing to dilute the implacability of their hatred for each other.

Hitler carried his message not only to the man in the street but also to the chimney barons who crowded the Düsseldorf Industry Club. "Bolshevism today," he declared, "is not merely a mob storming about in our streets in Germany but is a conception of the world which is on the point of subjecting to itself the entire Asiatic Continent, and . . . will gradually shatter the whole world and bring it down in ruins."[6] Nor did Hitler forget that he would need allies in his crusade against the Communist International: in an interview with a correspondent of a

British newspaper, the *Daily Express*, he urged an Anglo-German alliance against Russia, and to a corresponent for the *Daily Mail*, he described the Germany he intended to create as a nation with a mission to create an army solely for the task of destroying the Red Army and the Communist International. It was a prospect that a sector of the ruling classes of Britain, France, and the United States looked upon with favor. Alarmed by the appeal and vigor of what the American news magnate William Randolph Hearst called "the alien cult," leading personalities in that sector were soon expressing deep interest in what Hitler had to offer, an alliance that Hitler would call the Blue International.

With President von Hindenburg's term of office expiring in 1932, Hitler made a bid for power through the polls. With three other candidates, he stood against the old soldier for the office, forcing a runoff in which von Hindenburg amassed more than 19 million votes to Hitler's more than 13 million. In the wake of that indication that Hitler's strength was increasing, elections for the Reichstag in July 1932 brought 230 National Socialists into the assembly.

To Hitler, there was no question that he should be called upon to form a new government, for the Nazis had won almost 14 million votes, half a million more than the combined total of their two closest rivals, which included the Communists. Yet that was reckoning without the determination of the old gentleman, von Hindenburg; he would have no part of the upstart Austrian. Von Hindenburg finally proffered the post of vice chancellor, but Hitler refused it. He had dedicated himself to wiping out the Marxists, he said, and he could do that only if he controlled the government. When the news reached the streets, the storm troopers clamored for action, but Hitler in an impassioned plea convinced their leaders that a putsch would be disastrous, that power by legal means was soon to be achieved.

Such was the power of the Nazi delegates in the Reichstag that they were able to paralyze a new government under Chancellor Franz von Papen and force new elections in November 1932. When those results were in, many began to bemoan Hitler's failure to listen to the storm troopers, for in the new elections, the Nazis lost nearly 2 million votes and thirty-four of their assembly seats. The Communists, on the other hand, increased their seats by fourteen.

Yet again no single party nor any combination of parties was able to achieve a working majority in the Reichstag to form a new government. For all von Hindenburg's antipathy to the man he called "the Bohemian corporal," the aged president finally felt compelled to offer Hitler the chancellorship. Hardly had the news been announced on January 28, 1933, when rumors swept Berlin that the commander in chief of the Army, General Kurt von Hammerstein-Equord, had alerted the garrison at nearby Potsdam and to prevent Hitler from becoming chancellor, was planning to arrest von Hindenburg and establish a military dictatorship. Thaelmann added to the tension by calling on Communists and workers to stage a general strike beginning at dawn on the 30th, the day Hitler was to take the oath of office.

In response, brown-shirted troopers of the Sturmabteilung poured into Berlin from all parts of the country, but nothing happened. The Army made no move, and the general strike never materialized. There was not even a major street disturbance.

At 9:45 A.M. on January 30, 1933, Hitler and the members of his Cabinet filed through snow-covered ministerial gardens to the president's office. There von Hindenburg was abrupt, failing even to welcome the new Cabinet with a speech, and the swearing-in ceremony was soon concluded "in the style of a shotgun wedding."[7] As if dismissing troops in the field, von Hindenburg ended the audience with a wave of his hand: "And now, gentlemen, forward with God!"[8]

Berlin that night was one big gala. Troopers from the SA in their brown uniforms and from the SS in their black were out in force, surprised that the police greeted them not with nightsticks but with smiles. Some policemen even wore swastika bands. Starting at dusk, the troopers began a giant torchlight parade; passing by the presidential palace, they paid tribute to von Hindenburg, then marched past Hitler's new address, 77 Wilhelmstrasse, where the Führer watched from a balcony. Hour after hour, the troopers paraded, torches glowed hypnotically, drums beating thunderously, marchers chanting incessantly, 'Heil, Heil, Sieg Heil!' It was all staged by that master showman, Joseph Goebbels, who had the foresight to take over the radio stations throughout the country so that the burghers everywhere could be treated to eyewitness accounts of the demonstration.

As Hitler was aware, he still had to consolidate his power, but already he had assured that by insisting that there had yet to be another election for the Reichstag, and from his position as chancellor, he was confident of turning that election to his purposes. Thus there was little to detract from the sweetness of the triumph.

After a late supper with Goebbels, Rudolf Hess, Hermann Göring, and others of the inner circle, Hitler himself stayed up even later, engaging in a rambling monologue in which he recounted his triumphs, the consternation his achievement must have been for his Communist opponents, the necessity to achieve his goal of mastering the earth for the white man, the Aryan. It was, he said, the beginning of "the greatest Germanic racial revolution in world history."[9] That evening, said Hitler, "marks the end of the so-called 'Red Berlin.' People are only Red when they have no other way." Some "foreign source," he said, had called him "anti-Christ"; the only kind of "anti" he actually was, he said, was "anti-Lenin."[10]

Outside the Reichskanzlei and away from the mesmerizing flicker of the flares and the beat of marching feet, there were many who viewed the proceedings with grave misgivings. In the French Embassy in Berlin, for example, the counselor noted that as the marching bands approached, they stopped playing their Prussian marching songs, and in the wake of a roll of drums, broke into a soldier's air from the Great War: "Siegreich woll'n wir Frankreich schlagen" ("Victorious We Will Smash the French"). Von Hindenburg's old comrade in arms, General Ludendorff, who had long since become disillusioned with Hitler, sent his former colleague a telegram warning that "you have handed over our sacred German fatherland to one of the greatest demagogues of all time . . . this evil man will plunge our Reich into the abyss and will inflict immeasurable woe on our nation. Future generations will curse you in your grave for this action."[11]

## Chapter Thirty-Five

As time neared for the election campaign that Hitler intended to use to cement his power, there came a thunderbolt. Political police discovered that the two daughters of the commander of the Army, General von Hammerstein-Equord, had been spying on their father for the Communists. Everything he wrote and left in his desk, everything he said in their presence, all was faithfully reported to the editor of a Communist newspaper, *Rote Fahne*, Werner Hirsch, who had been the girls' tutor, and Hirsch had passed the material to the German representative of the Red Army's intelligence service.

It was an incident tailor-made for the Nazi press. It was symptomatic, intoned the press, of a state entwined by Bolshevik tentacles sucking the genius, loyalty, and devotion of the German people. The Nazi journal, *Der Angriff*, epitomized the outcry with a cartoon depicting an evil Bolshevik octopus slithering across a devastated landscape with a naked, nubile Saxon maiden in one tentacle, a bag of gold Reichsmarks in another, a Reichswehr general flailing helplessly in a third, the Reichstag in a fourth, that temple of conservatism, the Herrenclub, in a fifth, a chimney baron in a sixth, and so on to demonstrate that the Communist International had penetrated every treasured aspect of Germanic life. As depicted in the cartoon, the Marxist octopus was obedient only to the Jew, a long-haired, hook-nosed man in silk hat and morning coat who was leading the octopus through the gates of the Kremlin by a halter.

There was a measure of reality behind the representation, for Bolshevism's tentacles did indeed reach into a number of countries and most particularly into Germany where the Soviet agents and those of the Comintern had penetrated many segments of German society, especially in the industrial sector. Although the political police collapsed most of the organizations in the wake of the German October, new organizations soon took their place. By the late 1920s, so widespread was Communist industrial espionage that the Weimar Republic established a special branch of the police to fight it; in 1929 the branch prosecuted 330 cases of industrial espionage; in 1930, over a thousand. So, too, political agitation was rampant to the extent that in the year and a half beginning in June 1931, 111 people were brought to trial for treason.

There was also considerable evidence that the Comintern was using Berlin as a transit center for intelligence agents traveling to and from Moscow and other western countries. The police were soon aware that somewhere in Berlin the Comintern maintained a center for producing passports and other travel documents and that the Soviet trade delegation was financing Comintern operations throughout Western Europe and the Americas. Lacking incontrovertible proof and endeavoring to sustain the Spirit of Rapallo, the government for long tried to downplay the activities, but by 1932 so flagrant were they that the Reichstag enacted a "Decree for the Defense of the National Economy" aimed primarily at suppressing Soviet technical espionage. Adolf Hitler was to find that decree a convenient precedent for others.

On February 1, 1933, Hitler went to the microphones of Radio Berlin to open the election campaign. The speech was a masterpiece of Hitlerian oratory focused on the Red threat, its impact less in drama than in sexuality. That and Hitler's other oratorical triumphs appeared to be "surrogate actions of a churning sexuality unable to find its object. . . . The sound recordings of the period clearly convey the peculiarly obscene, copulatory character of mass meetings: the silence at the beginning, as of a whole multitude holding its breath; the short, shrill yappings; the minor climaxes; and then the ecstasies released by the finally unblocked oratorical orgasms." The speeches, another observer would note, were "like sex murders."[1]

Since "the days of treachery" in November 1918, Hitler began, "the Almighty has withheld his blessing from our people." Partisan strife, hatred, and chaos had transformed the German nation into "a confusion of political and personal opinions, economic interests, and ideological differences." He deplored the hunger, uncertainty, insecurity, misery, and inner decay of those "wasted years," which were attributable in large measure to "a powerful and insidious attack" by Communism. That "negative, destroying spirit," Hitler continued, had undermined the family, morality, faith, culture, business, justice, honor. Sounding much like the young Winston Churchill, Hitler cried: "Fourteen years of Marxism have ruined Germany; one year of Bolshevism would destroy her."

The policy of the new German government would be "to revive in the nation the spirit of unity and cooperation," to foster "Christianity as the foundation of our national morality, and the family as the basis of racial and political life." He intended to revive the economy by two great Four Year Plans and to restore Germany to a position of power capable of meeting what appeared to be "a constantly accelerating pace toward a new [world] conflict, the extreme solution of which is Bolshevism, whose essence and goal is the elimination and displacement of the hitherto leading social classes of humanity by international Jewry." No nation, he said, would be able "to avoid this historical conflict" in which "an ideologically divided democratic world faces a determined will to attack based on unified authoritarian ideology." Faced with such a dire challenge, his government, said Hitler, could not be bound by constitutional checks, could not "make the work of reconstruction dependent upon the approval of those who were responsible for the collapse. The Marxist parties and their leaders have had fourteen years to show what they can do. The result is a heap of ruins."[2]

As might have already been apparent to anybody who chose to look beneath the surface of Hitler's pronouncements, Hitler saw the threat of Communism as his ticket to total authority over the state. As a preliminary to that goal, he accepted an invitation on the fourth day of his chancellery, on February 3, 1933, to dine at the official residence of the commander in chief of the Army, General von Hammerstein-Equord, who had so recently been torn by the revelation that his beloved daughters had been subverted by the Bolsheviks. There Hitler told the leaders of the armed forces that the first requirement for Germany's regaining its position of power was internal stability, and that was to be achieved by "the ruthless extermination of Marxism." In a move to placate the generals, who had long been concerned about the increasing power of the SA and the SS, Hitler assured them that the German Army would be the sole bearer of arms in the new state. Yet the Army, he said, need have no concern for internal stability; he would achieve that through "a stringently authoritarian administration," leaving the Army free to concentrate on rearmament and an eventual "concentration of power for the conquest of new living space in the East and its ruthless Germanization."[3]

The next day, February 4, 1933, Hitler pushed through the Cabinet a Decree for the Protection of the German People. Proclaimed as a prophylactic against Bolshevism, the decree permitted him on the vaguest grounds to forbid political meetings and to proscribe the press of rival parties. When none of the non-Nazi members of the Cabinet lodged a protest, President von Hindenburg signed it, and Hitler used the decree almost immediately to shut down the Communist press. Two days later he pushed through a second decree enabling him to replace the Prussian state government on the grounds that the government harbored officials who consciously desired to harm Germany, while to the ex-fighter ace, Hermann Göring, he entrusted the task of purging the interior ministry of non-Nazi officials and establishing tight control over the state police, a task Göring accomplished in less than a fortnight, and then in time went on to establish the Geheime Staatspolizei, the Secret State Police, which would become known as the Gestapo.

The Communists tried to fight back. On February 21, 1933, the Union of Red Fighters demanded that the Red Brigades disarm the SA and the SS. "Every comrade a commander in the coming Red Army!" read the proclamation. "This is our oath for the Red soldiers of the Soviet Union. Our fight cannot be broken by machine guns or pistol-barrels or prison. We are the masters of tomorrow!"[4]

In response, Göring banned all Communist assemblies in Prussia, an edict that inspired bloody street fighting and provided him whatever excuse he needed to raid the headquarters of the German Communist Party at Karl Liebknecht House in Berlin. In a raid on February 24, 1933, the police claimed to have discovered "tons of treasonous materials" containing evidence, said Göring, of "a projected Communist revolution."[5] Yet no document verifying that intention was ever made public; that, said the Communists, was because they had abandoned the headquarters well in advance of the raid and no such documents existed.

As raids against other suspected Communist hideouts continued, Göring claimed to have uncovered the secret offices of the Comintern's Western Bureau and the Department for International Liaison, where a large stockpile of several thousand genuine and forged passports was discovered, as well as hundreds of official stamps from many nations and a collection of signatures from police and passport officials throughout Europe. Elsewhere the police found a printing shop belonging to the Comintern, which was equipped with modern lithography machines and process-engraving equipment. Although none of the evidence was ever made public, the *ratissages* were in themselves sufficient to drive many of the Comintern's agents and the headquarters of the Western European Bureau out of Germany.

There was enough evidence, Göring told Hitler, to outlaw the German Communist Party, but Hitler said no. To declare the party illegal would drive the entire left into the camp of his rivals and at the same time appear to eliminate the very threat that he needed in order to rally support for consolidating his power. The election campaign would have to come first.

Hitler opened the campaign with a mass meeting in the Sportspalast in Berlin. Bands, searchlights, swastikas, marching feet, Celtic drums and horns, orchestrated shouts of *"Sieg Heil!"* It was, declared Hitler, his "rockhard conviction that sooner or later the hour will come in which the millions who hate us today will stand behind us and together with us will hail what we have jointly created, toilsomely struggled for, bitterly paid for: the new German Reich of greatness and honor and power and glory and justice. Amen!" From the Sportspalast, Hitler went to the presidential palace for a meeting with leaders of finance, industry, mining, and commerce; Bolshevism, he told them, could be overcome only by a tightly organized and controlled ideological state, for constitutional democracy provided the Communists with the tool they needed to penetrate and exploit the inner weaknesses of the nation. In response, the chimney barons contributed 3 million marks.

Hitler would have welcomed a Communist attempt at revolution as a worthy addition to his campaign. That was his "old dream: to be called in at the climax of a Communist uprising and annihilate the great foe in a single dramatc clash. Then he would be hailed by the nation as the restorer of order and granted legitimacy and respect." Yet as Rosa Luxemburg had cried after the failure of the Spartakus Revolution in 1919: "Where is the German proletariat?" The German proletariat had long been more interested in the *Bierlokal* than the barricades, and in awareness of that, the Comintern directed all party cells to lie low until the Hitler furor had passed, as they were convinced it would. There would thus be no attempted Communist revolution to help Hitler in his campaign, but that might not rule out the staging of a revolution. Or if not that, perhaps Hitler might take advantage of some dramatic event that could be pinned on the Communists.

On the evening of February 27, 1933, Hitler dined with his minister of propaganda and national enlightenment, Joseph Goebbels, at Goebbels' apartment in the Reichskanzlerplatz. At about nine o'clock, the two settled down to listen to a new recording of Gustav Mahler's *Kindertotenlieder*, those haunted songs of childhood death. The recording was nearing an end—*Ich bin der Welt abhanden gekommen*—when Hitler and Goebbels heard fire bells ringing in the streets. A few minutes later, the telephone rang. It was Hitler's old crony, Ernst Hanfstängel, breathless: the Reichstag was on fire!

Goebbels thought at first that the report was a prank, but when he went to a window, he could see that the undersides of the clouds over the Reichstag were tinged blood-red. Telephoning Göring's office, he confirmed that the Reichstag was, indeed, on fire. When he hurried back to the drawing room and told Hitler, Hitler bolted from his chair. "It's the Communists!" he exclaimed. "Now I have them!"

Rushing to Goebbels' large Mercedes tourer in the street below, Hitler and Goebbels tore down the Charlottenburger Chaussee toward the Reichstag. By the time they arrived, there was a bright red glow under the great dome of the building, and smoke poured from the windows. Making their way over coils of firehoses, they reached the grand lobby where they found Göring surrounded by newsmen; the fire, he was telling them, was "the beginning of the Communist uprising. Now they are going to strike. Not a minute must be lost!" As Hitler's face turned red from the heat and excitement, he took up the chorus. Although the chief of the Prussian political police, Rudolf Diels, told Hitler that the police had caught the arsonist, who swore that he had worked alone and denied any connection with the Communists, Hitler refused to listen. "This is a cunning and well-prepared plot," he insisted. "The only thing is that they have reckoned without us and without the German people. In their ratholes, from which they are now trying to crawl out, they cannot hear the jubilation of the masses."[6]

From the scene of the fire, Göring went to the police command telephone and placed the Prussian police force on emergency alert. That same night, the police arrested 4,000 people, most of them Communists, including the parliamentary party leader in the Reichstag, Ernst Torgler. Göring, meanwhile, was officially proclaiming that "The burning of the Reichstag was intended to be the signal for a bloody uprising and civil war." He claimed to have proof that the Communists planned large-scale pillaging to follow the fire and that acts of terrorism were scheduled throughout the country "against prominent individuals, against private property, against the lives and safety of the peaceful population, and general civil war was to be unleashed." He had ordered the arrest, he said, of two prominent Communist deputies to the Reichstag on suspicion of having been involved in setting the fire, while other Communist deputies and party functionaries were being taken into protective custody.

The next day Hitler proposed another restrictive decree in the Cabinet. Such was the concern over the Red threat as Hitler presented it that none of the non-Nazi members of the Cabinet protested other than to suggest the change of a word here and there, yet it was a decree that went beyond suspending civil rights to eliminating them outright: free speech, free press, sanctity of the home, secrecy of mail and telephone, freedom to assemble, inviolability of private property. While the non-Nazi members, including the former chancellor, Franz von Papen, could hardly have been unaware of the extent of the powers involved in the decree, they were conscious that they still held a majority in the Cabinet and assumed that once the Communist crisis was over, they would be able to relax or repeal the decree. Yet that was reckoning without the determination of Hitler and the National Socialists to retain any power once gained, to use the power itself to maintain it.

In view of the extraordinary powers conferred by the decree, it was widely believed, particularly by the foreign press, that Göring had engineered the fire to enable Hitler to seize power. By Göring's account, the arrested arsonist, a young Dutchman, Martin van der Lubbe, who appeared to be mentally deficient and who professed to have resigned in disgust from the Communist Party four years earlier because of the party's inaction, confessed to having set the fire, twenty-four blazes in all; but shortly before discovery of the fire, van der Lubbe was seen conferring with the parliamentary Communist Party leader in the Reichstag, Ernst Torgler. Foreign observers found it hard to believe that one man could have set twenty-four separate fires before discovery, but Göring would go to his death denying any connection with the fire.

On March 4, 1933, the eve of the election for the Reichstag, the Nazis celebrated with a magnificent ceremony in Northeast Prussia at Königsberg, once the seat of the Grand Master of the Teutonic Knights and after them the coronation city of the kings of Prussia. Only recently an SS newspaper had woven the castle at Königsberg into Nazi legend by running a serialized account telling of a seventeen-year-old girl who had been lured there by a Jew for midnight bathing in the nude but had been rescued from a fate worse than death by the timely arrival of a patrol of SS troopers. In the historic setting of Königsberg, the ceremony was to consecrate Hitler as the new spiritual and temporal leader of the Reich, the reincarnation of Friedrich Barbarossa. *"Hitler ist der Sieg!"* ("Hitler Is Victory Itself!") proclaimed a hundred blood-red posters on the ancient Hanseatic walls. Down ancient cobbled streets reverberated the incantations of the storm troopers: *"Deutschland erwache! Ju–da ver–recke!"* ("Germany awake! Perish Judah!") A great crowd of *Herrenvolk* beneath the floodlit castle chanted a Nazi liturgy: "You are nothing—your nation is everything!"

The ceremony was well along when the last of a group of preliminary but eloquent speakers declared: "Now he approaches, he whom the voices of our poets and sages have summoned, the liberator of the German genius." As Hitler approached in the brown uniform of the SA, wearing a glistening black Sam Browne and burnished boots and leggings and with an Iron Cross Second Class pinned to his chest, the speaker concluded: "He has removed the blindfold from our eyes, and . . . has enabled us to see and love again the one essential thing, our unity of blood, our German self, the *homo germanus.*"

The fury of the applause at Hitler's appearance drowned out the speaker's last words. Mounting the tribunal, Hitler gave the *Hitlergruss*—the stiff-armed Nazi salute—and at the precise moment when he began to speak, bonfires on every hilltop along every frontier of the Reich burst into flame, a signal and warning that Germany had awakened. Through synchronized radio hookups, Hitler's hoarse, mesmeric voice wafted to every corner of the nation. For the twenty-eight and one-half minutes that he spoke, all ordinary activities ceased. As the conductor Wilhelm Furtwängler would recall, such was the moment that he stopped the Berlin Philharmonic in mid-concerto to permit the packed audience to hear the broadcast.

"Now hold your heads high and proud, once again!" Hitler concluded. "Now you are no longer enslaved and unfree; now you are free again! By God's gracious aid you are free!" At that moment bands and a massed choir burst into the choral hymn *"Nun danket Alle Gott,"* sung always during great occasions of state in Germany ever since Frederick the Great's victory over the Austrians at Leuthen in 1757. As the choir reached the last stanza, the bells in Königsberg Cathedral began to peal, their ringing carried by radio throughout the land.

The outcome of the elections on the morrow proved to be less satisfying to the National Socialists than the grandeur of their election-eve ceremony would have indicated. Of more than 39 million votes cast, the Nazis received more than 17 million, more by far than any other single party, but the Center Party and the Social Democrats maintained their strength, and it would require the collaboration of fifty-two delegates of the Nationalist Party for Hitler to achieve a bare majority in the Reichstag.

The fact was hardly to be discerned by the party's official proclamations. He had won, Hitler declared, "a colossal victory," while Goebbels pronounced that the vote provided "the basis for the historic mission—to execute the verdict that the people have passed upon Marxism." Nor were Hitler's early political moves the work of a man doubting his mandate: on the day after the election he placed on von Hindenburg's desk for signature a proclamation replacing the black, red, and gold flag of the Weimar Republic with the black, red, and white of the German Empire, which thenceforth would fly from all public buildings with the hooked cross of the Nazi Party, the swastika flag, alongside it. Renunciation of the Treaty of Versailles, including its disarmament and reparations requirements, was soon to follow, along with termination of the military arrangement with the Red Army, but Hitler would carefully maintain the Treaty of Berlin, for he had no wish at that point to alarm the parvenus in the Kremlin.

Across the seas, the rise of a beer-hall fighter to be chancellor of Germany invoked little attention or alarm in the United States, for that nation had turned inward in hope of finding relief from the debacle of the Great Depression. In the European states, there was considerably more concern but no action. Hitler nevertheless sought to salve the concern, particularly in Britain. At his direction, Goebbels emphasized the national rather than the Socialist nature of the new government, its traditional rather than its revolutionary attitudes, and to show the

British crown that Hitler was the protector rather than the usurper of monarchy, he pointed up the fact that King George V's great-nephew, the old kaiser's son, Prince August Wilhelm, had joined the Sturmabteilung and hinted that if Hitler's chancellery prospered, the Hohenzollerns might be restored to the throne.

Yet as Hitler recognized, a bow to European monarchy—even British monarchy—was but a formality. What mattered was not royalty but industry and finance, and with that truth in mind, he sought out the financial wizard who had stemmed inflation and had lately become a Nazi acolyte, Hjalmar Schacht. Schacht's mission was to convince the world's industrial and financial circles that Hitler was no wild-eyed revolutionary but rather a German nationalist with a profound concern about Bolshevism whom the German people had elected as the only man capable of stemming the onrushing political tide of Bolshevik Russia. If supported, Schacht was to explain, Hitler would prove to be Europe's principal bulwark against the alien cult.

Schacht was hardly likely to fail in his mission. The European and American financial communities—the gnomes of London, Zurich, and New York—had since 1923 formed a high regard for Schacht's abilities in stabilizing the German economy. In the City of London, a community largely conservative in attitude, few would also fail to note how the German monarchy and nobility had been justly recompensed for the expropriation of their assets. Of particular importance, Schacht was considered reliable by that formidable figure of world finance, Montagu Norman, governor of the Bank of England, which was one of the world's most powerful and most secretive institutions.

When on March 17, 1933, Hitler chose Schacht as president of the Reichsbank, Norman and his colleagues could hardly have looked upon it with anything but approval. With Schacht at the financial helm, the international leaders of finance and industry were convinced that Hitler's government would create a Germany that would no longer be an international liability, nor a nation that would succumb to Bolshevism, and of greater importance, "an entirely peace-loving country following the leadership of a great man," functioning, as was President Franklin D. Roosevelt, with "no other purpose than to regain national prosperity after a period of crisis and depression."[7] Largely through the influence of Schacht, Hitler would soon become *salonfähig* (socially acceptable) among many in the ruling circles in Britain and France, in Britain in particular, where some would try to convince successive British governments to abandon their gentlemanly, leisurely approach toward world events and adopt instead some of the new Teutonic dynamism that Hitler demonstrated.

In Berlin, Hitler prepared the final decree that he considered necessary to ensure the power and durability of his regime: the Enabling Act, the title of which tended to obscure the immense power that it entailed. By arresting or otherwise excluding the eighty-one Communist deputies in the Reichstag and by buying the deputies of the Nationalist and Centrist parties with promises, Hitler easily achieved passage of legislation that effectively turned the government into an uncontested dictatorship. Under the Enabling Act, power passed to the chancellor—to Hitler—to produce legislation by decree without consultation either with the president or with the Reichstag, to make changes unilaterally in the constitution, and to negotiate treaties with foreign states. Although the validity of the act and the existence of the government were limited to four years, that would hardly prove to be an obstacle for a government once firmly installed under the other conditions of the act. Along with the decree, enacted the day after the Reichstag fire, the Enabling Act passed the total power of the state into the hands of one man, Adolf Hitler, who in the wake of the death of von Hindenburg in 1934, would merge the offices of president and chancellor under the title Führer und Reichskanzler.

In Hitler's view, the First German Reich was the Holy Roman Empire; the Second Reich was that created in 1871 by Bismarck. On the first day of spring, 1933, Hitler created the Third Reich.

The staging of the ceremony was, as usual, largely in the hands of Joseph Goebbels, a man who single-handedly possessed the ceremonial and propaganda skills of a master to compare with those of the British court and the Holy See. He chose the first day of spring because that was the day on which Bismarck established the Hohenzollerns as the emperors of the Second Reich, a choice bound to appeal to Monarchists, Nationalists, the Junkerdom, generals and admirals alike. He called it the Day of the National Rising, a day on which Germany symbolically awakened from the sloth and despair of the Weimar Republic to resume its rightful position in historic greatness. He as carefully chose the site of the ceremony: Potsdam, an island formed by the river Havel, on which had stood the royal residence since the days of Frederick the Great, the seat of the lord lieutenant of the Mark of Brandenburg, the spiritual home of the Great German General Staff and of the German Army. Although the weather would remain the province of God, the almanacs showed that for a hundred years the sun had shone at Potsdam on the first day of spring. So it was that except for the weather, all was carefully stage-managed.

As it turned out, Goebbels might have ordered the weather as well: the sun was bright and a stiff breeze kept flags unfurled in all their Wotan brilliance. The old streets were packed with scrubbed *Herrenvolk*, pensioners, bands, choirs, storm troopers carrying standards bearing Nazi eagles with the globe in their claws, notables in the full ceremonial of the Guards or in morning dress with high silk hats. Von Hindenburg arrived in the full-dress uniform of the 3rd Regiment of the Guards, carrying his field marshal's baton and wearing the same *Pickelhaube* (spiked helmet) that he had worn when he and Ludendorff had destroyed the Russians at Tannenberg. Hitler arrived in his giant state Mercedes and behind him, vehicles bearing his bodyguard, the Leibstandarte Adolf Hitler, led by Heinrich Himmler in uniform of black and silver and jackboots and wearing pince-nez.

They gathered at the Town Hall. Escorted by the 3rd Regiment and with

President von Hindenburg and Chancellor Hitler leading the way, the procession marched the short distance to the Nikolaikirche for a brief Cromwellian service. With all the bells of Potsdam chiming and pealing, Hitler appeared just before noon on the steps of the Garrison Church. Precisely at midday, von Hindenburg arrived and shook Hitler's hand, symbolizing the unity of the aristocracy and the proletariat, whereupon the two entered the early-eighteenth-century church, which was filled with leaders of the old and new Reichs and with representatives of foreign governments. As they walked down the aisle, Hitler bowed to the crown prince, who was in the dress uniform of the Death's Head Hussars, and von Hindenburg with his baton saluted the empty seat of the kaiser. Together they proceeded to the marble altar beneath which lay the bones of Frederick the Great.

The service opened with *"Nun danket Alle Gott,"* performed by a mighty organ, trumpets, and choir. Then von Hindenburg took out a pair of tortoise-shell glasses and began to read his speech. The tasks facing the new government, he said, were many and difficult, but he asked the Reichstag deputies to support the new government, invoked "the old spirit of this shrine," and called upon the Almighty to bless "a free, proud Germany united within herself." Hitler responded in equally solemn and measured words, summarizing the legacy of economic depression and unemployment that had followed a war that he said was forced upon Germany and the kaiser and espousing his faith in the "eternal foundations" of German life and spirit and in the traditions of German culture. To von Hindenburg, he spoke of "the great-hearted decision" that had made possible "this union between the symbols of old greatness and youthful strength." Looking at the old field marshal as if he were still his military commander, Hitler said he considered it "a blessing to have your consent to the work of the German rising."

As Goebbels would note in his diary, von Hindenburg rose and walked toward the entrance to the crypt of Frederick the Great. "I am sitting close to Hindenburg and see tears filling his eyes. All rise from their seats and jubilantly pay homage to the gray-haired Field Marshal, who is extending his hand to the young Chancellor. A historic moment. The shield of German honor is once again washed clean. The standards with our eagles rise high."

For a few minutes, von Hindenburg disappeared to say prayers over Frederick the Great's sarcophagus, then reappeared and, with Hitler at his side, left the Garrison Church for the Plantage. "Now the trumpets sound," Goebbels recorded. "The President of the Reich stands upon a podium, Field Marshal's baton in hand." Drawn up before him were Teuton phalanxes of Reichswehr, Sturmab-teilung, and Schutzstaffel. In the role of parade master, Heinrich Himmler ordered war flags lowered in salute. Swords flashed, cannon boomed, bells rang. As von Hindenburg saluted with his baton, the battalions goose-stepped past the podium to the light infantry pace beat out by the horse-drummers.

# PART VI

## The Russian Cockpit

*Chapter Thirty-Six*

At the request of the Soviet government in March 1922, a distinguished German doctor, Professor Felix Klemperer, accompanied by a neurologist, Dr. Ottfried R. Foerster, visited Moscow to examine Lenin in an effort to diagnose the cause of lethargy and persistent headaches. To a correspondent for the New York *Times*, Klemperer stated after the examination that he and his colleague had "found only a moderate neurasthenia, the result of overwork." He had prescribed, said Klemperer, exercise, diet, and a holiday.[1]

Yet there were strong doubts whether Professor Klemperer was telling all. Nor was he. He had actually concluded that Lenin's ills were attributable to lead poisoning from two of Fanny Kaplan's bullets that had remained in his body since the near-fatal shooting the evening of August 30, 1918. He prescribed surgery to remove the bullets.

The Russian surgeon who had saved Lenin's life that fateful night at the Kremlin, Vladimir N. Rozanov, disagreed with the diagnosis. Because the body had developed tight fibrous sacs around the bullets, Rozanov maintained, lead from the bullets could not possibly be poisoning Lenin. When a German surgeon, Professor Moritz Borchardt, arrived to perform the operation, Dr. Rozanov agreed to removal of the bullet which was lodged in the neck and which could be felt with the fingertips, but he continued to object to removing the other, which was embedded deep in the left shoulder and would require "an extensive and painful dissection."[2]

A decision made to remove only the bullet in the neck, Professor Borchardt invited Dr. Rozanov to perform the operation, but Rozanov elected instead to serve as assistant surgeon. On April 23, 1922, the bullet was removed without complications and Lenin kept under observation for a day. Lenin then left for a period of rest at his dacha in Gorki. When a few days later Dr. Rozanov asked how he felt, Lenin replied: "In general, not so bad, but I have a headache at times, don't sleep well, and my mood is bad."

Twenty-three days after the operation, Dr. Rozanov received an urgent telephone call from Lenin's sister, Maria. Her brother, she said, was having severe stomach pains and was vomiting. When Rozanov and a team of doctors arrived, they found in attendance a local doctor, who reported that the vomiting had stopped but that Lenin had a persistent headache. In the end, the diagnosis was paresis, or partial paralysis, affecting the right leg and right arm, and there was evidence of speech impairment. Dr. Rozanov would record his reaction: "Death for the first time clearly wagged its finger."

Yet for a while it appeared that death might only be playing a game, for by late October 1922 Lenin had recovered sufficiently to return to Moscow and resume his duties. Dr. Rozanov and the other doctors in Lenin's attendance nevertheless continued to worry, and on December 12, 1922, fearful lest Lenin overwork, they confined him to his private apartment in the Kremlin for a rest. Four days later, at about eleven P.M., he had a second and more serious stroke that left his entire right side paralyzed.

Incapacitated, Lenin nevertheless remained in full possession of his faculties. Lying in bed in the quiet of his apartment, he found time to contemplate the state of Socialism in Russia, and what he discerned plunged him into deep anxiety. "He saw ahead not a communist paradise but a pit of errors and sufferings."[3] In a remarkably short time since the revolution, the apparatus of both the party and the Socialist state had become entangled in the red tape and incompetence of a monstrous bureaucracy with power centralized perilously in the hands of a few, and vocal and strong opposition to it had arisen. Lenin was disturbed, too, by the chauvinism that leading Bolsheviks were displaying toward the non-Russian minorities as he had set about reorganizing the state into a federal system, the Union of Soviet Socialist Republics, a reorganization of which Stalin disapproved but in which as commissar of nationalities he was deeply involved.

Like other leading Bolsheviks, Lenin had long seen Stalin as innocuous, little more than a faithful disciple and able organizer. Since the man was obviously no intellectual, his peers assumed that he was also unintelligent. Yet as Lenin lay alone in the Kremlin with his thoughts, he began to see Stalin differently.

As commissar of nationalities, Stalin had control over the sixty-five million non-Russians out of the country's population of 140 million, and as commissar for state control, he had a hand on the machinery of government. To those posts, he had in April 1922 added a newly created position, that of general secretary of the party's Central Committee. Concerned lest some predominant figure arise out of the Russian Revolution as had Napoleon Bonaparte out of the French Revolution—and that figure might be Trotsky—Lenin himself and Zinoviev and Kamenev had acquiesced in the appointment; it gradually became apparent that in that position Stalin commanded the Orgburo, the party's secretariat, which controlled the party through preparing agendas and minutes, making appointments, and exercising the other dreary activities of the administrator, and which also controlled the Central Control Commission, responsible for party discipline at home and abroad. When added together, control of the Orgburo and the Central Control Commission also meant control of the secret police, the OGPU. For almost a year, operating quietly and in the background, Stalin had been, in effect, the ruler of Russia.

Although the long-faithful Zinoviev might see himself as the heir-apparent to Lenin's crown, it became clear to Lenin in the clairvoyance of approaching death that there were two heirs-apparent and that Zinoviev was not one of them. There was the obvious candidate, Trotsky, and there was Stalin.

On Christmas Day 1922, nine days after his second stroke, Lenin voiced his first written concern about Stalin as he dictated to his secretaries a memorandum for the Congress of Soviets; it would later become known as his testament. Expressing fears about the stability of the party, he noted that the immediate danger was a split in the Central Committee between adherents of Trotsky and Stalin. "Having become General Secretary," said Lenin, "Comrade Stalin has concentrated boundless power in his hands, and I am not certain he can always use this power with sufficient caution." Trotsky, on the other hand, he noted, was "distinguished not only by his remarkable abilities—personally, I think, he is the most able person in the present Central Committee—but he also has an exceptionally extensive self-confidence and an exceptional fascination for the purely administrative aspects of power." The qualities of the two men in juxtaposition, noted Lenin, "might inadvertently lead to a split, and if our party does not take measures to prevent it, the split might arise unexpectedly."

Although Lenin neither suggested any action to prevent a schism nor expressed a specific preference between Trotsky and Stalin, he obviously leaned toward Trotsky. Not quite a fortnight later, on January 4, 1923, he dictated a postscript to his testament to make his position clear:

> Stalin is too rude, and this fault, quite tolerable in the company of communists and among us, becomes intolerable for one who holds the office of General Secretary. Therefore I propose to the comrades to consider a means of removing Stalin from that post and appointing another person to this position who in all respects differs from Stalin only in superiority, namely, more patient, more loyal, more polite, and more attentive to comrades, less capricious, and so forth.

Since the testament and addendum were known at the time only to Lenin's wife, Krupskaya, and to his secretaries, the members of the Politburo were unaware of Stalin's fall from grace. The first inkling they had of it was an article written by Lenin and despite Stalin's efforts to prevent publication, published on March 4, 1923, in *Pravda*. It was a severe condemnation of one of Stalin's subagencies, th People's Commissariat of Workers' and Peasants' Inspection. Lenin also sent a letter to dissident leaders in Georgia promising to support them against Stalin as the commissar of nationalities in the Twelfth Party Congress, due to convene shortly, and as an afterthought, recognizing that he probably would be unable to attend the congress, he dictated a letter to Trotsky, taken down in longhand by Krupskaya, asking Trotsky to support his views and "not to trust any 'rotten compromise' that Stalin might propose."[4]

Learning of the letter to Trotsky and worried that Lenin might be out to destroy him (which, Krupskaya would reveal later, he was), Stalin telephoned Krupskaya and in her words "allowed himself . . . an unusually rude outburst directed at me." Stalin accused her of disturbing her ailing husband with official trivia and threatened to bring charges against her before the Central Control Commission. Upon learning of the encounter, Lenin was furious. An affront to his wife, he wrote Stalin, was an affront to him personally. "I ask you therefore whether you are agreeable to withdrawing your words and apologizing or whether you prefer to break off relations between us."[5] Stalin promptly apologized.

Close on that episode, Lenin, on March 9, 1923, suffered a third and still more severe stroke. Dr. Rozanov found him with dimmed consciousness, high fever, complete paralysis of the right side, partial paralysis of the left, and aphasia. He could explain his condition to Rozanov only by gestures. Three days later the government took the ominous step of issuing daily bulletins, but as the month wore on, an international panel of doctors came to the opinion that Lenin's illness was such that "complete restoration of health is possible." Removed to a rest home in Gorki, he did appear to begin to recover and by September, with the help of orthopedic shoes, was able to walk, but he was still unable to speak.

On the theory that for Lenin politics was therapy, the doctors permitted visits from leaders of the Comintern in Italy, Britain, and Germany, but Lenin took no real part in either party, Comintern, or state affairs; but in late October 1923 he insisted on being driven to Moscow, where he roamed about his office in the Kremlin, touching books and other familiar objects. At last, seemingly having taken a final farewell, he shuffled down the stairs and rode back to his dacha.

In late morning of January 21, 1924, while Krupskaya was away in Moscow, Lenin began to experience severe body spasms, and when his cook, Gavril Volkov, brought his lunch, he passed him a note: "I've been poisoned . . . go fetch Nadya [Krupskaya] at once . . . tell Trotsky . . . tell everyone you can."[6] (Trotsky would later state that Lenin had been poisoned and that Stalin was responsible, but there was no proof, and nobody ever claimed to have seen Lenin's note except Volkov.) At six o'clock that evening, Lenin died of cerebral arteriosclerosis.

Later that evening, Stalin, Zinoviev, Kamenev, Bukharin, Kalinin, and another leading Bolshevik, M. P. Tomsky, rode in sleighs through a cold moonlit night to Gorki to view the body, laid out on a table banked with flowers and fir branches. (Having contracted malaria during a duck shooting weekend in marshy countryside outside Moscow, Trotsky was en route by train to recuperate at the Black Sea spa of Sukhumi.) Two days later the leaders returned to escort the body to Moscow where it lay in state in the old Nobleman's Club while 360,000 people, despite the coldest January in sixty years, paid their respects.

At Stalin's direction, the corpse was then taken to a laboratory where Lenin's brain was removed for inspection and a postmortem conducted. There was no evidence of poison, but many of his organs were in a state of such calcification that when tapped by the faithful Rozanov with a surgical hammer, they rang like stone. After embalming, the body was placed in a special mausoleum erected beside the Kremlin wall near the graves of the Bolshevik heroes who had died in the revolution.

The battle for the succession, long since under way, emerged at that point in full fray.

Well aware that Trotsky was Lenin's choice as successor, Stalin had already moved to isolate Trotsky within the Politburo, a relatively easy task since all— particularly the ambitious Zinoviev—continued to be cautious in case Trotsky should emerge as a Napoleon. During the Twelfth Congress, as Lenin had lain suffering from his third stroke, Stalin could plead the necessity for maintaining party unity in order to defeat an opposition that grew ever more vocal as famine and economic crisis racked the country. Making common cause with Zinoviev and Kamenev, Stalin proposed a triumvirate, or troika, to rule the party until Lenin should recover. Sharing the alarm over the growing opposition, Trotsky too was anxious for unity and made no effort to oppose the troika.

Stalin moved physically and intellectually, his contemporaries would note later, with the speed of a tortoise, but a tortoise with a deadly bite. Having created the ruling troika, he assured himself time by engineering reappointment as general secretary of the party. At that point, through his personal posts and through his connivance with Zinoviev and Kamenev, Stalin maintained direct or indirect control of the all-powerful Politburo, of the Soviet Communist Party and its organizing and disciplinary organs, of the important Moscow and Petrograd soviets, and of the Comintern, and from that point he would work to remove his rivals. "To choose one's victim, to prepare one's plans minutely, to slake an implacable vengeance and then to go to bed," he told Kamenev and Feliks Derzhinski one evening over bottles of Khahetian wine at his dacha, "there is nothing sweeter in the world."[7]

Aside from personal differences that arose during the revolution and culminated in ambition for the succession, the basic conflict between Trotsky and Stalin could even in the Byzantine affairs of the Kremlin be explained simply. Trotsky wanted to be head of a genuine workers' democracy, and he wanted, as always, to achieve through the Comintern a world revolution of the proletariat. Stalin wanted instead to head a dictatorship of the Russian proletariat, closely controlled by the Kremlin and served by a Comintern bound ever more closely to the Soviet state for the defense of the Socialist fatherland. The two positions were irreconcilable.

In June 1923, as Lenin was still ailing in the rest home in Gorki, Stalin tried to insert himself in Trotsky's beloved War Commissariat. As Zinoviev suggested at a Politburo meeting, Trotsky was an extremely busy statesman; would it not be wise, would it not serve to heal wounds, if Trotsky accepted Stalin as a controller within the Commissariat? Trotsky replied that Stalin, too, was a busy man. Conscious of the mess Stalin had made whenever he dabbled in military affairs, Trotsky said flatly there was no need for a controller in the War Commissariat and walked out of the meeting. To Trotsky's defense sprang the chief political commissar of the Red Army, Alexander Antonov-Ovseenko. The Red Army, he declared, would stand up "like one man" for Trotsky, "the leader, organizer, and inspirer of the Revolution's victories." Hardly had Stalin left the meeting than he began plotting to relieve Antonov-Ovseenko of his post while at the same time filing away in the back of his mind the possibility that the Red Army might some day constitute a personal threat.

Upon Lenin's death, Stalin demonstrated the petty personal connivance of which he was capable. Learning the news upon arrival at the Tiflis Station en route to Sukhumi, Trotsky telephoned Stalin to ask when the funeral was to be. Stalin replied that it would be held in two days, on January 26, 1924, and since Trotsky was already two and a half days away from Moscow by train, Stalin advised him to continue his journey, enjoy the sunshine at Sukhumi, and return when he had fully recovered. As Stalin well knew, since he personally was in charge of arrangements, the funeral was set for the 27th, which could have afforded ample time for Trotsky to return. As it was, only one of the two heirs-apparent would be present.

On the 26th, the Politburo conducted a memorial service for Lenin, at which the membership decreed that thenceforth Petrograd would be named Leningrad. Stalin, once a seminary student in his native Georgia, delivered a powerful eulogy couched "in a form of commands and responses echoing the Orthodox liturgy even to the point of using biblical wording," a performance that stirred the great majority of the members who, like Stalin himself, were "rooted in the Russian soil" and found a speech "redolent of old Russia . . . moving and memorable."[8] Stalin needed the support that the performance brought him, for when the Politburo went into secret session, the question at issue was what to do about Lenin's testament, a copy of which Krupskaya had provided in a sealed envelope. Having apparently learned something of the embarrassment the contents posed for him, Stalin moved that the testament be filed with his Secretariat to await Trotsky's return.

Suspicious that Stalin was trying to suppress the document, Krupskaya confronted him. "It's a matter of Vladimir Ilyich's last testament of his last wishes," Krupskaya stormed. "The Party must be told of them. I warn you that if you don't read the testament when the Central Committee meets, I shall publish it myself."[9]

Aware that Krupskaya was probably well able to carry out her threat—she had in fact five copies of the testament and the postscript—Stalin himself produced the document at a plenary session of the Central Committee. According to a member of the Secretariat, Boris Bazhanov, who shortly thereafter defected to Britain, the reading caused considerable embarrassment: "Stalin sitting on the steps of the rostrum looked small and miserable. . . . In spite of his self-control and show of calm, it was clearly evident that his fate was at stake."

Yet so menacing was the specter of Trotsky—not Stalin—as a Bonaparte that Zinoviev rose to Stalin's defense. "Comrades," he declared, "we have sworn to fulfill anything the dying Ilyich ordered us to do." On the other hand, he declared, "You have all witnessed our harmonious cooperation [with Stalin] in the last few months, and, like myself, you will be happy to say that Lenin's fears [about Stalin] have proved baseless." Although Stalin dutifully offered to resign as general secretary, the second member of the troika, Kamenev, waved his gesture away. When both Zinoviev and Kamenev moved that the testament be withheld from the full party membership, the committee voted thirty to ten not only to withhold the testament but also to invite Stalin to remain as general secretary. With that accomplished by the ruling body, there was nothing Krupskaya could do.

Although Stalin was still destined to pass through many perilous interludes in that predatory world which he inhabited, his future was from that moment assured. Quietly but assiduously he began to work to undermine Trotsky by playing on the necessity, now that the great Lenin was gone, to maintain party unity, and in the process, he portrayed Trotsky as the epitome of discord.

In the campaign, Stalin had ready help from Zinoviev and Kamenev, who still feared Trotsky while unaware of Stalin's wiles. At the Thirteenth Party Congress opening on May 23, 1924, for example, Zinoviev called on the opposition— meaning Trotsky—"to liquidate the controversy and come to the congress and say, 'I made a mistake and the party was right!'"[10] With that demand, Zinoviev was going beyond the accepted principle of submission to the will of the party and developing a new policy of recantation, a policy he and others were destined at a later date to rue. Yet Trotsky, while accepting submission, refused recantation. That set him up for a powerful attack by Stalin and for a final resolution by the congress extolling the Central Committee for taking a firm stand against "petty bourgeois deviations." In the circumlocutory language of Communism, that was a preliminary to an eventual sentence of disgrace for the deviationist.

Working closely with Zinoviev, Stalin also connived to convince the Comintern that Trotsky had sinned. Zinoviev had already prepared the way by inviting several prominent members of European Communist parties to sit on the tribunal during the Thirteenth Congress, and by the time the Comintern held its Fifth Congress in Moscow in late June and early July 1924, American, British, French, and German delegates were eager to echo Trotsky's condemnation. When the Comintern called on Trotsky to appear to justify himself, he declined; a true believer in party unity, he saw no point in continuing a debate that could do no good for the party and might even lead to his expulsion. With that development, Stalin had not only sealed Trotsky's eventual end, but he had taken a first step toward recasting the Comintern from a visionary instrument of international Communism into a submissive pawn of Russian Communism existing solely for the service and benefit of the Soviet state.

Under the strain, Trotsky's frail health began to deteriorate. Although doctors recommended rest in a warm climate, he refused to leave his apartment in the Kremlin, seemingly resigned to his fate. A few days before a meeting of the Central Committee on January 20, 1925, he wrote what became known as his letter of resignation, again expressing his loyalty and submission to the party and suggesting that he resign as war commissar but again declining to confess error.

As the Central Committee sat, Kamenev demanded Trotsky's dismissal from the Politburo, others his expulsion from the party, others his arrest. Always the sly master of the situation, Stalin declined to go along. "Obviously," he declared, "Trotsky does not understand that the Party demands . . . not diplomatic evasions, but an honest admission of kes." Yet he asked only what Trotsky himself had offered, his resignation as war commissar, a step Stalin obviously saw as vital lest Trotsky's acquiescent attitude in time might fade and he should lead a military coup d'état. Although relieved of that post, Trotsky continued as a member of the Central Committee and of the Politburo, but it was clear to all—including himself—that he survived on sufferance.

Stalin's next step was to dispense with Zinoviev and Kamenev. As he turned the hot breath of his intrigue upon them, such was his success that they turned in desperation to Trotsky, the man they had connived to destroy. The common front they established disturbed Stalin not at all. "Ah!" he exclaimed. "They have granted themselves a mutual amnesty."[11]


## Chapter Thirty-Seven


On the evening on July 20, 1926, Feliks Derzhinski, the founder and head of the Cheka and the head of its successor, the OGPU, addressed a meeting of the Soviet Economic Commission. For nearly a hundred minutes, he spoke with vibrant passion about the evils of Bonapartism, a word that had come to be accorded to Trotsky's violent, egoistic, impatient—if brilliant—policies and manners. In midsentence Derzhinski suddenly stopped, gripped the sides of the tribunal, collapsed to the floor, and died of a heart attack.

The fates had removed Stalin's most powerful ally in his campaign against the

Trotskyite opposition. The man who had secured Lenin's revolution through a combination of icy devotion to the minutiæ of police work and the slashing saber of the purge, who had seen Stalin through the perilous early days of the transition with pitiless efficiency, was no more. At age forty-five, overworked, he had died in the service of the cause.

The passing of Derzhinski provoked the most solemn outpourings from those on Stalin's side. Stalin himself wrote of "this most perfect Jacobin who insured the safety of the toilers and the masses during the revolution of the Great Lenin," while Zinoviev, in what would turn out to be among his last duties as president of the Comintern, called upon the proletariat of the world to spare a moment's thought "for the great Derzhinski."[1]

In the search for a successor to Derzhinski, Stalin soon found a faithful adherent: Derzhinski's second-in-command, Vyaschlev R. Menzhinsky, former head of the Secret Political Department of the Cheka and chief of the Extraordinary Department of the OGPU, responsible for foreign intelligence, counterespionage within the Comintern, and liquidations. Menzhinsky was an accomplished pianist, and prisoners crossing the inner courtyard of the Lubyanka often heard the strains of Chopin or Grieg coming from his office.[2] Like Derzhinski, he was the son of a petty Polish baron; like Bukharin, he was a faceless theorist; but unlike Bukharin, he had no love for Stalin personally yet was such a devout old Bolshevik that he would devote every energy to the party's command.

With the immense apparatus of the OGPU thus as firmly in hand as ever, Stalin renewed his moves against his political enemies. The first to feel his iron hand was the vice-commissar of the War Commissariat, General Mikhail Lasevitch, who like most of the officer corps of the Red Army was pro-Trotsky. He was dismissed from his post and expelled from the Central Committee.

Next: Gregori Zinoviev, a man whom an American Communist writer, Max Eastman, described as one whose record of "switched allegiances and belly-crawling and sleekly gliding in and out would look like acrobatics to a water snake."[3] He who sought to get rid of such a man would find many a supporter, as Stalin was aware. Upon Stalin's accusation that Zinoviev had committed crimes against the statutes of the party and had aided Trotsky in forming a party within the party, Zinoviev was expelled from the Politburo, discharged as head of the Comintern (to be replaced by Bukharin), and relieved of his post as head of the Leningrad branch of the party, which had long shown leanings toward Trotsky. All that was left to Zinoviev was his party card and his position on the Central Committee.

Stalin also engineered Trotsky's and Kamenev's expulsion from the Politburo, but over the next few months, indications developed that he might be moving too fast. As shown by the collapse of Borodin's operations in China and the ruptured relations with Britain, all was not right with Stalin's stewardship of the Soviet realm. In a strong gesture of defiance, eighty-three leading Bolsheviks put their names to a public statement attacking Stalin for contributing to the international crisis by what was in Communist circles a high crime and misdemeanor: "inefficiency and lack of foresight."

Such was the force of the attack that Stalin felt compelled to respond publicly. The oppositionists "hurl abuse at Stalin," he declared, "because Stalin knows all the opposition's tricks." To the oft-repeated charge that Lenin in his political testament had suggested replacing him as general secretary, Stalin pointed out that Lenin had proposed his replacement only because of his rudeness. "Yes, comrades," he declared, "I am rude to those who grossly and perfidiously wreck and split the party." Yet when he had offered his resignation to the plenum of the Central Committee, "all the delegates, including Comrade Trotsky, Comrade Kamenev, and Comrade Zinoviev, unanimously *obliged* Stalin to remain at his post." What would they have had him do after such an endorsement? "Leave my post? That is not in my nature."[5]

Having played on the acute dread of the rank-and-file for any rift within the party, Stalin deflected the criticism, but it drove the opposition members to a daring step. Believing that they would be allowed no opportunity to present their views at the Fifteenth Party Congress, scheduled in December 1927, they prepared a pamphlet for distribution to the delegates, criticizing Stalin for dictatorial methods and lack of support for the Comintern and the international revolution. Although the pamphlet was printed secretly, copies of it and the printing press were in the hands of agents of the OGPU within days. Trotsky and Kamenev were expelled immediately from the Central Committee, leaving them, like Zinoviev, with little more to show for their long devotion to the cause than their party cards.

Trotsky's next move was an act of desperation, and just what he hoped to accomplish by it would never be clear. Did he intend merely to dramatize his cause, to force a hearing and serious consideration of his complaints before the Fifteenth Congress? Or did he actually intend to capture the Soviet state?

An Italian Communist writer, Curzio Malaparte, who was in Moscow soon after the Fifteenth Congress, would assert in 1932 that he had definite information that Trotsky did, indeed, intend to overthrow Stalin's regime.[6] Trotsky planned to achieve it, he maintained, in the same way that he had successfully deposed the Kerensky government in 1917, by employing small, carefully trained bands in Moscow and Leningrad to seize such key installations as railways, streetcars, power plants, newspapers, telephones, radio stations, gas, water, telegraph, and government offices. With those facilities in hand, the government would be crippled.

According to Malaparte, Trotsky himself was to lead the revolution in Moscow while Zinoviev was to direct the takeover in Leningrad. They were to strike on November 7, 1927, while the workers were in the streets celebrating the tenth anniversary of the revolution.

What they failed to take into account was a basic difference in the situation in November 1917 and November 1927. The Kerensky government had lacked vigilance; not so the Stalin government and particularly Menzhinsky's OGPU, which was well prepared to counter an invisible attack with an invisible defense.

Hardly anywhere either in Moscow or Leningrad did the attacks on key installations succeed, reducing the attempted takeover to little more than small groups of supporters demonstrating in the streets, watched lethargically by the crowds until at last the police organized mobs to break their ranks. On Stalin's orders, both Trotsky and Zinoviev were expelled from the party, the ultimate disgrace and the penultimate step before the execution chamber.

At the direction of Stalin, Menzhinsky called the opposition leaders to his office in the Lubyanka to demand from them declarations disavowing further antiparty activity and denouncing their views as anti-Leninist. "Do you understand, Comrade Menzhinsky," Kamenev said, "what those tactics are leading up to? You'll end by shooting the lot of us in your cellar." Menzhinsky rose abruptly, went behind a screen, sat down at his piano, and began to play the opening bars of Solveig's Song from Grieg's *Peer Gynt*. "Stop playing!" Kamenev shouted. "Stop! I insist you tell me as an old bolshevik if you believe that Stalin after shooting us could by himself insure the final victory of our Party in its struggle for world power." Menzhinsky returned to his desk. "Why did you ever allow him to obtain the immense power which he is wielding already?" he asked his old comrades. "Now it's too late."[7]

Kamenev, Zinoviev, most of the other leaders, and some 30,000 party members signed the declarations, but Trotsky refused to sink so low. On January 19, 1928, he was banished to Alma-Ata, a terminal of the Turkistan-Siberian Railroad in the foothills of the Central Asian mountain chain of the Trans-Ili Ala-Tau, while over 3,000 others were expelled from the party and many of them deported or jailed. "If Lenin were alive now," said his widow, "he would probably be in one of Stalin's jails."[8]

Trotsky's banishment to Alma-Ata brought no end to his opposition to Stalin. He soon learned that Bukharin had deserted Stalin and joined Zinoviev and Kamenev in a new opposition; when an intermediary brought a message asking Trotsky's support, Trotsky replied with a single word sent in the clear by telegraph: "Agree!" Intercepted by a reluctant but dutiful Menzhinsky, that telegram brought agents of the OGPU to Alma-Ata in the middle of the night.

Trotsky, his wife, and their eldest son, Lev Sedov, who was living with them, were put aboard a special coach attached to a train that arrived at Odessa the evening of February 10, 1928. There they were transferred, the only passengers, to a steamer, the *Ilyich*. Aboard ship, an official of the Extraordinary Department handed Trotsky papers signed by Stalin proclaiming him an enemy of the people and banishing him from Russia forever. He also handed him an envelope that contained the equivalent of $1,500; on that, presumably, he was to begin a new life. As the official disembarked, the ship sailed away, dark, silent, bearing the man who had led the Bolshevik Revolution, who had created the Red Army, who had fought and won on fifteen different fronts during the civil war, who had inspired the formation of the Comintern, and who had been Lenin's heir-apparent.

The *Ilyich* made its way to Constantinople, where the Trotskys were housed temporarily in the Russian Consulate while negotiations proceeded for residence on Turkish territory, on one of the Princes Islands in the Sea of Marmara, where a decade earlier the British prime minister, Lloyd George, had hoped to arrange a Truce of God between the Reds and the Whites. On the island, the co-founder of the Soviet state made his home in a shabby villa rented from a bankrupt pasha.

Apart from the $1,500, Trotsky had no funds, no hidden bank accounts, no chamois bags of noble metals or precious stones in the safe of some acolyte. His only assets were his beloved wife, Natalya, his son, Lev Sedov, a remarkable brain, an equally remarkable pen, good health, and will. Almost immediately he began to receive requests for books and articles from western editors, which brought large fees and royalties. With those fees, he was able to launch a newspaper in Paris, *Bulletin Oppozitsii*, to help finance pro-Trotsky Communist newspapers in Europe and the United States, and to organize his followers in a worldwide, often violent conspiracy against the Comintern and the Stalin regime. He named it the Fourth International.

For that effort, Trotsky could call upon his moral authority, his good name, the legend of invincible generalship, omniscient clandestinity and absolute victory that was little diminished by the seemingly inexplicable defeat at the hands of Stalin. Indeed, his name took on a new richness that came with martyrdom. His followers were many, and even though the Fourth International would never become as large as the Comintern, it was a viable force that would for long remain at the center of Stalin's thoughts and actions, often prompting Stalin to direct against Trotsky "such immense resources of power and propaganda" as were probably never employed "against a single individual."[9] Yet for all Stalin's efforts, the Fourth International would survive as a world revolutionary organization well beyond the Third International. As late as 1964, long after Stalin's death, the Fourth International would still be officially proscribed in Russia, and as late as 1975 its activities would be sufficiently energetic and mischievous to trouble an investigative committee of the United States Senate.[10]

As soon as Trotsky was financially able, he sent his son, a slight, tubercular youth of twenty-four, to Paris, there to manage the *Bulletin Oppozitsii* and to organize what became known as the International Secretariat. Headed by the former French representative to the Executive Committee of the Comintern, Alfred Rosmer, it resembled that committee in structure and functions, consisting of representatives of Trotskyite parties in Europe and the United States and possessing a system of couriers that penetrated all Comintern cells, including the headquarters in Russia.

The committee's principal method of attack was political warfare: charges that Stalin was financing Hitler; that he was creating a vast bureaucracy with which to smother pure Marxism and create instead a personal dictatorship; that Stalin had no interest in Lenin's heritage, the world dictatorship of the proletariat; that he was sacrificing the high ideals of the revolution to promote and protect his own power. Wounded and infuriated by those barbs, Stalin came to conclude that as long as Trotsky lived he constituted as real a threat to his existence as Lenin and Trotsky together had represented to the czar's.

Almost from the start of Trotsky's exile, the shadow of the assassin hung over the Princes Islands. With congeries of acolytes trooping to the island to sit at the feet of the master, agents of the OGPU had little difficulty infiltrating the household. In the first year alone, two agents worked their way in: a Latvian named Franck became a bodyguard; another Latvian named Sobolevicius, who would be arrested thirty years later in the United States as a Soviet spy with the alias of Jack Sobel, was a house guest. Both posed as supporters, and through their hands passed much of Trotsky's correspondence with his supporters in Russia.

By early 1933, Trotsky had become depressed over the suicide of his daughter, Zina, a brilliant if unstable young woman. She had killed herself, Trotsky believed, as a protest against the disappearance of her husband and several other members of the Trotsky family in Russia. Trotsky considered that unless he took extraordinary precautions, it would be but a matter of time before Stalin's agents killed him and Natalya. By that time, too, the Fourth International was well established; by going elsewhere, he might take a more active role in the movement, which he hoped to invigorate by capitalizing on the cruelties that Stalin was perpetrating in forcing an inhuman scheme of collectivization of farms, in the process murdering millions of peasants. Appealing to France for asylum, he received approval on the condition that he eschew any form of politics.

On July 17, 1933, Trotsky and Natalya left the Princes Island for France, where they went into hiding, moving from one obscure village to the next. Always they moved suddenly and secretly, often in disguise and always under a false name. So furtive and mysterious were his movements that the world press was mesmerized. The wildest rumors spread as to his whereabouts, including several that he was living in the United States.

However much Trotsky might have wanted to come to the United States—he once asked an American journalist wistfully, "Do you think it is a Utopian dream to think that I should be able to work in one of the great American libraries for two or three months?" [11]—he was actually living in the modest home of a Monsieur Beau, much of the time with an ear glued to an old Telefunken radio, listening to the transmissions from Moscow. From them he learned of new actions against members of his family inside Russia: his sons-in-law, having earlier been committed to remote prison settlements, had their terms extended indefinitely; his first wife, Alexandra, then over sixty, was banished to Omsk; and his youngest son, Sergei, a scientist, disappeared.

Depressed by the news, Trotsky saw a parallel in his own situation to the fate of a revered Russian priest of the seventeenth century, Protopop Avakuum, who had been defrocked and jailed for exposing the corruption of the hierarchs, released, then hounded, and eventually burned at the stake. To his wife, Natalya, Trotsky told of how Avakuum in his autobiography wrote of stumbling through the snows of Siberia with his wife, who kept falling in the drifts. "And I came up and she, poor soul, began to reproach me, saying, 'How long, Archpriest, is this suffering to be?' And I said, 'Markovna, unto our very death.' And she, with a sigh, answered: 'So be it, Petrovich, let us be getting on our way.' " [12]

When in the spring of 1935 France and Russia signed an alliance, an alarmed Trotsky asked and received asylum from the then Socialist state of Norway. There, while continuing through his phantomas the work of the Fourth International, he wrote an indictment of Stalinism, *The Revolution Betrayed.*

From time to time there were ominous flickers of news from inside Russia. In June 1935, the preeminent Russian literary figure Maxim Gorky died at the age of sixty-eight at his dacha outside Moscow on the eve of departing for a writers' conference, a death attributable—so word reaching Trotsky had it—to poison. Just over a year later, on July 7, 1936, Trotsky learned that the former foreign commissar, Georgi Chicherin, long since replaced by Litvinov, had died in the Kremlin hospital, ostensibly of diabetes, but Chicherin's death also appeared to have unnatural aspects. [13]

A few weeks later, in August 1936, the thunderbolt. While on a holiday fishing for salmon in a Norwegian fjord, Trotsky heard over a little portable radio his host had installed in a fisherman's cabin that Zinoviev and Kamenev had been tried, sentenced to death, and executed.

A single pistol shot, which Stalin himself was said to have engineered, set off Stalin's purge to eliminate his Trotskyite opposition. Just after four o'clock in the afternoon of December 1, 1934, at the Smolny Convent, a young unemployed Communist malcontent shot and killed Sergei Kirov, secretary of the Communist Party's Central Committee, a member of the Politburo, first secretary of the Leningrad party organization, and one of Stalin's closest comrades.

Stalin himself hastened to Leningrad to supervise the investigation. In tones reminiscent of the hysteria, savagery, and vengeance that flowed from the murder of Uritsky and the attempt on Lenin's life in 1918, the press and radio began a campaign calling upon all party members and the state as a whole to be on the alert for "loathsome, hateful agents of the class enemy," which meant the supporters of Trotsky or anybody who might stand in the way of Stalin's consolidating his authority. Three days following the murder, a government decree amended the criminal code, providing for those accused of terrorism immediate trial and execution without right of appeal.

On December 29, 1934, Moscow radio announced that those who had plotted Kirov's assassination had been caught, found guilty of "working for foreign powers proposing to change the regime in the USSR by armed forces from abroad," and shot. A witness to the executions reported "prisoners queuing up by the elevator and being taken down, one by one, to the cellar and shot at intervals of two to two and a half minutes throughout the night. In the morning 200 corpses lay in the cellar." [14]

There followed a reign of terror and savagery unparalleled even in the time of the civil war and the collectivization of the farms, a terror directed for the first time at the party itself. Among the hundreds of thousands who were arrested, many of them executed, others committed to forced labor, Stalin reserved a special venom for the old Bolsheviks who had helped Lenin—not Stalin—come to power. Nowhere was that venom more apparent for a shocked world to see than at the trial, which opened just past midday on August 19, 1936, of Zinoviev, Kamenev, and fourteen others accused of plotting against Stalin's life and the state.

The presiding judge was a fat man with a soft, oily voice and large pouches encasing sharp little eyes, V. V. Ulrikh. Flanked by two other judges, he sat high above the court on a tribune, looking out over some 150 Soviet observers and thirty-odd foreign diplomats and journalists. Appearing careworn, the defendants sat in a dock to Ulrikh's right, guarded by secret police of the Commissariat of Internal Affairs, commonly known as the NKVD, which two years earlier had absorbed the successor agency of the Cheka, the OGPU.

As the proceedings unfolded, they were marked by an eerie, stagelike evolution that suggested less a trial than a well-rehearsed political drama. It was clear that while Zinoviev, Kamenev, and the others well might pay with their lives, their trial was incidental to a juridical play intended to procure the final indictment of Trotsky. In essence, the charges were that the leftist leaders of the Bolshevik movement, including Zinoviev and Kamenev, had conspired under Trotsky's leadership to kill Stalin and other rightist leaders of the state, that they intended to seize the power of the state, that they had collaborated with the German secret police, and that—a charge of particular importance in Stalin's plans—there were many others, including high officers of the Army, who were also involved.

One of Lenin's principal phantomas, a member of the first Politburo, and with Stalin and Zinoviev one of the troika that had headed the Soviet state after Lenin's death, Lev Kamenev made no attempt to repudiate the principal charges against him. His testimony early made it clear that he and Zinoviev, in exchange for their lives, were to implicate other of Stalin's enemies. Kamenev dutifully named a number of old Bolsheviks, including the theoretician who had succeeded Zinoviev as president of the Comintern but had broken with Stalin, Nikolai Bukharin.

When Gregori Zinoviev came to the stand on the second day, he looked cowed, "puffy and grey," and gasped "asthmatically."[15] The man whom Lenin had personally selected to export the Bolshevik elysium to other lands made a full confession, admitting to all the charges and detailing various schemes and plots allegedly devised by Trotsky from afar.

On the morning of August 22, 1936, the prosecutor, Andrei Vishinsky, began his summary with a violent attack on Zinoviev and Kamenev. He accused "these mad dogs of capitalism" of trying "to tear limb from limb the best of our Soviet land." Then something appeared to have gone wrong with the prearranged scenario, for Vishinski demanded that "these dogs gone mad should be shot."

As the time arrived for Zinoviev, Kamenev, and their co-defendants to make final statements to the court, Zinoviev and Kamenev were abject. Rising, Kamenev said he was "a dreg" who deserved no mercy. Sitting down, he rose again quickly to ask if he might make a statement directed at his two sons. When Judge Ulrikh granted permission, Kamenev declared: "No matter what my sentence will be, I in advance consider it just. Don't look back. Go forward. Together with the Soviet people, follow Stalin." As he sat again, he buried his face in his hands. Zinoviev in turn told the court: "My defective Bolshevism became transformed into anti-Bolshevism, and through Trotskyism I arrived at Fascism. Trotskyism is a variety of Fascism, and Zinovievism is a variety of Trotskyism."

At 2:30 A.M. on August 23, 1936, Judge Ulrikh pronounced that all were guilty as charged and that all were sentenced to death. As he finished, one of the condemned shrieked hysterically: "Long live the cause of Marx, Engels, Lenin, and Stalin!" In police wagons heading for the Lubyanka, Zinoviev and Kamenev could hardly have been unaware that the bargain they had struck with Stalin for their lives was worthless.

When guards took Kamenev from his cell, he "made no complaint and appeared stunned. He was executed by an hysterical NKVD lieutenant who kicked his body as it fell and shot him again." Once the most powerful voice in international Bolshevism after Lenin and Trotsky, Zinoviev died less gracefully. Unwell and feverish, he was taken from his cell by a group of guards who told him he was only being moved to another cell, but Zinoviev sensed the truth, fell to the floor, and sobbed appeal after appeal to Stalin. The NKVD officer in charge of the detail produced his revolver and shot him, an action for which the officer subsequently received a medal for having displayed presence of mind.

There could be no question but that Joseph Stalin intended, by whatever means, to establish an iron control over the entire apparatus of the Soviet state.

*Book Two*

# WAR STATIONS: 1933–1939

# PART VII

## The American Station

---

*Chapter Thirty-Eight*

When Franklin Delano Roosevelt succeeded Herbert Hoover as president of the United States early in 1933, few men had ever entered high office at a more disastrous time: the capitalist world was deep into its worst economic depression; 15 million Americans were unemployed, and *Fortune* magazine estimated that out of 140 million Americans 34 million had no income whatsoever. The gross national product had fallen from $104 billion to $56 billion; such was the state of American agriculture that there was real doubt whether the farmers could continue to feed the nation; stocks and shares were worth only 11 percent of their 1929 value; and America's confidence in its business community had been totally shattered. Wags recited a jingle that summed up the people's attitude toward government and finance:

> Mellon pulled the whistle,
> Hoover rang the bell,
> Wall Street gave the signal,
> And the country went to hell.[1]

And when a reporter asked the British economist John Maynard Keynes whether there had ever been anything like it before, Keynes replied: "Yes, it was called the Dark Ages, and it lasted four hundred years."[2]

In contrast to Communism, which decreed complete ownership and control by the state of all raw materials and means of production, capitalism involved an economy essentially unfettered by state control. Thus, as disaster struck the capitalist states, capitalism itself appeared to be on trial, and the Communist International had no hesitation in rejoicing at the predicament of its principal adversaries, Britain, France, Germany, and the United States. Nor did the Comintern fail to point out loudly and frequently that the Soviet economy was healthy and expanding. Millions of Americans came to believe that the Russian economic system, at least, was superior.

The eventual outcome of events of the years from 1922 through 1929, the years in which the roots of the Great Depression developed, encouraged a widespread belief that the American system might be but a ramshackle outgrowth of the Industrial Revolution that time had rendered perilous and obsolete. In those years, there was a rising tide of prosperity sustained by a marked expansion in the manufacture of durable consumer goods and by a boom in construction and real estate. A warning signal first developed in 1926 with the collapse of a real estate boom in Florida, followed the next year by indications of unusual declines in home construction and in automobile purchases. Yet the aura of prosperity continued for a while, only to dissolve with unprecedented fury in the collapse of the stock market in late 1929.

In a series of calamities in which error, greed, and speculation were conspicuously present, by mid-1932 $75 billion in the market value of listed stocks had been wiped out. The American banking system began to experience severe runs; hoarding was widespread; and between 1930 and the eve of Roosevelt's inauguration, 5,504 banks with total deposits of almost $3½ billion closed their doors. By Inauguration Day, almost every bank in the United States was either shut or under restrictions by state proclamations.

Such was the gravity of the situation that Roosevelt felt compelled to call a special session of the Congress to enact emergency legislation. While awaiting the opening of the session on March 9, 1933, he declared a four-day national banking moratorium, suspending all transactions by the Federal Reserve and other banks, trust companies, credit unions, and building and loan associations. When accompanied by the printing of new currency based on tangible assets in the banks and by special measures against hoarders, that action restored a measure of sanity and discipline to the money market, but there was no such dramatic stimulant for other areas of the economy. For all Roosevelt's unprecedented efforts, such was the degree of the economic disaster that as late as 1939 some 10 million people would still be unemployed; and based upon a national income in 1929 of $81 billion, the estimated loss of national income between 1930 and 1938 would be more than $132,600,000,000, four times the amount that the nation had spent on the World War.

In simplest terms, if the disaster reflected the inherent problems of a free economy—overproduction and underconsumption—then, plainly, new markets had to be found. To anyone with a map or a general knowledge of the world, new markets were obvious in the vast reaches of the Union of Soviet Socialist Republics. In one of Roosevelt's early decisions, he let it be known that he intended without delay to extend diplomatic relations, to include financial and industrial intercourse, to Russia.

Maxim Litvinov, Chicherin's successor as foreign commissar, had repeatedly dangled promises of huge orders if the United States would but recognize the Soviet regime. Even without recognition and despite political differences, Litvinov pointed out, American exports to Russia had increased from a value of $4.5 million in 1923 to over $114 million in 1930. They would have risen even more, he told American diplomats in Riga, but for difficulties in obtaining credits in the United States and for official American restrictions on importing Russian goods. The chief of Amtorg, the official Soviet trading agency in New York, Peter A. Bogdanov, conducted much the same kind of campaign among American business leaders, emphasizing in speeches across the country that if the United States wanted Russian markets to help itself out of the depression, then the American government would have to recognize the Soviet government.

Yet how was Russia to pay for American goods? The Russian economy was no healthier than America's. American diplomatic outposts in the Baltic States were reporting that to meet obligations in Germany, the Soviet government was obliged to borrow $50 million from the German government. On July 26, 1933, the American consul at Riga, Felix Cole, warned Secretary of State Cordell Hull that while Russian overtures stressed recognition, what the Russians really wanted was credit, and "there has never been a time . . . when conditions were worse for granting of credits to Russia and when the risk involved was greater."[3]

Having emphasized during the political campaign a need for innovations in government in order to restore economic health, President Roosevelt was inclined to pay little attention to those alarms. What really concerned him, he told the acting secretary of the treasury, Henry J. Morgenthau, was that if the United States recognized Russia, would the Russians agree "to cease to direct the activities of the American Communist Party?"[4] How doubtful that might be was demonstrated, even as the president prepared to make his first cautious overtures toward recognition, by the case of Corporal Robert Osman, United States Army.

The attorney general charged Osman with "stealing documents containing secrets vital to the defense of the Panama Canal"[5] and others containing the U.S. Army's industrial and manpower mobilization plans. Admitting the charges, Osman said he supplied the documents to a group of New York Communists who paid him a total of $200 in $50 bills.

Roosevelt was nevertheless inclined to dismiss Soviet espionage operations in the United States as pinpricks not to be accorded undue importance. On October 10, 1933, only six weeks after Osman's sentencing, Roosevelt wrote to Soviet President Kalinin, stating that he desired "to end the present abnormal relationship" between the two countries. He invited Kalinin to send "any representative you may designate to explore with me personally all questions outstanding between our countries."[6]

A week later Kalinin accepted Roosevelt's proposal. An indication of the importance the Russians attached to it was apparent in the choice of the Russian representative, the new foreign commissar himself, Maxim Litvinov.

Litvinov arrived in New York on November 7, 1933, accompanied by one whose credentials listed him as "Chief of the Press Bureau of the Commissariat of Foreign Affairs," Konstantin Oumansky. It would turn out that Oumansky had less to do with the Foreign Commissariat than he had to do with the OGPU.

At the dockside, Litvinov announced that he expected to be able to reach agreement with President Roosevelt "in a half hour, perhaps less."[7] As he explained to the press, he expected to be called upon to settle only the matter of diplomatic relations and that other questions would be approached later. But once he was in Washington, Secretary of State Hull made it clear that other matters came first, diplomatic recognition later. The other matters included Communist propaganda in the United States, legal and religious rights of American citizens in Russia, Russian debts to the United States, Soviet claims against the United States, and Communist economic espionage.

Litvinov first called at the State Department on the day after his arrival in New York, and by cocktail time the next day it was apparent that the negotiations were foundering. "The Soviet laws as reasonably interpreted and administered," said Litvinov, "and the institutions of our Government afford American nationals all the protection they can desire." He gave the same kind of lofty and vague assurances on every issue, so that Undersecretary R. Walter Moore finally told Hull's special assistant and the ambassador-designate to Moscow, William C. Bullitt, to place on the table before Litvinov a timetable of steamship departures from New York to Leningrad. Tell him, Moore said, to sign a treaty or go home.

Perceiving the implications immediately, Litvinov was happy the next day to answer a summons to the White House to see the president. Yet at the White House, too, there was no question of "a half hour, perhaps less," but extended negotiations. Only on the sixth day, November 16, 1933, did Roosevelt and Litvinov finally reach a degree of agreement.

In regard to establishing diplomatic relations, the two exchanged almost identical letters expressing the niceties long familiar to diplomats around the world. The crucial issue was noninterference in internal affairs. On that matter, the letter to which Litvinov put his signature reflected long deliberations and careful wording proscribing any Soviet organization or any organization supported or countenanced in any way by the Soviet Union "from any act overt or covert liable in any way whatsoever to injure the tranquility, prosperity, order, or security of the whole or any part of the United States," to include specifically agitation or propaganda aimed either at "armed intervention" or at "bringing about by force of a change in the political or social order" of the United States.[8]

On paper, at least, that was an agreement hardly to be misunderstood.

Although Roosevelt had insisted throughout the lengthy negotiations that the agreement was to apply specifically to the Comintern, as well as to the Soviet intelligence services, Litvinov maintained that he could not mention the Comintern by name in the letter because the Comintern had no government standing. Yet the State Department official who drafted the letter, Robert J. Kelley, stated that the understanding was that the agreement proscribed all activities of all organizations, the Comintern specifically. If in no other way, the Comintern was included as a recipient of financial assistance from the Soviet government.

Hardly had Litvinov left the White House before he made it clear that his understanding of the agreement was different. After he had addressed the National Press Club in Washington on November 17, 1933, a reporter asked how the agreement would affect the Communist Party. "What Communist Party?" Litvinov shot back. "The Communist Party of Russia doesn't concern America. The Communist Party of America does not concern Russia." Then how would the agreement, asked another newsman, affect the Comintern? "The [Comintern]," replied Litvinov, "is not mentioned in the documents. You should not read more into the documents than was intended."[9]

Even if one might see that response as evasive, there was nothing indirect about Litvinov's remarks a short while later at a secret meeting in New York with members of the Secretariat of the American Communist Party and New York-based agents of the OGPU. According to an ex-Comintern agent, Benjamin Gitlow, a former secretary-general of the American Communist Party, Litvinov "assured the frightened Communists that they had nothing to worry about." The agreement, he said, was between governments and had no connection with the Comintern. "After all, comrades," he said, "you should know by this time how to handle the fiction of the tie-up between the Comintern and the Soviet Government. Don't worry about the letter. It is a scrap of paper which will soon be forgotten in the realities of Soviet-American relations."[10]

President Roosevelt's nominee to be ambassador to Moscow, William C. Bullitt, was a wealthy Philadelphia dilettante who had been deeply impressed by Soviet leaders and Bolshevism when he had traveled from Versailles to Moscow as Woodrow Wilson's representative in 1920. Bullitt was immediately acceptable to the Russians but not so acceptable to an American patriotic organization, the Daughters of the American Revolution, prominent members of which also belonged to the strongly anticommunist American Defense Society; they opposed his appointment, partly because he had married "Louise Bryant Reed, wife of the late John Reed, a communist who lies in the walls of the Kremlin and was given highest military honors by the Soviet Government for his work in directing communist propaganda."[11]

It was true that Bullitt had married Louise Bryant Reed, but in 1930 they had been divorced. Weighing the matter carefully, the State Department established that although the couple had produced a daughter, Bullitt had no relations with his ex-wife that might embarrass the department. Nor did he have any association with the woman with whom Louise Bryant Reed Bullitt was living in a Paris hotel, Angelika Balabanov, the woman who had been the first secretary-general of the Comintern but who had recanted the faith.

Assured of confirmation, Bullitt set out for Moscow on a reconnaissance. When he arrived on December 11, 1933, the American flag was flying above the entrance to the National Hotel near Red Square, and a red carpet covered the steps. Litvinov received him immediately, and the next day he lunched with the foreign commissar's family, a rare honor for a foreign ambassador.

On the third day, Bullitt presented his credentials to the Russian president, Mikhail Kalinin, who took him aside after the ceremony to declare that "he felt as if he were welcoming someone he had known a long time."[12]

There followed a formal dinner hosted by Litvinov and an evening at the ballet. At a dinner in the Kremlin given by the commissar of defense, Voroshilov, Stalin himself received him. "I want you to understand," said Stalin, "that if you want to see me at any time, day or night, you have only to let me know and I will see you at once."[13] Bullitt returned to Washington "flushed with the welcome he had received and the many kindnesses the Soviet officials had showered upon him."[14]

He went back to Moscow early in 1934 to assume his post, taking with him as a military attaché a man who would play a role of some importance in future relationships between the United States and the Soviet Union, Colonel Phillip R. Faymonville. Like Bullitt's other principal assistant, a young foreign service officer, George F. Kennan, Colonel Faymonville had conscientiously prepared himself as an authority on Soviet Russia. As a junior officer he had studied the Russian language and in General Graves' expeditionary force in Siberia had served as an ordnance officer. He was a bachelor, a solitary man, an intellectual, devoted to the opera and ballet, not the pursuits of most members of the General Staff. Yet he was considered to be an outstanding officer, a graduate of both the Industrial and War colleges, and but for outspoken criticism of the Army's handling of the Bonus Marchers who encamped in Washington in 1932 would have become head of military intelligence. He became instead an aide-de-camp to President Roosevelt and a considerable influence with the president's closest adviser, Harry Hopkins, the president's wife, Eleanor, and the secretary of agriculture and future vice-president, Henry Wallace.

Almost from the start in Moscow most officials in the Embassy saw Colonel Faymonville as unduly sympathetic to the Russians. A junior official, Charles S. Bohlen, saw him as "the weak link in the staff." A "slender pink-faced man with a fringe of white hair," he invoked in both Ambassador Bullitt and his first secretary, Loy Henderson, "serious doubts as to his judgment and his impartiality wherever the Soviets are concerned." Once he was promoted, he would come to be known in some Washington circles as the "Red General," and one of

Roosevelt's most trusted executives, Admiral William H. Standley, who was destined to succeed Bullitt in Moscow, would denounce him as "a flaming fanny." Yet there were others who saw him as the best-informed American in Moscow; he was obviously liked and trusted by the Red Army's General Staff more than any other foreign military attaché.[15]

As Ambassador Bullitt discovered soon after returning to Moscow, ceremonial greetings and hard business bear little resemblance. The second time around there was no American flag, no red carpet.

Bullitt early saw Litvinov to discuss the matter of Russian debts, one of several problems that had been left for further discussion when Litvinov was in Washington. With accumulated interest, those debts, incurred by Czar Nicholas's government and the provisional government of Alexander Kerensky with the United States government and American firms and individuals but repudiated by Lenin, amounted to $771,159,000.15. Although the government was the principal single creditor, more than half the total was owed to private corporations.

In Washington Litvinov had offered at first to settle for a figure that American officials saw as absurd: $50 million, later raised to an almost equally absurd $75 million. Yet in Moscow Litvinov refused to increase the offer. As negotiations dragged on with no results, the Export-Import Bank, established largely to finance trade with Russia, announced that there were to be no credit transactions with the Soviet government "unless and until that government shall submit . . . an acceptable agreement respecting the Russian indebtedness to the Government of the United States and its nationals."[16]

Early in 1935, Secretary of State Hull summoned the Soviet ambassador, Alexander Troyanovsky, to the State Department for a conversation that was to last exactly four and one-half minutes. What, Hull asked, was the final position of the Soviet government on the debts? Troyanovsky replied apprehensively that his government, "while desiring to have friendly relations with the United States," was unable to go beyond the offer already submitted. To which Secretary Hull replied that he was "profoundly disappointed," that the United States had "gone to the limit to which it could go." He bade the ambassador good afternoon. Troyanovsky departed.

The secretary of state promptly acted to abolish the Export-Import Bank, withdraw the naval and air attachés (Faymonville remained), abolish the consulate-general, and in general reduce the size of the Embassy staff, all calculated to indicate that Washington at that point regarded Moscow as a minor post. In discussing those actions with the Soviet government, Hull told Bullitt, "you should endeavor to convey clearly the fact . . . that the Government of the United States is convinced that no real friendship can be developed so long as [Litvinov] adheres to his present attitude."[17]

For the United States, the Roosevelt-Litvinov Agreements of 1933 were intended to be the basis through which capitalism and Communism could live and work together on the same planet. Yet for all the careful wording so laboriously pursued in Washington, Stalin had within six weeks of the signing demonstrated that the agreements had no application to the Comintern.

An official organ of the Soviet Communist Party, *Bolshevik*, announced that since the United States "may be confronted by serious political strikes," the American Communist Party should "guide the incitement of the masses in this direction."[18] The vice-president of the American Federation of Labor soon presented the State Department with "a mass of evidence" showing that "Propagandist activities are carried on in Moscow in disregard of the pledge made by Mr. Litvinov to the President."[19] Then, in August 1934, Secretary of State Hull advised Bullitt in Moscow of what he considered to be hard evidence that Russia had violated the agreements in a serious manner: adoption by the Comintern in December 1933 of an American "program," consideration at a meeting of the Red Trades Union International in Moscow the same month of a report concerning "the organization of revolutionary elements" within the American Federation of Labor, and a message from the Comintern in January 1934 urging the *Daily Worker* in New York to become "a real collective agitator and organizer in the workers' struggle" in the United States.[20] By 1935 the Comintern was acting in complete and undisguised violation of both the spirit and the letter of the Roosevelt-Litvinov Agreements, as was clearly demonstrated by the Comintern's Seventh Congress in Moscow.

Seeking to establish from Soviet authorities whether American affairs were to be on the agenda of the congress, Bullitt encountered only obfuscation. When he asked Litvinov about the congress, Litvinov asked: "What? Is there to be one?" When Bullitt replied that it was to open on July 20, 1935, Litvinov said with a grin: "You know more about the Third International than I do."[21]

Five days later when Bullitt again approached Litvinov about the congress, Litvinov again denied any knowledge of it. When Bullitt reminded him of his promises to President Roosevelt, Litvinov responded with annoyance: "I remember I said I could not promise anything about the Third International." To which Bullitt replied that he "feared most serious consequences if the pledge of his Government should not be respected."[22]

Possibly because of Bullitt's strong representation, Litvinov advised Stalin to cancel the congress, but Stalin refused. When the Comintern met from July 25 through August 20, 1935, two American Communists—Earl Browder and William Z. Foster—were elected to the Presidium, Americans served on various working committees, and Browder, Foster, and another American delegate were elected to the all-powerful Executive Committee. The congress heard a report on the Washington Bonus March in which some 20,000 veterans had descended on the capital demanding passage of a bonus bill and had been evicted by troops under General Douglas MacArthur; Earl Browder reported on "the growth of factionalism" in the American Communist Party, which was contributing to a kind of gangland warfare in and around New York; and while discussing the United States, the new secretary-general, Georgi Dmitrov, proclaimed to "the thousands of . . . prisoners of capitalism and fascism" that the members of the Comintern would give "Every hour of our lives, every drop of our blood . . . for your liberation."[23]

To Secretary of State Hull, Ambassador Bullitt wrote that the congress "was a flagrant violation of Litvinov's pledge to the President," so flagrant that "the Government of the United States would be juridically and morally justified in severing diplomatic relations with the Soviet Government."[24] Yet Roosevelt was unprepared to take that step. He directed instead the sending of a note declaring that the United States anticipated "the most serious consequences" if the Soviet government was "unwilling, or unable, to take appropriate measures in disregard of the solemn pledge" given to the American government.[25]

Denying that the Soviet government had violated the 1933 agreements, the Russians repeated the old line that their government "has not taken upon itself obligations of any kind with regard to the Communist International," over which it professed to have no control. Thus the Soviet government was "obliged to decline" the American note.

It was ironic that it was William C. Bullitt, who as a young man in 1919 had been so favorably impressed with Soviet Russia and who had entered upon his office in Moscow with an idealist's high hopes of establishing close and enduring relations, who insisted on a hard line. Unless the United States took strong action, Bullitt declared, "all future dealings with the Soviet Government would be gravely prejudiced." The Soviet Foreign Office, said Bullitt, "does not understand the meaning of honor or fair dealing, but it does understand the meaning of acts."[26] Yet again Roosevelt declined to act, and in time a disillusioned Bullitt would ask to come home and would be replaced by a wealthy lawyer and Democratic politician, Joseph E. Davies.

In the wake of the Roosevelt-Litvinov Agreements, there was also no letup in Soviet intelligence activities in the United States. Indeed, as the United States gradually began to awaken to the threat posed by the totalitarian powers in Europe and Asia, the Soviet Union became ever more interested in what was happening in Washington and stepped up its intelligence activities under the aegis of the Comintern. Those activities were soon flourishing in the shadow of the capitol with the operatives functioning under two agencies known as Apparat A and Apparat B. The one concerned with political and military espionage was Apparat A, whose agents operated primarily in Washington, their efforts aimed at penetrating the government. It was controlled during its most flourishing years, from 1933 until 1945, by the leading Comintern functionary, J. Peters (born Alexander Golderberger, alias Alexander Stevens and other names), the man who was probably the chairman of the OO (Otdel Okhrany) in the United States.[27]

Peters' principal American lieutenant was Harold Ware, the son of a prominent and energetic Communist leader, Ella Reeve "Mother" Bloor. Recruited as a plenipotentiary of the Comintern while in Russia helping to organize collective farms, Ware returned to the United States at the request of the president of the Comintern, Zinoviev, to help Peters organize farm workers. In 1928, during the presidency of Calvin Coolidge, he became a consultant in the Department of Agriculture, from which time the department became a center of Comintern activity in Washington. That activity increased in the early years of Roosevelt's New Deal when the secretary of agriculture, Henry Wallace, established the Agricultural Adjustment Administration.

The name of Henry Agard Wallace would occur frequently in the history of Comintern activities in Washington and those of the OGPU to the extent that Wallace in time would become the subject of a major if cautious investigation by J. Edgar Hoover. Born in 1888, Wallace was reared in Ames, Iowa, the grandson of a Calvinist cleric and the son of a professor at the state agricultural college. Diligent, ascetic, inclined toward mysticism, he edited *Wallace's Farmer*, an influential agricultural periodical run by his family, and won recognition as an agrarian authority skilled in farm economics. Although he claimed to be apolitical, his ideas on agricultural administration were almost Marxist-Leninist in concept. When he became vice-president, he was clearly pro-Russian, and with or without his knowledge, some of his closest advisers and associates in government were active members of the Communist Party with strong links to both the Comintern and the Soviet intelligence services in the United States.

In creating the Agricultural Adjustment Administration, which became known as the Triple A, President Roosevelt intended to help farmers by reducing their dependence on staple crops and encouraging more diversified farming. Although there was nothing communistic about the Triple A, it nevertheless soon attracted Communists. Several of the acolytes in the Triple A went on to higher, more influential posts or started Comintern cells that spread their tentacles into areas of greater interest to the Soviet Union than agriculture.

The principal recruiter was Harold Ware, who held a first meeting of the Triple A group at a violin studio owned by his sister on Connecticut Avenue. At the start, the cell consisted only of Ware and three others, all attorneys: John Abt, Nathan Witt, and Lee Pressman; but from that microcosm there developed a shadow Soviet Government of America under the direction of J. Peters, the full range of which the Federal Bureau of Investigation would never be able to determine. That was accomplished despite the fact that in 1935, the director of the Agricultural Adjustment Administration, Chester C. Davis, broke up the cell there when he discovered that a group in the legal division, including a brilliant young lawyer, Alger Hiss, was interpreting laws pertaining to the Triple A "not in accordance with the intent of the Congress."

While Apparat A concentrated on political and military espionage, Apparat B devoted its activities to industrial espionage through the person of Jacob N. Golos, head of World Tourists, Incorporated, with offices in New York at 41 Union Square on the fringe of Greenwich Village. Of all the officials of the Comintern-OGPU systems in the United States, Jacob Golos was among the cleverest, the most mysterious, and the most powerful.

Jacob Golos, formerly Jacob Raisin, was born in Russia in 1890 in the Pale of the Settlement, that region to which Jews were confined by czarist law. He accompanied his parents to the United States in 1908, and became a naturalized citizen in 1915. By trade he was a printer, color-matcher, and chemist. During the World War he joined the extremist group within Louis Fraina's wing of the Communist Party and probably to avoid arrest, became known first as J. N. Davis and then as Jacob N. Golos. He subsequently submerged into the underground or illegal branch of the Communist Party.

Golos' first major espionage ventures were launched in accordance with a resolution passed by the Comintern's Executive Committee in Moscow on July 1, 1927, which came to be known as the "Resolution on the American Question." It laid down the principle that the economic system of the United States had outstripped that of Great Britain and that the United States was "contesting to an ever-greater degree the leading role of Great Britain." Thus the task of the Soviet Union as spelled out by the Comintern's Executive Committee was "to match and then eclipse the dominance of the United States." [28]

When World Tourists, Inc., was chartered on June 10, 1927, in the state of New York with an authorized capital of $50,000, Golos was appointed secretary. He and all other officers of the company were known Communists. The company's registration certificate showed that its foreign principal was the official Soviet travel agency, Intourist, and the nature of the business was selling Intourist travel and tourist documents on a commission basis and selling steamship passage to and from the United States and air and rail tickets for travel inside Russia. World Tourists was also authorized by Intourist "to organize on a broad scale" in the United States, Canada, and Mexico a system for forwarding parcels to "individuals residing in the USSR . . . for the personal use of addressees" containing such articles as were "permitted to be imported by parcel post into the USSR in conformity with Customs and other regulations of the USSR." [29] That proved a convenient way for Golos to forward documents and intelligence material calculated to assist Russia in realizing the objective of the Resolution on the American Question. When World Tourists made money, part of it was channeled to the Communist Party's East Coast newspaper, the *daily Worker*.

While remaining with World Tourists, Golos in 1934 became head of the Central Control Commission of the American Communist Party, a post resembling that of the former inquisitor-general of Spain in theory and sometimes in practice. Golos was to assure the faith and obedience of all members of the party but especially those in the Executive and the underground. As with Tomás de Torquemada and Isabella I of Spain, so with Golos and Stalin. In keeping with the principle laid down by Stalin that the Communist Party had to be "strong in its integration and iron in its discipline," the party through Golos asserted control over "every aspect of the lives of militant members," recognizing "no dividing line between the political and the personal."[30] It was Golos' responsibility either to exact the penitence of the heretic or to administer the punishment as determined by "pitiless trials." The worst apostates were almost always expelled from the party, the harshest of punishments.

Jacob Golos was at the height of his power in Communist circles in the United States when Stalin announced the first and second industrialization plans to build Russia's heavy industry and, under challenge from the west, to become self-reliant. The rising power of Fascism in Germany, Italy, and Japan imparted particular urgency and single-mindedness to those plans. That left no time for the slow process of developing industrial methods and formulae through Russia's own facilities; industrial secrets had to be obtained instead from other countries. Since the ultramodern industrial innovations and research and development then taking place in the United States were ideally suited for Russia's needs, the espionage service in the United States was expanded. Thus in 1934 and 1935 Golos and his comrades received the call to transform Russian espionage in the United States from a cottage industry to a major corporation.

As part of the expansion, Golos joined the secretary of the American Communist Party, Earl Browder, in founding the United States Shipping Corporation, located at 212 Fifth Avenue in New York. Browder provided $15,000 in seed money, which he obtained from the second secretary at the Soviet Embassy in Washington, Anatole B. Gromov, a Comintern agent known to the American Communist Party and American police alike as "Al."[31]

As specified by the corporation's charter, its purpose was "to carry on the business of forwarders, exporters, importers, ship brokers, and all other business incident to shipping and maritime work of every description." The corporation later became "the sole and exclusive agency for the issuance of licenses for imports to the Soviet Union from the United States, Canada, and Mexico."[32] The ties between United States Shipping and World Tourists were close, and at various times Golos served as either president or vice-president of both firms. Both United States Shipping and World Tourists flourished to the extent that they were able to donate to the Communist Party press "considerable sums of money" and to make loans to the party and the party press "running into the thousands of dollars."[34]

Success also created a need for additional employees, which led Jacob Golos into a fateful hiring. At the recommendation of the Communist Party executive, he added to the staff of World Tourists as secretary a Vassar graduate, Elizabeth Terrill Bentley, who had joined the party while taking postgraduate work at Columbia University.

Golos was at the time living alone, his wife, Celia, having gone to Moscow with their thirteen-year-old son, Milton, with no intention to return. In time, Golos and his new employee took an apartment on West 54th Street, where they lived as man and wife, and Bentley gradually became Golos' principal courier in his dealings with Apparats A and B and an investigator in control commission matters. In executing those duties, Bentley came to know almost as much about party personalities and affairs as did Golos, and the party Executive, while protesting from time to time, could do little about it: Golos was too powerful.

## Chapter Thirty-Nine

In July 1933, as President Roosevelt was completing the first part of his patchwork of legislation to produce relief and recovery from the Great Depression, a Comintern agent named Gerhardt Eisler arrived in New York to take charge of the entire Comintern *apparat* in North America. He was to prove to be by far the most efficient of all the Comintern plenipotentiaries sent by Moscow to the United States. A scientific—as opposed to utopian—Communist, Eisler was born in Leipzig in 1887 into a family of academics. Like his brother, Hans, who would become a film scriptwriter in the United States, and his sister, Elfriede, who would become an important functionary in the Comintern, he was early drawn to Communism. During the German October of 1923, he was secretary to Heinrich Brandler, the leader of the Communist movement in Saxony.

By 1924, Elfriede, who was always known to the Comintern by her underground name, Ruth Fischer, had become head of the German Communist Party, a deputy in the Reichstag, and a power in the Comintern, but she joined in the ideological fight between Trotsky and Stalin on the side of Trotsky and was soon expelled from all her posts in the Comintern and the party. Her expulsion led to a grave disturbance in the relationship between brother and sister, in which Fischer began to denounce Gerhardt not only to her associates but also to the police. So dangerous did Eisler consider her that for seven years after his arrival in the United States, he would connive successfully to prevent her from following.

Within the American Communist underground, Eisler's arrival in New York provoked unusually severe tremors of concern, for he was known throughout the international movement as a particularly intelligent and able clandestine and devout supporter of Stalin. The Communist International had sent such a capable and trusted plenipotentiary—so the theory had it—for two purposes: to bring discipline and unity once and for all to a badly fractured and unruly Communist leadership in the United States and to ready that leadership and the movement for seizing power in the insurrectionary disturbances that were expected to follow the anticipated collapse of Roosevelt's New Deal. In pursuit of party discipline, it was widely suspected—though never proven—that it was Eisler who was responsible in the mid-1930s for doing away with two prominent Communists in New York, Carlo Tresca and Juliet Stewart Poyntz.

Juliet Stewart Poyntz was a classic example of the bourgeois turned Bolshevik.[1] Tall, slender, somewhat masculine in appearance, she was a woman of fifty-one with superior gifts of intellect and oratory. Educated at Barnard College of Columbia University, she had spent a year at the London School of Economics and was for a time a professor of history at Hunter College. She was politically a fierce, pure Marxist-Leninist, had become a Comintern functionary, a leader of a Communist group within the New York Waist and Needleworkers' Union, the national organizer for the Women's Division of the American Communist Party, and an agent of the Soviet intelligence service. According to the editor of the *New Yorker Volkszeitung* and Trotsky's most intimate American associate, Ludwig Lore, she was "in charge of the 'illegal' section of the Communist party in this country" and a close associate of the head of the Control Commission, Golos. Having stood unsuccessfully for various political offices, including the U.S. Congress and attorney general for the State of New York, she became ultimately "among the first ten Communist leaders in the United States." She was at once a "blue stocking" and "a cop-baiting, street-demonstrating Union Square radical."

In 1934, Poyntz suddenly announced that "in order to pursue other interests," she had terminated her membership in the Communist Party, and the party accepted the resignation "with regret." Yet those announcements were not what they seemed: they merely marked the stage at which she ceased overt work for the party and began covert work for the illegal branch, which in accordance with a Comintern directive, was established when it appeared that the American Communist Party might be outlawed.

Early in 1936, Juliet Poyntz went to Moscow, apparently on party business. Other Americans reported seeing her at Comintern meetings in the company of a former Philadelphia taxi driver who was then an organizer in the National Maritime Union, George Mink, and it was widely whispered in party circles that the two were lovers. Yet when she returned to New York early in 1937, she told her close friends that Muscovy politics had disgusted her, especially the purges, and that she intended to cease all party work and join the Trotskyites. She also said she intended writing a book exposing Stalinism and the work of the Communist secret apparatus in the United States. Her recantation was apparently genuine.

On June 3, 1937, Juliet Poyntz received a telephone call in her room in the American Women's Association Club on West 57th Street in New York. Putting on her coat and picking up her handbag, she left the club and was never seen again.

When the New York *Herald-Tribune* on December 17, 1937, broke the story of Poyntz's disappearance, the editor of the *Daily Worker*, Clarence Hathaway, was quick to announce that Poyntz had ended her membership in the Communist Party near the end of 1934 "without any 'rift,' apparently to occupy herself with other interests." The director of public relations for the New York branch of the Communist Party, H. C. Adamson, made an even greater effort to disassociate the party from the case, telling the New York *World-Telegram* that "We have no record of the woman as a member of the Communist Party and no knowledge of her whereabouts for ten years."

A few weeks later, in early February 1938, a leading New York Anarchist, Carlo Tresca, informed Assistant United States Attorney Lester C. Dunigan that he had evidence Poyntz had been kidnapped by a former lover, Schachno Epstein. Tresca persisted in trying to find out what became of Poyntz for five years, until he was shot to death on January 11, 1943, on Fifth Avenue in New York by an unknown assassin. Yet before that fate befell Tresca, he had already provided the former secretary-general of the American Communist Party, Benjamin Gitlow, with such information as he had developed. By that time bitterly anticommunist, Gitlow revealed the information in a book published in 1948: *The Whole of Their Lives: Communism in America—A Personal History and Intimate Portrayal of Its Leaders.*

After visiting Moscow in 1936, according to Gitlow, Juliet Poyntz began to speak guardedly about her "disillusionment." When the Soviet intelligence service called her to account over rumors that she was writing about her experiences in the Communist underground, she gave evasive answers. Meeting in New York with officials of Golos' commission, Soviet intelligence officials decreed that Juliet Stewart Poyntz was to be liquidated.

The three killers who drew the assignment—one of whom was apparently George Mink—used Schachno Epstein as a decoy. A "coward who cringed in the presence of danger," according to Gitlow, Epstein was nevertheless so in fear of the Soviet intelligence service that he always did what the service directed. Telephoning "his former sweetheart," he told her he wanted "to talk over old times." As the two went for a walk through Central Park, "Schachno took her by the arm and led her up a side path, where a large black limousine hugged the edge of the walk. . . . Two men jumped out, grabbed Miss Poyntz, shoved her into the car, and sped away." They took her to a wood in Duchess County on bluffs overlooking the Hudson River, shot her, and buried her in a shallow grave.

"At the next meeting of the [Soviet intelligence] cell," wrote Gitlow, "the order of business was a report on the Poyntz case," which occasioned considerable merriment. As Gitlow quoted one of the killers: "The poor girl, I felt sorry for her. The way she pleaded for her life." She cried and "behaved awful, not at all like a communist. She was so afraid to die."

Under the leadership of Gerhardt Eisler, the Comintern in 1934 established a revolutionary commission in the United States to take advantage of the favorable political position deemed to have arisen as a result of the Great Depression. An underground group complete with safe houses, front organizations, dummy business corporations, clandestine shortwave radio connection with headquarters of the Comintern in Moscow, and all the other infrastructure usually developed by secret services engaged in hostile operations, Eisler's commission in some respects resembled the Military Revolutionary Committee with which Trotsky and his associates had seized control of Petrograd during the October Revolution: its cells were if anything better organized and more deeply rooted than Trotsky's had been, and the commission was extremely well financed.

In retrospect, Eisler's belief that revolutionary conditions were inherent in the economic collapse in the United States was misplaced, for it was reckoning without the strength of the American middle and upper classes, the depth of entrenchment of the local, state, and national governments, the power of the police forces, and a lack of full-scale commitment to revolution by the great majority of the intelligentsia. As a political realist, Eisler may well have discerned that his chances of success were few, yet he worked with the vigor of one who truly believed that even if he failed to create a revolution, he would at least shake loose the safe old bolts of capitalism for a long time to come.

Although the FBI successfully penetrated Eisler's commission, the identities of those serving on it were difficult to determine; for Eisler imposed from bottom to top a time-tested system of cells, each consisting of no more than five people with only the leader knowing the identity of anyone in another cell. Only the most trusted of senior organizers would know the assignments and identities either of people in other cells or of other officials, and then only his contact immediately above and the organizers of five cells below him. Provided none of the organizers became disaffected, the system was virtually impenetrable, and even if an organizer should defect, the amount of information he could reveal would be so limited as to leave the basic structure intact.

One of Eisler's closest associates at the top of the commission did become disaffected: a man identified as Joseph Weinkoop. Soon after the end of World War II, Weinkoop wrote—for what specific reason and for whom would remain obscure—a 400-page manuscript dealing with operations of the Comintern in the United States, including considerable information on Eisler's revolutionary commission.[2] To have written the manuscript, Weinkoop would have had to be a senior Communist official in the United States, but there would be no reference to anyone by that name in any history of Communist activities in the United States nor in any biographical dictionary of Communist officials. The name Weinkoop thus was probably the author's underground party name, a man, as revealed by the manuscript, who attended the Lenin School for tuition in covert action, who served in the highest councils of the Red Trades Union International, the Profintern, who was on occasion consulted by Stalin himself, and who was a close friend and associate of one of Lenin's principal conspirators and an intimate of Stalin, Abraham Lozovsky, the secretary-general of the Profintern.

As revealed by some remarks in the manuscript, Weinkoop may have been William Weinstone (sometimes Weinstein), a man who, within the Communist movement, was alleged to have been the informant for the FBI both within the Eisler commission and the party's Central Committee. Weinkoop and Weinstone were both born in 1897, but Weinkoop in his manuscript stated that he was born in Philadelphia of Dutch-Czech parents, whereas party literature showed that Weinstone was born in Lithuania. If not the same man, Weinkoop and Weinstone nevertheless made pilgrimages to Moscow at the same time, and both appeared to have been union organizers for the American Communist Party in Detroit at the same time. Yet from that point, similarities between the two diverged, for

Weinstone would remain a loyal party member at least as late as 1969, whereas Weinkoop in his manuscript noted that he became disillusioned with Communism as early as 1929 and left the party altogether in 1949.

Whatever Weinkoop's true identity, he revealed in his manuscript that Eisler's inner cabinet consisted of at least three whom he could name: George Alpi, known as Brown, "always in the background and the brain behind the organization techniques of the Party"; Herta Kuusinen, Eisler's specialist in foreign language propaganda to "new Americans" (émigrés) of Slavic origin; and Josef Pogany, the commissar for war in the short-lived government of Béla Kun in Hungary, who came to New York at about the same time as Eisler. The manuscript also provided sufficient indications to surmise the identities of two others in senior ranks of the Eisler commission: Max Bedacht, a German-born hairdresser who was a frequent representative of the American party at meetings of the Comintern in Moscow and a general secretary of the American Communist Party, and Alexander Trachtenberg, a Russo-American who founded International Publishers in New York, which specialized in Marxist literature. The cell system obviously had something to do with Weinkoop's failure to name but a few people; in addition, by 1935, as Weinkoop noted, "an increasing number of mysterious individuals appeared at the secret meetings of the Central Committee, and it became a habit not to ask who they were lest one be considered a government spy."

Gerhardt Eisler himself left no trace of his activities during that time. Few knew where he lived, where he ate, whom he saw, what his marital status or his social life were. He was secretive not only because of the police but also because of the acute ideological differences that beset the party in the era of Stalin versus Trotsky. The intraparty conflict had special concern for Eisler since his diligent, merciless sister, Ruth Fischer, had marked him for destruction. Knowledge of how Eisler's intricate world functioned would thus depend on the testimony of others, among them Whittaker Chambers.

While editor of the Socialist journal, *New Masses*, in the spring of 1934, Whittaker Chambers received a telephone call from the Communist organizer Max Bedacht, ordering him to report immediately to party headquarters on 12th Street in New York City. There Bedacht told Chambers that he had been selected for underground work; thus, according to the system, he was to create an incident that would appear to provide justification for his resigning from the party. Bedacht then took Chambers to the 14th Street subway station for a meeting with John Loomis Sherman, a man whom Chambers had known while employed on the editorial staff of the *Daily Worker* and whom Chambers had last seen hunched over his typewriter in tears because, he said, he had been expelled from the party. As was at that point apparent to Chambers, Sherman's expulsion had been a fiction.

At Sherman's direction, Chambers agreed to meet him that night on Riverside Drive near Grant's Tomb. At the rendezvous point, Sherman led Chambers to a large black automobile whose driver Chambers would come to know as Herbert. As Herbert drove the two back downtown, he questioned Chambers "very closely" about "his political background in the Communist Party," then told him that he was to be the *Verbindungsmensch*—he used the German word for liaison man—betwen "the bank" (the underground) and the party in the person of Max Bedacht. After providing Chambers $50 with which to buy better clothes, Herbert introduced him to his controller, Ulrich, whom Chambers would later identify from FBI photographs as a Soviet national, Alexander Petrovich Ulanovski, who was ostensibly employed at the time as a clerk with the Soviet trading agency, Amtorg, but who was in reality a senior officer of the OGPU.[3]

Ulrich soon introduced Chambers to two of the party's safe houses, one called "the Gallery," a brownstone belonging to an American lawyer who worked for the party underground, the other an apartment in another brownstone in Greenwich Village. The apartment contained a photographic workshop and "the base of operations for a communications system between the underground in the United States and Europe." At the apartment, the underground received messages transported by couriers who worked as stewards and seamen on various ships of the North German Lloyd and Hamburg American lines. Almost always in Russian, the messages were either on microfilm or in a primitive system of secret writing whereby the writing could be recovered by dipping the paper in a washbasin containing permanganate of potassium. Late in 1934, after the Gestapo uncovered the operation among the employees of the German shipping firms, the mesages arrived through employees of French flagships. Chambers' job all along was to deliver the messages to Ulrich.

Chambers was soon transferred to other courier work involving Communist penetration of military and weapons establishments. It was Chambers who served as the contact with the American corporal stationed in the Panama Canal Zone, Robert Osman, who was subsequently sentenced to prison for spying. Chambers also claimed to have acted as intermediary between a spy in the Picatinny Arsenal in New Jersey, who provided information on explosives; an Italian Communist working for the Electric Boat Company in New London, Connecticut, who supplied blueprints of submarines and their fittings; another contact at a torpedo base at Narragansett Bay near Boston; and yet another who worked in the plant of the Crucible Steel Company in New Jersey.

Chambers soon received another new assignment as a courier between the party in New York and Apparat A in Washington. His principal contact for delivery of the messages in New York was Jacob Golos' dentist, Dr. Phillip Rosenbliet, whose surgery was at the corner of 40th Street and Broadway. That Dr. Rosenbliet was deeply involved with the party was evident to Chambers when at his dental offices he encountered his former contact at the Picatinny Arsenal and on another occasion, the secretary of the Canadian Communist Party, Tim Buck. The dentist told Chambers that he had an important contact within the War Department, a general whom he identified only by the name Miller, who among other information was supplying data on a light tank under development that was expected to be capable of speeds up to 35 miles per hour. General Miller, said Rosenbliet, was "a man who loved his liquor and was kept well supplied with it by Soviet agents."

After a time, Chambers was assigned a new controller, the man who controlled Apparat A in Washington, J. Peters. Peters made Chambers the principal courier between the party headquarters in New York and Apparat A in Washington and introduced him to the man whom Chambers would describe as the "sparkplug" of the Washington underground, Harold Ware. Most of the members of Ware's *apparat*, Chambers learned, were in the New Deal agencies created by President Roosevelt in his effort to restore national economic health, while J. Peters' "dream," as he told Chambers, was "to penetrate the 'old line agencies,' such as Navy, State, Interior, etc." After studying Ware's *apparat* in detail, Chambers was to establish a parallel one in the old line agencies.

During the course of his stay in Washington, Chambers accompanied Ware to a meeting in the apartment of a government employee, Henry Hill Collins, who was known in Apparat A as Carl. From all that Chambers could discern, Apparat A engaged in no espionage operations, its objectives being to obtain new members to extend the *apparat* within the government and to try to influence governmental policy in the direction of Communist goals. "In this connection," Chambers would note, "I recall that Lee Pressman once spoke of trying to influence decisions regarding farm mortgages in Oklahoma." He also recalled "Nathan Witt once speaking of trying to swing a decision on the National Labor Relations Board to conform to the Communist Party line."

Chambers soon became aware that there were other Communist cells within the government not associated with Apparat A. Like Apparat A, and contrary to the normal cellular organization employed by the Communist underground, members were often known to each other. Since the members were in almost all cases enthusiastic idealists who yearned for recognition of their idealism, that served to some degree to provide a recognition otherwise denied by the clandestine nature of their operations; another method of providing them a sense of importance and contribution was through dues based on a percentage of a member's salary, collection of which, for transmission to Peters, was one of Chambers' responsibilities.

Soon after Chambers' first encounters with Apparat A, its leader, Harold Ware, died in a car accident in Pennsylvania. Although members of the *apparat* would speculate among themselves that the FBI was responsible, there was no evidence to that effect. As Ware's successor, Peters named Nathan Witt, who was at the time working in the National Labor Relations Board, an instrument of the government with important powers of control within industry and unions and in the field of employers' practices and collective bargaining. As Witt took control,

Chambers made the acquaintance of a man whom he would subsequently name as an important figure in the Washington underground: Alger Hiss.

Alger Hiss was one of the those golden young Americans who emerged during the depression years with bearing and examination papers marked with the assessment, "very superior." He was born in 1904 into a Maryland family of *haute bourgeoisie;* so absolutely did his father believe in American capitalism that in 1907, when the system appeared to have failed, he killed himself. Yet that awful event appeared in no way to have affected his son's development. In both the Johns Hopkins University and the Harvard Law School, he won all the honors, in the process giving an impression of effortless superiority.

Hiss seldom, if ever, revealed his political beliefs for public scrutiny. One of the times he came closest to doing so was in regard to the Sacco-Vanzetti case when the professor under whom he studied at the Harvard Law School, Felix Frankfurter, one of the leaders of contemporary American jurisprudence, became a vigorous defender of the two convicted Italian immigrants. A protégé of Professor Frankfurter, Hiss was a frequent visitor in the Frankfurter home at a time when Frankfurter was writing a book purporting to show that the men had been unfairly convicted and while Mrs. Frankfurter was editing the doomed men's letters for publication. Although it was apparent that Hiss sympathized with the protests that swept the campus of the Harvard Law School, he remained cool, guarded, opaque, and prim.

As with her other children, Hiss's mother, Minnie, had imbued her son with a desire "to strive and succeed . . . to exhibit . . . virtues, talents, and knowledge, and to be nice and especially pleasant to important people."[4] Hiss followed those precepts throughout his career, and when he became a corporation lawyer, he epitomized success. He married quite well, in the opinion of his colleagues, taking as his bride a product of Bryn Mawr, a Quaker School noted for bluestockings, its priceless collection of medieval incunabula, and its devotion to the system. Her name was Priscilla Fransler; she had studied literature at Yale University; she had been married before to a member of the New York literati; she had a son; and she was noted for a lively intelligence. Yet among her husband's friends, she was never genuinely popular; as one would recall, "She was a kind of wild-eyed do-gooder . . . They didn't trust her . . . She seemed to have some of the aspects of a *femme fatale.*"[5]

The Great Depression soon made a mark on Alger and his wife. While they were relatively prosperous and secure on Alger's salary as a corporation lawyer, they were all too conscious of the misery and squalor all around them and began to look for alternatives. While defending capitalist firms during the day, Hiss would spend his evenings quietly reading Karl Marx, while Priscilla joined a branch of the Socialist Party in New York and when the party opened soup kitchens with the Salvation Army on Broadway, she went to work with a ladle. Hiss joined the International Juridical Association, an organization which attracted liberals and

Communists, which published a bulletin devoted to labor law and civil liberty cases, and which attracted a number of crusading young lawyers, such as Nathan Witt and Lee Pressman. It was a first step along a path that, according to Whittaker Chambers, would lead the promising young man with the golden future in the capitalist world into active subterranean participation in support of another and contrary ideology.

According to Chambers' account to the FBI, one of the goals of the Comintern's *apparats* in Washington was "to bring to Washington Communist Party members from other cities, especially New York, and to secure Government positions for them." The primary objective of the parallel *apparat* that Chambers was to establish was to advance the careers of Communists in government, "particularly in the old line agencies."[6]

When Chambers and Alger Hiss first met, according to Chambers, Hiss had just left the Agricultural Adjustment Administration to become chief counsel for the Nye Committee, which was investigating the influence of the international arms industry on American foreign policy before, during, and after the World War, an assignment which, according to Chambers, Lee Pressman may have helped Hiss to obtain. Since Hiss had access through the Nye Committee to the confidential files of a number of government agencies, including the State Department, Chambers suggested to J. Peters that Hiss be named in his place to found the parallel apparatus that was to concern itself with the old line agencies. Peters agreed, and Hiss, said Chambers, was "perfectly agreeable" to it.

It was at about that time that Chambers and his family moved from New York to Baltimore. Chambers would recall that Priscilla and Alger Hiss were his guests on at least one occasion in Baltimore for dinner, and both he and his wife would remember that the Hisses also visited them while in Baltimore for the Preakness Ball, one of the leading social events for the blue-blooded horse fraternity of Maryland. Chambers' relationship with Hiss, according to Chambers, became so close that in the spring of 1935, after Priscilla and Alger moved into a furnished house on P Street in Washington, the Chambers family moved into the Hiss's apartment on 28th Street, NW, transferring their belongings in the Hiss's Ford. Although Chambers was drawing a salary from the Communist Party—$125 a month plus medical, telephone, and rental expenses—Hiss, said Chambers, charged him no rent.

While Hiss was still working with the Nye Committee, J. Peters learned of some State Department documents provided the committee and suggested that Chambers arrange to copy them. Chambers later told the FBI that Hiss brought the documents either to his home on P Street or to the apartment of a novelist, John Herman. Chambers said that he himself "photographed them with a Leica camera" and turned over the negatives, not more than ten, to J. Peters.

Following service with the Nye Committee, according to Chambers, Hiss was offered the post of assistant solicitor general in the Department of Justice. When

Peters learned of the offer, said Chambers, he directed "that Hiss should take this position though there was no immediate [party] purpose in view." Yet Hiss served in the position only briefly before an assistant secretary of state, Francis Sayre, offered him a position in the State Department. Although Hiss was reluctant, in view of the shortness of his stay in the Justice Department, to accept, Peters and Chambers, as Chambers told it, decided that "he should make this change."

Having begun work with the State Department, Hiss soon began, Chambers claimed, to bring State Department documents to his home in a zippered leather briefcase. Chambers would take the documents for photographing to the apartment of a party member in Baltimore whose name he was unable to recall. Although the quantity was at first small, they soon numbered about twenty in each transaction. With the increase, said Chambers, they were provided the services of a party photographer, Felix August Inslerman, who would collect the documents from Chambers at Union Station in Washington, photograph them, and return them to Chambers at the station. The number of documents provided by Hiss and seven other members of the *apparats* had become so large by 1937, said Chambers, that the party established a photographic workshop in an apartment in Washington on B or C Street, NE.

## Chapter Forty

Whittaker Chambers was bound to the Comintern by more than conviction and emotion; he was bound by a fundamental law of Bolshevism promulgated at the conception of the world revolution of the proletariat by Lenin himself and enforced through the years by a legion of inquisitors-general traveling the world to ensure the devotion and obedience of all who entered the fold. The edict of the Fourth Congress of the Communist International in 1922 was considered binding upon all members of all Communist parties: "In view of the fact that the USSR is the only fatherland of the international proletariat, the principal bulwark of its achievements, and the most important factor for its international emancipation, the international proletariat must, on its part, facilitate the success of the work of socialist construction in the USSR, and defend her against the attacks of the capitalist Powers by all means in its power." Nor was there any doubt that the American Communist Party subscribed to that edict, for in the early years, at least, the party required of its members an oath: "I pledge myself to rally the masses to defend the Soviet Union, the land of victorious Socialism."[1]

When in 1937 Chambers began to consider the possibility of defecting, he was aware that he would place himself in great peril, for the defection of such an important member as Chambers, especially one with Chambers' knowledge of the *apparats* in Washington, was bound to call down the full wrath of the Comintern plenipotentiary, Gerhardt Eisler, and the head of the Central Control Commission, Jacob Golos. Chambers assumed that they would use any means, including murder, to silence him.

As Chambers would subsequently tell the FBI, the reasoning that brought him to consider defecting was diverse. Nearly every Communist, he said, "that breaks with the party, breaks over the question of Russia." Since the Communist Party held up Russia as "the example of what Communists can do to make a better world, once a Communist begins to suspect that Russia is not a better world, but a monstrously worse world, he is on his way out of the party." Chambers himself began to believe that. From his first entry into the party, he had been "disturbed by its bureaucracy and its inability to act and think in a creative way," but upon Stalin's assuming power, that was the least of his concerns. He was upset by the fact that "all independent thought was strangled, and in Russia, this strangulation was enforced by the NKVD in forms that amounted to Fascism," a situation that "the purges lighted up . . . in a dreadful way." It seemed to Chambers that "either the Stalinists were deliberately killing out the whole generation of the most dedicated revolutionists, in which case the Communist Party was headed by monsters, or the crimes charged against the executed oppositionists were true, and in that case the Party had always been headed by monsters."[2]

A book by a Professor Chernavin, I Speak for the Silent, brought him, said Chambers, to the brink of final decision. It contained "a frightful revelation of conditions in northern prison camps run by the NKVD," conditions which Chambers "did not dream existed," a revelation that left him, he said, with two alternatives: he could either kill himself or "break with the Communist Party and actively fight it." Although he chose to break, it was "a desperate choice," for it meant "reversing the whole current of my life . . . trying to reintegrate myself into a society I had been working to change . . . cutting myself off from the only large group of people with whom I had long been in contact." How could he do it?

At that point, said Chambers, he began "groping painfully for the vital defect which made the Communist Party, whose purposes as understood by its most devoted adherents are for the ultimate good of mankind, a positive evil." The theory of Communism, he reasoned, was "the most logical expression of that rationalism which had more and more engulfed the western world for the last two hundred years," yet in the practice of Communism, something vital was missing. That, he finally concluded, was "the absence of God," for "man without God, no matter how intelligent he may be, or how dedicated, is inevitably a beast." Finding God for the first time as an adult, he found the strength "to do what I never could have done without that guidance." To his wife he said: "'You know that I am leaving the winning side and going over to the losing side, but it is better to die with free men than to live under the Communist Party.'"

Slowly, carefully, Chambers prepared for his break. Since Communist officials, he reasoned, would find it easier to kill a man who did not exist than one who obviously did, he determined to establish a record of Whittaker Chambers having existed in Washington in 1937. Talking with J. Peters, he asked him to get him a job in the government. Unaware of Chambers' motive, Peters agreed, noting conveniently that it was dangerous for Chambers to continue "to knock about Washington without some apparent occupation." Within less than a week—while

12 million other Americans remained unemployed—Chambers was hired by the National Research Project, a make-work program of the New Deal in which Chambers found himself preparing indexes of the American railroad system under the supervision of a member of Apparat A.

While continuing to act as courier for the Washington *apparats*, Chambers began to build up "insurance" that he hoped might provide pause to those whose decision it might be to liquidate him, or, if he was killed, that might be used to identify his killers. He began to save "the typed copies and summaries of original documents" that Alger Hiss gave him, he would tell the FBI, and also kept "certain handwritten notes which Alger Hiss occasionally made about documents he could not bring out of the State Department." He also retained strips of undeveloped and developed film.

Chambers also faced the problem of money. From his underground worker's salary, he had been able to save nothing, and if he were to vanish effectively, he would be unable to work for a long time. He solved the problem by stealing from party funds given him to maintain the *apparats*. Provided $2,000 to cover his wages, rent for the photographic workshop, sundry expenses, and $500 for repaying Hiss for a loan enabling him to buy an automobile, Chambers kept both the money and the car.

As to where to hide, Chambers reasoned that his Communist colleagues would expect him to get as far away from Washington and Baltimore as possible. He thus decided to live in Baltimore, moving from time to time from one quarter of the city or its environs to another. After moving with his wife and daughter into a single room in a house near Pikesville, Maryland, he defected simply by failing to appear at a scheduled meeting. For weeks thereafter he rarely emerged from his room, doing so finally in order to go to New York to find some kind of work in the publishing field that he could do at home. Through Paul Willert, an Englishman with the Oxford University Press, he obtained an assignment to translate a book by a German Communist, Gustav Regler, *The Great Crusade.*

With that work in hand, Chambers drove with his family to Florida where he rented a beach cottage. "I worked at the translation all night," he would recall, "so as always to be on guard, sleeping during the day." Returning to Baltimore after a month, Chambers concluded that whatever the danger, he had to come out of hiding and try to begin a normal life. As a precaution, he bought a shotgun and shells at a Montgomery Ward store.

Jacob Golos and his Central Control Commission, Chambers soon learned, were aware of his defection and were trying to do something about it. Through Paul Willert, who turned out to have been a Communist while serving as a diplomat with the British Embassy in Berlin and had broken with the party while remaining a fellow traveler, Chambers' former controller, Ulrich, sent word that he wanted to see him; but Chambers refused to acknowledge the message. He also learned that a Communist underground worker, Grace Hutchins, visited his brother-in-law, a New York lawyer, Reuben Schemitz, with word that Chambers "was to report to the Communist Party by a certain date 'or else.'" Again Chambers ignored the word. Returning to see Schemitz, Hutchins suggested that if he would agree to surrender Chambers, she would be able to guarantee the safety of his sister (Chambers' wife) and her daughter.

With the threat to his wife and daughter hanging over him, Chambers collected the films and documents he had amassed during his last weeks as a courier and turned them over in a brown envelope to his wife's nephew, Nathan Levine, who lived in New York, and Levine in turn hid them in the dumbwaiter shaft of his mother's home at 260 Rochester Avenue in Brooklyn. If anything happened to him, Chambers told Levine, he was "to make the contents of this envelope public in some way."

Whittaker Chambers' apostasy came at a time when, in faddish circles at least, it was smart to sympathize with and even embrace Communism. In America, an oft-repeated German aphorism had yet to take hold: he who has not been a Communist by the time he is twenty has no heart; he who is still a Communist after thirty has no brains. At elegant dinner parties in the upper Eighties in New York, "the most recent caller at the Communist Party's headquarters at 35 East Twelfth Street would be the cynosure of all artistic eyes."[3] Nor was that sentiment confined to the modish set: on a political platform in Cleveland, Robert Alphonsus Taft, the leader of the Republican right wing, seated the secretary-general of the American Communist Party, Earl Browder, thereby to demonstrate that no Fascist brush—whether wielded by Hitler or Mussolini—had tarred his conservative skin.

The evil ones were not the Communists but the Fascists: the Silver Shirts, Huey Long, Father Coughlin. When President Roosevelt in 1934 upgraded the Bureau of Investigation to become the Federal Bureau of Investigation, he charged J. Edgar Hoover with keeping an eye on the growing Fascist movement in the United States while making no mention of Communists. Not until 1938 did the president add Communists and the Comintern to the list of suspect political organizations, and even then there was widespread respect for Stalin as the only man who was standing up to Hitler and Mussolini. Thus it was that in the latter part of 1939, when Whittaker Chambers decided to inform the government in Washington of what he knew about the Comintern's *apparats* within its ranks, he found nobody particularly eager to hear his story.

Chambers first contacted a journalist who was regarded as an authority on communism, Isaac Don Levine. At Chambers' request, Levine went personally to the White House with a message that Chambers had a matter of major national importance to communicate but that he would do so only to the president himself and only if the president personally would assure him of immunity from prosecution. In response, the president's appointments secretary said that it would be impossible to arrange a meeting with the president on such short notice; he suggested instead that Chambers talk with the president's adviser on internal security, Adolf A. Berle, who was also undersecretary of state in charge of national and international intelligence matters.

When Chambers agreed, Berle entertained Chambers and Levine at dinner at his home in Washington on Saturday evening, September 2, 1939, the eve of the outbreak of World War II. After dinner, while it was still light, the three moved out onto the lawn where, as Chambers would tell the story, Berle took notes on what he had to say. When Chambers and Levine had gone, Berle that same evening typed up a rough transcript.

The notes plainly revealed that Chambers told Berle that by 1939 the Communist underground in Washington, the *apparats*, was heavily engaged not only in penetrating the government but also the military. There were clear identifications of individuals as Comintern agents: Lee Pressman, Harold Ware, Nathan Witt, John Abt, J. Peters, Alexander Trachtenberg, Alger Hiss, his brother, Donald, and others. It was also clear that a number of government agencies had been penetrated: the State Department, the Labor Department, the Securities and Exchange Commission, the Treasury, the Department of Justice.

From the notes alone, it was obvious that the information Chambers had provided was of the highest importance to the Federal Bureau of Investigation, yet Berle made no effort to pass it on to J. Edgar Hoover. Nor would he even mention Chambers to the FBI until February 28, 1941, after eighteen months had passed. Even then he would make only a request for "someone from the Bureau to contact him regarding Chambers" and make no mention of his meeting with Chambers or of his notes on what Chambers had told him.[4]

Yet by that time Hoover had heard about Chambers from another source: the prominent Communist Ludwig Lore, who told the FBI that "a former *OGPU* agent" had "delivered to the President of the United States through a trusted friend who had the necessary contact a list of persons in the Government who were Communists or pro-Soviet," but, said Lore, "nothing had been done about it."[5] The man to whom he referred had by that time come out of hiding and had become as associate editor of *Time* Magazine: Whittaker Chambers.

On August 18, 1941, J. Edgar Hoover directed an assistant "to institute a detailed investigation regarding Chambers to determine his character, background, activities and affiliations in a highly discreet and tactful manner." Upon conclusion of the investigation, "the feasibility of openly interviewing Chambers would be considered."[6] Yet not for another six months, until March 4, 1942, would the investigation get under way.

The delay was attributable in part to "a general investigative delinquency in the field during the period immediately prior to and subsequent to Pearl Harbor."[7] It was also attributable to the fact that the FBI's informant, Ludwig Lore, soon after telling the FBI about Chambers, died suddenly at his home on East 55th Street in New York. Various investigations into the disappearance of Juliet Stewart Poyntz were under way at the time, and according to the former secretary-general of the American Communist Party, Benjamin Gitlow, Lore had become "caught in a mesh of international intrigue" over the Poyntz case. Lore, said Gitlow, "knew all about the Poyntz affair, yet he dared not tell." He had "died suddenly, mysteriously, without any premonition of illness."[8]

Just over two months after beginning to investigate Whittaker Chambers, FBI agents on May 13, 1942, visited him. Chambers "advised that he had given all of the information which was in his possession to Mr. A. A. Berle of the State Department . . . in September, 1939, and before discussing any of the matters with the agents put through a long distance call to Mr. Berle at the latter's home." Would it be all right, Chambers asked Berle, if he passed on to two FBI agents the information he had earlier provided? Berle apparently agreed, "for Chambers thanked him and thereafter supplied considerable information which he indicated had been furnished previously to Mr. Berle."[9]

It was thus two and a half years after Whittaker Chambers had informed Adolfe Berle of Communists within the American government that the Federal Bureau of Investigation finally learned the specifics about it. Yet even then the FBI made no immediate effort to corroborate the information that its agents had obtained with that provided Berle nor to determine why Berle had failed to pass along the information he had received. Not for another year, until May 1943, when agents again interviewed Chambers, did the FBI decide to check its information against Berle's. Only then, more than three and a half years after Chambers talked with Berle, did the FBI's liaison section with the State Department in June 1943 obtain what turned out to be a four-page transcript of Chamber's statements.

"Do I understand correctly," asked Hoover, "that Chambers talked to Berle in 1939; we interviewed him first in May 1942; and Berle gave us information first in June 1943?"[10] That was indeed the case, and it produced not only a long apologia from Hoover's subordinates but also awkward questions for Adolf Berle both from the FBI and from the House Un-American Activities Committee.

Berle subsequently explained that "he did not feel free to divulge the contents of Chambers' conversation to the FBI inasmuch as Chambers had indicated that he did not so desire, . . . particularly if the source was to be revealed." If that occurred, said Berle, Chambers "would not back up the story."[11] Or, on the other hand, Chambers may have asked only a delay in the passing of the information until Berle could arrange his immunity from prosecution, something he asked Berle to do but which Berle failed to do.[12]

Whatever the case, the fact remained that the president's adviser on matters of internal security had for long months failed to inform the FBI or any other official agency about material he had obtained from Whittaker Chambers that would clearly have had a bearing on investigation into the Soviet intelligence and subversive apparatus in the United States and that in the end he had revealed the material only wen spcifically asked for it. It was conduct that would remain baffling. Those who believed that Berle had attempted to cover up for Alger Hiss in disbelief of Hiss's guilt—a disbelief that many a member of the establishment and many a liberal would long sustain—may have been right.

It was not until the second great world conflagration was long over and an anticommunist spasm was sweeping the United States that anybody began to take Chambers' accusations really seriously, and even then the doubters would be legion. When Chambers would at last begin to name names before the Un-American Activities Committee in late summer of 1948, the statute of limitations would have run out on the people he accused, but one man—Alger Hiss—would rush to deny Chambers' accusations and in the process make himself vulnerable to a charge of perjury and set himself up as a cause célèbre with few parallels on the American scene.

As developed before the Un-American Activities Committee, Chambers knew too many intimate details about Alger Hiss, had too much knowledge about life in the house on P Street and about documents typed on an old Woodstock typewriter and a Bokhara carpet delivered in a parking lot, as well as commanding too many details about the espionage he accused Hiss of to be lying. Before a Baltimore court he produced the documents that his wife's nephew, Nathan Levine, had hidden for him in the dumbwaiter of his mother's home in Brooklyn. He also led investigators of the Un-American Activities Committee to a farm he had purchased outside Westminster, Maryland, where he removed the top of a pumpkin and pulled out the film that had also been a part of the package entrusted to Levine. After two sensational trials, in the first of which some of the jurors would have as much trouble as did most members of the establishment in believing that such a golden boy of capitalism as Alger Hiss might spy on his government for the Soviet Union, Hiss would at last go to jail, convicted on two counts of perjury.

## Chapter Forty-One

Soon after Gerhardt Eisler arrived in New York in 1933 as plenipotentiary for the Comintern in North America, he received from headquarters of the Comintern in Moscow an order to begin to organize American "white collar workers, municipal, government, and office employees, etc., with particular emphasis on technical and laboratory personnel." Having been "considered 'servants of the bourgeoisie,'" those groups "had hitherto been ignored," but Moscow saw "the possibility of obtaining political intelligence by organizing government employees" and "of obtaining technical intelligence by organizing technicians and laboratory person-nel."[1] Gerhardt Eisler put a member of the American Communist Party's Central Committee, Joseph Weinkoop, in charge of organizing those two groups.

Weinkoop soon discovered "a small independent union of civil engineers, employed by New York City," which he ordered "all Party members in that profession to join, and in due time they took it over." It was the start, according to Weinkoop, of the Federation of Architects, Chemists, and Technicians, an affiliate of the Congress of Industrial Organizations, the CIO. The party took over an independent union of radio operators in the same way, an organization that later became, Weinkoop maintained, the CIO's Communications Workers Union. At his direction, Weinkoop related, party members moved into the Independent Subway Workers Union in New York City and another union "operating within the General Electric Plants in Schenectady, New York, which in later years became the United Electrical Radio and Equipment Workers, CIO." Party members who were clerical workers infiltrated a small union affiliated with the American Federation of Labor, the AF of L, split the union, and, according to Weinkoop, founded what would become the United Office and Professional Workers, CIO. By the end of 1934, said Weinkoop, membership in the independent unions under party control totaled 32,000, while there were 3,600 party members in left-wing groups within the AF of L.

At that point, Eisler sent Weinkoop to Cleveland to organize independent unions in the party's Midwestern administrative area. As Weinkoop would record, "The only labor union contact [upon his arrival] was a lazy little group in one of the painter's locals," and the union's headquarters consisted of nothing more than an "old dilapidated desk in a dingy office." Weinkoop promptly rented a suite in a building on Paine Avenue, which he named "Headquarters for the Council of Independent Industrial Unions." To give the suite an appearance of activity, he borrowed a secretary and a typewriter from headquarters of the Communist Party in Cleveland and allowed the Unemployed Councils, an organization of unemployed men and women, to use one of the rooms as a food distribution center.

Registering all Communists who then worked or had worked in plants and factories in Cleveland, he used them to begin to organize cells within the plants and factories. For nine months, Weinkoop had only limited success, but when the National Recovery Administration was created, providing collective bargaining machinery for 22 million workers in 500 fields of industry, "things began to happen." Calls began to come in volume to headquarters of the Council of Independent Industrial Unions—it became known as the CIIU—asking for someone to speak on behalf of workers in such plants as Fisher Bodies, White Motors, Republic Steel, and Otis Elevator. Weinkoop invited the more malcontent among the callers to his offices, provided them propaganda leaflets and placards promoting the CIIU, and organized them into "strike committees" to solicit membership in the CIIU.

Thus did Weinkoop, by his own account, became the artful dodger of the trade union movement in Cleveland. Considering his membership to be sufficiently strong, he called a strike in a truck body plant. When the management refused to negotiate, Weinkoop accompanied the strike committee from the plant to the local headquarters of the National Recovery Administration, which forced the plant's management to arbitrate. The management finally met the strikers' demands, whereupon "contacts," claimed Weinkoop, "piled into the CIIU headquarters from other plants."

As Weinkoop's strike committees demonstrated their strength, he reported to Earl Browder, the AF of L in Cleveland, "one of the most ossified and sleepy outfits, began to wake up," and its local officials sent alarming reports to their respective international unions that "the Communists through the Council of Independent Industrial Unions are taking over in Cleveland." According to Weinkoop, the AF of L "sent in organizers by the dozens." In plants where he considered that the workers would swing to the AF of L, he instructed his men to join the unions. The AF of L's organizers, wrote Weinkoop, "were unaccustomed to such deceptive techniques and boasted about the increased membership only to discover that they had paid for the organizing and often the strike expenses, but the Communists had the union."

So successful was Weinkoop's work that the party's Central Committee called him to New York to make a special report and congratulated him for using "the best principles of Lenin technique"; but while he was away, a goon squad—which, he said, belonged to the AF of L—wrecked the CIIU's headquarters. Returning immediately to Cleveland, Weinkoop lined up 600 members of the CIIU and the Unemployed Councils, armed them "with lead pipes and brick bats," and challenged the AF of L to a showdown fight. When no members of the AF of L showed up, the press, duly invited to the confrontation, duly reported it, and according to Weinkoop, "the CIIU was really established as the rival union of the AFL in Cleveland."

Weinkoop was by that time well known to the police as a Communist, as well as to Better America, Inc., a private intelligence organization funded by industry and the oil companies to identify Communist organizers and their tactics. Using aliases, Weinkoop nevertheless continued and expanded his activities. Reviving a Revolutionary War flag—a snake with the motto: "Don't Tread on Me"—he used the banner as a symbol to organize mass marches that profoundly troubled a number of Midwestern industrial cities. He turned next to the Civilian Conservation Corps, a New Deal program to provide work for unemployed young men, eighteen to twenty-five, in reforestation, flood control, road building, and anti-soil erosion. From the Unemployed Councils, he sent young men to enroll in the work camps, where they drew their $30 per month salary while at the same time propagating the faith among men who were destined soon either to be serving in war industries or the armed forces.

Still operating from headquarters of the CIIU, Weinkoop decided on a step that he hoped would expand the class war in Cleveland, to infiltrate an organization in the Kinsman section of the city, the Association of Small Homes and Land Owners, which was designed to assist and protect mortgaged home and land owners. The object, Weinkoop noted, was to fight the banks and to bring those "temples of capitalism" into ridicule, contempt, and hatred. Within fifteen months the association had 23,000 members, mostly industrial workers. "Whenever the banks tried to take over a house," he wrote, "all association members with tin lizzies fender to fender, for blocks around, would prevent the police from executing the order."

In some circles, Weinkoop was regarded as a kind of Midwestern Robin Hood.

Capitalizing on that reputation, he began to organize industrial workers in Cincinnati and Dayton and to expand into other fields: the food trades, slaughterhouses, textile plants, the cafeteria and restaurant trades, and furniture manufacturers. "Secret organizing groups," he wrote, "were even formed in some of the huge steel mills operated by Republic and Carnegie Steel and in the lodges of the Railroad Brotherhoods." When called back to New York "to build up front groups among the Negroes, Women, and Youth," he left behind a relatively small but highly disciplined organization that had representatives in plants and factories throughout Ohio. By means of a system of workers' correspondents—*rabcors*—first established by Lenin in France, the CIIU performed an important intelligence function; little of import in social, political, technical, and military matters could develop in Ohio without the party's Central Committee and the representatives of the Comintern and the Soviet special services in New York being informed. That situation, Weinkoop claimed, was in time duplicated throughout the United States.

The American Communist Party's campaign to organize—which was to say, revolutionize—the American black people developed as a result of a detailed "Resolution of the Communist International on the Negro Question in the United States," promulgated in October of 1930. Although most Comintern resolutions concerning the United States were couched in careful language to avoid legal actions for incitement, conspiracy, or sedition and to maintain a fiction of compliance with the Roosevelt-Litvinov Agreements of 1933, the Comintern's resolution on blacks in America, which antedated the agreement, constituted a clear directive to the American Communist Party to foment a black rebellion and to establish a separate black nation in what the Comintern called the "Black Belt."[2]

The party's "constant call to the Negro masses" was to be: "*Revolutionary struggle against the ruling white bourgeoisie through a fighting alliance with the revolutionary white proletariat.*" [Italics in the original]. A successful revolution by the American blacks would "establish a common tie" for "the revolutionary struggle of race and national liberation from imperialist domination of the Negroes in various parts of the world," especially in South Africa, Liberia, and the black colonies of the British and French empires.

As a first step, the party was to form a Trade Union Unity League, which was to organize blacks into unions and conduct "an aggressive struggle" against the AF of L. Special attention was to be paid to "the Negro workers' organizations, such as the Brotherhood of Sleeping Car Porters, Chicago Asphalt Workers' Union, and so on." Ridiculing existing American black organizations—the National Association for the Advancement of Colored People and the Pan-African Congress—as "bourgeois," the directive demanded that the league become "the champions in the struggle for the rights of the Negroes in the old unions, and in the organizing of new unions for both Negroes and whites, as well as separate Negro unions."

On the theory that properly indoctrinated black organizers were needed, the American Communist Party in August 1931 booked twenty-five young blacks aboard the Cunard Line's *Aquitania,* traveling ostensibly as Bible students on the way to Jerusalem, but upon reaching Cherbourg, they turned not right toward the Holy Land but left toward Moscow. There they enrolled in the Lenin School.

Administered jointly by the Comintern and the Russian Communist Party, the Lenin School was located in four buildings on Voroskia Street, enclosed by a fence on three sides and a brick wall facing the street. The "terms ranged from one to four years and ran continuously," and the curriculum consisted of: Philosophy (dialectic materialism), Marxist Economics, History of the Labor Movement and Trade Unionism, History of the Comintern and the Russian Communist Party, Party Organization, Conspiracy (which included civil warfare, standard arms, code, sabotage, and international propaganda), and Socialism in Russia. One Chinese instructor and several Russians taught "underground work and partisan fighting," and there was target practice, swimming, horseback riding, rowing, rescue work, grenade practice, and hiking in gas masks. At the conclusion of the course, each student was given an academic and political "characterization."

Hardly had the Americans begun their academic work when "the student body, especially the Americans, was torn apart." The issues were manifold and obscure, but to the American Communist, Joseph Weinkoop, who was in Moscow at the time, the immediate cause of the disturbance was a resentment by the blacks of "white chauvinism" within the Comintern and objections to the founding of a separate black nation within the United States. When one of the black students, William Nowell, complained to a representative of the Comintern's Executive Committee, the Comintern established a commission which produced a resolution condemning the actions of the Americans and denying that any form of chauvinism existed in "the land of socialism."

Incensed by that brushoff, the American blacks, joined by their white student colleagues, marched on the headquarters of the Russian Communist Party, much to the alarm of the Lenin School's proctor. There a representative of the party authorized them to present their grievances "in documentary form," but in the end party headquarters merely referred the protest to the Comintern's Political Secretariat, which did nothing. Nowell was in time pulled from the school, confined temporarily to a Red Army barracks at Gorki, and then sent to Batum, where—word reaching the other American students had it—he died, either from tuberculosis or by drowning.

Further angered by that word, the other blacks became so unruly that the Comintern broke up the class and ordered the Americans home. Back in the United States, the report of Nowell's death proved to be unfounded, for he, too, in time returned.

The unhappy outcome of the attempt to indoctrinate American blacks at the Lenin School was the story in microcosm of the early efforts to revolutionize blacks in the United States. When Joseph Weinkoop created a new front organization, the League of Struggle for Negro Rights, and the party press began to propagandize for a separate Negro republic, "the Negro intellectuals ridiculed it so effectively" that it almost brought the black revolutionary movement to an end. The Comintern was reduced for a time to sponsoring a black front movement outside the boundaries of the United States, the International Negro Workers Committee, in Hamburg, Germany.

The black revolutionary movement in the United States might have collapsed at the start had it not been for what came to be known as the Scottsboro Case, an incident in 1931 in which nine black youths were indicted and tried in Scottsboro, Alabama, on charges of raping two white girls while all, as was the custom of many during the depression, were hitching rides on a freight train. Found guilty, eight of the nine youths were sentenced to death and the other to life imprisonment.

Having learned much in propagandizing alleged injustice in the Sacco-Vanzetti Case, the Comintern was quick to take up the cause of the Scottsboro Boys. The American Communist Party led the chorus of protest, assisted by the International Negro Workers Committee, which had been forced out of Hamburg by the Gestapo, relocated in New York, and renamed the National Negro Congress, with some distinguished membership including the great black actor and singer Paul Robeson.

In 1932 the Supreme Court agreed to review the Scottsboro Case and overturned the verdict, ruling that the youths had been afforded inadequate counsel. At a retrial, one of the girls recanted her testimony, maintaining that she and her companion had encouraged and acquiesced in the sexual acts; and when the jury again returned a verdict of guilty, the judge, James Edwin Horton, set it aside as contrary to the weight of the evidence, an act that soon cost him his job at the polls. Although yet a third trial again produced a verdict of guilty, the Supreme Court in 1935 overturned it on the grounds that the State of Alabama had systematically excluded blacks from jury service. Another jury was quick to convict again.

Largely because of the work of Communist lawyers and a massive international demand for a general pardon, in large measure generated by an unceasing campaign orchestrated by the Comintern, a compromise reached in 1937 set four of the men free and reduced the sentences of the other five to prison terms ranging from twenty years to life. Between 1943 and 1950, four would be released on parole, and in 1948, when the last escaped and made his way to Michigan, that state refused to extradite him. Almost two decades later, in 1966, Judge Horton would finally reveal theretofore confidential information conclusively proving the innocence of all of the nine.

In the course of the campaign to free—or at least capitalize on—the Scottsboro Boys, the National Negro Congress came into vocal and sometimes violent conflict with the NAACP. That association, which had built a strength and prestige among the broad mass of American blacks, clearly stood in the way of the

Comintern's design. To the task of penetrating and gaining control of the organization, the American Communist Party named Joseph Weinkoop.

"Before long," according to Weinkoop, "infiltration was in full swing"; but Weinkoop would never be able to infiltrate enough Communists or Communist sympathizers into the organization to come anywhere near gaining control. Thus the seeming gains of the black revolutionary movement during the years of agitation over the Scottsboro Boys proved to be illusory and fleeting, and the movement would never gain real strength. For any real success in organizing Americans for the Comintern's goals, Weinkoop would have to be content with his achievements among American workers and in yet another direction, among American youth.

The Comintern's propaganda wizard, Willi Muenzenberg, founded the Communist Youth International in Germany in 1919, and three years later, in 1922, recognized an American adjunct, the Young Communist League. At the Sixth Congress of the Communist International in Moscow on August 29, 1928, a senior Comintern functionary, Otto Kuusinen, reported on the tactics of the young Communists while at the same time appealing to adult Communist parties to support them. "The American young comrades," he declared, had learned to penetrate the large bourgeois youth organizations and "in the course of not quite a year" had "succeeded in creating 175 factions in these mass organizations." It was vital, he said, to educate the youth everywhere so they would not "be dragged into the war by deceit," and if the Comintern was "to attack our class enemies in the rear when they start the war against the Soviet Union," the support of the youth was essential."[3]

For all that and similar exhortations, by the time Weinkoop began his efforts to organize American youth, the Young Communist League had made few converts. Upon return to New York from Cleveland, Weinkoop attempted to change that by adopting new tactics, which could be summed up in a phrase: using the adult to snare the child.

"Throughout the country," Weinkoop would relate, "adult members of the party were asked to invite sympathetic students to a meeting in the member's home, where all the current troubles were to be discussed and the blame fixed upon the capitalist system, particularly where the depression and the rise of fascism was concerned." Among teachers and faculty, party organizers, feigning interest in their problems and grievances, formed secret groups with the real purpose of indoctrinating the adults in order to get at the minds of the students. "It took some time before the Central Committee recognized all the possibilities of this approach," noted Weinkoop, "but when they did, special training schools for teachers and faculty were formed in which every method was taught to introduce the Communist view into the classrooms and text books." Under Weinkoop's direction, the party also began to infiltrate Parent-Teacher Associations in an effort "to get at the youth below the college level."

On college and university campuses, according to Weinkoop, students formed clubs which took up "student grievances . . . thus . . . combining immediate demands and ultimate aims into whatever Party line was then in vogue." Those clubs, at the direction of the Young Communist League, supported the Oxford Oath, the resolution adopted in 1933 by the Oxford Union, the debating society of Oxford University in England, declaring that "The House would under no circumstances fight for King and Country." In a manifesto issued in 1934, the Young Communist League proclaimed: "Youth of America! Serve notice on the bosses' government that you are through serving as cannon fodder. . . . We must turn our guns on our real enemies—not the workers of other countries but our own bosses in this country! Fight for a Soviet USA!"

On many a campus, the Reserve Officers' Training Corps became a special target. At New York's City College, for example, according to Weinkoop, party members or sympathizers organized a "social problems club" and under prolonged agitation, students were soon picketing with placards demanding "an end to ROTC and military training." In some institutions, students formed antimilitary organizations called Veterans of Future Wars. At City College, the campaign was so successful that the college dropped ROTC.

Through the years, the Young Communist League vividly mirrored the chameleonlike changes in Comintern policy. When, for example, civil war began in Spain in 1936 and the Soviet government supported the leftist government, the general secretary of the Young Communist League, Gil Green, speaking at the Eighth National Convention, reversed the league's adherence to the Oxford Oath: "If we in this country face the same conditions as the young people of Spain, we would not hesitate for one second in defending democracy against fascism to the last drop of our blood."[4]

With the signing in 1939 of a Nazi-Soviet Nonaggression Pact between Hitler and Stalin, an unholy alliance between Fascism and Communism that could but imperil the world's democracies, the league proclaimed: "Every increase in the armed forces of the United States is but a step toward preparing this country for entry into the European War. . . . The armed forces must not be expanded. American youth must not be militarized! . . . Support the Peace Policies of the Soviet Union!"

Throughout the country, the Young Communist League joined in a campaign to undermine the fighting ability of the armed forces—until Hitler attacked Russia in 1941. At that point, there would no longer be "an imperialist war." As the league declared: "All of us stand ready to lay down our lives in defense of our nation, our people, and our democratic heritage . . . it is a just war to destroy fascism. It is a people's war for national liberation. We will resolutely combat the treacherous conspiracies of the fascists, defeatists, and their fifth column."

There was no determining the exact extent of the influence of the Young Communist League, but many an official considered the league's infiltration of the school system to be serious. In 1941, for example, Mayor Fiorello La Guardia appointed a New York City Subcommittee Relative to Subversive Activity Among Students in Public High Schools and Colleges of the City of New York, which found that the league used secret writing and codes in its communications; that it maintained "an elaborate system of conniving, masquerading, interlocking directorates, agitation and propaganda"; that of fifty-two members of the National Council of the American Youth Congress, twenty-two, while posing as representatives of religious groups, were identified as Communists; that the league was no "spontaneous or indigenous movement" but one "carefully cultivated and directed from outside"; that from 1935 to 1939 "the high schools and colleges of the country were afflicted with an epidemic of Communist-staged 'peace strikes'"; and that there were "numerous examples of teacher and student cooperation in Communist projects."

In a post-World War II investigation, the House Committee on Un-American Activities would note that American Youth for Democracy, the name which the Young Communist League adopted in 1943 as the United States was fighting alongside the Soviet Union, claimed sixty chapters in fourteen states and a total membership of 16,194. By its own admission, the Young Communist League thus was never large, but its influence far exceeded its size. That had been demonstrated as early as 1934 when at Gerhardt Eisler's direction, the first American Youth Congress convened. As Joseph Weinkoop recorded, "the liberals even to the First Lady [Mrs. Roosevelt] fronted for the Communists. . . . Almost every youth organization except those of the Catholic Church and the American Legion were [sic] affiliated." So successful was the congress from the viewpoint of the Comintern that Moscow changed the name of the Communist Youth International to the World Youth Congress. In the meantime, as chapters of the American Youth Congress multiplied, young Communists meager in numbers but strong in influence subtly established control in many of them. As late as 1947, the Un-American Activities Committee would declare that "The fact that forces hostile to American democracy and seeking its destruction are penetrating our schools and colleges in an effort to subvert the great body of American students is . . . a matter of major national concern."

## Chapter Forty-Two

In 1938, as the great nations of the world began to go to war stations, the Communist Party of America published its first manifesto. In that document, the party renounced as "Trotskyist" the old Bolshevik proposition that a Communist state could be created in the United States only through an armed revolution of the proletariat against the bourgeoisie to overthrow the government. Citing quotations from Lenin and Stalin to show that the Marxist notion of the inevitability of civil war between the classes in America had become obsolete, the party leader, Earl Browder, implied—although he made no categorical disavowal—that thenceforth the party would employ "the means of capitalism," by which he meant lawyers and legalism, to bring about the Communist elysium in the western hemisphere.

Such a basic and drastic revision in Communist doctrine was hardly to be promulgated without the advice and consent of the Comintern, which probably specifically directed it, for to Stalin it had become evident that when Hitler attacked Russia—as Stalin was convinced he would eventually do—the Soviet Union would require the industrial assistance of the United States. If capitalist industry were to help Russia obtain the means to resist, the methods of the Comintern had to change—at least overtly—from inciting class warfare to doing other things that would benefit the security of Russia. The new objective of the Comintern thus was to form an alliance with capitalism against Fascism, so that clandestine operations in the United States were at that point to focus on liquidating elements in the country hostile to Stalin and his concept of national Communism.

That kind of proposition held a certain attraction for wide sectors of American capitalism, for it removed the irritant of the Comintern's unremitting attempts to provoke class warfare while at the same time providing orders for American industry. To those who believed that the United States would inevitably be drawn into any new European war, it also held out the prospect of victory without the United States' having to incur the enormous casualties that would result if its own troops had to fight a land campaign in Europe.

To such Marxist purists as the former secretary-general of the Comintern, Angelika Balabanov, who was then in the United States, having mysteriously been permitted to leave Russia for ideological reasons and equally mysteriously having been permitted to make an exile's home in the United States, Browder's manifesto was heresy and treason. Balabanov spoke words of warning: once the manifesto had accomplished its purposes, she said, Stalin would return the international Communist movement to the old form of Communist imperialism. The Comintern, her pen cried from a coldwater flat in New York, had capitulated "on successive occasions to capitalism, militarism, nationalism, and obscurantism, in their most obnoxious forms"; the manifesto had "destroyed the political and economic organizations of the underprivileged masses" and had "shattered the faith and hopes of millions in the future of humanity and Socialism."[1]

Yet the voice of Angelika Balabanov, once so powerful, was at that point no more influential than that of any other aging, impecunious exile living bitterly and hopelessly far from the Kremlin. The Communist movement in the United States, for the most part, swung obediently to the dictate of the manifesto, many members doing so with relief, for they had felt the hot breath of the police, but in the activities of the underground *apparats*, the shift meant no decrease in operations, merely a change in direction. Whereas subversion had always been the underlying principle behind all activities, greater attention turned to trying to influence the government's policies, to fighting the activities of the Fascist powers in the United

States and neutralizing their attempts to influence the American government, and to focusing espionage primarily on weapons technology.

At the FBI, J. Edgar Hoover, seeing no reason to alter his agency's policy toward the Communists just because of a few pretty words, continued to treat the American Communist Party as an institution bent upon employing violence and armed revolution to overthrow the government of the republic. That he was justified appeared to be evident from word provided by his informant within the party's Central Committee, who revealed that the Soviet secret services were more active than ever in the United States and that within various American organizations—labor, youth, blacks, teachers, the Russian Orthodox Church in America—Communists obedient to their oaths to defend the Soviet Union were as diligent as ever. They were spreading pacifist and antiwar ideas to such an extent that Hoover considered that if the United States became involved in a war, it would be difficult to raise reliable armed forces.

In that atmosphere, the Department of Justice moved to test the attitudes of American courts toward the new Communist doctrine as implied in Browder's manifesto. There was no concern about such a basic issue as espionage, for on that the law was clear; the question was: did the American Communist Party constitute a conspiracy intent on using armed violence to overthrow the government of the United States?

Although there had been numerous trials in the United States involving Communists, the body of available law and precedent under which Communists suspected of subversive activities could be indicted was thin. In most cases, Communists had been indicted for such peripheral offenses as making a false declaration to obtain a passport or, having pledged allegiance to the United States, behaving in such a manner as to indicate continuing allegiance to a foreign power. Members of the American Communist Party and the Communist International consciously tried to avoid public statements that might be construed as seditious and thus result in indictment or new legislation. When indictments did occur, the party and the Comintern relied on statements by such leaders as Lenin and Stalin to show that a policy of violent change of government had been rendered obsolete and that while individuals associated with the party might make revolutionary or seditious statements, the policy of the party was to work within the laws of the United States.

In prosecuting Communists, the sterner practitioners of American law relied heavily on the case of *Gitlow* v. *New York*, which was heard in 1919 and lasted with appeals until 1925.

Born in New York City in 1891 to Russian immigrant parents, Benjamin Gitlow had become a leading Communist militant at the time the Comintern was formed. On information provided by a committee which had been created by the New York State Senate investigating organizations suspected of revolutionary activity aimed at the government of the United States, Gitlow was arrested on November

8, 1919, in the course of a roundup that led to the *Buford* deportations of such agitators as Emma Goldman. Gitlow and three others were accused of sedition in an action brought under the New York Criminal Anarchy Statute and received sentences of from five to ten years in prison. When Gitlow challenged the constitutionality of the indictment, the matter eventually came before the New York Supreme Court. At issue was whether "certain statements such as the advocacy of the violent overthrow of government are constitutionally punishable under any and all circumstances and without waiting until there is a danger that it will be successful."[2]

In its judgment, the court upheld the constitutionality of the finding of the lower court, declaring that:

> . . . utterances inciting to the overthrow of organized government by unlawful means present a sufficient danger of substantive evil to bring their punishment within the range of legislative discretion. . . . Such utterances, by their very nature, involve danger to the public peace and to the security of the State. . . . [The State] cannot reasonably be required to defer the adoption of measures for its own peace and safety until the revolutionary utterances lead to actual disturbance of the public peace or . . . its own destruction; but it may, in the exercise of its judgment, suppress the threatening danger in its incipiency.[3]

That ruling was of marked importance as a precedent for courts hearing cases against individual Communists, but it had little validity for those who sought to show that the American Communist Party was seditious and should be proscribed. Although the legal testing of that was tried on occasion, no clear precedent would be established until much later, in 1943, when the United States and the Soviet Union were allied in a war against Germany. That case involved a man named Schneiderman, who appealed to the United States Supreme Court to overturn a proceeding against him canceling his certificate of naturalization and citizenship on the grounds that he had fraudulently obtained American citizenship by swearing he was a man of good moral character "attached to the principles of the Constitution." The government contended that at the time Schneiderman took the oath, he was a member of the American Communist Party and thus was not attached to the principles of the Constitution; the lower court agreed and ordered Schneiderman deported.

Hearing the appeal, the Supreme Court held that the government had failed to prove at the time of Schneiderman's naturalization, that either the petitioner or the Communist Party advocated the overthrow of the American government by force. Schneiderman had been naturalized in 1938, the court noted, at a time when the Browder manifesto had been proclaimed, and in the documentary evidence on party objectives submitted by the government, there was conflict. According to the court:

The 1938 Constitution of the Communist Party of the United States, which [Schneiderman] claimed to be the first and only written constitution ever officially adopted by the Party and which he asserted enunciated the principles of the Party as he understood them from the beginning of his membership, ostensibly eschews resort to force and violence as an element of Party tactics. A tenable conclusion from the foregoing is that the Party in 1938 desired to achieve its purpose by peaceful and democratic means, and as a theoretical matter justified the use of force and violence only as a method of preventing an attempted forcible counter-overthrow once the Party had obtained control in a peaceful manner, or as a method of last resort to enforce the majority will if at some indefinite future time because of peculiar circumstances constitutional or peaceful channels were no longer open.[4]

As landmark as was that decision, it was reached at a time when the Congress had enacted legislation enabling the government to deal with Communists by indirection and without running the risks implicit in any action that might or might not result in the party being declared illegal. On June 28, 1940, for example, the Congress enacted the Alien Registration Act, commonly called the Smith Act, which strengthened existing laws governing the admission and deportation of aliens and required the fingerprinting of all aliens residing in the United States, a measure directed primarily at checking subversive activities by foreign-born members of the Comintern and by agents of the Soviet secret services. Any who failed to comply with the new law or were found to be acting in a manner that even suggested that they were engaged in activities inimical to the interests and safety of the United States faced criminal penalties. That legislation caught at least one big Soviet fish, an official of Amtorg, Gaik Ovakiminian, who was in charge of industrial and technological espionage in the United States. When he failed to register as required, he was arrested and deported.

Aroused by what Weinkoop would call "the obvious loyalty of the American Communist Party to Moscow, by the Party's anti-American propaganda, and by the Party's activities in promoting strikes to interfere with the War Effort," the Congress also passed the Voorhis Act, which required Americans acting as agents of a foreign agency or power to register. As Weinkoop would write, "This legislation was a serious threat to the Party, in that in complying with the law, it would be publicly admitting that it and its officers were agents of Moscow." The law also required all Americans acting as agents for foreign institutions or governments to file financial statements, and "the public disclosure of finances would also be embarrassing."[5] The party would either have to comply with the law, which would impair its effectiveness, or, in keeping with one of Lenin's dictums "to resort to any stratagem, deceit, or lie, so long as the Party could accomplish its objectives," disavow its relationship with the Comintern.

At a special convention in the Oddfellows Hall in Manhattan on November 16,

1940, the party membership voted to retire from the Comintern. As Weinkoop would note, the leaders admitted "very frankly that the affiliation was cancelled to meet the requirements of the Voorhis Act." The disaffiliation, Secretary-General Earl Browder told the convention, was "a pretext"; the party would continue to "uphold the higher spirit and tradition of our International teachers and exemplars, Marx, Engels, Lenin, and Stalin," and "reaffirm the principles of proletarian Internationalism . . . which offers the only road to the future for suffering humanity."[6]

The Voorhis Act nevertheless netted some important Soviet agents. Among them was Jacob Golos, the head of World Tourists, Inc., which for so many years had been a front organization for intelligence and political warfare activities in the United States. After failing to register as an American serving as an agent of a foreign power, Golos was fined $500.

Yet another act was designed to inhibit Communist penetration of the federal and state governments. The Hatch Act, enacted in August 1939, prohibited federal employees from membership in any organization that advocated the overthrow of the government by force, but enforcement against membership in the American Communist Party could prove to be difficult because of the failure of the Supreme Court to hold that the party did, indeed, advocate force and violence toward that goal. Another portion of the act, which provided for withholding federal funds from states where state employees engaged in political activities, was challenged but held to be constitutional.

Even though the Supreme Court had yet to rule definitively on the intentions of the American Communist Party, the government in 1942 moved to act against federal employees who were Communists. In a memorandum to all federal agencies, the Interdepartmental Committee of Investigations, chaired by J. Edgar Hoover, directed that "Whether or not a showing is made as to the advocacy of force or violence, it would seem that a member of the party or the [German-American] Bund is by reason of that fact alone subject to removal from Federal employment under section 652 of title 5 of the United States Code, which provides for removal 'for such cause as will promote the efficiency of said service.'" Even stricter controls, said the committee, should be exercised in the armed forces. "There can be no doubt," the committee concluded, "that Congress regards the dismissal of Communists and Bundists from the Federal service as not only desirable but mandatory."[7]

Throughout those years of Soviet intrigue and breaching of the Roosevelt-Litvinov Agreements, the State Department from time to time considered breaking diplomatic relations with the Soviet Union, expelling all Soviet diplomatic, consular, and trade missions, withdrawing American missions from the Soviet Union, and resuming that state of ostracization that had formed the American attitude toward Soviet Russia between 1917 and 1933. Yet there was a powerful reason not to take those steps, as George Kennan had notified Secretary of State Cordell Hull from the American Embassy in Moscow in 1937. "The situation in many countries—and particularly in the United States—is such," wrote Kennan, "that it is an easy matter for Moscow to circumvent the governments of those countries and to deal directly with private individuals, firms, and organizations. It has its trade delegations, its local communist parties, its foreign newspaper correspondents, and its various disguised agents to help in these efforts. Thus the Soviet leaders have been able to proceed to curb the scope of activity of the Moscow diplomatic corps, confident that no retaliatory measures which might follow could effectively disturb their own business with the outside world."[8]

What Kennan was saying in effect was that the United States would lose more by breaking relations than would the Soviet Union. Yet there were others who felt so strongly about Soviet duplicity that they would take that chance.

When in 1939 Russia attacked Finland, demands for breaking relations increased. The chairman of the Senate Foreign Relations Committee, Senator Key Pittman, passed to Cordell Hull a resolution proposed by a powerful member of the Senate, Arthur Vandenburg, asking the president, "if not incompatible with the public interest," to report to the Senate whether Russia had "fulfilled the obligations of the Litvinov agreements of November 16, 1933, upon which our diplomatic relations . . . [with Russia] were then and are now made wholly contingent."[9]

In reply, Secretary of State Hull declared that relations with Russia were not "wholly contingent" upon "the fulfillment by the Soviet Government of the obligations set forth in these agreements." That failed to silence Senator Pittman, who forwarded another resolution requesting that in view of Russia's attack on Finland, diplomatic relations be broken. Again Hull rejected a breach on the ground that to break relations would be to shut the only American window on Russian affairs, the American Embassy in Moscow, whereas Russia would still have open windows for observing the United States.

Hull nevertheless proposed a hard line in dealing with Russia: to treat any Russian approaches with reserve; to make no concessions without "a strict *quid pro quo* . . . the principle of reciprocity"; to make clear "that the United States considered an improvement in relations to be just as important, if not more so, to Russia than to the United States."[10]

Yet that policy made no provision for dealing with the vexing and omnipresent question of Soviet clandestine activities in the United States; that was the province of Assistant Secretary of State Adolf Berle, the enigmatic presidential adviser on internal security affairs. Berle proposed a policy just as firm as that advocated by Hull: to tell the Russians that the United States was "sick and tired of the pretense that the Russian government has nothing to do with [the Comintern] here . . . of the whole farce of Russia's insisting that she be treated in all respects as a friendly nation while she left-handedly carries on a campaign plainly hostile to the system in this country." Until the Soviet Union began in good faith to carry out the terms of the Roosevelt-Litvinov Agreements, Berle wanted to demonstrate that the United States had "no interest whatever in assisting the Soviet government"; had "no reason to permit a Soviet engineer or any other kind of Soviet visitor to visit our plants"; had no reason to afford the Soviet Union a favored position in exports; and had "every reason to take obvious measures for internal and external defense . . . against Soviet intrigues." [11]

Those words bespoke a firm policy, a policy which was, in fact, adopted, but whether it would turn out to be mere words or whether it would have any effect would never be determined, for its adoption came just before Nazi Germany attacked Russia. The United States was shortly to find itself in alliance with Communism's mother country. That would change everything.

## Chapter Forty-Three

In New York City just before Christmas of 1937, an ominous shadow fell across the headquarters of the Fourth International in North America at 116 University Place. It was cast by Dr. Gregory Rabinovich, a senior official of the Soviet secret service who had come from Berlin where he had reorganized Communist intelligence networks that had been demolished in the *ratissages* of Hitler's rule. Dr. Rabinovich had arrived in New York to take charge of the operation to kill Leon Trotsky.

An operative of great ability and stealth, Rabinovich would leave few traces of himself other than a number of corpses. Although aware that some important new clandestine had arrived in New York, the FBI was unable either to determine his name or to locate him, thereby prompting J. Edgar Hoover to assign his dossier the title: "Unsub John," for "Unknown Subject John." The editor of the *Daily Worker*, Louis Budenz, whom Jacob Golos had designated as Rabinovich's contact with the Stalinist wing of the American Communist Party, would provide one of the few descriptions of the elusive Rabinovich: "there was a sadness but also an intelligence in his deep brown eyes that immediately impressed me. His excellently tailored but conservative clothes enhanced his appearance of stability and solidity. He might easily be some recently arrived European business man— and that was supposedly his role, I was afterwards informed." [1]

As Rabinovich began his work, his quarry, Leon Trotsky, had recently been granted permanent asylum by the Socialist president of Mexico, Lázaro Cárdenas, and had arrived in Coyoacán, a suburb of Mexico City, to live as a guest in the Blue House, owned by the great Mexican muralist Diego Rivera. Residing at the Blue House was to Trotsky like coming from the labyrinth of madness into some Pierian spring, for it was a place of brilliant sunlight, flowers, lawns, paintings, objects of Mexican and Indian art, fruit, vegetables, and warm hosts. Yet as Trotsky soon discovered, the Pierian spring would be hard to hold on to, for Stalin was determined to exterminate him, his sons, and the Fourth International.

Only sixteen days after Trotsky took up residence in the Blue House, the official

Soviet news agency, Tass, announced that his younger son, Sergei, the scientist whose disappearance had earlier been reported, had been arrested in Western Siberia and charged with poisoning Soviet workers. That was a charge for which there was only one penalty, but Trotsky was never to know whether Sergei actually paid it, for Sergei simply vanished.

Just over a year later, on February 8, 1938, Trotsky's elder son, Lev Sedov, still residing in Paris as the European organizer of the Fourth International, suddenly collapsed with acute appendicitis. After an operation, he was well on the way to recovery when he had a visit from a Soviet agent, Mark Zborowski; soon after the visit, Lev Sedov turned violently ill and died, leaving a strong presumption of death by poisoning. A few weeks later, the secretary of the Fourth International, Rudolf Klement, disappeared.

As Dr. Rabinovich began to devise Stalin's vengeance against Trotsky himself, the Fourth International was soon to hold its founding congress in Paris. That provided a setting for him to use the services of an American dissident who planned to attend, a tiny blonde just five feet tall named Sylvia Ageloff.

Twenty-nine years of age at the time, Sylvia Ageloff was one of two daughters of a Russian-born Jew who had become a wealthy real estate promoter in Brooklyn. She had studied at the Washington Square College of New York University and at Columbia, where she specialized in child psychology, and was currently employed as a social investigator with the city's Welfare Department. She was a plain woman who wore good clothes untidily and whose bobbed hair gave her something of a masculine appearance. Intelligent, well-spoken, and self-assured, she nevertheless was nervous and bore an aureole of loneliness. She had become a Communist on the theory that only Stalin and the Comintern could protect the Jews from the Nazis, but out of disgust with the purges, she had joined a Trotskyite cell and by 1938 was employed as a courier carrying messages and propaganda between New York and the headquarters of other Trotskyite cells elsewhere in North America and in Europe.[2]

In the spring of 1938, soon after German troops occupied Austria, Sylvia Ageloff revealed to friends at a meeting of Trotskyites that she was going to Europe, although she gave no indication why she was making the trip. When the news reached Dr. Rabinovich and his colleague, Louis Budenz, they called in a member of the Stalinist wing, Ruby Weill, whom they knew to be a friend and former co-worker of Sylvia's. Rabinovich told Weill to prepare herself for a mission to Paris having to do with the task of "halting the infiltration of Trotskyites into Soviet Russia and thus preventing Stalin's assassination."[3]

Weill was first to report to an address in Greenwich Village in New York to meet a woman named Gertrude, who told her that she would establish contact after Weill reached Paris. Meanwhile, she was to get in touch with Sylvia Ageloff and arrange to travel on the same ship. The two not only sailed together but in Paris lodged at the same hotel.

Soon after reaching Paris, Ruby Weill received a telephone call from Gertrude, instructing her to go to a small café. There Gertrude introduced her to an unusually handsome man, Jacques Mornard van Dendreschd, whom she was to present to Sylvia Ageloff as Jacques Mornard, "the wealthy son of a Belgian count."[4]

Ageloff found Mornard to be "a personable, generous, warm-hearted individual . . . a playboy type who seemed to have plenty of money and never worked." He spoke French "like a native" and "never evidenced any interest in Trotskyism or any other political ideology." She "thoroughly enjoyed his company." As Louis Budenz would note, he "swept Sylvia off her feet with his attentions, pretending to fall in love with her at first sight." The two were soon lovers.[5]

On September 3, 1938, Ageloff attended the founding congress of the Fourth International, held in a village near Paris in the home of Alfred and Marguerite Rosmer. The event was as small—thirty-eight delegates attended—as the founding congress of the Third International nearly twenty years earlier, and as with the Third International, the congress met under the shadow of martyrs: Lev Sedov was dead, and police had found a remnant of Rudolf Klement's corpse in the Seine with head, arms, and feet cut off.

Security was elaborate. To deflect the attention of any special commission that might seek to liquidate the Rosmers, the minutes carried the notation that the congress took place in Lausanne, Switzerland. Despite an agenda lengthy enough to occupy most assemblies for a week, the congress met for only a day, from just after daybreak to just before sunset, so that the delegates could get away before dark. During the meeting, Ageloff served as an interpreter, while Jacques Mornard "hovered somewhere outside the conference room, pretending to take no interest in the highly secret gathering and waiting only for Sylvia to come out."[6]

The principal business was to vote that the Comintern was "morally dead" and to argue a motion by Polish delegates that with war looming, the Fourth International could serve no purpose. The first was readily handled, the second eventually defeated on the grounds that no war threatened the United States and that New York had supplanted Paris as the center of Trotskyism.

At the Blue House, in Coyoacán, Mexico, late in 1939, a severe quarrel erupted between Trotsky and his host, Diego Rivera. Rumor had it that the dispute arose over an affair between Trotsky and Rivera's wife, Frida Kahlo, "herself a painter of delicate melancholy . . . and a woman of exquisite beauty . . . exotic grace and dreaminess" who wore long, colorfully embroidered Mexican robes to conceal a deformed leg.[7] The rumor was probably a product of Trotsky's enemies, for the argument actually appeared to be over ideological obscurities. Yet the dispute was nevertheless irreparable, which compelled Trotsky at a time of considerable financial difficulty to find another residence. He somehow managed to borrow enough money first to rent and later to buy a villa on the Avenida Viena at the end of a deserted street on the outskirts of Coyoacán. Built of old stone, the villa was spacious and sturdy and stood on its own grounds.

Trotsky's bodyguards, mostly idealistic young Americans of the moneyed class, began immediately to fortify the walls against the assassination attempt that all knew must eventually come. Six Americans guarded the house itself, and at all times there were five Mexican policemen outside the walls in the dusty street, while other police and soldiers patrolled neighboring shantytowns. Infrared signaling devices were installed along the walls to sound the alarm if prowlers approached, and in time a wooden main gate was replaced by another of bulletproof steel with sliding visors for observation.

While the headquarters of the Fourth International on University Place in New York constituted Trotskyism's principal field office, the little fortress on the Avenida Viena became the world headquarters for the movement. To the villa came a steady stream of visitors: publishers, politicians, refugees, phantomas, pilgrims. Trotsky himself seldom left the villa except for sudden, secret trips to collect rare cacti from the foothills of nearby mountains and volcanoes. With the harvest in the trunk, his car would speed back through Mexico City with Trotsky prone on the floor.

Trotsky also resumed work on a book to be called "Stalin." So riddled with Marxist ideology that it was almost unreadable, the work accused Stalin of having poisoned Lenin and called him the "Super-Cain" of the Bolshevik movement. With a touch of prophecy, Trotsky noted that after the suicide of the Roman emperor Nero, the people smashed his statues, execrated his memory, and erased his name, a fate, he said, which Stalin was also destined to incur. "The vengeance of history is more powerful than the vengeance of the most powerful General Secretary," wrote Trotsky, a fact that he found "consoling."[8] Although he hoped that by exposing Stalin's malversations, his book would become a powerful political instrument, his publishers were to find it politically inexpedient to bring it out until after the end of World War II, by which time the accusations had lost their force.

Even aside from the prospect of assassination, Trotsky was convinced that he had not much longer to live. Suspecting that he had advanced arteriosclerosis, he had no intention of enduring paralysis, incapacity, or mental incompetency. If such a fate threatened, he hoped that he might die suddenly of a brain hemorrhage, but if not, he intended to "cut short" the "too slow process of dying."[9]

In his will, which he began to write on February 27, 1940, he paid tribute to his wife, Natalya, for giving him her "inexhaustible . . . love, magnanimity, and tenderness." Having for forty-three years been a revolutionary, with forty-two of them "under the banner of Marxism," he would wish no change. "I shall die a proletarian revolutionary, a Marxist, a dialectical materialist, and consequently an irreconcilable atheist. My faith in the communist future of mankind is not less ardent, indeed it is firmer today, than it was in the days of my youth."[10]

Everything about the gray eminence of the Soviet secret service, Dr. Gregory Rabinovich, was gray: his hair, skin, eyes, suit, overcoat, hat, tie, even the velvet on the collar of his coat. As he learned that Trotsky was well along on the writing of his book, he began to move his last pieces. As in chess, the opening and middle games had been played; the end game was to follow. The knight was Jacques Mornard, the queen Sylvia Ageloff, the object to eliminate the king.

On September 9, 1939, six days after Britain and France had declared war on Germany, Jacques Mornard disembarked from the SS *Ile de France* in New York. The entry papers he filled out with a blunt pencil showed: *Name: Frank Jacson.* His final destination was to be Montreal, Canada, via Rouses Point, New York. Seeing no cause for suspicion, the customs official duly stamped the passport: "Admitted to the United States, Transit, period of admission: 28 days."[11]

Waiting at the quayside, Sylvia Ageloff took the man whom she knew as Jacques Mornard to her home at 50 Livingston Street in Brooklyn. Disturbed when she learned he had changed his identity, she readily accepted his explanation that he had done it and come to the United States to escape military service and "the horrors of the war in Europe."[12] Yet as the days passed and Jacson—she learned to call him by the new name—continued to live with her, she again became concerned: while he professed to be on his first visit to New York, he appeared to know the city well. Yet again her unease disappeared when Jacson invited her to join him for a holiday in Mexico City. He had been offered a position there, he said, with a British import-export company trading in oil, copper, sugar, and old iron. Jacson departed in October 1939, and after obtaining a leave of absence for two months on the pretense of needing treatment for an acute throat and sinus infection, Sylvia Ageloff in January 1940 left by rail to join him.

In Mexico City, Jacson and Ageloff shared a room at the Hotel Montejo. As Dr. Rabinovich had no doubt calculated, it was not long before Ageloff called upon her idol, Trotsky, whom she had never met, both to worship at the shrine and to present a report on the Trotsky movement in New York. Granted an audience, she offered to help with Trotsky's secretarial work and began to go each day to the villa on the Avenida Viena. Jacson usually drove her and in the evening waited for her at the gate. Although the guards "came to know him and often chatted with him," he made no effort to venture into the compound. Yet through Sylvia, he met Alfred and Marguerite Rosmer, who had come from France for a visit, and "they presently became familiar with him as the 'obliging young man, Sylvia's husband.'" Jacson invited the couple to dinner in Mexico City and "took them out into the country on sightseeing trips."[13]

Sylvia Ageloff was as enraptured with her life with Frank Jacson as she had been when she had known him as Jacques Mornard; but in March 1940, an incident occurred that again made her suspicious. While Jacson was out of the city "on business," she received word that her sister, Ruth, had fallen ill in New York and would require surgery; Sylvia was needed to look after the family's affairs. Making plans to go home, she telephoned a number that Jacson had given her, supposedly that of his employers in Room 820 in the Edificio Ermita, a building in the Tacubaya district of Mexico City. Nobody at that number, she found, knew a

Frank Jacson. Assuming she had taken down the number incorrectly, she went to the building, but nobody in the building, she discovered, knew a Frank Jacson, and there was neither a British import-export company nor a Room 820 in the Edificio Ermita. Her lover, she decided, "was in the service of the British Government as an agent of the Intelligence Service."[14]

When Sylvia Ageloff told Marguerite Rosmer of her suspicion, Madame Rosmer advised her not to worry, that whatever Jacson was doing in Mexico City, it could hardly have to do with Trotsky. Yet Ageloff continued to be concerned, and when Jacson returned, she demanded an explanation. As nimbly as ever, Jacson explained that he had made a mistake and had given her the wrong address; he provided another that, when she checked it, appeared to be truthful. Ageloff reasoned that the first address must have been that of associates of some kind.

Had she pursued her inquiries at the Edificio Ermita, she might have found that it was, indeed, the address of associates of some kind, for one of the offices there had been taken over by a Mexican painter, David Alfaro Siqueiros, who headed a special commission, which included an American, George Mink, Carlos Contreras, and others who had had experience as executioners during the Spanish Civil War. Dr. Rabinovich had dispatched the special commission to Mexico City to murder Trotsky.

As Sylvia Ageloff left for New York, she apparently felt satisfied that her lover's business in Mexico City was legitimate. She did take the precaution of extracting a promise from Jacson that he would make no effort to see Trotsky or to enter the Trotsky compound, and she would later maintain that she had advised Trotsky personally that Jacson might be a British intelligence agent.

The opportunity for Jacson to enter the compound on the Avenida Viena came soon after Ageloff had departed when Marguerite Rosmer telephoned to say that her husband, Alfred, was ill. Despite the fact that there were cars and drivers available within the compound, she asked Jacson to drive her husband to the French hospital in Mexico City, buy any medicines that were required, and return him to the compound.

As ready as ever to be of help, Jacson drove into the compound to collect Alfred Rosmer. Having achieved that entrance, he became over the next three months a familiar figure at Trotsky's villa, although during that time he never encountered Trotsky himself. In the course of his frequent visits, he established friendship with one of the guards, a sandy-haired, blue-eyed American, Robert Sheldon Harte, a twenty-five-year-old New Yorker.

During those months, the tenor of accusations against Trotsky by the Stalinist press and party spokesmen had become steadily more virulent. To the familiar charges—that Trotsky was at once a German agent, a British agent, and the principal behind terrorist plots inside Russia—was added a new allegation calculated to inflame anti-American sentiment in Mexico: that Trotsky was an American spy charged with overthrowing the Cárdenas government and replacing it with another better disposed toward American capital, one that would restore to the United States petroleum concessions that Cárdenas had recently nationalized.

Although that accusation was obviously spurious, Trotsky did have some American contacts. He apparently enjoyed the company on a number of occasions of the American consul general in Mexico City, Robert MacGregor, and near the end of 1939 he had agreed to go at some point to Washington to testify before the Un-American Activities Committee in regard to a continuing investigation of Soviet intelligence activities in the United States. He also negotiated with officials of Harvard University, agreeing in early May 1940 to sell part of his archives to the university for $3,000.

That portion of the archives appeared to have little contemporary political importance, for it consisted primarily of letters exchanged by Lenin and Trotsky during the revolutionary periods of 1905 and 1917 and Trotsky's correspondence as Lenin's foreign commissar with all the major powers, including the United States. Yet hardly had the sale been announced publicly when the special commission in the Edificio Ermita decided to act.

Was there something in those archives that Stalin wanted to protect? Or was it that the special commission wanted to prevent Trotsky from testifying in Washington?

By the early spring of 1940, Trotsky was conscious, in view of increasingly vituperative attacks against him in Stalinist newspapers and by Stalinist spokesmen, that violence might be imminent. As he remarked early in May: "People write like this only when they are ready to change the pen for the machine gun." [15] The defenses of the villa on the Avenida Viena were strengthened: ten Mexican policemen were on duty day and night just outside the compound; patrols of the Mexican Army came and went unpredictably; inside the compound, the American guards set up machine guns covering the approaches to the house; and in addition to the steel door at the entrance to the compound, there had been added electric fences and warning equipment.

On the night of May 23, 1940, between the hours of midnight and dawn of the 24th, the main sentry inside the compound was to be Jacson's acquaintance, Sheldon Harte, who was a fairly recent arrival—April 7, 1940. Early in Harte's duty, Trotsky himself had reprimanded the youth when he saw him give the key to the front gate to a builder who was doing work inside the compound; Trotsky saw Harte as "a warm-hearted and devoted but rather gullible and feckless creature." [16] Yet that creature was to be responsible, should something happen, to give the alarm that was supposed to bring the other five guards rushing from their quarters with weapons at the ready. Nobody knew it at the time, but that infinite trust rested in a young man who, his father would later reveal, had "a picture of Stalin prominently displayed" in his bedroom in New York City. [17]

When Sheldon Harte took his post at the gate of the compound, he was wearing the uniform of adherents of the Fourth International: black beret, windbreaker, corduroy riding breeches, boots, and leather leggings. He was armed with two hand grenades and a Schmeisser-type machine pistol; in his lapel was a police whistle. The night was dark but starlit. Because heavy rains had turned the nearby fields into a morass, any attack on the compound would have to come down the Avenida Viena.

Inside the villa, Trotsky and Natalya had retired late; when Trotsky found he was unable to sleep, he arose and took a heavy sleeping potion. Also in the villa were Trotsky's two male secretaries, a few servants, Alfred and Marguerite Rosmer, and one of the few survivors in the Trotsky family, a twelve-year-old grandson, Zina's son, Seva, who had been living with the Rosmers in France.

At about the same hour that Sheldon Harte took up his post and Trotsky retired, a member of the special commission, David Siqueiros, arrived at a house near the center of Mexico City, where he joined twenty other men. Before leaving the house, Siqueiros put on the uniform of a major in the Mexican Army, while the others put on police uniforms. They were armed with a variety of submachine guns, pistols, and bombs. Traveling in several cars and taking different routes, they headed for a rendezvous near the Avenida Viena. On the way, Siqueiros tried to calm a nervous chauffeur; "the way," he said, "has been prepared" and "one of the guards has been bought."[18]

At about 4:30 A.M. on May 24, 1940, Siqueiros and his men stole up on the guards outside the compound and succeeded in gagging the police without raising an alarm. From the police, they took a key to the gate; they either opened it themselves or Harte opened it for them. Harte neither cried out "nor did he shoot."[19]

The raiders surprised the other guards in their beds and threatened them into silence with submachine guns. In less than five minutes, Siqueiros held the guards and the compound and was ready to storm the villa. Positioning some men to provide covering fire, he himself prepared to lead the others in an assault on the side of the villa he already knew to contain Trotsky's study and bedroom.

Under heavy fire from the covering submachine guns, the assault began. Despite the sleeping potion Trotsky had taken, the firing awakened him; drowsy, he thought the Mexicans were celebrating some kind of holiday with firecrackers. Natalya was more alert. Rolling Trotsky out of the bed onto the floor between the bed and the wall, she threw her body over him just as fire from Siqueiros and the assault team poured into the room—police would later count more than seventy rounds fired into and around the bed—while elsewhere in the house three bombs went off, one of them an incendiary. The only human sound was a cry from young Seva: "Grandpapa!"

In little more than twenty minutes, the raid was over. When the guards determined that the raiders had gone, they rushed to the villa, and the household assembled on the terrace. The only person hurt was Seva, who had been nicked in a toe, apparently by a ricochet bullet. Trotsky himself was calm and directed the guards to search for Harte. He had disappeared with the attackers, the word came back, his arms pinioned behind him by two of Siqueiros' men.

Within half an hour, the chief of the Mexican Secret Service, Colonel L. A. S. Salazar, was on the scene. He found it hard to believe that, as Trotsky charged, Stalin had engineered the attack. Trotsky and his wife seemed too relaxed. Seventy-three bullet holes in the vicinity of Trotsky's bed, yet neither he nor his wife even wounded! Had Trotsky staged the attack as some kind of stunt in his feud with Stalin? Detaining the police who had been on duty, the guards, and the male secretaries, he questioned them at length but finally came to the conclusion that Trotsky was indeed telling the truth, that the attack had been a genuine attempt on his life; but Salazar departed convinced that Harte had been suborned and had been a party to the attack.

In the search for Trotsky's attackers, the Mexican police and Salazar's agents made their first arrests on June 8, 1940, in Vera Cruz. Several men seized there confessed taking part and implicated Siqueiros, two Mexican artists known as the Arenal brothers, and the American, Sheldon Harte. Ten days later the police uncovered Siqueiros hiding in a village near Guadalajara in the state of Jalisco. Although Siqueiros admitted financing and organizing the attack, he denied that the Soviet secret service had had anything to do with it. Nor was the objective to kill Trotsky; it was instead to seize the archives that Trotsky was sending to Harvard. While revealing that Harte had been murdered, Siqueiros denied that he had ordered it or had had anything to do with it. Although Siqueiros was jailed on nine charges, including attempted murder and murder, he was eventually released on bail, jumped it, and slipped out of the country. The Arenal brothers in the meantime escaped to New York City, where they went into hiding.

In a shallow grave on a small farm that the brothers had been renting at San Angel, outside Mexico City, the authorities found the corpse of Robert Sheldon Harte. They determined that one of the brothers had executed him as he lay sleeping, presumably to prevent him from laying evidence against the brothers and the other attackers.

Whether Harte had any role in cooperating with the attackers was never determined. To the end, Trotsky refused to believe that one of his guards would have betrayed him. When he went to the farm at San Angel to identify Harte's body, there were tears in his eyes. To Harte's family, he sent a message of condolence reflecting what appeared to be deep and genuine sadness, and he directed that a bronze plaque be placed in the courtyard of the villa bearing a single word: Bob.

To the State Department and the FBI, both of which had sought to avoid involvement in the matter of Trotsky's asylum in Mexico, the death of an American citizen and the fact that the killers were being harbored on American territory prompted a reconsideration. When Trotsky told the American consul general, Robert MacGregor, that he "suspected" that "the orders for this attempt on his life had come from the Soviet ambassador in Washington, [Konstantin] Oumanski," who was, said Trotsky, an agent of the Soviet intelligence service, it appeared to represent another grave infringement of the 1933 agreement by which diplomatic relations had been established with Soviet Russia.

Shortly after the attack on the villa on the Avenida Viena, Trotsky began to prepare a series of articles entitled "Him, I Accuse," [20] in which he defined the relationship of the Stalin regime and its secret police to the Comintern. The NKVD, he declared, was "the instrument of the totalitarian domination . . . over the USSR and the Comintern." Although not a part of the Comintern, the NKVD was "inextricably connected" with it and dominated it. Together the two organizations were dedicated to eliminating, by murder if necessary, Trotsky himself, the Fourth International, and anybody who might oppose Stalin at home or abroad, including Britain and the United States. The tools were terror and lies: "They commit a crime, deny that they did it, and then blame their political adversaries." The Stalin regime, Trotsky wrote, was financing the combined operations of the NKVD and the Comintern at home and abroad. From an organization seeking the international solidarity of workers, Stalin had transformed the Comintern into a "personal dictatorship."

Since the NKVD controlled the Comintern's funds, they were dispensed to foreign Communist parties primarily in exchange for espionage on behalf of the Soviet government, not only with the foreign parties' own countries but within other countries as well. As proof, Trotsky offered a notarized letter from the former secretary-general of the American Communist Party, Benjamin Gitlow, in which Gitlow stated that even though the American Communist Party had always disclaimed any connection with the Soviet government, the truth was that "the American Communist Party is in the same relationship with the Soviet Government as the Nazi agents in the United States are with the government of the Third Reich." Nor did the American operatives confine their activities to the United States; they operated "in a wide area, including China, Japan, Germany, Mexico, and in the countries of Central and South America."

Trotsky also cited an affidavit from the former head of the Soviet military intelligence service in Western Europe, Walter Krivitsky. Through the International Secretariat of the Comintern, Krivitsky declared, the NKVD controlled "a whole network of permanent agents stretched across the world" with sufficient power "to intimidate the leaders of the Communist Party in whichever countries they are stationed." Stalin was using those agents, said Trotsky, to deal with "cases of treason against Stalin" both by Russians living abroad and by members of foreign Communist parties.

The investment by the NKVD through the medium of the Comintern amounted in the United States alone, wrote Trotsky, to some $3 million annually, and the Kremlin owned 95 percent of the party press in New York, Chicago, and San Francisco. The Soviet Treasury, he alleged, working through the International Secretariat of the Comintern, funded all Comintern-NKVD operations.

However self-serving Trotsky's articles, they had important, even vital ramifications for the western nations. Yet they burst upon the world at a time when newsmen were concerned with an even more dramatic and portentous issue: the onset of a second world war. Since attention to the political conflict between Trotsky and Stalin was being submerged in the concern about a world holocaust, Trotsky had lost the power of the last political instrument left to him: the pen. Nothing that he could say at that point could alter the basic fact that the second man and tactical leader of the Russian revolution, the man who had raised twenty-two armies and defeated the seemingly overwhelming forces of the counterrevolution, the man who had matched wits with and had defeated the greatest generals and statesmen of his time, was at that point no more than an aging, failing old Bolshevik revolutionary hiding in Mexico while awaiting the Black Widow.

Trotsky knew that he was doomed and said so. "Yes, Natalya," he had remarked to his wife just after the attack at the villa on the Avenida Viena, "we have had a reprieve."[21]

## Chapter Forty-Four

Four days after the attempt on Trotsky's life, as Trotsky fed his rabbits in their hutches on the terrace of his villa, he came face to face for the first time with Frank Jacson. Having arranged to drive Marguerite and Alfred Rosmer to Vera Cruz, where they were to board a ship for New York, Jacson had arrived early and was waiting outside the villa until the Rosmers were ready. Jacson and Trotsky shook hands and exchanged pleasantries, during which Jacson explained that he was Sylvia Ageloff's husband. Excusing himself, Jacson sought out the grandson, Seva, to whom he gave a toy glider and explained how it worked. At Trotsky's suggestion, Natalya invited Jacson to join the family and the Rosmers for breakfast.

Following the trip to Vera Cruz, Jacson made no appearance at the Trotsky villa until a fortnight later, on June 12, 1940, when he called on one of Trotsky's secretaries, Otto Schussler, a tough young Austrian Jew who had been with Trotsky since the Princes Islands, to explain that he was traveling to New York on business and to ask Schussler to take care of his Buick while he was away. When Schussler agreed, Jacson invited him to use the car if he wished, then went away.

Up to the time of the raid on the villa, Jacson's assignment had been to provide details about the household, its guards, and its defenses, but with the failure of the attack, his assignment had changed. That was why Jacson was headed for New York, probably to get final instructions from Dr. Rabinovich, but primarily to establish an alibi that in the event he escaped after murdering Trotsky, would fix him somewhere else at the time of the murder.

Before leaving for New York, Jacson went to the American Consulate in Mexico City, where he produced an airline ticket for Montreal by way of New York and a tourist card that had been issued him before he entered Mexico on October 12, 1939, from Laredo, Texas. Shown that documentation, a clerk issued him a transit visa that would enable him to stop briefly in New York en route to his "home" in Montreal. That officially established his intention to leave Mexico, and the fact that he had actually departed would be officially established when he passed through immigration in New York.

Landing in New York on June 14, 1940, Jacson went to the Hotel Pierpont in Brooklyn, there to be joined by Sylvia Ageloff. They stayed in the hotel for just over a fortnight, during which time they made seven telephone calls, one of which was to headquarters of the Trotskyite Workers' Party on West 14th Street. Explaining that he had come to New York "to attend to some financial details for [his employer] at the British consul's office," [1] Jacson apparently was registering his presence in New York with the Trotskyites.

After checking out of the hotel and saying goodbye to Sylvia Ageloff on June 30, 1940, Jacson flew to New Orleans. From there he left by air the next day for Houston, from where he took a train on July 2, 1940, to Laredo. Declaring himself at the frontier to be a day tourist and thus avoiding any record of his entering Mexico, he walked across the International Bridge spanning the Rio Grande. At Nuevo Laredo on the Mexican side of the border, he boarded a train for Mexico City, using as a document to enable him to purchase a ticket the tourist card which he had employed when he first entered Mexico on October 12, 1939.

On July 4, 1940, Frank Jacson was back in Mexico City with neither American nor Mexican authorities aware of his presence. His alibi established on the official record to the effect that he had left Mexico on June 14, 1940, he began the process of ingratiating himself with the Trotskys and their guards.

For that, he decided in time that he needed the help of Sylvia Ageloff. Saying that he had fallen ill, he telegraphed her to join him. Taking three weeks' holiday time owed her by the New York City Department of Welfare, she left La Guardia Airport on August 8, 1940, for Brownsville, Texas. When she arrived by train in Mexico City, she apparently accepted the fact of Jacson's remarkably quick recovery without suspicion and the two again lived together at the Hotel Montejo. Soon after her arrival, at the invitation of the Trotskys, she and Jacson went to the villa on the Avenida Viena for tea. [2]

After that visit, Jacson saw Trotsky only a few more times, but that "was enough for him to survey the scene, to take the measure of his victim, and to put the finishing touches on his plan." He behaved "unobtrusively, obligingly, innocuously," sometimes bringing a bouquet or a box of chocolates as "'gifts from Sylvia'" for Natalya. In talking with the guards, he gave the impression that he was an ardent Trotskyite, but in Trotsky's and Natalya's presence, he played the role of "an outsider who was just being converted into a 'sympathizer.'" [3]

Yet however clever Jacson was in avoiding suspicion, his behavior soon began to raise questions. He was often "in a brooding mood . . . his face twitched, his hands trembled." Then he might suddenly turn gay and garrulous, boasting to Trotsky's secretaries of his powerful physical strength and to Trotsky offering through his "boss" who was "a financial genius" to undertake speculative operations on the Stock Exchange on behalf of the Fourth International. Since

Trotsky detested any form of financial speculation, that suggestion annoyed him. "Who is this very rich 'boss'?" he asked Natalya. "One should find out." In Jacson, he had begun to sense "something sinister" and suggested to Natalya that "it might be better for us not to receive Sylvia's husband any more."[4]

But Trotsky failed to pursue his suspicions. Neither did he speak of them to Sylvia Ageloff, his secretaries, or his guards, and he received Jacson when on August 17, 1940, Jacson paid a call that was a dress rehearsal for murder.

Knowing Trotsky's bent for instructing and advising young followers, Jacson came with an article, which he asked Trotsky to do him the honor of evaluating. Reluctantly, Trotsky led Jacson into his study. In ten or fifteen minutes, they emerged, and Trotsky showed his guest to the door.

Finding Natalya, Trotsky told her that he never wanted to see Jacson again. It was not because the man's essay was naive, but rather his manner. As they discussed the article, Jacson had seated himself on a corner of the desk, his hat still on his head, his overcoat still on and clutched tightly, and there he had remained. Trotsky had a strong feeling that the man was a mountebank. Throughout the meeting, he had acted decidedly unlike a Belgian raised in France. If he was deceiving them about his nationality, why? What was he hiding? To Natalya, it seemed that Trotsky had perceived something ominous about Jacson but had yet to make up his mind what it was. Although Trotsky also confided his suspicions to his principal secretary, an American, Joseph Hansen, he issued no instructions to stop Jacson from calling again.

Trotsky had every reason to be suspicious. Jacson had kept on his overcoat and clutched it closely because in it he had concealed a pistol, a dagger, and an alpenstock, a mountain climber's ice-ax with a sharp steel point, the same weapons he intended to bring with him to perform the act of murder. In further preparation for the deed, Jacson began to prepare a letter that, should he fail to escape, would explain "to public opinion the motives which impelled me to perform the act of justice."[5] Writing at great length, Jacson declared that he had become a devout Trotskyite in Paris and had gone to Mexico "for the purpose of making Leon Trotsky's acquaintance," but instead of finding "a political chief who directed the struggle for liberation of the working class," he had met "a man who desired nothing more than to satisfy his needs and desire for vengeance and hate."

Trotsky proposed, wrote Jacson, that Jacson go to Russia "to organize underground a series of attempts against various persons," including Stalin. That, he declared, "was against all the principles of a struggle which until then I had considered frank and loyal, and was contrary to all my own principles." Yet Jacson had concealed his reaction in order to find out more. He soon found that Trotsky had "the support of a great Nation" and "also that of a certain foreign Parliamentary Committee" and that the money that had enabled Trotsky to turn his compound on the Avenida Viena into a miniature fortress had come "from the consul of a great foreign nation who visits him," an obvious reference to the American consul general, Robert MacGregor. Those revelations, wrote Jacson, convinced him "that Trotsky had no other purpose in life but to make use of his partisans to satisfy his personal and mean ends."

Jacson's next step was to remove from Trotsky's villa the Austrian Jew, Otto Schussler, whom he considered to be the most formidable opponent he was likely to encounter inside the compound. Having earlier established a relationship with Schussler by lending him his Buick, he invited him and his wife to lunch on August 20, 1940, a day when Schussler, Jacson knew, would be off duty. Accepting, Schussler and his wife met Jacson and Sylvia Ageloff at the Hotel Montejo around two o'clock in the afternoon.

During lunch, Jacson confided that his employer wanted him to go to New York on business, which meant that he would have to leave the table early to collect his visa. Apologizing, he said it would take but a short time and urged the Schusslers and Sylvia to linger over their meal, whereupon he would join them later for drinks. When Schussler agreed, Jacson left the table around three o'clock.

At the villa on the Avenida Viena on August 20, 1940, "exceptional peace and serenity" prevailed.[6] "The Old Man emanated calm, confidence, and energy." Upon arising, he quipped in a manner that had become something of a commonplace: "You see, they did not kill us last night."

It had been "a long time since I felt so well," Trotsky told Natalya, and he anticipated "a really good day's work." Going first to the patio, he attended to his rabbits, then retired to his study. Following a light lunch and brief siesta, he returned to his study until five o'clock, when he went back to the hutches to attend his rabbits. While he was on the patio, Jacson appeared. "Here he is again," Natalya was to recall her startled reaction when she saw Jacson. "Why has he begun to come so often?"

Going onto the patio, Natalya asked Jacson why he was wearing a coat and hat on such a hot day. "His face was grey-green," she would recall, "his gestures nervous and jerky." Jacson replied that "It might rain." Asking Natalya for a glass of water, he declined her offer of a cup of tea: "No, no, I dined too late and I feel the food up to here. It's choking me."

Would Trotsky consent, asked Jacson, as he had promised, to look at the revised text of his article? When he produced several pages of typed manuscript, Trotsky silently and reluctantly led Jacson toward the study. At the door Natalya left them to fetch Jacson's glass of water.

Seated at his desk, Trotsky had finished reading the first of the typed pages when Jacson brought his alpenstock down on Trotsky's head with all the strength he could muster. Although he expected the sharp point of the alpenstock to kill Trotsky quietly and silently, enabling him to escape to his Buick, parked nearby, the blow failed either to kill, to stun, or to silence Trotsky. He let out "a terrible piercing cry."

As Jacson would later tell the police, "His yell was 'aaaaa!' . . . very long, infinitely long, and even now it seems that such a yell is still penetrating my brain." Trotsky leaped from his chair like "a crazy man and let himself go at me, biting my hand." Jacson said that he pushed Trotsky "and made him fall to the floor; he arose as best he could and, running or stumbling, I do not know how, he left the room; I was left dumbfounded, without knowing what to do."[7]

The terrible cry raised Natalya; the secretary, Hansen; and the guards. Rushing to the study, they found Trotsky in the adjacent dining room leaning against a doorway leading onto a balcony, his face covered with blood. Uttering one word, "Jacson," he collapsed slowly to the floor. To Natalya, he said, "Natasha, I love you." To Hansen, he said in English, "This is the end." In the study, the guards had pinioned Jacson and were beating him fiercely. "Tell the boys not to kill him," said Trotsky. "He must be made to talk."

By the time doctors and the police arrived, paralysis had begun to set in. Inside an ambulance, going to the Green Cross Emergency Station in Coyoacán, Natalya covered him with a white shawl and held his bleeding head between her hands. To Hansen, Trotsky whispered that Jacson was "a political assassin . . . a member of the NKVD[8] . . . or a fascist. More likely the NKVD . . . but possibly aided by Gestapo."

For a time in the emergency station, as attendants shaved Trotsky's head and began undressing him in preparation for surgery, he tried to dictate to Hansen in laborious English, his words blurred and often indistinct. He seemed to want to record his own version of Jacson's attack while at the same time leaving some kind of political testament, but in time he became so weak that he stopped and turned his attention to Natalya. He wanted her to finish undressing him. She kissed him several times. Each time he responded.

The surgeons had yet to begin their work when at about 7:30 P.M., Trotsky sank into a coma. Five surgeons trepanned his skull and established that the wound was almost three inches deep. The right parietal bone was shattered and the splinters embedded in his brain; the meninges were destroyed and part of the brain ruptured. Although death was inevitable, it came slowly. For just over twenty-two hours Natalya, "dry-eyed, hands clenched," watched over him until at last the four-kind son of a bitch, but the greatest Jew since Jesus Christ, died.

Wearing black berets, windbreakers, corduroy breeches, and boots with leather leggings, Trotsky's followers bore his coffin through the streets of Mexico City, making a point of passing through working-class quarters. Laid out in the Alcazar Funeral Parlor, the corpse became something of a shrine attended by thousands of Mexicans, a fact duly noted by officials of the American Consulate.

When Natalya Ivanovna asked the Consulate for permission to bury Trotsky's body in the United States, she gave no reason for the request, but officials again noted that the funds for shipment and burial were to be provided by a person or persons unknown in New York City. "This presents a difficult choice," noted the head of the State Department's Division of American Republics, Ellis Briggs, to Undersecretary of State Sumner Welles, "since were we to permit it, an effort might be made to convert the grave into a Communist or anti-Communist shrine with resulting difficulties and disorders."[9]

At the direction of the State Department, the American Consulate in Mexico City stated that while "the matter had been given sympathetic consideration, . . . it would not be appropriate in all the circumstances for burial to be authorized in [the United States]."[10] Natalya at that point directed that her husband be cremated and the ashes buried in the compound of the villa on the Avenida Viena close to the plaque erected in honor of Robert Sheldon Harte.

## Chapter Forty-Five

J. Edgar Hoover, ordered the FBI to carry out a major investigation into Trotsky's murder. By "an exhaustive and comprehensive inquiry into the background and contacts" of Jacques Mornard van Dendreschd, alias Frank Jacson, and Sylvia Ageloff, he hoped to determine "the identities of those responsible for directing the death of Trotsky."[1] That in turn, he hoped, would enable him to uncover and destroy the apparatus of the Soviet intelligence service in the United States.

It would prove to be a difficult assignment, for like most Communist phantomas, Jacson refused to talk except about his personal background. Sylvia Ageloff, whom Mexican authorities detained for a time on suspicion of complicity in the murder, could tell little other than her own experiences with Jacson; and eventually she was released, returned to New York, adopted a pseudonym, and passed into obscurity.

Inquiries into the origin of Jacson's Canadian passport turned up the fact that it had been issued to one Tony Babich, a Canadian volunteer killed in the Civil War in Spain in 1937.[2] Since the Soviet intelligence service made a practice of using cobbled passports belonging to men killed in the Spanish Civil War, that pointed to what almost everybody already believed, that Jacson was a Soviet agent.

The International Bureau of the Fourth International in Paris determined that Jacson was in Paris at the time of the death of Trotsky's son, Lev Sedov, and also at the time of the disappearance of Rudolf Klement, whose dismembered body was found in the Seine. The leadership of the Fourth International believed—as did the Mexican police and the FBI—that Jacson had participated in the raid on Trotsky's villa on May 24, 1940, and "It may have been he who convinced Robert Sheldon Harte to open the door for the assassins that night."[3]

As the FBI's investigation was in progress, Mexican police intercepted three letters written to Jacson from a Sylvia Rosenberg in The Bronx. The letters were replete with misspellings, errors in punctuation, and inexplicable references, seemingly the ramblings of someone demented. On the chance that they might be written in some kind of code, both American and Mexican cryptographers examined them but could turn up nothing. Although FBI agents found no Sylvia Rosenberg at the address given on the letters, they found a woman by that name at another Bronx address who turned out to be a sane twenty-five-year-old American citizen; but before agents could arrange an interview, she was found dead on a New York street, having "died by either jumping or falling from a window."[4]

The FBI was never able to establish the true identity of Jacques Mornard van Dendreschd, alias Frank Jacson, and conclusive evidence that Jacson had killed Trotsky at the order of the Soviet intelligence service would be definitely established only in 1944 when the FBI would uncover and neutralize a plot to free Jacson from his cell in Mexico City. The investigation into Trotsky's murder thus failed to accomplish what J. Edgar Hoover had hoped it would, to uncover the Soviet intelligence network in the United States. Yet Hoover's sense of frustration in that failure was destined soon to be alleviated by information that would threaten almost the entire secret Soviet system in the United States, including Apparats A and B. The information came from a defector, the man who had headed the Soviet military intelligence service in Western Europe and thus had intimate knowledge of the identities of many of the phantomas serving the Soviet intelligence service in Europe and the United States—General Walter Krivitsky.

Ignace Reiss, a Polish Jew born in 1899, had served as an agent for the Comintern, with the Red Army of the Ruhr in Germany, and for five years after that as a Comintern plenipotentiary in Vienna. Appointed to the Soviet intelligence service abroad, he was deeply involved in forming the *rabcors* in France. Reiss's superiors regarded him as a devout and wholly reliable Marxist-Leninist. Yet that was before the expulsion of Leon Trotsky, whom Reiss deeply admired, and the trial and execution of Kamenev and Zinoviev, who as head of the Comintern had long been Reiss's director.

On May 29, 1937, Reiss called at 32 Celebesstraat in The Hague, which bore a plaque beside the door: *Dr. Martin Lessner, Austrian Art Dealer.* Reiss and the man whom that identity concealed, General Krivitsky, were old friends from the days when both had served in the Communist underground in Warsaw during the Russo-Polish War. To Krivitsky, Reiss spoke "of his crushing disillusionment, of his desire to drop everything and go off to some remote corner where he could be forgotten."[5]

Krivitsky prevailed upon Reiss not to defect but to reconsider for some weeks until the two might meet again in Paris. That meeting occurred six weeks later, but Krivitsky was pressed and suggested that Reiss telephone him the next morning at the Hôtel Napoléon, when he would arrange to talk at length. Yet that was not to be, for that evening Krivitsky received a telephone call instructing him to go to the Mexican pavillion at the Paris Exposition, to meet the inspector general of the Soviet secret and counterespionage service, Alexander Shpigelglas. To Krivitsky that meant that something serious was in the offing, for Shpigelglas normally came to a foreign capital only at the head of one of the special commissions. Who, pondered Krivitsky, was to be the victim?

At the exposition grounds, Shpigelglas showed Krivitsky a letter from Reiss to

Stalin. In it, Reiss professed that he should have written it the day Zinoviev and Kamenev "were murdered in the cellars of the Lubianka at the command of the Father of Nations [Stalin]." He had kept silent then, Reiss wrote, "and for this I bear a large responsibility. My guilt is great, but I shall try to make up for it quickly, and to ease my conscience." Up to the point of writing the letter, said Reiss, "I had followed you. From now on, not a step further. Our ways part! He who keeps silent at this hour becomes an accomplice of Stalin and a traitor to the cause of the working class and of Socialism."[6]

It would later emerge that Reiss had been finally persuaded to defect at a meeting with Trotsky's son, Lev Sedov, then the head of the International Bureau of the Fourth International in Paris. At that meeting—of which Shpigelglas was informed almost as soon as it had taken place—Reiss had warned Lev Sedov that he and his father, Trotsky, were in grave peril. "It has been decided," said Reiss, "to use every means against you. I repeat: every means."[7]

Krivitsky, ordered Shpigelglas, was to find Reiss and, using the oblique language of the trade in such matters, "resolve the problem." Yet Krivitsky could not bring himself to kill Reiss. "At that moment," he would later write, " I realized that my lifelong service to the Soviet government was ended." Although he had "taken an oath to serve the Soviet Union" and had lived by that oath, "to take a hand in these wholesale murders was beyond my powers."[8]

Over the next six weeks, while appearing to be settling his affairs in preparation for a visit to Moscow, Krivitsky made his own plans to defect. He still had arrangements to make when on the morning of September 5, 1937, he opened the Paris newspaper Le Matin and saw a dispatch from Switzerland reporting that a man's corpse had been found on a road near Chamblandes. There were five bullets in the man's head and seven in his body; in the dead man's pockets were a rail ticket for Paris and a Czechoslovakian passport in the name of Hans Eberhardt. Eberhardt, Krivitsky knew, was the cover name for Ignace Reiss.

Since Krivitsky had failed to follow his orders to kill Reiss, he concluded that he too was marked for assassination. On October 6, 1937, he left Paris by car with his wife and son for Dijon, the capital of Burgundy, where he took a train for some distance, then arranged for another car to complete his journey to the Côte d'Azur and the resort town of Hyères-les-Palmiers. They paused only for Krivitsky to make a brief call to his secretary in Paris, informing her "of my break with the Soviet government."[9]

For nearly three months, Krivitsky and his family hid in the quiet little resort, Krivitsky departing only once for a trip to Paris where he sought "advice and comradeship" from Lev Sedov. "I learned to admire this son of Leon Trotsky," he would relate later, "as a personality in his own right." He found him "charming, well-informed, efficient," and contrary to testimony at the Zinoviev-Kamenev trial that he had received vast sums of money from Hitler and the Japanese, living "the life of a revolutionist, toiling all day in the cause of the opposition, in actual need of better food and clothing."[10]

Krivitsky and his family soon crossed the Atlantic by steamer to Montreal, waiting there briefly for a visa to enter the United States and arriving in New York in December 1938. There Krivitsky engaged a lawyer prominent in handling left-wing causes, Louis Waldman, in an attempt to make an agreement with the State Department's visa section: if granted the green card of a resident alien, he would tell all.

The details of what happened in regard to that proposal would remain obscure, for sometime in 1946, Krivitsky's file would somehow vanish either from the State Department or from the National Archives. Since Krivitsky remained on the books as an alien on a 120-day visa, subject to renewal upon application, his proposal was apparently rejected. Ignored, he was left to join the foreign flotsam and jetsam on New York's Lower East Side.

Nor did the government provide him any protection, so that when it was announced publicly that he was writing his memoirs for a New York publishing house as well as a series of articles for *The Saturday Evening Post*, he became especially vulnerable. An attack on his life appeared to be in the making when on March 7, 1939, he lunched at a Child's restaurant on 42nd Street just off Times Square with the editor of a labor daily in New York, David Schub, a former Russian revolutionary who was later to become a biographer of Lenin. Hardly had they begun their meal when three men sat down at the next table. Krivitsky recognized one of them immediately: an agent in the United States from Krivitsky's own former service, the Fourth Department of the Red Army General Staff, Sergei Basov.

Beckoning Schub, Krivitsky rose immediately, but as he made his way across the crowded restaurant to the cashier, Basov and his colleagues followed. At the cashier's desk, Krivitsky challenged Basov directly: had he come to shoot him down? No, indeed, replied Basov calmly, he only wanted to have "a friendly chat."[11] Replying that he had no time for friendly chats, Krivitsky left the restaurant and headed for the nearby offices of the New York *Times*, but as he entered the building, Basov followed. Krivitsky went to the office of an acquaintance on the staff and in front of the acquaintance told Basov he wanted to see nothing more of him. Although Basov departed, he remained outside the *Times* building, occasionally relieved by one of his two colleagues. For almost six hours, Krivitsky stayed in the building, departing at last in the company of a group of fellow émigrés whom he summoned by telephone. They merged quickly in the throng of theatergoers that descended upon Times Square after nightfall.

Krivitsky's articles in *The Saturday Evening Post* revealed a thorough knowledge of secret Soviet affairs, and in one he made what at the time seemed to be an incredible prophecy that the Soviet and Nazi governments would soon sign a pact of friendship and nonaggression. Yet despite his obvious knowledge, the State Department took no notice of him except for an invitation from a functionary, Raymond E. Murphy, head of a small Soviet research section in the Department, to come to Washington for a talk. They met on June 29, 1938. Surviving files would indicate that Krivitsky passed along no particularly valuable information, possibly because he was still trying to barter his knowledge for the green card that would enable him to reside permanently in the United States. On the same visit to Washington, he also saw the head of the State Department's passport and visa section, Ruth Shipley, but no record of the interview survived the disappearance of the Krivitsky file.

A short while later, in a conversation with the journalist, Isaac Don Levine, Krivitsky revealed that there was a Soviet agent operating in the communications and cipher department of the British Foreign Office in London. When Levine passed the information to Undersecretary of State Adolf Berle, Berle arranged for Levine to see the British ambassador in Washington, Lord Lothian, who passed the word to London. Since there were only sixteen employees in the communications and cipher department, it was relatively easy for British authorities to identify the traitor, a clerk named John Herbert King.

The success in uncovering King having proved Krivitsky's soundness as an informer, the British brought him to London in a submarine that had been refitting in Newfoundland. Although unable to provide names except in a few instances, Krivitsky revealed that there were more than a hundred Soviet agents working directly against British interests either in Britain or in the empire. Of those inside Britain, six were "legal" spymasters, Soviet citizens operating under the cover of official positions either in the Russian Embassy or in the Russian trade mission, Arcos. He said there were twenty so-called apparatus workers in Britain, whose task was to provide the administrative infrastructure on which any espionage network depends: couriers, keepers of safe houses, photographers. There were also thirty-five espionage agents inside Britain, such as King, of whom sixteen were British subjects. Of those sixteen, eight were "active in politics," six were in the civil service, and two were journalists. One of the civil servants, said Krivitsky, was "a foreign office man who wore a cape." [12]

Returning to New York, Krivitsky found at least some American officials at last beginning to display an interest in him. Called to Capitol Hill to testify before the Un-American Activities Committee, which was investigating Soviet intelligence and propaganda activities in the United States, he delivered what was considered to be at the time grave testimony.

All Communists everywhere, said Krivitsky, were agents of Joseph Stalin, and Stalin thus was the actual head of the American Communist Party. As one of Stalin's representatives abroad, he said, one of his own principal duties had been to ensure that all Communists obeyed the Stalinist dogma. Local Communists in every country helped Stalin's military and political intelligence services to obtain military, industrial, and political intelligence about their home countries. "The *NKVD* has its agents planted in all institutions, governmental and industrial," and, he said, "undoubtedly has its agents in the army and navy of the United States." [13]

Contrary to prior testimony given the committee by the head of the American Communist Party, Earl Browder, Krivitsky declared that the Soviet hierarchy, not the Comintern, decided international Communist policies. To assure that local Communist parties obeyed the party line as transmitted by the Russian Communist Party through the Comintern, Comintern representatives in each country controlled funds—sometimes up to 90 percent of all expenditures—that Moscow provided local parties. The money, he said, was usually transmitted either through Soviet diplomatic channels or through such trade agencies as Amtorg.

The NKVD, said Krivitsky, controlled the Red Army and the Soviet diplomatic service and operated in every country of the world to supervise local Communist parties. Since the secret police were "interested in the entire economic and political life of this country," he said, "its agents are planted in all institutions." In addition to espionage, he said, the agents conducted "activities beginning with discrediting people who are regarded as dangerous to the Soviet Union and ending with kidnapping and murdering them."[14]

To the Un-American Activities Committee, Krivitsky explained that he was withholding much of his information until the State Department gave him a green card, which prompted the committee to ask the State Department to grant him resident alien status. While that possibility was under consideration, Krivitsky, fearful for his life, withdrew from the hearings.

Learning that one of the gunmen involved in the murder of Ignace Reiss had arrived in New York, Krivitsky determined to arm himself, even though as a temporary resident alien, he was forbidden by law from buying a weapon in New York State. Having friends in Virginia, a former German Army officer named Lobertov and his wife, he set out on February 5, 1941, by train for Washington, where he stayed overnight and then went on to Charlottesville. Using the name Walter Paref, which he intended to adopt legally if he could obtain resident status, he purchased, a .38 caliber revolver and fifty bullets at Charles Henshaw's hardware store in Charlottesville. The night of February 8, 1941, he spent at the farm home of his friends, the Lobertovs, and the next day, Mrs. Lobertov drove him to Washington. She dropped him at about 6:30 P.M. at the Hotel Bellevue across from Union Station.

Checking in, Krivitsky went directly to his room on the fifth floor, and from all accounts, remained in the room for the rest of the night. He made no telephone calls, asked for no room service, and had no known visitors.

At about 9:30 A.M. on February 10, 1941, a maid knocking on Krivitsky's door received no answer. After knocking several times, she tried to use her passkey but to no avail; the door had been secured from the inside. When the police arrived and broke down the door, they found Walter Krivitsky dead on his bed. He had been shot once in the head with the pistol he had bought at Henshaw's hardware. The bullet was from the carton he had also purchased.

Mrs. Krivitsky, Louis Waldman, Isaac Don Levine, and another friend, Suzanne

La Follette, all charged that Krivitsky had been murdered, probably by the agent who had approached him earlier in New York, Sergei Basov. Even though Krivitsky had been constantly concerned about assassination, they said, he had been in good spirits and on occasion had warned a number of associates that if ever he should be found dead, they were not to believe that he had killed himself.

Since there was no indication of interstate involvement and thus no federal jurisdiction involved, the FBI was unable to enter the case, leaving it to the Washington police. They established that not only was the door to the hotel room locked from the inside, but also the only other entrance, a window. The window was distant from the roof and the pavement and gave out neither to a fire escape nor a ledge. To support a theory of suicide, there were three notes, one in German, one in English, and one in Russian, and all in Krivitsky's handwriting. The notepaper bore the country address of the Lobertovs.

The letter in German was addressed to the attorney, Louis Waldman:

> Dear Mr. Waldman:
> My wife and my boy will need your help. Please do for them what you can.
>
> > (s) WALTER KRIVITSKY.
>
> P.S. I went to Virginia because I knew there I could get a gun. If my friends should have any trouble, please help them, they did not know why I bought the gun.[15]

The letter in English was to Suzanne La Follette:

> Dear Suzanne:
> I trust that you are well, and I am dying with the hope that you will help Tanya and my poor boy. You were a friend.
>
> > Yours,
> > WALTER
>
> P.S. I also think about your brother and Dorothy.

The third letter, in Russian, was to his wife and son but apparently directed only to his wife:

> Dear Tanya and Alek:
> It is very difficult but I want to live very badly. But it is impossible. I love you, my only one.
> It is difficult to write, but think about me and you will understand that I have to go. Don't tell Alek yet where his father is going. I believe that in time you will tell him, because it will be best for him.
> Forgive, it is very hard to write. Take care of him and be a good mother to him and be always quiet and never get angry at him. He is

very good and always very pale. Good people will help you, but not enemies. I think my sins are big. I see you, Tanya and Alek. I embrace you.

Yours,<br>VELLA

P.S. On the farm I wrote this yesterday, but I did not have any strength in New York. I did not have any business in Washington. I went to see Lobertov because that is the only place I could get firearms.

Were those the final words of a man about to shoot himself? Did they express genuine anguish and mental turmoil? If so, how could a man preparing for the act of suicide have kept at least one of them in his pocket for many hours, as the letter to Tanya indicated, and still have shown no signs of depression or intent to kill himself? The last person known to have seen him alive, Mrs. Lobertov, was adamant in that Krivitsky was composed and happy when he spent the night at the farm, through the next morning, during the drive to Washington, and when she dropped him at the Hotel Bellevue.

Why would a suicide write: "It is very difficult but I want to live very badly. But it is impossible"? Why would a suicide say: "It is difficult to write, but think about me and you will understand that I have to go"? Think about me. "Don't tell Alek yet" but "I believe that in time you will tell him." "It is very hard to write." "Good people will help you, but not enemies." Were those not clues composed while staring at the barrel of a gun to draw the attention of a wife to a statement often made, that if ever he were found dead, to discount suicide?

So Mrs. Krivitsky, Suzanne La Follette, Levine, and Waldman insisted. Waldman pointed out inconsistencies of style and calligraphy in the letters, maintaining that they were forgeries. Nor was the coroner fully convinced that General Krivitsky had taken his own life; while officially declaring the death a suicide, he stated that if further evidence developed, he would empanel a jury.

Yet there would be no further evidence—not for the moment. At the Fresh Pond Crematory in Queens, New York, after dark so that the identities of the mourners might be concealed, the body was cremated. Krivitsky's wife and son then went into hiding on the Maryland farm of Whittaker Chambers, the former Comintern agent turned both Quaker and informer, who even then was at work trying to warn the United States that some of its most trusted officials were Soviet agents.

Six years later, with World War II at an end, the Krivitsky case would be suddenly reopened when the State Department in 1947 received intelligence that Krivitsky had been shadowed in the United States by an agent of the German intelligence bureau in Buenos Aires named Stein. By that time, American officials were aware that upon the signing of the Nazi-Soviet Nonaggression Pact in 1939,

German and Russian secret police had agreed to assist each other in their operations.

Digging into the ruins of the Foreign Ministry's archives in Berlin, American investigators were able to trace the path of an agent named Stein from Washington to Buenos Aires, Moscow, and Berlin. Yet there was no evidence that either Stein or five other Steins who were in the German intelligence service before the war had been in Washington at the time of Krivitsky's death. On the other hand, Hitler's government restored the German nationality, previously revoked, of Krivitsky's friends in Charlottesville, the Lobertovs.

What was established was that on Monday morning, the day after Krivitsky arrived at the Hotel Bellevue, he had planned to go to Capitol Hill, where, regardless of whether he received a green card, he intended to lay information before the Un-American Activities Committee exposing Soviet agents in the United States. One whom he intended to expose was the all-powerful head of the Central Control Commission, Jacob Golos. Although Krivitsky may for long have been marked for eventual extermination, that may have been the matter that actually triggered it; for despite the appearance of suicide, Krivitsky had been murdered. He had warned too many people that he would never kill himself, and in the NKVD there was a professional saying: "Any fool can commit a murder, but it takes an artist to commit a natural death." [16]

## Chapter Forty-Six

Alexander Sachs was one of the brainiest, ablest, and most courtly of the American economists of the 1930s and 1940s. As he strolled each morning from his home on West 57th Street in New York to the offices of the Lehman Corporation, he had a touch of the boulevardier about him; he wore morning dress, vicuna spats, and a Prince Edward hat over long, curly hair and carried a cane of malacca and gold that he said had been given him as a present by the maharajah of Cooch Behar. Born in Russia in 1893, he had come to the United States when he was eleven and received a scientific degree from Columbia University when he was nineteen. In 1914, he was again at Columbia as a graduate student in philosophy, and in 1916, he was made a Frances Parkman Fellow in philosophy at Harvard University and later a Henry Rogers Fellow in jurisprudence and sociology.

Having established a reputation as a leading international specialist in the economics of oil, Sachs was retained as an economic adviser to a number of important investors. In 1936 he had become vice-president in charge of economic research at the Lehman Corporation, one of those impenetrable organizations wholly devoted to money, its study, its movement, its power, and above all its whereabouts. He made a first move into government as organizer and chief of the economic research and policy section of the National Recovery Administration, the agency which President Roosevelt established with no less an assignment than to lift the country out of the Great Depression and restore its economic health. As World War II came, he became a consultant to the War Emergency Pipelines Corporation, which built petroleum pipelines from the Pacific coast to the Atlantic; to the Petroleum Industry War Council, which the Petroleum Administrator, Harold Ickes, formed to coordinate and oversee the business of the oil companies; and to the Office of Strategic Services, where he pelted the director, Major General William J. Donovan, with lengthy, almost incomprehensibly complex advice about German oil.

Alexander Sachs' greatest weakness was that he was extraordinarily prolix. His memoranda, letters, and speeches were incredibly long and studded with obscure phrases, such as: "the scleroticism of the Right and the infantilism of the Left" and "instrument of divisiveness among the survived triad of hegemonous powers."

Prolixity notwithstanding, it fell to Dr. Sachs to explain to President Roosevelt, a man hardly noted for his patience as a listener, the complex nuclear physics theories of Albert Einstein, Leo Szilard, and Enrico Fermi.

In early spring of 1939, at about the time that Hitler seized Czechoslovakia, the great Hungarian nuclear physicist Leo Szilard summed up in a report entitled "Instantaneous Emission of Slow Neutrons with Uranium" work that he and his Italian colleague, Enrico Fermi, had performed at Columbia University on the theories of fission. After Einstein read the report in the *Physical Review* of April 15, 1939, he and Szilard, joined by Professor Eugene P. Wigner, a Princeton University physicist, and Sachs, all of whom were friends, began to discuss the role an atomic bomb might have on a world that appeared headed for war.

Through sources available to Einstein, the four men knew that Germany had stopped exporting the ore that yields radium, uranium, and pitchblende from the Joachimstal mines in Czechoslovakia and that uranium research was proceeding at a fast pace at the Kaiser Wilhelm Institute in Berlin. The four agreed that the potential peril of the Nazis obtaining an atomic bomb was so great that the matter should be brought to the attention of the president. Since Sachs had a prior relationship with the president, Szilard and Einstein agreed that he was the right person "to make the relevant elaborate scientific material intelligible to Mr. Roosevelt." He took with him to the White House a letter from Einstein warning of the extraordinary explosive power to be obtained from a critical mass of uranium.

At the White House on October 11, 1939, Dr. Sachs' performance came close to disaster. He talked ad infinitum, and for fear that Einstein's letter might get lost in the shuffle of papers on the president's desk, he insisted on reading it aloud. The session went on so long that Roosevelt finally cut Sachs short. He thought, said Roosevelt, that government interest in the matter might be premature.

Shocked and alarmed, Sachs begged for another meeting at breakfast the next morning. When the president agreed, Sachs stayed up much of the night trying to think of a way to dramatize the importance of uranium to the president.

At breakfast, Sachs reminded the president that Robert Fulton had taken his steamboat invention to Napoleon, who had dismissed it as impractical, thus missing out on a development that might have enabled the French to invade England. The president at last was impressed. Producing a bottle of Napoleon brandy, he poured a little into two glasses, lifted his glass to Sachs, and said: "Alex, what you are after is to see that the Nazis don't blow us up." "Precisely," replied Sachs with a rare succinctness. At that, Roosevelt called in his military aide, Major General Edwin "Pa" Watson, handed him Einstein's letter and supporting documents that Sachs had brought with him, and announced: "Pa! This requires action!"[1]

So began the American exploration of the atomic bomb, but it began with something less than the urgency indicated by the president's words. It took nine days to form a guiding group, the Uranium Committee, and on the tenth day $6,000 was transferred from Army and Navy funds to buy four tons of graphite and fifty tons of uranium oxide, a paltry initial outlay for a project that would in the end cost almost $3 billion. Yet the pace picked up, and although Sachs served for a time on the Uranium Committee, he in time moved on to other pursuits and more mundane directors took over in what came to be known as the supersecret S-1 Project, whose managers dealt in more concise memoranda than did Sachs. One of those, entitled "Possibilities of an Explosive Fission Reaction with U-235," marked the end of one era in human development and the beginning of another, for it was instrumental in a presidential decision to proceed on a full-scale effort, in concert with Britain and Canada, whose work in the field was already substantial, to produce an atomic bomb. It also led to a decision to assign management and support of the project to the United States Army with a general officer in charge of what would become known as the Manhattan Project, while the scientific part of the program would be under the direction of a civilian scientist: Dr. J. Robert Oppenheimer.

Julius Robert Oppenheimer was born on April 22, 1904, in New York City, the son of a German-born naturalized citizen who had realized the American dream by making a fortune importing textiles. He attended Harvard University, spent a year at the Cavendish Laboratory at Cambridge University performing research in atomic structure, then, at the invitation of the distinguished German physicist Professor Max Born, studied at the University of Göttingen, receiving his doctorate in physics in 1927. In 1929 he moved to the University of California at Berkeley and soon held a joint professorship there and at the California Institute of Technology. His early research concerned the quantum theory and nuclear physics, and with Professor Born, he wrote a milestone paper contributing to the quantum theory of molecules. With the rise of Hitler and a growing concern in scientific circles that the Nazis might be the first to construct a nuclear bomb, Oppenheimer began research into the process of separating uranium-235 from natural uranium and the critical mass of uranium needed to make a bomb. After the U.S. Army assumed the task of organizing and administering the effort to construct an atomic bomb, Oppenheimer headed the radiation laboratory at which atomic research was conducted at Berkeley and became the scientific director of laboratories established at Los Alamos, New Mexico.

J. Robert Oppenheimer was thus one of the premier nuclear physicists of the world. He was also a man of strong liberal bent, which would in time lead to official investigation into his "activities, contacts, and associates,"[2] including association with Communists and Communist front organizations. That association was not unlike that of many thousands of intellectuals who came to regard Russia as the only breakwater against the tide of Nazism and Fascism and attendant anti-Semitism. From information obtained by the FBI up until 1940, he was clearly no Communist, nor had he materially aided the Communist cause. The FBI's interest in him might not have extended beyond that point had not an organizer for the American Communist Party, Steve Nelson, returned from the Spanish Civil War and in 1940 begun to work as an organizer in Alameda County, California, where Oppenheimer lived and worked.

When Nelson telephoned Oppenheimer's home, Oppenheimer knew at once who he was, a man who had consoled and befriended his wife, Katherine, when her first husband had been killed in the Spanish Civil War. Oppenheimer invited Nelson to his home, and a number of visits followed. The visits, said Oppenheimer, were "friendly," but never did Nelson approach him "for any information regarding the experiments that were being conducted at the Radiation Laboratory."

As Dr. Oppenheimer was beginning to explore that nebulous, murky, and perilous dividing line between national loyalty and political conscience, a small cast of characters was assembling that was destined to become closely involved in a drama focused on the atomic bomb project that he headed. One who was destined to play a major role was then in Britain, a refugee from Nazism, Emil Julius Klaus Fuchs.

Klaus Fuchs owed his escape from Nazi Germany and perhaps his life to International Red Aid, an agency that had been established in 1922 on orders of the Comintern. When Hitler promulgated his Decree for the Protection of the People and the State and began a roundup of suspected enemies of the state in what became known as the Brown Terror, thereby precipitating a mass flight of intellectuals from Germany, especially Jewish intellectuals, International Red Aid began its first major operation, passing wanted German Communists by the scores across the western German frontier into the forests of the Belgian Ardennes. One of those whom the agency assisted was Fuchs, a young man of exceptional ability both as a physicist and as a Communist theoretician. Active in the Communist street struggle with the Nazis, he was attending a conference of the Young Communist International at Berlin University when he learned that a warrant was out for his arrest.

Fuchs turned to International Red Aid, which by that time, through the work of a leading Comintern clandestine, Henri Robinson, had established an efficient underground railway leading to the western border city of Aachen, where fugitives were collected for transportation through the Ardennes to one of the Channel ports and on to London. Fuchs appeared to have been a special case, for when he arrived in Aachen, Robinson himself was there to assist him onward. As yet another refugee from Nazism, Fuchs attracted little attention from British immigration authorities and police, and after a few formalities, the authorities granted him refuge. Fuchs immediately established contact with a small group of German Communist émigrés at the London School of Economics, which had coalesced around a lecturer, René Robert Kuczynski, and his son, Jürgen, who were Comintern agents controlled by a shadowy Soviet intelligence official known only as Harry II.[3]

Soon after arriving in Britain, Fuchs made application to continue his studies at a British university and despite a warning from the German consul in Bristol that he was a Communist, was admitted for advanced studies at Bristol University in fields connected with nuclear physics. It would be established later that while in Bristol, Fuchs openly joined such Communist front organizations as the Society for Cultural Relations with the Union of Soviet Socialist Republics.

That was a time when a team of physicists at Cambridge University, led by Sir James Chadwick, had discovered the neutron, a key to atomic fission. Thus when Fuchs moved on for further study at Edinburgh University, there was considerable appreciation in scientific circles of his emerging genius as a theoretical physicist. There was less enthusiasm for his politics, for Fuchs made no secret of the fact that he was a member of the German Communist Party and again openly attended meetings of Communist front groups. Less openly, he became a member of "an underground section of the German Communist Party," of which Jürgen Kuczynski was regarded as the head.[4]

Yet another member of the cast was at about the same time taking steps in Philadelphia and New York that were in time to lead him, too, into close association with the atomic bomb program. That man was Harry Gold.

A bookish, talkative, introspective man, Gold was born to Sam Golodnitsky and his wife in December 1910 in Switzerland as the couple was emigrating from Russia to the United States. The family came to live in the 2600 block of South Phillip Street in a poor neighborhood of Philadelphia known as "The Neck." Establishing a reputation of being decent, thrifty, devout, and loyal to their new country, the Golodnitskys became naturalized citizens and anglicized the family name.

Sam Gold obtained work as a cabinetmaker with the Victor Talking Machine Company, which was later absorbed by the Radio Corporation of America. He enjoyed his work until in 1920 a change from handcraft to mass production brought an influx of new employees, many of whom proved to be anti-Semitic.

One of only a few Jewish employees, Sam Gold was a ready target. The other workers made life miserable for him; they "stole his chisels, put glue on his tools and his good clothes," and put liquid wood into the fillings of his sandwiches. A new foreman assigned him a job hand-sanding cabinets on a fast production line so that Sam Gold would come home at night "with his fingertips raw." During lunch breaks his fellow workmen would talk loudly about "kikes" and "yids."[5]

Sam's son, Harry, meanwhile did well at school, eventually entering the University of Pennsylvania and obtaining a degree in chemical engineering at Drexel Night School. At various times he took courses in psychology and economics and did some graduate work in chemistry at Xavier University in Cincinnatti. During the course of his education, he frequently encountered anti-Semitism and through those experiences and those of his father developed a hatred for Anglo-Saxon society.

The fees for Harry Gold's studies were far in excess of what Sam Gold might have been thought to be able to pay. Which led to subsequent speculation that the American Communist Party paid at least part of them, for Jacob Golos made it a practice to help with the education of young people who might later be of use to the party. If Golos did, in fact, help Harry Gold, it was one of the best investments in an individual ever made by the Comintern.

Gold's first direct contact with the Communist Party came late in 1932 while he was working as a laboratory assistant at the Pennsylvania Sugar Company in Philadelphia for a kindly old chemist, Dr. Gustav Reich, who had invented a nonbacterial sugar process. Gold having expressed some interest in Socialism, a fellow chemist, Thomas L. Black, invited him to attend Communist Party meetings. Gold went but was unimpressed. "The members were a shabby and shoddy lot," he would recall, "run through with informers and opportunists." Thus he chose not to join the party, which made him the more attractive as an agent since he had no police record as a member of the party.

Late in 1933, at about the time Litvinov signed the noninterference agreement, Gold's colleague, Black, took Gold to a party in a flat in Greenwich Village. Over spaghetti and oysters, a man who called himself Paul Smith told Gold that Roosevelt had negotiated the agreement in order to get American industry moving again. If Gold could supply information about projects under way at Pennsylvania Sugar, said Smith, that might enable Amtorg to decide what contracts to offer the company. Aware of Gold's sensitivity about anti-Semitism, Smith said Russia was the only country in which there was no anti-Semitism and that Russia was the only country opposing the anti-Semitic powers, Germany and Italy. If Gold helped Russia, he would be helping both the United States and the Jewish people.

The party over, Smith walked with Gold to Pennsylvania Station where Gold was to take a train back to Philadelphia. While they were waiting together on the platform, Smith confided to Gold that Amtorg was immensely interested in Dr. Reich's research into the manufacture of absolute ethyl alcohol, which could be used to "cut" petroleum. If Gold could obtain the formula, that would enable

Amtorg to know what to cite in applying to Pennsylvania Sugar for the license to develop the process in Russia. That information, said Smith, would save Russia time and money, help the Russian government raise the standard of living of Russian workers, and also help Russia to defend Socialism and the Jews against Fascism.

Gold said he would see what he could do. In due course, he stole not only the formula for absolute ethyl alcohol but also that for Dr. Reich's nonbacterial sugar process. He turned them over to Black for transmittal to Smith. Although Harry Gold was destined never to meet Jacob Golos, he was at that point trapped into becoming an industrial spy for Golos; if he backed down, Black told him, the party would inform Pennsylvania Sugar about what he had done.

Gold needed no coercion to continue. Over the next two years he stole a succession of formulae: solvents for lacquers and varnishes, paper fillers, a local anesthetic known as ethyl chloride, vitamin D concentrate obtained from fish oils, and synthetic detergents. Never did he accept any money for his services other than occasional reimbursement for expenses. That totaled about $2,000 over his entire period of spying, which averaged less than $250 a year.

Later in 1935, for reasons that escaped Gold, his controllers became ecstatic when he handed over details of a process to make phosphoric acid from waste bone black and waste sulphuric acid. Hinting that he might be in line for a medal, they urged him to expand his work. Over the next few years he provided a variety of industrial and pharmaceutical processes and blueprints, such as a process for production of lanolin, a formula for production of synthetic rubber, a process of carbon-dioxide recovery, blueprints for a magnesium powder plant, an early aerosol dispenser, blueprints for a 1,000-gallon cooled resin plant, the Eastman Kodak color-photography process, blueprints of a system for production of aerial camera film, a method of "subbing" photographic paper, a nylon production process, and the formula for RDX, a superpowerful explosive.

Gold's controllers in time awarded him the Red Star for "conspicuous service to the Soviet Union in time of peace and war." He had become Jacob Golos' most productive agent in all the *apparats*.

# PART VIII
## The British Station

## Chapter Forty-Seven

In 1933, one of those years when, as Lord Byron wrote, "the Fates change horses, making history change its tune," the fate of the world in the great struggle between Fascism and Communism rested to a considerable degree in London. As the coalition government of J. Ramsay MacDonald ruled insecurely and uneasily, Winston Churchill was only a backbencher in the House of Commons, but his antipathy for Bolshevism remained as strong as ever. Yet Churchill's prospects of enjoying high office again were remote; for his unrestrained public utterances had appalled both Socialists and Tories alike, as in 1927, at a time of rising anxiety about the intentions of Hitler and Mussolini, Churchill had told a press conference in Rome following a meeting with Mussolini: "If I had been an Italian, I am sure I should have been whole-heartedly with you from the start to finish in your triumphant struggle against the bestial appetites and passions of Leninism. But in England we have not yet had to face this danger in the same deadly form. We have our own way of doing things. But that we shall succeed in grappling with Communism and choking the life out of it—of that I am absolutely sure." In cracking down on the Bolsheviks, Churchill concluded, Italy had rendered "service to the whole world."[1]

Those remarks produced an uproar, particularly among liberals. "We had always suspected," declared a revered liberal journalist, C. P. Scott, in *The New Leader*, "that Mr. Winston Churchill was a Fascist at heart. Now he has openly avowed it." Not that Churchill in any case had enjoyed much popularity with the working classes, and particularly with the trade unions, ever since his private war on Bolshevism in 1918–1921.

In 1933, Churchill delivered a speech before the fifteenth anniversary meeting of the Anti-Socialist and Anti-Communist Union in London soon after the world-famous debating society at Oxford University, the Oxford Union, had passed its resolution declaring "That this House refuses in any circumstances to fight for King and Country." It was an incident, Churchill would write later, promoting "the idea of a decadent, degenerate Britain" that "took deep root and swayed many calculations" in Germany, Russia, Italy, and Japan.[2] To the Anti-Socialist and Anti-Communist Union, Churchill called it "that abject, squalid, shameless avowal" and noted that "We are told we ought not to treat it seriously. 'The Times' talks of the Children's House [a current radio program for tiny tots]. I disagree. It is a very disquieting and disgusting symptom." He looked "across the narrow waters of the Channel and the North Sea," he said, and saw Germany "with its splendid clear-eyed youth marching forward . . . burning to suffer and die for their fatherland." He saw Italy with its "ardent Fascisti, renowned Chief, and stern sense of national duty." He also saw France, "pacifist to the core, but armed to the teeth and determined to survive as a great nation of the world." "One can almost feel the curl of contempt upon the lips of the manhood of all these peoples," he said, "when they read this message sent out by Oxford University in the name of young England."[3]

In the course of the speech, Churchill praised "the Roman genius" of Mussolini, whom he called, for his anticommunist stand, "the greatest law-giver among living men." As for Japan, whose Army had occupied Manchuria in 1931 and was preparing to advance into the Chinese province of Jehol, "we should try in England to understand a little the position of Japan, an ancient state with the highest sense of national honour and patriotism and with a teeming population and a remarkable energy"; Japan, he said, saw on one side "the dark menace of Soviet Russia," on the other "the chaos of China, four or five provinces of which are actually now being tortured under Communist rule."[4]

Although Churchill mitigated his remarks by dismissing the notion of Fascism for Britain, that did little to dilute the calamitous impact of his other words. Yet Churchill cared not. For him, his personal *bête noire* and that of the world, in his opinion, was Bolshevik Russia.

Yet even at that moment there was emerging to intrude upon Churchill's cyclops-eyed view of the world events a new menace: Hitler's Germany. Hitler had just promulgated the Enabling Act, the legislation that afforded him dictatorial powers, and despite a specific prohibition of the Treaty of Versailles, Göring had just announced the establishment of the Luftwehr, a military aviation service, the precursor of the Luftwaffe. Churchill watched "with surprise and distress the tumultuous insurgence of ferocity and war spirit, the pitiless ill-treatment of minorities, the denial of the normal protections of civilized society to large numbers of individuals solely on the ground of race." For the moment, he said, "one cannot help feeling glad that the fierce passions that are raging in Germany have not, as yet, any outlet but upon Germans." Yet that might well change, and how was Britain preparing to meet it? By a device that to Churchill was anathema: by disarmament.

In the *Daily Mail,* Churchill declared that the interminable efforts of the League of Nations to create a world brotherhood where arms and armies were no longer necessary had produced only "Mush, slush, and gush!" The league was even proposing, Churchill declared to the House of Commons, a maximum period of military service in all European armies of only eight months; no cannon larger than 105 mm.; no tank to exceed sixteen tons unladen, twenty tons laden; land forces to be restricted to 500,000 men in Russia, 200,000 in Germany, France, Italy, and Poland, and all other European states to have even smaller armies; aerial bombardment to be prohibited and no country to have more than 500 aircraft, none to exceed twelve tons in weight.

Those proposals came at a time, Churchill noted, when Hitler had repudiated the league's disarmament conference and the league itself, yet the British prime minister had only recently gone again to Geneva to propose that France disarm; France, a nation confronted by German invasion three times in less than a century, a nation "with less than forty millions faced by Germany with sixty millions." How could anybody expect France "to deprive herself of the mechanical aids and appliances on which she relies to prevent a fourth invasion?" What, too, of the new states of Northern and Eastern Europe, such as Finland, Latvia, Lithuania, and Poland; how were they "to protect themselves from being submerged in a ferocious deluge from Russia?" The league's disarmament program, he declared, was "a problem smothered with hypocrisy," from which the only real victor would be Russia, which would emerge "smelling of phlox" while at the same time preparing "a deadly combination of arms through which to spread her vile philosophy."

No, Churchill declared, peace was not to be had that way. Peace would be achieved, he said, "only when in a favourable atmosphere half a dozen great men, with as many first class powers at their backs, are able to lift world affairs out of their present confusion." With that eventual goal in mind, "Out first supreme object is not to go to war. To that end we must do our best to prevent others from going to war."[5]

There was surely little news emerging at the time from Germany to suggest that that glorious millennium was about to occur. Hitler had suppressed the entire democratic, Socialist, and Communist press; he had dismissed the Prussian state government and formally imposed Nazi rules on the governments of all the German states; he had removed all Jews from public office and directed local organizations throughout Germany to begin anti-Jewish propaganda; he had placed all youth organizations under the labor ministry to begin paramilitary programs; he had established concentration camps; he had banned all trade unions and sent most of the former leaders of them to the camps. On May 10, 1933, the Nazis staged a first mass public burning of books of which they disapproved; soon thereafter aircraft from the Luftwehr flew across the Austrian frontier to drop leaflets abusing the Austrian government and extolling Nazism; and on June 15, 1933, President von Hindenburg signed a special decree abolishing all political parties except the National Socialist Party. All funds and property of other parties were confiscated; and the Weimar Republic, established on a bright spring day in 1919 on the tulip-decked stage of the Weimar opera house, ended ignominiously with its leading politicians marching through the streets on the way to concentration camps.

On August 12, 1933, Churchill warned his constituents in Theydon Bois that Europe lay under "an evil and dangerous" storm cloud. "Nobody," he declared, "can watch the events which are taking place in Germany without increasing anxiety about what their outcome will be." There was, he said, "grave reason to believe that Germany is arming herself, or seeking to arm herself, contrary to the solemn treaties exacted from her in her hour of defeat."[6]

Yet as Churchill would reveal later, he sympathized with the German people, who constituted "one of the most gifted, learned, and scientific, and formidable nations in the world"; for some of the responsibility for the rise of Hitler lay with the Allied governments and the policy they dictated through the Treaty of Versailles. The Allied governments, he wrote, had made "no sincere attempts . . . to reach agreement with the various moderate governments of Germany." For long the French had "foolishly believed that they could demand tremendous reparations of Germany as compensation for the devastation of the war," and French occupation of the Ruhr and the Inter-Allied Commission for long "controlled the international payments of Germany intensified and prolonged the utmost embitterment of the defeated nation." The Allies, he wrote, had done little "to redress grievances arising from [Versailles], and Hitler in his campaigns could constantly point to a number of absurdities and injustices in the territorial policies of Europe. These fed the sources from which he drew his power."[7] No one could know, he would write in 1935, "whether Hitler is the man who one day will drag Germany into a new war, in which civilization will suffer final defeat, or whether he will go down in history as the man who restored honor and peace to the great German nation and led her back, helpful and strong, into the European family of nations."

That day in 1933 in Theydon Bois, Churchill nevertheless urged the government and its ministers "to realize how grave is their responsibility," to "make sure that the forces of the crown are kept in a proper state of efficiency, with the supplies and the munitions factories which they require." Yet there was little reason to feel confident that that would be the case: Britain had failed even to complete a program started in 1923 to modernize the Royal Air Force. It was as if the government intended to rely on the strength of others, for as was usual in times of rising peril in Europe, the British statesmen, generals, and admirals began to search the horizons for powerful, dependable allies. If Hitler had his way, one of those allies would be the apparent source of Europe's peril: Germany itself.

There was no question but that Hitler admired Britain. He admired Britain's history, which he saw as a concatenation of romance and achievement that had lasted over a thousand years. He admired the British Empire, the largest in the history of the world. He admired the unity, doggedness, and genius of the British people, their courtliness, the stateliness of their institutions, and he admired the pageantry, the grandeur, the power of the Royal Navy.

Some of Hitler's admiration for Britain dated from 1912 when as an impressionable youth of twenty-three, he had visited England. In that year, Hitler's brother, Alois, had married a young actress, Bridget Elizabeth Dowling, and was living in a small flat in Toxteth Park, a respectable lower middle-class suburb of the great port of Liverpool. In early autumn of 1912, Alois sent his sister, Angela Raubal, money to make the trip from Austria to visit him in Liverpool, but when he and his wife met the train from London, it was not Angela who disembarked but Alois' brother, Adolf. "A pale, haggard, shifty-eyed young man without any luggage came down the platform," Bridget would recall, "took Alois by the hand, and began agitatedly whispering in German."[8]

In the days that followed, Bridget thought Adolf Hitler was ill; he slept on the living room sofa and some days lay on it "all day long, like an invalid." Bridget was concerned that he might intend to stay permanently; but he gradually seemed to get better, and in his improved condition, he discoverd the Merseyside docks, the principle entrepôt between Britain, the empire, and the Americas, where there was "a vast procession of ships. Not even in London or at the royal dockyards was there such a pageant of shipping, from the great Cunarders to the small squat merchant steamers trading with Africa and the Pacific Islands. Ships of every flag steamed up the Mersey past the huge towers of the Customs House, but by far the greater number of them flew the white ensign." Hitler for the first time in his life "was confronted with the gleaming instruments of modern power, huge, deafening, and strangely beautiful."

For more than four months, "Adolf Hitler lived in England like a ghost, solitary and unknown, haunting the docks and shipyards." Although he "learned almost nothing about the English and made no English friends, to the very end of his life he retained an abiding respect for the English," and on his mind was "indelibly impressed . . . the supremacy of British maritime power."

Hitler next encountered the British on the battlefields of Flanders, where as an infantryman with the List Regiment he participated in the great German attacks against the British front in the vicinity of Ypres in 1914 and won his first Iron Cross for gallantry for his part in an epic action against the Brigade of Guards at Hill 60. On various occasions in the future, Hitler would pay tribute to the heroism and tenacity of that Praetorian Guard, from which he drew the idea first for the Sturmabteilung and then for the Schutzstaffel. He remained opposite the British sector for most of the rest of the war until the gas attack that temporarily blinded him.

Following Germany's defeat, Hitler never associated the harsh terms of the Treaty of Versailles and the requirement for reparations with the British in the same degree that he associated them with the French. For the French, he developed a personal embitterment and hatred to be compared only with his feelings toward the Jews and Bolsheviks. The British, he said on a number of occasions, were people he could do business with, and when he gained power, he would reveal an intent to negotiate an alliance with the British Empire against Soviet Russia. The first overture came in June 1935, when Ramsay MacDonald's government fell and was replaced by a new coalition led by Stanley Baldwin.

Hitler appointed Joachim von Ribbentrop as "special representative with plenipotentiary powers" to negotiate an alliance between Britain and Germany, and it was probably with Hitler's approval that von Ribbentrop chose as intermediary the Duke of Saxe-Coburg-Gotha, a German subject but an Englishman at birth and a grandson of Queen Victoria, who had attended the "Blessed College of St. Mary's at Eton" and who had been a knight of that most illustrious of all British orders, the Garter. During the years following the World War, he was to be found in the membership of many of the most reactionary and militaristic of all German right-wing organizations and eventually drifted into the Sturmabteilung; but despite—or perhaps because of—his right-wing connections in Germany, he remained a familiar and popular figure in British aristocratic and conservative political circles. He was welcome at Buckingham Palace, and in 1936 he would be staying at Kensington Palace with his sister, Princess Alice, Countess of Athlone.

Princess Alice was the wife of the Earl of Athlone, personal aide-de-camp to King George V and soon to become the Gold Stick—head of the bodyguard—to the king's successor, King Edward VIII. In a world where to know a duke was to know enough, those connections were of considerable political importance. As Grand Master of "The Most Distinguished Order of St. Michael and St. George," an award usually conferred upon British subjects for distinguished services to the crown in the empire, the Earl of Athlone maintained good relations with the Foreign Office, where the honor of the Knight Commander of St. Michael and St. George—the KCMG—was regarded so highly that it was called from its acronym as the "Kindly Call Me God" and the highest rank of the order, the Grand Cross of St. Michael and St. George—the GCMG—was known as the "God Calls Me God."

According to Princess Alice, the Duke of Saxe-Coburg-Gotha came to England for a rugby match between national teams of England and Germany; according to the duke himself, as president of the Anglo-German Fellowship, a strongly pro-German, anticommunist British organization, he was "hoping to engage in consultations with a view to strengthening the Fellowship arrangements and extending them to other countries," presumably into the dominions and the empire.[9] What was more certain was that the duke was influential with the heir to the British throne, the Prince of Wales, who was a strong advocate of an alliance between Britain and Germany against the Soviet Union, and who shared the duke's opinion that it was the Bolsheviks, not the Nazis, who represented a peril to Europe and the British Empire. It was to be noted, also, that the duke was the prince's cousin once removed.

It would later be deduced that it was through the Duke of Saxe-Coburg-Gotha that von Ribbentrop sent a message asking for an audience with Prime Minister Baldwin, who as a liberal conservative well understood the perils of extreme Socialism and who thus might have been expected to entertain the possibility of an alliance with Germany against the Soviet Union. Yet Baldwin was first and foremost a conservative and disliked extremism whether of the left or of the right. While he was aware of general talk that the Prince of Wales admired Hitler, that was apt to influence him more against an alliance than for one.

When von Ribbentrop's emissary approached Baldwin at the official prime minister's residence at No. 10 Downing Street to propose a meeting between Baldwin and Hitler as a prelude to an alliance, he "had great difficulty in getting the Prime Minister to look up from his evening game of patience and hear out his proposal." Although the proposal excited some enthusiasm among the prime minister's aides, Baldwin "was no more concerned with this fellow Hitler than he was with the rest of Europe," of which, as Churchill bitingly commented, "he knew little and disliked what he knew." Yet he failed to rule out a meeting, "but if there had to be a meeting, let Hitler come to see him; he did not like either planes or travelling by boat. The thing was not to make any great fuss about it." He suggested that perhaps Hitler could come in August, and they might meet "in the mountains or in the Lake District." With that, Baldwin drank "a drop of Malvern soda water and to bed."[10]

Hitler "'beamed with joy' at the thought of the impending meeting," for he strongly wanted British cooperation in plans for what he called an Anti-Comintern Pact. All that Britain would have to do was "keep quiet" in Eastern Europe and the Far East while Hitler concluded an alliance with Japan and then "Germany and Japan together, each secure in her rear, could attack the Soviet Union from two sides and destroy it." That would free the British Empire of the acute threat of the Comintern while at the same time "extirpating the sworn enemy of the existing order of Old Europe" and securing for the Germans *Lebensraum.*[11]

But nothing was to come of the proposed encounter with Stanley Baldwin; although there was some talk of meeting on a ship in the North Sea, it never developed. Not to be thwarted by Baldwin's procrastination, Hitler proposed the plan early in 1936 to Lord Londonderry, the Lord Privy Seal, the Leader of the House of Lords, head of the Conservative Party, member of the Anglo-German Fellowship, and one of England's largest landowners and richest men. Hitler also discussed the plan with the director of studies at the Royal Institute of International Affairs, Arnold Toynbee, a leading British historian with a long record of intelligence connnections in a country where the intelligence community was often as influential—and right wing—as the nobility.

Hitler accompanied his efforts to attract Britain by a highly charged war of words against Communism, presumably to impress the British with the wisdom and advantages of an alliance. The outbreak of the Spanish Civil War provided his propagandists with a multitude of arguments and visions of a world in the terrible embrace of Bolshevism; they painted lurid word pictures of leftist atrocities in Spain, of "the brutal mass slaughter of [rightist] officers," of setting them afire with gasoline and "slaughtering the children and babies of nationalist parents." For France, which had recently concluded a military alliance with Russia, Hitler predicted similar horrors and prophesied that under the Bolsheviks Europe would "drown in a sea of blood and tears." He himself and his Third Reich, he declared, afforded the only fortress against the fulfillment of the apocalypse: "The whole world may begin to burn around us, but the National Socialist State will tower like platinum out of the Bolshevistic fire." [12]

Although Prime Minister Baldwin himself found an alliance with Hitler unattractice, the more formidable opposition came from his foreign secretary, Anthony Eden. For centuries, Britain had waged wars not for ideological reasons but to assure Britain's safety by maintaining a balance of power in Europe. However deplorable a Bolshevik Russia, Russia had insufficient power at the moment to upset that balance of power; and while the Russians might have to be dealt with in the future, the immediate threat to the balance of power in Europe was Nazi Germany, for Hitler was making no secret of the fact that when sufficiently strong, he intended to attack both France and Russia. While Eden might raise no objections no matter what Hitler did to Russia, he could tolerate no threat to France; France was Britain's eastern bulwark.

So the official British policy. Yet there was still a sizable segment of the bourgeoisie and the nobility in Britain that saw not Hitler but Stalin as the more dangerous enemy. As had been the case with noblemen since the American Revolution, they forever worried that every bell that tolled might be sounding their last hour, so that both inside and outside Parliament they propounded the view that a war between Britain and Germany would be a disaster that could benefit but one power: Soviet Russia.

## Chapter Forty-Eight

The man appointed by Hitler to try to bring Britain into the Anti-Comintern Pact, Joachim von Ribbentrop, was an odd, unpleasant character. Few people except Hitler—who regarded him as a "genius" and a "second Bismarck"—had anything good to say about him, and even the London haut monde regarded him as an impossible, insufferable, pretentious, and in some ways sinister snob and oaf. "The salient features of von Ribbentrop's personality," the Jewish psychiatrists who would examine his Rorschach blots before an American master sergeant hanged him at Nürnberg would write, "appear . . . to have been compensation, both gaudy and sinister, for his inner emptiness; there was very little of a person underneath the actor's make-up."[1]

Born in 1893 as Joachim Ribbentrop—the aristocratic "von" was acquired through a wealthy aunt who adopted him at his own suggestion in 1926—he married well and became head of a wine-importing firm in Berlin. Joining the National Socialist Party in 1926, he impressed Hitler with his knowledge of foreign languages and countries, became an advisor to the Führer on foreign affairs, and in 1933, a Nazi deputy in the Reichstag. In 1936, Hitler made him ambassador to the Court of St. James's and two years later was to name him foreign minister. A devout Nazi, he was admitted by Reichsführer-SS Himmler to the SS Order in the rank of Obergruppenführer-SS, the equivalent in the U.S. Army of a lieutenant general. Yet despite von Ribbentrop's impressive career, not even his wife's mother liked him. "Of all my sons-in-law," she would say, "the most foolish became the most prominent." When Hitler defended his appointment as ambassador to Britain on the grounds that he knew many of the leading figures in British social and political life, Göring remarked: "Yes, but they know him, too."

Yet for all von Ribbentrop's shortcomings, he had measured the interests and psychology of the British ruling class—particularly the Tories with their financial, industrial, territorial, and land interests—with considerable accuracy. He knew that few of them would endorse going to war merely to restore Europe to its pre-Hitler state; he knew that a certain segment in high places admired Hitler's suppression of the Communists; and he knew that if a war between Germany and the Soviet Union meant no war between Britain and Germany, many of them would welcome it.

Von Ribbentrop also counted on the antibolshevism of the heir to the throne, the Prince of Wales, who in his view had also shown every indication of being intensely pro-German (he was almost completely German genetically with but a dash of Greek and English). Von Ribbentrop made his first attempt to bring the Prince of Wales into the Nazi embrace in late 1934 or early 1935 when he called on the Prince and Princess of Hanover to suggest that they arrange a marriage between their daughter and the Prince of Wales; but because the Hanovers were concerned about the age difference between the two, the overture came to nothing. Yet von Ribbentrop's disappointment was brief, for he soon began to believe that his goal might be achieved for him through the Prince of Wales' relationship with an American woman who was living in London, Mrs. Wallis Warfield Simpson, who was also considered to have pro-German views.

The issues and problems that were to face Edward Albert Christian George Andrew Patrick David, Prince of Wales, had been clearly expressed even at the time of his christening. "The young Prince," declared the *Times*, "is heir to a noble inheritance, not only to a station of unequalled dignity, but more than all to the affection of a loyal people, which it will be his office to keep and make his own. Our heartfelt prayer is that he may prove worthy of so great a trust."[2] At the other end of the political spectrum, an ex-coal miner who had become a labor leader and member of Parliament, Keir Hardie, rose in the Commons to make what turned out to be a remarkable prophecy: "From his childhood onward this boy will be surrounded by sycophants and flatterers by the score and will be taught to believe himself as of a superior creation . . . he will be sent on a tour around the world, and probably rumors of a morganatic alliance will follow . . . and the end of it all will be the country will be called upon to pay the bill."[3]

Through some forty years following those remarks, British political attitudes toward the monarchy changed little: editorial writers of the *Times* would continue to treat the question of monarchy judiciously while the Socialists would continue to be vaguely critical but rarely to the point of demanding an end to knighthoods, earldoms, and Orders of the British Empire. Although a small sect of shrill-voiced Bolsheviks would from time to time advocate a republic, their influence following the riots of 1918–1919 was small. In the wake of a flurry of concern for the monarchy as other great dynasties were swept away, the throne of King George V appeared to be as safe as any throughout the long history of the British royal house.

Yet there was no denying the existence of multiple pressures posed by Bolshevism, Fascism, depression, Socialism, the demands of some of the nations within the empire for independence, the apparent arrival of an age of the common man. If the great perils facing the empire were to be resisted, argued the Praetorians of the monarch, the man who mounted the throne would have to be of the highest ability and probity. Did Edward, Prince of Wales, have those attributes? His father, the king, thought not, for as he had remarked to Prime Minister Baldwin: "After I am dead, the boy will ruin himself in twelve months."[4]

The prince was a bachelor with a long history of restlessness and idle pursuits that—as Keir Hardie had predicted—had been skillfully concealed from the public by an adulatory court and press. Something of a dandy—he was given to wearing plaid suits, two-tone shoes, boaters, and boutonnieres and to tying his cravat in a way that would be called the Windsor knot—he had a hint of the racetrack about him. He was educated at the naval academies at Osborne and Dartmouth, where because of his small stature he was known as "Sardine"; he was a midshipman at sea on the battleship *Hindostan;* and as the Prince of Wales he was at Magdalen College, Oxford, which was known less for academics than for producing "Rolls-Royce minds."[5] Not expected to graduate, he spent much time riding with the South Oxfordshire Hounds and playing polo. He liked tap-dancing, strumming a ukulele, nightclubbing, yachting, speedboating, and he was also keenly interested in young women; like James I, his fingers were "ever . . . fiddling about his codpiece."[6] He was often irritable, haughty, willful, and self-indulgent. During the war, much was made of his presence in France with the 1st Life Guards, but the reality was that the heir was kept away from the front; he spent much of his time attached to the staff of the commander in chief of the British Expeditionary Force, Field Marshal Sir John French. Demobilized in February 1919, Edward began to go on foreign tours—as Keir Hardie had predicted—and—again in accord with Hardie's prophecy—there were rumors of "morganatic alliances," especially in the United States; and he fell in love three times.

In 1930, the Prince of Wales met Bessie Wallis Warfield Spencer Simpson, the daughter of a Baltimore clerk "of good family but small means,"[7] the divorced wife of an American naval officer, and at the time the wife of an Anglo-American businessman, Ernest Simpson; she was a woman who, in her own words, was of an age when in her own country she would have been considered "securely on the shelf."[8] There followed invitations to the Simpsons to dinner at the prince's country retreat near Virginia Water and Windsor Castle, Fort Belvedere. Then there were return invitations to the prince for cocktails and dinner at the Simpsons' flat in London. In time there was an invitation to Biarritz and a trip in a yacht along the Spanish and Portuguese coasts that Ernest Simpson was unable to accept but which Wallis Simpson could. With a play on the title of a drama by Oscar Wilde, the British peerage would soon be making remarks about "The Unimportance of Being Ernest."[9]

The prince and his mistress were soon to be seen almost nightly at the theater or fox-trotting into the small hours at the Embassy Club. Mrs. Simpson's jewels and expensive clothes were the talk of London: she was seen variously "dripping" with diamonds or "glittering" with rubies and emeralds.[10] Even in public, she would straighten the prince's tie, rearrange his breast-pocket handkerchief and his boutonniere, and she forbade him to smoke between acts. "He was made for domination, while she was made to dominate."[11] They went on holiday together to Europe, the Mediterranean, winter sports at Kitzbühel, waltzes in Vienna, violins and czardas in Budapest. When the prince took his consort to Buckingham Palace to meet his father, the old king showed an immediate dislike for the small, dark American woman with bright but hard eyes, plucked eyebrows, and hair parted severely in the middle; but the romance went on.

By decision of the newspaper proprietors in the empire, all news and gossip about the romance was suppressed, but it leaked out from the United States, where the press leaped on the story like lions at dinner. In Britain, the scandal would have been of little but prurient interest except for the fact that it involved the future king of England and emperor of the world's greatest empire; princes were permitted a few wild oats, provided they were discreet, and, in England, provided they did not become involved with married women. As it was, the future king's behavior threatened the dignity and majesty of the throne, and that was unforgivable. The scandal also came at a time of severe international tensions, at a time when British institutions everywhere were under attack from the Comintern, and at a time of acute social and economic distress. The events also prompted many to recall the prince's outspoken statements of admiration for Hitler,

Mussolini, and the Fascist system and of contempt for Stalin and Communism. Within the very powerful left-wing circles in Britain, the conclusion was widespread that the Prince of Wales was an incipient if not an actual Fascist.

Within the government, the concern was all the greater because of Mrs. Simpson's alleged German sympathies. She had, it was said, ties to von Ribbentrop, who had on occasion given dinner parties in her honor. An eminent historian who later became the royal archivist, Sir John W. Wheeler-Bennett, would later assert that "Ribbentrop *used* Mrs. Simpson," and, he said, the *Times* had proofs. Although the supposed proofs were never produced publicly, it was a fact that at the time Edward was often "under the surveillance of security officers" and that "Mrs. Simpson was the primary object of these attentions." In view of "her unrivalled opportunities for securing information . . . for the first and last time in history papers were screened in the Foreign Office before the red [dispatch] boxes went off to [Edward]." [12]

On January 20, 1936, His Most Excellent Majesty King George the Fifth, "by the Grace of God, of the United Kingdom of Great Britain, Ireland, and of the British Dominions Beyond the Seas, King, Defender of the Faith, Emperor of India," died peacefully in his sleep at Sandringham Castle. As the death watch ended and the bells began to toll, Queen Mary took Edward's hand, kissed it, and as ritual demanded, declared: "The King is dead; long live the King." At the age of forty-one, the Prince of Wales thus had succeeded to the British throne, the thirty-eighth monarch to reign since the Norman Conquest of 1066. He immediately signed the proclamations of his accession for transmittal to the leaders of the world powers, including "a high and mighty testimonial" on an immense sheet of black-bordered parchment conveyed by a King's Messenger to the president of the United States, that pledged to continue "relations of friendship and good understanding." The relations of which Edward wrote were even then exemplified by the presence in London of an American naval officer for secret talks with the Admiralty concerning joint operations in the event that Japanese military adventures in the Pacific became intolerable. It was also exemplified by the warmth of President Roosevelt's reply, couched in the protocol of the republic, although the last phrase contained an inadvertent slip: "May God have Your Majesty and His Majesty's family in his safe and holy keeping." [13]

The president's gaffe was but the first mishap to mar the new sovereign's reign, for as the dead king was brought in his coffin to London and then placed on a gun carriage for the funeral march from Liverpool Street Station to Palace Yard, outside Westminster Hall, the Privileged Bodies witnessed "a most terrible omen." [14] The Maltese Cross on the top of the Royal Crown fell to the street. For what seemed an age, that ancient symbol of empire, set with two hundred diamonds from the Yukon, the Rand, and the North-West Territory and with a great sapphire from the Burmese hills, lay in a drizzle on the cobbles until at last a grenadier picked it up. The new king-emperor, who saw the cross fall, was heard to exclaim: "Christ! What will happen next!" A member of Parliament remarked to a companion: "A fitting motto for the coming reign."[15]

On January 22, 1936, the day of the Proclamation of the Accession of Edward the Eighth at St. James's Palace, von Ribbentrop's predecessor as German ambassador, Leopold von Hoesch, advised von Ribbentrop, who was then Hitler's adviser on foreign affairs, that Edward "quite generally feels warm sympathy for Germany." Although the new king would "naturally have to impose restrictions on himself at first, especially in questions of foreign policy, which are so very delicate," von Hoesch was convinced that "his friendly attitude toward Germany might in time come to exercise a certain amount of influence on the shaping of British foreign policy."[16] That prompted von Ribbentrop to direct the Duke of Saxe-Coburg-Gotha, who was again in London still trying to arrange a meeting between Prime Minister Baldwin and Chancellor Hitler, to seek an audience with Edward; and the duke soon reported back that Edward had told him: "An alliance [of] Germany-Britain is for him an urgent necessity and a guiding principle for British foreign policy." Furthermore, von Hoesch reported, the king's close friend, Sir Henry "Chips" Channon, had declared that Edward was "going the dictator way, and is pro-German, against Russia and against too much slipshod democracy. I shouldn't wonder if he aimed at making himself a mild dictator."[17]

When Adolf Hitler on March 7, 1936, launched his first military operation as Führer, one that he would call his "most daring undertaking," he would have already had those advices in hand. On that date, the German Army marched into a Rhineland that had been demilitarized by the provisions of the Treaty of Versailles, thereby providing a bridgehead for any subsequent campaign against France. "Nervously," Hitler's architect and later munitions minister, Albert Speer, would write, "Hitler waited for the first reactions [from Britain and France]." For, as Hitler told Speer, the German Army was no match even for the Polish Army, let alone the combined armies of Britain and France; if even the French alone took action, said Hitler, Germany would be defeated in a few days.[18]

France immediately called on Britain to join in mounting an expedition to eject the Germans, and the League of Nations and the Cabinets of both countries met in emergency session in an atmosphere of war crisis; but Prime Minister Baldwin advised the British Cabinet against intervention. Britain and France, said Baldwin, "might succeed in crushing Germany" but only "with the use of Russia," and that, he said, "would probably only result in Germany going Bolshevik."[19] Britain would not act, and without British support, neither would France.

That denouement would lead later to charges that Edward VIII personally intervened to prevent Britain from marching with France. Although the king's position in any political matter was limited constitutionally virtually to giving advice and signing papers and proclamations, the allegation gained some weight when a representative of the German News Agency, Fritz Hesse, recalled how the German ambassador, von Hoesch, waited during the crisis for a telephone call from the king. When the telephone rang, said Hesse, "Hoesch whispered to me: 'The King!' and handed the second receiver to me, so that I could listen to the conversation." The voice on the wire said: "'David speaking. Do you know who's speaking?'" To which von Hoesch replied: "'Of course I do.'" The voice continued: "'I sent for the Prime Minister and gave him a piece of my mind. I told the old so-and-so that I would abdicate if he made war. There was a frightful scene. But you needn't worry. There won't be a war.'" Putting down the receiver, von Hoesch "jumped up and danced around the room. 'I've done it! I've outwitted them all; there won't be a war! *Herr* Hesse, we've done it!'"[20]

Although some would later dispute Hesse's account, there was little doubt either that an exchange similar to that described by Hesse took place or that the king did exercise direct influence to prevent his government's using force in the Rhineland. The London correspondent for the *Berliner Tageblatt*, for example, telephoned his editor: "The King is taking an extraordinarily active part in the whole affair; he has caused a number of important people in the Government to come and see him and has said to them: 'This is a nice way to start my reign.' The King won't hear of there being a war . . . In view of the tremendous influence possessed by the King and his immense energy, due importance must be attached to this where Germany is concerned."[21]

Ambassador von Hoesch on March 11, 1936, telegraphed von Ribbentrop: "Today I got into direct touch with the Court [and] . . . there is understanding for the German point of view." He said that "the directive given to the Government" by the court was "to the effect that, no matter how the details of the affair are dealt with, complications of a serious nature are in no circumstances to be allowed to develop."[22]

It was also clear that Hitler himself saw Edward as a friendly intermediary, for as Speer would relate: "I can recall that in Hitler's entourage the peaceful conclusion was attributable to the influence of the King of England. 'At last!' exclaimed Hitler, 'The King of England will not intervene. He is keeping his promise. That means it can all go well.'"[23]

Prime Minister Baldwin and his government were markedly concerned by that and other instances of the king's intruding into foreign affairs. The government was kept fully informed of the king's liaison with the Germans through the Government Code and Cipher School, which was intercepting and decrypting German diplomatic cipher traffic;[24] and Foreign Secretary Eden later told the Czechoslovakian ambassador in London, Jan Masaryk, that the Foreign Office was "worried" over the king's "increasing and disturbing intervention in foreign affairs," and that if it continued, there were "ways and means of compelling him to abdicate."[25]

On October 30, 1936, King Edward VIII received the new German ambassador, von Ribbentrop, in a full-dress ceremony at Buckingham Palace, a gesture intended to impress and flatter, for no such ceremony had yet been accorded any other new ambassador during the king's brief reign. Soon thereafter, as von

Ribbentrop set about trying to cement cordial relations between the two countries, he called on Winston Churchill, whom he hoped he might count on as a member of the pro-Hitler faction in the Tory Party. To Churchill he outlined the terms of membership in the Anti-Comintern Pact, which Germany had recently concluded with Japan and Italy; Britain, he said, had but "to give Germany a free hand in the East of Europe," for Germany had to have *"Lebensraum,* or living space, for her increasing population." That meant incorporating Poland, White Russia, and the Ukraine in a Greater German Reich. "Nothing less," said von Ribbentrop, "would suffice." If Britain would promise not to interfere, Germany in turn "would stand guard for the British Empire in all its greatness and extent."[26]

Churchill responded emphatically that even though it was true that Britain "hated Communism as much as Hitler did," Britain, "would never disinterest herself in the fortunes of the Continent to an extent which would enable Germany to gain the domination of Central and Eastern Europe." "In that case," said von Ribbentrop sharply, "war is inevitable. There is no way out. The *Führer* is resolved. Nothing will stop him and nothing will stop us."

When Churchill reported the conversation to the Foreign Office, Foreign Secretary Eden took von Ribbentrop's words as nothing more than an empty threat. On the other hand, he felt compelled to try to ensure that the German ambassador would be prevented from influencing the king in favor of the German policy. The first step in doing that would be to get rid of Wallis Warfield Simpson.

## Chapter Forty-Nine

The confrontation between Ernest Simpson and King Edward VIII occurred in June 1936 in York House, the king's residence in St. James's. Mrs. Simpson, said her husband, would have to choose between them. Was Edward planning to marry his wife? Rising from his chair, the king declared: "Do you really think that I would be crowned without Wallis by my side?"[1]

Mrs. Simpson was quick to prepare the way. Filing for divorce, she charged her husband had committed adultery at a society hotel on the Thames at Bray in Berkshire, the Café de Paris, with Buttercup Kennedy. That done, she and the king set off on another yachting cruise in the Mediterranean, where they were careful to avoid some of their old haunts, for civil war had broken out in Spain, Italy had shocked the world by overrunning Ethiopia, and in France, where Léon Blum had established a Popular Front government, civil war threatened, and within sight of the palatial villas along the Côte d'Azur where the couple was wont to visit, red flags flew.

For long, Prime Minister Stanley Baldwin had tried to avoid involvement in his sovereign's private life; but when it appeared to be obvious that the king intended to marry Mrs. Simpson, he saw it his constitutional duty as the monarch's principal adviser to intervene. He conferred first with Anthony Eden, then with the archbishop of Canterbury, Cosmo Lang, who as Primate of All-England would have to crown Edward as king and, if he were married, Mrs. Simpson as queen. Lang would later record that "the thought of my having to consecrate *him* as King weighed on me as a heavy burden," for as he saw it, "the monarchy was being vulgarized and degraded, that mud was being thrown on sacred things."[2]

With other powerful voices joining Eden and Lang in urging the prime minister to act, Baldwin called on the king on October 21, 1936, at Fort Belvedere. Fatigued and highly nervous about his assignment, the prime minister fortified himself with a strong whiskey and soda, then reminded his sovereign of his duties and responsibilities. Fervent factions for and against the king, he warned, might emerge and crystallize at a time when international perils demanded a strong and trusted monarch as a unifying force for the nation and for the empire. In the hope that a separation might prompt the king to reconsider, he urged the king to ask Mrs. Simpson to leave the country for six months. Yet to all the prime minister's pleadings, Edward was adamant. Mrs. Simpson, he said, was for him "the only woman in the world, and I cannot live without her."[3] To the prime minister, the foreign secretary, the archbishop of Canterbury, the king's powerful private secretary, and to many others of the Privileged Bodies, there appeared to be at that point no recourse but to compel Edward to abdicate the throne, and that would precipitate a constitutional crisis without precedent in British history.

On November 13, 1936, Major Alexander Hardinge, the private secretary, wrote to Edward to warn of the "calamitous" situation that was arising. The government, wrote Hardinge, might resign, and "in view of the feeling prevalent among members of the House of Commons of all parties," the king might find it impossible to form a new government. In that case, Parliament would be dissolved and a general election called, in which the chief issue would be "Your Majesty's personal affairs." While many, noted Hardinge, might "sympathize with Your Majesty as an individual," they "would deeply resent the damage which would inevitably be done to the Crown, the corner-stone on which the whole empire rests." There was only one solution: "for Mrs. Simpson to go abroad *without further delay.*"[4]

A group of senior members of the government drafted an ultimatum that they pressed the prime minister to present to Edward. "Unless steps are taken promptly to allay the widespread and growing misgivings among the people," the draft noted, "the feelings of respect, esteem and affection which Your Majesty has evoked among them will disappear in a revulsion of so grave and perilous a character as possibly to threaten the stability of the nation and the Empire." There could be but one course: "namely to put an end to Your Majesty's association with Mrs. Simpson."[5]

Those officials obviously were concerned that at a time when the Comintern and its agents were trying to bring about the downfall of all monarchies, and with Hitler and Mussolini about to try new adventures while Britain was distracted,

Edward's conduct was subjecting the British imperial system to ridicule and contempt among the king's subjects at home and abroad. That was particularly apparent in India, where Edward's behavior was being interpreted by intensely moralistic religious leaders as evidence of the decadence of their masters. From Australia, the high commissioner, Stanley Bruce, informed the prime minister bluntly that "The people of this country and of the Dominions would not accept this woman as Queen"; he urged Baldwin to inform the king that if he persisted in his association with Mrs. Simpson, "there would be a demand for his abdication that he would find it impossible to resist."[6] From Singapore, the American consul reported "a very strong undercurrent of resentment over the whole matter"; as one newspaper put it, "while it is for the King to say who shall be his partner for life, it is for Parliament to decide who shall be Queen,"[7] but from Canada, the American ambassador, Norman Armour, reported that some newspapers were reflecting a widely held belief that the real issue was not the king's relationship with Mrs. Simpson but his admiration for Nazi Germany and Fascist Italy and the fact that he had "offended vested interests" by advocating social reforms.[8]

In mid-November 1936 at Fort Belvedere, Prime Minister Baldwin again called upon the king to break off his relationship with Mrs. Simpson. "The position of the King's wife," said Baldwin, "was different from the position of any other citizen in the country; it was part of the price which the King has to pay. His wife becomes Queen; the Queen becomes the Queen of the country; and, therefore, in the choice of a Queen, the voice of the people must be heard."[9]

Edward for a time stood silently. At length, in measured words, he declared: "I want you to be the first to know that I have made up my mind and nothing will alter it—I have looked at it from all sides—and I mean to abdicate and marry Mrs. Simpson."[10]

So it was. On December 10, 1936, in the presence of the three royal dukes, Edward VIII signed the Instrument of Abdication, and the crown, scepter, and orb passed to the Duke of York, who became King George VI.

Having undertaken to go into exile and to return to England only with the consent of the king and the government of the day, Edward addressed the nation over the BBC: "A few hours ago," he said, "I discharged my last duty as King and Emperor, and now that I have been succeeded by my brother, the Duke of York, my first words must be to declare my allegiance to him. This I do with all my heart." He explained that "you must believe me when I tell you that I have found it impossible to carry the heavy burden of responsibility and to discharge my duties as King as I would wish to do without the help and support of the woman I love." He concluded: "And now we all have a new King. I wish him, and you, his people, happiness and prosperity with all my heart. God bless you. God save the King."[11]

The same evening, the man known at that point as His Royal Highness, Prince Edward, Duke of Windsor, left Fort Belvedere for the last time, for Austria, where he would wait out the remainder of the six months until Mrs. Simpson's divorce decree became final, during which time, by requirement of British law, he was not to see her. As he departed, the archbishop of Canterbury noted: "From God he had received a high and sacred trust. . . . Yet by his own will he has abdicated— he has surrendered the trust." His motive: "a craving for private happiness. Strange and sad it must be that for such a motive, however strongly it pressed upon his heart, he should have disappointed hopes so high and abandoned a trust so great."[12]

The lords spiritual had passed judgment: it was the turn of the lords temporal. In an age when Fascists and Communists alike were proclaiming the dynamics of their systems, when Stakhanovites, Brown Shirts, Black Shirts, Silver Shirts were massing, the head of the world's mightiest democracy—as Britain then considered itself to be—had shown himself to be without spiritual stamina and without sense of personal sacrifice. As Stanley Baldwin would put it: "I have never in my life met anyone so completely lacking in any sense of the—the—well, what is *beyond*. And he kept on repeating over and over again: 'I can't do my job without her—I am going to marry her, and I will *go*.' There was simply no moral struggle. It appalled me."[13]

What the lasting effect of Edward's bewitchment would be, remained to be seen. An American diplomat reporting from the West Country of England thought that "the crisis will pass over quietly and eventually be forgotten. The Kings of England will reign for more than one generation to come—they are the very life of the people."[14] Prime Minister Baldwin was less sure. In a private moment shortly before his death, he remarked that Edward had done Britain more harm than any king in its history.

In any event, the omen of the broken crown had come to pass. Although the government hoped fervently that the affair was at an end, that no more would be heard from the fallen monarch, that was not to be.

On June 3, 1937, at the Château de Cande, near Touraine in the valley of the Loire, the woman who would have been queen married the man who only briefly had been king. To at least one observer, the ceremony was marked by Mrs. Simpson's coldness: "The effect is of a woman unmoved by the infatuated love of a younger man," wrote the duke's friend, Major Edward "Fruity" Metcalfe, to his wife. "Let's hope that she lets up in private with him, otherwise it must be grim."[15]

The man whose château served as the wedding site, a millionaire French-American Fascist, Charles Bedaux, was "one of those strange manic types who appear from time to time on the financial or industrial scene, make a large fortune and a brilliant reputation very quickly, and end, as often as not, in trouble."[16] Although the Duke of Windsor met Bedaux only upon arrival at the Château de Cande, the two soon became friends. When Edward expressed an interest in surveying labor conditions in Germany, Bedaux offered to arrange the trip. What he failed to tell the duke was that he himself had had a business enterprise in Germany, which the Nazis had forced him to close. Since that time, Bedaux had worked for approval to reconstitute his business, and in the summer of 1937, in the wake of the publicity he had enjoyed as host to the Windsor wedding, he had succeeded. For a price. He would have to put up $50,000 in American currency, $30,000 of which would go into coffers of the Nazi Party, and he would have to give a cut of any profits to a prominent German labor leader, Dr. Robert Ley.

Charles Bedaux saw two ways by which he might benefit from association with the Duke of Windsor. In a view shared by many others at the time, he had become convinced that the duke would in time become a factor in British politics, which could put Bedaux in an enviable position. Meanwhile, by accompanying the duke to Germany under the auspices of Dr. Ley, he might capitalize on the delight of the Nazis in embarrassing the British government and obtain a lessening of the restrictions Hitler's government had imposed on his reestablishing his business.

As Bedaux anticipated, the British government was upset even by the prospect of the Duke of Windsor visiting Germany. Although many within the British establishment still favored joining Germany in the Anti-Comintern Pact, the government opposed Hitler without condition. Lord Beaverbrook flew to Paris to advise the duke to have nothing to do either with Germany or with Bedaux, but the duke and his duchess went ahead with their plans, arriving by train at the Friedrichstrasse Station in Berlin on October 11, 1937. The platform and the red carpet were crowded with Nazi eminences, including Dr. Ley. Yet only a junior representative of the British Embassy was among them; he bore a letter noting that the ambassador, Sir Nevile Henderson, had been "unexpectedly" called away from Berlin.

Although the duchess would maintain later that Bedaux had assured the duke that the tour would be private, the German propaganda minister, Dr. Goebbels, from the first turned the duke's visits to farms, factories, hospitals, and housing developments into what looked to be an endorsement of the Nazi Party. However the duke himself viewed his visit, the Nazi officials saw him as the one man who could arrange an alliance between Britain and Germany.

He was entertained lavishly: by Dr. Goebbels; by the chief of the Gestapo and founder of the SS, Heinrich Himmler; by the deputy Führer, Rudolf Hess; and by Hermann Göring. In Nüremberg, the Duke of Coburg feted the couple at a gala dinner in the house of a leader of the Nazi Party, Julius Streicher. Ceremonial troops of the Nazi Praetorian Guard, the SS, provided military honors befitting a British royal duke and field marshal. On at least two occasions, the duke gave the stiff-armed Nazi salute, once on the last day of his visit when he and the duchess went to meet Hitler at his residence at Berchtesgaden.

Hitler's interpreter, Paul Schmidt, would later note that in the course of the meeting, the Duke of Windsor avoided politics and ideology. "There was nothing whatever to indicate whether the Duke of Windsor really sympathized with the ideology and practices of the Third Reich, as Hitler seemed to assume he did." He did have "some appreciative words for the measures taken in Germany in the field of social welfare," but other than that, the "duke was noncommital." [17]

A correspondent covering the duke's tour for the New York *Times* saw Edward's behavior differently. The duke's decision to visit Germany, wrote the *Times*, and "his gestures and remarks" had "demonstrated adequately that the Abdication did rob Germany of a firm friend, if not indeed a devoted admirer, on the British throne. He has lent himself, perhaps unconsciously but easily, to National Socialist propaganda." He was reported, said the *Times*, "to have become very critical of English politics" and viewed "British ministers of today and their possible successors" as "no match for the German or Italian dictators." [18]

Hitler regarded the abdication of Edward VIII as one of his most serious political defeats. "I am certain that through him permanent friendly relations with England could have been achieved," he told his confidant, Albert Speer. "If he had stayed, everything would have been different." [19]

The man whose tactical specialty was suborning the weak links in aristocracy, Joachim von Ribbentrop, the new ambassador in London, had little hope of penetrating the court of the new monarch, George VI; nor was there hope of influencing the monarch through his queen, Elizabeth, whose family constituted a deeply entrenched tree of dukes' relatives, directors, bankers, and clergymen who regarded von Ribbentrop as a social interloper. Yet there were still powerful individuals in the aristocracy, the ruling class, and in the House of Parliament who might be relied upon to swing Britain behind the Anti-Comintern Pact that Hitler desired so fervently as a precursor to war with the Soviet Union. Indicative of the attitude of that group was that of the former prime minister, David Lloyd George, age seventy-three, who after calling on Hitler on September 5, 1936, declared that he was "the greatest German of the age," a man who had restored Germany's honor and made the world acknowledge "her equality of rights." [20]

Within the right wing of the Conservative Party, the prevailing attitude was still that Stalin, not Hitler, was mankind's greatest enemy; and to give effect to that belief, a number of powerful and influential right-wingers had formed pro-Fascist organizations, of which the most prominent was the Anglo-German Fellowship, which the Duke of Saxe-Coburg-Gotha headed. The first annual report of the Anglo-German Fellowship noted that "the work of the Fellowship is divorced from party politics; its principal purpose is to promote fellowship between the two peoples, but however much such a purpose is non-political, its fulfillment must inevitably have important consequences on policy." The secretary of the fellowship, Elwin Wright, put it more directly: "It isn't numbers that matter. We want 'names,' otherwise how can we have any influence with the Government or the Foreign Office?" [21]

There were names to be had, starting with the Marquess of Londonderry, Sir Charles Stewart Henry Vane-Tempest-Stewart, who was related by blood, marriage, money, or politics to almost the entire aristocracy. Lord Londonderry's family had developed a reputation for having been in the forefront of resistance to every western revolution of note: the American, the French, the Russian; and few found it surprising that he was a guest of Hermann Göring in Germany, that von Ribbentrop was a guest at the family seat, Mount Stewart in County Down, and that one of his closest associates in the Anglo-German Fellowship was the Duke of Saxe-Coburg-Gotha. On every anniversary of Hitler's coming to power, London-derry sent his congratulations.

Among other names in the fellowship were: Lord Mount Temple, a brother-in-law of Lord Louis Mountbatten; Lord Redesdale, father of Unity Mitford, an intimate of Hitler's; the Earls of Airlie and Malmesbury, former lords-in-waiting to King George V; the Marquess of Carisbrooke, a grandson of Queen Victoria; the Marquess of Lothian, a former secretary to Lloyd George and a subsequent ambassador to the United States; the Duke of Wellington, the descendant of the British general who defeated Napoleon at Waterloo. Twenty-nine prominent Tory members of Parliament also belonged, as did the directors of almost all the major British banks, almost all the major insurance companies, and various railway and industrial companies.

Time after time members of the fellowship made unbridled pro-Fascist public statements. In speaking of the war in Ethiopia, for example, Lord Mottistone called the Ethiopians "bloodthirsty tyrants," the Italians, "the honourable and humane army." Lord Esher saw the Japanese invasion of China as a logical search for "a large trading area." Sir Arnold Wilson, Captain Victor Cazalet, Sir Henry Page Croft, and Captain A. H. M. Ramsay, all members of Parliament, praised the Fascist leader in Spain, Francisco Franco, for such feats as "leading a crusade for all that we in England hold dear." Sir Thomas Moore warned that if Britain should isolate Germany and discredit Hitler, the German people would "seek another God . . . [and] there is only one, the anti-Christ of Communism."

Some members of the fellowship, such as Lord Londonderry and Lord Mount Temple, and some acolytes, such as Lord Halifax, who was soon to replace Anthony Eden as foreign secretary, visited Germany as guests of the state. They hunted the chamois with Reichsführer-SS Himmler, the deer with Field Marshal Göring, or attended concerts with Hitler himself.

It was inevitable that the activities of the fellowship would in time provoke the attention of the police and intelligence authorities. The home secretary soon authorized the Special Branch of Scotland Yard to open a file on the organization, while Admiral Sir Hugh Sinclair's British Secret Intelligence Service also began to keep an eye on the members, even though Sir Hugh himself was not wholly without sympathy for some of the fellowship's views. Nor was there any inclination on the part of the service to upset existing intelligence contacts with the Germans, such as that between Squadron Leader Frederick W. Winter-botham, who had struck up a fruitful relationship with the German foreign minister, Alfred Rosenberg, entertained him, and introduced him to many of the members of the anti-Soviet coterie in British society.[22]

Behind the fellowship stood an organization called the Link, of which the chairman was Admiral Sir Barry Domville, a newly retired naval officer with a powerful influence in that most influential of all British lobbies, the Admiralty; he was married into a leading German family, von der Heydt, which had close connections with the German General Staff. The vice-chairman was Professor Sir Charles Raymond Beazley, historian, geographer, vice-president of the Royal Historical Society, and a member of the council of the Royal Geographic Society. The Link's journal, the *Anglo-German Review*, which existed primarily to influence Parliament, was consistently pro-Fascist and pro-Nazi, was heavily subsidized by German advertisers, and was thought to receive funds from the Nazi Party's secret foreign intelligence service, the Sicherheitsdienst; and, indeed, Admiral Domvile would later be arrested under the Defense of the Realm Act largely because of having been founder and chairman of the Link. The organization's activities became particularly suspect when in mid-1936 an associate of the Link and a member of the Anglo-German Fellowship, Douglas Jerrold, was identified as a central figure in opening events of the Spanish Civil War, which would provide the first active battlefield pitting forces of Nazi Germany against those of Soviet Russia.

## Chapter Fifty

On Thursday afternoon, July 9, 1936, Luis Bolin, the London correspondent of a Spanish Monarchist newspaper, *ABC*, approached Olley Airways, a small charter company at Croydon Airport in the London suburbs. He wanted, said Bolin, to charter a Rapide twin-engine biplane to fly him and a group of friends to the Canaries, a group of seven islands off the Atlantic coast of Spanish Morocco, for a holiday. What he actually intended was to fly to the Canaries to pick up a Spanish staff officer, General Francisco Franco y Bahamonde, and transport him to Tetuán, the capital of Spanish Morocco, where Franco was to seize command of the Spanish Army of Africa and lead it in a revolution of the Spanish right against the leftist government in Madrid.

As the pilot of the Rapide lifted off from Croydon Airport on July 11, 1936—it was a Saturday, when British airport authorities were less vigilant than usual—aboard the aircraft in addition to Bolin were four Britons: Major Hugh B. C. Pollard, a retired officer with connections to the intelligence branch of the Imperial General Staff at the War Office; Douglas Jerrold, chairman of a London publishing company, Eyre and Spottiswoode, who had been connected with British naval intelligence during the World War at Gallipoli and in France; and two striking blonde women, who were apparently along to give verisimilitude to the cover of going for a holiday in the Canaries.

Although the nature of Jerrold's and Pollard's connection with Bolin would not be defined, there could be no question that Bolin was involved in the Franco conspiracy, for in chartering the aircraft, he had received his authority, orders, and finance from his editor, Luca de Tena, a prominent figure in the plot, who received his orders from a colonel in the Spanish Air Force, Alfredo Kindelan, who was closely associated with the ringleaders. There would also be evidence that the foreign intelligence services of Germany and Italy were aware in advance of the plans for the uprising, and there would be speculation that Jerrold, Pollard, and the Link acted as intermediaries for the Spanish conspirators and the Germans in obtaining the charter from Olley Airways. Whatever the truth, the Rapide did, indeed, collect Franco in the Canaries and fly him to Spanish Morocco, where he assumed command of the Army of Africa and broadcast the radio signal for the start of the rebellion: "A cloudless sky hangs over all of Spain."

Beginning with the end of the World War, Spain had become a political caldron. In hope of preventing civil war, King Alfonso XIII had left the country in 1931, and a series of unstable governments had followed, culminating early in 1936 with victory at the polls by a leftist coalition calling itself a Popular Front with the liberal Republican Party constituting the largest contingent. Yet the victory was by the narrowest of margins, some of the parties that had helped form the Popular Front refused to participate in this government, and a form of anarchy racked the country. Spain had become perilously polarized: on the right, the aristocracy, the Catholic church, a powerful plutocracy, an ancient oligarchy, a fearful bourgeoisie, the military, and a miasma of Fascism; on the left, the intellectuals, the proletariat, the trade unions, Socialists of many persuasions including revolutionaries, a small but cohesive Communist Party, and a miasma of Communism. To confuse the political spectrum further, there were lesser groups of Trotskyites, Anarchists, Syndicalists, Freethinkers, Freemasons, tribal and religious groups, and secession-minded Catalans and Basques. As the left feared Fascism, so the right feared what the Socialist leader Francisco Largo Caballero called a dictatorship of the proletariat. It was soon evident that power in the state would eventually pass to the side strong enough to seize and maintain it.

The impending tragedy in Spain was made the more inevitable by the ideological warfare between Nazis and Communists with an assist from the immense concern of Britain and France about what the outcome might be, whichever the direction. A Fascist government in Spain allied with Hitler and Mussolini sitting virtually atop the fortress of Gibraltar, the entry point to the Mediterranean through which ran Britain's links to the empire? A Fascist government in Spain constituting for France a Fascist state on yet a third frontier? On the other hand, a Communist state in Western Europe with a window on the Atlantic? Yet whatever the concerns, with Franco's radio message of July 17, 1936, Spain exploded.

Public reaction in Britain to the outbreak of war was passionate but sharply divided. "General Franco," declared Captain A. H. M. Ramsay, the Tory Member of Parliament for Peebles, Scotland, and a member of the Link, "is fighting the cause of Christianity against the Anti-Christ."[1] On the other side, the Labour Party swiftly passed a resolution pledging "all practical support" for the Republicans; Spain, declared the poet Stephen Spender, "offered the twentieth century an 1848."[2]

Yet no politician was prepared to buck the strong pacifist sentiment in the country to urge intervention on behalf of either side. As Winston Churchill had put it, the supreme object of British policy should be to avoid going to war. Aware that representatives of both sides were already touring the European capitals trying to line up support, Foreign Secretary Eden began to press his counterparts in the other capitals to agree to a policy of nonintervention in order to keep the conflict confined to the Iberian Peninsula. He would run into opposition in France, where the leftist government of Léon Blum's Popular Front was anxious to help the Republicans, but there was a way to handle that: if France failed immediately to ban sending war materials to Spain, the British ambassador in Paris, Sir George Clark, told the Blum government, and Germany should attack France in retaliation, Britain would consider its obligations to aid France under the Treaty of Locarno to be absolved.

France in the end took the lead in negotiating a treaty of nonintervention. Just about everybody agreed to it; across the seas even the Roosevelt administration, while strongly favoring the Republicans, proclaimed that the United States, too, would pursue a policy of nonintervention.

As would soon develop, the agreement was worth little except that in the end it would have the effect of confining the war to Spain and postponing another general world war, for few of the powers would enforce either the spirit or the letter of the agreement. Indeed, even as negotiations to reach a nonintervention agreement were under way, several countries had already made their commitments.

On the evening of July 25, 1936, Adolf Hitler was in Bavaria, in an ecstatic mood after listening in the course of the annual Wagner festival to a part of *Der Ring des Nibelungen,* at the Festspielhaus in Bayreuth. When couriers arrived with a letter from Franco asking help in Spain, Hitler saw every reason to respond favorably. His old enemy, France, had signed an alliance with the Soviet Union plainly directed at confronting Germany with a united opposition on two fronts; the French electorate had installed a Popular Front government that might in time propel the country into the Soviet orbit; and the French government had built powerful fortifications fronting Germany, the Maginot Line. When the time came to move eastward to gain *Lebensraum,* that situation at his rear would be intolerable.

Almost in a flash, the Spanish Civil War had provided a means to further his ends. If, with the help of Mussolini, he could prevent Russia from establishing a client state in Spain and instead establish a Fascist state, it would be France, not Germany, that would be confronted with enemies on two (even three) sides, compelling France to divert military forces to its southwestern frontier, and Germany, not Russia, would sit astride Britain's communications with its vast empire. Directives were soon on the way to Hermann Göring of the Air Force and Werner von Blomberg of the Army to give Franco all reasonable help.

Göring promptly dispatched several squadrons of Junkers 52 troop transports to airlift Franco's Riff Legionnaires from Tetuán to the mainland, and other help soon followed: a hundred fighter-bombers in what was called the Kondor Legion and some of the latest German tanks and cannon, including the 88 mm multipurpose gun that was to prove to be the workhorse of German field pieces in World War II. Mussolini in the meantime prepared and later sent an expeditionary force of 50,000 men equipped with artillery and light tanks.

When the Socialist leader, Largo Caballero appealed to Russia for help for the Republicans, Stalin moved with caution. Far from being a product of Comintern intrigue, the civil war in Spain was for Stalin in some ways an embarrassment. The lines between left and right were so clearly drawn in Spain as to be difficult for Stalin to ignore, and when both Hitler and Mussolini appeared to be ready to aid Franco, the embarrassment increased. Yet Stalin was a firm believer in Lenin's dictum: "Accept all the obligations that are demanded of us, but when the hour of decision sounds, do not forget that the honor of a communist consists in not fulfilling them except in the measures in which they answer to the interests of the proletariat." For Stalin, the proletariat had come to mean the Soviet state, so that when on July 26, 1936—the day after Franco's messengers reached Hitler at Bayreuth—the Comintern's Executive Committee convened secretly in Prague with Soviet military and diplomatic officials, the decisions that would emerge would reflect less the agony of the Spanish proletariat than the realpolitik of the Kremlin:

Since the Red Army was not yet strong enough to protect Russia against Germany, the Comintern would do nothing in Spain that might provoke a German attack on Russia.

At the same time, Franco could not be allowed to win, for that would confront France with Fascist enemies on three sides, which might encourage Germany to attack Russia without fear of French attack from the rear.

So, too, victory by the Spanish Communists was, for the moment, not to be countenanced, for that might prompt Britain and France to make common cause with Germany and Italy against Russia.

On the other hand, Russia had to provide enough help to keep the Spanish Communists from losing, so that the war would continue until such time as Russia might turn it to advantage, perhaps in time to provoke a general European war that would leave the Western European nations exhausted and impotent and Russia the dominant power on the Continent.

After frequent and lengthy telegraphic conversations with Stalin, the Executive Committee determined to supply the Madrid government with enough food, raw materials, and medical supplies to sustain the fight, but with an eye both to

Germany and the western democracies, the aid was to be provided not by the Soviet government directly but by the Comintern and by the Russian trade unions, whose members would pay for the supplies by subscribing a billion rubles from their paychecks. Not until a little over two months later did Stalin agree to provide arms and ammunition and even then he made it a cash-and-carry proposition, providing only such munitions as the Spaniards were able to pay for and again under the aegis of the Comintern. The Red Army would send not fighting men but "observers"—with strict orders to avoid capture—and in conjunction with the Comintern, the Soviet diplomatic service would establish a "general staff" to "guide" the Spanish government and assure that Madrid did nothing that might involve Russia in a confrontation with either the Fascist or the democratic powers.

The Comintern's contribution to the General Staff was impressive: the head of the Italian Communist Party, Palmiro Togliatti, who was a member of the Comintern's Presidium and head of the Secretariat for Western Europe; a leading member of the French party, Jacques Duclos, who was a member of the Comintern's Executive Committee; a former head of the Italian bureau of the American party and founder of the Communist newspaper in Chicago, *Il Lavoratore*, Vittorio Vidali, alias Carlos Contreras; and a sinister and ruthless Ernö Gerö, who had served in Béla Kun's government of the glorious light, was at the time a Comintern organizer in France, and would later become interior minister in Hungary.

The General Staff operated primarily outside Spain. Inside the country, a political and military mission functioned under the overall direction of a new ambassador, the former Soviet ambassador in London, Marcel Rosenberg. Heading the military mission was the former chief of the Soviet military intelligence service, General Jan Berzin, an expert in clandestine supply and underground revolutionary warfare. To Spain's second city, Barcelona, went V. A. Antonov-Ovseenko, who had led the Red Guard that captured the Winter Palace during the October Revolution, and a large staff that included an officer of the NKVD, Artur Stashevsky, charged with disciplining the Spanish trade unions and getting the port working to receive Soviet supplies.

Settling into the Gaylord Hotel in a parklike setting in Madrid, Rosenberg and his staff soon controlled almost every function of the Spanish government. Either Rosenberg's men or their Spanish nominees filled the key posts in the Army, Navy, Air Force, police, and supply and communications systems, and they created a Spanish secret police force with its own staff of agents, interrogators, and executioners. A man of advanced years, Largo Caballero would nevertheless continue to resist Rosenberg's more dictatorial demands but with an underlying realization that when the Russians chose, they would find a way of getting rid of him.

Close on the decision to assist the Republicans in Spain, the Comintern embarked on a campaign to enlist volunteers throughout the western world to fight in International Brigades in Spain under the slogan: "Spain shall be the grave of European Fascism."[3] The call in time produced a movement among young Communists, Socialists, liberals, idealists, and freethinkers as filled with passion as were the crusades of the European Christians between the eleventh and fourteenth centuries to recover the Holy Land from Islam, and those 40,000 men who in time responded saw the cause in much the same terms: a campaign by the forces of light and decency against those of darkness and evil, a fight not for a nation but for an ideal. W. H. Auden, who himself served briefly in Spain in an ambulance unit, captured the spirit of it:

> Many have heard it on remote peninsulas,
> On sleepy plains, in the aberrant fishermen's islands
>   Or the corrupt heart of a city,
> Have heard and migrated like gulls or the seeds of a flower.
>
> They clung like burrs to the long expresses that lurch
> Through the unjust lands, through the night, through
>   the alpine tunnel;
>     They floated over the oceans;
> They walked the passes: they came to present their lives.

The volunteers came from almost every western nation but none from the Soviet Union, which by a decree of February 20, 1937, prohibited Russians from volunteering. Yet it was the Comintern that commanded the movement: a Comintern agent known by the party name of Tito received the men in Paris and arranged their passage to Spain; the Comintern provided the arms, money, food; the Comintern through a system of political commissars gave the orders; and the Comintern in most cases even named the battalions making up the seven brigades, usually after Communist heroes of fact or myth.

Although perhaps as many as a fourth of the men were French, they represented all together fifty-three nationalities. The first, who arrived in time to help stop Franco's forces before Madrid in November 1936, would be characterized by a Hungarian Communist writer, Sandor Voros, as "the multitudes found in every society since the dawn of history, who were born to the dry teat and destined for the bottom of the heap."[4] Yet other segments of society also contributed: among 3,000 Americans, for example, almost every major college and university was represented, and there was at least one member of the European aristocracy in the person of Esmond Romilly, son of a colonel of the Scots Guards and the Egyptian Camel Corps, and a nephew of Winston Churchill.

Among the volunteers, approximately 60 percent were Communists, and another 20 percent—of those that survived; 60 percent died—would eventually become Communists. For every volunteer there were hundreds of thousands of sympathizers who failed to heed the martial call but nevertheless worked actively for the cause: made speeches, wrote articles, gave or collected money, sent ambulances and medical supplies. With the active support of the Comintern, Communist front organizations sprang up everywhere, particularly in Britain and the United States, dedicated to the saving of the Spanish Republic. Support was particularly strong among intellectuals: academics, scientists, the literati. Ernest Hemingway wrote a play sympathetic to the Republican cause, *The Fifth Column*, even as Nationalist artillery was bombarding Madrid and scoring thirty-two hits on his hotel, the Florida, as well as a best-selling novel, *For Whom the Bell Tolls*.

When Stalin in early fall of 1936 made the decision to begin providing arms and munitions for the Republicans, he also intensified the work in Spain of the NKVD. To assist in that assignment, a new head of the NKVD, Nikolai Yeshov, had the services of an agent with impressive credentials, General Walter G. Krivitsky, born Samuel Ginzburg in the Western Ukraine, who at the time was operating as chief of Soviet military intelligence in Western Europe. Despite an impressive record as a revolutionary, Krivitsky, according to one of his agents, Paul Wohl, was "not a ruthless fanatic, not an underground leader"; he was instead "a sensitive, nervous intellectual" whose career had brought him into contact both with Russia and Western Europe, a man "who knew both worlds: the walled-up, one-purpose world of the communist militants and the vacillating, capricious world of personal venture and ambition." At the age of seventeen, he had walked into the October Revolution "like young girls into the month of May," had "leaped to the sacrifice" like the French Jacobins or the German Anabaptists";[5] but unknown to the Kremlin, Krivitsky by 1936 was beginning to have second thoughts because of two profound disappointments with the cause: Lenin's New Economic Policy that followed the Kronstadt Rebellion and Stalin's treatment of Trotsky and his supporters. Walter Krivitsky was close to becoming an apostate.

Yet that point was still to be reached when in August 1936 he received a message from Moscow: "Extend your operations immediately to cover the Spanish Civil War. Mobilize all available agents and facilities for prompt creation of a system to purchase and transport arms to Spain."[6] Krivitsky began immediately to establish business houses in all the capitals of Europe to be used to purchase arms and send them to Spain, thereby concealing the fact that Russia was behind the venture. In every case an agent of the NKVD was "a silent partner," who "furnished the funds and controlled all transactions."[7]

There was no true generosity or altruism behind the Russian support, for Moscow made sure that all credits to the government in Madrid were secured by the gold reserves in the Spanish national treasury. That assignment fell to an adviser to the Spanish government on matters pertaining to intelligence, counterintelligence, and guerrilla warfare, General Alexander Orlov, an official of the NKVD. At a time when it appeared that Franco would seize Madrid, Orlov on October 20, 1936, received a telegram from Yeshov with instructions from Stalin directing him to "arrange with the head of the Spanish government, Caballero, for the shipment of the gold reserves of Spain to the Soviet Union," an operation to "be carried out with the utmost secrecy." If Largo Caballero demanded a receipt, said Stalin's instructions, Orlov was to refuse. "I repeat, refuse to sign anything, and say that a formal receipt will be issued in Moscow by the State Bank."[8]

Orlov approached the Spanish finance minister, Juan Negrín. While stressing that the transfer of the gold would be only for safekeeping, he urged secrecy for fear that the transaction might set off "a tremendous political scandal all over the world, and it might even create an internal revolution."[9] After consulting with Largo Caballero, Negrín approved the transfer, and some 7,900 crates of gold, each weighing 125 pounds, were soon loaded aboard four Soviet freighters at the Mediterranean port of Cartagena, the loading done at night by recently arrived Soviet tank crews. The total amount was 510 metric tons, representing a total value at 1936 rates of $600 to $700 million.

When the crates were unloaded at Odessa, a hundred were found to be missing, which Orlov assumed that Stalin sequestered to pay for "some Comintern work or for something else." According to Orlov, once the gold was safely in Moscow, Stalin declared that "The Spaniards will never see their gold again."[10] Yet, years later, when the story of the transfer of the gold came to light, Moscow Radio announced that the gold was intended all along as payment for Soviet arms delivered to the Spanish Republican government, which "frequently asked the Soviet Central State Bank to make payments abroad from it. The payments became so frequent that the money soon was all gone."[11]

The gold was worth, said Moscow Radio, $420 million. For it, the Spaniards received from Russian arsenals, according to Soviet figures, 250 aircraft, 731 tanks, 1,386 trucks, 69,200 tons of war materials, 29,125 tons of ammunition, some 500 howitzers, 32,278 tons of crude oil, 4,650 tons of lubricants, 187 tractors, uncountable assignments of individual arms and ammunition, and the services of 920 advisers. In addition, the Comintern purchased large amounts of arms and munitions from other than Russian sources (some of which was defective, fed to Krivitsky's purchasing organizations by the German and Italian intelligence services). The Spanish Republican government, said the Kremlin, still owed Russia some $57 million.

As Stalin's ideological conflict with Trotsky made a harsh and indelible imprint on Communists and their activities throughout the world, so it intruded on the conflict in Spain. There the NKVD used the war as an excuse to wage its own war against what it maintained was a strong Trotskyite movement. The order went out through the medium of the Comintern's Executive Committee: since the Trotskyites, "in the interests of Fascism, are carrying on subversion in the rear of the republican troops, the Presidium approves the policy of the party of the complete and final destruction of Trotskyism in Spain as essential to the victory over Fascism."[12] It was a license for murder.

It was no true anti-Trotskyite campaign, for, in reality, Trotskyites in Spain were few; Stalin was really out to eliminate the Partido Obrero de Unificación

Marxista, or the POUM, an alliance of Revolutionary Socialists, Anarchists, and Syndicalists opposed to Communist methods. From time to time, the head of the Comintern's mission, Ambassador Rosenberg, had informed Prime Minister Largo Caballero that the POUM had to be liquidated, but Largo Caballero, in one of his courageous acts of defiance, had consistently refused. In early 1937, Rosenberg informed Jesús Hernández, one of two Communists in Largo Caballero's Cabinet, that the Soviet mission would provide an alternative method to get rid of the POUM: the NKVD would stage a provocation, and if Largo Caballero refused to go along, he would be replaced as head of the government.

The scene of the provocation was to be Barcelona, the capital of Catalonia, a nation-state in Northeastern Spain which had a history dating from the fifteenth century of rejection of outside rule, which had obtained autonomy in the early 1930s, but which had been caught up in the struggle against Franco. Catalonia, and especially Barcelona, was the stronghold of the POUM.

On May 3, 1937, a subservient Spanish Communist whom the Comintern's mission had intruded into the leadership of the Catalan police, Rodríguez Sala, seized the Barcelona telephone exchange from Anarchist-Syndicalist trade unions that had controlled it since the war began. The noncommunist leftists, including members of the POUM, fought back. For four days fighting raged in the port city, ending only when platoons of Comintern-advised police were brought in from outside Catalonia. Pointing to the fighting in Barcelona as an example of the opposition of the POUM to the government, the two Communist ministers in the Cabinet demanded that the POUM be suppressed and Socialists and Communists merged into a single party.

Largo Caballero adamantly refused, but it would be his last refusal. Unless he resigned, Rosenberg told him, in favor of his finance minister, Negrín, whom the NKVD's man in Barcelona, Stashevsky, had been carefully cultivating, the Spanish Communist Party would withdraw its support from the government, which might bring the government down, and Russian aid would cease, which would mean that the war would be lost.

When the aging premier at last backed down and resigned, the Comintern was at that point in full control of the Spanish government. The POUM was outlawed and a campaign to exterminate its members as alleged Trotskyites began. Squads of killers, constituting in a way another international brigade consisting mainly of Germans and Italians but including some recruited from among the goon squads of the waterfronts of New York and other east coast American ports, began a campaign of systematic murder, a war within the civil war. The head of the POUM, Andrés Nin, former secretary of the Red Trades Union International in Moscow, was arrested, accused of being Hitler's personal spy and a British secret agent, subjected to cruel interrogation that left his face "no more than a formless mass,"[13] and when he still refused to confess, was executed by ten Germans manning machine guns. On the orders of the head of the NKVD in Spain, Alexander Orlov, forty members of the POUM's Executive Committee were arrested and disappeared. Hundreds, perhaps thousands, were murdered or briefly imprisoned and then executed, including some members of the International Brigades, for the NKVD carried its purge to deviationists in the ranks of the foreign troops.

In time, as Hitler and Mussolini poured aid to Franco's forces in amounts that Stalin was unwilling to match and a Fascist victory became inevitable, Stalin lost interest in the war in Spain, and the executioners became in turn new victims. Stalin had sent many of them to Spain in the first place to get them out of the way while he conducted his vast purges of the politicians and the military, and an inhospitable reception awaited them on their return. The Kremlin accused almost all senior officials who served in Spain of being Trotskyites, spies, saboteurs, or agents-provocateur for Hitler and Mussolini. The head of the Comintern's commission, Ambassador Rosenberg; the senior military official, General Berzin; the Comintern's man in Barcelona, Antonov-Ovseenko, who long years before had stood up in defense of Leon Trotsky—those and others simply vanished. Alexander Orlov escaped by defecting to the United States. Even those Spanish Communists who fled to find sanctuary in the Soviet Union, while welcomed at first as heroes, were in time banished to labor camps. In the case of General Valentín Gonzáles, a Communist hero known as El Campesino, he found himself subjected to brutal interrogation and imprisonment and for long dug earth for the Moscow subway before being banished to a labor camp, and the secretary-general of the Spanish Communist Party, José Díaz, died in Moscow when he either jumped or was pushed from an upper-story window.

# PART IX

## The German Station

---

## Chapter Fifty-One

After Hitler came to power in 1933, the Sturmabteilung raided the Soviet trade mission at 14 Lindenstrasse and arrested several Soviet commercial officials on suspicion of espionage and subversion. That raid and Hitler's quick decimation of the German Communist Party brought an end to the Spirit of Rapallo that for over a decade had sustained—however shakily—Russo-German relations. Yet Hitler still extended the hand of friendship. "The fight against Communism in Germany," he declared before the Reichstag, "is our internal affair in which we will never permit interference from outside." On the other hand, he added, "Our political relations with other powers to whom we are bound by common interests will not be affected thereby." His government, he said, was "ready to cultivate with the Soviet Union friendly relations profitable to both parties."[1]

Hitler gave substance to his words by extending the Berlin Treaty of 1926 and the conciliation convention of 1929, but that did little to lessen the Kremlin's concern for his real objective. It was Hitler's plan, the Comintern warned its adherents on May 14, 1933, to negotiate an alliance with Britain and Italy against the USSR with the purpose of turning European Russia "into a 'bourgeois' state under the aegis of Germany" and opening Siberia "for German colonization and enterprise."[2] Like Hitler, representatives of the Kremlin nevertheless spoke in conciliatory terms. Noted the current head of the Comintern, Vyacheslav Molotov, speaking as a vice-commissar of the Foreign Commissariat, "Of course we sympathize with the sufferings of our German comrades, but we as Marxists are the last who can be reproached with allowing sentiment to prevail over policy. The entire world knows that we can and do maintain good relations with Capitalist States, whatever their regime, even if it is fascist."[3]

In practice, relations steadily deteriorated. Although commercial interchange continued, military collaboration began to dwindle as early as the late months of 1933, and by 1935 it had ceased altogether, including joint manufacture of aircraft and weapons. That upset the vice-commissar of defense, Marshal Mikhail N. Tukhachevsky, who was also commander in chief of the Red Army: "Don't forget, my friend," he told a German official in late 1933, "it is politics, your politics alone, which separate us, not our feelings, our most friendly feelings for the *Reichswehr.*"[4] The sentiment of that statement would come back to haunt Tukhachevsky.

The young Napoleon of the revolution and a man who owed his high position both to his considerable ability and to his former relationship with Leon Trotsky, the founder of the Red Army, Marshal Tukhachevsky on January 15, 1936, warned the Russian Communist Party's Central Executive Committee of growing German military strength. "In preparing her imperialist plans," said Tukhachevsky, ". . . Germany has in point of fact been converted into a military camp." The German aircraft industry, he said, had made such "gigantic strides" that Britain and France had moved to rebuild their air power. German munitions factories, he said, were producing 500 artillery pieces a month and "no less than 200 tanks," and the Army was carrying out a plan "at a feverish pace and far more rapidly than was at first intended" to create twelve army corps and thirty-six divisions.[5]

Tukhachevsky noted also that the German Army was concentrating on flexibility and rapid movement in order to be able "to carry out sudden attacks." Using Nazi Party functions as rationalization, the Army was "practicing mass transfers of troops both by automobile and rail." To speed deployments by road, he said, the Germans were building almost 5,000 miles of superhighways (*Autobahnen*), which Tukhachevsky defined as "perfected roads which are free of intersecting roads and which provide tremendous opportunities for uninterrupted and unobstructed movement of troops," three of which connected Germany's eastern and western frontiers. "In all," he concluded, "vast preparations are being made by the German militarists for war on land and sea and in the air which . . . cannot but compel us to pay serious attention to the protection of our western frontiers." On the eastern frontiers, he warned, the situation was "just as serious," for "Japanese imperialism each year presents us with new proofs that its intentions are far from peaceful."

Like military men everywhere when seeking to increase their budgets, Tukhachevsky had no inclination to understate the peril; he wanted funds, he said, that would enable Soviet military forces to hit an attacker with a blow that would be "at once crushing and victorious." Yet probably nobody on the Central

Executive Committee questioned the fact that the danger as outlined by Tukhachevsky was real. The only question, one which concerned foreign governments as well, was: how strong was the Red Army and Soviet Russia?

Few astute foreign observers doubted that in terms of raw materials, the Soviet Union was the richest country in the world. Yet as Stalin transmuted the country from an agrarian to an industrial society, could the new Socialist administration and the new society function efficiently enough to produce the weapons, munitions, and materials required to win a war that well might involve a coalition of enemies on east and west? Had Russian industry and the Red Army been able to fulfill a mandate given them by Stalin in 1934: that the Red Army had to be stronger than any possible combination of arms that might be raised against the Soviet Union?

Most observers would answer both questions no. The general view was that for either a long war against Germany or against Germany and Japan together, Russia would be "severely handicapped by its inability to produce essential sinews of war" in the same quantities as its adversaries. Although the armed forces had "accumulated a tremendous reservoir of military engines and weapons," the country's ability to replenish that reservoir "was still insufficient to enable it to wage successfully a long war *without importation of war materials in large quantities from abroad.*" That fact alone would make it desirable for Russia "to postpone as long as possible the day of conflict with these formidable enemies."[6]

There would be yet another reason for the Soviet Union "to postpone as long as possible the day of conflict with these formidable enemies." That emerged on June 12, 1937, with a banner headline in *Pravda*: FOR ESPIONAGE AND TREASON TO THE FATHERLAND—EXECUTION BY SHOOTING. Among a list of officers who had been shot for having "violated their military oath, for treason to the Red Army, and for treason to the Fatherland" was the name of Mikhail Nikolayevich Tukhachevsky.[7]

The execution of Marshal Tukhachevsky and those listed with him was but the start of a vast purge that reached into every corner of the Soviet military and naval establishments and appeared to have left the Soviet armed forces, at a critical time, divested of experienced leadership. Among those executed were:

3 of the 5 marshals
14 of the 16 army commanders
6 of the 8 admirals
60 of the 67 corps commanders
136 of the 199 division commanders
211 of the 397 brigade commanders
11 of the 11 vice-commissars of defense
75 of the 80 members of the Supreme Military Soviet[8]

In the lower ranks, approximately half of the officer corps, some 35,000 in all, were either shot or imprisoned, including almost all of the regimental commanders.

The world would long seek to know what lay behind that dreadful affair. For years it would appear to have been only one more of those gigantic, bloody spasms that periodically shook revolutionary Russia; but after World War II, two senior SS officers, Brigadeführer-SS Walter Schellenberg, chief of the foreign secret intelligence branch of the Sicherheitsdienst, and Obergruppenführer-SS Wilhelm Hoettl, chief of Schellenberg's service in Southeastern Europe, stated independently that the bloodbath was the result of a plot commissioned by Himmler and Hitler and executed by Heydrich in order to weaken the Red Army as a prelude to an attack on the Soviet Union. According to Schellenberg and Hoettl, the chief of the Sicherheitsdienst, Heydrich, was provided in 1935 with a small extra budget for operations to produce an indictment of the Comintern to be used should Hitler require an excuse for attacking the Soviet Union. Heydrich employed a number of Russian émigrés living in Berlin who had contacts with the Russian Inter-Forces Union, General Wrangel's counterrevolutionary organization formed in 1923 with headquarters in Paris, whose aim was to restore the Romanov dynasty to power in Russia. The Inter-Forces Union was of particular interest to Heydrich because it maintained a network of agents inside Russia.

One of the senior officials at headquarters of the Inter-Forces Union was General Rudolf Skoblin, who, as Heydrich was aware, was also an agent of the NKVD. Heydrich's emissary approached Skoblin with the proposal that he work also for the Sicherheitsdienst. Skoblin accepted and toward the end of 1936 informed Heydrich that Marshal Tukhachevsky was planning to seize power in Russia and get rid of Stalin and the Bolshevik regime. If that was true, it was logical that Tukhachevsky would welcome and even actively solicit German help.

When told by Heydrich about Tukhachevsky's alleged scheme, Himmler and Hitler saw two courses open to them: either support Tukhachevsky and help him to destroy Stalin and the Bolsheviks or betray him to Stalin and thereby destroy the leadership of the Red Army. Hitler had no interest in the first course, for he saw Tukhachevsky as one who was as Bolshevik as Stalin; but he sanctioned the second.

Heydrich confined information about any part of his plan to a small group of senior officers within the SS. The only one to whom he confided the entire plan was a close friend, Standartenführer-SS Hermann Behrends, head of the Eastern Branch of the Sicherheitsdienst, who later, while serving as chief of the SS in Yugoslavia, told the story to Hoettl. Behrends would not live to tell the story again; when he was captured near the end of World War II by forces of Marshal Tito of Yugoslavia, Soviet authorities asked that he be turned over to them, and they shot him.

To prepare the documents that would be needed to show that Tukhachevsky was scheming with the Germans, Heydrich established a laboratory in the basement of the Gestapo's offices in the Delbrückstrasse in Berlin. Using signatures, paper, and typewriter specimens drawn from the files of correspondence between the German and Russian high commands during the years of military collaboration following the Treaty of Rapallo, the forgers prepared a number of letters purporting to show that Tukhachevsky had been in treasonable correspondence with General von Seeckt, with General Kurt von Hammerstein, and with the head of German military intelligence, Captain Wilhelm Canaris. The letter bearing Canaris's signature included thanks to Marshal Tukhachevsky and several Russian generals for the helpful information they had provided on the Red Army.

When the forgers had completed their task, Heydrich briefed Hitler and received his approval to place the file in the hands of the NKVD. Heydrich passed the documents to a known agent of the NKVD in Berlin with no mention or expectation of getting money for them. After a look at the documents, the agent flew to Moscow and returned with a special agent representing the head of the NKVD, Nicolai Yeshov, who offered 3 million rubles for the documents. Heydrich gratefully accepted the money and passed it to Behrends' Eastern Branch, but the money was either counterfeit or marked, for those agents who used the notes while on operations inside Russia were lost. The forged documents, on the other hand, "functioned with deadly infallibility."

There was little doubt that Hitler authorized the operation, that there were forged documents, and that they were placed in the hands of the NKVD. It was also clear that the forged documents were at least in part responsible for the terrible fate that befell the Russian General Staff and the officer corps. Yet matters in the Kremlin were rarely that simple and straightforward, and in the case of Tukhachevsky and his colleagues, there was a second—and yet a third—story of events seemingly connected in some way with Heydrich's scheme.

If there was one man after the departure of Leon Trotsky who had the popularity and the power to overthrow Stalin, it was Marshal Tukhachevsky. By birth, education, demeanor, and professional accomplishment, he was superior to the gray wolf in the Kremlin. The product of an age when an Army officer was expected not only to know about howitzers and movement tables but also to be accomplished in the drawing room, Tukhachevsky had broad intellectual and cultural interests, and music—particularly playing the violin—was his passion. He had served with distinction in the Semonovsky Guards Regiment, an excellent provincial regiment staffed by the sons of young noblemen and bourgeois farmers; although captured by the Germans, he had escaped and walked nearly 700 miles back to Russia. Embracing Bolshevism in 1917, Tukhachevsky at the age of only twenty-five formed the 1st Red Army, which defeated White armies east and south of Moscow and the Poles in the Ukraine. He was, Trotsky believed, a man in the mold of the First Consul; and as Napoleon had overthrown the Directory by the coup d'état of the 18th Brumaire on November 9, 1799, so Stalin feared that Tukhachevsky might overthrow the Central Executive Committee of the October Revolution.

There was even more to Stalin's animosity toward Tukhachevsky than fears for his regime; the two had come into severe professional conflict. The first incident involved the defeat of the Red Army outside Warsaw during the Russo-Polish War of 1920.

That was the occasion when Tukhachevsky was leading the main thrust of the Red Army into Central Poland in a drive aimed at Warsaw, while General Semon Budyenny's 1st Cavalry Army was conducting a feint into Southern Poland toward Lvov. Although the feint drew off Polish forces, enabling Tukhachevsky to get within twelve miles of Warsaw, when the Poles counterattacked, Tukhachevsky needed help. He ordered Budyenny to come to his assistance, but Stalin as chief political officer of the Revolutionary Military Council countermanded the order and told Budyenny to take Lvov. Without Budyenny's help, Tukhachevsky had had to fall back in the retreat that turned into a rout and ended in Russia's losing the war. Stalin, Tukhachevsky maintained, was solely responsible.

After defecting to the United States, the man who had been chief of the NKVD in Spain and who had served with Tukhachevsky during the Russo-Polish War, Alexander Orlov, explained Stalin's motive: "Overshadowed by more brilliant men, he wanted to gain a place in the limelight" by taking Lvov even as Tukhachevsky took Warsaw. "He had long been resenting the secondary role he was playing in military affairs. He resented the leadership of Trotsky and of newcomers like Tukhachevsky."[9] Even after it became obvious what the Poles intended to do, according to Orlov, Stalin still insisted that Budyenny continue the drive on Lvov.

The defeat provoked severe repercussions within the party and the Central Executive Committee to the point that it appeared for a time that Stalin's career— if not his neck—might not survive the criticism leveled at him. All that saved Stalin was the intervention of Lenin, who ordered the matter dropped.

Stalin to that point had no quarrel with Tukhachevsky personally, but he did have after Tukhachevsky discussed the disaster in a lecture at the Frunze Military Academy, the senior college of the Soviet armed forces, and later published the lecture as a book. Tukhachevsky compared Stalin's action with that of Pavel Rennenkampf, the czarist commander who was held responsible for the calamitous defeat of the Imperial Army at Tannenberg, when he had failed to come to the support of the main Russian force. It was an odious comparison, for the proletarian generals considered the incident to be the prime example of the incompetence of their imperial predecessors.

The next disagreement between Stalin and Tukhachevsky developed after Lenin's death and Trotsky's exile when Stalin set out to modernize Russian agriculture through collectivization, a process by which landowners were dispossessed and the land gathered into large collective farms adaptable to mechanized agriculture. It was a brutal process. Hundreds of thousands of peasants were moved off land to which they had ties for generations and to which most had obtained possession only through the October Revolution, and whoever resisted was either sent to labor camps or killed. Such was the scale of misery and death that Stalin himself would tell Churchill during one of their conferences during

World War II that of all of Soviet Russia's early agonies, that of the forced collectivization of the farms was the greatest. For an army whose soldiers were almost all of the peasantry, the cruel program had special meaning; morale plummeted; many deserted to go back home to try to help their families. If the Red Army were to survive, Tukhachevsky and other senior officers told Stalin, the policy had to be modified to provide the peasants the right to own at least some land. Unsure of himself in those days and reluctant to challenge luminaries of the revolution directly, Stalin relented, but he never forgave the generals who forced him to do it.

Yet that and the incident in the Russo-Polish War were but contributing factors to Stalin's determination to rid himself of Marshal Tukhachevsky and his colleagues. Even after Trotsky's exile, Stalin was convinced that the military leadership remained loyal to Trotsky and that if the regime were not to be challenged by that leadership, it had to be replaced by officers of the proletarian generation. Yet even autocracies as dictatorial as Stalin's need a reason for wiping out an entire class; so it was—according to the second theory about what lay behind the mass execution of the officer corps—that the NKVD at Stalin's bidding set out to manufacture a reason. But according to the defector Alexander Orlov, there was already a reason.

Before defecting, said Orlov, he had learned that Tukhachevsky was planning with a number of other senior officer to overthrow Stalin and bring an end to the mammoth purge that had followed the trial of Zinoviev and Kamenev and was leading to a general liquidation of all the old Bolsheviks who had participated in the October Revolution. The ostensible reason for the revolt was evidence that during the revolution, Stalin had been a spy for the czarist secret police, the Okhrana. According to Orlov, documents providing that evidence had emerged in the course of a routine search of czarist police files in Leningrad. An officer of the NKVD named Stein was supposed to have come across a secret file kept by the vice-director of the Okhrana, which contained reports and letters to the vice-director in Stalin's handwriting and which established without question that before 1912, Stalin worked for the Okhrana as a secret agent, principally against the Bolsheviks.

Shocked at the import of the discovery, Stein was afraid to turn over the documents to his superiors. He instead went to Kiev and gave them to his closest friend, Viktor A. Balitsky, chief of the NKVD in Kiev, who, according to Orlov, was in league with Tukhachevsky against Stalin. Balitsky in turn called in Orlov's cousin, Zinovi B. Katsnelson, who was also involved in the plot. Convinced of the authenticity of the documents, the two decided to inform one of Tukhachevsky's most trusted accomplices, General Yon E. Yakir.

According to Orlov, General Yakir flew to Moscow and conferred with Tukhachevsky, who in turn "took into his confidence" several colleagues; but when the conspirators attempted to bring into their ranks the commandant of the Kuibyshev military district, General Pal Dybenko, he made his way to Moscow and told Stalin all that he knew. Stalin proclaimed a state of limited emergency and brought in troops of the NKVD to guard him, his quarters, the Kremlin, and all key public buildings. At the same time, he began to weave a plot to enable him to arrest and charge Tukhachevsky not only with treason against the party and the nation but also with connivance with a foreign power. That was where the two versions of the origins of the bloodbath began to converge.

Yet a third version had it that the NKVD—not the Sicherheitsdienst— fabricated the documents showing that Tukhachevsky had collaborated with and spied for Germany and that at Stalin's order, they were planted on General Skoblin, the triple agent with the Russian Inter-Forces Union in Paris. Skoblin sold them to Heydrich, who passed them through Behrends to the president of Czechoslovakia, Dr. Eduard Beneš, who had recently signed a mutual aid treaty with Russia. Anxious to be seen by Stalin as loyal to the spirit as well as to the letter of the treaty—so the story had it—Beneš reputedly passed the documents to Stalin. It was at that point that Stalin called in the troops of the NKVD to make it appear that there was a crisis.

Whatever the case—story one, story two, or story three, or a combination of parts of all three—the dreadful purge of the military leadership unfolded. The general staffs of every country watched it with horrified, even morbid fascination and incredulity. The General Staff in Germany watched most closely of all, and in due course, the Eastern Branch of the Sicherheitsdienst sent a report to Heydrich entitled, "Political Situation in the Red Army," which included these sentences: "The new arrivals will inevitably take time to overcome the effects of so far-reaching a purge in the higher ranks of the Soviet Army. The new commanders are inadequately trained and prematurely promoted; it is difficult to underestimate their efficiency." [10]

## Chapter Fifty-Two

At 4:30 P.M. on November 5, 1937, Adolf Hitler met secretly with a group of the most powerful men in the Third Reich at the fireside of the Little Cabinet Room in the chancellery on the Wilhelmstrasse. Present at the most secret meeting were the foreign minister, Konstantin Baron von Neurath; the war minister, Field Marshal Werner von Blomberg; the commander in chief of the Luftwaffe, General Hermann Göring; the commander in chief of the Army, General Werner Baron von Fritsch; and the commander in chief of the Navy, Grand Admiral Erich Raeder. When the men had settled into big club chairs under the oil portrait of the Iron Chancellor, Bismarck, Hitler swore them to secrecy, and as a wintry gloom descended outside the French windows, began to talk. The words he uttered spelled doom for a continent.

He began portentously by asking those present to regard his remarks as his "testamentary bequest in case of decease." In the course of four hours of nonstop monologue, he went on to say that he had made certain decisions "as the result of detailed considerations and the experiences of four and a half years as head of government."[1] In reality, he was doing little more than reiterating the design he had developed while writing *Mein Kampf* in Landsberg Fortress.

If the goal of German policy, he said, was safeguarding, preserving, and increasing the body of the nation, the problem of space had to be confonted at the start; all Germany's problems—economic, social, racial—could be conquered only by mastering the problem of *Lebensraum*. It had once been possible, he said, to alleviate the problem by overseas colonies, but since that outlet no longer existed, the only solution was to gain *Lebensraum* within Eurasia. While admitting that there were dangers involved—for "the aggressor always comes up against the possessor"—the goal of a Greater German Reich ruled by "a solid racial nucleus" justified taking high risks. "For the solution of the German question," he declared emphatically, "all that remains is the way of force."

Having made that decision, there remained a matter of timing. To delay much longer, he said, would be to allow time for Britain, France, and Russia to develop their strength. Thus he had decided to "solve the question of German space between 1943–1945 at the latest." If any opportunity arose before that time, such as Britain or France getting involved somewhere militarily, he was "unalterably resolved" to take advantage of it.

In any case, he continued, Austria was to be the first target and Czechoslovakia the second. By those two conquests, Germany would acquire manpower for twelve new divisions, food for 5 to 6 million people, and "a spring-board for far-reaching imperialist aims." By that he meant European Russia.

The way to *Anschluss*—federation of Germany and Austria—had been prepared by a sinister incident that had occurred in 1934. After months of Nazi agitation by the Austrian Legion, 150 of its gunmen forced their way into the chancellery in Vienna. Among them was a member of Heydrich's Sicherheitsdienst, Ernst Kaltenbrunner, himself an Austrian and, in time, Heydrich's successor. Either Kaltenbrunner or one of the legionnaires shot the chancellor, Engelbert Dollfuss. Dollfuss collapsed, badly but not mortally wounded, although he was bleeding profusely. Kaltenbrunner was said to have ordered all others from the room and to have remained alone with him. When Kaltenbrunner at last came out of the room, Dollfuss was dead; Kaltenbrunner had deliberately allowed him to bleed to death while trying to extract some kind of information from him.

Dollfuss's death created an extreme crisis that appeared to his successor, Kurt von Schuschnigg, to be a prelude to a coup d'état. The man said to have inherited whatever secret it was that Kaltenbrunner had tried to extract from the bleeding Dollfuss, von Schuschnigg sought to gain time in order to forestall a coup and try to line up support from other nations. With that in mind, he accepted an invitation in February 1938 to talk with Hitler at his residence outside Berchtesgaden, the Berghof.

If von Schuschnigg had hoped to achieve any kind of rapport with Hitler, the hope was misplaced. Hitler launched immediately into a tirade. Austria's whole history, he declared, was "a continuous betrayal of the people . . . And let me tell you this, Herr Schuschnigg: I am firmly determined to put an end to all of it." He had "a historic mission," he said, and he was "going to fulfill it because Providence" had appointed him "to do so."

Throughout much of the day, Hitler continued to rail at his guest. He demanded that all imprisoned Austrian National Socialists, including the gunmen who had raided the chancellery and killed Dollfuss, be set free and that all Austrian Nazis who had been dismissed from the government or the miltary be reinstated. A Nazi sympathizer, Artur von Seyss-Inquart, was to be appointed interior minister with full control over the nation's police forces. For long von Schuschnigg resisted, in the process gaining concessions in a few minor demands, but in the end, he felt compelled to give in. It was the beginning of the end for Austria.

With Seyss-Inquart in control of the police, Nazi hoodlums were soon freely parading in the streets of the old capital and crossing the Danube Canal to invade the Jewish quarter with shouts of *"Sieg heil!"* and *"Heil Hitler!"* The Austrian chancellor nevertheless took heart from the obvious concern of the great bulk of the people and determined to concede nothing else. From the rostrum of the Parliament, decorated with tulips in the Austrian colors of red-white-red, he declared: "We have gone to the very limit of concessions, where we must call a halt and say, 'Thus far and no further.'"[2] The nation would fight, he declared, and Austria would remain free. Members of the Parliament rose in frenzied applause, while crowds outside, listening to the proceedings over amplifiers, joined the chorus. A great enthusiasm swept the streets.

The enthusiasm carried all the way to Paris, where the French government composed a note asking Britain to join in a protest to Berlin. The note arrived at an inauspicious time, for Foreign Secretary Anthony Eden had just resigned his post, leaving the Foreign Ministry temporarily leaderless. In any case, as von Ribbentrop reported to Berlin, "England was not in the least disposed to fight for this troublesome leftover of the Versailles Treaty." As with Hitler's march into the Rhineland, France would not act without British support.

In Vienna, buoyed by the public response to his speech of defiance, von Schuschnigg decided to hold a national plebiscite to determine the issue of giving in or fighting back. In that heart of Austrian nationalism, the Tyrol, von Schuschnigg on March 9, 1938, mounted a rostrum in the main square in Innsbruck to announce his decision. "Tyroleans and Austrians," he cried, "say 'Yes' to Tyrol. Say 'Yes' to Austria!" He ended his speech with the words in the Tyrolean dialect of the patriot Andreas Hofer, calling for volunteers to fight Napoleon: *"Marde, 's ischt Zut!* (Men, the time has come!)"[3]

That step prompted Hitler to move swiftly to tighten the screw. To the consternation of the German General Staff, which as yet had prepared no plan for invading Austria, he ordered on March 10, 1938, that the Army be ready to march by noon of the 12th. German newspapers published banner headlines declaring that Communist flags were flying in Vienna and mobs were shouting, "Heil Moskau! Heil Schuschnigg!"[4] In midmorning of the 11th, von Schuschnigg got the word he had been dreading: Hitler demanded that the plebiscite be postponed and that von Schuschnigg resign. As von Schuschnigg delayed, the demands increased: not only was he to resign, but Seyss-Inquart was to take his place, and the government was to send a telegram asking Germany for help.

When last-minute appeals to Britain and Italy yielded nothing and a chanting Nazi mob took over the streets of Vienna and headed for the chancellery, von Schuschnigg went to a microphone set up only a few feet from the spot where Dollfuss had met his death. President Miklas, he said, had asked him to tell his people that Austria had been compelled to give in to force so that no blood would be spilled. Orders had gone to the Army, he said, to withdraw before German invasion without resistance.

To the end, the government refused to accept Seyss-Inquart as chancellor, but as the mob outside the chancellery swelled to more than 100,000 and the mood grew ugly, he simply took over and sent a telegram asking the German Army to enter Austria "to help restore order." As Austrian Nazis began occupying public buildings, the Wehrmacht, as the German armed forces had come to be called, began at eight o'clock on the morning of March 12, 1938, to march into Hitler's homeland. The march displayed none of the efficiency of blitzkrieg as practiced on the steppes of Russia—tanks and trucks broke down, traffic jammed at the bridges over the Inn River—but it mattered little, for it was a battle of flowers. At some points local inhabitants themselves dismantled the frontier barriers; women and children attired in native costume bombarded the troops with flowers; swastika flags decorated public buildings and dwellings alike. Where were all those people who had cheered the chancellor's plan for a plebiscite, secure in the knowledge that independence would win? They were nowhere to be seen, not in the villages, not in the cities, not in the capital.

So clogged were the roads with military traffic that Hitler himself was unable to cross the frontier before midafternoon, but then to the peal of bells, his car inched into Braunau, his birthplace, amid a jubilant crowd "struggling to touch the vehicle as if it were some religious relic."[5] As the procession continued, tens of thousands lined the road, and in every village, the streets were bedecked with flowers. In the capital, so tumultuous was his reception when he addressed a crowd of 200,000 in the Heldenplatz that he went beyond his original plan for Anschluss and fully absorbed Austria into the Greater German Reich.

As the German Army moved into Austria in the spring of 1938, Adolf Hitler had become to many a diety, and his public appearances had taken on the atmosphere of a religious revival. When he entered a party rally, there were searchlights, massed rolling drums, and modern interpretations of ancient Saxon rites to create a supernatural and religious atmosphere more befitting a god than a man, a "procession of the modern Messiah incarnate."[6]

The world had never seen anything quite like it. The Teuton magic of Saxon horns and Celtic runes appealed not only in the country districts, where in living memory blood sacrifices had taken place, but in the great cities as well. One of the largest and most sophisticated art shops on the Unter den Linden, the principal shopping street in Berlin, exhibited a large portrait of Hitler in the center of its display window, entirely surrounded, as if by a halo, by portraits of Christ. In Munich, as early as the autumn of 1936, there were to be seen everywhere color portraits of Hitler in the silver garments of a Knight of the Grail; at the party rally in Nuremberg in 1937 there was a gigantic floodlit picture of Hitler seemingly hanging in the sky with the inscription: IN THE BEGINNING WAS THE WORD. The mayor of Hamburg reputedly said: "We need no priests or parsons. We communicate direct with God through Adolf Hitler. He has many Christ-like qualities." A newspaperwoman, Dorothy Thompson, quoted a fellow American who had attended a performance of the Passion Play at Oberammergau: "They think Hitler is God. Believe it or not, a German woman sat next to me at the Passion Play and when they hoisted Jesus on to the Cross, she said, 'There he is. That is our *Führer*, our Hitler.'"[7]

The trappings impressed foreign observers as well, as noted by the French ambassador, André François-Poncet, when invited to visit the Eagle's Nest, Hitler's teahouse retreat atop the Bavarian Alps outside Berchtesgaden. A twentieth-century fortress, he called it, inhabited by a solitary reincarnation of a knight of Friedrich Barbarossa: ". . . a strong and massive building containing a gallery with Roman pillars, an immense circular hall with windows all around. . . . It gives the impression of being suspended in space, an almost over-hanging wall of bare rock rises up abruptly. The whole, bathed in the twilight of an autumn evening, is grandiose, wild, almost hallucinating."[8]

The British ambassador, Sir Nevile Henderson, attended the rally at Nuremburg in 1937, was invited to dine with Reichsführer-SS Himmler "in a great tent in Herr Himmler's SS Police Camp" where "a chorus of blackshirts" sang, followed by "a tattoo for the lowering of the Swastika camp flag." As Sir Nevile wrote, "the camp in the darkness, dimly lit by flares, with the black uniforms in the silent background and the skull and crossbones on the drums and trumpets lent to the scene a sinister and menacing impression." He felt, he said, "as if I were back in the days of Wallenstein and the Thirty Years' War in the seventeenth century."[9]

That Wotan instinct, the parades of hundreds of thousands, the lutes, the worship of flaxen hair and slim, muscular young bodies—there was something terrifying about that Hitlerian world, something diabolical. What, for example, of the somber casualty rate among Hitler's close female associates: a film actress, Renate Müller, after a nocturnal visit to Hitler's bedchamber, killed herself; the woman he was eventually to marry as Berlin burned, Eva Braun, twice tried to kill herself; the daughter of a British aristocrat, Unity Mitford, who was often at Berchtesgaden in the years 1937 to 1939, also tried to commit suicide; and Hitler's niece, Geli Raubal, a girl for whom Hitler maintained an intense passion and kept in the style of a mistress, was found dead from a bullet from Hitler's pistol, fired by her own hand.

"Most loathsome of all," wrote Hermann Rauschning, one of Hitler's political associates who became president of the Danzig Senate until he fled first to Britain and then to the United States, "is the reeking miasma of furtive, unnatural sexuality that fills and fouls the whole atmosphere around [Hitler] like an evil emanation."[10] Yet, as Field Marshal von Ludendorff had predicted, Germany had found its Messiah to defend the Reich against the forces of darkness and evil to the east.

Hitler in 1936 commissioned a young German architect, Albert Speer, to redesign the heart of Berlin as the center of a great Germanic empire to be known as Germania. Each building was to be larger than any other comparable building in other world capitals, and at the center was to be a palace befitting the German Messiah. The entire complex of government offices, private dwellings, memorials, railway stations, and parks was to be grouped around a boulevard that was to be far wider and five times longer than the Champs-Elysées. As Speer would record, the complex was "to spell out in architecture the political, military, and economic power of Germany."[11]

The final expression of Hitler's ambition, Germania was to consist of a system of German protectorates and subject states extending from the Atlantic at least as far as the Volga and possibly to the Urals. Whether the Volga or the Urals, the frontier was to be defended by a deep interlocking system of fortified villages, populated by the pure of thought and blood, the Aryans of the SS, and constituting "a gigantic wall to shield the new East against the Central Asiatic masses."[12]

In the end, there was to be a Great Germanic Empire of the German Nation, an imperium of 200 million "racially conscious" and blood-pure people living under the SS in a single, economically independent state. Eliminating what Hitler called "the rubbish heap of small countries," the new empire was to include Norway, Denmark, the Netherlands, Belgium, Alsace-Lorraine, the Paris basin, Burgundy, and the Franche-Comté up to Lake Geneva. From the center of the empire, Berlin, there would extend "a dense network of garrisons, party citadels, temples of art, camps and watchtowers, in whose shadow a generation of master personalities would pursue the Aryan blood cult and the breeding of the new god-man."[13]

# PART X

## The Russian Station

---

*Chapter Fifty-Three*

In Moscow, whenever Joseph Stalin chose to survey his horizons, he could note that internally he was basically secure. He had defeated and exiled his principal rival, Trotsky; he had taken the first steps toward the purge that would in time eradicate not only those who remained loyal to Trotsky but almost all the old Bolsheviks except those few whom he could infinitely trust; and he had successfully imposed his industrial and agricultural modernization schemes on a people who sometimes had to be bludgeoned into acceptance, but there had been no counterrevolution. In the early 1930s, nevertheless, none of those gigantic programs was complete, and until they were, peril to him and his regime would remain. Yet the principal danger at that point was from the outside, from a possible alliance of the militaristic Fascist states, backed either directly or tacitly by such capitalist countries as Great Britain and the United States.

Stalin's answer to that threat was to seek to create a system of alliances, to construct a buffer between Russia and the hostile powers, and to employ nimble diplomacy in order to procure that most priceless of assets: time. Time in which to develop the Red Army to a point where it could defend the country simultaneously in Europe and Asia; time in which also to develop Russia's vast national resources to the point of self-sufficiency.

In the early years of the decade, Japan appeared to be the most immediate threat. Japanese armies had occupied Manchuria and begun to march into North

China, and everywhere—so it seemed from a look at the maps—Japanese armies were aimed toward Russia's vital lifeline, the Trans-Siberian Railroad linking Moscow with Vladivostok. When in February 1933 the Japanese walked out of the League of Nations, Stalin had every reason to feel as did the American ambassador in Tokyo, Joseph C. Grew, who reported to Washington: "This step indicates the complete supremacy of the military and a fundamental defeat for the moderate elements in the country." Large segments of the Japanese people, reported Grew, considered that war with Russia or America, or both, was inevitable, and that for that war, "the military and naval machines are in a state of high efficiency."[1]

A few months later, Grew reported that most foreign observers in Tokyo considered a Russo-Japanese war to be inevitable, possibly as early as 1935 or 1936. "Russo-Japanese relations," noted an American intelligence survey, involved "antagonistic tendencies: the Japanese dreams of expansion toward Siberia, and the Soviet attempts to prevent Japan from becoming uncontrollable in her ambitious designs in Asia."[2]

Indeed, in the years since 1925, there had been more than 2,000 military clashes of lesser or greater degree between Japanese and Russian military forces in Asia, and all the while the Japanese were engaged in clandestine operations on a grand scale to try to incite Soviet Muslims into launching a jihad against Moscow's rule. Those operations were conducted primarily through the mystical patriotic societies, long a feature of Japanese life, the most active of which at the time was the Black Dragon Society. The Black Dragon and other patriotic societies constituted "powerful, ever-present groups behind Japanese aggression, permeating the political life of the nation."[3] The Black Dragon Society drew "a zealous membership . . . from every walk of life." Some members were trained in languages, others in subversion, while others would simply pursue such mundane professions as "shopkeepers, tourists, students of Islam, salesmen of literature, fishermen, wrestling teachers, businessmen, professors, priests, archaeologists" while at the same time busily collecting information.

During Lenin's revolution and the Civil War, there were several examples of Japanese intrigues against the Bolshevik government, including Baron Ungern von Sternberg's mad dream of a Mongol Empire, and between 1925 and 1935, there was evidence of Japanese schemes to stir discontent among the natives of Soviet Central Asia and Buriat-Mongolia, to blow up railways, to wreck highway construction, and generally to impede Soviet development of the Muslim lands between the Urals and the Pacific. Between 1933 and 1939, the Russian counterespionage service would identify at least fifty-four Japanese organizations with intelligence agents working inside the Soviet Union.

With Hitler's rise to power in 1933, the threat from the east took on a new and darker complexion through a possible link with the rapidly growing threat from the west. When intelligence revealed that the Nazi chancellor was seeking a military alliance with Japan, an alliance unabashedly directed against Russia, that made Russian alliances with other powers all the more essential. Yet what nation would ally itself with the power behind the Comintern? Because Italy, too, was Fascist and because the United States had retreated into isolationism, leaving old Europe to its humors and intrigues, there remained of the major powers only Russia's old capitalist enemies, Britain and France. They, too, were menaced by the new Teuton furor, yet even so, in view of all that had happened through the instigation of the Comintern, would either agree to negotiate an alliance with Communism?

There was a possibility that two new faces on the diplomatic scene might change the relationship with Britain. Those were a new foreign commissar, Maxim Litvinov, whose "chubby and unproletarian figure radiated an aura of robust and businesslike common sense that was in striking contrast to the enigmatic brutality of the Politburo and the conspiratorial noisiness of the Comintern,"[4] and on the other side, a new British ambassador in Moscow, Aretas Akers-Douglas, the 2nd Viscount Chilston, Knights Grand Cross of the Most Distinguished Order of St. Michael and St. George. When on June 21, 1934, the proletarian foreign minister and the bourgeois ambassador met to talk about an alliance, they were evenly matched, for each doubted the sincerity of the other: both men nevertheless talked earnestly about negotiating a collective security pact between Russia, Britain, France, and the lesser nations of Eastern Europe.

Another meeting followed in London between the permanent undersecretary at the Foreign Office, Sir Robert G. Vansittart, and the Soviet ambassador, Ivan Maisky. Maisky, "earnestly desired" better relations with Britain and frankly admitted that the desire was "motivated largely by fear of Germany." Russia was suspicious of Britain, he said, because of British policy in regard to Germany but particularly because of British policy in regard to Japan: there was, he said, "a genuine apprehension . . . regarding the Far Eastern Policy of His Majesty's Government." To which Vansittart replied that "no well-informed person . . . could for a moment credit so fantastic a tale as that of a British desire for warfare in the Far East." Britain wanted to be on good terms with Japan, of course, but primarily for commercial reasons, as Britain also hoped that Russia "should be on as good terms as possible with Japan." British interests in the Far East were "far too great for any other attitude to be possible."[5]

With regard to Europe, Vansittart assured Maisky that His Majesty's Government favored a security pact with Russia and was also prepared to welcome Russia into the League of Nations, which soon developed. Maisky appeared to be jubilant. "Both in London and in Moscow," he remarked excitedly to the American ambassador in Moscow, William C. Bullitt, "we are now discussing all the problems of the world freely in the most friendly manner."[6]

Yet Britain made no overtures for a defensive alliance. Pressing for that, Stalin invited the British foreign secretary, Sir John Simon, to come to Moscow to discuss the implications of Germany's rearmament in defiance of the Treaty of Versailles. Declining because of "the pressure of business," the foreign secretary suggested sending in his place the Lord Privy Seal, Anthony Eden. When Stalin readily accepted Eden as a substitute, it provided striking evidence of his immense concern, for Eden was only a junior minister and in the past Stalin had declined, with the exception of the American ambassador, to see even heads of missions. As Eden made his way toward Moscow, Ambassador Maisky accorded him the signal honor of meeting him in Berlin to escort him to Moscow in what had been the czar's imperial railroad coach.

At the conference, Eden's impression of Stalin was from the first favorable and would remain so through a long association. "As we entered," he would record, "I saw standing there a short, thick-set man with hair *en brosse*. He was in a grey tunic, with rather baggy dark trousers and calf-length black boots. . . . He always appeared well laundered and neatly dressed." His personality, wrote Eden, "made itself felt without effort or exaggeration." Although Eden "knew the man to be without mercy," he "respected the quality of his mind and even felt a sympathy," a sympathy which he was never able "entirely to analyze." Perhaps, he wrote: "this was because of Stalin's pragmatic approach. It was easy to forget that I was talking to a Party man; certainly no one could have been less doctrinaire. I cannot believe that Stalin ever had any affinity with Marx; he never spoke of him as if he did."

During that meeting and others that would follow in later years, Eden "found the encounter stimulating, grey and stern though the agenda often had to be." He was a man, wrote Eden, who handled himself superbly in conference. "Well informed on all points that were of concern to him, Stalin was prudent but not slow." He seldom raised his voice; he was "a good listener, prone to doodling," whom Eden found "the quietest dictator" he ever met. "Yet the strength," he wrote, "was there, unmistakeably."[7]

As Eden opened his first conference with Stalin, he directed his first words indirectly at the Comintern. He trusted, he said, that the Soviet government intended to conduct relations with the United Kingdom "in the spirit of collaboration and non-interference which was inherent in our common membership of the League of Nations." In yet another remark directed at the Comintern, he said that the British government was confident that Russia "recognized that the continued, integrity, tranquility, and prosperity of British territories were an advantage to peace." The Soviet government, Molotov interrupted to say, had "no desire to interfere in any way in the internal affairs of the British Empire." To which Stalin nodded his agreement.[8]

When Stalin spoke, he immediately called Eden's attention to the situation in Europe. It was, he said, "fundamentally worse" than it had been on the eve of the World War. Then there had been but one aggressor: Germany; in 1935 there were two: Germany and Japan. Yet Stalin directed most of his attention to Germany, a nation composed, he said, of "a great and capable people with exceptional powers of organisation and great industrial strength" but a people strongly influenced by a sense of injury over the Treaty of Versailles. "We must expect," he said, "that they will be actuated by motives of revenge." The only way to restrain Germany, Stalin continued, was by a system of pacts, to force Germany to recognize "that if she attacked any other nation, she would have Europe against her." If the League of Nations was too weak to maintain peace, then it was up to the Europeans themselves to ensure it through collective security. So sincere did Stalin sound that Eden concluded that whatever else Stalin might be, he was no warmaker.

Rising, Stalin walked to a map on the wall and with one hand made a sweep across the areas marked in red: the British Empire. The influence and power of so small an island as Great Britain, he said, was remarkable. "That little island, if she chooses, can stop Germany by refusing her raw materials without which she cannot pursue aggressive designs." Much would depend upon that little island, said Stalin, and the part its government was prepared to play in the system of pacts with which Russia wished to be associated. "It would be fatal to let events drift," Stalin warned. "If a check is to be placed upon a potential aggressor, there is no time to lose."[9]

Amid renewed expressions of cordiality, the meeting ended. That night when Eden and Lord Chilston attended a gala performance at the Bolshoi Theater of *Swan Lake*, the orchestra played "God Save the King," the first time the British national anthem had been played in Russia since the October Revolution, and the audience rose in respect. When it came time for Eden to leave Moscow, he walked across a red carpet laid from the czar's former waiting room to the czar's railroad coach, and again Ambassador Maisky joined him for the long leg of his trip, the journey from Moscow to Berlin.

Yet for all Stalin's courtship, there would be no treaty between Britain and the Soviet Union. It was probably foredoomed in any event, for as Prime Minister Baldwin and Foreign Secretary Simon maintained in the House of Commons, there was no reason, just because of the rise of Hitler, to believe that the element of sincerity had entered Soviet diplomacy. There might have been pressure from the British public in favor of a treaty nevertheless had not one of those events occurred that appeared to illustrate—as so often in Russian relations with Britain—that one hand of the Soviet government was disposed to ignore—if not to sabotage—what the other hand was seemingly trying to accomplish.

Not long after Anthony Eden's visit, the NKVD arrested six British engineers employed by the Metropolitan Vickers Electrical Company to work on construction projects for the Soviet government and charged them with sabotaging the Soviet economy. Although there was reason to believe that at least some of the men were, as the Russians charged, informants for the British Secret Intelligence Service, the reaction of the British government was firm: unless a satisfactory settlement was forthcoming immediately, the Anglo-Russian commercial trade agreement, which was up for renegotiation, would not be renewed, an embargo would be imposed on all trade, and diplomatic relations would again be broken.

Although Stalin ordered the men released on bail, the trial proceeded. All six were found guilty as charged: four were ordered deported and two were sentenced to jail for two- and three-year terms. The British government promptly imposed a trade embargo, and within three months the two men were pardoned and deported; but the damage had been done. If it be true that statesmanship, like war, is mainly a catalogue of blunders, what was known as the Metropolitan Vickers trial was a clear example of the aphorism; it made an Anglo-Russian alliance against Fascism impossible at the very time when it might have proved effective.

Rebuffed by Britain, Stalin found more willing partners in Czechoslovakia and France, countries which shared common frontiers with Hitler's Germany and saw obvious peril in Hitler's pronouncements in Mein Kampf and in his bombastic speeches in the months since he had come to power. Both nations signed military alliances with Russia in 1935, and as Stalin continued to pursue insurance against the threats posed by Germany and Japan, the Comintern abruptly reversed its long-standing policy of implacable hostility to the capitalist powers. There was suddenly to be found virtue in all foreign Communist parties joining hands with bourgeois, religious, liberal, radical, Socialist, and even conservative elements to create what the Comintern called a Popular Front of all political parties, classes, and nations. It was a time, in keeping with Lenin's dictum on the necessity for resilience, to adjust, to bend, to compromise, to temporize. The policy produced remarkable about-faces in Communist parties around the world, and in two countries—France and Spain—it produced Popular Front governments.

Through those methods, Stalin gained at least a measure of security, but in Adolf Hitler he faced a foe who recognized to no degree less than did Stalin the necessity for allies. That Hitler and his diplomats were just as busy behind the scenes as were Stalin and his, burst upon the world when on November 25, 1936, Berlin Radio announced what was tantamount to the establishing of a counter-force to the Communist International, a Fascist International, or as Hitler called it, the Blue International: "This noon the Royal Japanese Ambassador in Berlin, Vicomte Mushakoji, under direction of the Emperor of Japan, and the Special Ambassador of the German Reich, Joachim von Ribbentrop, by order of the Führer and Reich Chancellor, signed an agreement against the Communist International." [10]

Convinced "that the toleration of Communist International interference in the internal affairs of nations not only endangers their inner peace and social welfare but world peace as a whole," Germany and Japan had agreed "to confer on the required defense measures and carry these out in close cooperation." When they issued an open invitation to other countries to join the pact, Italy's Mussolini acceded immediately and called on other powers to join, Britain, in particular; but in Britain there was little sympathy in that direction. Nor did any other countries come forward.

The belief that Japan might attack Russia gained added credence from two border battles that occurred in 1938 and 1939. The first took place in the Maritime Province of Siberia in mountainous country near Lake Khasan, where the borders of Manchuria, Korea, and Russia meet. Known as the Battle of

Changkufeng Hill, it involved large forces on both sides. As the fighting progressed, the Comintern and the Soviet government opened a sharp propaganda offensive designed to show that the United States was helping the Japanese and was hoping for a major war of attrition that would leave both countries so weakened that the United States would emerge as the dominant power in the Far East. "American monopolists," an official Soviet history would later state, "hurried to give their Japanese partners large loans." [11]

Although the Battle of Changkufeng Hill ended on August 10, 1938, with the Russians still holding the hill, the "Japanese imperialists," wrote the official Soviet historians, continued their aggression, beginning operations in May 1939 by the 6th Kwantung Army along the Khalkin Gol (river) on the frontier between Manchuria and the People's Republic of Mongolia, with which the Soviet Union had a defense pact. According to the official history, the Soviets quickly sent 12,500 troops to help the Mongolians. Bolstered by Anglo-American support, the historians would maintain, the Japanese eventually increased their forces to 75,000 men, but the Russians also brought up reinforcements and wiped out early Japanese gains. "The Army," the history would conclude, "gave the Japanese invaders a crushing blow at Khalkin Gol," in the process dealing "the Anglo-American imperialists" a defeat. [12]

What the official Russian history failed to note was that Changkufeng Hill and the country along the Khalkin Gol were border territories long in dispute and that before the Japanese attacks, the Russians at Changkufeng Hill and the Mongolians along the Khalkin Gol had occupied the territories and built fortifications. Casualties were considerably less than the Russians claimed: some 18,000 men on both sides. Yet in the context of the world conflict then taking shape, the two battles had a singular importance: through them the Japanese gained a healthy respect for the Red Army. It followed that in the wake of those experiences, the Japanese might choose not to move against Siberia but to seek softer targets among colonial possessions to the south. An indication of that possibility would arise a little later when Ambassador Grew in Tokyo telegraphed Secretary of State Cordell Hull: "A member of the Embassy was told by my [Filipino] colleague that from many quarters, including a Japanese one, he had heard that a surprise attack on Pearl Harbor was planned by the Japanese military forces, in case of 'trouble' between Japan and the United States; that the attack would involve the use of all the Japanese military facilities. My colleague said that he was prompted to pass this on because it had come to him from many sources, although the plan seemed fantastic." [13]

## Chapter Fifty-Four

As Adolf Hitler began the buildup of German military power, the head of the Red Army Military Intelligence Service, General Ivan Pavlovich Berzin, was at the height of his influence and power. Although appointed to the post by Trotsky,

Berzin had survived the first purges that followed the struggle for power between Stalin and Trotsky, and with the NKVD in large measure preoccupied with guarding the regime against its internal enemies, the Red Army Military Intelligence Service, in concert with the Comintern, was chiefly responsible for providing secret intelligence about the outside world.

Other than that Berzin was not Russian but Latvian, little was known about him personally, which was probably by design. Nor was much known about the Red Army Military Intelligence Service, for like the British, the Russians would never acknowledge officially that they maintained any secret intelligence services. As noted by the Sicherheitsdienst in a report to Hitler, the Russians followed Lenin's dictum in regard to secret organizations: "Their eyes fixed on one common aim, they alter the places and methods of their activity, synchronizing their means and weapons with the shifting phases and conditions of the struggle." As of the moment, the Sicherheitsdienst noted, "the Soviet organization appears to consist of a multitude of commands, administrations, groups, sections, and clubs of all kinds and forms, including military, state, and party agencies of a public or secret character, on Russian soil as well as abroad." Those organizations appeared "to be synchronized and directed in a centralized manner by the leadership of the Soviet Union, reportedly vested in the 'Polit Bureau' of the Communist Party."[1]

As the possibility of war with Germany and Japan increased, Stalin directed General Berzin to expand his *apparats* and create new cover organizations with which to wage the secret war. He specifically named to head the critical Soviet war station in Western Europe a man known as Leopold Trepper, "an old-time intelligence officer who had mastered his craft completely," a man whose "actions were disciplined by careful deliberation," a man "completely at home in the West; there was little chance that he would betray his Soviet and Eastern European background."[2]

He was born Leiba ben Zeharya Trepper on February 23, 1902, in Neumark, near Zakopane, Poland, a product of the Pale of the Settlement, one of ten children of a Neumark merchant. While still in his teens, he was forced by economic conditions to leave school to work in the iron mines. A devout Communist by the age of twenty-two, he was arrested by the Polish secret police for leading a revolt at Dombrova, a rail and industrial town on a tributary of the Vistula in Southeastern Poland. Having spent eight months in jail, he elected to go to Palestine where he "became acquainted with the Grand Mufti of Jerusalem" and "began his apprenticeship as a spy."

By 1928 Trepper had become a member of an organization in Paris known as the Rabcors, which by 1932 had become so dangerous an instrument of Soviet intelligence that the renowned French counterespionage *commissaire*, Charles Faux-pas-Bidet, moved to break it up. Although the leaders were arrested, Trepper escaped to Moscow, where he entered the Red Army Academy. There he was taught two principles that were motivating large numbers of Jews to continue to serve Soviet intelligence even as the NKVD was liquidating the Jewish leaders in the Soviet state in the great purge: "that only by supporting Stalin and the Communist cause could the Jewish demands [for a national homeland] be realized" and that "the war against Fascism and Nazism could be successfully waged only under the guidance of Communism and [thus] that the support of the Soviet anti-Fascist movement was obligatory for the Jewish masses."

As Léon Blum established the Popular Front government in France, part of the worldwide movement promoted by the Comintern to weld all the parties of the left into a single whole to fight Fascism, Trepper was sent back to France. His assignment was to kill a man who had betrayed the leaders of the Rabcors, Robert Switz-Gordon, whom the Federal Bureau of Investigation had turned into a double agent during inquiries into the case of Robert Osman, the U.S. Army corporal sentenced in 1933 for spying for the Russians in Panama.

Unable to find Switz-Gordon, Trepper was diverted to establishing a new intelligence net in France. In the process, he operated under at least twenty aliases, including Adam Mikler, Léopold de Winter, Vladislav Ivanovich Ivanowski, Le Grand Chef, and Le Général, and was known to have used Austrian, Polish, Luxemburgian, French, and Canadian passports. Such was his requirement for false papers that he was assigned a specialist in their manufacture, Mikhail Makarov.

When directed by Berzin to create new nets and cover organizations for Soviet intelligence, Trepper went first to Brussels, where he contacted a long-term Comintern agent, Leon Grossvogel, a Polish Jew from Lodz with whom Trepper had been associated in anti-British espionage for a Zionist organization in Palestine. Grossvogel was at the time a member of the board of directors of a rainwear manufacturing company, the King of Raincoats Corporation. Although his activities as a Communist sometimes disturbed the other three directors of the company, he was retained largely because the wife of one of the directors, Louis Kapelowitz, was Grossvogel's sister.

Trepper convinced Grossvogel to work for "the expansion of the raincoat company's overseas business" by setting up "an independent (or subsidiary) company in the same line of business" to be called the Foreign Excellent Raincoat Company. Because of Grossvogel's Communist activities, his codirectors were pleased at the thought of his moving on to a separate firm. When Grossvogel put up half the capital for the new company, some $8,000 to $10,000, all provided by Trepper, the other three directors and a friend put up the other half. Aside from retailing the rainwear manufactured by the King of Raincoats Corporation, the purpose of the Foreign Excellent Raincoat Company was to establish "a network of outlet stores throughout Europe . . . as fronts for members of a Soviet espionage network."

After setting up a first branch of the company at Ostend, managed by Grossvogel's Belgian wife, Trepper invested $10,000 in the Foreign Excellent Raincoat Company in his own name and thus became a full partner. Having established himself as a member of that most respected class of Bruxellois, the bourgeois businessman, he set out to make a penetration of that next most respected class of Bruxellois, the civil service.

Trepper's penetration was made through Jean-Claude Spaak, a dignified figure known as a revolutionary in a dinner jacket. "The confidence which Trepper reposed in Spaak," a British secret service report would note, suggested that Spaak "was a well-known and well-tried friend of the USSR if not of the [Soviet intelligence service]." Just what use Trepper made of Spaak or whether the Soviet intelligence service obtained any benefit from the association would be impossible to say. What could be said was that Trepper had chosen his contact well, for Jean-Claude was a brother of a man who would become one of Belgium's most illustrious sons, Paul-Henri Spaak. In the years just before the start of World War II, Paul-Henri Spaak was Belgium's Socialist prime minister, and after the war he would hold a number of important posts, such as president of the Council of Europe, president of the United Nations, chairman of the Council for European Recovery, and secretary-general of the North Atlantic Treaty Organization. In a postwar report, the Central Intelligence Agency would note: "A source believed reliable advised that the [Soviet intelligence service] had an important contact in Paris with access to files of the NATO Political and Military Committees. This contact produced photographs of NATO documents and reportedly had access to Paul-Henri Spaak."

That was hardly an indictment of connivance by Paul-Henri Spaak, acting either wittingly or unwittingly. Yet whatever Trepper's success or lack of it within the Belgian civil service, he formed altogether seventeen networks in Belgium, Britain, Bulgaria, Canada, Czechoslovakia, France, Germany, Holland, Italy, Rumania, Sweden, Switzerland, and Yugoslavia, almost all linked in one way or another to the Foreign Excellent Raincoat Company. The link between the European and American arms of the Soviet intelligence service was probably Jacob Golos' World Tourist Bureau.

The most important of the branches of the Foreign Excellent Raincoat Company was that established in Berlin, to the founding of which the Comintern assigned a senior official from its headquarters in Moscow, Alexander Rado. In time, Rado established two major intelligence nets, which came to have at least 283 agents.

The first was headed by Harro Schulze-Boysen, a great-nephew of Grand Admiral Alfred von Tirpitz, the founder of the modern Imperial German Navy. Schulze-Boysen's wife was of the nobility, a granddaughter of Princess Eulenburg, wife of a principal diplomatic adviser to Emperor Wilhelm II. Among the social élite of Nazi Germany, the Schulze-Boysens numbered among their closest friends the president of Prussia, founder of the Gestapo, and head of the Luftwaffe, Hermann Göring. Despite the fact that Schulze-Boysen had spent three months in jail in 1933 for having headed an antinazi resistance group, Göring arranged a position for him in the news department of the Air Ministry.

The second group was built around Dr. Arvid Harnack, the son of Otto

Harnack, noted German historian, and nephew of Adolf von Harnack, German theologian. With an advanced degree from the University of Wisconsin, Dr. Harnack lectured in economics and philosophy at the University of Berlin and was a consultant at the foreign ministry. His wife, Mildred Fish, whom he had met while studying in Wisconsin, was also involved in Harnack's espionage activities. Among their agents were Adam and Margarete Kuckhoff, close friends of the American ambassador to Germany between 1933 and 1937; a former minister of culture, Adolf Grimm; a professor at the University of Giessen, Friedrich Bernard Hermann Lenz; and a socially prominent Berliner, Erika von Brockdorff, a member of a leading German diplomatic family and a relative of Count Ulrich von Brockdorff-Rantzau, who had headed the German delegation at the peace treaty negotiations at Versailles and then was the first postwar German ambassador to Moscow.

Known to the Gestapo collectively as the Rote Kapelle (Red Orchestra), the German branch of the Foreign Excellent Raincoat Company thus was an organization involving a large number of influential and socially prominent Germans; and it represented a major penetration of the German establishment.

As Leopold Trepper and Alexander Rado established the new Soviet intelligence system on the Continent, another leading Soviet spymaster set out to do the same thing in Britain. The man was Henri Robinson, who according to the files of the Central Intelligence Agency, "was probably a German Jew and identical with Henri Baumann, born on May 8, 1897, in Frankfurt-am-Main, Germany," but files of the Gestapo, spelling the name Robinsohn, listed him as having been born in St. Gilles, Belgium. Robinson conversed fluently in several languages, and "was about 5 ft 8 inches tall with a dark complexion, black greying hair, a high forehead, deep-set eyes, a big curved nose, full lips, wore glasses and pince-nez, dressed well, [and] had a quiet appearance."

During the World War, Robinson studied in Geneva, where he moved on the fringes of Zinoviev's group of Bolshevik exiles who were with Lenin before the October Revolution. After the war, he went to Berlin, where he began to associate with Goebbels' rival as a master propagandist, Willi Muenzenberg. Robinson joined the agile and brilliant Muenzenberg in forming the International Communist Youth Movement, predecessor of the Young Communist League, and during the German October of 1923, he commanded the underground AM (military) *apparat* in the Rhineland. From Germany, he soon moved on to Moscow where he succeeded Muenzenberg as head of the Comintern's Communist Youth International, but he held that post only briefly before assignment in Berne as technical chief of the AM *apparat* for Central and Eastern Europe.

By 1928, Robinson was in France as principal Comintern assistant to the chief of Red Army military intelligence in France, "General Muraille," a man to whom "direct action—war, revolution, barricades—was everything."[3] At the direction of General Berzin, Muraille and Robinson proceeded to build up a network of military intelligence specialists that penetrated almost every corner of France and beyond. After the Sécurité arrested and deported Muraille in 1931, Robinson became chief of the BB (political) *apparat* in France, and it was in that capacity that he acquired a Red Army military intelligence agent known as Harry II.

Harry II was the founder of a network of spies in Britain that would include some of the era's more prominent names in espionage: Anthony Blunt, Guy Burgess, Klaus Fuchs, Donald MacLean, and Allan Nunn May. Based in Paris, Harry II operated in London through a "cut-out"—intelligence jargon for an intermediary—known as Ernest Weiss, who concentrated upon a small group of the sons of the higher British bourgeoisie who attended Eton or some similarly exclusive school and went on to either Oxford or Cambridge. Weiss appeared suddenly in London in 1927, the year in which the bullfrog's chorus—the rumors of war between Britain and the Soviet Union—was alive. It was probable that Weiss was a homosexual, for one of his earliest converts was Guy Francis de Moncy Burgess, one of the most beautiful, most intelligent, wittiest, and most notorious homosexuals of the period.

Guy Burgess was noted for bawdy songs ("Little boys are cheap today, cheaper than yesterday") and outlandish remarks (he could never fly on a commercial airliner because he would feel compelled to seduce the pilot). He was so outspoken in his admiration for Communism that hardly anybody took him seriously. His police record would show that he sometimes wandered through Mayfair at two o'clock in the morning brandishing a bottle of beer, one arm around a boyfriend, crying, "I am a Comintern agent."[4]

The epitome of the upper-class British establishment rebel who became embroiled in the Comintern's conspiracies, Burgess went to Eton, that school which for over two centuries had produced seventeen of Britain's prime ministers and was known, above all, for its loyalty to the throne. When Burgess went up to Trinity College, Cambridge, to read history, the principal topic for discussion had become politics, especially Communism. Burgess quickly fell in with another future Comintern agent, Kim Philby, the son of Harry St. John Bridger Philby, an explorer who had recently foresworn allegiance to the muddled grandeur of British Monarchism for the stern world of a Saudi Arabian muslim. Both Burgess and Philby quickly joined the Communist cell at Cambridge.

Kim Philby was ready-made for conversion: it was in the blood. His father before him had experienced a mystical transformation upon arrival at Trinity; from a pure Christian and a devout imperial administrator, he had embraced, as he himself put it, "agnosticism, atheism, anti-imperialism, socialism, and general progressive revolt against the philosophical and political canons in which I was brought up."[5] So with his son, who began to develop the political ambiguity associated with his namesake, Rudyard Kipling's Kim:

Something I owe to the soil that grew—
More to the life that fed—
But most to Allah, Who gave me two
Separate sides to my head.

One side of Philby's head was British: cricket, P. G. Wodehouse, the *Times*, and what Evelyn Waugh called "reformed dress, . . . heraldry, madrigals, regional cookery, Devonshire teas."[6] The other side of his head was Communist, which involved a devotion to the Kremlin at the very time that the Comintern was engaged in a determined campaign to supplant the institutions of British life that the other side of Philby loved the most. Although that schizophrenia would never be satisfactorily explained, Philby grew up at a time when many British intellectuals were coming to the conclusion that the British Empire should be swept away in the interests of peace and progress and when youths were searching for a young man's politics, which Communism seemed to offer, evoking visions of "fresh faced young comrades marching together to smash the bastions of privilege, the banks and barracks of the old men."[7]

Guy Burgess left Philby and Cambridge in the spring of 1935 to experience that bittersweet loneliness peculiar to English university men who came down to London without a job. After being turned down by the Foreign Office, the BBC, the *Times*, and the office of the Conservative Party, Burgess finally found a minor job as a financial adviser to Mrs. Charles Rothschild, who employed him on a retainer of £100 a month. He also became a secretary and traveling companion to Captain John Macnamara, a Tory member of Parliament who was also a prominent member of the Anglo-German Fellowship and a homosexual.

In 1938, Burgess announced that he had turned Fascist, which probably marked the point at which he became a Comintern agent working against the Fellowship and the Link. Through connections provided by a friend, Burgess subsequently obtained a job on the *Times*, then with the BBC, then finally with the secret service. To help Burgess establish himself, the Comintern regularly fed him tidbits of information. All the while he continued to say openly that he was a Comintern agent, as on one evening when he arrived fairly drunk at the flat of Morgan Goronwy Rees, a Fellow of All Souls College, announced "with a good deal of weight and seriousness" that he was a Comintern agent, and proceeded to try to recruit Rees.[8]

It was apparently the very audacity of Burgess's declarations that kept people from believing him. In any case, two facets of his personality, his drunkenness and his homosexuality, made him useful to a service that existed, as the phrase went, to gather all the secrets of all the princes of Europe. Many of the princes were homosexuals who engaged in pillow talk with the same avidity as other types of lovers. Appointed to the service as a principal officer in Section D, the department given over to sabotage and subversion, Burgess's assignment was to engage in pillow talk.

Burgess lived for a time in a flat in Bentinck Street, where the British journalist Malcolm Muggeridge found on one occasion a future minister of food, John Strachey; the crystallographic expert John Desmond Bernal; the art critic Anthony Blunt; and several counterintelligence officials. The scene appalled Muggeridge. Burgess himself gave Muggeridge the impression of "being morally afflicted in some way . . . as though he had some consuming illness—like the galloping consumption . . . or leprosy." The scene to Muggeridge seemed to represent "the end of a class, of a way of life."[9]

The British counterintelligence service, MI-5, could hardly have been unaware of what went on at the flat in Bentinck Street. A "prominent feature of the establishment was the presence of working-class boys, who participated in homosexual stripteases and drink-and-drug orgies," while Burgess took compromising photographs, collected compromising letters, and blackmailed those who could be useful to him.

Through John Macnamara, who was a frequent visitor to the flat when he was not visiting Hitler Youth camps in Germany, Burgess late in 1939 obtained information that he believed he might use to ensure his full acceptance in the world of British intelligence and counterespionage. It involved an American, Tyler Gatewood Kent, who worked as a code clerk for the American ambassador, Joseph P. Kennedy. Kent had previously served in the American Embassy in Moscow, where he had developed "a maniacally hostile attitude towards the Soviet regime, and an extra hatred of Roosevelt and his policies, besides fortifying his anti-semitism."[10]

Soon after arriving in London, Kent had fallen in love with Anna Volkov, the daughter of the czar's last naval attaché at the Court of St. James's, who was as Fascist as was Kent. To further the cause of Fascism and to frustrate what Kent perceived to be a British plot to involve the United States in a war against Germany, Kent began removing secret documents from the Embassy and passing them to Anna Volkov, who transmitted copies through the Rumanian Embassy to Italy and Germany.

Through the information supplied by Burgess, Kent and Volkov were arrested and tried for espionage at the Old Bailey. Both were convicted, Volkov sentenced to ten years, Kent to seven.

When Kim Philby returned to London after covering the Spanish Civil War for the *Times,* he thus found his old friend Guy Burgess seemingly securely ensconced in the British secret service. He himself had established a right-wing record that he hoped would provide him also with an entrée: he had reported the war from Franco's side, he had been wounded, and his current inamorata was Lady Margaret Vane-Tempest-Stewart, a daughter of the Marquess of Londonderry, whom Philby had met at a dinner party for the Duke and Duchess of Brunswick, the pro-Nazi daughter and son-in-law of Kaiser Wilhelm II. Philby tried first for a position with the Government Code and Cypher School but without success. However, when Guy Burgess put in a word for him, he obtained a post with the British Secret

Intelligence Service, there to rise rapidly until he became chief of the branch formed to watch the activities of the Soviet secret service.

Throughout the period 1933–1937, Burgess's controller, Henri Robinson, was in and out of London, using at least four different passports, none of which was his. Although his network of agents was plainly extensive, the full range of it would never be determined. Some of his papers would fall into the hands of Allied agents at the end of World War II, but they were passed to Philby as head of the Soviet section of the British Secret Intelligence Service and soon vanished from their file in the service's central registry. Duplicates of some of the papers held by American and French services nevertheless provided some information. Of the case officers of the three networks, one was identified by what appeared to be his real name, Ernest David Weiss; the others were known only as Harry II and "Jean," the latter having become Robinson's principal agent in Britain whose handwriting and the syntax and phraseology of his letters indicated him to be a British male. The papers also revealed that all three networks concentrated upon government espionage, including the operations of the British secret agencies, science and technology, and agents-of-influence operating in high places.

The papers and subsequent blunders of some of Robinson's agents revealed that Robinson had made a very accurate assessment of the morals and political attitudes of the first postwar generation of bourgeois Englishmen of good families who would in time take over their fathers' high offices and estates. Partly because of the process of ordinary political evolution, partly because of the exotic nature of the morals and manners of their class, and partly because of the dread evoked by the terrible casualties of the World War, they were fundamentally in rebellion against society. It was a society with one foot in the twilight of Britain's greatest epoch, the Victorian Age, and the other in a dawning Russo-American epoch, a society beset by various pressures that led many youths within it to accept the dictates of political conscience over the traditional demands of disciplines of national loyalty, and to rebel against parental authority. A classic case was the Prince of Wales; another was Oliver Baldwin, son of the Conservative leader and prime minister, Stanley Baldwin, who refused to speak to his father and became first a Socialist and then a Fascist and was "spoilt, unstable, homosexual, and naive."[11]

All the men recruited by Henri Robinson were affected in one degree or another with similar rebellion against their class and the attitudes of their fathers. It was particularly striking in the case of Philby; it was similarly startling in the case of a good friend of Guy Burgess', Anthony Frederick Blunt, who would become Knight Commander of the Royal Victorian Order, Légion d'Honneur, and Commander of the Order of Orange of Nassau.

One of London's most golden youths, Anthony Blunt went to Marlborough College and then to Trinity College, Cambridge, where in time he entered the Soviet service. When he came down from Trinity in 1932 at the age of twenty-five, he joined the staff of the Warburg Institute and began a career that was to establish him as one of the world's leading—or perhaps one of the most fashionable—art experts. During World War II, he would become a major in the Special Operations Executive, that branch of the British secret services responsible for raising secret armies, committing sabotage, and waging political warfare. Out of uniform, he became a professor of art history at London University and director of the Courtauld's Institute. Honors and posts were showered down upon him: the most important one of all, art adviser first to King George VI and then to Queen Elizabeth II. Many years were to pass before Blunt would be challenged, and when faced with exposure, he turned double agent for the British against the Russians in London during the Cold War, rendering such important services that his earlier file was closed without criminal proceedings being taken against him. The London establishment closed ranks around him and kept his confidence until in 1979 his secret life at last came to light.

When exposed, Blunt talked freely. To a British television audience, he confided that he had been invited to settle in Russia but had decided against it because he would rather have one month of life in London than fifty years in Moscow. Yet he appeared to have no regret over having spied for the Comintern and the Soviet Union; to the *Sunday Times*, he spoke in a parable: "The Florentine Army was fighting the Papal Army, and Benvenuto Cellini was on the Florentine side. During a lull in the battle, a voice came from the Papal lines: 'Benvenuto. The Pope wants you to work for him.' Cellini threw away his weapons, went over to the Papal Army, and became a silversmith for the Pope. When he had finished his work, he returned to Florence, where he was received with honor and rejoicing because he was a great artist."


## Chapter Fifty-Five

Willi Muenzenberg was the phenomenon of the Communist International, the Communist world's Hearst and Lord Beaverbrook in one. In the gray, dreary constellation of Comintern functionaries, he was the kingfisher that flashes across the lifeless pool, leaving in the mind's eye a streak of vivid color to enliven a monochrome world of drab, obedient clerks. With his ability to sell a product, he would have made a million dollars a year on Madison Avenue, for it was he who achieved the seemingly impossible: he made Communism's turgid jargon and thesis understandable to the working classes of the world. Through his publications—by the time he was thirty-eight, he was a press baron with concealed financial interests in almost all Communist news outlets around the world—he made the words "bourgeoisie," "capitalists," and "Fascists" the passionate epithets of the class war. He was the Spyros P. Skouras of the world revolution of the proletariat.

Muenzenberg was born in Erfurt, that ancient German city where another evangelist, Martin Luther, once studied, on August 14, 1887, four years before the

Erfurt Declaration by the German Social Democratic Party, one of the milestones in the history of the introduction of Marxism to Germany. At twenty-seven, Muenzenberg became secretary-general of Georgi Chicherin's Socialist antiwar organization, the Sozialistische Jugendverband, which as the World War began was operating in Switzerland.

There he began his career as the Bolshevik hot gospeler after becoming acquainted with Lenin; Lenin's wife, Krupskaya; Gregori Zinoviev; Karl Radek; and Dimitri Manuilisky, who would become the "owl of Minerva" behind Zinoviev and Dimitrov at headquarters of the Comintern. His first publishing enterprise was the journal of the Sozialistische Jugendverband, for which he persuaded Lenin to write the lead article for the first issue. When Lenin left for Petrograd to overthrow the Kerensky government, he told Muenzenberg of his plans to form the Communist International and invited him to join as a publicist. Although Muenzenberg accepted, he stayed behind in Switzerland as one of Lenin's phantomas.

Tiring of the incessant intrigues of the revolutionary microbes, the Swiss government began in 1918 to expel them, including Muenzenberg. Put across the frontier into Germany, he went to Stuttgart to reform the Sozialistische Jugendverband, and a year later that organization emerged in Berlin under Muenzenberg's presidency as the Communist Youth International, independent of the Communist International but conforming to the same political line. He dressed a host of ragged Berlin youths like Boy Scouts, except that they wore the badge of the Comintern—a brawny workingman smiting his chains and exclaiming, "Workers of the World, Unite!"—sang songs of praise about Marx rather than Sir Robert Baden-Powell, and held meetings and organized camps that looked to be preparation for guerrilla warfare.

In hope of obtaining funds for the new organization, Muenzenberg attended the Comintern's Second Congress in 1920 but was unsuccessful. The movement nevertheless prospered; with a hint of the Manhattan hyperbole that characterized him, Muenzenberg claimed a membership of 800,000.[1]

When the Communist Youth International held its second congress in Jena in April 1921, Zinoviev suddenly came alive to its possibilities; he ordered the seat of the congress transferred to Moscow, which meant funding by the Comintern and glory for Zinoviev for adopting such a useful device. As a reward, the Comintern's Central Executive Committee provided Muenzenberg a seat, but Zinoviev soon arranged to remove him from that control position by assigning him to organize an international campaign to promote famine relief in Russia. It was then that Muenzenberg began "his fruitful career as a promoter of Comintern front organizations."[2]

In that work, Muenzenberg displayed the imagination that was to characterize his career as the Barnum of Bolshevism. Nobody, he reasoned, would listen to an appeal for help from such a dyspeptic hermit as Chicherin; nor would the capitalist world listen to anyone considered so murderous as Lenin. What was needed was a trusted, well-known voice not identified in the public mind with the October Revolution. The choice was brilliant: the great Russian novelist, Maxim Gorki, social realist and humanist, illustrious friend of Chekhov, a man known to be philosophically at odds with Lenin. When Gorki appealed for help, the capitalists, particularly in the United States, responded as Muenzenberg anticipated: they lined up to donate their money. Muenzenberg had invented the fellow traveler.

Going to Oslo, he persuaded Fridtjof Nansen, renowned Norwegian explorer, humanist, natural historian, nutritionist, zoologist, oceanographer, and high commissioner for refugees of the League of Nations, to head an international relief committee. With Muenzenberg in attendance, Nansen established the Council for Russian Relief in Geneva under the auspices of the International Red Cross. Muenzenberg had invented the Communist front, and the grain poured in.

Returning to Berlin, he set up yet another organization with himself as chairman, the International Workers' Aid Committee, one of the first of what he called his "Innocents' Clubs," which employed "a new technique based on the simple observation that it is possible to persuade people to assist a cause in such a way that they become emotionally involved." Workers were asked to donate a day's pay or some item that their factory produced, "not as an act of charity towards the Russian people but rather as a gesture of solidarity with them." Aside from a tangible contribution to relief of the famine, the process had "a propaganda value . . . out of all proportion to that of money collected or goods supplied."

Quick to recognize the value of the technique employed with the International Workers' Aid Committee, Zinoviev was almost as quick to appropriate it. While Zinoviev basked in glory, Muenzenberg seethed.

Yet anger did nothing to lessen the bubble and froth of Muenzenberg's ideas. After the famine ended, the International Workers' Aid Committee, at his suggestion, continued, and its paraphernalia of soup kitchens and mobile canteens appeared wherever Communist propaganda might be gleaned: in Germany during the horrendous inflation, in Japan during the strikes of 1925, in Britain during the general strike of 1926, in New York, in Detroit, in Chicago during the first years of the Great Depression.

Muenzenberg also went back into the newspaper business and in time formed an amalgam of publications that would be known as the Muenzenberg Trust. His various publications, including two daily newspapers in Berlin, *Berlin am Morgen* and *Welt am Abend,* and a weekly modeled on *Life* Magazine, *Berliner Illustrierte,* were far more lively than the various official publications of the Comintern, which employed such dry names as *World News and Views* and *International Press Correspondence,* so that in time Muenzenberg became known in Europe and North America as the voice of the Comintern. Counting both newspapers and magazines, he was said to control no less than nineteen publications in Japan and, moreover, made them pay. He had extensive interests in the Communist press in the United States, in Socialist minority newspapers in Eastern Europe, and in the publishing worlds of France and Britain. He provided the seed money for the Left

Book Club in London, a brilliantly managed publishing house that became an institution of the British left. He also established a company with exclusive rights to distribute Soviet films, with agents in London, Paris, Rome, Amsterdam, and New York. The entire "elaborate apparatus linked up with banks, commercial, and other institutions which not only propagated the Party line but also earned large sums for the movement."

Burly, dark-haired, well-dressed, charming, Muenzenberg was forever rushing between Copenhagen and Constantinople, between Berlin and London, buying, selling, encouraging new talent, launching new enterprises, severing moribund ones; and he never seemed to run out of ideas. After Zinoviev stole away the Communist Youth International and International Workers' Aid, he soon founded the League Against Imperialism, which employed a small host of hungry young writers in London and Paris to dig out the records of the aristocracy and bourgeoisie to show their inequities and greed in imperial lands. The league attracted "many well-intentioned persons who were unaware that it was being used as a cover for all sorts of Comintern activities"; and when a police raid on the league's headquarters in Berlin in 1931 turned up evidence that put the league out of business, it was not long before branches of a new organization called the Colonial Information Bureau, taking the place of the league, sprang up around the world. As one of Muenzenberg's associates, a prominent Communist writer, Arthur Koestler, would remark, his chief could produce committees as a conjuror pulls rabbits from a hat.

To confront the rising tide of Nazism in Germany and Fascism in Italy and Japan and to depict the Soviet Union as the only law-abiding, antifascist, peace-loving nation among the great powers, the Comintern early in 1932 decided to hold a gigantic World Congress Against War.[3] The assignment to organize and conduct it went predictably to Willi Muenzenberg. He promptly turned the congress into another of his Innocents' Clubs by appealing, in particular, to intellectuals of international fame. They responded admirably: such eminences as the French writers Romain Rolland and Henri Barbusse; the Soviet writer Maxim Gorki; the German novelist Heinrich Mann; the scientist Albert Einstein; the Chinese women's leader Madame Sun Yat Sen; the American writers Upton Sinclair and Theodore Dreiser. Those and many more agreed either to attend the congress or to lend their names to the sponsoring committee.

That committee, the Committee for Struggle Against War, which Muenzenberg formed and administered, sent out invitations to thousands: Socialists, Communists, trade union leaders, capitalists, churchmen, national leaders. The announcement was at once an invitation and a document condemning the disarmament policies of the great powers in the League of Nations, which Russia had yet to join. Nowhere, other than in the stylized language of the document and the focus of the Soviet Union, was there any clue that the sponsoring committee was a tool of the Comintern. It mattered little, in any case, for at the time there was a flood of admiration among the world's intellectuals, and particularly those of Europe, for Soviet achievements in science, literature, art, medicine, and architecture. There was considerable excitement when the Committee for Struggle Against War announced that Gorki would tear himself away from his greatest work, *The Life of Klim Samgin,* to attend the congress and serve as chairman.

With the announcement that the congress was to open on August 27, 1932, in Amsterdam, the Dutch police were quickly on the alert. Aware of the true sponsor of the congress, Dutch authorities notified Moscow that neither Gorki nor anybody else representing the Comintern or Russia would be permitted past the frontier.

That failed to prevent hundreds of other delegates from turning up; although Muenzenberg's literature would subsequently claim that there were 2,196 delegates from twenty-seven countries representing 30 million people, only about half that number actually attended. At the opening ceremonies, those who did attend were treated at the outset to a demonstration of Muenzenberg's great sense of theater, a performance to rival that in the Royal Albert Hall in London on Empire Day.

The great convention hall was in darkness except for a single spotlight dwelling upon a mezzo-soprano in Ukrainian peasant costume attended by a brawny swain and singing the "Internationale" to the swelling accompaniment of a great orchestra and massed workers' brass bands. At the conclusion of the song, the hall suddenly filled with dazzling light, revealing myriads of waving red flags and banners, while the bands broke into a medley of revolutionary songs: the French "Carmagnole," the Czech "Scarlet Banner," the Chinese "March of the Red Army," the Italian "Red Bands," the German "Red Wedding." As the last notes died away, a roll of drums, a blast of an organ, and a summons by an announcer for the delegates to stand in a moment of silence and remembrance for a long list of proletarian heroes, including Sacco and Vanzetti, the Scottsboro Boys, and a California labor agitator, Tom Mooney, who was still in jail for having blown up and killed a number of people in San Francisco in 1916.

With a mighty cheer for "Stalin, the Great Leader," the congress began its deliberation with a welcome by Henri Barbusse, who announced that the sponsors had intended the congress to convene in Geneva, "but this was prevented because the League of Nations found itself embarrassed at the proximity of a Congress which planned *real* action against war." Calling for "workers' unity" in defense of "the country that guarantees socialism, the Soviet Union," Barbusse added: "The toiling masses are not only the source of power for social progress; they are also the power for intellectual progress."

With regret, said Barbusse, he had to announce that Romain Rolland, the 1915 winner of the Nobel Prize for literature, was unable to attend; but he had sent a telegram. As Barbusse read it at length, one sentence in particular drew "wild 'hurrahs.' . . . We reject no one, except the cowards, except the pusillanimous sleepers who satisfy themselves with declamations never translated into action; except, in a word, all those who seek, without confessing it, to find a pretext for not acting at all." Nobody appeared to notice that Rolland himself had found "a pretext for not acting at all," and in a letter to the French daily, *Figaro*, Rolland would later deny that he had sent the telegram; he said that Muenzenberg had composed it.

There followed a lavish ceremony honoring the man whom the Dutch authorities had prevented from attending: Maxim Gorki. Then came a long procession of speeches, among them:

> "A *striking Belgian miner*" told "dramatically" that one month ago, "when the army was called out and ordered to fire on the striking miners, the soldiers refused to obey. One corporal even broke his gun as a sign of protest."
>
> "A *German marine transport worker*" urged that "the fight be carried on, not only in the munitions industries, but in all key industries." He "pledged the active support of his union in preventing the transport of munitions."
>
> "An *anonymous British sailor who had saved up his leave and money to come here*" spoke "vibrantly" about the "brutalities" of the British government in suppressing a naval "mutiny" at Invergordon in 1931.
>
> "*Joe Gardner, American Negro miner and ex-serviceman* and Mrs. *Wright, mother of two of the Negro boys condemned to death at Scottsboro*, received a memorable ovation when they arose to greet the Congress; a vigorous resolution was adopted demanding the immediate release of the innocent boys."
>
> "*Sherwood Anderson, American author*, deplored the exploitation of authors in time of war—men of talent are bought over to serve for the propagation of hatred and lies. Anderson assured the Congress that an increasing number of American writers . . . stand ready to use their talents to expose war."
>
> "*Professor H. W. L. Dana, of Harvard University*, briefly described the mass unemployment and hunger in America and the consequent unrest which the ruling class attempts to sidetrack through war."

There followed what the official report called "the most stirring, breathtaking demonstration . . . in honor of an unexpected speaker whose name we shall never know."

The chairman stepped forward, and in an electrically vibrant voice he cried out, "Comrades! I have an extraordinarily important announcement to make! The sailors of the *Italian warship* now in the harbor of Amsterdam have heard of this Congress, and one of them has come to bring you greetings from his comrades! But first let me warn you: take no pictures! This boy's life is doomed if his picture gets into the hands of the police. And now I present him to you [roll of drums]—a *nameless sailor* of the Italian fleet." Instantly the Congress was on its feet as one man, and the *Internationale* rang out from thousands of throats.

Where the sailor came from, nobody knew; for the only Italian warship to call at Amsterdam for some time had sailed four days before the congress opened. In any event, as the official report had it, a

> sun-browned sailor in the dazzling white uniform of the Italian navy . . . described the absolutism of the Fascist dictatorship which, he said, makes revolution the only possible means of change. . . . All Italians realize that they are being driven into an imperialist war, with every avenue of protest closed to them. Nevertheless there are small groups in the army and navy who are aware of the true course of events, and they are preparing for the only possible resistance when the crucial moment comes. The speaker concluded: *"Abbasso il Fascismo! Viva la rivoluzione sociale!"*

With the long roll call of speakers completed, the congress turned to the presentation and dutiful acceptance of a number of resolutions, one of which stressed a familiar theme:

> The Congress points out that all capitalist powers treat the Soviet Union as a common enemy which they are attempting to undermine and overthrow. There have been direct wars of intervention, encirclement and blockades, armed attacks supported by Western imperialism, arming of White Guards, attempts at destruction by sabotage within the Soviet Union, unprecedented campaigns of calumny and defamation, all carried on under flimsy cover of diplomatic relations established merely for the sake of immediate financial advantage. . . . The Congress points to the steadfast peace policy systematically pursued by the Soviet Union and repudiates the legend of "red imperialism," the only object of which is to justify and mask the persistent attacks against the Republic of workers and peasants.

The congress also condemned the League of Nations, the capitalist, imperialist, and Fascist powers, and all other instrumentalities that failed to accept Communism as a political doctrine and pledged to mobilize the politically potent intelligentsia into the service of the world revolution.

In an atmosphere of jamboree, the congress adjourned, to be followed by a session of an international committee established by the congress with headquarters at Aumont, France, composed of 133 representatives from twenty-seven countries. Twelve of them were Americans, including Theodore Dreiser, John Dos Passos, Upton Sinclair, and Ella Reeve Bloor, the mother of the founder of the Soviet intelligence service's first major *apparat* in Washington, Harold Ware. Within a year, world events provided the committee with a clear cause—Hitler came to power, and Germany, Italy, and Japan left the League of Nations—and also with a change of name: the League Against War and Fascism.

While the official Communist parties throughout the world tried "to capture the masses by frontal assault," Muenzenberg's front organizations, such as the League Against War and Fascism, sought to influence "by indirect means that section of society which Soviet propaganda describes as the 'progressive bourgeoisie.'" That was to say, the intellectuals, a class long given to embracing presumably liberal causes, and among that class Muenzenberg's clubs achieved considerable success; in at least one country, France, such success as to contribute to a marked lessening of the country's capacity to conduct military operations in its own defense.

Many who took part did so unwittingly out of a genuine revulsion to war or to Fascism. Yet it was also true that the intellectual class furnished a preponderance of the hard-core collaborators, the subversives, the spies. Why, asked a British journalist, Claude Cockburn, himself a Marxist in the 1930s who founded and edited an "extreme left-wing news sheet," *The Week*, while at the same time acting as a stringer for *Time*, *Fortune*, and *Pravda*, would "so many members of the affluent class—a bunch of gilded popinjays, one might say"—choose that course? One who chose the course, Guy Francis de Moncy Burgess, answered Cockburn's question "with casual candor." As Cockburn told it: "'After all,' he once said to me, 'as an English Catholic in the days of Elizabeth I, I would certainly have seen nothing disgraceful in spying against the English in the interests of the Vatican.'"[4]

Like a Trojan Horse, the League Against War and Fascism came to New York in September 1933. The first congress in its official report noted that "The delegates to this historic assembly represented trade union, farm, women's, fraternal, youth, religious, Negro, veterans', political, and cultural organizations." Yet the affair lacked the spirit of the Amsterdam congress, and the largest delegation appeared to be from the FBI. The second congress, held in Chicago in September 1934, was also listless; but the third, held in Cleveland over three days beginning on January 3, 1936, was different. Muenzenberg himself was present as "the representative of the European League" and of "Reichstag deputies exiled by Hitler" but probably also as organizer or the power behind whoever was the organizer. Some 2,070 delegates from 1,840 organizations claiming to represent 3,291,096 people in thirty states took part, and none but astute students of Communism could have discerned that the Communist Party or the Comintern were in any way affiliated.[5]

As the delegates took their seats in the Cleveland Public Auditorium, a massed choir of 300 voices drawn from various singing societies throughout Cleveland sang three American folk songs to do with the plow, the seasons, and the hearth. The chairman was the respected and respectable Dr. Paul Rogers of Oberlin College, an institution known for its Christian good works, and the mayor of Cleveland, Harold H. Burton, officially welcomed the delegates in the name of the City Council; but the star of the opening session was Major General Smedley Butler, United States Marine Corps, Retired:

> War is a racket! It is conducted for the benefit of the very few at the expense of the very many. . . . A second World War is gathering in Europe and the Far East. . . . Now is the time to tie your government in a strait-jacket so it can't go to war. And every time you feel like slackening up your effort, look at your son and imagine him in the condition in which I have seen boys on the battlefield—killed and wounded, with arms and legs shot away. And all for nothing, too!

After "thunderous applause and loud hurrahs" for General Butler, the congress elected a president, the noncommunist Dr. Harry Ward, a professor at the Union Theological Seminary, and an executive committee consisting in the main of noncommunist delegates but including a black member of the party, Clarence Hathaway.

The proceedings continued with the solemn reading of a telegram from the incarcerated labor agitator, Tom Mooney:

> Your fight against war and fascist terror . . . are commendable beyond words. Twenty years ago I fell victim to such terror in preparation for American entry into the World War. . . . Hope your Congress will remember Tom Mooney buried alive for twenty years in capitalism's dungeon because of militant loyalty to working class and active aggressive opposition to war.

The day's proceedings ended with the singing by a chorus of ethnic Hungarians of "The People's Song," written for the congress to the tune of "Song of the Vagabonds" by Hans Eisler, a Hollywood librettist who was the brother of the chief of the Comintern in the United States, Gerhardt Eisler:

> War is coming nearer,
> Fascist trends grow clearer,
> Nations rushing to their fall.
> But the people waken,
> From their slumber shaken,
> Form their ranks and heed the call.
>
> CHORUS:
> Forward! Onward! One united throng!
> Onward! Onward! Raise the people's song!
> Stop the mad war-breeders,
> Halt the fascist leaders,
> Peace and Freedom shall prevail!

By 1939, the League Against War and Fascism would claim that 16,128,000 Americans were associated either directly or indirectly with it.

Like most idea men, Willi Muenzenberg was not always popular with those for whom he worked, for idea men tend to generate jealousy and distrust in their more pedantic employers. So it was beginning in 1928 when Stalin, with Molotov as intermediary, assumed active direction of the Comintern. After Muenzenberg became a member of the Central Committee of the German Communist Party, Stalin's suspicions became pronounced, for here was a man who was running, very much as a free-lance, what almost amounted to a private Comintern of his own, and one which was mushrooming in every direction.

Yet those suspicions had generated no reprisal when with the rise of Hitler to power, Muenzenberg disappeared. Soon after the Reichstag fire in February 1933, he turned up in Paris, where he obtained a residency permit from the Popular Front government, which took a kindlier attitude toward Comintern agents on the run than had predecessor governments. The Hitler regime condemned both Muenzenberg and his wife, Babette, a woman with propagandistic skills to complement those of her husband, to death in absentia, and Heydrich sent agents of the Sicherheitsdienst to France to try to kill Muenzenberg; but those steps were insufficient to silence him. He soon formed the Committee for the Relief of the Victims of German Fascism with branches over much of Europe, an organization that had far less to do with charity than with intelligence and subversion and with which the German nuclear physicist who had been transplanted to Edinburgh, Klaus Fuchs, was associated, along with any number of people who had no Communist leanings, "had never heard of Muenzenberg, and believed the Comintern to be a bogey invented by Goebbels."

It was in large measure to assist that committee that Muenzenberg founded Editions Carrefour, which published mainly propaganda literature, the most sensational of which was *The First Brown Book of the Hitler Terror and the Burning of the Reichstag*. Dreamed up amid considerable laughter and popping of champagne corks in Muenzenberg's apartment on the Boulevard Montparnasse and written by Muenzenberg's first lieutenant, Otto Katz, a talented journalist, it was translated into many languages. The thesis was that Hitler and Göring had ordered the Reichstag set afire by goons of the Sturmabteilung in order to fix the blame on the German Communist Party and provide a rationale for the harsh restrictive decree which Hitler used to ravage the party. Although "the evidence . . . was scarcely conclusive enough to warrant the categorical statements made," the book "was aimed at that large class of reader which is not very interested in the distinction between assertion and proof, especially if its sympathies are already engaged."

To supplement the propaganda of the book, Muenzenberg went to London and persuaded the Duchess of Atholl to convene a shadow court in London to "try" those whom the Nazis had accused of setting the fire. Lawyers with international reputations were persuaded to give their services *pro bono*. Employing accusations and alleged evidence as made public by the Hitler regime, the shadow court successfully implanted the image of Göring as a corpulent satyr in a toga playing the role of Nero and "acquitted" all of the defendants, in the process so convincing public opinion in most countries of their innocence that not the London trial but a trial staged by the Nazis in Leipzig looked to be the greater travesty. Through a combination of the book and the London show trial, Muenzenberg successfully beclouded the facts about the Reichstag fire at the time and for decades to follow, and he did it without the Duchess of Atholl realizing that he was a Comintern agent or that she was serving a Comintern cause.

Yet for all Willi Muenzenberg's triumphs, doubts about the cause which he served so nimbly and assiduously were beginning to beset him. As he reflected, for example, on the Comintern's policy of violence against the Nazis as they were coming to power, he saw it as contributing to the decimation and collapse of the German Communist movement. In Paris, he began for the first time to study anti-Marxist–Leninist literature. While there was as yet no apparent weakening of his belief in Communism, he remained adamant in a belief that he had to oppose Nazism and renascent German militarism by every means at his disposal; and with the advent of the Popular Front as official policy of the Comintern, it seemed to Muenzenberg that the Comintern was nothing more than an instrument of Soviet nationalism and imperialism. Under those circumstances, was the Comintern really capable of fighting Nazism and German militarism? Indeed, was Russia under Stalin strong enough to resist Hitler?

Those doubts were in Muenzenberg's mind when he went to Moscow for the Comintern's Seventh Congress, upon the conclusion of which Stalin staged the trial of Zinoviev, Kamenev, and their colleagues. Rumors quickly spread that Muenzenberg, whose ideas in regard to Communist youth and workers' aid Zinoviev had appropriated, had provided some of the stories that had led to Zinoviev's indictment. Whatever the truth behind the rumors, they marked a turning point in Muenzenberg's career. Called back to Moscow, he arrived there in September 1936, while at the same time, a Czechoslovakian Communist of the Comintern, Bohumir Smeral, a member of the International Control Commission of the Comintern, the body responsible for ensuring the loyalty and discipline of Comintern agents, turned up in Paris "to make himself thoroughly acquainted with Muenzenberg's affairs."

In Moscow, Muenzenberg was requested to respond to questions about several members of the staff in his Paris office, in particular about a secretary named Liane, whom the control commission suspected was a spy for Franco. That was of special concern because Muenzenberg had established the Committee for War Relief for Republican Spain, which like his other organizations, was less concerned with philanthropy than with intelligence and espionage and which, like them, worked closely with Red Army military intelligence and the NKVD. Finding it hard to believe that the Control Commission was serious, Muenzenberg at first refused to talk about Liane, but it gradually became clear that the NKVD was seriously disturbed over the possibility that Franco might have an agent working where she might learn of the NKVD's operations. As rumor spread that Muenzenberg had offended against "revolutionary vigilance," other guests at the Hotel Luxe, where all visiting Comintern representatives stayed when in Moscow, began to avoid him. As an old Communist hand, Muenzenberg could hardly have failed to read the portent, and at last the dreaded order arrived: he was not to be permitted to leave the Soviet Union.

There was some consolation for him in that the head of the Secretariat for Western Europe, Palmiro Togliatti, offered him the post of propagandist for the Communist Youth International; but unable to believe that he was actually going to be prevented from leaving Russia, Muenzenberg appealed to Stalin's personal representative on the Comintern's Executive Committee, Dimitri Manuilisky, who promised that Muenzenberg and his wife would be granted exit visas. Yet when they arrived at the railroad station to pick them up, they found that they had been denied.

Thus thwarted, Muenzenberg went back to Togliatti and assured him that he was quite willing to accept the post proffered him in Moscow but that he first had to clear up his affairs in Paris. As inexplicably as in many another Communist about-face, the officials at that point granted the exit visas.

Returning to Paris, Muenzenberg was thoroughly alarmed. The problem over the exit visas would have been upsetting in any case; it was the more so because of the extreme political terror that was gripping Moscow in the wake of the Zinoviev-Kamenev trial. He was all the more taken aback when he found the representative of the International Control Commission, Smeral, awaiting him in Paris.

Whatever the two had to say to each other, Muenzenberg soon after their meeting took a precautionary step. In the habit of obtaining receipts for heavy expenditures of Comintern funds, many of which might be seriously questioned, he had hidden the receipts before leaving for Moscow; at that point, he retrieved them and gave them to his wife who turned them over to a Catholic press agency with the promise that they would be held in confidence and made public only if something untoward happened to Muenzenberg or her.

That action strongly suggested that Muenzenberg had decided to part company with the Comintern. Yet to Smeral he insisted that he was putting his affairs in order in preparation for returning to Moscow to assume the position with the Communist Youth International, but as the time to depart approached, he suddenly had a nervous breakdown.

Muenzenberg went to a clinic run by a Professor Chateaubriand, a clinic to which Nikolai Bukharin had gone for treatment when he realized that his number was up; but Muenzenberg and Babette at that point vanished. They apparently remained in or around Paris, and in July 1937, a White Russian émigré newspaper, *Poslyedniya Novost*, announced that Muenzenberg had severed his connections with the Comintern. In a second story, the newspaper reported that Moscow had summoned him to return to Russia on several occasions, threatening to expel him from the Comintern and the party if he refused, but Muenzenberg had refused. He also refused, according to the newspaper, a demand from the Comintern plenipotentiary and fellow German, Wilhelm Pieck, to hand over extensive bank accounts held in his name in Amsterdam, Strasbourg, and Basel, although he apparently did turn over financial details of his publishing empire, the Muenzenberg Trust, which soon collapsed. The newspaper also reported that Muenzenberg had threatened to publish all that he knew—and few men knew more—about the Comintern's activities in Western Europe.

By Christmas of 1937, Babette Muenzenberg would later state, her husband's break with the Comintern and the party was complete. A few months later, on May 23, 1938, the Central Committee of the German Communist Party announced that Muenzenberg had been "excluded" from the party for "action contrary to party principles and for breaches of discipline." The Soviet press announced that he had been disciplined—the equivalent in Communist parlance of excommunication—for "intriguing against the Popular Front policy and with refusing to carry out the party's directives."

It would emerge later that all along, Muenzenberg's friend and deputy, Otto Katz, had been an NKVD plant and that he had been providing information indicating that Muenzenberg was misusing party funds for his own purposes and that he had been engaging in activities, such as frequent consort with titled women, that were inimical to party policy. Summoned to Moscow to receive the Order of the Red Banner for work against "anti-party elements," Katz vanished; his name would reappear only in 1952 when the Soviet press would announce that he had been found to be a British spy and a Zionist agent and had been executed.

Muenzenberg, in the meantime, back in Paris, started a weekly German-language newspaper, *Die Zukunft,* edited by his writer friend Arthur Koestler, who was at the time at work on a brilliant indictment of Soviet politics and the Comintern that would be published under the title *Darkness at Noon.* The newspaper's editorial policy was strongly antinazi and anti-Soviet.

As World War II began in September 1939, French police took no step at first to intern Muenzenberg, but when the German Army achieved a massive breakthrough into Belgium and France in the late spring of 1940, that changed. The Sécurité at that point picked him up and sent him to a detention camp near Lyons, but his stay there would be short. With the continued advance of the German columns, he was released and with three companions, known to be Communists, made his way toward Marseilles where, he said, a rich Rumanian friend would provide money and documents for flight to Britain; the Rumanian, it would be said later, was part of an escape chain for European politicians set up by the British Secret Intelligence Service.

As Muenzenberg and his three companions reached the village of St. Antoine, a stronghold of militant French Communists, he learned that a car was waiting for them in a nearby hamlet. The four men set out for the hamlet along a path through the woods, but Muenzenberg never made it. Some weeks later his corpse would be found lying under a tree, one end of a length of piano wire attached to a broken bough and the other tied around his throat. Nothing further was ever heard of his three companions.

## Chapter Fifty-Six

When the world parliament, the League of Nations, admitted the Soviet Union into its ranks in 1934, the head of the Soviet delegation was Meer Genokh Moisseevitch Wallach, alias Maxim Litvinov, born on July 17, 1876, at Belostok in the Pale of the Settlement, the son of a produce merchant who dealt in potatoes, rye, oats, flax, wheat, and hemp. When Litvinov was five, the czar's secret police upset the family's comfortable bourgeois existence by arresting the father in the dead of night and accusing him of having "foreign connections with elements hostile to Russia."[1] The authorities in time admitted that a commercial rival had concocted the charge and released Wallach to go about his business, but Litvinov would say later that the incident affected him as deeply as Lenin had been affected by the execution of his brother for political offenses against the state. Almost from that moment, Litvinov became a revolutionary.

Following a brief service in the Imperial Army, Litvinov before reaching the age of twenty went to work in Kiev in a sugar factory and in time became the manager. He also joined the Social Democratic Labor Party, the leftist party that later split into the two factions of Mensheviks and Bolsheviks. Since the czar outlawed the party, Litvinov thus became a member of the Russian political underground. Such was his devotion to the party's revolutionary program that he spent his savings and all that he could borrow to purchase a small printing press. After working at the sugar factory during the day, he joined fellow party members in the evenings to operate the printing press—until he was betrayed, arrested, and sentenced to two years in jail. While in prison in Kiev, he read a copy of Lenin's revolutionary newspaper, *Iskra,* and from that moment became devoted to the concept of the world revolution of the proletariat.

Fashioning a rope ladder from bedsheets, Litvinov during the night of August 18, 1902, escaped over the wall of the prison. It was while he was on the run from czarist police that he assumed the name Maxim Litvinov, which he drew from a novel by his favorite author, Ivan Turgenev, whose masterpiece, *Fathers and Sons,* dealt with the philosophy of Nihilism and personal and social rebellion. Making his way to Switzerland, Litvinov tried to contact Lenin in Geneva but received no response to his letters; but he did make the acquaintance of one of the cofounders of *Iskra,* Georgi Valentinovich Plekhanov, known as the father of Russian Marxism, who suggested that Litvinov become the clandestine distributor of *Iskra* in Berlin. Using the alias Gustav Graf, Litvinov took up residence in a cheap lodging house in the Neustädtische Kirchstrasse and performed his underground duties so efficiently that in 1903, when he visited London, Lenin received him cordially in the two shabby little rooms at 30 Holford Square that he and his wife then occupied.

Impressed with Litvinov, Lenin made him an assistant and took him along to the congress in Brussels in midsummer of 1903 where the split in the party occurred. Although the basic issue was Lenin's desire for a small, elite membership as opposed to an all-encompassing organization, there was also friction over a small Jewish segment and its demand for authority in all matters related to the Jewish proletariat. To Litvinov, all religion was an "opiate" that stifled "realistic thinking"; he stayed with Lenin and the Bolsheviks.

Impressed with Litvinov's competence, dependability, common sense, and calm, Lenin appointed him to a seven-man Committee for Organization of the Bolshevik Party, which would be active not only in forming the party but also in staging the October Revolution. While acting as Lenin's agent in Riga in 1905, Litvinov ran guns and explosives to revolutionaries in the Russian capital of St. Petersburg; and after Czar Nicholas II granted a considerable degree of civil liberties in hope of warding off revolution, Litvinov accepted an invitation from one of Lenin's inner circle, Leonid Krassin, to go to St. Petersburg to found a newspaper for the Social Democratic Party, *Novaya Zhizn (The New Life)*, which the czarist government authorized on the condition that the paper eschew revolutionary propaganda. Under an alias, Ludwig Vilhelmovitch Nietz, and posing as an engineer, Litvinov went to St. Petersburg and with an original capital of 15,000 rubles provided by Gorki assembled an editorial staff, engaged a printshop, and established an efficient distribution system. So successful was the newspaper that it was soon financially self-sufficient.

In the issue of December 2, 1905, Litvinov violated the agreement against publishing revolutionary propaganda. "The government is on the verge of bankruptcy," the newspaper stated. "It has changed this country into a mass of ruins and covered it with corpses." The czarist political police reacted swiftly, banning publication of the newspaper and coming calling for "Engineer Nietz." As Litvinov would recall later, he "decided not to trifle with my luck." Gathering together important documents, he "went out though the back door."

Litvinov surfaced in Paris where he posed as a Belgian, Pierre Dubreil, who was buying arms for the government of Ecuador. He was, in reality, buying arms for the revolutionary movement inside Russia and in the course of the assignment made such an ostentatious display of wealth as to provoke multiple rumors as to the source of his funds. He was, according to one account, "swimming in money," and according to another, he "ate only in the best restaurants, insisted that his champagne be very dry and cold, invited his hungry comrades and always paid their bills." There were stories that he got his money through highway robberies and that he headed a band of counterfeiters.

It was more likely that Litvinov actually obtained his funds from the Bolshevik Party, for under the leadership of Stalin, Bolshevik gunmen and bombers on June 13, 1907, had robbed the Imperial State Bank in Tiflis and made off with currency and securities valued at 300,000 gold rubles. The police of all Western Europe having been alerted to the robbery, the Paris police found Litvinov buying railroad tickets for London at the Gare du Nord and arrested him on suspicion. As the police discovered, he had on his person twelve 500-ruble notes whose serial numbers matched twelve of those stolen in Tiflis; but as Litvinov pointed out, he had been in Paris when the robbery occurred, and he had received the notes from the party treasury with no knowledge of where they had originally come from. Since he had been about to depart for London when arrested, the Paris police solved their problem by hastening him on his way.

When he arrived in London in January 1908, Litvinov produced a letter from Gorki to the director of the London Library, who found Litvinov a position with a London publishing house, Williams and Norgate. At age thirty-two, Litvinov soon appeared by day to be just another member of the bourgeoisie, known as Maxim Harrison, earning a livelihood in the publishing trade, but by night he was Maxim Litvinov, representative of the Bolshevik Party and Lenin's plenipotentiary at the underground International Socialist Bureau in London. Rising steadily in the publishing world, Litvinov became an executive with the old conservative house of John Murray, but with the outbreak of the World War, he joined the Russian Purchasing Commission in London, a post in which he had access to "considerable information of value," which he transmitted "direct to the Bolshevik Party." He extended his range of connections considerably when he accepted an assignment to tutor a high official of the Political Intelligence Department of the Foreign Office, Rex Leeper, in the Russian language and when he married a rising young English novelist of considerable beauty, Ivy Low, the daughter of H. G. Wells' collaborator on the *Educational Times.*

Mrs. Litvinov was recuperating in a London nursing home from delivery of the couple's first child when revolution erupted in Petrograd and the Provisional Government established control. At Lenin's direction, Litvinov remained in London, and once the Bolsheviks had staged the October Revolution, Lenin appointed him the Soviet "representative" at the Court of St. James's. As Litvinov soon discovered, appointment and practice were two different things, for the Foreign Office refused to recognize his position and continued to maintain relations with the ambassador of the Provisional Government at the Embassy in Chatham House. Undaunted, Litvinov opened a "People's Embassy" in a dingy working-class district at 21 Victoria Street, near Parliament Square.

As Litvinov began his stewardship, he had neither funds, staff, instructions, nor recognition from his host government. Following Fanny Kaplan's attempt to assassinate Lenin in August 1918, he nevertheless protested to the Foreign Office that the British agent Robert Bruce Lockhart was involved. The protest availed nothing, and Litvinov soon found that instead of enying the elegant prerogatives of diplomacy in the capital of capitalism, he would experience life inside Brixton Prison in a cell that bore the sign: "Reserved for the Military Guests of His Majesty." He was charged with unlawful agitation in trying to raise stevedores against loading ships carrying supplies to British forces in Russia, and he would be released only after the agreement reached by the British government to exchange him for Lockhart.

So it was that Litvinov ended his brief career as Soviet representative at the Court of St. James's, unaccepted to the end. The British government looked upon him as a dangerous dreamer who combined politics with crime, and anybody familiar with his dossier well might have wondered if Litvinov would ever become socially acceptable in a world of diplomacy framed according to the manners and morals laid down at the Congress of Vienna.

The assembly, or main body, of the League of Nations met in Geneva in Reformation Hall, a gaunt building with turrets and battlements alongside Lake Geneva that resembled in architecture and spirit an enormous Scottish castle on some remote and misty moor. It was a place of rectitude and prudence devoted to good works and—it seemed to ordinary people—inhabited by powerful people who were vaguely mad. Yet as the British writer Malcolm Muggeridge observed: "The League of Nations in those days focused the hopes of the enlightened everywhere; all eyes were upon it in the confident expectation that it would succeed in making war as obsolete as duelling, and armed forces as unnecessary to nations as wearing a sword had become to individual citizens."[2]

The pariahs of Europe—Germany and Soviet Russia—were at first excluded from membership, but after accepting the Soviet embrace at Rapallo, Germany was admitted in the hope of the capitalist powers that having Germany as an ally would help them deal with Russia. Even had Soviet Russia been invited to join, Lenin would have refused, partly because he regarded the league as nothing more than a capitalist cabal planning war against the Socialist fatherland and partly because he had publicly vowed that no Soviet envoy would set foot on Swiss soil so long as the murderers of Vatislav Vorovsky remained unpunished; but when Germany, Italy, and Japan walked out of the league, Lenin was dead, and when the hierarchs of the temple of peace invited Russia to join in order to raise for Germany the old specter of a two-front war, Stalin's government accepted.

The other major power not belonging to the league was the country of its principal advocate, Woodrow Wilson. As Wilson's own Democratic Party put it in its campaign platform of 1920, the league was "the surest, if not the only practicable means of maintaining the peace of the world and terminating the insufferable burden of great military and naval establishments." The Republican Party, on the other hand, maintained "the traditional American policy of noninterference in the political affairs of other nations," and when it came to ratifying American membership in the league by the U.S. Senate, the Republican view prevailed. There would be many over the years who would attribute the weakness, lack of resolution, and eventual demise of the League of Nations to the decision of the United States to stand aloof. But in the final analysis, the league could only be as strong as the will of the individual member states to forgo national interest and privilege in favor of the common good, and as the record would show, that will was never strong.

Upon Fascist Italy's invasion of Ethiopia, for example, Litvinov warned the assembly that failure to act against Italy would "stimulate new conflicts more directly affecting the whole of Europe," and the league did, indeed, condemn Italy as an aggressor and impose sanctions, but in great part because Britain and France were trying to maintain good relations with Mussolini as a bulwark against Hitler, the sanctions were almost meaningless. When Hitler marched into the Rhineland, thereby in effect denouncing both the Treaty of Versailles and the Locarno Pact, and the league's Council met at the British government's invitation in London, Litvinov warned that "if we close our eyes to the violation of these treaties or confine ourselves to verbal protests without taking more effective measures," the League of Nations would appear to be "ridiculous"; yet largely at the instigation of the Baldwin government, the Council declined to do more than refer the matter to the International Court of Justice at The Hague.

When Litvinov succeeded Chicherin as foreign commissar in July 1930, three mighty forces were at work to shape Soviet diplomacy: a consolidation of Stalin's power inside Russia by brutal and murderous methods; a need to keep faith with the world proletariat if only as a force for the protection of the Soviet Union; and a need to come to terms with capitalism in order to prevent the capitalist nations from uniting with Fascism in a crusade against Communism. As an official of the Soviet Union, Litvinov would have few prerogatives to pursue his personal conceptions, but he would exert an influence on those policies that Stalin and the Politburo adopted, and in the process, one misstep might consign him to the same grim fate that befell many of the old Bolsheviks.

Nowhere were Soviet tactics during the Litvinov period more consistent—or, in retrospect, more obvious—than in the matter of disarmament. While Stalin's Russia rearmed in secret with German help, Chicherin and then Litvinov appeared at the great international conferences to propagate pacifism and disarmament publicly while the Comintern did the same thing more covertly but no less energetically.

As noted in a report prepared in the U.S. State Department, the Soviets at all the various disarmament conferences between 1921 and 1932 "energetically stressed the urgent need for total disarmament."[3] In 1923, when the League of Nations asked the Soviet government to comment on a Draft Treaty of Mutual Assistance, an attempt to guarantee the security of each state as a preliminary to disarmament, the Russians responded in considerable detail and remarked that "The reduction of armaments is the most serious and immediate task of all governments." In keeping with the usual snail-like pace of the League of Nations, the next development came only in 1927 when a Preparatory Commission for a General Disarmament Conference began its work. Finally agreeing to appear before the commission after considerable procrastination and disagreement,

Litvinov declared that the only way to disarm was to disarm totally. He proposed that over a period of four years, all armies, navies, air forces, and fortresses be abolished in all countries along with military schools, military budgets, and any scientific research directed toward military ends. To supervise the disarmament process, Litvinov proposed a Permanent International Commission of Control, which would exercise overall authority over Commissions of Control in each contracting state and over local commissions within the state.

Litvinov could hardly have been unaware that his proposal had virtually no chance of acceptance, for aside from being utopian and thus impractical, it would establish an authority, as the British delegate pointed out, that would "transcend the League structure." There was also a matter that went largely unspoken: given Bolshevik skill in establishing control of unwary institutions, what would be the effect if the Russians succeeded in dominating or controlling either the International Commission or the national commissions, or both? With that proposal rejected, Litvinov submitted an alternative, but the control measures he proposed were even more rigid than those for his first proposal.

To the authors of the State Department study on Russian participation in disarmament proceedings, the Soviet record appeared on the surface to be "clear" and "forthright." Yet as the Soviets were presenting that front to the other states, what were they saying in Communist circles?

The authors of the State Department study looked back to Lenin's views on disarmament as expressed in his book *The State and Revolution.* Since the modern state was an instrument of the capitalist class, wrote Lenin, the armed services of those states were "instruments devised and used by the Capitalists to maintain their domination." The future Socialist state, on the other hand, would need no armies, navies, nor any state organ which then existed "only to oppress the proletariat." Thus, with the coming "of the Socialist classless society, the states and organs of oppression will no longer be needed and therefore will 'wither away.'" Yet in achieving the first step toward a Socialist world, establishing the dictatorship of the proletariat, it would be necessary to "break by violence" the hold that the capitalists maintained on society, and to do that, wrote Lenin, "many of the existing state organs can be turned against the oppressors and utilized to protect the proletarian revolution and the proletarian state against the remaining Capitalistic world." Therefore, "until the internal contradictions of the remaining Capitalistic states provoke imperialist war and violent revolution and eventual world socialism," the Soviet state would have to "remain strong and use the 'Communized' armies to defend the Socialist Fatherland." That dogma, noted the State Department's study, comprised the essence of a resolution approved by the Sixth Congress of the Communist International in the summer of 1928, "only four months after the Litvinoff proposals were made in the Preparatory Commission."

If such was, indeed, the Soviet view, why did Soviet Russia participate in the conferences and consistently propose disarmament? The State Department study eventually concluded that the Soviets presented their proposals "as a sharp weapon to cut away the camouflage and disclose to the world the insincerity of the capitalist states." In making disarmament proposals, the Soviets were careful to phrase them so that they had no chance of being accepted, for Lenin's thesis still prevailed: the Communists themselves needed "certain arms," including those of the capitalist military forces, to be used at the proper time "against the Capitalistic class in order to bring about the revolution." Only with the coming of a Socialist classless society established in the wake of the world revolution of the proletariat was disarmament to be countenanced.

By the time Litvinov became the Soviet Union's foreign commissar, he was already well known for the strong hand he had taken in foreign affairs as deputy to the ailing Chicherin. To some, "his chubby and unproletarian figure radiated an aura of robust and businesslike common sense that was in striking contrast to the enigmatic brutality of the Politburo or the conspiratorial noisiness of the Comintern,"[4] and when he waddled along the shore of Lake Geneva with his three immense, thuggy bodyguards, he conveyed a sense that all was right with the world. The fact that he had an English wife reinforced the view that he was somehow different from the intransigent revolutionaries.

There was none of that acceptance in Germany; for not only was Litvinov a Bolshevik, he was also a Jew, and on a visit to Berlin in December 1933, he calculatedly ignored a suggestion by the German foeign minister, Konstantin von Neurath, that he call on Adolf Hitler. Nazi diatribes against Litvinov were soon pathological in their fury. A seemingly unending spume of invective arose from Goebbels' propaganda mills to denounce the "Jew Litvinoff Meer Wallack Finkelstein" (Finkelstein being a term which the Nazis seemed to believe embodied all that they found objectionable in "Judeo-Marxism"). Using language unheard of in modern times between powers maintaining diplomatic and trade relations, Goebbels called Litvinov a "criminal," a "Yiddish conspirator," a known murderer with a large file at the Berlin *Polizei*, an *Untermensch* (subhuman).

It fell to Litvinov to carry out Stalin's new policy of countering the threat of Fascism by diverging from Leninism and the theory of international Bolshevism in favor of using every facility, including the Comintern, to assure the safety of the cradle of Socialism, the Soviet Union. It would come to be known as a policy of collective security aimed primarily at securing the frontiers in the west in order to be able to meet the threat from the east. The policy would in time produce treaties of nonaggression with Poland, Estonia, Latvia, Lithuania, Afghanistan, Persia, Rumania, Turkey, Yugoslavia, Czechoslovakia, and Italy and the treaties of friendship and mutual assistance with France and Czechoslovakia. It would also lead to the Comintern's call for the Popular Front.

Litvinov executed his assignment with energy and magnificent oratory while at his back Stalin was executing his old Bolshevik colleagues in the Great Purge and drastically cutting into the membership of the Foreign Commissariat. Either through demotion, fear-imposed defection, exile, imprisonment, or execution, Stalin got rid of the ambassadors to China, Denmark, Japan, Poland, and Turkey; the ministers to Lithuania, Finland, Hungary, Bulgaria, Latvia, Norway, and Afghanistan; a principal undersecretary at the League of Nations; the chargé d'affaires in Athens; a senior member of the legation in Bucharest; two of Litvinov's assistant commissars, his private secretary, most of the departmental heads in the Commissariat, and numbers of lesser officials and workers, including translators and secretaries.

Except in one instance, as that tidal wave swept through the diplomatic service, Litvinov revealed no emotion. The exception was in the case of an assistant commissar, Nikolai Nikolaievitch Krestinsky, who confessed at his trial to having taken money from the German General Staff. Having known Krestinsky since the days when the two worked together on Lenin's newspaper, *Iskra*, Litvinov was inclined to give him the benefit of the doubt, and when Krestinsky repudiated his confession, Litvinov was delighted. Yet when Krestinsky then withdrew his recantation and confessed everything, Litvinov said nothing. In a speech in Leningrad in late 1937, he indirectly praised Stalin's purge by declaring that no aggressor would ever find a "fifth column" on Soviet territory, for "the People's Commissariat of Internal Affairs [the NKVD]" was "unwilling to let such plans come to fruition" and was "vigilant and strong enough to destroy the Trotsky-Fascist organization of spies and wreckers in embryo."

In regard to the Comintern, Litvinov was faithful to the official line. In January 1919, while the peace conference at Versailles was in session, he declared emphatically that once Allied troops left Russian soil, all propaganda against Allied governments would cease; Soviet propaganda, in any case, he said, had nothing to do with creating a world revolution of the proletariat but was instead "an act of self-defense." "The prospect of world revolution," he told the American writer Louis Fischer, "disappeared on November 11, 1918." Even while professing to President Harding in 1921 that the Soviet Union desired nothing more than "intimate and solid ties . . . between the two republics," he was engaged with Washington B. Vanderlip in trying to create a trade war among the capitalist powers. The Comintern, he consistently maintained, was no agency of the Soviet government, and the Soviet government had no more authority over the Communist parties at home and abroad than did the governments of Britain, France, and the United States over the political parties in their countries.

For all the concern about the threat from the east, Litvinov saw Hitler and Nazi Germany as the greater peril. That hardly required any great prescience, for it was there to be read in *Mein Kampf* or to be heard in any number of Hitler's speeches. There was always the "Judeo-Marxist danger" and Germany's requirement for *Lebensraum*. Litvinov also watched warily as German bankers and industrialists visited Britain and the United States in apparent efforts to create a united front of capitalism against Communism, and there was no mistaking the sentiment of many in Britain for an alliance with Hitler against Russia. If assured of the support of the Wehrmacht, would not those same Englishmen who had tried to destroy the infant Soviet Republic in 1918 try again?

It was in large measure to obtain a forum for trying to create a united front against Fascism that the Soviet Union entered the League of Nations. That also explained Litvinov's strong stand against Mussolini's aggression in Ethiopia and Germany's march into the Rhineland. When Britain and France failed to react with comparable determination, that was to Litvinov proof that the two western democracies—and Britain, in particular—favored alliance with the Fascist states, which along with fear of Nazi Germany was in large measure responsible for the Comintern's abrupt shift in policy.

With the departure of Ambassador Bullitt from Moscow in the wake of the disagreements with the United States over the Seventh Congress of the Comintern in August 1935 and the arrival of his replacement, the millionaire lawyer, Joseph E. Davies, Litvinov hoped for improved relations with the United States. Davies would, indeed, prove to be a more cooperative emissary, and Litvinov and Davies would in time establish a "Max and Joe" relationship. Yet that relationship would in the long run do little to improve relations between the two countries.

Except for membership in the League of Nations and the treaty with France, the Soviet Union thus was still isolated from the other great powers when on November 25, 1936, Germany announced the Anti-Comintern Pact with Japan. The provisions of the pact that Germany made public were essentially innocuous, not even mentioning the Soviet Union by name, but when the head of Red Army military intelligence in Western Europe, Walter Krivitsky, managed to obtain copies of the correspondence between the two countries leading to conclusion of the pact, the threat to the Soviet Union was clear. The pact, Litvinov told the Eighth All-Union Congress of the Soviets on November 28, 1936, contained a secret military agreement directed against Russia.

In Moscow, the feeling that Russia was beleagured from east and west was acute, and to ease it, Litvinov tried to turn the Anti-Comintern Pact into an instrument for frightening the western democracies into cooperation with Russia. The Germans, he said, were "bent on a brutal policy of gangsterism" and would bring "those contemptible peoples, the Japanese and Italians," along with them. It would not be the Soviet Union that would suffer, he said, for "we have the Red Army and a vast extent of territory"; it would instead be "the rich capitalist countries that will fall an easy prey. The British and French people are soft under leaders who are blind.

"Hitler and his generals who control Germany," Litvinov continued, "read history. They know that Bismarck warned against war on two fronts . . . They believe the Kaiser lost the first world war because he forgot Bismarck's admonitions." When the Germans were ready "to embark upon their new adventures," he concluded, "these bandits will come to Moscow to ask us for a pact."[5]

In a further effort to inveigle the western democracies into cooperation, Litvinov hammered the theme that Hitler was less interested in destroying the ideology of Communism than in gaining "tin, zinc, mercury, copper, and other minerals" and acquiring Lebensraum. That theme was designed to disarm those of the right wing who saw alliance with the Fascists as the way to get rid of Communism, and the theme was also aimed at arousing the proletariat in the democracies against leaders who displayed sympathy with Mussolini and Hitler. In Britain, the approach was clearly effective in raising suspicions against Prime Minister Chamberlain, the "Cliveden set" around Nancy, Lady Astor, and an anti-Soviet group around the American ambassador, Joseph P. Kennedy. The most damaging and persistent of Litvinov's rumors was that Hitler and Chamberlain were actually in league and by 1938 had reached agreement on giving Germany a free hand in Eastern Europe and Russia in return for a pledge of noninterference with the British Empire.

Yet when Britain and France tacitly accepted Hitler's conquest of Austria and handed over Czechoslovakia at the Munich conference, about which the Soviet government was neither consulted nor informed, it was clear that Litvinov's policy had failed. Fascism, he said, would soon dominate all Europe except for Britain on the west and Russia on the east. On September 21, 1938, at Geneva, he declared that the League of Nations had failed and called for its dissolution. "The Soviet Government," he said, "bears no responsibility for the events now taking place and for the fatal consequences which may inexorably ensue."[6]

As Litvinov saw it, time was running out. All hope of support from the west seemingly having failed, it was time to turn to the final possibility for saving the Socialist fatherland: to make accommodation with the archenemy, Nazi Germany. But that was no assignment for the "Jew Litvinoff Meer Wallack Finkelstein." On May 3, 1939, Tass announced that Litvinov had asked permission to resign for reasons of health. His successor was one of his closest friends in the Soviet hierarchy and sometime head of the Comintern, Vyacheslav Mikhailovich Molotov, who was also the premier. Under Molotov, the Soviet government would make yet a final effort to conclude a mutual assistance pact with the capitalist powers, but there would be little hope that the effort would be successful. In the meantime, Moscow would be making stronger overtures to Berlin.

# PART XI

## "The Second Imperialist War"

*Chapter Fifty-Seven*

Prime Minister three times since 1923 and when not in office, leader of the opposition or of the Socialist Party, Stanley Baldwin on April 11, 1937, retired, his last major task to supervise the coronation of King George VI. The grateful sovereign created him the 1st Earl Baldwin of Bewdley, a Knight of the Garter, and a Privy Councillor. Departing on a long holiday cruise to South America, the new earl dropped dead of apoplexy on the captain's bridge as the liner steamed past the Abrolhos Rocks. Baldwin's successor as prime minister was a man who was almost as idle in office as the earl had been but considerably less charming, a man destined to go down in British political history as the most regrettable instrument since the mongrel Parliament of 1681: Arthur Neville Chamberlain.

In a revolutionary era, Chamberlain's antecedents were important, for he epitomized the class that the Communists detested: the bourgeoisie. Born in 1869, Chamberlain was a member of "an extraordinary, almost unique family,"[1] representing "a new and important element in the Conservative Party, the well-to-do middle class. They were men of property. They were as solid as their silver."[2]

In the House of Commons, a place noted for the cruelty of its wit, the members referred to Chamberlain as "the coroner." Not without reason. He never appeared in public wearing anything but black, with winged collar, frock coat, and tall silk hat; the only color ever to be seen about him was a heavy gold chain across his waistcoat joining his fob to what many believed was a Masonic relic. "He had a sardonic, not to say contemptuous, look and spoke with a harsh and rasping voice," and he had "a curiously stiff appearance, like those old daguerreotypes of the host's father or grandfather which hung about in the passages and gun-rooms of country houses." In the House, he took no trouble "to make himself agreeable even to his supporters, still less to his opponents." He "always gave the impression that he looked on the Labour Party as dirt," and members of the Labour Party reciprocated. His only relaxation, they said, was to play musical chairs at Cliveden, the stately home of Nancy, Lady Astor, which had given its name to a political cabal favoring an "understanding" with Hitler against Stalin. Back-benchers complained that there was a whiff of formaldehyde or carbolic about him, similar to that encountered in the vicinity of Westminster Mortuary on the Horseferry Road.

Hardly had Chamberlain succeeded to the post of prime minister than he came into conflict with his foreign secretary, Anthony Eden, that symbol of British masculine good looks, good manners, good breeding, and accomplishment. The issue was basic: Eden advocated a policy of firmness and strength in dealing with the dictators; much influenced by the pro-German, anti-Soviet sentiments of the Cliveden Set and probably admiring of the dynamics and industry of Hitler's resurgent Germany just so long as its attentions remained focused on Moscow, Chamberlain favored a policy of what he called conciliation. Whereas Eden had been impressed by Stalin and thought that under certain circumstances an alliance with Russia—or at least an understanding—might serve to deter all the dictators, Chamberlain was adamantly opposed even to contemplation of an alliance with "the bolshies."

At rather sharp odds with the foreign secretary, Chamberlain ignored him. Rather than establish that close partnership between both sides of Downing Street that was essential "if confusion and something worse" were to be avoided, Chamberlain "either did not understand or willfully set aside even the outward form of loyalty to his Foreign Secretary." On foreign policy matters, he worked not through the Foreign Office but through a small group of like-minded politicians and government officials: Lord Halifax, Sir John Simon, Sir Samuel Hoare, and Sir Robert Vansittart. Watching from the back benches, a member of Parliament and a later prime minister, Harold Macmillan, observed that with those men at his side, Chamberlain began to deal with the dictators "as if they were foreign business men with whom . . . he was doing some deal." He had no conception "that there could be such a man as Hitler, absolutely ruthless and quite regardless of any promises or pledged word."

As a part of that dealing, one of Chamberlain's close associates, Lord Halifax, the Lord President of the Council, the sovereign's panel of advisers or privy councillors, paid a visit to Germany. The visit grew out of an ostensibly private invitation from Reich Master Huntsman Hermann Göring to Lord Halifax as Master of the Middleton Hounds to attend an international hunting exposition in

Berlin. Since Göring held out a promise that Halifax would be able to talk with Hitler, Chamberlain urged acceptance.

The German press provided a warm reception, stressing the bluebloodedness of the guest: that his father was a viscount, his mother the daughter of an earl, his wife also the daughter of an earl and a lady of the bedchamber to Queen Elizabeth, and he himself a lord of the manor. The press made no mention that the visit had anything to do with diplomacy; with a play on the word *Halali*—the German equivalent of Tallyho!—the press nicknamed him Lord *Halalifax*.

As Göring had promised, Hitler received Lord Halifax on November 19, 1937, at the Berghof. Speaking candidly, Halifax said he had brought no new proposals from Chamberlain; he had "chiefly come to ascertain the German government's views on the existing political situation, and to see what possibilities of a solution there might be."[3] Hitler used that as a point of departure to criticize the British press, which he claimed had tried to sabotage Halifax's visit by publishing a list of so-called German demands. He had no demands, Hitler said; all he wanted was a close relationship with Austria, an end to the persecution of ethnic Germans in the Czechoslovakian Sudetenland, return of Germany's prewar colonies, and an end to interference by the western powers with the extension of German trade in Southeastern and Eastern Europe. As Hitler's voice rose, Lord Halifax tried to be conciliatory: England, he said, was always open to any solution not based on force. Force, Hitler shouted back, was never a consideration; were not the Austrian people demanding *Anschluss* with Germany?

Lasting much of the day, the meeting was for Lord Halifax genuinely unpleasant. He came away seriously perturbed, worried that there was no way to conciliate the volatile German leader. After a long talk with Göring, who assured him that under no circumstances would Germany use force, Halifax nevertheless left the country convinced that all would be well in the end. The Germans, he reported back to the British Cabinet, "had no policy of immediate adventure. They were too busy building up their country, which was still in a state of revolution." What Lord Halifax could not know was that—wittingly or unwittingly—he had given Hitler the impression that Britain would prove no obstacle to his plans. "I have always said," Hitler remarked after Halifax left, "that the English will get under the same eiderdown with me; in their politics they follow the same guidelines as I do, namely, the overriding necessity to annihilate Bolshevism."[4]

As Lord Halifax rode by train for Calais and London, he made notes on his impressions of his meeting with Hitler. "What we want is assurance that Germany is *not out for war*," he wrote. "We want an understanding, we will have to pay, and colonies are our only money."[5]

It was what Prime Minister Chamberlain also had in mind. Soon after Lord Halifax's return, he arranged a conference with French officials in London "to determine if it would be opportune to attempt appeasing the German dictator by making important propositions and if so, what they were to be." The French were at first firmer than the British, declaring that to allow the Germans to act with impunity in Eastern Europe would lead inevitably to "rapid German domination of Europe." Yet how to stop Hitler without going to war? It soon developed, as Lord Halifax had put it, that colonies were the only money, but the British had grown accustomed to those former German colonies that they were ruling by mandate of the Treaty of Versailles and were loath to give them up. It was at that point that it became clear to the French that a paranoid dread of war had driven the British leaders to a strange new definition of honor; perhaps, the British suggested, Hitler might settle for the Belgian Congo.[6]

That the British government was reluctant to take a firm stand against fascism could have come as no surprise to Hitler or to his partner, Mussolini, for in those early years of Fascist aggression, as British authorities were soon to discover, the British Embassy in Rome had kept the Fascist leaders well informed of the British government's views. The events occurred in the period when His Britannic Majesty's Ambassador Extraordinary and Plenipotentiary to the Italian Empire was one of Scotland's greatest noblemen, the Earl of Perth, a cool, stately figure much given to dry witticisms about the personality and character of his host, Benito Mussolini.

Lord Perth was assisted in representing his government by frequent telegrams from London, often of a highly personal and confidential nature and consisting of advices concerning the objectives, intentions, strategies, and tactics practiced by the government to achieve its end. There were also summaries of the intelligence upon which the British government made its decisions and copies of much of the material exchanged between the Foreign Office and other major embassies, such as those in Paris, Berlin, Moscow, and Washington, including the most important interdepartmental correspondence relating to affairs concerning the empire, the armed forces, and other vital agencies of state.

The material was known collectively as "the Print." Since most of it was sensitive and secret, it was transmitted in a special cipher, and when a communication was either too long or too sensitive to entrust to the wires, a man known as the King's Messenger, usually a retired Army officer with a record of devoted service and reliability, brought it personally from London. When moved between offices, the Print was transported in locked dispatch boxes emblazoned with the royal coat of arms and when not in use, it was secured in a special safe within the Embassy.

The great central issue between Britain and Italy during much of Lord Perth's tenure was Italian presence in Abyssinia, that remote, undeveloped kingdom on the Red Sea, where Italian presence appeared to threaten the British Empire in Arabia, East Africa, and, on occasions, India. At the same time, major expansion of the Italian Fleet seemed to foreshadow Italian attack on British mercantile marine communications running through the Mediterranean from Britain to the empire. As ringing proclamations from the balcony of the Palazzo Venezia made amply clear, Mussolini was in an imperial mood.

For almost a half-century, Abyssinia had stirred Italian emotions, for there in

1896 tribesmen had defeated an Italian army of 20,000 men, a defeat that had a lasting and shattering impact on Italian society. Thus when Fascist representatives in the Chamber proposed in 1934 that an imperial expedition to Abyssinia might solve Italy's economic and unemployment problems and at the same time enable Fascism to fulfill its mission, the proposal was received with enthusiasm and emotion. As a first step toward mounting such an expedition, Mussolini in December 1934 engineered an incident near Walwal on the ill-defined frontier between Abyssinia and Italian Somaliland, but Abyssinia appealed to the League of Nations and while the league deliberated, Mussolini stayed his hand. When the league in September 1935 returned a verdict absolving both sides of blame, it became clear that Mussolini had delayed not out of respect or concern for the league but because he needed time to prepare the immense army he intended to deploy to take the country.

In the face of mounting evidence that Mussolini was about to act, the Abyssinian emperor, Haile Selassie, the King of Kings and Lion of Judah, again appealed to the League of Nations, but the league was still at work preparing a report on the crisis when on October 3, 1935, the Italian Army struck. Coming on the eve of a general election in Britain, the invasion produced a strong reaction. In an election manifesto, the Tories proclaimed that "there will be no wavering of our support for the League," while the Labourites professed a similar determination. The foreign secretary at the time, Sir Samuel Hoare, declared that Britain stood with the league "for the collective maintenance of the Covenant in its entirety, and particularly for the steady and collective resistance to all acts of unprovoked aggression," while the French government professed support for the British position "without reservation or fear."[7]

That failed to deter Mussolini. What had Britain and France done when Hitler had repudiated the disarmament clauses of the Treaty of Versailles? Nothing. More than that, Mussolini had a source of information that told him that should the League of Nations demand Italian withdrawal, neither Britain nor France would take any military or naval action to enforce it.

To Mussolini's surprise, the League of Nations did impose economic sanctions against Italy. Literally applied, the decision required members of the league to sever all trade and financial relations with Italy, to prohibit financial dealings with Italian nationals, and to prevent all personal, financial, and commercial relations between Italians and the nationals of any other state, whether the state belonged to the league or not. As a first step, member states were to ban loans and exports to and imports from Italy. It looked like a strong measure, particularly if it meant an embargo on oil and closing of the Suez Canal to Italian shipping, either of which might wreck Mussolini's operations in Abyssinia; yet again Mussolini had a special source of information that put his mind at rest. For fear of throwing Italy into the arms of Germany, he learned, Britain would not take those steps, nor would the British government strictly enforce the other economic sanctions.

In Britain, in the meantime, the Tories and Stanley Baldwin won an overwhelming victory in the general election, mainly on the strength of a strong pro-league stance. It was thus with the most profound shock that the electorate soon learned that the foreign secretary, Sir Samuel Hoare, had been conferring with the French foreign minister, Pierre Laval, about a plan to settle the Abyssinian crisis by splitting the country between the Abyssinians and the Italians, that the British Cabinet had approved the plan, and that it was soon to be presented to the League of Nations. The public outcry was emotional and strong, for Britain had taken the lead in imposing sanctions; the Italians were using tanks, bombers, even poison gas against virtually defenseless tribesmen; why would the government back down? So strong was the outcry that Hoare was forced to resign.

Yet the furor in Britain did nothing to save Abyssinia. In May 1936, as all resistance collapsed, the world was treated to pictures of the bearded King of Kings and Lion of Judah boarding a British cruiser at Djibouti for exile, while there were reports of widespread Italian looting.

The Italian triumph would have a decisive effect on the future of the League of Nations. For the first time, the league had imposed strong sanctions, but the noble declarations of the leading league powers, Britain and France, turned out to be hollow. That undermined virtually all faith in the determination of the two major European democracies, so that Hitler and the other dictators might expect with considerable confidence that the democracies would back down again and again.

The new foreign secretary, Anthony Eden, tried to fight the policy in Britain, but he had little success against the determination of his prime minister, Neville Chamberlain, to pursue a policy o appeasement. After Chamberlain sent Lord Halifax to confer with Hitler in 1937 and then tried to bring Mussolini into an alliance with Britain, Eden resigned. To many who shared Eden's concern about appeasement, it was a hard blow. As Churchill put it, he lay in his bed "consumed by emotions of sorrow and fear." Eden appeared to Churchill to have been "one strong young figure standing up against long, dismal, drawling tides of drift and surrender, of wrong measurements and feeble impulses," one who seemed "to embody the life-hope of the British nation, the grand old British race that had done so much for men, and had yet some more to give." Yet at that point Eden had departed. "I watched the daylight slowly creep in through the windows," Churchill was to write, "and saw before me in mental gaze the vision of Death." [7]

It was not long after that, early in 1938, when the British ambassador, Lord Perth, and his wife attended a state function in Rome, at which Lady Perth, as usual, wore her tiara. Upon return to the Embassy, she asked the counselor to put it away for safekeeping, and since he was going to the safe containing the Print, he put it there for the night. When Lady Perth a few days later asked for the tiara, it was not to be found. Since the counselor had forgotten to retrieve it from the safe, it had obviously been stolen. A check revealed that the combination of the safe was so rudimentary that any half-skilled safecracker could negotiate it and that, on occasion, whenhe combination failed to work, some Embassy employees had been leaving it open.

Security officials soon determined that the thief was an Italian clerk in the central registry at the Embassy. Under interrogation, he confessed to having stolen the tiara, and he returned it. He also admitted that for five years he had been opening the safe regularly, usually when the Embassy staff was at siesta or the beach, and taking secret items from the Print to a branch office of SIM, the Italian secret intelligence service, located in a nearby police station. Once the intelligence agents had photographed the Print, he returned it to the safe.

During that critical five-year period, 1933-1938, which included the crisis over Abyssinia, Mussolini had thus been kept reliably informed of Lord Perth's transactions with the British government, and it would emerge later that the clerk had sold copies of the Print to a representative of the Soviet secret service in Rome. It had to be assumed that during that period, Mussolini and Stalin, and possibly Hitler as well, had had an inside track to the innermost policies of His Britannic Majesty's government.

## Chapter Fifty-Eight

In Britain, those last months before the start of another world war were bittersweet and haunted. The crown still exercised its magic, and proletarian families still rose in their parlors and stood at attention when the national anthem came over the BBC at the end of the day's programs. As was usual in Britain in times of great crisis, the aristocracy and bourgeoisie came forward to advise and lead the masses, issuing appeals such as Lady Reading's call to "every kind of woman in every kind of sphere of life" to prepare "patiently and thoroughly a protection for our loved ones and our homes."[1] The youth of the upper classes, who had so recently vowed not to fight for king or country, were spending considerable time at lectures in fire stations or at civil defense meetings, discussing such matters as tourniquets, splints, and gas masks. The skies above the capital were crowded with fat antiaircraft barrage balloons lolling listlessly under the cumulus. Stalin having signed a nonagression pact with Hitler, many members of the Anglo-German Fellowship and the Link were joining the Society of Friends of the Soviet Union or the Left Book Club of Victor Gollancz; while in the working-class flats of the Peabody Estate at Clapham Junction, the great Southern Railway entrepôt in a grimy quarter that lay ten miles—and light-years in thought—to the south of Whitehall, Communist cell leaders forswore their lectures on Marxist dialectics to organize the digging of air raid shelters and trenches, taking the opportunity in the process to sell copies of Soviet Russia Today, a brightly colored magazine full of pictures of dams, hydroelectric plants, and ballerinas.

The man of the hour in those last months of 1938 and 1939 was to many Winston Churchill, out of office and sixty-three years of age, the leader of a small group of the Privileged Bodies who advocated a determined and vigorous restraint upon Germany. Although numbers of Churchill's friends anticipated that he would soon be called to high office, they worried about his physical condition, concerned that he drank too much. A London press baron, Harold Harnsworth,

Lord Rothermere, wagered Churchill $3,000 in an effort to get him to give up brandy for a year, for "Everyone, including especially myself, will wish you to be in the finest fettle when the day arrives."[2] Another friend suggested that he get away on a cruise, but Churchill refused to go, for to his mind it was no time to leave England. "Everything is overshadowed," he wrote to his old chief, David Lloyd George, "by the impending trial of will-power which is developing in Europe. I think we shall have to choose in the next few weeks between war and shame, and I have very little doubt what the decision will be."[3]

Yet no great power resided with the rotund, sly Churchill; it rested instead with the coroner, Neville Chamberlain, who was beginning—although he did not know it at the time—to die of cancer of the colon. The symbol of Tory probity, a man who seemed not to have a single thermal unit of liveliness about him, a man imbued with the effortless superiority of his class, Chamberlain appeared to be incapable of a single courageous decision. In the middle of the night, he nevertheless suddenly rose from his bed at No. 10 Downing Street, switched on the lights, called his private secretary, and dictated a memorandum for the foreign secretary, who had succeeded Eden, Lord Halifax: he would, he declared, go at once to Berchtesgaden and talk with Hitler as one reasonable man to another.

When the news of Chamberlain's proposed trip broke, it electrified the world. "Nothing so daring or dramatic had been seen in the annals of British diplomacy." So dread was the prospect of another great war and so fervent the hope that Chamberlain would succeed that "at Westminster Abbey the nave around the grave of the Unknown Warrior was ordered set aside for unbroken prayers." All churches urged their congregations to join in prayer "for the blessing of God upon the Prime Minister's journey to Germany."[4] King George VI and President Roosevelt hurriedly returned to their capitals. At Berchtesgaden, Hitler reacted to a telegram from Chamberlain proposing a conference with astonishment: "*Ich bin vom Himmel gefallen!*" ("I was utterly amazed.")

As intelligence reports indicated that Hitler would invade Czechoslovakia with a million and a half troops on November 25, 1938, Neville Chamberlain, who was nearly seventy and had never flown before, took off from the Royal Air Force station at Heston in Kent aboard a Lockheed Lodestar, a small craft that heaved, shuddered, and bumped across Europe in a flight lasting nearly seven hours. Such was Hitler's confidence that he declined to go to the Munich airport to greet his guest, preferring instead to sit on the sundeck of the Berghof.

As the principal dancers in a *menuet macabre* were about to come face to face at Berchtesgaden, Hitler saw his British opponents in much the same way as did his colleague, Mussolini. "These men," Mussolini had said to Hitler, "are not made of the same stuff as the Francis Drakes and the other magnificent adventurers who created the empire. These . . . are the tired sons of a long line of rich men, and they will lose their empire."[5]

Upon return to London after the last of three conversations with Hitler, Chamberlain in the evening of September 30, 1938, appeared on a balcony of the prime minister's residence at No. 10 Downing Street. To a crowd assembled below, he waved a piece of paper and declared that he had secured with Germany "peace with honour." There would be "peace in our time."[6]

As the crowd cheered, he proceeded to read a joint declaration which he and Hitler had signed that morning in Munich:

> We, the German Führer and Chancellor and the British Prime Minister, . . . are agreed in recognising that the question of Anglo-German relations is of the first importance for the two countries and for Europe. . . . We are resolved that the method of consultation shall be the method adopted to deal with any other question that may concern our two countries and we are determined to continue our efforts to remove possible sources of difference and thus to contribute to the assurance of peace in Europe.
>
> (s) A. HITLER<br>NEVILLE CHAMBERLAIN.[7]

In the general relief with which an anxious world received the news, few paused to note that the piece of paper said nothing specific. What appeared to matter at the time was that as Chamberlain had predicted, two reasonable men had settled their differences and produced an agreement that would end the war crisis and bring a lasting peace to long-embattled Europe; but the reality was far different and warranted no celebration. Chamberlain had sold Czechoslovakia to Hitler for what would prove to be but a year of peace, and by March of 1939, the Czechoslovak state created at Versailles in large measure by the very power that at that point had betrayed it would cease to exist. "These men," Mussolini had told Hitler, "are not made of the same stuff as the Francis Drakes and the other magnificent adventurers who created the empire."

Mussolini's remark reflected a widespread belief that the British ruling class was disintegrating and that Britain, compared to the authoritarian states, had already become a second-rate power. Britain at times clearly gave that impression, that the old heroic values of the Victorian Calm—empire, service, sacrifice, discipline, patriotism—were giving way to decadence, class warfare, modernism, and antipaternalism. The great institutions of learning—especially Eton, Oxford, and Cambridge, long said to have more influence over the soul of England than did the archbishop of Canterbury—still maintained the highest academic standards, yet in reaction to the bloodletting of the Great War, they had become what many regarded as "a hot spring of anarchy bubbling out of the rocks."[8] No longer were the great institutions just for learning and training the sons of the ruling class in the arts of maintaining Britain's supremacy; within the historic walls, there was eroticism, drugs, cults, politics, "exuberant, anarchic, fantasizing hedonism." From that bewitched world, squads of fresh-faced young bluebloods emerged, some to take over the process of ruling a world empire, but others, through the embrace of Fascism or Communism, to try to destroy it. Among them, Kim Philby, Guy

Burgess, and others, including one who would come to be called "the greatest mole of them all." He was Walter Krivitsky's man who wore a cape.

Donald Duart Maclean was a son of a solicitor and politician from Tyree, Argyllshire, Sir Donald Maclean. A liberal (in the British sense), Sir Donald was a member of Parliament who helped found the National Society for Prevention of Cruelty to Children and was a lay preacher—a Gladstonian highland Presbyterian—who regularly held family prayers. In 1931, the year Donald Duart entered Trinity College, Cambridge, a place second only to Oxford's Balliol in producing cabinet ministers, bankers, and colonial administrators, Sir Donald became president of the Board of Education. The relationship between father and son, it was said, was typical of the antipaternalism of the times.

Descriptions of Maclean at Trinity were hard to come by, but one applied to another might well have applied to him: "He was a man with a drawl marked by sickliness, jaded mannerisms, long hair, an ebony cane, and timid prurience." Confused sexually and politically, he was soon seduced in both directions by Guy Burgess, who was later heard to joke that going to bed with Donald Maclean's "great white body" reminded him of what it would be like to sleep with the operatic diva Dame Nellie Melba.

Slightly under six feet, with pale eyes, sallow complexion, and a somewhat exotic taste in dress, Maclean in 1933 dismissed capitalism in the *Cambridge Left* as "a crack-brained criminal mess" that was doomed to be swept away. By 1935, when he obtained a First, he was a confirmed member of the Communist cell at Trinity. Yet the party was legal and his membership in it failed to preclude his entering the Foreign Service, where, after training and probation, he was posted to the British Embassy in Paris.

There Maclean entered a world not unlike the one he had just left at Trinity College: clubby, secretive, insular, privileged. As a student of the man and the period would write: "The embassies established private worlds, exempt from the laws obeyed by the greater society." British ambassadors seemed "to have been notorious for eccentricities like homosexuality and transvestism," which made them welcome such men as Maclean. They tended toward "a curious melange of literary and libertine elements" in which "the mingling of moral anarchy and political authority was very intimate."

With that quick eye for ability and presence that also characterized ambassadors of the time, the British ambassador in Paris, Sir Ronald Campbell, soon saw in Maclean a man of promise. At that critical time—an emerging Hitler, Italian adventures in Abyssinia, the Spanish Civil War—Maclean was soon undertaking duties and responsibilities not usually entrusted to a third secretary. Among them was looking after the Print. Maclean was thus in a position to supply the Soviet intelligence service with a most detailed and comprehensive picture of British diplomacy at work in a difficult period. The mole had begun his burrow.

## Chapter Fifty-Nine

The emergence of Fascism as a major aggressive force in Europe produced a quaint relationship between Winston Churchill, man of the purple, and Ivan Mikhailovitch Maisky, man of the red. The old Bolshevik who planned and carried out the Comintern's first successful conquest, Outer Mongolia in the days of the mad Baron von Ungern-Sternberg, Maisky had made an early appearance in London diplomatic circles as an assistant to the People's Representative, Maxim Litvinov, and had spent time for sedition in no less than four British jails. In the 1930s, Maisky's credentials were better, for in 1932 he presented them to King George V and was duly accredited as the ambassador of the Union of Soviet Socialist Republics at the Court of St. James's.

In an era when most ambassadors were drawn from the aristocracy, Maisky was in manner and appearance—not to mention in politics—an anomaly. At fifty-five years of age, he was rolypoly and even in the most critical of times wore an Oriental smile. He was, in fact, an Asiatic, born the son of a Jewish doctor and a Gentile mother at Omsk. Although he appeared to do his best to conform to the fastidious world of London diplomacy, he never quite overcame a vague air of disrepute. Yet he was likable, the one among all Russian diplomats who seemed to comprehend the western viewpoint. "I rather like Maisky," noted Sir Alexander Cadogan, the permanent undersecretary of state for foreign affairs, "although—or perhaps because—he's such a crook."[1]

To the world of British diplomacy that put great store by an embassy's foods and wines, Maisky's table was little short of criminal. As one London politician noted after attending an important luncheon in 1936, the Embassy was "in a grim Victorian mansion in Kensington Palace Gardens." Let in by "a gentleman in a soft collar and stubby yellow moustache," the guest "was ushered into a room of unexampled horror" where Ambassador Maisky greeted him "with effusion." "We stood in this grim ante-room," the guest noted, "while we were given corked sherry, during which time the man with the yellow moustache and a moujik's unappetising daughter carried tableware and bananas into the room beyond." At table, the first course was caviar, "which was all to the good," but then there was "a little wet dead trout," followed by "chicken in slabs surrounded by a lavish display of water-cress." Then there was "what in nursing homes is called 'fruit jelly.'" As the guest noted, Maisky was playing at being European; "One felt sorry for the little beast."[2]

Winston Churchill had far less concern for inelegancies; his concern was for some kind of alliance to counter the rising power of Germany and Italy. The capitalist world's leading anticommunist spokesman, he nevertheless declared that if forced to choose between Communism and Nazism, he would become a Communist. "Mortal quarrels are afoot," he would write, "and I had my station in them."[3]

At the beginning of April 1936, Churchill lunched with Maisky and soon began to see him regularly. Maisky was quite willing to be wooed, for it was clear from Stalin's reception of Anthony Eden in Moscow the year before, that Stalin was prepared to accept an alliance between Communism and capitalism against Fascism. Although Churchill was concerned whether Russia could be relied upon as an ally, he was also so concerned about the danger from Germany that, as a colleague put it, he "buried his violent and anti-Russian complex of former days and is apparently a bosom friend of M. Maisky."[4] In the House of Commons, replying to criticism by Lady Violet Bonham Carter of his espousal of a relationship with Russia, Churchill on May 23, 1936, asserted that he "would marshall all the countries including Soviet Russia from the Baltic southward right round to the Belgian coast, all agreeing to stand by any victim of unprovoked aggression. I would put combined pressure upon every country neighbouring to Germany to subscribe to this and to guarantee a quota of armed force."[5]

Yet for all Churchill's eloquence and other endearing qualities, he was out of office, and to some critics, he had merely replaced the Reds that had once infested his brain with Nazis. While amused and entertained by him, few were prepared to accept his imperial rhetoric. As the prime minister, Stanley Baldwin, said to a colleague in that month of May 1936, he intended some day to make a speech about Churchill:

> I am going to say that when Winston Churchill was born, lots of fairies swooped down on his cradle bearing gifts—imagination, eloquence, industry, ability—and then came a fairy who said, 'No one person has a right to so many gifts,' picked him up and gave him such a shake and twist that with all these gifts he was denied judgment and wisdom. And that is why while we delight to listen to him in this House, we do not take his advice.[6]

By September 1938 and the onset of the crisis over Czechoslovakia, Churchill and Maisky, having met at least once a month to discuss the gathering storm in Europe, had established such a mutual confidence that Maisky consulted Churchill on British foreign policy even though Churchill was out of office, and on a promise of strict confidence, Churchill provided such assistance as he could. How well Maisky kept the confidence could be discerned from the fact that the Comintern, while attacking almost every other prominent Tory for pusillanimity or pro-Nazism, never once mentioned the name of Churchill, once one of its most loudly proclaimed enemies.

As the year of 1939 opened, the list of Fascist conquests was growing ever longer: Manchuria, North China, Abyssinia, Austria, the Sudetenland. The talk was where they might strike next: the Germans against Holland, Poland, Rumania? the Italians against Egypt, the Sudan, Tunisia? the Japanese against Russia? While Churchill continued relentlessly from his back bench in Parliament to challenge Chamberlain's attempts to make friends with the dictators and to urge instead a pact with Russia, Chamberlain just as relentlessly pursued his own policy while implacably refusing all suggestions that he bring Churchill into the government.

As the first day of spring neared, the next objective became apparent: the rest of Czechoslovakia. Through a combination of promises and threats, Nazi agents stimulated the Slovaks to secede from the state. Convinced that Britain and France would do nothing, Hitler had only one concern: Soviet Russia; but Stalin quickly took care of that. Addressing the Eighteenth Party Congress, he declared that Russia had to be careful to avoid letting the western powers trap the Soviet Union into a war with Germany in order to pull their chestnuts out of the fire; Russia's pact with Czechoslovakia, he said, required Russian aid only if France moved first. Russia, he concluded, wanted "peace and business relations with all countries." [7]

Provided that assurance, Hitler threatened President Emil Hácha, the successor to Beneš, with immediate invasion and Luftwaffe bombs. The aging Hácha, who suffered from a heart ailment, gave in and signed a document placing the fate of the Czech people in Hitler's hands. It was, in effect, surrender, and on March 14, 1939, German columns marched into the country. The democratic state created by the Treaty of Versailles had lasted only twenty years.

In London, Prime Minister Chamberlain announced that Britain's guarantee of the new Czechoslovakian frontier, established following the ceding of the Sudetenland to Germany, did not apply, for the secession of Slovakia had already destroyed the state "whose frontier we had proposed to guarantee. His Majesty's Government cannot accordingly hold themselves any longer bound by that obligation." Chamberlain added not a word of reproach for Hitler or sympathy for the Czechs, but such was the anger of the House that a few days later he felt compelled to issue a warning: "No greater mistake could be made than to suppose that because it believes war to be a senseless and cruel thing, this nation has so lost its fibre that it will not take part to the utmost of its power in resisting such a challenge if ever it were made." [8]

Chamberlain attempted to give substance to the warning by announcing on March 31, 1939, a British guarantee to Poland. By that guarantee, he stated, Britain promised Poland all possible support "in the event of any action which clearly threatened Polish independence, and which the Polish Government accordingly considered it vital to resist"; but the next day, a headline in the *Times*, which at that period served as a mouthpiece for the Chamberlain government, called attention to the specific wording of the guarantee. The obligation, the *Times* pointed out, did not bind Britain "to defend every inch of the present frontiers of Poland. The key word in the statement is not integrity but 'independence.'" [9]

That propelled Churchill to the attack. The "sinister passage" in the *Times*, he declared, was "similar to that which foreshadowed the ruin of Czechoslovakia." Britain, he told the House, should have no concern "with particular rights of places, but to resist by force of arms further acts of violence, or pressure, or of intrigue . . . our first duty is to re-establish the authority of law and public faith in Europe." The "slightest sign of weakness," Churchill warned, would "only serve to aggravate the dangers, not only for Britain but for the whole world." Above all, he declared, "the Soviet Union must be encouraged to come forward as a partner in the gathering together of all threatened States." [10]

For all the mounting fervor of Churchill's campaign to bring Russia into an alliance against Hitler, Chamberlain remained unconvinced. Yet as Churchill recognized, the world was running out of time, and such was the crisis that, in his view, Britain could afford to put aside no potential ally. That was made the more evident when on April 7, 1939, the Italian Army invaded the tiny Adriatic state of Albania, and again Chamberlain did nothing. Nor did Chamberlain do anything when a few days later, on April 27, 1939, Hitler announced that he "no longer considered the Anglo-German Naval Agreement [which conceded naval superiority to Britain] to be binding on Germany." [11]

There was no question that during this period, Chamberlain honestly believed he could do business with Hitler, that Hitler would hold to a bargain once struck. There was also the dread fear that another generation of young Englishmen might die like the generation before them on the Somme and Aisne; and there was also the state of Britain's arms. Unlike France, which had maintained a degree of readiness for war, Britain had come late to the rearmament race, and the country's deficiencies were frightening. In the spring of 1939, for example, when the Royal Air Force tested a new 250-pound bomb, eleven out of twenty-eight failed to explode. The entire Fighter Command was in much the same state as 29 Squadron, which was supposed to have twenty-one aircraft but actually had only sixteen, and the number of those capable of taking to the air was three. After only 120 hours of flying time, the aircraft had to be grounded for six weeks for maintenance. To Churchill, facts like these made all the more essential an alliance with Soviet Russia, particularly as Hitler began to employ the same kind of war of nerves against Poland that he had earlier employed against Austria and Czechoslovakia.

Churchill's constant badgering, as Chamberlain called it, and public exhortations from Ambassador Maisky finally prompted Chamberlain to reconsider the possibility of an alliance, but he remained dubious. As he confided in a letter to his sister, "I have deep suspicions of Soviet aims and profound doubts as to her military capacity even if she honestly desired and intended to help." [12] But the pressure in the end nevertheless proved too much for Chamberlain, and he dispatched, along with the French government, a military mission to Moscow to explore the possibility of a tripartite alliance. The heads of the mission were Admiral the Right Honourable Sir Reginald Aylmer Ranfurly Plunkett-Ernle-Erle-Drax, Knight Commander of the Bath, Companion of the Most Excellent Order of St. Stanislaus of Imperial Russia, and Général d'Armée Joseph Edouard Doumenc, who had seen service with Admiral Kolchak in 1919 at Omsk.

Yet at the same time, one of Chamberlain's top advisers, Sir Horace Wilson, called to his home in West Kensington the German journalist Fritz Hesse, whom the Foreign Office correctly looked upon as Ribbentrop's undercover representative in London. To an astounded Hesse, Sir Horace announced that Prime Minister Chamberlain was prepared to offer the Führer a twenty-five-year defensive alliance to include economic advantages for Germany and a return by stages of the colonies taken from Germany by the Treaty of Versailles. Hitler, for his part, was to promise no more aggression in Europe.

Elated, Hesse promptly transmitted the offer to the Wilhelmstrasse, then took a special plane to Berlin with a summary of Wilson's offer in writing. Von Ribbentrop, like Hesse, was impressed. Would the British call off their negotiations in Moscow? Would they really come to Germany's aid if Russia should attack? Hesse was convinced that they would.

Hitler, too, was ecstatic, "transported with joy." It was, he declared, "the greatest news I've had for a long time!"[13] But his ecstasy was short-lived. The British were setting a trap, Hitler declared, to save Poland, and he wanted no interference with his efforts to force the Poles to capitulate. What guarantee, in any case, that the English would keep their word? As the days passed, Hitler became more and more convinced that it was a British trick, that if Britain would go to war over such a trivial matter as the demands he had thus far made on Poland, then war with England was inevitable in any case. In time, von Ribbentrop sent Hesse back to London with no commitment. "I have just come from the *Führer*," he said. "He is, unfortunately, not in a position to discuss Chamberlain's offer. He has quite different intentions." On the other hand, the offer was not to be discarded; "We shall return to it when the time has come."[14]

In the meantime, the very way by which the members of the Drax-Doumenc Mission were proceeding to Russia would indicate that Chamberlain had no real heart for the mission to Moscow; the group traveled not in a stately procession of modern warships that might excite admiration as they steamed in line astern under the guns at Kronstadt but at thirteen knots aboard a merchantman. The Russians responded in kind, greeting their visitors upon their arrival in Leningrad the night of August 9, 1939, as if they were passengers in steerage.

The opening session in Moscow began inauspiciously when the Soviet defense commissar, Voroshilov, produced an official document authorizing the Soviet delegation to negotiate and sign a military agreement; did his visitors, he asked, have similar documents? Although General Doumenc produced an order authorizing him to sign a draft agreement, he had to confess that the draft would have no bearing until ratified by the French government; and Admiral Ernle-Erle-Drax had to admit that he had no written authority at all. The Soviet government, said Voroshilov, attached great importance to such matters but would nevertheless proceed with the discussions pending receipt of the credentials.

Discussions at the first working session on August 13, 1939, were nearing an end when Voroshilov introduced a subject that was destined to loom ever more crucial to the outcome of the negotiations: if forces of the Soviet Union were to operate against Germany, they would have to pass through Poland and possibly Rumania; how did Britain and France propose to obtain authority for that movement? That subject occupied almost the entire second day of the discussions. Neither the British nor the French governments had approached either Warsaw or Bucharest, said Admiral Drax and General Doumenc; would not the simplest procedure be for the Soviet government to deal directly with the Polish and Rumanian governments?

After a long recess, Voroshilov came back with his government's answer in writing. France already had a treaty with Poland, the note said, and Britain had guaranteed Polish independence, but the Soviet Union had no military agreement with either country. Since those agreements existed and "since the danger of aggression in Europe is most likely to affect Poland, Rumania, France, and England," the governments of France and Britain should arrange for the passage of Soviet forces directly with the Polish and Rumanian governments. "Without a solution to this question," the note concluded, "the Soviet Military Mission cannot recommend to its Government to take part in an enterprise so obviously doomed to failure."[15]

When Admiral Drax and General Doumenc agreed to ask their governments to consult with the Polish and Rumanian governments, Voroshilov agreed to proceed the next day with a presentation of Soviet military plans. Although the plans were vague and replete with problematical conditions, the British and French delegations were anxious to proceed with drafting an agreement based on them, but Voroshilov refused. First, the cardinal point had to be settled: the question of transit rights for the Red Army through Poland and Rumania. If the British and French delegations were unable to obtain indications of the attitudes of the governments of those two countries within the next twenty-four hours, there would be no point in continuing the discussions. When that proved to be impossible, Voroshilov declared that since the visiting delegations had displayed no consideration for "such an elementary matter as the passage and action of Soviet armed forces against the troops of the aggressor, on the territory of Poland and Rumania, with which countries France and Britain have corresponding military and political agreements," the Soviet delegation had to conclude "that there are reasons to doubt their desire to come to serious and effective cooperation with the USSR."[16]

The Soviet performance was for the moment baffling. The British and French delegations—and Winston Churchill back in London—had no way of knowing at the time that all the prior Soviet protestations in support of Czechoslovakia had been false; that Ambassador Maisky's overtures to Winston Churchill were, at best, no more than fishing expeditions; that Russian willingness to engage in talks aimed at a tripartite military alliance was a maneuver designed with other ends in mind; that even as Admiral Drax and General Doumenc were negotiating with Voroshilov, Russian officials were preparing to receive another foreign delegation also seeking a treaty. It would be a treaty that would jolt the world.

## Chapter Sixty

On August 22, 1929, the most senior commanders of the Wehrmacht assembled in Berchtesgaden. Chauffeurs drawn from the Führer's bodyguard, the Leibstandarte-SS Adolf Hitler, drove them through the picturesque streets of the old town and upon reaching the outskirts, turned sharply left up a steep, winding road, the Kehlsteinstrasse, past an occasional farmhouse and an old church and then a group of barracks which housed the SS bodyguards, passing at last beneath a great stone terrace and coming to a halt at the foot of a flight of stone steps leading up to Hitler's residence, the Berghof. It was a big, white washed, chalet-type structure with a steeply pitched roof and with a balcony on the second floor.

Mounting the steps, the officers entered the side of the house into a small anteroom, bare except for Hitler's collection of Nymphenburg and Frankenthal pottery. For what seemed an interminable time, they waited, until at last a blond giant of a man in the uniform of the SS opened the doors to a great, elongated reception chamber. At one end a huge window framed a breathtaking view of the Bavarian Alps, sun-filled valleys, villages, and the houses and steeples of Salzburg. At the other end was a raised dais with table and chairs.

Striding into the hall, Hitler took a seat behind a large desk and motioned for the officers to be seated. From the first, it was plain that there was to be no conference but a lecture. "There will probably never again in the future be a man with more authority that I have," he said. "My existence is therefore a factor of great value." On the other hand, some criminal or lunatic could eliminate him at any time. Therefore: "War must come in my lifetime."[1]

Like a thunderclap, Hitler made the announcement he had called his commanders to hear. That very day in Moscow, he revealed, the Soviet Union had agreed to sign with Germany a Treaty of Friendship and Nonaggression. He paused for the rustle that came as his listeners absorbed the momentous news. He had at that point, he continued, honored his vow to von Hindenburg that there would be no two-front war. Relations with Poland had become so unbearable, he said, that Germany either had to strike or eventually be destroyed, but in view of the bargain he had made with the Soviet Union, he had eliminated any threat the western democracies might pose. Blockade the Reich? What did it matter, for the Soviet Union could supply the grain, cattle, coal, lead, zinc, all the food and raw materials that Germany needed. "Our enemies are little worms: I saw them at Munich. I am only afraid that at the last minute some *Schweinehund* will produce a plan of mediation!"

Led by Hermann Göring, the commanders applauded enthusiastically, a strange departure, for almost to a man they opposed war on the grounds that Germany was as yet ill-prepared. Nor would there be any word of criticism or protest from the field commanders when in the afternoon, they, too, arrived at the Berghof for an inspirational address.

Case White, the invasion of Poland, Hitler declared, was to be put into effect. X-Day was August 26, 1939. Zero hour was 0430. "Have no pity! Brutal attitude! Eight million people must get what is their right!" When both delegations of officers had departed, he spent the evening looking at motion pictures of the Red Army.

Ever since June 30, 1934—the "Night of the Long Knives"—when Hitler had consolidated his power in Germany with a brutal blood purge, Stalin had been convinced that Hitler was the real power in Europe. With an eye toward obtaining *peredyshka* (breathing space) to provide time to rebuild the Red Army and expand Russian industry, Stalin over the next six years worked singlemindedly toward arranging some kind of pact with Hitler. While he sought the hand of France, flirted with Poland, and courted Britain, he was legitimately trying to improve Russian security, but all the while he had "an eye upon Berlin." He was determined "to get into such a position that Hitler would find it advantageous to meet his advances."[2]

It would be clear in retrospect that Foreign Commissar Litvinov's retirement in May 1939 and his replacement by Molotov were a step toward Stalin's objective. Molotov was a man whom Churchill saw as a statesman of "outstanding ability and cold-blooded ruthlessness" whose "cannon-ball head, black moustache, and comprehending eyes, his slab face, his verbal adroitness and imperturbable demeanour, were appropriate manifestations of his qualities and skill."[3] He was also a man known to be an advocate of an alliance with Germany.

At about the time Molotov assumed his new office, a new Soviet ambassador to Berlin, Alexei Merekalov, asked to call upon the senior state secretary in the German Foreign Ministry, Ernst Freiherr von Weizsäcker. After discussing the overture with Foreign Minister von Ribbentrop, Count von Weizsäcker invited the ambassador to tea.

Ambassador Merekalov ostensibly wanted to talk about trade. Now that the Skoda arms works in Czechoslovakia were in German hands, he asked, would the German government permit fulfillment of Russian orders? Von Weizsäcker replied that "even with good will on our side," the antinazi, pro-British declarations by the Communist International had not made "the atmosphere exactly favorable for making deliveries of war materials to Soviet Russia." In response, Merekalov asked bluntly what von Weizsäcker thought of German-Russian relations. Germany, von Weizsäcker replied, "had always wished to live in a mutually satisfactory condition of economic exchanges with Russia." As far as Russia was concerned, responded the ambassador, there was no reason not to live "on a normal footing" with Germany, "and out of normal relations could grow increasingly improved relations."[4]

In the wake of that dialogue, it seemed to Foreign Minister von Ribbentrop that there might be no war at all: France was too degenerate, Britain too decadent, the United States too far away and disinterested, and Russia apparently amenable to some kind of agreement. On August 16, 1939, with the plans and most preparations for Case White completed, the German ambassador in Moscow, Count Werner von der Schulenburg, conveyed a suggestion from his government for a nonaggression pact that, if Russia desired, might be made irrevocable for a quarter of a century; the German foreign minister, he said, was prepared to fly to Moscow at any time with full powers to sign the pact.

A few days later, on August 19, 1939, Foreign Commissar Molotov handed the German ambassador the draft of a nonaggression treaty and noted that the Soviet government was prepared to receive Herr von Ribbentrop on either the 26th or 27th of August. Since the German Army was under orders to march at dawn on August 26, the suggested dates threw Hitler into a state of agitation. Would not Stalin agree, he asked by telegraph, to permit von Ribbentrop to fly to Moscow without further delay? Presumably unaware of Hitler's reason for urgency, Stalin agreed to receive von Ribbentrop on the 23rd.

At noon on August 23, 1939, Foreign Minister von Ribbentrop arrived at Khodynka Airport in the northern outskirts of Moscow in Hitler's private four-engine Kondor aircraft, the Grenzpark, followed shortly by a staff of thirty in a Junkers 52. Although von Ribbentrop had already received Stalin's assurance that the Russians would sign the treaty, neither he nor anybody else in his delegation totally trusted the Russian promise. There was encouragement nevertheless from the fact that the swastika was flying side by side with the hammer and sickle at the airport, that there was a guard of honor from the Red Air Force, and that an Air Force band played the national anthems, "Deutschland über Alles" and the "Internationale."

When at the Embassy, Count von der Schulenburg advised von Ribbentrop to allow himself plenty of time in the discussions, above all to give no indication that he was in a hurry, von Ribbentrop dismissed him with a wave of the hand. Tell the Russians, he said, that he had to be back in Berlin within twenty-four hours.

Shortly after six P.M., von Ribbentrop faced an impassive Foreign Commissar Molotov and an affable Joseph Stalin in Molotov's office. Noting that he was speaking with full powers, von Ribbentrop announced that the Führer desired to settle the problem of Russo-German relations for "the longest possible time." From Stalin's speech to the Eighteenth Party Congress in March, said von Ribbentrop, in which Stalin had declared the Soviet Union's aversion to being dragged into a war with Germany by the western powers and the desire for amiable relations with all countries, the Führer had discerned that Stalin felt the same. Unlike the British and French, said von Ribbentrop with disdain, he had not come to ask military assistance in the event war came; the German armed forces were sufficiently strong to protect the nation against any enemy or any combination of enemies. Germany wanted nothing more than a treaty of friendship and nonaggression.

Stalin by his opening words revealed that he was as anxious for an agreement as was Hitler. For years, he said, Russia and Germany had "poured buckets of filth" over each other, but there was no reason why their differences could not be settled. Noting Germany's "proud attitude by rejecting at the outset any armed assistance from the Soviets," he said it was of considerable interest to have "a strong Germany as a neighbour, and in the case of an armed showdown between Germany and the western democracies, the interests of the Soviet Union and of Germany would certainly run parallel to each other." The Soviet Union would "never stand for Germany getting into a difficult position."

On the basis of those amiable and reassuring remarks, a treaty of friendship and nonaggression seemed to be quickly assured, but Stalin wanted more: he wanted a secret protocol to the treaty establishing the spheres of influence of the two nations in Central Europe. Producing a map and a child's coloring pencil, he drew a line through Eastern Europe: on the Russian side of it lay part of Finland, most of two of the Baltic States, Estonia and Latvia, eastern portions of Poland, and the Rumanian provinces of Bessarabia and Bukovina.

Von Ribbentrop appeared to have come prepared for demands of some kind. Since Poland was becoming increasingly aggressive, he said, he thought it a "good idea" to establish a line within Poland that would "exclude" German and Russian interests from conflicting. As finally determined, the line in Poland generally followed the Narew, upper Vistula, and San rivers, thereby consigning to Russia almost half of Poland. As for the Baltic States, Stalin wanted specific approval of including in the Russian sphere the Latvian ports of Libau (Lepaya) and Windau (Ventspils), thereby providing convenient windows on the Baltic. For that, von Ribbentrop asked a brief recess to enable him to confer with Hitler.

A telephone call to the Wilhelmstrasse and another from there to the Berghof took little time. Hitler was obviously anxious to conclude the pact. "Answer is yes. Agreed."[5]

There was no question of delay; drafts of the pact and of the secret protocol were initialed immediately and once secretaries had produced final copies, they would be signed immediately. While awaiting the final copies, toast followed toast, to "the new era of German-Russian relations," to "the German nation which has given the world illustrious scientists and brilliant writers and musicians," to "the great achievements" of the Soviet people under their "wise and great leader, Josef Stalin."

As the talk continued, "So much vodka and champagne were consumed that it was surprising that anyone could stand up when the necessary documents in their final form were produced for Molotov and Ribbentrop to sign."[6] Although the documents were dated August 23, 1939, the signing actually took place at 2:40 A.M. on the 24th. The Treaty of Friendship and Nonaggression was a clear, concise contract binding both governments to refrain "from any act of violence, any aggressive action, or any attack" on the other, to lend no support to a third party should either "become the object of belligerent action" by a third party, and to join in no "grouping of Powers whatsoever which is aimed directly or indirectly at the other Party." The treaty was to be in effect for ten years and continue for another five unless renounced by either party a year in advance of termination.

The signing concluded, Stalin told von Ribbentrop that "The Soviet Government takes the new pact very seriously. I can guarantee on my word of honor that the Soviet Union will not betray its partner." It was Stalin who proposed the last toast. "I know how much the German nation loves its *Führer*," he said. "I should like therefore to drink to his health. *Prost! Zur Gesundheit!*" In Berlin, when Hitler learned that at last he had a piece of paper with Molotov's signature on it, he exclaimed: "Now, I have the world in my pocket!"[7]

Even though there was no revelation of the secret protocol, the Nazi-Soviet Nonaggression Pact produced amazement in bourgeois and Communist worlds alike. Reflecting the importance of the event, the New York *Times* devoted the whole of page one of its issue of August 24, 1939, to the arrangement. In Germany, the pact represented an about-face without precedent in the history of National Socialism, producing widespread consternation; but it was among the Communists and the adherents of the Comintern that the pact produced the greatest bewilderment. Had not the Seventh Congress of the Comintern in 1935 declared class war on the Fascist states? Had not the Fascist states through the Anti-Comintern Pact declared political war on the Communist International?

In many cases, it proved impossible to reverse the Comintern's propaganda machines soon enough to adjust to the about-face, for Comintern propaganda was still referring to the impending war as the Second Imperialist War. In the United States, the Communist leader Earl Browder had just posted a letter to President Roosevelt on behalf of himself and 650 other party leaders stating that "the immediate instigators and perpetrators of war" were "the bloody fascist dictator-ships of Germany, Japan, and Italy."[8] Even after announcement of the pact, the German Communist Party ordered its cadres "to intensify the struggle against the Nazi dictatorship." The British and French parties also reaffirmed their intention to continue to wage class war against Fascist elements within their countries, and even in Russia the proletariat displayed confusion over the new coalition. As Ambassador von der Schulenburg advised Berlin, the Soviet Union, which had always "shown a masterly ability to guide the opinion of the population in the direction desired," was having great difficulty in getting Russian Communists to accept the new party attitude toward the Third Reich. "This sudden switch in the Soviet government's policy after years of insistent propaganda against the German aggressor is not being very well understood by the people at the moment."[9] Throughout the world, thousands of Communists were soon burning their party cards or joining the Trotskyites and the Fourth International.

On August 31, 1939, the secretary-general of the Comintern, Dimitrov, hastened to the microphones of Radio Moscow to make a declaration intended to provide guidance. It had been essential for Russia to sign the pact with Germany, he declared, because the British prime minister, Chamberlain, had been trying to trick Germany and Russia into a war from which the western democracies might emerge triumphant. Russia had signed the pact, he said, to demonstrate that "all ideas of making the Soviet Union into a catspaw to take British chestnuts out of the fire would have to be abandoned."[10]

To party leaders over the world went instructions in question-and-answer form for dissemination to the faithful:

> Have the basic aims of the Comintern changed? No, as heretofore the purpose of the Comintern is to bring about a world revolution of the proletariat.
>
> Is a world revolution possible now? No, all efforts to kindle a revolution have so far been unsuccessful.
>
> Cannot the beginning of a revolution be hastened by agitation? No, as this is dependent upon the conditions in the different countries.
>
> What are the natural prerequisites to a revolution? A prolonged war, as expounded in the writings of Marx, Engels, and Lenin.
>
> Is a war in Europe in the interests of the Comintern? Yes, since it must bring nearer the moment when the temper of the masses explodes.
>
> Would a pact between the USSR and England and France hasten the outbreak of war? No, because a union between those countries would cause Germany to refrain from a military venture.
>
> Would a pact between the USSR and Germany hasten the outbreak of war? Yes, with the USSR as a neutral power, Germany would be able to carry through with her plans.
>
> What, therefore, must the attitude of the USSR be to hasten a world revolution? To assist Germany in a sufficient degree so that she will begin a war and to take measures to insure that this war will drag on.[11]

The two principals themselves had no illusions about the pact. As Stalin guardedly remarked to the Latvian foreign minister, Wilhelm Munters: "Now an unexpected turn took place; that happens often in the course of history. But one cannot rely upon it . . . Perhaps German pretensions can awaken again." Much more blatantly, Hitler told a foreign visitor to the Berghof: "Everything I am doing is directed *against* Russia; if the West is too stupid and too blind to grasp this, I shall be forced to . . . strike at the West, and then after its defeat turn against the Soviet Union with my assembled forces."[12]

In Britain, Chamberlain saw the Nazi-Soviet Nonagression Pact as Stalin's granting of a free hand to Hitler to do whatever he wanted with Poland and recognized at that point that Hitler was certain that Britain would not honor its guarantee to Poland. No doubt stung by the enormous diplomatic defeat that the western democracies had sustained in Moscow, Chamberlain wrote personally to the Führer, warning him that if Germany attacked Poland, Britain would fight; and that same day, August 25, 1939, the British government concluded with the Polish government a pact of mutual assistance that eliminated the equivocations that had been a part of the earlier guarantee to Poland.

In France, the French Communist Party reacted swiftly to the news of the Russo-German pact with a new slogan to guide the proletariat: *"Mourir pour*

*Danzig?* (Why die for Danzig?)," but the French government, stiffened by Chamberlain's changed stance, reacted firmly. Escorted into Hitler's office during the afternoon of the 25th, the French ambassador, Robert Coulondre, was as firm as was Chamberlain in his letter: "I give you my word of honor as a French officer that the French Army will fight by the side of Poland if that country should be attacked."[13]

As that day of August 25, 1939, wore on, the British military attaché, Colonel Dennis Daly, reported that several special military trains were formed at the marshaling yards at Wedding, a suburb of Berlin, and that the operations staff of the Oberkommando der Wehrmacht had boarded and departed, ostensibly for celebrations in East Prussia of the great victory of the German Army over the Imperial Russian Army at Tannenberg. Hardly had he transmitted that intelligence when all telephone communications between Berlin and London and Paris were severed, and all foreign air, naval, and military attachés received instructions that they were to leave Berlin only with the approval of the War Ministry. Except for regularly scheduled airlines flying on approved routes, all German air space and airports were closed to foreign traffic.

In early afternoon, Hitler summoned the British ambassador, Sir Nevile Henderson, to the chancellery. As Henderson prepared to go, he carefully inserted a red carnation in his lapel, a symbol which the Germans had come to assume meant that the British ambassador was optimistic that the current crisis could be solved. Henderson found Hitler in a conciliatory mood. The motive was soon apparent; he was prepared, said Hitler, to make a final effort to secure good relations with Britain, "to make a move as regards England which should be as decisive as the move towards Russia. . . ."[14] As it would develop, he was playing on Chamberlain's recent secret offer of an alliance, the offer that Hitler had declined but had not discarded.

He had "always wanted an Anglo-German understanding," said Hitler, but the German-Polish problem, despite England's guarantee to Poland, "must be solved and will be solved." Should England resort to war, it would be far bloodier than that of 1914–1918, and in contrast to that war, Germany would no longer have to fight on two fronts. "Agreement with Russia was unconditional. . . . Russia and Germany would never again take up arms against each other," and the agreement "would also render Germany secure economically for the longest possible period of war."

Yet once the Polish problem was solved, Hitler continued, he was "prepared and determined" to "approach England once more with a large comprehensive offer." Accepting the reality of the British Empire, he was "ready to pledge himself personally for its continued existence and place the power of the German Reich at its disposal." His conditions, he said, were few. If the British government would accept them, Hitler concluded, "a blessing" for both the British Empire and Germany would result. "If it rejects those ideas, there will be war." In order that the ambassador might discuss the proposal with his government, said Hitler, he was making available a Junkers 52 to fly the ambassador to London immediately.

No sooner had the ambassador left the room than Hitler sent for the head of the Oberkommando der Wehrmacht, General Wilhelm Keitel, and confirmed the order given at the Berghof to launch Case White against Poland before dawn the next day, August 26, 1939. As the British ambassador prepared to avail himself of the offer of a plane to fly to London, he learned of the order in a manner that struck Henderson as ironic: he, an agent of—by Comintern definition—an imperialist power, informed by an agent of the Comintern's German Communist underground, the Rote Kapelle, whose governing force, the Soviet Union, had so recently concluded a pact with the anticommunist Nazi state.

Hitler had begun that fateful day of August 25, 1939, by dispatching a letter to his ally, Mussolini, explaining that he hoped Il Duce would understand why he had had to take such a drastic step as making a pact with Stalin. It embarrassed Hitler, particularly because much of his long-standing admiration for Mussolini came from Mussolini's deft handling of the problem of Bolshevism in Italy. Over the years, Hitler had developed "a deep friendship for this extraordinary man." As recently as August 22, 1939, when he was telling his generals and admirals at the Berghof of his own importance, he noted that Mussolini's existence also was decisive. "If anything happened to him, the loyalty of Italy to the alliance would be no longer secure." [15] The alliance to which he referred was the Pact of Steel by which Germany and Italy agreed unconditionally to go to the assistance of the other in the event of war.

Even as Hitler was delivering his order to General Keitel to begin Case White, his ambassador in Rome, Hans Georg von Mackensen, was entering the Palazzo Venezia with Hitler's letter for Mussolini. Although Mussolini could appreciate Hitler's need for a pact with Russia in order to avoid the German nemesis of a two-front war, he had no appreciation for the ruthlessness with which Hitler had broken the basic tenet of Fascism, which was anticommunism, or with Hitler's risk of immediate war with Britain and France. So profound was Mussolini's dismay that after brooding over the matter, he would write Hitler a stern letter:

> You cannot abandon the anti-Semitic and anti-Bolshevist banners which you have flown for twenty years and for which so many of your comrades died; you cannot abjure your gospel, which the German people have blindly believed . . . The solution for your *Lebensraum* is in Russia and nowhere else. Russia has twenty-one million square kilometers and nine inhabitants per kilometer. It is outside Europe, in Asia—and this is not just some theory of [Oswald] Spengler's. [16]

Not until the Fascist dictators had eradicated Bolshevism would they have kept faith with their revolution, and then—and only then—should they contemplate war with the great democracies.

Yet, at the moment, Mussolini vacillated. The threat of war troubled him mightily, for his army had demonstrated in Albania that its shortcomings in training and morale were too serious to risk entering a major war; but on the other hand, if war came, he wanted, like some battlefield hyena, some of the spoils. To Ambassador von Mackensen, he pledged his support for Hitler "unconditionally and with all his resources,"[17] yet hardly had the German ambassador departed than he was composing a personal telegram to Hitler, explaining that Italy was still unready for war and could participate only if Germany were able to deliver immediately sufficient military and raw materials to enable him to withstand the inevitable attack by Britain and France. He implored Hitler to seek a solution by negotiation so that "the rhythm of your magnificent creations will not be interrupted."[18]

Mussolini's warning came to Hitler on top of the other hard news of the day: Chamberlain's new stance, including the change of the Anglo-Polish agreement to a full mutual assistance treaty, and the unequivocal position of French Ambassador Coulondre; but Mussolini's telegram hit him hardest of all, for it was, in effect, the defection of a trusted and respected ally. In view of all that had happened, should he postpone or even cancel Case White? Quite clearly, he could obtain his immediate demands through negotiation: the port of Danzig and the Polish Corridor; in time, he could also probably get back the colonies taken away at Versailles, and the British prime minister seemed in a mood—if Hitler would but stay his hand in Poland—to come to some kind of grand settlement. So, too, Hitler knew that the war he might be getting, which was war with Britain and France, was not the war that he wanted, which was war with Russia. He summoned General Keitel: "Stop everything at once . . . I need time for negotiations."[19]

All that happened after that was a travesty.

Nevile Henderson flew aboard the Junkers trimotor to Croydon Airport outside London on August 26, 1939, conferred for almost three days in Whitehall, and flew back to Berlin late on the 28th. He called at the Reichschancellery that evening, his red carnation in place, and made the same old arguments for peace and new elaborations of them. While the British government was anxious for good relations with Germany, everything turned, said Henderson, upon "the nature of the settlement" that Hitler required from Poland as a prerequisite and upon "the method by which it is reached." It would be impossible for the British government to "acquiesce in a settlement which put in jeopardy the independence of a State to whom they have given their guarantee."

When Henderson, again with red carnation in place, returned to the Reichschancellery the next day for Hitler's answer, he "immediately sensed on Hitler's part a distinctly more uncompromising attitude than on the previous evening." Although doubtful of results, said the Führer, the German government was prepared to begin direct negotiations with Poland "solely out of desire to ensure lasting friendship with Britain," but he could afford Poland only twenty-four hours in which to send a representative with full powers. To Henderson, it was clear that Hitler was delivering an ultimatum, for it would be impossible for the Polish government to meet that deadline.

The final British effort to achieve peace occurred at midnight on August 30, 1939, when Henderson—sans red carnation—called on Foreign Minister von Ribbentrop. That meeting removed any doubt Henderson still might have held that Hitler intended to settle the issue of Poland by force. Fatigued by the long days and nights of peregrinations and attempted negotiations—he was living with the secret that he was dying of cancer of the colon—Henderson found von Ribbentrop rude and overbearing, and the two came close to blows. The confrontation accomplished nothing.

Just after midday on August 31, 1939, Adolf Hitler signed Directive No. 1 for the Conduct of the War. At nine o'clock that evening, all German radio stations broadcast sixteen points which the announcers said had been presented to the Polish government as a basis for a peaceful settlement. In fact, they had never been presented, but von Ribbentrop at the midnight conference with Ambassador Henderson and at a separate conference with Ambassador Coulondre had read them off at such high speed that neither ambassador, both of whom spoke excellent German, could decipher much of what the points contained. They had been fabricated not as an attempt at peace but as an excuse for war, the last-minute, fairly reasonable approach that the Poles never saw but which Hitler could tell the German people that the Polish government had rejected.

In Moscow on August 31, 1939, the Supreme Soviet met to go through the ritual of ratifying the Nazi-Soviet Nonaggression Pact. As the delegates convened at midday, it seemed to foreign observers that after more than a week of delay in taking up the matter, the Soviet government was suddenly in a hurry to push the ratification through.

Preceding the vote, Foreign Commissar Molotov spoke. In a lengthy presentation, he declared that in seeking cooperation from the Soviet Union, Britain and France had blundered badly; and by the time he was finished, he had eliminated any faint hope that the western democracies still might have held that the Soviet Union "might yet find loopholes or excuses for joining them at some subsequent date in resisting German aggression against Poland." The wording of the pact, said Molotov, was "precise in its definition of Soviet obligations to refrain from participating on the side of Great Britain and France in any war against Germany." At great length, he attacked "charges of inconsistency against Communist Russia for embracing Fascist Germany" and insisted "on the inevitability of friendship 'not merely between the governments but also the peoples' of Germany and Russia."[20]

In Berlin that evening, von Ribbentrop delivered to Hitler a comforting message from Ambassador von der Schulenburg in Moscow. The Supreme Soviet, said the message, had ratified the treaty with Germany after a particularly brilliant speech by Molotov.

## Chapter Sixty-One

During the predawn twilight of September 1, 1939, without declaration of war, the Wehrmacht invaded Poland in great strength and with great violence. Employing a million and a quarter men in sixty divisions, nine of them panzer divisions, and protected by fleets of tactical aircraft, the German Army struck across sunbaked plains while some 1,600 medium and dive-bombers of the Luftwaffe struck principal cities, including the capital, Warsaw. For the first time, the world witnessed the harsh military efficiency of blitzkrieg: synchronized operations by tanks, planes, and mobile infantry and artillery. The plans, procedures, and weapons first tried out on the Soviet steppe under the terms of the Treaty of Rapallo had reached maturity in a burst of military precision and scientifically applied force such as the world had never seen.

At ten o'clock on the morning of the attack, Hitler addressed the Reichstag in its temporary quarters in the pillared hall of the Kroll Opera House. He wore a plain field-gray tunic and black trousers and on his left breast, the Iron Cross Second Class. Over the last weeks and months, he declared, the Polish government had looked the other way while agitators attacked and persecuted the minority of ethnic Germans inside Poland. Then there had developed a series of costly border provocations culminating during the night of August 31, 1939, when "for the first time Polish regular soldiers fired on our territory." Since 5:45 A.M., said Hitler, "we have been returning the fire, and from now onwards bombs will be met with bombs." He himself from that moment, he said, wanted to be "the first soldier of the Reich." He had "once more put on that coat that was most sacred and dear to me," and he would not "take it off again until victory is secured, or I will not survive the outcome."[1]

Alluding to the defense agreements between Poland and Britain and France, Hitler warned London and Paris not to "confuse my patience for cowardice." He had "offered England friendship," he said, "and, if necessary, close cooperation"; so that at that point the matter of European security and peace was for England to decide, for Germany had "no interests in the west other than peace and friendship." As for Russia, "any war between our peoples would be no profit to either," and for that reason Russia and Germany had resolved "to exclude the use of force for all time to come."

"If I now call upon the German people to make sacrifices," Hitler concluded, "it is because I have a right to do so. I am ready to make every personal sacrifice on my part. I expect nothing from any German but what I would also do myself and would always be prepared to do. My life belongs to my people."

In Britain, Winston Churchill worked until the first hours of the morning of September 1, 1939, at his home in Kent on the half-million-word manuscript of his *History of the English Speaking Peoples*. Having finished a section on William

Pitt, the prime minister during the French Revolution and the Napoleonic Wars, he laid down his pen and retired for the night. He was still asleep when the telephone rang at 8:30 A.M.; it was the Polish ambassador, Count Raczynski, with news that the Germans had struck.

Arising immediately, Churchill telephoned the chief of the Imperial General Staff, Sir Edmund Ironside, who had commanded the North Russian Expeditionary Force during Mr. Churchill's private war. "Warsaw and Cracow are being bombed now," Ironside told him. With that news, Churchill began to dress and prepare to drive to London, where the obvious question before the House of Commons that day would be whether Britain and France were to honor their guarantees to Poland and declare war.[2]

Hardly had Churchill begun to dress when the telephone rang again. It was Prime Minister Chamberlain's secretary asking Churchill to see the prime minister before the House of Commons convened. Driving to London, two hours away, Churchill called on Chamberlain at No. 10 Downing Street. He "saw no hope of averting war with Germany," said Chamberlain and asked Churchill to serve in a small war cabinet that he intended to form. Remarking to himself that Chamberlain had made no mention of a declaration of war, Churchill accepted, left the residence, and walked down the foreign office steps across Parliament Square to the Palace of Westminster. It was a hot day without a breath of wind.

Meanwhile, in the Foreign Office, Lord Halifax drafted a note to the German government and sent it across to No. 10 Downing Street for Chamberlain's approval. In final form, the note read:

> Unless the German government are prepared to give His Majesty's Government satisfactory assurances that the German Government have suspended all aggressive action against Poland and are prepared promptly to withdraw their forces from Polish territory, His Majesty's Government in the United Kingdom will without hesitation fulfill their obligation to Poland.[3]

When the German government made no response to the note, Ambassador Henderson was able to inform his government of that in time for Chamberlain to make a statement in the House of Commons at six o'clock that evening. "The responsibility for this terrible catastrophe," Chamberlain said, "lies on the shoulders of one man, the German Chancellor, who has not hesitated to plunge the world into misery in order to serve his own senseless ambition." [Loud cheers from all benches.] The sixteen points which Hitler claimed that the Polish government had rejected, said Chamberlain, had never been communicated to the Polish government. [A gasp of astonishment. Lady Astor exclaims: "Well, I never did!"] After fiddling with a sheaf of papers, Chamberlain produced a document and began to read it slowly; it was the note presented earlier to the German government and ignored by Hitler, but Chamberlain made no mention of that.

Some officials were getting anxious, among them Winston Churchill. Shortly after midnight, he wrote a note to the prime minister in which he expressed concern over rumors he had heard that the French government was dispatching another note to Berlin, not an ultimatum. "The Poles have now been under heavy attack for 30 hours," Churchill wrote. "I trust you will be able to announce our Joint Declaration of War at *latest* when Parliament meets this afternoon. I remain here at your disposal." As it turned out, he would wait all day, "pacing up and down like a lion in a cage. He was expecting a call, but the call never came."[4]

What was wrong? The treaty with Poland called unequivocally for an immediate declaration of war; had the prime minister decided not to honor the treaty?

It was an accepted fact among the French *poilus* that before the start of every great battle during the Great War, a grim battlefield ghost wearing an enigmatic smile, the Angels of Rheims, appeared in the sky, beckoning the soldiers in the manner of the Valkyries, the maidens of Odin who chose those who were to die in battle and conducted them to Valhalla. To many a French official, and, in particular, to the prime minister, Edouard Daladier, it seemed in those first days of September 1939 that the Angel of Rheims was beckoning all of France.

No nation had suffered more in the Great War than had France: a generation of young Frenchmen wiped from the earth, the northern part of the country turned into a wasteland, the soil in some regions so torn and convoluted by shells and mines that it would never again support more than scrub growth. There were wounds that had never healed, would never heal. Of a population of 38 million, France had called 8.5 million to serve the Tricolor, and 5 million of those had become casualties, of which 1.4 million had died in battle. As a consequence, the generation that had to provide the manpower for the French Army of 1939 was so weakened that it was unable to sustain the annual demands for the call to arms: between 1936 and 1940, the response to the yearly call fell from 240,000 to 120,000; marriages in the decade of the 1930s fell by half; and after 1934, the number of deaths among the population exceeded the number of births.

Although Daladier's sense of honor demanded that he join the British immediately in a joint declaration of war, the Angel of Rheims was beckoning at his shoulder, and throughout the first two hot, airless days of September 1939, as the Poles collapsed, Daladier brooded. There were many in France, as Daladier was aware, who were concerned not only about the carnage that might again be visited upon France but about fighting the wrong war: the old adage from the Napoleonic era, "The Cossack will rule Europe!", had taken hold. So troubled were many with the threat from the left that "even in the most justified social demands the diabolical figure of Bolshevism" appeared to be involved, "for the elimination of which even Hitler, that scourge of God, would be welcome; the watchword was 'better Hitler than [Léon] Blum.'"[5]

The irony of it, as would be apparent in retrospect, was that if Daladier had acted with determination and if the French Army had marched out of its forts and crossed the Rhine, the French would have defeated such German units as were left in the west, for on the western front the French had 110 divisions available, while there were only thirty German divisions defending a 300-mile frontier, only twelve of them at full strength. Furthermore, while the Wehrmacht had enough war materiel on hand for only eight weeks of operations, the French had stockpiled enough for a full year. At worst, the French Army could have forced German withdrawal from Poland, but more likely, the French would have defeated Germany and deposed Adolf Hitler.

Yet the specter of the Angel of Rheims assured that there would be no resolution, no swift strike across the Rhine. A banner hanging over the French lines at Saarbrücken told the story: "We won't fire the first shot." Neither—until ready—would Hitler.

In early evening of September 2, 1939, the German newspaperman in London, Fritz Hesse, received a telephone call from the Wilhelmstrasse. It was Foreign Minister von Ribbentrop. "You know who is speaking," he said and told Hesse not to say his name. "Please go immediately to your confidant—you know who I mean [he was referring to Chamberlain's close adviser, Sir Horace Wilson]—and tell him this: the *Führer* is prepared to move out of Poland and to offer reparation damages provided that we receive Danzig and a road through the corridor, if England will act as mediator in the German-Polish conflict. You are empowered by the *Führer* to submit this proposal to the British cabinet and initiate negotiations immediately."[6]

Convinced that the British would go to war over Poland, Hesse was stunned but delighted. Assured by von Ribbentrop that he was acting at the express direction of Hitler, Hesse telephoned No. 10 Downing Street, only to learn that Sir Horace would be unavailable for some time. Wilson was, in fact, on his way to the House of Commons, where members of Parliament and another packed gallery anxiously awaited a speech by the prime minister. Hesse fretted. When he saw Sir Horace, would it be too late?

He need have had no concern. At 7:44 P.M., Prime Minister Chamberlain walked into the House of Commons, where the members waited "exactly like a court awaiting the verdict of the jury," but the verdict would be delayed. Chamberlain made no mention of an ultimatum but spoke instead of the possibility of further negotiations. The Germans still had not replied to the British government's note of the previous day, he said, possibly because they were considering an Italian proposal for a big-power conference to discuss a possible settlement of the crisis. "If the German Government should agree to withdraw their forces," he said, "then His Majesty's Government would be willing to regard the position as being the same as it was before the German forces crossed the Polish frontier."[7]

The House was aghast. "Speak for England, Arthur!" cried several members of the opposition, and the opposition leader, Arthur Greenwood, sprang to his feet: "I wonder," he cried, "how long we are prepared to vacillate . . . when Britain and all that Britain stands for, and human civilization, are in peril."[8] As a conservative member, Leopold Amery, would recall: "For two whole days the wretched Poles had been bombed and massacred, and we were still considering within what time limit Hitler should be invited to tell us whether he felt like relinquishing his prey! . . . Was all this havering the prelude to another Munich?"[9] Churchill saw it the same way: "There was no doubt that the temper of the House was for war. I deemed it even more resolute and united than in the similar scene on August 3, 1914."[10] Even Chamberlain's colleagues in the Cabinet were seriously concerned that the prime minister would go back on Britain's pledge to Poland, and five of them went to Chamberlain's office in the House to demand that the government dispatch an ultimatum at once.

At about ten P.M. Fritz Hesse arrived at No. 10 Downing Street to see Sir Horace Wilson, but Wilson found it almost impossible to believe that Hitler would back down. Would Hitler publicly apologize for the assault on Poland? "If this proposal fails merely because Hitler won't apologize," said Hesse, "then the world will believe that Chamberlain wanted the war, inasmuch as he had the chance of avoiding it." With that, Wilson agreed to transmit the proposal to the Cabinet, but he had yet to depart when a servant knocked at the door and handed him a piece of paper. After reading it, Wilson held it over the flame of a candle, then turned to Hesse. "I cannot forward your suggestion to the Cabinet," he said.[11] It was too late; the mood of the House of Commons had gotten through to Neville Chamberlain. A short while later, at 11:30 P.M., Chamberlain told the Cabinet that he was instructing Sir Nevile Henderson to see Foreign Minister von Ribbentrop at 9:00 A.M. the next day, Sunday, September 3, 1939, and inform him that unless Hitler gave a favorable reply to the British note by 11:00 A.M., "a state of war would exist between England and Germany as from that hour."[12]

In Berlin the next morning, the ailing Sir Nevile Henderson arrived at the Wilhelmstrasse shortly before nine to find Hitler's interpreter, Paul Schmidt, authorized to receive the British note. Within minutes, Schmidt was at the Reichchancellery and pushed his way past a crowd gathering outside the Führer's office. As he entered the office, Hitler at his desk and von Ribbentrop by the window "looked up tensely." As he finished translating the ultimatum, "Hitler sat immobile, staring into space." After what "seemed an eternity" to Schmidt, Hitler turned to von Ribbentrop and in an accusing tone asked abruptly: "What now?" Replied von Ribbentrop: "I assume that within the hour the French will hand us a similar ultimatum."[13] When the French ambassador, Robert Coulondre, did arrive, he had tears in his eyes.

At ten o'clock that Sunday morning, the BBC alerted the British public to expect an important official announcement shortly. For an hour and a quarter, the people sat by their radios, listening to a selection from *Princess Ida*, to Parry Jones singing "The Passionate Shepherd," and to a recorded talk entitled, "Making the Most of Tinned Foods."[14] Then finally came the tired, sad voice of the prime minister: "I am speaking to you from the Cabinet Room at No. 10 Downing Street." Telling of the final note handed the German government and the hour of expiration of eleven o'clock, he continued: "I have to tell you now that no such undertaking has been received, and that consequently this country is at war with Germany." A situation, he said, "in which no word given by the German ruler could be trusted and no people or country could feel itself safe, had become intolerable. Now we have resolved to finish it . . . May God bless you all.[15]

At Chamberlain's request, Churchill called on the prime minister in his office in the House of Commons. After Chamberlain offered and Churchill accepted the post in the War Cabinet of First Lord of the Admiralty, the Board of the Admiralty sent a signal to all ships: "Winston is back!" Calling at the Admiralty, Churchil went straight to the First Lord's room, walked to a cupboard in the paneling, opened it, and pulled out a large rolled map showing the disposition of all German ships on the day he had been forced to resign from the Admiralty for his part in the naval disaster in the Dardanelles. As Churchill would later relate, he felt: ". . . a serenity of mind and a kind of uplifted detachment from human and personal affairs. The glory of old England, peace-loving and ill-prepared as she was, but instant and fearless at the call of honour, thrilled my being and seemed to lift our fate to those spheres far removed from earthly facts and physical sensation . . . Once again we must fight for life and honour against all the might and fury of the valiant, disciplined, and ruthless German race. Once again! So be it."[16]

In Moscow, the German attack on Poland and the British and French declarations of war took the Kremlin by surprise. To the last, Stalin had believed that Hitler would get what he was after by some kind of compromise. When on the evening of September 3, 1939, von Ribbentrop sent a telegram to the German ambassador, von der Schulenburg, directing him to invite the Russians to join in the attack, the Kremlin did nothing. Hitler thought Stalin was stalling until the last possible moment in order to keep Russian casualties down, which may have been a factor, but the main reason was that the Red Army was not ready to march. Not until shortly before dawn on September 17, 1939—only ten days before Poland's final collapse, and in disregard for the Russo-Polish Nonaggression Pact executed in 1932 and renewed, at Russian insistence, in 1934—would the first Russian troops cross Poland's eastern frontier.

"The Polish-German War," Molotov explained over Moscow Radio, "has revealed the internal bankruptcy of the Polish State," which had made of Poland "a suitable field for all manner of hazards and surprises, which may constitute a threat to the Soviet Union." Moreover, said Molotov, "the Soviet Government cannot view with indifference the fact that kindred Ukrainian and White Russian people, who live on Polish territory and who are at the mercy of Fate, are left defenceless." Thus the Soviet government had ordered the Red Army, "to cross the frontier and to take under their protection the life and property of the population of Western Ukraine and Western White Russia."[17] The people of those provinces, Molotov declared, were "giving a joyous and enthusiastic welcome to the heroic Red Army, which is freeing them from the nationalistic yoke of the Polish landowners."[18]

As Comintern plenipotentiaries throughout the world parroted that line, the Polish ambassador in Moscow, Waclaw Grybowski, rejected Molotov's diplomatic note; it was "a lying document" with so few parallels in the history of diplomacy that he refused to communicate it to his government. He accused the Soviet government of "stabbing Poland in the back" and demanded that the Red Army cease operations and withdraw. So ferociously did he speak that he awed the deputy foreign commissar, Vladimir Potemkin, but to no end.[19]

The Poles having committed most of their troops against the Germans, the Red Army encountered little resistance, having more problems in shepherding Germans out of the assigned Soviet zone. Advancing as far west as the Bug, the Red Army nevertheless took 217,000 prisoners. The men in the ranks and the noncommissioned officers were soon shipped to penal work colonies in the frozen Komi Republic and the Kola Peninsula, while the officers and cadet officers, men drawn mainly from the middle and upper classes, were held in three widely separated prisoner-of-war camps: at Kozelsk, at Ostashkov near Kalinin, and at Starobelsk near Kharkov.

At Kozelsk, in a filthy, dungeonlike former Orthodox monastery encased in barbed wire and guarded by sentry boxes and machine gun posts were 4,500 officers and cadet officers. Just before Christmas 1939, the NKVD removed all priests from the prison; only one priest was ever heard from again. Three months later, in March 1940, guards removed 245 men seemingly selected at random, including a general officer. Although none who remained knew at the time why those men were taken away, it turned out that they joined 203 others culled from the other two camps; they had been selected as political reliables who might benefit from Communist indoctrination and eventually form the cadre of an officer corps for a Polish Red Army to be formed in Russia.

Among the prisoners remaining at Kozelsk, rumor spread that the camps were to be broken up and the prisoners returned to Poland, for each man had to fill out a form indicating the region he came from and where he would like to be released. When the first prisoners were culled one or two at a time from the various cell blocs early in April 1940, the men were hopeful yet at the same time concerned: why were men about to be released herded by platoons of NKVD guards with rifles, bayonets, and machine pistols at the ready? Those who followed in subsequent shipments found inscriptions on the walls of the train compartments they traveled in, etched with pencils or burnt matches, such as: "Two stations beyond Smolensk. We get out. We are loaded."

Jammed into tiny barred compartments aboard the trains, less than half the men were able to sit. After three days and nights, they arrived at the village of Gniezno on the fringe of a sandy-floored forest of pines, birches, sorbs, and alders. That particular stretch of woodland was the Kosy Gory, or Goat Hills; the entire region was known as the Katyn Forest. Before the revolution, some wealthy noble had built a summer dacha of native lumber in the Goat Hills looking down upon a picturesquely curving Dnieper River. Since 1929, the OGPU and its successor, the NKVD, had used the dacha to house execution squads and the surrounding forest to liquidate convicts and political prisoners.

From the trains the men were loaded into prison vans called "black ravens" and driven into the woods of the Goat Hills. Their wrists tied with wire, prodded with bayonets, they were marched to the edge of a huge pit where half of each group of thirty was forced to get into the pit and lie face forward on the ground. As the other fifteen watched, NKVD guards shot each man at the base of the skull with a pistol. Machine guns cut down any man who tried to bolt. First one tier, then fifteen more men forced to lie atop the dead; then, as another van unloaded, another tier, and yet another. The deed done, the guards filled in the pit and planted saplings on top of it. When later discovered, the pit would be found to contain the bodies of 4,143 men.

Nobody ever learned what happened to the officers who had been held at the other two camps at Ostashkov and Starobelsk; their fate was presumably the same as that of the men from the camp at Kozelsk. If so, that meant that the NKVD had executed approximately 15,000 Polish officers and officer cadets, a start on what would grow to be a systematic program to eliminate those who might develop into bourgeois leaders in a Polish state.

## Chapter Sixty-Two

From the moment Churchill took over the First Lord's office at the Admiralty, a building in Whitehall where the Sea Lords had directed the imperial destiny from behind a façade of sea horses since the time of George I, his principal weapon against the Third Reich was the naval blockade, which in four great wars over two hundred years had effectively wrecked the economies of Britain's enemies. The principle of the blockade was the same as that laid down by the Virgin Queen in 1601 in the war with Phillip II of Spain: "The stopping, hindrance, and impeaching of all commerce and traffick with him in his territories . . . will quickly in likelihood give an end to these bloudie warres which disturb the generall peace and quiet of all these parts of Christendome."[1]

As with Elizabeth I in 1601, so with George VI in 1939, for the enemy was particularly vulnerable to the weapon of blockade. Even in peacetime, Germany produced adequate quantities of only four out of thirty-four raw materials considered essential for modern warfare. With the post–World War I increase in German population, the standard of nourishment of the German people was below that of 1916, and production of such basic foodstuffs as meat and grains was well below the need. Naval blockade might quickly bring about a military collapse or internal rebellion.

Yet a naval blockade to be effective had to be accompanied by a campaign to stop those powers with land access to Germany from supplying war materials and foodstuffs: most notably, the Soviet Union. If that campaign should fail, no matter how effective the naval blockade, Germany would be capable of sustaining a long war and possibly of winning it, and even if in the end Germany fell, Britain might be left so exhausted as to be no more than a second-class power. That was a fate feared in London with almost as much dread as defeat.

On the day that Warsaw surrendered—September 27, 1939—the German foreign minister, Joachim von Ribbentrop, was again aboard Hitler's private plane, the *Grenzpark*, bound for Moscow to clear up odds and ends in regard to the division of Eastern Europe as spelled out in the Nazi-Soviet Nonaggression Pact and to tighten the agreement between the two countries in order to assure the kind of support from Russia that Britain feared. At Khodynka Airport, the reception provided by the new foreign commissar, Molotov, was even warmer than the one accorded von Ribbentrop when he had come to sign the Nonaggression Pact; that boded well for the outcome of the negotiations.

To support the war against Britain and France, von Ribbentrop told Stalin, Hitler required the oil fields in Southeastern Poland that had fallen inside the Russian sphere. Because Stalin had plans to incorporate that region into the Ukraine, he demurred, but he agreed to supply from Russian fields the 300,000 barrels that Hitler would have realized annually from the Polish fields. On the condition, Stalin added, that Hitler concede to Russia the third of the Baltic States, Lithuania. A telephone call to Berlin produced that concession except for a small corner of the country, while the Russians in return conceded to Germany the Polish city of Lublin. The Polish carcass thoroughly picked over, large-scale maps were produced, demarcation lines drawn, and final copies of the treaties and protocols sent to the typists. Signatures were to be affixed at one of those odd hours inexplicably favored by the Kremlin—5:00 A.M.—while the night before, festivities were to reign.

The festivities opened with a banquet given by Molotov in von Ribbentrop's honor in the Grand Palace within the Kremlin amid whose "splendid and majestic halls" the czars resided and held their receptions when they were in Moscow. As the lavish meal proceeded, toast followed toast, and "each time Stalin himself stood at the chair of the person addressed to drink his health."[2] Following the banquet, von Ribbentrop and his party were escorted to the Bolshoi Theater for a special performance of *Swan Lake*, which von Ribbentrop watched from the same distinguished visitors' box that Anthony Eden had occupied during the brief Anglo-Russian flirtation in 1935.

After but a brief rest, von Ribbentrop arrived before daylight the next morning, September 29, 1939, for the signing. First to be signed was a German-Soviet Boundary and Friendship Treaty, which formally carved up Poland and Lithuania, to which was attached a secret protocol pledging both countries to put down any "Polish agitation" that might arise. Next was a joint Peace Appeal of the German and Soviet Governments addressed to Britain and France in an effort to end the war with Germany. Then came the pact that most concerned Britain: a trade pact in which Russia undertook to provide Germany with the war materials that would enable Germany, despite an Anglo-French blockade, to pursue the war.

Throughout the ceremony, Stalin watched with "evident satisfaction." The signing over, von Ribbentrop remarked that "the Germans and Russians must never be allowed to fight each other," to which Stalin replied: "This ought to be the case." As if to emphasize the point, von Ribbentrop asked the interpreter to repeat Stalin's reply. Perhaps, he suggested, Stalin might be inclined to go beyond the friendship agreement and conclude an alliance for the coming battle with the western powers. Although Stalin had no intention of getting involved in that conflict, he did agree to a passage in the official communiqué, which noted that "in case of the continuation of the war, the Governments of Germany and of the USSR shall engage in mutual consultations with regard to necessary measures." [3]

For Stalin, the ceremony of September 29, 1939, was but a formality, for from the first he saw the war between Germany and the western democracies in terms of the long-range advantages for Soviet Russia. With that in mind, he began from the onset of war to assist the Third Reich. Russia, for example, promptly provided sanctuary at Murmansk for the German liner *Bremen* and a host of merchantmen. Stalin also allowed German ships to unload their cargoes at Russian ports and move them by rail to Germany. The Soviet government also agreed to allow and assist converting German merchantmen in Russian harbors into armed merchant cruisers and offered Teriberka Harbor in the Gulf of Motovska as a German anchorage "sufficiently isolated for German ships and submarines to carry out repairs in Russian territorial waters without being observed." [4]

In late October 1939, the Russians allowed all German vessels to depart Murmansk while detaining the ships of other countries until the German ships had gotten away. The next day the Russians delivered "a sharp protest" against British blockade of the Baltic, and a few days later in a major foreign policy pronouncement, Molotov proclaimed "lasting friendship" with Germany and denounced the blockade as "contrary to international law."

Just over a fortnight later, Stalin submitted a bill for services rendered. He wanted three of the most modern and powerful ships of the German fleet, the cruisers *Lützow*, *Seydlitz*, and *Prinz Eugen*; the plans of the most powerful warships in the occident at the time, the battleships *Bismarck* and *Tirpitz*; material for constructing in Soviet yards four 15,000-ton cruisers; the plans and equipment for two heavy cruisers of the *Admiral Hipper* class, to be built in Soviet yards with German technical assistance; and the plans for the battle cruiser *Scharnhorst* and aircraft carrier *Graf Zeppelin*, with options to purchase all equipment needed to make copies of the ships operational. He also placed huge orders for ammunition, turrets, submarine periscopes, fire control equipment, rangefinders, mines, minelayers, minesweepers, torpedoes, torpedo-firing equipment, and navigational aids and for light, medium, heavy, and very heavy artillery, including massive 405 mm coastal guns. Stalin was clearly trying to obtain almost the entire inventory of modern German naval technology.

Although Hitler's first reaction was to turn down the request, Grand Admiral Raeder reminded the Führer that "Russian economic assistance is of decisive importance to enable us to see this war through to the end" and rule out "any success of the British economic blockade." As noted by the Supreme Command, the Oberkommando der Wehrmacht, "fulfillment of these demands shall depend in general on the extent to which we are dependent upon Russian reciprocal aid." As all knew, that dependence was tremendous. In a Russo-German Economic Agreement, signed on February 11, 1940, under terms of which Russia was to complete its deliveries in seventeen months and the Germans theirs in just over two years, the Russians undertook to provide many of those items that Germany lacked and required for circumventing the British blockade.

It was soon evident in London and Paris that as a result of massive Russian assistance, the naval blockade against Germany was ineffective. Seeing that assistance as a hostile act, the British and French reacted with a hint of the belligerence they had shown during Mr. Churchill's private war. At French instigation, they developed plans for bombing the great Russian oil installations at Batum and Baku in order to deny Germany the oil promised under the Nazi-Soviet Economic Agreement of February 1940. Conscious of a great buildup of German forces in what looked to be a preliminary to a major offensive against France, the commander of the French Army, General Maurice Gamelin, advised that if the bombing were conducted on a sufficient scale, it would so reduce Russian oil shipments to Germany as to deter German ability to conduct a major offensive. Gamelin also noted that in view of the dependence of Soviet agriculture on tractors, "successful air strikes against the oil fields could bring the USSR to the verge of collapse in a few months."[5]

When the British War Cabinet authorized participation in the planning, the commander of the Royal Air Force in the Middle East, Air Marshal Sir William Mitchell, visited the French Army's commander in Syria, General Maxime Weygand, to reconnoiter possible bases from which to send his bombers against Batum and Baku. A few days later, on February 25, 1940, the chief of the Imperial General Staff, General Ironside, directed the commander of British land forces in the Middle East to examine with Weygand the feasibility of ground operations in Transcaucasia, the Russian region in which two British divisions during Mr. Churchill's private war had seized Batum and Baku and the railroad connecting them. At the same time, Churchill and the First Sea Lord, Admiral Sir Dudley Pound, directed the British naval commander in the Meditteranean, Admiral Sir Andrew Cunningham, to examine the possibility of submarine operations against Russian shipping in the Black Sea. As British aircraft began photographic reconnaissance over Batum and Baku, the Anglo-French High Command entered into staff conversations at French headquarters in Aleppo, Syria, with Turkey, which had indicated a possibility of joining an Anglo-French expedition against Russia.

Informing the Germans that there was evidence the British were reconnoitering the approaches to Murmansk, the Soviet government noted that it might be necessary to obtain magnetic mines from Germany in order to seed the approaches both to Murmansk and Odessa against British naval action. Both the Soviet government and the Comintern declared that General Weygand was creating Anglo-French armies in the Middle East and warned against "extensive and suspicious activity" there. "We must exercise vigilance," declared *Pravda*, lest the Anglo-French troops be used "for purposes hostile to the Soviet Union." Britain and France, warned *Pravda*, were "playing with fire."

In the late winter of 1939–1940, another military collision between Soviet Russia and the western allies thus appeared possible, even likely. Yet events were soon to occur on the western front that would rule it out.

Russia had yet another resource to put at the disposal of its newfound ally: the Communist International; for despite the disillusionment of many a foreign Communist with the unholy alliance with Fascism, many others duly accepted it as they had the various other abrupt shifts in policy over the years. On September 30, 1939, the day after von Ribbentrop and Molotov had signed the second round of agreements implementing the Nazi-Soviet Nonaggression Pact, the Comintern issued a new party line instructing the British and French Communist Parties to work for an immediate peace with Germany and calling upon the proletariat of the world to act against "the reactionary imperialists of Britain and France" and their "unjust imperialist war." [6]

In the United States, the Comintern's campaign had little impact until November 1939, when in a special session Congress repealed the nation's embargo on exports of arms and munitions to permit "cash-and-carry" purchases by the belligerent powers, which for all practical purposes, because of the Allied naval blockade, meant sales only to Britain and France. The Comintern immediately ordered a slowdown in manufacture of arms and ammunition, a campaign to prevent loading of Allied ships, and agitation to induce the crews to refuse to sail or to desert their ships. [6]

Within weeks, the campaign had gained sufficient momentum to prompt FBI Director J. Edgar Hoover to warn the president's adviser on internal security affairs, Adolf Berle, about it; but the campaign proved more irritating than serious, partly because of intense vigilance on the part of the FBI, port police, and military intelligence authorities and partly because Communist labor organizers found it difficult to sell the contention that in using the war materials against Germany, which most longshoremen would applaud, Britain and France were hurting the Soviet Union. When the Red Army invaded Finland, that virtually ended the campaign, for American reaction was almost universally hostile.

The Comintern also devoted some effort to playing on the views of many Americans that the British and French had tricked the United States into entering World War I, and worked at length to reinforce the strong isolationist sentiment that had long gripped the country. The theme, constantly reiterated, was: "The Yanks are NOT coming this time!"

The gist of the party line was apparent in a speech by the secretary general of the American Communist Party, Earl Browder, at a celebration of the twenty-second anniversary of the October Revolution on November 5, 1939, in Symphony Hall in Boston. The war, Browder declared, was "a family quarrel of rival capitalist imperialisms, who cannot agree upon the division of the world among themselves," a war fomented by "ruling classes" which could "settle their quarrels" only by mobilizing "the millions of their populations and sending them out to slaughter one another." The American people, Browder declared, should resist the imperialist efforts to drag them into the war, stop the shipment of munitions to Britain and France, and indict the Allied leaders as war criminals. Although the American Communist Party, he said, appeared "small and weak" in comparison to "the gigantic tasks" it faced, yet "we must never forget that twenty-five years ago the Russian Bolsheviks appeared even weaker, a persecuted and outlawed group," but "out of the struggle against the first imperialist World War, the working class and the toiling people rose to power on one-sixth of the earth's surface and proceeded to abolish capitalism and build a glorious new society of socialism."[7]

Not long after that speech, Browder was arrested for passport fraud in connection with false papers used in attending prewar meetings of the Comintern and was convicted and sentenced to four years in prison. By the time he had served fourteen months of the sentence and obtained parole, the Comintern would have changed its view of the second imperialist war.

As revealed by a defecting Comintern courier, Jan Valtin, in a book published in 1941, *Out of the Night*, the Comintern assigned leadership of the antiwar activities in American labor and industry to two employees of the Red Trades Union International, the Profintern. One was relatively unknown, Tom Ray; the other was the former Philadelphia taxi driver, George Mink, who had worked for the Comintern as a hired gun liquidating Trotskyites in Spain and who was peripherally involved in the murder of Trotsky. In addition to their full-time salaries, Ray and Mink were provided funds to establish a seamen's and port workers' newspaper, to maintain International Seamen's Clubs in nine American ports, and to establish the Marine Workers Industrial Union.

In instructions to Ray, Mink, and the American Communist Party, the Comintern directed that to avoid anything that might be considered treasonable, antiwar activities were to be conducted under the guise of normal agitation for higher wages and better working conditions. The workers were "to assert their right to strike and picket . . . build and strengthen the trade unions, organize the unorganized, fight . . . for civil liberties to include all groups, fight for the rights of Communists, and fight for the release of Earl Browder, the symbol of the unity of the working class." Workers were also to oppose industrial mobilization and "the huge government expenditures for expanding the naval, air, and army forces."[8]

As the Comintern agent and member of Gerhardt Eisler's commission in New York, Joseph Weinkoop, was later to note, he and other agents were successful in producing a number of strikes, of which the most successful was at the Allis Chalmers plant in West Allis, Wisconsin, where 12,000 employees worked to produce "precision instruments and equipment essential for the building of destroyers, submarines, mine-sweepers, etc."[9] According to Weinkoop, the Communists controlled Local 248 of the United Autombile Workers, CIO. In voting on a call to strike on January 22, 1941, Communists in the local "marked 2,200 ballots out of the total of about 7,000 in order to insure a majority vote for a strike," a fact subsequently verified by handwriting experts. As the strike progressed and the workers grew restive, the Communists concentrated "a large force of their goons to keep it going." That led to "one of the biggest riots in American Labor history. The windows of the plant were smashed by bricks, the Governor's car was overturned, and tear gas was used against both the strikers and the police, many of whom were wounded." The Communists deliberately provoked the riot in order "to get the sort of publicity Party Headquarters wanted, and to impress Berlin." When those opposing the strike tried to organize, "the Party goons invaded their meetings and beat them up so severely that many were hospitalized." Although opposition leaders appealed to the International Union in Detroit, "since it too was Communist-dominated, they got no redress." The strike lasted seventy-six days.

Another major strike hit the North American Aviation Corporation in Inglewood, California, where the strikers went back to work only under the prodding of U.S. Army bayonets. Other strikes hit the manufacturer of aircraft engines, Vultee, and the airframe industry, and there were scores of smaller strikes throughout the country, particularly in small but vulnerable firms building parts for the larger manufacturers. There might have been many more had not the Comintern's period of antiwar agitation been so brief.

In the meantime, Communist activity continued against what was becoming a burgeoning new industry: atomic research. Since that day in the early fall of 1939, when Alexander Sachs had nearly bungled a first effort to convince President Roosevelt of the necessity of building an atomic bomb, intelligence obtained from the British had imparted a rare sense of urgency to the program. Although it was known early that a large part of the Kaiser Wilhelm Institute in Berlin had been set aside for the study of uranium, the British Secret Intelligence Service developed more alarming information: the Germans in Norway, the British learned, were producing several kilograms a day of heavy water, a product essential for a nuclear reaction. What would happen if Germany got an atomic bomb first was all too obvious.

One of the early centers of research in what would become known as the Manhattan Project was the Radiation Laboratory of the University of California at Berkeley, where many of the scientific employees were members of the International Federation of Architects, Engineers, Chemists, and Technicians, CIO. Only after World War II was over would the extent of Communist domination in that union be revealed, exposed by a Joint Fact-Finding Committee of the 57th California Legislature.[10]

Known by the acronym FAECT, the federation was founded in 1931 by a Communist candidate for alderman in the 37th district of Brooklyn, Marcel

Scherer. The president as World War II approached was Lewis Alan Berne, who denied membership in the Communist Party but admitted to membership in a number of front organizations. Chapter 25 was the branch of the FAECT that was active at the Radiation Laboratory at Berkeley. Its journal, *Bulletin*, quickly adopted the new Comintern line following the signing of the Nazi-Soviet Nonaggression Pact in August 1939.

Soon after the government began expanding its atomic research program, national officials of the FAECT visited Chapter 25. Alerted by the visit of officials who "had shown much evidence of Communist sympathies," informants for the Legislative Committee of the California Legislature infiltrated Chapter 25 and learned that all scientists who were members of the FAECT and sought employment at the laboratory were "interviewed beforehand" by the FAECT's founder, Scherer, "who had an office on the campus." It was "not too far-fetched to say," according to the informants, "that just about all applicants are either members of the FAECT or have to become members before or after they are accepted as employees for the Lab." It was also noted that some of the scientists who were engaged in research at the laboratory and who were members of Chapter 25 lectured on scientific subjects at the California Labor School in San Francisco, whose director, David Jenkins, "was observed going to and from the Soviet Consulate in San Francisco" and "admitted that he was a registered Communist in New York." It was a branch of the Comintern's activities in the United States that would long continue.

In Britain, too, the Comintern's espionage in the atomic energy program continued, but in the program of antiwar agitation, the Comintern was even less successful than in the United States, partly because the British Communist Party had always been nationally oriented but mainly because there could be no questioning the fact that Nazi Germany posed a peril to Britain's very existence. Some Communist extremists were detained under various emergency power acts; the *Daily Worker* was suppressed for a time; and among some Army regiments recruited primarily from urban slums, there were a few minor incidents; but that was all. In France, the story was tragically different.

That the French Army was peculiarly sensitive to revolutionary agitation had been demonstrated in the great mutiny in the spring of 1917 when sixteen army corps rebelled and entire regiments marched on Paris to demand that the government open peace negotiations; it took firing squads working overtime— 8,000 ringleaders were said to have been shot—to quell the uprising, and even then as men returned to the attack, they went forward bleating like sheep going to slaughter. The mutiny followed the czar's abdication and the first revolution in Petrograd, and it was to some degree attributable to Bolshevik propaganda emanating from 15,000 Russians whom the czar had sent to fight in France "to pay for French munitions sold to Russia."[11] There were later insurrections among French troops at Archangel and among soldiers and sailors in the Crimea.

Although the original concept of undermining the bourgeoisie and capitalist states by subverting the Army was attributable to Marx—he had at hand a clear example of the danger to a proletarian revolution in the French Army's defeat of the Paris Commune in 1871—it was Lenin who made the concept official dogma when in 1920 he personally wrote Article 4 of the 21 Points for Admission to the Communist International: "Persistent and systematic propaganda and agitation must be carried on in the Army where Communist groups should be formed in every military organization. Wherever, owing to repressive legislation, agitation becomes impossible, it is necessary to carry on such agitation illegally."

Prior to the proclamation of the Seventh Congress of the Comintern in 1935 creating the popular front against Fascism, the French Communist Party had depended not on vast numbers but on "a very hard core of well-indoctrinated leaders who would carry out to the best of their ability any order received,"[12] but the proclamation had brought large numbers of Frenchmen, possessed of an almost paranoid fear of Germany, flocking to the party. When in May 1935 France signed the treaty of friendship with Russia aimed at restraining Germany, that brought more Frenchmen to the party, and Communist leaders began to agitate for the "democratization" of the French Army, which in time led to widespread replacement of bourgeois officers with others drawn from the proletariat.

In the months following the Allied declarations of war, while the French and German armies faced each other without fighting, a period that became known as the "Phony War," Comintern activists bombarded the troops and the people with propaganda in pursuit of the new party line, the gist of which was: "The Government, supported by the reaction and by the Socialist leaders, argues that it is waging a war of freedom against fascism. Nothing could be farther from the truth. As in 1914, it is capitalist interests which are at stake, and it is the workers and peasants who are being sent to slaughter to defend interests which are not theirs."

In the strange atmosphere of the Phony War, German "fraternization patrols" often crossed into French lines, parroting the Comintern's propaganda. When Foreign Commissar Molotov in a speech on October 31, 1939, put the blame for the war on "French and British capitalists and warmongers," German planes dropped leaflets carrying the speech over French positions. By the spring of 1940, the French Army for a variety of reasons—the war-weariness carrying over from World War I, a feeling that France was safe behind the big forts of the Maginot Line, and a lassitude induced by the years under the Popular Front government, by the Phony War, and by the Comintern's propaganda—was "a nerveless, soulless body, a castle made out of cards."[13]

That was particularly true of the 9th Army, under General André Georges Corap, whose soldiers were in large measure reservists drawn mainly from the so-called "red belt" of Paris, the working class *arrondissements* in the southern reaches of the capital, and whose "lower officers consisted primarily of intellectuals who were either members of the Communist Party or fellow-travelers." Because the 9th Army was admittedly one of France's weakest, the High Command reserved for it an assignment not expected to be difficult: to defend the line of the Meuse running through the Belgian Ardennes, a semimountainous, heavily forested region with a limited, twisting road-net that French generals expected the armor-heavy German forces would avoid. It was a decision that was to have a marked effect on the ultimate fate of France.

## Chapter Sixty-Three

For all the eagerness that Stalin displayed in arranging the alliance of the Soviet Union and Nazi Germany and for all the felicity he exhibited in assuring its consummation, he never wavered in his conviction that at some point his political bedfellow would put a knife in his back or a vial of poison in his soup. Should Britain and France come to terms with Germany, as the lack of fighting on the western front would appear to foreshadow, that time might not be far off. To Stalin, there could be no delay in adding to the buffer zone along Russia's western frontier.

In mid-September 1939, Soviet export-import authorities in Moscow informed the Estonian Embassy that they wanted to increase Soviet shipments through the port of Tallinn, the Estonian capital. In view of the fact that the Russians were already using the port for some shipments and that Russia had no ice-free access to the Baltic, the request appeared to be reasonable; and on September 24, 1939, the Estonian foreign minister, Karl Selter, came to Moscow to sign an agreement.

Upon arrival, Selter encountered an amiable Foreign Commissar Molotov, who suggested that "in view of these uncertain times," Estonia might consider a treaty of mutual assistance with Russia, by means of which the Soviet Union would maintain air and naval bases and up to 25,000 troops in Estonia. The proposal shocked Selter, for like all Russia's neighbors through the years, Estonia believed in the dictum that once Russian troops arrived, it was impossible to get them out. When Salter declined, a still amiable Molotov placed a hand on Salter's knee; "I beg you," he said, "not to compel the Soviet Government to use other, more radical methods of safeguarding its security."[1] Once Selter determined through the British and German ambassadors in Tallinn that Estonia could count on no help from either Britain or Germany, he returned to Moscow and gave in.

Latvia received the next invitation, its foreign minister, Wilhelm Munters, arriving on October 1, 1939. Although Latvia had a nonaggression treaty with Germany, Munters had already made inquiries at the Germany Embassy in Riga and knew that he had to accept whatever the Russians demanded. Stalin personally assured him that "We do not encroach upon either your constitution, organs, ministries, foreign policy, financial policy, or economic system"; the Soviet Union only wanted access to and use of Latvian ports and authority to put in troops and installations to defend them. Although Stalin suggested 50,000 troops, Munters, after what he called "real Asiatic haggling," got the number cut by half.

Lithuania was next. The foreign minister, Juozas Urbys, arrived at the Kremlin on October 3, 1939. Although both Stalin and Molotov insisted that the Soviet Union had no wish to see Lithuania "sovietized," it was essential to move 20,000 Red Army troops into the country in order to defend the ports.

Within less than a year of their concessions to Russia, Estonia, Latvia, and Lithuania, along with Eastern Poland, would become a part of the Soviet Union, to which Stalin would add in the summer of 1940 the Rumanian province of Bessarabia and the northern portion of Bukovina. As in Poland, a process of depopulation in the new territories began. Declared to be enemies of the people, the leaders of the bourgeoisie and most of the officer class—as the authorizing directive of the deputy people's commissar of public security put it, "of anti-Soviet elements"—were deported to the Russian Arctic and Asiatic Russia.

The directive was specific and detailed, covering every eventuality to ensure that no "demonstrations or other excesses" would occur. Agents and soldiers of the NKVD were to descend on the household to be deported just at daybreak, and if the occupants refused to admit them, "the doors should be broken down." The agents provided the family a list of personal items that each member was allowed to carry, the father's to be packed separately on the pretense that at the train the men would undergo a separate "sanitary inspection" but actually because they would be packed into separate railway cars. The directive provided a grim testament to the efficiency of the NKVD. [2]

With no more than minimal expenditure, the Union of Soviet Socialist Republics obtained dominion over 286,000 square miles of territory and 20 million people and proceeded immediately to "resettle" 1,230,000 Poles, approximately 200,000 Bessarabians and Bukovinians, 34,000 Lithuanians, 15,000 Latvians, and just under 60,000 Estonians. How many of the people survived would probably never be known, but some figures eventually became available in regard to the Polish deportees: within eighteen months, approximately 25 percent were dead of execution, hunger, exhaustion, and disease; of 140,000 Polish children deported, 35 percent died in that first eighteen months; and of Polish Army officers, 95 percent, and those few who survived did so only by changing into the uniforms of private soldiers.

With control of Eastern Poland and the Baltic States assured, Stalin had the makings of a substantial buffer zone against the German attack that he knew would eventually be coming, but he wanted more. He wanted to close the door to Russia from the north. He wanted Finland.

On November 13, 1939, a hierarch of the Comintern, Otto Kuusinen, a Finnish philogist, sent a letter to a friend and cofounder of the Finnish Communist Party, Arvo Tuominen, who received the letter from the hand of a Comintern courier at a clandestine meeting in a café on the island of Kungsholmen. In the letter, Kuusinen revealed that on that day, Finnish delegates had walked out of diplomatic talks in Moscow; they had steadfastly refused the same kind of overtures that had led to Russian takeover of the Baltic States and specifically declined to cede territory the Russians wanted in order to improve their northern defenses: islands in the Gulf of Finland—the sea route to Leningrad—and the bulk of the Karelian Isthmus—the land bridge to Leningrad— where the Finnish frontier was within artillery range of Russia's second capital. The time had come, wrote Kuusinen, when "more forceful measures would have to be taken, measures Finnish Communists had long hoped for."

Since war between Russia and Finland had become inevitable, Kuusinen wrote, the Comintern at the instruction of the Soviet government was forming a Finnish government-in-exile. Kuusinen was to be president and Tuominen prime minister. Once formed, the government was to appeal to Moscow for protection and mutual assistance, thereby giving an aura of legitimacy to the forthcoming attack by the Red Army. In order that arrangements might be quickly completed, Kuusinen urged Tuominen to hasten to Moscow.

Tuominen had seen too many of his friends vanish while on operational missions to Moscow; in any event, he had become disenchanted and was about to desert the cause. He informed the courier to explain that he was ill and that his physician had forbidden him to travel.

Kuusinen was not to be easily put off. Three times he sent the courier back. When Tuominen each time refused to go to Moscow, the messenger at last informed him that unless he obeyed the summons, he would be expelled from the Communist Party and the Comintern, with all that that might entail. Still refusing, Tuominen moved to a town near the western frontier from which, if required, he might flee into Sweden; but his refusal to cooperate with the Comintern had no apparent effect on Russian plans.

On November 26, 1939, seven rounds of artillery fire fell upon Red Army positions near the village of Mainila on the Karelian Isthmus just to the north of Leningrad. Declaring that the fire had come from Finnish guns and had killed seven Red Army soldiers and wounded four, Premier and Foreign Commissar Molotov demanded that the Finns pull back their troops between twelve and fifteen miles from the frontier. When the Finns refused, Molotov abrogated the nonaggression pact between the two countries, broke diplomatic relations, and on November 30, 1939, declared that "the Red Army must be prepared for any eventualities."[3]

The Russian assault began the same day with a heavy aerial bombardment of the capital, Helsinki, and the port of Viipuri (Vyborg); and as Red Army troops rolled up against the Finns amid the forests and lakes, icefields and tundra, Kuusinen announced creation of a People's Democratic Government of Finland and called on the Soviet government for a treaty of mutual assistance. Molotov and Kuusinen signed the treaty on December 2, 1939, and when the legitimate government of Finland the next day asked for an armistice, Molotov refused; he "preferred to deal with the government of President Kuusinen." To charges by the western democracies of armed aggression, Molotov replied that Russia was intervening in the Finnish "problem" at the request of the popular government of Finland. When a near-moribund League of Nations in one of the few forceful acts of its existence expelled the Soviet Union, the Russian reaction was to warn the world that "much had changed since the civil war," that the Red Army had become "a gigantic force" that "would make intervention very dangerous."[4]

As was soon demonstrated, the fact was far different. Outnumbered five to one overall and far more than that wherever the attacking Red divisions chose to concentrate, the Finns nevertheless exacted a terrible retribution. In the Gulf of Finland, the Russians occupied a few islands the Finns had elected to evacuate and on the Karelian Isthmus seized a few miles of undefended territory, but then they came up against a line of bunkers housing machine guns that stretched all the way across the seventy miles of the isthmus, the Mannerheim Line, named after Finland's revered military commander, Marshal Carl Gustaf Baron von Mannerheim. In minefields and under Finnish machine gun fire, Russians died by the thousands without breaking the line. In the great Arctic wastes between Lake Ladoga and Murmansk, Finnish troops in white camouflage suits and on skis roamed everywhere amid the larches and birches, severing Russian supply lines, marauding with hit-and-run tactics, cutting entire Russian divisions into small encirclements and annihilating them. The subzero landscape was dotted with the corpses of Soviet soldiers frozen in grotesque positions, and by Christmas 1939, the Red Army's drive was at a standstill.

While the Red Army was reforming for the next round of fighting, the Comintern sought to justify the attack. As Molotov put it, Finland was a threat to Russia, because "Finland is really the key to Leningrad and Leningrad is the key to Moscow, and one who wishes to defeat the Soviet Union must have Finland at its disposal."[5] After Soviet Russia granted Finland its independence in 1918, the party line had it, "the White Guards seized control of the country," and ever since that time it had been "a handy base for imperialist assaults against the Soviet Union, many of them aided by American funds." Once the White Guards were defeated, "the new People's Democratic Republic of Finland, headed by Otto Kuusinen" would "restore self-determination to the Finnish people" and "put an end to imperialist intrigues in Finland and stop once and for all the use of the Finnish Government as a war weapon of world imperialism against the Soviet Union."

The Comintern also sought to rationalize the Red Army's difficulties. They were attributable to "execrable transportation," "difficult national terrain," "impossible weather," and the fact that "for many years past Great Britain and other imperialist powers have been busy fortifying and arming Finland against the USSR," thereby making the Mannerheim Line "one of the most heavily fortified areas in the world." In that line, said the Comintern, 300,000 men could easily hold off a million, and "the entire Russian invading force numbered only 200,000 men."

Over twenty years later, official Soviet historians would be following a similar line, maintaining that France and Britain furnished Finland hundreds of artillery pieces and thousands of mines, bombs, machine guns, shells, and grenades and that the United States provided a thousand fighter pilots.[6] Yet the reality was far different, for even though the plight and pluck of Finland excited the sympathy and admiration of the entire western world, help was minimal. The U.S. Congress appropriated $30 million for nonmilitary aid, and to deny Russia the assets of the Baltic States in the United States, President Roosevelt froze them and in protest against Russian bombing of Finnish cities, invoked a "moral embargo" on trade in aircraft and aircraft parts. Although there was official talk in London and Paris of sending an expeditionary force variously projected at from 6,000 to 57,000 men, the battle would be over before any components of the force sailed. So, too, a French decision to send a hundred bombers and a British decision to send fifty would be made too late, and even though recruiting stations for foreign volunteers opened in Sweden, Britain, and the United States, only two battalions of Swedes and a lone company of Finnish-Americans reached Finland, and they got there just before the end.

Despite the Comintern's efforts to rationalize the Red Army's difficulties, they produced within the Kremlin the severest strains. A member of the Politburo and of the Soviet Communist Party's Central Committee, Nikita Khrushchev, would later recall a manifestation of them. At a dinner at Stalin's dacha, Khrushchev later wrote, Stalin blamed Defense Commissar Marshal Klementi Voroshilov, which made Voroshilov "boiling mad." Voroshilov "leaped up, turned red," and shouted: "'You have only yourself to blame for all this! You're the one who annihilated the Old Guard of the army; you had our best generals killed!'" When "Stalin rebuffed him," Voroshilov "picked up a platter with a roast suckling pig on it and smashed it on the table." Voroshilov, noted Khrushchev, "ended up by being relieved of his duties as People's Commissar of Defense."[7]

Yet how the adventure in Finland would ultimately end was never really in doubt, for how was a nation of 3,658,000 to stand up indefinitely against one of 140 million? As Stalin ordered a resumption of the attack, there would be no stinting on resources. Artillery pieces lined up hub-to-hub pounded the Mannerheim Line with incessant barrages while waves of bombers hit railroads, communications centers, troop concentrations, towns, cities. In the relatively narrow sector of the Karelian Isthmus, fifty-four Russian divisions rose to the attack, and in time, the incessant pounding produced the inevitable breakthrough. On March 12, 1940, the Finns accepted Stalin's harsh terms.

The terms were less harsh than they might have been, for by their fortitude and gallantry, the Finns had created the possibility that they might refuse Stalin's demands and resume the war. Quietly dissolving the Kuusinen government, from which no more would be heard, Stalin demanded basically only what he needed to secure Leningrad and Murmansk, but that included the islands in the Gulf of Finland, the Finnish naval base at Hango, all of the Karelian Isthmus, Viipuri (the country's second city), an enclave between Lake Ladoga and Murmansk that would afford access—when needed—to a railroad traversing the waist of the country, and territory giving Russia control of the Arctic port of Petsamo.

Despite the final victory, the ineptitude of the Red Army had been exposed for all the world to see, and general staffs everywhere were inclined to discount Russia as a major factor on the world scene. Few noted, as did the American military attaché in Moscow, Colonel Faymonville, that there were, indeed, special factors involved in Finland, not the least of which was that in expecting swift Finnish collapse, the Russians at first had used reserve divisions hastily called to arms and ill-equipped for winter warfare. The Red Army, said Faymonville, might better be judged by its strong showing in the recent border battles with the Japanese, where the Russians had introduced a new tank, the T-34, superior to that of any other power, and a new general of exceptional ability, Georgi Zhukov. Yet even Colonel Faymonville's own General Staff, long inured to his pro-Soviet reports, would pay little attention, and in Berlin the tendency to discount the Red Army was especially strong. As Hitler remarked to the chief of the German General Staff, General Franz Halder, the Red Army was "a paralytic on crutches having difficulty in wading through a quagmire of blood."[8]

## Chapter Sixty-Four

Pulled into war with the western powers by Britain's and France's reaction to the invasion of Poland, Hitler moved to get it over with quickly so that he might turn to his primary objective, conquering the Soviet Union, To ensure a supply of essential iron ore from Scandinavia and to gain ports from which the Germany Navy might circumvent the Allied naval blockade, he moved first against Denmark and Norway. The Germans struck on April 9, 1940. Denmark capitulated immediately; and despite commitment of limited numbers of Briish and French troops at Norway's northern ports, most of Norway was also soon in hand. By early May 1940, the Wehrmacht was free to concentrate for a great surge against the western allies.

Such was the shock of the German conquests that discontent against Neville Chamberlain's government mounted in the House of Commons. In the midst of a stormy debate, Chamberlain heard the imperious words first uttered by Oliver Cromwell at the Long Parliament: "You have sat too long here for any good you have been doing. Depart, I say, and let us have done with you. In the name of God, go!" One of the most dramatic and wounding attacks in the history of the ancient House, it turned the debate into a discussion of censure that ended in what Churchill called "a violent manifestation of want of confidence in Mr. Chamberlain and his Administration."[1]

Chamberlain was still holding on to his office when at dawn on May 10, 1940, German paratroopers and glidermen descended on the Netherlands and Belgium, and infantry, motorized, and panzer divisions, the vanguard of a force of two and a half million men, crossed the frontiers into Belgium, Holland, and Luxembourg.

When it finally became clear to Chamberlain that the Labour Party would refuse to support him in a National Coalition government, he prepared to carry out his final duty as prime minister, to select his successor for the assent of the sovereign. His first choice was his foreign secretary, Lord Halifax, but when Chamberlain invited him to form a government, there was "a very long pause." Halifax had been one of the principal architects of appeasement; he had displayed considerable sympathy with the Fascist movement; and the left had consistently denounced him as a reactionary. Could such a man bind and lead the government, the Parliament, and the country at so desperate a moment? At length, Halifax broke the silence; as a peer of the realm, he said, with no seat in the Commons, he would find great difficulty leading the country. As Churchill would recall, "He spoke for some minutes in this sense, and by the time he had finished it was clear that the duty would fall on me—had in fact fallen upon me."[2]

Declining to have contact with any of the parties until after receiving the King's Commission to form a government, Churchill withdrew to his office at the Admiralty, a short way up Whitehall from Downing Street. There he found tumult and the first personification of the magnitude of the disaster that had befallen Western Europe: the ministers of the Dutch government were in his office. "Haggard and worn, with horror in their eyes, they had just flown over from Amsterdam. Their country had been attacked without the slightest pretext or warning. The avalanche of fire and steel had rolled across the frontiers, and . . . an overwhelming onslaught was made from the air."[3]

A message soon arrived instructing Churchill to be at Buckingham Palace at 6:00 P.M. for an audience with King George VI. There the sovereign asked if he was prepared to accept the ministry and form a government. "Sire," replied Churchill, "I will certainly do so." The new premier and his monarch talked briefly, then Churchill and the king kissed hands, and Churchill, bowing low and walking backward out of the audience chamber, departed.

Professing to have "nothing to offer but blood, toil, tears, and sweat," Churchill two days later asked the House of Commons for a vote of confidence:

> You ask, What is our policy? I will say: It is to wage war, by sea, land, and air, with all our might and with all the strength that God can give us: to wage war against a monstrous tyranny, never surpassed in the dark, lamentable catalogue of human crimes. That is our policy.
> You ask, What is our aim? I can answer in one word: Victory—victory at all costs, victory in spite of all terror; victory, however long and hard the road may be; for without victory there is no survival.[4]

There were numerous reasons for the swift success of the German blitzkrieg in the west. There was the efficacy of the blitzkrieg itself: the use of paratroopers and glider troops to seize fortifications, bridges, communications centers behind the Allied lines; sympathizers and soldiers masquerading as civilians—what became known as a "Fifth Column"—to spread panic among the people and send them scurrying in flight and blocking the movement of Allied reserves; intimate coordination between motorized infantry, tanks, and Stuka dive-bombers, whose screeching dives with machine guns blazing terrified unseasoned troops. There was a lack of prior coordination between the British and French General Staffs and that of Belgium, occasioned by what turned out to be a futile effort on the part of the Belgian government to assure survival by maintaining a strict neutrality, which meant that British and French troops could enter Belgium only after the Germans had invaded. Nor had the British and French staffs come to appreciate fully the role of the tank in modern warfare as other than an infantry support weapon, and the French had failed to see tactical aircraft as other than a defense against enemy aircraft. Wary of subjecting the provinces that had been devastated by World War I to a new siege of position warfare, the French government had failed to extend the mammoth fortifications of the Maginot Line along the frontier with Belgium, counting instead on carrying the war into Belgium; but the blitzkrieg was too swift for that. Despite a number of intelligence slips by the Germans, the Allies were the victims of strategic surprise, and they were the victims of tactical surprise as well when the Germans delivered their *Schwerpunkt* (main effort) through the border region known for its inhospitable terrain, the Ardennes.

There was yet another explanation, a broad malaise, hard to define, that played at least a part in all of Hitler's early victories. It flowed from a curious amalgam of beliefs: that the German armies were invincible; that Hitler did, indeed, represent Europe's future; that the true enemy was not Hitler and the right but as the incessant burrowing of the Comintern over twenty years had demonstrated, the true enemy was Stalin and the left; and that Hitler and his powerful military forces represented the only meaningful bulwark against the westward spread of Communism.

By the evening of May 12, 1940, the end of the third day, seven panzer divisions comprising the *Schwerpunkt* had brushed aside a screen of French and Belgian horsemen in the Ardennes and closed up to the Meuse, there to face the reservists of General André Corap's 9th Army, whose weak divisions had been assigned to that sector because the French General Staff expected no major German attack there. The heaviest blow, led personally by the Inspector-General of Armored Forces, Generalleutnant Heinz Guderian, hit the southern hinge of Corap's line near Sedan, the site of a catastrophic French defeat in the Franco-Prussian War. Under an incessant pounding from the guns of German tanks, from self-propelled artillery, and from machine guns and bombs of screeching Stukas, the reservists, whose morale had been so weakened by the Comintern's propaganda, collapsed. By late afternoon of the 13th, the blitzkrieg was past the last major obstacle into the heart of Belgium and France.

In a letter to a friend in the United States, a Frenchwoman captured the surreal atmosphere generated by the assault:

> Do you know how France was invaded? First of all, hundreds of motorcyclists appeared on the roads, all camouflaged—we thought we were watching the arrival of panthers or tigers on machines, because the men were all dressed in camouflaged waterproof capes covered with

splashes of yellow, green, brown, black. Their motor-bikes and their helmets were camouflaged too, and they wore huge goggles which hid half their faces. They came like that, in lines, one behind the other, without moving or turning their heads, followed by sidecars with machine guns, also camouflaged. Then came hundreds of motor cars, transporting blond men who had a dull, stupid air, dressed in grey-green with high black boots, and behind them again, trucks of supplies. They came like lightning, dull grey cars with no nickel showing, racing at 200 kilometers an hour. We wondered what we had seen—was it just a grey vapor? a phantom? The cars were absolutely silent, and out of them stepped tall individuals dressed in grey-green with gloves of imitation leather like their capes—and all with high, black leather boots; and they clicked their heels with a noise like a pistol shot. The officers were different, tall, thin, with faces of steel and intelligent, piercing gaze—faces implacable and hard . . . All France is invaded by grey-green beasts in black boots.[5]

By May 21, 1940, only eleven days after the German drive began, tanks of the 7th Panzer Division under a then obscure general, Erwin Rommel, reached the French coast in the vicinity of Boulogne. The British Expeditionary Force, the Belgian Army, and the best divisions of the French Army were trapped, soon to be pinned against the sea. The Dutch had already surrendered, their stand weakened by Dutch Nazis aiding the conqueror. In the early evening of May 26, 1940, the new Churchill government authorized the British commander, Lord Gort, to evacuate British troops through the sole remaining port of Dunkirk, and on May 28, 1940, the king of the Belgians, Leopold III, surrendered unconditionally.

As British troops fell back on the little port of Dunkirk, the fate of the British Expeditionary Force and French troops fighting with it appeared to be sealed, for German tanks were fast closing on the port. The British would later call the evacuation of their troops "the miracle of Dunkirk"; but the true miracle, the miracle that allowed the evacuation to proceed, happened before the evacuation began: in a seemingly inexplicable move, Hitler on May 24, 1940, ordered the five panzer divisions that were closing in to halt. The panzer divisions were to be withdrawn from the line, regrouped and prepared for the next phase of the battle: the drive southward to deliver the coup de grâce to France. It was a step that would long remain one of the great controversies of the war, for it seemed to many at the time and to almost every student of the war since that had the panzer divisions continued to attack, few British soldiers would have made it back to England and the Germans would have staged a mammoth Cannae, perhaps, as General Keitel would suggest, "the greatest encirclement battle in history."[6]

The German field commander, General Karl Rudolf Gerd von Rundstedt, would later disclaim all responsibility for the order. Yet it was von Rundstedt himself who provided Hitler a pessimistic picture at a time when Hitler and the Oberkommando der Wehrmacht were seriously concerned about the long German flank stretching 300 miles from the Meuse to the sea. The very success of the blitzkrieg had unnerved them, for surely the powerful French Army would have withheld strong reserves that even at that moment would be preparing to hit that extended flank. Already the panzer divisions had incurred heavy losses (some as many as half their tanks), and to commit them in the low-lying mucky fields of Flanders with their patchwork of canals, drainage ditches, and inundations— terrain which Hitler knew well from his service in World War I—might make it impossible for them to repulse the expected French counterattack and proceed with the drive to finish off France. The proud, vain chief of the Luftwaffe, Hermann Göring, boasted in any case that his aircraft would deal with the English.

There was yet another possible—even likely—explanation: Hitler's long-standing admiration for Great Britain and his desire for peace in the west so that he might get on with his great ambition, the extermination of the Marxist world view. The most convincing evidence of the part that played in Hitler's reckoning was provided by von Rundstedt's operations officer, General Günther Blumentritt, who was present when Hitler talked with von Rundstedt and issued the order to halt the tanks:

> [He] gave us the opinion that the war would be finished in six weeks. After that he wished to conclude a reasonable peace with France, and then the way would be free for an agreement with Britain.
>
> He then astonished us by speaking with admiration of the British Empire, of the necessity for its existence, and of the civilization that Britain had brought into the world . . . He compared the British Empire with the Catholic Church—saying that both were essential elements of stability in the world. He said that all he wanted from Britain was that she should acknowledge Germany's position on the Continent. The return of Germany's colonies would be desirable but not essential. . . .
>
> He concluded by saying that his aim was to make peace with Britain on a basis that she would regard as compatible with her honour to accept.[7]

There would be some indications that as Britain achieved the miracle of Dunkirk—extricating 338,226 men (225,000 of them British, the rest French and Belgian) but virtually none of their tanks, cannon, or transport—Hitler stayed the full fury of the Luftwaffe, though the Luftwaffe's failure may have been attributable to the proximity of British fighter bases just across the Channel. Yet when the British had at last taken off their troops and ended a drama that at once shocked and stirred the world, Hitler again reiterated his wish for peace with Britain. Yet his aim of peace would receive no encouragement from Churchill, for on June 4, 1940, while smoke from fires burning in Dunkirk could still be seen from the cliffs of Dover, Churchill spoke before the House of Commons:

> We shall go on to the end, we shall fight in France, we shall fight on
> the seas and oceans, we shall fight . . . in the air, we shall defend our
> island . . . we shall fight on the beaches, we shall fight on the landing-
> grounds, we shall fight in the fields and in the streets, we shall fight in
> the hills; we shall never surrender, and even if . . . this island . . .
> were subjugated and starving, then our Empire beyond the seas, armed
> and guarded by the British Fleet, would carry on the struggle, until, in
> God's good time, the New World, with all its power and might, steps
> forth to the rescue and the liberation of the Old.[8]

A week later, on June 11, 1940, Churchill flew to a small landing field outside Briare, near Orléans, for a meeting in the Château de Muguet with the Supreme Allied War Council. The German drive southward had begun six days before, and as early as nightfall of the second day, Marshal Henri Pétain, the vice-premier, was telling the British liaison officer in Paris, General Sir Edward Spears: "C'est sans espoir (there is no hope)."[9] On the 10th, in order to get "a few thousand dead so as to be able to attend the peace conference as a belligerent,"[10] Mussolini threw Italian divisions against the French rear along the mountainous frontier between the two countries. Even as Churchill arrived at the Château de Muguet, the French government was relocating from Paris southward to Tours.

As the war council began at seven o'clock to deliberate, "The Frenchmen sat with set white faces, their eyes on the table. They looked for all the world like prisoners hauled up from some deep dungeon to hear the inevitable verdict."[11] There was, said the French commander in chief, General Maxime Weygand, "nothing to prevent the enemy reaching Paris . . . I cannot intervene for I have no reserves; there are no reserves." It was, he concluded, "la dislocation (the break-up)."[12]

In an effort to inspire some kind of action, Churchill turned to Pétain, reminding him of the nights they had spent together in the marshal's train at Beauvais in 1918 after the Kaiserschlacht had destroyed the British 5th Army, how Pétain had restored the front, and how the French premier, Georges Clemenceau, had declared: "I will fight in front of Paris, in Paris, and behind Paris." Would it not be possible to draw the German Army into the great conurbation of Paris, to utilize "the enormous absorbing power of the house-to-house defence of a great city upon an invading army?" Pétain replied "very quietly and with dignity" that in 1918 there had been sixty British divisions in the line and he had had a reserve of another sixty divisions; but in 1940, there was no reserve, and even though he did not mention it, there were only three British divisions left in France. "Making Paris a ruin," he said, "would not affect the final event."[13]

A hint of acrimony crept into the conversations. It was time, said General Weygand, to commit everything to the battle, including every British fighter squadron. "Here," he said, "is the decisive point . . . It is therefore wrong to keep any squadrons back in England." Although sharply conscious of how unfairly divided the losses to that point had been between Britain and France, Churchill refused to concede. "This is not the decisive point and this is not the decisive moment," he said. "That moment will come when Hitler hurls his Luftwaffe against Great Britain. If we can keep command of the air, and if we can keep the seas open, as we certainly shall keep them open, we will win it all back for you." Britain had twenty-five fighter squadrons left, and nothing could convince Churchill to give them up, for to do so would "destroy our chance of life."

Into the evening and over dinner, the discussions continued, with one French commander after another providing dismal reports while Churchill urged one strategy after another. To no avail. As the officials left the table, Reynaud told Churchill that Pétain had informed him that France would have to seek an armistice and had put it in writing but was "still ashamed" to hand it to him.

The next day, as Churchill prepared to fly home and took leave of his hosts, he called aside the commander in chief of the French Navy, Admiral Jean François Darlan. As would be apparent by Churchill's terse remark, Britain's fear above all else, if France should fall, was that the powerful French Fleet would go over to Germany, at one step transforming Germany from essentially a land power into a terrible threat to Britain on the high seas. "Darlan," said Churchill, "you must never let them get the French Fleet." Darlan promised solemnly, Churchill would recall, that he would never do so.

As Parisians wept, the conqueror entered the capital on June 14, 1940. Two days later, Churchill took a constitutional step without precedent in modern times: he offered France not an alliance but full union with the British Empire. He composed the proposal with the approval of a young *général de brigade*, Charles de Gaulle, whom Churchill had regarded with interest during the deliberations in the Château de Muguet and who had accompanied Churchill to London in his capacity as undersecretary of state for national defense. The proposal stated in part:

> The two governments declare that France and Great Britain shall no longer be two nations, but one Franco-British Union. . . .
>
> Every citizen of France will enjoy immediately citizenship of Great Britain; every British subject will become a citizen of France. . . .
>
> During the war there shall be a single War Cabinet, and all the forces of Britain and France, whether on land, sea, or in the air, will be placed under its direction. It will govern from wherever it best can. The two Parliaments will be formally associated. The nations of the British Empire are already forming new armies. France will keep her available forces in the field, on the sea, and in the air. . . .
>
> The Union will concentrate its whole energy against the power of the enemy, no matter where the battle may be.
>
> And thus we shall conquer.

Yet that grand appeal would have no effect, for it arrived at the new site of the French government at the southwestern port of Bordeaux as a crisis beset the French Cabinet. Although Premier Reynaud was endeavoring to uphold his government's pledge to Britain to make no separate peace, he was up against powerful opponents: Pétain, the central figure among a band of defeatists who were resolved at all costs to stop the war; his military commander, General Weygand, who wanted his government to surrender so as to spare him the stigma of military surrender in the field; and a sinister figure, the former premier, Pierre Laval, a wily politician who had made his way to Bordeaux to surround himself with agitated senators and deputies offering a simple solution to France's agony: France should not only make peace with Germany; France should join the German side.

Confronted with that opposition, Reynaud felt compelled to ask the Germans the terms of an armistice, which would be tantamount to accepting one, for news of the request would surely destroy any morale left in the French Army; but Reynaud would consent only if the British government agreed. The Churchill government's answer was prompt: yes, but only on the condition that the French fleet took refuge in British ports.

That measure generated little discussion, for it emerged at a time when the Cabinet was hotly debating Churchill's offer of a Franco-British Union. Although the effect of the offer on Reynaud himself was "like a tonic," the defeatists around him rejected it from the first as a trick by Perfidious Albion. It relegated France, some said, to the status of a dominion. In keeping with a prevailing view among the French military that "In three weeks, England will have her neck wrung like a chicken," Pétain declared that to form a union with Britain would be "fusion with a corpse." Said another: "Better be a Nazi province. At least we know what that means." The proposal collapsed without even coming to a vote, and the Cabinet never even heard the British proposition for safeguarding the French Fleet.

The opposition was too much for Reynaud; he resigned. The eighty-four-year-old Marshal of France, Henri Philippe Pétain, the hero of Verdun, promptly undertook to form a new government. In the new Cabinet, General Weygand, to whom all was already lost, became the minister of defense; Admiral Darlan became the minister of marine; and Pierre Laval became the minister of state, eventually to become the premier, the *éminence grise* of the Pétain government, and the architect of a policy of collaboration with Hitler's New Order of Europe. Those and others in the Cabinet were all passionate French nationalists, but in their view, Adolf Hitler had already established hegemony over the Continent with no power capable of challenging him; to that reality, France had to accommodate itself. Yet even in the misery and ignominy of defeat at the hands of Nazi Germany, there were consolations: like so many of their class—the businessmen, the bankers, the clergy, the still-influential remnants of the aristocracy, the rentier classes—the men in Pétain's Cabinet could see in Hitler a relief from the nightmare of a Communist France. Hitler had demonstrated that he knew how to deal with the Communist menace; he could be expected to help eradicate it in France; and only Hitler had the power to stand up to the Soviet Union. As Charles de Gaulle, with British connivance, fled to London to continue the fight (in time to be condemned to death in absentia by the Pétain government), the new French government pursued overtures submitted as early as June 17, 1940, through Madrid, for a statement of armistice terms.

## Chapter Sixty-Five

Hitler personally directed that the French surrender take place in the same old wooden dining car in the forest of Compèigne the French had preserved as a national monument, in which, in 1918, emissaries of the kaiser had been forced to accept defeat. After the Führer's motorcade arrived at 3:15 P.M. on the afternoon of June 21, 1940, Hitler paused briefly at a granite block that, as an inscription indicated, had been erected as a reminder of "the criminal pride of the German Empire—vanquished by the free people which it tried to enslave." His face "afire with scorn, anger, hate, revenge, triumph,"[1] he muttered something and walked on to enter the railway car.

When a three-man French delegation arrived, Field Marshal Wilhelm Keitel read the terms. They were elastic enough to appear compassionate, strict enough to ensure subjugation. When Keitel finished, Hitler rose and with his party departed, leaving others to spell out the details. At Hitler's personal direction, the terms were not to require surrender of the French Fleet; by taking over the Fleet, he recognized, Germany would pose a challenge to British supremacy of the seas and thereby steel British determination to continue the fight, and seizing proud vessels that had not been defeated in battle might make it more difficult to obtain French collaboration, which was a basic goal, for he wanted France's cooperation in the coming showdown with Bolshevism. In any event, most of the capital ships were in North African ports, out of reach. As finally decided, that part of the Fleet considered unnecessary for administering the French colonies was in time "to be collected in ports to be specified and there demobilized and disarmed under German or Italian control."[2]

Before daylight on the 23rd, Hitler flew from his headquarters at Bruly-le-Pêche in Belgium to Le Bourget and motored in the early morning sunlight into the French capital. Through nearly deserted streets, the party went first to the Opéra, then to the Eiffel Tower, the Arc de Triomphe, and Les Invalides, where Hitler gazed bareheaded upon Napoleon's sarcophagus and instructed an aide to have the bones of Napoleon's young son transferred from Vienna to lie beside those of his father, a gesture directed at the French people. The tour ended on the heights of Montmartre at the Sacré-Coeur. "It was the dream of my life to be permitted to see Paris," he said to his architect, Albert Speer. "I cannot say how happy I am to have that dream fulfilled."[3] Speer, he directed, was to begin work immediately rebuilding Berlin into the monumental capital of Germania.

By terms of the armistice, France was divided into an occupied zone and an unoccupied zone, the latter embracing roughly the southern two-fifths of the country and governed by Pétain from Vichy, a spa in Central France previously known as a place to take the waters for such complaints as gout, liver trouble, catarrh, and rheumatism. There Pétain moved swiftly to establish a benevolent dictatorship, which many a Frenchman who revered the old war hero considered to be preferable to the dissident, impotent parliamentarianism of the old Third Republic.

Quickly reestablishing the American Embassy in Vichy, Ambassador William C. Bullitt found that Pétain believed one of the chief causes of the collapse of the French Army was that "the reserve officers who had been educated by school teachers who were Socialists and not patriots had deserted their men and shown no fighting spirit whatsoever," and if he had continued the war, there would sooner or later have been a Bolshevik government. Pétain and the other leaders, Bullitt observed, wanted "to cut loose from all that France has represented during the past two generations." So "absolute" was "their physical and moral defeat," Bullitt noted, "that they have accepted completely for France the fate of becoming a province of Nazi Germany."[4]

Vichy France under Pétain would be swiftly transformed into a Fascist state, ostensibly independent but controlled in large measure from behind the scenes by a Nazi *Polizeiführer*, a former art teacher, Karl Oberg. The new state gained endorsement by "a considerable body of Frenchmen who at that time believed in, or hoped for, a final German victory."[5] Still guided by the Comintern's dictates based on the Nazi-Soviet Nonaggression Pact, even the Communists cooperated.

There was little Britain could do at that point to influence the policies of Vichy France other than to offer refuge for Frenchmen who fled in order to continue the fight. What worried the Churchill government most in any case was not Vichy's policies but Admiral Darlan's promise in regard to the French Fleet, which to Churchill was an issue involving no less than the survival of democracy itself. The concern carried across the Atlantic to Washington where the U.S. Army's chief of staff, General George C. Marshall, and the chief of naval operations, Admiral Harold R. Stark, observed that if the French Fleet passed to German control, it would be necessary, however great the peril posed by Japan, to transfer the main American Fleet from the Pacific to the Atlantic. Under instructions from Washington, Ambassador Bullitt warned that if the French failed to keep the Fleet out of Hitler's hands, "the French Government will permanently lose the friendship and good-will of the United States."[6]

What disturbed Churchill particularly was the phrase in the armistice terms whereby the Fleet would be "collected in ports to be specified and there demobilized and disarmed under German or Italian control." To Churchill, that meant that "the French war vessels would pass into that control while fully armed." Although the Germans had pledged under terms of the armistice not to use the vessels, who could trust the word of Hitler? "At all costs," Churchill noted, "at all risks, in one way or another, we must make sure that the Navy of

France did not fall into wrong hands, and then perhaps bring us and others to ruin."[7]

The decision that Churchill faced was to him "a hateful decision, the most unnatural and painful in which I have ever been concerned," but he felt he had no alternative, particularly in view of the character of the French minister of marine, Admiral Darlan. In responding to a toast at a dinner in his honor at the Admiralty in 1939, Darlan had begun by reminding his hosts that his great-grandfather had died at British hands in the Battle of Trafalgar; he was, Churchill concluded, "one of those good Frenchmen who hate England." He was one of that "category of politicians, without doctrine and without character who plunged into the new [pro-German] policy for the sole purpose of profiting by the political changes."[8]

Churchill's thinking thus colored, he gave scant weight to the fact that if Darlan turned over the French Fleet to the Germans, he would be giving up the only power behind his political ambition and the only fulcrum that Vichy France possessed to influence the German masters. So, too, Churchill discounted the fact that most of the capital ships had sailed beyond German reach to French ports in North Africa or to the British-controlled Egyptian port of Alexandria; only a few remained in a mainland French port, at Toulon and Marseilles.

When British intelligence on July 1, 1940, intercepted a French naval signal revealing that Darlan "had requested accommodations for himself, a German officer, a certain Wielleman, and accompanying party in Algiers, it looked as if the French might be about to turn over the fleet."[9] Unless the French Fleet would proceed to French ports in the West Indies or to other ports under British control, Churchill decided, the Royal Navy would attack and destroy it. During the evening of July 2, 1940, Churchill himself went to the war room at the Admiralty to direct the operations.

In the British ports of Plymouth, Portsmouth, Falmouth, and Sheerness, where the old French battleships *Courbet* and *Paris*, two cruisers, four destroyers, seven submarines, and a host of lesser craft had taken refuge, British soldiers in soft-soled shoes crept abroad the vessels before daylight on July 3, 1940, seized or clubbed the deck watches, and subdued the sleeping crews. Only aboard a big submarine, *Surcouf*, did the surprised French fight back; a French sailor and three British soldiers were killed.

There was also little difficulty with French warships at Alexandria. There the British and French admirals, Sir Andrew Cunningham and Théodore Godefroy, reached a gentleman's agreement: in return for Cunningham's assurance that the British would make no use of the ships (a battleship, four cruisers, three destroyers, and a submarine), Admiral Godefroy agreed to remove vital parts, including the breech blocks from the guns, and reduce the crews to a fifth of the normal complement, sufficient to maintain the vessels but not to sail them.

The disaster as well as the real test of French will came at the big naval base at Mers-el-Kebir in French North Africa near Oran, the anchorage for the most powerful units of the French Fleet, including the *Dunkerque* and the *Strasbourg*, battle cruisers built with the express purpose of making them superior to the German *Scharnhorst* and *Gneisenau*. With them were two battleships, a seaplane tender, and a number of light cruisers and heavy destroyers, all under the flag of Admiral Marcel Gensoul. Before dawn on the morning of July 3, 1940, a British squadron consisting of an aircraft carrier, two battleships, a battle cruiser, two cruisers, and eleven destroyers appeared off Cape Falcon outside the base. The squadron was under Churchill's direct order by wireless from the Admiralty.

The British commander, Admiral Sir James Somerville, sent an emissary, Captain C. S. Holland, who had recently been the British naval attaché in Paris and had "keen French sympathies,"[10] to enter the anchorage aboard the destroyer *Foxhound*, to talk with Admiral Marcel Gensoul. When the *Foxhound* anchored in the outer harbor at about eight A.M., Gensoul's flag lieutenant, Lieutenant Charles de Vaisseau Dufay, an "old friend" of Holland's, came alongside in the admiral's barge; the admiral, said the lieutenant, regretted that he could not come to see Holland personally. To Lieutenant de Vaisseau Dufay, Captain Holland passed a sealed envelope containing a letter from Somerville to Gensoul that set out in detail the British position and offered Gensoul three options:

> Sail with us and continue to fight for victory against the Germans and Italians.
> Send his ships to a British port with reduced crews, which would be repatriated at the earliest possible moment.
> If Gensoul was bound by the terms of the armistice to prevent his ships from being used against the Germans and Italians, sail with reduced crews for the West Indies where the ships would be interned under the authority of the United States, the crews repatriated, and the ships returned at the end of the war.[11]

"If you refuse these fair offers," the letter concluded, "I must with profound regret require you to sink your ships within six hours. Finally, failing the above, I have the orders of His Majesty's Government to use whatever force may be necessary to prevent your ships from falling into German or Italian hands."

As Captain Holland awaited a reply, he noted that the French ships were furling awnings and raising steam, as if preparing for action at sea. A few minutes later, as de Vaisseau Dufay returned with a letter from Gensoul, Holland knew why. Gensoul vowed that no French warship would be allowed to fall intact to either Germans or Italians, but "in view of the meaning and form of expression, the veritable ultimatum which has been sent to Admiral Gensoul, French warships will meet force by force."

Captain Holland refused to accept that as the end to negotiations. The British, he told de Vaisseau Dufay, were reading Darlan's special code for communication with Gensoul, and although they knew from those signals that Darlan intended to honor his promise to the British government, "his hands were being tied by others" who were intent on turning over the French Fleet to the Germans. He "begged" the lieutenant to transmit to his admiral typewritten notes which he had prepared for use in talking with Gensoul, and the lieutenant agreed, but the reading of Captain Holland's typescript failed to move the French admiral. "Admiral Gensoul," the reply brought back by de Vaisseau Dufay stated, "wishes to draw Admiral Somerville's attention to the fact that the first shot fired against us will have the result of putting immediately the whole French Fleet against Great Britain."

The exchange of messages had by that time consumed the entire morning and the first hours of the afternoon, but Admiral Somerville determined to make another try to prevent bloodshed. At 2:19 P.M., he sent Gensoul a signal: if he accepted the terms, he was to fly a large square flag at the masthead of *Dunkerque*; otherwise, at 3:00 P.M., the British ships would open fire. That signal brought a favorable turn. Gensoul replied that he was "now ready to receive delegates for honourable discussion"; but at 4:15 P.M., as Captain Holland went aboard the *Dunkerque*, he noted that all the French warships were in an advanced state of readiness.

Receiving Holland "very formally," Admiral Gensoul was obviously "extremely indignant and angry at the course of events." "He would sink his ships to prevent them from falling into German or Italian hands," he said, but he refused to acquiesce to what he considered to be an ultimatum. While Gensoul was still deliberating, there came a signal from Somerville: if the terms were not accepted by 5:30 P.M., which was only fifteen minutes off, Somerville intended to sink the French ships. As Captain Holland departed, he had the impression that Gensoul did not wholly believe Somerville would actually fire; but as he went over the side to his motor launch, the *Dunkerque*'s bells were sounding action stations.

At 5:30 P.M., the British ships opened fire. For Gensoul, the results were calamitous. The *Bretagne* exploded and sank. The flagship *Dunkerque* was badly damaged and three days later would be sunk by British torpedo bombers. The seaplane carrier *Commandant Teste* caught fire. Badly hit, the battleship *Provence* got under way but ran aground. Although the battle cruiser *Strasbourg* cleared harbor and made for Toulon, British torpedo bombers would intercept it and inflict severe damage. All together, 1,300 French sailors were killed and over 4,000 wounded.

A few days later, a French aircraft flew over the British naval base at Gibraltar and dropped a packet containing souvenirs of wardroom parties with British officers. Attached to it was a black-bordered letter signed by officers of the *Dunkerque* who had survived the attack at Mers-el-Kebir:

> The commander and the officers of the *Dunkerque* announce the death, for the honor of their flag, of 9 officers and 200 men. They return to you the souvenirs, which they received from their comrades in war of the Royal Navy, and in whom they had placed all their trust. And they express to you on this occasion all their bitter sadness and their disgust, having seen that these comrades did not hesitate to soil

the glorious flag of St. George with an everlasting stain, that of an assassination.

For Adolf Hitler, the action at Mers-el-Kebir came as a jolt. If the British would do that to their ally, they obviously intended to continue the war. It was a reaction echoed in neutral capitals around the world, including Washington, a reaction that Churchill had hoped for. It would not end Hitler's efforts for peace with Britain, but it dealt his hopes a severe setback. It also planted in the Führer's mind the likelihood that even if he invaded and defeated his foe, the rulers of the little island would go off with their fleet to outposts of the empire and rule the seas from there.

Yet there was for Hitler a consolation, for France reacted with grief and fury. Already bitter over the British withdrawal at Dunkirk and Churchill's refusal to commit his last air squadrons, millions of Frenchmen saw the attack on the Fleet as yet another example of British perfidy to go along with Britain's extension of its naval blockade to all of German-dominated Western Europe, including the ports of France. A British intelligence survey found that many Frenchmen saw the Royal Navy's attack as "dastardly aggression," and there was "an overwhelming consensus . . . in both the occupied and unoccupied zones of France" in favor of the pro-German policies of the government of Marshal Pétain.[12] In one day, noted one Frenchman, "England killed more French sailors than Germany did during the whole war."[13] The reaction would for a long time help Pierre Laval and old Pétain to convince millions of Frenchmen to support their New Order and in the process materially strengthen the Third Reich for the bout with the Communist giant to the east.

In the capital of the Communist giant, spokesmen for the Comintern noted that as Lenin had predicted, the principal capitalist powers, England and France, had begun to make war on each other.[14]

# PART XII
## "The Great Patriotic War"

*Chapter Sixty-Six*

In an address before the House of Commons on June 18, 1940, Winston Churchill announced the imminence of the Battle of Britain:

> The whole fury and might of the enemy must very soon be turned on us. Hitler knows that he will have to break us in this island or lose the war. If we can stand up to him, all Europe may be free and the life of the world may move forward into broad, sunlit uplands. But if we fail, then the whole world, including the United States, including all that we have known and cared for, will sink into the abyss of a new Dark Age, made more sinister, and perhaps more protracted, by the lights of perverted science. Let us therefore embrace ourselves to our duties, and so bear ourselves that, if the British Empire and its Commonwealth last for a thousand years, men will say: 'This was their finest hour.'[1]

In view of the magnificent but defiant tone of the speech, it was widely expected that Hitler would respond with a violent air attack, such as he had unleashed on Warsaw at the start of the campaign in Poland and on Rotterdam at the start of the campaign in the west, attacks intended to demonstrate the invincibility of the Wehrmacht and the futility of resistance. But the great attack did not come. As if to demonstrate that the Luftwaffe was still to be reckoned with, seventy aircraft raided the South Wales Docks on July 10, 1940, other planes struck British shipping in the Narrow Seas, and there were occasional low-level sorties over the Kentish countryside; but there were no violent, prolonged attacks. Only later would the German tactics become evident: despite the determination the British had demonstrated in attacking the French Fleet, Hitler still hoped to beguile them into making peace.

During the month following the fall of France, several peace feelers reached Churchill, one delivered by Hitler in a radio address, others by way of the Vatican and Stockholm, and at least one through an American businessman named Stallworth, a confidant of Hermann Göring, who passed the feeler to the United States government. Churchill's reaction was to ignore all overtures. On July 14, 1940, in a broadcast over the BBC, he succinctly summed up the British position: " . . . be the ordeal sharp or long, or both, we shall seek no terms, we shall tolerate no parley, we may show mercy—we shall ask for none."[2]

While restraining the Luftwaffe, Hitler delayed his victory speech before the Reichstag in hope of being able to announce that Britain and Germany had come to terms, but at last, on July 19, 1940, he addressed the deputies. Even then he still offered reconciliation, feeling "duty bound before my conscience once again to direct an appeal to reason even in England."[3] Hitler still found Britain's rejecti of his overtures almost impossible to believe. "England's situation is hopeless," he said in a conference with his military commanders a few days later. "The war has been won by us. A reversal of the prospects of success is impossible." Perhaps the fault lay with Stalin, he mused; "Stalin is flirting with England to keep England at war and tie us down, to gain time for taking what he wants and what cannot be taken if peace breaks out."[4]

Yet if the British were to continue to refuse to come to terms, Hitler called for a quick end to the war. Plans and preparations for an invasion of the British Isles— Operation Sealion—were to begin immediately, and as a preliminary, the Luftwaffe was to open a massive air offensive. Yet even after giving that order, Hitler vacillated. England's stubbornness was preventing him from getting on with his holy war against Russia; if preparations for Sealion could not be "completed with certainty" by the beginning of September 1940, it would be necessary "to consider other plans."[5]

To all the world that late summer of 1940 it appeared that the German legions would soon come ashore in Britain and quickly subdue the feeble forces that had managed under the greatest adversity to get home from Dunkirk. No longer under restraint, the Luftwaffe began a persistent, terrible bombardment, while the fighter squadrons of the Luftwaffe and the Royal Air Force fought for mastery of the skies. From capitals around the world poured a stream of reports that three Germans armies were to land from a mighty armada between The Wash and the Isle of Wight before the equinoctial gales began in October. The moon and the tides, the British reckoned, would be at the most favorable for an invasion around the middle of September, a period when three centuries of records showed, the

Channel, one of the most fickle bodies of water in the world, was usually calm.

As August merged into September, the British Isles, Churchill recorded, "entered upon a period of extreme tension and vigilance."[6] Moon and tide conditions, the Admiralty determined, would be most favorable on the southeast coast between the 8th and 10th of September, and the defenders stood to their posts; but the invasion never came.

The fact was, Hitler never had any real heart for Operation Sealion, for the magnetism exercised on him by Soviet Russia was too powerful to resist. On July 1, 1940, on Hitler's order, the commander-in-chief of the Army, Field Marshal Walther von Brauchitsch instructed his chief of operations to begin preparing outline plans for an invasion of Russia and his chief of intelligence to prepare a detailed study of the strength, equipment, morale, commanders, and disposition of the Soviet military forces.

On July 29, 1940, only ten days after Hitler's victory speech and eight days after he directed planning and preparations to begin for Operation Sealion, the chief of the operations staff of the Oberkommando der Wehrmacht, General Alfred Jodl, met with other senior officers in a car of the Supreme Command's special train, *Atlas*, which was drawn up in the station at Bad Reichenhall near Berchtesgaden. Jodl first "went round ensuring that all doors and windows were closed and then, without any preamble, disclosed . . . that Hitler had decided to rid the world 'once and for all' of the danger of Bolshevism by a surprise attack on Soviet Russia to be carried out at the earliest possible moment, i.e., in May 1941."[7] Two days later at the Berghof, he told the chief of the German General Staff, General Franz Halder: *"Russia is the factor by which England sets the greatest store. . . . If Russia is beaten, England's last hope is gone. Germany is then master of Europe and the Balkans. . . . Decision: As a result of this argument, Russia must be dealt with. Spring 1941."*[8]

That decision obviously meant an end to Operation Sealion, the invasion of Britain, but nobody outside the highest official German circles was to know that. Once the autumn days during which an invasion might have been staged in 1940 had passed, German intelligence agencies immediately embarked on one of the grandest deceptions of the war, designed to show that (1) the Wehrmacht would invade Britain in the spring of 1941, and (2) whatever the signs and portents to the contrary, Hitler had no intention of attacking Russia. As trailed before the eyes of foreign intelligence agents, the main invasion was to be launched in the spring of 1941 across the Strait of Dover (codename: Shark) while a feint (code name: Harpoon) was directed against the northeast coast off England to draw off mobile British forces.

The plans were detailed and meticulous, to include occupation procedures, military government policies, even a list of British citizens to be rounded up and sent to concentration camps. Transports, barges, ferries, tugs, supplies began to assemble in the ports of Norway, the Low Countries, and the French Channel coast. Troops engaged in landing exercises; English-speaking officers were assigned to headquarters staffs; guidebooks and English phrase books were issued to the ranks; and the German press and radio were to be allowed to speculate freely about the invasion.

As an American naval intelligence study would disclose: " . . . by the spring of 1941, orders went out to the German commands to start moving for *Haifisch* [*Shark*] and *Harpune* [*Harpoon*]. These orders closely resembled those issued in the summer and fall under [*Sealion*] . . . the original plan for the invasion." Yet this time there was a difference: along with the orders went a sealed envelope "to be opened only on orders from the *Oberkommando der Wehrmacht*. This envelope contained the information that *Haifisch* and *Harpune* were deceptive movements and that the invasion was not directed against England but against the USSR." [9]

When the chief of the operations staff of the Oberkommando der Wehrmacht, General Jodl, first informed the senior German commanders of Hitler's decision to attack Russia, a chorus of protests had erupted. Was that not the two-front war that had always spelled problems for the German General Staff and had brought the nation's downfall in 1918? Yet Hitler, as conscious as his commanders of that, had not given up on his plans to neutralize Britain. There was surely some way to bring the British to terms. As Hitler pondered that equation, the name of a familiar figure began to appear in Foreign Minister von Ribbentrop's bulletins to the Führer: the Duke of Windsor.

As France fell, the Duke and Duchess of Windsor fled as ordinary refugees across the Spanish frontier to Madrid and then went to Lisbon. Concerned that the Germans might in some way try to use the Windsors, the British government offered to allow them to return to England, but when the duke made their going dependent upon his wife being granted a title earlier denied her, "Her Royal Highness," and George VI denied the request, the duke and duchess accepted an invitation to reside as guests in the Portuguese seaside resort of Estoril in the villa of a high official of the Vatican's Bank of the Holy Ghost, Ricardo Espirito Santo e Silva, who was also an informant of the Nazi diplomatic service.

In mid-July 1940, von Ribbentrop summoned to his presence the head of the foreign intelligence section of the Sicherheitsdienst, the intelligence service of the Nazi Party, SS-Brigadeführer Walter Schellenberg. Since the Duke of Windsor's abdication, noted von Ribbentrop, he had been under such close surveillance by "the British Secret Service" that he had come to feel "as if he were their prisoner." Yet the duke, said von Ribbentrop on the basis of reports from the German ambassador in Madrid, Eberhardt von Stöhrer, still maintained "sympathetic feelings toward Germany." If afforded the right circumstances, "he would not be averse to escaping from his present environment." [10]

Schellenberg was to proceed to Spain as Hitler's personal representative and contact the duke. If Edward was prepared to live in a country within the sphere of German economic, political, or military influence and make "some official gesture disassociating himself from the manoeuvres of the British Royal Family," the

Third Reich would place at his disposal in a Swiss bank a sum amounting to $50 million. At some point in the conversation, Hitler himself telephoned von Ribbentrop and with Schellenberg listening on an extension said that "Schellenberg should particularly bear in mind the importance of the Duchess's attitude and try as hard as possible to get her support," for she had "a great influence over the Duke."

Not a man to pay out $50 million just because somebody had indicated admiration for the Nazi regime, Hitler obviously wanted to hold the Duke of Windsor in readiness for whatever role he might play to serve Germany. That the Churchill government had survived under all the adversities that had already beset England was to Hitler illogical; as adversities built up and as Germany turned against Bolshevism, which so many Englishmen of the ruling class so clearly detested, surely the Churchill government would fall, to be replaced by someone more amenable to settlement with Germany, such as Lord Halifax or even the old prime minister, David Lloyd George. Even if the Duke of Windsor could not return to the throne, he might serve as a figurehead around whom those sympathetic to Germany and antipathetic to Soviet Russia might rally.

Hitler's scheme received an impetus when a leader of the Spanish Falangists, Miguel Primo de Rivera, reported to German agents that in two conversations with the Duke of Windsor, the duke said that he was "more and more distant from the King and the present British government" and was "considering making a public statement . . . disavowing English policy and breaking with his brother." When de Rivera suggested that the duke was still likely to be "called upon to play an important role in English policy and possibly to ascend the English throne," that "astonished both the duke and the duchess." According to the British constitution, they said, it would be impossible for a monarch who had abdicated to reoccupy the throne. Yet when de Rivera replied that "the course of the war might bring some changes even in the English constitution, the Duchess especially became very pensive."

Although thwarted in bringing the duke to England, Churchill had in the meantime been busily arranging to get him out of the way of German scheming by appointing him governor general of the Bahamas, which was remote from Europe and also a place where British intelligence agents could operate unimpeded. The duke was completing plans for his departure when von Ribbentrop sent a signal to the German ambassador in Lisbon, Baron Oswald Hoynegen-Huene, for "strictly confidential transmission" to the duke. "Germany" wired von Ribbentrop, "wants peace with the English people. The Churchill clique stands in the way of this peace." If the duke would "keep himself prepared for further developments . . . Germany would be prepared to cooperate most closely . . . and to clear the way for any desire expressed by the Duke, especially with a view to the assumption of the English throne by the Duke and Duchess." Even if the duke had "other plans" but was willing to cooperate in establishing amicable relations between Germany and Britain, Germany was prepared "to assure him and his wife of a subsistence which would permit him, either as a private citizen or in some other position, to lead a life suitable for a king." [11]

As Espirito Santo reported to the German ambassador, "The message which was conveyed to the Duke made the deepest impression on him." The Führer's desire for peace, reported Baron Hoynegen-Huene to Berlin, "was in complete agreement with his own point of view." He was "firmly convinced that if he had been King it would never have come to war" and that he agreed "gladly" to "cooperate at a suitable time in the establishment of peace." Yet that time, the duke believed, had still not arrived, for "there was as yet no inclination in England for an approach to Germany," and until the moment came, he was obliged "to follow the official orders of his government." On the other hand, when that moment came, "he was prepared for any personal sacrifice and would make himself available without the slightest personal ambition." Intending to remain in close communication with his Portuguese host, Espirito Santo, he had established with him a code word; upon receiving it, he would return immediately to Portugal.

As the Duke of Windsor and his duchess sailed on August 2, 1940, for the Bahamas, the duke was still reluctant to leave in case he might not be at hand "to step in at the decisive moment." His concern continued, for a fortnight later, he telegraphed his former host, Espirito Santo, "to send him a communication as soon as action was advisable." Even a year later, on August 5, 1941, a few weeks after the German invasion of Russia, Hoynegen-Huene informed von Ribbentrop that Espirito Santo had received a letter from the duke "confirming his opinion . . . that Britain had virtually lost the war already" and that the United States "would be better advised to promote peace, not war" between Britain and Germany. Even when the war had ended and the vast crimes of the Hitler regime exposed, the duke was said to have remarked to a British official in Washington, Sir John Balfour, that "had Hitler been differently handled, war with Germany might have been avoided in 1939."

By the standards of the emergency decrees in effect in Britain in 1940, if there was truth in the various accounts of the Duke of Windsor's conduct in Lisbon in the summer of 1940, he had committed treason in wartime, the gravest of offenses. Yet no sanctions in law were taken against him. Nor would verification or repudiation of the reports be possible even after he died, for in revising the law on public release of state documents, the British government specifically excluded papers relating to the duke; they were to remain closed for 101 years. The Supreme Allied Commander, General Dwight D. Eisenhower, cooperated in that policy by ordering his chief of intelligence, Major General Edwin L. Sibert, to hand over to him all documents found in archives captured by the United States Army which related to the Duke of Windsor, and Sibert subsequently passed along a small collection found in von Ribbentrop's home. The documents were either destroyed or their whereabouts concealed. [12]

There was no such control to be exercised over official Soviet documentation. Official Soviet historians would assert that as early as the summer of 1940, Hitler's deputy, Rudolf Hess, tried to get in touch with pro-German, anti-Soviet leaders in Britain in an attempt to arrange an understanding that would permit Hitler to invade Russia without interference from Britain. The Duke of Windsor, wrote the Soviet historians, established the British contacts when shortly before the German invasion of Russia, Hess made a sudden and mysterious flight to Britain.[13]

On the night of May 10, 1941, the Luftwaffe struck London with what was up to that time the largest air attack of the war. More than 700 bombers, each carrying some 2,000 pounds of bombs, hit the center of the capital in an attempt to re-create the catastrophe of 1666 when the Great Fire of London had almost obliterated the city.

Starting at about ten o'clock, the planes struck first with high explosive bombs to disrupt the water system. With that system wrecked and the Thames at low tide, denying water from the river to firefighters, the bombers deluged the half-timbered, medieval heart of the city with scores of thousands of two-pound magnesium and phosphorus bombs. By midnight some 2,000 major fires were raging, principally in and around the financial center, the City of London. The chamber of the House of Commons was consumed by flames; Westminster Abbey, Westminster Hall and School, the British Museum, St. Paul's Cathedral, the Mint, the Bank of England, and scores of other famous and noble buildings, many of them built by Sir Christopher Wren when he was restoring the city after the Great Fire, were damaged, many of them severely. When dawn came, hundreds of fires were still burning out of control, and three days later four would still be ablaze. Five docks and some forty factories were destroyed, and all but one of the capital's main railroad stations were blocked for weeks, the main rail lines through the city not to be reopened until early June. Three thousand people were killed or injured, more than 700 acres of the city virtually laid to waste.

As the Luftwaffe was creating that havoc, a radar post near Berwick-on-Tweed, along the border between England and Scotland, some 350 miles north of London, detected a twin-engined Messerschmitt 110, a long-range fighter-bomber. Tracking the craft as it flew due west at 180 miles per hour over Coldstream, Peebles, and Lanark, the radar post passed a warning to all civil and military authorities.

As officer of the Renfrewshire Constabulary, Lieutenant Tom Hyslop heard the alert over his police-band radio even as he heard the noise of an aircraft rapidly approaching the ground. Shortly before the plane hit and exploded, he caught a brief glimpse of an opening parachute. At about the same time, a plowman at Floors Farm, David McLean, also heard the roaring of the aircraft. Turning out the light and opening the blackout curtain, McLean saw a man coming to earth by parachute. Pulling a coat over his night clothes, McLean rushed into the night. As he approached the parachutist, the wind was billowing and thrashing the silk, dragging the hapless man across the ground. Grasping the shrouds, McLean collapsed the parachute.

When he demanded to know the identity of the parachutist, the man said he was German, Captain Horn of the Luftwaffe. He was unarmed, he said, and invited McLean to search him. Determining that he had no weapon but that he had injured an ankle, McLean helped him to his cottage, where his mother began to prepare a pot of tea. He had an urgent message for the Duke of Hamilton, said the German; would McLean help him to get to the duke's residence, Dungavel House?

At that point Lieutenant Hyslop arrived in company with several British soldiers. They took the German to the Home Guard post in the Boy Scouts Hall in nearby Busby and searched him. Although the German insisted that his captors contact the Duke of Hamilton, they took him first to the sick bay at nearby Maryhill barracks for treatment of his injured ankle.

That night the Duke of Hamilton, thirty-nine years of age and a squadron commander in the Royal Air Force, was at Drem airbase in North Berwick. Exhausted from four days and nights of almost continual flying, he had just turned in when the telephone rang. It was the operations controller asking that he report to air traffic control without delay. When he reached the command center, he learned that a German officer calling himself Alfred Horn, who had parachuted from his crashing aircraft, insisted on speaking with him. Although mystified, the duke chose to get some sleep first; he would drive to Maryhill barracks to see the man the next morning.

Douglas Douglas-Hamilton, 14th Duke of Hamilton and the 11th Duke of Brandon, was one of Britain's more prominent aristocrats, a conservative member of Parliament for East Renfrewshire, a member of the King's Bodyguard for Scotland, and Lord Steward of the king's household. A leading British flyer, he had come to know a number of Germans through the years, and in 1936, while attending the Olympic Games in Berlin, he had met, through an acquaintance, one of Hitler's closest advisers, Hitler's deputy, Rudolf Hess.

As the Duke of Hamilton confronted the German parachutist on the morning of May 11, 1940, at Maryhill barracks, the man announced that he and the duke had met in Germany some years earlier. He was, said the German, the deputy Führer of the Greater German Reich, Rudolf Hess.

Although the duke recognized Hess, he gave no indication of it. Departing, he notified his superiors, the Foreign Office, and the Cabinet Office and flew to London, where he put in a telephone call to Churchill, with whom he was acquainted. Hess, the duke told Churchill, had flown to Britain to arrange a peace with Germany.

Within a few days, Rudolf Hess was in the Tower of London, the medieval fortress in the heart of the City of London. Interrogated at length by some of the leading British Foreign Office and intelligence officials, Hess reiterated that he had flown to England to convince the British to make peace with Germany and confront the real enemy of mankind, Bolshevism. Hitler had not sent him, Hess insisted; indeed, Hitler had no knowledge of his coming.

As Churchill would note later, Hess "knew and was capable of understanding

Hitler's inner mind—his hatred of Soviet Russia, his lust to destroy Bolshevism, his admiration for Britain and earnest wish to be friends with the British Empire, his contempt for most other countries." Hess was convinced that "England had been wrested from her true intersts and policy of friendship, and above all from alliance against Bolshevism, by the war-mongers, of whom Churchill was the superficial manifestation." Hess believed that if only he "could get at the heart of Britain and make its King believe how Hitler felt," then "the malign forces that ruled this ill-starred island and had brought so many needless miseries upon it would be swept away." Hess had chosen the Duke of Hamilton as intermediary both because he had met him and because he thought that as the Lord Steward, Hamilton probably would be "dining every night with the King and have his private ear." [14]

To Stalin, the news of Hess's mission was yet another example of British perfidy. As he noted, the great air attack of May 10, 1941, was the last inflicted on Britain for almost two months, an obvious maneuver, thought Stalin, to give the British people time to choose between destruction and salvation, between Armageddon in a war with Germany and the glories of a crusade against Stalin, the anti-Christ. As the official Soviet history would profess, Stalin was convinced that "The English Government entered into talks with Hess" conducted by a "special representative of the government," Ivone Kirkpatrick, a former senior member of the British Embassy's staff in Berlin. Correctly reporting the terms that Hess offered, the Soviet historians maintained that in response the British government "strongly 'directed the attention' of Germany toward the Soviet Union," an oblique euphemism for urging that Germany attack Russia. German officials, the Soviet historians asserted, arranged through the Duke of Windsor for Hess's flight, which was designed "to attract the enemies of Germany to the anti-Soviet campaign . . . a general crusade against 'the Bolshevik peril.'" [15]

Nor were Stalin's suspicions to be allayed by an official German pronouncement that Hess "lived in a state of hallucination" that led him to believe that he personally could achieve "an understanding between England and Germany," nor by the knowledge that for Hitler Hess's flight was embarrassing, the kind of embarrassment, as Churchill put it, that he might experience should "my trusted colleague, the Foreign Secretary . . . , parachute from a stolen Spitfire into the grounds of Berchtesgaden." Even three years later, when Churchill was conversing face to face with Stalin, he concluded that Stalin continued to believe that "there had been some deep negotiation or plot for Germany and Britain to act together in an invasion of Russia, which had miscarried." Irritated when Stalin refused to believe him, Churchill said: "When I make a statement of facts within my knowledge, I expect it to be accepted." To which Stalin responded: "There are lots of things that happen even here in Russia which our Secret Service do not necessarily tell me about." [16]

At the White House, Hess's flight and rumors of peace conversations between Britain and Germany produced serious concern. If Britain capitulated or otherwise acquiesced, Roosevelt believed that it would be only a matter of time before the United States came under attack, probably by a German-Japanese combination. If Britain were to enter into league with Germany, then the military supplies being provided Britain should be withheld for the American armed forces.

Most people in the United States believed that Hess had in fact come to Britain with "specific and concrete peace proposals"; they also doubted that Hitler's close associate could have flown to Britain without the Führer's knowledge. As with Stalin, the failure of the Luftwaffe to strike again after the great raid of May 10, 1941, appeared to many to indicate that Hitler was counting on a pact with Britain. Yet the facts in the Hess case were, in reality, much as Churchill would report them to Roosevelt and as the president would soon learn from another source. That would be revealed only in 1979 when the United States government released the intercepts and descriptions of Japanese diplomatic radio traffic between Tokyo and Berlin, Rome, Vienna, and other major Japanese diplomatic outposts, material that was on hand in Washington almost as quickly as it was in Tokyo through means of a code-breaking operation known as Magic. When the Japanese ambassador in Berlin, Baron Hiroshi Oshima, transmitted an account of his briefing about Hess to Tokyo, he unwittingly reported it to Washington as well.

According to Oshima, von Ribbentrop said that Hess was "mentally and physically ill," and even though he occupied "a position of prominence in the Nazi Party," he "had no knowledge of current political policy in Germany."[17] Troubled for several years by a gallbladder ailment, Hess had turned in his pain to astrology, "frequently conjuring castles in the air out of his fancies." He had come to the conclusion that by "working upon the Fascist element of Great Britain," he could bring about Churchill's downfall and "the conclusion of the offensive against England with as little sacrifice and loss of life as possible." Although von Ribbentrop said that Hess had told Hitler about his plan, he flew to Scotland without Hitler's knowledge or authority. Aware that Hess's mind was "not normal," said von Ribbentrop, the German government did not "consider the facts of this unhappy official treasonable even to the slightest extent."[18]

As the furor over the Hess affair died down, Baron Oshima provided his government with yet another advice that was also almost immediately on President Roosevelt's desk. On June 3, 1941, Tokyo informed its diplomatic net that Berlin had reported: "There is no room for doubt that the beginning of a great battle is about to take place. The manner of carrying this out and the time of its execution are entirely a secret plan of Chancellor Hitler's. As yet it is still too early to know exactly the course of events."[19]

## Chapter Sixty-Seven

Joseph Stalin distrusted Winston Churchill and Great Britain beyond all other statesmen and powers, for he was convinced that the British prime minister was working secretly to incite a war between Germany and Russia so that the two would tear each other apart, leaving to Britain its traditional role of arbiter of Europe. With the fall of the Low Countries and France, which put virtually all the resources of Western Europe at Hitler's disposal, Stalin's suspicions intensified to the point of paranoia, but he was determined to stay out of the war until Britain and Germany had so weakened themselves that conditions would be right for establishing a dictatorship of the proletariat. Despite the Nazi-Soviet Nonaggression Pact, Stalin could not be sure that Churchill might not succeed in his stratagem, nor that Hitler might not turn of his own volition against the Soviet Union. For the Soviet Union, the pact was, after all, but a device to gain time to enable Russia to prepare for war. Stalin thus was compelled to maintain the friendliest relations with Hitler while at the same time trying to avoid alienating Churchill, with whom he would need an alliance should Hitler attack the Soviet Union. Churchill, for his part, saw Stalin's predicament clearly, which prompted him to pursue what he called "a patient policy of trying to re-establish relations of a confidential character with Russia, trusting to the march of events and to their fundamental antagonisms to Germany."[1] Both Churchill and Stalin were thus practicing the old and cynical game of diplomacy according to Cardinal Mazarin: "In statecraft there are no long term friends, no long term enemies, only short term interests."

To foster the new diplomacy, Churchill selected as Britain's new ambassador to Moscow one of the oddest men in Parliament, Sir Stafford Cripps. An extreme left-wing Socialist, austere in appearance and manner, with perceptions priestly, ethereal, prim, and severe, Cripps was difficult to understand and even more difficult to like. Yet he had had a distinguished career in public service, was quite selfless, and, as Churchill noted, "willingly accepted this bleak and unpromising task."[2]

Cripps arrived in Moscow with Churchill's first direct communication to Stalin, a letter in which Churchill briefly noted the geographical separation of the two countries and a similar wide separation between their systems of government, but, he said, a new factor had arisen that, in Churchill's opinion, made it "desirable" that the two countries reestablish close contact: "the prospect of Germany establishing a hegemony over the Continent." It was for the Soviet Union alone, of course, to decide how Germany's bid for hegemony affected their interests, but Churchill hoped that in any discussion with the new British ambassador, there would be "no misunderstanding as to the policy of His Majesty's Government or of their readiness to discuss fully with the Soviet Government any of the vast problems created by Germany's present attempt to pursue in Europe a methodical process by successive stages of conquest and absorption."[3]

Receiving Ambassador Cripps on July 1, 1940, Stalin said he "must honestly state that to the extent to which I have had the opportunity of discussing the question with the German representative, I have not noticed any signs of such a wish for domination."[4] Hardly had Sir Stafford left when Stalin's premier and foreign commissar, Molotov, sent for the German ambassador, Count von der

Schulenburg, to assure the German government that Stalin's meeting with the British ambassador was without significance; the principal business, he said, was Russia's interest in exchanging lumber for British rubber and tin. Von der Schulenburg in turn notified his government that there was "no reason for apprehension . . . no reason to doubt the loyal attitude of the Soviet Union towards us."[5]

In London, where the reality of Soviet policy was often measured in the rise and fall in the number of dinner parties that Ambassador Maisky gave for people to whom he otherwise never talked, it was concluded that the Soviet government was, in fact, very nervous. Maisky had begun once more to dine conservative leaders and politicians.

Aside from Maisky's behavior, there were other signs that what Churchill called the "fundamental antagonisms" between Nazism and Communism were at work to wreck the Nazi-Soviet Pact. Hitler guaranteed Rumania's frontiers and sent a military mission to Bucharest, a capital which Stalin regarded as one of the principal centers of "anti-Soviet reaction" in the Balkans. In a move that hardly could have escaped the attention of the Soviet *apparats* in Germany and Poland, headquarters of Field Marshal Fedor von Bock's army group moved from France to Posen in Poland to assume command of three armies containing six panzer and twenty-nine motorized and infantry divisions; but the German secret service, the Abwehr, as part of the Shark and Harpoon deceptions, spread the word that it had been necessary to remove most of those troops from France because of their impact on the French economy and that von Bock's forces were positioned to defend the Balkans and assure continued German access to Rumanian oil. Yet even if Stalin accepted those explanations, what of the successor to the Anti-Comintern Pact, the Tripartite Pact?

Aside from a traditional role as Russia's principal adversary in Asia, Japan by 1940 had become one of the most powerful and determined of the Soviet Union's ideological adversaries. Ever since 1918, it had become clear that Japan intended some day to move against the Asian possessions of the European powers in order to become the leading power in the Pacific, but a new complexity entered the equation when in 1936 Japan joined the Anti-Comintern Pact and signed a secret military understanding with Hitler. The terms of that understanding had been intercepted by the U.S. Navy's radio intelligence service and laid before the president. The secret clause read: "If one of the contracting powers is attacked or threatened with an attack, regardless of circumstances, the other must uphold her position and take whatever measures are necessary to uphold her position, and both nations will immediately confer on what measures are to be taken for the common good."[6]

While that clause was ambiguous and, at least on its face, less than a declaration that war against one Anti-Comintern power would constitute war against the other, it did provide, when related to the rest of the text of the pact, for a certain synchronization of operations between Germany, Japan, and later Italy. When one of the Anti-Comintern powers made a move, another would act soon afterward to take advantage of the international confusion and outrage created by the original action. Soon after the surrender of the Dutch in May 1940, for example, Germany advised Japan to proceed with plans to occupy the oil fields of the Dutch East Indies and then began pressuring the Dutch to accept the Japanese terms. When France surrendered in June 1940, the Japanese promptly asked the Germans to invite the new French government of Marshal Pétain to grant military, naval, and trade concessions in French Indochina.

As an extension of the Anti-Comintern Pact and Hitler's alliance with Mussolini, the Pact of Steel, Germany, Japan, and Italy on September 27, 1940, negotiated a new and fuller alliance, the Tripartite Pact. The principal covenants were:

> Japan recognizes and respects the leadership of Germany and Italy in the establishment of a New Order in Europe.
> Germany and Italy recognize and respect the leadership of Japan in the establishment of a New Order in Greater East Asia.
> Germany, Italy, and Japan agree to cooperate in their efforts on the aforesaid lines.
> Germany, Italy, and Japan affirm that the aforesaid terms do not in any way affect the political status which exists at the present as between each of the contracting parties and Soviet Russia.

From that agreement, it was plain that Japan intended soon to begin operations directed toward establishing the Greater East Asia Co-Prosperity Sphere, which would probably lead to war with all the great European powers except Germany and Italy. But which way would Japan strike first? The earliest indications were that they would attempt to carve out the empire that had narrowly eluded them during the intervention in Siberia between 1918 and 1922. Russian intelligence claimed to have obtained knowledge of a Japanese plan for war with Russia, codenamed Otsu, and as early as January 1937, the Red Army in Siberia was concerned about the strength of the Japanese Kwantung Army in Manchuria, estimating that the army had 250,000 men, 439 tanks, 500 aircraft, and 1,193 field guns.[7] The continuing presence of that army compelled the Russians to keep large forces in the east that were badly needed to meet the confused and turbulent conditions created by Hitler in the west and left them with little confidence that they could find the forces to defeat a synchronized attack from east and west.

To resolve what Moscow called "inconsistencies" in Russo-German relations, Molotov departed on his special train for Berlin in early November 1940. As he left, there were signs that Finland, Rumania, and Hungary might join the Tripartite Pact. There were also diplomatic reports that Germany was trying to persuade Greece and Yugoslavia to join, and Hitler himself had just completed a round of state visits: to General Franco in Spain, to Marshal Pétain in Vichy, France, and to Mussolini in Italy, who on the very day of Hitler's visit had suddenly invaded Greece. To a wary Molotov, all that activity was threatening. He went to Berlin determined to stand up to the Germans. In an opening discussion on November 12, 1940, von Ribbentrop found his guest stern and unbending. Seeking to placate him, he assured him "that England was beaten, and it was only a question of time when she would finally admit her defeat." Should continued bombing fail to bring the British to terms, Germany was prepared, "as soon as weather conditions permitted," to launch "a large-scale attack and thereby definitely crush England."[8] When that failed to thaw the frosty Molotov, von Ribbentrop took him to see Hitler, who reiterated von Ribbentrop's assurances about German determination, if the British refused to give in, to invade the British Isles.

Since Britain's fate was sealed, said Hitler, it was necessary "to clarify the political issues which would be of importance during and after this showdown." At that point, Hitler adopted his accustomed practice of haranguing his visitor. If Russia was concerned about the Tripartite Pact, which was nothing more than an alliance "to regulate conditions . . . as to the natural interests of the European countries," Russia should enter into the Tripartite Pact and also "designate her claims" in the Greater East Asia Co-Prosperity Sphere, as Japan was calling the New Order in Asia.[9]

When Hitler finally ceased, Molotov replied with such bluntness that Hitler's interpreter, Paul Schmidt, feared that the Führer might stalk from the room. There were certain points, said Molotov, that Stalin had specifically directed him to clarify. What about Finland? Russia wanted another stab at Finland; indeed, intended to occupy and annex the whole country. What about Hitler's guarantee of Rumania's frontiers and the presence of a German military mission in Bucharest? What about Russian interests in Bulgaria and Turkey? If Russia was to join the Tripartite Pact, he said, "the aim and object of the pact must be closely defined, and I must be more precisely informed about the boundaries of the Greater East Asia area." Disconcerted, Hitler suggested that they break off the discussion temporarily, "Otherwise we shall be caught by the air raid warning."[10]

The next day, Hitler reluctantly invited his guest to lunch—he disliked eating with foreigners—but the gesture did nothing to mellow Molotov. Why were there German troops in Finland? They were, said Hitler, only in transit to Northern Norway. When Molotov reminded Hitler that the Nazi-Soviet Nonaggression Pact accorded Finland to Russia's sphere of influence, Hitler agreed to send no more troops through the country, but he insisted that there could be no new war in Finland, for Germany required Finland's nickel and timber. As Hitler would reveal later, he was appalled at Molotov's arrogance: "He demanded that we give him military bases on Danish soil . . . He demanded Constantinople, Rumania, Bulgaria, and Finland—and *we* were supposed to be the victors!"[11] Again Hitler broke off the discussion on the pretext that there might be an air raid warning.

That night during a dinner in von Ribbentrop's honor at the Soviet Embassy, just as Molotov was proposing a toast, the air raid sirens sounded. At von Ribbentrop's invitation, Molotov went with his host to the foreign minister's own air raid shelter in the Wilhelmstrasse. There von Ribbentrop produced a draft of a four-power treaty between Germany, Italy, Japan, and Russia under which each of the powers would agree "to respect each other's natural spheres of influence. A secret protocol would partition the land grants: Germany would receive territory in central Africa, Italy in northern and northeastern Africa, Japan in Manchuria, and the Soviet Union in "the area of the Indian Ocean." [12]

Russia, said Molotov, was more interested in Europe and the Dardanelles than the Indian Ocean. There would have to be guarantees of Russian security and of other Russian interests, including Swedish neutrality and the fate of Rumania, Hungary, Bulgaria, Yugoslavia, Greece. Taken aback, von Ribbentrop insisted that the only point at issue was "whether the Soviet Union was prepared and in a position to cooperate with us in the liquidation of the British Empire." [13] As Stalin was to tell Churchill later in a period of improved relations between the two leaders, Molotov responded: "'What will England say?' 'England,' said Ribbentrop, 'is finished. She is no more use as a Power.' 'If that is so,' said Molotov, 'why are we in this shelter, and whose are these bombs which fall?'" [14]

Not quite a fortnight after the visit to Berlin, Molotov notified von Ribbentrop of the conditions under which Russia would enter the Tripartite Pact. The two principal points, that all German troops leave Finland and that Bulgaria conclude a pact granting Russia military bases within range of the Bosphorus, were hardly excessive, but they were still unacceptable to Hitler. Obviously having made up his mind to concede nothing to the Russians, he told von Ribbentrop to make no response.

At a conference in the Reichschancellery on December 5, 1940, at which the commander-in-chief of the Army, von Brauchitsch, and the chief of the German General Staff, General Halder, were present, Hitler declared that "Hegemony over Europe will be decided in battle against Russia." One need no longer consider an invasion of England, he said, except insofar as the invasion would serve to camouflage the operation against Russia. It was "more than doubtful," he said, "that the Red Army had digested the recent lessons presented to its military leadership," so that in the spring of 1941, Germany would have "an obvious and overwhelming superiority in leadership, matériel, and well-trained troops—the Russians an unmistakeable inferiority." As he would later tell General Jodl, Germany had to "settle all Continental problems in 1941 . . . since from 1942 on the United States would be in a position to intervene."

In the early morning of December 18, 1940, Hitler signed the order for the invasion of Russia, codenamed Operation Barbarossa (red beard), a name Hitler personally chose after Frederick I Barbarossa, who as emperor of the Holy Roman Empire had led the Third Crusade to liberate the Holy Land (and had died in the process). The final objective of the assault was "to establish a defense line against Asiatic Russia from a line running approximately from the Volga River to Archangel," and if required, "the last industrial area left to Russia in the Urals can be eliminated by the *Luftwaffe.*" Rumania and Finland were to be counted upon to protect the flanks of the operation from the start. Although the original order as drawn up by the Oberkommando der Wehrmacht specified that the first major objective was to capture Moscow, Hitler directed a change, specifying that a final drive on Moscow would be launched only after securing the Baltic States and Leningrad, thereby assuring a supply route by sea.[15]

The same day, von Ribbentrop talked with Japanese Ambassador Oshima. The time might come, von Ribbentrop told him, when Hitler would find it necessary to deal with Russia with other than diplomatic means, in which case Germany would be able to defeat the Red Army in eight weeks, so that there would be no need for Japanese help, nor should there be concern about Red Army action in Manchuria. What did concern Hitler was possible reaction by Britain and the United States. Japan could best serve the interests of the Tripartite Pact, said von Ribbentrop, by attacking Singapore and other European and American interests in the Pacific in order to divert American and British naval and military strength. Oshima replied that he would advise his government of the foreign minister's suggestion.

## Chapter Sixty-Eight

Adolf Hitler spent the Christmas season of 1940 on a tour of inspection of the Wehrmacht in France with the added objective of giving verisimilitude to the deception operations, Shark and Harpoon, that pointed to the invasion of Britain—not Russia—as Germany's next goal. Back at the Berghof by New Year's Eve, Hitler hosted a conference of his military chiefs and his foreign minister beginning on January 7, 1941, and ending on the ninth with a secret speech in which he reviewed the state of the war and the outlook for Operation Barbarossa.

There was no longer any question of invading Britain in 1941, Hitler said, unless the country should become so paralyzed that Germany could take over without a fight. Nor was there any point in maintaining the terror air raids, for they had shown little prospect of bringing the British to terms; they would be used only as part of the operations to conceal the buildup for Barbarossa. The Luftwaffe was to concentrate instead on reinforcing the submarine campaign against British shipping and on hitting bottlenecks in the British armaments industry. The Kriegsmarine was to intensity its naval warfare in the North Atlantic, to which end the thirty-eight submarines then in service were to be reinforced by about fifty others that were either in advanced stages of construction, were being refitted, or were being used for training. The U-boat campaign alone, he said, might eventually bring Britain's downfall.

In general, said Hitler, Germany's position was impregnable, for Germany could be defeated only on the Continent, and with the possible exception of Russia, there was no power left capable of doing that in the foreseeable future. Russia thus was the last hope for Britain, and he had come to the conclusion that the British would give in only when that last hope had been destroyed. If with Russia's defeat Britain still refused to come to terms, Germany would need to leave only a few divisions on occupation duty in Russia and still have sufficient strength to deal with Britain.

Russia, Hitler declared, had to be beaten while the Wehrmacht was at the height of its power and with a lightninglike campaign that would be over before the Russian winter set in. Although he was concerned about fighting a two-front war, he was convinced that the Wehrmacht could defeat the Red Army so swiftly that the war would be over before Britain could do anything in the west. At that point, Germany would be without challenge. "The vast spaces of Russia will yield hoards of incalculable wealth . . . Thus we will have all we need to be able to fight whole continents in the future, if need be; we will be invincible."[1]

To everybody but Hitler and his inner circle, the conundrum of the time was what Hitler intended to do next: did he really intend to invade Britain? or was he going to attack Soviet Russia?

The answers to those questions were obscured by Hitler's intense campaign of secrecy and deception, by the fact that Europe was in large measure cut off from communication with the rest of the world, and by the efficiency and omnipresence of the Gestapo, the Abwehr, and the Sicherheitsdienst. Yet there still existed some outlets for information, one of them supranational in its agents and its goals, a curious organization known at the Vatican as the Center of Information Pro Deo, a service that Hitler himself called "the black moles."

Pro Deo—For God—grew out of the establishment at a Catholic press exhibition in Cologne in 1926 of "an international center of information" designed to combat the "anti-God Communist International."[2] Six years later, it was expanded to struggle against "the Anti-Christ of Communism." By the time of Pope Pius XII, who in 1939 issued his first encyclical, *Summi pontificatus*, a general condemnation of all totalitarianism, Pro Deo claimed to have established bureaus in major cities throughout Europe and the Americas, and with war imminent, it abandoned its "former defensive attitude" to embrace an "offensive movement" of positive propaganda. From a main headquarters in Brussels run by a Jesuit priest, Pro Deo issued bulletins exposing both Fascist and Communist brutality.

As the German Army occupied Belgium, the Gestapo decimated Pro Deo's operatives, as it did those of all intelligence services; but the survivors fled to Lisbon, where with the help of the cardinal patriarch and Catholic Action leaders, a new headquarters staff was formed. With an overall objective "to re-establish God in public life," Pro Deo went into the business of military espionage, proving particularly effective in heavily Catholic areas of the Rhineland, Southern Germany, and Austria.

In the first weeks of 1941 Pro Deo established a Center of Information Pro Deo at 325 West 101st Street in New York, and a headquarters official, Charles Friediger, brought Pro Deo's files there from Lisbon "to insure their safety and to carry on the documentation and study services." Friediger informed representatives of the predecessor agency of the OSS, the Coordinator of Information, that he had the "sanction" of the Vatican "as well as the Cardinal of Portugal and the hierarchy in various Latin American countries." As reported to the head of the agency known as the Coordinator of Information, Colonel William J. Donovan, Friediger was "much more interested in political, military, and subversive information than he was, at the moment, in purely church affairs." Little time passed before Donovan's embryonic little secret intelligence service was passing along a small but regular stipend to the Center of Information Pro Deo in order to obtain, as the Elizabethan spymaster, Francis Walsingham, once put it, "all the secrets at all the girdles of all the princes of Europe."

The first prince of particular importance to Pro Deo had already arrived in the United States, ostensibly as a refugee from the war, and was residing at a Franciscan monastery at 1400 Quincy Street NE, in Washington. He was known as Father Odo, but before taking his vows as a Benedictine, he had been Charles, Duke of Württemberg, a son of King Charles of Württemberg, who had abdicated his throne during the general upheaval that beset European monarchies in the wake of the Bolshevik Revolution in Russia. He had arrived in Washington by way of Lisbon, where he had had contact with the British Secret Intelligence Service, which quickly determined that Father Odo had excellent contacts in his native Württemberg, including entrée to some of Württemberg's native sons who had entered the Germany Army, including the former head of Hitler's bodyguard, General Erwin Rommel. The British agents also determined that Father Odo had spent considerable time at the great Benedictine abbey of Beuron, which sometimes served as a retreat for Catholic officers of the German General Staff. Father Odo listed among his friends the chief of the German General Staff, General Franz Halder, and among the people whom British intelligence knew to be well disposed toward him were Pope Pius XII, the British queen mother, Queen Mary, and a confidential agent employed for many years by Sir Robert Vansittart, the permanent undersecretary at the Foreign Office.

The British Secret Intelligence Service nevertheless had reservations, for as the dossier on Odo noted, he was "characterized by a peculiar temperament. It is probable the disease of the thyroid from which he suffers contributes largely to this. He is difficult to get along with . . . especially as he is easily moved to anger." On the other hand, he had been wounded during the World War, which may have been the basis of his problem. At any rate, Father Odo also had occasional problems "on account of his morals."[3]

While at Beuron, Father Odo became involved in intrigues to dispossess Abbot Rafael Walser, whom some at the monastery saw as too friendly with Hitler's regime. When the *Gestapo* in 1934 murdered two of his friends on the General

Staff, Generals Kurt von Schleicher and Kurt von Bredow, Father Odo "found it convenient" to leave Beuron and work, at least briefly, for Admiral Wilhelm Canaris, the chief of the Abwehr, who was bitterly antinazi and antibolshevik and used the Pro Deo movement as a source of intelligence and recruits. Father Odo thus entered the ranks of the underground anti-Hitler organization within the General Staff that came to be called the Schwarze Kapelle (Black Orchestra), with which General Halder and several other senior officers were associated. Aside from attempting on three occasions to murder Hitler, the Schwarze Kapelle in later years sought through Vatican channels to inform western sources of Hitler's plans to take Austria, Czechoslovakia, and Poland and then to attack Western Europe.

By that time, Father Odo had left Germany, entering Switzerland, probably in the summer of 1937, and joined a monastery near Zurich. British intelligence determined that in April 1940, Odo was in contact with a known agent of the Abwehr, a lawyer, Hans Etscheit, who was involved in some manner with a peace feeler directed from Admiral Canaris to the British government. Etscheit, British intelligence noted, was "blackmailing him, not on account of his political activities, but because of certain moral delinquencies which had taken place before he left Germany," which "suggested the possibility that Father Odo was not in reality a political refugee from Germany but had fled the country for fear of exposure on other accounts." Threatened with deportation by the Swiss, he left voluntarily for Lisbon and thence in early October 1940 arrived in the United States.

In Washington, Father Odo called on several occasions at the British Embassy. There was talk on one occasion of some kind of "elaborate scheme to get in touch with German Generals in some obscure manner and secure their aid in overthrowing the Nazi regime," on another that Hitler was soon to march "to liberate Europe from the beast of Bolshevism and bring Stalin in chains to Berlin." Those with whom Odo talked generally discounted his information: he was vague, obscure, and possibly "a trifle mentally unbalanced."[4]

By the turn of the new year 1941, Father Odo had received more definite information:

The *Wehrmacht* was concentrating not in the area of the Channel and North Sea ports, which would be the case if an invasion of Britain was imminent, but in Eastern and Central Europe and in Norway and Finland, which indicated an attack on Russia. . . .

A conspiracy was developing within the German General Staff over Hitler's decision to attack Russia before defeating Britain, thereby creating a two-front war that unless the Red Army was quickly destroyed, which Odo's informants thought unlikely, would lead inevitably to a disaster for Germany of immeasurable proportions.

In providing that information to Father Odo, the Pro Deo center in Lisbon directed him to pass it to an associate of President Roosevelt, Myron Taylor, whom Odo had met during a conference on refugees at the Vatican in 1938; but when Odo contacted the State Department, he found that Taylor had become President Roosevelt's representative at the Holy See. Odo turned then to a friend, Paul Schwartz, who had a contact in U.S. Army military intelligence at Governors Island in New York. Since the military intelligence bureau thought— erroneously—that Schwartz was connected with a German Communist underground group in New York, Neue Beginnen, any information he passed along would be suspect at the start.

A quick check on Odo by military intelligence produced word that he was not a member of Pro Deo but instead a Nazi agent, which was probably an erroneous interpretation of Odo's former work for Admiral Canaris and the Abwehr. When military intelligence turned the matter over to the FBI, that agency's Special Defense Unit contacted British intelligence, which produced more accurate information on Odo; but the FBI's report summed up: "Father Odo's indiscretions have caused him some trouble and inconvenience. We believe that any information he gives should not be taken too seriously."[5]

Pro Deo's information, as passed through Father Odo, purporting to reveal a forthcoming attack on the Soviet Union and a serious rift within the German General Staff thereupon disappeared in the files. So did a second report that Odo obtained through Pro Deo: General Deutelmoser, head of the Wehrmacht's supply services in Finland, had sent word that Hitler intended to invade Russia on or about May 20, 1941—his original target date was in fact May 14, 1941—and that the Finnish Army would march with the Germans in Eastern Karelia to take Leningrad.

That dramatic intelligence would have had a happier reception had it reached the State Department, for three similar fragments of intelligence had begun to come in indicating that the apparently impending attack on Britain was but a feint for an assault on Russia. The fragments came from the Vatican, from London, from Vichy, and from Berlin, where America's diplomatic outpost was still open— specifically, from one Sam Edison Woods.

A native of Lubbock, Texas, Sam Edison Woods was in 1940 the commercial attaché at the American Embassy in Berlin. In the course of his governmental duties, he had established a friendship with a German diplomat, Hans Heinrich Herwarth von Bittenfeld, who in the mid and late 1930s had been secretary at the German Embassy in Moscow, where he had "cooperated very closely" with and provided "much valuable information" to the American Embassy. One-quarter Jewish, von Bittenfeld "never advanced in the Diplomatic Service after the Nazis took over Germany." When war seemed imminent in 1939, he resigned from the diplomatic service, and being part Jewish and thus having little choice of profession, he joined the German Army.[6]

After the war began, he began to pass along tidbits of military gossip to Sam Woods in Berlin, and in August 1940, the tidbits turned into meaty morsels. At

Hitler's order, von Bittenfeld told Woods, the German General Staff had begun to plan for war with Russia, and the preparations for an invasion of Britain were only a blind for the attack on Russia. In the early weeks of 1941, von Bittenfeld provided documentation: details of one of the directives for Operation Barbarossa. Assembling all the information von Bittenfeld had provided in "an impressive package of reports," the American Embassy sent them to Washington in the diplomatic pouch for the attention of Secretary of State Cordell Hull.[7]

The information presented a dilemma. Should the State Department, which was traditionally in the forefront of anti-Comintern and antibolshevik resistance in the United States, warn the Soviet Union? A warning might assure the survival of a detestable regime; on the other hand, if the United States failed to warn Stalin and Russia collapsed, Hitler would emerge as the master not only of Mackinder's heartland but of Eurasia, the chieftain of a bloc too vast and powerful for the United States or any coalition of surviving powers to defeat, in which case a direct attack on the United States would not be long in coming.

In the end, President Roosevelt made the decision on the basis of practicality. If the United States were to avoid the immense casualties that would be bound to ensue in a war with the Tripartite powers, it would plainly be to American advantage for the Russians to be in a position to put up at least enough of a fight to cut the forces of the Third Reich down to size.

On March 1, 1941, Hull instructed the American ambassador in Moscow, Laurence Steinhardt, to seek an interview with Foreign Commissar Molotov and pass on the information "orally and confidentially." Ambassador Steinhardt was still trying to arrange an interview with Molotov when in a meeting between Undersecretary of State Sumner Welles and the Soviet ambassador in Washington, Konstantin Oumansky, the conversation "took such a turn as to render it opportune for the under secretary to convey to the ambassador the information which the Department had suggested that you pass on to Molotov." When Oumansky read the reports, he "blanched"; he would send the information to Moscow at once.[8]

Hitler having offered Russia membership in the Tripartite Pact, the Japanese foreign minister, Yosuki Matsuoka, saw no reason for Japan not to negotiate its own treaty with the Soviet Union. In Moscow on April 13, 1941, he signed a pact which "guaranteed the preservation of peaceful and free relations with each other and promised not to violate each other's territory even though the other nation became involved in a war."[9] From the Russian viewpoint, the pact clearly reflected concern over a joint attack by Germany and Japan.

In Washington, news of the pact was received with dismay, for the implications were evident: the pact would "relieve Japan of considerable pressure from the north" and permit the Japanese "to concentrate on Pacific and southern problems." In London, it was viewed with even more alarm, for it appeared to be "an effort by the Russians to encourage the southward expansion of the Japanese" against British and other European colonies.[10]

Hardly had that intelligence ceased to reverberate when, three days later, Magic radio intercepts began to provide the Americans with confirmation of German plans against Russia. From Berlin, the Japanese ambassador, Baron Oshima, "humbly" reported that "perhaps Germany is planning first to defeat the Soviet, secure the rich stores of Russian war materials and thus having fortified herself, to attack England later."[11]

A few days later, Oshima's colleague in Vienna, Ambassador Yamaji, confirmed Oshima's speculation: "In preparation for a long drawn out war . . . Germany will take over the grain fields of Ukraine and Caucasus as soon as the harvest is ready. This means war with USSR about June."[12]

Magic was at that point silent on what the United States most wanted to know: what would the Japanese do? There was by that time no doubt of Japanese interest in a southward move, for Japanese diplomacy had already obtained some concessions from Thailand; the German-dominated Vichy government had granted the right of military occupation of Tonkin, the northernmost protectorate in Indochina, and the use of French airfields in Tonkin; and the Japanese were pressuring the Dutch for oil concessions in the Dutch East Indies. There was, too, a Magic report that the commander of the German Navy, Grand Admiral Erich Raeder, had "expressed his desire for a Japanese attack on Singapore,"[13] the British bastion at the tip of Malaya, and there was no indication in the Magic traffic that the Germans expected Japanese support in the attack on Russia. Yet once the German attack began, the Japanese might decide on their own to shift to a northern strategy, or they might do both, employing the Kwantung Army against Russia while sending air, naval, and amphibious forces against the European and American possessions.

The question at that point remained unanswered.

## Chapter Sixty-Nine

To the serried ranks of 250 senior officers of the Wehrmacht, assembled in the Reichschancellery on March 30, 1941, Adolf Hitler revealed something of his plans for empire. The first stage was completed, he said, with the occupation of Western Europe. The second stage—the drive for *Lebensraum*—was about to begin. It was to be "a struggle between two ideologies"; and Bolshevism, which was "equivalent to asocial criminality" and "a tremendous danger for the future," was to be destroyed.[1] Political authorities, commissars, and agents of the NKVD, said Hitler, were to be treated not as prisoners of war but as criminals. They were to be handed over to Special Action Groups to be formed by the security and intelligence service of the SS, the Sicherheitsdienst, and where possible, they were to be "shot on the spot." Commanders had to "overcome any scruples they might have," for "communism must be exterminated for all time."[2]

After the German defeat in the skies over England in late summer and early fall of 1940, Winston Churchill had no doubt that Russia, not Britain, was Hitler's next target, for Churchill had at his disposal a source of intelligence of remarkable authority. It was a product of the British code and cipher-breaking service and from the codename of that service, whose real title was the Government Code and Cypher School, was known as Ultra.

Situated in a Victorian mansion outside Bletchley, a grimy industrial town some forty miles north of London, the Government Code and Cypher School would come to represent what was until that time the zenith activity of wartime employment for intellectuals. In the entire war, no matter was more secret than Ultra, not even the development of the atomic bomb, for while Ultra could not win the war for Britain, its existence made it difficult for Britain—and later, the United States—to lose it.

Working through a combination of sheer intellectual and technological genius—the early computers owed their existence to the need for electromechanical machines to penetrate German codes and ciphers—the Ultra service by the time of the air war over Britain had developed the ability to read some of the German ciphers all of the time and all of them some of the time. That capability had, in general, enabled tacticians of Fighter Command to dispose their forces at the right places, the right altitudes, and the right times, and in the end the Luftwaffe had lost the Battle of Britain.

By December 1940, when Hitler issued the first Barbarossa directive, the Ultra cryptanalysts had provided the Royal Air Force an accurate and almost complete picture of the Luftwaffe's order of battle in Western Europe, where most Luftwaffe units were at the time still located. Although all elements of the Luftwaffe were of interest, the intelligence specialists paid particular attention to those forces that had spearheaded the air attacks against France and Britain, for those units were obviously the Luftwaffe's best and where they were would provide a clue to Hitler's intentions.

In late December 1940, Ultra revealed eastward movement of an airfield engineer construction unit. Some three weeks later, further intelligence revealed that the engineers had arrived in Rumania and were preparing facilities for 500 dive bombers, a number capable of providing tactical air support for between fifteen and twenty army divisions. If Hitler genuinely intended to invade Britain in the spring of 1941, why was he moving airfield construction units and tactical aircraft in the other direction? As time passed, evidence piled up indicating a general movement of Luftwaffe ground support aircraft to airfields in Rumania and Bulgaria. Since it was no mass movement, but unit by unit, that indicated secrecy.

The Ultra service also intercepted and unbuttoned a signal revealing that a senior Luftwaffe officer, a pioneer in the use of tactical aircraft and dive-bombing in support of blitzkrieg, General Wolfram Baron von Richthofen, was in Rumania.

Word had long had it that wherever Richthofen, there the main battle; his appearance in Rumania meant to air intelligence officers in London that whatever the German spring campaign, it was not to be against Britain.

Ultra picked up thousands of similar fragments of intelligence, all indicating that Hitler intended to attack somewhere in the southeast or east. Yet for all the flood of information showing a precise but secret movement of German power away from the Channel coast, there was little indication of exactly where the Germans intended to strike; but in the middle of February 1941, technology available for the attack on German ciphers suddenly and dramatically improved.

The man responsible was a young mathematical logician, Alan Mathison Turing, a product of King's College, Cambridge, and of the mathematics department of the Institute for Advanced Studies at Princeton University, who had revealed a unique genius with a paper entitled, "On Computable Numbers with an Application to the *Entscheidungsproblem.*" In the simplest terms, Turing maintained that a riddle created by one machine can best be solved by another machine that has been primed with proper information. In the Munich summer of 1938, the Government Code and Cypher School had engaged Turing to work at Bletchley on the mathematical theories involved in a special electromechanical machine which the British government hoped would provide the keys to ciphers used by Germany. The machine that Turing was to attack was the Enigma, a German enciphering machine named after Sir Edward Elgar's *Enigma Variations,* music in which descriptions of some of Elgar's friends—some of them none too favorable—were encoded. The Enigma was capable of producing an almost infinite number of ciphers, a factor that made the Germans so confident of its security that they introduced the machine into general service throughout their armed forces and even sold versions of it to their allies: Japan, Finland, and Rumania. They were to pay dearly for ignoring the fundamental law of cryptanalysis: a cipher made by a man can, given time, be undone by a man, especially if he has the assistance of a machine.

At the root of the problem of breaking the Enigma codes was the need to establish the keys being used, an almost impossible task in view of daily and sometimes thrice-daily changes in keys. Yet the British achieved at least a start on the problem when along with the French and Polish intelligence services, they had obtained several of the Enigma machines just before and just after the outbreak of war. That would enable them at least to determine how the machine worked; but at first it took months of the most intense application for teams of the best mathematical brains to determine the key that was used. It was not until January 17, 1940, for example, that a Polish team established the keys used by the Enigma almost three months earlier. Yet that changed shortly before the opening of the Battle of Britain when Alan Turing produced the first of what was destined to be a series of "engines."

Called the Mark I Heath Robinson, after a British cartoonist of the time who was known for drawings of weird, fanciful machines intended for all manner of extraordinary tasks, the engine greatly expanded the capacity of the teams at Bletchley to penetrate the Luftwaffe's ciphers. Once the enemy signals were intercepted and copied exactly on tape, the tape was fed into the Heath Robinson, or the *bombe*, as it was sometimes called. Working at a speed far beyond that of human thought, the Turing engine electromagnetically scrutinized the tape to establish which of 1,060,560 keys had been used to encipher the message. Although it took time—the different German services used different keys each day, and even within a particular service, different units might use different keys— the Turing engine usually came up with the proper key, at which time it was relatively simple to convert the cipher into its original German and then translate the German into English.

The military and political value of the Turing engine was obviously so vast as to be incalculable. It enabled Churchill, who regarded warfare as being mainly a catalogue of blunders, to steer clear of the reefs of blunders on which Britain might have foundered in 1940 and 1941.

As Ultra early in 1941 began to reveal German preparations for Barbarossa, Churchill promptly decided that he had to warn the Soviet Union, for if Russia fell, Britain's turn obviously would be next. Yet how to make clear to a distrustful Stalin that the intelligence was solid, incontrovertible? Churchill would quite obviously be unable to reveal his source, for that was the Ultra imperative. If the Germans even vaguely suspected that the British were reading their most secret signals, the source would dry up. How to tell and convince Stalin without Stalin's telling Hitler?

All war, wrote the German military theorist, Karl von Clausewitz, is deception. A particular power of Ultra was that it permitted the British to winnow deceptive intelligence deliberately sown by the enemy from the truth of his movements and designs. In the last weeks before Barbarossa, as Hitler's intelligence and security services spread a final miasma of deception to beguile Churchill and Stalin about the reality of German plans, never was that capability of more importance.

When Hitler on December 18, 1940, issued his first directive on Barbarossa, there were thirty-four German divisions in the east. For what he planned as a three-tined campaign against Leningrad, Moscow, and Kiev, it was necessary to increase that force more than threefold. It was also necessary to position troops and aerial and naval squadrons in Finland, Rumania, and Bulgaria. Yet all obviously had to be done without revealing to Stalin what Hitler had in mind, for without surprise, the Germans plainly would be unable to conclude the campaign before winter set in. The German solution was to represent all movements in terms of Britain. As German diplomatic and intelligence agents throughout the world were instructed, with orders to pass the word, the German movements were part of "the greatest decoy operation in the history of war for the purpose of diverting attention from the final preparations for the invasion of England."[3]

It was in countering that kind of false screen that Magic and Ultra complemented each other. Ultra revealed tactics: the movement of a headquarters, a general, the nature of construction work, or the rise or fall in the volume of railroad traffic. Magic exposed policy and strategy and thus provided material to show that information to indicate the reverse of that afforded by Ultra was nothing but "blossoming" and thus was to be ignored. As revealed by Ultra, the velocity of the movement of major German units away from France, the Low Countries, Norway, the interior of Germany, gave some indication of the timing of the new strategy, which also might be confirmed by Magic.

Overawed by Hitler's immense military, political, and diplomatic successes, the regent of Yugoslavia, Prince Paul, committed his country in March 1941 to membership in the Tripartite Pact. Hardly had the signing been publicly announced when a revolution erupted in Belgrade: the Yugoslav military forces overthrew Paul and replaced him with the youthful king, Peter II. Hitler's reaction was violent: he ordered an aerial bombardment of the capital, in which 17,000 people were killed, and invasion.

For some time the Ultra analysts had been watching the movement of five German panzer divisions from France proceeding toward Yugoslavia in order to influence Paul to join the Tripartite Pact; that accomplished, three of the divisions turned northward toward Crakow in Poland, while the other two headed for Greece, where Hitler felt compelled at last to salvage the bumbled invasion staged by his Italian ally, Mussolini.

Following the coup d'état in Belgrade, the German panzer divisions that had turned toward Poland headed back toward Yugoslavia, but that first shift had been enough for Churchill. The panzer divisions intended to concentrate in Southern Poland for an attack on Russia; why else would they have headed in that direction? Apart from that information, Ultra told Churchill that German troops equipped for winter warfare were landing in Finland, that the Germans were financing separatist movements in the Ukraine and the Caucasus, and that the Luftwaffe was strengthening the runways of its airfields in Poland and extending the length of them to accommodate heavy bombers. "It occurred to me," remarked the chairman of the British Joint Intelligence Committee, Victor Cavendish-Bentinck, "that this was not being done for the benefit of *Lufthansa* [the German commercial airline]!"[4]

Like officials in Washington, Churchill faced the dilemma of whether to warn Stalin, but for him the decision was far less complex than it was for President Roosevelt. Britain needed allies, any allies, even Communist allies, so that as Churchill himself would put it, he "cast about for some means of warning Stalin, and, by arousing him to his danger, establishing contacts with him like those I had made with President Roosevelt."[5]

Unaware at the time that Stalin despised British Socialists as much as he despised any other British politician, Churchill first tried through his Socialist ambassador in Moscow, Sir Stafford Cripps. He directed Cripps to inform Stalin personally about the move of the three panzer divisions toward Southern Poland, but Stalin failed even to acknowledge receipt of the message. Since Churchill had to assume that Stalin treated it with suspicion—another British attempt to involve the Soviet Union in a war with Germany?—the chief of the British Secret Intelligence Service, Colonel Stewart G. Menzies, who was also chief of the Ultra service, began to devise a stratagem designed to make Stalin accept the British warning.

Through Menzies' chief representative in Switzerland, Count Van den Heuvel, Menzies had taken an interest in and had established a relationship with a private intelligence agency, Bureau Ha, which operated from a villa in Teufen, near St. Gallen and Lake Constance. It was run by Colonel Roger Gallen and Major Hans Hausmann, who had affiliations with but were not employed by the Swiss intelligence service, the Nachrichtendienst, headed by General Henri Guisan, and even though Bureau Ha was "an unofficial center," it was "funded actually or nominally" by Guisan and "certain friends."[6] Among those friends, it would emerge, was Van den Heuvel.

Although Bureau Ha was credited in intelligence circles with having almost miraculous intelligence sources inside Germany, that was actually a fiction created by General Guisan to conceal the fact that Bureau Ha's basic source was two Berlin-Rome telecommunications trunk cables passing through Switzerland, the primary communications link between Germany and Italy, which also carried the "A-net," the separate communications system of the German intelligence service, the Abwehr. Although the Germans recognized that tapping was possible and would later build a second channel by way of Munich and Bolzano, they were so confident of the impenetrability of the Enigma machine and its multiple cipher converter keys that they believed that even if tapped, the traffic could not be read.[7]

In the summer of 1939, Bureau Ha employed a new agent who was destined to establish one of the most fabulous reputations in the history of espionage, a monkish man named Rudolf Roessler, alias Lucy, who was born in Kaufbeuren, the great Catholic center of learning in South Germany. For reasons that would remain obscure, Roessler constantly threw up a miasma of confusing stories about himself; he spread the word, for example, that he was a Czech, and in the years just after the war, had worked for the Czech intelligence service. In reality, he was editing a small newspaper in Augsburg. Then, around 1928, he went to Berlin to become general secretary of the Bühnenvolksbund, the Alliance of Stage People. Fleeing Germany as a political refugee in 1933, he settled in Lucerne, where he soon founded a publishing company, Vita Nova Verlag. It was widely assumed that Roessler was a vague Communist and that his house published Communist literature, but it was really "Christian anti-Fascist."

In the summer of 1939, a friend in Lucerne, Xavier Franz Josef Schneiper, suggested that Roessler work for Swiss intelligence. Roessler liked the idea, but his friend arranged a contact not with the official Swiss intelligence service but with the unofficial agency, Bureau Ha. Meeting with one of the bureau chiefs, Hans Hausmann, at Bureau Ha's headquarters, Roessler accepted an assignment as the contact for a British intelligence agent in Switzerland, named either Charles Simon or Simpson.

From that small beginning, Roessler was soon in the pay not only of Bureau Ha but also of the Swiss intelligence service and of the Soviet intelligence service and possibly of the British intelligence service as well. He did his work not for lofty political ideals but for money.

When recruited to work for the Rote Drei, the branch of the Foreign Excellent Raincoat Company in Switzerland, Roessler's contact was a British Comintern agent, Allan Alexander Foote. To Foote, who was widely believed both inside and outside the Comintern to have been a British penetration agent, Roessler began passing material for transmission to Moscow under the alias of Lucy.

The volume, nature, and immediacy of the material that Lucy passed along would raise his reputation as a master spy. He was reputed to have four excellent sources known as Werther, Teddy, Anna, and Olga, who were never positively identified. Yet no matter who they were, it would have been impossible for them to furnish the volume of material that Lucy passed to Foote for transmission or to have sent it to Lucy within the short period of time that it often took Lucy to come up with information. As Foote would later note, "One would normally think that a source producing information of this quality would take time to obtain it. No such delay occurred in the receipt of *Lucy*'s information. On most occasions it was received within twenty-four hours of its being known at the appropriate headquarters in Berlin." So voluminous and current was the material that Foote would later claim that the Red Army "very largely fought the war on *Lucy*'s messages."[8]

The volume and the currency of Lucy's intelligence plainly pointed to technical rather than human sources. As the CIA would note later: ". . . the widely accepted story that *Lucy* was a master spy is nothing but a myth."[9] And as one of the chiefs of radio intelligence in General Eisenhower's Supreme Allied Headquarters, Brigadier Walter Scott, would state: "*Lucy* and his sources were valuable for one thing only—cover for *Ultra.*"[10] *Lucy* was getting his rich material not from Werther, Teddy, Anna, and Olga but from the British agent for whom he was the contact for Bureau Ha, Charles Simon or Simpson. Winston Churchill had found his way of getting information to Stalin by a means that Stalin, he hoped, would trust.

On June 11, 1941, Lucy passed to Alexander Foote a critical message for transmission to Moscow: "A general assault on the territory occupied by Russia will start on Sunday, 22 June, at 3:15 A.M."[11]

A week later, on June 18, 1941, Japanese Ambassador Oshima, in Berlin, sent a long message to Foreign Minister Matsuoka in Tokyo, noting that "we may see the outbreak of war at any moment." The chief of the German General Staff, General Halder, he reported, considered that "war with Russia amounts to nothing more than a police action and that the whole thing should be over within four weeks."

At the same time, he said, the Germans appeared to be increasing their preparations for an invasion of Britain, so that "it may well be that the Reich will make a decisive attack upon the British Isles while in the midst of the Russian fray." Within the next several months, predicted Oshima, "the European situation will take a sudden turn, and the war . . . will end summarily." That being the case, "it is urgent that we adopt and adamantly stick to a policy assuring the establishment and maintenance of our area and rights of co-prosperity in Greater East Asia."[12] Intercepted and decrypted in Washington on the same day sent, the message was translated on the next, and there were indications that at least a summation of its contents was relayed that same night to the Soviet ambassador, Konstantin Oumansky.

Stalin had no lack of intelligence which, if properly evaluated and respected, would have provided ample warning that the Germans were going to attack the Soviet Union. Even when the first German divisions had begun to shift to the east, Soviet intelligence had picked up the movement, but Stalin placidly accepted Hitler's explanation that the shifts represented nothing more than a readjustment of forces following the victory in France, a relocation to better training grounds and a strengthening of the occupation forces in Poland. There was the warning in early March 1941 by Sumner Welles in Washington to Ambassador Oumansky, at least partly based on what Sam Woods had picked up in Berlin from his friend von Bittenfeld; there was Churchill's warning based on the peregrinations of German panzer divisions between Yugoslavia and Southern Poland; there was information provided by Leopold Trepper in Brussels that the German 4th Army under General Hans Günther von Kluge, which, as Moscow was aware, played prominent roles in the invasions of Poland and France, had left France for the vicinity of Brest Litovsk in Poland; and there was a warning on March 5, 1941, from a Russian spy in the German Embassy in Tokyo, Richard Sorge, who sent Moscow a microfilm of messages from Berlin indicating that the Germans would attack in mid-June 1941.

Yet Stalin appeared to take no heed of those warnings. After Sorge on April 10, 1941, reported from Tokyo that the German attack might begin at any time after the Japanese foreign minister, Matsuoka, returned from signing the neutrality pact in Moscow, Stalin at last authorized a state of "preliminary alertness" for military districts along the western frontier, but the alert carried no real urgency and was soon relaxed. Yet so thick were the rumors in the Russian capital of impending war that the German naval attaché in Moscow on April 25, 1941, warned Berlin to tighten security: "British Ambassador gives 22nd June as date of beginning the war."[13] When on May 22, 1941, an assistant military attaché in Berlin signaled that the Germans were to attack on June 15, Stalin authorized the Red Army General Staff to move two army headquarters, a mechanized corps, and a number of divisions from the interior toward the frontier, but all movement was to be secret; he was determined to afford Hitler "no pretext for the initiation of military action against us."[14]

Nor would Stalin accept the information that Lucy began to provide. The very precision and detail of it made the national intelligence headquarters, the Center, and Stalin himself suspect a British plot to destroy Stalin's reliance on the Nazi-Soviet Nonaggression Pact. Until events would prove otherwise, Stalin stamped the information provided by Lucy: "English provocation."[15]

It was the same when, at the end of May, Richard Sorge again reported, providing details of the German order of battle and the exact date of the attack. As with the information from Lucy, it was so precise that it was considered an Abwehr plant. That attitude persisted when the Center received information only sixteen days before the German target date that some 4 million German and Rumanian troops were concentrated near the Soviet frontier. It persisted when twelve days before the target date, the permanent undersecretary of the Foreign Office, Sir Alexander Cadogan, presented Ambassador Maisky in London with specific, detailed information: "On such-and-such a date two German motorized divisions passed through such-and-such a point in the direction of your frontier . . . During the whole of May there passed through such-and-such a point in the direction of your frontier twenty-five to thirty military trains a day."[16] Although Cadogan would not say so, that information was plainly based on Ultra.

The attitude still persisted when eleven days before the attack date, Lucy passed his specific warning that the attack would begin at 3:15 A.M. on Sunday, the 22d, and Stalin learned that the German ambassador in Moscow had been ordered to begin burning documents. It persisted when ten days before the attack date, the British foreign secretary, Anthony Eden, personally warned Ambassador Maisky of impending German attack. It still persisted when as the attack date drew even closer, Russian units picked up deserters from German ranks who identified their units and the specific date and time they were to attack.

Stalin's performance and that of his intelligence agencies was one of the strangest in history; it was hardly to be explained except through the paranoia of dictatorship. Stalin distrusted everybody: Churchill wanted to provoke him to action against Germany in order to destroy the Nazi-Soviet Nonaggression Pact and save Britain's hide; Hitler wanted to provoke him to action in order to have an excuse to destroy him. For Stalin, the Nonaggression Pact represented his only hope of survival: if through the pact and his appeasement policy he could forestall German attack at least until 1942, the Red Army would have improved to the point where there would be at least a hope of turning the Germans back.

Yet at that point there was no forestalling a reckoning; on the night of June 20, 1941, the Japanese ambassador in Berlin sent his counterpart in Moscow a telegram containing two words: "Very near."

## Chapter Seventy

During the evening of June 21, 1941, the commander of the German 4th Army, General Hans Günther von Kluge, was at his headquarters across the Bug River from Brest Litovsk. After dining with his chief of staff, von Kluge went for a walk in the starlit, purple-velvet night of the Polish prairie. All was quiet, Russian outposts across the Bug apparently unaware that a mighty force was about to descend upon them. As artillerymen of the assault divisions laid their guns on their targets, a brightly lit Berlin-Moscow express train passed incongruously but without incident through Brest Litovsk.

A man in the mold of Marshal Michel Ney, "the bravest of the brave," who had led one of Napoleon's armies in the march on Moscow in 1812, General von Kluge, like Ney in relation to Napoleon, had no love for Adolf Hitler. Neither was he blinded by the *Fahneneid,* the ancient oath with which Hitler had bound his commanders to his person as had the kaisers before him. The son of a *Junker,* the backbone of the German General Staff, von Kluge had been raised according to the ethic of the Prussian soldier. "Gentlemen," his tutor had told him and his classmates at the Red Den, the war college at Potsdam, "you have the highest aim in view. We teach you how to fulfill this aim. You are here to learn what gives your life its real meaning. You are here to learn how to die!"[1]

It was that precept that guided von Kluge, not the philosophy of the swastika. He was a soldier whose duty was to obey orders, and for doing that, Hitler would in time make him a marshal of Germany and give him a purse with which to purchase a baronial estate in Pomerania. In 1939 he had marched into Czechoslovakia and had also helped capture Warsaw; in 1940 his army had helped drive King Léopold of Belgium to surrender, pin the British against the sea at Dunkirk, break a last French line at Rouen, capture the Cotentin and Breton peninsulas, and drive down the Atlantic coast toward the Spanish frontier. In 1941 Günther von Kluge was to take Moscow.

Returning from his walk, von Kluge read for a while from the memoirs of Armand Augustin Louis, Marquis of Caulincourt, Duke of Vicenza, who had been Napoleon's aide-de-camp during the emperor's Russian campaign. Von Kluge in those days always had the memoirs close at hand, for they dealt at great length with Russian weather, Russian terrain, and the Russian character.

At three o'clock in the morning of June 22, 1941, a chauffeur drove him to the headquarters of the 31st Infantry Division, northwest of Brest Litovsk. On the way he stopped briefly at a forward airfield to watch squadrons of dive bombers taking off. As he reached the headquarters, the zero hour of 3:30 A.M. was approaching. "The sky began to lighten, turning to a curious yellow color. All still was quiet."[2]

Precisely at 3:30 A.M. that Sunday morning, June 22, 1941, 7,184 German artillery pieces opened fire to signal the start of the greatest land campaign in history; along a front of more than 2,000 miles extending from the Baltic in the north to the Black Sea in the south, 3,400 tanks and the men of 149 divisions, a total force of 3,050,000 men, leaped upon Red Army outposts. In addition, in the far north, the German Army of Norway with 67,000 men in four divisions crossed the Russian frontier in the direction of Murmansk and Archangel, while the vanguard of a Finnish Army of 500,000 men in fourteen divisions and three brigades struck in the Karelian Isthmus toward Leningrad, and a Rumanian Army of 150,000 men joined the fight in the south. In a special operation called Nightingale, squads of infiltrators behind Russian lines cut telephone wires, demolished bridges, and tried to assassinate Russian commanders. In swift, deadly blows against sixty-six Russian airfields previously photographed from high-altitude reconnaissance planes, 2,770 German aircraft delivered a paralyzing blow to the Red Air Force.

On the principal front between the Baltic and Black seas, the force consisted of three army groups: Army Group North under Field Marshal Wilhelm Ritter von Leeb, attacking out of East Prussia through the Baltic States toward Leningrad; Army Group Center under Field Marshal Fedor von Bock, thrusting across the Russo-Polish frontier through Minsk and Smolensk toward Moscow; and Army Group South under Field Marshal Gerd von Rundstedt, marching toward Kiev, capital of the Ukraine, and southeastward toward the great oil fields of the Caucasus.

Surprise—both strategic and tactical—was total. The day before, in London, Sir Stafford Cripps, at home for consultations, had told Ambassador Maisky that the Germans would attack the next day, and in response to Maisky's urgent coded message, Stalin had at last ordered the Red Army to the alert; but the order had reached most units too late to be of any help, and Stalin's own actions revealed that he still doubted that the Germans would attack: he was spending the weekend in his dacha outside Moscow. "We are being fired on," reported field commanders, wary of taking the wrong step for fear of the dreaded NKVD. "What shall we do?"[3]

In Moscow, Ambassador von der Schulenburg, unaware that a German attack was coming, had responded on the evening of the 21st to a summons from Molotov to explain reported German troop movements near the frontier. Returning to the German Embassy, Schulenburg found awaiting him instructions from von Ribbentrop to pass to Molotov a formal note that amounted to a declaration of war. He reached Molotov's office again at 5:30 Sunday morning, the 22nd, and as his instructions from Berlin directed, handed Molotov the note without comment.

After reading it, Molotov looked up sternly. "This is war," he said. "Do you believe that we deserved that?"[4] Summoning all the icy formality he could muster, he directed an assistant to show the ambassador out by a back door. Proceeding to the Kremlin, Molotov informed Stalin, who had returned from his dacha upon first news that there was trouble. Stalin sank into a chair and appeared to be lost in deep thought.

Through most of that morning, Moscow Radio broadcast its normal Sunday morning fare: a physical fitness program, items for children, reports concerning agriculture and industry. All the while rumors about what was happening were sweeping the country, but the only official voice the Russian people heard at first came over banned radios capable of picking up foreign broadcasts: Hitler's propaganda minister, Joseph Goebbels, speaking of a preventive war to smash "a conspiracy between the Jewish-Anglo-Saxon warmongers and the equally Jewish rulers of the Moscow center for bolshevism," a crusade for "the protection and salvation of Europe" from the menaces of the Communist International.[5]

Goebbels had set the official German line: the necessity to stamp out the activities of the Comintern. It was plainly an effort to cast Germany in the heroic role of saving Europe from Communism, to sound a clarion for all those nations of the world who since 1919 had been subjected to the Comintern's propaganda and subversion.

The first official Russian announcement of the German attack finally came shortly before noon when Molotov spoke over Moscow Radio. In a faltering voice and anxious tones, Molotov denounced this "unparalleled act of perfidy," this "act of robbery," this "faith-breaking deed." He employed phrases dropped from official pronouncements since the signing of the Nonaggression Pact: "Nazi assasins," "Fascist brigands covered with blood." Yet "Russia will win as it did against Napoleon in 1813." He called on the people "to rally even more closely around the glorious Bolshevik Party, around the Soviet Government and our great leader, Comrade Stalin." "Our cause is good," he declared. "The enemy will be smashed. Victory will be ours."[6]

Yet the people noted that "our great leader, Comrade Stalin," had not himself come to the microphones, "the great and brilliant Stalin," as the official press had been extolling him since the signing of the Nonaggression Pact, to whom all thanks were due that "our country has not known the horrors of war." At that point, it was clear that Stalin had not absolved the country of the horrors of war. The public's reaction "was one of stupefaction, almost disbelief."[7]

In official circles, there was also stupefaction, almost disbelief, for it was clear that the German legions were lancing and amputating the Red Army with surgical precision. It was also clear that there could be no reinforcement from the armies in the east, for what were Japan's intentions? Would Japan honor its treaty with Russia or attack in conjunction with its partner in the Tripartite Pact? There was also the dire question of whether the Russian soldiers and the people would put up a real fight for a Bolshevik Russia. There were already reports of entire villages greeting the German troops with the traditional gifts of welcome—bread and salt—and of Red soldiers throwing away their weapons and rushing to surrender.

On the evening of the German attack, as Stalin appeared in the operations room of the Commissariat of Defense, he seemed "clearly unhinged."[8] Why were the Russian troops retreating? So insistent was he on attacking to destroy the invaders and to retaliate by driving deeply into Poland that Marshal Timoshenko ordered the armored reserve, which constituted the second line of defense, to go over to the attack. German forces two nights later were a hundred miles or more inside Russia and the armored reserve was annihilated.

Stalin, meanwhile, had retreated again to his dacha outside the village of Kuntsevo, overlooking the Moscow River, and "for the next several days suffered from nervous prostration, which completely disabled him." It was a time when his marshals, generals, and commissars might have unseated him, for the nation had no guiding hand; but the dreadful purges had served their purpose well. The very magnitude of the disaster indicated that to remove the iron hand of the dictator would be to precipitate "an uncontrollable and irremediable panic,"[9] and the nation was still under the complete control of the NKVD. The very extent of Stalin's tyranny made him for the moment irreplaceable.

As Winston Churchill on Friday evening, June 20, 1941, set out from London to pass the weekend at Chequers, his official country residence in Buckinghamshire, his military and political fortunes appeared again to be at a near nadir. The Royal Navy had just lost its proudest battlecruiser, *Hood;* the Luftwaffe had swarmed to the offensive with the start of the spring campaigning season; the German intelligence services had established a beachhead for the Wehrmacht in Syria; and in Iraq, the grand mufti of Jerusalem had launched a jihad against British control of that oil-rich country. In North Africa, a panzer-heavy force under Rommel was preparing to march on Cairo and the great bastion of Alexandria; in the month of May 1941, another 500,000 tons of shipping had been sunk; and worst of all, the British Expeditionary Force in Greece had gone down to defeat. On the mainland, Britain had lost nearly 12,000 men, and when Hitler followed with an airborne assault on the island of Crete, another 18,000; along with the defeats on land had gone the loss of four cruisers and six destroyers, plus severe damage to a carrier and three battleships. And in Parliament, Churchill had barely survived a severe test.

There was nevertheless encouraging news in that President Roosevelt had declared an unlimited national emergency, which appeared to indicate that Britain would not much longer have to fight alone. Even more encouraging, his military advisers had told him that it was more certain than ever that Hitler was about to attack Russia. So sure was Churchill that the attack was coming that before leaving London he sent Roosevelt a signal advising him that "The German onslaught upon Russia was a matter of days or it might be hours."[10]

Soon after Churchill awoke on Sunday morning, Field Marshal Sir Alan Brooke, having hastened down from London, brought the news of the German attack. Brooke saw little chance for the Russians; they would be "rounded up in hordes," he said, and within six weeks, the Red Army would probably collapse.

Churchill spent most of the day composing a statement to be broadcast at nine o'clock that evening, but while he took a break and a stroll on the lawn, his private secretary, J. R. Colville, asked whether in supporting Russia, he, "the arch anti-Communist," was not "bowing down in the House of Rimmon." To which Churchill replied: "Not at all. I have only one purpose, the destruction of Hitler, and my life is much simplified thereby. If Hitler invaded Hell, I would make at least a favourable reference to the Devil in the House of Commons."[11] There would be many who would maintain that his real policy was to encourage Germany and Russia to destroy each other, but so long as Hitler lived, Churchill never deviated—publicly, at least—from his position of support for Russia.

As Churchill went before the microphones of the BBC that night, he submerged the bitterness and enmities of the past to the enormity of the challenge of the present. The past, the prime minister told his people and the world, "fades away before the spectacle which is now unfolding. The past, with its crimes, its follies, and its tragedies, flashes away." In a speech noteworthy for the fact that he mentioned Communism only once and never used the term "Soviet Union," always referring instead to Russia, Churchill declared: "No man has been a more consistent opponent of communism than I have been in the last twenty-five years. I will unsay no word that I have spoken about it." [12]

Yet at that point he saw "the Russian soldiers standing on the threshold of their native land, guarding the fields which their fathers have tilled from time immemorial." He saw them "guarding their homes where mothers and wives pray—ah, yes, for there are times when all pray—for the safety of their loved ones, the return of the bread-winner, of their champion, of their protector." Yet he also saw "advancing on all this in hideous onslaught the Nazi war machine, with its clanking, heel-clicking, dandified Prussian officers, its crafty expert agents fresh from the cowing and tying down of a dozen countries." He saw "the German bombers and fighters in the sky, still smarting from many a British whipping, delighted to find what they believe is an easier and safer prey."

Should Hitler succeed in his design to destroy Russia, said Churchill, he would "bring back the main strength of his Army and Air Force from the East and hurl it upon this island." British policy, he said, had "but one aim and one single, irrevocable purpose . . . to destroy Hitler and every vestige of the Nazi regime." Thus, "Any man or state who fights on against Nazidom will have our aid," and Britain would "give whatever help we can to Russia and the Russian people" and would "appeal to all our friends and allies . . . to take the same course and pursue it, as we shall, faithfully and steadfastly to the end."

Although Churchill's speech was one of the most important and most grandiloquent of his career, its effect was at first uncertain. It clearly failed to sweep away "the past, with its crimes, its follies, and its tragedies," and those troubles would continue to plague the new alliance long after it was formed. On both sides: for as Churchill could never forget the ills and near disaster that Russian participation in the Nonaggression Pact had helped visit on Western Europe and Britain and the subversions of the Comintern through the years, neither could Stalin forget Churchill's effort to strangle the Bolshevik state in its infancy and his persisting antagonisms. The first reaction in London to Churchill's call for a brotherhood with the Bolshevik state was decidedly cool: what effect would it have, for example, on American assistance to Britain? Yet that attitude failed to last long, for Hitler's attack on the Soviet Union was clearly a reprieve for Britain. Newspapers on both sides of the political spectrum were soon demanding a cleanout of anti-Soviets in high positions and an immediate invasion of Northern France to draw off a part of the Wehrmacht in an effort to assure the Red Army's survival.

In that change of attitude, the hand of the Comintern was readily apparent.

Yesterday's "Second Imperialist War" became overnight the "Great Patriotic War." No longer did the Comintern demand strikes and interference with the shipment of war materials; at that point, everybody was to dedicate himself to creating "a Second Front to destroy the Hitlerite-fascist hordes." [13]

Yet there were many, particularly among the bourgeoisie, who wondered why Britain did not stand aside and let the Nazis and Communists bleed themselves to death on the Russian steppe. A quip went the rounds in which one asked, What happened to the two wolves who had a fight? And the answer was, All they found of either was their tails. The minister of aircraft production, J. T. C. Moore-Brabazon, expressed at a private dinner a view widely held by the Conservatives; he hoped, he said, that "the German and Russian armies would destroy one another while the British Commonwealth in the meantime built up its forces to assure a dominating position in Europe." [14] Such indignation did the remark occasion when revealed at a meeting of the Trades Union Congress, that Churchill was compelled to state in Parliament that Moore-Brabazon's words had been misinterpreted and that he did, in fact, agree with the government's policy toward Russia.

That failed to convince many people in official Washington, in official Moscow, and among Churchill's own people. A belief would long persist—indeed, would never be completely hushed—that Churchill's policy was just that: to let the two wolves eat each other down to their tails. Even when Churchill made good on his pledge to help by sending war materials to Russia, there would be those who would maintain that he was doing it only to keep Russia in the fight long enough to assure a proper bloodletting. Churchill plainly had no great relish for supporting Russia: "We endured the unpleasant process of exposing our own vital security and projects to failure," he was later to write, "for the sake of our new ally—surly, snarling, grasping, and so lately indifferent to our survival." [15]

The doubts as to Churchill's ultimate goal were attributable in large measure to his policy toward an invasion of Western Europe, to establish what the Comintern early called for, a "second front." He believed that even a combination of American and British arms would be incapable of invading Western Europe while the German armed forces were still strong. From his earliest conversations with Roosevelt, he advocated a strategy of aerial bombardment, naval warfare, blockade, economic and political warfare, aid to underground resistance groups in occupied countries, and deception, and only after Germany was sufficiently weakened by those operations and by the land war with Russia would Anglo-American armies deliver the coup de grâce of invasion. As time passed, he would alter the strategy to include land operations on the periphery of Europe—North Africa, Norway, Sicily, Italy, the Balkans—but for long months extending into years he would consistently resist coming to grips directly with the German Army in France, an army which in the wake of the attack on Russia in 1941 was no more than a rear guard.

For Churchill, the first objective of the war was to defend the British Isles and the empire; the second was to develop ties with the United States to the point where, at least for military and military-industrial purposes, the two powers became a single nation; and the third was to keep the Red Army fighting as long as possible in order to prolong the period of respite granted Britain by the German invasion of Russia. As he noted in the course of a directive to the Admiralty, "The advantage we should reap if the Russians could keep the field and go on with the war, at any rate until the winter closes in, is measureless."

In the meantime, from Russia, there arose at first no great chorus of jubilation over Churchill's grandiloquent offer of assistance. *Pravda* printed parts of the speech and announced that the Soviet Union would ask British approval for sending a military mission to London, but that failed to conceal an air of intense suspicion. Had Germany attacked with British connivance? Was that the true meaning behind Rudolf Hess's flight to Britain? "The silence on the top level was oppressive," Churchill was to write, "and I thought it my duty to break the ice." In a personal letter to Stalin on July 7, 1941, Churchill advised that there was in Britain "genuine admiration" for the "bravery and tenacity of the soldiers and the people." The British, he wrote, would "do everything to help you that time, geography, and our growing resources allow"; the longer the war lasted, "the more help we can give." Britain had already launched a powerful aerial offensive against Germany, he said, with which "we hope to force Hitler to bring back some of his air power to the West and gradually take some of the strain off you." He mentioned the possibility of a naval operation in the Arctic, hoped that contact could be established immediately between the Red and Royal navies, declared that Britain would welcome the arrival of a Russian military mission, and through Ambassador Maisky arranged to send a British military mission to Moscow. Churchill also directed the Admiralty to prepare naval squadrons to sail for two ports well known to the Royal Navy: Murmansk and Archangel, but this time "to operate with the Russian naval forces."

Not quite a fortnight later, Stalin responded that he would welcome a joint declaration of purpose by the two governments which would state that:

> (1) The two Governments mutually undertake to render each other assistance of all kinds in the present war against Germany.
> (2) They further undertake that during this war they will neither negotiate nor conclude an armistice or treaty of peace except by mutual agreement.[16]

Stalin's second point, to make no separate peace, could have been a reflection of suspicions about British objectives, but to Churchill, whose goal was to keep Russia in the war as long as possible, and who well remembered Lenin's pullout in 1917, it was welcome.

The first joint operation undertaken by the two countries was launched at Churchill's suggestion: joint occupation of Iran. There the shah was falling increasingly under the influence of German agents, which posed a menace to Britain's supply of oil. And, by means of Iranian ports, British supplies might reach Russia through the Persian Gulf, thereby avoiding both winter ice and German U-boats on the route to Murmansk and Archangel. When British and Russian troops moved in, the Iranian Army resisted fiercely, but it was all over in three days.

In the meantime, Stalin made the first of what would turn out to be a long series of demands for a second front. "The military situation of the Soviet Union, as well as of Great Britain," he wrote Churchill, "would be considerably improved if there could be established a front against Hitler in the West—Northern France, and in the North—the Arctic." Since Hitler's forces were occupied in Russia but had yet to consolidate their position, he wrote, it was "a most propitious moment" to create a second front.

A few days later, on September 4, 1941, Stalin warned Churchill that the Soviet Union might not be able to hold on. The "relative stabilization of the front," he said, had just broken down through reinforcement by twenty Finnish and twenty-six Rumanian divisions and through the transfer to Russia from other sectors, principally France, of thirty to thirty-four fresh German divisions and "an enormous quantity of tanks and aircraft." The Germans were able to make the transfers, he said, because they considered "danger in the West a bluff" and were "convinced that no second front exists in the West and that none will exist." The only hope was for Britain to establish a second front before the year 1941 ended, either in France or the Balkans, "capable of drawing away from the Eastern Front 30 to 40 divisions," and at the same time "ensuring to the Soviet Union 30,000 tons of aluminum by the beginning of October next and a *monthly* minimum of aid amounting to 400 aircraft and 500 tanks (of small or medium size)."

Delivering the telegram personally to Churchill during the evening of September 4, 1941, Ambassador Maisky stayed to talk. He "emphasized in bitter terms how for the last eleven weeks Russia had been bearing the brunt of the German onslaught virtually alone." As Maisky continued, Churchill "sensed an underlying air of menace in his appeal." Angered, he responded: "Remember that only four months ago we in this Island did not know whether you were not coming in against us on the German side. Indeed, we thought it quite likely that you would. Even then we felt sure we would win in the end. We never thought our survival was dependent on your action either way. Whatever happens, and whatever you do, you of all people have no right to make reproaches to us."

When Maisky left, Churchill dictated a reply to Stalin in which he promised to send from British production half the aircraft and tanks that Stalin asked for, but, he said, there could be no invasion in 1941 and an invasion in 1942 depended upon "unforeseeable events." He also advised his ambassador in Moscow, Sir Stafford Cripps, that he had arranged with Canada to send Russia 5,000 tons of aluminum and 2,000 tons monthly thereafter to help Stalin rebuild his Air Force, and he spelled out in detail why there could be no second front:

If it were possible to make any successful diversion upon the French or Low Countries shore which would bring back German troops from Russia, we should order it even at the heaviest cost. All our generals are convinced that a bloody repulse is all that would be sustained. . . . The French coast is fortified to the limit, and *the Germans still have more divisions in the West than we have in Great Britain,* and formidable air support. The shipping available to transport a large army to the Continent does not exist. . . . The diversion of our flotillas to such an operation . . . might mean the loss of the Battle of the Atlantic and the starvation and ruin of the British Isles. Nothing that we could do or could have done would affect the struggle on the Eastern Front. From the first day when Russia was attacked, I have not ceased to press the Chiefs of Staff to examine every form of action. They are united in the views here expressed.

In conclusion, Churchill noted, "No one wants to recriminate, but it is not our fault that Hitler was enabled to destroy Poland before turning his forces against France, or to destroy France before turning them against Russia."

Stalin nevertheless persisted. If "a second front in the West" was at that time impossible, he said, "perhaps another method could be found to render to the Soviet Union an active military help." In view of the previous history of Russian reaction to foreign troops on Russian soil, Churchill found "the other method" staggering and at the same time illustrative of the depth of Stalin's despair. He proposed that Britain send twenty-five to thirty divisions to Iran or to Archangel to establish "military collaboration between the Soviet and British troops on the territory of the USSR." The unreality of Stalin's request also stunned Churchill; that many divisions would involve between 500,000 and 600,000 men, far more than existed in the British Isles.

## Chapter Seventy-One

Before Hitler attacked Russia, Winston Churchill informed President Roosevelt that if an attack came, he intended to support Russia and asked the president to do the same. Although Roosevelt agreed, he was hardly prepared for such a clarion call as Churchill had issued that Sunday evening. Ever since those auspicious days in 1933 when Roosevelt had granted diplomatic recognition to the Soviet Union and executed the Roosevelt-Litvinov agreements, he had been thoroughly frustrated by Soviet behavior. He understood well the secretiveness, the brutality, the lust for territory that pervaded the Soviet regime, yet, like Churchill, he saw Communist expansionism as a bugbear of the future, far less perilous at the moment than the demonstrated might and appetite of Adolf Hitler.

On the other hand, Roosevelt was all too conscious that his people had become far more inflamed over Communism and its insidious infiltration through the

Comintern than had the people of Britain, and his people faced no such immediate threat to survival that made a marriage of convenience with Communism acceptable. The long catalogue of recent Soviet intrigues and crimes was still much on American minds: the Nazi-Soviet Nonaggression Pact, the seizure of the Baltic States and parts of Poland and Rumania, the aggressive war against little Finland, the Russo-Japanese neutrality pact that gave the impression that hostile powers were pressing in on the United States. There was a recent revelation of the Comintern's cold hand in the strikes that beset the defense industry; as recently as May 6, 1941, a Soviet intelligence general operating under the cover of Amtorg, Gaik Ovakiminian, had been arrested and deported; the head of World Tourists, Jacob Golos, a high official of the Communist underground, had just been tried and fined for failing to register as an agent of a foreign government. Such was the government's concern about Comintern propaganda that almost on the eve of the German attack, the Treasury Department had frozen Russian assets in the United States of $39 million, in the process informing the Soviet Embassy that the funds would be released only upon assurance that "they would not be used for anti-American propaganda."[1]

Roosevelt was also conscious of the way the professionals in the State Department viewed helping Russia. On the eve of the German attack, the State Department advised that the United States should offer nothing "unless the Soviet Union approaches us" and then should act consistent with its own needs and those of Britain and help Russia only on the basis of "mutual advantage." Reflecting a general belief that Russia would not survive a German attack, the State Department recommended engaging "in no undertaking which might make it appear that we have not acted in good faith if later we should refuse to recognize a refugee Soviet Government or cease to recognize the Soviet Ambassador in Washington as the diplomatic representative of Russia."[2]

Loud were the voices of protest raised by Churchill's promise of aid to Russia. The head of the isolationist America First Committee, a retired general, Robert E. Wood, said that Americans could hardly be expected to "take up arms behind the Red flag of Stalin" and that aid to Britain should be reconsidered unless "some definite assurance" could be obtained that "everything we send will not be relayed to Stalin in accordance with Mr. Churchill's pledge." "Are we going to fight," asked a columnist for the New Republic, John T. Flynn, "to make Europe safe for Communism?" Recalling the bad grace with which Russia had accepted American aid during the great famine, Roosevelt's predecessor, Herbert Hoover, declared that aid to Russia would make "a gargantuan jest" of the thesis that the war was a struggle between democracy and totalitarianism; American aid would merely help Stalin fasten "the grip of communism on Russia" and "extend it over the world." Although the New York Times favored helping Russia, its editorial columns warned that "Stalin is on our side today," but where would he be tomorrow? Various patriotic, Catholic, and ethnic organizations produced a torrent of arguments opposing sympathy for a country that had so recently gobbled up its neighbors. Declared an obscure senator from Missouri, Harry S. Truman: "If we see that Germany is winning, we ought to help Russia, and if Russia is winning, we ought to help Germany. And that way let them kill as many as possible."[3]

Moving cautiously, Roosevelt fulfilled the letter of his pledge to Churchill by authorizing an indecisive declaration by the State Department denigrating both Fascism and Communism but declaring that the Fascist threat was so great that assistance to any anti-Hitler forces, regardless of the source, would benefit American security. At a press conference on June 24, 1941, he told newsmen that "of course we are going to give all the aid that we possibly can to Russia," but as yet there had been no request for assistance.[4]

The president nevertheless took two immediate steps to help Russia. He stretched his constitutional authority to rule against invoking the Neutrality Acts against Russia, thereby assuring a legal means of providing loans, credits, and arms should that be decided. He also lifted the freeze on the $39 million in Russian assets in the United States on the condition that none of the funds be used for anti-American propaganda, a condition the Comintern was happy to accept, for the new party line was for American Communists to do everything to support their government and increase arms production. Even if Russia in the end went down, Roosevelt told intimates, anything done to delay the collapse would buy time for Britain, buy time for American rearmament, and buy harmony in American defense plants. On the other hand, Roosevelt was conscious that little could be done immediately; "You can't just go around to Mr. Garfinckel's," he said, referring to a Washington department store, "and fill the order and take it away with you."[5]

There was also the matter of how Russia was to pay. The Treasury Department knew that Russia lacked the foreign exchange for extensive purchases, and to bring that country under the umbrella of Lend-Lease was, for the moment, out of the question. As a stopgap measure, Roosevelt authorized the Treasury to buy Soviet gold, paying $60 million as an advance on purchases, and directed his administrators to buy strategic raw materials from Russia, the proceeds from those transactions to pay for war goods going to Russia.

Although Roosevelt obviously intended to provide some aid, the extent of it remained undecided when in late July 1941 a cable arrived from his man Friday, Harry Hopkins, who was on a mission to London, asking if the president might not send him to Moscow. Despite the heavy Russian losses, said Hopkins, he might be able to convince Stalin to hold out by making clear to him "that we mean business on a long term supply job."[6]

In a Catalina flying boat provided by Churchill, a gaunt and ailing Hopkins arrived in Archangel on July 30, 1941, and the next day flew on to Moscow and met Stalin. He was strongly impressed. Stalin was "an austere, rugged, determined figure . . . built close to the ground, like a football coach's dream of a tackle . . . There was no waste of word, gesture, nor mannerism. It was like talking to a perfectly coordinated machine, an intelligent machine."[7]

Hopkins told Stalin that Roosevelt believed "the most important thing to be done in the world today was to defeat Hitler and Hitlerism," and thus he was determined "to extend all possible aid to the Soviet Union at the earliest possible time." Conscious of the feeling in the American Embassy and in Washington that Russia could not long survive, Hopkins watched carefully for indications that Stalin genuinely believed that the Red Army would in the end hold fast. What did Russia require immediately, he asked, and what were the requirements for a long war? Antiaircraft guns and antiaircraft ammunition, Stalin replied without hesitation, and machine guns and rifles. For the long term, high octane aviation gasoline and aluminum for building planes. "Give us anti-aircraft guns and the aluminum," he declared, "and we can fight for three or four years." [8]

In a second session, Stalin sketched the military situation in more optimistic terms than events appeared to warrant: the Red Army, he declared, would hold until the winter set in, and by the time the spring campaign started, Russia would have mobilized 350 divisions. Yet that was not what sent Hopkins away convinced that the Russians would survive. "A man," he was to write later, "who feared immediate defeat would not have put aluminum so high on the list of priorities." [9] In a cable to President Roosevelt, Hopkins urged that the United States provide all possible aid.

That recommendation ended any equivocation that might still have remained with Roosevelt. At a Cabinet meeting on August 1, 1941, he laced into his secretaries in a manner none had experienced before. They had been giving the Russians "the runaround," he said. "He did not want to hear what was on order; he wanted to hear what was on the water." [10] He wanted "whatever we are going to give them . . . to be over by the first of October, and the only answer I want to hear is that it is under way." [11]

Yet as Roosevelt surely knew, the governmental machinery of a great democracy is ponderous. The first American shipment to the Soviet Union, aviation fuel, left by tanker from Los Angeles bound for Vladivostok only on August 14, 1941, and for long weeks and months other consignments would be spotty. The country was still a long way from being the arsenal of democracy that Roosevelt had proclaimed, and there was still the priority of aid to Britain. Nor did the excessive shopping list submitted to the Office of Emergency Management by Ambassador Oumansky help; he asked, for example, for an amount of tank armor plate that would have consumed the entire American output for the next two years. He wanted 12,500 tons of toluol, used in the production of high octane aviation fuel, more than existed in the entire American stockpile, and he wanted early delivery of 180,000 tons of 250-pound bombs, far more than existed. The U.S. Army's chief of staff, General George C. Marshall, complained that Oumansky would "take everything if we submit to his criticism." [12]

There remained also the matter of how Russia over the long run was to pay. On that score, Roosevelt drew encouragement from a recent Gallup Poll which revealed that 70 percent of those sampled favored the *sale* of war materials to

Russia, then another poll showed that 49 percent approved the extension of credits. Yet on the matter of extending Lend-Lease to Russia, another Gallup Poll showed that the American people were sharply divided: 38 percent for, 39 percent against.

Lest Roosevelt jeopardize passage of a new appropriation for Lend-Lease, he made no effort to specifically include Russia, arranging instead a new advance of $150 million against Russian gold and raw materials and launching a public relations campaign on behalf of the need to help Russia. He and spokesmen for his administration stressed constantly the necessity for *realpolitik*, to help keep the Russians in the fight in order to keep American boys out. And in the end, the campaign paid off. On October 24, 1941, the new appropriation passed with every attempt to attach provisions specifically excluding Russia beaten down. On November 7, 1941—which, some might have noted, was the twenty-fourth anniversary of the October Revolution—the White House announced a $1 billion credit to Russia with repayment to be spread over ten years but not to begin until five years after the end of the war. Although aware that the terms were considerably less favorable than those granted Britain, Stalin accepted.

Aid to Russia nevertheless still failed to flow with the speed that all involved might have wished, for the old problems of priorities and inadequate supply remained. Thus by the end of 1941 Russia would have received only eighty-five American aircraft and sixteen American tanks. In time, American aid would amount to over $11 billion, but as the Red Army in December 1941 faced its crisis of survival before the gates of its capital, the fight would be conducted basically with Russia's own resources. Which would in time lead critics of American aid to maintain that the Soviet Union would have survived without American help, that American supplies merely ensured the Red Army's later advance into Central Europe and the rise of the Soviet Union as a great and menacing power.


Throughout those critical months of the summer and fall of 1941, Roosevelt faced not only concern about the fate of Britain and Russia but about the likelihood of an outbreak of war in the Pacific. In late November 1941, with the breakoff of prolonged conversations between Japanese and American representatives in Washington, a menacing radio silence descended on the Japanese Fleet. Through Magic intercepts, the government knew by November 30, 1941, that Japan might strike at any moment, and warnings went out to all Pacific commands. Every indication was that the attack would move southward against American and European possessions in the South Pacific and Southeast Asia.

As the Japanese Fleet continued to maintain radio silence, intelligence agencies in Washington began to pay close attention to Japanese commercial radio, for in mid-November 1941, the Office of Naval Intelligence in Singapore had obtained a copy of what came to be called the "winds code," a simple code that could be inserted, if need arose, in Japanese news broadcasts as a warning that a break in diplomatic relations and war were imminent. The code provided for three contingencies:

> If relations with the United States were about to break down, the signal would be: east wind, rain.
> If Russo-Japanese relations: north wind, cloudy.
> If Anglo-Japanese relations: west wind, clear.[13]

Monitors picked up a first suspicious message from a Tokyo station, JVW 3, on December 4, 1941, a forecast predicting the weather for Tokyo, Kanagawa, and Chiba, in each case predicting north wind, cloudy. That report caused consternation at naval intelligence headquarters in the Munitions Building on Constitution Avenue in Washington, for if not a deception, it meant that Japan would honor the Tripartite Pact and attack Russia. If that happened, Russia was sure to fall.

At 9:30 P.M. (Washington time) on December 5, 1941, monitors picked up a second message over JVW 3, concealed in the weather forecast at the end of the nine o'clock news: "TODAY NORTH WIND MORNING CLOUDY AFTERNOON BEGIN CLOUDY EVENING. TOMORROW NORTH WIND AND LATER FROM SOUTH."[14] That report added to the concern, for as specified in the winds code, the announcer repeated it three times. Again, it meant war with Russia.

Yet almost immediately, the monitors heard Tokyo stations JLG 4 and JZJ broadcast identical messages:

> THIS IS IN THE MIDDLE OF THE NEWS BUT TODAY, SPECIALLY AT THIS POINT, I WILL GIVE THE WEATHER FORECAST:
>
> WEST WIND, CLEAR.
> WEST WIND, CLEAR.
> WEST WIND, CLEAR.[15]

That meant a break in diplomatic relations and war with the British Empire. If the intercepts were not deceptions, Japan was thus about to go to war with both Russia and the British Empire. But what of the United States? There was no broadcast of the third winds code, no forecast of east wind, rain.

## Chapter Seventy-Two

It was not until July 3, 1941, twelve days after the Nazi military machine rolled across the Russian frontier, that Stalin at last went before the microphones of Radio Moscow to proclaim a Holy War for the defense of Mother Russia. He spoke with unaccustomed warmth: "Comrades, citizens, brothers and sisters, fighters of our Army and Navy! I am speaking to you, my friends!"[1]

While making no direct reference to the enormity of the German gains nor to the catastrophe that had befallen the Soviet armed forces, Stalin nevertheless proclaimed that "A serious threat hangs over our country." The Germans were not invincible, he declared; the armies of Napoleon and Kaiser Wilhelm had once been considered invincible, yet they had been defeated. That the Germans had achieved any gains at all was attributable to their perfidious violation of the Nonaggression Pact, a pact which he justified on the basis of the time it had given the Soviet Union to improve its defenses.

The Germans intended, said Stalin, "to restore the power of the landowners, re-establish Tsarism, and destroy the national culture of the peoples of the Soviet Union . . . and turn them into the slaves of German princes and barons." Not only the Red Army and Navy but "the whole Soviet people must fight to the last drop of blood for our towns and villages." If the Red Army were forced to retreat, nothing of use to the enemy was to be left behind, and those men and women trapped behind enemy lines were to begin a merciless partisan warfare. It was a campaign for the survival of Holy Russia. "All the strength of the people," he concluded, "must be used to smash the enemy. Onward to Victory!"

In the entire speech there was not a single reference to Bolshevism, not a single call to the nation to defend the ideology of the Communist Party, and only one reference to the party at all, a call to "rally round the Party of Lenin and Stalin." It was an appeal not to Communism but to nationalism, a call to join in prosecuting the Great Patriotic War.

When Lenin seized power in 1917, both he and Trotsky saw the Russian Orthodox clergy as inseparably linked to the czars. In the first years of the Bolshevik regime, many churches were closed and hundreds of priests exiled, jailed, or executed. By confiscating church property, the government helped finance the Comintern's operations overseas by sale of such church furniture as crosses, ikons, and altar bowls. A system of terror embraced the entire Orthodox clergy.

In 1923, possibly as a result of the battle for the succession to Lenin, the terror subsided, but in 1929 it began again, directed not only against the Orthodox Church but against all faiths. It subsided again in 1931, possibly because of American insistence on religious freedom in Russia as a precondition for diplomatic recognition.

In 1936, a new Soviet constitution solemnly proclaimed freedom of religion for all faiths, but less than a year later, as a corollary of the Great Purge, Orthodox priests were again subjected to persecution. Lacking priests and severely burdened by the taxes, almost a third of the existing parishes had to suspend all religious activities. Of 454 churches officiating in Moscow at the time of the revolution, only twenty-six were still operating twenty years later.

In 1938 came yet another shift in policy. At a special meeting between representatives of the government and of the Atheist Society, government spokesmen explained that persecution of religion constituted "a revival of the bourgeois period," and the Academy of Sciences proclaimed that "religion might form a positive basis for the history of the State" since "the Orthodox Church had played a progressive and cultural part in the education of the Russian people." Young Communists and members of the Communist Boy Scouts movement, the Pioneers, were forbidden to annoy or ridicule "their comrades wearing a cross."[2]

That abrupt shift was difficult to explain, but it coincided with issuance of a secret pastoral letter from the Metropolitan of Moscow, Sergei, to foreign episcopates in which Sergei urged the bishops to permit the NKVD to use the Orthodox Church's facilities, a tie-in soon uncovered in the United States by the FBI. Sergei was a nimble politician who, like the Vicar of Bray, was quite prepared to make a pact with the Devil if it meant the preservation of the faith; and as the Wehrmacht attacked Russia on June 22, 1941, and Russia's struggle for survival began, Sergei's time appeared to have come. "On behalf of our clergy and all believers of the Russian Orthodox Church, true children of our motherland," Sergei wrote to Stalin, "I heartily and prayerfully greet in your person the God-chosen leader of our military and cultural forces who leads us on to victory over the barbarous invasion."

Stalin was quick to see the advantages that religion offered for the imperiled state. Although Sergei never proclaimed fealty to Bolshevism, Stalin moved to bring the church into the struggle for survival. In a ceremony in Moscow Cathedral marked by much pomp and by the presence of Stalin, Molotov, other government dignitaries, and the metropolitans of Leningrad and Kiev, Stalin installed Sergei as the Patriarch of All-Russia. The official press carried a formal notice that the Soviet government recognized the new patriarch, and Stalin sanctioned re-establishing the Holy Synod to rule the Russian Orthodox Church "in Russia, in the Balkans, and throughout the world."[3] Soon there were "constitutional provisions concerning freedom of religion";[4] collective farms were permitted to deliver food and fuel to the clergy and the churches and workmen to repair the churches, and church taxes were reduced. The government appointed the metropolitan of Kiev and Galicia, Nikolai, to a state commission to investigate war crimes by the German Army, the first official post afforded an Orthodox clergyman since the October Revolution. The Ikon of the Holy Mother of Tver, one of the great relics of the Orthodox faith, which had vanished during the revolution, was somehow "found" and restored to the Moscow Cathedral.

The clergy, in turn, did its part. The Patriarch, Sergei, preached obedience to the state, which could "in no way misguide our conscience and our faith in Christ." Although the Religious Decree of 1929, which forbade both clergy and church to possess funds, had never been revoked, the church made large contributions to the Soviet Defense Fund, which the government accepted without question. The priesthood blessed the Red Army and its generals and called upon the laity everywhere to help defend the fatherland. Such was the reconciliation between state and church that in areas overrun by the German

Army, many priests joined the partisans despite a promise from Hitler to afford absolute religious freedom, few of the clergy collaborated with the conqueror.

The reconciliation between church and state also extended to the minority religions. Irinarkh, Old Believer Archbishop of Moscow and of All-Russia, appealed to his followers in occupied territory to pray for victory and at the same time to fight the Germans behind the lines. The Baptist and Evangelical Protestant Communities of Russia issued a manifesto, recalling the importance in the Evangelical Movement of Hus and the Moravian Brethren and of the Protestants of Britain and the United States and establishing a day of prayer for Soviet victory. The Central Ecclesiastical Council of Muhammadans called on all Muslims in the Soviet Union to fight the invaders. Tracts were issued in the various regional languages with such injunctions from the Koran as "Kill the enemy wherever thou findest him, drive him out. . . ." The Mufti and the Moslem Spiritual Promoter of Central Asia, the Moscow Jewish Community, the Catholicos Patriarch of Georgia, the Catholicos of All Armenians, Gevorkian—all pledged their support.

As the reaction of the people to the new religious freedom soon demonstrated, Lenin's and Stalin's campaigns to destroy religion had failed. Church attendance multiplied everywhere, and among "wounded or dying Red soldiers in hospital and on the battlefield," 20 percent "asked to have the last sacraments of the church administered to them." Yet Stalin could accept the evidence of that setback in return for the help that his pact with God provided in the struggle to save the fatherland. That pact accomplished, he moved to adjust to those other former enemies of the people, Churchill and the British.

As the Second Imperialist War became the Great Patriotic War, the Comintern chieftain, Georgi Dimitrov, in *World News and Views* of July 12, 1941, performed the feat of turning yesterday's "mercenaries of the City of London" into today's "gallant fighters for the freedom of the world." It was, Dimitrov wrote, "no longer a question of which of the two imperialist groups is going to rule the world. If the German Fascist attack on the Soviet Union were to succeed, there would be a Fascist empire from Lisbon to Vladivostok." Nothing would then be left to prevent the subjugation of all peoples by Germany. "The struggle for the defeat and destruction of the German Fascist war machine is therefore the common cause of all peoples."

The reaction of the world's Communist and Socialist parties to that declaration by the Comintern demonstrated that for all the disillusionment and wreckage caused by the exile of Trotsky and by the Nonaggression Pact, the Comintern still commanded loyalty and obedience. In Britain and the United States, the Communists began to agitate for increased war production, to stifle strikes, and to demand the opening of a second front; and in the German-occupied countries, a form of three-way civil war broke out in which the Communists fought the underground right and the Germans.

As the Germans battled that new enemy, Stalin took steps to tighten his hold on his military forces. He reintroduced a system generally abandoned following the Red Army's poor performance in Finland: political commissars, and gave them full authority to deal without mercy with "cowards, the creators of panic, and deserters."[5] Generals whose fronts collapsed were either submitted to drumhead courts or summarily shot. The Russian soldier himself faced two enemies: the Germans at his front and green-capped NKVD troops at his rear. Even bodies of troops that escaped from encirclement to return to Russian lines were interrogated by the NKVD before being absolved—or convicted—of treason.

There was also Secret Order No. 0019. Since, as Stalin himself admitted, "There are many elements . . . who even run to meet the foe and throw away their weapons on first contact with him,"[6] he decreed that any soldier who surrendered for whatever reason was a traitor to the state, whereupon the head of the NKVD, Lavrenti Beria, ordered reprisals against the families of anybody who allowed himself to fall into German hands.

That last would be a difficult order to execute with any regard to reality, for in the maelstrom of the broken front and in an army that had no more than a rudimentary casualty reporting system, who was to know who was captured and who died on the battlefield? One whose capture was soon revealed by German design was Stalin's elder son, Jacob Djugashvili; he had early incurred Stalin's wrath by a bungled attempt at suicide, adding to it by marrying a Jewess. A captain of artillery, he fell into German hands in the first days of the attack, and when the Germans offered to exchange him for a captured German officer, Stalin refused and ordered Jacob's wife arrested "to find out what was behind it."[7]

Yet there was one way of getting at those who surrendered. On at least two occasions, at Orel and at Novgorod-Seversky, Russian planes bombed camps where the Germans were holding Russian prisoners of war, other planes following to drop leaflets proclaiming: "So will it be with all those who betray the cause of Lenin and Stalin."[8]

By July 4, 1941, the day after Stalin finally broke his silence and less than two weeks after the start of the German offensive, the objective of destroying the Red Army appeared to have been achieved. "For all practical purposes," declared Hitler, "the enemy has lost this campaign."[9]

So convinced was Hitler of quick victory that he began to plan for "a fundamental readjustment" of the German armed forces. While proposing to increase the number of motorized and panzer divisions, he intended to reduce the overall size of the Army and restrict naval forces to those "immediately necessary for the conduct of the war against England" and, should it come to that, "against America."[10] The increase was to be in the Luftwaffe, which was to be provided short- and long-range rockets, jet aircraft, and very long range patrol aircraft and bombers capable of round-trip missions against the northeastern coast of the United States. There was also to be a greater concentration on producing an atomic bomb, which appeared feasible following acquisition of a Norwegian heavy water plant at Norsk Hydro and of uranium mines at Joachimstal in Czechoslovakia.

For the immediate objective of completing the conquest of Russia, Hitler as early as June 29, 1941, suggested that it was time to consider diverting the panzer armies from Army Group Center and the drive on Moscow until Leningrad could be taken and the grain and oil in South Russia obtained. The chief of the Oberkommando der Wehrmacht's Operations Staff, General Jodl, promptly objected; a detour by way of Leningrad, he said, would wear out the tanks and half-tracks, making it impossible for them to participate in a subsequent assault on the Russian capital. With that exchange, the line of conflict between Hitler and his generals was drawn.

To a military man, the first and vital objective of warfare is to destroy the enemy's armed forces, whereupon other objectives may be readily attained. For all the optimism engendered by the spectacular achievements of the opening fortnight of the campaign, the Red Army still might have sizable formations left, in which case Stalin would obviously employ them to defend his capital, thereby affording an opportunity to destroy them and inflict the decisive defeat. To a man, Hitler's military chiefs believed that the Army's central forces should push on to Moscow; a diversion of the armor to Leningrad would mean that no attack on the capital could be launched before September at the earliest and probably later.

To Hitler, to the contrary, Moscow for all its symbolism was but a place-name. Contemptuous of the "ossified brains"[11] of his generals, he was convinced that the fall of Moscow would have little effect but that the fall of Leningrad, the cradle of Bolshevism, might precipitate a complete Russian collapse. Even though Moscow itself was an industrial and communications center, the importance of Leningrad and the objectives in the south were to his mind paramount: opening the port of Leningrad would enable Germany to obtain vitally needed iron ore, and in the south, grain, coal, oil.

Since the tanks, in any case, had to be pulled from the line for two weeks for refitting, no decision had to be reached immediately. Yet even though the German generals continued such protests as delicate relations with their demanding Führer allowed, the decision in the end was Hitler's. On August 21, 1941, he directed an army on the south wing of Army Group Center to help the offensive in the south and the two panzer armies to turn toward Leningrad. That left only von Kluge's 4th Army still pointed toward Moscow, so that there was nothing for von Kluge to do but hold fast, ward off Russian counterattacks, and wait for the panzers to return.

Hitler, noted General Jodl, appeared to have "an instinctive aversion to treading the same path as Napoleon." Moscow, said Jodl, seemed to give Hitler "a sinister feeling," as if he saw in an attack on the city "a life and death struggle with bolshevism."

Almost from the start of the German campaign, Heydrich's SS Action Groups were doing their work behind German lines to rid the conquered territory of commissars and other Communist officials, NKVD agents, anybody associated with Communism, and—incidentally—Jews. In the first four months, Action Group A, for example, operating in rear of the German army group advancing on Leningrad, executed in Estonia, Latvia, and Lithuania 3,387 Communists and 123,930 Jews, and once inside Russia, another 2,000 and some 748 "lunatics," while SS forces operating in support of the Action Group liquidated 5,502 men and women. The total was 135,560.[12]

In the process, the commanders of the Action Groups encouraged the local population to move on their own against their Bolshevik masters and the Jews. "It had to be shown to the world," noted the commanding general of Action Group A, that the people themselves "took the first action by way of natural reaction against the terror exercised by the Communists." Also, he noted, "It was no less important in view of the future to establish the unshakable and provable fact that the liberated population themselves took the most severe measures against the Bolshevik and Jewish enemy quite on their own, so that the direction by German authorities could not be found out."[13]

Yet however much the German commanders wanted the local population to participate, the Action Groups did most of the work, and in most cases, the victims accepted their fate supinely and hopelessly. As one SS executioner wrote at the time, "Many times I have asked myself when one of these Russians sat there in front of me, vacant and apathetic. . . . . Is there nothing else in this human being, no hope, no love, no self-respect, personality, faith . . . the things that made a human being?"[14]

From the interrogation table to the death pit was but a short walk. There the plans of the SS for "special treatment," "sanitary measures," "change of residence" assumed grim reality. As one observer described it:

> The people who got off the trucks, men, women and children of every age, had to undress on orders from an SS man who held a riding whip or dog whip in his hand. They had to deposit their clothing, shoes, outer and underclothes separately, at certain places. . . .
> Without an outcry or weeping these people undressed, stood together in family groups, kissed and said goodbye to each other, and waited for the beckoning gesture of another SS man who stood at the pit and likewise held a whip in his hand.
> During a quarter of an hour that I stood by the pit, I heard no laments or pleas for mercy. I observed a family of some eight persons. . . . An old woman with snow-white hair held a year-old baby in her arms and sang something to it and tickled it. The child crowed with pleasure. The couple looked on with tears in their eyes. The father held a boy of about ten by the hand and spoke comfortingly to him in a low voice. The boy was fighting back his tears. The father pointed his finger up at the sky, caressed his head, and seemed to be explaining something to him.

At this point the SS man by the pit called out something to his fellow. The other man divided off about twenty persons and instructed them to go behind the mound of earth. The family I have been speaking of was among them. . . .

The completely naked people walked down a flight of steps that had been cut into the earthen wall of the pit, stumbled over the heads of those who were already lying there. . . . They lay down in front of the dead or wounded; some stroked those who were still living and murmured what seemed to be words of comfort. Then I heard a series of shots. I looked at the pit and saw the bodies twitching or the heads already lying still on the bodies in front. Blood ran from the backs of their necks.[15]

In those territories such as the Baltic States which Stalin had so recently annexed, but also inside liberated portions of the old Russia, masses of the people looked to the Germans as liberators. "Many peasants gladly helped the Germans, toasted the birth of a new nation in vodka, fashioned festive flower garlands, and worshipped with Te Deums the god that communism had so long denied."[16] In some villages, the people quickly organized local governments whose first step was to abolish the hated *kolkhozy* (collective farms) and redistribute land. Stalin's order for partisan warfare drew little support, and in the Ukraine there was soon the start of a liberation army under the auspices of the Organization of Ukrainian Nationalists. Cossacks, too, began to reform long-disbanded formations, and in Smolensk, the mayor and ten other notables signed a memorandum assuring the Germans that if they would guarantee independence, form a Russian liberation army, and install a new Russian regime, the people would overthrow the Communists. Since Heydrich's Action Groups focused their repression on Communist officials, the NKVD, and Jews, the repression produced little reaction against the Germans.

It was much the same in neighboring Belorussia. In that portion which had been a part of Poland, the Germans dissolved the collective farms, restored properties to their owners, and established what were accepted as legitimate local governments. While they took less radical steps in the Russian part, where German administrators supervised the collective farms and directed a highly centralized governmental system, the people still remained basically friendly. The "resettlement" of the Communist officials appeared to assure that.

In the Baltic States, the Germans found economic conditions chaotic. In Estonia, for example, the fleeing Russians had made off with the railroad rolling stock or destroyed what they were unable to take with them. Although conditions were less critical in Latvia and Lithuania, the people there as in Estonia welcomed the Germans, although cautiously, as liberators. In all three countries, there were numbers of people eager to cooperate. There remained one gnawing concern: the Germans never said what the status of the Baltic States would eventually be.

The Germans everywhere sought to exploit their welcome through propaganda. They quickly opened radio stations and soon sponsored newspapers, which the people seized avidly, hungry for news. Cinemas reopened to play German propaganda films to full houses. In the propaganda, the Germans stressed the need to fight Communist saboteurs and partisans, criticism of the collective farms with vague promises of impending land reform, and to attract Russian labor, the excellent working conditions inside Germany. However propagandistic the material, the people were eager to hear it, for too long they had been starved. Tell us, they would demand, all about the NKVD.

It could not last, for Adolf Hitler had not sent his legions into Russia or anywhere else as liberators; there was no possibility of cooperation in any form with a race of *Untermenschen.* A conquered Russia would exist solely to provide *Lebensraum* and material substance for the Greater German World Empire. Stalin's agents were soon everywhere among the people, stirring resistance, and each day that the German rule grew harsher, attracting more recruits. As the commander of a battalion of partisans put it: "We who are in the woods believe that communism—which 70 to 80 percent of us hate—will at least give us a chance to live, while the Germans . . . will either kill us outright or let us die of hunger." [17]

But in general, it at that point appeared that Hitler's vision of a world empire based upon Germania was not unrealistic. In every country there was at least a segment of strong support for Fascism, nodules of power, sometimes influential, that welcomed a New Order of Europe, and there was widespread acquiescence. Aside from the conquered countries, Hitler's power was also supreme in Rumania, Bulgaria, and Hungary, and his agents had begun to appear in Asia Minor and Arabia. At the same time, British influence was weakening markedly throughout the world, leaving vacuums which, so it seemed, only Germany had the power to fill.

Facing the emergence of a new empire vaster than Britain's own, Winston Churchill reacted by establishing what a British Socialist leader, Ernest Bevin, would come to call the "Democratic International." It was the Special Operations Executive, which had its headquarters next door to Sherlock Holmes' fictional residence in Baker Street in London. To the head of the new international, Colonel Colin Gubbins, a Hebridean with a long history of involvement in unorthodox warfare, Churchill's directive contrasted sharply with the wordy orders of the Comintern. It consisted of just seven words uttered in an elevator: "Now go out and set Europe ablaze." [18]

That Gubbins proceeded to do, establishing relations with every anti-German resistance movement in Europe, and to complete the circle of ironies that attended Anglo-Russian politics of the period, he formed an alliance with the Comintern. To Moscow he sent a representative to act as liaison between the British and Soviet intelligence services: Brigadier George Hill, who in the twenties had been the case officer of Sidney George Reilly and who wore on his dinner jacket the cross pattée of the Order of St. George of the Czar Nicholas II, awarded for conspicuous bravery in action against the enemy: the Bolsheviks. Hill was to arrange cooperation between the resistance groups of the Democratic International and the underground cells of the Communist International.

## Chapter Seventy-Three

By early autumn of 1941, the campaign in Russia had begun to drag at the very spirit of the German soldier and his commander. As one German general put it:

> The spaces seemed endless, the horizons nebulous. We were depressed by the monotony of the landscape, and the immensity of the stretches of forest, marsh, and plain. Good roads were so few, and bad tracks so numerous, while rain quickly turned the sand or loam into a morass. The villages looked wretched and melancholy, with their straw-thatched wooden houses. Nature was hard, and in her midst were human beings just as hard and insensitive—indifferent to the weather, hunger, and thirst, and almost as indifferent to life and losses, pestilence, and famine. The Russian civilian was tough, and the Russian soldier tougher. He seemed to have an illimitable capacity for obedience and endurance.[1]

While still decrying Hitler's shift of emphasis away from Moscow, the German generals could note that there had been a tremendous victory in the south near Kiev: perhaps as many as 700,000 Russians captured along with 900 tanks; that another German army was approaching the Crimea; and that in the north, Leningrad was encircled except for a slender lifeline across Lake Lodoga and could be left to succumb in time to starvation. That meant that at last the panzer armies could be returned to Army Group Center to launch the climactic drive on Moscow; and if the diaries of Napoleon's aide-de-camp, the Marquis of Caulain-court, were a proper guide—as they had been to that point—the typical winter trend of isotherms would not be fully established before late November. Thus despite what the generals saw as Hitler's blunder in delaying the march on Moscow, there still might be time.

The battle was to be joined in that area of European Russia known as Old Muscovy, a region slightly smaller than the British Isles, an island of plains, low hills, and farming and meadowland bordered by dark-green forests to the north and east, deciduous forests to the west, and a sea of golden grain to the south. The German commander was Field Marshal Fedor von Bock, a gaunt, bony, hard-bitten man known throughout the German Army as *"der Sterber* (a man who preaches death)" and of whom Hitler once said, "Nobody in the world but von Bock can teach soldiers to die." Von Bock's was a formidable force of three regular and three panzer armies totaling sixty-eight divisions, including eight motorized and fourteen panzer divisions with nearly 2,000 tanks, all concentrated on a 150-mile front and with von Kluge's 4th Army headed up the old Napoleonic route toward the capital.

Opposing that force were seventy to eighty Red Army divisions, but for the most part they were made up of raw levies, men who arrived at railroad stations behind the front in civilian clothes and with civilian valises, drew uniforms and rifles, and marched off to battle. In just over three months of fighting, the Red Army had lost at least 2,500,000 men and possibly as many as 18,000 tanks. To German commanders, it was incredible that the Army still fought and still had the means to fight with, for already the German Army had overrun territory in which 85 million people, 45 percent of the total population, lived and produced a third of all Russian goods.

With the panzer armies in the lead, the German attack began on September 30, 1941. Breakthrough of the thin crust of Russian positions was swift; on the first day, one of the panzer columns drove eighty miles, and two great encirclements quickly formed: one at Bryansk, 200 miles southwest of Moscow, the other at Vyazma, 120 miles southwest of the capital, the last major stop short of Moscow on the Berlin-Moscow railroad. Russian losses were tremendous: 663,000 prisoners, 1,200 tanks, over 5,000 field pieces. On the 12th of October, Kaluga fell; on the 14th, Kalinin, ninety miles northwest of Moscow and the northern hinge of a 110-mile horseshoe-shaped "Mozhaisk Defense Line," the principal defenses before the capital; only with immense difficulty did the Red Army prevent a breakthrough into the rear of the line. On the 15th, lead tanks of the 10th Panzer Division and the SS-Das Reich reached the hills at Borodino, only sixty-two miles from the Kremlin, the scene of the decisive battle that had turned back Napoleon on September 7, 1812.

With that news, Moscow's nerve snapped.

On October 15, 1941, the citizens of Moscow listened to a dolorous official communiqué: "During the night of October 14–15 the position on the Western Front became worse. The German-Fascist troops hurled against our troops large quantities of tanks and motorized infantry, and in one sector broke through our defenses."[2] Word quickly spread that the breakthrough had propelled German tanks to the hills around Borodino, and rumor swept the city that in early morning two German tanks had appeared at the northern suburb of Khimki, only twelve miles from the Kremlin; although, the story had it, they had been quickly destroyed, could others be far behind?

There began what would later be called the *bolshoi drap*, or big skedaddle.[3] Tens upon tens of thousands of people, with and without permits to leave, rushed the railroad stations and the eastern exits from the city; official cars, loaded with fleeing officials and their families, jammed the streets; offices and factories shut down; there was hardly a policeman in the streets; looting was rampant; so was hoarding; swastikas appeared on walls; handbills declaring "Death to the Communists" appeared in mailboxes; there was the occasional sound of gunfire in outlying districts. Foreign intelligence services reported to their governments that "dissatisfaction with Government is openly expressed" and "the stability of the Central Government is uncertain."[4] At least half Moscow's normal population fled toward the east.

The next day, the 16th, in keeping with Secret Order No. 022 for "the provisional relocation of Commissariats and Administrations," the government agencies began an exodus that would be accomplished over the next fortnight with more than two hundred trains. The NKVD, the Comintern, and the Defense and Transportation Commissariats settled in Kuybyshev; others went to Astrakhan, Saratov, Ulyanovsk, Kazan, Gorki, Kirov, Chelyabinsk, Orsk, and Chkalov; and government by telephone and telegraph soon collapsed the telecommunications system.

On October 17, 1941, Moscow Radio reported that the Kremlin had proclaimed a state of siege in the capital, which invoked a form of martial law administered by the NKVD. By the 19th, a semblance of calm had nevertheless returned to the city, and by that time, Stalin himself had found new hope.

Georgi Konstantinovich Zhukov was within a few days of his forty-fifth birthday when Stalin called him to take command of the defense of Moscow. A man who appeared to be built as broad as he was tall, Zhukov was a typical product of Trotsky's old Red Guard. He had been born to peasant parents living in a moss-covered shack with one room and two windows near Kaluga, southwest of Moscow. Too poor to keep their son in school, they apprenticed him at the age of eleven to an uncle, a Muscovy furrier, in whose home Zhukov was able to continue his studies in the evenings. In World War I, he began service in 1915 in the Czar's 10th Dragoon Novgorod Regiment and was twice awarded the Cross of St. George, for conspicuous bravery in battles along the Dniester. For all Zhukov's exemplary conduct, he came to resent what he considered to be the arrogance and stupidity of his officers, who were commissioned less in accordance with their ability than with their social standing.

Early in 1917, Zhukov joined a small "discussion group" in his regiment that focused on social equality, and when the czar abdicated and Zhukov's regiment turned Bolshevik, his squadron elected him the chairman of its soviet of soldiers, workers, and peasants. From that time, he served the new regime as loyally as he had the old. He came to admire Stalin, which turned out to serve him well during the Great Purge; and through the thinned ranks of Red Army command, he moved up rapidly and commanded in the border battles against the Japanese. Yet Zhukov was no ideologue: when the politicians spoke the jargon of the Bolshevik ideology, Zhukov responded in the harsh, salty language of the peasant. He was "tough, apparently nerveless, impassive, and often bitingly sarcastic," and he was "ruthless and even implacable, but with a certain charm and childlike vanity."[5]

When Zhukov arrived in Moscow in early October 1941, he met with Stalin in Stalin's command post under the Borovitsky Gate of the Kremlin. He "spoke brusquely, in a very authoritative way. The effect suggested that the senior officer here was Zhukov. And Stalin took it all for granted. At no time did any trace of annoyance cross his face."[6] The command of the capital had passed from the party to the Army, a step that in other times and under other circumstances would have led Zhukov to the Lubyanka.

In Zhukov, Stalin had found the man whom he could intrust with saving the capital. Yet what about troops and tanks? As Stalin told Zhukov in turning over to him the Red Army's tank reserve for use before Moscow, there were only fifteen tanks left in it, but on that very day, as Stalin and Zhukov were soon to learn, there appeared at Borodino the 32d Siberian Rifle Division. The troops were "tall, burly fellows in long greatcoats, with fur caps on their heads and high fur boots, most generously equipped . . . They fought impassively. There was never any panic. They stood fast and held on. They killed and let themselves be killed."[7]

Those were but the vanguard of a powerful force that was already speeding west along the Trans-Siberian Railroad. There were in all thirty Red Army divisions in Siberia, tough, hardy, well-trained, fully equipped. There were also three cavalry brigades and sixteen tank brigades with over 2,000 tanks. Yet in the first days of the fight for Moscow, even when it appeared that the capital might quickly fall, Stalin had felt compelled to leave those strong forces in Siberia, for if Japan should attack and there was nobody to oppose it, Moscow's fall would be but one catastrophe within a holocaust. Then, on October 4, 1941, Stalin had received a critical word from his man in Tokyo, Richard Sorge, a word that afforded new hope for Moscow.

Sorge was the son of a Russian mother and a German oil engineer; his paternal grandfather, Adolf, had been secretary to Karl Marx when Marx founded the First International in London in 1864.

While serving in the German Army as a private soldier during the Great War, Sorge was twice wounded, which left him with a pronounced limp. While studying for a doctoral degree in political science in Hamburg in 1919, he joined the German Communist party. An able linguist, he conversed readily in French, English, Russian, Japanese, and Chinese. Such were his intellectual capacities and his devotion to Bolshevism that in 1924 the Comintern inducted him as a secret agent. After attending the Lenin School in Moscow, Sorge traveled widely in Scandinavia and Western Europe as a Comintern agent, using journalism as a cover. In 1929, after transferring to the Red Army General Staff's intelligence directorate, the Fourth Department, he was sent to Shanghai to rebuild the combined intelligence nets of the Red Army and the Comintern in China, which had collapsed following the debacle that in 1927 had beset Mikhail Borodin.

With hostility increasing between Japan and Russia, Sorge was appointed the Red Army's intelligence plenipotentiary in Japan, arriving at Yokohama on September 6, 1933, with cover as correspondent for the leading German newspaper, the *Frankfürter Zeitung*. He took a house in Tokyo, left his card at the German Embassy, joined the German Club, and was quickly accepted into the German community of the Japanese capital.

A big man, tall but stocky, with brown hair, Dr. Sorge had "an arrogance and cruelty to the set of his eyes and the line of his mouth." Although "well-liked and deeply admired by those whose friendship he desired," he was "ruthless towards others and frankly detested by them." Many a Japanese newsman "saw him as the typically swashbuckling, arrogant Nazi and avoided him." A hard drinker, quick tempered, he "liked variety in his women." He had a wife in Russia and another, a schoolteacher, in the United States, and while serving in Japan was "known to have been intimate with some 30 women in Tokyo."[8]

Sorge's principal assistant was a Japanese journalist, Hotsumi Ozaki, son of the editor of the *Nichi Nichi Shimbun* in Taiwan, a confidant of Prince Konoye and adviser to the South Manchuria Railway, which was less a business than an empire and which maintained a wide intelligence network to keep abreast of all matters pertaining to Manchuria, including Russian and Chinese activities there.

Ozaki was also a Bolshevist. He first met Sorge through an American writer, Agnes Smedley, who was a Comintern agent in China. When Sorge asked if Ozaki would "collect and supply him with information on the internal Chinese situation and on Japanese policy toward China," Ozaki "consented without hesitation," for he was pleased to "be doing something worthwhile in cooperating with an intelligence group connected in some way with the Soviet Communist International."

By 1939 Sorge and Ozaki had recruited some forty men and women to work either directly for Sorge or through intermediaries. Organized into "inner" and "outer" rings, no member of either ring knew that he or she was working for the Red Army's intelligence service, and few had any direct connection with Sorge himself or knew that he was their chief.

Sorge, meanwhile, had become friendly with the assistant German military attaché, Eugen Ott, who served as liaison officer between the Japanese and German military intelligence services in any matter concerning the Anti-Comintern Pact, and was in time to become the ambassador. By early 1939, Sorge had so gained the trust of the current ambassador, Herbert von Dirksen, that he was appointed press attaché, which put him in an ideal position to employ his clandestine network to keep Stalin informed of Japanese and related German plans.

Through 1939, 1940, and into 1941, Sorge kept Moscow well informed of Japanese activities and, in many cases, Japanese intentions, including reports on the sang-froid with which the Japanese entered into the neutrality pact with Russia; but it was on June 22, 1941, the day the German legions crossed the Russian frontier, that Richard Sorge and what he could find out about the Japanese became vital to the survival of the Soviet Union. Rarely before in history had so much depended upon the information that a single man might provide.

Sorge's crucial work began two days later, on June 23, 1941 (Tokyo time), when the Japanese General Staff adopted as policy a paper entitled "Outline of Japan's National Policy to Meet Changes in the International Situation." That new policy, predicated upon the German invasion of Russia, proposed a "southern solution" and an "independent" settlement of the "northern question." A southern solution was quite clearly a move southward against American and

European possessions, but what did the staff mean by independent settlement of the northern question? Without further information, Sorge was compelled to assume that the Kwantung Army in Manchuria would attack the Soviet Union. Japanese troop movements and repeated requests from the German foreign minister, von Ribbentrop, for Japan to attack in conjunction with the German drive, to which Sorge was privy, seemed to reinforce that view.

As Sorge knew and had previously reported, the Japanese plan for war with Russia, called *Hachi-Go,* originally written in 1937, had been extensively revised in 1940; a "Guide to Operational Planning against the USSR for Fiscal Year 1941" had become operative on April 1, 1941; and the Japanese General Staff had conducted what was called a "special exercise" named *Kan-Toku-En,* in which the Kwantung Army was reinforced from 350,000 to 700,000 men and aircraft strength increased from 180 planes to 600. By the end of September 1941, all other Japanese forces on the Asian mainland had also been reinforced. Since the reinforcements had all been accomplished after the signing of the Russo-Japanese neutrality pact, that seemed to indicate that the Japanese might be more inclined toward honoring the Tripartite Pact, or, as Sorge learned, the reinforcements may have followed urging by the German ambassador, General Ott, that even if the Japanese chose not to attack Russia, they reinforce their troops in Manchuria in order to pin down Russian divisions. A final decision, Sorge learned, was to be made at an Imperial Conference in Tokyo on July 2, 1941.

It was at that point that Sorge called on his trusted agent, Hotsumi Ozaki. Despite Ozaki's connections, information on what was decided at the Imperial Conference proved hard to come by, but from all he was able to determine, and that mainly by rumor, the decision was against attacking Russia, which Sorge duly passed to the Kremlin, yet that was too uncertain to warrant Stalin taking the risk of transferring large numbers of troops from the east.

Aware of a prior order to the Kwantung Army in Manchuria to muster 3,000 railroad workers for support of an attack on Russia, Sorge sent Ozaki to Manchuria to determine the status of that order. Upon Ozaki's return, Sorge at last had the definite information he needed to resolve Stalin's quandary: there had been no implementing of the order to muster the railroad workmen. Sorge transmitted that information to Moscow along with a definitive assessment of Japanese intentions:

> According to information obtained from various Japanese official sources, if no satisfactory reply is received from the US to Japan's request for negotiations by the 15th or 16th of this month . . . there will be war with the US this month [July] or next month. . . .
>
> With respect to the Soviet Union, top-ranking elements are generally agreed that, if Germany wins, Japan can take over her gains in the Far East in the future and that therefore it is unnecessary for Japan to fight Russia. They feel that if Germany proves unable to destroy the Soviet Government and force it out of Moscow, Japan should bide her time until next spring. In any event, the American

issue and the question of the advance to the south are far more important than the northern problem.[9]

Other than the warning of the German attack on Russia, which Stalin had failed to heed, that was the most vital information Richard Sorge had ever passed to his controllers in the Kremlin. It was also the last. A week later, in a general anticommunist roundup, Japanese police arrested a member of Sorge's ring, who talked; three days later the police arrested Ozaki and the next morning took Sorge from his bed in pyjamas and slippers. At the police station, the German ambassador, General Ott, shaken by the news, came to see him. "Mr. Ambassador," said Sorge, "this is our final farewell. Give my regards to your wife and family."[10] Both Ozaki and Sorge were tried, sentenced to death, and hanged.

On November 6, 1941, the eve of the anniversary of the October Revolution, the remnants of the Moscow branch of the party, of the government, of the city administration, and of the military high command filled the great marble underground hall of the Mayakovsky subway station in Moscow to hear Stalin speak. "If they [the Germans] want a war of extermination," Stalin declared, "they shall have one." The German blitzkrieg, he said, had failed in its essential purpose—to take Moscow—because the Wehrmacht had incurred more than 4 million casualties. It had failed also, he said, because "the Hess mission" had not brought Britain and the United States into the war on the side of Germany; indeed, both countries were providing supplies to the Soviet Union. It had failed, too, because the Red Army remained unbroken. Although "certain German technical superiorities" had had "a telling effect," the Red Army had survived and would become "the terror of the German Army." England had yet to launch a second front, he concluded, but "unquestionably" it would be launched "within a very short time."[11]

It was true that the German Army's advance on the capital had slowed to a crawl, blunted not only by the reinforcements from Siberia but also by a morass of mud. Rain, rain, more rain. German divisions that had been accustomed to advancing as far as ten to thirty miles a day could advance no more than one to two. There were seemingly suicidal Russian counterattacks; occasionally one of the new, powerful T-34 tanks; mammoth bombardments by Katyusha rockets. Yet the advance, though slowed, continued, seemingly inexorable, and the SS panzer division Das Reich was less than fifty miles from the heart of Moscow.

Few who heard Stalin's speech that night could have shared their leader's apparent confidence. Of 4.3 million men serving in the Red Army in June 1941 and the tens of thousands of others that had joined the ranks afterward, almost 3 million were prisoners of the Germans, probably history's largest roundup of prisoners in so brief a time, and countless hordes had been killed or wounded or had simply wandered away from the battle. While conscription could refill the ranks, it could not replace training and experience. The great Russian tank armies—some fifty divisions—had been all but obliterated. The 54th Army before Moscow had one tank division but no tanks; the 21st Army had only 8 percent of normal strength in its rifle divisions; hardly any division, which normally contained 16,000 men, had more than 7,000, and many were down to 5,000 and even 2,000 men. The fate of Moscow hinged upon those forces hurrying down the Trans-Siberian Railroad.

The next evening, the twenty-fourth anniversary of the birth of the Soviet Union, party and government officials gathered at the Bolshoi Theater for the annual performance in honor of the October Revolution of *Swan Lake*. Only forty-three members of the Moscow Symphony Orchestra were on hand; only twenty-seven members of the ballet. Many of the boxes that in happier times had been filled by the leaders of the Bolshevik Revolution were empty, and the house was less than half full. Twice flights of Heinkel 111s flying down the Moscow River on reconnaissance interrupted the performance, and on a score of occasions the chandeliers guttered and tinkled from the concussion of antiaircraft artillery. There was no champagne afterward, for the members of the audience left hurriedly for their holes in the ground.

Yet when the people awoke the next morning, something occurred that to many demonstrated that Stalin had been right in compromising state ideology with the divinity. The wintry dawn twilight was yellow. That was the sign that the high-altitude winds from beyond the Aral Sea that brought the winter had arrived. That year Caulaincourt's memoirs, Field Marshal von Kluge's weather bible, was wrong. The winds came not late in the month; in the year of Bolshevism's supreme peril, the winds came early.


Adolf Hitler was supremely confident that he was about to accomplish the supreme goal of his existence: the extermination of the Marxist world view. The first reports from the drive on Moscow were exhilarating. He could even take confidence in the British and American reaction to the invasion of Russia: although they had proclaimed their intent to help Russia, so slow was the flow of supplies that it was almost as if both nations had adopted a policy of implied neutrality.

The time had come, Hitler decided, to speak to the German people. As he reached Berlin from a spartan headquarters established in the pine forests of East Prussia near Rastenberg, his reception enhanced his sense of mission and confidence. There had been no need for block wardens to bring out the people to greet their Führer; they came of their own free will and lined the streets. "It was the same atmosphere as at the most wonderful of our meetings during the years of struggle." In his speech at the Sportspalast on October 3, 1941, he spoke of the New Order he had created in Europe, of how he had unified Western Europe, Eastern Europe, Scandinavia, and of how Japan had "come closer" to Germany. "Unhappily," he said, "not the nation I have courted all my life: the British. Not that the British people as a whole bear the responsibility for this, but there are some people who in their pigheaded hatred and lunacy have sabotaged every such attempt at an understanding between us, with the support of that international enemy known to us all, international Jewry." He had tried through the years, he said, "to achieve understanding whatever the cost," but there was always Mr. Churchill, "who kept on shouting, 'I want a war!' Well, now he has it." [12]

A few days later, Hitler issued an order to the army group commander before Moscow, Field Marshal von Bock, forbidding him to accept Moscow's surrender. As he had earlier remarked, he intended to raze both Moscow and Leningrad, to remove both cities from the maps and replace them with gigantic reservoirs. Both were to be encircled and pummeled by artillery and air strikes to ease the final task of demolition, but avenues of escape were to be left for the people so that in their flight they might add to the disintegration of the Bolshevik system.

As the panic that had hit Moscow in mid-October 1941 subsided, more than a hundred thousand civilians, mostly women, worked in round-the-clock shifts to dig mile after mile of trenches and antitank ditches, to string barbed wire, to build pillboxes, while other workers denuded some 500 factories of their equipment and hauled it eastward by train, by truck, by oxcart toward the Urals and Siberia. Proclamations from the Great Stalin flooded the radio and plastered the walls of buildings, exhorting the people to fight for the survival of Mother Russia. Pilots of the Red Air Force knelt beside their planes to repeat an oath sometimes administered by an Orthodox priest, as it had been in the days of the czars and of Admiral Kolchak: "I swear to you my country and to you my native Moscow that I will fight relentlessly and destroy the Fascists." [13] So, too, the troops arriving from Siberia took an oath: "I, son of Russia, part of one nation indivisible, will fight and die to defend my capital, the capital of All-Russia, of the most Holy Russia." [14]

At the front on November 15, 1941, men of the Red Army crouched in their slit trenches in snow-covered fields as tanks of the 4th Panzer Army attacked toward the little town of Klin, a nondescript halt on the railway to Leningrad, forty-eight miles northwest of Moscow. The Red Army's losses were appalling: the 17th Cavalry Division, fighting as infantry, began the battle with 3,218 men; at dusk, only 790 were left. Three infantry divisions were "no longer in touch with Army HQ," a euphemism masking their extermination or disintegration. Klin fell, as did another railroad town, Solnech-Nogorsk, only thirty miles from Moscow. Zhukov's northwestern front was caving in, and unlike the defenses west of Moscow, there were no second and third lines. "It gets worse," Zhukov reported to Stalin by telephone, "from hour to hour." [15]

It was much the same to the southwest of the capital. There German tanks and infantry lapped up against the old city of Tula, the southern gateway to the capital, made an attack as if to take the city, then suddenly lunged and took another of those small but vital railway towns, a little place called Mikhailov. The German strategy was becoming clear: in addition to hitting the capital directly from the west, the Germans were sending pincers to north and south to encircle it.

Field Marshal von Bock, a victim of severe abdominal pains brought on by the stress of command, gave his orders from his command vehicle, lying on his back with a hot-water bottle between his breeches and his stomach. Beginning at five o'clock on the morning of December 1, 1941, while aircraft and artillery pummeled Russian positions, he sent von Kluge's 4th Army in a final break-through attack against the Mozhaisk Line along the shortest route to Red Square: down the Minsk-Moscow highway. Although von Kluge's infantry, supported by tanks and assault guns, chewed two miles out of the Russian defenses, the conditions of combat were almost impossible for man to endure. Temperatures were below minus 30 degrees; snow squalls hampered visibility; tank turrets froze; lubricating oil in artillery pieces froze; even antifreeze in vehicles froze. Many a man went mad from the cold, yet men still fought.

On the next day, December 2, 1941, a mixed unit made up of the 258th Infantry Division and the 2nd Panzer Division pushed beyond Klin and, virtually unopposed, reached the vicinity of Khimki, the northern suburb of the capital, only twelve miles from the Kremlin, the place, where rumor had it, two German tanks had appeared in October; the rumor had helped set off the *bolshoi drap*. A patrol from the 258th Infantry Division probed forward into the suburb. As a member of the patrol, Heinrich Haape, recalled it:

> There was deathly silence all around. In front of us lay the tramway shelter, and the telegraph poles silently pointed the way to the great city beyond the curtain of snow.
> 'Let's walk across and have a look at that tramway station,' Kageneck said. 'Then we can tell Neuhoff that we were only a tram ride from Moscow.'
> We walked silently down the road to the stone shed. There was not a movement around us as we stopped and stared at the wooden seats on which thousands of Muscovites had sat and waited for the tram to clang down the road to Moscow.

Reaching into a wooden bin on the wall of the shelter, the men pulled out handfuls of used tramway tickets. Pocketing some of them as souvenirs, they trudged back to their scout car. "Fischer turned the car round and we headed back along the white road. The snow was coming down a little more heavily now."

"It must fall," said Kageneck. Then he added: "Yet I wonder." [16]

# EPILOGUE

## One

In that first fortnight of December 1941, three great events in world affairs occurred on three consecutive days: the 6th, the 7th, and because of the time difference imposed by the international dateline, the 8th. On the 6th, giving substance to the doubts that the German soldier, Kageneck, expressed in the snow at the tramway station outside Moscow, the Red Army began a powerful counteroffensive that was to stop the German Army at the very gates of Moscow and in the end assure the survival of the Soviet Union and its emergence as a world superpower. On the 7th, the Japanese attacked the U.S. naval base at Pearl Harbor, which was destined to awaken the sleeping giant and in the end assure the collapse of the dream of a Japanese empire, enable the western democracies to prevail over Fascist Italy and Nazi Germany, help Russia to survive, and assure the emergence of the United States as—at least for a time—the world's foremost power. And on the 8th, Japanese troops landed on the Malay peninsula in Southeast Asia to seal the fate of Singapore, the island bastion of the British Empire at the tip of the peninsula, marking the symbolic end of the British Empire and leaving the empire, like France, no longer a major factor in world affairs.

For the Comintern, the onset of global war would mark the beginning of an end of sorts. Stalin had already changed it from an instrument for promoting the world revolution of the proletariat to a device for defense of the Soviet Union, and with the entry of the United States into the war, Stalin saw the Comintern as expendable, something that might be sacrificed to influence American policy.

Yet whatever the shifts in the objectives of the Comintern—or even if Stalin should choose to do away with it—there was one field in which Comintern agents would continue to function as they always had. That field was espionage, and if the Soviet Union were to achieve the status its leader demanded, the Comintern had to help Russia get the secrets of the atomic bomb. That meant a shift in emphasis from operations in Western Europe to North America. Which was just as well in any case, for under German vigilance, there were dire happenings to the Comintern's *apparats* in Western Europe.

.   .   .

611

In the summer of 1941, the German radio intelligence interception service in Berlin picked up a powerful illegal transmitter operating somewhere in Western Europe, apparently in Belgium. In November 1941, the intelligence service of the German General Staff, the Abwehr, sent to Brussels an expert in radio goniometry, Henry Peipe, who began a direction-finding operation, and gradually narrowed down the location of the transmitter to a house in the rue des Attrebates. On December 13, 1941, Peipe's men raided the house even as the radio operator, a Red Army intelligence lieutenant, Anton Danilov, was transmitting to the Center in Moscow. Although Danilov put up a fight and tried to kill himself by diving out an attic window, he was seriously injured and soon cornered.

The man who had been instrumental in establishing the intelligence networks based on the Foreign Excellent Raincoat Company, Leopold Trepper, escaped the German raid and in May of 1942 established a new communications post in a house in the district of Laeken. He chose the site because it was near an electric railroad, whose current confused the radiogoniometrical detection devices used by the Germans; but the detection expert, Peipe, brought in a mobile detection unit powerful enough not to be affected by the interference from the railroad and finally pinned down the location.

At three o'clock in the morning of June 29, 1942, Peipe and his agents struck. Breaking into the house, they found the transmitter still warm, but the operator escaped through an attic window onto the roof, where he blazed away with two pistols at Peipe's men in the street below. Leaping from rooftop to rooftop, the fugitive finally reached the end of the block; with nowhere else to go, he smashed a dormer window and disappeared into the last house. When Peipe and his agents entered the house, they discovered him cowering beneath an overturned bathtub in the basement. "He was a short, stocky, hard-featured man, about forty years old," Peipe would note later, "terribly working class."[1]

Peipe routinely committed the man to St. Gilles Prison, but when he reported to headquarters of the Abwehr the man's name—Johannes Wenzel, a German graduate of the Lenin School in Moscow—orders came back immediately to send him to Berlin. "You've caught one of the most prominent members of the prewar German Communist Party," Abwehr headquarters informed Peipe, "one of the chiefs of the Comintern's underground apparatus." As Peipe sent Wenzel off to Berlin, he noted that Wenzel was "out of his mind with fear, for obviously the *Gestapo* had old scores to settle with him." Under torture, he revealed all; and when next Peipe saw him in Brussels, he was hardly to be recognized, "a broken man."

Through a combination of the information obtained as a result of the two raids, the Abwehr had the keys to information carefully hidden in its files: folder after folder containing the coded messages that had been transmitted over the months from Brussels to Moscow. One of those messages, dated October 18, 1941, instructed Trepper's assistant, Victor Sukolov, when next in Berlin, to call on Harro Schulze-Boysen, the head of one of the two networks making up the intelligence organization which the Germans called collectively the Rote Kapelle, someone whom the Abwehr knew at the time only as a member of the aristocracy, an intimate of Reichsmarschall Hermann Göring, and the head of Luftwaffe counterintelligence. The Abwehr placed Schulze-Boysen under special surveillance, and even though agents had already searched Johannes Wenzel's apartment in Brussels while he was being interrogated, they went back again. That time they found an uncoded message, which had apparently been sent from Germany to Wenzel by courier, which gave precise details of a Luftwaffe operation to employ some 2,500 Junkers 52 transport aircraft to supply a beleagurered German 6th Army at Stalingrad. Only three people at Luftwaffe headquarters knew that a shortage of gasoline was the cause of the delay. The message gave precise details about the operation, including the fact that a shortage of gasoline was postponing its start.

The head of the Nazi Party's security service, the Sicherheitsdienst, Reichsführer-SS Himmler, and the head of the Luftwaffe, Reichsmarschall Göring, personally supervised the police investigation that followed. Schulze-Boysen was arrested on August 30, 1942, and after him 118 more prisoners were seized, including the leaders of all the component parts of Schulze-Boysen's *apparat*. They constituted virtually a shadow administration, including twenty-nine students and academicians, twenty government officials, twenty-one artists, writers, and journalists, and seventeen officers and men of the armed services, including a member of the German General Staff, Erwin Gehrts. There were also several who were prominent in society, including the Countess Erika von Brockdorff.

It was a serious blow to the Rote Kapelle, one that Nazi officials at the time saw as lethal, but that would fail to be the case. There was the other branch, that headed by Dr. David Harnack, and there were lesser members of Schulze-Boysen's group who remained at large. The Rote Kapelle was destined to survive the war and eventually to penetrate the postwar German secret intelligence service, the German government, and an international alliance created to oppose Communist expansion, the North Atlantic Treaty Organization.

As the Abwehr first began to move against the intelligence network in Brussels, Leopold Trepper fled to Paris, where he came under control of the Soviet military attaché with orders to build up an organization in France to obtain military intelligence. Trepper's principal assistants were Leon Grossvogel, the founder of the Foreign Excellent Raincoat Company, and a former Comintern agent in Palestine, Hillel Katz, who served as Trepper's secretary. Under an alias, Jean Gilbert, Trepper established a firm known as Simexco, which specialized in import and export operations in support of contracts arising from the German occupation; the firm dealt extensively, for example, with Organization Todt, a paramilitary German construction amalgam building formidable defenses, the Atlantic Wall. Having direct contact with the Germans, the firm's employees (Trepper's agents) were exposed to considerable military information and were free to move about in ordinarily restricted areas. Trepper himself established a reputation as "a solid businessman" who was "a welcomed and much respected personage in the Paris and Brussels business worlds." He soon controlled seven *réseaux* (intelligence nets) operating throughout France, including one headed by Leon Grossvogel's brother, André; another by Trepper's former assistant in Brussels, Victor Sukolov; and another by the Comintern official who had formerly headed Soviet intelligence in London, Henri Robinson.

As a corollary of the raids that netted Danilov, Wenzel, and Schulze-Boysen, the Germans in November 1942 decided that Simexco in Paris was involved in espionage. They seized the company and made wholesale arrests, but most of the officials, including "Jean Gilbert," eluded them. Through one captured official, the Sicherheitsdienst nevertheless learned that Gilbert had earlier asked the address of a dentist in the rue de Rivoli, located the dentist, and determined that a M. Gilbert had an appointment at 2:00 P.M. on December 5, 1942, and staked out the offices. Trepper was arrested as he sat in the dentist's chair.

At his first interrogation, he offered to collaborate fully with the Germans, to include exposing the entire Soviet intelligence network in France and participating in a *Funkspiel* (radio game) to feed false intelligence information to Moscow. Although he would name all his assistants, agents, and informants, some of them—whom Trepper himself proposed to designate—were to remain at large to give verisimilitude to the *Funkspiel*. He was eager to participate in the game, Trepper told his captors, for if it succeeded, the Germans would have to conceal the fact of his arrest from the Russians, thereby sparing his wife and child, who were in Russia, from retaliation by Soviet authorities.

To give evidence of his sincerity, Trepper betrayed his secretary, Hillel Katz, who, when arrested, also offered his services. Satisfied of Trepper's sincerity by that betrayal, the Sicherheitsdienst—with the specific approval of Himmler— agreed to the *Funkspiel*. It began on Christmas Day 1942 and would continue through mid-September 1943. (Among those whom Trepper exposed but did not ask to be left at large were his good friend Leon Grossvogel and the veteran Comintern agent Henri Robinson. Both men offered their services to the Germans but were said to have eventually been executed.)

To the Germans, the capture and defection of Trepper represented an intelligence coup, but what they failed to realize was that Trepper was, from all indications, a triple agent. Following the Abwehr's raids in Brussels, he obviously would have been concerned about his own safety, and in the time before his arrest, he would have had ample time to work out a plan with the Center in Moscow for a triple-cross. Two or three weeks after being arrested, Trepper told his Belgian acquaintance Claude Spaak that he was able to pass to the Center, through one of his agents whom he had failed to name to the Germans, a detailed account of his arrest and his plans.

To make absolutely certain that the Center would accept nothing that he sent as truth, Trepper persuaded the Germans that if he were to continue to be accepted by the Center, he would have to go on making his usual "recognition meetings," a system whereby an agent periodically demonstrates that he is safe, well, and reliable by appearing at a prearranged time and place to show his person to his controllers. Since it was to the Germans' advantage that no suspicions about Trepper arise in Moscow, they agreed, whereupon Trepper began to make his recognition meetings at the Pharmacie Bailly near the Gare St. Lazare. At one of those meetings, according to what Trepper told Claude Spaak, he provided a detailed account of the *Funkspiel* to a female agent whom he had not betrayed, possibly his former mistress, New York dancer Georgie de Winter.

Yet if Trepper was indeed a triple agent, to what gain for the Russians? Trusted by the Germans, he might obtain considerable information to be passed by surviving agents, yet that would appear to be of minor benefit in view of the fact that his preservation required the sacrifice of several hundred—perhaps as many as a thousand—agents and informers, virtually the entire intelligence network in France. What mattered more was the fact that by the time Trepper began to play his *Funkspiel,* the major military crisis had passed in Russia, leaving Stalin with little doubt that the Soviet Union would eventually triumph, so that by that time it was of less importance to protect the intelligence networks in Western Europe, whose day-to-day information had ceased to be critical, than it was to preserve the political underground that was to emerge, once the war was over, to help transmit Communism throughout Europe. The everyday operatives thus were expendable in order to deflect German counterintelligence resources from the operatives that mattered in the long run, the political underground. As it turned out, Trepper himself would survive, eventually escape from the Germans, and when the war ended, return to Moscow and like many another who loyally served the cause, enter Lubyanka prison.

On May 15, 1943, meeting in Moscow, the Communist International's Presidium dissolved the Communist International. There was no explanation for it, merely a statement in *Pravda* several days later announcing that the Comintern had been dissolved "as the directing centre of the international working class movement" and that foreign Communist parties were thus freed "from their obligations arising from the statutes and resolutions of the congresses of the Communist International." The dissolution, declared Stalin a few days later, "exposes the lie of the Hitlerites to the effect 'Moscow' allegedly intends to intervene in the life of other nations" and "exposes the calumny of the adversaries of Communism within the labour movement to the effect that Communist parties in various countries are allegedly acting not in the interests of their people but on orders from outside."[2]

Born in fiery rhetoric and weaned in almost a quarter-century of existence on dissimulation and criminality, the Comintern thus expired in obfuscation. Most western geopoliticians would come to believe that the name and bureaucracy of the Comintern had indeed been dissolved but that its functions and its objective—

world revolution of the proletariat—had been transferred to the Foreign Department of the NKVD and that as soon as the Grand Alliance of Great Britain, the Soviet Union, and the United States had served its purpose with the saving of the Soviet Union and the defeat of Germany, conspiracy would begin again. In any event, in the relations of the foreign Communist parties with Moscow, the dissolution of the Comintern made little difference; those parties "remained as they had always been—faithful, reliable, devoted servants of the Soviet Union, ready to carry out any duty which might seem to serve its interests, even to the point of self-destruction."[3]

It would be assumed that Stalin timed the dissolution to coincide with a meeting of Roosevelt and Churchill in Washington to debate the great decision of the war in Western Europe: where and when the Anglo-American armies were to invade the Continent. Stalin may have hoped that by removing the principal irritant in his relations with the United States and the British Empire—the Comintern—he might encourage the Allied leaders to move quickly to open a second front in France.

It was early apparent that the dissolution of the Comintern would bring no end to Soviet meddling, particularly in regard to states bordering on the Soviet Union. As early as 1943, it was clear from a survey of the Communist press in the United States, conducted by the OSS, successor agency to the Coordinator of Information, that in the postwar world, the question of the Baltic States would not be open to "discussion or bargaining"; that Finland would not again be allowed to serve as a base for attack on Russia; that only governments of neighboring Rumania, Hungary, and Poland that were friendly to the Soviet Union would be allowed to exist; that any future German government would be molded to assure that never again would Germany attack Russia; and that Russia would "prefer" similar governments in Bulgaria, Yugoslavia, Albania, and Czechoslovakia."[4]

That long-term Soviet international policy remained revolutionary was verified in 1944 when American military intelligence intercepted an instruction to the American Communist Party from the head of the NKVD, Lavrenti P. Beria, denouncing the Atlantic Charter, which Roosevelt and Churchill had adopted in August 1941 and to which the Soviet Union, desperate for help against Nazi Germany, had promptly acceded. Both the Atlantic Charter and the United Nations Declaration that followed from it renounced territorial aggrandizement, opposed territorial changes made against the wishes of the population, restored sovereign rights and self-government to those forcibly deprived of them, and recommended adoption of other social, political, and economic understandings that might be expected to remove the causes of war.

"It is the intention of the People of the Soviet Union," wrote Beria, "that no such provisions shall be imposed upon the Government of the Soviets or on any other people for that matter." The NKVD advised all foreign Communist parties, once the victory was won, to return to the policies earlier laid down by the Communist International. Those parties that did so would "be supported to the fullest extent of the Power still left to the [Soviet] Union."[5]

Once Germany was defeated, the Soviet Union thus intended to resume operations designed to achieve the world revolution of the proletariat; and that required that the Soviet Union be strong, which meant continuing and even stepping up the program of espionage aimed at obtaining the secrets of the new advanced weapons—particularly the secrets of the atomic bomb—upon which Russia expected the United States and Britain to base their postwar military systems. That program would produce what would be called "the steal of the century."[6]

## Two

In 1934, Peter Leonidovich Kapitsa, the son of a czarist general of engineers, was conducting research at the Cavendish Laboratories at Cambridge University on an expansion engine that liquefied helium. A scientist of such brilliance that he had become the first foreigner in two centuries to be elected a fellow of the Royal Society, Kapitsa received an invitation to attend a scientific conference in Moscow and accepted, but when the time came to return to England, Soviet authorities at Stalin's personal direction seized his passport and refused to allow him to leave. The next year he was made head of the Institute of Physical Problems of the Academy of Sciences of the USSR, provided a large flat in Moscow, a dacha, two cars, two chauffeurs, and such other accoutrements as were afforded the Soviet élite, and went to work on experiments to find temperature's absolute zero, that stage of refrigeration at which the thermal motion of atoms is slowed to the point where the scientist can observe their structure.

Despite that evidence of interest in nuclear research, Russian science by 1939 had achieved little progress. In that year, a Soviet scientist, A. I. Brodsky, published a paper on what would prove to be one of the key problems in making an atomic bomb—the separation of uranium isotopes. Soon thereafter, two other Russian scientists, G. N. Flerov and a certain Petrzhak, working under the leading Soviet nuclear physicist, Igor Kurchatov, discovered spontaneous fission. But when the American scientific journal *Physical Review*, on July 1, 1940, published their report on their findings, "the complete lack of any American response . . . was one of the factors which convinced the Russians that there must be a big secret project under way in the United States."[1]

Early in 1942, Flerov wrote to the Communist Party's highest war policy organization, the State Defense Committee, of which Stalin was chairman, to urge that "no time must be lost in making a uranium bomb," and to Kurchatov he noted that "urgent top secret work" on atomic bombs was under way in both Germany and the United States.[2] Yet, not until February 1943, after victory at Stalingrad, would Stalin allocate resources for a program to develop an atomic bomb, and at no time during the war years did he commit anywhere near the resources that the United States and Britain allotted. The total number of physicists said to have been involved was about twenty (against 1,500 in the

United States), and the total staff at the main laboratory never exceeded fifty.

Yet there was another way to obtain the secrets of the atomic bomb: steal them, and to that program Stalin committed infinite resources. The NKVD and the Comintern launched a greatly expanded industrial intelligence attack in the United States, with primary reliance on the Comintern's "government in being" in Washington, including Apparats A and B, which had been established by the American underground Communist chieftain, Jacob Golos, and a senior NKVD officer, Gaik Ovakiminian, masquerading as an official of the Soviet trading corporation, Amtorg. The Four Continents Book Corporation also played a part, combing the government, the press, and the publishing world, the universities and the libraries, for American publications in the field; and behind those organizations stood the Soviet military, diplomatic, and consular services, along with selected individuals among some 1,800 Soviet bureaucrats and technicians who entered the United States in conjunction with administration of the multimillion-dollar American aid program to Russia. Thus, as the military chief of the atomic bomb project, Major General Leslie R. Groves, would note, the program encountered "the most serious espionage activity," not from the enemy but from an ally, the Soviet Union, and Soviet agents, pleading "that the American government was withholding from them important information and thus delaying Allied victory . . . experienced little difficulty in recruiting many native Communists and fellow-travelers" to assist them in their intelligence attack.[3]

The most prominent of those who were alleged to have helped was the vice-president of the United States, Henry Wallace, who in a subsequent run for the presidency with Communist support would campaign for a closer relationship with Russia at the expense of the "special relationship" with Britain. According to the allegation, which originated with the counsel to the House Committee on Un-American Activities, Jay Sourwine, Wallace, while a member of the Top Policy Group, which supervised the atomic development program, furnished Russia with specimens of the isotope vital to the making of a bomb, U-235.

Sourwine noted that "Henry Wallace in 1943 or 1944 met a subversive agent in Philadelphia and that the subversive agent asked Wallace for additional data on the atomic bomb. Wallace is reported to have said to the subversive agent that he had gotten the U-235 for the agent and that should be enough."[4]

Pursuing the allegation, the FBI found that Wallace had had a meeting with a Soviet agent concerning the atomic bomb in Miami in 1941 and a meeting in Philadelphia in 1943 or 1944 with two men: C. B. "Beany" Baldwin and Leo Krzycki. The FBI called Krzycki "a Security Index subject who presently lives in Milwaukee, Wisconsin," and discovered that Baldwin "had been connected with numerous Communist Party fronts and was described as a Communist by a confidential informant." Baldwin was manager of Wallace's presidential campaign in 1948.

As part of the investigation, the FBI inquired into the activities of one of Wallace's friends, Boris Pregel, a Russian-born speculator with a considerable knowledge of fissile materials who had been trying to get a corner on the uranium-mining market. A former associate of Leopold Trepper's in the Foreign Excellent Raincoat Company in Brussels, Pregel telephoned or called upon Wallace frequently while Wallace was a member of the Top Policy Group. Although the FBI accumulated a thick file on Pregel, there was nothing to connect him with a meeting with an agent in Philadelphia. "The possibilities of locating the incident [in Philadelphia]," the FBI noted in closing its file on Wallace, "on the basis of information now available have been exhausted."[5]

Another allegation of help for the Russians involved the former American military attaché in Moscow, Colonel Faymonville, and was to lead to accusations against one of Faymonville's admirers in the White House, Harry Hopkins. The War Department had recalled Faymonville and posted him far from Washington to minimize his contacts with Mrs. Roosevelt, Henry Wallace, and Hopkins, but when the White House insisted on sending him back to Moscow as Lend-Lease representative, the War Department reluctantly agreed.

Hardly had Faymonville taken up his new post in Moscow when the same kind of clashes that had featured his earlier service developed. Even aside from his reputation, the seeds of friction were there, for with a new rank of brigadier general, he was senior to the military attaché, Colonel Joseph A. Michela; he lived apart from his colleagues in considerable comfort in the former residence of the German military attaché and had his own separate offices; the Russians clearly trusted him and catered to him in a manner denied all other western officials in Moscow; and he had private channels to the highest authorities in Washington, a privilege he was inclined to flaunt.

General Faymonville increased his circle of enemies when in late 1941 he supported Russian complaints about the amount of war materials reaching the Soviet Union from the United States. To Lend-Lease officials in Washington, he maintained that even though the Russians were doing most of the fighting against Germany, it was the British who were receiving the bulk of the American war materials. When the American ambassador, Admiral William H. Standley, learned of Faymonville's complaint, he called him to the Embassy. "You," he declared, "are not worthy of wearing the uniform you have on." To which Faymonville responded: "You mean that I am a traitor?" Standley: "That's just about what I mean."[6]

Others in the American colony held similar views. A member of the Embassy staff, Alexander Kirk, said that "You can't talk to Faymonville about Russia any more than you can talk to a man about his mother." A member of the military attaché's staff, Major Clinton Olson, declared that "Faymonville had ceased to be a soldier of the United States,"[7] a view shared by Colonel Michela. In Washington, Colonel Yeaton, then head of the Russian Section of the Military Intelligence Division, wondered if Faymonville's conduct was not the result of blackmail.

When Admiral Standley protested directly to President Roosevelt that Faymonville was giving the Russians "everything in the world they ask for, from a darning needle to a tire factory,"[8] the U.S. Army's chief of staff, General George C. Marshall, directed his chief of intelligence, Major General George V. Strong, to investigate Faymonville's conduct. In a thirty-five-page report, Strong noted that "General Faymonville is regarded by almost every American in Russia as pro-Soviet." While the report contained nothing sufficient to justify a court-martial, it was enough to prompt Marshall to order Faymonville home. Reduced to his permanent rank of colonel, he was relegated to an ordnance post in Arkansas, but he made occasional visits to Washington, where he met with Vice-President Wallace and such anti-British, pro-Russian State Department officials as Owen Lattimore and Lauchlin Currie, both of whom were to figure in investigations into subversion in government.

Lattimore and Currie would try to obtain Faymonville's appointment to accompany the vice-president on a mission to Siberia and China, but when Wallace approached General Marshall about it, "The General went straight up in the air. He said that Faymonville was a representative of the Russians, not of the United States." When Wallace went beyond Marshall to the president himself, Roosevelt said that "Marshall felt that Faymonville was a traitor" and that "Faymonville stood pretty low in the Army" at the time, so that "it would probably be best" not to include him in the mission.[9]

Only after the war ended would the principal allegation against Faymonville emerge. Two of the officers who had served with him in Moscow charged that through Harry Hopkins, Faymonville arranged to send the Russians specimens of uranium ore and salts and technical data related to the development of an atomic bomb. Faymonville maintained that he was justified in that the Russians needed the material and the information, that the United States was sharing its knowledge with Britain, and that Russia was as much an ally as was Britain. Investigating the charge, the counterespionage branch of the Army headquarters providing administrative support for the atomic bomb project, the Manhattan District, could find no evidence of Wallace's having provided data but did determine that the raw materials were shipped from the Lend-Lease air base at Great Falls, Montana, allegedly on the personal orders of Harry Hopkins. Yet it would be difficult to prove any offense in law, for the raw materials were at the time not under export prohibition.

Yet another case involved the scientific director of the atomic bomb project, J. Robert Oppenheimer.

When Oppenheimer and his associates determined that a special facility had to be built for going beyond the experimental stages to the actual development of the bomb, he himself selected the site of a boys' school, the Los Alamos Ranch School, on an isolated mesa about forty miles northwest of Santa Fe, New Mexico, there in time to found a scientific community based upon "the spirit of Athens, of

Plato, of an ideal republic." To the remote site came the best scientific minds of Britain and the United States to accomplish "the greatest single achievement of organized human effort in history."[10]

A brilliant man, Oppenheimer read Sanskrit and Dante, quoted from Proust and Dostoevsky. He was also a man of strong liberal bent, and the U.S. Army's Counter-Intelligence Corps soon had a thick file on his extensive prewar association with Communists in California, including the party organizer in San Francisco and later in Alameda County, Steve Nelson, and with the front groups that under Willi Muenzenberg's direction from Comintern headquarters in Paris sprang up at the time of the Spanish Civil War. The Counter-Intelligence Corps concluded that Oppenheimer was a dangerous security risk.

Yet the FBI determined, contrary to that finding, that "Oppenheimer [had] been inactive as a Communist Party member since commencing his work at Radiation Laboratory [Berkeley], and Communist Party executives [did not] consider him a Party member or as being a reliable source of information for the benefit of the Communist Party." Both the FBI and the Counter-Intelligence Corps nevertheless continued close surveillance and in 1943 determined that a former student of Oppenheimer's and an employee at Los Alamos, Joseph Woodrow Weinberg, had passed to Nelson what General Groves described as "the object and progress of the project, materials and means used, and the location of other installations engaged in [the project]."[11] FBI agents learned that Nelson passed the information on April 6, 1943, to the Soviet vice-consul in San Francisco, Peter Ivanov, and telephone taps showed that Ivanov in turn passed it to Vasili Zarubin, ostensibly third secretary of the Soviet Embassy in Washington but actually the head of the NKVD in North America. Weinberg was removed from the project, drafted into the Army, and posted to Alaska.

The incident prompted an agent of the Counter-Intelligence Corps, Boris Pash, to seek an interview with Oppenheimer. According to Pash's report of a meeting in Berkeley on August 26, 1943, Oppenheimer revealed that since the Soviet Union was an ally in the war, he favored giving atomic information to the Russians, but he said it should be done officially through the president. Of his own association with Communists and the Communist Party, he said that he "felt quite strongly that any association with the Communist movement was not compatible with the job of a secret war project, that the two loyalties just could not go together."[12] Already, said Oppenheimer, members of the Communist Party in California had approached him to provide information about the atomic bomb.

As Oppenheimer told the story to Pash, an employee of the Soviet Consulate in San Francisco (it turned out to be Ivanov, who was handling Oppenheimer's associate, Weinberg) approached an Englishman, George Charles Eltenton, who was employed by the Shell Development Laboratory at Emeryville, California, and was a Communist. Ivanov told Eltenton that "a staggering financial reward would be possible for anybody arranging to secure data on the secret work being done at the Radiation Laboratory."[13] Ivanov at first suggested that Eltenton approach

Oppenheimer with such a proposal, but when Eltenton replied that he did not know Oppenheimer well enough for that, Ivanov suggested that Eltenton enlist a Communist friend of Oppenheimer's, Haakon Chevalier. Chevalier apparently agreed, for while he and Oppenheimer were alone in the kitchen of Oppenheimer's home in Eagle Hill in Berkeley, mixing martinis, "Chevalier told Oppenheimer that Eltenton was interested in obtaining details of the work at the Radiation Laboratory and the work being planned or executed elsewhere in atomic installations." Eltenton had methods, said Chevalier, of sending that kind of information to Russia "secretly and safely." [14]

According to Oppenheimer, he used "strong words" in telling Chevalier that what he proposed was "treason" or "close to treason." [15] Yet as Oppenheimer continued to talk to Pash, he began to equivocate about his own story. Before the interview was over, he insisted that he had invented the story, that there had been no such contact. On a subsequent journey by train across the country to Washington in company with General Groves, he refused to talk about Chevalier; he had exaggerated the incident, he said, under the stress of a security interview.

In the end, the FBI concluded that Oppenheimer was "potentially dangerous to the United States since there was no certainty that he had permanently changed his sympathies or separated himself from his Communist Party associations"; but the FBI made no recommendation that he be relieved of his post. He was "indispensable to the project due to his ability in physics," and if kept on, "he would further separate himself from his Communist associations due to a feeling of responsibility which went with his position." [16]

When the war was over, Oppenheimer himself would corroborate some of the allegations against him. Until 1936, he said, he was "so naive regarding political matters that he wouldn't even vote," but beginning in 1936, when he was stirred emotionally by the Spanish Civil War antinazi sentiments, and extending into 1939, he "engaged in political matters in an amateurish way." His interest in Communism, he said, was confined to a desire to learn what "they proposed as a panacea for governmental ills of the United States." His brother, Frank, Frank's wife, and his own wife, Katherine, were all members of the party, he said, but although he had "at least an academic interest in the organization," he had never attended a closed meeting of the party, had never knowingly contributed funds to the party, had never been invited to join the party, and "never at any time was a dues-paying Communist" or otherwise a member of the party. He broke with the front groups, he said, because of cumulative "disgust" over Stalin's purge and the signing of the Nazi-Soviet Nonaggression Pact of 1939. [17]

In late 1953, while Oppenheimer was serving as chairman of the General Advisory Committee of the Atomic Energy Commission, a security hearing would determine that he was not guilty of treason but that he was a security risk and thus should have no access to military secrets, a ruling against which scientists around the world protested. In 1963, President Lyndon B. Johnson would, in effect, exonerate Oppenheimer by presenting him the prestigious Fermi Award of the Atomic Energy Commission.

## Three

When with the help of the Comintern relief organization, International Red Aid, the young physicist Emil Julius Klaus Fuchs escaped Nazi Germany and began graduate study at Bristol University in England, he openly joined Communist front organizations. Although the German consul in Bristol warned the local police that Fuchs was wanted in Germany as a Communist subversive, the police, on the theory that the word of the German consul was not to be trusted, took little notice. When in 1937 Fuchs left Bristol for further study at Edinburgh University, he continued to attend meetings of Communist front groups. It was at that time that he worked with a group of German refugees headed by Jürgen Kuczynski, the brother of Ursula Hamburger, at one time the controller of the Rote Drei in Switzerland; with Kuczynski's group, Fuchs engaged in underground activities in support of the German Communist Party.

In May 1940, British security authorities detained Fuchs as an enemy alien and sent him by ship to Canada, where he was interned, first at a center near Quebec known as Camp L, then at another near Montreal known as Camp N. Soon after Fuchs arrived at Camp L, a Comintern representative, Israel Halperin, visited him and began providing him with cigarettes and scientific magazines. Halperin also conveyed letters between Fuchs and his sister, Kristel Heinemann, who was then married to a scientist doing postgraduate work at Harvard.

Because of the insistence of scientific colleagues in Britain that Fuchs was too valuable to languish in a detention camp, he spent only a few months in Canada. Returned to Britain, he was released in January 1941 and at first went back to Edinburgh University for "non-secret academic work."[1] While he was so engaged, the British Security Service conducted an exhaustive security check on him as a preliminary to his beginning work in the atomic energy program at Birmingham University. Although the Security Service uncovered the warning of the German consul to the Bristol police and the association in Canada with Halperin, Fuchs was so strongly antinazi that the authorities expressed little concern. The enemy was not Russia but Germany.

Fuchs soon began work with a section of the highly secret atomic project headed by a renowned German-born, British-naturalized physicist, Rudolf Peierls. Having known Fuchs in Germany, Professor Peierls exacted from him a promise that while working for the British government, he would take no part in Communist activities. Fuchs agreed and began work with Peierls on the control of a diffusion cascade.

When Fuchs moved on to work in producing fissile materials, Professor Peierls, warning him that he was engaged in work vital to producing an atomic bomb, again exacted a promise to avoid Communist contacts and maintain the utmost secrecy. Yet when Hitler invaded Russia, Fuchs came to the conclusion that his duty lay not to Britain but to the greater cause of world Communism. Visiting London, he told Kuczynski that he wanted "to furnish information to the Soviet Union." Kuczynski put him in touch with a man whom Fuchs knew only as Alexander but who was the secretary to the Soviet military attaché in London, Simon Davidovitch Kremer. Fuchs met Alexander three times, including one occasion at the Soviet Embassy in Kensington Palace Gardens, and at each meeting provided Alexander with "written information concerning his work on atomic energy research" and handed over papers he had prepared in connection with the work.[2]

When Alexander became concerned—with reason—that he was being watched by British authorities, he feared that Fuchs might be comprised and turned him over to another contact, a woman, whose name Fuchs never learned. They met six times at Banbury, a market town between London and Birmingham, site of the Banbury Cross of nursery rhyme, where Fuchs provided additional information. As he would later note, his aim "was to aid in promoting atomic research and development in and for the advantage of the Soviet Union."[3]

Following a decision by Churchill and Roosevelt in May 1943 to combine the resources of Britain and the United States to produce an atomic bomb, Fuchs learned that he was to go to the United States as a senior member of a thirteen-man British mission. When he told his contact in Banbury about the assignment, she provided detailed instructions on how to contact a man who would be his controller in the United States.

Arriving in the United States on December 3, 1943, Fuchs and his scientific colleagues were briefed in Washington, then went to New York to join the staff of the British Mission. He soon began work, on the basis of his British security clearance, at the Kellex Corporation, a branch of the Kellogg Corporation involved in the Manhattan project. Fuchs's work clearly involved segments of the atomic program that would be of importance to any power only just starting out on a program. Thus as he set forth to meet his controller at the corner of Henry and Market streets on the Lower East Side, the Comintern's finest hour had begun.

In 1939, the most productive agent in Apparat B, Harry Gold, became disillusioned. He told his controllers that he was disgusted by Stalin's alliance with Hitler and by the intraparty warfare between the Stalinists and the Trotskyites; he had no wish, he said, to be associated with "gangsters."[4] On instructions, the man who had brought Gold into the party, Thomas Black, tried to change Gold's thinking, but with only lukewarm success. Gold's controllers thereupon ceased to call on him for industrial espionage assignments, allowing him to go about his ordinary business with the warning that if he talked, his employers would be informed of his party activities. For about eighteen months, Gold's work as a spy was suspended, but after the Germans attacked Russia in June 1941, the head of

World Tourists and the chairman of the Central Control Commission of the American Communist Party, Jacob Golos, reactivated him. Gold's new contact, known to him only as Sam, was Semen N. Semenov, at the time employed as a purchasing agent for Machinoport, a branch of the Soviet trade agency, Amtorg, which was his cover for his real work as an agent of the NKVD specializing in industrial and technical intelligence in the United States.

From that point, Harry Gold worked not as a spy but as a courier, collecting information and material from other industrial spies, paying them, and delivering the information to Sam. Rarely paid for his services, he nevertheless appeared to be at no loss for funds. While continuing to live with his family in Philadelphia— nobody in the family knew anything of his espionage activities—he helped found the Lecap Rainwear Corporation in New York and became associated with a firm, Abraham Brothman Associates of New York, which was a clearing house for Soviet technical espionage.

Late in November or early in December 1943, Gold received another signal for a meeting with Sam. Gold, said Sam, had been selected for "extremely important work." It was to be work "of so critical a nature" that he was "to think twice and even three times" before ever speaking a word about it to anybody or before making a move.[5] At a certain date and hour, Gold was to go to the Henry Hudson Settlement, a block of workers' flats on the Lower East Side at the corner of Henry and Market streets. Wearing gloves and carrying an extra pair in his right hand, he was to look for a tall, slim, youngish man who would be carrying a tennis ball. Gold was to ask the man, "Can you tell me the way to Grand Central Station?" The man was to respond with an absurd remark about the weather: if it was cold and gray, the man would say it was a nice day, or vice versa. Gold was then to arrange to meet at the man's convenience to collect information from him. The information, said Sam, would be called "the Candy" and the man would be known in conversation only as "the Candy Man." That man was to be Klaus Fuchs.

Summoning that combination of genius, vigor, imagination, and resources that had transmuted the United States from near economic collapse to superpower status in less than five years, the United States government, with British assistance, had in 1944 established an atomic bomb project that was the largest single scientific and industrial project in history. Such was the secrecy surrounding it that all involved took an oath to mention it to no one, not even wives, and members of the senior staff were removed from society; all their families knew of their work was an address: U.S. Army Post Office Box 1663. It was the task of Sam and Gold, working through the network established by the Comintern, to penetrate that secrecy.

The first meeting between Fuchs and Gold took place as arranged, just after New Year's Day of 1944. Over a hearty meal at Manny Wolf's Chop House on Third Avenue, Fuchs described the program of the Manhattan Engineer District, identified the men he was working with, and detailed the work going on at Kellex.

Having finished dinner, they made arrangements to meet again, then parted.

Gold was thoroughly impressed with Fuchs. "There is one word, an adjective," Gold would note later, "that pretty well sums up my estimate of the man, and that word is noble."[6] Fuchs was less impressed with Gold, whom he knew only by the code name Raymond. "At all times," said Fuchs, "Raymond's attitude was that of an inferior." Yet that made little difference to Fuchs, for he was motivated by only one goal, "a desire to aid the Soviet Union."[7]

Between January and August of 1944, Fuchs met Raymond four times at different places in Manhattan and The Bronx, where he passed to him documents obviously of high value, but nevertheless reflecting the limited scope of the work going on at Kellex. If Fuchs were to provide material of the utmost value, he needed to be at some nerve center of the Manhattan Project. That happened in August 1944 when suddenly and without prior notice, Fuchs was posted to Los Alamos.

His sudden departure caught Sam and Gold by surprise. For a time they thought he might have been arrested or sent back to Britain, in which case they themselves might be in danger. They could establish at first only that he had left no forwarding address other than U.S. Army Post Office Box 1663, and they dared not risk using that. Complicating matters, Sam was suddenly replaced by John, a man with "boyish features" and "a mincing but not effeminate walk,"[8] whose real identity, an assistant Soviet consul in New York, Anatoli Antonovitch Yakovlev, Gold would never learn. After Sam introduced Gold to John, John passed to Gold information that obviously came from Israel Halperin in Canada: the name of Fuchs's sister, Kristel Heinemann, and her address in Cambridge, Massachusetts. In an effort to learn what had become of Fuchs, Gold was to contact Mrs. Heinemann.

Gold called on Mrs. Heinemann at her home just before Christmas 1944. He represented himself as one of her brother's friends and asked where he might be reached. Mrs. Heinemann said she did not know but that he planned to visit her within a few weeks. When Gold asked if he might return at that time, Mrs. Heinemann agreed. Gold played briefly with the children, chatted about a recent snowstorm in Philadelphia and about his work as research scientist, and departed.

Learning in January 1945 that Fuchs was at Mrs. Heinemann's, Gold knocked at the door. Displaying some annoyance at Gold's appearance, Fuchs nevertheless invited him into a bedroom where they might talk in private. He had been sent so suddenly to Los Alamos, Fuchs told Gold, that he had had no time to communicate. He suggested that they meet the next day in the buffet of the North Station in Boston. There, Fuchs passed to Gold a written statement of six or more pages containing confidential and classified information dealing with the whole problem of making an atomic bomb from fissionable material as Fuchs understood it, specific information "as to the principle of the detonation of an atomic bomb," and considerable other related technical data.[9]

Even from the distance of thirty-five years, American scientists still gasp at the amount of priceless secret information that Fuchs passed to Gold that day. There in synthesis was laid out scientific knowledge that had cost the United States hundreds of millions of dollars in experimentation. "There was much in the list that they could have established for themselves," a leading nuclear scientist, Dr. J. Carson Mark, would observe, "but for a power in a hurry, it was of measureless value—especially the stuff telling them which way to go regarding the processing of uranium. We tried four ways at a cost of four hundred million dollars and found that only one way would really work. The Russians therefore had only to take that route and save themselves all the time—two years—that we had expended." [10]

Fuchs also told Gold the amount of uranium or plutonium that the Americans intended to use in each bomb, so that all the Russians needed to know to make a fairly accurate estimate of the atomic stockpile was to learn how much uranium and plutonium the United States was producing, which at that point became a primary intelligence target.

Before parting, Fuchs and Gold made arrangements to meet again in Santa Fe, then a small provincial city in the foothills of the Sangre de Cristo Mountains near Los Alamos. The time: an hour and a date in June 1945.

By June 1945, the atomic bomb was nearing the testing stage. All the essential scientific, technical, and engineering work was completed; the bomb was being built; and a site for the test explosion was being prepared in the Jornada del Muerto (Journey of Death), a stretch of mesa in the northwest corner of the Alamogordo bombing range. The date for the test was already fixed: July 16, 1945. In all those preparations, Klaus Fuchs was centrally involved, a member of an inner circle around J. Robert Oppenheimer of perhaps not more than a dozen men. As a scientist, his principal interest at that point was in the very secret method of detonating the bomb, which required him to live and work in the inner sanctum of the program on terms of closest intimacy with all the principal scientists at Los Alamos. Thus when in the first week of June 1945, about six weeks before the test bomb was to be exploded, Fuchs met with Gold in Santa Fe, he was well primed with information.

Having driven from Los Alamos in a two-seater touring car, Fuchs arrived at the meeting place, the Castillo Street Bridge, a few minutes after Gold. Fat and sweating, Gold climbed into the car, and Fuchs drove to a gravel track near Alameda Road. They stopped for a brief talk, during which they arranged another meeting for September, then Fuchs drove Gold back. As Gold got out of the car, Fuchs passed him an envelope containing, among other information, "a description of the plutonium bomb, which had been designed and was soon to be tested at Alamogordo test site and . . .the fact that the . . . test explosion was to be made, with the approximate site indicated, soon, in July 1945. . . ." [11]

On September 19, 1945, two months after man's first atomic explosion rocked the Jornada del Muerto, Klaus Fuchs drove his tourer out of the main gate of the reservation at Los Alamos and headed for Santa Fe. At about the same time, Gold arrived in Santa Fe by Greyhound bus. The two met at the Church of San Felipe de Neri, walked about the grounds, then drove off in Fuchs's car. Reaching an isolated spot overlooking the town, Fuchs stopped the car. That would be their last meeting, said Fuchs, for British participation in the bomb project was to be phased out, and he expected soon to receive orders to return to Britain. In which case, said Gold, there should be arrangements for someone to contact Fuchs in London. Fuchs suggested a meeting at the Mornington Crescent underground station; as an identification signal, the London contact should carry a bundle of five books tied with a string, and Fuchs would carry a copy of *Life* Magazine folded in half and tucked under his left arm.

By that time, atomic bombs had fallen on Hiroshima and Nagasaki, the war with Germany had been over since May, Japan too had surrendered, and there were awesome signs of tensions in the relationships of Britain and the United States with the Soviet Union. Fuchs said he was very concerned about the future. He was, he said, "rather awestricken by what had occurred," that he had "grievously underestimated the industrial potential of the United States in being able to complete such a gigantic undertaking," that he was "greatly concerned by the terrible destruction which the weapon had wrought."[12]

Below the two men the lights of Santa Fe were coming on. Fuchs started the car, drove Gold back into the town, and before parting, handed him an envelope containing the latest report on the Manhattan Project. Gold spent the night at the Hotel Hilton in Santa Fe, then left the next day for New York. At a meeting in a bar under the elevated railway at Flushing, he passed Fuchs's packet to John. Nine months later, on June 16, 1946, Fuchs left the United States to the plaudits of the American scientific community. The British government promptly appointed him head of experimental physics in the British atomic energy center at Harwell in Berkshire.

*Four*

Fulton is a town in Central Missouri remote from the great stages of world power, which in March 1946 had a population of about 11,000 people. On March 5, 1946, a new American president, Harry S. Truman, came to Fulton with a guest, Winston Churchill, who was to receive an honorary degree from Westminster College. In an address that followed the award, Churchill put Fulton, Missouri, on the news tickers of the world: "From Stettin in the Baltic to Trieste in the Adriatic, an iron curtain has descended across the continent . . . The Communist parties, which were very small in these eastern states of Europe, have been raised to pre-eminence and power far beyond their numbers and are seeking everywhere to obtain totalitarian control . . . Whatever conclusions may be drawn from these facts—and facts they are—this is certainly not the liberated Europe we fought to build up. Nor is it one that contains the essentials of permanent peace."[1]

Many aside from Russians and Communists bridled at Churchill's words, for the hope of peace and freedom for which so many had so recently died was still so fervent that it was often blinding of reality. As on other occasions, Churchill was ahead of the times, but he knew what he was talking about; for even before the guns fell silent in Europe, the Grand Alliance between Britain, Russia, and the United States had begun to break down. To the vast territory and millions of people absorbed in 1939, Russia had added 393,546 square miles and hegemony over 91.9 million people. Outnumbering Allied forces still in Europe by three to one, the Red Army was deep inside Germany, Poland, Austria, Czechoslovakia, Albania, Rumania, Bulgaria, and Hungary, seemingly intent on staying until satellite police states could be solidly entrenched. As the Joint Chiefs of Staff would soon note, "world communism" was driving "toward world conquest."

> The USSR had prevented the conclusion of peace treaties with Germany, Austria, and Japan; and has made impossible the international control of atomic energy and the effective functioning of the United Nations. Today Stalin has come close to achieving what Hitler attempted in vain. The Soviet world extends from the Elbe River and the Adriatic Sea on the west to Manchuria on the east, and embraces one-fifth of the land surface of the world. In addition, Soviet-directed world communism has faced the non-Soviet world with something new in history . . . the world-wide Fifth Column directed at frustrating foreign policy, dividing and confusing the people of a country, planting the seeds of disruption . . . , and subverting the freedom of democratic states.[2]

Nowhere was the Fifth Column of which the Joint Chiefs spoke more solidly established than in the United States, and at least one member of it was moving freely in high policy circles in Washington. That member was Donald Duart Maclean, then thirty-eight years of age and a diplomat of such apparent discretion, trust, loyalty, and social acceptability that he was in line for the post of His Britannic Majesty's ambassador in a major world capital, such as Paris or even Washington.

Donald Maclean arrived in the United States with his American-born wife, Melinda, in May 1944. By 1946 he was the third man in the British Embassy, which gave him complete access to all British policy decisions, including those related to the Anglo-American alliance, joint atomic policy matters, and joint politico-military affairs. As acting head of chancery during most of his assignment in Washington, Maclean alone among the Embassy staff in the great Tudor-style building on Massachusetts Avenue saw all incoming and outgoing cipher telegrams, and he was in charge of the Embassy's supersecret codes and ciphers room. In addition, he was the secretary of the Combined Policy Committee, an organization established in 1943 by Roosevelt and Churchill as "an overall policy making and coordinating group" for the Manhattan Project, a position which put him in the ranks of those who made the most important decisions in the American capital. Yet Maclean occupied yet another critical vantage point as assistant to the British representative, Sir Gordon Monroe, on the Combined Development Trust, which with American, British, and Canadian representation, was charged "to develop information concerning location and availability of raw materials [uranium, plutonium, thorium] for atomic production, negotiations for acquiring these raw materials, and the allocation of the raw materials amongst the three countries represented."[3]

In October 1947, Maclean participated in a three-day conference in Washington to declassify "atomic energy information held in common" by the United States, Britain, and Canada during the war.[4] To determine what to declassify and what to keep secret, the conferees had to have access to all atomic energy information developed during the war.

Maclean served, in effect, as "the liaison agent between the British and the Atomic Energy Commission."[5] He made frequent visits to the headquarters of the Atomic Energy Commission, where the chairman, Carroll J. Wilson, provided him a pass which enabled him to move about the building without an escort.

As subsequently determined, Maclean "did not have access to fissionable material production data," so that he could have arrived at only a rough estimate of "presently existing or prospective stockpile of fissionable materials."[6] Even such data as Maclean may have obtained would have been of no more than short-range benefit to the Russians, for the amount of fissionable material and the number of atomic bombs was constantly changing. Yet, when blended with the material provided by Klaus Fuchs, such information as was available to Maclean would have produced a fairly comprehensive picture of Allied as opposed to strictly American atomic capabilities. Of greater importance, the combination of Maclean and Fuchs was much like that of Magic and Ultra: like Magic, Maclean revealed policy and strategy; like Ultra, Fuchs provided the detail.

Maclean also had access, either directly, through his high position in the British Embassy, or indirectly, through association with members of the British Military Mission in the Pentagon, to planning for war with Russia conducted by the Joint Chiefs of Staff, which began seriously in 1947. Since all plans developed for war with Russia—such as war plan Broiler for the atomic destruction of the Soviet Union—involved use of bases in Britain and in parts of the empire, from which to launch an atomic air offensive, coordination with the British was essential.

Donald Maclean left Washington in late November 1948, covered with the admiration and good wishes of his friends and colleagues, and flew off to London to prepare for a new assignment in Cairo, leaving the task of spying for the Soviet Union within the British colony in Washington to a middle-level official in the Embassy, Guy Burgess, and a highly placed Harold Adrian Russell ("Kim") Philby, who had arrived in the American capital to serve as liaison between the British Secret Intelligence Service and the new American service, the Central Intelligence Agency.

Things began to go wrong for Maclean when in Cairo, among other transgressions, he got drunk and broke into and smashed up the apartment of an American woman employed by the American Embassy. Recalled to Britain, he was appointed to the post of chief of the American desk of the Foreign Office, a key assignment, but he was drinking heavily and engaging in an occasional homosexual dalliance when Kim Philby in Washington learned that the FBI was inquiring into Maclean's activities while serving in Washington. Philby promptly alerted Guy Burgess, who arranged to spirit Maclean to Moscow.

In Moscow, the Soviet authorities provided Burgess with a male dancer as a companion, and Burgess could be seen from time to time at the bar of the old Hotel Luxe, longtime haunt of Comintern phantomas, wearing his Gieves tweeds, his Eton tie, carrying a copy of the *Times*, and invariably displaying the effects of drink. Maclean led a quiet life doing some kind of secret work for the Soviet government. His wife, Melinda, soon joined him, and the little British refugee colony increased again when Kim Philby defected and arrived in Moscow. Melinda eventually moved in with Philby, leaving Maclean to lonely pursuits.

In Washington, the deputy director for intelligence in the Secretariat of the Joint Chiefs of Staff, Colonel Robert Totten, assessed the damage done by Maclean. Information in the fields of joint planning on atomic energy and on planning and policy in Europe "and all by-product information" up to the date—May 25, 1951—of Maclean's defection "undoubtedly reached Soviet hands, probably via the Soviet Embassy in London." At least a large part of joint high-level planning prior to the defection thus would have to be considered compromised along with all British and possibly some American diplomatic codes and ciphers. "Rather than attempt an estimate of how much damage has been done," declared Colonel Totten, "it might be more profitable to quietly inquire into just who may be taking the places of these two men in the apparatus at this time. It is inconceivable that the pipeline dried up and operations stopped on 25 May 1951."[7]

When Klaus Fuchs and Harry Gold met for the last time in September 1945 in Santa Fe, Fuchs remarked to Gold that an officer of the British Secret Intelligence Service had been in touch with him and that British officials were trying to contact Fuchs's father in the Russian-occupied part of Germany. Fuchs failed to tell Gold either why the British agents talked with him or why they wanted to talk with his father, but Fuchs was plainly concerned. As Gold would later relate, "Klaus told me that as far as he knew, the British had no inkling about his past as it related to his Communist activities, and he was anxious that this continue so," but "his father was very old and was given to talking rather freely about his son's past, meaning Klaus's activities in the Communist Party in Germany in the years 1932 and 1933."[8]

The contact between Fuchs and the British intelligence service would remain mysterious. As far as could be determined, Fuchs never mentioned it to any of his associates other than Gold, and there would be no reference to it in Fuchs's dossier in the FBI. Nor would there be reference in any of the papers relating to Fuchs's activities in the United States held by the Atomic Energy Commission. Yet what was clear was that the British Secret Intelligence Service knew more about Fuchs's Communist associations than Fuchs supposed.

Although British authorities had dismissed the information provided by the German consul in Bristol that Fuchs had been a Communist activist in Germany, the information had gone into Fuchs's security file, so that he was to some degree a man always under surveillance. British authorities turned up additional information on him when in May 1945 the British Army occupied Kiel. While searching the local Gestapo headquarters, British counterintelligence agents found two volumes listing Communists wanted by the police. From one of those volumes, the British learned that because of Communist activities, Klaus Fuchs had been classified as an enemy of the state. That information may have led to the contact with Fuchs that Fuchs told Harry Gold about.

When a representative of the FBI in London in early 1946 sent copies of the volumes to Washington, the FBI noted an entry on page 163 of Volume I: "FUCHS, Klaus, student of philosophy, Dec. 29, 1911, Russelheim, *RSHA 1VA2*, Gestapo Field Office Kiel." As the FBI determined, RSHA referred to headquarters of Reichsführer-SS Heinrich Himmler and 1VA2 referred to that department of the RHSA dealing with Communist sabotage and forgery. There was thus an implication that the Gestapo had wanted Fuchs on charges of either sabotage or forgery.

That information went into a dossier at FBI headquarters already containing two items. One was a list published in the German Communist journal, *Unsere Zeit*, of May 15, 1933, naming "scientists and artists who are political victims in Hitler Germany," which contained the notation: "Emil Fuchs of Kiel." The second was a similar list published by a journal called *USSR in Construction*, which contained an entry under university professors: "Aachen School of Technology. Prof. Fuchs (Physics)" and also "Kiel. 186. Prof. E. Fuchs."[9]

In September 1945, the FBI obtained yet a fourth indication of Fuchs's Communist connections when a cipher clerk employed at the Soviet Embassy in Ottawa, Igor Gouzenko, defected and sought political asylum in Canada. Gouzenko brought with him materials stolen from the safe of the head of the Soviet military intelligence service in Canada that showed that there was a close link between the Soviet espionage net in Canada and Jacob Golos' organization in New York, and that the Soviet service had thoroughly penetrated the Canadian branch of the Manhattan Project, and had gathered data almost at will on secret Allied military undertakings of all kinds in Canada, particularly those relating to research in explosives.

So important did the Canadian prime minister, W. Mackenzie King, consider the information that he went personally to Washington to inform President Truman and to London to inform Prime Minister Clement Attlee, and American and British security officers subsequently went to Ottawa to participate in the investigation, which turned up, among others, the Comintern official who had befriended Fuchs when he was interned in Canada, Israel Halperin. When the Canadians arrested Halperin on suspicion of espionage, they found on his person an address book with the entry: "Klaus Fuchs, Asst. to M. Born, 84 George Lane, Univ of Edinburgh, Scotland, Camp N. (Camp L)."[10]

By the time Fuchs prepared to leave the United States for Montreal and London in June 1946, the FBI clearly regarded him as a subject of security concern and held in its files sufficient indications of his Communist affiliation to warrant, in view of the intense concern for the security of the Manhattan Project, at least his questioning before he left for Britain. Although Fuchs was a British subject holding a British security clearance, the FBI on other occasions had sent British scientists or administrators back to Britain for security violations or unacceptable political attitudes. Yet they failed to do that. Was there some hidden reason why?

During World War II, it had been the practice of both the American and British intelligence services when uncovering a spy to attempt, as an alternative to shooting him, to turn him to work for the Allied cause, either with or without his knowledge. If that was the case in regard to Fuchs, what value could he be to Allied intelligence? Would not the danger of allowing him to continue his spying for the Russians far outweigh any advantages attained through his manipulation, either as a witting or unwitting subject? Before August 1945, when the first atomic bombs were used operationally against Hiroshima and Nagasaki, that might have been the case, but afterward, the greatest secret connected with the bomb was out: it worked. Thus at that point the critical intelligence for the United States and Britain was the state of the atomic art in Russia. Did the Russians have the knowledge and the resources to build a bomb? If so, where were they building it? How many could they build?

By 1946, the need for answers to those questions was less a matter of intelligence than of the highest state policy, and both the American and British governments would accept great sacrifices to find the answers. The reality which both governments were compelled to face was that the United States could hardly expect to keep the nuclear monopoly for long. Would it not be well to risk losing a secret that could not be kept in order to obtain intelligence of far greater value? Fuchs had already passed many of the most important secrets to the Russians in any case, and others might be purchased for a dollar in the form of a book by Professor Henry D. Smyth of Princeton University, *A General Account of the Development of Methods of Using Atomic Energy for Military Purposes under the Auspices of the United States Government, 1940–1945*, which the government published over the objections of the Joint Chiefs of Staff. Why lock the gate when somebody had already stolen the horse? Why not keep it open and try to find out what the thief was doing with the horse?

Upon Fuchs's return to Britain, his activities would suggest that he was a Soviet spy under the control of British security authorities, but whether with his knowledge and cooperation was problematical. When appointed head of the theoretical physics department of the British atomic weapons establishment at

Harwell, he was submitted to a routine but rigorous security investigation, which would have turned up at least as much derogatory information as that held by the FBI, yet Fuchs was still appointed to the post. That in itself was indicative; so too was the nature of his continuing espionage activities.

Because of intensified security following the Gouzenko defection in Canada, Fuchs, once back in London in mid-1946, decided against making the contact he had prearranged in Santa Fe with Harry Gold, under which he was to go to the underground station at Mornington Crescent carrying a folded copy of *Life* Magazine and his contact was to arrive with five books tied with a string. He tried instead, late in 1946, to get in touch with his old clandestine colleague, Jürgen Kuczynski, only to learn that Kuczynski had returned to Germany, but he did establish contact with a member of Kuczynski's movement, Johanna Klopstech. Fuchs asked Klopstech for a contact, and a few days later she instructed him to go to the Nags Head public house in the borough of Wood Green and carry with him a copy of a Socialist journal, *Tribune*. A man carrying a red book would approach him and "make some remark concerning a drink," whereupon Fuchs was "to make a suitable reply."[11]

Early in 1947, the contact took place as scheduled, and over the next two years, Fuchs met the Soviet agent, whose name he never learned, six times, either at a public house called the Spotted Horse or at the underground station at the Royal Botannical Gardens in the borough of Kew. Fuchs would later state that "he only delivered one or two actual reports to this contact . . . taken from his official position in connection with the Atomic Energy Research Plant at Harwell." He provided information relating to "the mechanics of assembly [of the atomic bomb]; he filled in the details on predetonation as he had learned them in the United States . . . [and] he furnished calculations from the two atomic bomb explosions in Japan, although he commented that his calculations . . . were not the officially accepted calculations."[12]

If that was indeed all the information passed by Fuchs, he was providing no more than "chicken feed," a term used by those engaged in manipulating agents, which meant valuable information—but not information of the first quality—in order to preserve the contact, to maintain the agent's usefulness and credibility, and, most importantly, to keep the arrangement going to encourage the contact to make requests for specific information. If that was the stratagem, it at least had the effect of preserving the contact. The Soviet agent in time invited Fuchs to go to Paris to meet the head of the Soviet scientific intelligence team in Western Europe, Vassili V. Soukhoumline, who "would be able more fully to understand scientific terms"; but Fuchs declined the invitation because of "restrictions placed on sterling for use in foreign travel,"[13] which would appear to have been a technical excuse to avoid the possibility of being kidnapped, as Peter Kapitsa had been before World War II and as many German scientists had been soon after the war.

A return trip to the United States that Fuchs made in 1947 would strengthen a case for his being under control. In the first place, the FBI made no effort to prevent his coming, and although he attended the declassification conference in Washington in which Donald Maclean participated, he was afforded, at the direction of the Atomic Energy Commission, no access to confidential materials. From Washington, Fuchs visited Cornell University to inspect the university's cyclotron, which was no secret, and when he visited the Argonne National Laboratory in Chicago and the General Electric plant in Schenectady, New York, the Atomic Energy Commission again directed that he be allowed to see no secret equipment or materials.

There was, nevertheless, one critical secret to which Fuchs had long been privy: the hydrogen bomb. He had been closely associated with early stages of that project, and had worked with and was a friend of the man who would be called "the father of the hydrogen bomb," Dr. Edward Teller. At Los Alamos, Fuchs had attended at least six top secret conferences on the hydrogen bomb, and as the Atomic Energy Commission would note, he "contributed heavily" to the state of thermonuclear concepts as they had advanced by 1946.[14] Would security authorities have risked playing a game in which their bait was capable of passing information about that terrible progression of the atomic bomb, a weapon so destructive that the scientists called it "the Super"? Either Fuchs was not, in fact, under control, or else his controllers were sure of their bait. Fuchs himself would maintain that such information as he passed to the Russians on the hydrogen bomb was at best "a confused picture."[15] If his recollections were factual, what he furnished was chicken feed.


On September 2, 1949, a B-29 of the United States Air Force flying from Japan to Alaska picked up signs of radioactivity that slightly exceeded the intensity necessary to constitute an official alert to the United States. When the information was passed to the Air Force Long Range Detection Center and to the Atomic Energy Commission, flights were sent up to check. Officials were soon convinced that four days earlier, on August 29, 1949, the Soviet Union had successfully tested an atomic bomb.

Only a few months before that momentous event, Klaus Fuchs had begun to have serious doubts about his allegiance to Communism. There had been some doubts ever since the signing of the Nazi-Soviet Nonaggression Pact, but until 1949, he had always been able to reconcile them. Early that year, he discovered that Communism could hit at him personally through his family, and at the time, at least, he was unable to reconcile that with his faith.

Intellectually brilliant, the Fuchs family had endured much tragedy. Fuchs's mother died in childbirth. One sister, Elizabeth, committed suicide; the other, Kristel Heinemann, was by 1949 committed to a mental institution in Massachusetts. His only brother, Gerhardt, was in a Swiss sanitorium with advanced tuberculosis. At seventy-six, his father was teaching social ethics and theology at

Leipzig University in East Germany, but he was infirm, and Fuchs was seriously concerned about him.

The East German police, Fuchs learned, were holding his father as a guarantee against Fuchs's continuing loyalty to Communism, an indication that Soviet officials suspected he might be under British control. Fuchs reacted to the news with immense bitterness. At first he began to skip meetings with his Soviet controller, then attended one and announced—as many a Communist before him had done and had come to regret—that he wanted to sever all connections with the Soviet intelligence service.

In Washington, in the meantime, the FBI had at last begun a detailed investigation of Fuchs and informed the British intelligence liaison officers in Washington—Kim Philby of the British Secret Intelligence Service and Geoffrey Patterson of the British Security Service—about it. When Patterson notified London, one of Britain's foremost spycatchers, J. James Skardon, interviewed Fuchs almost immediately, but what he learned, if anything, would remain an official British government secret.

There was no further word on Fuchs until January 27, 1950, when he confessed to spying for the Russians, and British authorities notified the FBI and the Atomic Energy Commission that he had been arrested. Although the British refused a request by the FBI to send agents to interview him, his arrest was soon publicly disclosed and within the scientific community in the United States created a rare consternation. As the science editor of the New York *Times*, William Laurence, who had been in the inner circle at Los Alamos, put it:

> And there in our midst stood Klaus Fuchs. There he was, this spy, standing right at the center of what we believed at the time to be the world's greatest secret. His associates at Los Alamos today sadly admit that Fuchs made it possible for Russia to develop her A-Bomb at least a year ahead of time. It is my conviction the information made it possible for the Russians to attain their goal at least three and possibly as much as ten years earlier.[16]

In retrospect, it would appear that up until the discovery of the Gestapo's notation on Fuchs in May 1945, he was an unsuspected Soviet spy but that after his return to Britain from the United States he became an unwitting double agent, his services as a scientist retained in a high post but his access to the innermost secrets of the atomic and hydrogen bomb projects limited, while all the while he was kept under the close surveillance that was easily maintained in the tight, closed world of nuclear research. When Fuchs became disillusioned over the treatment of his father, that would have been quickly detected by those who were watching him so closely, whereupon he was approached and agreed to work for Britain to establish the nature and extent of the Soviet atomic program, in that way to compensate at least to a degree for the damage he had done to Britain and the United States. Some of Fuchs's testimony at his trial would indicate that that was the case, as well as the wording of his indictment, for despite the fact that some of his most valuable spying for Russia was done in time of war, a capital offense, the government charged him with espionage in time of peace. The maximum sentence for that, which he received, was fourteen years in prison. Yet if Fuchs was, indeed, under control, why even that sentence? Probably because there appeared to be no alternative if the intelligence system and the alliance with the United States were to be maintained.

Whether the information gained through the gamble on Fuchs—if gamble there was—was worth it was problematical. If the gamble was to pay off, the requests for information that the Russians asked of him would have had to be detailed enough to reveal the weaknesses and the gaps in the Soviet atomic research and capabilities. That did not appear to be the case, for as an official of the FBI remarked, ". . . very few questions were ever asked of him to indicate what the Russians wanted, and when the questions were asked, they were general, such as furnishing information concerning the electromagnetic process, and these questions would not and did not indicate the progress which the Russians had made or were making in the development of the atomic bomb."[17]

The British government would in time provide Klaus Fuchs a parole that cut five years off his sentence, which would be another indication that he had in some way collaborated. Yet it would soon become apparent that Fuchs had never really repented his transgressions, for upon his release in 1959, he went to East Germany, where he was granted citizenship and appointed deputy director of the Central Institute for Nuclear Research. It would later be reported that he was working in the Soviet Union.

## Five

Jacob Golos, head of the Comintern's underground organization in the United States, died suddenly on November 25, 1943, at the New York home of his mistress, Elizabeth Terrill Bentley. From his death began to flow extraordinary events. They began almost from the moment an old Dodge truck deposited his pine coffin at the Bronx Crematorium and to the music of "The Red Flag," he was given a good worker's last rites.

The death of Golos had left Elizabeth Bentley, in her forties, alone. During the five years that she and Golos had been lovers, she had been his most trusted lieutenant in the Communist underground, the principal link between Golos as head of the Central Control Commission, the organization responsible for party discipline and for the underground, and the party's principal underground nets, Apparats A and B. Yet when Golos died, Elizabeth Bentley—as she herself would later put it—died as well, and so did her interest in and devotion to the Communist movement.

"Having worked with Mr. Golos, whom I considered to be a great idealist, a man who was working for the betterment of the world," she said, "I had been terrifically shielded from the realities behind this thing, and when he died I was thrown in direct contact with the Russians who had just come over from Russia." In general, she said, "they were about the cheapest type of person I have ever seen—the gangster type." She also found that men in the party who she had strongly admired, such as the secretary, Earl Browder, were "just cheap little men pulled by strings from Moscow." She decided that even though she might be putting her life in danger, she wanted "to abandon that way of life and [go back] to being a good American." As she saw it, she had two choices: "either to walk out and forget that it had happened, or go to the agency that was handling counterespionage, the FBI."[1]

Aware of the penetration of the United States government by Apparats A and B, Elizabeth Bentley was, she said, "like all people who get out . . . obsessed with the idea that Government bureaus are full of Communist spies." Rather than call at the offices of the FBI in New York or Washington, where she was afraid some Communist who knew her might spot her, she went instead, on August 21, 1945, to the bureau's small office in New Haven, Connecticut. She soon began to tell all that she knew about the Soviet intelligence services in the United States and about the Americans who were involved in Apparats A and B. Within a few days, the FBI asked her "to go back in again to the espionage network and see what further evidence" she might "dig up." She became, in effect, a double agent working for the FBI.

From time to time over the second half of 1945 and through 1946, FBI officials interrogated her at length. Between 1938 and 1945, she told them, some two dozen Washington officials had delivered secret official documents to her, among them a former senior assistant to President Roosevelt, Lauchlin Currie; a former assistant secretary of the Treasury, one of the founders of the World Bank, and a director of the International Monetary Fund, Harry Dexter White; and Whittaker Chambers.

Chambers soon appeared voluntarily before the Committee on Un-American Activities, where he repeated information given the FBI earlier about the underground organization in the government with which he had worked. He named names that by that time were familiar to the FBI—Nathan Witt, John Abt, Lee Pressman—but he also named others as members of the group, including "Alger Hiss, who, as a member of the State Department, later organized the conferences at Dumbarton Oaks, San Francisco, and the United States side of the Yalta Conference."[2] Between them, Chambers and Bentley named thirty-seven current or former government officials as Communists.

When taken in concert with information already obtained by the FBI, the Bentley-Chambers revelations led to the first major crackdown on Communism in the United States since the campaign of 1919 that culminated in the *Buford* deportations. It began with the Un-American Activities Committee, which called the government employees named by Chambers and Bentley to testify. Of the thirty-seven, Harold Ware had died in 1935 and seventeen others refused under oath to say whether they were Communists or had engaged in espionage. Of the remainder, two were not called to testify; two—John Abt and Lee Pressman— admitted to being Communists but denied having spied; a veteran State Department employee, Laurence Duggan, either jumped or was pushed from the sixteenth floor of a New York building; Harry Dexter White died of a heart attack; and twelve others testified under oath that the charges against them were false. Of those twelve, two were indicted for perjury: one, a bright star in the Department of Commerce, William T. Remington, was found guilty and was later murdered in prison, and the other was Alger Hiss.

In the fall of 1949, the Department of Justice charged eleven of thirteen members of the American Communist Party's National Board with having conspired "knowingly and willfully to advocate and teach the duty and necessity of overthrowing and destroying the Government of the United States by force and violence." Brought to trial under the provisions of the Smith Act, all were found guilty. In Washington, thirty-four suspected Communists were convicted of contempt of Congress for refusing to testify before the Un-American Activities Committee; in New York, five officials of the Soviet trade agency, Amtorg, were arrested for failing to register as agents of a foreign power; in California, sixteen people were convicted on charges of civil contempt for refusing to testify before a federal grand jury; in Denver, seven were convicted under the same charge. Other trials of so-called second- and third-string Communists followed, one of whom was Steve Nelson.

It was the start of a Red Scare that was to exceed that which had gripped the country at the start of the 1920s. Liberals would long maintain that hundreds of innocents were trapped by guilt by association, particularly in the entertainment industry; an obscure junior senator from Wisconsin, Joseph McCarthy, fashioned a meteoric career out of the hysteria but eventually drew the censure of his colleagues for his excesses; and to try to still the suspicion against government employees, President Harry S. Truman instituted a Federal Employee Loyalty Program. In the first two years of the program, the authorities screened almost two and a half million employees, of which 2,764 resigned while under investigation, 280 were dismissed, and six were indicted on various charges, including Alger Hiss for perjury, and a twenty-eight-year-old employee of the Department of Justice, Judith Coplon, for stealing government documents and passing them to an employee of the United Nations in New York, Valentin A. Gubitchev, who was a senior official of the Soviet Foreign Commissariat. To avoid reprisals against Americans in the Soviet Union, Gubitchev was allowed to leave the country.

In continuing talks with the FBI, Elizabeth Bentley suddenly recalled a name she had yet to mention: Abraham Brothman. Brothman's firm, Abraham Brothman Associates, she said, had been a collection center for blueprints obtained in the industrial espionage operations of Apparat B. Although Bentley acted as a courier from Brothman to Jacob Golos, she had no knowledge of where the blueprints came from, but she was aware that "the Soviets believed that the Brothman material was sufficiently important to turn over to Red Army Intelligence."[3] When she became involved in a dispute with Brothman over money, she asked Golos to use another courier, to which he agreed and selected a man from Philadelphia named Harry Gold.

When FBI agents Donald E. Shannon and Francis D. O'Brien called on Brothman, he insisted that the blueprints concerned only such items as "shafts, filter vats, and other things used in the manufacture of chemicals." He "emphatically denied that any of these blueprints were of a restricted or secret nature pertaining to the war effort of the United States."[4]

Shannon and O'Brien went to see Harry Gold, whom they found to be loquacious. After he was introduced to Jacob Golos in October 1940, said Gold, Golos informed him that he had "some connections with some individuals of a foreign country, not naming the country," and that a certain Brothman was "turning over to him certain blueprints which had a connection in the chemical field." He needed a qualified chemist, said Golos, "to evaluate these blueprints on a chemical basis." When offered the job, Gold accepted. Although told "that he would receive some reward for the work he was to perform," Gold said he ended up paying his own expenses, rewarded only occasionally by a $5 bill passed him by Brothman. When Agents Shannon and O'Brien returned to Brothman's offices, he again insisted that the blueprints were "very harmless"; he passed them first to Bentley and then later to Gold, he said, only in the hope that it might bring him contracts with Amtorg.[5]

In the view of the Department of Justice, there was sufficient evidence to seek an indictment of Brothman and Gold for espionage, but when the two men appeared on July 22 and 31, 1945, before a special grand jury in the Southern District of New York, the jury found the evidence insufficient for a true bill. After release, Gold obtained a job as a chemist at the Heart Station of Philadelphia General Hospital. He was by that time no longer sure of the rightness of Russia's cause, he would later declare, and no longer engaged in any activities for the Russians.

While living with his father and brother in Philadelphia, Gold in July 1949 received a letter bearing a Brooklyn postmark with the words "St. George Hotel" typed on the envelope. That was a prearranged code meaning that the Russians wanted to talk to him. Gold went to the appointed place, a seafood restaurant near the Broadway stop of the Astoria elevated railway, but nobody came. Returning to Philadelphia, he assumed that someone was merely testing whether the arrangements for a meeting would work.

Late on a Saturday night, September 24, 1949, soon after the FBI began to investigate Klaus Fuchs, there was a knock at the door of the Gold residence. Going to the door, Gold found a man whom he would later identify as an official of the Soviet Consulate in New York, Filipp Tikhonovich Sarytchev, who asked him, presumably as a means of establishing identification, if he remembered John, Gold's former controller, and "the Doctor," the latter a name sometimes used for Fuchs. He was there not for a conversation, said Sarytchev, but to arrange a rendezvous to talk about Gold's experience with the grand jury. Gold found it difficult to believe that after the passage of two years the Russians would suddenly become interested in the proceedings before the grand jury, but he agreed to a meeting on October 6, 1949, in New York.

At the meeting, Gold told Sarytchev that the jury had thought him to be "at the most, a well-meaning dupe." That may have been the case, replied Sarytchev, but he was convinced that American authorities saw him as much more deeply involved. He urged Gold to get out of the country immediately by way of Mexico and go to Czechoslovakia, for which ample funds would be provided. So insistent was Sarytchev that he should escape that Gold became convinced that something had developed that he knew nothing about, something that made him "dangerous to the Soviet Union."[6]

Breaking off the conversation, Sarytchev told Gold to be at the 180th Street station of the Bronx Park subway at 7:30 P.M. on October 23, 1949. Although Gold was there on time, nobody contacted him. It was, he decided, a recognition meeting designed to enable the Russians to determine whether he was still at liberty, for just as he arrived, he caught a brief glimpse of another spy whom he knew, Julius Rosenberg. Yet as soon as the two had exchanged glances, Rosenberg disappeared.

On the afternoon of February 2, 1950, Harry Gold was jolted by the lead story on the five o'clock news: the arrest of Klaus Fuchs in London as a Russian spy. Over the next few weeks, Gold waited day and night for the knock on his door that he was convinced would come, but it did not come, for the British government was refusing to allow representatives of the FBI to interview Fuchs. The British did pass to the FBI Fuchs's word that his contact in the United States was known to him as Raymond, that he was Jewish, and that in 1945 he would have been about forty years old, "fairly broad" in build with a round, full face, and about 5 feet 10 inches tall. Raymond was not a nuclear physicist, according to Fuchs, and was "not employed within the atomic energy plant," although he did have "knowledge of chemistry and engineering."[7]

On that slender information, the FBI launched what would become one of the most extensive investigations in its history. From the start, the primary suspect was not Gold but another Jewish industrial chemist with Communist leanings, Joseph Arnold Robbins of Manhattan. When it was eventually established that Robbins was not the man, the investigators turned their attention elsewhere.

Because Alexander Brothman was a Jewish industrial chemist, FBI agents made a routine check on him. To verify the type of work he was engaged in, Brothman produced a brochure which turned out to have been prepared by Gold as part of his efforts to use thermal diffusion in extracting valuable chemicals from industrial flues. With it was an attachment, which upon close examination appeared to have been obtained from "a highly confidential source."[8] When the agents asked where Gold might have obtained such a document, Brothman said they would have to ask Gold himself.

Checking the description of Raymond against a description of Gold, the agents noted considerable resemblance. Special Agent Joseph Walsh hurried that same day to the Heart Station in Philadelphia, where he found "a marked similarity in the appearance and actions of Gold with those of Joseph Arnold Robbins."[9] Both men had a pronounced stoop when they walked, wore earnest expressions, and moved with constant glances over their shoulders. Yet when still and motion pictures were taken surreptitiously of Gold and shown to Fuchs, he said that Gold was not Raymond. Complicating the investigation, the FBI found that there were at least nine Harry Golds in the United States who were industrial chemists or connected in some way with industrial chemistry; all had to be checked out before they could be eliminated.

On May 19, 1950, Special Agents Richard Brennan and Scott Miller went to see Gold and took him back over his entire life, with special attention to the period between 1943 and 1945 when Raymond was seeing Fuchs. Gold denied "ever having been west of the Mississippi," and when shown a photograph of Fuchs, responded: "This is a very interesting picture—that is the British spy, Dr. Emil Klaus Fuchs. It looks like a caricature. But I never met him. I've never been in Great Britain."[10]

After five hours, Brennan and Miller broke off the interview. "You're tired, Harry," one of them said. "Get some sleep. We'll come round to your house on Monday morning and clear this matter up. What time would be convenient with you?" When Gold suggested nine o'clock, the agents asked if he would allow them to search his house, reminding him that they could get a warrant if one was required. Gold said they could do as they wished; they would find nothing. They would find nothing, he thought to himself, because he would go straight home and destroy the incriminating material that he knew to be there.

As the agents departed, Gold suddenly thought of his experiment. Deciding that there was plenty of time to clear out his cupboards, he went back to his bench, became immersed in his work, slept on a camp bed, and returned to his house only at 5:00 A.M. on the Monday morning when the FBI agents were to call. He began hurriedly to look for and destroy incriminating material.

When at nine o'clock there was a knock at the door, Gold thought the task was complete. As he admitted Agents Brennan and Miller and they began their search, "At first, everything went well; there was a lot of stuff, but it was all school notes and lab and chemical literature references, and my books were all volumes of mathematics and physics and chemistry; then there were some 200 pocketbook editions of mystery stories."[11] Then came a blow. Thumbing through a book entitled *Principles of Chemical Engineering,* Brennan pulled out a yellowed tourist map of Santa Fe, which Gold had been aware that he had but which he had been unable to find. Holding up the map, Brennan asked: "What about it, Harry?"

Gold started to make up a story, then lowered himself wearily and heavily into a chair. "Yes," he said, "I am the man to whom Klaus Fuchs gave information on atomic energy."

Corroboration, though hardly needed, was soon forthcoming. From London came word that Fuchs had positively identified the latest photographs of Gold as the man he had known as Raymond; and from Albuquerque came word from an FBI agent that Harry Gold had had a reservation at the Hotel Hilton for the night of September 19, 1945, had listed his place of employment as Abraham Brothman Associates of New York, had been assigned room number 521, and had stayed the night.

On the personal instructions of J. Edgar Hoover, in an effort to keep Gold's arrest secret in hope of turning up his collaborators, the agents took Gold to the Benjamin Franklin Hotel in Philadelphia and registered him under a false name. In his hotel room, Gold began a confession that was to become majestic in content and length and spectacular in its effect, for in the process of it, he named one for whom he had served on a few occasions as a courier, a former sergeant in the United States Army who had worked in the inner circles of the atomic bomb project at Los Alamos, David Greenglass.

One of the trials of the century followed. Turning state's evidence, Greenglass named his sister, Ethel Rosenberg, and her husband, Julius, as spies for the Soviet Union who passed atomic secrets to the Soviet vice-consul in New York, Antol A. Yakovlyvev. He also linked the Rosenbergs with Klaus Fuchs. Convicted, they were sentenced to death, which set off a worldwide Communist propaganda campaign demanding clemency and accusing the United States of anti-Semitism. Exceeding in intensity the campaigns launched on behalf of Sacco and Vanzetti and the Scottsboro Boys, it would end only with the execution of Ethel and Julius Rosenberg, after numerous appeals and stays, on June 19, 1953.

As Harry Gold revealed in his confession, he was shocked at the reaction that the revelation of his espionage produced: "I thought that I would be helping a nation whose final aims I approved, along the road to industrial strength. . . . I felt that as an ally, I was only helping the Soviet Union obtain certain information that I thought it was entitled to."[12]

In the chambers of the U.S. District Judge in Philadelphia, James P. McGranery, Gold heard charges that he acted "against the peace and dignity of the United States of America, in time of war, unlawfully, willfully, knowingly, and feloniously" to receive "from one Emil Julius Klaus Fuchs documents, writings, sketches, notes, and information relating to the national defense and with intent and reason to believe that it was to be used to the injury of the United States and to the advantage of a foreign nation. . . ." The charge stunned Gold. That "horribly wrong statement in the complaint," he was to note later, "'With intent to harm and injure the United States.' No! Not this! This was not so! It was not true."[13]

# BIBLIOGRAPHY

As is apparent from the notes in this volume, the authors have made extensive use of the voluminous files of the United States Army's Military Intelligence Division, which were only recently declassified and have never previously been exploited for publication. The notes also provide an index to material obtained from the Atomic Energy Commission, Office of Naval Intelligence, State Department, Her Majesty's Documents Office, and through the Freedom of Information Act, the Federal Bureau of Investigation. In a special category is CIA, "Rote Kapelle: A Survey Report," prepared by the CIA in 1973, copy in the National Archives.

In addition, the authors have made extensive and unique use of the voluminous papers of the first head of the Office of Strategic Services, the late Major General William J. Donovan, a collection recently released by the CIA but not yet open to the public.

The secondary material applicable to the era and the subject is obviously so immense as to defy recitation in a single bibliography; those volumes listed below, along with others cited in the notes, constitute the works on which the authors have drawn extensively. As any student of the subject is soon aware, the authors of many works—of the left and of the right—have strewn the researcher's path with propagandistic obstacles designed to conceal or at least to confuse the truth.

## Official Publications

Committee on Foreign Relations, U.S. Senate, 68th Congress, 1st Session, *Recognition of Russia* (1924).

Committee on the Judiciary, U.S. Senate, 94th Congress, 1st Session, *Trotskyite Terrorist International* (1975).

Committee on Un-American Activities, House of Representatives, 80th Congress, 1st Session, *Report on American Youth for Democracy* (1947).

————, *The Communist Party of the United States as an Agent of a Foreign Power* (1947).

————, 81st Congress, 1st Session, *American Aspects of Assassination of Leon Trotsky* (1951).

Defense Dept, *The "Magic" Background of Pearl Harbor* (5 vols. with documentary annexes) (1977).

State Dept, *Germany: Auswärtiges Amt, Nazi-Soviet Relations, 1939–1941, Documents from the Archives of the German Foreign Office* (1948).

————, *Foreign Relations of the United States, 1918, Russia,* vol. 2, and *1940, General and Europe,* vol. 2.

Subcommittee to Investigate the Administration of the Internal Security Act and Other Internal Security Laws of the Committee of the Judiciary, U.S. Senate, 93d Congress, 1st Session, *The Legacy of Alexander Orlov* (1973).

U.S. Army Center of Military History, translation of *History of the Great Patriotic War of the Soviet Union, 1941–1945,* vol. 1, *Preparation for and Unleashing of the War by the Imperialistic Powers.* Moscow: Military Publishing House of the Ministry of Defense of the USSR.

## Memoirs, Diaries, Biographies, and Histories

Baldwin, Hanson, *The Crucial Years, 1939–1941.* New York: Harper and Row, 1976.

Bishop, Donald G., *The Roosevelt-Litvinov Agreements: The American View.* Syracuse: Syracuse University Press, 1965.

Blum, John Morton, *The Price of Vision: The Diary of Henry A. Wallace, 1942–1945.* Boston: Houghton Mifflin Co., 1973.

Bolloten, Burnett, *The Grand Camouflage: The Communist Conspiracy in the Spanish Civil War.* New York: Frederick A. Praeger, 1961.

Braunthal, Julius, *The History of the International.* New York: Frederick A. Praeger, 1967.

Bryan, J. III, and Charles J. V. Murphy, *The Windsor Story.* New York: William R. Murrow Co., 1979.

Burns, James MacGregor, *Roosevelt: The Soldier of Freedom, 1940–1945.* New York: Harcourt, Brace, Jovanovich, 1970.

Cante, David, *The Great Fear: The Anti-Communist Purge Under Truman and Eisenhower.* New York: Simon and Schuster, 1978.

Carrell, Paul, *Hitler Moves East, 1941–43.* Boston: Little, Brown and Co., 1963.

Churchill, Winston S., *The Gathering Storm*. Boston: Houghton Mifflin Co., 1948.

———, *The Grand Alliance*. Boston: Houghton Mifflin Co., 1950.

———, *The Great War*, vol. 3. London: Newnes, 1933.

———, *Their Finest Hour*. Boston: Houghton Mifflin Co., 1949.

Conquest, Robert, *The Great Terror: Stalin's Purge of the Thirties*. New York: The Macmillan Co., 1968.

Craig, Gordon A., and Felix Gilbert, eds., *The Diplomats, 1919–1939*. Princeton: Princeton University Press, 1953.

Crossman, R. H. S., ed., *The God That Failed*. New York: Harper Bros, 1950.

Dallin, David J., *Soviet Espionage*. New Haven: Yale University Press, 1955.

Deakin, F. W., *The Brutal Friendship*. New York: Harper and Row, 1962.

Deutscher, Isaac, *The Prophet Armed: Trotsky, 1879–1921*. London: Oxford University Press, 1952.

———, *The Prophet Outcast*. London: Oxford University Press, 1963.

Dilks, David, ed., *The Diaries of Sir Alexander Cadogan*. New York: G. P. Putnam's Sons, 1972.

Donaldson, Frances, *Edward VIII*. New York: J. B. Lippincott Co., 1974.

Draper, Theodore, *The Roots of American Communism*. New York: The Viking Press, 1957.

Erickson, John, *The Road to Stalingrad*. New York: Harper and Row, 1974.

———, *The Soviet High Command*. New York: St. Martin's Press, 1962.

Fest, Joachim, *Hitler*. New York: Harcourt, Brace, Jovanovich, 1974.

Fischer, Louis, *The Life of Lenin*. New York: Harper and Row, 1964.

Footman, David, *Civil War in Russia*. London: Faber and Faber, 1961.

Friedrich, Otto, *Before the Deluge: A Portrait of Berlin in the 1930s*. New York: Harper and Row, 1972.

Gilbert, Martin, *Winston S. Churchill*, vol. 4, *The Stricken World*, Boston: Houghton Mifflin Co., 1975, and vol. 5, *The Prophet of Truth*, Houghton Mifflin, 1977.

Goerlitz, Walter, *History of the German General Staff, 1657–1945*. New York: Frederick A. Praeger, 1952.

Gorodetsky, Gabriel, *The Precarious Truce: Anglo-Soviet Relations, 1924–1927*. Cambridge: Cambridge University Press, 1977.

Graves, Major General William S., *America's Siberian Adventure*. New York: Jonathan Cape and Harrison Smith, 1931.

Green, Martin, *Children of the Sun: A Narrative of "Decadence" in England after 1918*. New York: Basic Books, 1976.

Grey, Ian, *The First Fifty Years: Soviet Russia 1917–67*. New York: Coward-McCann, Inc., 1967.

Guillermaz, Jacques, *A History of the Chinese Communist Party, 1921–1949*. New York: Random House, 1972.

Hammond, Thomas T., and Robert Farrell, eds., *The Anatomy of Communist Takeovers*. New Haven: Yale University Press, 1975.

Henderson, Sir Nevile, *Failure of a Mission*. London: Hodder and Stoughton, 1940.

Hicks, Granville, with the assistance of John Stuart, *John Reed*. New York: The Macmillan Co., 1936.

Hulse, J. W., *The Forming of the Communist International*. Stanford: Stanford University Press, 1964.

Hyde, H. Montgomery, *Stalin: The History of a Dictator*. New York: Popular Library, 1971.

Ignotus, Paul, *Hungary*. New York: Frederick A. Praeger, 1972.

Irving, David, *Hitler's War*. New York: The Viking Press, 1977.

Kennan, George F., *Soviet-American Relations, 1917–1920*, vol. 1, *Russia Leaves the War*, Princeton: Princeton University Press, 1956, and vol. 2, *The Decision to Intervene*, Princeton University Press, 1958.

Kindall, Sylvian G., *American Soldiers in Siberia*. New York: Richard R. Smith, 1945.

Krivitsky, Walter G., *In Stalin's Secret Service*. New York: Harper Bros., 1939.

Lash, Joseph P., *Roosevelt and Churchill, 1939–1941*. New York: W. W. Norton Co., 1976.

Lazitch, Branko, and Milorad M. Drachkovitch, *Biographical Dictionary of the Comintern*. Stanford: Hoover Institution Press, 1973.

Leviné-Meyer, Rosa, *Leviné: The Life of a Revolutionary*. Farnborough: Saxon House, 1973.

Lockhart, Robin Bruce, *Ace of Spies*. New York: Stein and Day, 1967.

Lynam, R. W., *The First Labour Government*. London: Chapman and Hall, 1957.

Maddox, Robert J., *The Unknown War with Russia: Wilson's Siberian Intervention*. San Rafael, Cal: Presidio Press, 1977.

Manchester, William, *The Glory and the Dream: A Narrative History of America, 1932–1972*. Boston: Little, Brown and Co., 1973.

McSherry, James, *Stalin, Hitler, and Europe*, 2 vols. Arlington, Va: Open Door Press, 1968.

Morris, James, *The Pax Britannica Trilogy*, vol. 3, *Farewell to the Trumpets*. New York: Harcourt, Brace, Jovanovich, 1975.

Muggeridge, Malcolm, *Chronicles of Wasted Time*, vol. 2, *The Infernal Grove*. New York: William Morrow Co., 1973.

Nicolson, Nigel, ed., *Harold Nicolson: Diaries and Letters, 1930–1939*. New York: Atheneum Press, 1966.

Nollau, Gunther, *International Communism and World Revolution*. New York: Frederick A. Praeger, 1961.

Payne, Robert, *The Life and Death of Adolf Hitler*. New York: Frederick A. Praeger, 1973.

Pelling, Henry, *Winston Churchill*. New York: E. P. Dutton Co., 1974.

Petrie, Sir David, *Communism in India*. Calcutta: Saha, 1972.

Pick, Robert, *The Last Days of Imperial Vienna.* New York: Dial Press, 1976.

Pope, Arthur Upham, *Maxim Litvinoff.* New York: L. B. Fisher Co., 1943.

Rosenbaum, Kurt, *Community of Fate.* Syracuse: Syracuse University Press, 1965.

Sampson, Anthony, *Anatomy of Britain.* New York: Harper and Row, 1962.

Schellenberg, Walter, *The Schellenberg Memoirs.* London: Deutsch, 1956.

Schmidt, Paul, *Hitler's Interpreter.* London: Heinemann, 1951.

Sheridan, Clare, *The Naked Truth.* New York: Harper Bros., 1928.

———, *Russian Portraits.* London: Jonathan Cape, 1921.

Shirer, William L., *Berlin Diary.* New York: Alfred A. Knopf Co., 1941.

Sisson, Edgar G., *One Hundred Red Days.* New Haven: Yale University Press, 1931.

Speer, Albert, *Inside the Third Reich.* New York: Avon Books, 1970.

Stewart, George, *The White Armies of Russia.* New York: Russell and Russell, 1933.

Strasser, Roland, *The Mongolian Horde.* London: Jonathan Cape, 1930.

Taylor, A. P. J., ed., *Lloyd George: A Diary by Frances Stevenson.* New York: Harper and Row, 1971.

Thomas, Hugh, *The Spanish Civil War.* New York: Harper Bros., 1961.

Toland, John, *Adolf Hitler.* Garden City: Doubleday and Co., 1976.

———, *The Rising Sun: The Decline and Fall of the Japanese Empire, 1936–1945.* New York: Random House, 1970.

Trotsky, Leon, *The First Five Years of the Communist International,* vol. 1. New York: Pioneer Books, 1945.

———, *History of the Russian Revolution,* vol. 3, *The Triumph of the Soviets.* New York: Simon and Schuster, 1932.

Tuchman, Barbara W., *Stilwell and the American Experience in China, 1941–45.* New York: The Macmillan Co., 1971.

Ulam, Adam B., *Stalin: The Man and His Era.* New York: The Viking Press, 1973.

Ullman, Richard H., *Anglo-Soviet Relations, 1917–1921,* vol. 1, *Intervention and the War,* (Princeton: Princeton University Press, 1961, and vol. 2, ·*Britain and the Russian Civil War,* Princeton University Press, 1968.

Warlimont, General Walter, *Inside Hitler's Headquarters.* London: Weidenfeld and Nicolson, 1964.

Weinstein, Allen, *Perjury: The Hiss-Chambers Case.* New York: Alfred A. Knopf Co., 1978.

Werth, Alexander, *Russia at War, 1941–1945.* New York: Avon Books, 1965.

Wheeler-Bennett, J. W., *The Forgotten Peace.* New York: William R. Morrow Co., 1939.

———, *The Nemesis of Power: The German Army in Politics, 1918–1945.* New York: St. Martin's Press, 1954.

White, D. Fedotoff, *The Growth of the Red Army*. Princeton: Princeton University Press, 1944.

Woodcock, George, *Who Killed the British Empire?*. New York: Quadrangle Books, 1974.

Young, Kenneth, ed., *The Diaries of Sir Robert Bruce Lockhart, 1915–1938*. London: Macmillan, 1973.

# NOTES

## Prologue

1. Military Intelligence Division (MID), 10058–D–79–793, 17 Apr 18, Old Military Records (OMR), National Archives (NA). (Throughout MID files, there is often a discrepancy between date of origin of a document and date of filing, sometimes amounting to months and even years; to aid the researcher, the authors where possible use the date of filing.)

2. Col. Raymond Robins, at the time head of the American Red Cross in Russia, as cited in J. W. Wheeler-Bennett, *The Forgotten Peace*, p. 152.

3. Synopsis, Louis C. Fraina, Communist Party Leader, in MID, 10058–24, 20 Nov 20, OMR.

4. Leon Trotsky, *History of the Russian Revolution*, vol. 3, *The Triumph of the Soviets*, p. 119.

## Book One CONFRONTATION: 1917–1933
### PART I The Changing of the Guard

## Chapter One

1. Robert H. Ullman, *Anglo-Soviet Relations*, vol. 1, *Intervention and the War*, p. 45.

2. Kenneth Young, ed., *The Diaries of Sir Robert Bruce Lockhart, 1915–1938*, p. 9.

3. Ullman, *Anglo-Soviet Relations*, vol. 1, *Intervention*, p. 59.

4. Ibid., pp. 61–62.

5. J. W. Wheeler-Bennett, *The Forgotten Peace*, p. 152.

6. Ibid., p. 226.

7. Ibid., pp. 227, 243–44.

8. Rpt, American consul, Omsk, Siberia, to Sec State, History and Development of the Kolchak Government, vol. 2, Russia, Siberia, and Poland, 16 Aug 19, William J. Donovan Collection, the private papers of the former head of the Office of Strategic Services.

9. Harrison E. Salisbury, *Black Night, White Snow: Russia's Revolutions, 1905–1917* (Garden City, N.Y.: Doubleday and Co., 1978), p. 587.

10. Ian Grey, *The First Fifty Years: Soviet Russia 1917–1967*, p. 151.

11. Salisbury, *Black Night*, p. 589.

12. Robin Bruce Lockhart (Robert's son), *Ace of Spies*, p. 72.

13. Ullman, *Intervention*, p. 285.

14. MID, no file no., located in random MID papers, OMR. The top sheet begins: "Paraphrase of code message sent July 31, 1918, to American Embassy, Paris. No. 44—July 31—7 p.m. Lubly."

15. Ibid.

16. Salisbury, *Black Night*, p. 208.

17. Joachim Fest, *Hitler*, pp. 95–96.

18. Ullman, *Intervention*, p. 290.

19. *Pravda*, 9 Sep 18, in MID 20016, OMR.

## Chapter Two

1. Edgar G. Sisson, *One Hundred Red Days*, p. 27. Unless otherwise noted, quotations are from that source.

2. Sisson Rpt.

3. US Committee on Public Information, *The German-Bolshevik Conspiracy* (Washington: 20 Oct 18), pamphlet 20, doc 37A.

4. Statement by E. P. Semenov with notes by E. Sisson, MID, 10058–481–34–3284, 6 Jul 21, OMR.

5. See MID, 10058–481 for the complete file on the "Sisson Documents."

6. Statement by E. P. Semenov with notes by E. Sisson.

7. US Committee on Public Information, *The German-Bolshevik Conspiracy*.

8. George F. Kennan, *Soviet-American Relations, 1917–1920*, vol. 1, *Russia Leaves the War*, p. 448.

9. Ibid., vol. 2, *The Decision to Intervene*.

10. Philip Knightley, *The First Casualty* (New York: Harcourt, Brace, Jovanovich, 1975), p. 151.

11. US Committee on Public Information, *The German-Bolshevik Conspiracy*.

12. George Creel, *Rebel at Large: Recollections of 50 Crowded Years* (New York: G. P. Putnam's Sons, 1947), p. 183.

13. Creel, *Rebel at Large*, p. 184.

14. James R. Mock and Cedric Larson, *Words That Won the War: The Story of the Committee on Public Information* (Princeton: Princeton University Press, 1939), p. 319.

15. US Committee on Public Information, *German-Bolshevik Conspiracy*.

16. See Statement by E. P. Semenov with Notes by E. Sisson, MID, 10058–481–33, OMR.

17. Memorandum on Relations Between the Bolsheviks and the Imperial German Government in the Winter and Spring of 1918, MID, 10058–L–13, 2 Aug 21, OMR.

18. Ibid. Encl No. 2, Summary of Report of the Secretary of State dated July 1, 1920, by Two Handwriting Experts, as to the Genuineness of Thirty-nine Documents on File in the State Department.

19. Ibid. Notes Relating to Public Discussion and Criticism of the Genuineness of the Series of Documents Published by the Committee on Public Information.

20. MID, 2266–E–15, 17 Apr 18, OMR.

21. Creel, *Rebel at Large*, pp. 175 et seq.

## Chapter Three

1. Martin Gilbert, *Winston S. Churchill*, vol. 4, *The Stricken World, 1916–1922*, p. 221.

2. Winston S. Churchill, *The Great War*, vol. 3, p. 1334.

3. Maj Gen Wilds P. Richardson, "The North-Russian Expeditionary Force, 1918–1919," unpublished MS, Thomas files, US Army Center of Military History (CMH).

4. Kennan, *Soviet-American Relations*, vol. 2, *Decision to Intervene*, p. 395.

5. State Department, *Foreign Relations of the United States, 1918, Russia*, vol. 2, p. 288.

6. State Dept, *Foreign Relations, 1918, Russia*, vol. 2, p. 515.

7. Office of Naval Intelligence (ONI), Dr. Henry P. Beers, "US Naval Forces in North Russia (Archangel and Murmansk), 1918–1919," unpublished MS, Nov 43, OMR.

8. Ullman, *Anglo-Soviet Relations*, vol. 1, *Intervention*, p. 248–49.

9. Ibid., p. 251.

10. Beers, op. cit.

11. William S. Graves, *America's Siberian Adventure, 1918–1920*, p. 3.

12. Ibid., p. 4.

13. Ibid. pp. 55–56.

14. Sylvian G. Kindall, *American Soldiers in Siberia*, p. 16.

15. Ibid.

16. Graves, *America's Siberian Adventure*, p. 70.


## Chapter Four

1. GHQ, American Expeditionary Force, G-2 Sect, Report on Work of the Radio Station, Signal Corps, 25 Nov 18, in Special Collection of National Security Agent, OMR.

2. Gilbert, *Churchill*, vol. 4, *Stricken World*, pp. 78–79.

3. Churchill, *Great War*, p. 1123.

4. Ibid., p. 1133.

5. Ibid., p. 1130.

6. Gen Sir John Hackett, as cited in Anthony Sampson, *Anatomy of Europe* (New York: Harper and Row, 1962), p. 260.

7. Churchill, *Great War*, pp. 1318–19.

8. All quotations from Office of Naval Intelligence (ONI), The Massacre of the Russian Imperial Family, a report by Sir Basil Thomson of Scotland Yard, MID, 10058–949–2, 5 Jan 30, OMR.

9. J. W. Wheeler-Bennett, "Ludendorff: The Soldier and the Politician," *Virginia Quarterly Review*, spring 1938.

10. Barrie Pitt, *1918: The Last Act* (New York: W. W. Norton Co., 1962), p. 247.

11. J. W. Wheeler-Bennett, *The Nemesis of Power: The German Army in Politics 1918–1945*, p. 17.

12. Pitt, *Last Act*, p. 263, citing Capt. B. H. Liddell-Hart.

13. Julius Braunthal, *The History of the International*, p. 119n.

14. Lt Friedrich Fikentscher, "The Outbreak of the Revolution," *Deutsche Wehr*, 6 and 20 Nov 20, trans by ONI, OMR. All quotations are from that source.

15. Otto Friedrich, *Before the Deluge: A Portrait of Berlin in the 1930s*, pp. 35–37.

16. Walter Goerlitz, *History of the German General Staff, 1657–1945*, p. 202.

17. Wheeler-Bennett, *Nemesis of Power*, p. 3.

18. Robert Pick, *The Last Days of Imperial Vienna*, p. 16.

19. Ibid., p. 123.

20. Churchill, *Great War*, p. 1321.

21. Ibid., p. 1308.


## Chapter Five

1. Gilbert, *Churchill*, vol. 4, *Stricken World*, p. 227.

2. Josephus Daniels as cited by Elmer Bendiner, *A Time for Angels* (New York: Alfred A. Knopf, 1975), flyleaf.

3. Ltr, Pershing to President Wilson, 22 May 19, MID, 124–490–158, OMR.

4. Gilbert, *Churchill*, vol. 4, *Stricken World*, p. 245.

5. Ibid.

6. Henry Pelling, *Winston Churchill*, p. 255.

7. Churchill, *Great War*, p. 1397.

8. Richard H. Ullman, *Anglo-Soviet Relations*, vol. 2, *Britain and the Russian Civil War*, p. 147.

9. *Encyclopaedia Britannica*, Vol. 9, p. 546 (15th ed., 1974).

10. William E. Ironside, *Time Unguarded: The Ironside Diaries*, ed. Colonel Roderick M. McLeod and Denis Kelly (New York: David McKay Co., 1962), p. 27.

11. Maj Gen Wilds P. Richardson, "The North-Russia Expeditionary Force, 1918–1919."

12. Ibid.

13. C. J. Weeks and J. O. Baylen, "Admiral Kolchak's Visit to the United States, 10 September–9 November 1917," *Military Affairs*, April 1974.

14. Churchill, *Great War*, p. 1445.

15. State Dept, Russian Series No. 1, Exchange of Notes with Admiral Kolchak, telegram, Paris, 26 May 1919, in MID, 164–102, OMR.

16. State Dept, President of the French High Commission at Omsk to the French Foreign Office, repeated to the US Government, in Russian Series No. 1, MID, 164–102, OMR.

17. MID, 164–102, 8 Sep 19; R. O. Matheson, MID, 154–104, 26 May 20, both in OMR.

18. Ullman, *Anglo-Soviet Relations,* vol. 2, *Britain and the Russian Civil War*, p. 213.

19. Ullman, op. cit., War Cabinet, Minutes W.C. 588A, 4 Jul 19, Cab. 23/15, pp. 289–90.

## Chapter Six

1. Isaac Deutscher, *The Prophet Armed: Trotsky, 1879–1921*, p. 479.

2. D. Fedotoff White, *The Growth of the Red Army*, p. 115.

3. David Footman, *Civil War in Russia*, p. 197.

4. See Gen. A. Denikine, *The White Army* (Westport, Conn.: 1973—no publisher listed, but originally published by Jonathan Cape, London, 1930), p. 231.

5. Gilbert, *Churchill*, vol. 4, *Stricken World*, p. 309.

6. Ibid., p. 325.

7. Ullman, *Anglo-Soviet Relations*, vol. 1, *Britain and the Russian Civil War*, p. 222.

8. Gilbert, *Churchill*, vol. 4, *Stricken World*, p. 346.

9. Deutscher, *Prophet Armed*, p. 442.

10. Gilbert, *Churchill*, vol. 4, *Stricken World*, p. 351.

11. Ibid., p. 355.

12. Ibid., p. 356.

13. Ibid.

14. Churchill, *Great War*, p. 1263.

15. Footman, *Civil War*, p. 220.

16. Denikine, *White Army*, p. 327.

17. Gilbert, *Churchill*, vol. 4, *Stricken World*, p. 364.

18. Roland Gaucher, *Opposition in the USSR, 1917–1967* (New York: Funk and Wagnalls, 1969), p. 125.

19. MID, 1657–D–119, 12 Jun 20, OMR.

## PART II The Clarion

### Chapter Seven

1. Ceremonious Meeting of the First Gathering of the Third International in Moscow, in MID, 10058–S–510, 7 May 19, OMR.

2. R. H. S. Crossman, ed., *The God That Failed*, pp. 196–97.

3. Clare Sheridan, *The Naked Truth*, p. 179.

4. Gunther Nollau, *International Communism and World Revolution* (New York: Frederick A. Praeger, 1961), p. 162.

5. Sheridan, *Naked Truth*, pp. 180–81.

6. Ibid., p. 181.

7. Memo, Andor Klay to Gen Donovan, 26 Feb 47, item 32, William J. Donovan Collection.

8. This and subsequent quotations from Leon Trotsky, *The First Five Years of the Communist International*, vol. 1, pp. 19, 23–26.

### Chapter Eight

1. Braunthal, *History of International*, p. 168.

2. Paul Ignotus, *Hungary*, p. 147.

3. Ibid., p. 148n.

4. Ibid., p. 148.

5. Churchill, *Great War*, p. 1417.

6. Braunthal, *History of International*, p. 147.

7. Brit Govt, Home Office Directorate of Intelligence, Special Report: The Communist Revolution in Hungary by Sir Basil Thomson, no file no., locted in a general MID file with the document bearing the notation, "American Embassy, London, 2 June 1919." Unless otherwise noted, quotations are from that source.

8. Ignotus, *Hungary*, p. 149.

9. Ibid.

10. Fest, *Hitler*, p. 116.

11. Rosa Leviné-Meyer, *Leviné: The Life of a Revolutionary*, p. 180.

12. Leviné-Meyer, *Leviné*, p. 14.

13. Ibid., p. 95.

14. Ibid., p. 99.

15. Fest, *Hitler*, p. 87.

16. Leviné-Meyer, *Leviné*, pp. 107, 109.

17. John Toland, *Adolf Hitler*, p. 82.

18. Leviné-Meyer, *Leviné*, p. 153.

19. Sir Halford Mackinder, "The Geographical Pivot of History," in Sir Basil Liddell-Hart, *The Sword and the Pen: Selections from the World's Greatest Military Writings* (New York: Thomas Y. Crowell Co., 1976), pp. 240–41.

20. Friedrich, *Before the Deluge*, pp. 35–37.

21. Braunthal, *History of International*, p. 128.

22. Ibid., p. 129.

23. Ibid., p. 131.

24. Friedrich, *Before Deluge*, p. 43.

25. Ibid., p. 131.


## Chapter Nine

1. Washington *Post*, Dec. 24, 1920.

2. This and other Ludendorff quotes from MID, Ltr to Sec State for War and Air (British), 10058–L–15–6, Sec State to Director MID, undated, OMR.

3. Lloyd George papers, March 13, 1920, as cited in Gilbert, *Churchill*, vol. 4, *Stricken World*, p. 382.

4. Brit Govt, War Office Papers 32/6713, Public Records Office, London.

5. MID, 10058–8–342–3, Third Internationale, 88 Revolutionary, Report 2223, 1 Mar 20, OMR.

6. Report of the Visit of "The Doctor" to Scotland House, 14 Feb 20, MID, 10058–342–50–102, 30 Mar 20, OMR.

7. Warner Lerner, "Attempting a Revolution from Without: Poland in 1923" in Thomas T. Hammond and Robert Farrell, eds., *The Anatomy of Communist Takeovers*, p. 99.

8. Gilbert, *Churchill,* vol. 4, *Stricken World,* p. 414.

9. London *Evening News,* July 20, 1928.

10. Gilbert, *Churchill,* vol. 4, *Stricken World,* p. 421.

11. Braunthal, *History of International,* p. 188.

12. R. Ernst and Trevor N. Dupuy, *The Encyclopedia of Military History: From 3500 B.C. to the Present* (New York: Harper and Row, 1970), p. 991.

13. Churchill, *Great War,* pp. 1472–74.

14. ONI, Causes, Progress, and Results of Kronstadt Events, 28 Apr 21, 2657–D–381–3, OMR.

15. Ibid.

16. Resolutions in ONI, Conditions in Russia, 1921, Register No. 14230, OMR.

17. Robert Conquest, *The Great Terror: Stalin's Purge of the Thirties,* p. 545.

18. Events at Kronstadt, 6 May 21, MID, 10058–805–6–3286, OMR.

19. State Dept, H. B. Quarton to Sec State, Analysis of Foreign Assistance to the Cronstadt Revolution, 861.00/8619. OMR.

## Chapter Ten

1. George Stewart, *The White Armies of Russia,* p. 401.

2. Roland Strasser, *The Mongolian Horde,* p. 98.

3. Ibid., p. 102.

4. Stewart, *White Armies,* p. 123.

5. Thomas T. Hammond, "The Communist Takeover of Outer Mongolia: Model for Eastern Europe?" in Hammond and Farrell, *Anatomy of Communist Takeovers,* p. 118.

6. Ibid., p. 113.

7. Strasser, *Mongolian Horde,* p. 106.

8. Hammond, *Anatomy of Communist Takeovers,* p. 129.

## Chapter Eleven

1. New York *Times,* May 11, 1923.

2. Ibid.

3. State Dept, J. C. Grew to Sec State, 15 Nov 23, Diplomatic Branch (DB), 767.68119/739, NA. Unless otherwise noted, quotations are from the various Grew reports.

4. New York *Times,* May 11, 1933.

5. New York *Times,* May 20, 1923.

6. Ibid.

7. State Dept, J. C. Grew to Sec State, op. cit.

8. State Dept, F. W. B. Coleman, US Legation, Riga, Latvia, to Sec State, Comment in *Izvestia* re Appearance of Americans in the Lausanne Trial, 23 Nov 23, Diplomatic Branch, 767.68119/743.

## PART III *The American Cockpit*

### Chapter Twelve

1. Unless otherwise noted, all quotations are from the Case of Ludwig C. A. K. Martens, Self-styled "Ambassador" to the United States of the Russian Socialist Federal Republic, 10 Nov 20, MID 10110–1194–331, OMR.

2. MID, 10110–280, 20 Mar 19, OMR.

3. MID, 10110–1194–285, 5 Mar 20, OMR.

4. Ibid., US Treasury Dept, Customs Service, H. C. Stuart, Special Deputy Collector to Sec Treasury. Cf., Theodore Draper, *The Roots of American Communism*, pp. 337–38.

5. MID, 10058–25 Jun 20, OMR.

6. State Dept, Memorandum on The Bolshevist or Communist Party in Russia and Its Relation to the Third or Communist International and to the Russian Soviets, in ONI, PD 226–89, 20 Mar 20, OMR.

7. Brig Gen Churchill to Frank Burke, Asst Dir, Bureau of Investigation, MID, 10110–1194–283–102, 17 Feb 20, OMR.

8. This and subsequent quotations in regard to the subcommittee are from MID, 10110–1194–333, 13 Nov 20, Senate: Russian Propaganda Report, 12 Apr 21, OMR.

9. Brief of the Department of Justice upon the status of Ludwig Christian Alexander Karlovitch Martens under the Act of Congress, approved 16 Oct 18, submitted 7 Dec 20, MID, 10100–1194–334, OMR.

10. London *Daily Herald*, Feb. 21, 1925.

### Chapter Thirteen

1. State Dept, Memoranda on Problems Pertaining to Russian-American Relations, vol. 8, Statements by Litvinov on Matters of Foreign Policy that are of interest to the United States, p. 69, DB, NA.

2. Ibid., p. 70.

3. Special Report on Washington B. Vanderlip by the Bureau of Investigation, MID, 10058–822–21, 7 Dec 20, OMR.

4. Washington B. Vanderlip, Alleged commercial relations with Soviet government of Russia, 6 Dec 20, MID, 10058–822–25, OMR.

5. Quotations from State Dept, Cable msg from American minister at Copenhagen, August 31, 4 PM, 1920, No. 29, in MID, 10058–822–1, 8 Nov 20, OMR.

6. State Dept, Stockholm to Sec State, 15 Nov 20, Msg No. 213, in MID, 10058–822–9, OMR.

7. Weekly Situation Survey for Week Ending November 24, 1920, MID, 10058–822–X110, OMR.

8. MID, 10058–822–46, 22 Dec 20.

9. Louis Fischer, *The Life of Lenin*, p. 401.

10. Ibid., p. 407.

11. Tokyo to Sec State, Msg No. 575, 6 Nov 20, State Dept, in MID, 10058–822–6, OMR.

12. MID, 10058–822–42, Encl 2, OMR.

13. MID, 10058–822–48, OMR.

14. Fischer, *Life of Lenin*, p. 510.

15. Ltr, Sec Treasury to Sec State, MID, 2515–D–134, 2 Apr 28, OMR. See also ltr, Asst Sec Treasury to Sec State, Amtorg Trading Company, State Dept, ADT 661.1115 A.T.C./60, 11 Feb 31, DB, NA.

16. State Dept, Statements by Litvinov, op. cit., p. 77d.

17. Amtorg Information Dept, Address by Peter A. Bogdanov, Chairman, Board of Directors, Amtorg Trading Corporation, before The Institute of Politics, Williamstown, Mass., August 2, 1930, MID.

18. The Four Continents Book Corporation and Soviet Intelligence Procurement, State Dept IR Rpt 5157, 18 Jan 50, DB, NA.

*Chapter Fourteen*

1. MID, 164–A–39–17, 30 Apr 19, OMR.

2. WDGS, 16 Dec 20, OMR.

3. Ltr, J. Edgar Hoover, Actg Dir Bureau of Investigation to Dir, MID, 8 Dec 24, MID, 10110–2452–99, OMR.

4. Alexander Berkman, *Prison Memoirs of an Anarchist* (New York: Mother Earth, 1912), pp. 7–8.

5. Depts of Labor and Justice, Emma Goldman, in MID 10110–154, OMR.

6. New York *Times*, Goldman obit, May 15, 1940.

7. Depts of Labor and Justice, Emma Goldman, op. cit.

8. Washington *Post*, Dec. 22, 1919.

9. Ibid.

10. Fischer, *Life of Lenin*, pp. 410–11.

11. Ibid., p. 410.

## Chapter Fifteen

1. See *Commonwealth* v. *Nicola Sacco and Bartolomeo Vanzetti*, brief of facts brought out at the trial of the said two cases, in State Dept. 311.6521 Sa, 2 Nov 21, DB, NA.

2. Memorandum, Attorney General to Sec State, 5 Nov 21, in State Dept, 311.6521 Sa 1/41, DB, NA.

3. Ibid.

4. Ltr, Asst Attorney General to Sec State, 17 Oct 21, in State Dept, 311.6521 Sa 1/16, 2 Nov 21, DB, NA.

5. Memorandum, Attorney General to Sec State, 5 Nov 21.

6. Ltr, Ambassador Paris to Sec State, 12 Oct 21, in State Dept, 211.6521 Sa 1/8, DB, NA.

7. Manchester *Guardian*, Aug. 5, 1927.

8. Samuel Eliot Morison and Henry Steele Commager, *The Growth of the American Republic*, vol. 2. (New York: Oxford University Press, 1951), pp. 559–60.

9. Edna St. Vincent Millay, *Wine from These Grapes* (New York: Harper and Bros., 1934), p. 43.

10. State Dept, Memoranda on Problems Pertaining to Russian-American Relations, vol. 4, Question of "Communist Propaganda," Div of Eastern European Affairs, 30 Oct 33, DB, NA.

11. Ibid., citing *Stalin's Speeches on the American Communist Party*, as published by the Workers Library Publishers, New York.

12. Ibid., citing Ltr, Exec Com, Comintern, to the American Communist Party and the Communist Labor Party, as published in *The Communist International*, No. 11–12, Jun–Jul 20.

13. Ibid., citing Ltr, Exec Com, Comintern, to Communist Party of the United States of America, 21 Jan 31, as published in *The Communist International*, May 31.

## Chapter Sixteen

1. MID, 10058–94–86, 27 Apr 20, OMR.

2. Ltr, Hoover to Col. A. B. Cox, 14 Aug 20, in MID, 10058–94–128, 17 Aug 20, OMR.

3. MID, 10058–94–57, 11 Dec 19, OMR.

4. Ibid.

5. MID, 10038–24–82, 25 Feb 20, OMR.

6. MIS, 10058–24–111, Ltr, (J. Edgar) Hoover to Col Hicks (MID), 24 May 20, OMR.

7. MID, 10058–24–138, Stenographic Report of the "Trial" of L. C. Fraina, 24 Jan 21, OMR.

8. Draper, *Roots of American Communism*, p. 253, citing *The Communist*, No. 11 (1920).

9. Quotations from Lenin, *"Left-Wing" Communism: An Infantile Disorder*, in Draper, op. cit., pp. 248–49.

10. Granville Hicks, *John Reed*, p. 395.

11. W. B. Estes, "Prison and Hospital Life in Russia," an address to the Associated Physicians of Long Island, Oct 21, published as a pamphlet by the Beckwith Company, New York, as Beckwith Bulletin 2, in MID, 2657–D–687, 26 May 22, OMR.

12. Ibid.

13. Ibid.

14. Draper, *Roots of American Communism*, p. 285.

15. State Dept, American Bolshevist Dead, 5 Nov 20, in MID, 10058–94, 27 Nov 20, OMR.

16. Fischer, *Life of Lenin*, p. 411.

17. Draper, *Roots of American Communism*, pp. 287–88.

18. MID, 10058–94, 17 May 21, OMR.

19. Draper, *Roots of American Communism*, p. 289.

20. MID, 10058–24–145, 15 Mar 21, OMR.

21. MID, 10058–24, undated, OMR.

22. MID, 10058–24–156, 8 Sep 22, OMR.

## Chapter Seventeen

1. Clare Sheridan, *Russian Portraits*, p. 86.

2. Jacob Gruzenberg, alias Borodin, 1 Sep 20, MID 10058–0–3–66, OMR.

3. Campbell to Churchill, Bolshevist Propaganda, 26 May 20, MID 10058–0–3–9, OMR.

4. MID 10058–0–3–115, 27 Oct 20, OMR.

5. Senate Committee on Foreign Relations, 68th Congress, *Recognition of Russia* (Washington: GPO, 1924). Unless otherwise noted, quotations are from that source.

6. Draper, *Roots of American Communism*, p. 368. Subsequent quotations in this section are from that source.

7. See In Connection with the Affair 6-f, day and month illegible but year identifiable as 1925, MID 10058–K–18, OMR.

8. Ltr, Lt Col Mark Brooke, chief MI-4, to Director, Bureau of Investigation,

10 Apr 25, MID 10058–K–18–3, OMR. Subsequent quotations in this section are from that source.

9. Rpt of Interv with C. Fadiman by Special Agents Roy J. Barloga and John F. Sullivan, 22 Mar 49, in FBI Whittaker Chambers file, item no. 3059.

10. Chambers' consolidated statement, Item No. 3220, FBI.

## Chapter Eighteen

1. MID, 10058–600–43, 17 Sep 21, OMR.

2. MID, 10058–600–1, 28 Jun 20, OMR.

3. MID, 10058–600–T1, 28 Jun 20, OMR.

4. MID, 10058–600–43, 17 Sep 21, OMR.

5. See, for example, MID, Memorandum on British Secret Service Operations in This Country, 9771–945–45, 2 Nov 20, OMR.

6. MID, 10058–600–36, 4 Jul 21, OMR.

7. MID, 10058–372, p. 932, Wireless News, 3 May 21, OMR.

8. MID, 2655–D–10, Food Conditions in the Liberated Districts of Russia, 12 Dec 19, OMR.

9. H. H. Fisher, *The Famine in Soviet Russia 1919–1923—The Operations of the American Relief Administration* (Stanford: Stanford University Press, 1935), p. 42n.

10. Ibid., citing ltr, Martens to the Associate Editor of the Newspaper Enterprise Association, 18 Nov 20.

11. MID, 164–334–19, Russo-American Repatriations: Statement by Nuorteva, 12 Nov 20, OMR.

12. Fisher, *Famine in Soviet Russia*, p. 52.

13. Washington *Post*, Aug. 9, 1921.

14. MID, 2610–BB–8–1, 22 Sep 21, OMR.

15. Fisher, *Famine in Soviet Russia*, p. 66.

16. Ibid.

17. MID, 2657–D–538, Agreement Between Bolsheviks and American Relief Administration, Political Factor, 29 Aug 21, OMR.

18. Fisher, *Famine in Soviet Russia*, p. 61.

19. MID, 1657–D–538–3, 5 Oct 21, OMR.

20. Ibid., p. 398.

21. Baltimore *Sun*, Dec. 20, 1923.

## PART IV The British Cockpit

### Chapter Nineteen

1. Ullman, *Anglo-Soviet Relations*, vol. 1, *Intervention*, p. 233.

2. MID, 10058–384–4, 28 Feb 19, OMR.

3. ONI, Dr. Henry P. Beers, "US Naval Forces in North Russia (Archangel and Murmansk), 1918–1919," unpublished MS, Nov 43, OMR.

4. C. W. Purington to Col S. Heintzelman, The Ayan Corporation Ltd, MID, 164–397, 20 Jun 22, OMR.

5. The Hindu Conspiracy, no date, marked MI–4f, 61, MID 9771–B–70, and Memorandum of British Secret Service Activities in This Country, no date, MID 9771–949–45, OMR. Unless otherwise noted, quotations are from those sources.

6. Gilbert, *Churchill*, vol. 4, *Stricken World*, p. 405.

7. James Morris, *Pax Britannica Trilogy*, vol. 3, *Farewell to the Trumpets*, p. 274.

8. Ibid., p. 275.

9. Ibid., p. 282.

10. Gilbert, *Churchill*, vol. 4, *Stricken World*, p. 402.

11. Morris, *Pax Britannica*, p. 282.

12. Braunthal, *History of International*, p. 321.

13. Baku Conference: First Day (Sept 1, 1920), MID 10058–716–11, OMR.

14. Baku Conference, no date, MID 10058–716–14, OMR.

15. MID 10058–716–11–3284, 8 Nov 20, OMR.

16. Demonstrations of 3 Sept 20 in Baku, from the Baku newspaper, *Communist*, translated from the Russian, MID 10058–716–20, 26 Nov 20, OMR.

17. The Baku Conference of the Peoples of the Orient, Final Report from American Embassy, Constantinople, 22 Oct 20, MID 10058–716–42, OMR.

18. Ibid.

19. State Dept Press Notice: Baku Conference, 27 Sept 1920, MID 10058–716, OMR.

### Chapter Twenty

1. State Dept, Memoranda on Problems Pertaining to Russian-American Relations, vol. 4, Question of "Communist Propaganda," op. cit.

2. Quotations from Gilbert, *Churchill*, vol. 4, *The Stricken World* pp. 400, 423.

3. Christopher Andrew, The British Secret Service and Anglo-Soviet Relations in the 1920s, i, From the Trade Negotiations to the Zinoviev Letter, *The Historical*

*Journal*, Cambridge University Press, 20, 3 (1977), pp. 673–706, citing Lloyd George, "Memorandum on the proposal to expel Messrs. Kameneff and Krassin," 2 Sep 20, Lloyd George MSS F/203/1/4. Hereafter cited as Cambridge Rpt.

4. Cambridge Rpt, p. 684.

5. Gilbert, *Churchill*, vol. 4, *Stricken World*, p. 424.

6. Cambridge Rpt, pp. 424–25.

7. Cambridge Rpt, pp. 425–26.

8. Cambridge Rpt, p. 688.

9. Foreign Office Confidential Print 11861, Violations of the Russian Trade Agreement, Cambridge University Library. Hereafter cited as Violations Rpt.

10. David Piper, *London* (New York: Harper and Row, 1965), p. 350.

11. Violations Rpt, citing Secret Report No. 113 of 24 Mar 21, entitled, Bolshevik Help to Indian Revolutionaries.

12. Ibid.

13. Although the telegraphic extracts are not to be found in the MI-1C file, Violations Rpt, copies are in MID files, Telegrams No. 7245 and 7246, in Litvinov's Activities in Estonia, MID, 10058–680–323, 10 May 21, OMR.

14. Violations Rpt.

15. Ibid.

16. Brit Govt, Directorate of Intelligence (Home Office), A Monthly Review of Revolutionary Movements in British Dominions Overseas and Foreign Countries, No. 35, Sep 21, p. 24.

17. Violations Rpt, citing Soviet Report No. 293 of July 27, 1921, Programme of the Third International for 1921, 1922.

18. Ibid., File 33, Encl No. 1 to Note to Soviet Govt.

19. This and subsequent quotations from the Violations Rpt.

## Chapter Twenty-One

1. Sheridan, *Naked Truth*, p. 153. Unless otherwise noted, quotations are from that source.

2. Memo, Chief, Counter-Intelligence Branch, Col Matthew C. Smith, to director, subj: Mrs. Clare Sheridan, MID, 10058–U-28, 23 Apr 21, OMR. Another report noted Sheridan's apparent connection with the British Security Service and the opinion that "there is no harm in her." See ltr, W. F. Hurley to Under Sec State, MID, 10058–U–28–10, 16 May 21, OMR.

3. For this and subsequent quotations, see both Sheridan, *Naked Truth*, and excerpts from the Sheridan diary as published in the New York *Times* and the *Times* of London, Nov. 1920.

4. Ltr, Col Matthew C. Smith to W. D. Hurley, Under Sec State, MID, 10058–U–28–10, 16 May 21, OMR.

## Chapter Twenty-Two

1. MID, 245–71–1, 27 Nov 20, OMR.
2. MID, 245–71–5, Emigration of Undesirables to America, 18 Jan 21, OMR.
3. MID, 245–71–14, 24 Mar 21, OMR.
4. MID, 245–87, 18 Feb 21, OMR.
5. MID, 164–39, 30 Apr 19, OMR.
6. Quotations are from the *Morning Post,* July 12–19, 1920.
7. Chicago *Herald and Examiner,* Feb. 13, 1921.
8. Howard M. Sachar, *A History of Israel: From the Rise of Zionism to Our Time* (New York: Alfred A. Knopf, 1976), p. 9.

## Chapter Twenty-Three

1. Harold Nicolson, *King George the Fifth: His Life and Reign* (London: Collins, 1952), p. 384.
2. R. W. Lynam, *The First Labour Government* (London: Chapman and Hall, 1957), pp. 81–82.
3. *The Sunday Times,* Weekly Review: "The 'Red Letter' Forgers," Dec. 18, 1966.
4. Cambridge Rpt, p. 705.
5. Cambridge Rpt, p. 677.
6. Gabriel Gorodetsky, *The Precarious Truce, Anglo-Soviet Relations, 1924–1927,* p. 13, citing Brit Govt, FO 371 10465 N902/10/38: Rakovsky to MacDonald, 8 Feb 24.
7. Gorodetsky, *Precarious Truce,* p. 16.
8. Ibid., pp. 22–23.
9. Ibid., p. 32.
10. Cambridge Rpt, p. 700.
11. London *Daily Express,* Oct. 24, 1924.
12. Ibid.
13. London *Daily Mail,* Oct. 25, 1924.
14. N. Grant, "The Zinoviev Letter' Case," *Soviet Studies,* xix (1967–68), pp. 270–71.
15. Cambridge Rpt, p. 677.
16. Ibid.
17. Gilbert, *Churchill,* vol. 5, *The Prophet of Truth,* p. 59.
18. Cambridge Rpt.

## Chapter Twenty-Four

1. MID, 2657, OMR.
2. MID, 10058–890, Parts 1 and 2, 17 Dec 21, OMR.
3. Ltr from S. G. Reilly in MID, 10058–804–11, 23 Dec 21, OMR.
4. Ibid.
5. Both quotations from Gorodetsky, *Precarious Truce*, p. 38.
6. Cambridge Rpt.
7. Cambridge Rpt.
8. Lockhart, *Ace of Spies*, p. 133.
9. Ibid., p. 135.
10. In an interv with Anthony Cave Brown at Popham, Hampshire, in 1971.
11. Lockhart, *Ace of Spies*, pp. 150–51.
12. Ibid., p. 146.

## Chapter Twenty-Five

1. For this and subsequent quotations, see Gorodetsky, *Precarious Truce*.
2. Barbara W. Tuchman, *Stilwell and the American Experience in China, 1941–45*, p. 35.
3. Jacques Guillermaz, *A History of the Chinese Communist Party, 1921–1949*, p. 167.
4. Ibid., p. 78.
5. Tuchman, *Stilwell*, p. 93.
6. Guillermaz, *History of Chinese Communist Party*, pp. 94–95.
7. Ibid., p. 217.
8. Ibid., p. 218.

## Chapter Twenty-Six

1. Raid on Compound of Former Imperial Russian Legation Guard, MID, 2657–I–281, 11 Apr 27, OMR.
2. Ibid.
3. Ibid.
4. Guillermaz, *History of Chinese Communist Party*, p. 125.
5. Tuchman, *Stilwell*, p. 105.
6. Malcolm Muggeridge, *Chronicles of Wasted Time*, vol. 2, *The Infernal Grove*, p. 235.

7. Gorodetsky, *Precarious Truce*, p. 225.

8. British spy case, MID, 10058–M–34, 5 Dec 27, OMR.

9. Ibid.

10. This and following quotations are from US Mil Attaché, London, Rpt No. 19964, The Raid on Arcos Limited, in MID, 10058–M–34, 8 Jun 27.

11. State Dept, Ltr from J. B. Stetson to Sec State, No 1102, in MID, 2657–DD–514, 14 Jun 27, OMR.

12. Ibid.

13. State Dept, Ltr from Stetson to Sec State, 9 Jun 27, in MID, 2657–DD–514, OMR.

14. This and following quotations from the New York *Times*, June 11, 1927.

15. British Govt, Home Office, Report of Director of Intelligence on Singapore-Shanghai Raid of June 1931, item Fp/IPM 1932, located in Indian Govt archives, New Delhi.

## PART V The German Cockpit

### Chapter Twenty-Seven

1. Fest, *Hitler*, p. 80. Unless otherwise noted, quotations are from that source.

2. Walter C. Langer, Morale Operations Branch, OSS, with Prof. Henry A. Murray (Harvard Psychological Clinic), Dr. Ernest Kris (New School for Social Research), Dr. Bertram D. Lewis (New York Psychoanalytic Institute): "A Psychological Analysis of Adolph Hitler: His Life and Legend," in the William J. Donovan Collection. Dr. Langer in 1976 published a commercial version of the study.

3. Ibid., citing G. Ward Price, *I Know These Dictators* (London: Harrap, 1940).

4. Ibid., citing Dorothy Thompson and Edgar Mowrer.

5. Unless otherwise noted, quotations are from Fest, *Hitler*.

6. See papers of Col Carter W. Clarke, chief, Intelligence Group, MIS, OMR.

7. Interv, Maj Gen Edward L. Sibert, formerly G-2, 12th Army Group, with General of the Army Omar N. Bradley, Oct 77, as related to the authors by Sibert; and Walter Schellenberg, *The Schellenberg Memoirs*, p. 43.

8. Truman Smith Report, MID files, MMR, NA.

9. Ibid.

10. Ibid.

11. Program of German National Socialist Labor Party, from military attaché, Berlin, No. 16,402, 20 Jan 39, MID 2657–B–747–23, OMR.

12. Langer Study, op. cit.

13. Anti-Semitism in Germany, from military attaché, Berlin, No. 16,386, 12 Jan 38, MID 2657–B–801–5, OMR. Subsequent quotations are from that source.

## Chapter Twenty-Eight

1. Friedrich, *Before Deluge*, p. 53.
2. Kurt Rosenbaum, *Community of Fate*, p. 9.
3. Ibid., p. 10.
4. Fest, *Hitler*, p. 85.
5. Wheeler-Bennett, *Nemesis of Power*, p. 124.
6. Ibid., pp. 126–27.
7. Rosenbaum, *Community of Fate*, p. 17.
8. America's Refusal to Participate in the Genoa Conference, MID, 2657–D–538–10, 7 Apr 22, OMR.
9. A. P. J. Taylor, ed., *Lloyd George: A Diary by Frances Stevenson*, p. 266.
10. Harold Nicolson, *Curzon: The Last Phase, 1919–1925* (New York: Harper Bros., 1939), p. 397.
11. Fischer, *Life of Lenin*, p. 574.
12. Theodore H. von Laue, "Soviet Diplomacy: G. V. Chicherin, People's Commissar for Foreign Affairs, 1918–1930," in Gordon A. Craig and Felix Gilbert, eds., *The Diplomats, 1919–1939* (Princeton: Princeton University Press, 1953), p. 234.
13. Gordon A. Craig, "The British Foreign Office from Grey to Austen Chamberlain," in Craig and Gilbert, eds., *The Diplomats*, p. 27.
14. Taylor, *Lloyd George*, p. 236.

## Chapter Twenty-Nine

1. London *Morning Post*, May 12, 1922.
2. *Vossiche Zeitung*, 7 Oct 26, in Resignation of General Von Seeckt, Chief of the Army Directory, military attaché, Berlin, Rpt No. 8308, 13 Oct 26, MID 2016–1025–2, OMR.
3. See *"Rote Kapelle,"* a survey report, vol. 1, CIA, Aug 73, MMR.
4. Kenneth Macksey and John H. Batchelor, *Tank: A History of the Armored Fighting Vehicle* (London: Macdonald, 1970), p. 48.
5. Wheeler-Bennett, *Nemesis of Power*, p. 93.
6. Militarized Societies—The Black Reichswehr, US military attaché, Berlin, Rpt No. 8766, 7 May 27, MID 2016–1040–4–1, OMR.
7. ONI, Russo-German Naval Relations, Article 181, Versailles Treaty, OMR.
8. Leopold Heinemann to Gen of the Army D. D. Eisenhower, 20 Jul 45, Sect 10, Item 28, in War Dept, OPD 014.1, Germany, MMR.

9. The Navy's Battle Against the Treaty of Versailles, 1919–1935, rpt prepared by British Naval Intelligence Division, in Operational Archives Division, US Navy. All subsequent quotations are from that source.

## Chapter Thirty

1. Monarchistic Celebration, Rpt No. 3441, 27 Jun 22, MID 2657–B–530, OMR.
2. Friedrich, *Before Deluge,* p. 100.
3. Ibid., p. 102.
4. Ibid., p. 104.
5. The Assassination of Dr. Walther Rathenau, German Foreign Minister, on June 24, 1922, MID 2657–B–529, OMR.
6. Fest, *Hitler,* p. 162.
7. Friedrich, *Before Deluge,* p. 117.
8. Rosenbaum, *Community of Fate,* p. 48.
9. Ibid., p. 49.
10. Angelika Balabanov, former secretary of the Comintern, untitled, undated, and unpublished MS in the William J. Donovan Collection. Unless otherwise noted, quotations are from that source.
11. Rosenbaum, *Community of Fate,* p. 72.
12. Ibid.
13. Eugene Davidson, *The Making of Adolf Hitler* (New York: The Macmillan Co., 1977), p. 205.
14. Braunthal, *History of International,* vol. 2, p. 281.
15. Ibid., p. 282.
16. Fest, *Hitler,* p. 187.
17. Toland, *Adolf Hitler,* p. 151.
18. Fest, *Hitler,* pp. 192–93.
19. Toland, *Adolf Hitler,* p. 157.
20. Fest, *Hitler,* p. 187.
21. Toland, *Adolf Hitler,* p. 158.
22. Fest, *Hitler,* p. 195.
23. Toland, *Adolf Hitler,* p. 164.
24. Ibid., p. 167.
25. Ibid.
26. Arthur Möller van den Bruck, as cited in Toland, *Adolf Hitler,* p. 176.
27. Toland, *Adolf Hitler,* pp. 176–77.

## Chapter Thirty-One

1. All subsequent quotations are from Rosenbaum, *Community of Fate*.
2. Fest, *Hitler*, p. 214. All quotations are from that source.

## Chapter Thirty-Two

1. G-2 Rpt, Summary of the political situation for the month of May, 1925, MID, 2657–B–641, OMR.
2. Friedrich, *Before Deluge*, p. 187.
3. Muggeridge, *Chronicles of Wasted Time*, vol. 2, *Infernal Grove*, p. 13.
4. Rosenbaum, *Community of Fate*, p. 184. Subsequent quotations are from that source.

## Chapter Thirty-Three

1. Rosenbaum, *Community of Fate*, p. 247. Unless otherwise noted, quotations are from that source.
2. H. Montgomery Hyde, *Stalin: The History of a Dictator*, p. 277.

## Chapter Thirty-Four

1. Nevile Henderson, *Failure of a Mission*, pp. 27–28.
2. Heinz Höhne, *The Order of the Death's Head* (London: Secker and Warburg, 1969), pp. 44–45.
3. Ibid.
4. Ibid., p. 172.
5. Ibid.
6. Ibid., p. 322.
7. Toland, *Adolf Hitler*, p. 289.
8. Fest, *Hitler*, p. 381.
9. Ibid., p. 384.
10. Toland, *Adolf Hitler*, pp. 291–292.
11. Fest, *Hitler*, p. 427.

## Chapter Thirty-Five

1. Fest, *Hitler*, p. 337.
2. Ibid., pp. 404–05.
3. Ibid., p. 405.
4. Toland, *Adolf Hitler*, p. 297.
5. Fest, *Hitler*, p. 408. Subsequent unattributed quotations are from that source.
6. Toland, *Adolf Hitler* p. 300.
7. OSS, Research and Analysis Biographical Report on H. H. G. Schacht, Document No. 909, vol. 51, William J. Donovan Collection.

## PART VI The Russian Cockpit

## Chapter Thirty-Six

1. New York *Times*, April 6, 1922.
2. Fischer, *Life of Lenin*, pp. 598–99. Unattributed quotations are from that source.
3. Grey, *First Fifty Years*, p. 196.
4. Ibid., p. 197.
5. Hyde, *Stalin*, p. 201.
6. Elizabeth Lermolo, *Face of a Victim* (New York: Harper Bros., 1955), pp. 136–37.
7. Hyde, *Stalin*, p. 207.
8. Grey, *First Fifty Years*, p. 205.
9. Hyde, *Stalin*, p. 214.
10. Grey, *First Fifty Years*, p. 208.
11. Hyde, *Stalin*, p. 221.

## Chapter Thirty-Seven

1. New York *Times*, July 26, 1926.
2. Hyde, *Stalin*, p. 225.
3. Barbara Gelb, *So Short a Time: A Biography of John Reed and Louise Bryant* (New York: W. W. Norton Co., 1973), p. 256.

4. Hyde, *Stalin*, p. 223.

5. Ibid., p. 224. Italics in the original.

6. Curzio Malaparte, *Coup d'Etat: The Technique of Revolution* (New York: E. P. Dutton Co., 1932), pp. 79–80.

7. Hyde, *Stalin*, p. 226.

8. Ibid., p. 227.

9. Deutscher, *Prophet Armed*, pp. 125–26.

10. See Committee on the Judiciary, 94th Congress, 1st Session, *Trotskyite Terrorist International* (Washington: GPO, 1975).

11. Isaac Deutscher, *The Prophet Outcast*, p. 188.

12. Ibid., p. 289.

13. Office of Strategic Services (OSS), Chronology of Principal Events Relating to the USSR: From American Recognition of the USSR to the Soviet-German Conflict, 10 October 1933–21 June 1941, MMR. Hereafter cited as OSS Chronology.

14. Conquest, *Great Terror*, p. 52.

15. Ibid., p. 109. Unless otherwise noted, quotations about the trial are from that source.

## Book Two WAR STATIONS: 1933–1939

## PART VII The American Station

### Chapter Thirty-Eight

1. William Manchester, *The Glory and the Dream: A Narrative History of America, 1932–1972*, p. 43.

2. Ibid., p. 31.

3. State Dept, Cole to Sec State, 661.1115/551, 26 Jul 33, DB, NA.

4. William C. Bullitt, "How We Won the War and Lost the Peace," *Life*, Aug. 20, 1948.

5. Washington *Herald*, Aug. 31, 1933.

6. Donald G. Bishop, *The Roosevelt-Litvinov Agreements: The American View*, p. 11.

7. New York *Times*, Nov. 8, 1933.

8. Ltr, Litvinov to Roosevelt, 16 Nov 33, State Dept, *Foreign Relations of the United States, Russia*.

9. Washington *Post*, Nov. 18, 1933.

10. Earl Latham, *The Communist Controversy in Washington* (Cambridge: Harvard University Press, 1966), p. 36n.

11. Bishop, *Roosevelt-Litvinov Agreements*, p. 255.

12. Ibid., p. 211.

13. Ibid.

14. Ibid., p. 212.

15. War Dept Gen Staff, "The Influence of Brigadier General Phillip R. Faymonville on Soviet-American Relations," in the private papers of Maj Gen Watson, military aide to President Roosevelt, MS Dept, University of Virginia, Accession No. 9786, Box 29, "Intelligence Folder."

16. State Dept, Hull to Embassy, Moscow, 5 Apr 34, DB, NA.

17. State Dept, Hull to Embassy, Moscow, 31 Jan 35, DB, NA.

18. State Dept, Cole (Riga, Latvia) to Sec State, in 811.00B Party, Workers (Communist)/56, DB, NA.

19. Bishop, *Roosevelt-Litvinov Agreements*, p. 42.

20. Ibid.

21. Msg, Bullitt to Sec State, 8 Jul 35, State Dept, *Foreign Relations of the United States–Russia*, p. 222.

22. Ibid., Msg, Bullitt to Sec State, 13 Jul 35, p. 223.

23. Ibid., Msg, Bullitt to Sec State, 6 Aug 35, p. 224.

24. Ibid.

25. Ibid., State Dept press release, 25 Aug 35, p. 251.

26. Msg, Bullitt to Sec State, 29 Aug 35, in 711.61/542b, DB, NA.

27. Background and History of Alexander Stevens, item 3221, in the Hiss-Chambers file, FBI.

28. Final Text, Resolution on the American Question, Presidium ECCI, 1 Jul 27, in MID, 10058–349, OMR. (Also in file of Capt Harry C. Learn, MI–RES, OMR).

29. Dept of Justice, Registration Statement 485, in State Dept 861.01B11/11–447 CS/A, 4 Nov 27, DB, NA.

30. Maj Gen William J. Donovan and Mary Gardiner Jones, "Program for a Democratic Counterattack to Communist Penetration of Government Service," *The Yale Law Review*, July 1949.

31. Ltr, J. Edgar Hoover to Lt Gen Hoyt S. Vandenberg, G-2, 21 Feb 45, in FBI 61–6328–62.

32. Ibid.

33. World Tourists, Inc., Report of New York Confidential Informant T-1, Oct 54, 61–6328, New York file 97–13, FBI.

34. Foreign Agents' Registration Act: Statement by Elizabeth Terrill Bentley, in FBI 61–6328, sect 4, serials 91 through 135.

## Chapter Thirty-Nine

1. All quotations are from Poyntz file, FBI.

2. "Confessions of a Communist: The Life of Joseph Weinkoop," unpublished MS probably written around 1947, William J. Donovan Collection. Quotations are from that source.

3. Consolidated rpt of intervs by Special Agents Thomas G. Spencer and Francis X. Plant with Chambers "concerning his association with the Communist Party, the Communist Party underground, and the Communist Party espionage apparatus, 1924–April 1938," Item 3220, FBI. Unattributed quotations are from that source.

4. Ibid.

5. Allen Weinstein, *Perjury: The Hiss-Chambers Case*, p. 73.

6. Ibid., p. 96.

7. Item 3220, FBI. All quotations are from that source.

## Chapter Forty

1. House of Representatives, Committee on Un-American Activities, "The Communist Party of the United States as an Agent of a Foreign Power" (Washington: G.P.O, 1947).

2. Item 3220, FBI. Subsequent quotations in this section are from that source.

3. Manchester, *Glory and Dream*. p. 101.

4. Ladd to Hoover, 29 Dec 48, Item 659, FBI.

5. Ibid.

6. Ibid.

7. Ibid.

8. Norman Thomas to Director FBI, 15 Nov 48, in Juliet Stewart Poyntz, case no. 100–206603–20, page no. 2186, FBI.

9. Ladd to Hoover, Item 659.

10. Ibid.

11. Ibid.

12. Weinstein, *Perjury*, p. 330n.

## Chapter Forty-One

1. Weinkoop MS, op. cit. Unless otherwise noted, quotations are from that source.

2. "The Communist Position on the Negro Question, Self-Determination for

the Black Belt," pamphlet published Sep 32 by the Workers Library Publishers, New York, Item 2069, William J. Donovan Collection.

3. "Communism and the International Situation: Thesis on the International Situation and the Tasks of the Communist International," adopted at the Sixth World Congress of the Communist International, 1928 (New York: Workers Library Publishers, 1929), p. 30.

4. Committee on Un-American Activities, House of Representatives, 80th Congress, First Session, *Report on American Youth for Democracy* (Washington: GPO, 1947). Subsequent quotations are from that source.

## Chapter Forty-Two

1. Angelika Balabanov, untitled, undated MS of nine typewritten chapters, William J. Donovan Collection.

2. Statutes and Materials Relating to Subversive Activities, Vol. 43, Item 743, William J. Donovan Collection.

3. Ibid., citing *Gitlow v. New York*, 268 US 652 (1925).

4. Ibid., citing *Schneiderman v. United States*, 320 US 118 (21 Jun 43).

5. Weinkoop MS, op. cit.

6. Ibid.

7. Memo, Interdepartmental Committee of Investigations, FBI.

8. Memo by George Kennan, Nov. 24, 1937, in *Foreign Relations of the United States*, Russia, pp. 446–47.

9. Ltrs, Pittman-Hull and Hull-Pittman, 19 and 30 Jan 40, SD 711.61/704, DB, NA.

10. Cordell Hull, *Memoirs* (New York: The Macmillan Co., 1948), pp. 972–73.

11. Memo by Berle, 29 May 40, SD 711.61/732-1/2, DB, NA.

## Chapter Forty-Three

1. Louis Budenz, *This Is My Story* (New York: Whittlesey, 1947), pp. 254–55.

2. Rpt by Special Agent George J. Starr, in Frank Jacson and Sylvia Ageloff, file no. 62–6870, 3 Sep 40, and Interv with Sylvia Ageloff by Special Agent R. S. Garner, in Jacques Mornard van Dendreschd, file no. 100–7551, 5 Nov 42, both in FBI files.

3. Excerpt from Budenz, *Men Without Faces*, in Jacques Mornard et al., file no. 65–29162–193, 19 Jun 50, FBI.

4. Committee Print, *American Aspects of Assassination of Leon Trotsky*, Hearings before the Committee on Un-American Activities, House of Representatives, 81st Congress (Washington: GPO, 1951).

5. Ibid.

6. Deutscher, *Prophet Outcast,* p. 420.

7. Ibid., p. 359.

8. Leon Trotsky, *Stalin* (New York: Harper and Bros., 1946), pp. 416, 383.

9. Deutscher, *Prophet Outcast,* p. 478.

10. Ibid., p. 479.

11. Ltr, Special Agent B. E. Sackett to Director FBI, 30 Aug 40 in file no. 62–6870, FBI.

12. Memo, Re: Jacques Mornard van Dendreschd, 5 Sep 40, in case no. 65–29162, FBI.

13. Ltr, G. P. Shaw, US consul, Mexico City, to Sec State, Trotsky Case, 1 Sep 40, in 861.00 Trotsky, Leon/149: Extracts taken from the court record of the Trotsky Murder Case, Court of First Instance, Coyoacán, State Dept.

14. Ibid.

15. Deutscher, *Prophet Outcast,* p. 486.

16. Ibid., p. 487.

17. Rpt, G. P. Shaw, US consul, Mexico City, to Sec State, 28 May 40: Assault of Leon Trotsky and Disappearance of American citizen Sheldon Harte, in 861.00 Trotsky, Leon/114, DB, NA.

18. Rpt, G. P. Shaw, US consul, Mexico City, to Sec State, 11 Oct 40: Declarations of David Alfaro Siqueiros, Mexican Communist, Before the Judge of First Instance, in Connection with the Assault on the House of Leon Trotsky on May 24, 1940, in 861.00 Trotsky, Leon/183, DB, NA.

19. Memo, R. G. MacGregor to G. P. Shaw, 24 May 40, no file no. but in 861.00 Trotsky, Leon, DB, NA.

20. Ltr, J. Edgar Hoover to SAC New York transmitting memo from Adolf A. Berle re Jacques Mornard van Dendreschd, ESP-R: Translation of Articles by Leon Trotsky Entitled, "Him, I Accuse," 30 Oct 40, FBI. In the articles, Trotsky used the name for the Soviet secret police current at the time he left Russia, OGPU; the authors have substituted the designation then current, NKVD.

21. Deutscher, *Prophet Outcast,* p. 492.

## Chapter Forty-Four

1. Rpt by Special Agent R. S. Garner to Director FBI, 11 May 42, FBI.

2. Ibid.

3. Deutscher, *Prophet Outcast,* p. 496.

4. Ibid., pp. 497–98.

5. Quotations are from US Consul G. P. Shaw to Sec State, The Trotsky Case, 4 Sep 40, in 861.00 Trotsky, Leon/152, DB, NA.

6. Unless otherwise noted, quotations are from Deutscher, *Prophet Outcast,* pp. 500 ff.

7. Rpt, US Consul G. P. Shaw to Sec State, Statement of Jacques Mornard to Mexico City Police, in 861.00 Trotsky/Leon 152, DB, NA.

8. Trotsky used the old term, OGPU.

9. Memo, Briggs to Welles, 22 Aug 40, in 861.00 Trotsky, Leon/133, DB, NA.

10. Ibid.


## Chapter Forty-Five

1. Ltrs, Director FBI to SAC NY, 3 and 4 Sep 40, in file no. 56–29162–4 and –10, FBI.

2. Rpt, American Consul-General Vancouver, Application for Canadian Passport of Tony Babich, in 861.00 Trotsky, Leon/187, DB, NA.

3. Ibid., statement by Joseph Hansen, Encl to Dispatch No. 232 from American Consul-General, Mexico DF, 24 Aug 40.

4. Rpt on Jacques Mornard van Dendreschd by R. S. Garner, 11 May 42, in file no. 65–29162, item 150, FBI.

5. Walter G. Krivitsky, *In Stalin's Secret Service*, p. 252.

6. Ibid., pp. 254–55.

7. Gaucher, *Opposition in the USSR*, p. 274.

8. Krivitsky, *In Stalin's Secret Service*, p. 256.

9. Ibid., p. 266.

10. Ibid., p. 268.

11. Ibid., p. 273.

12. Gordon Brook-Shepherd, *The Stormy Petrels* (New York: Harcourt, Brace, Jovanovich, 1977), p. 169.

13. New York *Times*, Oct. 12, 1939. For OGPU, the authors have substituted NKVD.

14. Ibid.

15. All quotations from the New York *Times*, 12 Feb 41.

16. Arthur Koestler, *The Invisible Writing* (New York: The Macmillan Co., 1970), p. 483.


## Chapter Forty-Six

1. Geoffrey T. Hellman, "A Reporter At Large: The Contemporaneous Memoranda of Dr. Sachs," *The New Yorker*, Dec. 1, 1945.

2. Quotations are from Summary Memorandum containing the results of our investigation of Dr. J. Robert Oppenheimer, J. Edgar Hoover to the Hon Lewis L. Strauss, Chairman, Atomic Energy Commission, 18 Nov 53, FBI.

3. See dossier on Ursula Hamburger and R. R. Kuczynski in CIA Survey Report, *Rote Kapelle*, vol. 2, p. 334.

4. Rpt of H. H. Clegg and R. J. Lamphere covering interviews with Klaus Fuchs in London, Re: FOOCASE ESP-R, Item 1412, FBI.

5. All quotations from Harry Gold, unpublished memoir, "The Circumstances Surrounding My Work As a Soviet Agent," ESP-R, doc no. 798X, 5 Jul 51, FBI.

## PART VIII The British Station

### Chapter Forty-Seven

1. Gilbert, *Churchill*, vol. 5, *Prophet of Truth*, p. 226.

2. Churchill, *Gathering Storm*, p. 85.

3. Gilbert, *Churchill*, vol. 5, *Prophet of Truth*, p. 456.

4. Ibid., p. 457.

5. Ibid., p. 488.

6. Ibid.

7. Winston Churchill, "The Truth About Hitler," *Strand* Magazine, Nov. 1935.

8. Robert Payne, *The Life and Death of Adolf Hitler*, p. 94.

9. Frances Donaldson, *Edward VIII*, p. 211.

10. Fest, *Hitler*, p. 526.

11. Ibid., pp. 526–27.

12. Ibid., p. 527.

### Chapter Forty-Eight

1. Florence M. Miale and Michael Selzer, *The Nuremberg Mind: The Psychology of the Nazi Leaders* (New York: Quadrangle Books, 1975), p. 168 ff.

2. London *Times*, June 23, 1894.

3. Donaldson, *Edward VIII*, p. 19.

4. Keith Middlemas and John Barnes, *Baldwin* (London: Weidenfeld and Nicolson, 1969), p. 976.

5. Sampson, *Anatomy of Britain*, p. 227.

6. J. Bryan III and Charles J. V. Murphy, *The Windsor Story*, p. 61.

7. Marvin Barrett, *The Years Between: A Dramatic View of the Twenties and Thirties* (Boston: Little, Brown and Co., 1962), p. 151.

8. The Duchess of Windsor, *The Heart Has Its Reasons* (London: Michael Joseph, 1956), p. 201.

9. Barrett, *Years Between*, p. 153.

10. Donaldson, *Edward VIII*, p. 175.

11. Ibid., p. 181.

12. Donaldson, *Edward VIII*, pp. 203–4.

13. State Dept, 841.001 Edward VIII/109 GC, DB, NA.

14. Nigel Nicolson, ed., *Harold Nicolson: Diaries and Letters 1930–1939*, pp. 239–40.

15. Donaldson, *Edward VIII*, p. 192.

16. HMSO, *Documents on German Foreign Policy*, series v, vol. 7, doc 1506/E37133–35.

17. Donaldson, *Edward VIII*, p. 214.

18. Albert Speer, *Inside the Third Reich*, p. 113.

19. Gilbert, *Churchill*, vol. 5, *Prophet of Truth*, p. 712.

20. Fritz Hesse, *Hitler and the English* (London: Wingate, 1954), pp. 21–23.

21. HMSO, *Documents on German Foreign Policy*, series vii, vol. 4, doc no. 8015/E576522–4.

22. Ibid., doc no. HO 32069/70.

23. Speer, *Inside Third Reich*, p. 133.

24. Interv by Anthony Cave Brown with Maj Gen Sir Frederick de Guingand, at that period military secretary to British War Minister Leslie Hore-Belisha, later chief of staff to Field Marshal Sir Bernard L. Montgomery, 21st Army Group.

25. Donaldson, *Edward VIII*, p. 218.

26. This and subsequent quotations from Churchill, *Gathering Storm*, pp. 222–24.

## Chapter Forty-Nine

1. Donaldson, *Edward VIII*, p. 221.

2. J. G. Lockhart, *Cosmo Gordon Lang* (London: Hodder and Stoughton, 1949), p. 398.

3. Donaldson, *Edward VIII*, p. 242.

4. London *Times*, Nov. 29, 1936.

5. Donaldson, *Edward VIII*, p. 253.

6. Ibid., p. 257.

7. State Dept, Singapore, Straits Settlements, Constitutional Crisis, 5 Dec 36, in 841.000 Edward VIII, DB, NA.

8. State Dept, Canadian Reaction to Constitutional Crisis Between King and British Cabinet, 8 Dec 36, in 841.001 Edward VIII/67, DB, NA.

9. London *Times*, Dec. 10, 1936.

10. Donaldson, *Edward VIII*, p. 264.

11. Ibid., pp. 314–16.

12. London *Times*, Dec. 14, 1936.

13. Donaldson, *Edward VIII*, p. 323.

14. State Dept, 841.001/77, Edward VIII GMB, DB, NA.

15. Donaldson, *Edward VIII*, p. 347.

16. Ibid., p. 350.

17. Paul Schmidt, *Hitler's Interpreter*, p. 75.

18. New York *Times*, Oct. 23, 1937.

19. Speer, *Inside Third Reich*, p. 113.

20. Gilbert, *Churchill*, vol. 5, *Prophet of Truth*, p. 785.

21. Simon Haxey, *Tory MP* (London: Left Book Club, 1939), p. 199.

22. See Frederick W. Winterbotham, *The Nazi Connection* (New York: Harper and Row, 1978).

## Chapter Fifty

1. Haxey, *Tory MP*, p. 216.

2. Hugh Thomas, *The Spanish Civil War*, pp. 219, 221.

3. Ibid., p. 299.

4. Verle B. Johnstone, *Legions of Babel: The International Brigades in the Spanish Civil War* (Hoover Institution on War, Revolution, and Peace and the Pennsylvania State University Press, 1967), p. 91.

5. Paul Wohl, "Walter G. Krivitsky, A Study of a Man Whose Life Was Hidden Behind His Political Significance," *The Commonweal*, Feb. 28, 1941.

6. Krivitsky, *In Stalin's Secret Service*, pp. 81–82.

7. Ibid., p. 86.

8. *The Legacy of Alexander Orlov*, Hearings of the Subcommittee to Investigate the Administration of the Internal Security Act and Other Internal Security Laws of the Committee of the Judiciary, US Senate, 93d Congress, 1st Session (Washington: GPO, August 1973).

9. Ibid.

10. Ibid.

11. Washington *Post*, April 6, 1957.

12. Braunthal, *History of International*, p. 464.

13. Conquest, *Great Terror*, p. 439.

## PART IX The German Station

## Chapter Fifty-One

1. Norman H. Baynes, *The Speeches of Adolf Hitler* (London: Oxford University Press, 1942), vol. 2, p. 1019.

2. Library of Congress, "The Intensification of the Versailles Antagonisms and the Menace of the New Imperialist War," *Communist International*, vol. 10, no. 9, 15 May 33.

3. HMSO, *Documents on German Foreign Policy*, series C, vol. 2, pp. 334–35, 352.

4. Ibid., vol. 1, pp. 717, 833.

5. Quotes from Tukhachevsky are from M. N. Tukhachevsky, "Sentinel of Peace," his speech before the Central Executive Committee as published in Mar 36 by International Publishers, New York, Item 2069, William J. Donovan Collection.

6. White, *Growth of Red Army*, p. 352. Italics in the original.

7. *Pravda*, 12 Jun 37, copy in Faymonville to Asst G2, MID, 2655, OMRCofS, NA.

8. Conquest, *Great Terror*, p. 485.

9. Alexander Barmine, *One Who Served* (New York: G. P. Putnam's Sons, 1945), p. 79.

10. Head of SD Hauptamt 1938, *Die Politische Lage in der Roten Armee*, files of the Personal Staff of the Reichsführer-SS and Chief of the German Police, Microfilm Group 1–175, roll 467, William J. Donovan Collection.

## Chapter Fifty-Two

1. Fest, *Hitler*, p. 561. Unless otherwise noted, quotations are from that source.
2. Toland, *Adolf Hitler*, p. 438.
3. Ibid., p. 442.
4. Ibid., p. 444.
5. Ibid., p. 451.
6. William L. Shirer, *Berlin Diary*, p. 157.
7. Walter C. Langer study. See note 2, Chapter 2.
8. Ibid.
9. Henderson, *Failure of a Mission*, p. 74.
10. Ibid.
11. Speer, *Inside Third Reich*, p. 194.
12. Fest, *Hitler*, p. 109.
13. Ibid., p. 717.

## PART X  The Russian Station

### Chapter Fifty-Three

1. As cited in memo from John C. Hughes to Director, OSS, 19 Apr 43, A Survey of Russo-Japanese Relations, OSS, R&A, William J. Donovan Collection.

2. Memo from Hughes to Director, OSS, 19 Apr 43.

3. Japanese Attempts at Infiltration Among Muslims in Russia and Her Borderlands, Research and Analysis paper 890.2, Aug 44, OSS, DB, MMR, NA. All quotations are from that source.

4. Henry L. Roberts, "Maxim Litvinov," in Craig and Gilbert, eds., *The Diplomats, 1919–1939*, p. 344.

5. James McSherry, *Stalin, Hitler, and Europe*, vol. 1, p. 10.

6. Ibid., pp. 11–12.

7. The Earl of Avon, *The Eden Memoirs (2 vols.)*, vol. 2, *Facing the Dictators* (London: Heinemann, 1959), p. 155.

8. PRO: telegram, Eden to Northern Department and Sinon, FO, 30 Mar 35 in FO 371/19468.

9. Ibid.

10. The German-Japanese anti-Bolshevist Agreement, rpt no. 14,999 of the US military attaché, Berlin, 30 Nov 36, MID, 2657–B–792–1, OMR, NA.

11. US Army Center of Military History, translation of *History of the Great Patriotic War of the Soviet Union 1941–1945*, vol. 1, *Preparation for and Unleashing of the War by the Imperialistic Powers* (Moscow: Military Publishing House of the Ministry of Defense of the USSR), pp. 179–80.

12. Ibid., pp. 330–31.

13. *The "Magic" Background of Pearl Harbor* (Washington: GPO, 1979), vol. 1, Telegram from the Ambassador in Japan (Grew) to the Secretary of State, 27 Jan 41, State Dept 11, 134, p. 5.

### Chapter Fifty-Four

1. Excerpts from files of the German Naval Staff and from other captured German documents, in ONI, Espionage-Sabotage-Conspiracy.

2. Unless otherwise noted, all quotations are from CIA, *Rote Kapelle*: A Survey Report, vols. 1 and 2. For Trepper's own account of his activities, see Leopold Trepper, *The Great Game: Memoirs of the Spy Hitler Couldn't Silence* (New York: McGraw-Hill Book Co., 1977).

3. David J. Dallin, *Soviet Espionage*, p. 42.

4. Bruce Page, David Leitch, and Phillip Knightley, *The Philby Conspiracy* (Garden City: Doubleday and Co., 1968), p. 181.

5. Elizabeth Monroe, *Philby of Arabia* (New York: William R. Morrow Co.), 1973, p. 164.

6. Martin Green, *Children of the Sun: A Narrative of "Decadence" in England after 1918*, p. 229–30.

7. Ibid., p. 252.

8. Page, Leitch, and Knightley, *Philby Conspiracy*, p. 71.

9. Muggeridge, *Chronicles of Wasted Time*, vol. 2, *Infernal Grove*, pp. 106–7.

## Chapter Fifty-Five

1. R. N. Carew Hunt, "Willi Muenzenberg," an essay in St. Antony's Papers, No. 9, International Communism Edition, edited by David Footman and published in 1960 by Southern Illinois University Press. A leading British student of Russia, Carew Hunt served in the anti-Soviet section of the British Secret Intelligence Service; his essay provides one of the few biographical accounts of Muenzenberg, and unless otherwise noted, all quotations are from that source.

2. Lazitch and Drachkovitch, *Biographical Dictionary of the Comintern*, p. 282.

3. Unless otherwise noted, quotations are from The World Congress Against War, "Report on the Congress, Opening Address by Henri Barbusse, and the Manifesto," published by the American Committee for Struggle Against War, 1932, item 2069, William J. Donovan Collection.

4. Claud Cockburn, "Britain's Spy Serial," New York *Times*, Nov. 23, 1979.

5. Quotations are from Proceedings of the Third US Congress Against War and Fascism, "United Against Fascism for Peace," Cleveland, Ohio, 3–5 Jan 36, William J. Donovan Collection.

## Chapter Fifty-Six

1. Arthur Upham Pope, *Maxim Litvinoff*, p. 33. Unless otherwise noted, quotations are from that source.

2. Muggeridge, *Chronicles of Wasted Time*, vol. 2, *Infernal Grove*, p. 13.

3. State Dept, Regulation of Armaments Branch, Division of International Security Affairs, The USSR and Disarmament 1921–1932, item 202, vol. 5, William J. Donovan Collection. All quotations on disarmament are from that source.

4. Henry L. Roberts, "Maxim Litvinov," in Craig and Gilbert, *Diplomats*, p. 344.

5. Craig and Gilbert, *Diplomats*, p. 359.

6. Ibid., p. 362.

## PART XI *"The Second Imperialist War"*

### Chapter Fifty-Seven

1. Macmillan, *The Past Masters*, p. 126. Unless otherwise noted, quotations are from that source.

2. Ibid., citing Ian Macleod.

3. Schmidt, *Hitler's Interpreter*, p. 76.

4. Toland, *Adolf Hitler*, p. 425. See also B. H. Liddell-Hart, *History of the Second World War* (New York: G. P. Putnam's Sons, 1971), p. 8.

5. Telford Taylor, *Munich: The Price of Peace* (Garden City: Doubleday and Co., 1979), p. 311. Italics in the original.

6. Memo, John C. Wiley, Foreign Nationalities Branch, Coordinator of Information, British attitude before the *Anschluss*, 16 Feb 42, William J. Donovan Collection.

7. League of Nations *Official Journal*, special supplement 138, Library of Congress.

8. Churchill, *Gathering Storm*, pp. 257–58.

### Chapter Fifty-Eight

1. Norman Longmate, *How We Lived Then* (London: Hutchinson, 1971), p. 2.

2. Gilbert, *Churchill*, vol. 5, *Prophet of Truth*, p. 1088.

3. Ibid., p. 962.

4. New York *Times*, Sept. 15, 1938.

5. The Italian foreign minister, Count Ciano, as cited in David Dilks, ed., *The Diaries of Sir Alexander Cadogan, 1938–1945*, pp. 136–37.

6. As cited in Churchill, *Gathering Storm*, p. 286.

7. Ibid.

8. Green, *Children of Sun*, p. 180. Subsequent quotations are from that source.

## Chapter Fifty-Nine

1. Dilks, *Diaries of Sir Alexander Cadogan*, p. 363.
2. Nicolson, *Harold Nicolson: Diaries and Letters*, pp. 255–56.
3. Churchill, *Gathering Storm*, pp. 224–25.
4. Gilbert, *Churchill*, vol. 5, *Prophet of Truth*, pp. 723–24.
5. Ibid., p. 740.
6. Ibid., p. 741.
7. Toland, *Adolf Hitler*, p. 526.
8. Nicolson, *Harold Nicolson: Diaries and Letters*, pp. 387–88.
9. London *Times*, April 1, 1939.
10. Gilbert, *Churchill*, vol. 5, *Prophet of Truth*, p. 1053.
11. Ibid., p. 1056.
12. Ibid., p. 1073.
13. Toland, *Adolf Hitler*, p. 537.
14. Ibid., p. 539.
15. McSherry, *Stalin, Hitler, and Europe*, vol. 1, pp. 216–17.
16. Ibid.

## Chapter Sixty

1. Fest, *Hitler*, p. 619. Unless otherwise noted, quotations are from that source.
2. Krivitsky, *Inafl7Stalis Secret Service*, pp. 3–4.
3. Churchill, *Gathering Storm*, p. 330.
4. McSherry, *Stalin, Hitler and Europe*, vol. 1, pp. 141–42, citing *Documents on German Foreign Policy*, vol. 6, pp. 266–67.
5. Toland, *Adolf Hitler*, p. 547.
6. Hyde, *Stalin*, p. 396.
7. McSherry, *Stalin, Hitler and Europe*, vol. 1, p. 214.
8. Earl Browder, *America and the Second Imperialist War*, pamphlet issued by the New York State Committee of the Communist Party, item no. 2069, William J. Donovan Collection.
9. Braunthal, *History of International*, p. 498.
10. Report on Soviet-German Non-Aggression Pact by US military attaché, Riga, Latvia, MID Rpt No. 10501, 19 Sep 39, OMR, NA.
11. Ibid.
12. McSherry, *Stalin, Hitler, and Europe*, vol. 2, p. 15.
13. Toland, *Adolf Hitler*, p. 553.
14. Unless otherwise noted, subsequent quotations are from Henderson, *Failure of a Mission*, pp. 306–8.

15. Deakin, *The Brutal Friendship*, pp. 6–7.

16. David Irving, *Hitler's War*, p. 75.

17. Toland, *Adolf Hitler*, p. 553.

18. Deakin, *Brutal Friendship*, p. 7.

19. Toland, *Adolf Hitler*, p. 554.

20. New York *Times*, Sept. 1, 1939.

## Chapter Sixty-One

1. New York *Times*, Sept. 2, 1939; Fest, *Hitler*, p. 625.

2. Gilbert, *Churchill*, vol. 5, *Prophet of Truth*, p. 1106.

3. Ibid., p. 1107.

4. Ibid., p. 1108.

5. Herbert Luethy, *France Against Herself* (New York: Meridian Books, 1955), p. 82.

6. Toland, *Adolf Hitler*, p. 573.

7. *The Sunday Times*, Sept. 3, 1939.

8. Toland, *Adolf Hitler*, p. 574.

9. Gilbert, *Churchill*, vol. 5, *Prophet of Truth*, p. 1109.

10. Churchill, *Gathering Storm*, p. 362.

11. Toland, *Adolf Hitler*, p. 574.

12. Ibid., p. 575.

13. Schmidt, *Hitler's Interpreter*, p. 463.

14. Longmate, *How We Lived Then*, p. 25.

15. London *Times*, Sept. 4, 1939.

16. Churchill, *Gathering Storm*, p. 410.

17. *World News and Views*, Sept. 20, 1939.

18. Braunthal, *History of International*, p. 502.

19. McSherry, *Stalin, Hitler, and Europe*, vol. 2, p. 246.

## Chapter Sixty-Two

1. Proclamation by Elizabeth I, as cited in David L. Gordon and Royden Dangerfield, *The Hidden Weapon: The Story of Economic Warfare* (New York: Harper and Bros., 1947), p. 16.

2. Hyde, *Stalin*, p. 405.

3. McSherry, *Stalin, Hitler and Europe*, vol. 2, p. 10.

4. ONI, "Russo-German Naval Relations, 1926 to 1941," Historical Division, US Navy, citing German naval war diary entries for 1939. Unless otherwise noted, quotations are from that source.

5. Interview by Anthony Cave Brown with Col MacLeod, former ADC to Gen Ironside and co-editor of *The Ironside Diaries*, op. cit. See note 10, Chapter 5.

6. *World News and Views*, Oct. 7, 1939.

7. Earl Browder, *Stop the War*, pamphlet published by Workers Library Publishers, New York, Nov 39, item no. 2069, William J. Donovan Collection.

8. Israel Amter, *May Day, 1941*, pamphlet in the William J. Donovan Collection.

9. Weinkoop MS, op. cit. All unattributed quotations are from that source.

10. "Communists in Atomic Research," The International Federation of Architects, Engineers, Chemists and Technicians, CIO, data obtained from *Un-American Activities in California*, Third Report of the Joint Fact-Finding Committee to the 57th California Legislature, Sacramento, 1947, ch. 11, pp. 201–19, William J. Donovan Collection.

11. Churchill, *Great War*, p. 1004.

12. Lecture, Raymond E. Murphy, State Dept, "Revolutionary Defeatism," Army War College, 21 Jan 48, William J. Donovan Collection. Unattributed quotations are from that source.

13. Col A. Goutard, *The Battle of France 1940* (New York: Ives Washburn, Inc., 1959), p. 81.

## Chapter Sixty-Three

1. All unattributed quotations are from McSherry, *Stalin, Hitler and Europe*, vol. 2.

2. Instructions Regarding the Manner of Conducting the Deportation of Anti-Soviet Elements, item no. 424.41, vol. 2, William J. Donovan Collection.

3. OSS *Chronology*, 30 Nov 39.

4. Ibid., 4–10 Dec 39.

5. Quotations are from William Z. Foster, *The War Crisis: Questions and Answers*, pamphlet published by Workers Library Publishers, New York, Jan 40, item no. 2069, William J. Donovan Collection.

6. CMH translation, *Preparation for and Unleashing of the War*, p. 351. See note 11, Chapter 53.

7. Nikita Khruschev, *Khruschev Remembers* (Boston: Little, Brown and Co., 1970), p. 154.

8. US Forces European Theater, MS C-035, 3 Nov 48, Interv with Gen Franz Halder and Gen Ernst Koestring, Record Group 338, MMR, NA.

## Chapter Sixty-Four

1. Churchill, *Gathering Storm*, pp. 659–60.

2. Ibid., p. 663.

3. Ibid., pp. 663–64.

4. Churchill, *Their Finest Hour*, pp. 25–26.

5. Ltr from Cannes, 6 Sep 40, in British Security Coordination, Postal Censorship, Bermuda, Report on Conditions in France, 6 Jan 41, in "Balkan Trip of Wm. J. Donovan," vol. 1, William J. Donovan Collection.

6. As cited in Hanson Baldwin, *The Crucial Years 1939–1941*, p. 135.

7. As cited in B. H. Liddell-Hart, *History of the Second World War*, p. 83.

8. Churchill, *Their Finest Hour*, p. 118.

9. Baldwin, *Crucial Years*, p. 143.

10. Pietro Badoglio, *Italy in the Second World War* (Oxford: Oxford University Press, 1948), p. 97.

11. Sir Edward Spears, *The Fall of France* (London: Heinemann, 1954), p. 176.

12. Ibid.

13. Churchill, *Their Finest Hour*, pp. 153–54. Subsequent quotations are from that source.

## Chapter Sixty-Five

1. Shirer, *Berlin Diary*, p. 422.

2. Maxime Weygand, *Recalled to Service* (London: Heinemann, 1952), p. 124.

3. Speer, *Inside Third Reich*, p. 236.

4. William L. Langer, *Our Vichy Gamble* (New York: Alfred A. Knopf Co., 1947), p. 218.

5. Gen Henri Benouville et al., special memo for director, OSS, Lessons from the Resistance to the German Occupation of France, William J. Donovan Collection.

6. State Dept, *Foreign Relations of the United States, France*, June 17, 1940, pt. 2, p. 455.

7. Churchill, *Their Finest Hour*, pp. 221–22. Subsequent unattributed quotations are from that source.

8. Appreciation by J. C. Wiley to Col Donovan and Sec Navy Knox, no date, French Section, CIAP, William J. Donovan Collection.

9. Captain Holland, Narrative of Events on 3rd July, 1940, in "Balkan Trip of Wm. J. Donovan," vol. 1, William J. Donovan Collection.

10. Churchill, *Their Finest Hour*, p. 234.

11. These and subsequent quotations are from Holland, op. cit.

12. British Security Coordination, Bermuda: Report on Conditions in France, William J. Donovan Collection.

13. Toland, *Adolf Hitler*, p. 621.

14. *World News and Views*, July 12, 1940.

PART XII *"The Great Patriotic War"*

## Chapter Sixty-Six

1. New York *Times*, June 19, 1940.
2. New York *Times*, July 14, 1940.
3. Fest, *Hitler*, p. 664.
4. Toland, *Adolf Hitler*, pp. 622–23.
5. Ibid., p. 623.
6. Churchill, *Their Finest Hour*, p. 298.
7. Walter Warlimont, *Inside Hitler's Headquarters* (London: Weidenfeld and Nicolson, 1964), p. 111.
8. Franz Halder Diary as cited in Warlimont, p. 114. Italics in the original.
9. ONI, "Espionage-Sabotage-Conspiracy."
10. Schellenberg, *The Schellenberg Memoirs*, pp. 128 ff., for this and the next three unattributed quotations.
11. Donaldson, *Edward VIII*, p. 398, citing telegram from von Ribbentrop. The next two unattributed quotations are from Donaldson.
12. Interv by the authors with Sibert.
13. CMH trans, *Preparations for and Unleashing of the War*, p. 471. See note 11, Chapter 53.
14. Winston Churchill, *The Grand Alliance*, pp. 49–50.
15. CMH trans, *Preparation for an Unleashing of the War*, pp. 471–72. See note 11, Chapter 53.
16. Churchill, *Grand Alliance*, p. 550.
17. Department of Defense, *The "Magic" Background of Pearl Harbor*, vol. 2, p. 115, par. 134.
18. Ibid., vol. 2 (appendix), *Magic* no. 518, From Rome (Oshima) to Tokyo, 14 May 41.
19. Ibid., *Magic* no. 556, Tokyo to Nanking, Shanghai, Tientsin, Peking, and Hsinking, 3 Jun 41.

## Chapter Sixty-Seven

1. Churchill, *Their Finest Hour*, p. 134.
2. Ibid.
3. Ibid., pp. 135–36.

4. McSherry, *Stalin, Hitler, and Europe*, vol. 1, p. 150.

5. State Dept, *Foreign Relations of the United States, Nazi-Soviet Relations, 1939–1941*, p. 143.

6. *The "Magic" Background of Pearl Harbor*, vol. 1, Magic no. 235, From Tokyo (Arita) to Washington ("Utterly and Strictly Secret"), 14 Nov 36.

7. *Preparations for and Unleashing of the War*, p. 47.

8. "An Account of the Molotov-Ribbentrop Meeting in Berlin, 12 November–2 December 1940," prepared from captured German files for William L. Shirer, vol. 43, William J. Donovan collection.

9. Ibid.

10. Toland, *Adolf Hitler*, p. 644.

11. Irving, *Hitler's War*, pp. 195–6.

12. "An account of the Molotov-Ribbentrop meeting," op. cit.

13. Toland, *Adolf Hitler*, p. 646.

14. Churchill, *Their Finest Hour*, p. 586.

15. The full text of the order is to be found in Payne, *Life and Death of Adolf Hitler*, pp. 416–17.

## Chapter Sixty-Eight

1. Irving, *Hitler's War*, p. 215.

2. Unattributed quotations are from a secret memorandum from DeWitt Clinton Poole to Coordinator of Information, 4 Dec 41, William J. Donovan Collection.

3. Random memo from "YCD" entitled, Memorandum on Father Odo, OSB, Grand Duke of Württemberg, William J. Donovan Collection.

4. Memo from "Q" relayed to President Roosevelt and Adolf Berle entitled, Reverend Father Odo (Duke Charles of Württemberg), Rpt no. 639, 14 Apr 41, William J. Donovan Collection.

5. Rpt from "Q," op. cit.

6. Charles W. Thayer to Donovan, 21 Aug 45, "File 204," William J. Donovan Collection.

7. Barton S. Whaley, *Codename Barbarossa* (Cambridge, Mass.: Harvard University Press, 1968), p. 39.

8. John Erickson, *The Road to Stalingrad*, p. 74.

9. *The "Magic" Background of Pearl Harbor*, vol. 1, p. 46.

10. Ibid.

11. Ibid., Magic no. 366, 16 Apr 41.

12. Ibid., Magic no. 371, 21 Apr 41.

13. Ibid., Magic no. 376, 19 Mar 41.

## Chapter Sixty-Nine

1. Halder Diary, 30 Mar 41, as cited in Fest, *Hitler*, p. 676.
2. Warlimont, *Inside Hitler's Headquarters*, p. 161.
3. German Naval War Diary, entry of 6 Mar 41, in ONI, "Russo-German Naval Relations."
4. Ronald Lewin, *Ultra Goes to War* (New York: McGraw Hill Co., 1978), p. 109.
5. Churchill, *Grand Alliance*, p. 357.
6. CIA Survey Rpt, *Rote Kapelle*.
7. USFET MS P-108, "Germany and Her Allies in World War II," part 2, "The Coordination of Military Effort."
8. Alexander Foote, *Handbook for Spies* (London: Museum, 1964), pp. 196–97.
9. CIA Survey Rpt, *Rote Kapelle*, Swiss Section.
10. Interv by Anthony Cave Brown with Brig Walter Scott, Popham, Hampshire, Mar 70.
11. CIA Survey Rpt, *Rote Kapelle*.
12. *The "Magic" Background of Pearl Harbor*, vol. 2 (appendix), *Magic* no. 660, 18 Jun 41, p. A-335.
13. Paul Carrell, *Hitler Moves East, 1941–43* (Boston: Little, Brown and Co., 1963), p. 56.
14. Erickson, *Road to Stalingrad*, p. 91.
15. Ibid., p. 75.
16. Ivan Maisky, *Memoirs of a Soviet Ambassador* (London: Hutchinson, 1967), p. 149.

## Chapter Seventy

1. Gerd von Rundstedt et al., *OB West—A Study in Command*, MS No. B-633, CMH.
2. Günther Blumentritt, "Moscow," in Seymour Freiden and William Richardson, eds., *The Fatal Decisions* (New York: Berkley Medallion, 1956), p. 182.
3. Baldwin, *Critical Years*, p. 336.
4. Alexander Werth, *Russia At War, 1941–1945*, p. 140.
5. New York *Times*, June 23, 1941.
6. Hyde, *Stalin*, p. 436. See also Werth, *Russia at War*, pp. 167–68.
7. Hyde, *Stalin*, ibid.
8. Adam B. Ulam, *Stalin: The Man and His Era*, p. 539.
9. Ibid., p. 540.
10. Churchill, *Grand Alliance*, pp. 368–69.

11. Ibid.

12. Quotations from Churchill's speech are from ibid., pp. 371–73.

13. *World News and Views*, Sept. 15, 1941.

14. William Hardy McNeill, *America, Britain and Russia: Their Cooperation and Conflict 1941–1946* (London: Royal Institute of International Affairs and Oxford University Press, 1953), p. 51.

15. Churchill, *Grand Alliance*, p. 452. Unless otherwise noted, subsequent quotations are from that source.

16. Ibid., p. 342, and *Correspondence Between the Chairman of the Council of Ministers of the USSR and the Presidents of the USA and the Prime Ministers of Great Britain During the Great Patriotic War of 1941–1945*, vol. 1 (Foreign Languages Publishing House, Moscow), 1957, p. 12, in the Lawrence and Wishart edition, London, 1958.

## Chapter Seventy-One

1. OSS *Chronology*, 16 Jun 41.

2. *Foreign Relations of the United States, 1941 (Russia)*, pp. 766–67.

3. James MacGregor Burns, *Roosevelt: The Soldier of Freedom 1940–1945*, pp. 111–12.

4. New York *Times*, June 25, 1941.

5. George C. Herring, *Aid to Russia, 1941–1946* (New York: Columbia University Press, 1973), p. 9.

6. Burns, *Roosevelt*, p. 112.

7. Robert E. Sherwood, *Roosevelt and Hopkins* (New York: Harper Bros., 1948), pp. 343–44.

8. Ibid., p. 328.

9. Ibid., p. 330.

10. Burns, *Roosevelt*, p. 114.

11. Joseph P. Lash, *Roosevelt and Churchill*, p. 376.

12. Herring, *Aid to Russia*, p. 15.

13. The *"Magic"* History of Pearl Harbor, vol. 5, Special Study, p. 51.

14. *"Magic"* History, p. 53.

15. Ibid., p. 54.

## Chapter Seventy-Two

1. Quotations from the speech are from Werth, *Russia at War*, pp. 170–73.

2. OSS, "Religion as a Factor in Soviet Morale," *The Psychological Warfare Intelligence Weekly*, issue no. 1, 9 Apr 43, William J. Donovan Collection. Unattributed quotations are from that source.

3. Col I. D. Yeaton, "Reestablishment of Patriarchate of Russian Orthodox Church," 15 Sep 43, Military Intelligence Service, MMR, NA.

4. OSS *Chronology,* 30 Sep and 4, 5 Oct 41.

5. John Erickson, *The Soviet High Command,* p. 603.

6. Alexander Dallin, *German Rule in Russia* (New York: St. Martin's Press, 1958), p. 74n.

7. Ulam, *Stalin,* p. 549.

8. Intelligence and Evaluation Branch, Psychological Warfare Div, Planning for the Effective Use of Soviet Prisoners of War, 6 Dec 51, MMR, NA.

9. Warlimont, *Inside Hitler's Headquarters,* p. 180.

10. Ibid.

11. Baldwin, *Critical Years,* p. 344.

12. ONI, "Espionage—Sabotage—Conspiracy," ch. 55, p. 118.

13. Unless otherwise noted, quotations are from CIA, Special Study, "Intelligence and Counter Intelligence Activities on the Eastern Front and Adjacent Areas during World War II," RG 263, MMR, NA.

14. ONI, "Espionage—Sabotage—Conspiracy."

15. Fest, *Hitler,* p. 710.

16. Baldwin, *Critical Years,* p. 338.

17. OKW Documents, memo dtd 23 Feb 43, vol. 20, OKW/639, MMR, NA.

18. Interv by Anthony Cave Brown with Maj Gen Sir Colin Gubbins, Tarbut, Outer Hebrides, 1970.


## *Chapter Seventy-Three*

1. Liddell-Hart, *History of the Second World War,* p. 162, citing an anonymous German general.

2. Werth, *Russia at War,* p. 233.

3. Erickson, *Road to Stalingrad,* p. 220.

4. "Kuibyshev and Kazan," 21 Oct 41, MID, MMR, NA.

5. Baldwin, *Critical Years,* p. 352.

6. Erickson, *Road to Stalingrad,* p. 253.

7. Carrell, *Hitler Moves East,* p. 140.

8. Unless otherwise noted, quotations are from National Military Establishment, Dept of Army, rpt by GHQ, Far Eastern Command, Sorge Spy Ring, A Case Study in International Espionage in the Far East, CIA doc no. 829, 10 Feb 49, William J. Donovan Collection.

9. As cited in John Toland, *The Rising Sun: The Decline and Fall of the Japanese Empire, 1936–1945,* pp. 121–22.

10. Ibid., p. 122.

11. Erickson, *Road to Stalingrad,* p. 249.

12. Irving, *Hitler's War,* p. 349.

13. Alexander Boyd, *The Soviet Air Force* (New York: Stein and Day, 1977), p. 130.

14. "Kuibyshev and Kazan," op. cit.

15. Erickson, *Road to Stalingrad*, p. 258.

16. Heinrich Haape, *Moscow Tram Stop* (London: Collins, 1957), as cited in Desmond Flower and James Reeves, eds., *The Taste of Courage: The War, 1939–1945* (New York: Harper and Bros., 1960), p. 223.

## Epilogue

### One

1. CIA. *Rote Kapelle*: A Survey Report, vol. 1, for all unattributed quotations.

2. *World News and Views*, May 22 and June 5, 1943.

3. Braunthal, *History of International*, pp. 529–30.

4. OSS, OSS Weekly Survey, 10–17 Mar 43, William J. Donovan Collection.

5. Memo, CP in the USA, Brig Gen Clayton Bissell, G-2, to Lt Gen T. T. Handy, OPD Russia 1944, MMR, NA.

6. Statement to Anthony Cave Brown by a leading CIA official who took part in the Anglo-American investigation into Russian operations to obtain the atomic bomb, 1943–1946.

### Two

1. Herbert York, *The Advisers: Oppenheimer, Teller and the Superbomb* (San Francisco: W. H. Freeman, 1976), p. 29.

2. Ibid., p. 30.

3. Army Service Forces, *History of the Intelligence Division of the Manhattan Engineering District*, vol. 1, ch. 7, pp. 8–10, MMR.

4. Memo, D. M. Ladd to Director, 20 Oct 51, Wallace file, vol. 1, FBI.

5. Ibid.

6. WD Gen Staff, The Influence of Brigadier General Phillip R. Faymonville.

7. Ibid.

8. William H. Standley and Arthur A. Ageton, *Admiral Ambassador to Moscow* (Chicago: Henry Regnery Co., 1955), p. 93.

9. Langer, "The Red General."

10. Green, *Children of the Sun*, p. 330, citing British scientists James Tuck and Stephane Groueff, respectively.

11. Groves to President Roosevelt and Sec War: Summary, Russian Situation, Manhattan Project file, Army Service Forces, folder 12, Tab d, RG 77, MMR.

12. Oppenheimer dossier, FBI.

13. L. B. Nichols to Tolson: unpublished MS, Oliver Pilat, "The Atom Spies," 14 Dec 51, FBI.

14. Ibid.

15. Ibid.

16. Oppenheimer dossier, FBI.

17. Summary Memorandum, J. Edgar Hoover to the Hon Lewis L. Strauss, Chairman, Atomic Energy Commission, 18 Nov 53, FBI.

## Three

1. Extract from Security Conference, Notes prepared by UK representative concerning Tripartite Talks on Security Standards at Washington, 19–21 Jun 50, P1519, Atomic Energy Commission (AEC).

2. Rpt of H. H. Clegg and R. J. Lamphere covering interviews with Klaus Fuchs in London, re: FOOCASE ESP-R, item 1412, FBI.

3. Ibid.

4. Gold, "The Circumstances Surrounding My Work As a Soviet Agent." See note 5, Chapter 46.

5. Robert G. Jensen, Rpt of Interv with H. Gold, ESP-R, 31 May 50, FBI.

6. Ibid.

7. Clegg-Lamphere Rpt.

8. Gold, op. cit.

9. Clegg-Lamphere Rpt.

10. Intervs by the authors with Dr. Mark, Washington, DC, 1976.

11. Clegg-Lamphere Rpt.

12. Gold, op. cit.

## Four

1. As cited in McNeill, *America, Britain, and Russia,* p. 657.

2. NSC (National Security Council) 7, 30 mar 48, "The Position of the United States with Respect to Soviet-directed World Communism," MMR.

3. Telex rpt of interview with Carroll J. Wilson (chairman, Combined Development Trust), 11 Jun 51, FBI.

4. Ibid.

5. Interv with Roy B. Snapp (chief, Special Projects Div, AEC), 28 Jun 41, FBI.

6. Ibid.

7. Memo, Col Totten to Chairman, JCS, National security Implications Resulting from the Defection of British Diplomats, Donald Duart Maclean and Guy Fran deMoncy Burgess, 18 Oct 55, in Maclean file, FBI.

8. Gold, op. cit.

9. C. E. Hennrich to E. J. Van Loon, FOOCASE ESP-R, Search clips on Emil Julius Klaus Fuchs, together with the writeups of identifiable references, 21 Jun 50, document 213, FOOCASE file 3, FBI.

10. FOOCASE ESP-R, doc 200, FBI.

11. Clegg-Lamphere Rpt.

12. Ibid.

13. Ibid.

14. Undated, unsigned security note, CIAP, AEC.

15. Clegg-Lamphere Rpt.

16. Joint Committee on Atomic Energy, "Soviet Energy Espionage," p. 13, AEC Libray.

17. SAC Pittsburgh to Director FBI, Dr. Klaus Fuchs, Internal Security-R, 3 Jul 50, FOOCASE ESP-R, FBI.

## Five

1. File on E. T. Bentley in connection with the case of William W. Remington, William J. Donovan Collection. See also Elizabeth Terrill Bentley, File 61–6328, Sect 1, Serials 1–15, FBI.

2. House Committee on Un-American Activities (1), August–September 1948, pp. 564–66.

3. Rpt of Interv with Elizabeth Terrill Bentley by SA J. C. Walsh, 29 May 50, FBI.

4. Shannon and O'Brien, Interv with Abraham Brothman and Miriam Moskowitz, 22 May 47, FBI.

5. Ibid.

6. Gold Confession, consolidated rpt, Jan 51, FBI.

7. Harry Gold: Case History, doc 857, FBI.

8. Ladd to Director, 18 May 50, FBI.

9. Harry Gold, Case History.

10. Gold, op. cit.

11. Ibid.

12. Statement by H. Gold, 23 May 50, FBI.

13. Gold, op. cit.

# Index